America's Top-Rated Cities

In-Depth Statistics & Comparative Rankings of the Best Big Cities in America

2025
Thirty-second Edition

America's Top-Rated Cities

In-Depth Statistics & Comparative Rankings
of the Best Big Cities in America

Volume 4: Eastern Region

Cover images: Richmond, Virginia

PUBLISHER: Leslie Mackenzie
EDITORIAL DIRECTOR: Stuart Paterson
SENIOR EDITOR: David Garoogian

RESEARCHER & WRITER: Jael Bridgemahon; Laura Mars
MARKETING DIRECTOR: Jessica Moody

Grey House Publishing, Inc.
4919 Route 22
Amenia, NY 12501
518.789.8700 • Fax 845.373.6390
www.greyhouse.com
books@greyhouse.com

While every effort has been made to ensure the reliability of the information presented in this publication, Grey House Publishing neither guarantees the accuracy of the data contained herein nor assumes any responsibility for errors, omissions or discrepancies. Grey House accepts no payment for listing; inclusion in the publication of any organization, agency, institution, publication, service or individual does not imply endorsement of the editors or publisher.

Errors brought to the attention of the publisher and verified to the satisfaction of the publisher will be corrected in future editions.

Except by express prior written permission of the Copyright Proprietor no part of this work may be copied by any means of publication or communication now known or developed hereafter including, but not limited to, use in any directory or compilation or other print publication, in any information storage and retrieval system, in any other electronic device, or in any visual or audio-visual device or product.

This publication is an original and creative work, copyrighted by Grey House Publishing, Inc. and is fully protected by all applicable copyright laws, as well as by laws covering misappropriation, trade secrets and unfair competition.

Grey House has added value to the underlying factual material through one or more of the following efforts: unique and original selection; expression; arrangement; coordination; and classification.

Grey House Publishing, Inc. will defend its rights in this publication.

Copyright © 2025 Grey House Publishing, Inc.
All rights reserved

Thirty-second Edition
Printed in the U.S.A.

Publisher's Cataloging-in-Publication Data
(Prepared by The Donohue Group, Inc.)

America's top-rated cities. Vol. 4, Eastern region : in-depth statistics & comparative rankings of the best big cities in america. — 1992-

v. : ill. ; cm.
Annual, 1995-
Irregular, 1992-1993
ISSN: 1082-7102

1. Cities and towns—Ratings—Eastern States—Statistics—Periodicals. 2. Cities and towns—Eastern States—Statistics—Periodicals. 3. Social indicators—Eastern States—Periodicals. 4. Quality of life—Eastern States—Statistics—Periodicals. 5. Eastern States—Social conditions—Statistics—Periodicals. I. Title: America's top rated cities. II. Title: Eastern region

HT123.5.S6 A44
307.76/0973/05 95644648

4-Volume Set	ISBN: 979-8-89179-096-4
Volume 1	ISBN: 979-8-89179-098-8
Volume 2	ISBN: 979-8-89179-099-5
Volume 3	ISBN: 979-8-89179-100-8
Volume 4	**ISBN: 979-8-89179-101-5**

Table of Contents

Baltimore, Maryland

- **Background** 1
- **Rankings** 2
- **Business Environment** 4
  - Demographics 4
  - Economy 6
  - Income 6
  - Employment 7
  - City Finances 9
  - Taxes 9
  - Transportation 10
  - Businesses 11
- **Living Environment** 13
  - Cost of Living 13
  - Housing 13
  - Health 14
  - Education 17
  - Employers 18
  - Public Safety 19
  - Politics 20
  - Sports 20
  - Climate 20
  - Hazardous Waste 20
  - Air Quality 21

Boston, Massachusetts

- **Background** 23
- **Rankings** 24
- **Business Environment** 28
  - Demographics 28
  - Economy 30
  - Income 30
  - Employment 31
  - City Finances 33
  - Taxes 33
  - Transportation 34
  - Businesses 35
- **Living Environment** 37
  - Cost of Living 37
  - Housing 37
  - Health 38
  - Education 41
  - Employers 43
  - Public Safety 44
  - Politics 44
  - Sports 44
  - Climate 44
  - Hazardous Waste 45
  - Air Quality 45

Charlotte, North Carolina

- **Background** 47
- **Rankings** 48
- **Business Environment** 51
  - Demographics 51
  - Economy 53
  - Income 53
  - Employment 54
  - City Finances 56
  - Taxes 56
  - Transportation 57
  - Businesses 58
- **Living Environment** 59
  - Cost of Living 59
  - Housing 59
  - Health 60
  - Education 63
  - Employers 64
  - Public Safety 65
  - Politics 65
  - Sports 65
  - Climate 65
  - Hazardous Waste 66
  - Air Quality 66

Cincinnati, Ohio

- **Background** 69
- **Rankings** 70
- **Business Environment** 73
  - Demographics 73
  - Economy 75
  - Income 75
  - Employment 76
  - City Finances 78
  - Taxes 78
  - Transportation 79
  - Businesses 80
- **Living Environment** 81
  - Cost of Living 81
  - Housing 81
  - Health 82
  - Education 85
  - Employers 87
  - Public Safety 87
  - Politics 88
  - Sports 88
  - Climate 88
  - Hazardous Waste 88
  - Air Quality 89

Cleveland, Ohio

Background	91
Rankings	92
Business Environment	95
Demographics	95
Economy	97
Income	97
Employment	98
City Finances	100
Taxes	100
Transportation	101
Businesses	102
Living Environment	103
Cost of Living	103
Housing	103
Health	104
Education	107
Employers	108
Public Safety	108
Politics	109
Sports	109
Climate	109
Hazardous Waste	109
Air Quality	110

Columbus, Ohio

Background	113
Rankings	114
Business Environment	116
Demographics	116
Economy	118
Income	118
Employment	119
City Finances	121
Taxes	121
Transportation	122
Businesses	123
Living Environment	124
Cost of Living	124
Housing	124
Health	125
Education	128
Employers	129
Public Safety	130
Politics	131
Sports	131
Climate	131
Hazardous Waste	131
Air Quality	132

Durham, North Carolina

Background	135
Rankings	136
Business Environment	138
Demographics	138
Economy	140
Income	140
Employment	141
City Finances	143
Taxes	143
Transportation	144
Businesses	145
Living Environment	146
Cost of Living	146
Housing	146
Health	147
Education	150
Employers	151
Public Safety	152
Politics	152
Sports	152
Climate	153
Hazardous Waste	153
Air Quality	153

Greensboro, North Carolina

Background	155
Rankings	156
Business Environment	158
Demographics	158
Economy	160
Income	160
Employment	161
City Finances	163
Taxes	163
Transportation	164
Businesses	165
Living Environment	166
Cost of Living	166
Housing	166
Health	167
Education	169
Employers	171
Public Safety	171
Politics	171
Sports	172
Climate	172
Hazardous Waste	172
Air Quality	172

Lexington, Kentucky

Background	175
Rankings	176
Business Environment	178
Demographics	178
Economy	180
Income	180
Employment	181
City Finances	183
Taxes	183
Transportation	184
Businesses	185
Living Environment	186
Cost of Living	186
Housing	186
Health	187
Education	190
Employers	191
Public Safety	191
Politics	192
Sports	192
Climate	192
Hazardous Waste	192
Air Quality	192

Louisville, Kentucky

Background	195
Rankings	196
Business Environment	198
Demographics	198
Economy	200
Income	200
Employment	201
City Finances	203
Taxes	203
Transportation	204
Businesses	205
Living Environment	206
Cost of Living	206
Housing	206
Health	207
Education	209
Employers	211
Public Safety	211
Politics	212
Sports	212
Climate	212
Hazardous Waste	212
Air Quality	213

Manchester, New Hampshire

Background	215
Rankings	216
Business Environment	217
Demographics	217
Economy	219
Income	219
Employment	220
City Finances	222
Taxes	222
Transportation	223
Businesses	224
Living Environment	225
Cost of Living	225
Housing	225
Health	226
Education	228
Employers	229
Public Safety	230
Politics	230
Sports	230
Climate	230
Hazardous Waste	231
Air Quality	231

New York, New York

Background	233
Rankings	234
Business Environment	237
Demographics	237
Economy	239
Income	240
Employment	240
City Finances	242
Taxes	243
Transportation	244
Businesses	245
Living Environment	248
Cost of Living	248
Housing	248
Health	249
Education	255
Employers	257
Public Safety	258
Politics	259
Sports	259
Climate	259
Hazardous Waste	260
Air Quality	260

Philadelphia, Pennsylvania

Background	263
Rankings	264
Business Environment	266
Demographics	266
Economy	268
Income	268
Employment	269
City Finances	271
Taxes	271
Transportation	272
Businesses	273
Living Environment	275
Cost of Living	275
Housing	275
Health	276
Education	279
Employers	281
Public Safety	281
Politics	282
Sports	282
Climate	282
Hazardous Waste	283
Air Quality	283

Pittsburgh, Pennsylvania

Background	285
Rankings	286
Business Environment	289
Demographics	289
Economy	291
Income	291
Employment	292
City Finances	294
Taxes	294
Transportation	295
Businesses	296
Living Environment	297
Cost of Living	297
Housing	297
Health	298
Education	301
Employers	303
Public Safety	303
Politics	304
Sports	304
Climate	304
Hazardous Waste	304
Air Quality	304

Providence, Rhode Island

Background	307
Rankings	308
Business Environment	310
Demographics	310
Economy	312
Income	312
Employment	313
City Finances	315
Taxes	315
Transportation	316
Businesses	317
Living Environment	318
Cost of Living	318
Housing	318
Health	319
Education	321
Employers	323
Public Safety	323
Politics	323
Sports	324
Climate	324
Hazardous Waste	324
Air Quality	324

Raleigh, North Carolina

Background	327
Rankings	328
Business Environment	330
Demographics	330
Economy	332
Income	332
Employment	333
City Finances	335
Taxes	335
Transportation	336
Businesses	337
Living Environment	338
Cost of Living	338
Housing	338
Health	339
Education	341
Employers	343
Public Safety	343
Politics	344
Sports	344
Climate	344
Hazardous Waste	344
Air Quality	345

Richmond, Virginia

Background 347
Rankings 348
Business Environment 350
  Demographics 350
  Economy 352
  Income 352
  Employment 353
  City Finances 355
  Taxes 355
  Transportation 356
  Businesses 357
Living Environment 358
  Cost of Living 358
  Housing 358
  Health 359
  Education 362
  Employers 363
  Public Safety 364
  Politics 364
  Sports 364
  Climate 364
  Hazardous Waste 365
  Air Quality 365

Washington, D.C.

Background 387
Rankings 388
Business Environment 391
  Demographics 391
  Economy 393
  Income 393
  Employment 394
  City Finances 396
  Taxes 396
  Transportation 397
  Businesses 398
Living Environment 400
  Cost of Living 400
  Housing 400
  Health 401
  Education 404
  Employers 405
  Public Safety 406
  Politics 406
  Sports 407
  Climate 407
  Hazardous Waste 407
  Air Quality 407

Virginia Beach, Virginia

Background 367
Rankings 368
Business Environment 370
  Demographics 370
  Economy 372
  Income 372
  Employment 373
  City Finances 375
  Taxes 375
  Transportation 376
  Businesses 377
Living Environment 378
  Cost of Living 378
  Housing 378
  Health 379
  Education 381
  Employers 383
  Public Safety 383
  Politics 383
  Sports 384
  Climate 384
  Hazardous Waste 384
  Air Quality 384

Wilmington, North Carolina

Background 409
Rankings 410
Business Environment 411
  Demographics 411
  Economy 413
  Income 413
  Employment 414
  City Finances 416
  Taxes 416
  Transportation 417
  Businesses 418
Living Environment 419
  Cost of Living 419
  Housing 419
  Health 420
  Education 422
  Employers 423
  Public Safety 423
  Politics 424
  Sports 424
  Climate 424
  Hazardous Waste 425
  Air Quality 425

Winston-Salem, North Carolina

Background..................................... 427
Rankings...................................... 428
Business Environment.......................... 430
    Demographics................................ 430
    Economy.................................... 432
    Income..................................... 432
    Employment................................. 433
    City Finances.............................. 435
    Taxes...................................... 435
    Transportation............................. 436
    Businesses................................. 437
Living Environment............................ 438
    Cost of Living............................. 438
    Housing.................................... 438
    Health..................................... 439
    Education.................................. 441
    Employers.................................. 443
    Public Safety.............................. 443
    Politics................................... 443
    Sports..................................... 444
    Climate.................................... 444
    Hazardous Waste............................ 444
    Air Quality................................ 444

Appendixes

Appendix A: Comparative Statistics A-3
Appendix B: Metropolitan Area Definitions A-171
Appendix C: Government Type & Primary County .. A-175
Appendix D: Chambers of Commerce............. A-177
Appendix E: State Departments of Labor A-183

Introduction

This thirty-second edition of *America's Top-Rated Cities* is a concise, statistical, 4-volume work identifying America's top-rated cities with estimated populations of 100,000 or more. It profiles 97 cities that have received high marks for business and living based on our unique weighting system.

Each volume covers a different region of the country—Southern, Western, Central, Eastern—and includes a detailed Table of Contents, City Chapters, Appendices, and Maps. Each city chapter incorporates information from hundreds of resources to create the following major sections:

- **Background**—lively narrative of significant, up-to-date news for both businesses and residents. These combine historical facts with current developments, "known-for" annual events, and climate data.
- **Rankings**—fun-to-read, bulleted survey results from over 100 books, magazines, and online articles, ranging from general (Great Places to Live), to specific (Friendliest Cities), and everything in between.
- **Statistical Tables**—88 tables and detailed topics that offer an unparalleled view of each city's Business and Living Environments. They are carefully organized with data that is easy to read and understand.
- **Appendices**—five in all, appear at the end of each volume. These range from listings of Metropolitan Statistical Areas to Comparative Statistics for all 97 cities.

This new edition of *America's Top-Rated Cities* includes cities that not only surveyed well, but ranked highest using the following criteria: population growth, crime, household income, poverty, housing affordability, educational attainment, and unemployment. Part of the criteria, in most cases, is that it be the "primary" city in a given metropolitan area. For example, if the metro area is Raleigh-Cary, North Carolina, we would consider Raleigh, not Cary. This allows for a more equitable core city comparison. In general, the core city of a metro area is defined as having substantial influence on neighboring cities. A final consideration is location—we strive to include as many states in the country as possible.

You'll find that we have included several American cities despite having lower rankings in some categories. New York, Los Angeles, and Miami remain world-class cities despite challenges faced by many large urban centers. We also decided to include all major cities with historic or cultural significance. For example, Detroit, Michigan, the birthplace of the American automotive industry.

New to this edition are:
Volume 1: Midland, TX
Volume 2: Salem, OR
Volume 3: Green Bay, WI; St. Paul, MN

Praise for previous editions:

> "... [ATRC] has...proven its worth to a wide audience...from businesspeople and corporations planning to launch, relocate, or expand their operations to market researchers, real estate professionals, urban planners, job-seekers, students...interested in...reliable, attractively presented statistical information about larger U.S. cities."
> —ARBA

> "... For individuals or businesses looking to relocate, this resource conveniently reports rankings from more than 300 sources for the top 100 U.S. cities. Recommended..."
> —Choice

> "... While patrons are becoming increasingly comfortable locating statistical data online, there is still something to be said for the ease associated with such a compendium of otherwise scattered data. A well-organized and appropriate update..."
> —Library Journal

BACKGROUND
Each city begins with an informative Background that combines history with current events. These narratives often reflect changes that have occurred during the past year, and touch on the city's environment, politics, employment, cultural offerings, and climate, and include interesting trivia. For example: Tampa, Florida was known as the Cigar Capital of the World in the early 1900s; Wilmington, North Carolina was the site of one of the first rebellions in the United States'

revolt against British rule; and the first mail-order business, Montgomery Ward, was established in Chicago in 1872. Current events include: the most devastating fires recorded in the city of Los Angeles destroyed entire neighborhoods, including Pacific Palisades in January 2025; MARTA (Metropolitan Atlanta Rapid Transit Authority) unveiled its first state-of-the-art CQ400 railcar in early 2025; and Jaialdi, a large Basque festival held once every five years, is being held in Boise City in July 2025.

RANKINGS
This section has rankings from over 100 articles and reports. For easy reference, these Rankings are categorized into 16 topics including Business/Finance, Dating/Romance, and Health/Fitness.

The Rankings are presented in an easy-to-read, bulleted format and include results from both annual surveys and one-shot studies. **Fastest Job Growth** . . . **Best Drivers** . . . **Most Well-Read** . . . **Most Wired** . . . **Healthiest for Women** . . . **Best for Minority Entrepreneurs** . . . **Safest** . . . **Best to Retire** . . . **Most Polite** . . . **Best for Moviemakers** . . . **Most Frugal** . . . **Best for Bikes** . . . **Most Cultured** . . . **Least Stressful** . . . **Best for Families** . . . **Most Romantic** . . . **Most Charitable** . . . **Best for Telecommuters** . . . **Best for Singles** . . . **Nerdiest** . . . **Fittest** . . . **Best for Dogs** . . . **Most Tattooed** . . . **Best for Veterans** . . . **Best for Wheelchair Users**, and more.

Sources for these Rankings include both well-known magazines and other organizations, including *The Advocate*, *Condé Nast Traveler*, *Forbes*, *Kiplinger*, and *National Geographic*, as well as American Lung Association, Asthma & Allergy Foundation of America, National Civic League, People for the Ethical Treatment of Animals, and *Site Selection*.

Rankings cover a variety of geographic areas; see Appendix B for full geographic definitions.

STATISTICAL TABLES
Each city chapter includes 88 tables and detailed topics—45 in Business and 43 in Living. Over 90% of statistical data has been updated. This edition also includes new data on the economy from the U.S. Bureau of Economic Analysis and mortality rates from accidental poisonings and exposure to noxious substances.

Business Environment includes hard facts and figures on 8 major categories, including Demographics, Income, Economy, Employment, and Taxes. *Living Environment* includes 11 major categories, such as Cost of Living, Housing, Health, Education, Safety, and Climate.

To compile the Statistical Tables, editors have again turned to a wide range of sources, some well known, such as the Bureau of Labor Statistics, Centers for Disease Control and Prevention, Federal Bureau of Investigation, U.S. Census Bureau, and U.S. Environmental Protection Agency, plus others like The Council for Community and Economic Research, Federal Housing Finance Agency, and Texas A&M Transportation Institute.

APPENDIXES: Data for all cities appear in all volumes.
- **Appendix A**—*Comparative Statistics*
- **Appendix B**—*Metropolitan Area Definitions*
- **Appendix C**—*Government Type and County*
- **Appendix D**—*Chambers of Commerce and Economic Development Organizations*
- **Appendix E**—*State Departments of Labor and Employment*

Material provided by public and private agencies and organizations was supplemented by original research, numerous library sources and Internet sites. *America's Top-Rated Cities* is designed for a wide range of readers: private individuals considering relocating a residence or business; professionals considering expanding their businesses or changing careers; corporations considering relocating, opening up additional offices or creating new divisions; government agencies; general and market researchers; real estate consultants; human resource personnel; urban planners; investors; and urban government students.

Customers who purchase the four-volume set receive free online access to *America's Top-Rated Cities* allowing them to download city reports and sort and rank these cities by 50-plus data points.

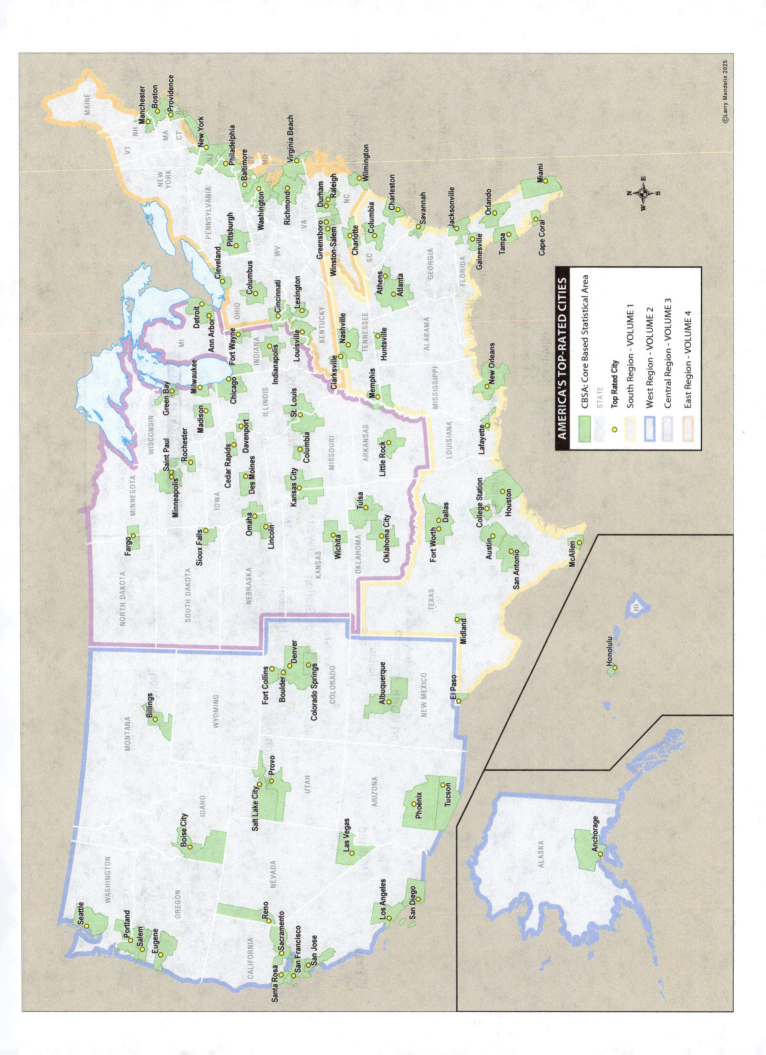

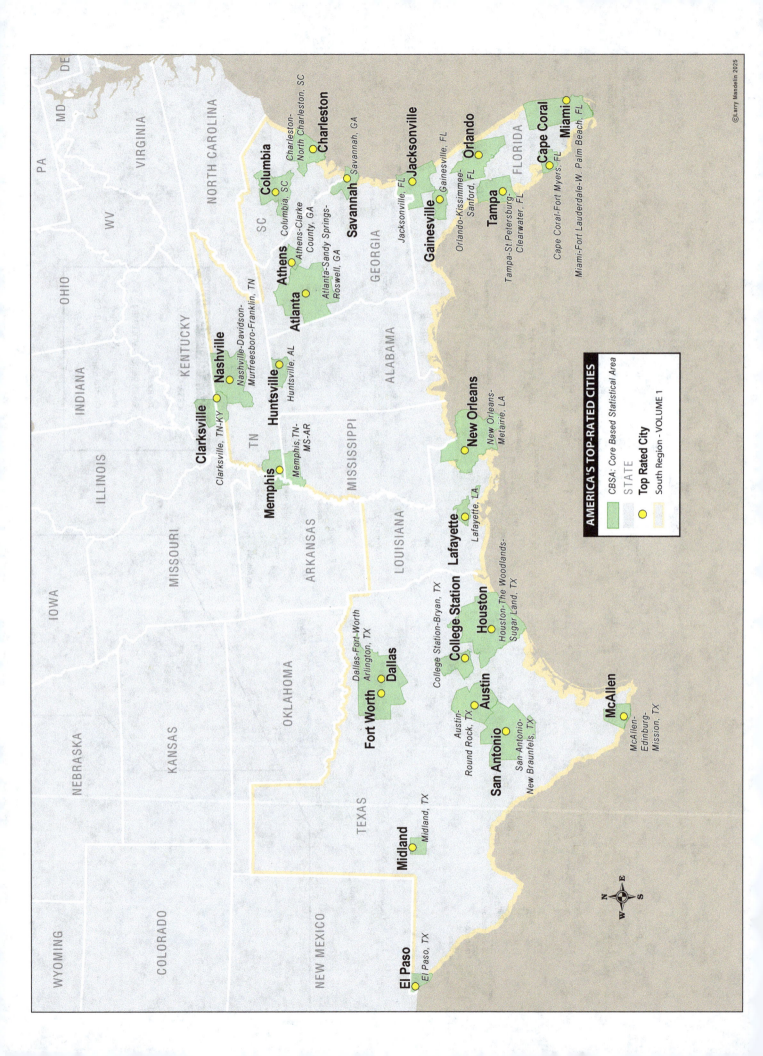

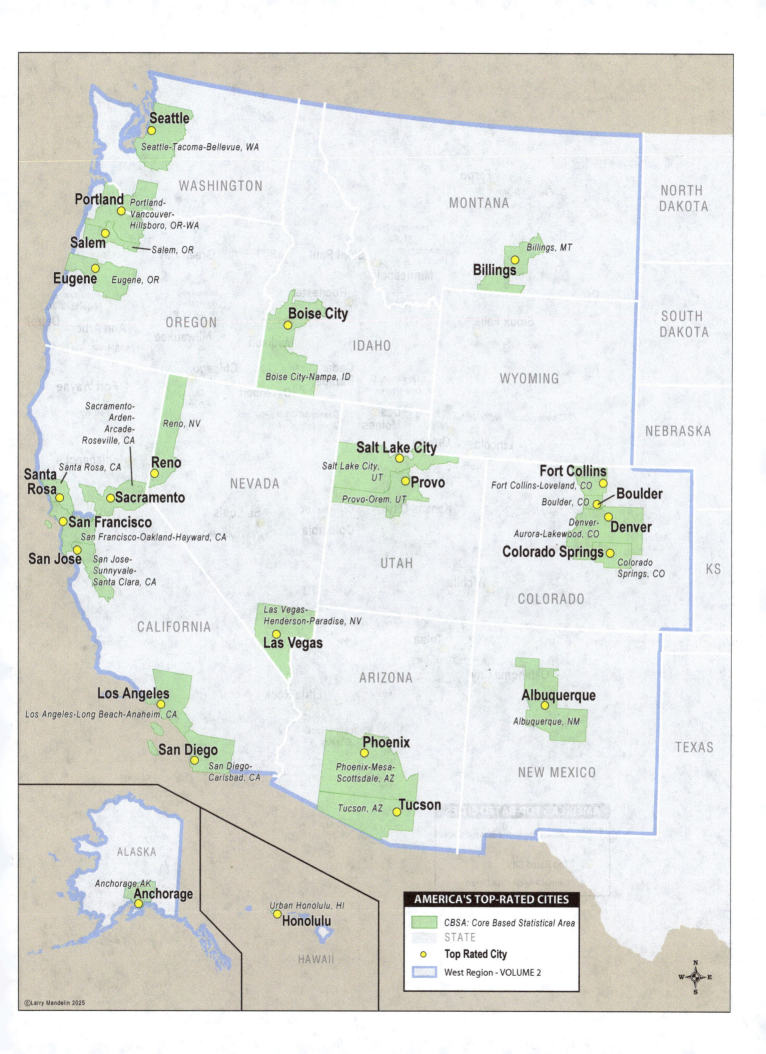

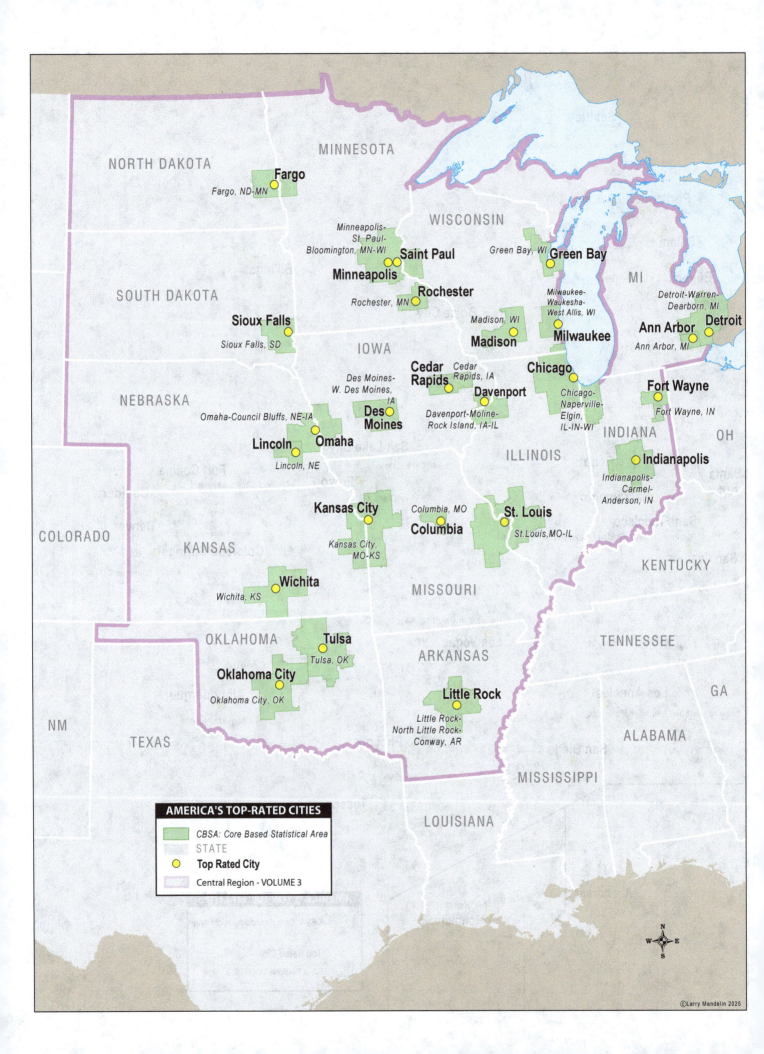

Baltimore, Maryland

Background

No one industry dominates Baltimore, but many of them have one thing in common: Baltimore's waterfront. The city's port facilities provide companies in Baltimore's municipal area with access to domestic and international markets. Not only that, but the port also has the advantage of being 150 miles closer to the Midwest than other eastern U.S. port cities.

With its easily accessible harbor, reached via a 42-foot-deep main channel from the Chesapeake Bay, Baltimore boasts strong roots in maritime commerce dating to the "Baltimore Clippers" built here that outran the British during wartime. The Port of Baltimore is ranked as the 9th largest port in the United States in terms of foreign cargo tonnage and 9th largest in terms of dollar value. Both state-owned public marine terminals and private terminals handled a record 52.3 million tons of foreign cargo worth $80 billion in 2023. On March 26, 2024, maritime access to and from the port was blocked by the collapse of the Francis Scott Key Bridge after it was hit by the MV *Dali*. A new bridge is expected in 2028.

The city was founded in 1729 and named for the Lords Baltimore, Cecil and Charles Calvert, the first proprietors of colonial Maryland in the seventeenth century. In 1812, poet and attorney Francis Scott Key wrote "The Star-Spangled Banner" while watching from a warship the bombardment of the city by the British. Baltimore is the site of the first Roman Catholic cathedral in the country, the Basilica of the Assumption of the Blessed Virgin Mary, which was designed by Benjamin H. Latrobe. The first telegraph line in the United States was installed in Baltimore, and the nation's first gas streetlamp was lit here.

Despite the urban decay experienced from the 1950s through the 1970s, reconstruction of many of the city's old areas in the ensuing years has brought people back to Baltimore neighborhoods such as the Inner Harbor, Fells Point, Federal Hill, and Canton. The upscale Harbor East neighborhood extends the walkability and attraction of the waterside area between the Inner Harbor and Fells Point, with dining, hotels, and shopping.

Healthcare and higher education are the city's major employers, with Johns Hopkins University, Johns Hopkins Hospital and Health System, the University of Maryland-Baltimore, and the University of Maryland Medical System providing nearly 60,000 jobs.

Baltimore's light rail transportation services the Hunt Valley corporate, hotel, and shopping area north of the city, and passes through downtown on its way to Oriole Park and Anne Arundel County. There is also service to Baltimore/Washington International Thurgood Marshall Airport and Amtrak's Baltimore Penn Station, as well as public subway and bus transportation.

The Baltimore waterfront area is a retail and entertainment district, and includes the renovated Pier Four Power Plant, which is listed on the National Register of Historic Places and is has been repurposed as a mixed-use space that includes businesses, restaurants, and cultural venues. Baltimore boasts many museums, including Port Discovery children's museum, the Edgar Allen Poe House and Museum, the Baltimore Museum of Art and the American Visionary Art Museum, to name a few. Some other attractions include the Baltimore Symphony Orchestra, Fort McHenry, Maryland Science Center, and the National Aquarium in Baltimore. The Peabody Conservatory, founded in 1857, is located north of the harbor in picturesque Mount Vernon Square, while the Maryland Institute College of Art boasts alumnae such as Jeff Koons. Of MICA's BFA graduates who take jobs immediately after graduation, nearly 90 percent work in an art-related field.

The first professional sports organization in the United States, The Maryland Jockey Club, was formed in Baltimore in 1743. The Preakness Stakes, the second race in the United States Triple Crown of Thoroughbred Racing, has been held every May at Pimlico Race Course in Baltimore since 1873. The city is also home to two professional sports teams, the Baltimore Orioles (MLB) and the Baltimore Ravens (NFL).

The region is subject to frequent changes in weather, although the mountains to the west, and the Chesapeake Bay and ocean to the east produce a more equable climate compared with other locations farther inland at the same latitude. In the summer, the area is under the influence of the high-pressure system commonly known as the "Bermuda High" which brings warm, humid air. In winter, snow is frequently mixed with rain and sleet, but seldom remains on the ground for more than a few days. Severe thunderstorms are generally confined to summer and fall, and hurricanes during the same period are possible.

Rankings

General Rankings

- To help military veterans find the best places in which to settle down, *WalletHub* compared the 100 largest U.S. cities across 19 key indicators of livability, affordability and veteran-friendliness. They range from the share of military skill-related jobs to veteran income growth to the availability of VA health facilities. Baltimore ranked #88. *Wallethub.com, "Best & Worst Places for Veterans to Live (2025)," November 7, 2024*

Business/Finance Rankings

- According to *Business Insider*, the Baltimore metro area is a prime place to run a startup or move an existing business to. The area ranked #15. More than 300 metro areas were analyzed for factors that were of top concern to new business owners. Data was based on the 2019 U.S. Census Bureau American Community Survey, statistics from the CDC, and University of Chicago analysis. Criteria: business formations; percentage of vaccinated population; percentage of households with internet subscriptions; median household income; and share of work that can be done from home. *BusinessInsider.com, "The 20 Best Cities for Starting a Business in 2022 Include Denver, Raleigh, and Olympia," June 7, 2022*

- Payscale.com ranked the 32 largest metro areas in terms of wage growth. The Baltimore metro area ranked #24. Criteria: quarterly changes in private industry employee and education professional wage growth from the previous year. *PayScale, "Wage Trends by Metro Area-4th Quarter," February 4, 2025*

- The Baltimore metro area appeared on the Milken Institute "2025 Best Performing Cities" list. Rank: #171 out of 200 large metro areas (based on performance category). Criteria: job growth; wage growth; high-tech growth and impact; community resilience; housing affordability; household broadband access. *Milken Institute, "Best-Performing Cities 2025," January 14, 2025*

Education Rankings

- Personal finance website *WalletHub* analyzed the 150 largest U.S. metropolitan statistical areas to determine where the most educated Americans are putting their degrees to work. Criteria: education levels; percentage of workers with degrees; education quality and attainment gap; public school quality rankings; quality and enrollment of each metro area's universities. Baltimore was ranked #20 (#1 = most educated city). *WalletHub.com, "Most & Least Educated Cities in America, 2025" July 2, 2024*

Health/Fitness Rankings

- For each of the 100 largest cities in the United States, the American Fitness Index®, compiled in partnership between the American College of Sports Medicine and the Elevance Health Foundation, evaluated community infrastructure and more than 30 health behaviors including preventive health, levels of chronic disease conditions, food insecurity, pedestrian safety, air quality, and community/environment resources that support physical activity. Baltimore ranked #58 for "community fitness." *americanfitnessindex.org, "2024 ACSM American Fitness Index Summary Report," July 23, 2024*

- The Baltimore metro area was identified as one of the worst cities for bed bugs in America by pest control company Orkin. The area ranked #16 out of 50 based on the number of bed bug treatments Orkin performed from December 2022 to November 2023. *Orkin, "Chicago Joins Paris In Global Bed Bug Spotlight Ranking As The Worst City On Orkin's U.S. Bed Bug Cities List," January 22, 2024*

- Baltimore was identified as a "2025 Allergy Capital." The area ranked #60 out of the nation's 100 largest metropolitan areas. Three groups of factors were used to identify the most challenging cities for people with allergies: annual tree, grass, and weed pollen scores; over the counter allergy medicine use; number of board-certified allergy specialists. *Asthma and Allergy Foundation of America, "2025 Allergy Capitals: The Most Challenging Places to Live with Allergies," March 18, 2025*

- Baltimore was identified as a "2024 Asthma Capital." The area ranked #8 out of the nation's 100 largest metropolitan areas. Criteria: estimated asthma prevalence; asthma-related mortality; and ER visits due to asthma. Risk factors analyzed but not factored in the rankings: annual air quality including pollution and ozone levels; public smoking laws; indoor air quality; access to asthma specialists; rescue and controller medication use; uninsured rate; pollen allergy; poverty rate. *Asthma and Allergy Foundation of America, "Asthma Capitals 2024: The Most Challenging Places to Live With Asthma," September 10, 2024*

Pet Rankings

- Baltimore was selected by *Sniffspot.com* as one of the most dog-friendly cities in the U.S., ranking #42 out of 50. Criteria: dog parks; hiking; sniffspots; public parks; dog-friendly businesses; housing; dog waste cleanliness; leash laws; dog services; and overall cost. *Sniffspot.com, "The Top 50 Most Dog-Friendly Cities in the U.S.," September 30, 2024*

Real Estate Rankings

- *WalletHub* compared the most populated U.S. cities to determine which had the best markets for real estate agents. Baltimore ranked #145 where demand was high and pay was the best. Criteria: sales per agent; annual median wage for real-estate agents; monthly average starting salary for real estate agents; real estate job density and competition; unemployment rate; home turnover rate; housing-market health index; and other relevant metrics. *WalletHub.com, "2021 Best Places to Be a Real Estate Agent," May 12, 2021*

- Baltimore was ranked #76 out of 176 metro areas in terms of cost of housing in 2024 by the National Association of Home Builders (#1 = most affordable). Criteria: the portion of an average family's income necessary to pay the mortgage on a median-priced home. *National Association of Home Builders®, NAHB-Wells Fargo Cost of Housing Index, 4th Quarter 2024*

Safety Rankings

- Allstate ranked the 100 most populous cities in America in terms of driver safety. Baltimore ranked #13. Criteria based on anonymized driving behavior data from Allstate's mobile app powered by Arity: high speed driving (over 80 mph), phone handling, and hard braking. The report helps increase the importance of safety and awareness behind the wheel. *Allstate, "16th Allstate America's Best Drivers Report®," July 11, 2024*

- Baltimore was identified as one of the most dangerous cities in America by NeighborhoodScout. The city ranked #18 out of 100 (#1 = most dangerous). Criteria: number of violent crimes per 1,000 residents. The editors evaluated cities with 25,000 or more residents. *NeighborhoodScout.com, "2023 Top 100 Most Dangerous Cities in the U.S.," January 12, 2023*

Women/Minorities Rankings

- Baltimore was listed as one of the most LGBTQ-friendly cities in America by *The Advocate*, as compiled by the real estate data site *Clever*. The city ranked #14 out of 15. Criteria, among many: Pride events; gay bars; LGBTQ-affirming healthcare options; state and local laws; number of PFLAG chapters; LGBTQ+ population. *The Advocate, "These Are the 15 Most LGBTQ-Friendly Cities in the U.S." November 1, 2023*

- Personal finance website *WalletHub* compared more than 180 U.S. cities across two key dimensions, "Hispanic Business-Friendliness" and "Hispanic Purchasing Power," to arrive at the most favorable conditions for Hispanic entrepreneurs. Baltimore was ranked #133 out of 182. Criteria includes: share of Hispanic-Owned Businesses; average growth of Hispanic Business revenues; Small Business-Friendliness score; affordability; and number of Hispanics with at least a bachelor's degree. *WalletHub.com, "Best Cities for Hispanic Entrepreneurs," September 4, 2024*

Miscellaneous Rankings

- *WalletHub* compared 148 of the most populated U.S. cities to determine their operating efficiency. A "Quality of Services" score was constructed for each city and then measured against the total budget per capita to reveal which were managed the best. Baltimore ranked #126. Criteria: financial stability; economy; education; safety; health; infrastructure and pollution. *WalletHub.com, "2025's Best- & Worst-Run Cities in America," June 18, 2024*

Business Environment

DEMOGRAPHICS

Population Growth

Area	1990 Census	2000 Census	2010 Census	2020 Census	2023 Estimate[2]	Population Growth 1990-2023 (%)
City	736,014	651,154	620,961	585,708	577,193	-21.6
MSA[1]	2,382,172	2,552,994	2,710,489	2,844,510	2,839,409	19.2
U.S.	248,709,873	281,421,906	308,745,538	331,449,281	332,387,540	33.6

Note: (1) Figures cover the Baltimore-Columbia-Towson, MD Metropolitan Statistical Area; (2) 2019-2023 5-year ACS population estimate
Source: U.S. Census Bureau, 1990 Census, 2000 Census, 2010 Census, 2020 Census, 2019-2023 American Community Survey 5-Year Estimates

Race

Area	White Alone[2] (%)	Black Alone[2] (%)	Asian Alone[2] (%)	AIAN[3] Alone[2] (%)	NHOPI[4] Alone[2] (%)	Other Race Alone[2] (%)	Two or More Races (%)
City	27.4	60.0	2.5	0.4	0.0	4.4	5.2
MSA[1]	54.8	29.0	5.8	0.3	0.0	3.6	6.4
U.S.	63.4	12.4	5.8	0.9	0.2	6.6	10.7

Note: (1) Figures cover the Baltimore-Columbia-Towson, MD Metropolitan Statistical Area; (2) Alone is defined as not being in combination with one or more other races; (3) American Indian and Alaska Native; (4) Native Hawaiian and Other Pacific Islander
Source: U.S. Census Bureau, 2019-2023 American Community Survey 5-Year Estimates

Hispanic or Latino Origin

Area	Total (%)	Mexican (%)	Puerto Rican (%)	Cuban (%)	Other (%)
City	7.9	1.6	1.0	0.4	4.8
MSA[1]	7.8	1.6	1.2	0.3	4.7
U.S.	19.0	11.3	1.8	0.7	5.2

Note: Persons of Hispanic or Latino origin can be of any race; (1) Figures cover the Baltimore-Columbia-Towson, MD Metropolitan Statistical Area
Source: U.S. Census Bureau, 2019-2023 American Community Survey 5-Year Estimates

Age

Area	Under Age 5	Age 5–19	Age 20–34	Age 35–44	Age 45–54	Age 55–64	Age 65–74	Age 75–84	Age 85+	Median Age
City	6.1	17.5	24.5	13.7	10.7	12.5	9.3	4.0	1.6	36.1
MSA[1]	5.8	18.8	19.8	13.5	12.3	13.4	9.7	4.7	1.9	38.9
U.S.	5.7	19.1	20.2	13.1	12.3	12.8	10.0	4.9	1.9	38.7

Note: (1) Figures cover the Baltimore-Columbia-Towson, MD Metropolitan Statistical Area
Source: U.S. Census Bureau, 2019-2023 American Community Survey 5-Year Estimates

Disability by Age

Area	All Ages	Under 18 Years Old	18 to 64 Years Old	65 Years and Over
City	16.5	5.7	14.6	40.0
MSA[1]	12.0	4.5	9.8	30.7
U.S.	13.0	4.7	10.7	32.9

Note: Figures show percent of the civilian noninstitutionalized population that reported having a disability. Disability status is determined from six types of difficulty: vision, hearing, cognitive, ambulatory, self-care, and independent living. For children under 5 years old, hearing and vision difficulty are used to determine disability status. For children between the ages of 5 and 14, disability status is determined from hearing, vision, cognitive, ambulatory, and self-care difficulties. For people aged 15 years and older, they are considered to have a disability if they have difficulty with any one of the six difficulty types; Note: (1) Figures cover the Baltimore-Columbia-Towson, MD Metropolitan Statistical Area
Source: U.S. Census Bureau, 2019-2023 American Community Survey 5-Year Estimates

Ancestry

Area	German	Irish	English	American	Italian	Polish	French[2]	European	Scottish
City	5.8	5.7	3.7	2.7	2.9	2.0	0.9	0.7	0.7
MSA[1]	13.7	10.9	8.6	4.4	5.5	3.6	1.3	1.4	1.4
U.S.	12.6	9.4	9.1	5.5	4.9	2.6	2.0	1.6	1.6

Note: Figures are the percentage of the total population reporting a particular ancestry. The nine most commonly reported ancestries in the U.S. are shown. Figures include multiple ancestries (e.g. if a person reported being Irish and Italian, they were included in both columns); (1) Figures cover the Baltimore-Columbia-Towson, MD Metropolitan Statistical Area; (2) Excludes Basque
Source: U.S. Census Bureau, 2019-2023 American Community Survey 5-Year Estimates

Foreign-born Population

Area	Percent of Population Born in								
	Any Foreign Country	Asia	Mexico	Europe	Caribbean	Central America[2]	South America	Africa	Canada
City	8.8	2.1	0.4	0.9	1.3	1.6	0.6	1.7	0.1
MSA[1]	11.2	4.4	0.4	1.2	0.8	1.5	0.7	2.1	0.1
U.S.	13.9	4.3	3.3	1.4	1.4	1.2	1.2	0.8	0.2

Note: (1) Figures cover the Baltimore-Columbia-Towson, MD Metropolitan Statistical Area; (2) Excludes Mexico.
Source: U.S. Census Bureau, 2019-2023 American Community Survey 5-Year Estimates

Household Size

Area	Persons in Household (%)							Average Household Size
	One	Two	Three	Four	Five	Six	Seven or More	
City	43.4	29.6	13.4	7.7	3.7	1.3	1.0	2.22
MSA[1]	30.0	32.8	15.7	13.0	5.3	2.1	1.2	2.51
U.S.	28.5	33.8	15.4	12.7	5.9	2.3	1.4	2.54

Note: (1) Figures cover the Baltimore-Columbia-Towson, MD Metropolitan Statistical Area
Source: U.S. Census Bureau, 2019-2023 American Community Survey 5-Year Estimates

Household Relationships

Area	Householder	Opposite-sex Spouse	Same-sex Spouse	Opposite-sex Unmarried Partner	Same-sex Unmarried Partner	Child[2]	Grandchild	Other Relatives	Non-relatives
City	42.9	9.6	0.3	3.3	0.3	24.9	3.7	5.8	6.1
MSA[1]	38.7	16.8	0.2	2.4	0.2	28.7	2.5	4.8	3.5
U.S.	38.3	17.5	0.2	2.5	0.2	28.3	2.4	4.8	3.4

Note: Figures are percent of the total population; (1) Figures cover the Baltimore-Columbia-Towson, MD Metropolitan Statistical Area; (2) Includes biological, adopted, and stepchildren of the householder
Source: U.S. Census Bureau, 2020 Census

Gender

Area	Males	Females	Males per 100 Females
City	268,932	308,261	87.2
MSA[1]	1,371,348	1,468,061	93.4
U.S.	164,545,087	167,842,453	98.0

Note: (1) Figures cover the Baltimore-Columbia-Towson, MD Metropolitan Statistical Area
Source: U.S. Census Bureau, 2019-2023 American Community Survey 5-Year Estimates

Marital Status

Area	Never Married	Now Married[2]	Separated	Widowed	Divorced
City	52.7	27.1	2.9	5.9	11.4
MSA[1]	36.4	46.2	1.8	5.7	9.9
U.S.	34.1	47.9	1.7	5.6	10.7

Note: Figures are percentages and cover the population 15 years of age and older; (1) Figures cover the Baltimore-Columbia-Towson, MD Metropolitan Statistical Area; (2) Excludes separated
Source: U.S. Census Bureau, 2019-2023 American Community Survey 5-Year Estimates

Religious Groups by Family

Area	Catholic	Baptist	Methodist	LDS[2]	Pentecostal	Lutheran	Islam	Adventist	Other
MSA[1]	12.4	3.2	4.4	0.6	1.2	1.4	3.3	1.2	11.7
U.S.	18.7	7.3	3.0	2.0	1.8	1.7	1.3	1.3	11.6

Note: Figures are the number of adherents as a percentage of the total population and cover the eight largest religious groups in the U.S; (1) Figures cover the Baltimore-Columbia-Towson, MD Metropolitan Statistical Area; (2) Church of Jesus Christ of Latter-day Saints
Sources: 2020 U.S. Religion Census, Association of Statisticians of American Religious Bodies; The Association of Religion Data Archives (ARDA)

Religious Groups by Tradition

Area	Catholic	Evangelical Protestant	Mainline Protestant	Black Protestant	Islam	Judaism	Hinduism	Orthodox	Buddhism
MSA[1]	12.4	10.6	5.9	3.3	3.3	1.7	0.1	0.5	0.1
U.S.	18.7	16.5	5.2	2.3	1.3	0.6	0.4	0.4	0.3

Note: Figures are the number of adherents as a percentage of the total population; (1) Figures cover the Baltimore-Columbia-Towson, MD Metropolitan Statistical Area
Sources: 2020 U.S. Religion Census, Association of Statisticians of American Religious Bodies; The Association of Religion Data Archives (ARDA)

ECONOMY

Real Gross Domestic Product (GDP)

Area	2017	2018	2019	2020	2021	2022	2023	Rank[3]
MSA[1]	198.3	200.4	201.6	194.8	204.8	210.2	213.5	19
U.S.[2]	17,619.1	18,160.7	18,642.5	18,238.9	19,387.6	19,896.6	20,436.3	—

Note: Figures are in billions of chained 2017 dollars; (1) Figures cover the Baltimore-Columbia-Towson, MD Metropolitan Statistical Area; (2) Figures cover real GDP within metropolitan areas; (3) Rank is based on 2023 data and ranges from 1 to 384
Source: U.S. Bureau of Economic Analysis

Economic Growth

Area	2014	2015	2016	2017	2018	2019	2020	2021	2022	2023
MSA[1]	1.6	2.0	3.4	2.1	1.0	0.6	-3.4	5.1	2.6	1.6
U.S.[2]	2.6	3.2	2.0	2.7	3.1	2.7	-2.2	6.3	2.6	2.7

Note: Figures are real gross domestic product growth rates and represent percent change from preceding period; (1) Figures cover the Baltimore-Columbia-Towson, MD Metropolitan Statistical Area; (2) Figures are the average growth rates within metropolitan areas
Source: U.S. Bureau of Economic Analysis

Metropolitan Area Exports

Area	2018	2019	2020	2021	2022	2023	Rank[2]
MSA[1]	6,039.2	7,081.8	6,084.6	8,200.6	7,820.0	10,196.2	43
U.S.	1,664,056.1	1,645,173.7	1,431,406.6	1,753,941.4	2,062,937.4	2,019,160.5	—

Note: Figures are in millions of dollars; (1) Figures cover the Baltimore-Columbia-Towson, MD Metropolitan Statistical Area; (2) Rank is based on 2023 data and ranges from 1 to 386
Source: U.S. Department of Commerce, International Trade Administration, Office of Trade and Economic Analysis, Industry and Analysis, Exports by Metropolitan Area, data extracted April 2, 2025

Building Permits

Area	Single-Family			Multi-Family			Total		
	2023	2024	Pct. Chg.	2023	2024	Pct. Chg.	2023	2024	Pct. Chg.
City	92	165	79.3	1,751	1,108	-36.7	1,843	1,273	-30.9
MSA[1]	3,798	3,849	1.3	3,741	2,435	-34.9	7,539	6,284	-16.6
U.S.	920,000	981,900	6.7	591,100	496,100	-16.1	1,511,100	1,478,000	-2.2

Note: (1) Figures cover the Baltimore-Columbia-Towson, MD Metropolitan Statistical Area; Figures represent new, privately-owned housing units authorized (unadjusted data)
Source: U.S. Census Bureau, Building Permits Survey (BPS), 2023, 2024

Bankruptcy Filings

Area	Business Filings			Nonbusiness Filings		
	2023	2024	% Chg.	2023	2024	% Chg.
Baltimore city County	35	43	22.9	1,502	1,656	10.3
U.S.	18,926	23,107	22.1	434,064	494,201	13.9

Note: Business filings include Chapter 7, Chapter 9, Chapter 11, Chapter 12, Chapter 13, Chapter 15, and Section 304; Nonbusiness filings include Chapter 7, Chapter 11, and Chapter 13
Source: Administrative Office of the U.S. Courts, Business and Nonbusiness Bankruptcy, County Cases Commenced by Chapter of the Bankruptcy Code, During the 12-Month Period Ending December 31, 2023 and Business and Nonbusiness Bankruptcy, County Cases Commenced by Chapter of the Bankruptcy Code, During the 12-Month Period Ending December 31, 2024

Housing Vacancy Rates

Area	Gross Vacancy Rate[3] (%)			Year-Round Vacancy Rate[4] (%)			Rental Vacancy Rate[5] (%)			Homeowner Vacancy Rate[6] (%)		
	2022	2023	2024	2022	2023	2024	2022	2023	2024	2022	2023	2024
MSA[1]	5.9	6.6	7.0	5.7	6.5	6.5	5.3	9.4	6.1	0.5	0.6	0.9
U.S.[2]	9.1	9.0	9.1	7.5	7.5	7.6	5.7	6.5	6.8	0.8	0.8	1.0

Note: (1) Figures cover the Baltimore-Columbia-Towson, MD Metropolitan Statistical Area; (2) Figures cover the 75 largest Metropolitan Statistical Areas; (3) The percentage of the total housing inventory that is vacant; (4) The percentage of the housing inventory (excluding seasonal units) that is year-round vacant; (5) The percentage of rental inventory that is vacant for rent; (6) The percentage of homeowner inventory that is vacant for sale
Source: U.S. Census Bureau, Housing Vacancies and Homeownership Annual Statistics: 2022, 2023, 2024

INCOME

Income

Area	Per Capita ($)	Median Household ($)	Average Household ($)
City	39,195	59,623	87,339
MSA[1]	51,146	97,300	128,719
U.S.	43,289	78,538	110,491

Note: (1) Figures cover the Baltimore-Columbia-Towson, MD Metropolitan Statistical Area
Source: U.S. Census Bureau, 2019-2023 American Community Survey 5-Year Estimates

Household Income Distribution

Area	Percent of Households Earning							
	Under $15,000	$15,000 -$24,999	$25,000 -$34,999	$35,000 -$49,999	$50,000 -$74,999	$75,000 -$99,999	$100,000 -$149,999	$150,000 and up
City	15.7	8.4	7.4	11.4	16.6	11.3	13.5	15.7
MSA[1]	7.6	4.9	5.0	8.3	13.3	12.0	18.8	30.1
U.S.	8.5	6.6	6.8	10.4	15.7	12.7	17.4	21.9

Note: (1) Figures cover the Baltimore-Columbia-Towson, MD Metropolitan Statistical Area
Source: U.S. Census Bureau, 2019-2023 American Community Survey 5-Year Estimates

Poverty Rate

Area	All Ages	Under 18 Years Old	18 to 64 Years Old	65 Years and Over
City	20.1	26.4	17.8	20.9
MSA[1]	9.9	12.0	9.0	10.2
U.S.	12.4	16.3	11.6	10.4

Note: Figures are percentage of people whose income during the past 12 months was below the poverty level;
(1) Figures cover the Baltimore-Columbia-Towson, MD Metropolitan Statistical Area
Source: U.S. Census Bureau, 2019-2023 American Community Survey 5-Year Estimates

EMPLOYMENT

Labor Force and Employment

Area	Civilian Labor Force			Workers Employed		
	Dec. 2023	Dec. 2024	% Chg.	Dec. 2023	Dec. 2024	% Chg.
City	276,136	279,771	1.3	267,011	268,805	0.7
MSA[1]	1,496,175	1,509,109	0.9	1,460,563	1,468,370	0.5
U.S.	166,661,000	167,746,000	0.7	160,754,000	161,294,000	0.3

Note: Data is not seasonally adjusted and covers workers 16 years of age and older; (1) Figures cover the Baltimore-Columbia-Towson, MD Metropolitan Statistical Area
Source: Bureau of Labor Statistics, Local Area Unemployment Statistics

Unemployment Rate

Area	2024											
	Jan.	Feb.	Mar.	Apr.	May	Jun.	Jul.	Aug.	Sep.	Oct.	Nov.	Dec.
City	4.2	4.2	4.0	3.6	3.8	4.5	4.8	4.8	4.0	4.3	4.2	3.9
MSA[1]	3.0	3.1	2.9	2.5	2.7	3.4	3.5	3.5	2.9	3.1	3.0	2.7
U.S.	4.1	4.2	3.9	3.5	3.7	4.3	4.5	4.4	3.9	3.9	4.0	3.8

Note: Data is not seasonally adjusted and covers workers 16 years of age and older; (1) Figures cover the Baltimore-Columbia-Towson, MD Metropolitan Statistical Area
Source: Bureau of Labor Statistics, Local Area Unemployment Statistics

Average Wages

Occupation	$/Hr.	Occupation	$/Hr.
Accountants and Auditors	44.96	Maintenance and Repair Workers	25.58
Automotive Mechanics	27.65	Marketing Managers	76.43
Bookkeepers	26.87	Network and Computer Systems Admin.	60.34
Carpenters	28.13	Nurses, Licensed Practical	34.04
Cashiers	16.18	Nurses, Registered	46.70
Computer Programmers	52.85	Nursing Assistants	20.15
Computer Systems Analysts	56.04	Office Clerks, General	22.45
Computer User Support Specialists	33.50	Physical Therapists	50.65
Construction Laborers	22.42	Physicians	111.79
Cooks, Restaurant	18.38	Plumbers, Pipefitters and Steamfitters	32.84
Customer Service Representatives	21.60	Police and Sheriff's Patrol Officers	38.57
Dentists	108.70	Postal Service Mail Carriers	28.82
Electricians	33.58	Real Estate Sales Agents	27.82
Engineers, Electrical	59.60	Retail Salespersons	17.59
Fast Food and Counter Workers	15.89	Sales Representatives, Technical/Scientific	44.15
Financial Managers	80.29	Secretaries, Exc. Legal/Medical/Executive	23.24
First-Line Supervisors of Office Workers	35.89	Security Guards	20.69
General and Operations Managers	61.48	Surgeons	171.05
Hairdressers/Cosmetologists	20.61	Teacher Assistants, Exc. Postsecondary[1]	18.88
Home Health and Personal Care Aides	18.43	Teachers, Secondary School, Exc. Sp. Ed.[1]	36.16
Janitors and Cleaners	18.03	Telemarketers	16.80
Landscaping/Groundskeeping Workers	19.36	Truck Drivers, Heavy/Tractor-Trailer	28.16
Lawyers	76.50	Truck Drivers, Light/Delivery Services	23.74
Maids and Housekeeping Cleaners	16.48	Waiters and Waitresses	19.68

Note: Wage data covers the Baltimore-Columbia-Towson, MD Metropolitan Statistical Area; (1) Hourly wages were calculated from annual wage data based on a 40 hour work week
Source: Bureau of Labor Statistics, Metro Area Occupational Employment & Wage Estimates, May 2024

Employment by Industry

Sector	MSA[1] Number of Employees	MSA[1] Percent of Total	U.S. Percent of Total
Construction, Mining, and Logging	79,500	5.4	5.5
Financial Activities	78,500	5.3	5.8
Government	244,400	16.6	14.9
Information	15,500	1.1	1.9
Leisure and Hospitality	123,800	8.4	10.4
Manufacturing	57,800	3.9	8.0
Other Services	54,700	3.7	3.7
Private Education and Health Services	294,000	20.0	16.9
Professional and Business Services	256,700	17.5	14.2
Retail Trade	132,300	9.0	10.0
Transportation, Warehousing, and Utilities	77,700	5.3	4.8
Wholesale Trade	53,700	3.7	3.9

Note: Figures are non-farm employment as of December 2024. Figures are not seasonally adjusted and include workers 16 years of age and older; (1) Figures cover the Baltimore-Columbia-Towson, MD Metropolitan Statistical Area
Source: Bureau of Labor Statistics, Current Employment Statistics, Employment, Hours, and Earnings

Employment by Occupation

Occupation Classification	City (%)	MSA[1] (%)	U.S. (%)
Management, Business, Science, and Arts	47.8	51.1	42.0
Natural Resources, Construction, and Maintenance	5.3	6.5	8.6
Production, Transportation, and Material Moving	11.4	9.3	13.0
Sales and Office	17.7	18.4	19.9
Service	17.8	14.6	16.5

Note: Figures cover employed civilians 16 years of age and older; (1) Figures cover the Baltimore-Columbia-Towson, MD Metropolitan Statistical Area
Source: U.S. Census Bureau, 2019-2023 American Community Survey 5-Year Estimates

Occupations with Greatest Projected Employment Growth: 2022 – 2032

Occupation[1]	2022 Employment	2032 Projected Employment	Numeric Employment Change	Percent Employment Change
Software Developers	34,970	45,890	10,920	31.2
General and Operations Managers	97,400	105,980	8,580	8.8
Home Health and Personal Care Aides	32,420	38,640	6,220	19.2
Cooks, Restaurant	20,110	25,450	5,340	26.6
Medical and Health Services Managers	15,250	19,840	4,590	30.1
Computer Occupations, All Other (SOC 2018)	22,760	26,980	4,220	18.5
Management Analysts	25,390	29,400	4,010	15.8
Project Management Specialists	36,080	40,000	3,920	10.9
Information Security Analysts (SOC 2018)	9,290	12,900	3,610	38.9
Stockers and Order Fillers	44,940	48,550	3,610	8.0

Note: Projections cover Maryland; (1) Sorted by numeric employment change
Source: www.projectionscentral.org, State Occupational Projections, 2022–2032 Long-Term Projections

Fastest-Growing Occupations: 2022 – 2032

Occupation[1]	2022 Employment	2032 Projected Employment	Numeric Employment Change	Percent Employment Change
Nurse Practitioners	5,240	7,450	2,210	42.2
Data Scientists	2,400	3,340	940	39.2
Information Security Analysts (SOC 2018)	9,290	12,900	3,610	38.9
Solar Photovoltaic Installers	660	900	240	36.4
Epidemiologists	500	670	170	34.0
Software Developers	34,970	45,890	10,920	31.2
Statisticians	3,060	4,010	950	31.0
Health Specialties Teachers, Postsecondary	9,280	12,130	2,850	30.7
Physical Therapist Assistants	1,880	2,450	570	30.3
Medical and Health Services Managers	15,250	19,840	4,590	30.1

Note: Projections cover Maryland; (1) Sorted by percent employment change and excludes occupations with numeric employment change less than 50
Source: www.projectionscentral.org, State Occupational Projections, 2022–2032 Long-Term Projections

CITY FINANCES

City Government Finances

Component	2022 ($000)	2022 ($ per capita)
Total Revenues	4,746,975	8,099
Total Expenditures	4,760,470	8,122
Debt Outstanding	4,354,835	7,430

Source: U.S. Census Bureau, State & Local Government Finances 2022

City Government Revenue by Source

Source	2022 ($000)	2022 ($ per capita)	2022 (%)
General Revenue			
From Federal Government	280,109	478	5.9
From State Government	1,230,473	2,099	25.9
From Local Governments	49,909	85	1.1
Taxes			
Property	1,061,193	1,811	22.4
Sales and Gross Receipts	175,463	299	3.7
Personal Income	491,092	838	10.3
Corporate Income	0	0	0.0
Motor Vehicle License	0	0	0.0
Other Taxes	210,335	359	4.4
Current Charges	526,262	898	11.1
Liquor Store	0	0	0.0
Utility	278,280	475	5.9

Source: U.S. Census Bureau, State & Local Government Finances 2022

City Government Expenditures by Function

Function	2022 ($000)	2022 ($ per capita)	2022 (%)
General Direct Expenditures			
Air Transportation	0	0	0.0
Corrections	0	0	0.0
Education	1,823,117	3,110	38.3
Employment Security Administration	0	0	0.0
Financial Administration	87,804	149	1.8
Fire Protection	351,425	599	7.4
General Public Buildings	1,679	2	0.0
Governmental Administration, Other	148,274	253	3.1
Health	190,953	325	4.0
Highways	99,403	169	2.1
Hospitals	0	0	0.0
Housing and Community Development	73,231	124	1.5
Interest on General Debt	36,868	62	0.8
Judicial and Legal	173,790	296	3.7
Libraries	27,282	46	0.6
Parking	7,692	13	0.2
Parks and Recreation	90,395	154	1.9
Police Protection	464,261	792	9.8
Public Welfare	3,065	5	0.1
Sewerage	296,260	505	6.2
Solid Waste Management	97,834	166	2.1
Veterans' Services	0	0	0.0
Liquor Store	0	0	0.0
Utility	264,334	451	5.6

Source: U.S. Census Bureau, State & Local Government Finances 2022

TAXES

State Corporate Income Tax Rates

State	Tax Rate (%)	Income Brackets ($)	Num. of Brackets	Financial Institution Tax Rate (%)[a]	Federal Income Tax Ded.
Maryland	8.25	Flat rate	1	8.25	No

Note: Tax rates for tax year 2024; (a) Rates listed are the corporate income tax rate applied to financial institutions or excise taxes based on income. Some states have other taxes based upon the value of deposits or shares.

Source: Federation of Tax Administrators, State Corporate Income Tax Rates, January 1, 2025

State Individual Income Tax Rates

State	Tax Rate (%)	Income Brackets ($)	Personal Exemptions ($)			Standard Ded. ($)	
			Single	Married	Depend.	Single	Married
Maryland	2.0 - 5.75	1,000 - 250,000 (l)	3,200	6,400	3,200	2,550	5,150 (aa)

Note: Tax rates for tax year 2024; Local- and county-level taxes are not included; Federal income tax is not deductible on state income tax returns; (l) The income brackets reported for Maryland are for single individuals. For married couples filing jointly, the same tax rates apply to income brackets ranging from $1,000, to $300,000; (aa) Standard deduction amounts reported are maximums, Maryland standard deduction is 15% of AGI with an increased deduction above $17,000 - S/$34,333 - MFJ in 2023; Montana, 20% of AGI.
Source: Federation of Tax Administrators, State Individual Income Tax Rates, January 1, 2025

Various State Sales and Excise Tax Rates

State	State Sales Tax (%)	Gasoline[1] ($/gal.)	Cigarette[2] ($/pack)	Spirits[3] ($/gal.)	Wine[4] ($/gal.)	Beer[5] ($/gal.)	Recreational Marijuana (%)
Maryland	6	0.46	5.00	5.46	1.64	0.60	(i)

Note: All tax rates as of January 1, 2025; (1) The American Petroleum Institute has developed a methodology for determining the average tax rate on a gallon of fuel. Rates may include any of the following: excise taxes, environmental fees, storage tank fees, other fees or taxes, general sales tax, and local taxes; (2) The federal excise tax of $1.0066 per pack and local taxes are not included; (3) Rates are those applicable to off-premise sales of 40% alcohol by volume (a.b.v.) distilled spirits in 750ml containers. Local excise taxes are excluded; (4) Rates are those applicable to off-premise sales of 11% a.b.v. non-carbonated wine in 750ml containers; (5) Rates are those applicable to off-premise sales of 4.7% a.b.v. beer in 12 ounce containers; (i) 9% excise tax (retail price)
Source: Tax Foundation, 2025 Facts & Figures: How Does Your State Compare?

State Tax Competitiveness Index

State	Overall Rank	Corporate Tax Rank	Individual Income Tax Rank	Sales Tax Rank	Property Tax Rank	Unemployment Insurance Tax Rank
Maryland	46	37	45	39	35	20

Note: The Tax Foundation's State Tax Competitiveness Index enables policymakers, taxpayers, and business leaders to gauge how their states' tax systems compare. A rank of 1 is best, 50 is worst. Rankings do not average to the total. States without a tax rank equally as 1. DC's scores and rankings do not affect other states. The report shows tax systems as of July 1, 2024 (the beginning of Fiscal Year 2025).
Source: Tax Foundation, State Tax Competitiveness Index 2025

TRANSPORTATION

Means of Transportation to Work

Area	Car/Truck/Van		Public Transportation			Bicycle	Walked	Other Means	Worked at Home
	Drove Alone	Car-pooled	Bus	Subway	Railroad				
City	56.8	6.9	9.3	1.0	0.8	0.6	5.6	3.1	15.9
MSA[1]	69.2	6.9	2.7	0.5	0.5	0.2	2.2	1.6	16.1
U.S.	70.2	8.5	1.7	1.3	0.4	0.4	2.4	1.6	13.5

Note: Figures are percentages and cover workers 16 years of age and older; (1) Figures cover the Baltimore-Columbia-Towson, MD Metropolitan Statistical Area
Source: U.S. Census Bureau, 2019-2023 American Community Survey 5-Year Estimates

Travel Time to Work

Area	Less Than 10 Minutes	10 to 19 Minutes	20 to 29 Minutes	30 to 44 Minutes	45 to 59 Minutes	60 to 89 Minutes	90 Minutes or More
City	7.2	24.8	24.3	24.3	8.5	6.9	4.0
MSA[1]	8.2	24.1	21.7	24.6	10.7	7.5	3.1
U.S.	12.6	28.6	21.2	20.8	8.1	6.0	2.8

Note: Note: Figures are percentages and include workers 16 years old and over; (1) Figures cover the Baltimore-Columbia-Towson, MD Metropolitan Statistical Area
Source: U.S. Census Bureau, 2019-2023 American Community Survey 5-Year Estimates

Key Congestion Measures

Measure	2000	2010	2015	2020	2022
Annual Hours of Delay, Total (000)	55,157	75,705	88,266	44,292	83,763
Annual Hours of Delay, Per Auto Commuter	41	47	55	27	54
Annual Congestion Cost, Per Auto Commuter ($)	963	1,051	1,133	614	1,145

Note: Figures cover the Baltimore MD urban area
Source: Texas A&M Transportation Institute, 2023 Urban Mobility Report

Freeway Travel Time Index

Measure	1985	1990	1995	2000	2005	2010	2015	2020	2022
Urban Area Index[1]	1.12	1.17	1.20	1.23	1.26	1.24	1.25	1.07	1.19
Urban Area Rank[1,2]	21	17	21	22	22	24	24	57	37

Note: Freeway Travel Time Index—the ratio of travel time in the peak period to the travel time at free-flow conditions. For example, a value of 1.30 indicates a 20-minute free-flow trip takes 26 minutes in the peak (20 minutes x 1.30 = 26 minutes); (1) Covers the Baltimore MD urban area; (2) Rank is based on 101 larger urban areas (#1 = highest travel time index)
Source: Texas A&M Transportation Institute, 2023 Urban Mobility Report

Public Transportation

Agency Name / Mode of Transportation	Vehicles Operated in Maximum Service[1]	Annual Unlinked Passenger Trips[2] (in thous.)	Annual Passenger Miles[3] (in thous.)
Maryland Transit Administration (MTA)			
Bus (directly operated)	642	45,734.0	183,667.6
Commuter Bus (purchased transportation)	92	1,188.4	22,143.9
Commuter Rail (purchased transportation)	149	3,376.8	93,614.7
Demand Response (directly operated)	11	11.7	128.7
Demand Response (purchased transportation)	457	1,911.2	18,622.0
Demand Response - Taxi	142	494.5	2,994.0
Heavy Rail (directly operated)	40	1,756.1	6,650.2
Light Rail (directly operated)	17	3,434.2	15,385.7

Note: (1) Number of revenue vehicles operated by the given mode and type of service to meet the annual maximum service requirement. This is the revenue vehicle count during the peak season of the year; on the week and day that maximum service is provided. Vehicles operated in maximum service (VOMS) exclude atypical days and one-time special events; (2) Number of passengers who boarded public transportation vehicles. Passengers are counted each time they board a vehicle no matter how many vehicles they use to travel from their origin to their destination. (3) Sum of the distances ridden by all passengers during the entire fiscal year.
Source: Federal Transit Administration, National Transit Database, 2023

Air Transportation

Airport Name and Code / Type of Service	Passenger Airlines[1]	Passenger Enplanements	Freight Carriers[2]	Freight (lbs)
Baltimore-Washington International (BWI)				
Domestic service (U.S. carriers only)	30	12,605,406	14	230,542,103
International service (U.S. carriers only)	9	384,136	3	309,343

Note: (1) Includes all U.S.-based major, minor and commuter airlines that carried at least one passenger during the year; (2) Includes all U.S.-based airlines and freight carriers that transported at least one pound of freight during the year.
Source: Bureau of Transportation Statistics, The Intermodal Transportation Database, Air Carriers: T-100 Domestic Market (U.S. carriers only), 2024; Bureau of Transportation Statistics, The Intermodal Transportation Database, Air Carriers: T-100 International Market (U.S. carriers only), 2024

BUSINESSES

Major Business Headquarters

Company Name	Industry	Rankings	
		Fortune[1]	Forbes[2]
Constellation Energy	Energy	165	-
Whiting-Turner Contracting	Construction	-	41

Note: (1) Companies that produce a 10-K are ranked 1 to 500 based on 2023 revenue; (2) All private companies with at least $2 billion in annual revenue through the end of their most current fiscal year are ranked 1 to 275; companies listed are headquartered in the city; dashes indicate no ranking
Source: Fortune, "Fortune 500," 2024; Forbes, "America's Largest Private Companies," 2024

Fastest-Growing Businesses

According to *Inc.*, Baltimore is home to one of America's 500 fastest-growing private companies: **Dobbs Defense Solutions** (#376). Criteria: must be an independent, privately-held, for-profit, U.S. corporation, proprietorship or partnership as of December 31, 2023; revenues must be at least $100,000 in 2020 and $2 million in 2023; must have four-year operating/sales history. *Inc., "America's 500 Fastest-Growing Private Companies," 2024*

According to *Initiative for a Competitive Inner City (ICIC)*, Baltimore is home to 10 of America's 100 fastest-growing "inner city" companies: **SCB Management Solutions Inc.** (#10); **Veltrust** (#11); **Maryland Energy Advisors** (#21); **Ease Painting And Construction** (#56); **Watkins Security Agency** (#66); **Nyla Technology Solutions** (#67); **All Pro Vending dba All Staffed Up** (#73); **Omni Strategy** (#78); **Lighting and Supplies** (#87); **AFRO American Newspapers** (#94). To be eligible for the IC100, companies have to be independently operated, privately held, for-profit businesses with revenues of at least $50,000 in 2019 and $500,000 in 2023, and headquartered in an under-resourced community. Recognizing that concentrated poverty exists within metropolitan areas outside of big cities (and that poverty overall is suburbanizing), ICIC defines under-resourced communities as large low-income, high-poverty areas located in the urban and suburban parts of all but the smallest metropolitan areas. Companies were ranked overall by revenue growth over the five-year period between 2019 and 2023. *Initiative for a Competitive Inner City (ICIC), "Inner City 100 Companies," 2024*

Living Environment

COST OF LIVING

Cost of Living Index

Composite Index	Groceries	Housing	Utilities	Transportation	Health Care	Misc. Goods/Services
100.5	102.8	86.5	110.6	104.2	94.2	108.4

Note: The Cost of Living Index measures regional differences in the cost of consumer goods and services, excluding taxes and non-consumer expenditures, for professional and managerial households in the top income quintile. It is based on more than 50,000 prices covering almost 60 different items for which prices are collected three times a year by chambers of commerce, economic development organizations or university applied economic centers in each participating urban area. The numbers shown should be read as a percentage above or below the national average of 100. For example, a value of 115.4 in the groceries column indicates that grocery prices are 15.4% higher than the national average. Small differences in the index numbers should not be interpreted as significant; Figures cover the Baltimore MD urban area.
Source: The Council for Community and Economic Research, Cost of Living Index, 2024

Grocery Prices

Area[1]	T-Bone Steak ($/pound)	Frying Chicken ($/pound)	Whole Milk ($/half gal.)	Eggs ($/dozen)	Orange Juice ($/64 oz.)	Coffee ($/11.5 oz.)
City[2]	15.52	1.44	4.64	3.35	4.34	5.56
Avg.	15.42	1.55	4.69	3.25	4.41	5.46
Min.	14.50	1.16	4.43	2.75	4.00	4.85
Max.	17.56	2.89	5.49	4.78	5.54	7.89

Note: (1) Values for the local area are compared with the average, minimum and maximum values for all 276 areas in the Cost of Living Index; (2) Figures cover the Baltimore MD urban area; **T-Bone Steak** (price per pound); **Frying Chicken** (price per pound, whole fryer); **Whole Milk** (half gallon carton); **Eggs** (price per dozen, Grade A, large); **Orange Juice** (64 oz. Tropicana or Florida Natural); **Coffee** (11.5 oz. can, vacuum-packed, Maxwell House, Hills Bros, or Folgers).
Source: The Council for Community and Economic Research, Cost of Living Index, 2024

Housing and Utility Costs

Area[1]	New Home Price ($)	Apartment Rent ($/month)	All Electric ($/month)	Part Electric ($/month)	Other Energy ($/month)	Telephone ($/month)
City[2]	390,678	1,695	-	134.88	101.43	201.97
Avg.	515,975	1,550	210.99	123.07	82.07	194.99
Min.	265,375	692	104.33	53.68	36.26	179.42
Max.	2,775,821	5,719	529.02	397.28	361.63	223.33

Note: (1) Values for the local area are compared with the average, minimum and maximum values for all 276 areas in the Cost of Living Index; (2) Figures cover the Baltimore MD urban area; **New Home Price** (2,400 sf living area, 8,000 sf lot, in urban area with full utilities); **Apartment Rent** (950 sf 2 bedroom/1.5 or 2 bath, unfurnished, excluding all utilities except water); **All Electric** (average monthly cost for an all-electric home); **Part Electric** (average monthly cost for a part-electric home); **Other Energy** (average monthly cost for natural gas, fuel oil, coal, wood, and any other forms of energy except electricity); **Telephone** (price includes the base monthly rate plus taxes and fees for three lines of mobile phone service).
Source: The Council for Community and Economic Research, Cost of Living Index, 2024

Health Care, Transportation, and Other Costs

Area[1]	Doctor ($/visit)	Dentist ($/visit)	Optometrist ($/visit)	Gasoline ($/gallon)	Beauty Salon ($/visit)	Men's Shirt ($)
City[2]	135.14	116.91	119.20	3.41	61.43	41.00
Avg.	143.77	117.51	129.23	3.32	48.57	38.14
Min.	36.74	58.67	67.33	2.80	24.00	13.41
Max.	270.44	216.82	307.33	5.28	94.00	63.89

Note: (1) Values for the local area are compared with the average, minimum and maximum values for all 276 areas in the Cost of Living Index; (2) Figures cover the Baltimore MD urban area; **Doctor** (general practitioners routine exam of an established patient); **Dentist** (adult teeth cleaning and periodic oral examination); **Optometrist** (full vision eye exam for established adult patient); **Gasoline** (one gallon regular unleaded, national brand, including all taxes, cash price at self-service pump if available); **Beauty Salon** (woman's shampoo, trim, and blow-dry); **Men's Shirt** (cotton/polyester dress shirt, pinpoint weave, long sleeves).
Source: The Council for Community and Economic Research, Cost of Living Index, 2024

HOUSING

Homeownership Rate

Area	2017 (%)	2018 (%)	2019 (%)	2020 (%)	2021 (%)	2022 (%)	2023 (%)	2024 (%)
MSA[1]	67.5	63.5	66.5	70.7	67.5	70.4	72.9	70.0
U.S.	63.9	64.4	64.6	66.6	65.5	65.8	65.9	65.6

Note: (1) Figures cover the Baltimore-Columbia-Towson, MD Metropolitan Statistical Area
Source: U.S. Census Bureau, Housing Vacancies and Homeownership Annual Statistics: 2017-2024

House Price Index (HPI)

Area	National Ranking[2]	Quarterly Change (%)	One-Year Change (%)	Five-Year Change (%)	Since 1991Q1 (%)
MSA[1]	113	0.13	5.59	41.90	246.61
U.S.[3]	–	1.43	4.51	57.13	327.82

Note: The HPI is a weighted repeat sales index. It measures average price changes in repeat sales or refinancings on the same properties. This information is obtained by reviewing repeat mortgage transactions on single-family properties whose mortgages have been purchased or securitized by Fannie Mae or Freddie Mac since January 1975; (1) Figures cover the Baltimore-Columbia-Towson, MD Metropolitan Statistical Area; (2) Rankings are based on annual percentage change for all metro areas containing at least 15,000 transactions over the last 10 years and ranges from 1 to 241; (3) figures based on a weighted average of Census Division estimates using a seasonally adjusted, purchase-only index; all figures are for the period ending December 31, 2024
Source: Federal Housing Finance Agency, Change in FHFA Metropolitan Area House Price Indexes, All Transactions Index, 2024Q4

Home Value

Area	Under $100,000	$100,000 -$199,999	$200,000 -$299,999	$300,000 -$399,999	$400,000 -$499,999	$500,000 -$999,999	$1,000,000 or more	Median ($)
City	15.5	28.6	26.5	13.5	6.5	7.8	1.5	219,300
MSA[1]	5.5	10.2	19.7	19.9	15.1	25.5	4.1	373,300
U.S.	12.1	17.8	19.5	14.4	10.5	19.1	6.5	303,400

Note: Figures are percentages except for median and cover owner-occupied housing units; (1) Figures cover the Baltimore-Columbia-Towson, MD Metropolitan Statistical Area
Source: U.S. Census Bureau, 2019-2023 American Community Survey 5-Year Estimates

Year Housing Structure Built

Area	2020 or Later	2010 -2019	2000 -2009	1990 -1999	1980 -1989	1970 -1979	1960 -1969	1950 -1959	1940 -1949	Before 1940	Median Year
City	0.3	4.3	4.1	4.1	4.6	5.8	8.6	15.3	11.6	41.1	1948
MSA[1]	0.6	7.2	9.6	13.0	13.4	12.8	10.3	12.4	6.0	14.6	1975
U.S.	1.2	8.9	13.6	12.8	13.0	14.4	10.0	9.7	4.5	11.9	1980

Note: Figures are percentages except for Median Year; Note: (1) Figures cover the Baltimore-Columbia-Towson, MD Metropolitan Statistical Area
Source: U.S. Census Bureau, 2019-2023 American Community Survey 5-Year Estimates

Gross Monthly Rent

Area	Under $500	$500 -$999	$1,000 -$1,499	$1,500 -$1,999	$2,000 -$2,499	$2,500 -$2,999	$3,000 and up	Median ($)
City	13.0	15.9	35.9	21.5	8.9	2.8	2.0	1,290
MSA[1]	6.9	10.5	29.1	28.1	15.8	5.6	3.9	1,562
U.S.	6.5	22.3	29.5	20.2	10.8	4.8	5.9	1,348

Note: Figures are percentages except for median; Gross rent is the contract rent plus the estimated average monthly cost of utilities (electricity, gas, and water and sewer) and fuels (oil, coal, kerosene, wood, etc.) if these are paid by the renter (or paid for the renter by someone else); (1) Figures cover the Baltimore-Columbia-Towson, MD Metropolitan Statistical Area
Source: U.S. Census Bureau, 2019-2023 American Community Survey 5-Year Estimates

HEALTH

Health Risk Factors

Category	MSA[1] (%)	U.S. (%)
Adults aged 18–64 who have any kind of health care coverage	93.8	90.8
Adults who reported being in good or better health	83.6	81.8
Adults who have been told they have high blood cholesterol	39.0	36.9
Adults who have been told they have high blood pressure	35.6	34.0
Adults who are current smokers	10.4	12.1
Adults who currently use e-cigarettes	5.6	7.7
Adults who currently use chewing tobacco, snuff, or snus	2.0	3.2
Adults who are heavy drinkers[2]	3.9	6.1
Adults who are binge drinkers[3]	14.0	15.2
Adults who are overweight (BMI 25.0 - 29.9)	34.6	34.4
Adults who are obese (BMI 30.0 - 99.8)	33.8	34.3
Adults who participated in any physical activities in the past month	77.2	75.8

Note: All figures are crude prevalence; (1) Figures cover the Baltimore-Columbia-Towson, MD Metropolitan Statistical Area; (2) Heavy drinkers are classified as adult men having more than 14 drinks per week and adult women having more than 7 drinks per week; (3) Binge drinkers are classified as males having five or more drinks on one occasion or females having four or more drinks on one occasion
Source: Centers for Disease Control and Prevention, Behaviorial Risk Factor Surveillance System, SMART: Selected Metropolitan Area Risk Trends, 2023

Acute and Chronic Health Conditions

Category	MSA[1] (%)	U.S. (%)
Adults who have ever been told they had a heart attack	3.7	4.2
Adults who have ever been told they have angina or coronary heart disease	3.9	4.0
Adults who have ever been told they had a stroke	3.2	3.3
Adults who have ever been told they have asthma	17.5	15.7
Adults who have ever been told they have arthritis	26.2	26.3
Adults who have ever been told they have diabetes[2]	12.8	11.5
Adults who have ever been told they had skin cancer	5.3	5.6
Adults who have ever been told they had any other types of cancer	8.3	8.4
Adults who have ever been told they have COPD	6.0	6.4
Adults who have ever been told they have kidney disease	3.6	3.7
Adults who have ever been told they have a form of depression	19.5	22.0

Note: All figures are crude prevalence; (1) Figures cover the Baltimore-Columbia-Towson, MD Metropolitan Statistical Area; (2) Figures do not include pregnancy-related, borderline, or pre-diabetes
Source: Centers for Disease Control and Prevention, Behavioral Risk Factor Surveillance System, SMART: Selected Metropolitan Area Risk Trends, 2023

Health Screening and Vaccination Rates

Category	MSA[1] (%)	U.S. (%)
Adults who have ever been tested for HIV	46.8	37.5
Adults who have had their blood cholesterol checked within the last five years	90.7	87.0
Adults aged 65+ who have had flu shot within the past year	71.9	63.4
Adults aged 65+ who have ever had a pneumonia vaccination	75.1	71.9

Note: All figures are crude prevalence; (1) Figures cover the Baltimore-Columbia-Towson, MD Metropolitan Statistical Area.
Source: Centers for Disease Control and Prevention, Behavioral Risk Factor Surveillance System, SMART: Selected Metropolitan Area Risk Trends, 2023

Disability Status

Category	MSA[1] (%)	U.S. (%)
Adults who reported being deaf	5.5	7.4
Are you blind or have serious difficulty seeing, even when wearing glasses?	3.9	4.9
Do you have difficulty doing errands alone?	6.1	7.8
Do you have difficulty dressing or bathing?	2.7	3.6
Do you have serious difficulty concentrating/remembering/making decisions?	11.4	13.7
Do you have serious difficulty walking or climbing stairs?	11.9	13.2

Note: All figures are crude prevalence; (1) Figures cover the Baltimore-Columbia-Towson, MD Metropolitan Statistical Area.
Source: Centers for Disease Control and Prevention, Behavioral Risk Factor Surveillance System, SMART: Selected Metropolitan Area Risk Trends, 2023

Mortality Rates for the Top 10 Causes of Death in the U.S.

ICD-10[a] Sub-Chapter	ICD-10[a] Code	Crude Mortality Rate[2] per 100,000 population	
		County[3]	U.S.
Malignant neoplasms	C00-C97	208.0	182.7
Ischaemic heart diseases	I20-I25	126.5	109.6
Provisional assignment of new diseases of uncertain etiology[1]	U00-U49	57.7	65.3
Other forms of heart disease	I30-I51	79.7	65.1
Other degenerative diseases of the nervous system	G30-G31	21.1	52.4
Other external causes of accidental injury	W00-X59	100.0	52.3
Cerebrovascular diseases	I60-I69	67.2	49.1
Chronic lower respiratory diseases	J40-J47	34.4	43.5
Hypertensive diseases	I10-I15	61.0	38.9
Organic, including symptomatic, mental disorders	F01-F09	45.5	33.9

Note: (a) ICD-10 = International Classification of Diseases 10th Revision; (1) Includes COVID-19, adverse effects to COVID-19 vaccines, SARS, and vaping-related disorders; (2) Crude mortality rates are a three-year average covering 2021-2023; (3) Figures cover Baltimore city.
Source: Centers for Disease Control and Prevention, National Center for Health Statistics. National Vital Statistics System, Mortality 2018-2023 on CDC WONDER Online Database

Mortality Rates for Selected Causes of Death

Cause of Death	ICD-10[a] Code	Crude Mortality Rate[1] per 100,000 population	
		County[2]	U.S.
Accidental poisoning and exposure to noxious substances	X40-X49	75.7	30.5
Alzheimer disease	G30	13.0	35.4
Assault	X85-Y09	42.3	7.3
COVID-19	U07.1	57.7	65.3
Diabetes mellitus	E10-E14	40.8	30.0
Diseases of the liver	K70-K76	17.6	20.8
Human immunodeficiency virus (HIV) disease	B20-B24	9.8	1.5
Influenza and pneumonia	J09-J18	10.5	13.4
Intentional self-harm	X60-X84	11.0	14.7
Malnutrition	E40-E46	1.8	6.0
Obesity and other hyperalimentation	E65-E68	3.7	3.1
Renal failure	N17-N19	15.2	16.4
Transport accidents	V01-V99	10.7	14.4

Note: (a) ICD-10 = International Classification of Diseases 10th Revision; (1) Crude mortality rates are a three-year average covering 2021-2023; (2) Figures cover Baltimore city; Data are suppressed when the data meet the criteria for confidentiality constraints; Crude mortality rates are flagged as unreliable when the rate would be calculated with a numerator of 20 or less.
Source: Centers for Disease Control and Prevention, National Center for Health Statistics. National Vital Statistics System, Mortality 2018-2023 on CDC WONDER Online Database

Health Insurance Coverage

Area	With Health Insurance	With Private Health Insurance	With Public Health Insurance	Without Health Insurance	Population Under Age 19 Without Health Insurance
City	94.2	58.5	46.8	5.8	3.8
MSA[1]	95.1	74.5	34.4	4.9	3.6
U.S.	91.4	67.3	36.3	8.6	5.4

Note: Figures are percentages that cover the civilian noninstitutionalized population; (1) Figures cover the Baltimore-Columbia-Towson, MD Metropolitan Statistical Area
Source: U.S. Census Bureau, 2019-2023 American Community Survey 5-Year Estimates

Number of Medical Professionals

Area	MDs[3]	DOs[3,4]	Dentists	Podiatrists	Chiropractors	Optometrists
City[1] (number)	7,108	206	500	45	95	94
City[1] (rate[2])	1,247.2	36.1	88.5	8.0	16.8	16.6
U.S. (rate[2])	302.5	29.2	74.6	6.4	29.5	18.0

Note: Data as of 2023 unless noted; (1) Data covers the city of Baltimore; (2) Number of medical professionals per 100,000 population; (3) Data as of 2022 and includes all active, non-federal physicians; (4) Doctor of Osteopathic Medicine
Source: U.S. Department of Health and Human Services, Health Resources and Services Administration, Bureau of Health Professions, Area Resource File (ARF) 2023-2024

Best Hospitals

According to *U.S. News,* the Baltimore-Columbia-Towson, MD metro area is home to three of the best hospitals in the U.S.: **Johns Hopkins Hospital** (Honor Roll/14 adult specialties and 11 pediatric specialties); **University of Maryland Medical Center** (2 adult specialties and 1 pediatric specialty); **Wilmer Eye Institute, Johns Hopkins Hospital** (14 adult specialties and 11 pediatric specialties). The hospitals listed were nationally ranked in at least one of 15 adult or 11 pediatric specialties. The number of specialties shown cover the parent hospital. Only 160 U.S. hospitals performed well enough to be nationally ranked in one or more specialties. Twenty hospitals in the U.S. made the Honor Roll. The Best Hospitals Honor Roll takes both the national rankings and the procedure and condition ratings into account. Hospitals received points if they were nationally ranked in one of the 15 adult specialties—the higher they ranked, the more points they got—and how many ratings of "high performing" they earned in the 20 procedures and conditions. *U.S. News Online, "America's Best Hospitals 2024-25"*

According to *U.S. News,* the Baltimore-Columbia-Towson, MD metro area is home to three of the best children's hospitals in the U.S.: **Johns Hopkins Children's Center** (11 pediatric specialties); **Johns Hopkins Children's Center-Kennedy Krieger Institute** (11 pediatric specialties); **University of Maryland Children's Hospital** (1 pediatric specialty). The hospitals listed were highly ranked in at least one of 11 pediatric specialties. One hundred five children's hospitals in the U.S. were nationally ranked in at least one specialty. Hospitals received points for being ranked in a specialty, and the 10 hospitals with the most points across the 11 specialties make up the Honor Roll. *U.S. News Online, "America's Best Children's Hospitals 2024-25"*

EDUCATION

Public School District Statistics

District Name	Schls	Pupils	Pupil/ Teacher Ratio	Minority Pupils[1] (%)	Total Rev. per Pupil ($)	Total Exp. per Pupil ($)
Baltimore City Public Schools	151	75,811	14.7	92.9	24,245	23,862
Baltimore County Public Schools	179	110,275	14.7	69.7	19,253	18,242

Note: Table includes school districts with 2,000 or more students; (1) Percentage of students that are not non-Hispanic white.
Source: U.S. Department of Education, National Center for Education Statistics, Common Core of Data, Local Education Agency (School District) Universe Survey: School Year 2023-2024; U.S. Department of Education, National Center for Education Statistics, Common Core of Data, School District Finance Survey (F-33): School Year 2021–22

Best High Schools

According to *U.S. News*, Baltimore is home to two of the top 500 high schools in the U.S.: **Eastern Technical High School** (#123); **Western School Of Technology** (#437). Nearly 25,000 public, magnet and charter schools were ranked based on their performance on state assessments and how well they prepare students for college. *U.S. News & World Report, "Best High Schools 2024"*

Highest Level of Education

Area	Less than H.S.	H.S. Diploma	Some College, No Deg.	Associate Degree	Bachelor's Degree	Master's Degree	Prof. School Degree	Doctorate Degree
City	12.8	27.9	18.4	5.5	18.1	11.7	3.1	2.5
MSA[1]	7.9	23.6	18.2	7.0	23.4	14.4	3.1	2.5
U.S.	10.6	26.2	19.4	8.8	21.3	9.8	2.3	1.6

Note: Figures cover persons age 25 and over; (1) Figures cover the Baltimore-Columbia-Towson, MD Metropolitan Statistical Area
Source: U.S. Census Bureau, 2019-2023 American Community Survey 5-Year Estimates

Educational Attainment by Race

Area	High School Graduate or Higher (%)					Bachelor's Degree or Higher (%)				
	Total	White	Black	Asian	Hisp.[2]	Total	White	Black	Asian	Hisp.[2]
City	87.2	92.9	85.7	92.2	70.0	35.4	62.2	20.0	73.3	31.3
MSA[1]	92.1	94.7	90.2	89.3	77.0	43.3	48.4	30.1	64.0	32.9
U.S.	89.4	92.9	88.1	88.0	72.5	35.0	37.7	24.7	57.0	19.9

Note: Figures shown cover persons 25 years old and over; (1) Figures cover the Baltimore-Columbia-Towson, MD Metropolitan Statistical Area; (2) People of Hispanic origin can be of any race
Source: U.S. Census Bureau, 2019-2023 American Community Survey 5-Year Estimates

School Enrollment by Grade and Control

Area	Preschool (%)		Kindergarten (%)		Grades 1 - 4 (%)		Grades 5 - 8 (%)		Grades 9 - 12 (%)	
	Public	Private	Public	Private	Public	Private	Public	Private	Public	Private
City	65.6	34.4	85.0	15.0	83.9	16.1	85.1	14.9	85.3	14.7
MSA[1]	47.0	53.0	82.9	17.1	84.6	15.4	84.0	16.0	84.2	15.8
U.S.	58.7	41.3	85.2	14.8	87.2	12.8	87.9	12.1	89.0	11.0

Note: Figures shown cover persons 3 years old and over; (1) Figures cover the Baltimore-Columbia-Towson, MD Metropolitan Statistical Area
Source: U.S. Census Bureau, 2019-2023 American Community Survey 5-Year Estimates

Higher Education

Four-Year Colleges			Two-Year Colleges			Medical Schools[1]	Law Schools[2]	Voc/ Tech[3]
Public	Private Non-profit	Private For-profit	Public	Private Non-profit	Private For-profit			
7	12	0	7	0	1	2	2	16

Note: Figures cover institutions located within the Baltimore-Columbia-Towson, MD Metropolitan Statistical Area and include main campuses only; (1) includes schools accredited by the Liaison Committee on Medical Education and the American Osteopathic Association's Commission on Osteopathic College Accreditation; (2) includes ABA-accredited schools, schools with provisional ABA accreditation, and state accredited schools; (3) includes all schools with programs that are less than 2 years.
Source: National Center for Education Statistics, Integrated Postsecondary Education System (IPEDS), 2023-24; Wikipedia, List of Medical Schools in the United States, accessed May 2, 2025; Wikipedia, List of Law Schools in the United States, accessed May 2, 2025

According to *U.S. News & World Report*, the Baltimore-Columbia-Towson, MD metro area is home to two of the top 200 national universities in the U.S.: **Johns Hopkins University** (#6 tie); **University of Maryland Baltimore County** (#144 tie). The indicators used to capture academic quality fall into a number of categories: assessment by administrators at peer institutions; retention of students; faculty resources; student selectivity; financial resources; alumni giving; high school counselor ratings of colleges; and graduation rate. *U.S. News & World Report, "America's Best Colleges 2025"*

According to *U.S. News & World Report,* the Baltimore-Columbia-Towson, MD metro area is home to two of the top 100 liberal arts colleges in the U.S.: **United States Naval Academy** (#4); **St. John's College (MD)** (#83 tie). The indicators used to capture academic quality fall into a number of categories: assessment by administrators at peer institutions; retention of students; faculty resources; student selectivity; financial resources; alumni giving; high school counselor ratings of colleges; and graduation rate. *U.S. News & World Report, "America's Best Colleges 2025"*

According to *U.S. News & World Report,* the Baltimore-Columbia-Towson, MD metro area is home to one of the top 100 law schools in the U.S.: **University of Maryland (Carey)** (#63 tie). The rankings are based on a weighted average of 12 measures of quality: peer assessment score; assessment score by lawyers/judges; median LSAT scores; median undergrad GPA; acceptance rate; employment rates for graduates; placement success; bar passage rate; faculty resources; expenditures per student; student/faculty ratio; and library resources. *U.S. News & World Report, "America's Best Graduate Schools, Law, 2025"*

According to *U.S. News & World Report,* the Baltimore-Columbia-Towson, MD metro area is home to one of the top medical schools for research in the U.S.: **University of Maryland 2** (Tier 2). *U.S. News* placed medical and osteopathic schools into tiers based on their research productivity, faculty and admissions data. Each school's tier was derived from its overall score, calculated by summing the weighted normalized values generated across several factors of academic quality, outlined below. There are four tiers, with tier 1 medical schools as the highest-performing and tier 4 as the lowest-performing. Only tier 1 and 2 schools are shown. Because of the tier presentation, *U.S. News* calculated overall scores based on their percentile performance among all rated schools instead of dividing against the rescaled score of the No. 1-performing schools. Tier 1 included schools with overall scores of 85 to 99. The cutoffs for tiers 2 through 4 were schools scoring 50 to 84, 15 to 49 and 1 to 14, respectively. The rankings are based on a weighted average of the following measures of quality: total research activity; average research activity per faculty member; total NIH research grants at the medical school and its affiliated hospitals; average NIH research grants per faculty; median MCAT total score; median undergraduate GPA; acceptance rate; and faculty resources. *U.S. News & World Report, "America's Best Graduate Schools, Medical, 2025"*

According to *U.S. News & World Report,* the Baltimore-Columbia-Towson, MD metro area is home to one of the top medical schools for primary care in the U.S.: **University of Maryland 2** (Tier 2). *U.S. News* placed medical and osteopathic schools into tiers based on their research productivity, faculty and admissions data. Each school's tier was derived from its overall score, calculated by summing the weighted normalized values generated across several factors of academic quality, outlined below. There are four tiers, with tier 1 medical schools as the highest-performing and tier 4 as the lowest-performing. Only tier 1 and 2 schools are shown. Because of the tier presentation, *U.S. News* calculated overall scores based on their percentile performance among all rated schools instead of dividing against the rescaled score of the No. 1-performing schools. Tier 1 included schools with overall scores of 85 to 99. The cutoffs for tiers 2 through 4 were schools scoring 50 to 84, 15 to 49 and 1 to 14, respectively. The rankings are based on a weighted average of the following measures of quality: graduates practicing in primary care specialties; graduates entering primary care residencies; median MCAT total score; median undergraduate GPA; acceptance rate; and faculty resources. *U.S. News & World Report, "America's Best Graduate Schools, Medical, 2025"*

EMPLOYERS

Major Employers

Company Name	Industry
Exelon	Energy products & services
FutureCare	Healthcare
Horseshoe Casino	Entertainment and recreation
Johns Hopkins Hospital & Health System	Healthcare
Johns Hopkins University	Educational services
Kennedy Krieger Institute	Healthcare
LifeBridge Health	Healthcare
Maryland Institute College of Art	Higher education
MedStar Health	Healthcare
Mercy Health Services	Healthcare
Morgan State University	Higher education
St. Agnes Healthcare	Healthcare
University of Maryland	Higher education
University of Maryland Medical System	Healthcare
Veterans Health Administration	Military/healthcare

Note: Companies shown are located within the Baltimore-Columbia-Towson, MD Metropolitan Statistical Area.
Source: Chambers of Commerce; State Departments of Labor; Wikipedia

Best Companies to Work For

Brightview Senior Living, headquartered in Baltimore, is among "The 100 Best Companies to Work For." To pick the best companies, *Fortune* partnered with the Great Place to Work Institute. Using their proprietary Trust Index™ survey, the core of what creates great a workplace is measured—key behaviors that drive trust in management, connection with colleagues, and loyalty to the company. To be eligible for the *Fortune* 100 Best Companies to Work For list, employers must have 1,000 or more employees in the U.S. and cannot be a government agency. *Fortune, "The 100 Best Companies to Work For," 2025*

Constellation Energy, headquartered in Baltimore, is among "Fortune's Best Workplaces for Parents." To pick the best companies, *Fortune* partnered with the Great Place to Work Institute. To be considered for the list, companies must be Great Place To Work-Certified and have at least 50 responses from parents in the US. The survey enables employees to share confidential quantitative and qualitative feedback about their organization's culture by responding to 60 statements on a 5-point scale and answering two open-ended questions. Collectively, these statements describe a great employee experience, defined by high levels of trust, respect, credibility, fairness, pride, and camaraderie. In addition, companies provide organizational data like size, location, industry, demographics, roles, and levels; and provide information about parental leave, adoption, flexible schedule, childcare and dependent health care benefits. *Fortune, "Best Workplaces for Parents," 2024*

Constellation Energy, headquartered in Baltimore, is among "Fortune's Best Workplaces for Women." To pick the best companies, *Fortune* partnered with the Great Place to Work Institute. To be considered for the list, companies must be Great Place To Work-Certified. Companies must also employ at least 50 women, at least 20% of their non-executive managers must be female, and at least one executive must be female. To determine the Best Workplaces for Women, Great Place To Work measured the differences in women's survey responses to those of their peers and assesses the impact of demographics and roles on the quality and consistency of women's experiences. Great Place To Work also analyzed the gender balance of each workplace, how it compared to each company's industry, and patterns in representation as women rise from front-line positions to the board of directors. *Fortune, "Best Workplaces for Women," 2024*

Johns Hopkins Medicine, headquartered in Baltimore, is among the "Best Places to Work in IT." To qualify, companies had to have a minimum of 100 total employees and five IT employees. The best places to work were selected based on DEI (diversity, equity, and inclusion) practices; IT turnover, promotions, and growth; IT retention and engagement programs; remote/hybrid working; benefits and perks (such as elder care and child care, flextime, and reimbursement for college tuition); and training and career development opportunities. *Computerworld, "Best Places to Work in IT," 2025*

PUBLIC SAFETY

Crime Rate

Area	Total Crime Rate	Violent Crime Rate				Property Crime Rate		
		Murder	Rape	Robbery	Aggrav. Assault	Burglary	Larceny-Theft	Motor Vehicle Theft
City	5,850.2	41.2	45.1	577.9	908.2	445.5	1,987.6	1,844.7
U.S.	2,290.9	5.7	38.0	66.5	264.1	250.7	1,347.2	318.7

Note: Figures are crimes per 100,000 population.
Source: FBI, Table 8, Offenses Known to Law Enforcement, by State by City, 2023

Hate Crimes

Area	Number of Quarters Reported	Number of Incidents per Bias Motivation					
		Race/Ethnicity/Ancestry	Religion	Sexual Orientation	Disability	Gender	Gender Identity
City[1]	4	23	6	10	1	0	2
U.S.	4	5,900	2,699	2,077	187	92	492

Note: (1) Figures include at least one incident reported with more than one bias motivation.
Source: Federal Bureau of Investigation, Hate Crime Statistics 2023

Identity Theft Consumer Reports

Area	Reports	Reports per 100,000 Population	Rank[2]
MSA[1]	8,940	315	58
U.S.	1,135,291	339	-

Note: (1) Figures cover the Baltimore-Columbia-Towson, MD Metropolitan Statistical Area; (2) Rank ranges from 1 to 401 where 1 indicates greatest number of identity theft reports per 100,000 population
Source: Federal Trade Commission, Consumer Sentinel Network Data Book 2024

Fraud and Other Consumer Reports

Area	Reports	Reports per 100,000 Population	Rank[2]
MSA[1]	52,648	1,854	20
U.S.	5,360,641	1,601	-

Note: (1) Figures cover the Baltimore-Columbia-Towson, MD Metropolitan Statistical Area; (2) Rank ranges from 1 to 401 where 1 indicates greatest number of fraud and other consumer reports per 100,000 population
Source: Federal Trade Commission, Consumer Sentinel Network Data Book 2024

POLITICS

2024 Presidential Election Results

Area	Trump (Rep.)	Harris (Dem.)	Stein (Green)	Kennedy (Ind.)	Oliver (Lib.)	Other
Baltimore City	12.1	84.6	1.4	0.8	0.4	0.7
U.S.	49.7	48.2	0.6	0.5	0.4	0.6

Note: Results are percentages and may not add to 100% due to rounding
Source: Dave Leip's Atlas of U.S. Presidential Elections

SPORTS

Professional Sports Teams

Team Name	League	Year Established
Baltimore Orioles	Major League Baseball (MLB)	1954
Baltimore Ravens	National Football League (NFL)	1996

Note: Includes teams located in the Baltimore-Columbia-Towson, MD Metropolitan Statistical Area.
Source: Wikipedia, Major Professional Sports Teams of the United States and Canada, May 1, 2025

CLIMATE

Average and Extreme Temperatures

Temperature	Jan	Feb	Mar	Apr	May	Jun	Jul	Aug	Sep	Oct	Nov	Dec	Yr.
Extreme High (°F)	75	79	87	94	98	100	104	105	100	92	86	77	105
Average High (°F)	41	44	53	65	74	83	87	85	79	68	56	45	65
Average Temp. (°F)	33	36	44	54	64	73	77	76	69	57	47	37	56
Average Low (°F)	24	26	34	43	53	62	67	66	58	46	37	28	45
Extreme Low (°F)	-7	-3	6	20	32	40	50	45	35	25	13	0	-7

Note: Figures cover the years 1950-1990
Source: National Climatic Data Center, International Station Meteorological Climate Summary, 9/96

Average Precipitation/Snowfall/Humidity

Precip./Humidity	Jan	Feb	Mar	Apr	May	Jun	Jul	Aug	Sep	Oct	Nov	Dec	Yr.
Avg. Precip. (in.)	2.9	3.0	3.5	3.3	3.7	3.7	3.9	4.2	3.4	3.0	3.2	3.3	41.2
Avg. Snowfall (in.)	6	7	4	Tr	Tr	0	0	0	0	Tr	1	4	21
Avg. Rel. Hum. 7am (%)	72	71	71	71	77	79	80	83	85	83	78	74	77
Avg. Rel. Hum. 4pm (%)	56	53	48	47	52	53	53	55	55	54	55	57	53

Note: Figures cover the years 1950-1990; Tr = Trace amounts (<0.05 in. of rain; <0.5 in. of snow)
Source: National Climatic Data Center, International Station Meteorological Climate Summary, 9/96

Weather Conditions

Temperature			Daytime Sky			Precipitation		
10°F & below	32°F & below	90°F & above	Clear	Partly cloudy	Cloudy	0.01 inch or more precip.	0.1 inch or more snow/ice	Thunderstorms
6	97	31	91	143	131	113	13	27

Note: Figures are average number of days per year and cover the years 1950-1990
Source: National Climatic Data Center, International Station Meteorological Climate Summary, 9/96

HAZARDOUS WASTE

Superfund Sites

The Baltimore-Columbia-Towson, MD metro area is home to nine sites on the EPA's Superfund National Priorities List (NPL) or Superfund Alternative Approach (SAA) list: **68th Street Dump/Industrial Enterprises** (Proposed NPL and SAA); **Aberdeen Proving Ground (Edgewood Area)** (Final NPL); **Aberdeen Proving Ground (Michaelsville Landfill)** (Final NPL); **Bear Creek Sediments** (Final NPL); **Bush Valley Landfill** (Final NPL); **Curtis Bay Coast Guard Yard** (Final NPL); **Fort George G. Meade** (Final NPL); **Kane & Lombard Street Drums** (Final NPL); **Sauer Dump** (Final NPL). The Superfund alternative approach uses the same investigation and cleanup process and standards that are used for sites listed on the National Priorities List. The SAA is an alternative to listing a site on the NPL; it is not an alternative to Superfund or the Superfund process. There are a total of 1,445 Superfund sites with a status of proposed or final on both lists in the United States. *U.S. Environmental Protection Agency, National Priorities List, May 1, 2025; U.S. Environmental Protection Agency, Superfund Alternative Approach Sites, May 1, 2025*

AIR QUALITY

Air Quality Trends: Ozone

	1990	1995	2000	2005	2010	2015	2020	2021	2022	2023
MSA[1]	0.100	0.103	0.088	0.089	0.084	0.073	0.064	0.071	0.066	0.073
U.S.	0.087	0.089	0.081	0.080	0.072	0.068	0.066	0.067	0.067	0.070

Note: (1) Data covers the Baltimore-Columbia-Towson, MD Metropolitan Statistical Area. The values shown are the composite ozone concentration averages among trend sites based on the highest fourth daily maximum 8-hour concentration in parts per million. These trends are based on sites having an adequate record of monitoring data during the trend period. Data from exceptional events are included.
Source: U.S. Environmental Protection Agency, Air Quality Monitoring Information, "Air Quality Trends by City, 1990-2023"

Air Quality Index

Area	Percent of Days when Air Quality was...[2]					AQI Statistics[2]	
	Good	Moderate	Unhealthy for Sensitive Groups	Unhealthy	Very Unhealthy	Maximum	Median
MSA[1]	55.1	40.3	3.6	0.8	0.3	205	49

Note: (1) Data covers the Baltimore-Columbia-Towson, MD Metropolitan Statistical Area; (2) Based on 365 days with AQI data in 2023. Air Quality Index (AQI) is an index for reporting daily air quality. EPA calculates the AQI for five major air pollutants regulated by the Clean Air Act: ground-level ozone, particle pollution (aka particulate matter), carbon monoxide, sulfur dioxide, and nitrogen dioxide. The AQI runs from 0 to 500. The higher the AQI value, the greater the level of air pollution and the greater the health concern. There are six AQI categories: "Good" AQI is between 0 and 50. Air quality is considered satisfactory; "Moderate" AQI is between 51 and 100. Air quality is acceptable; "Unhealthy for Sensitive Groups" When AQI values are between 101 and 150, members of sensitive groups may experience health effects; "Unhealthy" When AQI values are between 151 and 200 everyone may begin to experience health effects; "Very Unhealthy" AQI values between 201 and 300 trigger a health alert; "Hazardous" AQI values over 300 trigger warnings of emergency conditions (not shown).
Source: U.S. Environmental Protection Agency, Air Quality Index Report, 2023

Air Quality Index Pollutants

Area	Percent of Days when AQI Pollutant was...[2]					
	Carbon Monoxide	Nitrogen Dioxide	Ozone	Sulfur Dioxide	Particulate Matter 2.5	Particulate Matter 10
MSA[1]	0.0	1.1	54.5	(3)	44.4	0.0

Note: (1) Data covers the Baltimore-Columbia-Towson, MD Metropolitan Statistical Area; (2) Based on 365 days with AQI data in 2023. The Air Quality Index (AQI) is an index for reporting daily air quality. EPA calculates the AQI for five major air pollutants regulated by the Clean Air Act: ground-level ozone, particle pollution (also known as particulate matter), carbon monoxide, sulfur dioxide, and nitrogen dioxide. The AQI runs from 0 to 500. The higher the AQI value, the greater the level of air pollution and the greater the health concern; (3) Sulfur dioxide is no longer included in this table because SO_2 concentrations tend to be very localized and not necessarily representative of broad geographical areas like counties and CBSAs.
Source: U.S. Environmental Protection Agency, Air Quality Index Report, 2023

Maximum Air Pollutant Concentrations: Particulate Matter, Ozone, CO and Lead

	Particulate Matter 10 (ug/m^3)	Particulate Matter 2.5 Wtd AM (ug/m^3)	Particulate Matter 2.5 24-Hr (ug/m^3)	Ozone (ppm)	Carbon Monoxide (ppm)	Lead (ug/m^3)
MSA[1] Level	42	10.1	32	0.075	1	n/a
NAAQS[2]	150	15	35	0.075	9	0.15
Met NAAQS[2]	Yes	Yes	Yes	Yes	Yes	n/a

Note: (1) Data covers the Baltimore-Columbia-Towson, MD Metropolitan Statistical Area; Data from exceptional events are included; (2) National Ambient Air Quality Standards; ppm = parts per million; ug/m^3 = micrograms per cubic meter; n/a not available.
Concentrations: Particulate Matter 10 (coarse particulate)—highest second maximum 24-hour concentration; Particulate Matter 2.5 Wtd AM (fine particulate)—highest weighted annual mean concentration; Particulate Matter 2.5 24-Hour (fine particulate)—highest 98th percentile 24-hour concentration; Ozone—highest fourth daily maximum 8-hour concentration; Carbon Monoxide—highest second maximum non-overlapping 8-hour concentration; Lead—maximum running 3-month average
Source: U.S. Environmental Protection Agency, Air Quality Monitoring Information, "Air Quality Statistics by City, 2023"

Maximum Air Pollutant Concentrations: Nitrogen Dioxide and Sulfur Dioxide

	Nitrogen Dioxide AM (ppb)	Nitrogen Dioxide 1-Hr (ppb)	Sulfur Dioxide AM (ppb)	Sulfur Dioxide 1-Hr (ppb)	Sulfur Dioxide 24-Hr (ppb)
MSA[1] Level	15	45	n/a	4	n/a
NAAQS[2]	53	100	30	75	140
Met NAAQS[2]	Yes	Yes	n/a	Yes	n/a

Note: (1) Data covers the Baltimore-Columbia-Towson, MD Metropolitan Statistical Area; Data from exceptional events are included; (2) National Ambient Air Quality Standards; ppm = parts per million; ug/m^3 = micrograms per cubic meter; n/a not available.
Concentrations: Nitrogen Dioxide AM—highest arithmetic mean concentration; Nitrogen Dioxide 1-Hr—highest 98th percentile 1-hour daily maximum concentration; Sulfur Dioxide AM—highest annual mean concentration; Sulfur Dioxide 1-Hr—highest 99th percentile 1-hour daily maximum concentration; Sulfur Dioxide 24-Hr—highest second maximum 24-hour concentration
Source: U.S. Environmental Protection Agency, Air Quality Monitoring Information, "Air Quality Statistics by City, 2023"

Boston, Massachusetts

Background

Who would think that Boston, a city founded upon the Puritan principles of hard work, plain living, sobriety, and unyielding religious conviction, would be known for such a radical act of throwing tea overboard from a ship? The answer lies in ship trading—the industry upon which Boston gained its wealth. Boston sea captains reaped more profits from West Indies molasses, mahogany from Honduras, and slaves from Guinea than did the English, who decided to impose additional taxes upon her colonial subjects. In defiance, Samuel Adams led the Sons of Liberty to throw a precious cargo of tea, so dear to the English, overboard. Events escalated, and the American Revolution began.

After the Revolution, Boston continued to grow into the Yankee capital—and educational center—that it is today. According to recent numbers, the greater Boston area hosts more than 118 colleges and universities. Boston's largest universities are Boston University, Northeastern University, University of Massachusetts/Boston, and Boston College. Cambridge, across the Charles River, is home to both the Massachusetts Institute of Technology (MIT) and Harvard University, which also has a presence in nearby Allston.

Boston's moniker is "The Hub." The largest city in the six-state New England region, it has been recognized not only as a city of historic importance in the American Revolution, but as a leading educational and medical center and as a site for historic architecture and world class cultural institutions. Boston is also the largest biotechnology hub in the world.

Historic Faneuil Hall and the nearby Quincy Market have been renovated into a historical attraction and a festival marketplace of food and shopping. The Back Bay and fashionable Newbury Street offers art galleries, fashion boutiques, and open-air cafes, all of which draw tourists and residents alike. The Fenway neighborhood is home to the Boston Symphony Orchestra, Boston Pops, Berklee College of Music, Gardner Museum, and New England Conservatory. Along the city's downtown waterfront are the Museum of Science, New England Aquarium, and the Children's Museum.

Boston's historic buildings include Trinity Church, with its brilliant stained-glass windows, built in 1877. The African meeting house on Beacon Hill is the oldest surviving black church in North America. Christ Church (Old North Church) is the oldest church in Boston (1723) and was part of Paul Revere's ride. Modern architecture is represented by the John Hancock Tower by I.M. Pei and luxury hotels, including the Ritz Carlton Boston Common and the Four Seasons.

The TD Garden is home to the Boston Bruins and the Boston Celtics and a venue for concerts, shows and conventions. Gillette Stadium, a 68,000-seat outdoor coliseum hosts football, soccer, and other events in nearby Foxboro. Fenway Park, the oldest major league ballpark still in use, is home to the Boston Red Sox, 2018 World Series winners. Deep pride in their sports teams is a known characteristic of Bostonians. In addition to the Red Sox victory, the Celtics won the 2022 NBA Eastern conference title, and the New England Patriots won the NFL Super Bowl in 2019, after which superstar quarterback Tom Brady left the team after 20 seasons. Boston is one of 11 U.S. cities to host matches during the 2026 FIFA World Cup.

The Boston Marathon is the world's oldest annual marathon and best-known road racing event. During the 2013 race, two explosions occurred close to the end of the course, halting the race, and preventing many from finishing. Three spectators were killed and more than 200 people were injured. Two brothers, allegedly motivated by extremist Islamist beliefs, planted the two bombs. One brother was killed by police and the other was sentenced to death.

Boston's colleges and universities have a major impact on the city's economy, attracting high-tech industries including computer hardware and software and biotech companies. Boston receives the largest amount of annual funding from the National Institutes of Health of all cities in the United States.

In 2021, Asian American Michelle Wu was the first women and first person of color elected to lead the city as mayor. It was the first time in history that Boston did not elect a white man.

Boston's weather is influenced by both tropical and polar air masses, proximity to several low-pressure storm tracks, and by its moderating East Coast location. Summer heat is relieved by sea breezes. Cold winters are often alleviated by the relatively warm ocean.

Rankings

General Rankings

- To help military veterans find the best places in which to settle down, *WalletHub* compared the 100 largest U.S. cities across 19 key indicators of livability, affordability and veteran-friendliness. They range from the share of military skill-related jobs to veteran income growth to the availability of VA health facilities. Boston ranked #64. *Wallethub.com, "Best & Worst Places for Veterans to Live (2025)," November 7, 2024*

- The human resources consulting firm Mercer ranked 241 major cities worldwide in terms of overall quality of life. Boston ranked #32. Criteria: political and personal safety, social, and economic factors; medical and health considerations; schools and education; public services and transportation; recreation; connectivity; housing and infrastructure; and climate. *Mercer, "Mercer 2024 Quality of Living Survey," December 2024*

- Boston appeared on *Travel + Leisure's* list of "The 15 Best Cities in the United States." The city was ranked #14. Criteria: walkability; sights/landmarks; culture; food; friendliness; shopping; and overall value. *Travel + Leisure, "The World's Best Awards 2024" July 9, 2024*

- For its 37th annual "Readers' Choice Awards" survey, *Condé Nast Traveler* ranked its readers' favorite cities in the U.S. Whether it be a longed-for visit or the next big new thing, these are the places travelers loved best. The list was broken into large cities and cities under 250,000. Boston ranked #7 in the big city category. *Condé Nast Traveler, Readers' Choice Awards 2024, "Best Big Cities in the U.S." October 1, 2024*

Business/Finance Rankings

- According to *Business Insider*, the Boston metro area is a prime place to run a startup or move an existing business to. The area ranked #10. More than 300 metro areas were analyzed for factors that were of top concern to new business owners. Data was based on the 2019 U.S. Census Bureau American Community Survey, statistics from the CDC, and University of Chicago analysis. Criteria: business formations; percentage of vaccinated population; percentage of households with internet subscriptions; median household income; and share of work that can be done from home. *BusinessInsider.com, "The 20 Best Cities for Starting a Business in 2022 Include Denver, Raleigh, and Olympia," June 7, 2022*

- WalletHub's latest report ranked 182 cities by the average credit score of its residents. Boston was ranked #8 among the ten cities with the highest average credit score, based on WalletHub's 2024 fourth quarter data. *WalletHub.com, "2025's Cities With the Highest & Lowest Credit Scores," March 6, 2025*

- Payscale.com ranked the 32 largest metro areas in terms of wage growth. The Boston metro area ranked #10. Criteria: quarterly changes in private industry employee and education professional wage growth from the previous year. *PayScale, "Wage Trends by Metro Area-4th Quarter," February 4, 2025*

- For its annual survey of the "Most Expensive U.S. Cities to Live In," Kiplinger applied Cost of Living Index statistics developed by the Council for Community and Economic Research to U.S. Census Bureau population and median household income data for 265 urban areas. Boston ranked #9 among the most expensive in the country. *Kiplinger.com, "The 10 Most Expensive Cities to Live in the U.S.," February 3, 2025*

- Boston was cited as one of America's top metros for total corporate facility investment projects in 2024. The area ranked #9 in the Tier 1 (large) metro area category (population over 1 million). *Site Selection, "Top Metros of 2024," March 2025*

- The Boston metro area appeared on the Milken Institute "2025 Best Performing Cities" list. Rank: #119 out of 200 large metro areas (based on performance category). Criteria: job growth; wage growth; high-tech growth and impact; community resilience; housing affordability; household broadband access. *Milken Institute, "Best-Performing Cities 2025," January 14, 2025*

- Mercer Human Resources Consulting ranked 226 cities worldwide in terms of cost-of-living. Boston ranked #19 (the lower the ranking, the higher the cost-of-living). The survey measured the comparative cost of over 200 items (such as housing, food, clothing, domestic supplies, transportation, and recreation/entertainment) in each location. *Mercer, "2024 Cost of Living City Ranking," June 17, 2024*

Culture/Performing Arts Rankings

- Boston was selected as one of the 25 best cities for moviemakers in North America. Great film cities are places where filmmaking dreams can come true, that offer more creative space, lower costs, and great outdoor locations. NYC & LA were intentionally excluded. Criteria: film industry presence and culture; tax incentives; affordability; and proximity of festivals and schools. The city was ranked #18. *MovieMaker Magazine, "Best Places to Live and Work as a Moviemaker, 2025," January 29, 2025*

Dating/Romance Rankings

- *Apartment List* conducted its Annual Renter Satisfaction Survey and asked renters "how satisfied are you with opportunities for dating in your current city." The cities were ranked from highest to lowest based on their satisfaction scores. Boston ranked #2 out of 10 cities. *Apartment List, "Best Cities for Dating 2022 with Local Dating Insights from Bumble," February 7, 2022*

Education Rankings

- Personal finance website *WalletHub* analyzed the 150 largest U.S. metropolitan statistical areas to determine where the most educated Americans are putting their degrees to work. Criteria: education levels; percentage of workers with degrees; education quality and attainment gap; public school quality rankings; quality and enrollment of each metro area's universities. Boston was ranked #9 (#1 = most educated city). *WalletHub.com, "Most & Least Educated Cities in America, 2025" July 2, 2024*

Environmental Rankings

- The U.S. Environmental Protection Agency (EPA) released its list of U.S. metropolitan areas with the most ENERGY STAR certified buildings in 2023. The Boston metro area was ranked #12 out of 25. *U.S. Environmental Protection Agency, "2024 Energy Star Top Cities," May 22, 2024*

Health/Fitness Rankings

- For each of the 100 largest cities in the United States, the American Fitness Index®, compiled in partnership between the American College of Sports Medicine and the Elevance Health Foundation, evaluated community infrastructure and more than 30 health behaviors including preventive health, levels of chronic disease conditions, food insecurity, pedestrian safety, air quality, and community/environment resources that support physical activity. Boston ranked #14 for "community fitness." *americanfitnessindex.org, "2024 ACSM American Fitness Index Summary Report," July 23, 2024*

- Boston was identified as one of the 10 most walkable cities in the U.S. by Walk Score. The city ranked #3. Walk Score measures walkability by analyzing hundreds of walking routes to nearby amenities, and also measures pedestrian friendliness by analyzing population density and road metrics such as block length and intersection density. *WalkScore.com, April 13, 2021*

- Boston was identified as a "2025 Allergy Capital." The area ranked #100 out of the nation's 100 largest metropolitan areas. Three groups of factors were used to identify the most challenging cities for people with allergies: annual tree, grass, and weed pollen scores; over the counter allergy medicine use; number of board-certified allergy specialists. *Asthma and Allergy Foundation of America, "2025 Allergy Capitals: The Most Challenging Places to Live with Allergies," March 18, 2025*

- Boston was identified as a "2024 Asthma Capital." The area ranked #74 out of the nation's 100 largest metropolitan areas. Criteria: estimated asthma prevalence; asthma-related mortality; and ER visits due to asthma. Risk factors analyzed but not factored in the rankings: annual air quality including pollution and ozone levels; public smoking laws; indoor air quality; access to asthma specialists; rescue and controller medication use; uninsured rate; pollen allergy; poverty rate. *Asthma and Allergy Foundation of America, "Asthma Capitals 2024: The Most Challenging Places to Live With Asthma," September 10, 2024*

- The Sharecare Community Well-Being Index evaluates 10 individual and social health factors in order to measure what matters to Americans in the communities in which they live. The Boston metro area ranked #4 in the top 10 across all 10 domains. Criteria: access to healthcare, food, and community resources; housing and transportation; economic security; feeling of purpose; and physical, financial, social, and community well-being. *Sharecare.com, "Community Well-Being Index: 2020 Metro Area & County Rankings Report," August 30, 2021*

Pet Rankings

- Boston appeared on *The Dogington Post* site as one of the top cities for dog lovers, ranking #7 out of 15. The real estate marketplace, Zillow®, and Rover, the largest pet sitter and dog walker network, introduced a new list of "Top Emerging Dog-Friendly Cities" for 2021. Criteria: number of new dog accounts on the Rover platform; and rentals and listings that mention features that attract dog owners (fenced-in yards, dog houses, dog door or proximity to a dog park). *Dogingtonpost.com, "15 Cities Emerging as Dog-Friendliest in 2021," May 11, 2021*

Real Estate Rankings

- *WalletHub* compared the most populated U.S. cities to determine which had the best markets for real estate agents. Boston ranked #19 where demand was high and pay was the best. Criteria: sales per agent; annual median wage for real-estate agents; monthly average starting salary for real estate agents; real estate job density and competition; unemployment rate; home turnover rate; housing-market health index; and other relevant metrics. *WalletHub.com, "2021 Best Places to Be a Real Estate Agent," May 12, 2021*

- The Boston metro area was identified as one of the nations's 20 hottest housing markets in 2025. Criteria: unique listing views as an indicator of demand and number of days on the market as an indicator of pace. The area ranked #15. *Realtor.com, "January 2025 Top 20 Hottest Housing Markets," February 11, 2025*

- The Boston metro area was identified as one of the 10 worst condo markets in the U.S. in 2024. The area ranked #54 out of 63 markets. Criteria: year-over-year change of median sales price of existing apartment condo-coop homes between the 4th quarter of 2023 and the 4th quarter of 2024. *National Association of Realtors®, Median Sales Price of Existing Apartment Condo-Coops Homes for Metropolitan Areas, 4th Quarter 2024*

- The Boston metro area was identified as one of the 20 least affordable housing markets in the U.S. in 2024. The area ranked #212 out of 226 markets. Criteria: qualification for a mortgage loan with a 10 percent down payment on a typical home. *National Association of Realtors®, Qualifying Income Based on Sales Price of Existing Single-Family Homes for Metropolitan Areas, February 6, 2025*

- Boston was ranked #162 out of 176 metro areas in terms of cost of housing in 2024 by the National Association of Home Builders (#1 = most affordable). Criteria: the portion of an average family's income necessary to pay the mortgage on a median-priced home. *National Association of Home Builders®, NAHB-Wells Fargo Cost of Housing Index, 4th Quarter 2024*

Safety Rankings

- Allstate ranked the 100 most populous cities in America in terms of driver safety. Boston ranked #46. Criteria based on anonymized driving behavior data from Allstate's mobile app powered by Arity: high speed driving (over 80 mph), phone handling, and hard braking. The report helps increase the importance of safety and awareness behind the wheel. *Allstate, "16th Allstate America's Best Drivers Report®" July 11, 2024*

Transportation Rankings

- Boston was identified as one of the most congested metro areas in the U.S. The area ranked #9 out of 10. Criteria: yearly delay per auto commuter in hours. *Texas A&M Transportation Institute, "2023 Urban Mobility Report," June 2024*

- According to the INRIX "2024 Global Traffic Scorecard," Boston was identified as one of the most congested metro areas in the U.S. The area ranked #4 out of 10 in the country and among the top 25 most congested in the world. Criteria: average annual time spent in traffic and average cost of congestion per motorist. *Inrix.com, "Employees & Consumers Returned to Downtowns, Traffic Delays & Costs Grew," January 6, 2025*

Women/Minorities Rankings

- Personal finance website *WalletHub* compared more than 180 U.S. cities across two key dimensions, "Hispanic Business-Friendliness" and "Hispanic Purchasing Power," to arrive at the most favorable conditions for Hispanic entrepreneurs. Boston was ranked #181 out of 182. Criteria includes: share of Hispanic-Owned Businesses; average growth of Hispanic Business revenues; Small Business-Friendliness score; affordability; and number of Hispanics with at least a bachelor's degree. *WalletHub.com, "Best Cities for Hispanic Entrepreneurs," September 4, 2024*

Miscellaneous Rankings

- Boston was selected as a 2024 Digital Cities Survey winner. The city ranked #6 in the large city (500,000 or more population) category. The survey examined and assessed how city governments are utilizing new technology and modernized applications to provide residents an array of contactless services and conveniences. Survey questions focused on ten initiatives: cybersecurity; citizen experience; disaster recovery; business intelligence; IT personnel retention; data governance; business automation; AI/machine learning; application modernization; and IT collaboration. *Center for Digital Government, "2024 Digital Cities Survey," November 5, 2024*

- In its roundup of St. Patrick's Day parades, *Gayot* listed the best festivals and parades of all things Irish. The festivities in Boston as among the best in North America. *Gayot.com, "Best St. Patrick's Day Parades," March 2025*

- *WalletHub* compared 148 of the most populated U.S. cities to determine their operating efficiency. A "Quality of Services" score was constructed for each city and then measured against the total budget per capita to reveal which were managed the best. Boston ranked #67. Criteria: financial stability; economy; education; safety; health; infrastructure and pollution. *WalletHub.com, "2025's Best- & Worst-Run Cities in America," June 18, 2024*

Business Environment

DEMOGRAPHICS

Population Growth

Area	1990 Census	2000 Census	2010 Census	2020 Census	2023 Estimate[2]	Population Growth 1990-2023 (%)
City	574,283	589,141	617,594	675,647	663,972	15.6
MSA[1]	4,133,895	4,391,344	4,552,402	4,941,632	4,917,661	19.0
U.S.	248,709,873	281,421,906	308,745,538	331,449,281	332,387,540	33.6

Note: (1) Figures cover the Boston-Cambridge-Newton, MA-NH Metropolitan Statistical Area; (2) 2019-2023 5-year ACS population estimate
Source: U.S. Census Bureau, 1990 Census, 2000 Census, 2010 Census, 2020 Census, 2019-2023 American Community Survey 5-Year Estimates

Race

Area	White Alone[2] (%)	Black Alone[2] (%)	Asian Alone[2] (%)	AIAN[3] Alone[2] (%)	NHOPI[4] Alone[2] (%)	Other Race Alone[2] (%)	Two or More Races (%)
City	47.8	21.5	10.0	0.3	0.1	7.1	13.2
MSA[1]	69.2	7.5	8.5	0.2	0.0	5.5	9.1
U.S.	63.4	12.4	5.8	0.9	0.2	6.6	10.7

Note: (1) Figures cover the Boston-Cambridge-Newton, MA-NH Metropolitan Statistical Area; (2) Alone is defined as not being in combination with one or more other races; (3) American Indian and Alaska Native; (4) Native Hawaiian and Other Pacific Islander
Source: U.S. Census Bureau, 2019-2023 American Community Survey 5-Year Estimates

Hispanic or Latino Origin

Area	Total (%)	Mexican (%)	Puerto Rican (%)	Cuban (%)	Other (%)
City	18.9	1.2	4.4	0.4	13.0
MSA[1]	12.0	0.8	2.7	0.3	8.3
U.S.	19.0	11.3	1.8	0.7	5.2

Note: Persons of Hispanic or Latino origin can be of any race; (1) Figures cover the Boston-Cambridge-Newton, MA-NH Metropolitan Statistical Area
Source: U.S. Census Bureau, 2019-2023 American Community Survey 5-Year Estimates

Age

Area	Under Age 5	Age 5–19	Age 20–34	Age 35–44	Age 45–54	Age 55–64	Age 65–74	Age 75–84	Age 85+	Median Age
City	4.6	15.3	33.4	13.3	10.2	10.5	7.6	3.4	1.7	33.2
MSA[1]	5.1	17.2	21.6	13.2	12.6	13.5	9.8	4.7	2.1	39.3
U.S.	5.7	19.1	20.2	13.1	12.3	12.8	10.0	4.9	1.9	38.7

Note: (1) Figures cover the Boston-Cambridge-Newton, MA-NH Metropolitan Statistical Area
Source: U.S. Census Bureau, 2019-2023 American Community Survey 5-Year Estimates

Disability by Age

Area	All Ages	Under 18 Years Old	18 to 64 Years Old	65 Years and Over
City	12.1	5.8	9.1	37.2
MSA[1]	10.9	4.5	8.2	29.6
U.S.	13.0	4.7	10.7	32.9

Note: Figures show percent of the civilian noninstitutionalized population that reported having a disability. Disability status is determined from six types of difficulty: vision, hearing, cognitive, ambulatory, self-care, and independent living. For children under 5 years old, hearing and vision difficulty are used to determine disability status. For children between the ages of 5 and 14, disability status is determined from hearing, vision, cognitive, ambulatory, and self-care difficulties. For people aged 15 years and older, they are considered to have a disability if they have difficulty with any one of the six difficulty types; Note: (1) Figures cover the Boston-Cambridge-Newton, MA-NH Metropolitan Statistical Area
Source: U.S. Census Bureau, 2019-2023 American Community Survey 5-Year Estimates

Ancestry

Area	German	Irish	English	American	Italian	Polish	French[2]	European	Scottish
City	4.8	13.2	5.4	2.2	7.3	2.2	1.7	1.1	1.1
MSA[1]	5.7	19.8	10.0	3.2	12.0	3.0	3.9	1.3	2.0
U.S.	12.6	9.4	9.1	5.5	4.9	2.6	2.0	1.6	1.6

Note: Figures are the percentage of the total population reporting a particular ancestry. The nine most commonly reported ancestries in the U.S. are shown. Figures include multiple ancestries (e.g. if a person reported being Irish and Italian, they were included in both columns); (1) Figures cover the Boston-Cambridge-Newton, MA-NH Metropolitan Statistical Area; (2) Excludes Basque
Source: U.S. Census Bureau, 2019-2023 American Community Survey 5-Year Estimates

Foreign-born Population

Area	Percent of Population Born in								
	Any Foreign Country	Asia	Mexico	Europe	Caribbean	Central America[2]	South America	Africa	Canada
City	27.5	7.8	0.4	3.0	8.1	2.3	2.3	3.0	0.4
MSA[1]	19.7	6.4	0.2	3.1	3.5	1.7	2.5	1.8	0.4
U.S.	13.9	4.3	3.3	1.4	1.4	1.2	1.2	0.8	0.2

Note: (1) Figures cover the Boston-Cambridge-Newton, MA-NH Metropolitan Statistical Area; (2) Excludes Mexico.
Source: U.S. Census Bureau, 2019-2023 American Community Survey 5-Year Estimates

Household Size

Area	Persons in Household (%)							Average Household Size
	One	Two	Three	Four	Five	Six	Seven or More	
City	36.9	33.2	14.6	8.9	4.0	1.5	0.9	2.22
MSA[1]	28.0	33.2	16.7	14.0	5.5	1.7	0.9	2.47
U.S.	28.5	33.8	15.4	12.7	5.9	2.3	1.4	2.54

Note: (1) Figures cover the Boston-Cambridge-Newton, MA-NH Metropolitan Statistical Area
Source: U.S. Census Bureau, 2019-2023 American Community Survey 5-Year Estimates

Household Relationships

Area	Householder	Opposite-sex Spouse	Same-sex Spouse	Opposite-sex Unmarried Partner	Same-sex Unmarried Partner	Child[2]	Grandchild	Other Relatives	Non-relatives
City	41.4	10.4	0.5	3.1	0.4	20.6	1.7	5.3	9.7
MSA[1]	38.7	17.4	0.3	2.5	0.2	27.1	1.6	4.5	4.4
U.S.	38.3	17.5	0.2	2.5	0.2	28.3	2.4	4.8	3.4

Note: Figures are percent of the total population; (1) Figures cover the Boston-Cambridge-Newton, MA-NH Metropolitan Statistical Area; (2) Includes biological, adopted, and stepchildren of the householder
Source: U.S. Census Bureau, 2020 Census

Gender

Area	Males	Females	Males per 100 Females
City	319,182	344,790	92.6
MSA[1]	2,405,154	2,512,507	95.7
U.S.	164,545,087	167,842,453	98.0

Note: (1) Figures cover the Boston-Cambridge-Newton, MA-NH Metropolitan Statistical Area
Source: U.S. Census Bureau, 2019-2023 American Community Survey 5-Year Estimates

Marital Status

Area	Never Married	Now Married[2]	Separated	Widowed	Divorced
City	55.7	31.0	2.2	3.8	7.4
MSA[1]	37.5	47.6	1.5	4.9	8.6
U.S.	34.1	47.9	1.7	5.6	10.7

Note: Figures are percentages and cover the population 15 years of age and older; (1) Figures cover the Boston-Cambridge-Newton, MA-NH Metropolitan Statistical Area; (2) Excludes separated
Source: U.S. Census Bureau, 2019-2023 American Community Survey 5-Year Estimates

Religious Groups by Family

Area	Catholic	Baptist	Methodist	LDS[2]	Pentecostal	Lutheran	Islam	Adventist	Other
MSA[1]	37.0	1.0	0.7	0.5	0.7	0.2	2.2	0.9	7.1
U.S.	18.7	7.3	3.0	2.0	1.8	1.7	1.3	1.3	11.6

Note: Figures are the number of adherents as a percentage of the total population and cover the eight largest religious groups in the U.S; (1) Figures cover the Boston-Cambridge-Newton, MA-NH Metropolitan Statistical Area; (2) Church of Jesus Christ of Latter-day Saints
Sources: 2020 U.S. Religion Census, Association of Statisticians of American Religious Bodies; The Association of Religion Data Archives (ARDA)

Religious Groups by Tradition

Area	Catholic	Evangelical Protestant	Mainline Protestant	Black Protestant	Islam	Judaism	Hinduism	Orthodox	Buddhism
MSA[1]	37.0	3.4	3.2	0.3	2.2	1.1	0.3	0.9	0.4
U.S.	18.7	16.5	5.2	2.3	1.3	0.6	0.4	0.4	0.3

Note: Figures are the number of adherents as a percentage of the total population; (1) Figures cover the Boston-Cambridge-Newton, MA-NH Metropolitan Statistical Area
Sources: 2020 U.S. Religion Census, Association of Statisticians of American Religious Bodies; The Association of Religion Data Archives (ARDA)

ECONOMY

Real Gross Domestic Product (GDP)

Area	2017	2018	2019	2020	2021	2022	2023	Rank[3]
MSA[1]	433.8	451.3	467.4	463.3	495.9	507.8	515.4	8
U.S.[2]	17,619.1	18,160.7	18,642.5	18,238.9	19,387.6	19,896.6	20,436.3	—

Note: Figures are in billions of chained 2017 dollars; (1) Figures cover the Boston-Cambridge-Newton, MA-NH Metropolitan Statistical Area; (2) Figures cover real GDP within metropolitan areas; (3) Rank is based on 2023 data and ranges from 1 to 384
Source: U.S. Bureau of Economic Analysis

Economic Growth

Area	2014	2015	2016	2017	2018	2019	2020	2021	2022	2023
MSA[1]	2.1	4.0	1.7	2.3	4.0	3.6	-0.9	7.0	2.4	1.5
U.S.[2]	2.6	3.2	2.0	2.7	3.1	2.7	-2.2	6.3	2.6	2.7

Note: Figures are real gross domestic product growth rates and represent percent change from preceding period; (1) Figures cover the Boston-Cambridge-Newton, MA-NH Metropolitan Statistical Area; (2) Figures are the average growth rates within metropolitan areas
Source: U.S. Bureau of Economic Analysis

Metropolitan Area Exports

Area	2018	2019	2020	2021	2022	2023	Rank[2]
MSA[1]	24,450.1	23,505.8	23,233.8	32,084.2	33,101.8	34,519.4	12
U.S.	1,664,056.1	1,645,173.7	1,431,406.6	1,753,941.4	2,062,937.4	2,019,160.5	—

Note: Figures are in millions of dollars; (1) Figures cover the Boston-Cambridge-Newton, MA-NH Metropolitan Statistical Area; (2) Rank is based on 2023 data and ranges from 1 to 386
Source: U.S. Department of Commerce, International Trade Administration, Office of Trade and Economic Analysis, Industry and Analysis, Exports by Metropolitan Area, data extracted April 2, 2025

Building Permits

Area	Single-Family			Multi-Family			Total		
	2023	2024	Pct. Chg.	2023	2024	Pct. Chg.	2023	2024	Pct. Chg.
City	108	72	-33.3	1,943	1,717	-11.6	2,051	1,789	-12.8
MSA[1]	3,396	3,734	10.0	7,426	7,501	1.0	10,822	11,235	3.8
U.S.	920,000	981,900	6.7	591,100	496,100	-16.1	1,511,100	1,478,000	-2.2

Note: (1) Figures cover the Boston-Cambridge-Newton, MA-NH Metropolitan Statistical Area; Figures represent new, privately-owned housing units authorized (unadjusted data)
Source: U.S. Census Bureau, Building Permits Survey (BPS), 2023, 2024

Bankruptcy Filings

Area	Business Filings			Nonbusiness Filings		
	2023	2024	% Chg.	2023	2024	% Chg.
Suffolk County	53	63	18.9	233	316	35.6
U.S.	18,926	23,107	22.1	434,064	494,201	13.9

Note: Business filings include Chapter 7, Chapter 9, Chapter 11, Chapter 12, Chapter 13, Chapter 15, and Section 304; Nonbusiness filings include Chapter 7, Chapter 11, and Chapter 13
Source: Administrative Office of the U.S. Courts, Business and Nonbusiness Bankruptcy, County Cases Commenced by Chapter of the Bankruptcy Code, During the 12-Month Period Ending December 31, 2023 and Business and Nonbusiness Bankruptcy, County Cases Commenced by Chapter of the Bankruptcy Code, During the 12-Month Period Ending December 31, 2024

Housing Vacancy Rates

Area	Gross Vacancy Rate[3] (%)			Year-Round Vacancy Rate[4] (%)			Rental Vacancy Rate[5] (%)			Homeowner Vacancy Rate[6] (%)		
	2022	2023	2024	2022	2023	2024	2022	2023	2024	2022	2023	2024
MSA[1]	6.2	6.1	5.7	5.4	5.3	4.8	2.5	2.5	3.0	0.7	0.6	0.6
U.S.[2]	9.1	9.0	9.1	7.5	7.5	7.6	5.7	6.5	6.8	0.8	0.8	1.0

Note: (1) Figures cover the Boston-Cambridge-Newton, MA-NH Metropolitan Statistical Area; (2) Figures cover the 75 largest Metropolitan Statistical Areas; (3) The percentage of the total housing inventory that is vacant; (4) The percentage of the housing inventory (excluding seasonal units) that is year-round vacant; (5) The percentage of rental inventory that is vacant for rent; (6) The percentage of homeowner inventory that is vacant for sale
Source: U.S. Census Bureau, Housing Vacancies and Homeownership Annual Statistics: 2022, 2023, 2024

INCOME

Income

Area	Per Capita ($)	Median Household ($)	Average Household ($)
City	60,001	94,755	140,807
MSA[1]	61,389	112,484	155,005
U.S.	43,289	78,538	110,491

Note: (1) Figures cover the Boston-Cambridge-Newton, MA-NH Metropolitan Statistical Area
Source: U.S. Census Bureau, 2019-2023 American Community Survey 5-Year Estimates

Household Income Distribution

Area	Percent of Households Earning							
	Under $15,000	$15,000 -$24,999	$25,000 -$34,999	$35,000 -$49,999	$50,000 -$74,999	$75,000 -$99,999	$100,000 -$149,999	$150,000 and up
City	12.9	6.5	5.1	7.1	10.6	9.9	15.5	32.5
MSA[1]	7.2	4.9	4.5	6.7	11.2	10.5	17.7	37.2
U.S.	8.5	6.6	6.8	10.4	15.7	12.7	17.4	21.9

Note: (1) Figures cover the Boston-Cambridge-Newton, MA-NH Metropolitan Statistical Area
Source: U.S. Census Bureau, 2019-2023 American Community Survey 5-Year Estimates

Poverty Rate

Area	All Ages	Under 18 Years Old	18 to 64 Years Old	65 Years and Over
City	16.9	21.8	15.0	21.0
MSA[1]	8.9	9.7	8.3	10.3
U.S.	12.4	16.3	11.6	10.4

Note: Figures are percentage of people whose income during the past 12 months was below the poverty level;
(1) Figures cover the Boston-Cambridge-Newton, MA-NH Metropolitan Statistical Area
Source: U.S. Census Bureau, 2019-2023 American Community Survey 5-Year Estimates

EMPLOYMENT

Labor Force and Employment

Area	Civilian Labor Force			Workers Employed		
	Dec. 2023	Dec. 2024	% Chg.	Dec. 2023	Dec. 2024	% Chg.
City	403,771	411,958	2.0	390,365	395,765	1.4
MD[1]	1,158,650	1,182,153	2.0	1,119,472	1,135,105	1.4
U.S.	166,661,000	167,746,000	0.7	160,754,000	161,294,000	0.3

Note: Data is not seasonally adjusted and covers workers 16 years of age and older; (1) Figures cover the Boston, MA Metropolitan Division
Source: Bureau of Labor Statistics, Local Area Unemployment Statistics

Unemployment Rate

Area	2024											
	Jan.	Feb.	Mar.	Apr.	May	Jun.	Jul.	Aug.	Sep.	Oct.	Nov.	Dec.
City	3.7	3.7	3.5	3.2	3.8	4.3	4.6	4.4	3.8	3.9	3.9	3.9
MD[1]	3.9	4.0	3.7	3.2	3.8	4.2	4.5	4.3	3.7	3.9	3.9	4.0
U.S.	4.1	4.2	3.9	3.5	3.7	4.3	4.5	4.4	3.9	3.9	4.0	3.8

Note: Data is not seasonally adjusted and covers workers 16 years of age and older; (1) Figures cover the Boston, MA Metropolitan Division
Source: Bureau of Labor Statistics, Local Area Unemployment Statistics

Average Wages

Occupation	$/Hr.	Occupation	$/Hr.
Accountants and Auditors	49.79	Maintenance and Repair Workers	28.49
Automotive Mechanics	29.49	Marketing Managers	98.23
Bookkeepers	28.51	Network and Computer Systems Admin.	53.85
Carpenters	38.40	Nurses, Licensed Practical	37.85
Cashiers	17.37	Nurses, Registered	55.63
Computer Programmers	57.83	Nursing Assistants	22.73
Computer Systems Analysts	60.98	Office Clerks, General	25.39
Computer User Support Specialists	37.62	Physical Therapists	49.54
Construction Laborers	33.95	Physicians	104.76
Cooks, Restaurant	21.98	Plumbers, Pipefitters and Steamfitters	42.81
Customer Service Representatives	25.48	Police and Sheriff's Patrol Officers	39.16
Dentists	n/a	Postal Service Mail Carriers	29.71
Electricians	40.10	Real Estate Sales Agents	46.11
Engineers, Electrical	64.82	Retail Salespersons	19.71
Fast Food and Counter Workers	17.43	Sales Representatives, Technical/Scientific	54.45
Financial Managers	100.73	Secretaries, Exc. Legal/Medical/Executive	27.63
First-Line Supervisors of Office Workers	38.59	Security Guards	22.25
General and Operations Managers	78.73	Surgeons	161.25
Hairdressers/Cosmetologists	24.97	Teacher Assistants, Exc. Postsecondary[1]	20.03
Home Health and Personal Care Aides	19.58	Teachers, Secondary School, Exc. Sp. Ed.[1]	42.74
Janitors and Cleaners	21.75	Telemarketers	18.61
Landscaping/Groundskeeping Workers	24.09	Truck Drivers, Heavy/Tractor-Trailer	29.10
Lawyers	109.06	Truck Drivers, Light/Delivery Services	25.46
Maids and Housekeeping Cleaners	21.01	Waiters and Waitresses	22.07

Note: Wage data covers the Boston-Cambridge-Newton, MA-NH Metropolitan Statistical Area; (1) Hourly wages were calculated from annual wage data based on a 40 hour work week
Source: Bureau of Labor Statistics, Metro Area Occupational Employment & Wage Estimates, May 2024

Employment by Industry

Sector	MD[1] Number of Employees	MD[1] Percent of Total	U.S. Percent of Total
Construction, Mining, and Logging	52,200	4.1	5.5
Financial Activities	123,500	9.6	5.8
Government	156,400	12.2	14.9
Information	33,400	2.6	1.9
Leisure and Hospitality	134,200	10.5	10.4
Manufacturing	36,300	2.8	8.0
Other Services	45,900	3.6	3.7
Private Education and Health Services	316,000	24.6	16.9
Professional and Business Services	209,800	16.3	14.2
Retail Trade	100,200	7.8	10.0
Transportation, Warehousing, and Utilities	44,000	3.4	4.8
Wholesale Trade	31,900	2.5	3.9

Note: Figures are non-farm employment as of December 2024. Figures are not seasonally adjusted and include workers 16 years of age and older; (1) Figures cover the Boston, MA Metropolitan Division
Source: Bureau of Labor Statistics, Current Employment Statistics, Employment, Hours, and Earnings

Employment by Occupation

Occupation Classification	City (%)	MSA[1] (%)	U.S. (%)
Management, Business, Science, and Arts	56.4	54.0	42.0
Natural Resources, Construction, and Maintenance	3.2	6.1	8.6
Production, Transportation, and Material Moving	6.2	8.0	13.0
Sales and Office	16.8	17.4	19.9
Service	17.4	14.6	16.5

Note: Figures cover employed civilians 16 years of age and older; (1) Figures cover the Boston-Cambridge-Newton, MA-NH Metropolitan Statistical Area
Source: U.S. Census Bureau, 2019-2023 American Community Survey 5-Year Estimates

Occupations with Greatest Projected Employment Growth: 2022 – 2032

Occupation[1]	2022 Employment	2032 Projected Employment	Numeric Employment Change	Percent Employment Change
Home Health and Personal Care Aides	39,480	46,500	7,020	17.8
Software Developers	20,230	25,250	5,020	24.8
Cooks, Restaurant	10,330	13,400	3,070	29.7
Fast Food and Counter Workers	28,340	31,010	2,670	9.4
Registered Nurses	30,060	32,600	2,540	8.4
General and Operations Managers	38,270	40,770	2,500	6.5
Stockers and Order Fillers	16,870	19,200	2,330	13.8
Medical and Health Services Managers	6,820	8,870	2,050	30.1
Financial Managers	11,230	12,930	1,700	15.1
Computer and Information Systems Managers	8,500	9,790	1,290	15.2

Note: Projections cover Massachusetts; (1) Sorted by numeric employment change
Source: www.projectionscentral.org, State Occupational Projections, 2022–2032 Long-Term Projections

Fastest-Growing Occupations: 2022 – 2032

Occupation[1]	2022 Employment	2032 Projected Employment	Numeric Employment Change	Percent Employment Change
Nurse Practitioners	2,730	4,010	1,280	46.9
Solar Photovoltaic Installers	240	330	90	37.5
Statisticians	740	1,000	260	35.1
Epidemiologists	230	310	80	34.8
Data Scientists	2,520	3,380	860	34.1
Taxi Drivers	1,780	2,360	580	32.6
Medical and Health Services Managers	6,820	8,870	2,050	30.1
Physician Assistants	1,430	1,860	430	30.1
Information Security Analysts (SOC 2018)	1,600	2,080	480	30.0
Cooks, Restaurant	10,330	13,400	3,070	29.7

Note: Projections cover Massachusetts; (1) Sorted by percent employment change and excludes occupations with numeric employment change less than 50
Source: www.projectionscentral.org, State Occupational Projections, 2022–2032 Long-Term Projections

CITY FINANCES

City Government Finances

Component	2022 ($000)	2022 ($ per capita)
Total Revenues	5,100,266	7,375
Total Expenditures	5,126,187	7,413
Debt Outstanding	2,063,136	2,983

Source: U.S. Census Bureau, State & Local Government Finances 2022

City Government Revenue by Source

Source	2022 ($000)	2022 ($ per capita)	2022 (%)
General Revenue			
From Federal Government	27,096	39	0.5
From State Government	1,234,166	1,785	24.2
From Local Governments	2,477	4	0.0
Taxes			
Property	2,867,471	4,147	56.2
Sales and Gross Receipts	130,811	189	2.6
Personal Income	0	0	0.0
Corporate Income	0	0	0.0
Motor Vehicle License	0	0	0.0
Other Taxes	119,311	173	2.3
Current Charges	329,241	476	6.5
Liquor Store	0	0	0.0
Utility	176,649	255	3.5

Source: U.S. Census Bureau, State & Local Government Finances 2022

City Government Expenditures by Function

Function	2022 ($000)	2022 ($ per capita)	2022 (%)
General Direct Expenditures			
Air Transportation	0	0	0.0
Corrections	0	0	0.0
Education	1,876,589	2,713	36.6
Employment Security Administration	0	0	0.0
Financial Administration	70,735	102	1.4
Fire Protection	289,514	418	5.6
General Public Buildings	51,155	74	1.0
Governmental Administration, Other	23,649	34	0.5
Health	29,559	42	0.6
Highways	140,729	203	2.7
Hospitals	364,470	527	7.1
Housing and Community Development	157,244	227	3.1
Interest on General Debt	66,860	96	1.3
Judicial and Legal	8,227	11	0.2
Libraries	66,414	96	1.3
Parking	2,195	3	0.0
Parks and Recreation	148,587	214	2.9
Police Protection	441,749	638	8.6
Public Welfare	6,815	9	0.1
Sewerage	68,592	99	1.3
Solid Waste Management	143,445	207	2.8
Veterans' Services	0	0	0.0
Liquor Store	0	0	0.0
Utility	63,315	91	1.2

Source: U.S. Census Bureau, State & Local Government Finances 2022

TAXES

State Corporate Income Tax Rates

State	Tax Rate (%)	Income Brackets ($)	Num. of Brackets	Financial Institution Tax Rate (%)[a]	Federal Income Tax Ded.
Massachusetts	8.0 (k)	Flat rate	1	9.0 (k)	No

Note: Tax rates for tax year 2024; (a) Rates listed are the corporate income tax rate applied to financial institutions or excise taxes based on income. Some states have other taxes based upon the value of deposits or shares; (k) Business and manufacturing corporations pay an additional tax of $2.60 per $1,000 on either taxable Massachusetts tangible property or taxable net worth allocable to the state (for intangible property corporations). The minimum tax for both corporations and financial institutions is $456.
Source: Federation of Tax Administrators, State Corporate Income Tax Rates, January 1, 2025

State Individual Income Tax Rates

State	Tax Rate (%)	Income Brackets ($)	Personal Exemptions ($)			Standard Ded. ($)	
			Single	Married	Depend.	Single	Married
Massachusetts	5.0 (m)	Flat rate	4,400	8,800	1,000	–	–

Note: Tax rates for tax year 2024; Local- and county-level taxes are not included; Federal income tax is not deductible on state income tax returns; (m) Short-term capital gains in Massachusetts is taxed is reduced to 8.5% from 12% rate. An additional tax of 4% on income of $1,053,750.
Source: Federation of Tax Administrators, State Individual Income Tax Rates, January 1, 2025

Various State Sales and Excise Tax Rates

State	State Sales Tax (%)	Gasoline[1] ($/gal.)	Cigarette[2] ($/pack)	Spirits[3] ($/gal.)	Wine[4] ($/gal.)	Beer[5] ($/gal.)	Recreational Marijuana (%)
Massachusetts	6.25	0.27	3.51	4.05	0.55	0.11	(j)

Note: All tax rates as of January 1, 2025; (1) The American Petroleum Institute has developed a methodology for determining the average tax rate on a gallon of fuel. Rates may include any of the following: excise taxes, environmental fees, storage tank fees, other fees or taxes, general sales tax, and local taxes; (2) The federal excise tax of $1.0066 per pack and local taxes are not included; (3) Rates are those applicable to off-premise sales of 40% alcohol by volume (a.b.v.) distilled spirits in 750ml containers. Local excise taxes are excluded; (4) Rates are those applicable to off-premise sales of 11% a.b.v. non-carbonated wine in 750ml containers; (5) Rates are those applicable to off-premise sales of 4.7% a.b.v. beer in 12 ounce containers; (j) 10.75% excise tax (retail price)
Source: Tax Foundation, 2025 Facts & Figures: How Does Your State Compare?

State Tax Competitiveness Index

State	Overall Rank	Corporate Tax Rank	Individual Income Tax Rank	Sales Tax Rank	Property Tax Rank	Unemployment Insurance Tax Rank
Massachusetts	41	33	41	20	46	47

Note: The Tax Foundation's State Tax Competitiveness Index enables policymakers, taxpayers, and business leaders to gauge how their states' tax systems compare. A rank of 1 is best, 50 is worst. Rankings do not average to the total. States without a tax rank equally as 1. DC's scores and rankings do not affect other states. The report shows tax systems as of July 1, 2024 (the beginning of Fiscal Year 2025).
Source: Tax Foundation, State Tax Competitiveness Index 2025

TRANSPORTATION

Means of Transportation to Work

Area	Car/Truck/Van		Public Transportation			Bicycle	Walked	Other Means	Worked at Home
	Drove Alone	Car-pooled	Bus	Subway	Railroad				
City	34.1	5.4	8.6	13.6	1.2	2.1	13.8	2.4	18.8
MSA[1]	58.6	6.3	2.6	4.6	1.4	1.0	4.7	2.0	18.7
U.S.	70.2	8.5	1.7	1.3	0.4	0.4	2.4	1.6	13.5

Note: Figures are percentages and cover workers 16 years of age and older; (1) Figures cover the Boston-Cambridge-Newton, MA-NH Metropolitan Statistical Area
Source: U.S. Census Bureau, 2019-2023 American Community Survey 5-Year Estimates

Travel Time to Work

Area	Less Than 10 Minutes	10 to 19 Minutes	20 to 29 Minutes	30 to 44 Minutes	45 to 59 Minutes	60 to 89 Minutes	90 Minutes or More
City	6.9	21.3	20.7	28.8	11.4	8.6	2.3
MSA[1]	9.4	22.9	19.3	24.4	11.2	9.6	3.1
U.S.	12.6	28.6	21.2	20.8	8.1	6.0	2.8

Note: Note: Figures are percentages and include workers 16 years old and over; (1) Figures cover the Boston-Cambridge-Newton, MA-NH Metropolitan Statistical Area
Source: U.S. Census Bureau, 2019-2023 American Community Survey 5-Year Estimates

Key Congestion Measures

Measure	2000	2010	2015	2020	2022
Annual Hours of Delay, Total (000)	126,792	154,889	179,172	122,348	165,890
Annual Hours of Delay, Per Auto Commuter	61	65	75	50	73
Annual Congestion Cost, Per Auto Commuter ($)	1,699	1,652	1,764	1,233	1,664

Note: Figures cover the Boston MA-NH-RI urban area
Source: Texas A&M Transportation Institute, 2023 Urban Mobility Report

Freeway Travel Time Index

Measure	1985	1990	1995	2000	2005	2010	2015	2020	2022
Urban Area Index[1]	1.15	1.19	1.21	1.26	1.27	1.26	1.28	1.12	1.22
Urban Area Rank[1,2]	15	12	16	13	18	19	19	10	28

Note: Freeway Travel Time Index—the ratio of travel time in the peak period to the travel time at free-flow conditions. For example, a value of 1.30 indicates a 20-minute free-flow trip takes 26 minutes in the peak (20 minutes x 1.30 = 26 minutes); (1) Covers the Boston MA-NH-RI urban area; (2) Rank is based on 101 larger urban areas (#1 = highest travel time index)
Source: Texas A&M Transportation Institute, 2023 Urban Mobility Report

Public Transportation

Agency Name / Mode of Transportation	Vehicles Operated in Maximum Service[1]	Annual Unlinked Passenger Trips[2] (in thous.)	Annual Passenger Miles[3] (in thous.)
Massachusetts Bay Transportation Authority (MBTA)			
Bus (directly operated)	624	76,628.0	193,886.8
Bus (purchased transportation)	234	2,860.0	10,722.2
Bus Rapid Transit (directly operated)	34	8,908.5	19,433.3
Commuter Rail (purchased transportation)	406	23,494.8	503,068.8
Demand Response (purchased transportation)	460	1,008.5	7,243.9
Ferryboat (purchased transportation)	10	1,009.6	7,652.2
Heavy Rail (directly operated)	312	84,030.2	275,137.4
Light Rail (directly operated)	128	37,035.9	86,273.0

Note: (1) Number of revenue vehicles operated by the given mode and type of service to meet the annual maximum service requirement. This is the revenue vehicle count during the peak season of the year; on the week and day that maximum service is provided. Vehicles operated in maximum service (VOMS) exclude atypical days and one-time special events; (2) Number of passengers who boarded public transportation vehicles. Passengers are counted each time they board a vehicle no matter how many vehicles they use to travel from their origin to their destination. (3) Sum of the distances ridden by all passengers during the entire fiscal year.
Source: Federal Transit Administration, National Transit Database, 2023

Air Transportation

Airport Name and Code / Type of Service	Passenger Airlines[1]	Passenger Enplanements	Freight Carriers[2]	Freight (lbs)
Logan International (BOS)				
Domestic service (U.S. carriers only)	30	16,855,500	14	151,812,611
International service (U.S. carriers only)	9	1,507,141	3	9,008,602

Note: (1) Includes all U.S.-based major, minor and commuter airlines that carried at least one passenger during the year; (2) Includes all U.S.-based airlines and freight carriers that transported at least one pound of freight during the year.
Source: Bureau of Transportation Statistics, The Intermodal Transportation Database, Air Carriers: T-100 Domestic Market (U.S. carriers only), 2024; Bureau of Transportation Statistics, The Intermodal Transportation Database, Air Carriers: T-100 International Market (U.S. carriers only), 2024

BUSINESSES

Major Business Headquarters

Company Name	Industry	Fortune[1]	Forbes[2]
American Tower	Real estate	363	-
BCG (Boston Consulting Group)	Business services & supplies	-	38
Bain & Company	Business services & supplies	-	88
Fidelity Investments	Diversified financials	-	9
General Electric	Industrial machinery	56	-
Goodwin Procter	Business services & supplies	-	256
Liberty Mutual Insurance Group	Insurance: property and casualty (stock)	87	-
New Balance	Retailing	-	98
Ropes & Gray	Services	-	212
State Street	Commercial banks	225	-
Suffolk	Construction	-	117
Vertex Pharmaceuticals	Pharmaceuticals	400	-
Wayfair	Internet services and retailing	346	-

Note: (1) Companies that produce a 10-K are ranked 1 to 500 based on 2023 revenue; (2) All private companies with at least $2 billion in annual revenue through the end of their most current fiscal year are ranked 1 to 275; companies listed are headquartered in the city; dashes indicate no ranking
Source: Fortune, "Fortune 500," 2024; Forbes, "America's Largest Private Companies," 2024

Fastest-Growing Businesses

According to *Inc.*, Boston is home to six of America's 500 fastest-growing private companies: **1upHealth** (#95); **LJV Development** (#115); **apiphani** (#173); **H2O Care Partners** (#322); **StemWave** (#326); **Fort Point Payments** (#439). Criteria: must be an independent, privately-held, for-profit, U.S. corporation, proprietorship or partnership as of December 31, 2023; revenues must be at least $100,000 in 2020 and $2 million in 2023; must have four-year operating/sales history. *Inc., "America's 500 Fastest-Growing Private Companies," 2024*

According to *Initiative for a Competitive Inner City (ICIC)*, Boston is home to five of America's 100 fastest-growing "inner city" companies: **LJV Development** (#3); **CAAN Fence** (#20); **Proverb** (#58); **Red's Best** (#83); **R&E dba My Grandma's Coffee Cakes of New England** (#86). To be eligible for the IC100, companies have to be independently operated, privately held, for-profit businesses with revenues of at least $50,000 in 2019 and $500,000 in 2023, and headquartered in an under-resourced community. Recognizing that concentrated poverty exists within metropolitan areas outside of big cities (and that poverty overall is suburbanizing), ICIC defines under-resourced communities as large low-income, high-poverty areas located in the urban and suburban parts of all but the smallest metropolitan areas. Companies were ranked overall by revenue growth over the five-year period between 2019 and 2023. *Initiative for a Competitive Inner City (ICIC), "Inner City 100 Companies," 2024*

According to Deloitte, Boston is home to 17 of North America's 500 fastest-growing high-technology companies: **Circle** (#17); **1upHealth** (#43); **Nift** (#109); **RapDev** (#171); **LinkSquares** (#174); **Hometap** (#208); **Wasabi Technologies** (#217); **SquareWorks Consulting** (#218); **DraftKings** (#238); **Fairmarkit** (#295); **Tango Therapeutics** (#310); **Toast** (#317); **Klaviyo** (#332); **G-P** (#396); **PathAI** (#420); **Ginkgo Bioworks Holdings** (#458); **Zone & Co** (#495). Companies are ranked by percentage growth in revenue over a four-year period. Criteria for inclusion: company must be headquartered within North America; must own proprietary intellectual property or technology that is sold to customers in products that contributes to a significant portion of the company's operating revenue; must have been in business for a minumum of four years with 2020 operating revenues of at least $50,000 USD/CD and 2023 operating revenues of at least $5 million USD/CD. *Deloitte, 2024 Technology Fast 500™*

Living Environment

COST OF LIVING

Cost of Living Index

Composite Index	Groceries	Housing	Utilities	Transportation	Health Care	Misc. Goods/Services
145.9	104.4	218.9	149.7	109.8	125.3	115.2

Note: The Cost of Living Index measures regional differences in the cost of consumer goods and services, excluding taxes and non-consumer expenditures, for professional and managerial households in the top income quintile. It is based on more than 50,000 prices covering almost 60 different items for which prices are collected three times a year by chambers of commerce, economic development organizations or university applied economic centers in each participating urban area. The numbers shown should be read as a percentage above or below the national average of 100. For example, a value of 115.4 in the groceries column indicates that grocery prices are 15.4% higher than the national average. Small differences in the index numbers should not be interpreted as significant; Figures cover the Boston MA urban area.
Source: The Council for Community and Economic Research, Cost of Living Index, 2024

Grocery Prices

Area[1]	T-Bone Steak ($/pound)	Frying Chicken ($/pound)	Whole Milk ($/half gal.)	Eggs ($/dozen)	Orange Juice ($/64 oz.)	Coffee ($/11.5 oz.)
City[2]	15.52	1.51	4.76	3.03	4.54	5.39
Avg.	15.42	1.55	4.69	3.25	4.41	5.46
Min.	14.50	1.16	4.43	2.75	4.00	4.85
Max.	17.56	2.89	5.49	4.78	5.54	7.89

Note: (1) Values for the local area are compared with the average, minimum and maximum values for all 276 areas in the Cost of Living Index; (2) Figures cover the Boston MA urban area; **T-Bone Steak** (price per pound); **Frying Chicken** (price per pound, whole fryer); **Whole Milk** (half gallon carton); **Eggs** (price per dozen, Grade A, large); **Orange Juice** (64 oz. Tropicana or Florida Natural); **Coffee** (11.5 oz. can, vacuum-packed, Maxwell House, Hills Bros, or Folgers).
Source: The Council for Community and Economic Research, Cost of Living Index, 2024

Housing and Utility Costs

Area[1]	New Home Price ($)	Apartment Rent ($/month)	All Electric ($/month)	Part Electric ($/month)	Other Energy ($/month)	Telephone ($/month)
City[2]	1,039,939	3,993	-	190.85	180.18	190.24
Avg.	515,975	1,550	210.99	123.07	82.07	194.99
Min.	265,375	692	104.33	53.68	36.26	179.42
Max.	2,775,821	5,719	529.02	397.28	361.63	223.33

Note: (1) Values for the local area are compared with the average, minimum and maximum values for all 276 areas in the Cost of Living Index; (2) Figures cover the Boston MA urban area; **New Home Price** (2,400 sf living area, 8,000 sf lot, in urban area with full utilities); **Apartment Rent** (950 sf 2 bedroom/1.5 or 2 bath, unfurnished, excluding all utilities except water); **All Electric** (average monthly cost for an all-electric home); **Part Electric** (average monthly cost for a part-electric home); **Other Energy** (average monthly cost for natural gas, fuel oil, coal, wood, and any other forms of energy except electricity); **Telephone** (price includes the base monthly rate plus taxes and fees for three lines of mobile phone service).
Source: The Council for Community and Economic Research, Cost of Living Index, 2024

Health Care, Transportation, and Other Costs

Area[1]	Doctor ($/visit)	Dentist ($/visit)	Optometrist ($/visit)	Gasoline ($/gallon)	Beauty Salon ($/visit)	Men's Shirt ($)
City[2]	222.77	144.00	161.33	3.33	66.76	39.88
Avg.	143.77	117.51	129.23	3.32	48.57	38.14
Min.	36.74	58.67	67.33	2.80	24.00	13.41
Max.	270.44	216.82	307.33	5.28	94.00	63.89

Note: (1) Values for the local area are compared with the average, minimum and maximum values for all 276 areas in the Cost of Living Index; (2) Figures cover the Boston MA urban area; **Doctor** (general practitioners routine exam of an established patient); **Dentist** (adult teeth cleaning and periodic oral examination); **Optometrist** (full vision eye exam for established adult patient); **Gasoline** (one gallon regular unleaded, national brand, including all taxes, cash price at self-service pump if available); **Beauty Salon** (woman's shampoo, trim, and blow-dry); **Men's Shirt** (cotton/polyester dress shirt, pinpoint weave, long sleeves).
Source: The Council for Community and Economic Research, Cost of Living Index, 2024

HOUSING

Homeownership Rate

Area	2017 (%)	2018 (%)	2019 (%)	2020 (%)	2021 (%)	2022 (%)	2023 (%)	2024 (%)
MSA[1]	58.8	61.0	60.9	61.2	60.7	59.4	59.9	60.7
U.S.	63.9	64.4	64.6	66.6	65.5	65.8	65.9	65.6

Note: (1) Figures cover the Boston-Cambridge-Newton, MA-NH Metropolitan Statistical Area
Source: U.S. Census Bureau, Housing Vacancies and Homeownership Annual Statistics: 2017-2024

House Price Index (HPI)

Area	National Ranking[2]	Quarterly Change (%)	One-Year Change (%)	Five-Year Change (%)	Since 1991Q1 (%)
MD[1]	123	0.36	5.29	50.28	365.78
U.S.[3]	—	1.43	4.51	57.13	327.82

Note: The HPI is a weighted repeat sales index. It measures average price changes in repeat sales or refinancings on the same properties. This information is obtained by reviewing repeat mortgage transactions on single-family properties whose mortgages have been purchased or securitized by Fannie Mae or Freddie Mac since January 1975; (1) Figures cover the Boston, MA Metropolitan Division; (2) Rankings are based on annual percentage change for all metro areas containing at least 15,000 transactions over the last 10 years and ranges from 1 to 241; (3) figures based on a weighted average of Census Division estimates using a seasonally adjusted, purchase-only index; all figures are for the period ending December 31, 2024
Source: Federal Housing Finance Agency, Change in FHFA Metropolitan Area House Price Indexes, All Transactions Index, 2024Q4

Home Value

Area	Under $100,000	$100,000 -$199,999	$200,000 -$299,999	$300,000 -$399,999	$400,000 -$499,999	$500,000 -$999,999	$1,000,000 or more	Median ($)
City	3.4	0.7	3.2	5.8	9.4	53.3	24.2	710,400
MSA[1]	2.6	1.9	5.8	10.4	15.0	48.7	15.6	610,900
U.S.	12.1	17.8	19.5	14.4	10.5	19.1	6.5	303,400

Note: Figures are percentages except for median and cover owner-occupied housing units; (1) Figures cover the Boston-Cambridge-Newton, MA-NH Metropolitan Statistical Area
Source: U.S. Census Bureau, 2019-2023 American Community Survey 5-Year Estimates

Year Housing Structure Built

Area	2020 or Later	2010 -2019	2000 -2009	1990 -1999	1980 -1989	1970 -1979	1960 -1969	1950 -1959	1940 -1949	Before 1940	Median Year
City	0.9	9.2	6.5	4.3	5.6	7.6	7.2	7.1	4.9	46.8	1947
MSA[1]	0.8	7.1	7.5	7.1	10.5	10.6	9.8	10.4	4.8	31.5	1963
U.S.	1.2	8.9	13.6	12.8	13.0	14.4	10.0	9.7	4.5	11.9	1980

Note: Figures are percentages except for Median Year; Note: (1) Figures cover the Boston-Cambridge-Newton, MA-NH Metropolitan Statistical Area
Source: U.S. Census Bureau, 2019-2023 American Community Survey 5-Year Estimates

Gross Monthly Rent

Area	Under $500	$500 -$999	$1,000 -$1,499	$1,500 -$1,999	$2,000 -$2,499	$2,500 -$2,999	$3,000 and up	Median ($)
City	12.2	9.1	9.8	15.4	18.7	13.2	21.6	2,093
MSA[1]	9.4	8.3	13.6	21.1	19.8	12.2	15.5	1,940
U.S.	6.5	22.3	29.5	20.2	10.8	4.8	5.9	1,348

Note: Figures are percentages except for median; Gross rent is the contract rent plus the estimated average monthly cost of utilities (electricity, gas, and water and sewer) and fuels (oil, coal, kerosene, wood, etc.) if these are paid by the renter (or paid for the renter by someone else); (1) Figures cover the Boston-Cambridge-Newton, MA-NH Metropolitan Statistical Area
Source: U.S. Census Bureau, 2019-2023 American Community Survey 5-Year Estimates

HEALTH

Health Risk Factors

Category	MD[1] (%)	U.S. (%)
Adults aged 18–64 who have any kind of health care coverage	96.5	90.8
Adults who reported being in good or better health	86.2	81.8
Adults who have been told they have high blood cholesterol	37.0	36.9
Adults who have been told they have high blood pressure	28.1	34.0
Adults who are current smokers	9.3	12.1
Adults who currently use e-cigarettes	6.4	7.7
Adults who currently use chewing tobacco, snuff, or snus	1.2	3.2
Adults who are heavy drinkers[2]	5.9	6.1
Adults who are binge drinkers[3]	18.3	15.2
Adults who are overweight (BMI 25.0 - 29.9)	36.8	34.4
Adults who are obese (BMI 30.0 - 99.8)	24.7	34.3
Adults who participated in any physical activities in the past month	79.1	75.8

Note: All figures are crude prevalence; (1) Figures cover the Boston, MA Metropolitan Division; (2) Heavy drinkers are classified as adult men having more than 14 drinks per week and adult women having more than 7 drinks per week; (3) Binge drinkers are classified as males having five or more drinks on one occasion or females having four or more drinks on one occasion
Source: Centers for Disease Control and Prevention, Behaviorial Risk Factor Surveillance System, SMART: Selected Metropolitan Area Risk Trends, 2023

Acute and Chronic Health Conditions

Category	MD[1] (%)	U.S. (%)
Adults who have ever been told they had a heart attack	2.9	4.2
Adults who have ever been told they have angina or coronary heart disease	3.4	4.0
Adults who have ever been told they had a stroke	2.0	3.3
Adults who have ever been told they have asthma	15.2	15.7
Adults who have ever been told they have arthritis	22.8	26.3
Adults who have ever been told they have diabetes[2]	8.5	11.5
Adults who have ever been told they had skin cancer	5.9	5.6
Adults who have ever been told they had any other types of cancer	8.3	8.4
Adults who have ever been told they have COPD	4.9	6.4
Adults who have ever been told they have kidney disease	3.5	3.7
Adults who have ever been told they have a form of depression	20.3	22.0

Note: All figures are crude prevalence; (1) Figures cover the Boston, MA Metropolitan Division; (2) Figures do not include pregnancy-related, borderline, or pre-diabetes
Source: Centers for Disease Control and Prevention, Behavioral Risk Factor Surveillance System, SMART: Selected Metropolitan Area Risk Trends, 2023

Health Screening and Vaccination Rates

Category	MD[1] (%)	U.S. (%)
Adults who have ever been tested for HIV	42.6	37.5
Adults who have had their blood cholesterol checked within the last five years	90.9	87.0
Adults aged 65+ who have had flu shot within the past year	69.0	63.4
Adults aged 65+ who have ever had a pneumonia vaccination	72.3	71.9

Note: All figures are crude prevalence; (1) Figures cover the Boston, MA Metropolitan Division.
Source: Centers for Disease Control and Prevention, Behavioral Risk Factor Surveillance System, SMART: Selected Metropolitan Area Risk Trends, 2023

Disability Status

Category	MD[1] (%)	U.S. (%)
Adults who reported being deaf	5.5	7.4
Are you blind or have serious difficulty seeing, even when wearing glasses?	2.6	4.9
Do you have difficulty doing errands alone?	5.9	7.8
Do you have difficulty dressing or bathing?	2.5	3.6
Do you have serious difficulty concentrating/remembering/making decisions?	11.9	13.7
Do you have serious difficulty walking or climbing stairs?	10.5	13.2

Note: All figures are crude prevalence; (1) Figures cover the Boston, MA Metropolitan Division.
Source: Centers for Disease Control and Prevention, Behavioral Risk Factor Surveillance System, SMART: Selected Metropolitan Area Risk Trends, 2023

Mortality Rates for the Top 10 Causes of Death in the U.S.

ICD-10[a] Sub-Chapter	ICD-10[a] Code	Crude Mortality Rate[2] per 100,000 population	
		County[3]	U.S.
Malignant neoplasms	C00-C97	131.5	182.7
Ischaemic heart diseases	I20-I25	53.3	109.6
Provisional assignment of new diseases of uncertain etiology[1]	U00-U49	30.8	65.3
Other forms of heart disease	I30-I51	45.6	65.1
Other degenerative diseases of the nervous system	G30-G31	18.9	52.4
Other external causes of accidental injury	W00-X59	58.9	52.3
Cerebrovascular diseases	I60-I69	26.1	49.1
Chronic lower respiratory diseases	J40-J47	21.8	43.5
Hypertensive diseases	I10-I15	18.9	38.9
Organic, including symptomatic, mental disorders	F01-F09	42.9	33.9

Note: (a) ICD-10 = International Classification of Diseases 10th Revision; (1) Includes COVID-19, adverse effects to COVID-19 vaccines, SARS, and vaping-related disorders; (2) Crude mortality rates are a three-year average covering 2021-2023; (3) Figures cover Suffolk County.
Source: Centers for Disease Control and Prevention, National Center for Health Statistics. National Vital Statistics System, Mortality 2018-2023 on CDC WONDER Online Database

Mortality Rates for Selected Causes of Death

Cause of Death	ICD-10[a] Code	Crude Mortality Rate[1] per 100,000 population	
		County[2]	U.S.
Accidental poisoning and exposure to noxious substances	X40-X49	44.8	30.5
Alzheimer disease	G30	16.4	35.4
Assault	X85-Y09	4.9	7.3
COVID-19	U07.1	30.8	65.3
Diabetes mellitus	E10-E14	19.8	30.0
Diseases of the liver	K70-K76	11.1	20.8
Human immunodeficiency virus (HIV) disease	B20-B24	1.6	1.5
Influenza and pneumonia	J09-J18	6.4	13.4
Intentional self-harm	X60-X84	6.5	14.7
Malnutrition	E40-E46	2.8	6.0
Obesity and other hyperalimentation	E65-E68	2.1	3.1
Renal failure	N17-N19	16.2	16.4
Transport accidents	V01-V99	5.5	14.4

Note: (a) ICD-10 = International Classification of Diseases 10th Revision; (1) Crude mortality rates are a three-year average covering 2021-2023; (2) Figures cover Suffolk County; Data are suppressed when the data meet the criteria for confidentiality constraints; Crude mortality rates are flagged as unreliable when the rate would be calculated with a numerator of 20 or less.
Source: Centers for Disease Control and Prevention, National Center for Health Statistics. National Vital Statistics System, Mortality 2018-2023 on CDC WONDER Online Database

Health Insurance Coverage

Area	With Health Insurance	With Private Health Insurance	With Public Health Insurance	Without Health Insurance	Population Under Age 19 Without Health Insurance
City	97.0	69.9	35.8	3.0	1.9
MSA[1]	97.2	76.4	33.5	2.8	1.6
U.S.	91.4	67.3	36.3	8.6	5.4

Note: Figures are percentages that cover the civilian noninstitutionalized population; (1) Figures cover the Boston-Cambridge-Newton, MA-NH Metropolitan Statistical Area
Source: U.S. Census Bureau, 2019-2023 American Community Survey 5-Year Estimates

Number of Medical Professionals

Area	MDs[3]	DOs[3,4]	Dentists	Podiatrists	Chiropractors	Optometrists
County[1] (number)	13,779	186	1,934	69	130	300
County[1] (rate[2])	1,797.9	24.3	251.7	9.0	16.9	39.0
U.S. (rate[2])	302.5	29.2	74.6	6.4	29.5	18.0

Note: Data as of 2023 unless noted; (1) Data covers Suffolk County; (2) Number of medical professionals per 100,000 population; (3) Data as of 2022 and includes all active, non-federal physicians; (4) Doctor of Osteopathic Medicine
Source: U.S. Department of Health and Human Services, Health Resources and Services Administration, Bureau of Health Professions, Area Resource File (ARF) 2023-2024

Best Hospitals

According to *U.S. News,* the Boston-Cambridge-Newton, MA-NH metro area is home to 10 of the best hospitals in the U.S.: **Beth Israel Deaconess Medical Center** (9 adult specialties); **Beth Israel Deaconess Medical Center/Joslin Diabetes Center** (9 adult specialties); **Boston Medical Center** (1 adult specialty); **Brigham and Women's Hospital** (Honor Roll/12 adult specialties); **Dana-Farber Brigham Cancer Center** (1 adult specialty and 1 pediatric specialty); **Mass Eye and Ear, Massachusetts General Hospital** (2 adult specialties); **Massachusetts General Hospital** (Honor Roll/13 adult specialties and 1 pediatric specialty); **McLean Hospital** (1 adult specialty); **New England Baptist Hospital** (1 adult specialty); **Spaulding Rehabilitation Hospital** (1 adult specialty). The hospitals listed were nationally ranked in at least one of 15 adult or 11 pediatric specialties. The number of specialties shown cover the parent hospital. Only 160 U.S. hospitals performed well enough to be nationally ranked in one or more specialties. Twenty hospitals in the U.S. made the Honor Roll. The Best Hospitals Honor Roll takes both the national rankings and the procedure and condition ratings into account. Hospitals received points if they were nationally ranked in one of the 15 adult specialties—the higher they ranked, the more points they got—and how many ratings of "high performing" they earned in the 20 procedures and conditions. *U.S. News Online, "America's Best Hospitals 2024-25"*

According to *U.S. News,* the Boston-Cambridge-Newton, MA-NH metro area is home to three of the best children's hospitals in the U.S.: **Boston Children's Hospital** (Honor Roll/11 pediatric specialties); **Dana-Farber/Boston Children's Cancer and Blood Disorders Center** (1 pediatric specialty); **MassGeneral Hospital for Children** (1 pediatric specialty). The hospitals listed were highly ranked in at least one of 11 pediatric specialties. One hundred five children's hospitals in the U.S. were nationally ranked in at least one specialty. Hospitals received points for being ranked in a specialty, and

EDUCATION

Public School District Statistics

District Name	Schls	Pupils	Pupil/ Teacher Ratio	Minority Pupils[1] (%)	Total Rev. per Pupil ($)	Total Exp. per Pupil ($)
Boston	109	45,742	10.4	85.2	37,558	47,393

Note: Table includes school districts with 2,000 or more students; (1) Percentage of students that are not non-Hispanic white.
Source: U.S. Department of Education, National Center for Education Statistics, Common Core of Data, Local Education Agency (School District) Universe Survey: School Year 2023-2024; U.S. Department of Education, National Center for Education Statistics, Common Core of Data, School District Finance Survey (F-33): School Year 2021–22

Best High Schools

According to *U.S. News*, Boston is home to one of the top 500 high schools in the U.S.: **Boston Latin School** (#27). Nearly 25,000 public, magnet and charter schools were ranked based on their performance on state assessments and how well they prepare students for college. *U.S. News & World Report, "Best High Schools 2024"*

Highest Level of Education

Area	Less than H.S.	H.S. Diploma	Some College, No Deg.	Associate Degree	Bachelor's Degree	Master's Degree	Prof. School Degree	Doctorate Degree
City	11.1	18.3	11.6	4.9	28.5	16.4	5.2	3.9
MSA[1]	7.7	20.8	13.3	7.0	27.5	16.4	3.6	3.7
U.S.	10.6	26.2	19.4	8.8	21.3	9.8	2.3	1.6

Note: Figures cover persons age 25 and over; (1) Figures cover the Boston-Cambridge-Newton, MA-NH Metropolitan Statistical Area
Source: U.S. Census Bureau, 2019-2023 American Community Survey 5-Year Estimates

Educational Attainment by Race

Area	High School Graduate or Higher (%)					Bachelor's Degree or Higher (%)				
	Total	White	Black	Asian	Hisp.[2]	Total	White	Black	Asian	Hisp.[2]
City	88.9	96.4	86.4	80.9	72.8	54.1	72.5	26.7	57.4	26.6
MSA[1]	92.3	95.8	87.4	87.0	74.8	51.2	54.8	31.8	65.0	26.6
U.S.	89.4	92.9	88.1	88.0	72.5	35.0	37.7	24.7	57.0	19.9

Note: Figures shown cover persons 25 years old and over; (1) Figures cover the Boston-Cambridge-Newton, MA-NH Metropolitan Statistical Area; (2) People of Hispanic origin can be of any race
Source: U.S. Census Bureau, 2019-2023 American Community Survey 5-Year Estimates

School Enrollment by Grade and Control

Area	Preschool (%)		Kindergarten (%)		Grades 1 - 4 (%)		Grades 5 - 8 (%)		Grades 9 - 12 (%)	
	Public	Private	Public	Private	Public	Private	Public	Private	Public	Private
City	46.4	53.6	83.7	16.3	86.5	13.5	85.2	14.8	85.4	14.6
MSA[1]	45.6	54.4	87.8	12.2	90.3	9.7	89.1	10.9	85.9	14.1
U.S.	58.7	41.3	85.2	14.8	87.2	12.8	87.9	12.1	89.0	11.0

Note: Figures shown cover persons 3 years old and over; (1) Figures cover the Boston-Cambridge-Newton, MA-NH Metropolitan Statistical Area
Source: U.S. Census Bureau, 2019-2023 American Community Survey 5-Year Estimates

Higher Education

Four-Year Colleges			Two-Year Colleges			Medical Schools[1]	Law Schools[2]	Voc/ Tech[3]
Public	Private Non-profit	Private For-profit	Public	Private Non-profit	Private For-profit			
8	51	0	8	4	2	3	7	20

Note: Figures cover institutions located within the Boston-Cambridge-Newton, MA-NH Metropolitan Statistical Area and include main campuses only; (1) includes schools accredited by the Liaison Committee on Medical Education and the American Osteopathic Association's Commission on Osteopathic College Accreditation; (2) includes ABA-accredited schools, schools with provisional ABA accreditation, and state accredited schools; (3) includes all schools with programs that are less than 2 years.
Source: National Center for Education Statistics, Integrated Postsecondary Education System (IPEDS), 2023-24; Wikipedia, List of Medical Schools in the United States, accessed May 2, 2025; Wikipedia, List of Law Schools in the United States, accessed May 2, 2025

According to *U.S. News & World Report,* the Boston-Cambridge-Newton, MA-NH metro area is home to 10 of the top 200 national universities in the U.S.: **Massachusetts Institute of Technology** (#2); **Harvard University** (#3); **Boston College** (#37 tie); **Tufts University** (#37 tie); **Boston University** (#41 tie); **Northeastern University** (#54 tie); **Brandeis University** (#63 tie); **University of**

New Hampshire (#109 tie); **University of Massachusetts—Lowell** (#152 tie); **Simmons University** (#165 tie). The indicators used to capture academic quality fall into a number of categories: assessment by administrators at peer institutions; retention of students; faculty resources; student selectivity; financial resources; alumni giving; high school counselor ratings of colleges; and graduation rate. *U.S. News & World Report, "America's Best Colleges 2025"*

According to *U.S. News & World Report*, the Boston-Cambridge-Newton, MA-NH metro area is home to one of the top 100 liberal arts colleges in the U.S.: **Wellesley College** (#7). The indicators used to capture academic quality fall into a number of categories: assessment by administrators at peer institutions; retention of students; faculty resources; student selectivity; financial resources; alumni giving; high school counselor ratings of colleges; and graduation rate. *U.S. News & World Report, "America's Best Colleges 2025"*

According to *U.S. News & World Report*, the Boston-Cambridge-Newton, MA-NH metro area is home to four of the top 100 law schools in the U.S.: **Harvard University 1** (#6 tie); **Boston University** (#22 tie); **Boston College** (#25); **Northeastern University** (#68 tie). The rankings are based on a weighted average of 12 measures of quality: peer assessment score; assessment score by lawyers/judges; median LSAT scores; median undergrad GPA; acceptance rate; employment rates for graduates; placement success; bar passage rate; faculty resources; expenditures per student; student/faculty ratio; and library resources. *U.S. News & World Report, "America's Best Graduate Schools, Law, 2025"*

According to *U.S. News & World Report*, the Boston-Cambridge-Newton, MA-NH metro area is home to one of the top medical schools for research in the U.S.: **Tufts University** (Tier 2). *U.S. News* placed medical and osteopathic schools into tiers based on their research productivity, faculty and admissions data. Each school's tier was derived from its overall score, calculated by summing the weighted normalized values generated across several factors of academic quality, outlined below. There are four tiers, with tier 1 medical schools as the highest-performing and tier 4 as the lowest-performing. Only tier 1 and 2 schools are shown. Because of the tier presentation, *U.S. News* calculated overall scores based on their percentile performance among all rated schools instead of dividing against the rescaled score of the No. 1-performing schools. Tier 1 included schools with overall scores of 85 to 99. The cutoffs for tiers 2 through 4 were schools scoring 50 to 84, 15 to 49 and 1 to 14, respectively. The rankings are based on a weighted average of the following measures of quality: total research activity; average research activity per faculty member; total NIH research grants at the medical school and its affiliated hospitals; average NIH research grants per faculty; median MCAT total score; median undergraduate GPA; acceptance rate; and faculty resources. *U.S. News & World Report, "America's Best Graduate Schools, Medical, 2025"*

According to *U.S. News & World Report*, the Boston-Cambridge-Newton, MA-NH metro area is home to one of the top medical schools for primary care in the U.S.: **Tufts University** (Tier 2). *U.S. News* placed medical and osteopathic schools into tiers based on their research productivity, faculty and admissions data. Each school's tier was derived from its overall score, calculated by summing the weighted normalized values generated across several factors of academic quality, outlined below. There are four tiers, with tier 1 medical schools as the highest-performing and tier 4 as the lowest-performing. Only tier 1 and 2 schools are shown. Because of the tier presentation, *U.S. News* calculated overall scores based on their percentile performance among all rated schools instead of dividing against the rescaled score of the No. 1-performing schools. Tier 1 included schools with overall scores of 85 to 99. The cutoffs for tiers 2 through 4 were schools scoring 50 to 84, 15 to 49 and 1 to 14, respectively. The rankings are based on a weighted average of the following measures of quality: graduates practicing in primary care specialties; graduates entering primary care residencies; median MCAT total score; median undergraduate GPA; acceptance rate; and faculty resources. *U.S. News & World Report, "America's Best Graduate Schools, Medical, 2025"*

According to *U.S. News & World Report*, the Boston-Cambridge-Newton, MA-NH metro area is home to six of the top 75 business schools in the U.S.: **Massachusetts Institute of Technology (Sloan)** (#5); **Harvard University** (#6 tie); **Boston College (Carroll)** (#46 tie); **Boston University (Questrom)** (#46 tie); **Northeastern University (D'Amore-McKim)** (#68 tie); **Babson College (Olin)** (#73 tie). The rankings are based on a weighted average of the following nine measures: quality assessment; peer assessment; recruiter assessment; placement success; mean starting salary and bonus; student selectivity; mean GMAT and GRE scores; mean undergraduate GPA; and acceptance rate. *U.S. News & World Report, "America's Best Graduate Schools, Business, 2025"*

EMPLOYERS

Major Employers

Company Name	Industry
Beth Israel Deaconess Med Ctr	General medical & surgical hospitals
Blue Cross Blue Shield of Massachusetts	Health insurance
Boston Children's Hospital	Specialty hospitals, except psychiatric
Boston University	Higher education
Brigham and Women's Hospital	Healthcare
Cambridge Innovation Center	Real estate services
City of Boston	Local government
City of Cambridge	Local government
Dan Farber Cancer Institute	Healthcare
Federal Reserve Bank of Boston	Banks
General Electric Company	Aircraft engines & engine parts
Google	Technology/computing
Harvard University	Higher education
Massachusetts General Hospital	Hospitals
Massachusetts Inst. Of Technology	Higher education
Raytheon Technologies	Software/IT
Stop & Shop	Grocery
TJX	Retail
Tufts Medical Center	Hospital management
University of Massachusetts	Higher education

Note: Companies shown are located within the Boston-Cambridge-Newton, MA-NH Metropolitan Statistical Area.
Source: Chambers of Commerce; State Departments of Labor; Wikipedia

Best Companies to Work For

Bain & Company; Vertex Pharmaceuticals, headquartered in Boston, are among "The 100 Best Companies to Work For." To pick the best companies, *Fortune* partnered with the Great Place to Work Institute. Using their proprietary Trust Index™ survey, the core of what creates great a workplace is measured—key behaviors that drive trust in management, connection with colleagues, and loyalty to the company. To be eligible for the *Fortune* 100 Best Companies to Work For list, employers must have 1,000 or more employees in the U.S. and cannot be a government agency. *Fortune, "The 100 Best Companies to Work For," 2025*

Bain & Company; CarGurus; ezCater; Shawmut Design and Construction, headquartered in Boston, are among "Fortune's Best Workplaces for Parents." To pick the best companies, *Fortune* partnered with the Great Place to Work Institute. To be considered for the list, companies must be Great Place To Work-Certified and have at least 50 responses from parents in the US. The survey enables employees to share confidential quantitative and qualitative feedback about their organization's culture by responding to 60 statements on a 5-point scale and answering two open-ended questions. Collectively, these statements describe a great employee experience, defined by high levels of trust, respect, credibility, fairness, pride, and camaraderie. In addition, companies provide organizational data like size, location, industry, demographics, roles, and levels; and provide information about parental leave, adoption, flexible schedule, childcare and dependent health care benefits. *Fortune, "Best Workplaces for Parents," 2024*

Bain & Company; ezCater; Vertex Pharmaceuticals; Zelis, headquartered in Boston, are among "Fortune's Best Workplaces for Women." To pick the best companies, *Fortune* partnered with the Great Place to Work Institute. To be considered for the list, companies must be Great Place To Work-Certified. Companies must also employ at least 50 women, at least 20% of their non-executive managers must be female, and at least one executive must be female. To determine the Best Workplaces for Women, Great Place To Work measured the differences in women's survey responses to those of their peers and assesses the impact of demographics and roles on the quality and consistency of women's experiences. Great Place To Work also analyzed the gender balance of each workplace, how it compared to each company's industry, and patterns in representation as women rise from front-line positions to the board of directors. *Fortune, "Best Workplaces for Women," 2024*

Liberty Mutual Insurance, headquartered in Boston, is among the "Best Places to Work in IT." To qualify, companies had to have a minimum of 100 total employees and five IT employees. The best places to work were selected based on DEI (diversity, equity, and inclusion) practices; IT turnover, promotions, and growth; IT retention and engagement programs; remote/hybrid working; benefits and perks (such as elder care and child care, flextime, and reimbursement for college tuition); and training and career development opportunities. *Computerworld, "Best Places to Work in IT," 2025*

PUBLIC SAFETY

Crime Rate

Area	Total Crime Rate	Violent Crime Rate				Property Crime Rate		
		Murder	Rape	Robbery	Aggrav. Assault	Burglary	Larceny-Theft	Motor Vehicle Theft
City	2,571.3	5.3	32.5	136.6	452.5	180.9	1,589.2	174.2
U.S.	2,290.9	5.7	38.0	66.5	264.1	250.7	1,347.2	318.7

Note: Figures are crimes per 100,000 population.
Source: FBI, Table 8, Offenses Known to Law Enforcement, by State by City, 2023

Hate Crimes

Area	Number of Quarters Reported	Number of Incidents per Bias Motivation					
		Race/Ethnicity/Ancestry	Religion	Sexual Orientation	Disability	Gender	Gender Identity
City[1]	4	100	44	41	5	3	21
U.S.	4	5,900	2,699	2,077	187	92	492

Note: (1) Figures include at least one incident reported with more than one bias motivation.
Source: Federal Bureau of Investigation, Hate Crime Statistics 2023

Identity Theft Consumer Reports

Area	Reports	Reports per 100,000 Population	Rank[2]
MSA[1]	19,929	405	20
U.S.	1,135,291	339	-

Note: (1) Figures cover the Boston-Cambridge-Newton, MA-NH Metropolitan Statistical Area; (2) Rank ranges from 1 to 401 where 1 indicates greatest number of identity theft reports per 100,000 population
Source: Federal Trade Commission, Consumer Sentinel Network Data Book 2024

Fraud and Other Consumer Reports

Area	Reports	Reports per 100,000 Population	Rank[2]
MSA[1]	59,918	1,218	123
U.S.	5,360,641	1,601	-

Note: (1) Figures cover the Boston-Cambridge-Newton, MA-NH Metropolitan Statistical Area; (2) Rank ranges from 1 to 401 where 1 indicates greatest number of fraud and other consumer reports per 100,000 population
Source: Federal Trade Commission, Consumer Sentinel Network Data Book 2024

POLITICS

2024 Presidential Election Results

Area	Trump (Rep.)	Harris (Dem.)	Stein (Green)	Kennedy (Ind.)	Oliver (Lib.)	Other
Suffolk County	22.2	74.3	1.1	0.0	0.4	2.0
U.S.	49.7	48.2	0.6	0.5	0.4	0.6

Note: Results are percentages and may not add to 100% due to rounding
Source: Dave Leip's Atlas of U.S. Presidential Elections

SPORTS

Professional Sports Teams

Team Name	League	Year Established
Boston Bruins	National Hockey League (NHL)	1924
Boston Celtics	National Basketball Association (NBA)	1946
Boston Red Sox	Major League Baseball (MLB)	1901
New England Patriots	National Football League (NFL)	1960
New England Revolution	Major League Soccer (MLS)	1996

Note: Includes teams located in the Boston-Cambridge-Newton, MA-NH Metropolitan Statistical Area.
Source: Wikipedia, Major Professional Sports Teams of the United States and Canada, May 1, 2025

CLIMATE

Average and Extreme Temperatures

Temperature	Jan	Feb	Mar	Apr	May	Jun	Jul	Aug	Sep	Oct	Nov	Dec	Yr.
Extreme High (°F)	72	70	85	94	95	100	102	102	100	90	83	73	102
Average High (°F)	36	38	46	56	67	76	82	80	73	63	52	41	59
Average Temp. (°F)	30	31	39	48	58	68	74	72	65	55	45	34	52
Average Low (°F)	22	23	31	40	50	59	65	64	57	47	38	27	44
Extreme Low (°F)	-12	-4	1	16	34	45	50	47	37	28	15	-7	-12

Note: Figures cover the years 1945-1990
Source: National Climatic Data Center, International Station Meteorological Climate Summary, 9/96

Average Precipitation/Snowfall/Humidity

Precip./Humidity	Jan	Feb	Mar	Apr	May	Jun	Jul	Aug	Sep	Oct	Nov	Dec	Yr.
Avg. Precip. (in.)	3.8	3.6	3.8	3.7	3.5	3.1	2.9	3.6	3.1	3.3	4.4	4.1	42.9
Avg. Snowfall (in.)	12	12	8	1	Tr	0	0	0	0	Tr	1	8	41
Avg. Rel. Hum. 7am (%)	68	68	69	68	71	72	73	76	79	77	74	70	72
Avg. Rel. Hum. 4pm (%)	58	57	56	56	58	58	58	61	61	59	61	60	59

Note: Figures cover the years 1945-1990; Tr = Trace amounts (<0.05 in. of rain; <0.5 in. of snow)
Source: National Climatic Data Center, International Station Meteorological Climate Summary, 9/96

Weather Conditions

Temperature			Daytime Sky			Precipitation		
5°F & below	32°F & below	90°F & above	Clear	Partly cloudy	Cloudy	0.01 inch or more precip.	0.1 inch or more snow/ice	Thunder-storms
4	97	12	88	127	150	253	48	18

Note: Figures are average number of days per year and cover the years 1945-1990
Source: National Climatic Data Center, International Station Meteorological Climate Summary, 9/96

HAZARDOUS WASTE

Superfund Sites

The Boston, MA metro division is home to five sites on the EPA's Superfund National Priorities List (NPL) or Superfund Alternative Approach (SAA) list: **Baird & McGuire** (Final NPL); **BJAT** (Final NPL); **Blackburn & Union Privileges** (Final NPL); **Lower Neponset River** (Final NPL); **South Weymouth Naval Air Station** (Final NPL). The Superfund alternative approach uses the same investigation and cleanup process and standards that are used for sites listed on the National Priorities List. The SAA is an alternative to listing a site on the NPL; it is not an alternative to Superfund or the Superfund process. There are a total of 1,445 Superfund sites with a status of proposed or final on both lists in the United States. *U.S. Environmental Protection Agency, National Priorities List, May 1, 2025; U.S. Environmental Protection Agency, Superfund Alternative Approach Sites, May 1, 2025*

AIR QUALITY

Air Quality Trends: Ozone

	1990	1995	2000	2005	2010	2015	2020	2021	2022	2023
MSA[1]	0.078	0.085	0.067	0.075	0.066	0.065	0.053	0.059	0.066	0.060
U.S.	0.087	0.089	0.081	0.080	0.072	0.068	0.066	0.067	0.067	0.070

Note: (1) Data covers the Boston-Cambridge-Newton, MA-NH Metropolitan Statistical Area. The values shown are the composite ozone concentration averages among trend sites based on the highest fourth daily maximum 8-hour concentration in parts per million. These trends are based on sites having an adequate record of monitoring data during the trend period. Data from exceptional events are included.
Source: U.S. Environmental Protection Agency, Air Quality Monitoring Information, "Air Quality Trends by City, 1990-2023"

Air Quality Index

Area	Percent of Days when Air Quality was...[2]					AQI Statistics[2]	
	Good	Moderate	Unhealthy for Sensitive Groups	Unhealthy	Very Unhealthy	Maximum	Median
MSA[1]	52.1	46.0	1.9	0.0	0.0	136	50

Note: (1) Data covers the Boston-Cambridge-Newton, MA-NH Metropolitan Statistical Area; (2) Based on 365 days with AQI data in 2023. Air Quality Index (AQI) is an index for reporting daily air quality. EPA calculates the AQI for five major air pollutants regulated by the Clean Air Act: ground-level ozone, particle pollution (aka particulate matter), carbon monoxide, sulfur dioxide, and nitrogen dioxide. The AQI runs from 0 to 500. The higher the AQI value, the greater the level of air pollution and the greater the health concern. There are six AQI categories: "Good" AQI is between 0 and 50. Air quality is considered satisfactory; "Moderate" AQI is between 51 and 100. Air quality is acceptable; "Unhealthy for Sensitive Groups" When AQI values are between 101 and 150, members of sensitive groups may experience health effects; "Unhealthy" When AQI values are between 151 and 200 everyone may begin to experience health effects; "Very Unhealthy" AQI values between 201 and 300 trigger a health alert; "Hazardous" AQI values over 300 trigger warnings of emergency conditions (not shown).
Source: U.S. Environmental Protection Agency, Air Quality Index Report, 2023

Air Quality Index Pollutants

Area	Percent of Days when AQI Pollutant was...[2]					
	Carbon Monoxide	Nitrogen Dioxide	Ozone	Sulfur Dioxide	Particulate Matter 2.5	Particulate Matter 10
MSA[1]	0.0	0.5	36.7	(3)	62.7	0.0

Note: (1) Data covers the Boston-Cambridge-Newton, MA-NH Metropolitan Statistical Area; (2) Based on 365 days with AQI data in 2023. The Air Quality Index (AQI) is an index for reporting daily air quality. EPA calculates the AQI for five major air pollutants regulated by the Clean Air Act: ground-level ozone, particle pollution (also known as particulate matter), carbon monoxide, sulfur dioxide, and nitrogen dioxide. The AQI runs from 0 to 500. The higher the AQI value, the greater the level of air pollution and the greater the health concern; (3) Sulfur dioxide is no longer included in this table because SO_2 concentrations tend to be very localized and not necessarily representative of broad geographical areas like counties and CBSAs.
Source: U.S. Environmental Protection Agency, Air Quality Index Report, 2023

Maximum Air Pollutant Concentrations: Particulate Matter, Ozone, CO and Lead

	Particulate Matter 10 (ug/m^3)	Particulate Matter 2.5 Wtd AM (ug/m^3)	Particulate Matter 2.5 24-Hr (ug/m^3)	Ozone (ppm)	Carbon Monoxide (ppm)	Lead (ug/m^3)
MSA[1] Level	47	7.8	22	0.071	1	n/a
NAAQS[2]	150	15	35	0.075	9	0.15
Met NAAQS[2]	Yes	Yes	Yes	Yes	Yes	n/a

Note: (1) Data covers the Boston-Cambridge-Newton, MA-NH Metropolitan Statistical Area; Data from exceptional events are included; (2) National Ambient Air Quality Standards; ppm = parts per million; ug/m^3 = micrograms per cubic meter; n/a not available.
Concentrations: Particulate Matter 10 (coarse particulate)—highest second maximum 24-hour concentration; Particulate Matter 2.5 Wtd AM (fine particulate)—highest weighted annual mean concentration; Particulate Matter 2.5 24-Hour (fine particulate)—highest 98th percentile 24-hour concentration; Ozone—highest fourth daily maximum 8-hour concentration; Carbon Monoxide—highest second maximum non-overlapping 8-hour concentration; Lead—maximum running 3-month average
Source: U.S. Environmental Protection Agency, Air Quality Monitoring Information, "Air Quality Statistics by City, 2023"

Maximum Air Pollutant Concentrations: Nitrogen Dioxide and Sulfur Dioxide

	Nitrogen Dioxide AM (ppb)	Nitrogen Dioxide 1-Hr (ppb)	Sulfur Dioxide AM (ppb)	Sulfur Dioxide 1-Hr (ppb)	Sulfur Dioxide 24-Hr (ppb)
MSA[1] Level	11	45	n/a	5	n/a
NAAQS[2]	53	100	30	75	140
Met NAAQS[2]	Yes	Yes	n/a	Yes	n/a

Note: (1) Data covers the Boston-Cambridge-Newton, MA-NH Metropolitan Statistical Area; Data from exceptional events are included; (2) National Ambient Air Quality Standards; ppm = parts per million; ug/m^3 = micrograms per cubic meter; n/a not available.
Concentrations: Nitrogen Dioxide AM—highest arithmetic mean concentration; Nitrogen Dioxide 1-Hr—highest 98th percentile 1-hour daily maximum concentration; Sulfur Dioxide AM—highest annual mean concentration; Sulfur Dioxide 1-Hr—highest 99th percentile 1-hour daily maximum concentration; Sulfur Dioxide 24-Hr—highest second maximum 24-hour concentration
Source: U.S. Environmental Protection Agency, Air Quality Monitoring Information, "Air Quality Statistics by City, 2023"

Charlotte, North Carolina

Background

Charlotte was settled by Scotch-Irish and German migrants from Pennsylvania, New Jersey, and Virginia in 1750, and named for Charlotte Sophia of Mecklenburg-Strelitz, queen to England's King George III. The county in which Charlotte lies was named for Queen Charlotte Sophia's duchy of Mecklenburg. In 1775 the citizens of Charlotte signed the Mecklenburg Resolves, a document invalidating the power of the king and the English Parliament over their lives. The British General Lord Cornwallis found subduing the rebels so difficult, he called Charlotte a "hornet's nest of rebellion."

Today, a better-behaved Charlotte is a sophisticated metropolitan area, its thriving economy based in banking and finance, manufacturing, retail, education, government, health care, transportation, and telecommunications. Known as a center for the banking industry, Charlotte is the nucleus of the Carolinas crescent, an industrial arc extending from Raleigh, North Carolina, to Greenville, South Carolina. Thirteen Fortune 500 companies have a presence in the Charlotte area.

The Charlotte region is home to a significant number of energy-oriented organizations and is known as "Charlotte USA—The New Energy Capital." The region includes nearly 300 energy related companies, employing more than 30,000. The University of North Carolina at Charlotte has a reputation in energy education and research; its Energy Production and Infrastructure Center (EPIC) trains energy engineers and conducts research in the energy sector. Charlotte is also listed as a "gamma" global city by the Globalization and World Cities Research Network.

Charlotte offers exciting cultural and nightlife scenes, and part of the film "Talladega Nights" were filmed in and around Charlotte. Sports in the city include the NFL's Carolina Panthers and the NBA's Charlotte Hornets. Charlotte is also a center of NASCAR racing and the NASCAR Hall of Fame opened in Charlotte in 2010. In 2019, MLS awarded Charlotte its expansion team and the Charlotte FC began play in 2022 as the league's 28th franchise.

Attractions include the Blumenthal Performing Arts Center, which offers Broadway theater, ballet, and music productions; the U.S. National Whitewater Center, the world's largest artificial whitewater river; ImaginOn: The Joe & Joan Martin Educational Center; and the Mint Museum of Art and Discovery Place, one of America's top hands-on science museums with a planetarium and IMAX® Dome theater. The Levine Museum of the New South offers the nation's most comprehensive exhibits on post-Civil War southern society.

The Yiasou Greek Festival began in 1978 and since become one of Charlotte's largest cultural events. The Yiasou (Greek for hello, goodbye, and cheers) Greek Festival features Hellenic cultural exhibits, authentic Greek cuisine and homemade pastries, entertainment, live music and dancing, wine tastings, art, and shopping.

Significant institutions of higher education in the region include Queens University, the University of North Carolina at Charlotte, Davidson College and nearby Winthrop University.

Charlotte is located in the Piedmont of the Carolinas, a transitional area of rolling country between the mountains to the west and the Coastal Plain to the east. The city enjoys a moderate climate, characterized by cool winters and warm summers. Winter weather is changeable, with occasional cold periods, but extreme cold is rare. Snow is infrequent. Summer afternoons can be hot. Rainfall is evenly distributed throughout the year. The city took a direct hit from Hurricane Hugo in 1989, which caused massive damage. In 2002, Charlotte, and much of central North Carolina experienced an ice storm that resulted in 1.3 million people without power for weeks.

Rankings

General Rankings

- To help military veterans find the best places in which to settle down, *WalletHub* compared the 100 largest U.S. cities across 19 key indicators of livability, affordability and veteran-friendliness. They range from the share of military skill-related jobs to veteran income growth to the availability of VA health facilities. Charlotte ranked #26. *Wallethub.com, "Best & Worst Places for Veterans to Live (2025)," November 7, 2024*

- *US News & World Report* conducted a survey of more than 3,500 people and analyzed the 150 largest metropolitan areas to determine what matters most when selecting the next place to live. Charlotte ranked #5 out of the top 25 as having the best combination of desirable factors. Criteria: cost of living; quality of life and education; climate; job market; desirability; and other factors. *realestate.usnews.com, "Best Places to Live in the U.S. in 2024-2025," May 21, 2024*

Business/Finance Rankings

- Payscale.com ranked the 32 largest metro areas in terms of wage growth. The Charlotte metro area ranked #4. Criteria: quarterly changes in private industry employee and education professional wage growth from the previous year. *PayScale, "Wage Trends by Metro Area-4th Quarter," February 4, 2025*

- The Charlotte metro area appeared on the Milken Institute "2025 Best Performing Cities" list. Rank: #24 out of 200 large metro areas (based on performance category). Criteria: job growth; wage growth; high-tech growth and impact; community resilience; housing affordability; household broadband access. *Milken Institute, "Best-Performing Cities 2025," January 14, 2025*

Education Rankings

- Personal finance website *WalletHub* analyzed the 150 largest U.S. metropolitan statistical areas to determine where the most educated Americans are putting their degrees to work. Criteria: education levels; percentage of workers with degrees; education quality and attainment gap; public school quality rankings; quality and enrollment of each metro area's universities. Charlotte was ranked #45 (#1 = most educated city). *WalletHub.com, "Most & Least Educated Cities in America, 2025" July 2, 2024*

Environmental Rankings

- The U.S. Environmental Protection Agency (EPA) released its list of U.S. metropolitan areas with the most ENERGY STAR certified buildings in 2023. The Charlotte metro area was ranked #20 out of 25. *U.S. Environmental Protection Agency, "2024 Energy Star Top Cities," May 22, 2024*

Health/Fitness Rankings

- For each of the 100 largest cities in the United States, the American Fitness Index®, compiled in partnership between the American College of Sports Medicine and the Elevance Health Foundation, evaluated community infrastructure and more than 30 health behaviors including preventive health, levels of chronic disease conditions, food insecurity, pedestrian safety, air quality, and community/environment resources that support physical activity. Charlotte ranked #50 for "community fitness." *americanfitnessindex.org, "2024 ACSM American Fitness Index Summary Report," July 23, 2024*

- The Charlotte metro area was identified as one of the worst cities for bed bugs in America by pest control company Orkin. The area ranked #9 out of 50 based on the number of bed bug treatments Orkin performed from December 2022 to November 2023. *Orkin, "Chicago Joins Paris In Global Bed Bug Spotlight Ranking As The Worst City On Orkin's U.S. Bed Bug Cities List," January 22, 2024*

- Charlotte was identified as a "2025 Allergy Capital." The area ranked #18 out of the nation's 100 largest metropolitan areas. Three groups of factors were used to identify the most challenging cities for people with allergies: annual tree, grass, and weed pollen scores; over the counter allergy medicine use; number of board-certified allergy specialists. *Asthma and Allergy Foundation of America, "2025 Allergy Capitals: The Most Challenging Places to Live with Allergies," March 18, 2025*

- Charlotte was identified as a "2024 Asthma Capital." The area ranked #93 out of the nation's 100 largest metropolitan areas. Criteria: estimated asthma prevalence; asthma-related mortality; and ER visits due to asthma. Risk factors analyzed but not factored in the rankings: annual air quality including pollution and ozone levels; public smoking laws; indoor air quality; access to asthma specialists; rescue and controller medication use; uninsured rate; pollen allergy; poverty rate. *Asthma and Allergy Foundation of America, "Asthma Capitals 2024: The Most Challenging Places to Live With Asthma," September 10, 2024*

Pet Rankings

- Charlotte appeared on *The Dogington Post* site as one of the top cities for dog lovers, ranking #4 out of 15. The real estate marketplace, Zillow®, and Rover, the largest pet sitter and dog walker network, introduced a new list of "Top Emerging Dog-Friendly Cities" for 2021. Criteria: number of new dog accounts on the Rover platform; and rentals and listings that mention features that attract dog owners (fenced-in yards, dog houses, dog door or proximity to a dog park). *Dogingtonpost.com, "15 Cities Emerging as Dog-Friendliest in 2021," May 11, 2021*

- Charlotte was selected by *Sniffspot.com* as one of the most dog-friendly cities in the U.S., ranking #8 out of 50. Criteria: dog parks; hiking; sniffspots; public parks; dog-friendly businesses; housing; dog waste cleanliness; leash laws; dog services; and overall cost. *Sniffspot.com, "The Top 50 Most Dog-Friendly Cities in the U.S.," September 30, 2024*

Real Estate Rankings

- *WalletHub* compared the most populated U.S. cities to determine which had the best markets for real estate agents. Charlotte ranked #26 where demand was high and pay was the best. Criteria: sales per agent; annual median wage for real-estate agents; monthly average starting salary for real estate agents; real estate job density and competition; unemployment rate; home turnover rate; housing-market health index; and other relevant metrics. *WalletHub.com, "2021 Best Places to Be a Real Estate Agent," May 12, 2021*

- According to Penske Truck Rental, the Charlotte metro area was named the #3 moving destination in 2023, based on one-way consumer truck rental reservations made through Penske's website, rental locations, and reservations call center. *gopenske.com, "Penske Truck Rental's 2023 Top Moving Destinations," May 7, 2024*

- Charlotte was ranked #96 out of 176 metro areas in terms of cost of housing in 2024 by the National Association of Home Builders (#1 = most affordable). Criteria: the portion of an average family's income necessary to pay the mortgage on a median-priced home. *National Association of Home Builders®, NAHB-Wells Fargo Cost of Housing Index, 4th Quarter 2024*

Safety Rankings

- Allstate ranked the 100 most populous cities in America in terms of driver safety. Charlotte ranked #69. Criteria based on anonymized driving behavior data from Allstate's mobile app powered by Arity: high speed driving (over 80 mph), phone handling, and hard braking. The report helps increase the importance of safety and awareness behind the wheel. *Allstate, "16th Allstate America's Best Drivers Report®" July 11, 2024*

Seniors/Retirement Rankings

- Charlotte made the 2024 *Forbes* list of "25 Best Places to Retire." Criteria, focused on overall affordability as well as quality of life indicators, include: housing/living costs compared to the national average and taxes; air quality; crime rates; median home prices; risk associated with climate-change/natural hazards; availability of medical care; bikeability; walkability; healthy living. *Forbes.com, "The Best Places to Retire in 2024: Las Cruces and Other Unexpected Hot Spots," May 10, 2024*

Women/Minorities Rankings

- Personal finance website *WalletHub* compared more than 180 U.S. cities across two key dimensions, "Hispanic Business-Friendliness" and "Hispanic Purchasing Power," to arrive at the most favorable conditions for Hispanic entrepreneurs. Charlotte was ranked #66 out of 182. Criteria includes: share of Hispanic-Owned Businesses; average growth of Hispanic Business revenues; Small Business-Friendliness score; affordability; and number of Hispanics with at least a bachelor's degree. *WalletHub.com, "Best Cities for Hispanic Entrepreneurs," September 4, 2024*

Miscellaneous Rankings

- Charlotte was selected as a 2024 Digital Cities Survey winner. The city ranked #8 in the large city (500,000 or more population) category. The survey examined and assessed how city governments are utilizing new technology and modernized applications to provide residents an array of contactless services and conveniences. Survey questions focused on ten initiatives: cybersecurity; citizen experience; disaster recovery; business intelligence; IT personnel retention; data governance; business automation; AI/machine learning; application modernization; and IT collaboration. *Center for Digital Government, "2024 Digital Cities Survey," November 5, 2024*

- *WalletHub* compared 148 of the most populated U.S. cities to determine their operating efficiency. A "Quality of Services" score was constructed for each city and then measured against the total budget per capita to reveal which were managed the best. Charlotte ranked #113. Criteria: financial stability; economy; education; safety; health; infrastructure and pollution. *WalletHub.com, "2025's Best- & Worst-Run Cities in America," June 18, 2024*

Business Environment

DEMOGRAPHICS

Population Growth

Area	1990 Census	2000 Census	2010 Census	2020 Census	2023 Estimate[2]	Population Growth 1990-2023 (%)
City	428,283	540,828	731,424	874,579	886,283	106.9
MSA[1]	1,024,331	1,330,448	1,758,038	2,660,329	2,712,818	164.8
U.S.	248,709,873	281,421,906	308,745,538	331,449,281	332,387,540	33.6

Note: (1) Figures cover the Charlotte-Concord-Gastonia, NC-SC Metropolitan Statistical Area; (2) 2019-2023 5-year ACS population estimate
Source: U.S. Census Bureau, 1990 Census, 2000 Census, 2010 Census, 2020 Census, 2019-2023 American Community Survey 5-Year Estimates

Race

Area	White Alone[2] (%)	Black Alone[2] (%)	Asian Alone[2] (%)	AIAN[3] Alone[2] (%)	NHOPI[4] Alone[2] (%)	Other Race Alone[2] (%)	Two or More Races (%)
City	41.5	34.1	6.4	0.4	0.0	8.8	8.9
MSA[1]	60.2	22.2	4.2	0.4	0.0	5.5	7.5
U.S.	63.4	12.4	5.8	0.9	0.2	6.6	10.7

Note: (1) Figures cover the Charlotte-Concord-Gastonia, NC-SC Metropolitan Statistical Area; (2) Alone is defined as not being in combination with one or more other races; (3) American Indian and Alaska Native; (4) Native Hawaiian and Other Pacific Islander
Source: U.S. Census Bureau, 2019-2023 American Community Survey 5-Year Estimates

Hispanic or Latino Origin

Area	Total (%)	Mexican (%)	Puerto Rican (%)	Cuban (%)	Other (%)
City	17.0	6.0	1.2	0.5	9.3
MSA[1]	12.0	4.9	1.1	0.4	5.6
U.S.	19.0	11.3	1.8	0.7	5.2

Note: Persons of Hispanic or Latino origin can be of any race; (1) Figures cover the Charlotte-Concord-Gastonia, NC-SC Metropolitan Statistical Area
Source: U.S. Census Bureau, 2019-2023 American Community Survey 5-Year Estimates

Age

Area	Percent of Population									Median Age
	Under Age 5	Age 5–19	Age 20–34	Age 35–44	Age 45–54	Age 55–64	Age 65–74	Age 75–84	Age 85+	
City	6.5	19.1	25.5	14.8	12.8	10.7	6.7	2.8	1.2	34.4
MSA[1]	5.9	19.9	20.1	13.9	13.7	12.2	8.7	4.1	1.4	37.9
U.S.	5.7	19.1	20.2	13.1	12.3	12.8	10.0	4.9	1.9	38.7

Note: (1) Figures cover the Charlotte-Concord-Gastonia, NC-SC Metropolitan Statistical Area
Source: U.S. Census Bureau, 2019-2023 American Community Survey 5-Year Estimates

Disability by Age

Area	All Ages	Under 18 Years Old	18 to 64 Years Old	65 Years and Over
City	8.3	2.8	7.0	28.3
MSA[1]	10.6	3.4	8.7	31.0
U.S.	13.0	4.7	10.7	32.9

Note: Figures show percent of the civilian noninstitutionalized population that reported having a disability. Disability status is determined from six types of difficulty: vision, hearing, cognitive, ambulatory, self-care, and independent living. For children under 5 years old, hearing and vision difficulty are used to determine disability status. For children between the ages of 5 and 14, disability status is determined from hearing, vision, cognitive, ambulatory, and self-care difficulties. For people aged 15 years and older, they are considered to have a disability if they have difficulty with any one of the six difficulty types; Note: (1) Figures cover the Charlotte-Concord-Gastonia, NC-SC Metropolitan Statistical Area
Source: U.S. Census Bureau, 2019-2023 American Community Survey 5-Year Estimates

Ancestry

Area	German	Irish	English	American	Italian	Polish	French[2]	European	Scottish
City	7.4	6.7	7.7	4.7	3.5	1.5	1.2	1.1	1.6
MSA[1]	10.2	8.4	10.3	8.3	3.9	1.7	1.4	1.5	2.0
U.S.	12.6	9.4	9.1	5.5	4.9	2.6	2.0	1.6	1.6

Note: Figures are the percentage of the total population reporting a particular ancestry. The nine most commonly reported ancestries in the U.S. are shown. Figures include multiple ancestries (e.g. if a person reported being Irish and Italian, they were included in both columns); (1) Figures cover the Charlotte-Concord-Gastonia, NC-SC Metropolitan Statistical Area; (2) Excludes Basque
Source: U.S. Census Bureau, 2019-2023 American Community Survey 5-Year Estimates

Foreign-born Population

Area	Percent of Population Born in								
	Any Foreign Country	Asia	Mexico	Europe	Caribbean	Central America[2]	South America	Africa	Canada
City	18.1	4.9	2.7	1.5	1.2	3.8	1.7	2.1	0.2
MSA[1]	11.4	3.2	2.0	1.2	0.7	1.8	1.2	1.0	0.2
U.S.	13.9	4.3	3.3	1.4	1.4	1.2	1.2	0.8	0.2

Note: (1) Figures cover the Charlotte-Concord-Gastonia, NC-SC Metropolitan Statistical Area; (2) Excludes Mexico.
Source: U.S. Census Bureau, 2019-2023 American Community Survey 5-Year Estimates

Household Size

Area	Persons in Household (%)							Average Household Size
	One	Two	Three	Four	Five	Six	Seven or More	
City	35.1	31.7	14.8	11.2	4.7	1.5	1.0	2.42
MSA[1]	28.0	34.2	15.9	13.2	5.6	1.9	1.1	2.55
U.S.	28.5	33.8	15.4	12.7	5.9	2.3	1.4	2.54

Note: (1) Figures cover the Charlotte-Concord-Gastonia, NC-SC Metropolitan Statistical Area
Source: U.S. Census Bureau, 2019-2023 American Community Survey 5-Year Estimates

Household Relationships

Area	House-holder	Opposite-sex Spouse	Same-sex Spouse	Opposite-sex Unmarried Partner	Same-sex Unmarried Partner	Child[2]	Grand-child	Other Relatives	Non-relatives
City	40.6	15.2	0.2	2.8	0.2	28.0	2.1	4.9	4.2
MSA[1]	38.9	18.3	0.2	2.4	0.2	29.2	2.4	4.2	2.8
U.S.	38.3	17.5	0.2	2.5	0.2	28.3	2.4	4.8	3.4

Note: Figures are percent of the total population; (1) Figures cover the Charlotte-Concord-Gastonia, NC-SC Metropolitan Statistical Area; (2) Includes biological, adopted, and stepchildren of the householder
Source: U.S. Census Bureau, 2020 Census

Gender

Area	Males	Females	Males per 100 Females
City	427,869	458,414	93.3
MSA[1]	1,323,612	1,389,206	95.3
U.S.	164,545,087	167,842,453	98.0

Note: (1) Figures cover the Charlotte-Concord-Gastonia, NC-SC Metropolitan Statistical Area
Source: U.S. Census Bureau, 2019-2023 American Community Survey 5-Year Estimates

Marital Status

Area	Never Married	Now Married[2]	Separated	Widowed	Divorced
City	42.9	41.1	2.1	3.8	10.1
MSA[1]	33.6	49.4	2.0	4.9	10.0
U.S.	34.1	47.9	1.7	5.6	10.7

Note: Figures are percentages and cover the population 15 years of age and older; (1) Figures cover the Charlotte-Concord-Gastonia, NC-SC Metropolitan Statistical Area; (2) Excludes separated
Source: U.S. Census Bureau, 2019-2023 American Community Survey 5-Year Estimates

Religious Groups by Family

Area	Catholic	Baptist	Methodist	LDS[2]	Pentecostal	Lutheran	Islam	Adventist	Other
MSA[1]	12.1	13.9	7.0	0.7	2.2	1.1	1.7	1.4	15.9
U.S.	18.7	7.3	3.0	2.0	1.8	1.7	1.3	1.3	11.6

Note: Figures are the number of adherents as a percentage of the total population and cover the eight largest religious groups in the U.S; (1) Figures cover the Charlotte-Concord-Gastonia, NC-SC Metropolitan Statistical Area; (2) Church of Jesus Christ of Latter-day Saints
Sources: 2020 U.S. Religion Census, Association of Statisticians of American Religious Bodies; The Association of Religion Data Archives (ARDA)

Religious Groups by Tradition

Area	Catholic	Evangelical Protestant	Mainline Protestant	Black Protestant	Islam	Judaism	Hinduism	Orthodox	Buddhism
MSA[1]	12.1	26.4	9.5	3.4	1.7	0.2	0.2	0.4	0.1
U.S.	18.7	16.5	5.2	2.3	1.3	0.6	0.4	0.4	0.3

Note: Figures are the number of adherents as a percentage of the total population; (1) Figures cover the Charlotte-Concord-Gastonia, NC-SC Metropolitan Statistical Area
Sources: 2020 U.S. Religion Census, Association of Statisticians of American Religious Bodies; The Association of Religion Data Archives (ARDA)

ECONOMY

Real Gross Domestic Product (GDP)

Area	2017	2018	2019	2020	2021	2022	2023	Rank[3]
MSA[1]	168.1	171.6	177.5	179.1	190.5	197.3	206.5	21
U.S.[2]	17,619.1	18,160.7	18,642.5	18,238.9	19,387.6	19,896.6	20,436.3	—

Note: Figures are in billions of chained 2017 dollars; (1) Figures cover the Charlotte-Concord-Gastonia, NC-SC Metropolitan Statistical Area; (2) Figures cover real GDP within metropolitan areas; (3) Rank is based on 2023 data and ranges from 1 to 384
Source: U.S. Bureau of Economic Analysis

Economic Growth

Area	2014	2015	2016	2017	2018	2019	2020	2021	2022	2023
MSA[1]	3.3	4.2	3.0	3.7	2.1	3.4	0.9	6.4	3.6	4.7
U.S.[2]	2.6	3.2	2.0	2.7	3.1	2.7	-2.2	6.3	2.6	2.7

Note: Figures are real gross domestic product growth rates and represent percent change from preceding period; (1) Figures cover the Charlotte-Concord-Gastonia, NC-SC Metropolitan Statistical Area; (2) Figures are the average growth rates within metropolitan areas
Source: U.S. Bureau of Economic Analysis

Metropolitan Area Exports

Area	2018	2019	2020	2021	2022	2023	Rank[2]
MSA[1]	14,083.2	13,892.4	8,225.6	10,554.3	12,223.1	11,470.3	34
U.S.	1,664,056.1	1,645,173.7	1,431,406.6	1,753,941.4	2,062,937.4	2,019,160.5	—

Note: Figures are in millions of dollars; (1) Figures cover the Charlotte-Concord-Gastonia, NC-SC Metropolitan Statistical Area; (2) Rank is based on 2023 data and ranges from 1 to 386
Source: U.S. Department of Commerce, International Trade Administration, Office of Trade and Economic Analysis, Industry and Analysis, Exports by Metropolitan Area, data extracted April 2, 2025

Building Permits

Area	Single-Family			Multi-Family			Total		
	2023	2024	Pct. Chg.	2023	2024	Pct. Chg.	2023	2024	Pct. Chg.
City	n/a	n/a	n/a	n/a	n/a	n/a	n/a	n/a	n/a
MSA[1]	19,146	18,954	-1.0	10,273	6,981	-32.0	29,419	25,935	-11.8
U.S.	920,000	981,900	6.7	591,100	496,100	-16.1	1,511,100	1,478,000	-2.2

Note: (1) Figures cover the Charlotte-Concord-Gastonia, NC-SC Metropolitan Statistical Area; Figures represent new, privately-owned housing units authorized (unadjusted data)
Source: U.S. Census Bureau, Building Permits Survey (BPS), 2023, 2024

Bankruptcy Filings

Area	Business Filings			Nonbusiness Filings		
	2023	2024	% Chg.	2023	2024	% Chg.
Mecklenburg County	69	60	-13.0	577	689	19.4
U.S.	18,926	23,107	22.1	434,064	494,201	13.9

Note: Business filings include Chapter 7, Chapter 9, Chapter 11, Chapter 12, Chapter 13, Chapter 15, and Section 304; Nonbusiness filings include Chapter 7, Chapter 11, and Chapter 13
Source: Administrative Office of the U.S. Courts, Business and Nonbusiness Bankruptcy, County Cases Commenced by Chapter of the Bankruptcy Code, During the 12-Month Period Ending December 31, 2023 and Business and Nonbusiness Bankruptcy, County Cases Commenced by Chapter of the Bankruptcy Code, During the 12-Month Period Ending December 31, 2024

Housing Vacancy Rates

Area	Gross Vacancy Rate[3] (%)			Year-Round Vacancy Rate[4] (%)			Rental Vacancy Rate[5] (%)			Homeowner Vacancy Rate[6] (%)		
	2022	2023	2024	2022	2023	2024	2022	2023	2024	2022	2023	2024
MSA[1]	7.4	7.6	8.1	7.0	7.4	7.7	5.9	6.6	6.7	0.7	0.4	0.9
U.S.[2]	9.1	9.0	9.1	7.5	7.5	7.6	5.7	6.5	6.8	0.8	0.8	1.0

Note: (1) Figures cover the Charlotte-Concord-Gastonia, NC-SC Metropolitan Statistical Area; (2) Figures cover the 75 largest Metropolitan Statistical Areas; (3) The percentage of the total housing inventory that is vacant; (4) The percentage of the housing inventory (excluding seasonal units) that is year-round vacant; (5) The percentage of rental inventory that is vacant for rent; (6) The percentage of homeowner inventory that is vacant for sale
Source: U.S. Census Bureau, Housing Vacancies and Homeownership Annual Statistics: 2022, 2023, 2024

INCOME

Income

Area	Per Capita ($)	Median Household ($)	Average Household ($)
City	49,991	78,438	119,473
MSA[1]	44,995	80,201	113,387
U.S.	43,289	78,538	110,491

Note: (1) Figures cover the Charlotte-Concord-Gastonia, NC-SC Metropolitan Statistical Area
Source: U.S. Census Bureau, 2019-2023 American Community Survey 5-Year Estimates

Household Income Distribution

Area	Percent of Households Earning							
	Under $15,000	$15,000 -$24,999	$25,000 -$34,999	$35,000 -$49,999	$50,000 -$74,999	$75,000 -$99,999	$100,000 -$149,999	$150,000 and up
City	7.0	5.6	6.2	11.6	17.6	12.7	16.9	22.5
MSA[1]	6.8	6.1	6.5	10.9	16.7	13.0	17.7	22.2
U.S.	8.5	6.6	6.8	10.4	15.7	12.7	17.4	21.9

Note: (1) Figures cover the Charlotte-Concord-Gastonia, NC-SC Metropolitan Statistical Area
Source: U.S. Census Bureau, 2019-2023 American Community Survey 5-Year Estimates

Poverty Rate

Area	All Ages	Under 18 Years Old	18 to 64 Years Old	65 Years and Over
City	11.7	16.9	10.1	10.4
MSA[1]	10.5	14.2	9.4	9.3
U.S.	12.4	16.3	11.6	10.4

Note: Figures are percentage of people whose income during the past 12 months was below the poverty level;
(1) Figures cover the Charlotte-Concord-Gastonia, NC-SC Metropolitan Statistical Area
Source: U.S. Census Bureau, 2019-2023 American Community Survey 5-Year Estimates

EMPLOYMENT

Labor Force and Employment

Area	Civilian Labor Force			Workers Employed		
	Dec. 2023	Dec. 2024	% Chg.	Dec. 2023	Dec. 2024	% Chg.
City	531,420	537,158	1.1	513,465	519,577	1.2
MSA[1]	1,472,294	1,492,625	1.4	1,424,686	1,443,425	1.3
U.S.	166,661,000	167,746,000	0.7	160,754,000	161,294,000	0.3

Note: Data is not seasonally adjusted and covers workers 16 years of age and older; (1) Figures cover the Charlotte-Concord-Gastonia, NC-SC Metropolitan Statistical Area
Source: Bureau of Labor Statistics, Local Area Unemployment Statistics

Unemployment Rate

Area	2024											
	Jan.	Feb.	Mar.	Apr.	May	Jun.	Jul.	Aug.	Sep.	Oct.	Nov.	Dec.
City	3.8	3.9	3.6	3.2	3.4	3.8	4.1	3.9	3.2	3.3	3.5	3.3
MSA[1]	3.6	3.8	3.5	3.1	3.4	3.8	4.0	3.9	3.3	3.4	3.5	3.3
U.S.	4.1	4.2	3.9	3.5	3.7	4.3	4.5	4.4	3.9	3.9	4.0	3.8

Note: Data is not seasonally adjusted and covers workers 16 years of age and older; (1) Figures cover the Charlotte-Concord-Gastonia, NC-SC Metropolitan Statistical Area
Source: Bureau of Labor Statistics, Local Area Unemployment Statistics

Average Wages

Occupation	$/Hr.	Occupation	$/Hr.
Accountants and Auditors	47.13	Maintenance and Repair Workers	25.50
Automotive Mechanics	27.27	Marketing Managers	77.80
Bookkeepers	24.68	Network and Computer Systems Admin.	48.36
Carpenters	25.51	Nurses, Licensed Practical	30.80
Cashiers	14.02	Nurses, Registered	42.86
Computer Programmers	44.72	Nursing Assistants	19.15
Computer Systems Analysts	57.50	Office Clerks, General	20.94
Computer User Support Specialists	30.08	Physical Therapists	48.26
Construction Laborers	21.52	Physicians	150.06
Cooks, Restaurant	17.64	Plumbers, Pipefitters and Steamfitters	27.07
Customer Service Representatives	21.55	Police and Sheriff's Patrol Officers	32.47
Dentists	106.87	Postal Service Mail Carriers	29.03
Electricians	27.55	Real Estate Sales Agents	30.17
Engineers, Electrical	58.48	Retail Salespersons	16.65
Fast Food and Counter Workers	14.27	Sales Representatives, Technical/Scientific	63.70
Financial Managers	91.39	Secretaries, Exc. Legal/Medical/Executive	20.49
First-Line Supervisors of Office Workers	33.22	Security Guards	19.12
General and Operations Managers	66.57	Surgeons	248.26
Hairdressers/Cosmetologists	20.12	Teacher Assistants, Exc. Postsecondary[1]	14.49
Home Health and Personal Care Aides	15.34	Teachers, Secondary School, Exc. Sp. Ed.[1]	27.70
Janitors and Cleaners	16.27	Telemarketers	19.21
Landscaping/Groundskeeping Workers	18.72	Truck Drivers, Heavy/Tractor-Trailer	27.14
Lawyers	89.69	Truck Drivers, Light/Delivery Services	21.73
Maids and Housekeeping Cleaners	16.06	Waiters and Waitresses	16.65

Note: Wage data covers the Charlotte-Concord-Gastonia, NC-SC Metropolitan Statistical Area; (1) Hourly wages were calculated from annual wage data based on a 40 hour work week
Source: Bureau of Labor Statistics, Metro Area Occupational Employment & Wage Estimates, May 2024

Employment by Industry

Sector	MSA[1]		U.S.
	Number of Employees	Percent of Total	Percent of Total
Construction, Mining, and Logging	81,900	5.9	5.5
Financial Activities	123,000	8.8	5.8
Government	180,600	12.9	14.9
Information	26,300	1.9	1.9
Leisure and Hospitality	151,600	10.9	10.4
Manufacturing	107,500	7.7	8.0
Other Services	55,700	4.0	3.7
Private Education and Health Services	154,900	11.1	16.9
Professional and Business Services	225,700	16.2	14.2
Retail Trade	139,500	10.0	10.0
Transportation, Warehousing, and Utilities	84,500	6.1	4.8
Wholesale Trade	65,000	4.7	3.9

Note: Figures are non-farm employment as of December 2024. Figures are not seasonally adjusted and include workers 16 years of age and older; (1) Figures cover the Charlotte-Concord-Gastonia, NC-SC Metropolitan Statistical Area
Source: Bureau of Labor Statistics, Current Employment Statistics, Employment, Hours, and Earnings

Employment by Occupation

Occupation Classification	City (%)	MSA[1] (%)	U.S. (%)
Management, Business, Science, and Arts	47.1	43.8	42.0
Natural Resources, Construction, and Maintenance	7.2	8.3	8.6
Production, Transportation, and Material Moving	12.0	13.7	13.0
Sales and Office	20.3	20.7	19.9
Service	13.5	13.6	16.5

Note: Figures cover employed civilians 16 years of age and older; (1) Figures cover the Charlotte-Concord-Gastonia, NC-SC Metropolitan Statistical Area
Source: U.S. Census Bureau, 2019-2023 American Community Survey 5-Year Estimates

Occupations with Greatest Projected Employment Growth: 2022 – 2032

Occupation[1]	2022 Employment	2032 Projected Employment	Numeric Employment Change	Percent Employment Change
Software Developers	57,190	75,660	18,470	32.3
Cooks, Restaurant	47,710	66,050	18,340	38.4
Registered Nurses	106,190	123,650	17,460	16.4
Home Health and Personal Care Aides	62,750	77,390	14,640	23.3
Stockers and Order Fillers	92,790	105,710	12,920	13.9
Laborers and Freight, Stock, and Material Movers, Hand	121,680	133,850	12,170	10.0
General and Operations Managers	94,010	105,400	11,390	12.1
Fast Food and Counter Workers	65,320	75,130	9,810	15.0
First-Line Supervisors of Food Preparation and Serving Workers	41,690	49,690	8,000	19.2
Waiters and Waitresses	71,300	79,060	7,760	10.9

Note: Projections cover North Carolina; (1) Sorted by numeric employment change
Source: www.projectionscentral.org, State Occupational Projections, 2022–2032 Long-Term Projections

Fastest-Growing Occupations: 2022 – 2032

Occupation[1]	2022 Employment	2032 Projected Employment	Numeric Employment Change	Percent Employment Change
Nurse Practitioners	8,200	12,750	4,550	55.5
Solar Photovoltaic Installers	950	1,400	450	47.4
Statisticians	1,580	2,270	690	43.7
Data Scientists	5,430	7,720	2,290	42.2
Medical and Health Services Managers	12,880	17,860	4,980	38.7
Cooks, Restaurant	47,710	66,050	18,340	38.4
Physician Assistants	7,440	10,170	2,730	36.7
Information Security Analysts (SOC 2018)	5,920	8,070	2,150	36.3
Occupational Therapy Assistants	1,310	1,780	470	35.9
Wind Turbine Service Technicians	140	190	50	35.7

Note: Projections cover North Carolina; (1) Sorted by percent employment change and excludes occupations with numeric employment change less than 50
Source: www.projectionscentral.org, State Occupational Projections, 2022–2032 Long-Term Projections

CITY FINANCES

City Government Finances

Component	2022 ($000)	2022 ($ per capita)
Total Revenues	2,363,548	2,625
Total Expenditures	2,937,673	3,263
Debt Outstanding	4,352,968	4,835

Source: U.S. Census Bureau, State & Local Government Finances 2022

City Government Revenue by Source

Source	2022 ($000)	2022 ($ per capita)	2022 (%)
General Revenue			
From Federal Government	314,302	349	13.3
From State Government	62,412	69	2.6
From Local Governments	28,919	32	1.2
Taxes			
Property	533,544	593	22.6
Sales and Gross Receipts	241,487	268	10.2
Personal Income	0	0	0.0
Corporate Income	0	0	0.0
Motor Vehicle License	38,127	42	1.6
Other Taxes	64,885	72	2.7
Current Charges	783,803	871	33.2
Liquor Store	0	0	0.0
Utility	206,983	230	8.8

Source: U.S. Census Bureau, State & Local Government Finances 2022

City Government Expenditures by Function

Function	2022 ($000)	2022 ($ per capita)	2022 (%)
General Direct Expenditures			
Air Transportation	464,670	516	15.8
Corrections	0	0	0.0
Education	0	0	0.0
Employment Security Administration	0	0	0.0
Financial Administration	34,191	38	1.2
Fire Protection	160,981	178	5.5
General Public Buildings	12,778	14	0.4
Governmental Administration, Other	50,559	56	1.7
Health	9,729	10	0.3
Highways	130,800	145	4.5
Hospitals	0	0	0.0
Housing and Community Development	171,545	190	5.8
Interest on General Debt	157,069	174	5.3
Judicial and Legal	3,936	4	0.1
Libraries	3	< 1	< 0.1
Parking	387	< 1	< 0.1
Parks and Recreation	124,373	138	4.2
Police Protection	330,419	367	11.2
Public Welfare	397	< 1	< 0.1
Sewerage	419,816	466	14.3
Solid Waste Management	71,434	79	2.4
Veterans' Services	0	0	0.0
Liquor Store	0	0	0.0
Utility	710,356	789	24.2

Source: U.S. Census Bureau, State & Local Government Finances 2022

TAXES

State Corporate Income Tax Rates

State	Tax Rate (%)	Income Brackets ($)	Num. of Brackets	Financial Institution Tax Rate (%)[a]	Federal Income Tax Ded.
North Carolina	2.5	Flat rate	1	2.5	No

Note: Tax rates for tax year 2024; (a) Rates listed are the corporate income tax rate applied to financial institutions or excise taxes based on income. Some states have other taxes based upon the value of deposits or shares.
Source: Federation of Tax Administrators, State Corporate Income Tax Rates, January 1, 2025

State Individual Income Tax Rates

State	Tax Rate (%)	Income Brackets ($)	Personal Exemptions ($)			Standard Ded. ($)	
			Single	Married	Depend.	Single	Married
North Carolina	4.5	Flat rate	None	None	None	12,750	25,500

Note: Tax rates for tax year 2024; Local- and county-level taxes are not included; Federal income tax is not deductible on state income tax returns
Source: Federation of Tax Administrators, State Individual Income Tax Rates, January 1, 2025

Various State Sales and Excise Tax Rates

State	State Sales Tax (%)	Gasoline[1] ($/gal.)	Cigarette[2] ($/pack)	Spirits[3] ($/gal.)	Wine[4] ($/gal.)	Beer[5] ($/gal.)	Recreational Marijuana (%)
North Carolina	4.75	0.41	0.45	18.23	1.00	0.62	Not legal

Note: All tax rates as of January 1, 2025; (1) The American Petroleum Institute has developed a methodology for determining the average tax rate on a gallon of fuel. Rates may include any of the following: excise taxes, environmental fees, storage tank fees, other fees or taxes, general sales tax, and local taxes; (2) The federal excise tax of $1.0066 per pack and local taxes are not included; (3) Rates are those applicable to off-premise sales of 40% alcohol by volume (a.b.v.) distilled spirits in 750ml containers. Local excise taxes are excluded; (4) Rates are those applicable to off-premise sales of 11% a.b.v. non-carbonated wine in 750ml containers; (5) Rates are those applicable to off-premise sales of 4.7% a.b.v. beer in 12 ounce containers.
Source: Tax Foundation, 2025 Facts & Figures: How Does Your State Compare?

State Tax Competitiveness Index

State	Overall Rank	Corporate Tax Rank	Individual Income Tax Rank	Sales Tax Rank	Property Tax Rank	Unemployment Insurance Tax Rank
North Carolina	12	3	21	16	20	7

Note: The Tax Foundation's State Tax Competitiveness Index enables policymakers, taxpayers, and business leaders to gauge how their states' tax systems compare. A rank of 1 is best, 50 is worst. Rankings do not average to the total. States without a tax rank equally as 1. DC's scores and rankings do not affect other states. The report shows tax systems as of July 1, 2024 (the beginning of Fiscal Year 2025).
Source: Tax Foundation, State Tax Competitiveness Index 2025

TRANSPORTATION

Means of Transportation to Work

Area	Car/Truck/Van		Public Transportation			Bicycle	Walked	Other Means	Worked at Home
	Drove Alone	Car-pooled	Bus	Subway	Railroad				
City	61.0	8.1	1.4	0.1	0.0	0.2	1.7	2.0	25.5
MSA[1]	69.3	8.1	0.7	0.1	0.0	0.1	1.2	1.5	19.0
U.S.	70.2	8.5	1.7	1.3	0.4	0.4	2.4	1.6	13.5

Note: Figures are percentages and cover workers 16 years of age and older; (1) Figures cover the Charlotte-Concord-Gastonia, NC-SC Metropolitan Statistical Area
Source: U.S. Census Bureau, 2019-2023 American Community Survey 5-Year Estimates

Travel Time to Work

Area	Less Than 10 Minutes	10 to 19 Minutes	20 to 29 Minutes	30 to 44 Minutes	45 to 59 Minutes	60 to 89 Minutes	90 Minutes or More
City	9.1	29.7	27.1	23.2	6.1	3.0	1.9
MSA[1]	9.8	27.9	22.9	23.4	9.2	4.9	2.0
U.S.	12.6	28.6	21.2	20.8	8.1	6.0	2.8

Note: Note: Figures are percentages and include workers 16 years old and over; (1) Figures cover the Charlotte-Concord-Gastonia, NC-SC Metropolitan Statistical Area
Source: U.S. Census Bureau, 2019-2023 American Community Survey 5-Year Estimates

Key Congestion Measures

Measure	2000	2010	2015	2020	2022
Annual Hours of Delay, Total (000)	21,924	35,734	46,235	23,138	44,957
Annual Hours of Delay, Per Auto Commuter	38	45	52	24	48
Annual Congestion Cost, Per Auto Commuter ($)	882	1,145	1,368	654	1,226

Note: Figures cover the Charlotte NC-SC urban area
Source: Texas A&M Transportation Institute, 2023 Urban Mobility Report

Freeway Travel Time Index

Measure	1985	1990	1995	2000	2005	2010	2015	2020	2022
Urban Area Index[1]	1.10	1.14	1.17	1.20	1.23	1.24	1.23	1.06	1.17
Urban Area Rank[1,2]	27	26	29	29	28	24	29	75	44

Note: Freeway Travel Time Index—the ratio of travel time in the peak period to the travel time at free-flow conditions. For example, a value of 1.30 indicates a 20-minute free-flow trip takes 26 minutes in the peak (20 minutes x 1.30 = 26 minutes); (1) Covers the Charlotte NC-SC urban area; (2) Rank is based on 101 larger urban areas (#1 = highest travel time index)
Source: Texas A&M Transportation Institute, 2023 Urban Mobility Report

Public Transportation

Agency Name / Mode of Transportation	Vehicles Operated in Maximum Service[1]	Annual Unlinked Passenger Trips[2] (in thous.)	Annual Passenger Miles[3] (in thous.)
Charlotte Area Transit System (CATS)			
Bus (purchased transportation)	153	7,852.3	34,214.3
Commuter Bus (purchased transportation)	35	254.2	3,835.4
Demand Response (directly operated)	55	186.5	2,150.3
Light Rail (directly operated)	20	5,084.6	24,678.3
Streetcar Rail (directly operated)	5	604.3	654.0
Vanpool (directly operated)	28	45.2	1,999.3

Note: (1) Number of revenue vehicles operated by the given mode and type of service to meet the annual maximum service requirement. This is the revenue vehicle count during the peak season of the year; on the week and day that maximum service is provided. Vehicles operated in maximum service (VOMS) exclude atypical days and one-time special events; (2) Number of passengers who boarded public transportation vehicles. Passengers are counted each time they board a vehicle no matter how many vehicles they use to travel from their origin to their destination. (3) Sum of the distances ridden by all passengers during the entire fiscal year.
Source: Federal Transit Administration, National Transit Database, 2023

Air Transportation

Airport Name and Code / Type of Service	Passenger Airlines[1]	Passenger Enplanements	Freight Carriers[2]	Freight (lbs)
Charlotte-Douglas International (CLT)				
Domestic service (U.S. carriers only)	28	26,172,279	11	142,365,742
International service (U.S. carriers only)	6	2,211,009	3	11,654,107

Note: (1) Includes all U.S.-based major, minor and commuter airlines that carried at least one passenger during the year; (2) Includes all U.S.-based airlines and freight carriers that transported at least one pound of freight during the year.
Source: Bureau of Transportation Statistics, The Intermodal Transportation Database, Air Carriers: T-100 Domestic Market (U.S. carriers only), 2024; Bureau of Transportation Statistics, The Intermodal Transportation Database, Air Carriers: T-100 International Market (U.S. carriers only), 2024

BUSINESSES

Major Business Headquarters

Company Name	Industry	Rankings	
		Fortune[1]	Forbes[2]
Albemarle	Chemicals	412	-
Bank of America	Commercial banks	18	-
Belk	Retailing	-	215
Duke Energy	Utilities: gas and electric	148	-
Honeywell International	Industrial machinery	114	-
Nucor	Metals	124	-
Sonic Automotive	Automotive retailing, services	296	-
Truist Financial	Commercial banks	132	-

Note: (1) Companies that produce a 10-K are ranked 1 to 500 based on 2023 revenue; (2) All private companies with at least $2 billion in annual revenue through the end of their most current fiscal year are ranked 1 to 275; companies listed are headquartered in the city; dashes indicate no ranking
Source: Fortune, "Fortune 500," 2024; Forbes, "America's Largest Private Companies," 2024

Fastest-Growing Businesses

According to *Inc.*, Charlotte is home to six of America's 500 fastest-growing private companies: **Top Tier Solar Solutions** (#4); **DebtBook** (#39); **Already Autism Health** (#132); **Lucid Bots** (#143); **Five Star Parks & Attractions** (#299); **LeadZod** (#329). Criteria: must be an independent, privately-held, for-profit, U.S. corporation, proprietorship or partnership as of December 31, 2023; revenues must be at least $100,000 in 2020 and $2 million in 2023; must have four-year operating/sales history. *Inc.*, "America's 500 Fastest-Growing Private Companies," 2024

According to Deloitte, Charlotte is home to one of North America's 500 fastest-growing high-technology companies: **MedShift** (#339). Companies are ranked by percentage growth in revenue over a four-year period. Criteria for inclusion: company must be headquartered within North America; must own proprietary intellectual property or technology that is sold to customers in products that contributes to a significant portion of the company's operating revenue; must have been in business for a minumum of four years with 2020 operating revenues of at least $50,000 USD/CD and 2023 operating revenues of at least $5 million USD/CD. *Deloitte, 2024 Technology Fast 500*™

Living Environment

COST OF LIVING

Cost of Living Index

Composite Index	Groceries	Housing	Utilities	Transportation	Health Care	Misc. Goods/Services
98.9	101.1	84.8	101.3	94.4	99.6	110.0

Note: The Cost of Living Index measures regional differences in the cost of consumer goods and services, excluding taxes and non-consumer expenditures, for professional and managerial households in the top income quintile. It is based on more than 50,000 prices covering almost 60 different items for which prices are collected three times a year by chambers of commerce, economic development organizations or university applied economic centers in each participating urban area. The numbers shown should be read as a percentage above or below the national average of 100. For example, a value of 115.4 in the groceries column indicates that grocery prices are 15.4% higher than the national average. Small differences in the index numbers should not be interpreted as significant; Figures cover the Charlotte NC urban area.
Source: The Council for Community and Economic Research, Cost of Living Index, 2024

Grocery Prices

Area[1]	T-Bone Steak ($/pound)	Frying Chicken ($/pound)	Whole Milk ($/half gal.)	Eggs ($/dozen)	Orange Juice ($/64 oz.)	Coffee ($/11.5 oz.)
City[2]	15.53	1.61	4.69	3.30	4.33	5.36
Avg.	15.42	1.55	4.69	3.25	4.41	5.46
Min.	14.50	1.16	4.43	2.75	4.00	4.85
Max.	17.56	2.89	5.49	4.78	5.54	7.89

Note: (1) Values for the local area are compared with the average, minimum and maximum values for all 276 areas in the Cost of Living Index; (2) Figures cover the Charlotte NC urban area; **T-Bone Steak** (price per pound); **Frying Chicken** (price per pound, whole fryer); **Whole Milk** (half gallon carton); **Eggs** (price per dozen, Grade A, large); **Orange Juice** (64 oz. Tropicana or Florida Natural); **Coffee** (11.5 oz. can, vacuum-packed, Maxwell House, Hills Bros, or Folgers).
Source: The Council for Community and Economic Research, Cost of Living Index, 2024

Housing and Utility Costs

Area[1]	New Home Price ($)	Apartment Rent ($/month)	All Electric ($/month)	Part Electric ($/month)	Other Energy ($/month)	Telephone ($/month)
City[2]	398,825	1,562	213.43	-	-	189.47
Avg.	515,975	1,550	210.99	123.07	82.07	194.99
Min.	265,375	692	104.33	53.68	36.26	179.42
Max.	2,775,821	5,719	529.02	397.28	361.63	223.33

Note: (1) Values for the local area are compared with the average, minimum and maximum values for all 276 areas in the Cost of Living Index; (2) Figures cover the Charlotte NC urban area; **New Home Price** (2,400 sf living area, 8,000 sf lot, in urban area with full utilities); **Apartment Rent** (950 sf 2 bedroom/1.5 or 2 bath, unfurnished, excluding all utilities except water); **All Electric** (average monthly cost for an all-electric home); **Part Electric** (average monthly cost for a part-electric home); **Other Energy** (average monthly cost for natural gas, fuel oil, coal, wood, and any other forms of energy except electricity); **Telephone** (price includes the base monthly rate plus taxes and fees for three lines of mobile phone service).
Source: The Council for Community and Economic Research, Cost of Living Index, 2024

Health Care, Transportation, and Other Costs

Area[1]	Doctor ($/visit)	Dentist ($/visit)	Optometrist ($/visit)	Gasoline ($/gallon)	Beauty Salon ($/visit)	Men's Shirt ($)
City[2]	157.61	120.57	92.08	3.12	79.44	57.64
Avg.	143.77	117.51	129.23	3.32	48.57	38.14
Min.	36.74	58.67	67.33	2.80	24.00	13.41
Max.	270.44	216.82	307.33	5.28	94.00	63.89

Note: (1) Values for the local area are compared with the average, minimum and maximum values for all 276 areas in the Cost of Living Index; (2) Figures cover the Charlotte NC urban area; **Doctor** (general practitioners routine exam of an established patient); **Dentist** (adult teeth cleaning and periodic oral examination); **Optometrist** (full vision eye exam for established adult patient); **Gasoline** (one gallon regular unleaded, national brand, including all taxes, cash price at self-service pump if available); **Beauty Salon** (woman's shampoo, trim, and blow-dry); **Men's Shirt** (cotton/polyester dress shirt, pinpoint weave, long sleeves).
Source: The Council for Community and Economic Research, Cost of Living Index, 2024

HOUSING

Homeownership Rate

Area	2017 (%)	2018 (%)	2019 (%)	2020 (%)	2021 (%)	2022 (%)	2023 (%)	2024 (%)
MSA[1]	64.6	67.9	72.3	73.3	70.0	68.7	64.8	62.7
U.S.	63.9	64.4	64.6	66.6	65.5	65.8	65.9	65.6

Note: (1) Figures cover the Charlotte-Concord-Gastonia, NC-SC Metropolitan Statistical Area
Source: U.S. Census Bureau, Housing Vacancies and Homeownership Annual Statistics: 2017-2024

House Price Index (HPI)

Area	National Ranking[2]	Quarterly Change (%)	One-Year Change (%)	Five-Year Change (%)	Since 1991Q1 (%)
MSA[1]	175	0.39	4.07	71.74	349.74
U.S.[3]	—	1.43	4.51	57.13	327.82

Note: The HPI is a weighted repeat sales index. It measures average price changes in repeat sales or refinancings on the same properties. This information is obtained by reviewing repeat mortgage transactions on single-family properties whose mortgages have been purchased or securitized by Fannie Mae or Freddie Mac since January 1975; (1) Figures cover the Charlotte-Concord-Gastonia, NC-SC Metropolitan Statistical Area; (2) Rankings are based on annual percentage change for all metro areas containing at least 15,000 transactions over the last 10 years and ranges from 1 to 241; (3) figures based on a weighted average of Census Division estimates using a seasonally adjusted, purchase-only index; all figures are for the period ending December 31, 2024
Source: Federal Housing Finance Agency, Change in FHFA Metropolitan Area House Price Indexes, All Transactions Index, 2024Q4

Home Value

Area	Under $100,000	$100,000 -$199,999	$200,000 -$299,999	$300,000 -$399,999	$400,000 -$499,999	$500,000 -$999,999	$1,000,000 or more	Median ($)
City	4.4	13.0	22.8	19.2	12.6	20.8	7.2	351,500
MSA[1]	8.7	15.9	21.8	18.3	12.5	18.3	4.4	319,400
U.S.	12.1	17.8	19.5	14.4	10.5	19.1	6.5	303,400

Note: Figures are percentages except for median and cover owner-occupied housing units; (1) Figures cover the Charlotte-Concord-Gastonia, NC-SC Metropolitan Statistical Area
Source: U.S. Census Bureau, 2019-2023 American Community Survey 5-Year Estimates

Year Housing Structure Built

Area	2020 or Later	2010 -2019	2000 -2009	1990 -1999	1980 -1989	1970 -1979	1960 -1969	1950 -1959	1940 -1949	Before 1940	Median Year
City	1.8	16.9	20.9	17.3	13.9	10.2	8.2	5.8	2.4	2.6	1994
MSA[1]	2.2	16.8	21.6	17.2	12.3	10.0	7.2	5.8	2.9	4.1	1994
U.S.	1.2	8.9	13.6	12.8	13.0	14.4	10.0	9.7	4.5	11.9	1980

Note: Figures are percentages except for Median Year; Note: (1) Figures cover the Charlotte-Concord-Gastonia, NC-SC Metropolitan Statistical Area
Source: U.S. Census Bureau, 2019-2023 American Community Survey 5-Year Estimates

Gross Monthly Rent

Area	Under $500	$500 -$999	$1,000 -$1,499	$1,500 -$1,999	$2,000 -$2,499	$2,500 -$2,999	$3,000 and up	Median ($)
City	2.7	10.1	36.9	33.9	10.9	3.2	2.3	1,504
MSA[1]	3.8	18.7	36.7	27.1	9.1	2.5	2.0	1,377
U.S.	6.5	22.3	29.5	20.2	10.8	4.8	5.9	1,348

Note: Figures are percentages except for median; Gross rent is the contract rent plus the estimated average monthly cost of utilities (electricity, gas, and water and sewer) and fuels (oil, coal, kerosene, wood, etc.) if these are paid by the renter (or paid for the renter by someone else); (1) Figures cover the Charlotte-Concord-Gastonia, NC-SC Metropolitan Statistical Area
Source: U.S. Census Bureau, 2019-2023 American Community Survey 5-Year Estimates

HEALTH

Health Risk Factors

Category	MSA[1] (%)	U.S. (%)
Adults aged 18–64 who have any kind of health care coverage	88.6	90.8
Adults who reported being in good or better health	80.4	81.8
Adults who have been told they have high blood cholesterol	35.0	36.9
Adults who have been told they have high blood pressure	34.2	34.0
Adults who are current smokers	11.8	12.1
Adults who currently use e-cigarettes	9.6	7.7
Adults who currently use chewing tobacco, snuff, or snus	3.1	3.2
Adults who are heavy drinkers[2]	5.6	6.1
Adults who are binge drinkers[3]	13.9	15.2
Adults who are overweight (BMI 25.0 - 29.9)	37.0	34.4
Adults who are obese (BMI 30.0 - 99.8)	31.2	34.3
Adults who participated in any physical activities in the past month	76.9	75.8

Note: All figures are crude prevalence; (1) Figures cover the Charlotte-Concord-Gastonia, NC-SC Metropolitan Statistical Area; (2) Heavy drinkers are classified as adult men having more than 14 drinks per week and adult women having more than 7 drinks per week; (3) Binge drinkers are classified as males having five or more drinks on one occasion or females having four or more drinks on one occasion
Source: Centers for Disease Control and Prevention, Behavioral Risk Factor Surveillance System, SMART: Selected Metropolitan Area Risk Trends, 2023

Acute and Chronic Health Conditions

Category	MSA[1] (%)	U.S. (%)
Adults who have ever been told they had a heart attack	4.9	4.2
Adults who have ever been told they have angina or coronary heart disease	6.2	4.0
Adults who have ever been told they had a stroke	3.1	3.3
Adults who have ever been told they have asthma	13.0	15.7
Adults who have ever been told they have arthritis	26.1	26.3
Adults who have ever been told they have diabetes[2]	12.0	11.5
Adults who have ever been told they had skin cancer	4.9	5.6
Adults who have ever been told they had any other types of cancer	8.0	8.4
Adults who have ever been told they have COPD	7.1	6.4
Adults who have ever been told they have kidney disease	3.9	3.7
Adults who have ever been told they have a form of depression	23.0	22.0

Note: All figures are crude prevalence; (1) Figures cover the Charlotte-Concord-Gastonia, NC-SC Metropolitan Statistical Area; (2) Figures do not include pregnancy-related, borderline, or pre-diabetes
Source: Centers for Disease Control and Prevention, Behavioral Risk Factor Surveillance System, SMART: Selected Metropolitan Area Risk Trends, 2023

Health Screening and Vaccination Rates

Category	MSA[1] (%)	U.S. (%)
Adults who have ever been tested for HIV	41.6	37.5
Adults who have had their blood cholesterol checked within the last five years	89.6	87.0
Adults aged 65+ who have had flu shot within the past year	59.6	63.4
Adults aged 65+ who have ever had a pneumonia vaccination	68.2	71.9

Note: All figures are crude prevalence; (1) Figures cover the Charlotte-Concord-Gastonia, NC-SC Metropolitan Statistical Area.
Source: Centers for Disease Control and Prevention, Behavioral Risk Factor Surveillance System, SMART: Selected Metropolitan Area Risk Trends, 2023

Disability Status

Category	MSA[1] (%)	U.S. (%)
Adults who reported being deaf	6.7	7.4
Are you blind or have serious difficulty seeing, even when wearing glasses?	4.9	4.9
Do you have difficulty doing errands alone?	6.9	7.8
Do you have difficulty dressing or bathing?	4.2	3.6
Do you have serious difficulty concentrating/remembering/making decisions?	13.2	13.7
Do you have serious difficulty walking or climbing stairs?	12.3	13.2

Note: All figures are crude prevalence; (1) Figures cover the Charlotte-Concord-Gastonia, NC-SC Metropolitan Statistical Area.
Source: Centers for Disease Control and Prevention, Behavioral Risk Factor Surveillance System, SMART: Selected Metropolitan Area Risk Trends, 2023

Mortality Rates for the Top 10 Causes of Death in the U.S.

ICD-10[a] Sub-Chapter	ICD-10[a] Code	Crude Mortality Rate[2] per 100,000 population	
		County[3]	U.S.
Malignant neoplasms	C00-C97	117.7	182.7
Ischaemic heart diseases	I20-I25	46.8	109.6
Provisional assignment of new diseases of uncertain etiology[1]	U00-U49	38.4	65.3
Other forms of heart disease	I30-I51	51.7	65.1
Other degenerative diseases of the nervous system	G30-G31	49.5	52.4
Other external causes of accidental injury	W00-X59	38.5	52.3
Cerebrovascular diseases	I60-I69	36.3	49.1
Chronic lower respiratory diseases	J40-J47	19.8	43.5
Hypertensive diseases	I10-I15	19.2	38.9
Organic, including symptomatic, mental disorders	F01-F09	21.6	33.9

Note: (a) ICD-10 = International Classification of Diseases 10th Revision; (1) Includes COVID-19, adverse effects to COVID-19 vaccines, SARS, and vaping-related disorders; (2) Crude mortality rates are a three-year average covering 2021-2023; (3) Figures cover Mecklenburg County.
Source: Centers for Disease Control and Prevention, National Center for Health Statistics. National Vital Statistics System, Mortality 2018-2023 on CDC WONDER Online Database

Mortality Rates for Selected Causes of Death

Cause of Death	ICD-10[a] Code	Crude Mortality Rate[1] per 100,000 population	
		County[2]	U.S.
Accidental poisoning and exposure to noxious substances	X40-X49	25.8	30.5
Alzheimer disease	G30	28.0	35.4
Assault	X85-Y09	9.1	7.3
COVID-19	U07.1	38.4	65.3
Diabetes mellitus	E10-E14	20.3	30.0
Diseases of the liver	K70-K76	13.6	20.8
Human immunodeficiency virus (HIV) disease	B20-B24	2.9	1.5
Influenza and pneumonia	J09-J18	6.6	13.4
Intentional self-harm	X60-X84	10.6	14.7
Malnutrition	E40-E46	9.0	6.0
Obesity and other hyperalimentation	E65-E68	2.6	3.1
Renal failure	N17-N19	14.7	16.4
Transport accidents	V01-V99	10.8	14.4

Note: (a) ICD-10 = International Classification of Diseases 10th Revision; (1) Crude mortality rates are a three-year average covering 2021-2023; (2) Figures cover Mecklenburg County; Data are suppressed when the data meet the criteria for confidentiality constraints; Crude mortality rates are flagged as unreliable when the rate would be calculated with a numerator of 20 or less.
Source: Centers for Disease Control and Prevention, National Center for Health Statistics. National Vital Statistics System, Mortality 2018-2023 on CDC WONDER Online Database

Health Insurance Coverage

Area	With Health Insurance	With Private Health Insurance	With Public Health Insurance	Without Health Insurance	Population Under Age 19 Without Health Insurance
City	87.1	67.8	26.5	12.9	8.3
MSA[1]	89.9	70.0	29.9	10.1	5.9
U.S.	91.4	67.3	36.3	8.6	5.4

Note: Figures are percentages that cover the civilian noninstitutionalized population; (1) Figures cover the Charlotte-Concord-Gastonia, NC-SC Metropolitan Statistical Area
Source: U.S. Census Bureau, 2019-2023 American Community Survey 5-Year Estimates

Number of Medical Professionals

Area	MDs[3]	DOs[3,4]	Dentists	Podiatrists	Chiropractors	Optometrists
County[1] (number)	4,041	239	839	43	433	169
County[1] (rate[2])	352.8	20.9	72.1	3.7	37.2	14.5
U.S. (rate[2])	302.5	29.2	74.6	6.4	29.5	18.0

Note: Data as of 2023 unless noted; (1) Data covers Mecklenburg County; (2) Number of medical professionals per 100,000 population; (3) Data as of 2022 and includes all active, non-federal physicians; (4) Doctor of Osteopathic Medicine
Source: U.S. Department of Health and Human Services, Health Resources and Services Administration, Bureau of Health Professions, Area Resource File (ARF) 2023-2024

Best Hospitals

According to *U.S. News,* the Charlotte-Concord-Gastonia, NC-SC metro area is home to two of the best hospitals in the U.S.: **Atrium Health Carolinas Medical Center** (10 pediatric specialties); **Atrium Health Carolinas Rehabilitation** (1 adult specialty). The hospitals listed were nationally ranked in at least one of 15 adult or 11 pediatric specialties. The number of specialties shown cover the parent hospital. Only 160 U.S. hospitals performed well enough to be nationally ranked in one or more specialties. Twenty hospitals in the U.S. made the Honor Roll. The Best Hospitals Honor Roll takes both the national rankings and the procedure and condition ratings into account. Hospitals received points if they were nationally ranked in one of the 15 adult specialties—the higher they ranked, the more points they got—and how many ratings of "high performing" they earned in the 20 procedures and conditions. *U.S. News Online,* "America's Best Hospitals 2024-25"

According to *U.S. News,* the Charlotte-Concord-Gastonia, NC-SC metro area is home to one of the best children's hospitals in the U.S.: **Levine Children's Hospital** (10 pediatric specialties). The hospital listed was highly ranked in at least one of 11 pediatric specialties. One hundred five children's hospitals in the U.S. were nationally ranked in at least one specialty. Hospitals received points for being ranked in a specialty, and the 10 hospitals with the most points across the 11 specialties make up the Honor Roll. *U.S. News Online,* "America's Best Children's Hospitals 2024-25"

EDUCATION

Public School District Statistics

District Name	Schls	Pupils	Pupil/ Teacher Ratio	Minority Pupils[1] (%)	Total Rev. per Pupil ($)	Total Exp. per Pupil ($)
Charlotte-Mecklenburg Schools	186	144,116	16.0	76.4	13,266	15,997

Note: Table includes school districts with 2,000 or more students; (1) Percentage of students that are not non-Hispanic white.
Source: U.S. Department of Education, National Center for Education Statistics, Common Core of Data, Local Education Agency (School District) Universe Survey: School Year 2023-2024; U.S. Department of Education, National Center for Education Statistics, Common Core of Data, School District Finance Survey (F-33): School Year 2021–22

Best High Schools

According to *U.S. News*, Charlotte is home to one of the top 500 high schools in the U.S.: **Providence High School** (#500). Nearly 25,000 public, magnet and charter schools were ranked based on their performance on state assessments and how well they prepare students for college. *U.S. News & World Report, "Best High Schools 2024"*

Highest Level of Education

Area	Less than H.S.	H.S. Diploma	Some College, No Deg.	Associate Degree	Bachelor's Degree	Master's Degree	Prof. School Degree	Doctorate Degree
City	10.4	16.6	17.5	8.0	30.4	12.8	2.9	1.3
MSA[1]	9.6	22.6	19.4	9.5	25.4	10.4	2.1	1.1
U.S.	10.6	26.2	19.4	8.8	21.3	9.8	2.3	1.6

Note: Figures cover persons age 25 and over; (1) Figures cover the Charlotte-Concord-Gastonia, NC-SC Metropolitan Statistical Area
Source: U.S. Census Bureau, 2019-2023 American Community Survey 5-Year Estimates

Educational Attainment by Race

Area	High School Graduate or Higher (%)					Bachelor's Degree or Higher (%)				
	Total	White	Black	Asian	Hisp.[2]	Total	White	Black	Asian	Hisp.[2]
City	89.6	95.9	91.6	85.3	60.5	47.4	63.1	33.3	61.3	20.5
MSA[1]	90.4	93.4	90.6	88.0	67.0	39.0	42.6	30.0	61.9	21.4
U.S.	89.4	92.9	88.1	88.0	72.5	35.0	37.7	24.7	57.0	19.9

Note: Figures shown cover persons 25 years old and over; (1) Figures cover the Charlotte-Concord-Gastonia, NC-SC Metropolitan Statistical Area; (2) People of Hispanic origin can be of any race
Source: U.S. Census Bureau, 2019-2023 American Community Survey 5-Year Estimates

School Enrollment by Grade and Control

Area	Preschool (%)		Kindergarten (%)		Grades 1 - 4 (%)		Grades 5 - 8 (%)		Grades 9 - 12 (%)	
	Public	Private	Public	Private	Public	Private	Public	Private	Public	Private
City	50.8	49.2	86.8	13.2	88.6	11.4	87.4	12.6	88.8	11.2
MSA[1]	50.5	49.5	86.2	13.8	87.8	12.2	87.3	12.7	88.6	11.4
U.S.	58.7	41.3	85.2	14.8	87.2	12.8	87.9	12.1	89.0	11.0

Note: Figures shown cover persons 3 years old and over; (1) Figures cover the Charlotte-Concord-Gastonia, NC-SC Metropolitan Statistical Area
Source: U.S. Census Bureau, 2019-2023 American Community Survey 5-Year Estimates

Higher Education

Four-Year Colleges			Two-Year Colleges			Medical Schools[1]	Law Schools[2]	Voc/ Tech[3]
Public	Private Non-profit	Private For-profit	Public	Private Non-profit	Private For-profit			
3	12	2	7	0	3	0	0	7

Note: Figures cover institutions located within the Charlotte-Concord-Gastonia, NC-SC Metropolitan Statistical Area and include main campuses only; (1) includes schools accredited by the Liaison Committee on Medical Education and the American Osteopathic Association's Commission on Osteopathic College Accreditation; (2) includes ABA-accredited schools, schools with provisional ABA accreditation, and state accredited schools; (3) includes all schools with programs that are less than 2 years.
Source: National Center for Education Statistics, Integrated Postsecondary Education System (IPEDS), 2023-24; Wikipedia, List of Medical Schools in the United States, accessed May 2, 2025; Wikipedia, List of Law Schools in the United States, accessed May 2, 2025

According to *U.S. News & World Report*, the Charlotte-Concord-Gastonia, NC-SC metro area is home to one of the top 200 national universities in the U.S.: **University of North Carolina at Charlotte** (#152 tie). The indicators used to capture academic quality fall into a number of categories: assessment by administrators at peer institutions; retention of students; faculty resources; student selectivity; financial resources; alumni giving; high school counselor ratings of colleges; and graduation rate. *U.S. News & World Report, "America's Best Colleges 2025"*

According to *U.S. News & World Report*, the Charlotte-Concord-Gastonia, NC-SC metro area is home to one of the top 100 liberal arts colleges in the U.S.: **Davidson College** (#14 tie). The indicators used to capture academic quality fall into a number of categories: assessment by administrators at peer institutions; retention of students; faculty resources; student selectivity; financial resources; alumni giving; high school counselor ratings of colleges; and graduation rate. *U.S. News & World Report, "America's Best Colleges 2025"*

EMPLOYERS

Major Employers

Company Name	Industry
American Airlines Group Inc	Airline
Atrium Health	Healthcare
Bank of America Corp.	Financial services
Cardinal Logistics Management	Logistics
CaroMont Health	Healthcare
Cato Corporation	Women's fashion
City of Charlotte	Local government
Dillard's	Retail and wholesale
Honeywell	Manufacturing
Lending Tree	Financial services
NASCAR	Motorsports entertainment
Novant Health Inc.	Healthcare
Parkdale Mills Inc.	Textile manufacturing
Wells Fargo	Financial services
Westrock Coffee Company	Supplier

Note: Companies shown are located within the Charlotte-Concord-Gastonia, NC-SC Metropolitan Statistical Area.
Source: Chambers of Commerce; State Departments of Labor; Wikipedia

Best Companies to Work For

Bank of America, headquartered in Charlotte, is among "The 100 Best Companies to Work For." To pick the best companies, *Fortune* partnered with the Great Place to Work Institute. Using their proprietary Trust Index™ survey, the core of what creates great a workplace is measured—key behaviors that drive trust in management, connection with colleagues, and loyalty to the company. To be eligible for the *Fortune* 100 Best Companies to Work For list, employers must have 1,000 or more employees in the U.S. and cannot be a government agency. *Fortune, "The 100 Best Companies to Work For," 2025*

Bank of America, headquartered in Charlotte, is among "Fortune's Best Workplaces for Parents." To pick the best companies, *Fortune* partnered with the Great Place to Work Institute. To be considered for the list, companies must be Great Place To Work-Certified and have at least 50 responses from parents in the US. The survey enables employees to share confidential quantitative and qualitative feedback about their organization's culture by responding to 60 statements on a 5-point scale and answering two open-ended questions. Collectively, these statements describe a great employee experience, defined by high levels of trust, respect, credibility, fairness, pride, and camaraderie. In addition, companies provide organizational data like size, location, industry, demographics, roles, and levels; and provide information about parental leave, adoption, flexible schedule, childcare and dependent health care benefits. *Fortune, "Best Workplaces for Parents," 2024*

Bank of America, headquartered in Charlotte, is among "Fortune's Best Workplaces for Women." To pick the best companies, *Fortune* partnered with the Great Place to Work Institute. To be considered for the list, companies must be Great Place To Work-Certified. Companies must also employ at least 50 women, at least 20% of their non-executive managers must be female, and at least one executive must be female. To determine the Best Workplaces for Women, Great Place To Work measured the differences in women's survey responses to those of their peers and assesses the impact of demographics and roles on the quality and consistency of women's experiences. Great Place To Work also analyzed the gender balance of each workplace, how it compared to each company's industry, and patterns in representation as women rise from front-line positions to the board of directors. *Fortune, "Best Workplaces for Women," 2024*

Atrium Health, headquartered in Charlotte, is among the "Best Places to Work in IT." To qualify, companies had to have a minimum of 100 total employees and five IT employees. The best places to work were selected based on DEI (diversity, equity, and inclusion) practices; IT turnover, promotions, and growth; IT retention and engagement programs; remote/hybrid working; benefits and perks (such as elder care and child care, flextime, and reimbursement for college tuition); and training and career development opportunities. *Computerworld, "Best Places to Work in IT," 2025*

PUBLIC SAFETY

Crime Rate

Area	Total Crime Rate	Violent Crime Rate				Property Crime Rate		
		Murder	Rape	Robbery	Aggrav. Assault	Burglary	Larceny-Theft	Motor Vehicle Theft
City	4,562.0	9.4	25.4	128.4	563.0	430.0	2,578.2	827.7
U.S.	2,290.9	5.7	38.0	66.5	264.1	250.7	1,347.2	318.7

Note: Figures are crimes per 100,000 population.
Source: FBI, Table 8, Offenses Known to Law Enforcement, by State by City, 2023

Hate Crimes

Area	Number of Quarters Reported	Number of Incidents per Bias Motivation					
		Race/Ethnicity/Ancestry	Religion	Sexual Orientation	Disability	Gender	Gender Identity
City[1]	4	20	4	6	0	0	0
U.S.	4	5,900	2,699	2,077	187	92	492

Note: (1) Figures include at least one incident reported with more than one bias motivation.
Source: Federal Bureau of Investigation, Hate Crime Statistics 2023

Identity Theft Consumer Reports

Area	Reports	Reports per 100,000 Population	Rank[2]
MSA[1]	10,144	374	28
U.S.	1,135,291	339	-

Note: (1) Figures cover the Charlotte-Concord-Gastonia, NC-SC Metropolitan Statistical Area; (2) Rank ranges from 1 to 401 where 1 indicates greatest number of identity theft reports per 100,000 population
Source: Federal Trade Commission, Consumer Sentinel Network Data Book 2024

Fraud and Other Consumer Reports

Area	Reports	Reports per 100,000 Population	Rank[2]
MSA[1]	48,136	1,774	25
U.S.	5,360,641	1,601	-

Note: (1) Figures cover the Charlotte-Concord-Gastonia, NC-SC Metropolitan Statistical Area; (2) Rank ranges from 1 to 401 where 1 indicates greatest number of fraud and other consumer reports per 100,000 population
Source: Federal Trade Commission, Consumer Sentinel Network Data Book 2024

POLITICS

2024 Presidential Election Results

Area	Trump (Rep.)	Harris (Dem.)	Stein (Green)	Kennedy (Ind.)	Oliver (Lib.)	Other
Mecklenburg County	32.5	65.2	0.7	0.0	0.5	1.1
U.S.	49.7	48.2	0.6	0.5	0.4	0.6

Note: Results are percentages and may not add to 100% due to rounding
Source: Dave Leip's Atlas of U.S. Presidential Elections

SPORTS

Professional Sports Teams

Team Name	League	Year Established
Carolina Panthers	National Football League (NFL)	1995
Charlotte FC	Major League Soccer (MLS)	2022
Charlotte Hornets	National Basketball Association (NBA)	2004

Note: Includes teams located in the Charlotte-Concord-Gastonia, NC-SC Metropolitan Statistical Area.
Source: Wikipedia, Major Professional Sports Teams of the United States and Canada, May 1, 2025

CLIMATE

Average and Extreme Temperatures

Temperature	Jan	Feb	Mar	Apr	May	Jun	Jul	Aug	Sep	Oct	Nov	Dec	Yr.
Extreme High (°F)	78	81	86	93	97	103	103	103	104	98	85	77	104
Average High (°F)	51	54	62	72	80	86	89	88	82	72	62	53	71
Average Temp. (°F)	41	44	51	61	69	76	79	78	72	61	51	43	61
Average Low (°F)	31	33	40	48	57	65	69	68	62	50	40	33	50
Extreme Low (°F)	-5	5	4	25	32	45	53	53	39	24	11	2	-5

Note: Figures cover the years 1948-1990
Source: National Climatic Data Center, International Station Meteorological Climate Summary, 9/96

Average Precipitation/Snowfall/Humidity

Precip./Humidity	Jan	Feb	Mar	Apr	May	Jun	Jul	Aug	Sep	Oct	Nov	Dec	Yr.
Avg. Precip. (in.)	3.6	3.8	4.5	3.0	3.7	3.4	3.9	3.9	3.4	3.2	3.1	3.4	42.8
Avg. Snowfall (in.)	2	2	1	Tr	0	0	0	0	0	0	Tr	1	6
Avg. Rel. Hum. 7am (%)	78	77	78	78	82	83	86	89	89	87	83	79	82
Avg. Rel. Hum. 4pm (%)	53	49	46	43	49	51	54	55	54	50	50	54	51

Note: Figures cover the years 1948-1990; Tr = Trace amounts (<0.05 in. of rain; <0.5 in. of snow)
Source: National Climatic Data Center, International Station Meteorological Climate Summary, 9/96

Weather Conditions

Temperature			Daytime Sky			Precipitation		
10°F & below	32°F & below	90°F & above	Clear	Partly cloudy	Cloudy	0.01 inch or more precip.	0.1 inch or more snow/ice	Thunder-storms
1	65	44	98	142	125	113	3	41

Note: Figures are average number of days per year and cover the years 1948-1990
Source: National Climatic Data Center, International Station Meteorological Climate Summary, 9/96

HAZARDOUS WASTE

Superfund Sites

The Charlotte-Concord-Gastonia, NC-SC metro area is home to 13 sites on the EPA's Superfund National Priorities List (NPL) or Superfund Alternative Approach (SAA) list: **Bypass 601 Ground Water Contamination** (Final NPL); **Carolawn, Inc.** (Final NPL); **Davis Park Road Tce** (Final NPL); **FCX, Inc. (Statesville Plant)** (Final NPL); **Hemphill Road Tce** (Final NPL); **Henry's Knob** (Pre-proposal SAA); **Jadco-Hughes Facility** (Final NPL); **Leonard Chemical Co., Inc.** (Final NPL); **National Starch & Chemical Corp.** (Final NPL); **North Belmont Pce** (Final NPL); **Ram Leather Care Site** (Final NPL); **Rock Hill Chemical Co.** (Final NPL); **Sigmon's Septic Tank Service** (Final NPL). The Superfund alternative approach uses the same investigation and cleanup process and standards that are used for sites listed on the National Priorities List. The SAA is an alternative to listing a site on the NPL; it is not an alternative to Superfund or the Superfund process. There are a total of 1,445 Superfund sites with a status of proposed or final on both lists in the United States. *U.S. Environmental Protection Agency, National Priorities List, May 1, 2025; U.S. Environmental Protection Agency, Superfund Alternative Approach Sites, May 1, 2025*

AIR QUALITY

Air Quality Trends: Ozone

	1990	1995	2000	2005	2010	2015	2020	2021	2022	2023
MSA[1]	0.094	0.091	0.099	0.089	0.082	0.071	0.060	0.067	0.068	0.072
U.S.	0.087	0.089	0.081	0.080	0.072	0.068	0.066	0.067	0.067	0.070

Note: (1) Data covers the Charlotte-Concord-Gastonia, NC-SC Metropolitan Statistical Area. The values shown are the composite ozone concentration averages among trend sites based on the highest fourth daily maximum 8-hour concentration in parts per million. These trends are based on sites having an adequate record of monitoring data during the trend period. Data from exceptional events are included.
Source: U.S. Environmental Protection Agency, Air Quality Monitoring Information, "Air Quality Trends by City, 1990-2023"

Air Quality Index

Area	Percent of Days when Air Quality was...[2]					AQI Statistics[2]	
	Good	Moderate	Unhealthy for Sensitive Groups	Unhealthy	Very Unhealthy	Maximum	Median
MSA[1]	39.7	58.1	2.2	0.0	0.0	150	53

Note: (1) Data covers the Charlotte-Concord-Gastonia, NC-SC Metropolitan Statistical Area; (2) Based on 365 days with AQI data in 2023. Air Quality Index (AQI) is an index for reporting daily air quality. EPA calculates the AQI for five major air pollutants regulated by the Clean Air Act: ground-level ozone, particle pollution (aka particulate matter), carbon monoxide, sulfur dioxide, and nitrogen dioxide. The AQI runs from 0 to 500. The higher the AQI value, the greater the level of air pollution and the greater the health concern. There are six AQI categories: "Good" AQI is between 0 and 50. Air quality is considered satisfactory; "Moderate" AQI is between 51 and 100. Air quality is acceptable; "Unhealthy for Sensitive Groups" When AQI values are between 101 and 150, members of sensitive groups may experience health effects; "Unhealthy" When AQI values are between 151 and 200 everyone may begin to experience health effects; "Very Unhealthy" AQI values between 201 and 300 trigger a health alert; "Hazardous" AQI values over 300 trigger warnings of emergency conditions (not shown).
Source: U.S. Environmental Protection Agency, Air Quality Index Report, 2023

Air Quality Index Pollutants

Area	Percent of Days when AQI Pollutant was...[2]					
	Carbon Monoxide	Nitrogen Dioxide	Ozone	Sulfur Dioxide	Particulate Matter 2.5	Particulate Matter 10
MSA[1]	0.0	0.0	45.8	(3)	54.2	0.0

Note: (1) Data covers the Charlotte-Concord-Gastonia, NC-SC Metropolitan Statistical Area; (2) Based on 365 days with AQI data in 2023. The Air Quality Index (AQI) is an index for reporting daily air quality. EPA calculates the AQI for five major air pollutants regulated by the Clean Air Act: ground-level ozone, particle pollution (also known as particulate matter), carbon monoxide, sulfur dioxide, and nitrogen dioxide. The AQI runs from 0 to 500. The higher the AQI value, the greater the level of air pollution and the greater the health concern; (3) Sulfur dioxide is no longer included in this table because SO_2 concentrations tend to be very localized and not necessarily representative of broad geographical areas like counties and CBSAs.
Source: U.S. Environmental Protection Agency, Air Quality Index Report, 2023

Maximum Air Pollutant Concentrations: Particulate Matter, Ozone, CO and Lead

	Particulate Matter 10 (ug/m^3)	Particulate Matter 2.5 Wtd AM (ug/m^3)	Particulate Matter 2.5 24-Hr (ug/m^3)	Ozone (ppm)	Carbon Monoxide (ppm)	Lead (ug/m^3)
MSA[1] Level	51	10	26	0.073	2	n/a
NAAQS[2]	150	15	35	0.075	9	0.15
Met NAAQS[2]	Yes	Yes	Yes	Yes	Yes	n/a

Note: (1) Data covers the Charlotte-Concord-Gastonia, NC-SC Metropolitan Statistical Area; Data from exceptional events are included; (2) National Ambient Air Quality Standards; ppm = parts per million; ug/m^3 = micrograms per cubic meter; n/a not available.
Concentrations: Particulate Matter 10 (coarse particulate)—highest second maximum 24-hour concentration; Particulate Matter 2.5 Wtd AM (fine particulate)—highest weighted annual mean concentration; Particulate Matter 2.5 24-Hour (fine particulate)—highest 98th percentile 24-hour concentration; Ozone—highest fourth daily maximum 8-hour concentration; Carbon Monoxide—highest second maximum non-overlapping 8-hour concentration; Lead—maximum running 3-month average
Source: U.S. Environmental Protection Agency, Air Quality Monitoring Information, "Air Quality Statistics by City, 2023"

Maximum Air Pollutant Concentrations: Nitrogen Dioxide and Sulfur Dioxide

	Nitrogen Dioxide AM (ppb)	Nitrogen Dioxide 1-Hr (ppb)	Sulfur Dioxide AM (ppb)	Sulfur Dioxide 1-Hr (ppb)	Sulfur Dioxide 24-Hr (ppb)
MSA[1] Level	11	37	n/a	2	n/a
NAAQS[2]	53	100	30	75	140
Met NAAQS[2]	Yes	Yes	n/a	Yes	n/a

Note: (1) Data covers the Charlotte-Concord-Gastonia, NC-SC Metropolitan Statistical Area; Data from exceptional events are included; (2) National Ambient Air Quality Standards; ppm = parts per million; ug/m^3 = micrograms per cubic meter; n/a not available.
Concentrations: Nitrogen Dioxide AM—highest arithmetic mean concentration; Nitrogen Dioxide 1-Hr—highest 98th percentile 1-hour daily maximum concentration; Sulfur Dioxide AM—highest annual mean concentration; Sulfur Dioxide 1-Hr—highest 99th percentile 1-hour daily maximum concentration; Sulfur Dioxide 24-Hr—highest second maximum 24-hour concentration
Source: U.S. Environmental Protection Agency, Air Quality Monitoring Information, "Air Quality Statistics by City, 2023"

Cincinnati, Ohio

Background

Cincinnati is located on the northern side of the confluence of the Licking and Ohio Rivers. After the American Revolution, former Continental Army soldiers formed a fraternal organization called the Society of Cincinnati, for Roman General Lucius Quinctius Cincinnatus. In 1790, General Arthur St. Clair, a member of that society and the first governor of the Northwest Territory, named the city Cincinnati and the county in which Cincinnati lies, Hamilton, after his fellow fraternal member Alexander Hamilton.

Since its incorporation as a city in 1819, the Miami and Erie canals have played great roles in Cincinnati's economic growth, giving farmers the transportation necessary to sell their produce in town. From there, businesses processed the farmers' wares such as corn, pigs, and wheat into whiskey, pork, and flour.

The South, which was Cincinnati's greatest market for pork, made the city's loyalties difficult to declare during the Civil War. Cincinnati chose sides when it became a major station of the Underground Railroad, as well as the haven where Harriet Beecher Stowe would write her classic, *Uncle Tom's Cabin.* The National Underground Railroad Freedom Center in the city offers programs and exhibits highlighting the Railroad's true stories of courage in the quest for freedom.

Today, the city's major economic sectors include aerospace, automotive, chemistry and plastics, financial services, advanced energy and consumer products. The city is home to the University of Cincinnati, Xavier University, and several Fortune 500 corporate headquarters. Major employers headquartered in the city include Proctor & Gamble and The Kroger Company. Five interstate highways converge at Cincinnati, providing present-day transportation access just as the canals did early in the city's growth. New Amtrak routes linking Cincinnati, Cleveland, Columbus, and Dayton are in the planning stages.

The city blends Old World charm with modern business savvy. Investments of more than $700 million in the first decades of the 21st century are drawing tourists, conventioneers, and residents downtown thanks to the Cincinnati Center City Development Corp., charged with supporting the area's renaissance. Improvements include new entertainment districts, called The Banks and Over the Rhine. Hotels that have opened in recent years include 21c Museum Hotel with an 8,000 square-foot art museum. Horseshoe Casino Cincinnati boasts a 31-table World Series Poker Room in addition to entertainment venues and restaurants. Not far from these are the Duke Energy Convention Center and the city's two professional sports stadiums; the Cincinnati Reds MLB team plays at the Great American Ball Park and the NFL's Cincinnati Bengals call Paycor Stadium home. In 2019, MLS (Major League Soccer) created FC Cincinnati and the city's third professional sports team.

The arts thrive in Cincinnati. The Rosenthal Center for Contemporary Art celebrated its 80th anniversary in 2019 and is housed in an acclaimed, Zaha Hadid-designed building; she won the Pritzker Architecture Award in 2004, the year after the building opened. The famed Cincinnati Opera, founded in 1920 and the second-oldest opera company in the U.S., features a complete season of productions as well as a summer program. The Cincinnati Symphony Orchestra, founded in 1905, is the nation's fifth-oldest orchestra. Both organizations perform in the historic Music Hall, whose Springer Auditorium is renowned for its acoustics.

To celebrate its German heritage, Cincinnati hosts the second largest Oktoberfest in the world. One of the city's most celebrated tradition is its chili, mostly served over spaghetti or on a hotdog. A "coney" dog, as it's called, is a staple in many city restaurants, including Skyline Chili, Empress, and Gold Star.

Cincinnati is at the southern limit of the humid continental climate zone, bordering the humid subtropical climate zone. Summers are hot and humid, with significant rainfall in each month, often with high dew points and humidity. Winters tend to be cold and moderately snowy. While snow in Cincinnati is not as intense as many of the cities located closer to the Great Lakes, there have been notable cases of severe snowfall, including the Great Blizzard of 1978, and more notable snow storms in 1994, 1999, 2007, 2021, and 2025. Severe thunderstorms are common in the warmer months, and tornadoes, while infrequent, are not unknown, with such events striking the metropolitan Cincinnati area most recently in 1974, 1999, 2012, and 2017.

Rankings

General Rankings

- To help military veterans find the best places in which to settle down, *WalletHub* compared the 100 largest U.S. cities across 19 key indicators of livability, affordability and veteran-friendliness. They range from the share of military skill-related jobs to veteran income growth to the availability of VA health facilities. Cincinnati ranked #49. *Wallethub.com, "Best & Worst Places for Veterans to Live (2025)," November 7, 2024*

- Cincinnati was selected as one of the happiest places to live in America by *Outside Magazine*. Criteria centered on overall well being; effect of climate change; inclusivity; affordability; outdoor access; and other demographic and population figures. Local experts shared highlights from hands-on experience in each location. *Outside Magazine, "The 15 Happiest Places to Live in the U.S.," September 18, 2023*

- Cincinnati was selected as one of the best places to live in the United States by *Money* magazine. The city placed among the top 50. This year's list focused on cities built around community spirit, thoughtful policy and civic engagement. Instead of relying on a predetermined dataset, the cities and towns were grouped according to their strengths and chosen due their affordability, good schools and strong job markets. *Money, "The 50 Best Places to Live in the U.S., 2024" April 8, 2024*

- In their annual survey, Livability.com looked at data for more than 2,000 mid-sized U.S. cities to assign a "Livability Score"for each. The top 100 scoring cities make up Livability's "Top 100 Best Places to Live in the U.S." in 2025. Cincinnati was placed among the top 100 of the customizable list. Criteria: housing and economy; cost of living; environment; education; health care options; transportation; safety; and community amenities. *Livability.com, "Top 100 Best Places to Live in the U.S. in 2025" April 15, 2025*

Business/Finance Rankings

- Payscale.com ranked the 32 largest metro areas in terms of wage growth. The Cincinnati metro area ranked #30. Criteria: quarterly changes in private industry employee and education professional wage growth from the previous year. *PayScale, "Wage Trends by Metro Area-4th Quarter," February 4, 2025*

- Cincinnati was cited as one of America's top metros for total corporate facility investment projects in 2024. The area ranked #5 in the Tier 1 (large) metro area category (population over 1 million). *Site Selection, "Top Metros of 2024," March 2025*

- The Cincinnati metro area appeared on the Milken Institute "2025 Best Performing Cities" list. Rank: #114 out of 200 large metro areas (based on performance category). Criteria: job growth; wage growth; high-tech growth and impact; community resilience; housing affordability; household broadband access. *Milken Institute, "Best-Performing Cities 2025," January 14, 2025*

Culture/Performing Arts Rankings

- Cincinnati was selected as one of the 25 best cities for moviemakers in North America. Great film cities are places where filmmaking dreams can come true, that offer more creative space, lower costs, and great outdoor locations. NYC & LA were intentionally excluded. Criteria: film industry presence and culture; tax incentives; affordability; and proximity of festivals and schools. The city was ranked #11. *MovieMaker Magazine, "Best Places to Live and Work as a Moviemaker, 2025," January 29, 2025*

Dating/Romance Rankings

- *Apartment List* conducted its Annual Renter Satisfaction Survey and asked renters "how satisfied are you with opportunities for dating in your current city." The cities were ranked from highest to lowest based on their satisfaction scores. Cincinnati ranked #1 out of 10 cities. *Apartment List, "Best Cities for Dating 2022 with Local Dating Insights from Bumble," February 7, 2022*

Education Rankings

- Personal finance website *WalletHub* analyzed the 150 largest U.S. metropolitan statistical areas to determine where the most educated Americans are putting their degrees to work. Criteria: education levels; percentage of workers with degrees; education quality and attainment gap; public school quality rankings; quality and enrollment of each metro area's universities. Cincinnati was ranked #57 (#1 = most educated city). *WalletHub.com, "Most & Least Educated Cities in America, 2025" July 2, 2024*

Environmental Rankings

- Cincinnati was highlighted as one of the 25 metro areas most polluted by year-round particle pollution (Annual PM 2.5) in the U.S. during 2021 through 2023. The area ranked #14. *American Lung Association, "State of the Air 2025," April 23, 2025*

Health/Fitness Rankings

- For each of the 100 largest cities in the United States, the American Fitness Index®, compiled in partnership between the American College of Sports Medicine and the Elevance Health Foundation, evaluated community infrastructure and more than 30 health behaviors including preventive health, levels of chronic disease conditions, food insecurity, pedestrian safety, air quality, and community/environment resources that support physical activity. Cincinnati ranked #62 for "community fitness." *americanfitnessindex.org, "2024 ACSM American Fitness Index Summary Report," July 23, 2024*

- The Cincinnati metro area was identified as one of the worst cities for bed bugs in America by pest control company Orkin. The area ranked #12 out of 50 based on the number of bed bug treatments Orkin performed from December 2022 to November 2023. *Orkin, "Chicago Joins Paris In Global Bed Bug Spotlight Ranking As The Worst City On Orkin's U.S. Bed Bug Cities List," January 22, 2024*

- Cincinnati was identified as a "2025 Allergy Capital." The area ranked #88 out of the nation's 100 largest metropolitan areas. Three groups of factors were used to identify the most challenging cities for people with allergies: annual tree, grass, and weed pollen scores; over the counter allergy medicine use; number of board-certified allergy specialists. *Asthma and Allergy Foundation of America, "2025 Allergy Capitals: The Most Challenging Places to Live with Allergies," March 18, 2025*

- Cincinnati was identified as a "2024 Asthma Capital." The area ranked #37 out of the nation's 100 largest metropolitan areas. Criteria: estimated asthma prevalence; asthma-related mortality; and ER visits due to asthma. Risk factors analyzed but not factored in the rankings: annual air quality including pollution and ozone levels; public smoking laws; indoor air quality; access to asthma specialists; rescue and controller medication use; uninsured rate; pollen allergy; poverty rate. *Asthma and Allergy Foundation of America, "Asthma Capitals 2024: The Most Challenging Places to Live With Asthma," September 10, 2024*

Pet Rankings

- Cincinnati was selected by *Sniffspot.com* as one of the most dog-friendly cities in the U.S., ranking #26 out of 50. Criteria: dog parks; hiking; sniffspots; public parks; dog-friendly businesses; housing; dog waste cleanliness; leash laws; dog services; and overall cost. *Sniffspot.com, "The Top 50 Most Dog-Friendly Cities in the U.S.," September 30, 2024*

Real Estate Rankings

- *WalletHub* compared the most populated U.S. cities to determine which had the best markets for real estate agents. Cincinnati ranked #111 where demand was high and pay was the best. Criteria: sales per agent; annual median wage for real-estate agents; monthly average starting salary for real estate agents; real estate job density and competition; unemployment rate; home turnover rate; housing-market health index; and other relevant metrics. *WalletHub.com, "2021 Best Places to Be a Real Estate Agent," May 12, 2021*

- The Cincinnati metro area was identified as one of the 10 worst condo markets in the U.S. in 2024. The area ranked #58 out of 63 markets. Criteria: year-over-year change of median sales price of existing apartment condo-coop homes between the 4th quarter of 2023 and the 4th quarter of 2024. *National Association of Realtors®, Median Sales Price of Existing Apartment Condo-Coops Homes for Metropolitan Areas, 4th Quarter 2024*

- Cincinnati was ranked #40 out of 176 metro areas in terms of cost of housing in 2024 by the National Association of Home Builders (#1 = most affordable). Criteria: the portion of an average family's income necessary to pay the mortgage on a median-priced home. *National Association of Home Builders®, NAHB-Wells Fargo Cost of Housing Index, 4th Quarter 2024*

Safety Rankings

- Allstate ranked the 100 most populous cities in America in terms of driver safety. Cincinnati ranked #17. Criteria based on anonymized driving behavior data from Allstate's mobile app powered by Arity: high speed driving (over 80 mph), phone handling, and hard braking. The report helps increase the importance of safety and awareness behind the wheel. *Allstate, "16th Allstate America's Best Drivers Report®" July 11, 2024*

Women/Minorities Rankings

- Personal finance website *WalletHub* compared more than 180 U.S. cities across two key dimensions, "Hispanic Business-Friendliness" and "Hispanic Purchasing Power," to arrive at the most favorable conditions for Hispanic entrepreneurs. Cincinnati was ranked #155 out of 182. Criteria includes: share of Hispanic-Owned Businesses; average growth of Hispanic Business revenues; Small Business-Friendliness score; affordability; and number of Hispanics with at least a bachelor's degree. *WalletHub.com, "Best Cities for Hispanic Entrepreneurs," September 4, 2024*

Miscellaneous Rankings

- *WalletHub* compared 148 of the most populated U.S. cities to determine their operating efficiency. A "Quality of Services" score was constructed for each city and then measured against the total budget per capita to reveal which were managed the best. Cincinnati ranked #99. Criteria: financial stability; economy; education; safety; health; infrastructure and pollution. *WalletHub.com, "2025's Best- & Worst-Run Cities in America," June 18, 2024*

Business Environment

DEMOGRAPHICS

Population Growth

Area	1990 Census	2000 Census	2010 Census	2020 Census	2023 Estimate[2]	Population Growth 1990-2023 (%)
City	363,974	331,285	296,943	309,317	309,595	-14.9
MSA[1]	1,844,917	2,009,632	2,130,151	2,256,884	2,255,257	22.2
U.S.	248,709,873	281,421,906	308,745,538	331,449,281	332,387,540	33.6

Note: (1) Figures cover the Cincinnati, OH-KY-IN Metropolitan Statistical Area; (2) 2019-2023 5-year ACS population estimate
Source: U.S. Census Bureau, 1990 Census, 2000 Census, 2010 Census, 2020 Census, 2019-2023 American Community Survey 5-Year Estimates

Race

Area	White Alone[2] (%)	Black Alone[2] (%)	Asian Alone[2] (%)	AIAN[3] Alone[2] (%)	NHOPI[4] Alone[2] (%)	Other Race Alone[2] (%)	Two or More Races (%)
City	49.4	38.7	2.8	0.1	0.0	2.0	7.0
MSA[1]	78.0	11.9	2.9	0.1	0.1	1.7	5.5
U.S.	63.4	12.4	5.8	0.9	0.2	6.6	10.7

Note: (1) Figures cover the Cincinnati, OH-KY-IN Metropolitan Statistical Area; (2) Alone is defined as not being in combination with one or more other races; (3) American Indian and Alaska Native; (4) Native Hawaiian and Other Pacific Islander
Source: U.S. Census Bureau, 2019-2023 American Community Survey 5-Year Estimates

Hispanic or Latino Origin

Area	Total (%)	Mexican (%)	Puerto Rican (%)	Cuban (%)	Other (%)
City	5.4	1.6	0.9	0.2	2.6
MSA[1]	4.3	1.8	0.5	0.2	1.9
U.S.	19.0	11.3	1.8	0.7	5.2

Note: Persons of Hispanic or Latino origin can be of any race; (1) Figures cover the Cincinnati, OH-KY-IN Metropolitan Statistical Area
Source: U.S. Census Bureau, 2019-2023 American Community Survey 5-Year Estimates

Age

Area	Under Age 5	Age 5–19	Age 20–34	Age 35–44	Age 45–54	Age 55–64	Age 65–74	Age 75–84	Age 85+	Median Age
City	6.3	18.7	28.1	12.5	10.0	11.1	8.2	3.4	1.7	33.0
MSA[1]	6.0	20.0	19.7	12.8	12.1	13.1	9.9	4.5	1.8	38.2
U.S.	5.7	19.1	20.2	13.1	12.3	12.8	10.0	4.9	1.9	38.7

Note: (1) Figures cover the Cincinnati, OH-KY-IN Metropolitan Statistical Area
Source: U.S. Census Bureau, 2019-2023 American Community Survey 5-Year Estimates

Disability by Age

Area	All Ages	Under 18 Years Old	18 to 64 Years Old	65 Years and Over
City	13.6	6.0	12.6	31.7
MSA[1]	12.7	5.1	10.8	31.5
U.S.	13.0	4.7	10.7	32.9

Note: Figures show percent of the civilian noninstitutionalized population that reported having a disability. Disability status is determined from six types of difficulty: vision, hearing, cognitive, ambulatory, self-care, and independent living. For children under 5 years old, hearing and vision difficulty are used to determine disability status. For children between the ages of 5 and 14, disability status is determined from hearing, vision, cognitive, ambulatory, and self-care difficulties. For people aged 15 years and older, they are considered to have a disability if they have difficulty with any one of the six difficulty types; Note: (1) Figures cover the Cincinnati, OH-KY-IN Metropolitan Statistical Area
Source: U.S. Census Bureau, 2019-2023 American Community Survey 5-Year Estimates

Ancestry

Area	German	Irish	English	American	Italian	Polish	French[2]	European	Scottish
City	17.5	9.8	6.9	3.0	3.7	1.4	1.2	1.2	1.0
MSA[1]	25.7	12.9	11.4	5.6	3.9	1.6	1.6	1.6	1.8
U.S.	12.6	9.4	9.1	5.5	4.9	2.6	2.0	1.6	1.6

Note: Figures are the percentage of the total population reporting a particular ancestry. The nine most commonly reported ancestries in the U.S. are shown. Figures include multiple ancestries (e.g. if a person reported being Irish and Italian, they were included in both columns); (1) Figures cover the Cincinnati, OH-KY-IN Metropolitan Statistical Area; (2) Excludes Basque
Source: U.S. Census Bureau, 2019-2023 American Community Survey 5-Year Estimates

Foreign-born Population

Area	Percent of Population Born in								
	Any Foreign Country	Asia	Mexico	Europe	Caribbean	Central America[2]	South America	Africa	Canada
City	7.1	2.1	0.3	0.7	0.2	1.0	0.3	2.2	0.1
MSA[1]	5.7	2.3	0.5	0.7	0.2	0.6	0.2	0.9	0.2
U.S.	13.9	4.3	3.3	1.4	1.4	1.2	1.2	0.8	0.2

Note: (1) Figures cover the Cincinnati, OH-KY-IN Metropolitan Statistical Area; (2) Excludes Mexico.
Source: U.S. Census Bureau, 2019-2023 American Community Survey 5-Year Estimates

Household Size

Area	Persons in Household (%)							Average Household Size
	One	Two	Three	Four	Five	Six	Seven or More	
City	44.9	30.5	10.7	8.5	3.0	1.4	1.0	2.07
MSA[1]	29.7	34.2	14.5	12.8	5.6	2.1	1.2	2.46
U.S.	28.5	33.8	15.4	12.7	5.9	2.3	1.4	2.54

Note: (1) Figures cover the Cincinnati, OH-KY-IN Metropolitan Statistical Area
Source: U.S. Census Bureau, 2019-2023 American Community Survey 5-Year Estimates

Household Relationships

Area	Householder	Opposite-sex Spouse	Same-sex Spouse	Opposite-sex Unmarried Partner	Same-sex Unmarried Partner	Child[2]	Grandchild	Other Relatives	Non-relatives
City	45.1	10.2	0.3	3.4	0.3	24.6	2.2	3.4	5.3
MSA[1]	39.5	18.1	0.2	2.7	0.1	28.9	2.3	3.2	2.9
U.S.	38.3	17.5	0.2	2.5	0.2	28.3	2.4	4.8	3.4

Note: Figures are percent of the total population; (1) Figures cover the Cincinnati, OH-KY-IN Metropolitan Statistical Area; (2) Includes biological, adopted, and stepchildren of the householder
Source: U.S. Census Bureau, 2020 Census

Gender

Area	Males	Females	Males per 100 Females
City	148,944	160,651	92.7
MSA[1]	1,113,237	1,142,020	97.5
U.S.	164,545,087	167,842,453	98.0

Note: (1) Figures cover the Cincinnati, OH-KY-IN Metropolitan Statistical Area
Source: U.S. Census Bureau, 2019-2023 American Community Survey 5-Year Estimates

Marital Status

Area	Never Married	Now Married[2]	Separated	Widowed	Divorced
City	53.4	29.8	1.8	4.5	10.6
MSA[1]	33.2	49.0	1.3	5.5	11.0
U.S.	34.1	47.9	1.7	5.6	10.7

Note: Figures are percentages and cover the population 15 years of age and older; (1) Figures cover the Cincinnati, OH-KY-IN Metropolitan Statistical Area; (2) Excludes separated
Source: U.S. Census Bureau, 2019-2023 American Community Survey 5-Year Estimates

Religious Groups by Family

Area	Catholic	Baptist	Methodist	LDS[2]	Pentecostal	Lutheran	Islam	Adventist	Other
MSA[1]	17.0	5.7	2.3	0.6	1.5	0.8	1.1	0.7	21.8
U.S.	18.7	7.3	3.0	2.0	1.8	1.7	1.3	1.3	11.6

Note: Figures are the number of adherents as a percentage of the total population and cover the eight largest religious groups in the U.S; (1) Figures cover the Cincinnati, OH-KY-IN Metropolitan Statistical Area; (2) Church of Jesus Christ of Latter-day Saints
Sources: 2020 U.S. Religion Census, Association of Statisticians of American Religious Bodies; The Association of Religion Data Archives (ARDA)

Religious Groups by Tradition

Area	Catholic	Evangelical Protestant	Mainline Protestant	Black Protestant	Islam	Judaism	Hinduism	Orthodox	Buddhism
MSA[1]	17.0	24.9	4.1	2.0	1.1	0.4	0.3	0.3	0.1
U.S.	18.7	16.5	5.2	2.3	1.3	0.6	0.4	0.4	0.3

Note: Figures are the number of adherents as a percentage of the total population; (1) Figures cover the Cincinnati, OH-KY-IN Metropolitan Statistical Area
Sources: 2020 U.S. Religion Census, Association of Statisticians of American Religious Bodies; The Association of Religion Data Archives (ARDA)

ECONOMY

Real Gross Domestic Product (GDP)

Area	2017	2018	2019	2020	2021	2022	2023	Rank[3]
MSA[1]	145.2	145.3	152.3	149.5	155.9	157.4	160.1	29
U.S.[2]	17,619.1	18,160.7	18,642.5	18,238.9	19,387.6	19,896.6	20,436.3	—

Note: Figures are in billions of chained 2017 dollars; (1) Figures cover the Cincinnati, OH-KY-IN Metropolitan Statistical Area; (2) Figures cover real GDP within metropolitan areas; (3) Rank is based on 2023 data and ranges from 1 to 384
Source: U.S. Bureau of Economic Analysis

Economic Growth

Area	2014	2015	2016	2017	2018	2019	2020	2021	2022	2023
MSA[1]	3.6	2.9	3.7	3.1	0.0	4.8	-1.8	4.3	1.0	1.7
U.S.[2]	2.6	3.2	2.0	2.7	3.1	2.7	-2.2	6.3	2.6	2.7

Note: Figures are real gross domestic product growth rates and represent percent change from preceding period; (1) Figures cover the Cincinnati, OH-KY-IN Metropolitan Statistical Area; (2) Figures are the average growth rates within metropolitan areas
Source: U.S. Bureau of Economic Analysis

Metropolitan Area Exports

Area	2018	2019	2020	2021	2022	2023	Rank[2]
MSA[1]	27,396.3	28,778.3	21,002.2	23,198.7	29,285.0	31,216.2	14
U.S.	1,664,056.1	1,645,173.7	1,431,406.6	1,753,941.4	2,062,937.4	2,019,160.5	—

Note: Figures are in millions of dollars; (1) Figures cover the Cincinnati, OH-KY-IN Metropolitan Statistical Area; (2) Rank is based on 2023 data and ranges from 1 to 386
Source: U.S. Department of Commerce, International Trade Administration, Office of Trade and Economic Analysis, Industry and Analysis, Exports by Metropolitan Area, data extracted April 2, 2025

Building Permits

Area	Single-Family			Multi-Family			Total		
	2023	2024	Pct. Chg.	2023	2024	Pct. Chg.	2023	2024	Pct. Chg.
City	117	110	-6.0	514	114	-77.8	631	224	-64.5
MSA[1]	3,714	4,025	8.4	2,527	3,064	21.3	6,241	7,089	13.6
U.S.	920,000	981,900	6.7	591,100	496,100	-16.1	1,511,100	1,478,000	-2.2

Note: (1) Figures cover the Cincinnati, OH-KY-IN Metropolitan Statistical Area; Figures represent new, privately-owned housing units authorized (unadjusted data)
Source: U.S. Census Bureau, Building Permits Survey (BPS), 2023, 2024

Bankruptcy Filings

Area	Business Filings			Nonbusiness Filings		
	2023	2024	% Chg.	2023	2024	% Chg.
Hamilton County	32	42	31.3	1,286	1,619	25.9
U.S.	18,926	23,107	22.1	434,064	494,201	13.9

Note: Business filings include Chapter 7, Chapter 9, Chapter 11, Chapter 12, Chapter 13, Chapter 15, and Section 304; Nonbusiness filings include Chapter 7, Chapter 11, and Chapter 13
Source: Administrative Office of the U.S. Courts, Business and Nonbusiness Bankruptcy, County Cases Commenced by Chapter of the Bankruptcy Code, During the 12-Month Period Ending December 31, 2023 and Business and Nonbusiness Bankruptcy, County Cases Commenced by Chapter of the Bankruptcy Code, During the 12-Month Period Ending December 31, 2024

Housing Vacancy Rates

Area	Gross Vacancy Rate[3] (%)			Year-Round Vacancy Rate[4] (%)			Rental Vacancy Rate[5] (%)			Homeowner Vacancy Rate[6] (%)		
	2022	2023	2024	2022	2023	2024	2022	2023	2024	2022	2023	2024
MSA[1]	6.8	5.4	5.8	6.3	5.2	5.5	6.3	7.2	6.1	0.3	0.2	0.8
U.S.[2]	9.1	9.0	9.1	7.5	7.5	7.6	5.7	6.5	6.8	0.8	0.8	1.0

Note: (1) Figures cover the Cincinnati, OH-KY-IN Metropolitan Statistical Area; (2) Figures cover the 75 largest Metropolitan Statistical Areas; (3) The percentage of the total housing inventory that is vacant; (4) The percentage of the housing inventory (excluding seasonal units) that is year-round vacant; (5) The percentage of rental inventory that is vacant for rent; (6) The percentage of homeowner inventory that is vacant for sale
Source: U.S. Census Bureau, Housing Vacancies and Homeownership Annual Statistics: 2022, 2023, 2024

INCOME

Income

Area	Per Capita ($)	Median Household ($)	Average Household ($)
City	38,878	51,707	83,146
MSA[1]	43,371	79,490	107,457
U.S.	43,289	78,538	110,491

Note: (1) Figures cover the Cincinnati, OH-KY-IN Metropolitan Statistical Area
Source: U.S. Census Bureau, 2019-2023 American Community Survey 5-Year Estimates

Cincinnati, Ohio

Household Income Distribution

Area	Percent of Households Earning							
	Under $15,000	$15,000 -$24,999	$25,000 -$34,999	$35,000 -$49,999	$50,000 -$74,999	$75,000 -$99,999	$100,000 -$149,999	$150,000 and up
City	16.9	10.2	8.7	12.9	15.0	10.3	11.8	14.2
MSA[1]	8.4	6.5	6.7	10.4	15.5	13.0	18.7	20.9
U.S.	8.5	6.6	6.8	10.4	15.7	12.7	17.4	21.9

Note: (1) Figures cover the Cincinnati, OH-KY-IN Metropolitan Statistical Area
Source: U.S. Census Bureau, 2019-2023 American Community Survey 5-Year Estimates

Poverty Rate

Area	All Ages	Under 18 Years Old	18 to 64 Years Old	65 Years and Over
City	24.5	34.2	22.8	17.1
MSA[1]	11.6	14.7	11.1	9.2
U.S.	12.4	16.3	11.6	10.4

Note: Figures are percentage of people whose income during the past 12 months was below the poverty level;
(1) Figures cover the Cincinnati, OH-KY-IN Metropolitan Statistical Area
Source: U.S. Census Bureau, 2019-2023 American Community Survey 5-Year Estimates

EMPLOYMENT

Labor Force and Employment

Area	Civilian Labor Force			Workers Employed		
	Dec. 2023	Dec. 2024	% Chg.	Dec. 2023	Dec. 2024	% Chg.
City	150,446	153,060	1.7	145,104	146,196	0.8
MSA[1]	1,154,630	1,170,746	1.4	1,116,229	1,123,236	0.6
U.S.	166,661,000	167,746,000	0.7	160,754,000	161,294,000	0.3

Note: Data is not seasonally adjusted and covers workers 16 years of age and older; (1) Figures cover the Cincinnati, OH-KY-IN Metropolitan Statistical Area
Source: Bureau of Labor Statistics, Local Area Unemployment Statistics

Unemployment Rate

Area	2024											
	Jan.	Feb.	Mar.	Apr.	May	Jun.	Jul.	Aug.	Sep.	Oct.	Nov.	Dec.
City	4.3	4.4	4.3	4.1	4.5	5.2	5.3	5.0	4.6	4.3	4.6	4.5
MSA[1]	4.1	4.2	4.2	3.8	4.0	4.6	4.6	4.3	4.1	3.9	4.1	4.1
U.S.	4.1	4.2	3.9	3.5	3.7	4.3	4.5	4.4	3.9	3.9	4.0	3.8

Note: Data is not seasonally adjusted and covers workers 16 years of age and older; (1) Figures cover the Cincinnati, OH-KY-IN Metropolitan Statistical Area
Source: Bureau of Labor Statistics, Local Area Unemployment Statistics

Average Wages

Occupation	$/Hr.	Occupation	$/Hr.
Accountants and Auditors	41.81	Maintenance and Repair Workers	26.32
Automotive Mechanics	24.64	Marketing Managers	72.86
Bookkeepers	24.76	Network and Computer Systems Admin.	48.96
Carpenters	27.72	Nurses, Licensed Practical	29.78
Cashiers	14.23	Nurses, Registered	41.93
Computer Programmers	56.17	Nursing Assistants	19.66
Computer Systems Analysts	52.48	Office Clerks, General	21.56
Computer User Support Specialists	28.23	Physical Therapists	48.99
Construction Laborers	26.28	Physicians	137.38
Cooks, Restaurant	15.92	Plumbers, Pipefitters and Steamfitters	32.13
Customer Service Representatives	21.20	Police and Sheriff's Patrol Officers	38.17
Dentists	103.59	Postal Service Mail Carriers	29.19
Electricians	30.46	Real Estate Sales Agents	24.40
Engineers, Electrical	51.81	Retail Salespersons	17.19
Fast Food and Counter Workers	14.06	Sales Representatives, Technical/Scientific	57.27
Financial Managers	77.39	Secretaries, Exc. Legal/Medical/Executive	23.98
First-Line Supervisors of Office Workers	32.81	Security Guards	19.14
General and Operations Managers	58.30	Surgeons	n/a
Hairdressers/Cosmetologists	20.06	Teacher Assistants, Exc. Postsecondary[1]	17.09
Home Health and Personal Care Aides	15.99	Teachers, Secondary School, Exc. Sp. Ed.[1]	33.20
Janitors and Cleaners	17.45	Telemarketers	16.50
Landscaping/Groundskeeping Workers	18.59	Truck Drivers, Heavy/Tractor-Trailer	30.56
Lawyers	69.29	Truck Drivers, Light/Delivery Services	24.16
Maids and Housekeeping Cleaners	15.43	Waiters and Waitresses	18.39

Note: Wage data covers the Cincinnati, OH-KY-IN Metropolitan Statistical Area; (1) Hourly wages were calculated from annual wage data based on a 40 hour work week
Source: Bureau of Labor Statistics, Metro Area Occupational Employment & Wage Estimates, May 2024

Employment by Industry

Sector	MSA[1] Number of Employees	MSA[1] Percent of Total	U.S. Percent of Total
Construction, Mining, and Logging	54,000	4.6	5.5
Financial Activities	80,000	6.8	5.8
Government	135,400	11.6	14.9
Information	13,200	1.1	1.9
Leisure and Hospitality	123,600	10.6	10.4
Manufacturing	121,900	10.4	8.0
Other Services	41,900	3.6	3.7
Private Education and Health Services	186,100	15.9	16.9
Professional and Business Services	178,300	15.3	14.2
Retail Trade	104,600	9.0	10.0
Transportation, Warehousing, and Utilities	67,800	5.8	4.8
Wholesale Trade	61,400	5.3	3.9

Note: Figures are non-farm employment as of December 2024. Figures are not seasonally adjusted and include workers 16 years of age and older; (1) Figures cover the Cincinnati, OH-KY-IN Metropolitan Statistical Area
Source: Bureau of Labor Statistics, Current Employment Statistics, Employment, Hours, and Earnings

Employment by Occupation

Occupation Classification	City (%)	MSA[1] (%)	U.S. (%)
Management, Business, Science, and Arts	45.5	43.6	42.0
Natural Resources, Construction, and Maintenance	3.5	6.8	8.6
Production, Transportation, and Material Moving	13.1	14.2	13.0
Sales and Office	19.5	20.3	19.9
Service	18.4	15.2	16.5

Note: Figures cover employed civilians 16 years of age and older; (1) Figures cover the Cincinnati, OH-KY-IN Metropolitan Statistical Area
Source: U.S. Census Bureau, 2019-2023 American Community Survey 5-Year Estimates

Occupations with Greatest Projected Employment Growth: 2022 – 2032

Occupation[1]	2022 Employment	2032 Projected Employment	Numeric Employment Change	Percent Employment Change
Home Health and Personal Care Aides	95,690	108,260	12,570	13.1
Cooks, Restaurant	48,380	57,540	9,160	18.9
Stockers and Order Fillers	125,650	131,710	6,060	4.8
Nurse Practitioners	11,020	15,710	4,690	42.6
Medical and Health Services Managers	18,720	23,310	4,590	24.5
Registered Nurses	131,390	135,860	4,470	3.4
Financial Managers	26,630	30,720	4,090	15.4
General and Operations Managers	132,340	136,170	3,830	2.9
Heavy and Tractor-Trailer Truck Drivers	98,350	102,030	3,680	3.7
Market Research Analysts and Marketing Specialists	31,720	35,170	3,450	10.9

Note: Projections cover Ohio; (1) Sorted by numeric employment change
Source: www.projectionscentral.org, State Occupational Projections, 2022–2032 Long-Term Projections

Fastest-Growing Occupations: 2022 – 2032

Occupation[1]	2022 Employment	2032 Projected Employment	Numeric Employment Change	Percent Employment Change
Nurse Practitioners	11,020	15,710	4,690	42.6
Taxi Drivers	2,490	3,480	990	39.8
Wind Turbine Service Technicians	170	230	60	35.3
Data Scientists	3,760	5,000	1,240	33.0
Statisticians	420	540	120	28.6
Medical and Health Services Managers	18,720	23,310	4,590	24.5
Physician Assistants	3,210	3,990	780	24.3
Semiconductor Processors	870	1,080	210	24.1
Epidemiologists	260	320	60	23.1
Speech-Language Pathologists	6,340	7,740	1,400	22.1

Note: Projections cover Ohio; (1) Sorted by percent employment change and excludes occupations with numeric employment change less than 50
Source: www.projectionscentral.org, State Occupational Projections, 2022–2032 Long-Term Projections

Cincinnati, Ohio

CITY FINANCES

City Government Finances

Component	2022 ($000)	2022 ($ per capita)
Total Revenues	1,014,051	3,330
Total Expenditures	845,984	2,778
Debt Outstanding	1,307,351	4,293

Source: U.S. Census Bureau, State & Local Government Finances 2022

City Government Revenue by Source

Source	2022 ($000)	2022 ($ per capita)	2022 (%)
General Revenue			
From Federal Government	13,325	44	1.3
From State Government	2,373	8	0.2
From Local Governments	1,364	4	0.1
Taxes			
Property	73,739	242	7.3
Sales and Gross Receipts	26,502	87	2.6
Personal Income	366,906	1,205	36.2
Corporate Income	47,842	157	4.7
Motor Vehicle License	4,375	14	0.4
Other Taxes	112,236	369	11.1
Current Charges	113,694	373	11.2
Liquor Store	0	0	0.0
Utility	176,755	580	17.4

Source: U.S. Census Bureau, State & Local Government Finances 2022

City Government Expenditures by Function

Function	2022 ($000)	2022 ($ per capita)	2022 (%)
General Direct Expenditures			
Air Transportation	525	1	0.1
Corrections	0	0	0.0
Education	0	0	0.0
Employment Security Administration	0	0	0.0
Financial Administration	62,185	204	7.4
Fire Protection	76,139	250	9.0
General Public Buildings	10,366	34	1.2
Governmental Administration, Other	29,235	96	3.5
Health	58,568	192	6.9
Highways	44,333	145	5.2
Hospitals	0	0	0.0
Housing and Community Development	30,943	101	3.7
Interest on General Debt	16,366	53	1.9
Judicial and Legal	0	0	0.0
Libraries	0	0	0.0
Parking	8,495	27	1.0
Parks and Recreation	67,206	220	7.9
Police Protection	167,905	551	19.8
Public Welfare	1,020	3	0.1
Sewerage	20,477	67	2.4
Solid Waste Management	20,799	68	2.5
Veterans' Services	0	0	0.0
Liquor Store	0	0	0.0
Utility	201,886	662	23.9

Source: U.S. Census Bureau, State & Local Government Finances 2022

TAXES

State Corporate Income Tax Rates

State	Tax Rate (%)	Income Brackets ($)	Num. of Brackets	Financial Institution Tax Rate (%)[a]	Federal Income Tax Ded.
Ohio	(r)	–	–	(r)	No

Note: Tax rates for tax year 2024; (a) Rates listed are the corporate income tax rate applied to financial institutions or excise taxes based on income. Some states have other taxes based upon the value of deposits or shares; (r) Ohio no longer levies a tax based on income (except for a particular subset of corporations), but instead imposes a Commercial Activity Tax (CAT). For tax periods beginning on and after January 1, 2024, the CAT annual minimum tax is eliminated, and the exclusion amount is increased from $1 million to $3 million. Therefore, taxpayers with taxable gross receipts of $3 million or less per calendar year will no longer be subject to the CAT. For those few corporations for whom the franchise tax
Source: Federation of Tax Administrators, State Corporate Income Tax Rates, January 1, 2025

State Individual Income Tax Rates

State	Tax Rate (%)	Income Brackets ($)	Personal Exemptions ($)			Standard Ded. ($)	
			Single	Married	Depend.	Single	Married
Ohio (a)	0.0 - 3.5	26,050 - 115,300	1,200	2,400	1,200 (u)	–	–

Note: Tax rates for tax year 2024; Local- and county-level taxes are not included; Federal income tax is not deductible on state income tax returns; (a) 16 states have statutory provision for automatically adjusting to the rate of inflation the dollar values of the income tax brackets, standard deductions, and/or personal exemptions. Oregon does not index the income brackets for $125,000 and over See: INFL and SPEC above; (u) Ohio suspends the annual inflation indexing adjustment of income tax brackets and personal exemption amounts for taxable years beginning in 2023 and 2024. Business income taxes at a flat 3% rate for individuals with income over $125,000S/$250,000MFJ.
Source: Federation of Tax Administrators, State Individual Income Tax Rates, January 1, 2025

Various State Sales and Excise Tax Rates

State	State Sales Tax (%)	Gasoline[1] ($/gal.)	Cigarette[2] ($/pack)	Spirits[3] ($/gal.)	Wine[4] ($/gal.)	Beer[5] ($/gal.)	Recreational Marijuana (%)
Ohio	5.75	0.39	1.60	12.33	0.32	0.18	(s)

Note: All tax rates as of January 1, 2025; (1) The American Petroleum Institute has developed a methodology for determining the average tax rate on a gallon of fuel. Rates may include any of the following: excise taxes, environmental fees, storage tank fees, other fees or taxes, general sales tax, and local taxes; (2) The federal excise tax of $1.0066 per pack and local taxes are not included; (3) Rates are those applicable to off-premise sales of 40% alcohol by volume (a.b.v.) distilled spirits in 750ml containers. Local excise taxes are excluded; (4) Rates are those applicable to off-premise sales of 11% a.b.v. non-carbonated wine in 750ml containers; (5) Rates are those applicable to off-premise sales of 4.7% a.b.v. beer in 12 ounce containers; (s) 10% excise tax (retail price)
Source: Tax Foundation, 2025 Facts & Figures: How Does Your State Compare?

State Tax Competitiveness Index

State	Overall Rank	Corporate Tax Rank	Individual Income Tax Rank	Sales Tax Rank	Property Tax Rank	Unemployment Insurance Tax Rank
Ohio	35	45	25	43	6	14

Note: The Tax Foundation's State Tax Competitiveness Index enables policymakers, taxpayers, and business leaders to gauge how their states' tax systems compare. A rank of 1 is best, 50 is worst. Rankings do not average to the total. States without a tax rank equally as 1. DC's scores and rankings do not affect other states. The report shows tax systems as of July 1, 2024 (the beginning of Fiscal Year 2025).
Source: Tax Foundation, State Tax Competitiveness Index 2025

TRANSPORTATION

Means of Transportation to Work

Area	Car/Truck/Van		Public Transportation			Bicycle	Walked	Other Means	Worked at Home
	Drove Alone	Car-pooled	Bus	Subway	Railroad				
City	66.2	7.5	5.7	0.0	0.0	0.3	5.3	1.8	13.2
MSA[1]	75.0	7.7	1.3	0.0	0.0	0.2	1.8	1.1	12.9
U.S.	70.2	8.5	1.7	1.3	0.4	0.4	2.4	1.6	13.5

Note: Figures are percentages and cover workers 16 years of age and older; (1) Figures cover the Cincinnati, OH-KY-IN Metropolitan Statistical Area
Source: U.S. Census Bureau, 2019-2023 American Community Survey 5-Year Estimates

Travel Time to Work

Area	Less Than 10 Minutes	10 to 19 Minutes	20 to 29 Minutes	30 to 44 Minutes	45 to 59 Minutes	60 to 89 Minutes	90 Minutes or More
City	11.2	34.5	26.3	19.1	3.8	2.8	2.2
MSA[1]	10.7	28.7	25.2	23.3	6.9	3.4	1.7
U.S.	12.6	28.6	21.2	20.8	8.1	6.0	2.8

Note: Note: Figures are percentages and include workers 16 years old and over; (1) Figures cover the Cincinnati, OH-KY-IN Metropolitan Statistical Area
Source: U.S. Census Bureau, 2019-2023 American Community Survey 5-Year Estimates

Key Congestion Measures

Measure	2000	2010	2015	2020	2022
Annual Hours of Delay, Total (000)	37,540	44,108	53,591	28,436	52,750
Annual Hours of Delay, Per Auto Commuter	38	41	50	26	49
Annual Congestion Cost, Per Auto Commuter ($)	1,169	1,092	1,226	680	1,257

Note: Figures cover the Cincinnati OH-KY-IN urban area
Source: Texas A&M Transportation Institute, 2023 Urban Mobility Report

Freeway Travel Time Index

Measure	1985	1990	1995	2000	2005	2010	2015	2020	2022
Urban Area Index[1]	1.06	1.11	1.15	1.17	1.17	1.16	1.17	1.06	1.15
Urban Area Rank[1,2]	53	42	36	36	49	54	46	75	54

Note: Freeway Travel Time Index—the ratio of travel time in the peak period to the travel time at free-flow conditions. For example, a value of 1.30 indicates a 20-minute free-flow trip takes 26 minutes in the peak (20 minutes x 1.30 = 26 minutes); (1) Covers the Cincinnati OH-KY-IN urban area; (2) Rank is based on 101 larger urban areas (#1 = highest travel time index)
Source: Texas A&M Transportation Institute, 2023 Urban Mobility Report

Public Transportation

Agency Name / Mode of Transportation	Vehicles Operated in Maximum Service[1]	Annual Unlinked Passenger Trips[2] (in thous.)	Annual Passenger Miles[3] (in thous.)
Southwest Ohio Regional Transit Authority (SORTA/Metro)			
Bus (directly operated)	252	12,902.1	68,980.6
Demand Response (directly operated)	40	181.7	1,864.4

Note: (1) Number of revenue vehicles operated by the given mode and type of service to meet the annual maximum service requirement. This is the revenue vehicle count during the peak season of the year; on the week and day that maximum service is provided. Vehicles operated in maximum service (VOMS) exclude atypical days and one-time special events; (2) Number of passengers who boarded public transportation vehicles. Passengers are counted each time they board a vehicle no matter how many vehicles they use to travel from their origin to their destination. (3) Sum of the distances ridden by all passengers during the entire fiscal year.
Source: Federal Transit Administration, National Transit Database, 2023

Air Transportation

Airport Name and Code / Type of Service	Passenger Airlines[1]	Passenger Enplanements	Freight Carriers[2]	Freight (lbs)
Cincinnati-Northern Kentucky International (CVG)				
Domestic service (U.S. carriers only)	27	4,357,453	22	1,198,884,483
International service (U.S. carriers only)	9	68,859	10	164,070,588

Note: (1) Includes all U.S.-based major, minor and commuter airlines that carried at least one passenger during the year; (2) Includes all U.S.-based airlines and freight carriers that transported at least one pound of freight during the year.
Source: Bureau of Transportation Statistics, The Intermodal Transportation Database, Air Carriers: T-100 Domestic Market (U.S. carriers only), 2024; Bureau of Transportation Statistics, The Intermodal Transportation Database, Air Carriers: T-100 International Market (U.S. carriers only), 2024

BUSINESSES

Major Business Headquarters

Company Name	Industry	Fortune[1]	Forbes[2]
American Financial Group	Insurance: property and casualty (stock)	470	-
Cintas	Diversified outsourcing services	437	-
Fifth Third Bancorp	Commercial banks	321	-
Kroger	Food & drug stores	25	-
Procter & Gamble	Household and personal products	50	-
Western & Southern Financial Group	Insurance: life, health (mutual)	284	-

Note: (1) Companies that produce a 10-K are ranked 1 to 500 based on 2023 revenue; (2) All private companies with at least $2 billion in annual revenue through the end of their most current fiscal year are ranked 1 to 275; companies listed are headquartered in the city; dashes indicate no ranking
Source: Fortune, "Fortune 500," 2024; Forbes, "America's Largest Private Companies," 2024

Fastest-Growing Businesses

According to *Initiative for a Competitive Inner City (ICIC)*, Cincinnati is home to two of America's 100 fastest-growing "inner city" companies: **Swath Design** (#50); **SURE Mechanical** (#69). To be eligible for the IC100, companies have to be independently operated, privately held, for-profit businesses with revenues of at least $50,000 in 2019 and $500,000 in 2023, and headquartered in an under-resourced community. Recognizing that concentrated poverty exists within metropolitan areas outside of big cities (and that poverty overall is suburbanizing), ICIC defines under-resourced communities as large low-income, high-poverty areas located in the urban and suburban parts of all but the smallest metropolitan areas. Companies were ranked overall by revenue growth over the five-year period between 2019 and 2023. *Initiative for a Competitive Inner City (ICIC), "Inner City 100 Companies," 2024*

Living Environment

COST OF LIVING

Cost of Living Index

Composite Index	Groceries	Housing	Utilities	Trans-portation	Health Care	Misc. Goods/ Services
96.0	100.7	87.3	99.6	96.2	94.8	100.4

Note: The Cost of Living Index measures regional differences in the cost of consumer goods and services, excluding taxes and non-consumer expenditures, for professional and managerial households in the top income quintile. It is based on more than 50,000 prices covering almost 60 different items for which prices are collected three times a year by chambers of commerce, economic development organizations or university applied economic centers in each participating urban area. The numbers shown should be read as a percentage above or below the national average of 100. For example, a value of 115.4 in the groceries column indicates that grocery prices are 15.4% higher than the national average. Small differences in the index numbers should not be interpreted as significant; Figures cover the Cincinnati OH urban area.
Source: The Council for Community and Economic Research, Cost of Living Index, 2024

Grocery Prices

Area[1]	T-Bone Steak ($/pound)	Frying Chicken ($/pound)	Whole Milk ($/half gal.)	Eggs ($/dozen)	Orange Juice ($/64 oz.)	Coffee ($/11.5 oz.)
City[2]	15.52	1.74	4.74	3.73	4.36	5.67
Avg.	15.42	1.55	4.69	3.25	4.41	5.46
Min.	14.50	1.16	4.43	2.75	4.00	4.85
Max.	17.56	2.89	5.49	4.78	5.54	7.89

Note: (1) Values for the local area are compared with the average, minimum and maximum values for all 276 areas in the Cost of Living Index; (2) Figures cover the Cincinnati OH urban area; **T-Bone Steak** (price per pound); **Frying Chicken** (price per pound, whole fryer); **Whole Milk** (half gallon carton); **Eggs** (price per dozen, Grade A, large); **Orange Juice** (64 oz. Tropicana or Florida Natural); **Coffee** (11.5 oz. can, vacuum-packed, Maxwell House, Hills Bros, or Folgers).
Source: The Council for Community and Economic Research, Cost of Living Index, 2024

Housing and Utility Costs

Area[1]	New Home Price ($)	Apartment Rent ($/month)	All Electric ($/month)	Part Electric ($/month)	Other Energy ($/month)	Telephone ($/month)
City[2]	443,467	1,416	-	116.95	90.88	189.55
Avg.	515,975	1,550	210.99	123.07	82.07	194.99
Min.	265,375	692	104.33	53.68	36.26	179.42
Max.	2,775,821	5,719	529.02	397.28	361.63	223.33

Note: (1) Values for the local area are compared with the average, minimum and maximum values for all 276 areas in the Cost of Living Index; (2) Figures cover the Cincinnati OH urban area; **New Home Price** (2,400 sf living area, 8,000 sf lot, in urban area with full utilities); **Apartment Rent** (950 sf 2 bedroom/1.5 or 2 bath, unfurnished, excluding all utilities except water); **All Electric** (average monthly cost for an all-electric home); **Part Electric** (average monthly cost for a part-electric home); **Other Energy** (average monthly cost for natural gas, fuel oil, coal, wood, and any other forms of energy except electricity); **Telephone** (price includes the base monthly rate plus taxes and fees for three lines of mobile phone service).
Source: The Council for Community and Economic Research, Cost of Living Index, 2024

Health Care, Transportation, and Other Costs

Area[1]	Doctor ($/visit)	Dentist ($/visit)	Optometrist ($/visit)	Gasoline ($/gallon)	Beauty Salon ($/visit)	Men's Shirt ($)
City[2]	158.21	98.92	97.57	3.18	39.43	41.70
Avg.	143.77	117.51	129.23	3.32	48.57	38.14
Min.	36.74	58.67	67.33	2.80	24.00	13.41
Max.	270.44	216.82	307.33	5.28	94.00	63.89

Note: (1) Values for the local area are compared with the average, minimum and maximum values for all 276 areas in the Cost of Living Index; (2) Figures cover the Cincinnati OH urban area; **Doctor** (general practitioners routine exam of an established patient); **Dentist** (adult teeth cleaning and periodic oral examination); **Optometrist** (full vision eye exam for established adult patient); **Gasoline** (one gallon regular unleaded, national brand, including all taxes, cash price at self-service pump if available); **Beauty Salon** (woman's shampoo, trim, and blow-dry); **Men's Shirt** (cotton/polyester dress shirt, pinpoint weave, long sleeves).
Source: The Council for Community and Economic Research, Cost of Living Index, 2024

HOUSING

Homeownership Rate

Area	2017 (%)	2018 (%)	2019 (%)	2020 (%)	2021 (%)	2022 (%)	2023 (%)	2024 (%)
MSA[1]	65.7	67.3	67.4	71.1	72.1	67.1	69.6	72.3
U.S.	63.9	64.4	64.6	66.6	65.5	65.8	65.9	65.6

Note: (1) Figures cover the Cincinnati, OH-KY-IN Metropolitan Statistical Area
Source: U.S. Census Bureau, Housing Vacancies and Homeownership Annual Statistics: 2017-2024

House Price Index (HPI)

Area	National Ranking[2]	Quarterly Change (%)	One-Year Change (%)	Five-Year Change (%)	Since 1991Q1 (%)
MSA[1]	93	0.82	6.08	61.42	247.18
U.S.[3]	—	1.43	4.51	57.13	327.82

Note: The HPI is a weighted repeat sales index. It measures average price changes in repeat sales or refinancings on the same properties. This information is obtained by reviewing repeat mortgage transactions on single-family properties whose mortgages have been purchased or securitized by Fannie Mae or Freddie Mac since January 1975; (1) Figures cover the Cincinnati, OH-KY-IN Metropolitan Statistical Area; (2) Rankings are based on annual percentage change for all metro areas containing at least 15,000 transactions over the last 10 years and ranges from 1 to 241; (3) figures based on a weighted average of Census Division estimates using a seasonally adjusted, purchase-only index; all figures are for the period ending December 31, 2024
Source: Federal Housing Finance Agency, Change in FHFA Metropolitan Area House Price Indexes, All Transactions Index, 2024Q4

Home Value

Area	Under $100,000	$100,000 -$199,999	$200,000 -$299,999	$300,000 -$399,999	$400,000 -$499,999	$500,000 -$999,999	$1,000,000 or more	Median ($)
City	14.9	31.5	20.8	12.4	7.1	10.7	2.6	215,300
MSA[1]	10.2	28.0	26.6	15.7	8.7	9.3	1.5	240,200
U.S.	12.1	17.8	19.5	14.4	10.5	19.1	6.5	303,400

Note: Figures are percentages except for median and cover owner-occupied housing units; (1) Figures cover the Cincinnati, OH-KY-IN Metropolitan Statistical Area
Source: U.S. Census Bureau, 2019-2023 American Community Survey 5-Year Estimates

Year Housing Structure Built

Area	2020 or Later	2010 -2019	2000 -2009	1990 -1999	1980 -1989	1970 -1979	1960 -1969	1950 -1959	1940 -1949	Before 1940	Median Year
City	0.5	4.4	4.1	4.0	6.3	9.3	12.0	10.9	8.3	40.3	1951
MSA[1]	0.9	6.6	12.1	13.5	10.7	13.4	10.4	11.3	4.7	16.5	1975
U.S.	1.2	8.9	13.6	12.8	13.0	14.4	10.0	9.7	4.5	11.9	1980

Note: Figures are percentages except for Median Year; Note: (1) Figures cover the Cincinnati, OH-KY-IN Metropolitan Statistical Area
Source: U.S. Census Bureau, 2019-2023 American Community Survey 5-Year Estimates

Gross Monthly Rent

Area	Under $500	$500 -$999	$1,000 -$1,499	$1,500 -$1,999	$2,000 -$2,499	$2,500 -$2,999	$3,000 and up	Median ($)
City	11.8	43.6	26.9	11.1	3.9	1.5	1.3	953
MSA[1]	8.2	37.8	34.1	12.7	4.4	1.5	1.4	1,047
U.S.	6.5	22.3	29.5	20.2	10.8	4.8	5.9	1,348

Note: Figures are percentages except for median; Gross rent is the contract rent plus the estimated average monthly cost of utilities (electricity, gas, and water and sewer) and fuels (oil, coal, kerosene, wood, etc.) if these are paid by the renter (or paid for the renter by someone else); (1) Figures cover the Cincinnati, OH-KY-IN Metropolitan Statistical Area
Source: U.S. Census Bureau, 2019-2023 American Community Survey 5-Year Estimates

HEALTH

Health Risk Factors

Category	MSA[1] (%)	U.S. (%)
Adults aged 18–64 who have any kind of health care coverage	92.7	90.8
Adults who reported being in good or better health	82.3	81.8
Adults who have been told they have high blood cholesterol	34.6	36.9
Adults who have been told they have high blood pressure	35.7	34.0
Adults who are current smokers	15.4	12.1
Adults who currently use e-cigarettes	8.0	7.7
Adults who currently use chewing tobacco, snuff, or snus	2.5	3.2
Adults who are heavy drinkers[2]	6.6	6.1
Adults who are binge drinkers[3]	18.4	15.2
Adults who are overweight (BMI 25.0 - 29.9)	34.6	34.4
Adults who are obese (BMI 30.0 - 99.8)	34.5	34.3
Adults who participated in any physical activities in the past month	76.8	75.8

Note: All figures are crude prevalence; (1) Figures cover the Cincinnati, OH-KY-IN Metropolitan Statistical Area; (2) Heavy drinkers are classified as adult men having more than 14 drinks per week and adult women having more than 7 drinks per week; (3) Binge drinkers are classified as males having five or more drinks on one occasion or females having four or more drinks on one occasion
Source: Centers for Disease Control and Prevention, Behavioral Risk Factor Surveillance System, SMART: Selected Metropolitan Area Risk Trends, 2023

Acute and Chronic Health Conditions

Category	MSA[1] (%)	U.S. (%)
Adults who have ever been told they had a heart attack	4.4	4.2
Adults who have ever been told they have angina or coronary heart disease	5.4	4.0
Adults who have ever been told they had a stroke	3.7	3.3
Adults who have ever been told they have asthma	14.0	15.7
Adults who have ever been told they have arthritis	27.6	26.3
Adults who have ever been told they have diabetes[2]	12.0	11.5
Adults who have ever been told they had skin cancer	5.8	5.6
Adults who have ever been told they had any other types of cancer	7.9	8.4
Adults who have ever been told they have COPD	6.7	6.4
Adults who have ever been told they have kidney disease	4.3	3.7
Adults who have ever been told they have a form of depression	24.0	22.0

Note: All figures are crude prevalence; (1) Figures cover the Cincinnati, OH-KY-IN Metropolitan Statistical Area; (2) Figures do not include pregnancy-related, borderline, or pre-diabetes
Source: Centers for Disease Control and Prevention, Behaviorial Risk Factor Surveillance System, SMART: Selected Metropolitan Area Risk Trends, 2023

Health Screening and Vaccination Rates

Category	MSA[1] (%)	U.S. (%)
Adults who have ever been tested for HIV	33.0	37.5
Adults who have had their blood cholesterol checked within the last five years	87.4	87.0
Adults aged 65+ who have had flu shot within the past year	63.2	63.4
Adults aged 65+ who have ever had a pneumonia vaccination	68.3	71.9

Note: All figures are crude prevalence; (1) Figures cover the Cincinnati, OH-KY-IN Metropolitan Statistical Area.
Source: Centers for Disease Control and Prevention, Behaviorial Risk Factor Surveillance System, SMART: Selected Metropolitan Area Risk Trends, 2023

Disability Status

Category	MSA[1] (%)	U.S. (%)
Adults who reported being deaf	5.9	7.4
Are you blind or have serious difficulty seeing, even when wearing glasses?	3.3	4.9
Do you have difficulty doing errands alone?	6.6	7.8
Do you have difficulty dressing or bathing?	3.0	3.6
Do you have serious difficulty concentrating/remembering/making decisions?	11.9	13.7
Do you have serious difficulty walking or climbing stairs?	11.0	13.2

Note: All figures are crude prevalence; (1) Figures cover the Cincinnati, OH-KY-IN Metropolitan Statistical Area.
Source: Centers for Disease Control and Prevention, Behaviorial Risk Factor Surveillance System, SMART: Selected Metropolitan Area Risk Trends, 2023

Mortality Rates for the Top 10 Causes of Death in the U.S.

ICD-10[a] Sub-Chapter	ICD-10[a] Code	Crude Mortality Rate[2] per 100,000 population	
		County[3]	U.S.
Malignant neoplasms	C00-C97	185.1	182.7
Ischaemic heart diseases	I20-I25	94.7	109.6
Provisional assignment of new diseases of uncertain etiology[1]	U00-U49	61.4	65.3
Other forms of heart disease	I30-I51	82.9	65.1
Other degenerative diseases of the nervous system	G30-G31	50.2	52.4
Other external causes of accidental injury	W00-X59	59.1	52.3
Cerebrovascular diseases	I60-I69	62.5	49.1
Chronic lower respiratory diseases	J40-J47	40.2	43.5
Hypertensive diseases	I10-I15	35.9	38.9
Organic, including symptomatic, mental disorders	F01-F09	37.2	33.9

Note: (a) ICD-10 = International Classification of Diseases 10th Revision; (1) Includes COVID-19, adverse effects to COVID-19 vaccines, SARS, and vaping-related disorders; (2) Crude mortality rates are a three-year average covering 2021-2023; (3) Figures cover Hamilton County.
Source: Centers for Disease Control and Prevention, National Center for Health Statistics. National Vital Statistics System, Mortality 2018-2023 on CDC WONDER Online Database

Mortality Rates for Selected Causes of Death

Cause of Death	ICD-10[a] Code	Crude Mortality Rate[1] per 100,000 population	
		County[2]	U.S.
Accidental poisoning and exposure to noxious substances	X40-X49	43.4	30.5
Alzheimer disease	G30	44.3	35.4
Assault	X85-Y09	11.6	7.3
COVID-19	U07.1	61.4	65.3
Diabetes mellitus	E10-E14	31.5	30.0
Diseases of the liver	K70-K76	18.1	20.8
Human immunodeficiency virus (HIV) disease	B20-B24	1.9	1.5
Influenza and pneumonia	J09-J18	15.1	13.4
Intentional self-harm	X60-X84	14.2	14.7
Malnutrition	E40-E46	13.2	6.0
Obesity and other hyperalimentation	E65-E68	3.0	3.1
Renal failure	N17-N19	24.0	16.4
Transport accidents	V01-V99	10.8	14.4

Note: (a) ICD-10 = International Classification of Diseases 10th Revision; (1) Crude mortality rates are a three-year average covering 2021-2023; (2) Figures cover Hamilton County; Data are suppressed when the data meet the criteria for confidentiality constraints; Crude mortality rates are flagged as unreliable when the rate would be calculated with a numerator of 20 or less.
Source: Centers for Disease Control and Prevention, National Center for Health Statistics. National Vital Statistics System, Mortality 2018-2023 on CDC WONDER Online Database

Health Insurance Coverage

Area	With Health Insurance	With Private Health Insurance	With Public Health Insurance	Without Health Insurance	Population Under Age 19 Without Health Insurance
City	92.4	61.1	40.3	7.6	5.7
MSA[1]	94.5	72.3	33.5	5.5	3.8
U.S.	91.4	67.3	36.3	8.6	5.4

Note: Figures are percentages that cover the civilian noninstitutionalized population; (1) Figures cover the Cincinnati, OH-KY-IN Metropolitan Statistical Area
Source: U.S. Census Bureau, 2019-2023 American Community Survey 5-Year Estimates

Number of Medical Professionals

Area	MDs[3]	DOs[3,4]	Dentists	Podiatrists	Chiropractors	Optometrists
County[1] (number)	5,469	297	638	86	179	193
County[1] (rate[2])	662.9	36.0	77.1	10.4	21.6	23.3
U.S. (rate[2])	302.5	29.2	74.6	6.4	29.5	18.0

Note: Data as of 2023 unless noted; (1) Data covers Hamilton County; (2) Number of medical professionals per 100,000 population; (3) Data as of 2022 and includes all active, non-federal physicians; (4) Doctor of Osteopathic Medicine
Source: U.S. Department of Health and Human Services, Health Resources and Services Administration, Bureau of Health Professions, Area Resource File (ARF) 2023-2024

Best Hospitals

According to *U.S. News*, the Cincinnati, OH-KY-IN metro area is home to two of the best children's hospitals in the U.S.: **Cincinnati Children's** (Honor Roll/11 pediatric specialties); **Cincinnati Children's and Kentucky Children's Hospital Joint Heart Program** (11 pediatric specialties). The hospitals listed were highly ranked in at least one of 11 pediatric specialties. One hundred five children's hospitals in the U.S. were nationally ranked in at least one specialty. Hospitals received points for being ranked in a specialty, and the 10 hospitals with the most points across the 11 specialties make up the Honor Roll. *U.S. News Online, "America's Best Children's Hospitals 2024-25"*

EDUCATION

Public School District Statistics

District Name	Schls	Pupils	Pupil/ Teacher Ratio	Minority Pupils[1] (%)	Total Rev. per Pupil ($)	Total Exp. per Pupil ($)
Cincinnati Public Schools	66	34,860	16.2	79.5	21,277	20,319
Forest Hills Local	9	6,935	17.1	15.1	13,768	14,336
Great Oaks Career Campuses	5	2,939	10.2	27.3	32,876	40,631
Indian Hill Exempted Village	4	2,222	14.6	24.6	26,129	25,398
Mt Healthy City	6	2,842	14.3	89.0	19,696	21,237
Northwest Local	11	8,465	18.5	61.8	15,565	14,893
Oak Hills Local	9	7,485	22.2	20.7	11,674	12,869
Princeton City	11	5,940	16.2	83.1	20,257	17,767
West Clermont Local	9	7,887	18.7	16.4	14,333	13,479
Winton Woods City	6	3,916	16.3	92.9	17,979	18,786

Note: Table includes school districts with 2,000 or more students; (1) Percentage of students that are not non-Hispanic white.
Source: U.S. Department of Education, National Center for Education Statistics, Common Core of Data, Local Education Agency (School District) Universe Survey: School Year 2023-2024; U.S. Department of Education, National Center for Education Statistics, Common Core of Data, School District Finance Survey (F-33): School Year 2021–22

Best High Schools

According to *U.S. News,* Cincinnati is home to three of the top 500 high schools in the U.S.: **Walnut Hills High School** (#118); **Madeira High School** (#212); **Indian Hill High School** (#310). Nearly 25,000 public, magnet and charter schools were ranked based on their performance on state assessments and how well they prepare students for college. *U.S. News & World Report, "Best High Schools 2024"*

Highest Level of Education

Area	Less than H.S.	H.S. Diploma	Some College, No Deg.	Associate Degree	Bachelor's Degree	Master's Degree	Prof. School Degree	Doctorate Degree
City	10.3	24.1	17.0	7.3	23.2	11.7	3.8	2.5
MSA[1]	7.7	28.8	18.0	8.6	22.7	10.4	2.2	1.6
U.S.	10.6	26.2	19.4	8.8	21.3	9.8	2.3	1.6

Note: Figures cover persons age 25 and over; (1) Figures cover the Cincinnati, OH-KY-IN Metropolitan Statistical Area
Source: U.S. Census Bureau, 2019-2023 American Community Survey 5-Year Estimates

Educational Attainment by Race

Area	High School Graduate or Higher (%)					Bachelor's Degree or Higher (%)				
	Total	White	Black	Asian	Hisp.[2]	Total	White	Black	Asian	Hisp.[2]
City	89.7	94.6	83.8	93.1	81.1	41.3	57.9	16.2	80.1	36.2
MSA[1]	92.3	93.5	87.9	88.6	76.7	36.9	38.1	22.8	63.4	31.1
U.S.	89.4	92.9	88.1	88.0	72.5	35.0	37.7	24.7	57.0	19.9

Note: Figures shown cover persons 25 years old and over; (1) Figures cover the Cincinnati, OH-KY-IN Metropolitan Statistical Area; (2) People of Hispanic origin can be of any race
Source: U.S. Census Bureau, 2019-2023 American Community Survey 5-Year Estimates

School Enrollment by Grade and Control

Area	Preschool (%)		Kindergarten (%)		Grades 1 - 4 (%)		Grades 5 - 8 (%)		Grades 9 - 12 (%)	
	Public	Private	Public	Private	Public	Private	Public	Private	Public	Private
City	60.9	39.1	77.2	22.8	78.5	21.5	78.9	21.1	81.8	18.2
MSA[1]	50.7	49.3	79.1	20.9	81.9	18.1	82.2	17.8	83.0	17.0
U.S.	58.7	41.3	85.2	14.8	87.2	12.8	87.9	12.1	89.0	11.0

Note: Figures shown cover persons 3 years old and over; (1) Figures cover the Cincinnati, OH-KY-IN Metropolitan Statistical Area
Source: U.S. Census Bureau, 2019-2023 American Community Survey 5-Year Estimates

Higher Education

Four-Year Colleges			Two-Year Colleges			Medical Schools[1]	Law Schools[2]	Voc/ Tech[3]
Public	Private Non-profit	Private For-profit	Public	Private Non-profit	Private For-profit			
8	11	4	1	1	5	1	2	14

Note: Figures cover institutions located within the Cincinnati, OH-KY-IN Metropolitan Statistical Area and include main campuses only; (1) includes schools accredited by the Liaison Committee on Medical Education and the American Osteopathic Association's Commission on Osteopathic College Accreditation; (2) includes ABA-accredited schools, schools with provisional ABA accreditation, and state accredited schools; (3) includes all schools with programs that are less than 2 years.
Source: National Center for Education Statistics, Integrated Postsecondary Education System (IPEDS), 2023-24; Wikipedia, List of Medical Schools in the United States, accessed May 2, 2025; Wikipedia, List of Law Schools in the United States, accessed May 2, 2025

According to *U.S. News & World Report,* the Cincinnati, OH-KY-IN metro area is home to two of the top 200 national universities in the U.S.: **Miami University—Oxford** (#136 tie); **University of Cincinnati** (#152 tie). The indicators used to capture academic quality fall into a number of categories: assessment by administrators at peer institutions; retention of students; faculty resources; student selectivity; financial resources; alumni giving; high school counselor ratings of colleges; and graduation rate. *U.S. News & World Report, "America's Best Colleges 2025"*

According to *U.S. News & World Report,* the Cincinnati, OH-KY-IN metro area is home to one of the top 100 law schools in the U.S.: **University of Cincinnati** (#71 tie). The rankings are based on a weighted average of 12 measures of quality: peer assessment score; assessment score by lawyers/judges; median LSAT scores; median undergrad GPA; acceptance rate; employment rates for graduates; placement success; bar passage rate; faculty resources; expenditures per student; student/faculty ratio; and library resources. *U.S. News & World Report, "America's Best Graduate Schools, Law, 2025"*

According to *U.S. News & World Report,* the Cincinnati, OH-KY-IN metro area is home to one of the top medical schools for research in the U.S.: **University of Cincinnati** (Tier 2). *U.S. News* placed medical and osteopathic schools into tiers based on their research productivity, faculty and admissions data. Each school's tier was derived from its overall score, calculated by summing the weighted normalized values generated across several factors of academic quality, outlined below. There are four tiers, with tier 1 medical schools as the highest-performing and tier 4 as the lowest-performing. Only tier 1 and 2 schools are shown. Because of the tier presentation, *U.S. News* calculated overall scores based on their percentile performance among all rated schools instead of dividing against the rescaled score of the No. 1-performing schools. Tier 1 included schools with overall scores of 85 to 99. The cutoffs for tiers 2 through 4 were schools scoring 50 to 84, 15 to 49 and 1 to 14, respectively. The rankings are based on a weighted average of the following measures of quality: total research activity; average research activity per faculty member; total NIH research grants at the medical school and its affiliated hospitals; average NIH research grants per faculty; median MCAT total score; median undergraduate GPA; acceptance rate; and faculty resources. *U.S. News & World Report, "America's Best Graduate Schools, Medical, 2025"*

According to *U.S. News & World Report,* the Cincinnati, OH-KY-IN metro area is home to one of the top medical schools for primary care in the U.S.: **University of Cincinnati** (Tier 2). *U.S. News* placed medical and osteopathic schools into tiers based on their research productivity, faculty and admissions data. Each school's tier was derived from its overall score, calculated by summing the weighted normalized values generated across several factors of academic quality, outlined below. There are four tiers, with tier 1 medical schools as the highest-performing and tier 4 as the lowest-performing. Only tier 1 and 2 schools are shown. Because of the tier presentation, *U.S. News* calculated overall scores based on their percentile performance among all rated schools instead of dividing against the rescaled score of the No. 1-performing schools. Tier 1 included schools with overall scores of 85 to 99. The cutoffs for tiers 2 through 4 were schools scoring 50 to 84, 15 to 49 and 1 to 14, respectively. The rankings are based on a weighted average of the following measures of quality: graduates practicing in primary care specialties; graduates entering primary care residencies; median MCAT total score; median undergraduate GPA; acceptance rate; and faculty resources. *U.S. News & World Report, "America's Best Graduate Schools, Medical, 2025"*

According to *U.S. News & World Report,* the Cincinnati, OH-KY-IN metro area is home to one of the top 75 business schools in the U.S.: **University of Cincinnati (Lindner)** (#73 tie). The rankings are based on a weighted average of the following nine measures: quality assessment; peer assessment; recruiter assessment; placement success; mean starting salary and bonus; student selectivity; mean GMAT and GRE scores; mean undergraduate GPA; and acceptance rate. *U.S. News & World Report, "America's Best Graduate Schools, Business, 2025"*

Cincinnati, Ohio

EMPLOYERS

Major Employers

Company Name	Industry
Cincinnati Children's Hospital Medical Ctr	Medical centers
Cleveland Clinic Foundation	Medical centers
General Electric Company	Conglomerate
Giant Eagle	Grocery stores
Golden Gate Capital LP/Bob Evans	Restaurants
Home Depot	Retail
Honda Motor Co.	Automotive
JP Morgan Chase & Co.	Banking and financial services
Kettering Health Network	Healthcare
Kroger Co.	Grocery stores
Mercy Health	Healthcare
Nationwide Mutual Insurance Company	Insurance
Ohio Health	Healthcare
Ohio State University	Colleges & universities
Premier Health Partners	Healthcare
ProMedica Health System	Healthcare
United Parcel Service	Package delivery services
University Hospitals Health System	Healthcare
Wal-Mart Stores	Retail
Wright-Patterson Air Force Base	Military

Note: Companies shown are located within the Cincinnati, OH-KY-IN Metropolitan Statistical Area.
Source: Chambers of Commerce; State Departments of Labor; Wikipedia

Best Companies to Work For

Cincinnati Children's Hospital Medical Center; Ensemble Health Partners, headquartered in Cincinnati, are among "Best Workplaces in Health Care." To determine the Best Workplaces in Health Care list, Great Place To Work analyzed the survey responses of over 185,000 employees from Great Place To Work-Certified companies in the health care industry. Survey data analysis and company-provided datapoints are then factored into a combined score to compare and rank the companies that create the most consistently positive experience for all employees in this industry. *Fortune, "Best Workplaces in Health Care," 2024*

The Kroger Company; Total Quality Logistics, headquartered in Cincinnati, are among the "Best Places to Work in IT." To qualify, companies had to have a minimum of 100 total employees and five IT employees. The best places to work were selected based on DEI (diversity, equity, and inclusion) practices; IT turnover, promotions, and growth; IT retention and engagement programs; remote/hybrid working; benefits and perks (such as elder care and child care, flextime, and reimbursement for college tuition); and training and career development opportunities. *Computerworld, "Best Places to Work in IT," 2025*

PUBLIC SAFETY

Crime Rate

Area	Total Crime Rate	Violent Crime Rate				Property Crime Rate		
		Murder	Rape	Robbery	Aggrav. Assault	Burglary	Larceny-Theft	Motor Vehicle Theft
City	4,956.6	22.0	71.4	208.4	426.2	617.2	2,416.3	1,195.2
U.S.	2,290.9	5.7	38.0	66.5	264.1	250.7	1,347.2	318.7

Note: Figures are crimes per 100,000 population.
Source: FBI, Table 8, Offenses Known to Law Enforcement, by State by City, 2023

Hate Crimes

Area	Number of Quarters Reported	Number of Incidents per Bias Motivation					
		Race/Ethnicity/Ancestry	Religion	Sexual Orientation	Disability	Gender	Gender Identity
City	4	5	1	3	0	0	0
U.S.	4	5,900	2,699	2,077	187	92	492

Source: Federal Bureau of Investigation, Hate Crime Statistics 2023

Identity Theft Consumer Reports

Area	Reports	Reports per 100,000 Population	Rank[2]
MSA[1]	4,477	199	157
U.S.	1,135,291	339	-

Note: (1) Figures cover the Cincinnati, OH-KY-IN Metropolitan Statistical Area; (2) Rank ranges from 1 to 401 where 1 indicates greatest number of identity theft reports per 100,000 population
Source: Federal Trade Commission, Consumer Sentinel Network Data Book 2024

Fraud and Other Consumer Reports

Area	Reports	Reports per 100,000 Population	Rank[2]
MSA[1]	24,149	1,071	178
U.S.	5,360,641	1,601	-

Note: (1) Figures cover the Cincinnati, OH-KY-IN Metropolitan Statistical Area; (2) Rank ranges from 1 to 401 where 1 indicates greatest number of fraud and other consumer reports per 100,000 population
Source: Federal Trade Commission, Consumer Sentinel Network Data Book 2024

POLITICS

2024 Presidential Election Results

Area	Trump (Rep.)	Harris (Dem.)	Stein (Green)	Kennedy (Ind.)	Oliver (Lib.)	Other
Hamilton County	41.7	56.5	0.4	0.0	0.6	0.8
U.S.	49.7	48.2	0.6	0.5	0.4	0.6

Note: Results are percentages and may not add to 100% due to rounding
Source: Dave Leip's Atlas of U.S. Presidential Elections

SPORTS

Professional Sports Teams

Team Name	League	Year Established
Cincinnati Bengals	National Football League (NFL)	1968
Cincinnati Reds	Major League Baseball (MLB)	1882
FC Cincinnati	Major League Soccer (MLS)	2019

Note: Includes teams located in the Cincinnati, OH-KY-IN Metropolitan Statistical Area.
Source: Wikipedia, Major Professional Sports Teams of the United States and Canada, May 1, 2025

CLIMATE

Average and Extreme Temperatures

Temperature	Jan	Feb	Mar	Apr	May	Jun	Jul	Aug	Sep	Oct	Nov	Dec	Yr.
Extreme High (°F)	74	72	84	89	93	102	103	102	102	89	81	75	103
Average High (°F)	38	42	52	64	74	82	86	85	78	67	53	42	64
Average Temp. (°F)	30	33	43	54	63	72	76	74	68	56	44	34	54
Average Low (°F)	21	24	33	43	52	61	65	63	56	45	35	26	44
Extreme Low (°F)	-25	-15	-11	17	27	39	47	43	33	16	0	-20	-25

Note: Figures cover the years 1948-1990
Source: National Climatic Data Center, International Station Meteorological Climate Summary, 9/96

Average Precipitation/Snowfall/Humidity

Precip./Humidity	Jan	Feb	Mar	Apr	May	Jun	Jul	Aug	Sep	Oct	Nov	Dec	Yr.
Avg. Precip. (in.)	3.2	2.9	3.9	3.5	4.0	3.9	4.2	3.1	2.8	2.8	3.4	3.1	40.9
Avg. Snowfall (in.)	7	5	4	1	Tr	0	0	0	0	Tr	2	4	23
Avg. Rel. Hum. 7am (%)	79	78	77	76	79	82	85	87	87	83	79	79	81
Avg. Rel. Hum. 4pm (%)	65	60	55	50	51	53	54	52	52	51	58	65	55

Note: Figures cover the years 1948-1990; Tr = Trace amounts (<0.05 in. of rain; <0.5 in. of snow)
Source: National Climatic Data Center, International Station Meteorological Climate Summary, 9/96

Weather Conditions

Temperature			Daytime Sky			Precipitation		
10°F & below	32°F & below	90°F & above	Clear	Partly cloudy	Cloudy	0.01 inch or more precip.	0.1 inch or more snow/ice	Thunderstorms
14	107	23	80	126	159	127	25	39

Note: Figures are average number of days per year and cover the years 1948-1990
Source: National Climatic Data Center, International Station Meteorological Climate Summary, 9/96

HAZARDOUS WASTE

Superfund Sites

The Cincinnati, OH-KY-IN metro area is home to six sites on the EPA's Superfund National Priorities List (NPL) or Superfund Alternative Approach (SAA) list: **Armco Incorporation-Hamilton Plant** (Proposed NPL); **Chem-Dyne** (Final NPL); **Milford Contaminated Aquifer** (Final NPL); **Peters Cartridge Factory** (Final NPL); **Pristine, Inc.** (Final NPL); **Skinner Landfill** (Final NPL). The Superfund alternative approach uses the same investigation and cleanup process and standards that are used for sites listed on the National Priorities List. The SAA is an alternative to listing a site on the NPL; it is not an alternative to Superfund or the Superfund process. There are a total of 1,445 Superfund sites with a status of proposed or final on both lists in the United States. *U.S. Environmental Protection Agency, National Priorities List, May 1, 2025; U.S. Environmental Protection Agency, Superfund Alternative Approach Sites, May 1, 2025*

AIR QUALITY

Air Quality Trends: Ozone

	1990	1995	2000	2005	2010	2015	2020	2021	2022	2023
MSA[1]	0.083	0.082	0.074	0.075	0.069	0.069	0.067	0.065	0.068	0.072
U.S.	0.087	0.089	0.081	0.080	0.072	0.068	0.066	0.067	0.067	0.070

Note: (1) Data covers the Cincinnati, OH-KY-IN Metropolitan Statistical Area. The values shown are the composite ozone concentration averages among trend sites based on the highest fourth daily maximum 8-hour concentration in parts per million. These trends are based on sites having an adequate record of monitoring data during the trend period. Data from exceptional events are included.
Source: U.S. Environmental Protection Agency, Air Quality Monitoring Information, "Air Quality Trends by City, 1990-2023"

Air Quality Index

Area	Percent of Days when Air Quality was...[2]					AQI Statistics[2]	
	Good	Moderate	Unhealthy for Sensitive Groups	Unhealthy	Very Unhealthy	Maximum	Median
MSA[1]	25.2	68.2	5.2	1.4	0.0	197	57

Note: (1) Data covers the Cincinnati, OH-KY-IN Metropolitan Statistical Area; (2) Based on 365 days with AQI data in 2023. Air Quality Index (AQI) is an index for reporting daily air quality. EPA calculates the AQI for five major air pollutants regulated by the Clean Air Act: ground-level ozone, particle pollution (aka particulate matter), carbon monoxide, sulfur dioxide, and nitrogen dioxide. The AQI runs from 0 to 500. The higher the AQI value, the greater the level of air pollution and the greater the health concern. There are six AQI categories: "Good" AQI is between 0 and 50. Air quality is considered satisfactory; "Moderate" AQI is between 51 and 100. Air quality is acceptable; "Unhealthy for Sensitive Groups" When AQI values are between 101 and 150, members of sensitive groups may experience health effects; "Unhealthy" When AQI values are between 151 and 200 everyone may begin to experience health effects; "Very Unhealthy" AQI values between 201 and 300 trigger a health alert; "Hazardous" AQI values over 300 trigger warnings of emergency conditions (not shown).
Source: U.S. Environmental Protection Agency, Air Quality Index Report, 2023

Air Quality Index Pollutants

Area	Percent of Days when AQI Pollutant was...[2]					
	Carbon Monoxide	Nitrogen Dioxide	Ozone	Sulfur Dioxide	Particulate Matter 2.5	Particulate Matter 10
MSA[1]	0.0	0.5	25.5	(3)	72.1	1.9

Note: (1) Data covers the Cincinnati, OH-KY-IN Metropolitan Statistical Area; (2) Based on 365 days with AQI data in 2023. The Air Quality Index (AQI) is an index for reporting daily air quality. EPA calculates the AQI for five major air pollutants regulated by the Clean Air Act: ground-level ozone, particle pollution (also known as particulate matter), carbon monoxide, sulfur dioxide, and nitrogen dioxide. The AQI runs from 0 to 500. The higher the AQI value, the greater the level of air pollution and the greater the health concern; (3) Sulfur dioxide is no longer included in this table because SO_2 concentrations tend to be very localized and not necessarily representative of broad geographical areas like counties and CBSAs.
Source: U.S. Environmental Protection Agency, Air Quality Index Report, 2023

Maximum Air Pollutant Concentrations: Particulate Matter, Ozone, CO and Lead

	Particulate Matter 10 (ug/m^3)	Particulate Matter 2.5 Wtd AM (ug/m^3)	Particulate Matter 2.5 24-Hr (ug/m^3)	Ozone (ppm)	Carbon Monoxide (ppm)	Lead (ug/m^3)
MSA[1] Level	111	12.2	44	0.077	1	n/a
NAAQS[2]	150	15	35	0.075	9	0.15
Met NAAQS[2]	Yes	Yes	No	No	Yes	n/a

Note: (1) Data covers the Cincinnati, OH-KY-IN Metropolitan Statistical Area; Data from exceptional events are included; (2) National Ambient Air Quality Standards; ppm = parts per million; ug/m^3 = micrograms per cubic meter; n/a not available.
Concentrations: Particulate Matter 10 (coarse particulate)—highest second maximum 24-hour concentration; Particulate Matter 2.5 Wtd AM (fine particulate)—highest weighted annual mean concentration; Particulate Matter 2.5 24-Hour (fine particulate)—highest 98th percentile 24-hour concentration; Ozone—highest fourth daily maximum 8-hour concentration; Carbon Monoxide—highest second maximum non-overlapping 8-hour concentration; Lead—maximum running 3-month average
Source: U.S. Environmental Protection Agency, Air Quality Monitoring Information, "Air Quality Statistics by City, 2023"

Maximum Air Pollutant Concentrations: Nitrogen Dioxide and Sulfur Dioxide

	Nitrogen Dioxide AM (ppb)	Nitrogen Dioxide 1-Hr (ppb)	Sulfur Dioxide AM (ppb)	Sulfur Dioxide 1-Hr (ppb)	Sulfur Dioxide 24-Hr (ppb)
MSA[1] Level	18	49	n/a	21	n/a
NAAQS[2]	53	100	30	75	140
Met NAAQS[2]	Yes	Yes	n/a	Yes	n/a

Note: (1) Data covers the Cincinnati, OH-KY-IN Metropolitan Statistical Area; Data from exceptional events are included; (2) National Ambient Air Quality Standards; ppm = parts per million; ug/m^3 = micrograms per cubic meter; n/a not available.
Concentrations: Nitrogen Dioxide AM—highest arithmetic mean concentration; Nitrogen Dioxide 1-Hr—highest 98th percentile 1-hour daily maximum concentration; Sulfur Dioxide AM—highest annual mean concentration; Sulfur Dioxide 1-Hr—highest 99th percentile 1-hour daily maximum concentration; Sulfur Dioxide 24-Hr—highest second maximum 24-hour concentration
Source: U.S. Environmental Protection Agency, Air Quality Monitoring Information, "Air Quality Statistics by City, 2023"

Cleveland, Ohio

Background

Cleveland has 31 miles of frontage on the south shore of Lake Erie in northeastern Ohio and is bisected by the Cuyahoga River. It was founded in 1796 by General Moses Cleveland, on what was known as the Western Reserve of Connecticut. The completion of the Erie and Ohio canals brought people and industry to the area and, by the 1840s, the population had grown by 500 percent from the prior decade. While neighborhoods fell along racial and ethnic lines, the children of the city's immigrants intermarried and surpassed their parents on socioeconomic levels. Cleveland was a place where the American dream could be realized.

During World War I, a new wave of job seekers, largely African Americans from Southern rural areas, and poor whites from Kentucky, Tennessee, and West Virginia flooded Cleveland, filling in for a shortage of workers in war goods production. After the war, job seekers were unskilled without the same opportunities as their predecessors. Lack of employment led to collapsing economic conditions, setting the stage for the urban unrest of the 1960s.

In the 1990s, Cleveland enjoyed an economic renaissance with several projects representing more than $9 billion in capital investment. A public-private partnership was responsible for a new downtown Gateway sports complex (1994), the Rock & Roll Hall of Fame (1998) designed by I.M. Pei, and a vibrant new entertainment district.

The biomed/biotechnology industry has been important in recent years, with the Cleveland Clinic recording over 15 million patient visits in 2024, and employing 83,000, alongside other area universities and foundations. A leading national research center, it receives millions of dollars annually from the National Institutes of Health and is ranked as one of the nation's best hospitals by *U.S. News and World Report*.

The Port of Cleveland is the largest for overseas general cargo on Lake Erie, and the third largest on any of the Great Lakes. It generates over a billion dollars annually in trade.

Progressive Field is home to the MLB Cleveland Guardians (formerly the Cleveland Indians), and the Rocket Mortgage FieldHouse hosts the Cavaliers basketball team. Both venues were extensively improved in recent years, and both teams have seen recent success, with the Guardians advancing to the World Series in 2016 and the Cavaliers playing in the NBA Finals every year from 2015 to 2018, winning a championship in 2016, behind superstar forward LeBron James. In 2024, Cleveland hosted the Pan American Masters Games.

Increasingly, the northeastern Ohio economy is driven by research and specialized service industries, and Cleveland is considered one of the best metro areas in the U.S. for attracting expanded business facilities. Cleveland is especially prominent in health-related technology, with nearly 200 tech companies operating in the Cleveland area, including OnShift, MRI Software, and Bravo Wellness. Other fields in which the city's economy thrives include banking, education, insurance, and healthcare. Cleveland's two largest employers are Cleveland Clinic and University Hospitals.

Few cities of its size offer the array of arts and cultural opportunities afforded by the Greater Cleveland area. The University Circle area is home to more than 70 cultural, educational, science, medical, and religious institutions, including the renowned Cleveland Orchestra. Playhouse Square offers Broadway shows, plays, opera, ballet, and contemporary performing arts. Cleveland also has one of the six Second City comedy theaters in the nation, and is where James Gunn's 2025 movie, Superman, was filmed. In 2022, the city started the Cleveland Silent Film Festival in addition to the Cleveland International Film Festival which began in 1977.

The city is home to the Cleveland Museum of Natural History, and the Cleveland Metroparks Zoo has the biggest collection of primates in North America and an indoor rainforest. Nearby is the Great Lakes Science center, which features an OMNIMAX(r) theater, and the Museum of Contemporary Art (MoCA).

Cleveland experiences a continental-like climate with four distinct seasons. Summers are hot and humid, while winters are cold and snowy. East of the mouth of the Cuyahoga, the land elevation rises rapidly in the south. This formation, together with the prevailing winds off Lake Erie, contributes to the lake-effect snow that is typical in Cleveland (especially on the city's East Side) from mid-November until the surface of the lake freezes, usually in late January or early February.

Rankings

General Rankings

- To help military veterans find the best places in which to settle down, *WalletHub* compared the 100 largest U.S. cities across 19 key indicators of livability, affordability and veteran-friendliness. They range from the share of military skill-related jobs to veteran income growth to the availability of VA health facilities. Cleveland ranked #67. *Wallethub.com, "Best & Worst Places for Veterans to Live (2025)," November 7, 2024*

- The human resources consulting firm Mercer ranked 241 major cities worldwide in terms of overall quality of life. Cleveland ranked #71. Criteria: political and personal safety, social, and economic factors; medical and health considerations; schools and education; public services and transportation; recreation; connectivity; housing and infrastructure; and climate. *Mercer, "Mercer 2024 Quality of Living Survey," December 2024*

Business/Finance Rankings

- Payscale.com ranked the 32 largest metro areas in terms of wage growth. The Cleveland metro area ranked #11. Criteria: quarterly changes in private industry employee and education professional wage growth from the previous year. *PayScale, "Wage Trends by Metro Area-4th Quarter," February 4, 2025*

- The Cleveland metro area appeared on the Milken Institute "2025 Best Performing Cities" list. Rank: #185 out of 200 large metro areas (based on performance category). Criteria: job growth; wage growth; high-tech growth and impact; community resilience; housing affordability; household broadband access. *Milken Institute, "Best-Performing Cities 2025," January 14, 2025*

- Mercer Human Resources Consulting ranked 226 cities worldwide in terms of cost-of-living. Cleveland ranked #84 (the lower the ranking, the higher the cost-of-living). The survey measured the comparative cost of over 200 items (such as housing, food, clothing, domestic supplies, transportation, and recreation/entertainment) in each location. *Mercer, "2024 Cost of Living City Ranking," June 17, 2024*

Culture/Performing Arts Rankings

- Cleveland was selected as one of the 25 best cities for moviemakers in North America. Great film cities are places where filmmaking dreams can come true, that offer more creative space, lower costs, and great outdoor locations. NYC & LA were intentionally excluded. Criteria: film industry presence and culture; tax incentives; affordability; and proximity of festivals and schools. The city was ranked #16. *MovieMaker Magazine, "Best Places to Live and Work as a Moviemaker, 2025," January 29, 2025*

Education Rankings

- Personal finance website *WalletHub* analyzed the 150 largest U.S. metropolitan statistical areas to determine where the most educated Americans are putting their degrees to work. Criteria: education levels; percentage of workers with degrees; education quality and attainment gap; public school quality rankings; quality and enrollment of each metro area's universities. Cleveland was ranked #82 (#1 = most educated city). *WalletHub.com, "Most & Least Educated Cities in America, 2025" July 2, 2024*

Environmental Rankings

- *Niche* compiled a list of the nation's snowiest cities, based on the National Oceanic and Atmospheric Administration's 30-year average snowfall data. Among cities with a population of at least 50,000, Cleveland ranked #9. *Niche.com, Top 25 Snowiest Cities in America, December 10, 2018*

- Cleveland was highlighted as one of the 25 metro areas most polluted by year-round particle pollution (Annual PM 2.5) in the U.S. during 2021 through 2023. The area ranked #9. *American Lung Association, "State of the Air 2025," April 23, 2025*

Health/Fitness Rankings

- For each of the 100 largest cities in the United States, the American Fitness Index®, compiled in partnership between the American College of Sports Medicine and the Elevance Health Foundation, evaluated community infrastructure and more than 30 health behaviors including preventive health, levels of chronic disease conditions, food insecurity, pedestrian safety, air quality, and community/environment resources that support physical activity. Cleveland ranked #48 for "community fitness." *americanfitnessindex.org, "2024 ACSM American Fitness Index Summary Report," July 23, 2024*

- The Cleveland metro area was identified as one of the worst cities for bed bugs in America by pest control company Orkin. The area ranked #4 out of 50 based on the number of bed bug treatments Orkin performed from December 2022 to November 2023. *Orkin, "Chicago Joins Paris In Global Bed Bug Spotlight Ranking As The Worst City On Orkin's U.S. Bed Bug Cities List," January 22, 2024*

- Cleveland was identified as a "2025 Allergy Capital." The area ranked #96 out of the nation's 100 largest metropolitan areas. Three groups of factors were used to identify the most challenging cities for people with allergies: annual tree, grass, and weed pollen scores; over the counter allergy medicine use; number of board-certified allergy specialists. *Asthma and Allergy Foundation of America, "2025 Allergy Capitals: The Most Challenging Places to Live with Allergies," March 18, 2025*

- Cleveland was identified as a "2024 Asthma Capital." The area ranked #6 out of the nation's 100 largest metropolitan areas. Criteria: estimated asthma prevalence; asthma-related mortality; and ER visits due to asthma. Risk factors analyzed but not factored in the rankings: annual air quality including pollution and ozone levels; public smoking laws; indoor air quality; access to asthma specialists; rescue and controller medication use; uninsured rate; pollen allergy; poverty rate. *Asthma and Allergy Foundation of America, "Asthma Capitals 2024: The Most Challenging Places to Live With Asthma," September 10, 2024*

Real Estate Rankings

- *WalletHub* compared the most populated U.S. cities to determine which had the best markets for real estate agents. Cleveland ranked #141 where demand was high and pay was the best. Criteria: sales per agent; annual median wage for real-estate agents; monthly average starting salary for real estate agents; real estate job density and competition; unemployment rate; home turnover rate; housing-market health index; and other relevant metrics. *WalletHub.com, "2021 Best Places to Be a Real Estate Agent," May 12, 2021*

- The Cleveland metro area was identified as one of the 20 best housing markets in the U.S. in 2024. The area ranked #6 out of 226 markets. Criteria: year-over-year change of median sales price of existing single-family homes between the 4th quarter of 2023 and the 4th quarter of 2024. *National Association of Realtors®, Median Sales Price of Existing Single-Family Homes for Metropolitan Areas, 4th Quarter 2024*

- The Cleveland metro area was identified as one of the 10 best condo markets in the U.S. in 2024. The area ranked #7 out of 63 markets. Criteria: year-over-year change of median sales price of existing apartment condo-coop homes between the 4th quarter of 2023 and the 4th quarter of 2024. *National Association of Realtors®, Median Sales Price of Existing Apartment Condo-Coops Homes for Metropolitan Areas, 4th Quarter 2024*

- Cleveland was ranked #16 out of 176 metro areas in terms of cost of housing in 2024 by the National Association of Home Builders (#1 = most affordable). Criteria: the portion of an average family's income necessary to pay the mortgage on a median-priced home. *National Association of Home Builders®, NAHB-Wells Fargo Cost of Housing Index, 4th Quarter 2024*

Safety Rankings

- To identify the most dangerous cities in America, *24/7 Wall St.* focused on violent crime categories—murder, non-negligent manslaughter, rape, robbery, and aggravated assault—as reported for every 100,000 residents using data from the FBI's 2020 annual Uniform Crime Report. For cities with populations over 25,000, Cleveland was ranked #12. *247wallst.com, "America's Most Dangerous Cities" November 12, 2021*

- Allstate ranked the 100 most populous cities in America in terms of driver safety. Cleveland ranked #11. Criteria based on anonymized driving behavior data from Allstate's mobile app powered by Arity: high speed driving (over 80 mph), phone handling, and hard braking. The report helps increase the importance of safety and awareness behind the wheel. *Allstate, "16th Allstate America's Best Drivers Report®" July 11, 2024*

- Cleveland was identified as one of the most dangerous cities in America by NeighborhoodScout. The city ranked #11 out of 100 (#1 = most dangerous). Criteria: number of violent crimes per 1,000 residents. The editors evaluated cities with 25,000 or more residents. *NeighborhoodScout.com, "2023 Top 100 Most Dangerous Cities in the U.S.," January 12, 2023*

Women/Minorities Rankings

- Personal finance website *WalletHub* compared more than 180 U.S. cities across two key dimensions, "Hispanic Business-Friendliness" and "Hispanic Purchasing Power," to arrive at the most favorable conditions for Hispanic entrepreneurs. Cleveland was ranked #180 out of 182. Criteria includes: share of Hispanic-Owned Businesses; average growth of Hispanic Business revenues; Small Business-Friendliness score; affordability; and number of Hispanics with at least a bachelor's degree. *WalletHub.com, "Best Cities for Hispanic Entrepreneurs," September 4, 2024*

Miscellaneous Rankings

- Despite a wide range of popular international destinations, plugged-in travel influencers and experts continue to rediscover their local regions. Cleveland appeared on a *Forbes Advisor* list of places in the U.S. designed to showcase a large variety of destinations. Whether it be discovery of hidden gems, delicious food, or outdoor exploring and daytrips, these places are a must-see. *Forbes.com, "Top 18 Places To Travel In the U.S. In 2024," February 7, 2024*

- *MoveHub* ranked 446 hipster cities across 20 countries, using its new and improved alternative Hipster Index and Cleveland came out as #36 among the top 50. Criteria: population over 150,000; number of vintage boutiques; density of tattoo parlors; vegan places to eat; coffee shops; and density of vinyl record stores. *MoveHub.com, "The Hipster Index: Brighton Pips Portland to Global Top Spot," July 28, 2021*

- In its roundup of St. Patrick's Day parades, *Gayot* listed the best festivals and parades of all things Irish. The festivities in Cleveland as among the best in North America. *Gayot.com, "Best St. Patrick's Day Parades," March 2025*

- *WalletHub* compared 148 of the most populated U.S. cities to determine their operating efficiency. A "Quality of Services" score was constructed for each city and then measured against the total budget per capita to reveal which were managed the best. Cleveland ranked #143. Criteria: financial stability; economy; education; safety; health; infrastructure and pollution. *WalletHub.com, "2025's Best- & Worst-Run Cities in America," June 18, 2024*

Business Environment

DEMOGRAPHICS

Population Growth

Area	1990 Census	2000 Census	2010 Census	2020 Census	2023 Estimate[2]	Population Growth 1990-2023 (%)
City	505,333	478,403	396,815	372,624	367,523	-27.3
MSA[1]	2,102,219	2,148,143	2,077,240	2,088,251	2,171,978	3.3
U.S.	248,709,873	281,421,906	308,745,538	331,449,281	332,387,540	33.6

Note: (1) Figures cover the Cleveland, OH Metropolitan Statistical Area; (2) 2019-2023 5-year ACS population estimate
Source: U.S. Census Bureau, 1990 Census, 2000 Census, 2010 Census, 2020 Census, 2019-2023 American Community Survey 5-Year Estimates

Race

Area	White Alone[2] (%)	Black Alone[2] (%)	Asian Alone[2] (%)	AIAN[3] Alone[2] (%)	NHOPI[4] Alone[2] (%)	Other Race Alone[2] (%)	Two or More Races (%)
City	36.7	46.8	2.3	0.4	0.0	4.6	9.2
MSA[1]	70.5	18.6	2.3	0.2	0.0	1.9	6.4
U.S.	63.4	12.4	5.8	0.9	0.2	6.6	10.7

Note: (1) Figures cover the Cleveland, OH Metropolitan Statistical Area; (2) Alone is defined as not being in combination with one or more other races; (3) American Indian and Alaska Native; (4) Native Hawaiian and Other Pacific Islander
Source: U.S. Census Bureau, 2019-2023 American Community Survey 5-Year Estimates

Hispanic or Latino Origin

Area	Total (%)	Mexican (%)	Puerto Rican (%)	Cuban (%)	Other (%)
City	12.8	1.7	8.8	0.2	2.2
MSA[1]	6.5	1.5	3.6	0.1	1.3
U.S.	19.0	11.3	1.8	0.7	5.2

Note: Persons of Hispanic or Latino origin can be of any race; (1) Figures cover the Cleveland, OH Metropolitan Statistical Area
Source: U.S. Census Bureau, 2019-2023 American Community Survey 5-Year Estimates

Age

Area	Percent of Population									Median Age
	Under Age 5	Age 5–19	Age 20–34	Age 35–44	Age 45–54	Age 55–64	Age 65–74	Age 75–84	Age 85+	
City	5.6	18.2	24.4	12.2	11.2	13.4	9.3	4.1	1.6	36.3
MSA[1]	5.3	17.9	18.9	12.1	12.2	14.2	11.5	5.6	2.4	41.6
U.S.	5.7	19.1	20.2	13.1	12.3	12.8	10.0	4.9	1.9	38.7

Note: (1) Figures cover the Cleveland, OH Metropolitan Statistical Area
Source: U.S. Census Bureau, 2019-2023 American Community Survey 5-Year Estimates

Disability by Age

Area	All Ages	Under 18 Years Old	18 to 64 Years Old	65 Years and Over
City	19.9	9.8	18.5	40.7
MSA[1]	14.6	5.6	12.2	32.1
U.S.	13.0	4.7	10.7	32.9

Note: Figures show percent of the civilian noninstitutionalized population that reported having a disability. Disability status is determined from six types of difficulty: vision, hearing, cognitive, ambulatory, self-care, and independent living. For children under 5 years old, hearing and vision difficulty are used to determine disability status. For children between the ages of 5 and 14, disability status is determined from hearing, vision, cognitive, ambulatory, and self-care difficulties. For people aged 15 years and older, they are considered to have a disability if they have difficulty with any one of the six difficulty types; Note: (1) Figures cover the Cleveland, OH Metropolitan Statistical Area
Source: U.S. Census Bureau, 2019-2023 American Community Survey 5-Year Estimates

Ancestry

Area	German	Irish	English	American	Italian	Polish	French[2]	European	Scottish
City	9.4	8.4	3.5	2.5	4.4	3.7	0.8	0.5	0.7
MSA[1]	18.5	13.3	8.6	4.1	9.1	6.9	1.4	1.1	1.5
U.S.	12.6	9.4	9.1	5.5	4.9	2.6	2.0	1.6	1.6

Note: Figures are the percentage of the total population reporting a particular ancestry. The nine most commonly reported ancestries in the U.S. are shown. Figures include multiple ancestries (e.g. if a person reported being Irish and Italian, they were included in both columns); (1) Figures cover the Cleveland, OH Metropolitan Statistical Area; (2) Excludes Basque
Source: U.S. Census Bureau, 2019-2023 American Community Survey 5-Year Estimates

Foreign-born Population

Area	Percent of Population Born in								
	Any Foreign Country	Asia	Mexico	Europe	Caribbean	Central America[2]	South America	Africa	Canada
City	6.1	2.3	0.4	1.1	0.5	0.5	0.3	0.9	0.1
MSA[1]	5.8	2.2	0.3	2.0	0.2	0.2	0.3	0.5	0.2
U.S.	13.9	4.3	3.3	1.4	1.4	1.2	1.2	0.8	0.2

Note: (1) Figures cover the Cleveland, OH Metropolitan Statistical Area; (2) Excludes Mexico.
Source: U.S. Census Bureau, 2019-2023 American Community Survey 5-Year Estimates

Household Size

Area	Persons in Household (%)							Average Household Size
	One	Two	Three	Four	Five	Six	Seven or More	
City	46.4	28.4	11.9	7.4	3.4	1.7	0.9	2.11
MSA[1]	35.3	33.7	13.6	10.5	4.4	1.6	0.9	2.29
U.S.	28.5	33.8	15.4	12.7	5.9	2.3	1.4	2.54

Note: (1) Figures cover the Cleveland, OH Metropolitan Statistical Area
Source: U.S. Census Bureau, 2019-2023 American Community Survey 5-Year Estimates

Household Relationships

Area	House-holder	Opposite-sex Spouse	Same-sex Spouse	Opposite-sex Unmarried Partner	Same-sex Unmarried Partner	Child[2]	Grand-child	Other Relatives	Non-relatives
City	45.0	8.5	0.2	3.5	0.3	27.0	3.3	5.0	3.8
MSA[1]	42.5	17.1	0.1	2.7	0.1	27.7	2.1	3.3	2.3
U.S.	38.3	17.5	0.2	2.5	0.2	28.3	2.4	4.8	3.4

Note: Figures are percent of the total population; (1) Figures cover the Cleveland, OH Metropolitan Statistical Area; (2) Includes biological, adopted, and stepchildren of the householder
Source: U.S. Census Bureau, 2020 Census

Gender

Area	Males	Females	Males per 100 Females
City	177,863	189,660	93.8
MSA[1]	1,057,990	1,113,988	95.0
U.S.	164,545,087	167,842,453	98.0

Note: (1) Figures cover the Cleveland, OH Metropolitan Statistical Area
Source: U.S. Census Bureau, 2019-2023 American Community Survey 5-Year Estimates

Marital Status

Area	Never Married	Now Married[2]	Separated	Widowed	Divorced
City	53.7	23.7	2.8	6.1	13.7
MSA[1]	35.7	44.2	1.5	6.4	12.1
U.S.	34.1	47.9	1.7	5.6	10.7

Note: Figures are percentages and cover the population 15 years of age and older; (1) Figures cover the Cleveland, OH Metropolitan Statistical Area; (2) Excludes separated
Source: U.S. Census Bureau, 2019-2023 American Community Survey 5-Year Estimates

Religious Groups by Family

Area	Catholic	Baptist	Methodist	LDS[2]	Pentecostal	Lutheran	Islam	Adventist	Other
MSA[1]	26.1	4.3	2.3	0.4	1.5	1.8	1.1	1.3	16.8
U.S.	18.7	7.3	3.0	2.0	1.8	1.7	1.3	1.3	11.6

Note: Figures are the number of adherents as a percentage of the total population and cover the eight largest religious groups in the U.S; (1) Figures cover the Cleveland, OH Metropolitan Statistical Area; (2) Church of Jesus Christ of Latter-day Saints
Sources: 2020 U.S. Religion Census, Association of Statisticians of American Religious Bodies; The Association of Religion Data Archives (ARDA)

Religious Groups by Tradition

Area	Catholic	Evangelical Protestant	Mainline Protestant	Black Protestant	Islam	Judaism	Hinduism	Orthodox	Buddhism
MSA[1]	26.1	15.1	5.6	3.5	1.1	1.3	0.3	0.8	0.2
U.S.	18.7	16.5	5.2	2.3	1.3	0.6	0.4	0.4	0.3

Note: Figures are the number of adherents as a percentage of the total population; (1) Figures cover the Cleveland, OH Metropolitan Statistical Area
Sources: 2020 U.S. Religion Census, Association of Statisticians of American Religious Bodies; The Association of Religion Data Archives (ARDA)

Cleveland, Ohio

ECONOMY

Real Gross Domestic Product (GDP)

Area	2017	2018	2019	2020	2021	2022	2023	Rank[3]
MSA[1]	128.6	130.6	134.0	129.2	136.3	139.1	139.9	36
U.S.[2]	17,619.1	18,160.7	18,642.5	18,238.9	19,387.6	19,896.6	20,436.3	—

Note: Figures are in billions of chained 2017 dollars; (1) Figures cover the Cleveland, OH Metropolitan Statistical Area; (2) Figures cover real GDP within metropolitan areas; (3) Rank is based on 2023 data and ranges from 1 to 384
Source: U.S. Bureau of Economic Analysis

Economic Growth

Area	2014	2015	2016	2017	2018	2019	2020	2021	2022	2023
MSA[1]	2.3	0.8	0.1	2.4	1.6	2.6	-3.6	5.5	2.1	0.6
U.S.[2]	2.6	3.2	2.0	2.7	3.1	2.7	-2.2	6.3	2.6	2.7

Note: Figures are real gross domestic product growth rates and represent percent change from preceding period; (1) Figures cover the Cleveland, OH Metropolitan Statistical Area; (2) Figures are the average growth rates within metropolitan areas
Source: U.S. Bureau of Economic Analysis

Metropolitan Area Exports

Area	2018	2019	2020	2021	2022	2023	Rank[2]
MSA[1]	9,382.9	8,829.9	7,415.8	8,560.4	9,561.2	10,206.2	42
U.S.	1,664,056.1	1,645,173.7	1,431,406.6	1,753,941.4	2,062,937.4	2,019,160.5	—

Note: Figures are in millions of dollars; (1) Figures cover the Cleveland, OH Metropolitan Statistical Area; (2) Rank is based on 2023 data and ranges from 1 to 386
Source: U.S. Department of Commerce, International Trade Administration, Office of Trade and Economic Analysis, Industry and Analysis, Exports by Metropolitan Area, data extracted April 2, 2025

Building Permits

Area	Single-Family			Multi-Family			Total		
	2023	2024	Pct. Chg.	2023	2024	Pct. Chg.	2023	2024	Pct. Chg.
City	161	234	45.3	644	662	2.8	805	896	11.3
MSA[1]	2,500	2,980	19.2	991	1,309	32.1	3,491	4,289	22.9
U.S.	920,000	981,900	6.7	591,100	496,100	-16.1	1,511,100	1,478,000	-2.2

Note: (1) Figures cover the Cleveland, OH Metropolitan Statistical Area; Figures represent new, privately-owned housing units authorized (unadjusted data)
Source: U.S. Census Bureau, Building Permits Survey (BPS), 2023, 2024

Bankruptcy Filings

Area	Business Filings			Nonbusiness Filings		
	2023	2024	% Chg.	2023	2024	% Chg.
Cuyahoga County	37	60	62.2	3,437	4,054	18.0
U.S.	18,926	23,107	22.1	434,064	494,201	13.9

Note: Business filings include Chapter 7, Chapter 9, Chapter 11, Chapter 12, Chapter 13, Chapter 15, and Section 304; Nonbusiness filings include Chapter 7, Chapter 11, and Chapter 13
Source: Administrative Office of the U.S. Courts, Business and Nonbusiness Bankruptcy, County Cases Commenced by Chapter of the Bankruptcy Code, During the 12-Month Period Ending December 31, 2023 and Business and Nonbusiness Bankruptcy, County Cases Commenced by Chapter of the Bankruptcy Code, During the 12-Month Period Ending December 31, 2024

Housing Vacancy Rates

Area	Gross Vacancy Rate[3] (%)			Year-Round Vacancy Rate[4] (%)			Rental Vacancy Rate[5] (%)			Homeowner Vacancy Rate[6] (%)		
	2022	2023	2024	2022	2023	2024	2022	2023	2024	2022	2023	2024
MSA[1]	7.0	7.6	7.5	6.8	7.2	7.4	3.2	4.7	5.8	1.0	0.5	0.4
U.S.[2]	9.1	9.0	9.1	7.5	7.5	7.6	5.7	6.5	6.8	0.8	0.8	1.0

Note: (1) Figures cover the Cleveland, OH Metropolitan Statistical Area; (2) Figures cover the 75 largest Metropolitan Statistical Areas; (3) The percentage of the total housing inventory that is vacant; (4) The percentage of the housing inventory (excluding seasonal units) that is year-round vacant; (5) The percentage of rental inventory that is vacant for rent; (6) The percentage of homeowner inventory that is vacant for sale
Source: U.S. Census Bureau, Housing Vacancies and Homeownership Annual Statistics: 2022, 2023, 2024

INCOME

Income

Area	Per Capita ($)	Median Household ($)	Average Household ($)
City	27,078	39,187	56,900
MSA[1]	41,791	68,507	96,273
U.S.	43,289	78,538	110,491

Note: (1) Figures cover the Cleveland, OH Metropolitan Statistical Area
Source: U.S. Census Bureau, 2019-2023 American Community Survey 5-Year Estimates

Household Income Distribution

Area	Percent of Households Earning							
	Under $15,000	$15,000 -$24,999	$25,000 -$34,999	$35,000 -$49,999	$50,000 -$74,999	$75,000 -$99,999	$100,000 -$149,999	$150,000 and up
City	22.1	12.6	10.7	14.2	16.0	9.2	8.9	6.4
MSA[1]	10.1	7.6	7.8	11.6	16.9	12.5	16.0	17.3
U.S.	8.5	6.6	6.8	10.4	15.7	12.7	17.4	21.9

Note: (1) Figures cover the Cleveland, OH Metropolitan Statistical Area
Source: U.S. Census Bureau, 2019-2023 American Community Survey 5-Year Estimates

Poverty Rate

Area	All Ages	Under 18 Years Old	18 to 64 Years Old	65 Years and Over
City	30.8	45.3	27.4	24.5
MSA[1]	13.6	19.3	12.6	10.6
U.S.	12.4	16.3	11.6	10.4

Note: Figures are percentage of people whose income during the past 12 months was below the poverty level;
(1) Figures cover the Cleveland, OH Metropolitan Statistical Area
Source: U.S. Census Bureau, 2019-2023 American Community Survey 5-Year Estimates

EMPLOYMENT

Labor Force and Employment

Area	Civilian Labor Force			Workers Employed		
	Dec. 2023	Dec. 2024	% Chg.	Dec. 2023	Dec. 2024	% Chg.
City	154,882	158,055	2.0	148,680	151,454	1.9
MSA[1]	1,067,052	1,088,179	2.0	1,033,451	1,051,761	1.8
U.S.	166,661,000	167,746,000	0.7	160,754,000	161,294,000	0.3

Note: Data is not seasonally adjusted and covers workers 16 years of age and older; (1) Figures cover the Cleveland, OH Metropolitan Statistical Area
Source: Bureau of Labor Statistics, Local Area Unemployment Statistics

Unemployment Rate

Area	2024											
	Jan.	Feb.	Mar.	Apr.	May	Jun.	Jul.	Aug.	Sep.	Oct.	Nov.	Dec.
City	5.0	5.8	5.2	4.7	5.0	5.5	5.5	4.7	4.1	3.8	4.0	4.2
MSA[1]	4.0	4.7	4.2	3.6	3.9	4.4	4.4	3.7	3.3	3.0	3.2	3.3
U.S.	4.1	4.2	3.9	3.5	3.7	4.3	4.5	4.4	3.9	3.9	4.0	3.8

Note: Data is not seasonally adjusted and covers workers 16 years of age and older; (1) Figures cover the Cleveland, OH Metropolitan Statistical Area
Source: Bureau of Labor Statistics, Local Area Unemployment Statistics

Average Wages

Occupation	$/Hr.	Occupation	$/Hr.
Accountants and Auditors	41.49	Maintenance and Repair Workers	25.41
Automotive Mechanics	26.14	Marketing Managers	67.80
Bookkeepers	24.08	Network and Computer Systems Admin.	46.55
Carpenters	29.35	Nurses, Licensed Practical	30.00
Cashiers	14.16	Nurses, Registered	43.24
Computer Programmers	44.94	Nursing Assistants	19.22
Computer Systems Analysts	47.53	Office Clerks, General	22.21
Computer User Support Specialists	28.26	Physical Therapists	48.56
Construction Laborers	27.82	Physicians	117.07
Cooks, Restaurant	17.24	Plumbers, Pipefitters and Steamfitters	33.28
Customer Service Representatives	22.13	Police and Sheriff's Patrol Officers	37.16
Dentists	81.41	Postal Service Mail Carriers	28.67
Electricians	32.62	Real Estate Sales Agents	23.45
Engineers, Electrical	49.77	Retail Salespersons	17.25
Fast Food and Counter Workers	14.06	Sales Representatives, Technical/Scientific	47.42
Financial Managers	76.95	Secretaries, Exc. Legal/Medical/Executive	22.52
First-Line Supervisors of Office Workers	33.00	Security Guards	19.46
General and Operations Managers	57.91	Surgeons	n/a
Hairdressers/Cosmetologists	17.62	Teacher Assistants, Exc. Postsecondary[1]	17.13
Home Health and Personal Care Aides	15.55	Teachers, Secondary School, Exc. Sp. Ed.[1]	37.67
Janitors and Cleaners	17.41	Telemarketers	15.51
Landscaping/Groundskeeping Workers	18.91	Truck Drivers, Heavy/Tractor-Trailer	28.14
Lawyers	71.42	Truck Drivers, Light/Delivery Services	21.75
Maids and Housekeeping Cleaners	15.21	Waiters and Waitresses	18.81

Note: Wage data covers the Cleveland, OH Metropolitan Statistical Area; (1) Hourly wages were calculated from annual wage data based on a 40 hour work week
Source: Bureau of Labor Statistics, Metro Area Occupational Employment & Wage Estimates, May 2024

Employment by Industry

Sector	MSA[1] Number of Employees	MSA[1] Percent of Total	U.S. Percent of Total
Construction, Mining, and Logging	40,900	3.7	5.5
Financial Activities	71,200	6.5	5.8
Government	137,100	12.5	14.9
Information	14,100	1.3	1.9
Leisure and Hospitality	103,400	9.5	10.4
Manufacturing	126,400	11.6	8.0
Other Services	38,600	3.5	3.7
Private Education and Health Services	215,900	19.7	16.9
Professional and Business Services	151,800	13.9	14.2
Retail Trade	99,400	9.1	10.0
Transportation, Warehousing, and Utilities	41,800	3.8	4.8
Wholesale Trade	53,500	4.9	3.9

Note: Figures are non-farm employment as of December 2024. Figures are not seasonally adjusted and include workers 16 years of age and older; (1) Figures cover the Cleveland, OH Metropolitan Statistical Area
Source: Bureau of Labor Statistics, Current Employment Statistics, Employment, Hours, and Earnings

Employment by Occupation

Occupation Classification	City (%)	MSA[1] (%)	U.S. (%)
Management, Business, Science, and Arts	33.5	42.0	42.0
Natural Resources, Construction, and Maintenance	5.8	6.8	8.6
Production, Transportation, and Material Moving	17.7	14.4	13.0
Sales and Office	20.2	20.8	19.9
Service	22.9	16.0	16.5

Note: Figures cover employed civilians 16 years of age and older; (1) Figures cover the Cleveland, OH Metropolitan Statistical Area
Source: U.S. Census Bureau, 2019-2023 American Community Survey 5-Year Estimates

Occupations with Greatest Projected Employment Growth: 2022 – 2032

Occupation[1]	2022 Employment	2032 Projected Employment	Numeric Employment Change	Percent Employment Change
Home Health and Personal Care Aides	95,690	108,260	12,570	13.1
Cooks, Restaurant	48,380	57,540	9,160	18.9
Stockers and Order Fillers	125,650	131,710	6,060	4.8
Nurse Practitioners	11,020	15,710	4,690	42.6
Medical and Health Services Managers	18,720	23,310	4,590	24.5
Registered Nurses	131,390	135,860	4,470	3.4
Financial Managers	26,630	30,720	4,090	15.4
General and Operations Managers	132,340	136,170	3,830	2.9
Heavy and Tractor-Trailer Truck Drivers	98,350	102,030	3,680	3.7
Market Research Analysts and Marketing Specialists	31,720	35,170	3,450	10.9

Note: Projections cover Ohio; (1) Sorted by numeric employment change
Source: www.projectionscentral.org, State Occupational Projections, 2022–2032 Long-Term Projections

Fastest-Growing Occupations: 2022 – 2032

Occupation[1]	2022 Employment	2032 Projected Employment	Numeric Employment Change	Percent Employment Change
Nurse Practitioners	11,020	15,710	4,690	42.6
Taxi Drivers	2,490	3,480	990	39.8
Wind Turbine Service Technicians	170	230	60	35.3
Data Scientists	3,760	5,000	1,240	33.0
Statisticians	420	540	120	28.6
Medical and Health Services Managers	18,720	23,310	4,590	24.5
Physician Assistants	3,210	3,990	780	24.3
Semiconductor Processors	870	1,080	210	24.1
Epidemiologists	260	320	60	23.1
Speech-Language Pathologists	6,340	7,740	1,400	22.1

Note: Projections cover Ohio; (1) Sorted by percent employment change and excludes occupations with numeric employment change less than 50
Source: www.projectionscentral.org, State Occupational Projections, 2022–2032 Long-Term Projections

CITY FINANCES

City Government Finances

Component	2022 ($000)	2022 ($ per capita)
Total Revenues	1,496,030	3,952
Total Expenditures	1,258,405	3,324
Debt Outstanding	1,726,268	4,560

Source: U.S. Census Bureau, State & Local Government Finances 2022

City Government Revenue by Source

Source	2022 ($000)	2022 ($ per capita)	2022 (%)
General Revenue			
From Federal Government	31,821	84	2.1
From State Government	115,385	305	7.7
From Local Governments	3,333	9	0.2
Taxes			
Property	39,079	103	2.6
Sales and Gross Receipts	22,364	59	1.5
Personal Income	429,087	1,133	28.7
Corporate Income	0	0	0.0
Motor Vehicle License	12,356	33	0.8
Other Taxes	48,542	128	3.2
Current Charges	215,958	570	14.4
Liquor Store	0	0	0.0
Utility	522,120	1,379	34.9

Source: U.S. Census Bureau, State & Local Government Finances 2022

City Government Expenditures by Function

Function	2022 ($000)	2022 ($ per capita)	2022 (%)
General Direct Expenditures			
Air Transportation	51,126	135	4.1
Corrections	4,009	10	0.3
Education	0	0	0.0
Employment Security Administration	0	0	0.0
Financial Administration	19,831	52	1.6
Fire Protection	133,811	353	10.6
General Public Buildings	8,408	22	0.7
Governmental Administration, Other	31,198	82	2.5
Health	9,113	24	0.7
Highways	6,565	17	0.5
Hospitals	0	0	0.0
Housing and Community Development	1,820	4	0.1
Interest on General Debt	24,658	65	2.0
Judicial and Legal	54,928	145	4.4
Libraries	0	0	0.0
Parking	0	0	0.0
Parks and Recreation	39,489	104	3.1
Police Protection	221,479	585	17.6
Public Welfare	0	0	0.0
Sewerage	32,531	85	2.6
Solid Waste Management	35,348	93	2.8
Veterans' Services	0	0	0.0
Liquor Store	0	0	0.0
Utility	449,882	1,188	35.8

Source: U.S. Census Bureau, State & Local Government Finances 2022

TAXES

State Corporate Income Tax Rates

State	Tax Rate (%)	Income Brackets ($)	Num. of Brackets	Financial Institution Tax Rate (%)[a]	Federal Income Tax Ded.
Ohio	(r)	–	–	(r)	No

Note: Tax rates for tax year 2024; (a) Rates listed are the corporate income tax rate applied to financial institutions or excise taxes based on income. Some states have other taxes based upon the value of deposits or shares; (r) Ohio no longer levies a tax based on income (except for a particular subset of corporations), but instead imposes a Commercial Activity Tax (CAT). For tax periods beginning on and after January 1, 2024, the CAT annual minimum tax is eliminated, and the exclusion amount is increased from $1 million to $3 million. Therefore, taxpayers with taxable gross receipts of $3 million or less per calendar year will no longer be subject to the CAT. For those few corporations for whom the franchise tax
Source: Federation of Tax Administrators, State Corporate Income Tax Rates, January 1, 2025

State Individual Income Tax Rates

State	Tax Rate (%)	Income Brackets ($)	Personal Exemptions ($)			Standard Ded. ($)	
			Single	Married	Depend.	Single	Married
Ohio (a)	0.0 - 3.5	26,050 - 115,300	1,200	2,400	1,200 (u)	–	–

Note: Tax rates for tax year 2024; Local- and county-level taxes are not included; Federal income tax is not deductible on state income tax returns; (a) 16 states have statutory provision for automatically adjusting to the rate of inflation the dollar values of the income tax brackets, standard deductions, and/or personal exemptions. Oregon does not index the income brackets for $125,000 and over See: INFL and SPEC above; (u) Ohio suspends the annual inflation indexing adjustment of income tax brackets and personal exemption amounts for taxable years beginning in 2023 and 2024. Business income taxes at a flat 3% rate for individuals with income over $125,000S/$250,000MFJ.
Source: Federation of Tax Administrators, State Individual Income Tax Rates, January 1, 2025

Various State Sales and Excise Tax Rates

State	State Sales Tax (%)	Gasoline[1] ($/gal.)	Cigarette[2] ($/pack)	Spirits[3] ($/gal.)	Wine[4] ($/gal.)	Beer[5] ($/gal.)	Recreational Marijuana (%)
Ohio	5.75	0.39	1.60	12.33	0.32	0.18	(s)

Note: All tax rates as of January 1, 2025; (1) The American Petroleum Institute has developed a methodology for determining the average tax rate on a gallon of fuel. Rates may include any of the following: excise taxes, environmental fees, storage tank fees, other fees or taxes, general sales tax, and local taxes; (2) The federal excise tax of $1.0066 per pack and local taxes are not included; (3) Rates are those applicable to off-premise sales of 40% alcohol by volume (a.b.v.) distilled spirits in 750ml containers. Local excise taxes are excluded; (4) Rates are those applicable to off-premise sales of 11% a.b.v. non-carbonated wine in 750ml containers; (5) Rates are those applicable to off-premise sales of 4.7% a.b.v. beer in 12 ounce containers; (s) 10% excise tax (retail price)
Source: Tax Foundation, 2025 Facts & Figures: How Does Your State Compare?

State Tax Competitiveness Index

State	Overall Rank	Corporate Tax Rank	Individual Income Tax Rank	Sales Tax Rank	Property Tax Rank	Unemployment Insurance Tax Rank
Ohio	35	45	25	43	6	14

Note: The Tax Foundation's State Tax Competitiveness Index enables policymakers, taxpayers, and business leaders to gauge how their states' tax systems compare. A rank of 1 is best, 50 is worst. Rankings do not average to the total. States without a tax rank equally as 1. DC's scores and rankings do not affect other states. The report shows tax systems as of July 1, 2024 (the beginning of Fiscal Year 2025).
Source: Tax Foundation, State Tax Competitiveness Index 2025

TRANSPORTATION

Means of Transportation to Work

Area	Car/Truck/Van Drove Alone	Car/Truck/Van Carpooled	Public Transportation Bus	Public Transportation Subway	Public Transportation Railroad	Bicycle	Walked	Other Means	Worked at Home
City	65.4	10.0	6.3	0.4	0.0	0.5	5.3	1.9	10.1
MSA[1]	74.3	7.4	1.9	0.1	0.0	0.2	2.1	1.3	12.6
U.S.	70.2	8.5	1.7	1.3	0.4	0.2	2.4	1.6	13.5

Note: Figures are percentages and cover workers 16 years of age and older; (1) Figures cover the Cleveland, OH Metropolitan Statistical Area
Source: U.S. Census Bureau, 2019-2023 American Community Survey 5-Year Estimates

Travel Time to Work

Area	Less Than 10 Minutes	10 to 19 Minutes	20 to 29 Minutes	30 to 44 Minutes	45 to 59 Minutes	60 to 89 Minutes	90 Minutes or More
City	10.5	35.0	27.3	19.4	3.3	2.6	1.9
MSA[1]	12.0	28.7	25.7	22.7	6.4	2.8	1.7
U.S.	12.6	28.6	21.2	20.8	8.1	6.0	2.8

Note: Note: Figures are percentages and include workers 16 years old and over; (1) Figures cover the Cleveland, OH Metropolitan Statistical Area
Source: U.S. Census Bureau, 2019-2023 American Community Survey 5-Year Estimates

Key Congestion Measures

Measure	2000	2010	2015	2020	2022
Annual Hours of Delay, Total (000)	37,731	43,033	49,262	33,300	51,997
Annual Hours of Delay, Per Auto Commuter	35	39	44	29	48
Annual Congestion Cost, Per Auto Commuter ($)	1,130	1,024	1,082	767	1,125

Note: Figures cover the Cleveland OH urban area
Source: Texas A&M Transportation Institute, 2023 Urban Mobility Report

Freeway Travel Time Index

Measure	1985	1990	1995	2000	2005	2010	2015	2020	2022
Urban Area Index[1]	1.04	1.08	1.14	1.14	1.14	1.14	1.15	1.08	1.13
Urban Area Rank[1,2]	81	62	41	62	73	71	67	44	71

Note: Freeway Travel Time Index—the ratio of travel time in the peak period to the travel time at free-flow conditions. For example, a value of 1.30 indicates a 20-minute free-flow trip takes 26 minutes in the peak (20 minutes x 1.30 = 26 minutes); (1) Covers the Cleveland OH urban area; (2) Rank is based on 101 larger urban areas (#1 = highest travel time index)
Source: Texas A&M Transportation Institute, 2023 Urban Mobility Report

Public Transportation

Agency Name / Mode of Transportation	Vehicles Operated in Maximum Service[1]	Annual Unlinked Passenger Trips[2] (in thous.)	Annual Passenger Miles[3] (in thous.)
The Greater Cleveland Regional Transit Authority (GCRTA)			
Bus (directly operated)	220	15,963.5	64,887.3
Bus Rapid Transit (directly operated)	7	1,714.1	4,782.2
Demand Response (directly operated)	59	303.0	2,617.3
Demand Response (purchased transportation)	70	300.4	2,642.2
Heavy Rail (directly operated)	16	3,472.3	24,757.8
Light Rail (directly operated)	8	662.1	3,151.8

Note: (1) Number of revenue vehicles operated by the given mode and type of service to meet the annual maximum service requirement. This is the revenue vehicle count during the peak season of the year; on the week and day that maximum service is provided. Vehicles operated in maximum service (VOMS) exclude atypical days and one-time special events; (2) Number of passengers who boarded public transportation vehicles. Passengers are counted each time they board a vehicle no matter how many vehicles they use to travel from their origin to their destination. (3) Sum of the distances ridden by all passengers during the entire fiscal year.
Source: Federal Transit Administration, National Transit Database, 2023

Air Transportation

Airport Name and Code / Type of Service	Passenger Airlines[1]	Passenger Enplanements	Freight Carriers[2]	Freight (lbs)
Cleveland-Hopkins International (CLE)				
Domestic service (U.S. carriers only)	27	4,830,320	13	77,065,875
International service (U.S. carriers only)	5	66,105	1	22,842

Note: (1) Includes all U.S.-based major, minor and commuter airlines that carried at least one passenger during the year; (2) Includes all U.S.-based airlines and freight carriers that transported at least one pound of freight during the year.
Source: Bureau of Transportation Statistics, The Intermodal Transportation Database, Air Carriers: T-100 Domestic Market (U.S. carriers only), 2024; Bureau of Transportation Statistics, The Intermodal Transportation Database, Air Carriers: T-100 International Market (U.S. carriers only), 2024

BUSINESSES

Major Business Headquarters

Company Name	Industry	Rankings	
		Fortune[1]	Forbes[2]
Cleveland-Cliffs	Metals	185	-
Jones Day	Services	-	225
KeyCorp	Commercial banks	386	-
Parker-Hannifin	Industrial machinery	216	-
Sherwin-Williams	Chemicals	176	-

Note: (1) Companies that produce a 10-K are ranked 1 to 500 based on 2023 revenue; (2) All private companies with at least $2 billion in annual revenue through the end of their most current fiscal year are ranked 1 to 275; companies listed are headquartered in the city; dashes indicate no ranking
Source: Fortune, "Fortune 500," 2024; Forbes, "America's Largest Private Companies," 2024

Fastest-Growing Businesses

According to *Initiative for a Competitive Inner City (ICIC)*, Cleveland is home to two of America's 100 fastest-growing "inner city" companies: **Muse Content Group** (#64); **Redmond Waltz Electric** (#91). To be eligible for the IC100, companies have to be independently operated, privately held, for-profit businesses with revenues of at least $50,000 in 2019 and $500,000 in 2023, and headquartered in an under-resourced community. Recognizing that concentrated poverty exists within metropolitan areas outside of big cities (and that poverty overall is suburbanizing), ICIC defines under-resourced communities as large low-income, high-poverty areas located in the urban and suburban parts of all but the smallest metropolitan areas. Companies were ranked overall by revenue growth over the five-year period between 2019 and 2023. *Initiative for a Competitive Inner City (ICIC), "Inner City 100 Companies," 2024*

Living Environment

COST OF LIVING

Cost of Living Index

Composite Index	Groceries	Housing	Utilities	Transportation	Health Care	Misc. Goods/Services
91.4	99.8	81.2	85.5	96.7	92.2	96.1

Note: The Cost of Living Index measures regional differences in the cost of consumer goods and services, excluding taxes and non-consumer expenditures, for professional and managerial households in the top income quintile. It is based on more than 50,000 prices covering almost 60 different items for which prices are collected three times a year by chambers of commerce, economic development organizations or university applied economic centers in each participating urban area. The numbers shown should be read as a percentage above or below the national average of 100. For example, a value of 115.4 in the groceries column indicates that grocery prices are 15.4% higher than the national average. Small differences in the index numbers should not be interpreted as significant; Figures cover the Cleveland OH urban area.
Source: The Council for Community and Economic Research, Cost of Living Index, 2024

Grocery Prices

Area[1]	T-Bone Steak ($/pound)	Frying Chicken ($/pound)	Whole Milk ($/half gal.)	Eggs ($/dozen)	Orange Juice ($/64 oz.)	Coffee ($/11.5 oz.)
City[2]	15.51	1.42	4.58	3.24	4.44	5.24
Avg.	15.42	1.55	4.69	3.25	4.41	5.46
Min.	14.50	1.16	4.43	2.75	4.00	4.85
Max.	17.56	2.89	5.49	4.78	5.54	7.89

Note: (1) Values for the local area are compared with the average, minimum and maximum values for all 276 areas in the Cost of Living Index; (2) Figures cover the Cleveland OH urban area; **T-Bone Steak** (price per pound); **Frying Chicken** (price per pound, whole fryer); **Whole Milk** (half gallon carton); **Eggs** (price per dozen, Grade A, large); **Orange Juice** (64 oz. Tropicana or Florida Natural); **Coffee** (11.5 oz. can, vacuum-packed, Maxwell House, Hills Bros, or Folgers).
Source: The Council for Community and Economic Research, Cost of Living Index, 2024

Housing and Utility Costs

Area[1]	New Home Price ($)	Apartment Rent ($/month)	All Electric ($/month)	Part Electric ($/month)	Other Energy ($/month)	Telephone ($/month)
City[2]	391,639	1,431	-	83.27	78.55	189.85
Avg.	515,975	1,550	210.99	123.07	82.07	194.99
Min.	265,375	692	104.33	53.68	36.26	179.42
Max.	2,775,821	5,719	529.02	397.28	361.63	223.33

Note: (1) Values for the local area are compared with the average, minimum and maximum values for all 276 areas in the Cost of Living Index; (2) Figures cover the Cleveland OH urban area; **New Home Price** (2,400 sf living area, 8,000 sf lot, in urban area with full utilities); **Apartment Rent** (950 sf 2 bedroom/1.5 or 2 bath, unfurnished, excluding all utilities except water); **All Electric** (average monthly cost for an all-electric home); **Part Electric** (average monthly cost for a part-electric home); **Other Energy** (average monthly cost for natural gas, fuel oil, coal, wood, and any other forms of energy except electricity); **Telephone** (price includes the base monthly rate plus taxes and fees for three lines of mobile phone service).
Source: The Council for Community and Economic Research, Cost of Living Index, 2024

Health Care, Transportation, and Other Costs

Area[1]	Doctor ($/visit)	Dentist ($/visit)	Optometrist ($/visit)	Gasoline ($/gallon)	Beauty Salon ($/visit)	Men's Shirt ($)
City[2]	117.00	111.33	110.47	3.21	40.20	39.79
Avg.	143.77	117.51	129.23	3.32	48.57	38.14
Min.	36.74	58.67	67.33	2.80	24.00	13.41
Max.	270.44	216.82	307.33	5.28	94.00	63.89

Note: (1) Values for the local area are compared with the average, minimum and maximum values for all 276 areas in the Cost of Living Index; (2) Figures cover the Cleveland OH urban area; **Doctor** (general practitioners routine exam of an established patient); **Dentist** (adult teeth cleaning and periodic oral examination); **Optometrist** (full vision eye exam for established adult patient); **Gasoline** (one gallon regular unleaded, national brand, including all taxes, cash price at self-service pump if available); **Beauty Salon** (woman's shampoo, trim, and blow-dry); **Men's Shirt** (cotton/polyester dress shirt, pinpoint weave, long sleeves).
Source: The Council for Community and Economic Research, Cost of Living Index, 2024

HOUSING

Homeownership Rate

Area	2017 (%)	2018 (%)	2019 (%)	2020 (%)	2021 (%)	2022 (%)	2023 (%)	2024 (%)
MSA[1]	66.6	66.7	64.4	66.3	64.7	63.0	63.1	65.6
U.S.	63.9	64.4	64.6	66.6	65.5	65.8	65.9	65.6

Note: (1) Figures cover the Cleveland, OH Metropolitan Statistical Area
Source: U.S. Census Bureau, Housing Vacancies and Homeownership Annual Statistics: 2017-2024

House Price Index (HPI)

Area	National Ranking[2]	Quarterly Change (%)	One-Year Change (%)	Five-Year Change (%)	Since 1991Q1 (%)
MSA[1]	71	0.34	6.77	57.08	194.72
U.S.[3]	—	1.43	4.51	57.13	327.82

Note: The HPI is a weighted repeat sales index. It measures average price changes in repeat sales or refinancings on the same properties. This information is obtained by reviewing repeat mortgage transactions on single-family properties whose mortgages have been purchased or securitized by Fannie Mae or Freddie Mac since January 1975; (1) Figures cover the Cleveland, OH Metropolitan Statistical Area; (2) Rankings are based on annual percentage change for all metro areas containing at least 15,000 transactions over the last 10 years and ranges from 1 to 241; (3) figures based on a weighted average of Census Division estimates using a seasonally adjusted, purchase-only index; all figures are for the period ending December 31, 2024
Source: Federal Housing Finance Agency, Change in FHFA Metropolitan Area House Price Indexes, All Transactions Index, 2024Q4

Home Value

Area	Under $100,000	$100,000 -$199,999	$200,000 -$299,999	$300,000 -$399,999	$400,000 -$499,999	$500,000 -$999,999	$1,000,000 or more	Median ($)
City	53.4	31.8	8.1	3.0	1.6	1.7	0.5	94,100
MSA[1]	16.6	33.1	23.9	12.6	6.4	6.4	1.0	201,000
U.S.	12.1	17.8	19.5	14.4	10.5	19.1	6.5	303,400

Note: Figures are percentages except for median and cover owner-occupied housing units; (1) Figures cover the Cleveland, OH Metropolitan Statistical Area
Source: U.S. Census Bureau, 2019-2023 American Community Survey 5-Year Estimates

Year Housing Structure Built

Area	2020 or Later	2010 -2019	2000 -2009	1990 -1999	1980 -1989	1970 -1979	1960 -1969	1950 -1959	1940 -1949	Before 1940	Median Year
City	0.6	3.8	3.8	2.9	3.0	5.6	7.8	12.1	10.8	49.6	1940
MSA[1]	0.5	4.0	7.0	8.8	7.1	12.5	13.3	17.0	7.3	22.6	1962
U.S.	1.2	8.9	13.6	12.8	13.0	14.4	10.0	9.7	4.5	11.9	1980

Note: Figures are percentages except for Median Year; Note: (1) Figures cover the Cleveland, OH Metropolitan Statistical Area
Source: U.S. Census Bureau, 2019-2023 American Community Survey 5-Year Estimates

Gross Monthly Rent

Area	Under $500	$500 -$999	$1,000 -$1,499	$1,500 -$1,999	$2,000 -$2,499	$2,500 -$2,999	$3,000 and up	Median ($)
City	17.2	43.0	26.0	9.4	2.6	0.9	0.8	894
MSA[1]	9.8	40.6	34.0	10.8	2.6	0.9	1.3	996
U.S.	6.5	22.3	29.5	20.2	10.8	4.8	5.9	1,348

Note: Figures are percentages except for median; Gross rent is the contract rent plus the estimated average monthly cost of utilities (electricity, gas, and water and sewer) and fuels (oil, coal, kerosene, wood, etc.) if these are paid by the renter (or paid for the renter by someone else); (1) Figures cover the Cleveland, OH Metropolitan Statistical Area
Source: U.S. Census Bureau, 2019-2023 American Community Survey 5-Year Estimates

HEALTH

Health Risk Factors

Category	MSA[1] (%)	U.S. (%)
Adults aged 18–64 who have any kind of health care coverage	93.3	90.8
Adults who reported being in good or better health	80.6	81.8
Adults who have been told they have high blood cholesterol	39.5	36.9
Adults who have been told they have high blood pressure	37.3	34.0
Adults who are current smokers	13.1	12.1
Adults who currently use e-cigarettes	5.4	7.7
Adults who currently use chewing tobacco, snuff, or snus	2.6	3.2
Adults who are heavy drinkers[2]	7.8	6.1
Adults who are binge drinkers[3]	17.7	15.2
Adults who are overweight (BMI 25.0 - 29.9)	32.8	34.4
Adults who are obese (BMI 30.0 - 99.8)	34.1	34.3
Adults who participated in any physical activities in the past month	76.1	75.8

Note: All figures are crude prevalence; (1) Figures cover the Cleveland, OH Metropolitan Statistical Area; (2) Heavy drinkers are classified as adult men having more than 14 drinks per week and adult women having more than 7 drinks per week; (3) Binge drinkers are classified as males having five or more drinks on one occasion or females having four or more drinks on one occasion
Source: Centers for Disease Control and Prevention, Behavioral Risk Factor Surveillance System, SMART: Selected Metropolitan Area Risk Trends, 2023

Acute and Chronic Health Conditions

Category	MSA[1] (%)	U.S. (%)
Adults who have ever been told they had a heart attack	3.9	4.2
Adults who have ever been told they have angina or coronary heart disease	3.4	4.0
Adults who have ever been told they had a stroke	3.3	3.3
Adults who have ever been told they have asthma	17.7	15.7
Adults who have ever been told they have arthritis	29.4	26.3
Adults who have ever been told they have diabetes[2]	12.2	11.5
Adults who have ever been told they had skin cancer	4.3	5.6
Adults who have ever been told they had any other types of cancer	9.1	8.4
Adults who have ever been told they have COPD	6.7	6.4
Adults who have ever been told they have kidney disease	5.2	3.7
Adults who have ever been told they have a form of depression	24.3	22.0

Note: All figures are crude prevalence; (1) Figures cover the Cleveland, OH Metropolitan Statistical Area; (2) Figures do not include pregnancy-related, borderline, or pre-diabetes
Source: Centers for Disease Control and Prevention, Behavioral Risk Factor Surveillance System, SMART: Selected Metropolitan Area Risk Trends, 2023

Health Screening and Vaccination Rates

Category	MSA[1] (%)	U.S. (%)
Adults who have ever been tested for HIV	40.2	37.5
Adults who have had their blood cholesterol checked within the last five years	87.9	87.0
Adults aged 65+ who have had flu shot within the past year	69.4	63.4
Adults aged 65+ who have ever had a pneumonia vaccination	76.2	71.9

Note: All figures are crude prevalence; (1) Figures cover the Cleveland, OH Metropolitan Statistical Area.
Source: Centers for Disease Control and Prevention, Behavioral Risk Factor Surveillance System, SMART: Selected Metropolitan Area Risk Trends, 2023

Disability Status

Category	MSA[1] (%)	U.S. (%)
Adults who reported being deaf	5.9	7.4
Are you blind or have serious difficulty seeing, even when wearing glasses?	4.1	4.9
Do you have difficulty doing errands alone?	8.7	7.8
Do you have difficulty dressing or bathing?	3.1	3.6
Do you have serious difficulty concentrating/remembering/making decisions?	11.9	13.7
Do you have serious difficulty walking or climbing stairs?	13.8	13.2

Note: All figures are crude prevalence; (1) Figures cover the Cleveland, OH Metropolitan Statistical Area.
Source: Centers for Disease Control and Prevention, Behavioral Risk Factor Surveillance System, SMART: Selected Metropolitan Area Risk Trends, 2023

Mortality Rates for the Top 10 Causes of Death in the U.S.

ICD-10[a] Sub-Chapter	ICD-10[a] Code	Crude Mortality Rate[2] per 100,000 population	
		County[3]	U.S.
Malignant neoplasms	C00-C97	218.6	182.7
Ischaemic heart diseases	I20-I25	141.0	109.6
Provisional assignment of new diseases of uncertain etiology[1]	U00-U49	75.9	65.3
Other forms of heart disease	I30-I51	102.7	65.1
Other degenerative diseases of the nervous system	G30-G31	42.1	52.4
Other external causes of accidental injury	W00-X59	73.2	52.3
Cerebrovascular diseases	I60-I69	59.0	49.1
Chronic lower respiratory diseases	J40-J47	44.9	43.5
Hypertensive diseases	I10-I15	41.7	38.9
Organic, including symptomatic, mental disorders	F01-F09	58.5	33.9

Note: (a) ICD-10 = International Classification of Diseases 10th Revision; (1) Includes COVID-19, adverse effects to COVID-19 vaccines, SARS, and vaping-related disorders; (2) Crude mortality rates are a three-year average covering 2021-2023; (3) Figures cover Cuyahoga County.
Source: Centers for Disease Control and Prevention, National Center for Health Statistics. National Vital Statistics System, Mortality 2018-2023 on CDC WONDER Online Database

Mortality Rates for Selected Causes of Death

Cause of Death	ICD-10[a] Code	Crude Mortality Rate[1] per 100,000 population	
		County[2]	U.S.
Accidental poisoning and exposure to noxious substances	X40-X49	47.0	30.5
Alzheimer disease	G30	30.1	35.4
Assault	X85-Y09	18.3	7.3
COVID-19	U07.1	75.9	65.3
Diabetes mellitus	E10-E14	31.6	30.0
Diseases of the liver	K70-K76	21.9	20.8
Human immunodeficiency virus (HIV) disease	B20-B24	1.6	1.5
Influenza and pneumonia	J09-J18	13.1	13.4
Intentional self-harm	X60-X84	14.3	14.7
Malnutrition	E40-E46	5.4	6.0
Obesity and other hyperalimentation	E65-E68	2.7	3.1
Renal failure	N17-N19	25.4	16.4
Transport accidents	V01-V99	9.9	14.4

Note: (a) ICD-10 = International Classification of Diseases 10th Revision; (1) Crude mortality rates are a three-year average covering 2021-2023; (2) Figures cover Cuyahoga County; Data are suppressed when the data meet the criteria for confidentiality constraints; Crude mortality rates are flagged as unreliable when the rate would be calculated with a numerator of 20 or less.
Source: Centers for Disease Control and Prevention, National Center for Health Statistics. National Vital Statistics System, Mortality 2018-2023 on CDC WONDER Online Database

Health Insurance Coverage

Area	With Health Insurance	With Private Health Insurance	With Public Health Insurance	Without Health Insurance	Population Under Age 19 Without Health Insurance
City	92.3	43.8	57.2	7.7	3.7
MSA[1]	94.4	67.4	40.0	5.6	3.9
U.S.	91.4	67.3	36.3	8.6	5.4

Note: Figures are percentages that cover the civilian noninstitutionalized population; (1) Figures cover the Cleveland, OH Metropolitan Statistical Area
Source: U.S. Census Bureau, 2019-2023 American Community Survey 5-Year Estimates

Number of Medical Professionals

Area	MDs[3]	DOs[3,4]	Dentists	Podiatrists	Chiropractors	Optometrists
County[1] (number)	9,880	915	1,364	232	253	224
County[1] (rate[2])	799.3	74.0	110.6	18.8	20.5	18.2
U.S. (rate[2])	302.5	29.2	74.6	6.4	29.5	18.0

Note: Data as of 2023 unless noted; (1) Data covers Cuyahoga County; (2) Number of medical professionals per 100,000 population; (3) Data as of 2022 and includes all active, non-federal physicians; (4) Doctor of Osteopathic Medicine
Source: U.S. Department of Health and Human Services, Health Resources and Services Administration, Bureau of Health Professions, Area Resource File (ARF) 2023-2024

Best Hospitals

According to *U.S. News,* the Cleveland, OH metro area is home to seven of the best hospitals in the U.S.: **Cleveland Clinic Rehabilitation Hospital** (1 adult specialty); **Cleveland Clinic** (Honor Roll/13 adult specialties and 11 pediatric specialties); **Cole Eye Institute, Cleveland Clinic** (13 adult specialties and 11 pediatric specialties); **MetroHealth Medical Center** (1 adult specialty); **University Hospitals Cleveland Medical Center** (3 adult specialties); **University Hospitals Harrington Heart & Vascular Institute** (3 adult specialties); **University Hospitals Seidman Cancer Center** (3 adult specialties). The hospitals listed were nationally ranked in at least one of 15 adult or 11 pediatric specialties. The number of specialties shown cover the parent hospital. Only 160 U.S. hospitals performed well enough to be nationally ranked in one or more specialties. Twenty hospitals in the U.S. made the Honor Roll. The Best Hospitals Honor Roll takes both the national rankings and the procedure and condition ratings into account. Hospitals received points if they were nationally ranked in one of the 15 adult specialties—the higher they ranked, the more points they got—and how many ratings of "high performing" they earned in the 20 procedures and conditions. *U.S. News Online,* "America's Best Hospitals 2024-25"

According to *U.S. News,* the Cleveland, OH metro area is home to two of the best children's hospitals in the U.S.: **Cleveland Clinic Children's Hospital** (11 pediatric specialties); **Rainbow Babies and Children's Hospital** (11 pediatric specialties). The hospitals listed were highly ranked in at least one of 11 pediatric specialties. One hundred five children's hospitals in the U.S. were nationally ranked in at least one specialty. Hospitals received points for being ranked in a specialty, and the 10 hospitals with the most points across the 11 specialties make up the Honor Roll. *U.S. News Online,* "America's Best Children's Hospitals 2024-25"

EDUCATION

Public School District Statistics

District Name	Schls	Pupils	Pupil/Teacher Ratio	Minority Pupils[1] (%)	Total Rev. per Pupil ($)	Total Exp. per Pupil ($)
Cleveland Municipal	93	33,841	15.9	86.4	25,680	24,085
Ohio Connections Academy Inc	1	5,305	39.2	30.8	8,147	8,622
Orange City	4	2,019	14.3	30.7	31,627	29,285

Note: Table includes school districts with 2,000 or more students; (1) Percentage of students that are not non-Hispanic white.
Source: U.S. Department of Education, National Center for Education Statistics, Common Core of Data, Local Education Agency (School District) Universe Survey: School Year 2023-2024; U.S. Department of Education, National Center for Education Statistics, Common Core of Data, School District Finance Survey (F-33): School Year 2021–22

Highest Level of Education

Area	Less than H.S.	H.S. Diploma	Some College, No Deg.	Associate Degree	Bachelor's Degree	Master's Degree	Prof. School Degree	Doctorate Degree
City	16.5	33.5	21.6	7.1	12.5	5.8	2.2	0.9
MSA[1]	8.3	29.0	20.4	8.8	20.0	9.6	2.5	1.4
U.S.	10.6	26.2	19.4	8.8	21.3	9.8	2.3	1.6

Note: Figures cover persons age 25 and over; (1) Figures cover the Cleveland, OH Metropolitan Statistical Area
Source: U.S. Census Bureau, 2019-2023 American Community Survey 5-Year Estimates

Educational Attainment by Race

Area	High School Graduate or Higher (%)					Bachelor's Degree or Higher (%)				
	Total	White	Black	Asian	Hisp.[2]	Total	White	Black	Asian	Hisp.[2]
City	83.5	87.5	82.3	78.8	70.9	21.3	31.8	12.7	55.6	10.6
MSA[1]	91.7	93.6	87.0	87.8	78.0	33.4	36.9	18.3	63.6	19.0
U.S.	89.4	92.9	88.1	88.0	72.5	35.0	37.7	24.7	57.0	19.9

Note: Figures shown cover persons 25 years old and over; (1) Figures cover the Cleveland, OH Metropolitan Statistical Area; (2) People of Hispanic origin can be of any race
Source: U.S. Census Bureau, 2019-2023 American Community Survey 5-Year Estimates

School Enrollment by Grade and Control

Area	Preschool (%)		Kindergarten (%)		Grades 1 - 4 (%)		Grades 5 - 8 (%)		Grades 9 - 12 (%)	
	Public	Private	Public	Private	Public	Private	Public	Private	Public	Private
City	68.9	31.1	68.7	31.3	78.2	21.8	77.9	22.1	77.6	22.4
MSA[1]	53.0	47.0	75.5	24.5	80.6	19.4	80.7	19.3	82.4	17.6
U.S.	58.7	41.3	85.2	14.8	87.2	12.8	87.9	12.1	89.0	11.0

Note: Figures shown cover persons 3 years old and over; (1) Figures cover the Cleveland, OH Metropolitan Statistical Area
Source: U.S. Census Bureau, 2019-2023 American Community Survey 5-Year Estimates

Higher Education

Four-Year Colleges			Two-Year Colleges			Medical Schools[1]	Law Schools[2]	Voc/Tech[3]
Public	Private Non-profit	Private For-profit	Public	Private Non-profit	Private For-profit			
4	12	2	2	2	10	1	2	13

Note: Figures cover institutions located within the Cleveland, OH Metropolitan Statistical Area and include main campuses only; (1) includes schools accredited by the Liaison Committee on Medical Education and the American Osteopathic Association's Commission on Osteopathic College Accreditation; (2) includes ABA-accredited schools, schools with provisional ABA accreditation, and state accredited schools; (3) includes all schools with programs that are less than 2 years.
Source: National Center for Education Statistics, Integrated Postsecondary Education System (IPEDS), 2023-24; Wikipedia, List of Medical Schools in the United States, accessed May 2, 2025; Wikipedia, List of Law Schools in the United States, accessed May 2, 2025

According to *U.S. News & World Report,* the Cleveland, OH metro area is home to one of the top 200 national universities in the U.S.: **Case Western Reserve University** (#51 tie). The indicators used to capture academic quality fall into a number of categories: assessment by administrators at peer institutions; retention of students; faculty resources; student selectivity; financial resources; alumni giving; high school counselor ratings of colleges; and graduation rate. *U.S. News & World Report,* "America's Best Colleges 2025"

According to *U.S. News & World Report,* the Cleveland, OH metro area is home to one of the top 100 liberal arts colleges in the U.S.: **Oberlin College** (#55 tie). The indicators used to capture academic quality fall into a number of categories: assessment by administrators at peer institutions; retention of students; faculty resources; student selectivity; financial resources; alumni giving; high school counselor ratings of colleges; and graduation rate. *U.S. News & World Report,* "America's Best Colleges 2025"

According to *U.S. News & World Report*, the Cleveland, OH metro area is home to one of the top medical schools for research in the U.S.: **Case Western Reserve University** (Tier 1). *U.S. News* placed medical and osteopathic schools into tiers based on their research productivity, faculty and admissions data. Each school's tier was derived from its overall score, calculated by summing the weighted normalized values generated across several factors of academic quality, outlined below. There are four tiers, with tier 1 medical schools as the highest-performing and tier 4 as the lowest-performing. Only tier 1 and 2 schools are shown. Because of the tier presentation, *U.S. News* calculated overall scores based on their percentile performance among all rated schools instead of dividing against the rescaled score of the No. 1-performing schools. Tier 1 included schools with overall scores of 85 to 99. The cutoffs for tiers 2 through 4 were schools scoring 50 to 84, 15 to 49 and 1 to 14, respectively. The rankings are based on a weighted average of the following measures of quality: total research activity; average research activity per faculty member; total NIH research grants at the medical school and its affiliated hospitals; average NIH research grants per faculty; median MCAT total score; median undergraduate GPA; acceptance rate; and faculty resources. *U.S. News & World Report, "America's Best Graduate Schools, Medical, 2025"*

EMPLOYERS

Major Employers

Company Name	Industry
Case Western Reserve University	Educational services
City of Cleveland	Municipal government
Cleveland Clinic	Healthcare
Cleveland Metropolitan School District	Educational services
Cuyahoga County	Government
KeyCorp	Finance
Metro Health System	Healthcare
Sherwin-Williams Co.	Retail
U.S. Office of Personnel Management	Government
University Hospitals	Healthcare

Note: Companies shown are located within the Cleveland, OH Metropolitan Statistical Area.
Source: Chambers of Commerce; State Departments of Labor; Wikipedia

Best Companies to Work For

Cleveland Clinic; The Center for Health Affairs, headquartered in Cleveland, are among "Best Workplaces in Health Care." To determine the Best Workplaces in Health Care list, Great Place To Work analyzed the survey responses of over 185,000 employees from Great Place To Work-Certified companies in the health care industry. Survey data analysis and company-provided datapoints are then factored into a combined score to compare and rank the companies that create the most consistently positive experience for all employees in this industry. *Fortune, "Best Workplaces in Health Care," 2024*

PUBLIC SAFETY

Crime Rate

Area	Total Crime Rate	Violent Crime Rate				Property Crime Rate		
		Murder	Rape	Robbery	Aggrav. Assault	Burglary	Larceny-Theft	Motor Vehicle Theft
City	6,515.8	38.8	119.5	448.1	1,096.8	894.3	2,475.2	1,443.0
U.S.	2,290.9	5.7	38.0	66.5	264.1	250.7	1,347.2	318.7

Note: Figures are crimes per 100,000 population.
Source: FBI, Table 8, Offenses Known to Law Enforcement, by State by City, 2023

Hate Crimes

Area	Number of Quarters Reported	Number of Incidents per Bias Motivation					
		Race/Ethnicity/Ancestry	Religion	Sexual Orientation	Disability	Gender	Gender Identity
City[1]	4	32	5	3	1	2	13
U.S.	4	5,900	2,699	2,077	187	92	492

Note: (1) Figures include at least one incident reported with more than one bias motivation.
Source: Federal Bureau of Investigation, Hate Crime Statistics 2023

Identity Theft Consumer Reports

Area	Reports	Reports per 100,000 Population	Rank[2]
MSA[1]	7,115	328	50
U.S.	1,135,291	339	-

Note: (1) Figures cover the Cleveland, OH Metropolitan Statistical Area; (2) Rank ranges from 1 to 401 where 1 indicates greatest number of identity theft reports per 100,000 population
Source: Federal Trade Commission, Consumer Sentinel Network Data Book 2024

Fraud and Other Consumer Reports

Area	Reports	Reports per 100,000 Population	Rank[2]
MSA[1]	31,336	1,443	67
U.S.	5,360,641	1,601	-

Note: (1) Figures cover the Cleveland, OH Metropolitan Statistical Area; (2) Rank ranges from 1 to 401 where 1 indicates greatest number of fraud and other consumer reports per 100,000 population
Source: Federal Trade Commission, Consumer Sentinel Network Data Book 2024

POLITICS

2024 Presidential Election Results

Area	Trump (Rep.)	Harris (Dem.)	Stein (Green)	Kennedy (Ind.)	Oliver (Lib.)	Other
Cuyahoga County	33.6	64.7	0.5	0.0	0.4	0.8
U.S.	49.7	48.2	0.6	0.5	0.4	0.6

Note: Results are percentages and may not add to 100% due to rounding
Source: Dave Leip's Atlas of U.S. Presidential Elections

SPORTS

Professional Sports Teams

Team Name	League	Year Established

No teams are located in the metro area
Source: Wikipedia, Major Professional Sports Teams of the United States and Canada, May 1, 2025

CLIMATE

Average and Extreme Temperatures

Temperature	Jan	Feb	Mar	Apr	May	Jun	Jul	Aug	Sep	Oct	Nov	Dec	Yr.
Extreme High (°F)	73	69	82	88	92	104	100	102	101	89	82	77	104
Average High (°F)	33	36	46	58	69	79	83	81	74	63	50	38	59
Average Temp. (°F)	26	28	37	49	59	68	73	71	64	54	43	31	50
Average Low (°F)	19	20	28	38	48	58	62	61	54	44	35	24	41
Extreme Low (°F)	-19	-15	-5	10	25	31	41	38	34	19	3	-15	-19

Note: Figures cover the years 1948-1990
Source: National Climatic Data Center, International Station Meteorological Climate Summary, 9/96

Average Precipitation/Snowfall/Humidity

Precip./Humidity	Jan	Feb	Mar	Apr	May	Jun	Jul	Aug	Sep	Oct	Nov	Dec	Yr.
Avg. Precip. (in.)	2.4	2.3	3.1	3.4	3.5	3.5	3.5	3.4	3.2	2.6	3.2	2.9	37.1
Avg. Snowfall (in.)	13	12	10	2	Tr	0	0	0	0	1	5	12	55
Avg. Rel. Hum. 7am (%)	79	79	78	76	77	78	81	85	84	81	78	78	79
Avg. Rel. Hum. 4pm (%)	70	67	62	56	54	55	55	58	58	58	65	70	61

Note: Figures cover the years 1948-1990; Tr = Trace amounts (<0.05 in. of rain; <0.5 in. of snow)
Source: National Climatic Data Center, International Station Meteorological Climate Summary, 9/96

Weather Conditions

Temperature			Daytime Sky			Precipitation		
5°F & below	32°F & below	90°F & above	Clear	Partly cloudy	Cloudy	0.01 inch or more precip.	0.1 inch or more snow/ice	Thunderstorms
11	123	12	63	127	175	157	48	34

Note: Figures are average number of days per year and cover the years 1948-1990
Source: National Climatic Data Center, International Station Meteorological Climate Summary, 9/96

HAZARDOUS WASTE

Superfund Sites

The Cleveland, OH metro area is home to six sites on the EPA's Superfund National Priorities List (NPL) or Superfund Alternative Approach (SAA) list: **Big D Campground** (Final NPL); **Chemical Recovery Systems** (SAA); **Fields Brook** (Final NPL); **Ford Rd Ind Ldfl** (SAA); **New Lyme Landfill** (Final NPL); **Old Mill** (Final NPL). The Superfund alternative approach uses the same investigation and cleanup process and standards that are used for sites listed on the National Priorities List. The SAA is an alternative to listing a site on the NPL; it is not an alternative to Superfund or the Superfund process. There are a total of 1,445 Superfund sites with a status of proposed or final on both lists in the United States. *U.S. Environmental Protection Agency, National Priorities List, May 1, 2025; U.S. Environmental Protection Agency, Superfund Alternative Approach Sites, May 1, 2025*

AIR QUALITY

Air Quality Trends: Ozone

	1990	1995	2000	2005	2010	2015	2020	2021	2022	2023
MSA[1]	0.084	0.090	0.079	0.084	0.074	0.069	0.069	0.066	0.068	0.071
U.S.	0.087	0.089	0.081	0.080	0.072	0.068	0.066	0.067	0.067	0.070

Note: (1) Data covers the Cleveland, OH Metropolitan Statistical Area. The values shown are the composite ozone concentration averages among trend sites based on the highest fourth daily maximum 8-hour concentration in parts per million. These trends are based on sites having an adequate record of monitoring data during the trend period. Data from exceptional events are included.
Source: U.S. Environmental Protection Agency, Air Quality Monitoring Information, "Air Quality Trends by City, 1990-2023"

Air Quality Index

Area	Percent of Days when Air Quality was...[2]					AQI Statistics[2]	
	Good	Moderate	Unhealthy for Sensitive Groups	Unhealthy	Very Unhealthy	Maximum	Median
MSA[1]	31.5	64.1	3.0	1.1	0.3	285	57

Note: (1) Data covers the Cleveland, OH Metropolitan Statistical Area; (2) Based on 365 days with AQI data in 2023. Air Quality Index (AQI) is an index for reporting daily air quality. EPA calculates the AQI for five major air pollutants regulated by the Clean Air Act: ground-level ozone, particle pollution (aka particulate matter), carbon monoxide, sulfur dioxide, and nitrogen dioxide. The AQI runs from 0 to 500. The higher the AQI value, the greater the level of air pollution and the greater the health concern. There are six AQI categories: "Good" AQI is between 0 and 50. Air quality is considered satisfactory; "Moderate" AQI is between 51 and 100. Air quality is acceptable; "Unhealthy for Sensitive Groups" When AQI values are between 101 and 150, members of sensitive groups may experience health effects; "Unhealthy" When AQI values are between 151 and 200 everyone may begin to experience health effects; "Very Unhealthy" AQI values between 201 and 300 trigger a health alert; "Hazardous" AQI values over 300 trigger warnings of emergency conditions (not shown).
Source: U.S. Environmental Protection Agency, Air Quality Index Report, 2023

Air Quality Index Pollutants

Area	Percent of Days when AQI Pollutant was...[2]					
	Carbon Monoxide	Nitrogen Dioxide	Ozone	Sulfur Dioxide	Particulate Matter 2.5	Particulate Matter 10
MSA[1]	0.5	0.0	27.1	(3)	71.2	1.1

Note: (1) Data covers the Cleveland, OH Metropolitan Statistical Area; (2) Based on 365 days with AQI data in 2023. The Air Quality Index (AQI) is an index for reporting daily air quality. EPA calculates the AQI for five major air pollutants regulated by the Clean Air Act: ground-level ozone, particle pollution (also known as particulate matter), carbon monoxide, sulfur dioxide, and nitrogen dioxide. The AQI runs from 0 to 500. The higher the AQI value, the greater the level of air pollution and the greater the health concern; (3) Sulfur dioxide is no longer included in this table because SO_2 concentrations tend to be very localized and not necessarily representative of broad geographical areas like counties and CBSAs.
Source: U.S. Environmental Protection Agency, Air Quality Index Report, 2023

Maximum Air Pollutant Concentrations: Particulate Matter, Ozone, CO and Lead

	Particulate Matter 10 (ug/m^3)	Particulate Matter 2.5 Wtd AM (ug/m^3)	Particulate Matter 2.5 24-Hr (ug/m^3)	Ozone (ppm)	Carbon Monoxide (ppm)	Lead (ug/m^3)
MSA[1] Level	147	12.8	40	0.075	5	0.04
NAAQS[2]	150	15	35	0.075	9	0.15
Met NAAQS[2]	Yes	Yes	No	Yes	Yes	Yes

Note: (1) Data covers the Cleveland, OH Metropolitan Statistical Area; Data from exceptional events are included; (2) National Ambient Air Quality Standards; ppm = parts per million; ug/m^3 = micrograms per cubic meter; n/a not available.
Concentrations: Particulate Matter 10 (coarse particulate)—highest second maximum 24-hour concentration; Particulate Matter 2.5 Wtd AM (fine particulate)—highest weighted annual mean concentration; Particulate Matter 2.5 24-Hour (fine particulate)—highest 98th percentile 24-hour concentration; Ozone—highest fourth daily maximum 8-hour concentration; Carbon Monoxide—highest second maximum non-overlapping 8-hour concentration; Lead—maximum running 3-month average
Source: U.S. Environmental Protection Agency, Air Quality Monitoring Information, "Air Quality Statistics by City, 2023"

Maximum Air Pollutant Concentrations: Nitrogen Dioxide and Sulfur Dioxide

	Nitrogen Dioxide AM (ppb)	Nitrogen Dioxide 1-Hr (ppb)	Sulfur Dioxide AM (ppb)	Sulfur Dioxide 1-Hr (ppb)	Sulfur Dioxide 24-Hr (ppb)
MSA[1] Level	9	44	n/a	27	n/a
NAAQS[2]	53	100	30	75	140
Met NAAQS[2]	Yes	Yes	n/a	Yes	n/a

Note: (1) Data covers the Cleveland, OH Metropolitan Statistical Area; Data from exceptional events are included; (2) National Ambient Air Quality Standards; ppm = parts per million; ug/m^3 = micrograms per cubic meter; n/a not available.
Concentrations: Nitrogen Dioxide AM—highest arithmetic mean concentration; Nitrogen Dioxide 1-Hr—highest 98th percentile 1-hour daily maximum concentration; Sulfur Dioxide AM—highest annual mean concentration; Sulfur Dioxide 1-Hr—highest 99th percentile 1-hour daily maximum concentration; Sulfur Dioxide 24-Hr—highest second maximum 24-hour concentration
Source: U.S. Environmental Protection Agency, Air Quality Monitoring Information, "Air Quality Statistics by City, 2023"

Columbus, Ohio

Background

Columbus is the capital of Ohio, and centrally located in the watershed of the Ohio River. The largest city in the state, it was not the first choice for the capital, but in 1812, residents of Franklinton, a county seat in the heart of Ohio, offered the government 1,200 acres of land and $50,000 to build a capitol building and state penitentiary.

Columbus grew steadily throughout the nineteenth century, its prosperity bolstered by the construction of a feeder link into the Ohio and Erie canals, which connected the town to the Great Lakes system and the Ohio River. By 1834, Columbus had attained a population of about 20,000. The railroad was established in 1850, bringing trade opportunities from the East.

Columbus became a major staging area for Union armies during the Civil War and was also home to Camp Chase, the largest military prison for Rebel soldiers. Both before and after the war, manufacturing in the city developed dramatically, based primarily on agricultural processing and packing, shoes, hardware, and heavy equipment. A specialty of Columbus was the buggy, and the Iron Buggy Company was the largest of its kind in the world.

Ohio State University, originally Ohio Agricultural and Mechanical University (1870), is in Columbus, and other colleges and universities include Franklin University (1902), Capital University (1830), Ohio Dominican University (1911), the Columbus College of Art and Design (1879), and Pontifical College Josephinum (1888). One of the first schools for the blind in the U.S., the Ohio State School for the Blind, was founded in Columbus in 1832.

Cultural resources include the Wexner Center for the Arts of Ohio State University, noted for its innovative architecture, and the Columbus Museum of Art, housing one of the nation's finest collections of 19th and 20th-century paintings. Columbus is also home to a symphony orchestra, and opera and ballet companies. The Columbus Zoo is nationally famous both for its success in the breeding of endangered species and for its large coral reef aquarium. A National Veteran's Memorial and Museum opened in 2018.

Columbus fans support Ohio State University's Buckeye football, a major league soccer team (Columbus Crew), an expansion National Hockey League franchise (Columbus Blue Jackets), and a minor league baseball team (Columbus Clippers). The Clippers played in Cooper Stadium from 1977 to the 2008 season. April 2009 marked the opening of the new ballpark, Huntington Park. Bodybuilding has long played an important role in Columbus sports, and the Arnold Fitness Weekend bodybuilding and fitness competition is an annual event, named for actor/politician Arnold Schwarzenegger.

The largest employers in Columbus are state government and Ohio State University. Other major employers include Nationwide Insurance, and Proctor & Gamble Company. Columbus is a digital city, home to the Online Computer Library Center, CompuServe (a subsidiary of AOL) and the world's largest databases of chemical information. The area's multi-jurisdictional 315 Research + Technology Corridor was designed to achieve national and international recognition like Research Triangle Park in North Carolina.

Columbus has a widespread municipal bus service. New Amtrak routes linking Cincinnati, Cleveland, Columbus, and Dayton are in the planning stages. Through partnership with the Mid-Ohio Regional Planning Commission, the city will add three more rapid transit corridors by 2030, with a total of five by 2050.

Columbus International Airport, built in the 1920s, today serves national and international carriers. Rickenbacker Airport, named for famed Columbus resident Eddie Rickenbacker, World War I ace and airline pioneer, is a major center for air cargo. Columbus has also been home to other famous Americans, most notably Red Barber, beloved sports announcer, and James Thurber, perhaps the nation's most widely read humorist after Mark Twain. In *More Alarms at Night*, Thurber wrote of Columbus: "It's a town in which almost anything is likely to happen, and in which almost everything has."

The city's climate is humid continental transitional with humid subtropical to the south characterized by warm, muggy summers and cold, dry winters. Winter snowfall is relatively light, since the city is not in the typical path of strong winter lows, such as the Nor'easters that strike cities farther east. It is also too far south and west for lake-effect snow from Lake Erie to have much effect, although the lakes to the north contribute to long stretches of cloudy spells in winter. Columbus is subject to severe weather typical to the Midwestern United States. Severe thunderstorms can bring lightning, large hail and on rare occasions tornadoes, especially during the spring and sometimes through fall. Floods, blizzards and ice storms can also occur from time to time.

Rankings

General Rankings

- To help military veterans find the best places in which to settle down, *WalletHub* compared the 100 largest U.S. cities across 19 key indicators of livability, affordability and veteran-friendliness. They range from the share of military skill-related jobs to veteran income growth to the availability of VA health facilities. Columbus ranked #41. *Wallethub.com, "Best & Worst Places for Veterans to Live (2025)," November 7, 2024*

- *Insider* listed 23 places in the U.S. that travel industry trends reveal would be popular destinations in 2023. This year the list trends towards cultural and historical happenings, sports events, wellness experiences and invigorating outdoor escapes. According to the website insider.com Columbus is a place to visit in 2023. *Insider, "23 of the Best Places You Should Travel to in the U.S. in 2023," December 17, 2022*

- For its 37th annual "Readers' Choice Awards" survey, *Condé Nast Traveler* ranked its readers' favorite cities in the U.S. Whether it be a longed-for visit or the next big new thing, these are the places travelers loved best. The list was broken into large cities and cities under 250,000. Columbus ranked #9 in the big city category. *Condé Nast Traveler, Readers' Choice Awards 2024, "Best Big Cities in the U.S." October 1, 2024*

Business/Finance Rankings

- Columbus was cited as one of America's top metros for total corporate facility investment projects in 2024. The area ranked #8 in the Tier 1 (large) metro area category (population over 1 million). *Site Selection, "Top Metros of 2024," March 2025*

- The Columbus metro area appeared on the Milken Institute "2025 Best Performing Cities" list. Rank: #109 out of 200 large metro areas (based on performance category). Criteria: job growth; wage growth; high-tech growth and impact; community resilience; housing affordability; household broadband access. *Milken Institute, "Best-Performing Cities 2025," January 14, 2025*

Education Rankings

- Personal finance website *WalletHub* analyzed the 150 largest U.S. metropolitan statistical areas to determine where the most educated Americans are putting their degrees to work. Criteria: education levels; percentage of workers with degrees; education quality and attainment gap; public school quality rankings; quality and enrollment of each metro area's universities. Columbus was ranked #44 (#1 = most educated city). *WalletHub.com, "Most & Least Educated Cities in America, 2025" July 2, 2024*

Environmental Rankings

- Sperling's *BestPlaces* assessed the 50 largest metropolitan areas of the United States for the likelihood of dangerously extreme weather events or earthquakes. In general the Southeast and South-Central regions have the highest risk of weather extremes and earthquakes, while the Pacific Northwest enjoys the lowest risk. Of the least risky metropolitan areas, the Columbus metro area was ranked #10. *Bestplaces.net, "Avoid Natural Disasters: BestPlaces Reveals The Top 10 Safest Places to Live," October 25, 2017*

Health/Fitness Rankings

- For each of the 100 largest cities in the United States, the American Fitness Index®, compiled in partnership between the American College of Sports Medicine and the Elevance Health Foundation, evaluated community infrastructure and more than 30 health behaviors including preventive health, levels of chronic disease conditions, food insecurity, pedestrian safety, air quality, and community/environment resources that support physical activity. Columbus ranked #66 for "community fitness." *americanfitnessindex.org, "2024 ACSM American Fitness Index Summary Report," July 23, 2024*

- The Columbus metro area was identified as one of the worst cities for bed bugs in America by pest control company Orkin. The area ranked #11 out of 50 based on the number of bed bug treatments Orkin performed from December 2022 to November 2023. *Orkin, "Chicago Joins Paris In Global Bed Bug Spotlight Ranking As The Worst City On Orkin's U.S. Bed Bug Cities List," January 22, 2024*

- Columbus was identified as a "2025 Allergy Capital." The area ranked #48 out of the nation's 100 largest metropolitan areas. Three groups of factors were used to identify the most challenging cities for people with allergies: annual tree, grass, and weed pollen scores; over the counter allergy medicine use; number of board-certified allergy specialists. *Asthma and Allergy Foundation of America, "2025 Allergy Capitals: The Most Challenging Places to Live with Allergies," March 18, 2025*

- Columbus was identified as a "2024 Asthma Capital." The area ranked #20 out of the nation's 100 largest metropolitan areas. Criteria: estimated asthma prevalence; asthma-related mortality; and ER visits due to asthma. Risk factors analyzed but not factored in the rankings: annual air quality including pollution and ozone levels; public smoking laws; indoor air quality; access to asthma specialists; rescue and controller medication use; uninsured rate; pollen allergy; poverty rate. *Asthma and Allergy Foundation of America, "Asthma Capitals 2024: The Most Challenging Places to Live With Asthma," September 10, 2024*

Pet Rankings

- Columbus was selected by *Sniffspot.com* as one of the most dog-friendly cities in the U.S., ranking #28 out of 50. Criteria: dog parks; hiking; sniffspots; public parks; dog-friendly businesses; housing; dog waste cleanliness; leash laws; dog services; and overall cost. *Sniffspot.com, "The Top 50 Most Dog-Friendly Cities in the U.S.," September 30, 2024*

Real Estate Rankings

- *WalletHub* compared the most populated U.S. cities to determine which had the best markets for real estate agents. Columbus ranked #116 where demand was high and pay was the best. Criteria: sales per agent; annual median wage for real-estate agents; monthly average starting salary for real estate agents; real estate job density and competition; unemployment rate; home turnover rate; housing-market health index; and other relevant metrics. *WalletHub.com, "2021 Best Places to Be a Real Estate Agent," May 12, 2021*

- Columbus was ranked #76 out of 176 metro areas in terms of cost of housing in 2024 by the National Association of Home Builders (#1 = most affordable). Criteria: the portion of an average family's income necessary to pay the mortgage on a median-priced home. *National Association of Home Builders®, NAHB-Wells Fargo Cost of Housing Index, 4th Quarter 2024*

Safety Rankings

- Allstate ranked the 100 most populous cities in America in terms of driver safety. Columbus ranked #14. Criteria based on anonymized driving behavior data from Allstate's mobile app powered by Arity: high speed driving (over 80 mph), phone handling, and hard braking. The report helps increase the importance of safety and awareness behind the wheel. *Allstate, "16th Allstate America's Best Drivers Report®" July 11, 2024*

Women/Minorities Rankings

- Personal finance website *WalletHub* compared more than 180 U.S. cities across two key dimensions, "Hispanic Business-Friendliness" and "Hispanic Purchasing Power," to arrive at the most favorable conditions for Hispanic entrepreneurs. Columbus was ranked #28 out of 182. Criteria includes: share of Hispanic-Owned Businesses; average growth of Hispanic Business revenues; Small Business-Friendliness score; affordability; and number of Hispanics with at least a bachelor's degree. *WalletHub.com, "Best Cities for Hispanic Entrepreneurs," September 4, 2024*

Miscellaneous Rankings

- In *Condé Nast Traveler* magazine's 2024 Readers' Choice Survey, Columbus made the top ten list of friendliest American cities. Columbus ranked #7. *Condé Nast Traveler, "The Friendliest Cities in the U.S., According to Our Readers" October 28, 2024*

- *WalletHub* compared 148 of the most populated U.S. cities to determine their operating efficiency. A "Quality of Services" score was constructed for each city and then measured against the total budget per capita to reveal which were managed the best. Columbus ranked #73. Criteria: financial stability; economy; education; safety; health; infrastructure and pollution. *WalletHub.com, "2025's Best- & Worst-Run Cities in America," June 18, 2024*

Business Environment

DEMOGRAPHICS

Population Growth

Area	1990 Census	2000 Census	2010 Census	2020 Census	2023 Estimate[2]	Population Growth 1990-2023 (%)
City	648,656	711,470	787,033	905,748	906,480	39.7
MSA[1]	1,405,176	1,612,694	1,836,536	2,138,926	2,151,847	53.1
U.S.	248,709,873	281,421,906	308,745,538	331,449,281	332,387,540	33.6

Note: (1) Figures cover the Columbus, OH Metropolitan Statistical Area; (2) 2019-2023 5-year ACS population estimate
Source: U.S. Census Bureau, 1990 Census, 2000 Census, 2010 Census, 2020 Census, 2019-2023 American Community Survey 5-Year Estimates

Race

Area	White Alone[2] (%)	Black Alone[2] (%)	Asian Alone[2] (%)	AIAN[3] Alone[2] (%)	NHOPI[4] Alone[2] (%)	Other Race Alone[2] (%)	Two or More Races (%)
City	53.3	29.0	5.8	0.3	0.0	3.4	8.2
MSA[1]	70.3	15.8	4.8	0.2	0.0	2.2	6.7
U.S.	63.4	12.4	5.8	0.9	0.2	6.6	10.7

Note: (1) Figures cover the Columbus, OH Metropolitan Statistical Area; (2) Alone is defined as not being in combination with one or more other races; (3) American Indian and Alaska Native; (4) Native Hawaiian and Other Pacific Islander
Source: U.S. Census Bureau, 2019-2023 American Community Survey 5-Year Estimates

Hispanic or Latino Origin

Area	Total (%)	Mexican (%)	Puerto Rican (%)	Cuban (%)	Other (%)
City	7.9	3.7	1.1	0.1	3.0
MSA[1]	5.3	2.5	0.8	0.1	2.0
U.S.	19.0	11.3	1.8	0.7	5.2

Note: Persons of Hispanic or Latino origin can be of any race; (1) Figures cover the Columbus, OH Metropolitan Statistical Area
Source: U.S. Census Bureau, 2019-2023 American Community Survey 5-Year Estimates

Age

Area	Percent of Population									Median Age
	Under Age 5	Age 5–19	Age 20–34	Age 35–44	Age 45–54	Age 55–64	Age 65–74	Age 75–84	Age 85+	
City	6.7	18.6	28.6	13.8	10.9	10.5	6.9	2.9	1.2	33.0
MSA[1]	6.3	19.8	21.6	14.0	12.4	11.9	8.7	3.9	1.5	36.6
U.S.	5.7	19.1	20.2	13.1	12.3	12.8	10.0	4.9	1.9	38.7

Note: (1) Figures cover the Columbus, OH Metropolitan Statistical Area
Source: U.S. Census Bureau, 2019-2023 American Community Survey 5-Year Estimates

Disability by Age

Area	All Ages	Under 18 Years Old	18 to 64 Years Old	65 Years and Over
City	12.2	5.3	10.9	34.7
MSA[1]	12.1	5.0	10.4	32.3
U.S.	13.0	4.7	10.7	32.9

Note: Figures show percent of the civilian noninstitutionalized population that reported having a disability. Disability status is determined from six types of difficulty: vision, hearing, cognitive, ambulatory, self-care, and independent living. For children under 5 years old, hearing and vision difficulty are used to determine disability status. For children between the ages of 5 and 14, disability status is determined from hearing, vision, cognitive, ambulatory, and self-care difficulties. For people aged 15 years and older, they are considered to have a disability if they have difficulty with any one of the six difficulty types; Note: (1) Figures cover the Columbus, OH Metropolitan Statistical Area
Source: U.S. Census Bureau, 2019-2023 American Community Survey 5-Year Estimates

Ancestry

Area	German	Irish	English	American	Italian	Polish	French[2]	European	Scottish
City	14.9	10.0	8.0	3.4	4.6	2.1	1.3	1.5	1.6
MSA[1]	20.0	12.4	11.1	5.3	5.1	2.2	1.6	1.8	2.1
U.S.	12.6	9.4	9.1	5.5	4.9	2.6	2.0	1.6	1.6

Note: Figures are the percentage of the total population reporting a particular ancestry. The nine most commonly reported ancestries in the U.S. are shown. Figures include multiple ancestries (e.g. if a person reported being Irish and Italian, they were included in both columns); (1) Figures cover the Columbus, OH Metropolitan Statistical Area; (2) Excludes Basque
Source: U.S. Census Bureau, 2019-2023 American Community Survey 5-Year Estimates

Foreign-born Population

Area	Any Foreign Country	Percent of Population Born in							
		Asia	Mexico	Europe	Caribbean	Central America[2]	South America	Africa	Canada
City	14.4	4.7	1.3	0.8	0.7	0.9	0.7	5.1	0.1
MSA[1]	9.5	3.8	0.8	0.7	0.4	0.5	0.4	2.7	0.1
U.S.	13.9	4.3	3.3	1.4	1.4	1.2	1.2	0.8	0.2

Note: (1) Figures cover the Columbus, OH Metropolitan Statistical Area; (2) Excludes Mexico.
Source: U.S. Census Bureau, 2019-2023 American Community Survey 5-Year Estimates

Household Size

Area	Persons in Household (%)							Average Household Size
	One	Two	Three	Four	Five	Six	Seven or More	
City	36.5	32.2	13.4	9.7	4.9	2.0	1.3	2.29
MSA[1]	29.4	33.6	15.1	12.7	5.8	2.2	1.2	2.46
U.S.	28.5	33.8	15.4	12.7	5.9	2.3	1.4	2.54

Note: (1) Figures cover the Columbus, OH Metropolitan Statistical Area
Source: U.S. Census Bureau, 2019-2023 American Community Survey 5-Year Estimates

Household Relationships

Area	House-holder	Opposite-sex Spouse	Same-sex Spouse	Opposite-sex Unmarried Partner	Same-sex Unmarried Partner	Child[2]	Grand-child	Other Relatives	Non-relatives
City	42.2	12.9	0.3	3.6	0.3	26.2	2.1	4.4	5.2
MSA[1]	39.4	17.4	0.2	2.9	0.2	28.5	2.0	3.5	3.3
U.S.	38.3	17.5	0.2	2.5	0.2	28.3	2.4	4.8	3.4

Note: Figures are percent of the total population; (1) Figures cover the Columbus, OH Metropolitan Statistical Area; (2) Includes biological, adopted, and stepchildren of the householder
Source: U.S. Census Bureau, 2020 Census

Gender

Area	Males	Females	Males per 100 Females
City	445,564	460,916	96.7
MSA[1]	1,066,090	1,085,757	98.2
U.S.	164,545,087	167,842,453	98.0

Note: (1) Figures cover the Columbus, OH Metropolitan Statistical Area
Source: U.S. Census Bureau, 2019-2023 American Community Survey 5-Year Estimates

Marital Status

Area	Never Married	Now Married[2]	Separated	Widowed	Divorced
City	45.8	36.3	2.0	4.2	11.7
MSA[1]	35.0	47.4	1.6	4.8	11.2
U.S.	34.1	47.9	1.7	5.6	10.7

Note: Figures are percentages and cover the population 15 years of age and older; (1) Figures cover the Columbus, OH Metropolitan Statistical Area; (2) Excludes separated
Source: U.S. Census Bureau, 2019-2023 American Community Survey 5-Year Estimates

Religious Groups by Family

Area	Catholic	Baptist	Methodist	LDS[2]	Pentecostal	Lutheran	Islam	Adventist	Other
MSA[1]	11.7	3.4	3.0	0.8	1.9	1.7	2.1	0.9	17.5
U.S.	18.7	7.3	3.0	2.0	1.8	1.7	1.3	1.3	11.6

Note: Figures are the number of adherents as a percentage of the total population and cover the eight largest religious groups in the U.S; (1) Figures cover the Columbus, OH Metropolitan Statistical Area; (2) Church of Jesus Christ of Latter-day Saints
Sources: 2020 U.S. Religion Census, Association of Statisticians of American Religious Bodies; The Association of Religion Data Archives (ARDA)

Religious Groups by Tradition

Area	Catholic	Evangelical Protestant	Mainline Protestant	Black Protestant	Islam	Judaism	Hinduism	Orthodox	Buddhism
MSA[1]	11.7	18.1	6.8	1.5	2.1	0.4	0.4	0.5	0.2
U.S.	18.7	16.5	5.2	2.3	1.3	0.6	0.4	0.4	0.3

Note: Figures are the number of adherents as a percentage of the total population; (1) Figures cover the Columbus, OH Metropolitan Statistical Area
Sources: 2020 U.S. Religion Census, Association of Statisticians of American Religious Bodies; The Association of Religion Data Archives (ARDA)

ECONOMY

Real Gross Domestic Product (GDP)

Area	2017	2018	2019	2020	2021	2022	2023	Rank[3]
MSA[1]	129.9	131.5	135.7	134.2	143.6	145.5	148.0	34
U.S.[2]	17,619.1	18,160.7	18,642.5	18,238.9	19,387.6	19,896.6	20,436.3	—

Note: Figures are in billions of chained 2017 dollars; (1) Figures cover the Columbus, OH Metropolitan Statistical Area; (2) Figures cover real GDP within metropolitan areas; (3) Rank is based on 2023 data and ranges from 1 to 384
Source: U.S. Bureau of Economic Analysis

Economic Growth

Area	2014	2015	2016	2017	2018	2019	2020	2021	2022	2023
MSA[1]	3.6	2.1	2.1	4.4	1.2	3.2	-1.1	7.0	1.3	1.8
U.S.[2]	2.6	3.2	2.0	2.7	3.1	2.7	-2.2	6.3	2.6	2.7

Note: Figures are real gross domestic product growth rates and represent percent change from preceding period; (1) Figures cover the Columbus, OH Metropolitan Statistical Area; (2) Figures are the average growth rates within metropolitan areas
Source: U.S. Bureau of Economic Analysis

Metropolitan Area Exports

Area	2018	2019	2020	2021	2022	2023	Rank[2]
MSA[1]	7,529.5	7,296.6	6,304.8	6,557.9	7,597.3	8,418.9	47
U.S.	1,664,056.1	1,645,173.7	1,431,406.6	1,753,941.4	2,062,937.4	2,019,160.5	—

Note: Figures are in millions of dollars; (1) Figures cover the Columbus, OH Metropolitan Statistical Area; (2) Rank is based on 2023 data and ranges from 1 to 386
Source: U.S. Department of Commerce, International Trade Administration, Office of Trade and Economic Analysis, Industry and Analysis, Exports by Metropolitan Area, data extracted April 2, 2025

Building Permits

Area	Single-Family			Multi-Family			Total		
	2023	2024	Pct. Chg.	2023	2024	Pct. Chg.	2023	2024	Pct. Chg.
City	943	828	-12.2	4,340	5,256	21.1	5,283	6,084	15.2
MSA[1]	5,364	6,094	13.6	6,076	7,868	29.5	11,440	13,962	22.0
U.S.	920,000	981,900	6.7	591,100	496,100	-16.1	1,511,100	1,478,000	-2.2

Note: (1) Figures cover the Columbus, OH Metropolitan Statistical Area; Figures represent new, privately-owned housing units authorized (unadjusted data)
Source: U.S. Census Bureau, Building Permits Survey (BPS), 2023, 2024

Bankruptcy Filings

Area	Business Filings			Nonbusiness Filings		
	2023	2024	% Chg.	2023	2024	% Chg.
Franklin County	43	81	88.4	2,330	2,671	14.6
U.S.	18,926	23,107	22.1	434,064	494,201	13.9

Note: Business filings include Chapter 7, Chapter 9, Chapter 11, Chapter 12, Chapter 13, Chapter 15, and Section 304; Nonbusiness filings include Chapter 7, Chapter 11, and Chapter 13
Source: Administrative Office of the U.S. Courts, Business and Nonbusiness Bankruptcy, County Cases Commenced by Chapter of the Bankruptcy Code, During the 12-Month Period Ending December 31, 2023 and Business and Nonbusiness Bankruptcy, County Cases Commenced by Chapter of the Bankruptcy Code, During the 12-Month Period Ending December 31, 2024

Housing Vacancy Rates

Area	Gross Vacancy Rate[3] (%)			Year-Round Vacancy Rate[4] (%)			Rental Vacancy Rate[5] (%)			Homeowner Vacancy Rate[6] (%)		
	2022	2023	2024	2022	2023	2024	2022	2023	2024	2022	2023	2024
MSA[1]	5.6	6.6	7.4	5.4	6.5	7.3	3.8	5.8	7.3	0.8	0.8	0.3
U.S.[2]	9.1	9.0	9.1	7.5	7.5	7.6	5.7	6.5	6.8	0.8	0.8	1.0

Note: (1) Figures cover the Columbus, OH Metropolitan Statistical Area; (2) Figures cover the 75 largest Metropolitan Statistical Areas; (3) The percentage of the total housing inventory that is vacant; (4) The percentage of the housing inventory (excluding seasonal units) that is year-round vacant; (5) The percentage of rental inventory that is vacant for rent; (6) The percentage of homeowner inventory that is vacant for sale
Source: U.S. Census Bureau, Housing Vacancies and Homeownership Annual Statistics: 2022, 2023, 2024

INCOME

Income

Area	Per Capita ($)	Median Household ($)	Average Household ($)
City	37,189	65,327	85,919
MSA[1]	43,665	79,847	108,257
U.S.	43,289	78,538	110,491

Note: (1) Figures cover the Columbus, OH Metropolitan Statistical Area
Source: U.S. Census Bureau, 2019-2023 American Community Survey 5-Year Estimates

Household Income Distribution

Area	Percent of Households Earning							
	Under $15,000	$15,000 -$24,999	$25,000 -$34,999	$35,000 -$49,999	$50,000 -$74,999	$75,000 -$99,999	$100,000 -$149,999	$150,000 and up
City	10.0	7.1	7.4	13.3	18.5	13.5	16.6	13.5
MSA[1]	7.6	5.8	6.4	11.0	16.6	12.9	18.2	21.5
U.S.	8.5	6.6	6.8	10.4	15.7	12.7	17.4	21.9

Note: (1) Figures cover the Columbus, OH Metropolitan Statistical Area
Source: U.S. Census Bureau, 2019-2023 American Community Survey 5-Year Estimates

Poverty Rate

Area	All Ages	Under 18 Years Old	18 to 64 Years Old	65 Years and Over
City	17.8	25.9	16.1	12.1
MSA[1]	12.2	16.5	11.4	8.7
U.S.	12.4	16.3	11.6	10.4

Note: Figures are percentage of people whose income during the past 12 months was below the poverty level; (1) Figures cover the Columbus, OH Metropolitan Statistical Area
Source: U.S. Census Bureau, 2019-2023 American Community Survey 5-Year Estimates

EMPLOYMENT

Labor Force and Employment

Area	Civilian Labor Force			Workers Employed		
	Dec. 2023	Dec. 2024	% Chg.	Dec. 2023	Dec. 2024	% Chg.
City	490,638	493,589	0.6	474,627	473,223	-0.3
MSA[1]	1,134,646	1,141,335	0.6	1,099,340	1,096,249	-0.3
U.S.	166,661,000	167,746,000	0.7	160,754,000	161,294,000	0.3

Note: Data is not seasonally adjusted and covers workers 16 years of age and older; (1) Figures cover the Columbus, OH Metropolitan Statistical Area
Source: Bureau of Labor Statistics, Local Area Unemployment Statistics

Unemployment Rate

Area	2024											
	Jan.	Feb.	Mar.	Apr.	May	Jun.	Jul.	Aug.	Sep.	Oct.	Nov.	Dec.
City	4.0	4.0	4.0	3.8	4.0	4.5	4.5	4.3	4.2	3.9	4.2	4.1
MSA[1]	3.9	3.9	3.9	3.6	3.8	4.3	4.3	4.1	4.0	3.7	4.0	4.0
U.S.	4.1	4.2	3.9	3.5	3.7	4.3	4.5	4.4	3.9	3.9	4.0	3.8

Note: Data is not seasonally adjusted and covers workers 16 years of age and older; (1) Figures cover the Columbus, OH Metropolitan Statistical Area
Source: Bureau of Labor Statistics, Local Area Unemployment Statistics

Average Wages

Occupation	$/Hr.	Occupation	$/Hr.
Accountants and Auditors	44.22	Maintenance and Repair Workers	25.88
Automotive Mechanics	27.22	Marketing Managers	70.72
Bookkeepers	24.48	Network and Computer Systems Admin.	48.31
Carpenters	29.44	Nurses, Licensed Practical	30.09
Cashiers	14.46	Nurses, Registered	42.87
Computer Programmers	48.11	Nursing Assistants	19.72
Computer Systems Analysts	49.66	Office Clerks, General	22.35
Computer User Support Specialists	30.19	Physical Therapists	47.24
Construction Laborers	27.99	Physicians	129.01
Cooks, Restaurant	16.81	Plumbers, Pipefitters and Steamfitters	32.38
Customer Service Representatives	22.27	Police and Sheriff's Patrol Officers	42.38
Dentists	78.07	Postal Service Mail Carriers	29.11
Electricians	31.75	Real Estate Sales Agents	25.57
Engineers, Electrical	49.68	Retail Salespersons	17.40
Fast Food and Counter Workers	14.24	Sales Representatives, Technical/Scientific	54.37
Financial Managers	75.71	Secretaries, Exc. Legal/Medical/Executive	23.47
First-Line Supervisors of Office Workers	33.43	Security Guards	19.81
General and Operations Managers	60.59	Surgeons	n/a
Hairdressers/Cosmetologists	18.45	Teacher Assistants, Exc. Postsecondary[1]	16.73
Home Health and Personal Care Aides	15.89	Teachers, Secondary School, Exc. Sp. Ed.[1]	38.26
Janitors and Cleaners	17.74	Telemarketers	15.60
Landscaping/Groundskeeping Workers	19.22	Truck Drivers, Heavy/Tractor-Trailer	30.84
Lawyers	72.24	Truck Drivers, Light/Delivery Services	23.64
Maids and Housekeeping Cleaners	15.53	Waiters and Waitresses	19.12

Note: Wage data covers the Columbus, OH Metropolitan Statistical Area; (1) Hourly wages were calculated from annual wage data based on a 40 hour work week
Source: Bureau of Labor Statistics, Metro Area Occupational Employment & Wage Estimates, May 2024

Employment by Industry

Sector	MSA[1] Number of Employees	MSA[1] Percent of Total	U.S. Percent of Total
Construction, Mining, and Logging	53,400	4.5	5.5
Financial Activities	80,700	6.9	5.8
Government	195,000	16.6	14.9
Information	18,100	1.5	1.9
Leisure and Hospitality	106,800	9.1	10.4
Manufacturing	77,100	6.5	8.0
Other Services	44,500	3.8	3.7
Private Education and Health Services	181,900	15.5	16.9
Professional and Business Services	191,700	16.3	14.2
Retail Trade	107,800	9.2	10.0
Transportation, Warehousing, and Utilities	78,400	6.7	4.8
Wholesale Trade	41,900	3.6	3.9

Note: Figures are non-farm employment as of December 2024. Figures are not seasonally adjusted and include workers 16 years of age and older; (1) Figures cover the Columbus, OH Metropolitan Statistical Area
Source: Bureau of Labor Statistics, Current Employment Statistics, Employment, Hours, and Earnings

Employment by Occupation

Occupation Classification	City (%)	MSA[1] (%)	U.S. (%)
Management, Business, Science, and Arts	43.7	45.9	42.0
Natural Resources, Construction, and Maintenance	5.2	6.1	8.6
Production, Transportation, and Material Moving	14.8	13.7	13.0
Sales and Office	20.1	19.6	19.9
Service	16.3	14.8	16.5

Note: Figures cover employed civilians 16 years of age and older; (1) Figures cover the Columbus, OH Metropolitan Statistical Area
Source: U.S. Census Bureau, 2019-2023 American Community Survey 5-Year Estimates

Occupations with Greatest Projected Employment Growth: 2022 – 2032

Occupation[1]	2022 Employment	2032 Projected Employment	Numeric Employment Change	Percent Employment Change
Home Health and Personal Care Aides	95,690	108,260	12,570	13.1
Cooks, Restaurant	48,380	57,540	9,160	18.9
Stockers and Order Fillers	125,650	131,710	6,060	4.8
Nurse Practitioners	11,020	15,710	4,690	42.6
Medical and Health Services Managers	18,720	23,310	4,590	24.5
Registered Nurses	131,390	135,860	4,470	3.4
Financial Managers	26,630	30,720	4,090	15.4
General and Operations Managers	132,340	136,170	3,830	2.9
Heavy and Tractor-Trailer Truck Drivers	98,350	102,030	3,680	3.7
Market Research Analysts and Marketing Specialists	31,720	35,170	3,450	10.9

Note: Projections cover Ohio; (1) Sorted by numeric employment change
Source: www.projectionscentral.org, State Occupational Projections, 2022–2032 Long-Term Projections

Fastest-Growing Occupations: 2022 – 2032

Occupation[1]	2022 Employment	2032 Projected Employment	Numeric Employment Change	Percent Employment Change
Nurse Practitioners	11,020	15,710	4,690	42.6
Taxi Drivers	2,490	3,480	990	39.8
Wind Turbine Service Technicians	170	230	60	35.3
Data Scientists	3,760	5,000	1,240	33.0
Statisticians	420	540	120	28.6
Medical and Health Services Managers	18,720	23,310	4,590	24.5
Physician Assistants	3,210	3,990	780	24.3
Semiconductor Processors	870	1,080	210	24.1
Epidemiologists	260	320	60	23.1
Speech-Language Pathologists	6,340	7,740	1,400	22.1

Note: Projections cover Ohio; (1) Sorted by percent employment change and excludes occupations with numeric employment change less than 50
Source: www.projectionscentral.org, State Occupational Projections, 2022–2032 Long-Term Projections

CITY FINANCES

City Government Finances

Component	2022 ($000)	2022 ($ per capita)
Total Revenues	2,498,947	2,765
Total Expenditures	2,389,564	2,644
Debt Outstanding	4,805,511	5,317

Source: U.S. Census Bureau, State & Local Government Finances 2022

City Government Revenue by Source

Source	2022 ($000)	2022 ($ per capita)	2022 (%)
General Revenue			
From Federal Government	190,921	211	7.6
From State Government	69,666	77	2.8
From Local Governments	42,581	47	1.7
Taxes			
Property	60,953	67	2.4
Sales and Gross Receipts	28,371	31	1.1
Personal Income	1,037,278	1,148	41.5
Corporate Income	0	0	0.0
Motor Vehicle License	0	0	0.0
Other Taxes	32,258	36	1.3
Current Charges	465,426	515	18.6
Liquor Store	0	0	0.0
Utility	298,458	330	11.9

Source: U.S. Census Bureau, State & Local Government Finances 2022

City Government Expenditures by Function

Function	2022 ($000)	2022 ($ per capita)	2022 (%)
General Direct Expenditures			
Air Transportation	0	0	0.0
Corrections	0	0	0.0
Education	11,337	12	0.5
Employment Security Administration	0	0	0.0
Financial Administration	66,443	73	2.8
Fire Protection	283,049	313	11.8
General Public Buildings	19,051	21	0.8
Governmental Administration, Other	52,364	57	2.2
Health	69,953	77	2.9
Highways	212,165	234	8.9
Hospitals	0	0	0.0
Housing and Community Development	56,374	62	2.4
Interest on General Debt	123,990	137	5.2
Judicial and Legal	54,770	60	2.3
Libraries	0	0	0.0
Parking	24,526	27	1.0
Parks and Recreation	206,626	228	8.6
Police Protection	356,502	394	14.9
Public Welfare	483	<1	<0.1
Sewerage	236,813	262	9.9
Solid Waste Management	50,579	56	2.1
Veterans' Services	0	0	0.0
Liquor Store	0	0	0.0
Utility	309,980	343	13.0

Source: U.S. Census Bureau, State & Local Government Finances 2022

TAXES

State Corporate Income Tax Rates

State	Tax Rate (%)	Income Brackets ($)	Num. of Brackets	Financial Institution Tax Rate (%)[a]	Federal Income Tax Ded.
Ohio	(r)	—	—	(r)	No

Note: Tax rates for tax year 2024; (a) Rates listed are the corporate income tax rate applied to financial institutions or excise taxes based on income. Some states have other taxes based upon the value of deposits or shares; (r) Ohio no longer levies a tax based on income (except for a particular subset of corporations), but instead imposes a Commercial Activity Tax (CAT). For tax periods beginning on and after January 1, 2024, the CAT annual minimum tax is eliminated, and the exclusion amount is increased from $1 million to $3 million. Therefore, taxpayers with taxable gross receipts of $3 million or less per calendar year will no longer be subject to the CAT. For those few corporations for whom the franchise tax
Source: Federation of Tax Administrators, State Corporate Income Tax Rates, January 1, 2025

State Individual Income Tax Rates

State	Tax Rate (%)	Income Brackets ($)	Personal Exemptions ($)			Standard Ded. ($)	
			Single	Married	Depend.	Single	Married
Ohio (a)	0.0 - 3.5	26,050 - 115,300	1,200	2,400	1,200 (u)	–	–

Note: Tax rates for tax year 2024; Local- and county-level taxes are not included; Federal income tax is not deductible on state income tax returns; (a) 16 states have statutory provision for automatically adjusting to the rate of inflation the dollar values of the income tax brackets, standard deductions, and/or personal exemptions. Oregon does not index the income brackets for $125,000 and over See: INFL and SPEC above; (u) Ohio suspends the annual inflation indexing adjustment of income tax brackets and personal exemption amounts for taxable years beginning in 2023 and 2024. Business income taxes at a flat 3% rate for individuals with income over $125,000S/$250,000MFJ.
Source: Federation of Tax Administrators, State Individual Income Tax Rates, January 1, 2025

Various State Sales and Excise Tax Rates

State	State Sales Tax (%)	Gasoline[1] ($/gal.)	Cigarette[2] ($/pack)	Spirits[3] ($/gal.)	Wine[4] ($/gal.)	Beer[5] ($/gal.)	Recreational Marijuana (%)
Ohio	5.75	0.39	1.60	12.33	0.32	0.18	(s)

Note: All tax rates as of January 1, 2025; (1) The American Petroleum Institute has developed a methodology for determining the average tax rate on a gallon of fuel. Rates may include any of the following: excise taxes, environmental fees, storage tank fees, other fees or taxes, general sales tax, and local taxes; (2) The federal excise tax of $1.0066 per pack and local taxes are not included; (3) Rates are those applicable to off-premise sales of 40% alcohol by volume (a.b.v.) distilled spirits in 750ml containers. Local excise taxes are excluded; (4) Rates are those applicable to off-premise sales of 11% a.b.v. non-carbonated wine in 750ml containers; (5) Rates are those applicable to off-premise sales of 4.7% a.b.v. beer in 12 ounce containers; (s) 10% excise tax (retail price)
Source: Tax Foundation, 2025 Facts & Figures: How Does Your State Compare?

State Tax Competitiveness Index

State	Overall Rank	Corporate Tax Rank	Individual Income Tax Rank	Sales Tax Rank	Property Tax Rank	Unemployment Insurance Tax Rank
Ohio	35	45	25	43	6	14

Note: The Tax Foundation's State Tax Competitiveness Index enables policymakers, taxpayers, and business leaders to gauge how their states' tax systems compare. A rank of 1 is best, 50 is worst. Rankings do not average to the total. States without a tax rank equally as 1. DC's scores and rankings do not affect other states. The report shows tax systems as of July 1, 2024 (the beginning of Fiscal Year 2025).
Source: Tax Foundation, State Tax Competitiveness Index 2025

TRANSPORTATION

Means of Transportation to Work

Area	Car/Truck/Van		Public Transportation			Bicycle	Walked	Other Means	Worked at Home
	Drove Alone	Car-pooled	Bus	Subway	Railroad				
City	70.1	7.5	2.1	0.0	0.0	0.4	2.6	1.2	16.1
MSA[1]	72.2	6.8	1.1	0.0	0.0	0.2	1.9	1.1	16.6
U.S.	70.2	8.5	1.7	1.3	0.4	0.4	2.4	1.6	13.5

Note: Figures are percentages and cover workers 16 years of age and older; (1) Figures cover the Columbus, OH Metropolitan Statistical Area
Source: U.S. Census Bureau, 2019-2023 American Community Survey 5-Year Estimates

Travel Time to Work

Area	Less Than 10 Minutes	10 to 19 Minutes	20 to 29 Minutes	30 to 44 Minutes	45 to 59 Minutes	60 to 89 Minutes	90 Minutes or More
City	10.3	35.1	31.0	17.2	3.1	2.1	1.3
MSA[1]	11.7	29.8	27.5	20.7	5.8	3.1	1.5
U.S.	12.6	28.6	21.2	20.8	8.1	6.0	2.8

Note: Note: Figures are percentages and include workers 16 years old and over; (1) Figures cover the Columbus, OH Metropolitan Statistical Area
Source: U.S. Census Bureau, 2019-2023 American Community Survey 5-Year Estimates

Key Congestion Measures

Measure	2000	2010	2015	2020	2022
Annual Hours of Delay, Total (000)	25,284	35,331	43,524	26,055	47,611
Annual Hours of Delay, Per Auto Commuter	38	41	47	27	53
Annual Congestion Cost, Per Auto Commuter ($)	925	1,027	1,168	721	1,316

Note: Figures cover the Columbus OH urban area
Source: Texas A&M Transportation Institute, 2023 Urban Mobility Report

Freeway Travel Time Index

Measure	1985	1990	1995	2000	2005	2010	2015	2020	2022
Urban Area Index[1]	1.09	1.12	1.15	1.17	1.18	1.17	1.18	1.08	1.18
Urban Area Rank[1,2]	36	35	36	36	41	41	41	44	40

Note: Freeway Travel Time Index—the ratio of travel time in the peak period to the travel time at free-flow conditions. For example, a value of 1.30 indicates a 20-minute free-flow trip takes 26 minutes in the peak (20 minutes x 1.30 = 26 minutes); (1) Covers the Columbus OH urban area; (2) Rank is based on 101 larger urban areas (#1 = highest travel time index)
Source: Texas A&M Transportation Institute, 2023 Urban Mobility Report

Public Transportation

Agency Name / Mode of Transportation	Vehicles Operated in Maximum Service[1]	Annual Unlinked Passenger Trips[2] (in thous.)	Annual Passenger Miles[3] (in thous.)
Central Ohio Transit Authority (COTA)			
Bus (directly operated)	189	11,128.9	48,130.6
Demand Response (directly operated)	22	157.2	403.5
Demand Response (purchased transportation)	62	240.4	2,747.5

Note: (1) Number of revenue vehicles operated by the given mode and type of service to meet the annual maximum service requirement. This is the revenue vehicle count during the peak season of the year; on the week and day that maximum service is provided. Vehicles operated in maximum service (VOMS) exclude atypical days and one-time special events; (2) Number of passengers who boarded public transportation vehicles. Passengers are counted each time they board a vehicle no matter how many vehicles they use to travel from their origin to their destination. (3) Sum of the distances ridden by all passengers during the entire fiscal year.
Source: Federal Transit Administration, National Transit Database, 2023

Air Transportation

Airport Name and Code / Type of Service	Passenger Airlines[1]	Passenger Enplanements	Freight Carriers[2]	Freight (lbs)
Port Columbus International (CMH)				
Domestic service (U.S. carriers only)	32	4,350,403	12	4,693,970
International service (U.S. carriers only)	6	9,043	1	61,562

Note: (1) Includes all U.S.-based major, minor and commuter airlines that carried at least one passenger during the year; (2) Includes all U.S.-based airlines and freight carriers that transported at least one pound of freight during the year.
Source: Bureau of Transportation Statistics, The Intermodal Transportation Database, Air Carriers: T-100 Domestic Market (U.S. carriers only), 2024; Bureau of Transportation Statistics, The Intermodal Transportation Database, Air Carriers: T-100 International Market (U.S. carriers only), 2024

BUSINESSES

Major Business Headquarters

Company Name	Industry	Fortune[1]	Forbes[2]
American Electric Power	Utilities: gas and electric	217	-
Bath & Body Works	Specialty retailers: other	481	-
Huntington Bancshares	Commercial banks	375	-
Nationwide	Insurance: property and casualty (mutual)	75	-

Note: (1) Companies that produce a 10-K are ranked 1 to 500 based on 2023 revenue; (2) All private companies with at least $2 billion in annual revenue through the end of their most current fiscal year are ranked 1 to 275; companies listed are headquartered in the city; dashes indicate no ranking
Source: Fortune, "Fortune 500," 2024; Forbes, "America's Largest Private Companies," 2024

Fastest-Growing Businesses

According to Deloitte, Columbus is home to one of North America's 500 fastest-growing high-technology companies: **Beam Benefits** (#475). Companies are ranked by percentage growth in revenue over a four-year period. Criteria for inclusion: company must be headquartered within North America; must own proprietary intellectual property or technology that is sold to customers in products that contributes to a significant portion of the company's operating revenue; must have been in business for a minumum of four years with 2020 operating revenues of at least $50,000 USD/CD and 2023 operating revenues of at least $5 million USD/CD. *Deloitte, 2024 Technology Fast 500*™

Living Environment

COST OF LIVING

Cost of Living Index

Composite Index	Groceries	Housing	Utilities	Transportation	Health Care	Misc. Goods/Services
95.3	100.6	96.5	104.2	87.5	82.3	93.6

Note: The Cost of Living Index measures regional differences in the cost of consumer goods and services, excluding taxes and non-consumer expenditures, for professional and managerial households in the top income quintile. It is based on more than 50,000 prices covering almost 60 different items for which prices are collected three times a year by chambers of commerce, economic development organizations or university applied economic centers in each participating urban area. The numbers shown should be read as a percentage above or below the national average of 100. For example, a value of 115.4 in the groceries column indicates that grocery prices are 15.4% higher than the national average. Small differences in the index numbers should not be interpreted as significant; Figures cover the Columbus OH urban area.
Source: The Council for Community and Economic Research, Cost of Living Index, 2024

Grocery Prices

Area[1]	T-Bone Steak ($/pound)	Frying Chicken ($/pound)	Whole Milk ($/half gal.)	Eggs ($/dozen)	Orange Juice ($/64 oz.)	Coffee ($/11.5 oz.)
City[2]	15.51	1.72	4.72	3.39	4.39	5.52
Avg.	15.42	1.55	4.69	3.25	4.41	5.46
Min.	14.50	1.16	4.43	2.75	4.00	4.85
Max.	17.56	2.89	5.49	4.78	5.54	7.89

Note: (1) Values for the local area are compared with the average, minimum and maximum values for all 276 areas in the Cost of Living Index; (2) Figures cover the Columbus OH urban area; **T-Bone Steak** (price per pound); **Frying Chicken** (price per pound, whole fryer); **Whole Milk** (half gallon carton); **Eggs** (price per dozen, Grade A, large); **Orange Juice** (64 oz. Tropicana or Florida Natural); **Coffee** (11.5 oz. can, vacuum-packed, Maxwell House, Hills Bros, or Folgers).
Source: The Council for Community and Economic Research, Cost of Living Index, 2024

Housing and Utility Costs

Area[1]	New Home Price ($)	Apartment Rent ($/month)	All Electric ($/month)	Part Electric ($/month)	Other Energy ($/month)	Telephone ($/month)
City[2]	482,718	1,613	-	146.60	76.69	189.10
Avg.	515,975	1,550	210.99	123.07	82.07	194.99
Min.	265,375	692	104.33	53.68	36.26	179.42
Max.	2,775,821	5,719	529.02	397.28	361.63	223.33

Note: (1) Values for the local area are compared with the average, minimum and maximum values for all 276 areas in the Cost of Living Index; (2) Figures cover the Columbus OH urban area; **New Home Price** (2,400 sf living area, 8,000 sf lot, in urban area with full utilities); **Apartment Rent** (950 sf 2 bedroom/1.5 or 2 bath, unfurnished, excluding all utilities except water); **All Electric** (average monthly cost for an all-electric home); **Part Electric** (average monthly cost for a part-electric home); **Other Energy** (average monthly cost for natural gas, fuel oil, coal, wood, and any other forms of energy except electricity); **Telephone** (price includes the base monthly rate plus taxes and fees for three lines of mobile phone service).
Source: The Council for Community and Economic Research, Cost of Living Index, 2024

Health Care, Transportation, and Other Costs

Area[1]	Doctor ($/visit)	Dentist ($/visit)	Optometrist ($/visit)	Gasoline ($/gallon)	Beauty Salon ($/visit)	Men's Shirt ($)
City[2]	115.70	94.35	93.20	3.19	49.51	36.47
Avg.	143.77	117.51	129.23	3.32	48.57	38.14
Min.	36.74	58.67	67.33	2.80	24.00	13.41
Max.	270.44	216.82	307.33	5.28	94.00	63.89

Note: (1) Values for the local area are compared with the average, minimum and maximum values for all 276 areas in the Cost of Living Index; (2) Figures cover the Columbus OH urban area; **Doctor** (general practitioners routine exam of an established patient); **Dentist** (adult teeth cleaning and periodic oral examination); **Optometrist** (full vision eye exam for established adult patient); **Gasoline** (one gallon regular unleaded, national brand, including all taxes, cash price at self-service pump if available); **Beauty Salon** (woman's shampoo, trim, and blow-dry); **Men's Shirt** (cotton/polyester dress shirt, pinpoint weave, long sleeves).
Source: The Council for Community and Economic Research, Cost of Living Index, 2024

HOUSING

Homeownership Rate

Area	2017 (%)	2018 (%)	2019 (%)	2020 (%)	2021 (%)	2022 (%)	2023 (%)	2024 (%)
MSA[1]	57.9	64.8	65.7	65.6	64.6	61.5	58.6	61.5
U.S.	63.9	64.4	64.6	66.6	65.5	65.8	65.9	65.6

Note: (1) Figures cover the Columbus, OH Metropolitan Statistical Area
Source: U.S. Census Bureau, Housing Vacancies and Homeownership Annual Statistics: 2017-2024

House Price Index (HPI)

Area	National Ranking[2]	Quarterly Change (%)	One-Year Change (%)	Five-Year Change (%)	Since 1991Q1 (%)
MSA[1]	63	1.20	6.96	61.81	293.84
U.S.[3]	—	1.43	4.51	57.13	327.82

Note: The HPI is a weighted repeat sales index. It measures average price changes in repeat sales or refinancings on the same properties. This information is obtained by reviewing repeat mortgage transactions on single-family properties whose mortgages have been purchased or securitized by Fannie Mae or Freddie Mac since January 1975; (1) Figures cover the Columbus, OH Metropolitan Statistical Area; (2) Rankings are based on annual percentage change for all metro areas containing at least 15,000 transactions over the last 10 years and ranges from 1 to 241; (3) figures based on a weighted average of Census Division estimates using a seasonally adjusted, purchase-only index; all figures are for the period ending December 31, 2024
Source: Federal Housing Finance Agency, Change in FHFA Metropolitan Area House Price Indexes, All Transactions Index, 2024Q4

Home Value

Area	Under $100,000	$100,000 -$199,999	$200,000 -$299,999	$300,000 -$399,999	$400,000 -$499,999	$500,000 -$999,999	$1,000,000 or more	Median ($)
City	11.3	27.4	31.0	18.0	6.6	4.9	0.8	234,500
MSA[1]	9.2	20.9	26.3	18.4	10.8	12.8	1.6	274,300
U.S.	12.1	17.8	19.5	14.4	10.5	19.1	6.5	303,400

Note: Figures are percentages except for median and cover owner-occupied housing units; (1) Figures cover the Columbus, OH Metropolitan Statistical Area
Source: U.S. Census Bureau, 2019-2023 American Community Survey 5-Year Estimates

Year Housing Structure Built

Area	2020 or Later	2010 -2019	2000 -2009	1990 -1999	1980 -1989	1970 -1979	1960 -1969	1950 -1959	1940 -1949	Before 1940	Median Year
City	1.0	9.6	11.8	13.7	13.3	14.4	10.7	9.6	4.0	12.0	1980
MSA[1]	1.4	9.5	14.1	14.9	11.5	13.7	10.1	9.2	3.5	12.1	1981
U.S.	1.2	8.9	13.6	12.8	13.0	14.4	10.0	9.7	4.5	11.9	1980

Note: Figures are percentages except for Median Year; Note: (1) Figures cover the Columbus, OH Metropolitan Statistical Area
Source: U.S. Census Bureau, 2019-2023 American Community Survey 5-Year Estimates

Gross Monthly Rent

Area	Under $500	$500 -$999	$1,000 -$1,499	$1,500 -$1,999	$2,000 -$2,499	$2,500 -$2,999	$3,000 and up	Median ($)
City	4.5	22.1	46.5	19.4	5.3	1.2	0.9	1,224
MSA[1]	5.1	24.3	43.9	18.5	5.5	1.4	1.2	1,208
U.S.	6.5	22.3	29.5	20.2	10.8	4.8	5.9	1,348

Note: Figures are percentages except for median; Gross rent is the contract rent plus the estimated average monthly cost of utilities (electricity, gas, and water and sewer) and fuels (oil, coal, kerosene, wood, etc.) if these are paid by the renter (or paid for the renter by someone else); (1) Figures cover the Columbus, OH Metropolitan Statistical Area
Source: U.S. Census Bureau, 2019-2023 American Community Survey 5-Year Estimates

HEALTH

Health Risk Factors

Category	MSA[1] (%)	U.S. (%)
Adults aged 18–64 who have any kind of health care coverage	92.8	90.8
Adults who reported being in good or better health	83.4	81.8
Adults who have been told they have high blood cholesterol	36.4	36.9
Adults who have been told they have high blood pressure	32.6	34.0
Adults who are current smokers	12.5	12.1
Adults who currently use e-cigarettes	9.5	7.7
Adults who currently use chewing tobacco, snuff, or snus	3.3	3.2
Adults who are heavy drinkers[2]	5.8	6.1
Adults who are binge drinkers[3]	14.9	15.2
Adults who are overweight (BMI 25.0 - 29.9)	33.3	34.4
Adults who are obese (BMI 30.0 - 99.8)	33.6	34.3
Adults who participated in any physical activities in the past month	78.0	75.8

Note: All figures are crude prevalence; (1) Figures cover the Columbus, OH Metropolitan Statistical Area; (2) Heavy drinkers are classified as adult men having more than 14 drinks per week and adult women having more than 7 drinks per week; (3) Binge drinkers are classified as males having five or more drinks on one occasion or females having four or more drinks on one occasion
Source: Centers for Disease Control and Prevention, Behaviorial Risk Factor Surveillance System, SMART: Selected Metropolitan Area Risk Trends, 2023

Acute and Chronic Health Conditions

Category	MSA[1] (%)	U.S. (%)
Adults who have ever been told they had a heart attack	3.8	4.2
Adults who have ever been told they have angina or coronary heart disease	4.1	4.0
Adults who have ever been told they had a stroke	3.4	3.3
Adults who have ever been told they have asthma	15.0	15.7
Adults who have ever been told they have arthritis	26.3	26.3
Adults who have ever been told they have diabetes[2]	12.3	11.5
Adults who have ever been told they had skin cancer	4.7	5.6
Adults who have ever been told they had any other types of cancer	8.0	8.4
Adults who have ever been told they have COPD	5.8	6.4
Adults who have ever been told they have kidney disease	4.0	3.7
Adults who have ever been told they have a form of depression	25.3	22.0

Note: All figures are crude prevalence; (1) Figures cover the Columbus, OH Metropolitan Statistical Area; (2) Figures do not include pregnancy-related, borderline, or pre-diabetes
Source: Centers for Disease Control and Prevention, Behavioral Risk Factor Surveillance System, SMART: Selected Metropolitan Area Risk Trends, 2023

Health Screening and Vaccination Rates

Category	MSA[1] (%)	U.S. (%)
Adults who have ever been tested for HIV	35.0	37.5
Adults who have had their blood cholesterol checked within the last five years	87.9	87.0
Adults aged 65+ who have had flu shot within the past year	68.9	63.4
Adults aged 65+ who have ever had a pneumonia vaccination	78.1	71.9

Note: All figures are crude prevalence; (1) Figures cover the Columbus, OH Metropolitan Statistical Area.
Source: Centers for Disease Control and Prevention, Behavioral Risk Factor Surveillance System, SMART: Selected Metropolitan Area Risk Trends, 2023

Disability Status

Category	MSA[1] (%)	U.S. (%)
Adults who reported being deaf	5.4	7.4
Are you blind or have serious difficulty seeing, even when wearing glasses?	3.7	4.9
Do you have difficulty doing errands alone?	6.6	7.8
Do you have difficulty dressing or bathing?	3.2	3.6
Do you have serious difficulty concentrating/remembering/making decisions?	13.4	13.7
Do you have serious difficulty walking or climbing stairs?	11.4	13.2

Note: All figures are crude prevalence; (1) Figures cover the Columbus, OH Metropolitan Statistical Area.
Source: Centers for Disease Control and Prevention, Behavioral Risk Factor Surveillance System, SMART: Selected Metropolitan Area Risk Trends, 2023

Mortality Rates for the Top 10 Causes of Death in the U.S.

ICD-10[a] Sub-Chapter	ICD-10[a] Code	Crude Mortality Rate[2] per 100,000 population	
		County[3]	U.S.
Malignant neoplasms	C00-C97	146.4	182.7
Ischaemic heart diseases	I20-I25	72.3	109.6
Provisional assignment of new diseases of uncertain etiology[1]	U00-U49	46.4	65.3
Other forms of heart disease	I30-I51	54.7	65.1
Other degenerative diseases of the nervous system	G30-G31	41.6	52.4
Other external causes of accidental injury	W00-X59	80.5	52.3
Cerebrovascular diseases	I60-I69	41.1	49.1
Chronic lower respiratory diseases	J40-J47	37.2	43.5
Hypertensive diseases	I10-I15	40.1	38.9
Organic, including symptomatic, mental disorders	F01-F09	27.2	33.9

Note: (a) ICD-10 = International Classification of Diseases 10th Revision; (1) Includes COVID-19, adverse effects to COVID-19 vaccines, SARS, and vaping-related disorders; (2) Crude mortality rates are a three-year average covering 2021-2023; (3) Figures cover Franklin County.
Source: Centers for Disease Control and Prevention, National Center for Health Statistics. National Vital Statistics System, Mortality 2018-2023 on CDC WONDER Online Database

Mortality Rates for Selected Causes of Death

Cause of Death	ICD-10[a] Code	Crude Mortality Rate[1] per 100,000 population	
		County[2]	U.S.
Accidental poisoning and exposure to noxious substances	X40-X49	57.7	30.5
Alzheimer disease	G30	25.0	35.4
Assault	X85-Y09	13.4	7.3
COVID-19	U07.1	46.4	65.3
Diabetes mellitus	E10-E14	21.0	30.0
Diseases of the liver	K70-K76	16.5	20.8
Human immunodeficiency virus (HIV) disease	B20-B24	1.1	1.5
Influenza and pneumonia	J09-J18	10.6	13.4
Intentional self-harm	X60-X84	13.0	14.7
Malnutrition	E40-E46	8.0	6.0
Obesity and other hyperalimentation	E65-E68	2.3	3.1
Renal failure	N17-N19	13.3	16.4
Transport accidents	V01-V99	11.5	14.4

Note: (a) ICD-10 = International Classification of Diseases 10th Revision; (1) Crude mortality rates are a three-year average covering 2021-2023; (2) Figures cover Franklin County; Data are suppressed when the data meet the criteria for confidentiality constraints; Crude mortality rates are flagged as unreliable when the rate would be calculated with a numerator of 20 or less.
Source: Centers for Disease Control and Prevention, National Center for Health Statistics. National Vital Statistics System, Mortality 2018-2023 on CDC WONDER Online Database

Health Insurance Coverage

Area	With Health Insurance	With Private Health Insurance	With Public Health Insurance	Without Health Insurance	Population Under Age 19 Without Health Insurance
City	90.2	62.3	35.5	9.8	5.8
MSA[1]	92.6	70.0	32.5	7.4	4.5
U.S.	91.4	67.3	36.3	8.6	5.4

Note: Figures are percentages that cover the civilian noninstitutionalized population; (1) Figures cover the Columbus, OH Metropolitan Statistical Area
Source: U.S. Census Bureau, 2019-2023 American Community Survey 5-Year Estimates

Number of Medical Professionals

Area	MDs[3]	DOs[3,4]	Dentists	Podiatrists	Chiropractors	Optometrists
County[1] (number)	6,255	1,041	1,315	106	352	396
County[1] (rate[2])	473.2	78.8	99.2	8.0	26.5	29.9
U.S. (rate[2])	302.5	29.2	74.6	6.4	29.5	18.0

Note: Data as of 2023 unless noted; (1) Data covers Franklin County; (2) Number of medical professionals per 100,000 population; (3) Data as of 2022 and includes all active, non-federal physicians; (4) Doctor of Osteopathic Medicine
Source: U.S. Department of Health and Human Services, Health Resources and Services Administration, Bureau of Health Professions, Area Resource File (ARF) 2023-2024

Best Hospitals

According to *U.S. News,* the Columbus, OH metro area is home to three of the best hospitals in the U.S.: **Ohio State University James Cancer Hospital** (1 adult specialty); **Ohio State University Wexner Medical Center** (8 adult specialties); **OhioHealth Rehabilitation Hospital** (1 adult specialty). The hospitals listed were nationally ranked in at least one of 15 adult or 11 pediatric specialties. The number of specialties shown cover the parent hospital. Only 160 U.S. hospitals performed well enough to be nationally ranked in one or more specialties. Twenty hospitals in the U.S. made the Honor Roll. The Best Hospitals Honor Roll takes both the national rankings and the procedure and condition ratings into account. Hospitals received points if they were nationally ranked in one of the 15 adult specialties—the higher they ranked, the more points they got—and how many ratings of "high performing" they earned in the 20 procedures and conditions. *U.S. News Online, "America's Best Hospitals 2024-25"*

According to *U.S. News,* the Columbus, OH metro area is home to one of the best children's hospitals in the U.S.: **Nationwide Children's Hospital** (Honor Roll/11 pediatric specialties). The hospital listed was highly ranked in at least one of 11 pediatric specialties. One hundred five children's hospitals in the U.S. were nationally ranked in at least one specialty. Hospitals received points for being ranked in a specialty, and the 10 hospitals with the most points across the 11 specialties make up the Honor Roll. *U.S. News Online, "America's Best Children's Hospitals 2024-25"*

EDUCATION

Public School District Statistics

District Name	Schls	Pupils	Pupil/ Teacher Ratio	Minority Pupils[1] (%)	Total Rev. per Pupil ($)	Total Exp. per Pupil ($)
Columbus City School District	116	45,181	15.5	80.3	22,787	22,434
Hamilton Local	5	3,151	19.0	33.9	14,958	11,883
Hilliard City	24	16,164	16.5	33.8	16,175	15,401

Note: Table includes school districts with 2,000 or more students; (1) Percentage of students that are not non-Hispanic white.
Source: U.S. Department of Education, National Center for Education Statistics, Common Core of Data, Local Education Agency (School District) Universe Survey: School Year 2023-2024; U.S. Department of Education, National Center for Education Statistics, Common Core of Data, School District Finance Survey (F-33): School Year 2021–22

Highest Level of Education

Area	Less than H.S.	H.S. Diploma	Some College, No Deg.	Associate Degree	Bachelor's Degree	Master's Degree	Prof. School Degree	Doctorate Degree
City	10.2	25.2	19.2	7.2	24.1	10.2	2.1	1.8
MSA[1]	7.9	26.7	18.4	7.5	24.4	10.8	2.5	1.7
U.S.	10.6	26.2	19.4	8.8	21.3	9.8	2.3	1.6

Note: Figures cover persons age 25 and over; (1) Figures cover the Columbus, OH Metropolitan Statistical Area
Source: U.S. Census Bureau, 2019-2023 American Community Survey 5-Year Estimates

Educational Attainment by Race

Area	High School Graduate or Higher (%)					Bachelor's Degree or Higher (%)				
	Total	White	Black	Asian	Hisp.[2]	Total	White	Black	Asian	Hisp.[2]
City	89.8	93.6	86.6	82.8	71.2	38.2	45.8	21.1	57.8	25.2
MSA[1]	92.1	94.2	87.4	86.3	75.0	39.4	41.8	23.9	62.6	27.7
U.S.	89.4	92.9	88.1	88.0	72.5	35.0	37.7	24.7	57.0	19.9

Note: Figures shown cover persons 25 years old and over; (1) Figures cover the Columbus, OH Metropolitan Statistical Area; (2) People of Hispanic origin can be of any race
Source: U.S. Census Bureau, 2019-2023 American Community Survey 5-Year Estimates

School Enrollment by Grade and Control

Area	Preschool (%)		Kindergarten (%)		Grades 1 - 4 (%)		Grades 5 - 8 (%)		Grades 9 - 12 (%)	
	Public	Private	Public	Private	Public	Private	Public	Private	Public	Private
City	64.5	35.5	79.2	20.8	84.3	15.7	85.7	14.3	87.2	12.8
MSA[1]	56.4	43.6	81.4	18.6	87.0	13.0	88.1	11.9	88.9	11.1
U.S.	58.7	41.3	85.2	14.8	87.2	12.8	87.9	12.1	89.0	11.0

Note: Figures shown cover persons 3 years old and over; (1) Figures cover the Columbus, OH Metropolitan Statistical Area
Source: U.S. Census Bureau, 2019-2023 American Community Survey 5-Year Estimates

Higher Education

Four-Year Colleges			Two-Year Colleges			Medical Schools[1]	Law Schools[2]	Voc/ Tech[3]
Public	Private Non-profit	Private For-profit	Public	Private Non-profit	Private For-profit			
4	12	4	1	1	8	1	2	8

Note: Figures cover institutions located within the Columbus, OH Metropolitan Statistical Area and include main campuses only; (1) includes schools accredited by the Liaison Committee on Medical Education and the American Osteopathic Association's Commission on Osteopathic College Accreditation; (2) includes ABA-accredited schools, schools with provisional ABA accreditation, and state accredited schools; (3) includes all schools with programs that are less than 2 years.
Source: National Center for Education Statistics, Integrated Postsecondary Education System (IPEDS), 2023-24; Wikipedia, List of Medical Schools in the United States, accessed May 2, 2025; Wikipedia, List of Law Schools in the United States, accessed May 2, 2025

According to *U.S. News & World Report*, the Columbus, OH metro area is home to one of the top 200 national universities in the U.S.: **The Ohio State University** (#41 tie). The indicators used to capture academic quality fall into a number of categories: assessment by administrators at peer institutions; retention of students; faculty resources; student selectivity; financial resources; alumni giving; high school counselor ratings of colleges; and graduation rate. *U.S. News & World Report, "America's Best Colleges 2025"*

According to *U.S. News & World Report*, the Columbus, OH metro area is home to one of the top 100 liberal arts colleges in the U.S.: **Denison University** (#36 tie). The indicators used to capture academic quality fall into a number of categories: assessment by administrators at peer institutions; retention of students; faculty resources; student selectivity; financial resources; alumni giving; high school counselor ratings of colleges; and graduation rate. *U.S. News & World Report, "America's Best Colleges 2025"*

According to *U.S. News & World Report*, the Columbus, OH metro area is home to one of the top 100 law schools in the U.S.: **Ohio State University (Moritz)** (#28 tie). The rankings are based on a weighted average of 12 measures of quality: peer assessment score; assessment score by lawyers/judges; median LSAT scores; median undergrad GPA; acceptance rate; employment rates for graduates; placement success; bar passage rate; faculty resources; expenditures per student; student/faculty ratio; and library resources. *U.S. News & World Report, "America's Best Graduate Schools, Law, 2025"*

According to *U.S. News & World Report*, the Columbus, OH metro area is home to one of the top medical schools for research in the U.S.: **Ohio State University** (Tier 1). *U.S. News* placed medical and osteopathic schools into tiers based on their research productivity, faculty and admissions data. Each school's tier was derived from its overall score, calculated by summing the weighted normalized values generated across several factors of academic quality, outlined below. There are four tiers, with tier 1 medical schools as the highest-performing and tier 4 as the lowest-performing. Only tier 1 and 2 schools are shown. Because of the tier presentation, *U.S. News* calculated overall scores based on their percentile performance among all rated schools instead of dividing against the rescaled score of the No. 1-performing schools. Tier 1 included schools with overall scores of 85 to 99. The cutoffs for tiers 2 through 4 were schools scoring 50 to 84, 15 to 49 and 1 to 14, respectively. The rankings are based on a weighted average of the following measures of quality: total research activity; average research activity per faculty member; total NIH research grants at the medical school and its affiliated hospitals; average NIH research grants per faculty; median MCAT total score; median undergraduate GPA; acceptance rate; and faculty resources. *U.S. News & World Report, "America's Best Graduate Schools, Medical, 2025"*

According to *U.S. News & World Report*, the Columbus, OH metro area is home to one of the top medical schools for primary care in the U.S.: **Ohio State University** (Tier 2). *U.S. News* placed medical and osteopathic schools into tiers based on their research productivity, faculty and admissions data. Each school's tier was derived from its overall score, calculated by summing the weighted normalized values generated across several factors of academic quality, outlined below. There are four tiers, with tier 1 medical schools as the highest-performing and tier 4 as the lowest-performing. Only tier 1 and 2 schools are shown. Because of the tier presentation, *U.S. News* calculated overall scores based on their percentile performance among all rated schools instead of dividing against the rescaled score of the No. 1-performing schools. Tier 1 included schools with overall scores of 85 to 99. The cutoffs for tiers 2 through 4 were schools scoring 50 to 84, 15 to 49 and 1 to 14, respectively. The rankings are based on a weighted average of the following measures of quality: graduates practicing in primary care specialties; graduates entering primary care residencies; median MCAT total score; median undergraduate GPA; acceptance rate; and faculty resources. *U.S. News & World Report, "America's Best Graduate Schools, Medical, 2025"*

According to *U.S. News & World Report*, the Columbus, OH metro area is home to one of the top 75 business schools in the U.S.: **Ohio State University (Fisher)** (#24 tie). The rankings are based on a weighted average of the following nine measures: quality assessment; peer assessment; recruiter assessment; placement success; mean starting salary and bonus; student selectivity; mean GMAT and GRE scores; mean undergraduate GPA; and acceptance rate. *U.S. News & World Report, "America's Best Graduate Schools, Business, 2025"*

EMPLOYERS

Major Employers

Company Name	Industry
Abbott Labs, Ross Products Division	Manufacturing
American Electric Power	Utilities
AT&T Ohio	Information
Battelle Memorial Institute	Professional services
Big Lots	Corp. mgt./retail trade
City of Columbus	Municipal government
Columbus City Schools	Public education
Franklin County	Government
Honda of America Manufacturing	Manufacturing
Huntington Bancshares	Financial activities
JPMorgan Chase	Financial activities
Kroger Company	Retail grocery
Limited Brands	Corp. mgt./retail trade
Medco Health Solutions	Healthcare/wholesale trade
Mount Carmel Health System	Healthcare
Nationwide	Financial activities
Nationwide Children's Hospital	Healthcare
OhioHealth	Healthcare
Retail Ventures	Corp. mgt./retail trade
South-Western City School District	Public education

Note: Companies shown are located within the Columbus, OH Metropolitan Statistical Area.
Source: Chambers of Commerce; State Departments of Labor; Wikipedia

Best Companies to Work For

Nationwide Mutual Insurance Company, headquartered in Columbus, is among "The 100 Best Companies to Work For." To pick the best companies, *Fortune* partnered with the Great Place to Work Institute. Using their proprietary Trust Index™ survey, the core of what creates great a workplace is measured—key behaviors that drive trust in management, connection with colleagues, and loyalty to the company. To be eligible for the *Fortune* 100 Best Companies to Work For list, employers must have 1,000 or more employees in the U.S. and cannot be a government agency. *Fortune, "The 100 Best Companies to Work For," 2025*

Loop Returns; Nationwide Mutual Insurance Company, headquartered in Columbus, are among "Fortune's Best Workplaces for Parents." To pick the best companies, *Fortune* partnered with the Great Place to Work Institute. To be considered for the list, companies must be Great Place To Work-Certified and have at least 50 responses from parents in the US. The survey enables employees to share confidential quantitative and qualitative feedback about their organization's culture by responding to 60 statements on a 5-point scale and answering two open-ended questions. Collectively, these statements describe a great employee experience, defined by high levels of trust, respect, credibility, fairness, pride, and camaraderie. In addition, companies provide organizational data like size, location, industry, demographics, roles, and levels; and provide information about parental leave, adoption, flexible schedule, childcare and dependent health care benefits. *Fortune, "Best Workplaces for Parents," 2024*

Loop Returns; Nationwide Mutual Insurance Company, headquartered in Columbus, are among "Fortune's Best Workplaces for Women." To pick the best companies, *Fortune* partnered with the Great Place to Work Institute. To be considered for the list, companies must be Great Place To Work-Certified. Companies must also employ at least 50 women, at least 20% of their non-executive managers must be female, and at least one executive must be female. To determine the Best Workplaces for Women, Great Place To Work measured the differences in women's survey responses to those of their peers and assesses the impact of demographics and roles on the quality and consistency of women's experiences. Great Place To Work also analyzed the gender balance of each workplace, how it compared to each company's industry, and patterns in representation as women rise from front-line positions to the board of directors. *Fortune, "Best Workplaces for Women," 2024*

Avaap; Nationwide Mutual Insurance Company; Worthington Steel, headquartered in Columbus, are among the "Best Places to Work in IT." To qualify, companies had to have a minimum of 100 total employees and five IT employees. The best places to work were selected based on DEI (diversity, equity, and inclusion) practices; IT turnover, promotions, and growth; IT retention and engagement programs; remote/hybrid working; benefits and perks (such as elder care and child care, flextime, and reimbursement for college tuition); and training and career development opportunities. *Computerworld, "Best Places to Work in IT," 2025*

PUBLIC SAFETY

Crime Rate

Area	Total Crime Rate	Violent Crime Rate				Property Crime Rate		
		Murder	Rape	Robbery	Aggrav. Assault	Burglary	Larceny-Theft	Motor Vehicle Theft
City	3,089.1	10.5	115.3	117.5	141.8	412.2	1,553.0	738.9
U.S.	2,290.9	5.7	38.0	66.5	264.1	250.7	1,347.2	318.7

Note: Figures are crimes per 100,000 population.
Source: FBI, Table 8, Offenses Known to Law Enforcement, by State by City, 2023

Hate Crimes

Area	Number of Quarters Reported	Number of Incidents per Bias Motivation					
		Race/Ethnicity/Ancestry	Religion	Sexual Orientation	Disability	Gender	Gender Identity
City[1]	4	16	7	10	0	0	2
U.S.	4	5,900	2,699	2,077	187	92	492

Note: (1) Figures include at least one incident reported with more than one bias motivation.
Source: Federal Bureau of Investigation, Hate Crime Statistics 2023

Identity Theft Consumer Reports

Area	Reports	Reports per 100,000 Population	Rank[2]
MSA[1]	6,805	316	56
U.S.	1,135,291	339	-

Note: (1) Figures cover the Columbus, OH Metropolitan Statistical Area; (2) Rank ranges from 1 to 401 where 1 indicates greatest number of identity theft reports per 100,000 population
Source: Federal Trade Commission, Consumer Sentinel Network Data Book 2024

Fraud and Other Consumer Reports

Area	Reports	Reports per 100,000 Population	Rank[2]
MSA[1]	28,999	1,348	86
U.S.	5,360,641	1,601	-

Note: (1) Figures cover the Columbus, OH Metropolitan Statistical Area; (2) Rank ranges from 1 to 401 where 1 indicates greatest number of fraud and other consumer reports per 100,000 population
Source: Federal Trade Commission, Consumer Sentinel Network Data Book 2024

POLITICS

2024 Presidential Election Results

Area	Trump (Rep.)	Harris (Dem.)	Stein (Green)	Kennedy (Ind.)	Oliver (Lib.)	Other
Franklin County	34.9	63.0	0.6	0.0	0.6	0.9
U.S.	49.7	48.2	0.6	0.5	0.4	0.6

Note: Results are percentages and may not add to 100% due to rounding
Source: Dave Leip's Atlas of U.S. Presidential Elections

SPORTS

Professional Sports Teams

Team Name	League	Year Established
Columbus Blue Jackets	National Hockey League (NHL)	2000
Columbus Crew	Major League Soccer (MLS)	1996

Note: Includes teams located in the Columbus, OH Metropolitan Statistical Area.
Source: Wikipedia, Major Professional Sports Teams of the United States and Canada, May 1, 2025

CLIMATE

Average and Extreme Temperatures

Temperature	Jan	Feb	Mar	Apr	May	Jun	Jul	Aug	Sep	Oct	Nov	Dec	Yr.
Extreme High (°F)	74	73	82	89	93	101	104	101	100	90	80	76	104
Average High (°F)	36	39	50	62	73	82	85	83	77	65	51	40	62
Average Temp. (°F)	28	31	41	52	62	70	74	73	66	54	43	32	52
Average Low (°F)	20	22	31	40	50	59	63	62	55	43	34	24	42
Extreme Low (°F)	-19	-13	-6	14	25	35	43	39	31	17	-4	-17	-19

Note: Figures cover the years 1948-1990
Source: National Climatic Data Center, International Station Meteorological Climate Summary, 9/96

Average Precipitation/Snowfall/Humidity

Precip./Humidity	Jan	Feb	Mar	Apr	May	Jun	Jul	Aug	Sep	Oct	Nov	Dec	Yr.
Avg. Precip. (in.)	2.8	2.4	3.1	3.3	3.9	4.0	4.3	3.3	2.7	2.1	3.0	2.8	37.9
Avg. Snowfall (in.)	8	6	5	1	Tr	0	0	0	Tr	Tr	2	6	28
Avg. Rel. Hum. 7am (%)	78	78	76	76	79	81	84	87	87	83	80	79	81
Avg. Rel. Hum. 4pm (%)	66	62	55	51	52	53	53	54	53	53	61	68	57

Note: Figures cover the years 1948-1990; Tr = Trace amounts (<0.05 in. of rain; <0.5 in. of snow)
Source: National Climatic Data Center, International Station Meteorological Climate Summary, 9/96

Weather Conditions

Temperature			Daytime Sky			Precipitation		
5°F & below	32°F & below	90°F & above	Clear	Partly cloudy	Cloudy	0.01 inch or more precip.	0.1 inch or more snow/ice	Thunderstorms
10	118	19	72	137	156	136	29	40

Note: Figures are average number of days per year and cover the years 1948-1990
Source: National Climatic Data Center, International Station Meteorological Climate Summary, 9/96

HAZARDOUS WASTE

Superfund Sites

The Columbus, OH metro area is home to one site on the EPA's Superfund National Priorities List (NPL) or Superfund Alternative Approach (SAA) list: **Air Force Plant 85** (Proposed NPL). The Superfund alternative approach uses the same investigation and cleanup process and standards that are used for sites listed on the National Priorities List. The SAA is an alternative to listing a site on the NPL; it is not an alternative to Superfund or the Superfund process. There are a total of 1,445 Superfund sites with a status of proposed or final on both lists in the United States. *U.S. Environmental Protection Agency, National Priorities List, May 1, 2025; U.S. Environmental Protection Agency, Superfund Alternative Approach Sites, May 1, 2025*

AIR QUALITY

Air Quality Trends: Ozone

	1990	1995	2000	2005	2010	2015	2020	2021	2022	2023
MSA[1]	0.090	0.091	0.085	0.084	0.073	0.066	0.062	0.061	0.061	0.066
U.S.	0.087	0.089	0.081	0.080	0.072	0.068	0.065	0.067	0.067	0.070

Note: (1) Data covers the Columbus, OH Metropolitan Statistical Area. The values shown are the composite ozone concentration averages among trend sites based on the highest fourth daily maximum 8-hour concentration in parts per million. These trends are based on sites having an adequate record of monitoring data during the trend period. Data from exceptional events are included.
Source: U.S. Environmental Protection Agency, Air Quality Monitoring Information, "Air Quality Trends by City, 1990-2023"

Air Quality Index

Area	Percent of Days when Air Quality was...[2]					AQI Statistics[2]	
	Good	Moderate	Unhealthy for Sensitive Groups	Unhealthy	Very Unhealthy	Maximum	Median
MSA[1]	37.0	59.5	2.5	0.8	0.3	210	54

Note: (1) Data covers the Columbus, OH Metropolitan Statistical Area; (2) Based on 365 days with AQI data in 2023. Air Quality Index (AQI) is an index for reporting daily air quality. EPA calculates the AQI for five major air pollutants regulated by the Clean Air Act: ground-level ozone, particle pollution (aka particulate matter), carbon monoxide, sulfur dioxide, and nitrogen dioxide. The AQI runs from 0 to 500. The higher the AQI value, the greater the level of air pollution and the greater the health concern. There are six AQI categories: "Good" AQI is between 0 and 50. Air quality is considered satisfactory; "Moderate" AQI is between 51 and 100. Air quality is acceptable; "Unhealthy for Sensitive Groups" When AQI values are between 101 and 150, members of sensitive groups may experience health effects; "Unhealthy" When AQI values are between 151 and 200 everyone may begin to experience health effects; "Very Unhealthy" AQI values between 201 and 300 trigger a health alert; "Hazardous" AQI values over 300 trigger warnings of emergency conditions (not shown).
Source: U.S. Environmental Protection Agency, Air Quality Index Report, 2023

Air Quality Index Pollutants

Area	Percent of Days when AQI Pollutant was...[2]					
	Carbon Monoxide	Nitrogen Dioxide	Ozone	Sulfur Dioxide	Particulate Matter 2.5	Particulate Matter 10
MSA[1]	0.0	0.0	26.6	(3)	71.2	2.2

Note: (1) Data covers the Columbus, OH Metropolitan Statistical Area; (2) Based on 365 days with AQI data in 2023. The Air Quality Index (AQI) is an index for reporting daily air quality. EPA calculates the AQI for five major air pollutants regulated by the Clean Air Act: ground-level ozone, particle pollution (also known as particulate matter), carbon monoxide, sulfur dioxide, and nitrogen dioxide. The AQI runs from 0 to 500. The higher the AQI value, the greater the level of air pollution and the greater the health concern; (3) Sulfur dioxide is no longer included in this table because SO_2 concentrations tend to be very localized and not necessarily representative of broad geographical areas like counties and CBSAs.
Source: U.S. Environmental Protection Agency, Air Quality Index Report, 2023

Maximum Air Pollutant Concentrations: Particulate Matter, Ozone, CO and Lead

	Particulate Matter 10 (ug/m^3)	Particulate Matter 2.5 Wtd AM (ug/m^3)	Particulate Matter 2.5 24-Hr (ug/m^3)	Ozone (ppm)	Carbon Monoxide (ppm)	Lead (ug/m^3)
MSA[1] Level	97	10.9	36	0.069	1	0
NAAQS[2]	150	15	35	0.075	9	0.15
Met NAAQS[2]	Yes	Yes	No	Yes	Yes	Yes

Note: (1) Data covers the Columbus, OH Metropolitan Statistical Area; Data from exceptional events are included; (2) National Ambient Air Quality Standards; ppm = parts per million; ug/m^3 = micrograms per cubic meter; n/a not available.
Concentrations: Particulate Matter 10 (coarse particulate)—highest second maximum 24-hour concentration; Particulate Matter 2.5 Wtd AM (fine particulate)—highest weighted annual mean concentration; Particulate Matter 2.5 24-Hour (fine particulate)—highest 98th percentile 24-hour concentration; Ozone—highest fourth daily maximum 8-hour concentration; Carbon Monoxide—highest second maximum non-overlapping 8-hour concentration; Lead—maximum running 3-month average
Source: U.S. Environmental Protection Agency, Air Quality Monitoring Information, "Air Quality Statistics by City, 2023"

Maximum Air Pollutant Concentrations: Nitrogen Dioxide and Sulfur Dioxide

	Nitrogen Dioxide AM (ppb)	Nitrogen Dioxide 1-Hr (ppb)	Sulfur Dioxide AM (ppb)	Sulfur Dioxide 1-Hr (ppb)	Sulfur Dioxide 24-Hr (ppb)
MSA[1] Level	9	43	n/a	4	n/a
NAAQS[2]	53	100	30	75	140
Met NAAQS[2]	Yes	Yes	n/a	Yes	n/a

Note: (1) Data covers the Columbus, OH Metropolitan Statistical Area; Data from exceptional events are included; (2) National Ambient Air Quality Standards; ppm = parts per million; ug/m^3 = micrograms per cubic meter; n/a not available.
Concentrations: Nitrogen Dioxide AM—highest arithmetic mean concentration; Nitrogen Dioxide 1-Hr—highest 98th percentile 1-hour daily maximum concentration; Sulfur Dioxide AM—highest annual mean concentration; Sulfur Dioxide 1-Hr—highest 99th percentile 1-hour daily maximum concentration; Sulfur Dioxide 24-Hr—highest second maximum 24-hour concentration
Source: U.S. Environmental Protection Agency, Air Quality Monitoring Information, "Air Quality Statistics by City, 2023"

Durham, North Carolina

Background

Durham, on the Eno River in north-central North Carolina, is known as the "City of Medicine," and forms a corner of the region's famous Research Triangle, one of the nation's earliest and most successful planned centers for research and development. The economy is deeply interlinked with area universities and businesses specializing in medicine, biopharmaceuticals, computer technology and software, and telecommunications.

The original inhabitants of the area were Eno and Occaneechi Native Americans, who were mostly settled, horticulturist villagers. English explorer John Lawson visited the site in 1701, and called it the "flower of the Carolinas" for its scenic beauty. By the mid-eighteenth century, Scottish, Irish, and English settlers had established farms in the site of the present city.

Durham began as a station for the North Carolina Railroad, which had been built on land originally owned by the city's namesake, Bartlett Durham. Prior to the Civil War, several extensive plantations were established in the area.

Throughout the prewar period and beyond, Durham continued its growth as a center for tobacco farming and processing, with emphasis on "brightleaf" tobacco. Tobacco entrepreneur Washington Duke was of particular importance to the growth of Durham, and his efforts helped established Durham as a major regional economic center. The textile industry also grew and prospered Durham in the post-Civil War years, giving rise to many clothing innovations, including the nation's first denim and sheer hosiery mills.

In 1910, the popular B.C. Headache Powders were produced in Durham and the city's connection with health care deepened considerably when Duke University's Medical School opened in 1939. Durham's current economy is both high-tech and broad-based. Hundreds of private companies in the area employ thousands of highly skilled workers in a variety of high-technology enterprises.

Durham boasts a vibrant African American community, the center of which was an area once known as Hayti, just south of the center of town, where some of the most prominent and successful black-owned businesses in the country were established during the early 20th century. Portions of the Hayti district, along with large parts of other historic neighborhoods, were demolished for the construction of the Durham Freeway during the late 1960s. Although downtown revitalization heated up in the 1970s and 1980s, economic progress continues to compete with historic preservation.

Durham's downtown draws many residents and out-of-town visitors for its architecture, shops, and restaurants. Former tobacco warehouses and factories are converted to residential, office, retail, and entertainment uses. The American Tobacco Company Historic District now features historic preservation projects, as well as offices, restaurants, stores, and residences. At the center of Durham's cultural scene is The Carolina Theatre, a historic building currently owned by the city and maintained by The Carolina Theatre of Durham Inc. Durham is home to the renowned annual Full Frame Documentary Film Festival, which celebrates its 28th year in 2025.

Beyond the influence of the historic theater, Durham maintains a vibrant arts scene. Many of Durham's substantial cultural assets are linked to Duke University, including the Nasher Museum of Art at Duke University, whose Rafael Vinoly-designed building hosts traveling exhibitions from cutting-edge contemporary artists. Duke University also hosts The American Dance Festival each summer. The city is also home to North Carolina Central University (1910), the nation's first publicly supported liberal arts college for African Americans.

In 2020, Durham residents elected its first Muslim American women to the city commission.

Durham is serviced by the 5,000-acre Raleigh-Durham International Airport, one of the country's fastest-growing terminals, now with two passenger terminals.

Durham lies between coastal plain and piedmont plateau, giving it a moderate climate. The mountains to the west partially protect the area from excess cold winter winds, although temperatures fall below freezing some days. Summers are hot and humid. July and August see the most rain, often in the form of thunderstorms, while October and November see the least amount of rainfall.

Rankings

General Rankings

- To help military veterans find the best places in which to settle down, *WalletHub* compared the 100 largest U.S. cities across 19 key indicators of livability, affordability and veteran-friendliness. They range from the share of military skill-related jobs to veteran income growth to the availability of VA health facilities. Durham ranked #23. *Wallethub.com, "Best & Worst Places for Veterans to Live (2025)," November 7, 2024*

- Durham was selected as one of the best places to live in the United States by *Money* magazine. The city placed among the top 50. This year's list focused on cities built around community spirit, thoughtful policy and civic engagement. Instead of relying on a predetermined dataset, the cities and towns were grouped according to their strengths and chosen due their affordability, good schools and strong job markets. *Money, "The 50 Best Places to Live in the U.S., 2024" April 8, 2024*

- In their annual survey, Livability.com looked at data for more than 2,000 mid-sized U.S. cities to assign a "Livability Score"for each. The top 100 scoring cities make up Livability's "Top 100 Best Places to Live in the U.S." in 2025. Durham was placed among the top 100 of the customizable list. Criteria: housing and economy; cost of living; environment; education; health care options; transportation; safety; and community amenities. *Livability.com, "Top 100 Best Places to Live in the U.S. in 2025" April 15, 2025*

Business/Finance Rankings

- The Durham metro area appeared on the Milken Institute "2025 Best Performing Cities" list. Rank: #16 out of 200 large metro areas (based on performance category). Criteria: job growth; wage growth; high-tech growth and impact; community resilience; housing affordability; household broadband access. *Milken Institute, "Best-Performing Cities 2025," January 14, 2025*

Education Rankings

- Personal finance website *WalletHub* analyzed the 150 largest U.S. metropolitan statistical areas to determine where the most educated Americans are putting their degrees to work. Criteria: education levels; percentage of workers with degrees; education quality and attainment gap; public school quality rankings; quality and enrollment of each metro area's universities. Durham was ranked #4 (#1 = most educated city). *WalletHub.com, "Most & Least Educated Cities in America, 2025" July 2, 2024*

Health/Fitness Rankings

- For each of the 100 largest cities in the United States, the American Fitness Index®, compiled in partnership between the American College of Sports Medicine and the Elevance Health Foundation, evaluated community infrastructure and more than 30 health behaviors including preventive health, levels of chronic disease conditions, food insecurity, pedestrian safety, air quality, and community/environment resources that support physical activity. Durham ranked #31 for "community fitness." *americanfitnessindex.org, "2024 ACSM American Fitness Index Summary Report," July 23, 2024*

- The Durham metro area was identified as one of the worst cities for bed bugs in America by pest control company Orkin. The area ranked #24 out of 50 based on the number of bed bug treatments Orkin performed from December 2022 to November 2023. *Orkin, "Chicago Joins Paris In Global Bed Bug Spotlight Ranking As The Worst City On Orkin's U.S. Bed Bug Cities List," January 22, 2024*

- Durham was identified as a "2025 Allergy Capital." The area ranked #35 out of the nation's 100 largest metropolitan areas. Three groups of factors were used to identify the most challenging cities for people with allergies: annual tree, grass, and weed pollen scores; over the counter allergy medicine use; number of board-certified allergy specialists. *Asthma and Allergy Foundation of America, "2025 Allergy Capitals: The Most Challenging Places to Live with Allergies," March 18, 2025*

- Durham was identified as a "2024 Asthma Capital." The area ranked #91 out of the nation's 100 largest metropolitan areas. Criteria: estimated asthma prevalence; asthma-related mortality; and ER visits due to asthma. Risk factors analyzed but not factored in the rankings: annual air quality including pollution and ozone levels; public smoking laws; indoor air quality; access to asthma specialists; rescue and controller medication use; uninsured rate; pollen allergy; poverty rate. *Asthma and Allergy Foundation of America, "Asthma Capitals 2024: The Most Challenging Places to Live With Asthma," September 10, 2024*

Real Estate Rankings

- *WalletHub* compared the most populated U.S. cities to determine which had the best markets for real estate agents. Durham ranked #25 where demand was high and pay was the best. Criteria: sales per agent; annual median wage for real-estate agents; monthly average starting salary for real estate agents; real estate job density and competition; unemployment rate; home turnover rate; housing-market health index; and other relevant metrics. *WalletHub.com, "2021 Best Places to Be a Real Estate Agent," May 12, 2021*

- The Durham metro area was identified as one of the top 16 housing markets to invest in for 2025 by *Forbes*. Criteria: stable local economies with good population growth and increase in jobs providing good support for home prices and rents. *Forbes.com, "Best Local Markets For Real Estate Investing In 2025," November 6, 2024*

- Durham was ranked #125 out of 176 metro areas in terms of cost of housing in 2024 by the National Association of Home Builders (#1 = most affordable). Criteria: the portion of an average family's income necessary to pay the mortgage on a median-priced home. *National Association of Home Builders®, NAHB-Wells Fargo Cost of Housing Index, 4th Quarter 2024*

Safety Rankings

- Allstate ranked the 100 most populous cities in America in terms of driver safety. Durham ranked #81. Criteria based on anonymized driving behavior data from Allstate's mobile app powered by Arity: high speed driving (over 80 mph), phone handling, and hard braking. The report helps increase the importance of safety and awareness behind the wheel. *Allstate, "16th Allstate America's Best Drivers Report®" July 11, 2024*

Women/Minorities Rankings

- Personal finance website *WalletHub* compared more than 180 U.S. cities across two key dimensions, "Hispanic Business-Friendliness" and "Hispanic Purchasing Power," to arrive at the most favorable conditions for Hispanic entrepreneurs. Durham was ranked #102 out of 182. Criteria includes: share of Hispanic-Owned Businesses; average growth of Hispanic Business revenues; Small Business-Friendliness score; affordability; and number of Hispanics with at least a bachelor's degree. *WalletHub.com, "Best Cities for Hispanic Entrepreneurs," September 4, 2024*

Miscellaneous Rankings

- Durham was selected as a 2024 Digital Cities Survey winner. The city ranked #5 in the large city (250,000 to 499,999 population) category. The survey examined and assessed how city governments are utilizing new technology and modernized applications to provide residents an array of contactless services and conveniences. Survey questions focused on ten initiatives: cybersecurity; citizen experience; disaster recovery; business intelligence; IT personnel retention; data governance; business automation; AI/machine learning; application modernization; and IT collaboration. *Center for Digital Government, "2024 Digital Cities Survey," November 5, 2024*

- *WalletHub* compared 148 of the most populated U.S. cities to determine their operating efficiency. A "Quality of Services" score was constructed for each city and then measured against the total budget per capita to reveal which were managed the best. Durham ranked #6. Criteria: financial stability; economy; education; safety; health; infrastructure and pollution. *WalletHub.com, "2025's Best- & Worst-Run Cities in America," June 18, 2024*

Business Environment

DEMOGRAPHICS

Population Growth

Area	1990 Census	2000 Census	2010 Census	2020 Census	2023 Estimate[2]	Population Growth 1990-2023 (%)
City	151,737	187,035	228,330	283,506	288,465	90.1
MSA[1]	344,646	426,493	504,357	649,903	594,291	72.4
U.S.	248,709,873	281,421,906	308,745,538	331,449,281	332,387,540	33.6

Note: (1) Figures cover the Durham-Chapel Hill, NC Metropolitan Statistical Area; (2) 2019-2023 5-year ACS population estimate
Source: U.S. Census Bureau, 1990 Census, 2000 Census, 2010 Census, 2020 Census, 2019-2023 American Community Survey 5-Year Estimates

Race

Area	White Alone[2] (%)	Black Alone[2] (%)	Asian Alone[2] (%)	AIAN[3] Alone[2] (%)	NHOPI[4] Alone[2] (%)	Other Race Alone[2] (%)	Two or More Races (%)
City	43.9	34.4	5.6	0.5	0.1	6.8	8.6
MSA[1]	56.6	24.0	5.1	0.5	0.0	5.9	7.8
U.S.	63.4	12.4	5.8	0.9	0.2	6.6	10.7

Note: (1) Figures cover the Durham-Chapel Hill, NC Metropolitan Statistical Area; (2) Alone is defined as not being in combination with one or more other races; (3) American Indian and Alaska Native; (4) Native Hawaiian and Other Pacific Islander
Source: U.S. Census Bureau, 2019-2023 American Community Survey 5-Year Estimates

Hispanic or Latino Origin

Area	Total (%)	Mexican (%)	Puerto Rican (%)	Cuban (%)	Other (%)
City	14.7	6.6	0.9	0.5	6.7
MSA[1]	13.2	6.3	0.8	0.4	5.8
U.S.	19.0	11.3	1.8	0.7	5.2

Note: Persons of Hispanic or Latino origin can be of any race; (1) Figures cover the Durham-Chapel Hill, NC Metropolitan Statistical Area
Source: U.S. Census Bureau, 2019-2023 American Community Survey 5-Year Estimates

Age

Area	Percent of Population									Median Age
	Under Age 5	Age 5–19	Age 20–34	Age 35–44	Age 45–54	Age 55–64	Age 65–74	Age 75–84	Age 85+	
City	6.1	17.6	26.8	14.3	11.5	10.7	8.1	3.5	1.4	34.8
MSA[1]	5.3	18.5	22.6	13.0	12.2	12.1	10.0	4.7	1.7	37.6
U.S.	5.7	19.1	20.2	13.1	12.3	12.8	10.0	4.9	1.9	38.7

Note: (1) Figures cover the Durham-Chapel Hill, NC Metropolitan Statistical Area
Source: U.S. Census Bureau, 2019-2023 American Community Survey 5-Year Estimates

Disability by Age

Area	All Ages	Under 18 Years Old	18 to 64 Years Old	65 Years and Over
City	9.9	3.6	8.0	29.6
MSA[1]	10.4	3.7	8.1	28.1
U.S.	13.0	4.7	10.7	32.9

Note: Figures show percent of the civilian noninstitutionalized population that reported having a disability. Disability status is determined from six types of difficulty: vision, hearing, cognitive, ambulatory, self-care, and independent living. For children under 5 years old, hearing and vision difficulty are used to determine disability status. For children between the ages of 5 and 14, disability status is determined from hearing, vision, cognitive, ambulatory, and self-care difficulties. For people aged 15 years and older, they are considered to have a disability if they have difficulty with any one of the six difficulty types; Note: (1) Figures cover the Durham-Chapel Hill, NC Metropolitan Statistical Area
Source: U.S. Census Bureau, 2019-2023 American Community Survey 5-Year Estimates

Ancestry

Area	German	Irish	English	American	Italian	Polish	French[2]	European	Scottish
City	8.2	6.7	10.0	3.8	3.4	1.8	1.5	1.7	1.8
MSA[1]	9.3	8.2	12.5	5.0	3.7	1.9	1.7	1.9	2.3
U.S.	12.6	9.4	9.1	5.5	4.9	2.6	2.0	1.6	1.6

Note: Figures are the percentage of the total population reporting a particular ancestry. The nine most commonly reported ancestries in the U.S. are shown. Figures include multiple ancestries (e.g. if a person reported being Irish and Italian, they were included in both columns); (1) Figures cover the Durham-Chapel Hill, NC Metropolitan Statistical Area; (2) Excludes Basque
Source: U.S. Census Bureau, 2019-2023 American Community Survey 5-Year Estimates

Foreign-born Population

Area	Percent of Population Born in								
	Any Foreign Country	Asia	Mexico	Europe	Caribbean	Central America[2]	South America	Africa	Canada
City	15.3	4.1	2.8	1.4	0.8	3.4	0.8	1.7	0.3
MSA[1]	13.2	3.7	2.7	1.6	0.5	2.4	0.8	1.1	0.2
U.S.	13.9	4.3	3.3	1.4	1.4	1.2	1.2	0.8	0.2

Note: (1) Figures cover the Durham-Chapel Hill, NC Metropolitan Statistical Area; (2) Excludes Mexico.
Source: U.S. Census Bureau, 2019-2023 American Community Survey 5-Year Estimates

Household Size

Area	Persons in Household (%)							Average Household Size
	One	Two	Three	Four	Five	Six	Seven or More	
City	36.1	34.1	13.9	9.9	4.0	1.4	0.6	2.25
MSA[1]	31.7	35.8	14.8	10.9	4.6	1.5	0.6	2.33
U.S.	28.5	33.8	15.4	12.7	5.9	2.3	1.4	2.54

Note: (1) Figures cover the Durham-Chapel Hill, NC Metropolitan Statistical Area
Source: U.S. Census Bureau, 2019-2023 American Community Survey 5-Year Estimates

Household Relationships

Area	House-holder	Opposite-sex Spouse	Same-sex Spouse	Opposite-sex Unmarried Partner	Same-sex Unmarried Partner	Child[2]	Grand-child	Other Relatives	Non-relatives
City	42.0	14.8	0.4	2.9	0.3	24.6	1.8	4.4	4.6
MSA[1]	40.3	17.2	0.3	2.5	0.2	25.1	1.9	3.8	3.9
U.S.	38.3	17.5	0.2	2.5	0.2	28.3	2.4	4.8	3.4

Note: Figures are percent of the total population; (1) Figures cover the Durham-Chapel Hill, NC Metropolitan Statistical Area; (2) Includes biological, adopted, and stepchildren of the householder
Source: U.S. Census Bureau, 2020 Census

Gender

Area	Males	Females	Males per 100 Females
City	136,368	152,097	89.7
MSA[1]	285,396	308,895	92.4
U.S.	164,545,087	167,842,453	98.0

Note: (1) Figures cover the Durham-Chapel Hill, NC Metropolitan Statistical Area
Source: U.S. Census Bureau, 2019-2023 American Community Survey 5-Year Estimates

Marital Status

Area	Never Married	Now Married[2]	Separated	Widowed	Divorced
City	44.1	40.5	1.8	3.7	9.8
MSA[1]	38.3	46.2	1.7	4.5	9.3
U.S.	34.1	47.9	1.7	5.6	10.7

Note: Figures are percentages and cover the population 15 years of age and older; (1) Figures cover the Durham-Chapel Hill, NC Metropolitan Statistical Area; (2) Excludes separated
Source: U.S. Census Bureau, 2019-2023 American Community Survey 5-Year Estimates

Religious Groups by Family

Area	Catholic	Baptist	Methodist	LDS[2]	Pentecostal	Lutheran	Islam	Adventist	Other
MSA[1]	8.5	12.3	6.5	0.9	1.3	0.3	1.5	1.1	13.7
U.S.	18.7	7.3	3.0	2.0	1.8	1.7	1.3	1.3	11.6

Note: Figures are the number of adherents as a percentage of the total population and cover the eight largest religious groups in the U.S; (1) Figures cover the Durham-Chapel Hill, NC Metropolitan Statistical Area; (2) Church of Jesus Christ of Latter-day Saints
Sources: 2020 U.S. Religion Census, Association of Statisticians of American Religious Bodies; The Association of Religion Data Archives (ARDA)

Religious Groups by Tradition

Area	Catholic	Evangelical Protestant	Mainline Protestant	Black Protestant	Islam	Judaism	Hinduism	Orthodox	Buddhism
MSA[1]	8.5	20.0	8.8	4.3	1.5	0.5	0.1	0.3	0.1
U.S.	18.7	16.5	5.2	2.3	1.3	0.6	0.4	0.4	0.3

Note: Figures are the number of adherents as a percentage of the total population; (1) Figures cover the Durham-Chapel Hill, NC Metropolitan Statistical Area
Sources: 2020 U.S. Religion Census, Association of Statisticians of American Religious Bodies; The Association of Religion Data Archives (ARDA)

ECONOMY

Real Gross Domestic Product (GDP)

Area	2017	2018	2019	2020	2021	2022	2023	Rank[3]
MSA[1]	46.4	48.7	50.1	51.5	55.1	57.0	59.0	58
U.S.[2]	17,619.1	18,160.7	18,642.5	18,238.9	19,387.6	19,896.6	20,436.3	—

Note: Figures are in billions of chained 2017 dollars; (1) Figures cover the Durham-Chapel Hill, NC Metropolitan Statistical Area; (2) Figures cover real GDP within metropolitan areas; (3) Rank is based on 2023 data and ranges from 1 to 384
Source: U.S. Bureau of Economic Analysis

Economic Growth

Area	2014	2015	2016	2017	2018	2019	2020	2021	2022	2023
MSA[1]	-1.9	-1.7	-0.7	-0.5	4.9	2.8	2.8	7.0	3.4	3.5
U.S.[2]	2.6	3.2	2.0	2.7	3.1	2.7	-2.2	6.3	2.6	2.7

Note: Figures are real gross domestic product growth rates and represent percent change from preceding period; (1) Figures cover the Durham-Chapel Hill, NC Metropolitan Statistical Area; (2) Figures are the average growth rates within metropolitan areas
Source: U.S. Bureau of Economic Analysis

Metropolitan Area Exports

Area	2018	2019	2020	2021	2022	2023	Rank[2]
MSA[1]	3,945.8	4,452.9	3,359.3	3,326.4	4,071.8	4,898.7	65
U.S.	1,664,056.1	1,645,173.7	1,431,406.6	1,753,941.4	2,062,937.4	2,019,160.5	—

Note: Figures are in millions of dollars; (1) Figures cover the Durham-Chapel Hill, NC Metropolitan Statistical Area; (2) Rank is based on 2023 data and ranges from 1 to 386
Source: U.S. Department of Commerce, International Trade Administration, Office of Trade and Economic Analysis, Industry and Analysis, Exports by Metropolitan Area, data extracted April 2, 2025

Building Permits

Area	Single-Family			Multi-Family			Total		
	2023	2024	Pct. Chg.	2023	2024	Pct. Chg.	2023	2024	Pct. Chg.
City	1,687	1,822	8.0	2,678	971	-63.7	4,365	2,793	-36.0
MSA[1]	3,127	2,815	-10.0	4,083	1,043	-74.5	7,210	3,858	-46.5
U.S.	920,000	981,900	6.7	591,100	496,100	-16.1	1,511,100	1,478,000	-2.2

Note: (1) Figures cover the Durham-Chapel Hill, NC Metropolitan Statistical Area; Figures represent new, privately-owned housing units authorized (unadjusted data)
Source: U.S. Census Bureau, Building Permits Survey (BPS), 2023, 2024

Bankruptcy Filings

Area	Business Filings			Nonbusiness Filings		
	2023	2024	% Chg.	2023	2024	% Chg.
Durham County	14	42	200.0	162	195	20.4
U.S.	18,926	23,107	22.1	434,064	494,201	13.9

Note: Business filings include Chapter 7, Chapter 9, Chapter 11, Chapter 12, Chapter 13, Chapter 15, and Section 304; Nonbusiness filings include Chapter 7, Chapter 11, and Chapter 13
Source: Administrative Office of the U.S. Courts, Business and Nonbusiness Bankruptcy, County Cases Commenced by Chapter of the Bankruptcy Code, During the 12-Month Period Ending December 31, 2023 and Business and Nonbusiness Bankruptcy, County Cases Commenced by Chapter of the Bankruptcy Code, During the 12-Month Period Ending December 31, 2024

Housing Vacancy Rates

Area	Gross Vacancy Rate[3] (%)			Year-Round Vacancy Rate[4] (%)			Rental Vacancy Rate[5] (%)			Homeowner Vacancy Rate[6] (%)		
	2022	2023	2024	2022	2023	2024	2022	2023	2024	2022	2023	2024
MSA[1]	n/a	n/a	n/a	n/a	n/a	n/a	n/a	n/a	n/a	n/a	n/a	n/a
U.S.[2]	9.1	9.0	9.1	7.5	7.5	7.6	5.7	6.5	6.8	0.8	0.8	1.0

Note: (1) Figures cover the Durham-Chapel Hill, NC Metropolitan Statistical Area; (2) Figures cover the 75 largest Metropolitan Statistical Areas; (3) The percentage of the total housing inventory that is vacant; (4) The percentage of the housing inventory (excluding seasonal units) that is year-round vacant; (5) The percentage of rental inventory that is vacant for rent; (6) The percentage of homeowner inventory that is vacant for sale; n/a not available
Source: U.S. Census Bureau, Housing Vacancies and Homeownership Annual Statistics: 2022, 2023, 2024

INCOME

Income

Area	Per Capita ($)	Median Household ($)	Average Household ($)
City	47,246	79,234	108,538
MSA[1]	48,827	81,017	116,697
U.S.	43,289	78,538	110,491

Note: (1) Figures cover the Durham-Chapel Hill, NC Metropolitan Statistical Area
Source: U.S. Census Bureau, 2019-2023 American Community Survey 5-Year Estimates

Household Income Distribution

Area	Percent of Households Earning							
	Under $15,000	$15,000 -$24,999	$25,000 -$34,999	$35,000 -$49,999	$50,000 -$74,999	$75,000 -$99,999	$100,000 -$149,999	$150,000 and up
City	7.7	5.8	6.4	10.6	16.9	12.9	17.9	21.7
MSA[1]	7.8	6.2	6.4	10.3	16.0	12.0	17.3	23.9
U.S.	8.5	6.6	6.8	10.4	15.7	12.7	17.4	21.9

Note: (1) Figures cover the Durham-Chapel Hill, NC Metropolitan Statistical Area
Source: U.S. Census Bureau, 2019-2023 American Community Survey 5-Year Estimates

Poverty Rate

Area	All Ages	Under 18 Years Old	18 to 64 Years Old	65 Years and Over
City	12.2	16.9	11.5	8.2
MSA[1]	12.3	16.2	12.2	7.9
U.S.	12.4	16.3	11.6	10.4

Note: Figures are percentage of people whose income during the past 12 months was below the poverty level; (1) Figures cover the Durham-Chapel Hill, NC Metropolitan Statistical Area
Source: U.S. Census Bureau, 2019-2023 American Community Survey 5-Year Estimates

EMPLOYMENT

Labor Force and Employment

Area	Civilian Labor Force			Workers Employed		
	Dec. 2023	Dec. 2024	% Chg.	Dec. 2023	Dec. 2024	% Chg.
City	161,695	163,549	1.1	156,943	158,778	1.2
MSA[1]	323,131	326,577	1.1	313,852	317,268	1.1
U.S.	166,661,000	167,746,000	0.7	160,754,000	161,294,000	0.3

Note: Data is not seasonally adjusted and covers workers 16 years of age and older; (1) Figures cover the Durham-Chapel Hill, NC Metropolitan Statistical Area
Source: Bureau of Labor Statistics, Local Area Unemployment Statistics

Unemployment Rate

Area	2024											
	Jan.	Feb.	Mar.	Apr.	May	Jun.	Jul.	Aug.	Sep.	Oct.	Nov.	Dec.
City	3.3	3.3	3.2	2.8	3.1	3.4	3.6	3.5	2.9	2.9	3.1	2.9
MSA[1]	3.2	3.2	3.2	2.8	3.0	3.4	3.6	3.4	2.8	2.9	3.1	2.9
U.S.	4.1	4.2	3.9	3.5	3.7	4.3	4.5	4.4	3.9	3.9	4.0	3.8

Note: Data is not seasonally adjusted and covers workers 16 years of age and older; (1) Figures cover the Durham-Chapel Hill, NC Metropolitan Statistical Area
Source: Bureau of Labor Statistics, Local Area Unemployment Statistics

Average Wages

Occupation	$/Hr.	Occupation	$/Hr.
Accountants and Auditors	46.33	Maintenance and Repair Workers	25.50
Automotive Mechanics	26.94	Marketing Managers	82.71
Bookkeepers	26.20	Network and Computer Systems Admin.	53.21
Carpenters	24.03	Nurses, Licensed Practical	30.26
Cashiers	14.15	Nurses, Registered	n/a
Computer Programmers	51.55	Nursing Assistants	19.70
Computer Systems Analysts	54.64	Office Clerks, General	21.79
Computer User Support Specialists	32.70	Physical Therapists	44.30
Construction Laborers	22.51	Physicians	69.93
Cooks, Restaurant	17.45	Plumbers, Pipefitters and Steamfitters	28.13
Customer Service Representatives	22.07	Police and Sheriff's Patrol Officers	30.46
Dentists	96.79	Postal Service Mail Carriers	29.34
Electricians	29.52	Real Estate Sales Agents	28.62
Engineers, Electrical	58.62	Retail Salespersons	16.63
Fast Food and Counter Workers	14.66	Sales Representatives, Technical/Scientific	57.68
Financial Managers	87.22	Secretaries, Exc. Legal/Medical/Executive	23.09
First-Line Supervisors of Office Workers	34.76	Security Guards	21.40
General and Operations Managers	68.52	Surgeons	n/a
Hairdressers/Cosmetologists	24.56	Teacher Assistants, Exc. Postsecondary[1]	14.99
Home Health and Personal Care Aides	15.58	Teachers, Secondary School, Exc. Sp. Ed.[1]	27.78
Janitors and Cleaners	17.12	Telemarketers	17.39
Landscaping/Groundskeeping Workers	19.05	Truck Drivers, Heavy/Tractor-Trailer	26.62
Lawyers	73.55	Truck Drivers, Light/Delivery Services	21.88
Maids and Housekeeping Cleaners	17.00	Waiters and Waitresses	16.09

Note: Wage data covers the Durham-Chapel Hill, NC Metropolitan Statistical Area; (1) Hourly wages were calculated from annual wage data based on a 40 hour work week
Source: Bureau of Labor Statistics, Metro Area Occupational Employment & Wage Estimates, May 2024

Employment by Industry

Sector	MSA[1] Number of Employees	MSA[1] Percent of Total	U.S. Percent of Total
Construction, Mining, and Logging	11,100	3.1	5.5
Financial Activities	17,200	4.8	5.8
Government	68,600	19.3	14.9
Information	5,700	1.6	1.9
Leisure and Hospitality	27,800	7.8	10.4
Manufacturing	28,300	7.9	8.0
Other Services	13,200	3.7	3.7
Private Education and Health Services	77,600	21.8	16.9
Professional and Business Services	63,300	17.8	14.2
Retail Trade	24,600	6.9	10.0
Transportation, Warehousing, and Utilities	8,700	2.4	4.8
Wholesale Trade	10,000	2.8	3.9

Note: Figures are non-farm employment as of December 2024. Figures are not seasonally adjusted and include workers 16 years of age and older; (1) Figures cover the Durham-Chapel Hill, NC Metropolitan Statistical Area
Source: Bureau of Labor Statistics, Current Employment Statistics, Employment, Hours, and Earnings

Employment by Occupation

Occupation Classification	City (%)	MSA[1] (%)	U.S. (%)
Management, Business, Science, and Arts	57.2	55.4	42.0
Natural Resources, Construction, and Maintenance	6.0	7.0	8.6
Production, Transportation, and Material Moving	7.2	8.1	13.0
Sales and Office	15.5	15.6	19.9
Service	14.1	13.9	16.5

Note: Figures cover employed civilians 16 years of age and older; (1) Figures cover the Durham-Chapel Hill, NC Metropolitan Statistical Area
Source: U.S. Census Bureau, 2019-2023 American Community Survey 5-Year Estimates

Occupations with Greatest Projected Employment Growth: 2022 – 2032

Occupation[1]	2022 Employment	2032 Projected Employment	Numeric Employment Change	Percent Employment Change
Software Developers	57,190	75,660	18,470	32.3
Cooks, Restaurant	47,710	66,050	18,340	38.4
Registered Nurses	106,190	123,650	17,460	16.4
Home Health and Personal Care Aides	62,750	77,390	14,640	23.3
Stockers and Order Fillers	92,790	105,710	12,920	13.9
Laborers and Freight, Stock, and Material Movers, Hand	121,680	133,850	12,170	10.0
General and Operations Managers	94,010	105,400	11,390	12.1
Fast Food and Counter Workers	65,320	75,130	9,810	15.0
First-Line Supervisors of Food Preparation and Serving Workers	41,690	49,690	8,000	19.2
Waiters and Waitresses	71,300	79,060	7,760	10.9

Note: Projections cover North Carolina; (1) Sorted by numeric employment change
Source: www.projectionscentral.org, State Occupational Projections, 2022–2032 Long-Term Projections

Fastest-Growing Occupations: 2022 – 2032

Occupation[1]	2022 Employment	2032 Projected Employment	Numeric Employment Change	Percent Employment Change
Nurse Practitioners	8,200	12,750	4,550	55.5
Solar Photovoltaic Installers	950	1,400	450	47.4
Statisticians	1,580	2,270	690	43.7
Data Scientists	5,430	7,720	2,290	42.2
Medical and Health Services Managers	12,880	17,860	4,980	38.7
Cooks, Restaurant	47,710	66,050	18,340	38.4
Physician Assistants	7,440	10,170	2,730	36.7
Information Security Analysts (SOC 2018)	5,920	8,070	2,150	36.3
Occupational Therapy Assistants	1,310	1,780	470	35.9
Wind Turbine Service Technicians	140	190	50	35.7

Note: Projections cover North Carolina; (1) Sorted by percent employment change and excludes occupations with numeric employment change less than 50
Source: www.projectionscentral.org, State Occupational Projections, 2022–2032 Long-Term Projections

Durham, North Carolina

CITY FINANCES

City Government Finances

Component	2022 ($000)	2022 ($ per capita)
Total Revenues	571,306	1,998
Total Expenditures	580,643	2,031
Debt Outstanding	263,075	920

Source: U.S. Census Bureau, State & Local Government Finances 2022

City Government Revenue by Source

Source	2022 ($000)	2022 ($ per capita)	2022 (%)
General Revenue			
From Federal Government	31,976	112	5.6
From State Government	43,938	154	7.7
From Local Governments	12,639	44	2.2
Taxes			
Property	217,104	759	38.0
Sales and Gross Receipts	74,904	262	13.1
Personal Income	0	0	0.0
Corporate Income	0	0	0.0
Motor Vehicle License	3,366	12	0.6
Other Taxes	894	3	0.2
Current Charges	114,843	402	20.1
Liquor Store	0	0	0.0
Utility	60,438	211	10.6

Source: U.S. Census Bureau, State & Local Government Finances 2022

City Government Expenditures by Function

Function	2022 ($000)	2022 ($ per capita)	2022 (%)
General Direct Expenditures			
Air Transportation	13	< 1	< 0.1
Corrections	0	0	0.0
Education	0	0	0.0
Employment Security Administration	0	0	0.0
Financial Administration	9,784	34	1.7
Fire Protection	46,538	162	8.0
General Public Buildings	14,792	51	2.5
Governmental Administration, Other	24,969	87	4.3
Health	0	0	0.0
Highways	45,825	160	7.9
Hospitals	0	0	0.0
Housing and Community Development	47,799	167	8.2
Interest on General Debt	14,953	52	2.6
Judicial and Legal	2,270	7	0.4
Libraries	0	0	0.0
Parking	3,283	11	0.6
Parks and Recreation	29,442	103	5.1
Police Protection	78,549	274	13.5
Public Welfare	0	0	0.0
Sewerage	93,471	326	16.1
Solid Waste Management	27,206	95	4.7
Veterans' Services	0	0	0.0
Liquor Store	0	0	0.0
Utility	115,628	404	19.9

Source: U.S. Census Bureau, State & Local Government Finances 2022

TAXES

State Corporate Income Tax Rates

State	Tax Rate (%)	Income Brackets ($)	Num. of Brackets	Financial Institution Tax Rate (%)[a]	Federal Income Tax Ded.
North Carolina	2.5	Flat rate	1	2.5	No

Note: Tax rates for tax year 2024; (a) Rates listed are the corporate income tax rate applied to financial institutions or excise taxes based on income. Some states have other taxes based upon the value of deposits or shares.
Source: Federation of Tax Administrators, State Corporate Income Tax Rates, January 1, 2025

State Individual Income Tax Rates

State	Tax Rate (%)	Income Brackets ($)	Personal Exemptions ($)			Standard Ded. ($)	
			Single	Married	Depend.	Single	Married
North Carolina	4.5	Flat rate	None	None	None	12,750	25,500

Note: Tax rates for tax year 2024; Local- and county-level taxes are not included; Federal income tax is not deductible on state income tax returns
Source: Federation of Tax Administrators, State Individual Income Tax Rates, January 1, 2025

Various State Sales and Excise Tax Rates

State	State Sales Tax (%)	Gasoline[1] ($/gal.)	Cigarette[2] ($/pack)	Spirits[3] ($/gal.)	Wine[4] ($/gal.)	Beer[5] ($/gal.)	Recreational Marijuana (%)
North Carolina	4.75	0.41	0.45	18.23	1.00	0.62	Not legal

Note: All tax rates as of January 1, 2025; (1) The American Petroleum Institute has developed a methodology for determining the average tax rate on a gallon of fuel. Rates may include any of the following: excise taxes, environmental fees, storage tank fees, other fees or taxes, general sales tax, and local taxes; (2) The federal excise tax of $1.0066 per pack and local taxes are not included; (3) Rates are those applicable to off-premise sales of 40% alcohol by volume (a.b.v.) distilled spirits in 750ml containers. Local excise taxes are excluded; (4) Rates are those applicable to off-premise sales of 11% a.b.v. non-carbonated wine in 750ml containers; (5) Rates are those applicable to off-premise sales of 4.7% a.b.v. beer in 12 ounce containers.
Source: Tax Foundation, 2025 Facts & Figures: How Does Your State Compare?

State Tax Competitiveness Index

State	Overall Rank	Corporate Tax Rank	Individual Income Tax Rank	Sales Tax Rank	Property Tax Rank	Unemployment Insurance Tax Rank
North Carolina	12	3	21	16	20	7

Note: The Tax Foundation's State Tax Competitiveness Index enables policymakers, taxpayers, and business leaders to gauge how their states' tax systems compare. A rank of 1 is best, 50 is worst. Rankings do not average to the total. States without a tax rank equally as 1. DC's scores and rankings do not affect other states. The report shows tax systems as of July 1, 2024 (the beginning of Fiscal Year 2025).
Source: Tax Foundation, State Tax Competitiveness Index 2025

TRANSPORTATION

Means of Transportation to Work

Area	Car/Truck/Van		Public Transportation			Bicycle	Walked	Other Means	Worked at Home
	Drove Alone	Car-pooled	Bus	Subway	Railroad				
City	65.2	8.0	2.2	0.0	0.0	0.5	2.3	1.4	20.6
MSA[1]	65.1	7.4	2.2	0.0	0.0	0.7	2.5	1.5	20.6
U.S.	70.2	8.5	1.7	1.3	0.4	0.4	2.4	1.6	13.5

Note: Figures are percentages and cover workers 16 years of age and older; (1) Figures cover the Durham-Chapel Hill, NC Metropolitan Statistical Area
Source: U.S. Census Bureau, 2019-2023 American Community Survey 5-Year Estimates

Travel Time to Work

Area	Less Than 10 Minutes	10 to 19 Minutes	20 to 29 Minutes	30 to 44 Minutes	45 to 59 Minutes	60 to 89 Minutes	90 Minutes or More
City	10.2	37.8	25.1	17.8	4.8	2.6	1.6
MSA[1]	10.6	32.7	25.3	20.0	6.2	3.8	1.5
U.S.	12.6	28.6	21.2	20.8	8.1	6.0	2.8

Note: Note: Figures are percentages and include workers 16 years old and over; (1) Figures cover the Durham-Chapel Hill, NC Metropolitan Statistical Area
Source: U.S. Census Bureau, 2019-2023 American Community Survey 5-Year Estimates

Key Congestion Measures

Measure	2000	2010	2015	2020	2022
Annual Hours of Delay, Total (000)	n/a	n/a	11,811	6,841	12,316
Annual Hours of Delay, Per Auto Commuter	n/a	n/a	32	18	34
Annual Congestion Cost, Per Auto Commuter ($)	n/a	n/a	722	448	763

Note: n/a not available
Source: Texas A&M Transportation Institute, 2023 Urban Mobility Report

Freeway Travel Time Index

Measure	1985	1990	1995	2000	2005	2010	2015	2020	2022
Urban Area Index[1]	n/a	n/a	n/a	n/a	n/a	n/a	1.15	1.10	1.15
Urban Area Rank[1,2]	n/a	n/a	n/a	n/a	n/a	n/a	n/a	n/a	n/a

Note: Freeway Travel Time Index—the ratio of travel time in the peak period to the travel time at free-flow conditions. For example, a value of 1.30 indicates a 20-minute free-flow trip takes 26 minutes in the peak (20 minutes x 1.30 = 26 minutes); (1) Covers the Durham NC urban area; (2) Rank is based on 101 larger urban areas (#1 = highest travel time index); n/a not available
Source: Texas A&M Transportation Institute, 2023 Urban Mobility Report

Public Transportation

Agency Name / Mode of Transportation	Vehicles Operated in Maximum Service[1]	Annual Unlinked Passenger Trips[2] (in thous.)	Annual Passenger Miles[3] (in thous.)
Durham Area Transit Authority (DATA)			
Bus (purchased transportation)	34	5,616.1	17,765.0
Demand Response (purchased transportation)	34	101.3	896.8
Demand Response - Transportation Network Company	33	36.7	286.8

Note: (1) Number of revenue vehicles operated by the given mode and type of service to meet the annual maximum service requirement. This is the revenue vehicle count during the peak season of the year; on the week and day that maximum service is provided. Vehicles operated in maximum service (VOMS) exclude atypical days and one-time special events; (2) Number of passengers who boarded public transportation vehicles. Passengers are counted each time they board a vehicle no matter how many vehicles they use to travel from their origin to their destination. (3) Sum of the distances ridden by all passengers during the entire fiscal year.
Source: Federal Transit Administration, National Transit Database, 2023

Air Transportation

Airport Name and Code / Type of Service	Passenger Airlines[1]	Passenger Enplanements	Freight Carriers[2]	Freight (lbs)
Raleigh-Durham International (RDU)				
Domestic service (U.S. carriers only)	29	7,285,042	10	69,157,417
International service (U.S. carriers only)	9	86,141	1	1,274,372

Note: (1) Includes all U.S.-based major, minor and commuter airlines that carried at least one passenger during the year; (2) Includes all U.S.-based airlines and freight carriers that transported at least one pound of freight during the year.
Source: Bureau of Transportation Statistics, The Intermodal Transportation Database, Air Carriers: T-100 Domestic Market (U.S. carriers only), 2024; Bureau of Transportation Statistics, The Intermodal Transportation Database, Air Carriers: T-100 International Market (U.S. carriers only), 2024

BUSINESSES

Major Business Headquarters

Company Name	Industry	Rankings Fortune[1]	Rankings Forbes[2]
IQVIA Holdings	Health care: pharmacy and other services	275	-

Note: (1) Companies that produce a 10-K are ranked 1 to 500 based on 2023 revenue; (2) All private companies with at least $2 billion in annual revenue through the end of their most current fiscal year are ranked 1 to 275; companies listed are headquartered in the city; dashes indicate no ranking
Source: Fortune, "Fortune 500," 2024; Forbes, "America's Largest Private Companies," 2024

Fastest-Growing Businesses

According to Deloitte, Durham is home to two of North America's 500 fastest-growing high-technology companies: **BioCryst Pharmaceuticals** (#76); **HemoSonics** (#453). Companies are ranked by percentage growth in revenue over a four-year period. Criteria for inclusion: company must be headquartered within North America; must own proprietary intellectual property or technology that is sold to customers in products that contributes to a significant portion of the company's operating revenue; must have been in business for a minumum of four years with 2020 operating revenues of at least $50,000 USD/CD and 2023 operating revenues of at least $5 million USD/CD. *Deloitte, 2024 Technology Fast 500™*

Living Environment

COST OF LIVING

Cost of Living Index

Composite Index	Groceries	Housing	Utilities	Trans-portation	Health Care	Misc. Goods/Services
98.5	102.0	101.6	93.4	93.8	103.8	96.2

Note: The Cost of Living Index measures regional differences in the cost of consumer goods and services, excluding taxes and non-consumer expenditures, for professional and managerial households in the top income quintile. It is based on more than 50,000 prices covering almost 60 different items for which prices are collected three times a year by chambers of commerce, economic development organizations or university applied economic centers in each participating urban area. The numbers shown should be read as a percentage above or below the national average of 100. For example, a value of 115.4 in the groceries column indicates that grocery prices are 15.4% higher than the national average. Small differences in the index numbers should not be interpreted as significant; Figures cover the Durham NC urban area.
Source: The Council for Community and Economic Research, Cost of Living Index, 2024

Grocery Prices

Area[1]	T-Bone Steak ($/pound)	Frying Chicken ($/pound)	Whole Milk ($/half gal.)	Eggs ($/dozen)	Orange Juice ($/64 oz.)	Coffee ($/11.5 oz.)
City[2]	15.53	1.48	4.61	3.25	4.39	5.40
Avg.	15.42	1.55	4.69	3.25	4.41	5.46
Min.	14.50	1.16	4.43	2.75	4.00	4.85
Max.	17.56	2.89	5.49	4.78	5.54	7.89

Note: (1) Values for the local area are compared with the average, minimum and maximum values for all 276 areas in the Cost of Living Index; (2) Figures cover the Durham NC urban area; **T-Bone Steak** (price per pound); **Frying Chicken** (price per pound, whole fryer); **Whole Milk** (half gallon carton); **Eggs** (price per dozen, Grade A, large); **Orange Juice** (64 oz. Tropicana or Florida Natural); **Coffee** (11.5 oz. can, vacuum-packed, Maxwell House, Hills Bros, or Folgers).
Source: The Council for Community and Economic Research, Cost of Living Index, 2024

Housing and Utility Costs

Area[1]	New Home Price ($)	Apartment Rent ($/month)	All Electric ($/month)	Part Electric ($/month)	Other Energy ($/month)	Telephone ($/month)
City[2]	521,333	1,650	187.89	-	-	189.44
Avg.	515,975	1,550	210.99	123.07	82.07	194.99
Min.	265,375	692	104.33	53.68	36.26	179.42
Max.	2,775,821	5,719	529.02	397.28	361.63	223.33

Note: (1) Values for the local area are compared with the average, minimum and maximum values for all 276 areas in the Cost of Living Index; (2) Figures cover the Durham NC urban area; **New Home Price** (2,400 sf living area, 8,000 sf lot, in urban area with full utilities); **Apartment Rent** (950 sf 2 bedroom/1.5 or 2 bath, unfurnished, excluding all utilities except water); **All Electric** (average monthly cost for an all-electric home); **Part Electric** (average monthly cost for a part-electric home); **Other Energy** (average monthly cost for natural gas, fuel oil, coal, wood, and any other forms of energy except electricity); **Telephone** (price includes the base monthly rate plus taxes and fees for three lines of mobile phone service).
Source: The Council for Community and Economic Research, Cost of Living Index, 2024

Health Care, Transportation, and Other Costs

Area[1]	Doctor ($/visit)	Dentist ($/visit)	Optometrist ($/visit)	Gasoline ($/gallon)	Beauty Salon ($/visit)	Men's Shirt ($)
City[2]	179.33	112.78	133.40	3.38	54.35	30.66
Avg.	143.77	117.51	129.23	3.32	48.57	38.14
Min.	36.74	58.67	67.33	2.80	24.00	13.41
Max.	270.44	216.82	307.33	5.28	94.00	63.89

Note: (1) Values for the local area are compared with the average, minimum and maximum values for all 276 areas in the Cost of Living Index; (2) Figures cover the Durham NC urban area; **Doctor** (general practitioners routine exam of an established patient); **Dentist** (adult teeth cleaning and periodic oral examination); **Optometrist** (full vision eye exam for established adult patient); **Gasoline** (one gallon regular unleaded, national brand, including all taxes, cash price at self-service pump if available); **Beauty Salon** (woman's shampoo, trim, and blow-dry); **Men's Shirt** (cotton/polyester dress shirt, pinpoint weave, long sleeves).
Source: The Council for Community and Economic Research, Cost of Living Index, 2024

HOUSING

Homeownership Rate

Area	2017 (%)	2018 (%)	2019 (%)	2020 (%)	2021 (%)	2022 (%)	2023 (%)	2024 (%)
MSA[1]	n/a	n/a	n/a	n/a	n/a	n/a	n/a	n/a
U.S.	63.9	64.4	64.6	66.6	65.5	65.8	65.9	65.6

Note: (1) Figures cover the Durham-Chapel Hill, NC Metropolitan Statistical Area; n/a not available
Source: U.S. Census Bureau, Housing Vacancies and Homeownership Annual Statistics: 2017-2024

Durham, North Carolina

House Price Index (HPI)

Area	National Ranking[2]	Quarterly Change (%)	One-Year Change (%)	Five-Year Change (%)	Since 1991Q1 (%)
MSA[1]	150	0.26	4.76	67.43	344.03
U.S.[3]	–	1.43	4.51	57.13	327.82

Note: The HPI is a weighted repeat sales index. It measures average price changes in repeat sales or refinancings on the same properties. This information is obtained by reviewing repeat mortgage transactions on single-family properties whose mortgages have been purchased or securitized by Fannie Mae or Freddie Mac since January 1975; (1) Figures cover the Durham-Chapel Hill, NC Metropolitan Statistical Area; (2) Rankings are based on annual percentage change for all metro areas containing at least 15,000 transactions over the last 10 years and ranges from 1 to 241; (3) figures based on a weighted average of Census Division estimates using a seasonally adjusted, purchase-only index; all figures are for the period ending December 31, 2024
Source: Federal Housing Finance Agency, Change in FHFA Metropolitan Area House Price Indexes, All Transactions Index, 2024Q4

Home Value

Area	Under $100,000	$100,000 -$199,999	$200,000 -$299,999	$300,000 -$399,999	$400,000 -$499,999	$500,000 -$999,999	$1,000,000 or more	Median ($)
City	3.1	10.7	22.2	25.3	16.4	20.2	2.1	355,300
MSA[1]	6.8	12.7	19.0	19.3	14.3	23.7	4.1	359,400
U.S.	12.1	17.8	19.5	14.4	10.5	19.1	6.5	303,400

Note: Figures are percentages except for median and cover owner-occupied housing units; (1) Figures cover the Durham-Chapel Hill, NC Metropolitan Statistical Area
Source: U.S. Census Bureau, 2019-2023 American Community Survey 5-Year Estimates

Year Housing Structure Built

Area	2020 or Later	2010 -2019	2000 -2009	1990 -1999	1980 -1989	1970 -1979	1960 -1969	1950 -1959	1940 -1949	Before 1940	Median Year
City	2.6	21.5	17.1	14.2	14.0	9.6	7.1	5.3	3.4	5.2	1994
MSA[1]	2.3	17.4	17.1	16.3	14.5	11.4	7.5	5.9	2.9	4.7	1992
U.S.	1.2	8.9	13.6	12.8	13.0	14.4	10.0	9.7	4.5	11.9	1980

Note: Figures are percentages except for Median Year; Note: (1) Figures cover the Durham-Chapel Hill, NC Metropolitan Statistical Area
Source: U.S. Census Bureau, 2019-2023 American Community Survey 5-Year Estimates

Gross Monthly Rent

Area	Under $500	$500 -$999	$1,000 -$1,499	$1,500 -$1,999	$2,000 -$2,499	$2,500 -$2,999	$3,000 and up	Median ($)
City	4.9	15.5	37.1	29.7	8.9	2.1	1.8	1,412
MSA[1]	5.0	18.6	36.6	26.5	8.7	2.4	2.3	1,374
U.S.	6.5	22.3	29.5	20.2	10.8	4.8	5.9	1,348

Note: Figures are percentages except for median; Gross rent is the contract rent plus the estimated average monthly cost of utilities (electricity, gas, and water and sewer) and fuels (oil, coal, kerosene, wood, etc.) if these are paid by the renter (or paid for the renter by someone else); (1) Figures cover the Durham-Chapel Hill, NC Metropolitan Statistical Area
Source: U.S. Census Bureau, 2019-2023 American Community Survey 5-Year Estimates

HEALTH

Health Risk Factors

Category	MSA[1] (%)	U.S. (%)
Adults aged 18–64 who have any kind of health care coverage	n/a	90.8
Adults who reported being in good or better health	n/a	81.8
Adults who have been told they have high blood cholesterol	n/a	36.9
Adults who have been told they have high blood pressure	n/a	34.0
Adults who are current smokers	n/a	12.1
Adults who currently use e-cigarettes	n/a	7.7
Adults who currently use chewing tobacco, snuff, or snus	n/a	3.2
Adults who are heavy drinkers[2]	n/a	6.1
Adults who are binge drinkers[3]	n/a	15.2
Adults who are overweight (BMI 25.0 - 29.9)	n/a	34.4
Adults who are obese (BMI 30.0 - 99.8)	n/a	34.3
Adults who participated in any physical activities in the past month	n/a	75.8

Note: All figures are crude prevalence; (1) Figures for the Durham-Chapel Hill, NC Metropolitan Statistical Area were not available.
(2) Heavy drinkers are classified as adult men having more than 14 drinks per week and adult women having more than 7 drinks per week; (3) Binge drinkers are classified as males having five or more drinks on one occasion or females having four or more drinks on one occasion
Source: Centers for Disease Control and Prevention, Behaviorial Risk Factor Surveillance System, SMART: Selected Metropolitan Area Risk Trends, 2023

Acute and Chronic Health Conditions

Category	MSA[1] (%)	U.S. (%)
Adults who have ever been told they had a heart attack	n/a	4.2
Adults who have ever been told they have angina or coronary heart disease	n/a	4.0
Adults who have ever been told they had a stroke	n/a	3.3
Adults who have ever been told they have asthma	n/a	15.7
Adults who have ever been told they have arthritis	n/a	26.3
Adults who have ever been told they have diabetes[2]	n/a	11.5
Adults who have ever been told they had skin cancer	n/a	5.6
Adults who have ever been told they had any other types of cancer	n/a	8.4
Adults who have ever been told they have COPD	n/a	6.4
Adults who have ever been told they have kidney disease	n/a	3.7
Adults who have ever been told they have a form of depression	n/a	22.0

Note: All figures are crude prevalence; (1) Figures for the Durham-Chapel Hill, NC Metropolitan Statistical Area were not available.
(2) Figures do not include pregnancy-related, borderline, or pre-diabetes
Source: Centers for Disease Control and Prevention, Behavioral Risk Factor Surveillance System, SMART: Selected Metropolitan Area Risk Trends, 2023

Health Screening and Vaccination Rates

Category	MSA[1] (%)	U.S. (%)
Adults who have ever been tested for HIV	n/a	37.5
Adults who have had their blood cholesterol checked within the last five years	n/a	87.0
Adults aged 65+ who have had flu shot within the past year	n/a	63.4
Adults aged 65+ who have ever had a pneumonia vaccination	n/a	71.9

Note: All figures are crude prevalence; (1) Figures for the Durham-Chapel Hill, NC Metropolitan Statistical Area were not available.
Source: Centers for Disease Control and Prevention, Behavioral Risk Factor Surveillance System, SMART: Selected Metropolitan Area Risk Trends, 2023

Disability Status

Category	MSA[1] (%)	U.S. (%)
Adults who reported being deaf	n/a	7.4
Are you blind or have serious difficulty seeing, even when wearing glasses?	n/a	4.9
Do you have difficulty doing errands alone?	n/a	7.8
Do you have difficulty dressing or bathing?	n/a	3.6
Do you have serious difficulty concentrating/remembering/making decisions?	n/a	13.7
Do you have serious difficulty walking or climbing stairs?	n/a	13.2

Note: All figures are crude prevalence; (1) Figures for the Durham-Chapel Hill, NC Metropolitan Statistical Area were not available.
Source: Centers for Disease Control and Prevention, Behavioral Risk Factor Surveillance System, SMART: Selected Metropolitan Area Risk Trends, 2023

Mortality Rates for the Top 10 Causes of Death in the U.S.

ICD-10[a] Sub-Chapter	ICD-10[a] Code	Crude Mortality Rate[2] per 100,000 population	
		County[3]	U.S.
Malignant neoplasms	C00-C97	139.5	182.7
Ischaemic heart diseases	I20-I25	58.3	109.6
Provisional assignment of new diseases of uncertain etiology[1]	U00-U49	27.2	65.3
Other forms of heart disease	I30-I51	45.4	65.1
Other degenerative diseases of the nervous system	G30-G31	32.5	52.4
Other external causes of accidental injury	W00-X59	53.9	52.3
Cerebrovascular diseases	I60-I69	36.1	49.1
Chronic lower respiratory diseases	J40-J47	20.4	43.5
Hypertensive diseases	I10-I15	22.0	38.9
Organic, including symptomatic, mental disorders	F01-F09	39.1	33.9

Note: (a) ICD-10 = International Classification of Diseases 10th Revision; (1) Includes COVID-19, adverse effects to COVID-19 vaccines, SARS, and vaping-related disorders; (2) Crude mortality rates are a three-year average covering 2021-2023; (3) Figures cover Durham County.
Source: Centers for Disease Control and Prevention, National Center for Health Statistics. National Vital Statistics System, Mortality 2018-2023 on CDC WONDER Online Database

Mortality Rates for Selected Causes of Death

Cause of Death	ICD-10[a] Code	Crude Mortality Rate[1] per 100,000 population	
		County[2]	U.S.
Accidental poisoning and exposure to noxious substances	X40-X49	32.8	30.5
Alzheimer disease	G30	22.3	35.4
Assault	X85-Y09	12.6	7.3
COVID-19	U07.1	27.2	65.3
Diabetes mellitus	E10-E14	20.4	30.0
Diseases of the liver	K70-K76	12.4	20.8
Human immunodeficiency virus (HIV) disease	B20-B24	Unreliable	1.5
Influenza and pneumonia	J09-J18	6.1	13.4
Intentional self-harm	X60-X84	9.8	14.7
Malnutrition	E40-E46	6.0	6.0
Obesity and other hyperalimentation	E65-E68	2.1	3.1
Renal failure	N17-N19	14.4	16.4
Transport accidents	V01-V99	10.6	14.4

Note: (a) ICD-10 = International Classification of Diseases 10th Revision; (1) Crude mortality rates are a three-year average covering 2021-2023; (2) Figures cover Durham County; Data are suppressed when the data meet the criteria for confidentiality constraints; Crude mortality rates are flagged as unreliable when the rate would be calculated with a numerator of 20 or less.
Source: Centers for Disease Control and Prevention, National Center for Health Statistics. National Vital Statistics System, Mortality 2018-2023 on CDC WONDER Online Database

Health Insurance Coverage

Area	With Health Insurance	With Private Health Insurance	With Public Health Insurance	Without Health Insurance	Population Under Age 19 Without Health Insurance
City	88.4	70.6	27.4	11.6	8.6
MSA[1]	90.2	72.6	29.5	9.8	6.1
U.S.	91.4	67.3	36.3	8.6	5.4

Note: Figures are percentages that cover the civilian noninstitutionalized population; (1) Figures cover the Durham-Chapel Hill, NC Metropolitan Statistical Area
Source: U.S. Census Bureau, 2019-2023 American Community Survey 5-Year Estimates

Number of Medical Professionals

Area	MDs[3]	DOs[3,4]	Dentists	Podiatrists	Chiropractors	Optometrists
County[1] (number)	4,013	73	260	14	71	46
County[1] (rate[2])	1,206.3	21.9	77.2	4.2	21.1	13.7
U.S. (rate[2])	302.5	29.2	74.6	6.4	29.5	18.0

Note: Data as of 2023 unless noted; (1) Data covers Durham County; (2) Number of medical professionals per 100,000 population; (3) Data as of 2022 and includes all active, non-federal physicians; (4) Doctor of Osteopathic Medicine
Source: U.S. Department of Health and Human Services, Health Resources and Services Administration, Bureau of Health Professions, Area Resource File (ARF) 2023-2024

Best Hospitals

According to *U.S. News*, the Durham-Chapel Hill, NC metro area is home to two of the best hospitals in the U.S.: **Duke University Hospital** (Honor Roll/11 adult specialties and 9 pediatric specialties); **UNC Hospitals** (1 adult specialty and 9 pediatric specialties). The hospitals listed were nationally ranked in at least one of 15 adult or 11 pediatric specialties. The number of specialties shown cover the parent hospital. Only 160 U.S. hospitals performed well enough to be nationally ranked in one or more specialties. Twenty hospitals in the U.S. made the Honor Roll. The Best Hospitals Honor Roll takes both the national rankings and the procedure and condition ratings into account. Hospitals received points if they were nationally ranked in one of the 15 adult specialties—the higher they ranked, the more points they got—and how many ratings of "high performing" they earned in the 20 procedures and conditions. *U.S. News Online, "America's Best Hospitals 2024-25"*

According to *U.S. News*, the Durham-Chapel Hill, NC metro area is home to two of the best children's hospitals in the U.S.: **Duke Children's Hospital and Health Center** (9 pediatric specialties); **North Carolina Children's Hospital at UNC** (9 pediatric specialties). The hospitals listed were highly ranked in at least one of 11 pediatric specialties. One hundred five children's hospitals in the U.S. were nationally ranked in at least one specialty. Hospitals received points for being ranked in a specialty, and the 10 hospitals with the most points across the 11 specialties make up the Honor Roll. *U.S. News Online, "America's Best Children's Hospitals 2024-25"*

EDUCATION

Public School District Statistics

District Name	Schls	Pupils	Pupil/Teacher Ratio	Minority Pupils[1] (%)	Total Rev. per Pupil ($)	Total Exp. per Pupil ($)
Durham Public Schools	57	31,339	13.3	80.4	16,522	17,524
NC Connections Academy	1	2,523	17.9	56.4	8,963	8,974
NC Virtual Academy	1	2,959	22.9	57.3	8,014	7,460

Note: Table includes school districts with 2,000 or more students; (1) Percentage of students that are not non-Hispanic white.
Source: U.S. Department of Education, National Center for Education Statistics, Common Core of Data, Local Education Agency (School District) Universe Survey: School Year 2023-2024; U.S. Department of Education, National Center for Education Statistics, Common Core of Data, School District Finance Survey (F-33): School Year 2021–22

Highest Level of Education

Area	Less than H.S.	H.S. Diploma	Some College, No Deg.	Associate Degree	Bachelor's Degree	Master's Degree	Prof. School Degree	Doctorate Degree
City	8.6	15.4	13.7	6.6	28.8	16.9	4.5	5.5
MSA[1]	8.9	17.0	14.3	7.5	26.3	15.5	4.8	5.6
U.S.	10.6	26.2	19.4	8.8	21.3	9.8	2.3	1.6

Note: Figures cover persons age 25 and over; (1) Figures cover the Durham-Chapel Hill, NC Metropolitan Statistical Area
Source: U.S. Census Bureau, 2019-2023 American Community Survey 5-Year Estimates

Educational Attainment by Race

Area	High School Graduate or Higher (%)					Bachelor's Degree or Higher (%)				
	Total	White	Black	Asian	Hisp.[2]	Total	White	Black	Asian	Hisp.[2]
City	91.4	96.1	91.7	92.8	59.7	55.7	70.7	39.4	76.8	22.1
MSA[1]	91.1	95.0	90.1	92.2	59.9	52.3	60.5	35.3	77.4	23.4
U.S.	89.4	92.9	88.1	88.0	72.5	35.0	37.7	24.7	57.0	19.9

Note: Figures shown cover persons 25 years old and over; (1) Figures cover the Durham-Chapel Hill, NC Metropolitan Statistical Area; (2) People of Hispanic origin can be of any race
Source: U.S. Census Bureau, 2019-2023 American Community Survey 5-Year Estimates

School Enrollment by Grade and Control

Area	Preschool (%)		Kindergarten (%)		Grades 1 - 4 (%)		Grades 5 - 8 (%)		Grades 9 - 12 (%)	
	Public	Private	Public	Private	Public	Private	Public	Private	Public	Private
City	51.3	48.7	86.2	13.8	86.0	14.0	85.2	14.8	87.8	12.2
MSA[1]	43.5	56.5	80.2	19.8	85.4	14.6	85.0	15.0	89.7	10.3
U.S.	58.7	41.3	85.2	14.8	87.2	12.8	87.9	12.1	89.0	11.0

Note: Figures shown cover persons 3 years old and over; (1) Figures cover the Durham-Chapel Hill, NC Metropolitan Statistical Area
Source: U.S. Census Bureau, 2019-2023 American Community Survey 5-Year Estimates

Higher Education

Four-Year Colleges			Two-Year Colleges			Medical Schools[1]	Law Schools[2]	Voc/Tech[3]
Public	Private Non-profit	Private For-profit	Public	Private Non-profit	Private For-profit			
2	2	0	2	0	0	2	3	3

Note: Figures cover institutions located within the Durham-Chapel Hill, NC Metropolitan Statistical Area and include main campuses only; (1) includes schools accredited by the Liaison Committee on Medical Education and the American Osteopathic Association's Commission on Osteopathic College Accreditation; (2) includes ABA-accredited schools, schools with provisional ABA accreditation, and state accredited schools; (3) includes all schools with programs that are less than 2 years.
Source: National Center for Education Statistics, Integrated Postsecondary Education System (IPEDS), 2023-24; Wikipedia, List of Medical Schools in the United States, accessed May 2, 2025; Wikipedia, List of Law Schools in the United States, accessed May 2, 2025

According to *U.S. News & World Report*, the Durham-Chapel Hill, NC metro area is home to two of the top 200 national universities in the U.S.: **Duke University** (#6 tie); **University of North Carolina—Chapel Hill** (#27 tie). The indicators used to capture academic quality fall into a number of categories: assessment by administrators at peer institutions; retention of students; faculty resources; student selectivity; financial resources; alumni giving; high school counselor ratings of colleges; and graduation rate. *U.S. News & World Report, "America's Best Colleges 2025"*

According to *U.S. News & World Report*, the Durham-Chapel Hill, NC metro area is home to two of the top 100 law schools in the U.S.: **Duke University 1** (#6 tie); **University of North Carolina—Chapel Hill** (#18 tie). The rankings are based on a weighted average of 12 measures of quality: peer assessment score; assessment score by lawyers/judges; median LSAT scores; median undergrad GPA; acceptance rate; employment rates for graduates; placement success; bar passage rate; faculty resources; expenditures per student; student/faculty ratio; and library resources. *U.S. News & World Report, "America's Best Graduate Schools, Law, 2025"*

According to *U.S. News & World Report,* the Durham-Chapel Hill, NC metro area is home to one of the top medical schools for research in the U.S.: **University of North Carolina—Chapel Hill** (Tier 1). *U.S. News* placed medical and osteopathic schools into tiers based on their research productivity, faculty and admissions data. Each school's tier was derived from its overall score, calculated by summing the weighted normalized values generated across several factors of academic quality, outlined below. There are four tiers, with tier 1 medical schools as the highest-performing and tier 4 as the lowest-performing. Only tier 1 and 2 schools are shown. Because of the tier presentation, *U.S. News* calculated overall scores based on their percentile performance among all rated schools instead of dividing against the rescaled score of the No. 1-performing schools. Tier 1 included schools with overall scores of 85 to 99. The cutoffs for tiers 2 through 4 were schools scoring 50 to 84, 15 to 49 and 1 to 14, respectively. The rankings are based on a weighted average of the following measures of quality: total research activity; average research activity per faculty member; total NIH research grants at the medical school and its affiliated hospitals; average NIH research grants per faculty; median MCAT total score; median undergraduate GPA; acceptance rate; and faculty resources. *U.S. News & World Report, "America's Best Graduate Schools, Medical, 2025"*

According to *U.S. News & World Report,* the Durham-Chapel Hill, NC metro area is home to one of the top medical schools for primary care in the U.S.: **University of North Carolina—Chapel Hill** (Tier 1). *U.S. News* placed medical and osteopathic schools into tiers based on their research productivity, faculty and admissions data. Each school's tier was derived from its overall score, calculated by summing the weighted normalized values generated across several factors of academic quality, outlined below. There are four tiers, with tier 1 medical schools as the highest-performing and tier 4 as the lowest-performing. Only tier 1 and 2 schools are shown. Because of the tier presentation, *U.S. News* calculated overall scores based on their percentile performance among all rated schools instead of dividing against the rescaled score of the No. 1-performing schools. Tier 1 included schools with overall scores of 85 to 99. The cutoffs for tiers 2 through 4 were schools scoring 50 to 84, 15 to 49 and 1 to 14, respectively. The rankings are based on a weighted average of the following measures of quality: graduates practicing in primary care specialties; graduates entering primary care residencies; median MCAT total score; median undergraduate GPA; acceptance rate; and faculty resources. *U.S. News & World Report, "America's Best Graduate Schools, Medical, 2025"*

According to *U.S. News & World Report,* the Durham-Chapel Hill, NC metro area is home to two of the top 75 business schools in the U.S.: **Duke University (Fuqua)** (#13 tie); **University of North Carolina—Chapel Hill (Kenan-Flagler)** (#28). The rankings are based on a weighted average of the following nine measures: quality assessment; peer assessment; recruiter assessment; placement success; mean starting salary and bonus; student selectivity; mean GMAT and GRE scores; mean undergraduate GPA; and acceptance rate. *U.S. News & World Report, "America's Best Graduate Schools, Business, 2025"*

EMPLOYERS

Major Employers

Company Name	Industry
CISCO Systems	Data conversion equipment, media-to-media: computer
City of Durham	Municipal government
Duke University	Colleges & universities
Duke University Health System	General medical & surgical hospitals
Durham County Hospital Corporation	General medical & surgical hospitals
Environmental Protection Agency	Environmental protection agency, government
IBM	Computer peripheral equipment
National Institutes of Health	Environmental health program administration, govt
Netapp	Computer integrated systems design
North Carolina Central University	Colleges & universities
Patheon	Pharmaceutical preparations
Phyamerica Government Services	Hospital management
Research Triangle Institute	Commercial physical research
Sports Endeavors	Sporting goods & bicycle shops
University of NC at Chapel Hill	University
University of North Carolina Hospitals	General medical & surgical hospitals

Note: Companies shown are located within the Durham-Chapel Hill, NC Metropolitan Statistical Area.
Source: Chambers of Commerce; State Departments of Labor; Wikipedia

Best Companies to Work For

Blue Cross and Blue Shield of North Carolina, headquartered in Durham, is among "Best Workplaces in Health Care." To determine the Best Workplaces in Health Care list, Great Place To Work analyzed the survey responses of over 185,000 employees from Great Place To Work-Certified companies in the health care industry. Survey data analysis and company-provided datapoints are then factored into a combined score to compare and rank the companies that create the most consistently positive experience for all employees in this industry. *Fortune, "Best Workplaces in Health Care," 2024*

Blue Cross Blue Shield of North Carolina, headquartered in Durham, is among the "Best Places to Work in IT." To qualify, companies had to have a minimum of 100 total employees and five IT employees. The best places to work were selected based on DEI (diversity, equity, and inclusion) practices; IT turnover, promotions, and growth; IT retention and engagement programs; remote/hybrid working; benefits and perks (such as elder care and child care, flextime, and reimbursement for college tuition); and training and career development opportunities. *Computerworld, "Best Places to Work in IT," 2025*

PUBLIC SAFETY

Crime Rate

Area	Total Crime Rate	Violent Crime Rate				Property Crime Rate		
		Murder	Rape	Robbery	Aggrav. Assault	Burglary	Larceny-Theft	Motor Vehicle Theft
City	4,397.4	15.2	53.4	168.4	399.3	497.0	2,574.8	689.3
U.S.	2,290.9	5.7	38.0	66.5	264.1	250.7	1,347.2	318.7

Note: Figures are crimes per 100,000 population.
Source: FBI, Table 8, Offenses Known to Law Enforcement, by State by City, 2023

Hate Crimes

Area	Number of Quarters Reported	Number of Incidents per Bias Motivation					
		Race/Ethnicity/Ancestry	Religion	Sexual Orientation	Disability	Gender	Gender Identity
City	4	1	2	2	0	0	0
U.S.	4	5,900	2,699	2,077	187	92	492

Source: Federal Bureau of Investigation, Hate Crime Statistics 2023

Identity Theft Consumer Reports

Area	Reports	Reports per 100,000 Population	Rank[2]
MSA[1]	1,348	227	124
U.S.	1,135,291	339	-

Note: (1) Figures cover the Durham-Chapel Hill, NC Metropolitan Statistical Area; (2) Rank ranges from 1 to 401 where 1 indicates greatest number of identity theft reports per 100,000 population
Source: Federal Trade Commission, Consumer Sentinel Network Data Book 2024

Fraud and Other Consumer Reports

Area	Reports	Reports per 100,000 Population	Rank[2]
MSA[1]	7,936	1,335	87
U.S.	5,360,641	1,601	-

Note: (1) Figures cover the Durham-Chapel Hill, NC Metropolitan Statistical Area; (2) Rank ranges from 1 to 401 where 1 indicates greatest number of fraud and other consumer reports per 100,000 population
Source: Federal Trade Commission, Consumer Sentinel Network Data Book 2024

POLITICS

2024 Presidential Election Results

Area	Trump (Rep.)	Harris (Dem.)	Stein (Green)	Kennedy (Ind.)	Oliver (Lib.)	Other
Durham County	18.2	79.8	0.7	0.0	0.4	0.8
U.S.	49.7	48.2	0.6	0.5	0.4	0.6

Note: Results are percentages and may not add to 100% due to rounding
Source: Dave Leip's Atlas of U.S. Presidential Elections

SPORTS

Professional Sports Teams

Team Name	League	Year Established
Carolina Hurricanes	National Hockey League (NHL)	1997

Note: Includes teams located in the Durham-Chapel Hill, NC Metropolitan Statistical Area.
Source: Wikipedia, Major Professional Sports Teams of the United States and Canada, May 1, 2025

CLIMATE

Average and Extreme Temperatures

Temperature	Jan	Feb	Mar	Apr	May	Jun	Jul	Aug	Sep	Oct	Nov	Dec	Yr.
Extreme High (°F)	79	84	90	95	97	104	105	105	104	98	88	79	105
Average High (°F)	50	53	61	72	79	86	89	87	81	72	62	53	71
Average Temp. (°F)	40	43	50	59	67	75	78	77	71	60	51	42	60
Average Low (°F)	29	31	38	46	55	63	68	67	60	48	39	32	48
Extreme Low (°F)	-9	5	11	23	29	38	48	46	37	19	11	4	-9

Note: Figures cover the years 1948-1990
Source: National Climatic Data Center, International Station Meteorological Climate Summary, 9/96

Average Precipitation/Snowfall/Humidity

Precip./Humidity	Jan	Feb	Mar	Apr	May	Jun	Jul	Aug	Sep	Oct	Nov	Dec	Yr.
Avg. Precip. (in.)	3.4	3.6	3.6	2.9	3.9	3.6	4.4	4.4	3.2	2.9	3.0	3.1	42.0
Avg. Snowfall (in.)	2	3	1	Tr	0	0	0	0	0	0	Tr	1	8
Avg. Rel. Hum. 7am (%)	79	79	79	80	84	86	88	91	91	90	84	81	84
Avg. Rel. Hum. 4pm (%)	53	49	46	43	51	54	57	59	57	53	51	53	52

Note: Figures cover the years 1948-1990; Tr = Trace amounts (<0.05 in. of rain; <0.5 in. of snow)
Source: National Climatic Data Center, International Station Meteorological Climate Summary, 9/96

Weather Conditions

Temperature			Daytime Sky			Precipitation		
32°F & below	45°F & below	90°F & above	Clear	Partly cloudy	Cloudy	0.01 inch or more precip.	0.1 inch or more snow/ice	Thunder-storms
77	160	39	98	143	124	110	3	42

Note: Figures are average number of days per year and cover the years 1948-1990
Source: National Climatic Data Center, International Station Meteorological Climate Summary, 9/96

HAZARDOUS WASTE

Superfund Sites

The Durham-Chapel Hill, NC metro area is home to one site on the EPA's Superfund National Priorities List (NPL) or Superfund Alternative Approach (SAA) list: **GMH Electronics** (Final NPL). The Superfund alternative approach uses the same investigation and cleanup process and standards that are used for sites listed on the National Priorities List. The SAA is an alternative to listing a site on the NPL; it is not an alternative to Superfund or the Superfund process. There are a total of 1,445 Superfund sites with a status of proposed or final on both lists in the United States. *U.S. Environmental Protection Agency, National Priorities List, May 1, 2025; U.S. Environmental Protection Agency, Superfund Alternative Approach Sites, May 1, 2025*

AIR QUALITY

Air Quality Trends: Ozone

	1990	1995	2000	2005	2010	2015	2020	2021	2022	2023
MSA[1]	0.078	0.080	0.082	0.079	0.074	0.061	0.051	0.063	0.058	0.066
U.S.	0.087	0.089	0.081	0.080	0.072	0.068	0.066	0.067	0.067	0.070

Note: (1) Data covers the Durham-Chapel Hill, NC Metropolitan Statistical Area. The values shown are the composite ozone concentration averages among trend sites based on the highest fourth daily maximum 8-hour concentration in parts per million. These trends are based on sites having an adequate record of monitoring data during the trend period. Data from exceptional events are included.
Source: U.S. Environmental Protection Agency, Air Quality Monitoring Information, "Air Quality Trends by City, 1990-2023"

Air Quality Index

Area	Percent of Days when Air Quality was...[2]					AQI Statistics[2]	
	Good	Moderate	Unhealthy for Sensitive Groups	Unhealthy	Very Unhealthy	Maximum	Median
MSA[1]	69.5	29.4	1.1	0.0	0.0	121	44

Note: (1) Data covers the Durham-Chapel Hill, NC Metropolitan Statistical Area; (2) Based on 361 days with AQI data in 2023. Air Quality Index (AQI) is an index for reporting daily air quality. EPA calculates the AQI for five major air pollutants regulated by the Clean Air Act: ground-level ozone, particle pollution (aka particulate matter), carbon monoxide, sulfur dioxide, and nitrogen dioxide. The AQI runs from 0 to 500. The higher the AQI value, the greater the level of air pollution and the greater the health concern. There are six AQI categories: "Good" AQI is between 0 and 50. Air quality is considered satisfactory; "Moderate" AQI is between 51 and 100. Air quality is acceptable; "Unhealthy for Sensitive Groups" When AQI values are between 101 and 150, members of sensitive groups may experience health effects; "Unhealthy" When AQI values are between 151 and 200 everyone may begin to experience health effects; "Very Unhealthy" AQI values between 201 and 300 trigger a health alert; "Hazardous" AQI values over 300 trigger warnings of emergency conditions (not shown).
Source: U.S. Environmental Protection Agency, Air Quality Index Report, 2023

Air Quality Index Pollutants

Area	Percent of Days when AQI Pollutant was...[2]					
	Carbon Monoxide	Nitrogen Dioxide	Ozone	Sulfur Dioxide	Particulate Matter 2.5	Particulate Matter 10
MSA[1]	0.0	0.0	45.2	(3)	52.4	2.5

Note: (1) Data covers the Durham-Chapel Hill, NC Metropolitan Statistical Area; (2) Based on 361 days with AQI data in 2023. The Air Quality Index (AQI) is an index for reporting daily air quality. EPA calculates the AQI for five major air pollutants regulated by the Clean Air Act: ground-level ozone, particle pollution (also known as particulate matter), carbon monoxide, sulfur dioxide, and nitrogen dioxide. The AQI runs from 0 to 500. The higher the AQI value, the greater the level of air pollution and the greater the health concern; (3) Sulfur dioxide is no longer included in this table because SO_2 concentrations tend to be very localized and not necessarily representative of broad geographical areas like counties and CBSAs.
Source: U.S. Environmental Protection Agency, Air Quality Index Report, 2023

Maximum Air Pollutant Concentrations: Particulate Matter, Ozone, CO and Lead

	Particulate Matter 10 (ug/m^3)	Particulate Matter 2.5 Wtd AM (ug/m^3)	Particulate Matter 2.5 24-Hr (ug/m^3)	Ozone (ppm)	Carbon Monoxide (ppm)	Lead (ug/m^3)
MSA[1] Level	42	8	24	0.066	n/a	n/a
NAAQS[2]	150	15	35	0.075	9	0.15
Met NAAQS[2]	Yes	Yes	Yes	Yes	n/a	n/a

Note: (1) Data covers the Durham-Chapel Hill, NC Metropolitan Statistical Area; Data from exceptional events are included; (2) National Ambient Air Quality Standards; ppm = parts per million; ug/m^3 = micrograms per cubic meter; n/a not available.
Concentrations: Particulate Matter 10 (coarse particulate)—highest second maximum 24-hour concentration; Particulate Matter 2.5 Wtd AM (fine particulate)—highest weighted annual mean concentration; Particulate Matter 2.5 24-Hour (fine particulate)—highest 98th percentile 24-hour concentration; Ozone—highest fourth daily maximum 8-hour concentration; Carbon Monoxide—highest second maximum non-overlapping 8-hour concentration; Lead—maximum running 3-month average
Source: U.S. Environmental Protection Agency, Air Quality Monitoring Information, "Air Quality Statistics by City, 2023"

Maximum Air Pollutant Concentrations: Nitrogen Dioxide and Sulfur Dioxide

	Nitrogen Dioxide AM (ppb)	Nitrogen Dioxide 1-Hr (ppb)	Sulfur Dioxide AM (ppb)	Sulfur Dioxide 1-Hr (ppb)	Sulfur Dioxide 24-Hr (ppb)
MSA[1] Level	n/a	n/a	n/a	3	n/a
NAAQS[2]	53	100	30	75	140
Met NAAQS[2]	n/a	n/a	n/a	Yes	n/a

Note: (1) Data covers the Durham-Chapel Hill, NC Metropolitan Statistical Area; Data from exceptional events are included; (2) National Ambient Air Quality Standards; ppm = parts per million; ug/m^3 = micrograms per cubic meter; n/a not available.
Concentrations: Nitrogen Dioxide AM—highest arithmetic mean concentration; Nitrogen Dioxide 1-Hr—highest 98th percentile 1-hour daily maximum concentration; Sulfur Dioxide AM—highest annual mean concentration; Sulfur Dioxide 1-Hr—highest 99th percentile 1-hour daily maximum concentration; Sulfur Dioxide 24-Hr—highest second maximum 24-hour concentration
Source: U.S. Environmental Protection Agency, Air Quality Monitoring Information, "Air Quality Statistics by City, 2023"

Greensboro, North Carolina

Background

Greensboro is a quiet community in northern North Carolina. Along with Winston-Salem and High Point, it's part of an urban triangle. The city was the site of the Battle of Guilford Courthouse on March 15, 1781, during the American Revolution, as well as the birthplace of such notable Americans as Dolly Madison, wife of James Madison, the fourth president of the United States, and William Sydney Porter, known as author O. Henry.

During the mid- to late nineteenth century, the economy of the city was largely based upon textile production. While that still remains a vital role in Greensboro, petroleum, pharmaceutical products, and furniture have since come into prominence.

The birth of the American Civil Rights movement can be traced to 1960 in Greensboro when four students from the historically black North Carolina A&T State sat at the white-only lunch counter at Greensboro's downtown Woolworth's department store. Their violent removal led to sit-ins all over the south. In 1979, several Ku Klux Klan (KKK) members traded gunfire with members of the Communist Workers Party (CWP) who were holding an anti-KKK rally. Five CWP members were killed and the event became known as the Greensboro Massacre. Today, the former Woolworth Building houses the Civil Rights Center and Museum.

Greensboro is one of the anchors of the center for business opportunities in North Carolina, the Piedmont Triad. Along with Winston-Salem and High Point, it has become a major metro area for attracting new plants and facilities. FedEx has a Mid-Atlantic air-cargo package-sorting hub in Greensboro, which is also home to the Gateway University Research Park, consisting of two 75-acre campuses focusing on nanotechnology, biotechnology, biochemistry, electronics, artificial intelligence, environmental sciences, food and nutrition, health genetics, materials science and engineering, alternate and renewable energy and social sciences.

Greensboro has a thriving cultural scene. The Green Hill Center for North Carolina Art Gallery promotes the visual arts and includes ArtQuest, an interactive gallery. The Greensboro Ballet provides performances, educational programs, the Summer Ballet Festival, and houses student and professional studios. The Greensboro Symphony Orchestra's Masterworks and Chamber Series concerts feature guest artists from around the world.

Greensboro College, Guilford College, University of North Carolina at Greensboro, North Carolina A&T State, and Bennett College for Women all reside in Greensboro. The Eastern Music Festival and School, part of Guilford College, offers a summer concert series. Elon University School of Law is in the heart of downtown.

In the past 30 years, Greensboro has grown into an internationally diverse community. Today, the city is home to large populations of Vietnamese, West African, and Latino immigrants. Such diverse communities have contributed to the local cuisine and flavor, bringing authentic international specialty stores and restaurants.

Downtown development, such as the First National Bank Field minor league baseball stadium, and a variety of residential options, have helped transform the city center. The revitalized Southside neighborhood is touted as one of the best planned re-developments in the U.S. The city is famous to college sports fans as the home to the Atlantic Coast Conference. The annual ACC basketball tournament in March often airs from the Greensboro Coliseum Complex.

The Greensboro Parks & Recreation Department has acquired over 3,200 acres of land, with more than 170 parks and special facilities recognized internationally for their culturally diverse athletic, historical, and arts programs. The Bog Garden features more than 8,000 individually labeled trees, shrubs, ferns, bamboo, and wildflowers. Wet 'n' Wild Emerald Pointe Water Park offers one of only four tsunami (giant wave) pools in the U.S. Greensboro Historical Museum, located downtown in a building dating back to 1900, is listed on the National Register of Historic Places. The Battle of Guilford Courthouse National Military Park, with 220 acres of historic fields and forests, monuments, and graves, was the first national park established at a Revolutionary War site.

Greensboro is the largest city in the Piedmont Triad region. Both winter temperatures and rainfall are modified by the Blue Ridge Mountain barrier on the northwest. The summer temperatures vary with cloudiness and shower activity, but are generally mild. Northwesterly winds rarely bring heavy or prolonged winter rain or snow. Damaging storms are infrequent, however, strong tornadoes have struck the area in the late 1990s, 2008, 2010, and 2018.

Rankings

General Rankings

- To help military veterans find the best places in which to settle down, *WalletHub* compared the 100 largest U.S. cities across 19 key indicators of livability, affordability and veteran-friendliness. They range from the share of military skill-related jobs to veteran income growth to the availability of VA health facilities. Greensboro ranked #53. *Wallethub.com, "Best & Worst Places for Veterans to Live (2025)," November 7, 2024*

- *US News & World Report* conducted a survey of more than 3,500 people and analyzed the 150 largest metropolitan areas to determine what matters most when selecting the next place to live. Greensboro ranked #23 out of the top 25 as having the best combination of desirable factors. Criteria: cost of living; quality of life and education; climate; job market; desirability; and other factors. *realestate.usnews.com, "Best Places to Live in the U.S. in 2024-2025," May 21, 2024*

- In their annual survey, Livability.com looked at data for more than 2,000 mid-sized U.S. cities to assign a "Livability Score"for each. The top 100 scoring cities make up Livability's "Top 100 Best Places to Live in the U.S." in 2025. Greensboro was placed among the top 100 of the customizable list. Criteria: housing and economy; cost of living; environment; education; health care options; transportation; safety; and community amenities. *Livability.com, "Top 100 Best Places to Live in the U.S. in 2025" April 15, 2025*

Business/Finance Rankings

- The Greensboro metro area appeared on the Milken Institute "2025 Best Performing Cities" list. Rank: #187 out of 200 large metro areas (based on performance category). Criteria: job growth; wage growth; high-tech growth and impact; community resilience; housing affordability; household broadband access. *Milken Institute, "Best-Performing Cities 2025," January 14, 2025*

Education Rankings

- Personal finance website *WalletHub* analyzed the 150 largest U.S. metropolitan statistical areas to determine where the most educated Americans are putting their degrees to work. Criteria: education levels; percentage of workers with degrees; education quality and attainment gap; public school quality rankings; quality and enrollment of each metro area's universities. Greensboro was ranked #101 (#1 = most educated city). *WalletHub.com, "Most & Least Educated Cities in America, 2025" July 2, 2024*

Health/Fitness Rankings

- For each of the 100 largest cities in the United States, the American Fitness Index®, compiled in partnership between the American College of Sports Medicine and the Elevance Health Foundation, evaluated community infrastructure and more than 30 health behaviors including preventive health, levels of chronic disease conditions, food insecurity, pedestrian safety, air quality, and community/environment resources that support physical activity. Greensboro ranked #80 for "community fitness." *americanfitnessindex.org, "2024 ACSM American Fitness Index Summary Report," July 23, 2024*

- The Greensboro metro area was identified as one of the worst cities for bed bugs in America by pest control company Orkin. The area ranked #18 out of 50 based on the number of bed bug treatments Orkin performed from December 2022 to November 2023. *Orkin, "Chicago Joins Paris In Global Bed Bug Spotlight Ranking As The Worst City On Orkin's U.S. Bed Bug Cities List," January 22, 2024*

- Greensboro was identified as a "2025 Allergy Capital." The area ranked #10 out of the nation's 100 largest metropolitan areas. Three groups of factors were used to identify the most challenging cities for people with allergies: annual tree, grass, and weed pollen scores; over the counter allergy medicine use; number of board-certified allergy specialists. *Asthma and Allergy Foundation of America, "2025 Allergy Capitals: The Most Challenging Places to Live with Allergies," March 18, 2025*

- Greensboro was identified as a "2024 Asthma Capital." The area ranked #44 out of the nation's 100 largest metropolitan areas. Criteria: estimated asthma prevalence; asthma-related mortality; and ER visits due to asthma. Risk factors analyzed but not factored in the rankings: annual air quality including pollution and ozone levels; public smoking laws; indoor air quality; access to asthma specialists; rescue and controller medication use; uninsured rate; pollen allergy; poverty rate. *Asthma and Allergy Foundation of America, "Asthma Capitals 2024: The Most Challenging Places to Live With Asthma," September 10, 2024*

Real Estate Rankings

- *WalletHub* compared the most populated U.S. cities to determine which had the best markets for real estate agents. Greensboro ranked #161 where demand was high and pay was the best. Criteria: sales per agent; annual median wage for real-estate agents; monthly average starting salary for real estate agents; real estate job density and competition; unemployment rate; home turnover rate; housing-market health index; and other relevant metrics. *WalletHub.com, "2021 Best Places to Be a Real Estate Agent," May 12, 2021*

- The Greensboro metro area appeared on Realtor.com's list of hot housing markets to watch in 2025. The area ranked #10. Criteria: forecasted home price and sales growth; overall economy; population trends. *Realtor.com®, "Top 10 Housing Markets Positioned for Growth in 2025," December 10, 2024*

- The Greensboro metro area was identified as one of the 10 worst condo markets in the U.S. in 2024. The area ranked #56 out of 63 markets. Criteria: year-over-year change of median sales price of existing apartment condo-coop homes between the 4th quarter of 2023 and the 4th quarter of 2024. *National Association of Realtors®, Median Sales Price of Existing Apartment Condo-Coops Homes for Metropolitan Areas, 4th Quarter 2024*

- Greensboro was ranked #82 out of 176 metro areas in terms of cost of housing in 2024 by the National Association of Home Builders (#1 = most affordable). Criteria: the portion of an average family's income necessary to pay the mortgage on a median-priced home. *National Association of Home Builders®, NAHB-Wells Fargo Cost of Housing Index, 4th Quarter 2024*

Women/Minorities Rankings

- Personal finance website *WalletHub* compared more than 180 U.S. cities across two key dimensions, "Hispanic Business-Friendliness" and "Hispanic Purchasing Power," to arrive at the most favorable conditions for Hispanic entrepreneurs. Greensboro was ranked #91 out of 182. Criteria includes: share of Hispanic-Owned Businesses; average growth of Hispanic Business revenues; Small Business-Friendliness score; affordability; and number of Hispanics with at least a bachelor's degree. *WalletHub.com, "Best Cities for Hispanic Entrepreneurs," September 4, 2024*

Miscellaneous Rankings

- *WalletHub* compared 148 of the most populated U.S. cities to determine their operating efficiency. A "Quality of Services" score was constructed for each city and then measured against the total budget per capita to reveal which were managed the best. Greensboro ranked #27. Criteria: financial stability; economy; education; safety; health; infrastructure and pollution. *WalletHub.com, "2025's Best- & Worst-Run Cities in America," June 18, 2024*

Business Environment

DEMOGRAPHICS

Population Growth

Area	1990 Census	2000 Census	2010 Census	2020 Census	2023 Estimate[2]	Population Growth 1990-2023 (%)
City	193,389	223,891	269,666	299,035	298,564	54.4
MSA[1]	540,257	643,430	723,801	776,566	779,894	44.4
U.S.	248,709,873	281,421,906	308,745,538	331,449,281	332,387,540	33.6

Note: (1) Figures cover the Greensboro-High Point, NC Metropolitan Statistical Area; (2) 2019-2023 5-year ACS population estimate
Source: U.S. Census Bureau, 1990 Census, 2000 Census, 2010 Census, 2020 Census, 2019-2023 American Community Survey 5-Year Estimates

Race

Area	White Alone[2] (%)	Black Alone[2] (%)	Asian Alone[2] (%)	AIAN[3] Alone[2] (%)	NHOPI[4] Alone[2] (%)	Other Race Alone[2] (%)	Two or More Races (%)
City	40.4	42.2	5.0	0.5	0.0	4.5	7.5
MSA[1]	57.7	26.9	3.8	0.4	0.0	4.3	6.9
U.S.	63.4	12.4	5.8	0.9	0.2	6.6	10.7

Note: (1) Figures cover the Greensboro-High Point, NC Metropolitan Statistical Area; (2) Alone is defined as not being in combination with one or more other races; (3) American Indian and Alaska Native; (4) Native Hawaiian and Other Pacific Islander
Source: U.S. Census Bureau, 2019-2023 American Community Survey 5-Year Estimates

Hispanic or Latino Origin

Area	Total (%)	Mexican (%)	Puerto Rican (%)	Cuban (%)	Other (%)
City	10.5	4.5	1.7	0.2	4.1
MSA[1]	10.2	5.9	1.2	0.2	2.8
U.S.	19.0	11.3	1.8	0.7	5.2

Note: Persons of Hispanic or Latino origin can be of any race; (1) Figures cover the Greensboro-High Point, NC Metropolitan Statistical Area
Source: U.S. Census Bureau, 2019-2023 American Community Survey 5-Year Estimates

Age

Area	Under Age 5	Age 5–19	Age 20–34	Age 35–44	Age 45–54	Age 55–64	Age 65–74	Age 75–84	Age 85+	Median Age
City	5.7	21.4	24.2	12.4	11.6	10.8	8.2	3.9	1.9	34.1
MSA[1]	5.6	20.1	19.7	12.0	12.9	13.0	9.9	4.8	1.9	38.9
U.S.	5.7	19.1	20.2	13.1	12.3	12.8	10.0	4.9	1.9	38.7

Note: (1) Figures cover the Greensboro-High Point, NC Metropolitan Statistical Area
Source: U.S. Census Bureau, 2019-2023 American Community Survey 5-Year Estimates

Disability by Age

Area	All Ages	Under 18 Years Old	18 to 64 Years Old	65 Years and Over
City	11.8	5.4	9.9	31.4
MSA[1]	13.4	4.9	11.2	32.9
U.S.	13.0	4.7	10.7	32.9

Note: Figures show percent of the civilian noninstitutionalized population that reported having a disability. Disability status is determined from six types of difficulty: vision, hearing, cognitive, ambulatory, self-care, and independent living. For children under 5 years old, hearing and vision difficulty are used to determine disability status. For children between the ages of 5 and 14, disability status is determined from hearing, vision, cognitive, ambulatory, and self-care difficulties. For people aged 15 years and older, they are considered to have a disability if they have difficulty with any one of the six difficulty types; Note: (1) Figures cover the Greensboro-High Point, NC Metropolitan Statistical Area
Source: U.S. Census Bureau, 2019-2023 American Community Survey 5-Year Estimates

Ancestry

Area	German	Irish	English	American	Italian	Polish	French[2]	European	Scottish
City	6.5	5.3	9.4	4.5	2.4	0.8	1.2	1.6	1.7
MSA[1]	8.4	6.9	11.0	7.4	2.4	1.0	1.3	1.8	2.1
U.S.	12.6	9.4	9.1	5.5	4.9	2.6	2.0	1.6	1.6

Note: Figures are the percentage of the total population reporting a particular ancestry. The nine most commonly reported ancestries in the U.S. are shown. Figures include multiple ancestries (e.g. if a person reported being Irish and Italian, they were included in both columns); (1) Figures cover the Greensboro-High Point, NC Metropolitan Statistical Area; (2) Excludes Basque
Source: U.S. Census Bureau, 2019-2023 American Community Survey 5-Year Estimates

Foreign-born Population

Area	Percent of Population Born in								
	Any Foreign Country	Asia	Mexico	Europe	Caribbean	Central America[2]	South America	Africa	Canada
City	12.7	4.0	1.9	1.0	0.6	0.9	0.8	3.4	0.2
MSA[1]	9.5	2.9	2.3	0.7	0.4	0.7	0.5	1.7	0.1
U.S.	13.9	4.3	3.3	1.4	1.4	1.2	1.2	0.8	0.2

Note: (1) Figures cover the Greensboro-High Point, NC Metropolitan Statistical Area; (2) Excludes Mexico.
Source: U.S. Census Bureau, 2019-2023 American Community Survey 5-Year Estimates

Household Size

Area	Persons in Household (%)							Average Household Size
	One	Two	Three	Four	Five	Six	Seven or More	
City	36.4	30.7	15.3	9.8	4.8	1.5	1.5	2.33
MSA[1]	31.0	33.8	15.5	11.4	5.2	2.0	1.1	2.42
U.S.	28.5	33.8	15.4	12.7	5.9	2.3	1.4	2.54

Note: (1) Figures cover the Greensboro-High Point, NC Metropolitan Statistical Area
Source: U.S. Census Bureau, 2019-2023 American Community Survey 5-Year Estimates

Household Relationships

Area	Householder	Opposite-sex Spouse	Same-sex Spouse	Opposite-sex Unmarried Partner	Same-sex Unmarried Partner	Child[2]	Grand-child	Other Relatives	Non-relatives
City	40.9	13.6	0.2	2.6	0.2	26.4	2.0	4.1	3.6
MSA[1]	40.2	17.1	0.2	2.4	0.2	27.4	2.3	3.9	2.6
U.S.	38.3	17.5	0.2	2.5	0.2	28.3	2.4	4.8	3.4

Note: Figures are percent of the total population; (1) Figures cover the Greensboro-High Point, NC Metropolitan Statistical Area; (2) Includes biological, adopted, and stepchildren of the householder
Source: U.S. Census Bureau, 2020 Census

Gender

Area	Males	Females	Males per 100 Females
City	138,079	160,485	86.0
MSA[1]	374,844	405,050	92.5
U.S.	164,545,087	167,842,453	98.0

Note: (1) Figures cover the Greensboro-High Point, NC Metropolitan Statistical Area
Source: U.S. Census Bureau, 2019-2023 American Community Survey 5-Year Estimates

Marital Status

Area	Never Married	Now Married[2]	Separated	Widowed	Divorced
City	45.1	36.4	2.4	5.8	10.3
MSA[1]	35.2	45.3	2.3	6.2	11.0
U.S.	34.1	47.9	1.7	5.6	10.7

Note: Figures are percentages and cover the population 15 years of age and older; (1) Figures cover the Greensboro-High Point, NC Metropolitan Statistical Area; (2) Excludes separated
Source: U.S. Census Bureau, 2019-2023 American Community Survey 5-Year Estimates

Religious Groups by Family

Area	Catholic	Baptist	Methodist	LDS[2]	Pentecostal	Lutheran	Islam	Adventist	Other
MSA[1]	7.9	10.0	8.0	0.7	2.8	0.4	1.5	1.4	17.8
U.S.	18.7	7.3	3.0	2.0	1.8	1.7	1.3	1.3	11.6

Note: Figures are the number of adherents as a percentage of the total population and cover the eight largest religious groups in the U.S; (1) Figures cover the Greensboro-High Point, NC Metropolitan Statistical Area; (2) Church of Jesus Christ of Latter-day Saints
Sources: 2020 U.S. Religion Census, Association of Statisticians of American Religious Bodies; The Association of Religion Data Archives (ARDA)

Religious Groups by Tradition

Area	Catholic	Evangelical Protestant	Mainline Protestant	Black Protestant	Islam	Judaism	Hinduism	Orthodox	Buddhism
MSA[1]	7.9	24.9	10.1	3.5	1.5	0.3	0.3	0.1	0.1
U.S.	18.7	16.5	5.2	2.3	1.3	0.6	0.4	0.4	0.3

Note: Figures are the number of adherents as a percentage of the total population; (1) Figures cover the Greensboro-High Point, NC Metropolitan Statistical Area
Sources: 2020 U.S. Religion Census, Association of Statisticians of American Religious Bodies; The Association of Religion Data Archives (ARDA)

ECONOMY

Real Gross Domestic Product (GDP)

Area	2017	2018	2019	2020	2021	2022	2023	Rank[3]
MSA[1]	41.2	41.4	41.0	39.5	41.1	42.2	42.5	80
U.S.[2]	17,619.1	18,160.7	18,642.5	18,238.9	19,387.6	19,896.6	20,436.3	—

Note: Figures are in billions of chained 2017 dollars; (1) Figures cover the Greensboro-High Point, NC Metropolitan Statistical Area; (2) Figures cover real GDP within metropolitan areas; (3) Rank is based on 2023 data and ranges from 1 to 384
Source: U.S. Bureau of Economic Analysis

Economic Growth

Area	2014	2015	2016	2017	2018	2019	2020	2021	2022	2023
MSA[1]	-0.4	2.5	-1.1	0.5	0.5	-1.1	-3.6	4.0	2.8	0.5
U.S.[2]	2.6	3.2	2.0	2.7	3.1	2.7	-2.2	6.3	2.6	2.7

Note: Figures are real gross domestic product growth rates and represent percent change from preceding period; (1) Figures cover the Greensboro-High Point, NC Metropolitan Statistical Area; (2) Figures are the average growth rates within metropolitan areas
Source: U.S. Bureau of Economic Analysis

Metropolitan Area Exports

Area	2018	2019	2020	2021	2022	2023	Rank[2]
MSA[1]	3,053.5	2,561.8	2,007.3	2,356.2	2,375.6	2,239.4	108
U.S.	1,664,056.1	1,645,173.7	1,431,406.6	1,753,941.4	2,062,937.4	2,019,160.5	—

Note: Figures are in millions of dollars; (1) Figures cover the Greensboro-High Point, NC Metropolitan Statistical Area; (2) Rank is based on 2023 data and ranges from 1 to 386
Source: U.S. Department of Commerce, International Trade Administration, Office of Trade and Economic Analysis, Industry and Analysis, Exports by Metropolitan Area, data extracted April 2, 2025

Building Permits

Area	Single-Family 2023	Single-Family 2024	Pct. Chg.	Multi-Family 2023	Multi-Family 2024	Pct. Chg.	Total 2023	Total 2024	Pct. Chg.
City	704	618	-12.2	1,063	1,336	25.7	1,767	1,954	10.6
MSA[1]	2,368	2,337	-1.3	1,139	2,639	131.7	3,507	4,976	41.9
U.S.	920,000	981,900	6.7	591,100	496,100	-16.1	1,511,100	1,478,000	-2.2

Note: (1) Figures cover the Greensboro-High Point, NC Metropolitan Statistical Area; Figures represent new, privately-owned housing units authorized (unadjusted data)
Source: U.S. Census Bureau, Building Permits Survey (BPS), 2023, 2024

Bankruptcy Filings

Area	Business Filings 2023	Business Filings 2024	% Chg.	Nonbusiness Filings 2023	Nonbusiness Filings 2024	% Chg.
Guilford County	11	16	45.5	375	473	26.1
U.S.	18,926	23,107	22.1	434,064	494,201	13.9

Note: Business filings include Chapter 7, Chapter 9, Chapter 11, Chapter 12, Chapter 13, Chapter 15, and Section 304; Nonbusiness filings include Chapter 7, Chapter 11, and Chapter 13
Source: Administrative Office of the U.S. Courts, Business and Nonbusiness Bankruptcy, County Cases Commenced by Chapter of the Bankruptcy Code, During the 12-Month Period Ending December 31, 2023 and Business and Nonbusiness Bankruptcy, County Cases Commenced by Chapter of the Bankruptcy Code, During the 12-Month Period Ending December 31, 2024

Housing Vacancy Rates

Area	Gross Vacancy Rate[3] (%) 2022	2023	2024	Year-Round Vacancy Rate[4] (%) 2022	2023	2024	Rental Vacancy Rate[5] (%) 2022	2023	2024	Homeowner Vacancy Rate[6] (%) 2022	2023	2024
MSA[1]	8.7	6.1	7.8	8.7	5.7	6.0	10.2	5.7	5.5	0.7	0.1	0.5
U.S.[2]	9.1	9.0	9.1	7.5	7.5	7.6	5.7	6.5	6.8	0.8	0.8	1.0

Note: (1) Figures cover the Greensboro-High Point, NC Metropolitan Statistical Area; (2) Figures cover the 75 largest Metropolitan Statistical Areas; (3) The percentage of the total housing inventory that is vacant; (4) The percentage of the housing inventory (excluding seasonal units) that is year-round vacant; (5) The percentage of rental inventory that is vacant for rent; (6) The percentage of homeowner inventory that is vacant for sale
Source: U.S. Census Bureau, Housing Vacancies and Homeownership Annual Statistics: 2022, 2023, 2024

INCOME

Income

Area	Per Capita ($)	Median Household ($)	Average Household ($)
City	35,858	58,884	85,861
MSA[1]	35,569	63,083	87,043
U.S.	43,289	78,538	110,491

Note: (1) Figures cover the Greensboro-High Point, NC Metropolitan Statistical Area
Source: U.S. Census Bureau, 2019-2023 American Community Survey 5-Year Estimates

Household Income Distribution

Area	Percent of Households Earning							
	Under $15,000	$15,000 -$24,999	$25,000 -$34,999	$35,000 -$49,999	$50,000 -$74,999	$75,000 -$99,999	$100,000 -$149,999	$150,000 and up
City	11.7	8.0	9.0	13.8	17.8	12.2	15.0	12.6
MSA[1]	10.1	8.0	8.3	13.7	17.6	12.6	16.3	13.5
U.S.	8.5	6.6	6.8	10.4	15.7	12.7	17.4	21.9

Note: (1) Figures cover the Greensboro-High Point, NC Metropolitan Statistical Area
Source: U.S. Census Bureau, 2019-2023 American Community Survey 5-Year Estimates

Poverty Rate

Area	All Ages	Under 18 Years Old	18 to 64 Years Old	65 Years and Over
City	18.4	26.0	16.5	14.2
MSA[1]	15.3	21.4	14.1	11.6
U.S.	12.4	16.3	11.6	10.4

Note: Figures are percentage of people whose income during the past 12 months was below the poverty level;
(1) Figures cover the Greensboro-High Point, NC Metropolitan Statistical Area
Source: U.S. Census Bureau, 2019-2023 American Community Survey 5-Year Estimates

EMPLOYMENT

Labor Force and Employment

Area	Civilian Labor Force			Workers Employed		
	Dec. 2023	Dec. 2024	% Chg.	Dec. 2023	Dec. 2024	% Chg.
City	145,300	143,645	-1.1	139,667	137,971	-1.2
MSA[1]	366,503	362,230	-1.2	353,122	348,882	-1.2
U.S.	166,661,000	167,746,000	0.7	160,754,000	161,294,000	0.3

Note: Data is not seasonally adjusted and covers workers 16 years of age and older; (1) Figures cover the Greensboro-High Point, NC Metropolitan Statistical Area
Source: Bureau of Labor Statistics, Local Area Unemployment Statistics

Unemployment Rate

Area	2024											
	Jan.	Feb.	Mar.	Apr.	May	Jun.	Jul.	Aug.	Sep.	Oct.	Nov.	Dec.
City	4.4	4.4	4.3	3.7	4.0	4.8	5.2	4.9	4.0	3.9	4.2	4.0
MSA[1]	4.2	4.2	4.0	3.5	3.9	4.5	4.8	4.5	3.7	3.7	4.0	3.7
U.S.	4.1	4.2	3.9	3.5	3.7	4.3	4.5	4.4	3.9	3.9	4.0	3.8

Note: Data is not seasonally adjusted and covers workers 16 years of age and older; (1) Figures cover the Greensboro-High Point, NC Metropolitan Statistical Area
Source: Bureau of Labor Statistics, Local Area Unemployment Statistics

Average Wages

Occupation	$/Hr.	Occupation	$/Hr.
Accountants and Auditors	41.27	Maintenance and Repair Workers	23.70
Automotive Mechanics	25.40	Marketing Managers	80.15
Bookkeepers	22.80	Network and Computer Systems Admin.	41.61
Carpenters	21.70	Nurses, Licensed Practical	30.11
Cashiers	13.29	Nurses, Registered	41.93
Computer Programmers	43.91	Nursing Assistants	18.27
Computer Systems Analysts	50.14	Office Clerks, General	19.68
Computer User Support Specialists	26.94	Physical Therapists	44.25
Construction Laborers	20.44	Physicians	144.60
Cooks, Restaurant	16.19	Plumbers, Pipefitters and Steamfitters	25.64
Customer Service Representatives	20.71	Police and Sheriff's Patrol Officers	30.89
Dentists	85.23	Postal Service Mail Carriers	29.19
Electricians	26.42	Real Estate Sales Agents	31.36
Engineers, Electrical	53.13	Retail Salespersons	15.70
Fast Food and Counter Workers	13.39	Sales Representatives, Technical/Scientific	47.29
Financial Managers	82.48	Secretaries, Exc. Legal/Medical/Executive	21.42
First-Line Supervisors of Office Workers	31.23	Security Guards	17.81
General and Operations Managers	58.89	Surgeons	n/a
Hairdressers/Cosmetologists	18.93	Teacher Assistants, Exc. Postsecondary[1]	13.56
Home Health and Personal Care Aides	14.32	Teachers, Secondary School, Exc. Sp. Ed.[1]	25.65
Janitors and Cleaners	15.59	Telemarketers	16.15
Landscaping/Groundskeeping Workers	17.87	Truck Drivers, Heavy/Tractor-Trailer	26.84
Lawyers	68.03	Truck Drivers, Light/Delivery Services	21.55
Maids and Housekeeping Cleaners	14.93	Waiters and Waitresses	15.80

Note: Wage data covers the Greensboro-High Point, NC Metropolitan Statistical Area; (1) Hourly wages were calculated from annual wage data based on a 40 hour work week
Source: Bureau of Labor Statistics, Metro Area Occupational Employment & Wage Estimates, May 2024

Employment by Industry

Sector	MSA[1] Number of Employees	MSA[1] Percent of Total	U.S. Percent of Total
Construction, Mining, and Logging	19,500	5.3	5.5
Financial Activities	16,000	4.3	5.8
Government	46,600	12.6	14.9
Information	3,600	1.0	1.9
Leisure and Hospitality	36,700	9.9	10.4
Manufacturing	47,400	12.8	8.0
Other Services	13,700	3.7	3.7
Private Education and Health Services	55,000	14.9	16.9
Professional and Business Services	46,700	12.6	14.2
Retail Trade	41,700	11.3	10.0
Transportation, Warehousing, and Utilities	21,100	5.7	4.8
Wholesale Trade	21,400	5.8	3.9

Note: Figures are non-farm employment as of December 2024. Figures are not seasonally adjusted and include workers 16 years of age and older; (1) Figures cover the Greensboro-High Point, NC Metropolitan Statistical Area
Source: Bureau of Labor Statistics, Current Employment Statistics, Employment, Hours, and Earnings

Employment by Occupation

Occupation Classification	City (%)	MSA[1] (%)	U.S. (%)
Management, Business, Science, and Arts	38.3	37.0	42.0
Natural Resources, Construction, and Maintenance	5.7	8.1	8.6
Production, Transportation, and Material Moving	16.3	18.0	13.0
Sales and Office	22.7	21.0	19.9
Service	17.0	16.0	16.5

Note: Figures cover employed civilians 16 years of age and older; (1) Figures cover the Greensboro-High Point, NC Metropolitan Statistical Area
Source: U.S. Census Bureau, 2019-2023 American Community Survey 5-Year Estimates

Occupations with Greatest Projected Employment Growth: 2022 – 2032

Occupation[1]	2022 Employment	2032 Projected Employment	Numeric Employment Change	Percent Employment Change
Software Developers	57,190	75,660	18,470	32.3
Cooks, Restaurant	47,710	66,050	18,340	38.4
Registered Nurses	106,190	123,650	17,460	16.4
Home Health and Personal Care Aides	62,750	77,390	14,640	23.3
Stockers and Order Fillers	92,790	105,710	12,920	13.9
Laborers and Freight, Stock, and Material Movers, Hand	121,680	133,850	12,170	10.0
General and Operations Managers	94,010	105,400	11,390	12.1
Fast Food and Counter Workers	65,320	75,130	9,810	15.0
First-Line Supervisors of Food Preparation and Serving Workers	41,690	49,690	8,000	19.2
Waiters and Waitresses	71,300	79,060	7,760	10.9

Note: Projections cover North Carolina; (1) Sorted by numeric employment change
Source: www.projectionscentral.org, State Occupational Projections, 2022–2032 Long-Term Projections

Fastest-Growing Occupations: 2022 – 2032

Occupation[1]	2022 Employment	2032 Projected Employment	Numeric Employment Change	Percent Employment Change
Nurse Practitioners	8,200	12,750	4,550	55.5
Solar Photovoltaic Installers	950	1,400	450	47.4
Statisticians	1,580	2,270	690	43.7
Data Scientists	5,430	7,720	2,290	42.2
Medical and Health Services Managers	12,880	17,860	4,980	38.7
Cooks, Restaurant	47,710	66,050	18,340	38.4
Physician Assistants	7,440	10,170	2,730	36.7
Information Security Analysts (SOC 2018)	5,920	8,070	2,150	36.3
Occupational Therapy Assistants	1,310	1,780	470	35.9
Wind Turbine Service Technicians	140	190	50	35.7

Note: Projections cover North Carolina; (1) Sorted by percent employment change and excludes occupations with numeric employment change less than 50
Source: www.projectionscentral.org, State Occupational Projections, 2022–2032 Long-Term Projections

CITY FINANCES

City Government Finances

Component	2022 ($000)	2022 ($ per capita)
Total Revenues	699,998	2,350
Total Expenditures	725,113	2,434
Debt Outstanding	675,980	2,269

Source: U.S. Census Bureau, State & Local Government Finances 2022

City Government Revenue by Source

Source	2022 ($000)	2022 ($ per capita)	2022 (%)
General Revenue			
From Federal Government	58,390	196	8.3
From State Government	42,053	141	6.0
From Local Governments	6,467	22	0.9
Taxes			
Property	181,272	609	25.9
Sales and Gross Receipts	91,203	306	13.0
Personal Income	0	0	0.0
Corporate Income	0	0	0.0
Motor Vehicle License	1,376	5	0.2
Other Taxes	114	0	0.0
Current Charges	172,910	580	24.7
Liquor Store	58,368	196	8.3
Utility	71,776	241	10.3

Source: U.S. Census Bureau, State & Local Government Finances 2022

City Government Expenditures by Function

Function	2022 ($000)	2022 ($ per capita)	2022 (%)
General Direct Expenditures			
Air Transportation	0	0	0.0
Corrections	0	0	0.0
Education	0	0	0.0
Employment Security Administration	0	0	0.0
Financial Administration	9,112	30	1.3
Fire Protection	65,658	220	9.1
General Public Buildings	17,128	57	2.4
Governmental Administration, Other	11,186	37	1.5
Health	406	1	0.1
Highways	41,432	139	5.7
Hospitals	0	0	0.0
Housing and Community Development	42,321	142	5.8
Interest on General Debt	19,543	65	2.7
Judicial and Legal	1,385	4	0.2
Libraries	9,838	33	1.4
Parking	13,786	46	1.9
Parks and Recreation	99,196	333	13.7
Police Protection	88,401	296	12.2
Public Welfare	0	0	0.0
Sewerage	77,433	259	10.7
Solid Waste Management	59,183	198	8.2
Veterans' Services	0	0	0.0
Liquor Store	47,806	160	6.6
Utility	105,419	353	14.5

Source: U.S. Census Bureau, State & Local Government Finances 2022

TAXES

State Corporate Income Tax Rates

State	Tax Rate (%)	Income Brackets ($)	Num. of Brackets	Financial Institution Tax Rate (%)[a]	Federal Income Tax Ded.
North Carolina	2.5	Flat rate	1	2.5	No

Note: Tax rates for tax year 2024; (a) Rates listed are the corporate income tax rate applied to financial institutions or excise taxes based on income. Some states have other taxes based upon the value of deposits or shares.
Source: Federation of Tax Administrators, State Corporate Income Tax Rates, January 1, 2025

State Individual Income Tax Rates

State	Tax Rate (%)	Income Brackets ($)	Personal Exemptions ($)			Standard Ded. ($)	
			Single	Married	Depend.	Single	Married
North Carolina	4.5	Flat rate	None	None	None	12,750	25,500

Note: Tax rates for tax year 2024; Local- and county-level taxes are not included; Federal income tax is not deductible on state income tax returns
Source: Federation of Tax Administrators, State Individual Income Tax Rates, January 1, 2025

Various State Sales and Excise Tax Rates

State	State Sales Tax (%)	Gasoline[1] ($/gal.)	Cigarette[2] ($/pack)	Spirits[3] ($/gal.)	Wine[4] ($/gal.)	Beer[5] ($/gal.)	Recreational Marijuana (%)
North Carolina	4.75	0.41	0.45	18.23	1.00	0.62	Not legal

Note: All tax rates as of January 1, 2025; (1) The American Petroleum Institute has developed a methodology for determining the average tax rate on a gallon of fuel. Rates may include any of the following: excise taxes, environmental fees, storage tank fees, other fees or taxes, general sales tax, and local taxes; (2) The federal excise tax of $1.0066 per pack and local taxes are not included; (3) Rates are those applicable to off-premise sales of 40% alcohol by volume (a.b.v.) distilled spirits in 750ml containers. Local excise taxes are excluded; (4) Rates are those applicable to off-premise sales of 11% a.b.v. non-carbonated wine in 750ml containers; (5) Rates are those applicable to off-premise sales of 4.7% a.b.v. beer in 12 ounce containers.
Source: Tax Foundation, 2025 Facts & Figures: How Does Your State Compare?

State Tax Competitiveness Index

State	Overall Rank	Corporate Tax Rank	Individual Income Tax Rank	Sales Tax Rank	Property Tax Rank	Unemployment Insurance Tax Rank
North Carolina	12	3	21	16	20	7

Note: The Tax Foundation's State Tax Competitiveness Index enables policymakers, taxpayers, and business leaders to gauge how their states' tax systems compare. A rank of 1 is best, 50 is worst. Rankings do not average to the total. States without a tax rank equally as 1. DC's scores and rankings do not affect other states. The report shows tax systems as of July 1, 2024 (the beginning of Fiscal Year 2025).
Source: Tax Foundation, State Tax Competitiveness Index 2025

TRANSPORTATION

Means of Transportation to Work

Area	Car/Truck/Van		Public Transportation			Bicycle	Walked	Other Means	Worked at Home
	Drove Alone	Car-pooled	Bus	Subway	Railroad				
City	73.7	8.2	2.4	0.0	0.0	0.2	2.3	1.4	11.8
MSA[1]	76.6	8.9	1.0	0.0	0.0	0.1	1.6	1.6	10.3
U.S.	70.2	8.5	1.7	1.3	0.4	0.4	2.4	1.6	13.5

Note: Figures are percentages and cover workers 16 years of age and older; (1) Figures cover the Greensboro-High Point, NC Metropolitan Statistical Area
Source: U.S. Census Bureau, 2019-2023 American Community Survey 5-Year Estimates

Travel Time to Work

Area	Less Than 10 Minutes	10 to 19 Minutes	20 to 29 Minutes	30 to 44 Minutes	45 to 59 Minutes	60 to 89 Minutes	90 Minutes or More
City	13.4	40.9	22.3	14.6	3.5	3.0	2.4
MSA[1]	13.3	34.4	23.7	18.1	5.0	3.2	2.2
U.S.	12.6	28.6	21.2	20.8	8.1	6.0	2.8

Note: Note: Figures are percentages and include workers 16 years old and over; (1) Figures cover the Greensboro-High Point, NC Metropolitan Statistical Area
Source: U.S. Census Bureau, 2019-2023 American Community Survey 5-Year Estimates

Key Congestion Measures

Measure	2000	2010	2015	2020	2022
Annual Hours of Delay, Total (000)	4,218	6,517	7,508	5,320	7,876
Annual Hours of Delay, Per Auto Commuter	26	32	37	25	38
Annual Congestion Cost, Per Auto Commuter ($)	542	670	711	518	736

Note: Figures cover the Greensboro NC urban area
Source: Texas A&M Transportation Institute, 2023 Urban Mobility Report

Freeway Travel Time Index

Measure	1985	1990	1995	2000	2005	2010	2015	2020	2022
Urban Area Index[1]	1.02	1.03	1.07	1.08	1.09	1.10	1.12	1.11	1.12
Urban Area Rank[1,2]	96	96	87	97	98	98	92	20	81

Note: Freeway Travel Time Index—the ratio of travel time in the peak period to the travel time at free-flow conditions. For example, a value of 1.30 indicates a 20-minute free-flow trip takes 26 minutes in the peak (20 minutes x 1.30 = 26 minutes); (1) Covers the Greensboro NC urban area; (2) Rank is based on 101 larger urban areas (#1 = highest travel time index)
Source: Texas A&M Transportation Institute, 2023 Urban Mobility Report

Public Transportation

Agency Name / Mode of Transportation	Vehicles Operated in Maximum Service[1]	Annual Unlinked Passenger Trips[2] (in thous.)	Annual Passenger Miles[3] (in thous.)
Greensboro Transit Authority (GTA)			
Bus (purchased transportation)	38	2,091.6	8,129.6
Demand Response (purchased transportation)	37	171.6	1,345.7

Note: (1) Number of revenue vehicles operated by the given mode and type of service to meet the annual maximum service requirement. This is the revenue vehicle count during the peak season of the year; on the week and day that maximum service is provided. Vehicles operated in maximum service (VOMS) exclude atypical days and one-time special events; (2) Number of passengers who boarded public transportation vehicles. Passengers are counted each time they board a vehicle no matter how many vehicles they use to travel from their origin to their destination. (3) Sum of the distances ridden by all passengers during the entire fiscal year.
Source: Federal Transit Administration, National Transit Database, 2023

Air Transportation

Airport Name and Code / Type of Service	Passenger Airlines[1]	Passenger Enplanements	Freight Carriers[2]	Freight (lbs)
Piedmont Triad International (GSO)				
Domestic service (U.S. carriers only)	22	985,423	13	76,702,652
International service (U.S. carriers only)	0	0	1	3,906

Note: (1) Includes all U.S.-based major, minor and commuter airlines that carried at least one passenger during the year; (2) Includes all U.S.-based airlines and freight carriers that transported at least one pound of freight during the year.
Source: Bureau of Transportation Statistics, The Intermodal Transportation Database, Air Carriers: T-100 Domestic Market (U.S. carriers only), 2024; Bureau of Transportation Statistics, The Intermodal Transportation Database, Air Carriers: T-100 International Market (U.S. carriers only), 2024

BUSINESSES

Major Business Headquarters

Company Name	Industry	Rankings	
		Fortune[1]	Forbes[2]
No companies listed	-	-	-

Note: (1) Companies that produce a 10-K are ranked 1 to 500 based on 2023 revenue; (2) All private companies with at least $2 billion in annual revenue through the end of their most current fiscal year are ranked 1 to 275; companies listed are headquartered in the city; dashes indicate no ranking
Source: Fortune, "Fortune 500," 2024; Forbes, "America's Largest Private Companies," 2024

Living Environment

COST OF LIVING

Cost of Living Index

	Composite Index	Groceries	Housing	Utilities	Transportation	Health Care	Misc. Goods/Services
	n/a	n/a	n/a	n/a	n/a	n/a	n/a

Note: The Cost of Living Index measures regional differences in the cost of consumer goods and services, excluding taxes and non-consumer expenditures, for professional and managerial households in the top income quintile. It is based on more than 50,000 prices covering almost 60 different items for which prices are collected three times a year by chambers of commerce, economic development organizations or university applied economic centers in each participating urban area. The numbers shown should be read as a percentage above or below the national average of 100. For example, a value of 115.4 in the groceries column indicates that grocery prices are 15.4% higher than the national average. Small differences in the index numbers should not be interpreted as significant; n/a not available.
Source: The Council for Community and Economic Research, Cost of Living Index, 2024

Grocery Prices

Area[1]	T-Bone Steak ($/pound)	Frying Chicken ($/pound)	Whole Milk ($/half gal.)	Eggs ($/dozen)	Orange Juice ($/64 oz.)	Coffee ($/11.5 oz.)
City[2]	n/a	n/a	n/a	n/a	n/a	n/a
Avg.	15.42	1.55	4.69	3.25	4.41	5.46
Min.	14.50	1.16	4.43	2.75	4.00	4.85
Max.	17.56	2.89	5.49	4.78	5.54	7.89

Note: (1) Values for the local area are compared with the average, minimum and maximum values for all 276 areas in the Cost of Living Index; (2) Figures cover the Greensboro NC urban area; n/a not available; **T-Bone Steak** (price per pound); **Frying Chicken** (price per pound, whole fryer); **Whole Milk** (half gallon carton); **Eggs** (price per dozen, Grade A, large); **Orange Juice** (64 oz. Tropicana or Florida Natural); **Coffee** (11.5 oz. can, vacuum-packed, Maxwell House, Hills Bros, or Folgers).
Source: The Council for Community and Economic Research, Cost of Living Index, 2024

Housing and Utility Costs

Area[1]	New Home Price ($)	Apartment Rent ($/month)	All Electric ($/month)	Part Electric ($/month)	Other Energy ($/month)	Telephone ($/month)
City[2]	n/a	n/a	n/a	n/a	n/a	n/a
Avg.	515,975	1,550	210.99	123.07	82.07	194.99
Min.	265,375	692	104.33	53.68	36.26	179.42
Max.	2,775,821	5,719	529.02	397.28	361.63	223.33

Note: (1) Values for the local area are compared with the average, minimum and maximum values for all 276 areas in the Cost of Living Index; (2) Figures cover the Greensboro NC urban area; n/a not available; **New Home Price** (2,400 sf living area, 8,000 sf lot, in urban area with full utilities); **Apartment Rent** (950 sf 2 bedroom/1.5 or 2 bath, unfurnished, excluding all utilities except water); **All Electric** (average monthly cost for an all-electric home); **Part Electric** (average monthly cost for a part-electric home); **Other Energy** (average monthly cost for natural gas, fuel oil, coal, wood, and any other forms of energy except electricity); **Telephone** (price includes the base monthly rate plus taxes and fees for three lines of mobile phone service).
Source: The Council for Community and Economic Research, Cost of Living Index, 2024

Health Care, Transportation, and Other Costs

Area[1]	Doctor ($/visit)	Dentist ($/visit)	Optometrist ($/visit)	Gasoline ($/gallon)	Beauty Salon ($/visit)	Men's Shirt ($)
City[2]	n/a	n/a	n/a	n/a	n/a	n/a
Avg.	143.77	117.51	129.23	3.32	48.57	38.14
Min.	36.74	58.67	67.33	2.80	24.00	13.41
Max.	270.44	216.82	307.33	5.28	94.00	63.89

Note: (1) Values for the local area are compared with the average, minimum and maximum values for all 276 areas in the Cost of Living Index; (2) Figures cover the Greensboro NC urban area; n/a not available; **Doctor** (general practitioners routine exam of an established patient); **Dentist** (adult teeth cleaning and periodic oral examination); **Optometrist** (full vision eye exam for established adult patient); **Gasoline** (one gallon regular unleaded, national brand, including all taxes, cash price at self-service pump if available); **Beauty Salon** (woman's shampoo, trim, and blow-dry); **Men's Shirt** (cotton/polyester dress shirt, pinpoint weave, long sleeves).
Source: The Council for Community and Economic Research, Cost of Living Index, 2024

HOUSING

Homeownership Rate

Area	2017 (%)	2018 (%)	2019 (%)	2020 (%)	2021 (%)	2022 (%)	2023 (%)	2024 (%)
MSA[1]	61.9	63.2	61.7	65.8	61.9	70.0	69.4	67.0
U.S.	63.9	64.4	64.6	66.6	65.5	65.8	65.9	65.6

Note: (1) Figures cover the Greensboro-High Point, NC Metropolitan Statistical Area
Source: U.S. Census Bureau, Housing Vacancies and Homeownership Annual Statistics: 2017-2024

House Price Index (HPI)

Area	National Ranking[2]	Quarterly Change (%)	One-Year Change (%)	Five-Year Change (%)	Since 1991Q1 (%)
MSA[1]	65	0.24	6.92	68.92	226.57
U.S.[3]	—	1.43	4.51	57.13	327.82

Note: The HPI is a weighted repeat sales index. It measures average price changes in repeat sales or refinancings on the same properties. This information is obtained by reviewing repeat mortgage transactions on single-family properties whose mortgages have been purchased or securitized by Fannie Mae or Freddie Mac since January 1975; (1) Figures cover the Greensboro-High Point, NC Metropolitan Statistical Area; (2) Rankings are based on annual percentage change for all metro areas containing at least 15,000 transactions over the last 10 years and ranges from 1 to 241; (3) figures based on a weighted average of Census Division estimates using a seasonally adjusted, purchase-only index; all figures are for the period ending December 31, 2024
Source: Federal Housing Finance Agency, Change in FHFA Metropolitan Area House Price Indexes, All Transactions Index, 2024Q4

Home Value

Area	Under $100,000	$100,000 -$199,999	$200,000 -$299,999	$300,000 -$399,999	$400,000 -$499,999	$500,000 -$999,999	$1,000,000 or more	Median ($)
City	10.1	33.8	25.7	14.3	6.6	8.2	1.4	221,300
MSA[1]	15.0	33.0	23.9	13.1	6.3	7.9	1.0	207,600
U.S.	12.1	17.8	19.5	14.4	10.5	19.1	6.5	303,400

Note: Figures are percentages except for median and cover owner-occupied housing units; (1) Figures cover the Greensboro-High Point, NC Metropolitan Statistical Area
Source: U.S. Census Bureau, 2019-2023 American Community Survey 5-Year Estimates

Year Housing Structure Built

Area	2020 or Later	2010 -2019	2000 -2009	1990 -1999	1980 -1989	1970 -1979	1960 -1969	1950 -1959	1940 -1949	Before 1940	Median Year
City	0.8	9.8	14.7	14.5	15.6	13.9	11.0	10.1	3.8	5.7	1983
MSA[1]	0.9	9.0	15.8	16.5	14.4	14.3	10.1	8.9	4.1	6.0	1985
U.S.	1.2	8.9	13.6	12.8	13.0	14.4	10.0	9.7	4.5	11.9	1980

Note: Figures are percentages except for Median Year; Note: (1) Figures cover the Greensboro-High Point, NC Metropolitan Statistical Area
Source: U.S. Census Bureau, 2019-2023 American Community Survey 5-Year Estimates

Gross Monthly Rent

Area	Under $500	$500 -$999	$1,000 -$1,499	$1,500 -$1,999	$2,000 -$2,499	$2,500 -$2,999	$3,000 and up	Median ($)
City	4.8	31.8	45.3	12.5	3.2	0.8	1.5	1,114
MSA[1]	7.6	37.7	39.7	10.5	2.6	0.7	1.2	1,045
U.S.	6.5	22.3	29.5	20.2	10.8	4.8	5.9	1,348

Note: Figures are percentages except for median; Gross rent is the contract rent plus the estimated average monthly cost of utilities (electricity, gas, and water and sewer) and fuels (oil, coal, kerosene, wood, etc.) if these are paid by the renter (or paid for the renter by someone else); (1) Figures cover the Greensboro-High Point, NC Metropolitan Statistical Area
Source: U.S. Census Bureau, 2019-2023 American Community Survey 5-Year Estimates

HEALTH

Health Risk Factors

Category	MSA[1] (%)	U.S. (%)
Adults aged 18–64 who have any kind of health care coverage	n/a	90.8
Adults who reported being in good or better health	n/a	81.8
Adults who have been told they have high blood cholesterol	n/a	36.9
Adults who have been told they have high blood pressure	n/a	34.0
Adults who are current smokers	n/a	12.1
Adults who currently use e-cigarettes	n/a	7.7
Adults who currently use chewing tobacco, snuff, or snus	n/a	3.2
Adults who are heavy drinkers[2]	n/a	6.1
Adults who are binge drinkers[3]	n/a	15.2
Adults who are overweight (BMI 25.0 - 29.9)	n/a	34.4
Adults who are obese (BMI 30.0 - 99.8)	n/a	34.3
Adults who participated in any physical activities in the past month	n/a	75.8

Note: All figures are crude prevalence; (1) Figures for the Greensboro-High Point, NC Metropolitan Statistical Area were not available.
(2) Heavy drinkers are classified as adult men having more than 14 drinks per week and adult women having more than 7 drinks per week; (3) Binge drinkers are classified as males having five or more drinks on one occasion or females having four or more drinks on one occasion
Source: Centers for Disease Control and Prevention, Behaviorial Risk Factor Surveillance System, SMART: Selected Metropolitan Area Risk Trends, 2023

Acute and Chronic Health Conditions

Category	MSA[1] (%)	U.S. (%)
Adults who have ever been told they had a heart attack	n/a	4.2
Adults who have ever been told they have angina or coronary heart disease	n/a	4.0
Adults who have ever been told they had a stroke	n/a	3.3
Adults who have ever been told they have asthma	n/a	15.7
Adults who have ever been told they have arthritis	n/a	26.3
Adults who have ever been told they have diabetes[2]	n/a	11.5
Adults who have ever been told they had skin cancer	n/a	5.6
Adults who have ever been told they had any other types of cancer	n/a	8.4
Adults who have ever been told they have COPD	n/a	6.4
Adults who have ever been told they have kidney disease	n/a	3.7
Adults who have ever been told they have a form of depression	n/a	22.0

Note: All figures are crude prevalence; (1) Figures for the Greensboro-High Point, NC Metropolitan Statistical Area were not available.
(2) Figures do not include pregnancy-related, borderline, or pre-diabetes
Source: Centers for Disease Control and Prevention, Behavioral Risk Factor Surveillance System, SMART: Selected Metropolitan Area Risk Trends, 2023

Health Screening and Vaccination Rates

Category	MSA[1] (%)	U.S. (%)
Adults who have ever been tested for HIV	n/a	37.5
Adults who have had their blood cholesterol checked within the last five years	n/a	87.0
Adults aged 65+ who have had flu shot within the past year	n/a	63.4
Adults aged 65+ who have ever had a pneumonia vaccination	n/a	71.9

Note: All figures are crude prevalence; (1) Figures for the Greensboro-High Point, NC Metropolitan Statistical Area were not available.
Source: Centers for Disease Control and Prevention, Behavioral Risk Factor Surveillance System, SMART: Selected Metropolitan Area Risk Trends, 2023

Disability Status

Category	MSA[1] (%)	U.S. (%)
Adults who reported being deaf	n/a	7.4
Are you blind or have serious difficulty seeing, even when wearing glasses?	n/a	4.9
Do you have difficulty doing errands alone?	n/a	7.8
Do you have difficulty dressing or bathing?	n/a	3.6
Do you have serious difficulty concentrating/remembering/making decisions?	n/a	13.7
Do you have serious difficulty walking or climbing stairs?	n/a	13.2

Note: All figures are crude prevalence; (1) Figures for the Greensboro-High Point, NC Metropolitan Statistical Area were not available.
Source: Centers for Disease Control and Prevention, Behavioral Risk Factor Surveillance System, SMART: Selected Metropolitan Area Risk Trends, 2023

Mortality Rates for the Top 10 Causes of Death in the U.S.

ICD-10[a] Sub-Chapter	ICD-10[a] Code	Crude Mortality Rate[2] per 100,000 population	
		County[3]	U.S.
Malignant neoplasms	C00-C97	179.1	182.7
Ischaemic heart diseases	I20-I25	91.0	109.6
Provisional assignment of new diseases of uncertain etiology[1]	U00-U49	55.6	65.3
Other forms of heart disease	I30-I51	66.0	65.1
Other degenerative diseases of the nervous system	G30-G31	51.8	52.4
Other external causes of accidental injury	W00-X59	67.4	52.3
Cerebrovascular diseases	I60-I69	50.6	49.1
Chronic lower respiratory diseases	J40-J47	36.4	43.5
Hypertensive diseases	I10-I15	29.5	38.9
Organic, including symptomatic, mental disorders	F01-F09	50.0	33.9

Note: (a) ICD-10 = International Classification of Diseases 10th Revision; (1) Includes COVID-19, adverse effects to COVID-19 vaccines, SARS, and vaping-related disorders; (2) Crude mortality rates are a three-year average covering 2021-2023; (3) Figures cover Guilford County.
Source: Centers for Disease Control and Prevention, National Center for Health Statistics. National Vital Statistics System, Mortality 2018-2023 on CDC WONDER Online Database

Mortality Rates for Selected Causes of Death

Cause of Death	ICD-10[a] Code	Crude Mortality Rate[1] per 100,000 population	
		County[2]	U.S.
Accidental poisoning and exposure to noxious substances	X40-X49	37.6	30.5
Alzheimer disease	G30	41.4	35.4
Assault	X85-Y09	12.1	7.3
COVID-19	U07.1	55.6	65.3
Diabetes mellitus	E10-E14	33.0	30.0
Diseases of the liver	K70-K76	18.2	20.8
Human immunodeficiency virus (HIV) disease	B20-B24	2.3	1.5
Influenza and pneumonia	J09-J18	14.4	13.4
Intentional self-harm	X60-X84	11.3	14.7
Malnutrition	E40-E46	7.9	6.0
Obesity and other hyperalimentation	E65-E68	4.1	3.1
Renal failure	N17-N19	22.6	16.4
Transport accidents	V01-V99	14.7	14.4

Note: (a) ICD-10 = International Classification of Diseases 10th Revision; (1) Crude mortality rates are a three-year average covering 2021-2023; (2) Figures cover Guilford County; Data are suppressed when the data meet the criteria for confidentiality constraints; Crude mortality rates are flagged as unreliable when the rate would be calculated with a numerator of 20 or less.
Source: Centers for Disease Control and Prevention, National Center for Health Statistics. National Vital Statistics System, Mortality 2018-2023 on CDC WONDER Online Database

Health Insurance Coverage

Area	With Health Insurance	With Private Health Insurance	With Public Health Insurance	Without Health Insurance	Population Under Age 19 Without Health Insurance
City	90.9	65.5	35.7	9.1	4.1
MSA[1]	90.2	64.1	37.2	9.8	4.2
U.S.	91.4	67.3	36.3	8.6	5.4

Note: Figures are percentages that cover the civilian noninstitutionalized population; (1) Figures cover the Greensboro-High Point, NC Metropolitan Statistical Area
Source: U.S. Census Bureau, 2019-2023 American Community Survey 5-Year Estimates

Number of Medical Professionals

Area	MDs[3]	DOs[3,4]	Dentists	Podiatrists	Chiropractors	Optometrists
County[1] (number)	1,432	103	346	26	83	56
County[1] (rate[2])	262.2	18.9	62.9	4.7	15.1	10.2
U.S. (rate[2])	302.5	29.2	74.6	6.4	29.5	18.0

Note: Data as of 2023 unless noted; (1) Data covers Guilford County; (2) Number of medical professionals per 100,000 population; (3) Data as of 2022 and includes all active, non-federal physicians; (4) Doctor of Osteopathic Medicine
Source: U.S. Department of Health and Human Services, Health Resources and Services Administration, Bureau of Health Professions, Area Resource File (ARF) 2023-2024

Best Hospitals

According to *U.S. News,* the Greensboro-High Point, NC metro area is home to one of the best hospitals in the U.S.: **Moses H. Cone Memorial Hospital** (1 adult specialty). The hospital listed was nationally ranked in at least one of 15 adult or 11 pediatric specialties. The number of specialties shown cover the parent hospital. Only 160 U.S. hospitals performed well enough to be nationally ranked in one or more specialties. Twenty hospitals in the U.S. made the Honor Roll. The Best Hospitals Honor Roll takes both the national rankings and the procedure and condition ratings into account. Hospitals received points if they were nationally ranked in one of the 15 adult specialties—the higher they ranked, the more points they got—and how many ratings of "high performing" they earned in the 20 procedures and conditions. *U.S. News Online, "America's Best Hospitals 2024-25"*

EDUCATION

Public School District Statistics

District Name	Schls	Pupils	Pupil/ Teacher Ratio	Minority Pupils[1] (%)	Total Rev. per Pupil ($)	Total Exp. per Pupil ($)
Guilford County Schools	124	67,832	14.6	73.3	14,420	13,788

Note: Table includes school districts with 2,000 or more students; (1) Percentage of students that are not non-Hispanic white.
Source: U.S. Department of Education, National Center for Education Statistics, Common Core of Data, Local Education Agency (School District) Universe Survey: School Year 2023-2024; U.S. Department of Education, National Center for Education Statistics, Common Core of Data, School District Finance Survey (F-33): School Year 2021–22

Best High Schools

According to *U.S. News,* Greensboro is home to three of the top 500 high schools in the U.S.: **The Early College at Guilford** (#16); **STEM Early College at N.C. A&T** (#77); **Philip J. Weaver Ed Center** (#268). Nearly 25,000 public, magnet and charter schools were ranked based on their performance on state assessments and how well they prepare students for college. *U.S. News & World Report, "Best High Schools 2024"*

Highest Level of Education

Area	Less than H.S.	H.S. Diploma	Some College, No Deg.	Associate Degree	Bachelor's Degree	Master's Degree	Prof. School Degree	Doctorate Degree
City	9.9	21.5	20.1	8.7	24.2	11.3	2.3	2.1
MSA[1]	11.7	26.5	20.8	9.6	20.0	8.5	1.5	1.4
U.S.	10.6	26.2	19.4	8.8	21.3	9.8	2.3	1.6

Note: Figures cover persons age 25 and over; (1) Figures cover the Greensboro-High Point, NC Metropolitan Statistical Area
Source: U.S. Census Bureau, 2019-2023 American Community Survey 5-Year Estimates

Educational Attainment by Race

Area	High School Graduate or Higher (%)					Bachelor's Degree or Higher (%)				
	Total	White	Black	Asian	Hisp.[2]	Total	White	Black	Asian	Hisp.[2]
City	90.1	95.2	89.5	75.7	70.2	39.9	52.3	28.0	46.5	19.4
MSA[1]	88.3	91.1	88.5	78.6	63.3	31.4	34.4	24.7	49.1	16.3
U.S.	89.4	92.9	88.1	88.0	72.5	35.0	37.7	24.7	57.0	19.9

Note: Figures shown cover persons 25 years old and over; (1) Figures cover the Greensboro-High Point, NC Metropolitan Statistical Area; (2) People of Hispanic origin can be of any race
Source: U.S. Census Bureau, 2019-2023 American Community Survey 5-Year Estimates

School Enrollment by Grade and Control

Area	Preschool (%)		Kindergarten (%)		Grades 1 - 4 (%)		Grades 5 - 8 (%)		Grades 9 - 12 (%)	
	Public	Private	Public	Private	Public	Private	Public	Private	Public	Private
City	56.8	43.2	89.0	11.0	88.9	11.1	89.3	10.7	88.6	11.4
MSA[1]	56.8	43.2	86.7	13.3	85.9	14.1	85.7	14.3	87.9	12.1
U.S.	58.7	41.3	85.2	14.8	87.2	12.8	87.9	12.1	89.0	11.0

Note: Figures shown cover persons 3 years old and over; (1) Figures cover the Greensboro-High Point, NC Metropolitan Statistical Area
Source: U.S. Census Bureau, 2019-2023 American Community Survey 5-Year Estimates

Higher Education

Four-Year Colleges			Two-Year Colleges			Medical Schools[1]	Law Schools[2]	Voc/Tech[3]
Public	Private Non-profit	Private For-profit	Public	Private Non-profit	Private For-profit			
2	4	2	3	0	1	0	1	2

Note: Figures cover institutions located within the Greensboro-High Point, NC Metropolitan Statistical Area and include main campuses only; (1) includes schools accredited by the Liaison Committee on Medical Education and the American Osteopathic Association's Commission on Osteopathic College Accreditation; (2) includes ABA-accredited schools, schools with provisional ABA accreditation, and state accredited schools; (3) includes all schools with programs that are less than 2 years.
Source: National Center for Education Statistics, Integrated Postsecondary Education System (IPEDS), 2023-24; Wikipedia, List of Medical Schools in the United States, accessed May 2, 2025; Wikipedia, List of Law Schools in the United States, accessed May 2, 2025

According to *U.S. News & World Report,* the Greensboro-High Point, NC metro area is home to one of the top 200 national universities in the U.S.: **University of North Carolina—Greensboro** (#196 tie). The indicators used to capture academic quality fall into a number of categories: assessment by administrators at peer institutions; retention of students; faculty resources; student selectivity; financial resources; alumni giving; high school counselor ratings of colleges; and graduation rate. *U.S. News & World Report, "America's Best Colleges 2025"*

EMPLOYERS

Major Employers

Company Name	Industry
Bank of America	Financial services
CitiGroup	Financial services
City of Greensboro	Municipal government
City of High Point	Municipal government
Cone Denim	Denims
County of Guilford	County government
Daimler Trucks North America	Motor vehicles & car bodies
Gilbarco	Electronic computers
High Point Regional Health System	General medical & surgical hospitals
ITG Holdings	Denims
Kayser- Roth Corporation	Mens, boys, girls, hosiery
Klaussner Furniture Industries	Upholstered/household furniture
Lorillard Tobbacco Co	Cigarettes
NC Ag & Technical State University	University
Piedmont Express	Airline ticket offices
Ralph Lauren Corporation	Distribution/customer service
RF Micro Devices	Semiconductors & related devices
Technimark	Injection-molded plastics
The Fresh Market	Grocery stores
The Moses H Cone Memorial Hospital	General medical & surgical hospitals

Note: Companies shown are located within the Greensboro-High Point, NC Metropolitan Statistical Area.
Source: Chambers of Commerce; State Departments of Labor; Wikipedia

PUBLIC SAFETY

Crime Rate

Area	Total Crime Rate	Violent Crime Rate				Property Crime Rate		
		Murder	Rape	Robbery	Aggrav. Assault	Burglary	Larceny -Theft	Motor Vehicle Theft
City	4,560.5	24.7	24.4	164.9	612.1	555.0	2,682.7	496.6
U.S.	2,290.9	5.7	38.0	66.5	264.1	250.7	1,347.2	318.7

Note: Figures are crimes per 100,000 population.
Source: FBI, Table 8, Offenses Known to Law Enforcement, by State by City, 2023

Hate Crimes

Area	Number of Quarters Reported	Number of Incidents per Bias Motivation					
		Race/Ethnicity/ Ancestry	Religion	Sexual Orientation	Disability	Gender	Gender Identity
City[1]	4	10	2	2	0	0	0
U.S.	4	5,900	2,699	2,077	187	92	492

Note: (1) Figures include at least one incident reported with more than one bias motivation.
Source: Federal Bureau of Investigation, Hate Crime Statistics 2023

Identity Theft Consumer Reports

Area	Reports	Reports per 100,000 Population	Rank[2]
MSA[1]	1,880	241	108
U.S.	1,135,291	339	-

Note: (1) Figures cover the Greensboro-High Point, NC Metropolitan Statistical Area; (2) Rank ranges from 1 to 401 where 1 indicates greatest number of identity theft reports per 100,000 population
Source: Federal Trade Commission, Consumer Sentinel Network Data Book 2024

Fraud and Other Consumer Reports

Area	Reports	Reports per 100,000 Population	Rank[2]
MSA[1]	11,078	1,420	71
U.S.	5,360,641	1,601	-

Note: (1) Figures cover the Greensboro-High Point, NC Metropolitan Statistical Area; (2) Rank ranges from 1 to 401 where 1 indicates greatest number of fraud and other consumer reports per 100,000 population
Source: Federal Trade Commission, Consumer Sentinel Network Data Book 2024

POLITICS

2024 Presidential Election Results

Area	Trump (Rep.)	Harris (Dem.)	Stein (Green)	Kennedy (Ind.)	Oliver (Lib.)	Other
Guilford County	38.3	60.0	0.5	0.0	0.4	0.8
U.S.	49.7	48.2	0.6	0.5	0.4	0.6

Note: Results are percentages and may not add to 100% due to rounding
Source: Dave Leip's Atlas of U.S. Presidential Elections

Greensboro, North Carolina

SPORTS

Professional Sports Teams

Team Name	League	Year Established
No teams are located in the metro area		

Source: Wikipedia, Major Professional Sports Teams of the United States and Canada, May 1, 2025

CLIMATE

Average and Extreme Temperatures

Temperature	Jan	Feb	Mar	Apr	May	Jun	Jul	Aug	Sep	Oct	Nov	Dec	Yr.
Extreme High (°F)	78	81	89	91	96	102	102	103	100	95	85	78	103
Average High (°F)	48	51	60	70	78	84	87	86	80	70	60	50	69
Average Temp. (°F)	38	41	49	58	67	74	78	76	70	59	49	40	58
Average Low (°F)	28	30	37	46	55	63	67	66	59	47	37	30	47
Extreme Low (°F)	-8	-1	5	23	32	42	49	45	37	20	10	0	-8

Note: Figures cover the years 1948-1990
Source: National Climatic Data Center, International Station Meteorological Climate Summary, 9/96

Average Precipitation/Snowfall/Humidity

Precip./Humidity	Jan	Feb	Mar	Apr	May	Jun	Jul	Aug	Sep	Oct	Nov	Dec	Yr.
Avg. Precip. (in.)	3.2	3.4	3.7	3.1	3.7	3.8	4.5	4.2	3.4	3.4	2.9	3.3	42.5
Avg. Snowfall (in.)	4	3	2	Tr	0	0	0	0	0	0	Tr	1	10
Avg. Rel. Hum. 7am (%)	80	78	78	77	82	84	87	90	90	88	83	80	83
Avg. Rel. Hum. 4pm (%)	53	50	47	44	51	54	57	58	56	51	51	54	52

Note: Figures cover the years 1948-1990; Tr = Trace amounts (<0.05 in. of rain; <0.5 in. of snow)
Source: National Climatic Data Center, International Station Meteorological Climate Summary, 9/96

Weather Conditions

Temperature			Daytime Sky			Precipitation		
10°F & below	32°F & below	90°F & above	Clear	Partly cloudy	Cloudy	0.01 inch or more precip.	0.1 inch or more snow/ice	Thunder-storms
3	85	32	94	143	128	113	5	43

Note: Figures are average number of days per year and cover the years 1948-1990
Source: National Climatic Data Center, International Station Meteorological Climate Summary, 9/96

HAZARDOUS WASTE

Superfund Sites

The Greensboro-High Point, NC metro area has no sites on the EPA's Superfund Final National Priorities List (NPL) or Superfund Alternative Approach (SAA) list. The Superfund alternative approach uses the same investigation and cleanup process and standards that are used for sites listed on the National Priorities List. The SAA is an alternative to listing a site on the NPL; it is not an alternative to Superfund or the Superfund process. There are a total of 1,445 Superfund sites with a status of proposed or final on both lists in the United States. *U.S. Environmental Protection Agency, National Priorities List, May 1, 2025; U.S. Environmental Protection Agency, Superfund Alternative Approach Sites, May 1, 2025*

AIR QUALITY

Air Quality Trends: Ozone

	1990	1995	2000	2005	2010	2015	2020	2021	2022	2023
MSA[1]	0.097	0.089	0.089	0.082	0.076	0.064	0.057	0.066	0.063	0.067
U.S.	0.087	0.089	0.081	0.080	0.072	0.068	0.066	0.067	0.067	0.070

Note: (1) Data covers the Greensboro-High Point, NC Metropolitan Statistical Area. The values shown are the composite ozone concentration averages among trend sites based on the highest fourth daily maximum 8-hour concentration in parts per million. These trends are based on sites having an adequate record of monitoring data during the trend period. Data from exceptional events are included.
Source: U.S. Environmental Protection Agency, Air Quality Monitoring Information, "Air Quality Trends by City, 1990-2023"

Air Quality Index

Area	Percent of Days when Air Quality was...[2]					AQI Statistics[2]	
	Good	Moderate	Unhealthy for Sensitive Groups	Unhealthy	Very Unhealthy	Maximum	Median
MSA[1]	50.1	48.8	1.1	0.0	0.0	131	50

Note: (1) Data covers the Greensboro-High Point, NC Metropolitan Statistical Area; (2) Based on 365 days with AQI data in 2023. Air Quality Index (AQI) is an index for reporting daily air quality. EPA calculates the AQI for five major air pollutants regulated by the Clean Air Act: ground-level ozone, particle pollution (aka particulate matter), carbon monoxide, sulfur dioxide, and nitrogen dioxide. The AQI runs from 0 to 500. The higher the AQI value, the greater the level of air pollution and the greater the health concern. There are six AQI categories: "Good" AQI is between 0 and 50. Air quality is considered satisfactory; "Moderate" AQI is between 51 and 100. Air quality is acceptable; "Unhealthy for Sensitive Groups" When AQI values are between 101 and 150, members of sensitive groups may experience health effects; "Unhealthy" When AQI values are between 151 and 200 everyone may begin to experience health effects; "Very Unhealthy" AQI values between 201 and 300 trigger a health alert; "Hazardous" AQI values over 300 trigger warnings of emergency conditions (not shown).
Source: U.S. Environmental Protection Agency, Air Quality Index Report, 2023

Air Quality Index Pollutants

Area	Percent of Days when AQI Pollutant was...[2]					
	Carbon Monoxide	Nitrogen Dioxide	Ozone	Sulfur Dioxide	Particulate Matter 2.5	Particulate Matter 10
MSA[1]	0.0	0.0	31.8	(3)	66.8	1.4

Note: (1) Data covers the Greensboro-High Point, NC Metropolitan Statistical Area; (2) Based on 365 days with AQI data in 2023. The Air Quality Index (AQI) is an index for reporting daily air quality. EPA calculates the AQI for five major air pollutants regulated by the Clean Air Act: ground-level ozone, particle pollution (also known as particulate matter), carbon monoxide, sulfur dioxide, and nitrogen dioxide. The AQI runs from 0 to 500. The higher the AQI value, the greater the level of air pollution and the greater the health concern; (3) Sulfur dioxide is no longer included in this table because SO_2 concentrations tend to be very localized and not necessarily representative of broad geographical areas like counties and CBSAs.
Source: U.S. Environmental Protection Agency, Air Quality Index Report, 2023

Maximum Air Pollutant Concentrations: Particulate Matter, Ozone, CO and Lead

	Particulate Matter 10 (ug/m³)	Particulate Matter 2.5 Wtd AM (ug/m³)	Particulate Matter 2.5 24-Hr (ug/m³)	Ozone (ppm)	Carbon Monoxide (ppm)	Lead (ug/m³)
MSA[1] Level	39	9.8	25	0.067	n/a	n/a
NAAQS[2]	150	15	35	0.075	9	0.15
Met NAAQS[2]	Yes	Yes	Yes	Yes	n/a	n/a

Note: (1) Data covers the Greensboro-High Point, NC Metropolitan Statistical Area; Data from exceptional events are included; (2) National Ambient Air Quality Standards; ppm = parts per million; ug/m³ = micrograms per cubic meter; n/a not available.
Concentrations: Particulate Matter 10 (coarse particulate)—highest second maximum 24-hour concentration; Particulate Matter 2.5 Wtd AM (fine particulate)—highest weighted annual mean concentration; Particulate Matter 2.5 24-Hour (fine particulate)—highest 98th percentile 24-hour concentration; Ozone—highest fourth daily maximum 8-hour concentration; Carbon Monoxide—highest second maximum non-overlapping 8-hour concentration; Lead—maximum running 3-month average
Source: U.S. Environmental Protection Agency, Air Quality Monitoring Information, "Air Quality Statistics by City, 2023"

Maximum Air Pollutant Concentrations: Nitrogen Dioxide and Sulfur Dioxide

	Nitrogen Dioxide AM (ppb)	Nitrogen Dioxide 1-Hr (ppb)	Sulfur Dioxide AM (ppb)	Sulfur Dioxide 1-Hr (ppb)	Sulfur Dioxide 24-Hr (ppb)
MSA[1] Level	n/a	n/a	n/a	4	n/a
NAAQS[2]	53	100	30	75	140
Met NAAQS[2]	n/a	n/a	n/a	Yes	n/a

Note: (1) Data covers the Greensboro-High Point, NC Metropolitan Statistical Area; Data from exceptional events are included; (2) National Ambient Air Quality Standards; ppm = parts per million; ug/m³ = micrograms per cubic meter; n/a not available.
Concentrations: Nitrogen Dioxide AM—highest arithmetic mean concentration; Nitrogen Dioxide 1-Hr—highest 98th percentile 1-hour daily maximum concentration; Sulfur Dioxide AM—highest annual mean concentration; Sulfur Dioxide 1-Hr—highest 99th percentile 1-hour daily maximum concentration; Sulfur Dioxide 24-Hr—highest second maximum 24-hour concentration
Source: U.S. Environmental Protection Agency, Air Quality Monitoring Information, "Air Quality Statistics by City, 2023"

Lexington, Kentucky

Background

Lexington continues to combine the pace of a major city with the tempo of a small town without losing the traditions and gentility of its Southern heritage. It is situated in a scenic area of rolling plateaus and small creeks flowing into the Kentucky River.

Since its settlement in 1775, Lexington has grown to become Kentucky's second-largest city and the commercial center of the Bluegrass Region. The town was founded in 1779 and incorporated in 1832. Hemp was Lexington's major antebellum crop until the rope from which it was made was no longer used for ship rigging. After the Civil War the farmers in the area switched to tobacco as their primary crop. The city is also the chief producer of bluegrass seed and white barley in the United States.

Also manufactured in Lexington are paper products, air-conditioning and heating equipment, electric typewriters, metal products, and bourbon whiskey.

Lexington was once known as the "Athens of the West" when many early American artists, poets, musicians, and architects settled here, all leaving their imprint on the city. The Actor's Guild of Lexington and the Studio Players, Lexington's oldest community theater (1953) reside in the city, as does the Chamber Music Society of Kentucky. The 1898 Fayette County Courthouse, which operated from 1901 to 2001, has been transformed into the Lexington History Museum.

No discussion of Lexington would be complete without mention of horse racing. Kentucky is synonymous with horses, especially the American Saddlebred—Kentucky's only native breed. The region, with its fertile soil and excellent pastureland, is perfectly suited for breeding horses. Horse racing in Kentucky dates to 1789, when the first course was laid out in Lexington. In 1787, The Commons, a park-like block near Race Street in Lexington, was used for horse racing, but complaints by citizens led to the formal development of a race meet, organized by Kentucky statesman Henry Clay, who also helped form the commonwealth's first jockey club in the city, now known as the Kentucky Jockey Club. Lexington is also home to The Kentucky Horse Park, highlighting 50 horse breeds that visitors can pet and ride; the International Museum of the Horse, with artifacts and exhibits (both in person and online); and the American Saddle Horse Museum, with exhibits that show the role of the saddle horse in American history.

In addition to racecourses, Lexington boasts fine golf courses and many blues, country, and dance clubs for those who prefer musical nightlife. Lexington is home to a thriving cultural arts scene, with a professional orchestra, two ballet companies, and several museums including a basketball museum, several choral organizations, and a highly respected opera program at the University of Kentucky. There are more than 230 churches and synagogues in Lexington, representing 50 denominations.

Institutions of higher learning include the University of Kentucky, Lexington Theological Seminary, the National College of Business and Technology, Georgetown College, Kentucky State University, and Transylvania University. Since its opening in 1982, the Kentucky World Trade Center has organized high-profile trade programs featuring business and political leaders from Asia, Europe, and the Middle East. The Commonwealth of Kentucky has emerged as a leader among the 50 states in expanding its international trade.

Hosted annually in June by the Lexington Pride Center, the Lexington Pride Festival celebrates the LGBTQ community in Central Kentucky, offering live music, crafts, food, and informational booths from diverse service organizations; 2025 is the festival's 17th year. In 2010, Jim Gray was elected as the first openly gay mayor of Lexington. He proclaimed June 29, 2013, as Pride Day.

Lexington has a definite continental climate, temperate and well-suited to a varied plant and animal life. The area is subject to sudden and sweeping temperature changes, generally of short duration. Temperatures below zero and above 100 degrees are relatively rare.

Rankings

General Rankings

- To help military veterans find the best places in which to settle down, *WalletHub* compared the 100 largest U.S. cities across 19 key indicators of livability, affordability and veteran-friendliness. They range from the share of military skill-related jobs to veteran income growth to the availability of VA health facilities. Lexington ranked #35. *Wallethub.com, "Best & Worst Places for Veterans to Live (2025)," November 7, 2024*

- *US News & World Report* conducted a survey of more than 3,500 people and analyzed the 150 largest metropolitan areas to determine what matters most when selecting the next place to live. Lexington ranked #15 out of the top 25 as having the best combination of desirable factors. Criteria: cost of living; quality of life and education; climate; job market; desirability; and other factors. *realestate.usnews.com, "Best Places to Live in the U.S. in 2024-2025," May 21, 2024*

- Lexington was selected as one of the best places to live in the United States by *Money* magazine. The city placed among the top 50. This year's list focused on cities built around community spirit, thoughtful policy and civic engagement. Instead of relying on a predetermined dataset, the cities and towns were grouped according to their strengths and chosen due their affordability, good schools and strong job markets. *Money, "The 50 Best Places to Live in the U.S., 2024" April 8, 2024*

- Lexington was selected as an "All-America City" by the National Civic League. The All-America City Award recognizes civic excellence and in 2024 honored 10 communities that best exemplify the spirit of citizen engagement and cross-sector collaborative problem solving to address pressing and complex issues and create stronger community connections. This year's theme was: "Strengthening Democracy Through Local Action and Innovation." *National Civic League, "2024 All-America City Awards," June 7-9, 2024*

- For its 37th annual "Readers' Choice Awards" survey, *Condé Nast Traveler* ranked its readers' favorite cities in the U.S. Whether it be a longed-for visit or the next big new thing, these are the places travelers loved best. The list was broken into large cities and cities under 250,000. Lexington ranked #4 in the small city category. *Condé Nast Traveler, Readers' Choice Awards 2024, "Best Small Cities in the U.S." October 1, 2024*

Business/Finance Rankings

- Lexington was cited as one of America's top metros for total major capital investment facility projects in 2024. The area ranked #5 in the Tier 2 (mid-sized) metro area category (population 200,000 to 1 million). *Site Selection, "Top Metros of 2024," March 2025*

- The Lexington metro area appeared on the Milken Institute "2025 Best Performing Cities" list. Rank: #75 out of 200 large metro areas (based on performance category). Criteria: job growth; wage growth; high-tech growth and impact; community resilience; housing affordability; household broadband access. *Milken Institute, "Best-Performing Cities 2025," January 14, 2025*

Children/Family Rankings

- Lexington was selected as one of the best cities for newlyweds by *Rent.com*. The city ranked #14 of 15. Criteria: cost of living; availability of affordable rental inventory; annual household income; entertainment, culture and restaurant options; percentage of married couples; concentration of millennials; and safety. *Rent.com, "The 15 Best Cities for Newlyweds," September 2, 2021*

Education Rankings

- Personal finance website *WalletHub* analyzed the 150 largest U.S. metropolitan statistical areas to determine where the most educated Americans are putting their degrees to work. Criteria: education levels; percentage of workers with degrees; education quality and attainment gap; public school quality rankings; quality and enrollment of each metro area's universities. Lexington was ranked #24 (#1 = most educated city). *WalletHub.com, "Most & Least Educated Cities in America, 2025" July 2, 2024*

Health/Fitness Rankings

- For each of the 100 largest cities in the United States, the American Fitness Index®, compiled in partnership between the American College of Sports Medicine and the Elevance Health Foundation, evaluated community infrastructure and more than 30 health behaviors including preventive health, levels of chronic disease conditions, food insecurity, pedestrian safety, air quality, and community/environment resources that support physical activity. Lexington ranked #49 for "community fitness." *americanfitnessindex.org, "2024 ACSM American Fitness Index Summary Report," July 23, 2024*

- The Lexington metro area was identified as one of the worst cities for bed bugs in America by pest control company Orkin. The area ranked #50 out of 50 based on the number of bed bug treatments Orkin performed from December 2022 to November 2023. *Orkin, "Chicago Joins Paris In Global Bed Bug Spotlight Ranking As The Worst City On Orkin's U.S. Bed Bug Cities List," January 22, 2024*

Pet Rankings

- Lexington was selected by *Sniffspot.com* as one of the most dog-friendly cities in the U.S., ranking #20 out of 50. Criteria: dog parks; hiking; sniffspots; public parks; dog-friendly businesses; housing; dog waste cleanliness; leash laws; dog services; and overall cost. *Sniffspot.com, "The Top 50 Most Dog-Friendly Cities in the U.S.," September 30, 2024*

Real Estate Rankings

- *WalletHub* compared the most populated U.S. cities to determine which had the best markets for real estate agents. Lexington ranked #136 where demand was high and pay was the best. Criteria: sales per agent; annual median wage for real-estate agents; monthly average starting salary for real estate agents; real estate job density and competition; unemployment rate; home turnover rate; housing-market health index; and other relevant metrics. *WalletHub.com, "2021 Best Places to Be a Real Estate Agent," May 12, 2021*

- Lexington was ranked #40 out of 176 metro areas in terms of cost of housing in 2024 by the National Association of Home Builders (#1 = most affordable). Criteria: the portion of an average family's income necessary to pay the mortgage on a median-priced home. *National Association of Home Builders®, NAHB-Wells Fargo Cost of Housing Index, 4th Quarter 2024*

Seniors/Retirement Rankings

- Lexington made *Southern Living's* list of southern places—by the beach, in the mountains, or scenic city—to retire. From the incredible views and close knit communities, to the opportunities to put down new roots, and great places to eat and hike, these superb places are perfect for settling down. *Southern Living, "The Best Places to Retire in the South," March 9, 2024*

- Lexington made the 2024 *Forbes* list of "25 Best Places to Retire." Criteria, focused on overall affordability as well as quality of life indicators, include: housing/living costs compared to the national average and taxes; air quality; crime rates; median home prices; risk associated with climate-change/natural hazards; availability of medical care; bikeability; walkability; healthy living. *Forbes.com, "The Best Places to Retire in 2024: Las Cruces and Other Unexpected Hot Spots," May 10, 2024*

Women/Minorities Rankings

- *Travel + Leisure* listed the best cities in and around the U.S. for a memorable and fun girls' trip, even on a budget. Whether it is for a special occasion, to make new memories or just to get away, Lexington is sure to have something for all the ladies in your tribe. *Travel + Leisure, "25 Affordable Girls Weekend Getaways That Won't Break the Bank," January 30, 2025*

- Personal finance website *WalletHub* compared more than 180 U.S. cities across two key dimensions, "Hispanic Business-Friendliness" and "Hispanic Purchasing Power," to arrive at the most favorable conditions for Hispanic entrepreneurs. Lexington was ranked #159 out of 182. Criteria includes: share of Hispanic-Owned Businesses; average growth of Hispanic Business revenues; Small Business-Friendliness score; affordability; and number of Hispanics with at least a bachelor's degree. *WalletHub.com, "Best Cities for Hispanic Entrepreneurs," September 4, 2024*

Miscellaneous Rankings

- In *Condé Nast Traveler* magazine's 2024 Readers' Choice Survey, Lexington made the top ten list of friendliest American cities. Lexington ranked #2. *Condé Nast Traveler, "The Friendliest Cities in the U.S., According to Our Readers" October 28, 2024*

- *WalletHub* compared 148 of the most populated U.S. cities to determine their operating efficiency. A "Quality of Services" score was constructed for each city and then measured against the total budget per capita to reveal which were managed the best. Lexington ranked #2. Criteria: financial stability; economy; education; safety; health; infrastructure and pollution. *WalletHub.com, "2025's Best- & Worst-Run Cities in America," June 18, 2024*

Business Environment

DEMOGRAPHICS

Population Growth

Area	1990 Census	2000 Census	2010 Census	2020 Census	2023 Estimate[2]	Population Growth 1990-2023 (%)
City	225,366	260,512	295,803	322,570	321,122	42.5
MSA[1]	348,428	408,326	472,099	516,811	517,378	48.5
U.S.	248,709,873	281,421,906	308,745,538	331,449,281	332,387,540	33.6

Note: (1) Figures cover the Lexington-Fayette, KY Metropolitan Statistical Area; (2) 2019-2023 5-year ACS population estimate
Source: U.S. Census Bureau, 1990 Census, 2000 Census, 2010 Census, 2020 Census, 2019-2023 American Community Survey 5-Year Estimates

Race

Area	White Alone[2] (%)	Black Alone[2] (%)	Asian Alone[2] (%)	AIAN[3] Alone[2] (%)	NHOPI[4] Alone[2] (%)	Other Race Alone[2] (%)	Two or More Races (%)
City	69.9	14.4	4.2	0.2	0.0	3.5	7.8
MSA[1]	76.6	10.6	2.9	0.2	0.0	2.9	6.7
U.S.	63.4	12.4	5.8	0.9	0.2	6.6	10.7

Note: (1) Figures cover the Lexington-Fayette, KY Metropolitan Statistical Area; (2) Alone is defined as not being in combination with one or more other races; (3) American Indian and Alaska Native; (4) Native Hawaiian and Other Pacific Islander
Source: U.S. Census Bureau, 2019-2023 American Community Survey 5-Year Estimates

Hispanic or Latino Origin

Area	Total (%)	Mexican (%)	Puerto Rican (%)	Cuban (%)	Other (%)
City	9.2	5.9	0.7	0.3	2.4
MSA[1]	7.8	4.9	0.5	0.3	2.0
U.S.	19.0	11.3	1.8	0.7	5.2

Note: Persons of Hispanic or Latino origin can be of any race; (1) Figures cover the Lexington-Fayette, KY Metropolitan Statistical Area
Source: U.S. Census Bureau, 2019-2023 American Community Survey 5-Year Estimates

Age

Area	Percent of Population									Median Age
	Under Age 5	Age 5–19	Age 20–34	Age 35–44	Age 45–54	Age 55–64	Age 65–74	Age 75–84	Age 85+	
City	5.7	18.8	25.1	13.1	11.6	11.2	8.8	4.2	1.4	35.2
MSA[1]	5.8	19.3	22.7	12.9	12.1	11.9	9.2	4.4	1.5	36.6
U.S.	5.7	19.1	20.2	13.1	12.3	12.8	10.0	4.9	1.9	38.7

Note: (1) Figures cover the Lexington-Fayette, KY Metropolitan Statistical Area
Source: U.S. Census Bureau, 2019-2023 American Community Survey 5-Year Estimates

Disability by Age

Area	All Ages	Under 18 Years Old	18 to 64 Years Old	65 Years and Over
City	12.8	4.9	11.0	32.4
MSA[1]	13.9	5.4	12.2	33.8
U.S.	13.0	4.7	10.7	32.9

Note: Figures show percent of the civilian noninstitutionalized population that reported having a disability. Disability status is determined from six types of difficulty: vision, hearing, cognitive, ambulatory, self-care, and independent living. For children under 5 years old, hearing and vision difficulty are used to determine disability status. For children between the ages of 5 and 14, disability status is determined from hearing, vision, cognitive, ambulatory, and self-care difficulties. For people aged 15 years and older, they are considered to have a disability if they have difficulty with any one of the six difficulty types; Note: (1) Figures cover the Lexington-Fayette, KY Metropolitan Statistical Area
Source: U.S. Census Bureau, 2019-2023 American Community Survey 5-Year Estimates

Ancestry

Area	German	Irish	English	American	Italian	Polish	French[2]	European	Scottish
City	12.7	10.8	13.8	7.7	2.7	1.4	1.6	2.4	2.4
MSA[1]	12.3	11.3	14.6	10.4	2.5	1.3	1.5	2.3	2.3
U.S.	12.6	9.4	9.1	5.5	4.9	2.6	2.0	1.6	1.6

Note: Figures are the percentage of the total population reporting a particular ancestry. The nine most commonly reported ancestries in the U.S. are shown. Figures include multiple ancestries (e.g. if a person reported being Irish and Italian, they were included in both columns); (1) Figures cover the Lexington-Fayette, KY Metropolitan Statistical Area; (2) Excludes Basque
Source: U.S. Census Bureau, 2019-2023 American Community Survey 5-Year Estimates

Foreign-born Population

Area	Any Foreign Country	Percent of Population Born in							
		Asia	Mexico	Europe	Caribbean	Central America[2]	South America	Africa	Canada
City	11.0	3.8	2.3	1.0	0.4	0.8	0.5	2.0	0.2
MSA[1]	8.2	2.6	1.8	0.9	0.3	0.7	0.4	1.3	0.2
U.S.	13.9	4.3	3.3	1.4	1.4	1.2	1.2	0.8	0.2

Note: (1) Figures cover the Lexington-Fayette, KY Metropolitan Statistical Area; (2) Excludes Mexico.
Source: U.S. Census Bureau, 2019-2023 American Community Survey 5-Year Estimates

Household Size

Area	Persons in Household (%)							Average Household Size
	One	Two	Three	Four	Five	Six	Seven or More	
City	34.8	33.4	14.3	10.8	4.0	1.7	0.9	2.24
MSA[1]	31.6	34.5	15.2	11.6	4.3	1.9	0.9	2.35
U.S.	28.5	33.8	15.4	12.7	5.9	2.3	1.4	2.54

Note: (1) Figures cover the Lexington-Fayette, KY Metropolitan Statistical Area
Source: U.S. Census Bureau, 2019-2023 American Community Survey 5-Year Estimates

Household Relationships

Area	Householder	Opposite-sex Spouse	Same-sex Spouse	Opposite-sex Unmarried Partner	Same-sex Unmarried Partner	Child[2]	Grandchild	Other Relatives	Non-relatives
City	41.7	16.0	0.3	2.9	0.3	25.3	1.6	3.4	4.4
MSA[1]	40.5	17.4	0.2	2.8	0.2	26.5	2.0	3.4	3.7
U.S.	38.3	17.5	0.2	2.5	0.2	28.3	2.4	4.8	3.4

Note: Figures are percent of the total population; (1) Figures cover the Lexington-Fayette, KY Metropolitan Statistical Area; (2) Includes biological, adopted, and stepchildren of the householder
Source: U.S. Census Bureau, 2020 Census

Gender

Area	Males	Females	Males per 100 Females
City	158,152	162,970	97.0
MSA[1]	254,019	263,359	96.5
U.S.	164,545,087	167,842,453	98.0

Note: (1) Figures cover the Lexington-Fayette, KY Metropolitan Statistical Area
Source: U.S. Census Bureau, 2019-2023 American Community Survey 5-Year Estimates

Marital Status

Area	Never Married	Now Married[2]	Separated	Widowed	Divorced
City	38.8	43.1	1.4	4.6	12.0
MSA[1]	34.4	46.7	1.5	5.1	12.3
U.S.	34.1	47.9	1.7	5.6	10.7

Note: Figures are percentages and cover the population 15 years of age and older; (1) Figures cover the Lexington-Fayette, KY Metropolitan Statistical Area; (2) Excludes separated
Source: U.S. Census Bureau, 2019-2023 American Community Survey 5-Year Estimates

Religious Groups by Family

Area	Catholic	Baptist	Methodist	LDS[2]	Pentecostal	Lutheran	Islam	Adventist	Other
MSA[1]	5.8	14.9	5.5	1.2	1.6	0.3	0.5	1.2	16.6
U.S.	18.7	7.3	3.0	2.0	1.8	1.7	1.3	1.3	11.6

Note: Figures are the number of adherents as a percentage of the total population and cover the eight largest religious groups in the U.S; (1) Figures cover the Lexington-Fayette, KY Metropolitan Statistical Area; (2) Church of Jesus Christ of Latter-day Saints
Sources: 2020 U.S. Religion Census, Association of Statisticians of American Religious Bodies; The Association of Religion Data Archives (ARDA)

Religious Groups by Tradition

Area	Catholic	Evangelical Protestant	Mainline Protestant	Black Protestant	Islam	Judaism	Hinduism	Orthodox	Buddhism
MSA[1]	5.8	26.9	8.1	3.5	0.5	0.3	0.1	0.2	<0.1
U.S.	18.7	16.5	5.2	2.3	1.3	0.6	0.4	0.4	0.3

Note: Figures are the number of adherents as a percentage of the total population; (1) Figures cover the Lexington-Fayette, KY Metropolitan Statistical Area
Sources: 2020 U.S. Religion Census, Association of Statisticians of American Religious Bodies; The Association of Religion Data Archives (ARDA)

ECONOMY

Real Gross Domestic Product (GDP)

Area	2017	2018	2019	2020	2021	2022	2023	Rank[3]
MSA[1]	28.7	29.5	30.0	28.7	29.6	30.6	31.4	105
U.S.[2]	17,619.1	18,160.7	18,642.5	18,238.9	19,387.6	19,896.6	20,436.3	—

Note: Figures are in billions of chained 2017 dollars; (1) Figures cover the Lexington-Fayette, KY Metropolitan Statistical Area; (2) Figures cover real GDP within metropolitan areas; (3) Rank is based on 2023 data and ranges from 1 to 384
Source: U.S. Bureau of Economic Analysis

Economic Growth

Area	2014	2015	2016	2017	2018	2019	2020	2021	2022	2023
MSA[1]	2.6	3.9	2.2	1.2	2.8	1.9	-4.5	3.1	3.6	2.7
U.S.[2]	2.6	3.2	2.0	2.7	3.1	2.7	-2.2	6.3	2.6	2.7

Note: Figures are real gross domestic product growth rates and represent percent change from preceding period; (1) Figures cover the Lexington-Fayette, KY Metropolitan Statistical Area; (2) Figures are the average growth rates within metropolitan areas
Source: U.S. Bureau of Economic Analysis

Metropolitan Area Exports

Area	2018	2019	2020	2021	2022	2023	Rank[2]
MSA[1]	2,148.0	2,093.8	1,586.3	1,880.0	2,677.2	3,343.3	81
U.S.	1,664,056.1	1,645,173.7	1,431,406.6	1,753,941.4	2,062,937.4	2,019,160.5	—

Note: Figures are in millions of dollars; (1) Figures cover the Lexington-Fayette, KY Metropolitan Statistical Area; (2) Rank is based on 2023 data and ranges from 1 to 386
Source: U.S. Department of Commerce, International Trade Administration, Office of Trade and Economic Analysis, Industry and Analysis, Exports by Metropolitan Area, data extracted April 2, 2025

Building Permits

Area	Single-Family			Multi-Family			Total		
	2023	2024	Pct. Chg.	2023	2024	Pct. Chg.	2023	2024	Pct. Chg.
City	624	492	-21.2	774	544	-29.7	1,398	1,036	-25.9
MSA[1]	1,319	1,392	5.5	1,123	809	-28.0	2,442	2,201	-9.9
U.S.	920,000	981,900	6.7	591,100	496,100	-16.1	1,511,100	1,478,000	-2.2

Note: (1) Figures cover the Lexington-Fayette, KY Metropolitan Statistical Area; Figures represent new, privately-owned housing units authorized (unadjusted data)
Source: U.S. Census Bureau, Building Permits Survey (BPS), 2023, 2024

Bankruptcy Filings

Area	Business Filings			Nonbusiness Filings		
	2023	2024	% Chg.	2023	2024	% Chg.
Fayette County	13	14	7.7	468	540	15.4
U.S.	18,926	23,107	22.1	434,064	494,201	13.9

Note: Business filings include Chapter 7, Chapter 9, Chapter 11, Chapter 12, Chapter 13, Chapter 15, and Section 304; Nonbusiness filings include Chapter 7, Chapter 11, and Chapter 13
Source: Administrative Office of the U.S. Courts, Business and Nonbusiness Bankruptcy, County Cases Commenced by Chapter of the Bankruptcy Code, During the 12-Month Period Ending December 31, 2023 and Business and Nonbusiness Bankruptcy, County Cases Commenced by Chapter of the Bankruptcy Code, During the 12-Month Period Ending December 31, 2024

Housing Vacancy Rates

Area	Gross Vacancy Rate[3] (%)			Year-Round Vacancy Rate[4] (%)			Rental Vacancy Rate[5] (%)			Homeowner Vacancy Rate[6] (%)		
	2022	2023	2024	2022	2023	2024	2022	2023	2024	2022	2023	2024
MSA[1]	n/a	n/a	n/a	n/a	n/a	n/a	n/a	n/a	n/a	n/a	n/a	n/a
U.S.[2]	9.1	9.0	9.1	7.5	7.5	7.6	5.7	6.5	6.8	0.8	0.8	1.0

Note: (1) Figures cover the Lexington-Fayette, KY Metropolitan Statistical Area; (2) Figures cover the 75 largest Metropolitan Statistical Areas; (3) The percentage of the total housing inventory that is vacant; (4) The percentage of the housing inventory (excluding seasonal units) that is year-round vacant; (5) The percentage of rental inventory that is vacant for rent; (6) The percentage of homeowner inventory that is vacant for sale; n/a not available
Source: U.S. Census Bureau, Housing Vacancies and Homeownership Annual Statistics: 2022, 2023, 2024

INCOME

Income

Area	Per Capita ($)	Median Household ($)	Average Household ($)
City	42,272	67,631	98,429
MSA[1]	41,230	70,717	99,405
U.S.	43,289	78,538	110,491

Note: (1) Figures cover the Lexington-Fayette, KY Metropolitan Statistical Area
Source: U.S. Census Bureau, 2019-2023 American Community Survey 5-Year Estimates

Household Income Distribution

Area	Percent of Households Earning							
	Under $15,000	$15,000 -$24,999	$25,000 -$34,999	$35,000 -$49,999	$50,000 -$74,999	$75,000 -$99,999	$100,000 -$149,999	$150,000 and up
City	9.8	7.2	8.6	11.9	16.8	11.9	15.7	18.1
MSA[1]	9.1	6.8	8.1	11.7	17.0	12.5	17.0	17.6
U.S.	8.5	6.6	6.8	10.4	15.7	12.7	17.4	21.9

Note: (1) Figures cover the Lexington-Fayette, KY Metropolitan Statistical Area
Source: U.S. Census Bureau, 2019-2023 American Community Survey 5-Year Estimates

Poverty Rate

Area	All Ages	Under 18 Years Old	18 to 64 Years Old	65 Years and Over
City	15.7	19.3	16.3	7.7
MSA[1]	14.0	17.4	14.1	8.6
U.S.	12.4	16.3	11.6	10.4

Note: Figures are percentage of people whose income during the past 12 months was below the poverty level; (1) Figures cover the Lexington-Fayette, KY Metropolitan Statistical Area
Source: U.S. Census Bureau, 2019-2023 American Community Survey 5-Year Estimates

EMPLOYMENT

Labor Force and Employment

Area	Civilian Labor Force			Workers Employed		
	Dec. 2023	Dec. 2024	% Chg.	Dec. 2023	Dec. 2024	% Chg.
City	178,351	182,353	2.2	172,195	175,041	1.7
MSA[1]	278,181	284,384	2.2	268,513	272,804	1.6
U.S.	166,661,000	167,746,000	0.7	160,754,000	161,294,000	0.3

Note: Data is not seasonally adjusted and covers workers 16 years of age and older; (1) Figures cover the Lexington-Fayette, KY Metropolitan Statistical Area
Source: Bureau of Labor Statistics, Local Area Unemployment Statistics

Unemployment Rate

Area	2024											
	Jan.	Feb.	Mar.	Apr.	May	Jun.	Jul.	Aug.	Sep.	Oct.	Nov.	Dec.
City	3.9	4.3	4.2	3.5	3.9	4.5	4.7	4.4	4.1	4.0	4.1	4.0
MSA[1]	4.0	4.4	4.2	3.5	3.9	4.6	4.7	4.5	4.1	4.1	4.2	4.1
U.S.	4.1	4.2	3.9	3.5	3.7	4.3	4.5	4.4	3.9	3.9	4.0	3.8

Note: Data is not seasonally adjusted and covers workers 16 years of age and older; (1) Figures cover the Lexington-Fayette, KY Metropolitan Statistical Area
Source: Bureau of Labor Statistics, Local Area Unemployment Statistics

Average Wages

Occupation	$/Hr.	Occupation	$/Hr.
Accountants and Auditors	36.98	Maintenance and Repair Workers	22.68
Automotive Mechanics	22.15	Marketing Managers	59.96
Bookkeepers	23.60	Network and Computer Systems Admin.	41.66
Carpenters	25.79	Nurses, Licensed Practical	28.18
Cashiers	13.44	Nurses, Registered	40.98
Computer Programmers	52.20	Nursing Assistants	19.39
Computer Systems Analysts	41.98	Office Clerks, General	19.89
Computer User Support Specialists	27.96	Physical Therapists	44.65
Construction Laborers	21.98	Physicians	134.53
Cooks, Restaurant	15.85	Plumbers, Pipefitters and Steamfitters	31.89
Customer Service Representatives	20.23	Police and Sheriff's Patrol Officers	32.13
Dentists	86.12	Postal Service Mail Carriers	28.80
Electricians	27.82	Real Estate Sales Agents	31.80
Engineers, Electrical	50.32	Retail Salespersons	16.41
Fast Food and Counter Workers	13.35	Sales Representatives, Technical/Scientific	45.46
Financial Managers	70.52	Secretaries, Exc. Legal/Medical/Executive	21.53
First-Line Supervisors of Office Workers	31.52	Security Guards	17.37
General and Operations Managers	48.11	Surgeons	n/a
Hairdressers/Cosmetologists	21.66	Teacher Assistants, Exc. Postsecondary[1]	17.74
Home Health and Personal Care Aides	16.98	Teachers, Secondary School, Exc. Sp. Ed.[1]	30.50
Janitors and Cleaners	16.37	Telemarketers	n/a
Landscaping/Groundskeeping Workers	18.10	Truck Drivers, Heavy/Tractor-Trailer	29.78
Lawyers	57.22	Truck Drivers, Light/Delivery Services	22.45
Maids and Housekeeping Cleaners	14.59	Waiters and Waitresses	14.52

Note: Wage data covers the Lexington-Fayette, KY Metropolitan Statistical Area; (1) Hourly wages were calculated from annual wage data based on a 40 hour work week
Source: Bureau of Labor Statistics, Metro Area Occupational Employment & Wage Estimates, May 2024

Employment by Industry

Sector	MSA[1]		U.S.
	Number of Employees	Percent of Total	Percent of Total
Construction, Mining, and Logging	14,900	4.9	5.5
Financial Activities	12,200	4.0	5.8
Government	59,400	19.6	14.9
Information	3,100	1.0	1.9
Leisure and Hospitality	32,500	10.7	10.4
Manufacturing	32,000	10.5	8.0
Other Services	14,600	4.8	3.7
Private Education and Health Services	40,100	13.2	16.9
Professional and Business Services	41,100	13.5	14.2
Retail Trade	29,200	9.6	10.0
Transportation, Warehousing, and Utilities	12,900	4.2	4.8
Wholesale Trade	11,700	3.9	3.9

Note: Figures are non-farm employment as of December 2024. Figures are not seasonally adjusted and include workers 16 years of age and older; (1) Figures cover the Lexington-Fayette, KY Metropolitan Statistical Area
Source: Bureau of Labor Statistics, Current Employment Statistics, Employment, Hours, and Earnings

Employment by Occupation

Occupation Classification	City (%)	MSA[1] (%)	U.S. (%)
Management, Business, Science, and Arts	47.1	44.5	42.0
Natural Resources, Construction, and Maintenance	5.4	6.5	8.6
Production, Transportation, and Material Moving	11.2	13.3	13.0
Sales and Office	20.4	20.5	19.9
Service	15.8	15.2	16.5

Note: Figures cover employed civilians 16 years of age and older; (1) Figures cover the Lexington-Fayette, KY Metropolitan Statistical Area
Source: U.S. Census Bureau, 2019-2023 American Community Survey 5-Year Estimates

Occupations with Greatest Projected Employment Growth: 2022 – 2032

Occupation[1]	2022 Employment	2032 Projected Employment	Numeric Employment Change	Percent Employment Change
Laborers and Freight, Stock, and Material Movers, Hand	57,770	64,360	6,590	11.4
Stockers and Order Fillers	50,640	56,760	6,120	12.1
Home Health and Personal Care Aides	24,650	30,540	5,890	23.9
Cooks, Restaurant	16,680	21,580	4,900	29.4
General and Operations Managers	51,300	54,500	3,200	6.2
Registered Nurses	47,300	50,400	3,100	6.6
Medical and Health Services Managers	9,660	12,440	2,780	28.8
Heavy and Tractor-Trailer Truck Drivers	31,110	33,340	2,230	7.2
Light Truck or Delivery Services Drivers	16,590	18,790	2,200	13.3
Nurse Practitioners	4,730	6,870	2,140	45.2

Note: Projections cover Kentucky; (1) Sorted by numeric employment change
Source: www.projectionscentral.org, State Occupational Projections, 2022–2032 Long-Term Projections

Fastest-Growing Occupations: 2022 – 2032

Occupation[1]	2022 Employment	2032 Projected Employment	Numeric Employment Change	Percent Employment Change
Nurse Practitioners	4,730	6,870	2,140	45.2
Information Security Analysts (SOC 2018)	1,230	1,600	370	30.1
Cooks, Restaurant	16,680	21,580	4,900	29.4
Medical and Health Services Managers	9,660	12,440	2,780	28.8
Taxi Drivers	1,250	1,590	340	27.2
Physician Assistants	1,220	1,550	330	27.0
Computer and Information Research Scientists (SOC 2018)	260	330	70	26.9
Computer Numerically Controlled Tool Programmers	240	300	60	25.0
Physical Therapist Assistants	2,280	2,840	560	24.6
Software Developers	6,650	8,260	1,610	24.2

Note: Projections cover Kentucky; (1) Sorted by percent employment change and excludes occupations with numeric employment change less than 50
Source: www.projectionscentral.org, State Occupational Projections, 2022–2032 Long-Term Projections

CITY FINANCES

City Government Finances

Component	2022 ($000)	2022 ($ per capita)
Total Revenues	953,245	2,935
Total Expenditures	584,119	1,799
Debt Outstanding	565,797	1,742

Source: U.S. Census Bureau, State & Local Government Finances 2022

City Government Revenue by Source

Source	2022 ($000)	2022 ($ per capita)	2022 (%)
General Revenue			
From Federal Government	98,467	303	10.3
From State Government	27,209	84	2.9
From Local Governments	27,953	86	2.9
Taxes			
Property	100,230	309	10.5
Sales and Gross Receipts	74,282	229	7.8
Personal Income	236,607	729	24.8
Corporate Income	61,579	190	6.5
Motor Vehicle License	254	1	0.0
Other Taxes	5,041	16	0.5
Current Charges	309,265	952	32.4
Liquor Store	0	0	0.0
Utility	3,312	10	0.3

Source: U.S. Census Bureau, State & Local Government Finances 2022

City Government Expenditures by Function

Function	2022 ($000)	2022 ($ per capita)	2022 (%)
General Direct Expenditures			
Air Transportation	14,187	43	2.4
Corrections	31,807	97	5.4
Education	0	0	0.0
Employment Security Administration	0	0	0.0
Financial Administration	6,832	21	1.2
Fire Protection	74,037	228	12.7
General Public Buildings	0	0	0.0
Governmental Administration, Other	53,243	164	9.1
Health	26,296	81	4.5
Highways	15,742	48	2.7
Hospitals	0	0	0.0
Housing and Community Development	2,679	8	0.5
Interest on General Debt	18,893	58	3.2
Judicial and Legal	2,405	7	0.4
Libraries	14,889	45	2.5
Parking	2,923	9	0.5
Parks and Recreation	67,289	207	11.5
Police Protection	74,047	228	12.7
Public Welfare	12,021	37	2.1
Sewerage	56,120	172	9.6
Solid Waste Management	52,356	161	9.0
Veterans' Services	0	0	0.0
Liquor Store	0	0	0.0
Utility	26,378	81	4.5

Source: U.S. Census Bureau, State & Local Government Finances 2022

TAXES

State Corporate Income Tax Rates

State	Tax Rate (%)	Income Brackets ($)	Num. of Brackets	Financial Institution Tax Rate (%)[a]	Federal Income Tax Ded.
Kentucky	5.0	Flat rate	1	5.0	No

Note: Tax rates for tax year 2024; (a) Rates listed are the corporate income tax rate applied to financial institutions or excise taxes based on income. Some states have other taxes based upon the value of deposits or shares.
Source: Federation of Tax Administrators, State Corporate Income Tax Rates, January 1, 2025

State Individual Income Tax Rates

State	Tax Rate (%)	Income Brackets ($)	Personal Exemptions ($)			Standard Ded. ($)	
			Single	Married	Depend.	Single	Married
Kentucky	4.0	Flat rate	None	None	None	3,160	6,320

Note: Tax rates for tax year 2024; Local- and county-level taxes are not included; Federal income tax is not deductible on state income tax returns
Source: Federation of Tax Administrators, State Individual Income Tax Rates, January 1, 2025

Various State Sales and Excise Tax Rates

State	State Sales Tax (%)	Gasoline[1] ($/gal.)	Cigarette[2] ($/pack)	Spirits[3] ($/gal.)	Wine[4] ($/gal.)	Beer[5] ($/gal.)	Recreational Marijuana (%)
Kentucky	6	0.28	1.10	9.56	3.82	0.89	Not legal

Note: All tax rates as of January 1, 2025; (1) The American Petroleum Institute has developed a methodology for determining the average tax rate on a gallon of fuel. Rates may include any of the following: excise taxes, environmental fees, storage tank fees, other fees or taxes, general sales tax, and local taxes; (2) The federal excise tax of $1.0066 per pack and local taxes are not included; (3) Rates are those applicable to off-premise sales of 40% alcohol by volume (a.b.v.) distilled spirits in 750ml containers. Local excise taxes are excluded; (4) Rates are those applicable to off-premise sales of 11% a.b.v. non-carbonated wine in 750ml containers; (5) Rates are those applicable to off-premise sales of 4.7% a.b.v. beer in 12 ounce containers.
Source: Tax Foundation, 2025 Facts & Figures: How Does Your State Compare?

State Tax Competitiveness Index

State	Overall Rank	Corporate Tax Rank	Individual Income Tax Rank	Sales Tax Rank	Property Tax Rank	Unemployment Insurance Tax Rank
Kentucky	22	18	23	18	27	34

Note: The Tax Foundation's State Tax Competitiveness Index enables policymakers, taxpayers, and business leaders to gauge how their states' tax systems compare. A rank of 1 is best, 50 is worst. Rankings do not average to the total. States without a tax rank equally as 1. DC's scores and rankings do not affect other states. The report shows tax systems as of July 1, 2024 (the beginning of Fiscal Year 2025).
Source: Tax Foundation, State Tax Competitiveness Index 2025

TRANSPORTATION

Means of Transportation to Work

Area	Car/Truck/Van		Public Transportation			Bicycle	Walked	Other Means	Worked at Home
	Drove Alone	Car-pooled	Bus	Subway	Railroad				
City	74.8	8.4	1.3	0.0	0.0	0.5	3.0	1.0	10.9
MSA[1]	76.1	8.6	0.9	0.0	0.0	0.4	2.5	0.8	10.7
U.S.	70.2	8.5	1.7	1.3	0.4	0.4	2.4	1.6	13.5

Note: Figures are percentages and cover workers 16 years of age and older; (1) Figures cover the Lexington-Fayette, KY Metropolitan Statistical Area
Source: U.S. Census Bureau, 2019-2023 American Community Survey 5-Year Estimates

Travel Time to Work

Area	Less Than 10 Minutes	10 to 19 Minutes	20 to 29 Minutes	30 to 44 Minutes	45 to 59 Minutes	60 to 89 Minutes	90 Minutes or More
City	13.0	40.1	26.4	13.7	2.7	2.3	1.9
MSA[1]	14.4	35.7	24.4	16.8	4.4	2.5	1.8
U.S.	12.6	28.6	21.2	20.8	8.1	6.0	2.8

Note: Note: Figures are percentages and include workers 16 years old and over; (1) Figures cover the Lexington-Fayette, KY Metropolitan Statistical Area
Source: U.S. Census Bureau, 2019-2023 American Community Survey 5-Year Estimates

Key Congestion Measures

Measure	2000	2010	2015	2020	2022
Annual Hours of Delay, Total (000)	n/a	n/a	11,066	4,137	10,295
Annual Hours of Delay, Per Auto Commuter	n/a	n/a	36	13	34
Annual Congestion Cost, Per Auto Commuter ($)	n/a	n/a	868	344	810

Note: n/a not available
Source: Texas A&M Transportation Institute, 2023 Urban Mobility Report

Freeway Travel Time Index

Measure	1985	1990	1995	2000	2005	2010	2015	2020	2022
Urban Area Index[1]	n/a	n/a	n/a	n/a	n/a	n/a	1.19	1.08	1.18
Urban Area Rank[1,2]	n/a	n/a	n/a	n/a	n/a	n/a	n/a	n/a	n/a

Note: Freeway Travel Time Index—the ratio of travel time in the peak period to the travel time at free-flow conditions. For example, a value of 1.30 indicates a 20-minute free-flow trip takes 26 minutes in the peak (20 minutes x 1.30 = 26 minutes); (1) Covers the Lexington-Fayette KY urban area; (2) Rank is based on 101 larger urban areas (#1 = highest travel time index); n/a not available
Source: Texas A&M Transportation Institute, 2023 Urban Mobility Report

Public Transportation

Agency Name / Mode of Transportation	Vehicles Operated in Maximum Service[1]	Annual Unlinked Passenger Trips[2] (in thous.)	Annual Passenger Miles[3] (in thous.)
Lexington Transit Authority (LexTran)			
Bus (directly operated)	52	3,524.3	15,763.0
Demand Response (purchased transportation)	37	155.0	1,041.0
Vanpool (purchased transportation)	14	53.7	1,069.9

Note: (1) Number of revenue vehicles operated by the given mode and type of service to meet the annual maximum service requirement. This is the revenue vehicle count during the peak season of the year; on the week and day that maximum service is provided. Vehicles operated in maximum service (VOMS) exclude atypical days and one-time special events; (2) Number of passengers who boarded public transportation vehicles. Passengers are counted each time they board a vehicle no matter how many vehicles they use to travel from their origin to their destination. (3) Sum of the distances ridden by all passengers during the entire fiscal year.
Source: Federal Transit Administration, National Transit Database, 2023

Air Transportation

Airport Name and Code / Type of Service	Passenger Airlines[1]	Passenger Enplanements	Freight Carriers[2]	Freight (lbs)
Bluegrass Airport (LEX)				
Domestic service (U.S. carriers only)	17	776,163	5	19,684
International service (U.S. carriers only)	1	13	0	0

Note: (1) Includes all U.S.-based major, minor and commuter airlines that carried at least one passenger during the year; (2) Includes all U.S.-based airlines and freight carriers that transported at least one pound of freight during the year.
Source: Bureau of Transportation Statistics, The Intermodal Transportation Database, Air Carriers: T-100 Domestic Market (U.S. carriers only), 2024; Bureau of Transportation Statistics, The Intermodal Transportation Database, Air Carriers: T-100 International Market (U.S. carriers only), 2024

BUSINESSES

Major Business Headquarters

Company Name	Industry	Rankings Fortune[1]	Forbes[2]
Gray	Construction	-	176

Note: (1) Companies that produce a 10-K are ranked 1 to 500 based on 2023 revenue; (2) All private companies with at least $2 billion in annual revenue through the end of their most current fiscal year are ranked 1 to 275; companies listed are headquartered in the city; dashes indicate no ranking
Source: Fortune, "Fortune 500," 2024; Forbes, "America's Largest Private Companies," 2024

Living Environment

COST OF LIVING

Cost of Living Index

Composite Index	Groceries	Housing	Utilities	Transportation	Health Care	Misc. Goods/Services
91.9	100.5	77.2	84.4	97.3	97.6	99.7

Note: The Cost of Living Index measures regional differences in the cost of consumer goods and services, excluding taxes and non-consumer expenditures, for professional and managerial households in the top income quintile. It is based on more than 50,000 prices covering almost 60 different items for which prices are collected three times a year by chambers of commerce, economic development organizations or university applied economic centers in each participating urban area. The numbers shown should be read as a percentage above or below the national average of 100. For example, a value of 115.4 in the groceries column indicates that grocery prices are 15.4% higher than the national average. Small differences in the index numbers should not be interpreted as significant; Figures cover the Lexington KY urban area.
Source: The Council for Community and Economic Research, Cost of Living Index, 2024

Grocery Prices

Area[1]	T-Bone Steak ($/pound)	Frying Chicken ($/pound)	Whole Milk ($/half gal.)	Eggs ($/dozen)	Orange Juice ($/64 oz.)	Coffee ($/11.5 oz.)
City[2]	15.52	1.44	4.69	3.40	4.30	5.70
Avg.	15.42	1.55	4.69	3.25	4.41	5.46
Min.	14.50	1.16	4.43	2.75	4.00	4.85
Max.	17.56	2.89	5.49	4.78	5.54	7.89

Note: (1) Values for the local area are compared with the average, minimum and maximum values for all 276 areas in the Cost of Living Index; (2) Figures cover the Lexington KY urban area; **T-Bone Steak** (price per pound); **Frying Chicken** (price per pound, whole fryer); **Whole Milk** (half gallon carton); **Eggs** (price per dozen, Grade A, large); **Orange Juice** (64 oz. Tropicana or Florida Natural); **Coffee** (11.5 oz. can, vacuum-packed, Maxwell House, Hills Bros, or Folgers).
Source: The Council for Community and Economic Research, Cost of Living Index, 2024

Housing and Utility Costs

Area[1]	New Home Price ($)	Apartment Rent ($/month)	All Electric ($/month)	Part Electric ($/month)	Other Energy ($/month)	Telephone ($/month)
City[2]	380,651	1,239	-	82.51	72.69	194.48
Avg.	515,975	1,550	210.99	123.07	82.07	194.99
Min.	265,375	692	104.33	53.68	36.26	179.42
Max.	2,775,821	5,719	529.02	397.28	361.63	223.33

Note: (1) Values for the local area are compared with the average, minimum and maximum values for all 276 areas in the Cost of Living Index; (2) Figures cover the Lexington KY urban area; **New Home Price** (2,400 sf living area, 8,000 sf lot, in urban area with full utilities); **Apartment Rent** (950 sf 2 bedroom/1.5 or 2 bath, unfurnished, excluding all utilities except water); **All Electric** (average monthly cost for an all-electric home); **Part Electric** (average monthly cost for a part-electric home); **Other Energy** (average monthly cost for natural gas, fuel oil, coal, wood, and any other forms of energy except electricity); **Telephone** (price includes the base monthly rate plus taxes and fees for three lines of mobile phone service).
Source: The Council for Community and Economic Research, Cost of Living Index, 2024

Health Care, Transportation, and Other Costs

Area[1]	Doctor ($/visit)	Dentist ($/visit)	Optometrist ($/visit)	Gasoline ($/gallon)	Beauty Salon ($/visit)	Men's Shirt ($)
City[2]	144.23	113.73	92.42	3.19	60.23	44.97
Avg.	143.77	117.51	129.23	3.32	48.57	38.14
Min.	36.74	58.67	67.33	2.80	24.00	13.41
Max.	270.44	216.82	307.33	5.28	94.00	63.89

Note: (1) Values for the local area are compared with the average, minimum and maximum values for all 276 areas in the Cost of Living Index; (2) Figures cover the Lexington KY urban area; **Doctor** (general practitioners routine exam of an established patient); **Dentist** (adult teeth cleaning and periodic oral examination); **Optometrist** (full vision eye exam for established adult patient); **Gasoline** (one gallon regular unleaded, national brand, including all taxes, cash price at self-service pump if available); **Beauty Salon** (woman's shampoo, trim, and blow-dry); **Men's Shirt** (cotton/polyester dress shirt, pinpoint weave, long sleeves).
Source: The Council for Community and Economic Research, Cost of Living Index, 2024

HOUSING

Homeownership Rate

Area	2017 (%)	2018 (%)	2019 (%)	2020 (%)	2021 (%)	2022 (%)	2023 (%)	2024 (%)
MSA[1]	n/a	n/a	n/a	n/a	n/a	n/a	n/a	n/a
U.S.	63.9	64.4	64.6	66.6	65.5	65.8	65.9	65.6

Note: (1) Figures cover the Lexington-Fayette, KY Metropolitan Statistical Area; n/a not available
Source: U.S. Census Bureau, Housing Vacancies and Homeownership Annual Statistics: 2017-2024

House Price Index (HPI)

Area	National Ranking[2]	Quarterly Change (%)	One-Year Change (%)	Five-Year Change (%)	Since 1991Q1 (%)
MSA[1]	147	-0.02	4.79	58.94	282.27
U.S.[3]	–	1.43	4.51	57.13	327.82

Note: The HPI is a weighted repeat sales index. It measures average price changes in repeat sales or refinancings on the same properties. This information is obtained by reviewing repeat mortgage transactions on single-family properties whose mortgages have been purchased or securitized by Fannie Mae or Freddie Mac since January 1975; (1) Figures cover the Lexington-Fayette, KY Metropolitan Statistical Area; (2) Rankings are based on annual percentage change for all metro areas containing at least 15,000 transactions over the last 10 years and ranges from 1 to 241; (3) figures based on a weighted average of Census Division estimates using a seasonally adjusted, purchase-only index; all figures are for the period ending December 31, 2024
Source: Federal Housing Finance Agency, Change in FHFA Metropolitan Area House Price Indexes, All Transactions Index, 2024Q4

Home Value

Area	Under $100,000	$100,000 -$199,999	$200,000 -$299,999	$300,000 -$399,999	$400,000 -$499,999	$500,000 -$999,999	$1,000,000 or more	Median ($)
City	5.4	22.4	29.2	18.8	10.0	11.8	2.4	272,100
MSA[1]	6.9	24.4	28.6	17.8	9.1	10.7	2.5	258,900
U.S.	12.1	17.8	19.5	14.4	10.5	19.1	6.5	303,400

Note: Figures are percentages except for median and cover owner-occupied housing units; (1) Figures cover the Lexington-Fayette, KY Metropolitan Statistical Area
Source: U.S. Census Bureau, 2019-2023 American Community Survey 5-Year Estimates

Year Housing Structure Built

Area	2020 or Later	2010 -2019	2000 -2009	1990 -1999	1980 -1989	1970 -1979	1960 -1969	1950 -1959	1940 -1949	Before 1940	Median Year
City	1.1	10.0	14.5	15.6	13.0	14.5	13.4	8.5	2.7	6.7	1983
MSA[1]	1.2	10.3	15.9	16.7	13.1	14.2	10.8	7.5	2.8	7.5	1985
U.S.	1.2	8.9	13.6	12.8	13.0	14.4	10.0	9.7	4.5	11.9	1980

Note: Figures are percentages except for Median Year; Note: (1) Figures cover the Lexington-Fayette, KY Metropolitan Statistical Area
Source: U.S. Census Bureau, 2019-2023 American Community Survey 5-Year Estimates

Gross Monthly Rent

Area	Under $500	$500 -$999	$1,000 -$1,499	$1,500 -$1,999	$2,000 -$2,499	$2,500 -$2,999	$3,000 and up	Median ($)
City	4.4	36.0	40.3	13.9	3.8	1.2	0.5	1,101
MSA[1]	5.5	38.0	38.7	13.0	3.1	1.1	0.5	1,070
U.S.	6.5	22.3	29.5	20.2	10.8	4.8	5.9	1,348

Note: Figures are percentages except for median; Gross rent is the contract rent plus the estimated average monthly cost of utilities (electricity, gas, and water and sewer) and fuels (oil, coal, kerosene, wood, etc.) if these are paid by the renter (or paid for the renter by someone else); (1) Figures cover the Lexington-Fayette, KY Metropolitan Statistical Area
Source: U.S. Census Bureau, 2019-2023 American Community Survey 5-Year Estimates

HEALTH

Health Risk Factors

Category	MSA[1] (%)	U.S. (%)
Adults aged 18–64 who have any kind of health care coverage	n/a	90.8
Adults who reported being in good or better health	n/a	81.8
Adults who have been told they have high blood cholesterol	n/a	36.9
Adults who have been told they have high blood pressure	n/a	34.0
Adults who are current smokers	n/a	12.1
Adults who currently use e-cigarettes	n/a	7.7
Adults who currently use chewing tobacco, snuff, or snus	n/a	3.2
Adults who are heavy drinkers[2]	n/a	6.1
Adults who are binge drinkers[3]	n/a	15.2
Adults who are overweight (BMI 25.0 - 29.9)	n/a	34.4
Adults who are obese (BMI 30.0 - 99.8)	n/a	34.3
Adults who participated in any physical activities in the past month	n/a	75.8

Note: All figures are crude prevalence; (1) Figures for the Lexington-Fayette, KY Metropolitan Statistical Area were not available.
(2) Heavy drinkers are classified as adult men having more than 14 drinks per week and adult women having more than 7 drinks per week; (3) Binge drinkers are classified as males having five or more drinks on one occasion or females having four or more drinks on one occasion
Source: Centers for Disease Control and Prevention, Behaviorial Risk Factor Surveillance System, SMART: Selected Metropolitan Area Risk Trends, 2023

Acute and Chronic Health Conditions

Category	MSA[1] (%)	U.S. (%)
Adults who have ever been told they had a heart attack	n/a	4.2
Adults who have ever been told they have angina or coronary heart disease	n/a	4.0
Adults who have ever been told they had a stroke	n/a	3.3
Adults who have ever been told they have asthma	n/a	15.7
Adults who have ever been told they have arthritis	n/a	26.3
Adults who have ever been told they have diabetes[2]	n/a	11.5
Adults who have ever been told they had skin cancer	n/a	5.6
Adults who have ever been told they had any other types of cancer	n/a	8.4
Adults who have ever been told they have COPD	n/a	6.4
Adults who have ever been told they have kidney disease	n/a	3.7
Adults who have ever been told they have a form of depression	n/a	22.0

Note: All figures are crude prevalence; (1) Figures for the Lexington-Fayette, KY Metropolitan Statistical Area were not available.
(2) Figures do not include pregnancy-related, borderline, or pre-diabetes
Source: Centers for Disease Control and Prevention, Behavioral Risk Factor Surveillance System, SMART: Selected Metropolitan Area Risk Trends, 2023

Health Screening and Vaccination Rates

Category	MSA[1] (%)	U.S. (%)
Adults who have ever been tested for HIV	n/a	37.5
Adults who have had their blood cholesterol checked within the last five years	n/a	87.0
Adults aged 65+ who have had flu shot within the past year	n/a	63.4
Adults aged 65+ who have ever had a pneumonia vaccination	n/a	71.9

Note: All figures are crude prevalence; (1) Figures for the Lexington-Fayette, KY Metropolitan Statistical Area were not available.
Source: Centers for Disease Control and Prevention, Behavioral Risk Factor Surveillance System, SMART: Selected Metropolitan Area Risk Trends, 2023

Disability Status

Category	MSA[1] (%)	U.S. (%)
Adults who reported being deaf	n/a	7.4
Are you blind or have serious difficulty seeing, even when wearing glasses?	n/a	4.9
Do you have difficulty doing errands alone?	n/a	7.8
Do you have difficulty dressing or bathing?	n/a	3.6
Do you have serious difficulty concentrating/remembering/making decisions?	n/a	13.7
Do you have serious difficulty walking or climbing stairs?	n/a	13.2

Note: All figures are crude prevalence; (1) Figures for the Lexington-Fayette, KY Metropolitan Statistical Area were not available.
Source: Centers for Disease Control and Prevention, Behavioral Risk Factor Surveillance System, SMART: Selected Metropolitan Area Risk Trends, 2023

Mortality Rates for the Top 10 Causes of Death in the U.S.

ICD-10[a] Sub-Chapter	ICD-10[a] Code	Crude Mortality Rate[2] per 100,000 population	
		County[3]	U.S.
Malignant neoplasms	C00-C97	156.6	182.7
Ischaemic heart diseases	I20-I25	68.0	109.6
Provisional assignment of new diseases of uncertain etiology[1]	U00-U49	44.5	65.3
Other forms of heart disease	I30-I51	70.8	65.1
Other degenerative diseases of the nervous system	G30-G31	45.5	52.4
Other external causes of accidental injury	W00-X59	63.9	52.3
Cerebrovascular diseases	I60-I69	41.0	49.1
Chronic lower respiratory diseases	J40-J47	40.9	43.5
Hypertensive diseases	I10-I15	31.5	38.9
Organic, including symptomatic, mental disorders	F01-F09	41.5	33.9

Note: (a) ICD-10 = International Classification of Diseases 10th Revision; (1) Includes COVID-19, adverse effects to COVID-19 vaccines, SARS, and vaping-related disorders; (2) Crude mortality rates are a three-year average covering 2021-2023; (3) Figures cover Fayette County.
Source: Centers for Disease Control and Prevention, National Center for Health Statistics. National Vital Statistics System, Mortality 2018-2023 on CDC WONDER Online Database

Mortality Rates for Selected Causes of Death

Cause of Death	ICD-10[a] Code	Crude Mortality Rate[1] per 100,000 population	
		County[2]	U.S.
Accidental poisoning and exposure to noxious substances	X40-X49	47.2	30.5
Alzheimer disease	G30	29.9	35.4
Assault	X85-Y09	10.6	7.3
COVID-19	U07.1	44.5	65.3
Diabetes mellitus	E10-E14	23.9	30.0
Diseases of the liver	K70-K76	20.8	20.8
Human immunodeficiency virus (HIV) disease	B20-B24	Unreliable	1.5
Influenza and pneumonia	J09-J18	10.3	13.4
Intentional self-harm	X60-X84	13.7	14.7
Malnutrition	E40-E46	5.1	6.0
Obesity and other hyperalimentation	E65-E68	4.4	3.1
Renal failure	N17-N19	15.0	16.4
Transport accidents	V01-V99	11.0	14.4

Note: (a) ICD-10 = International Classification of Diseases 10th Revision; (1) Crude mortality rates are a three-year average covering 2021-2023; (2) Figures cover Fayette County; Data are suppressed when the data meet the criteria for confidentiality constraints; Crude mortality rates are flagged as unreliable when the rate would be calculated with a numerator of 20 or less.
Source: Centers for Disease Control and Prevention, National Center for Health Statistics. National Vital Statistics System, Mortality 2018-2023 on CDC WONDER Online Database

Health Insurance Coverage

Area	With Health Insurance	With Private Health Insurance	With Public Health Insurance	Without Health Insurance	Population Under Age 19 Without Health Insurance
City	93.2	69.8	34.5	6.8	2.9
MSA[1]	93.9	69.8	36.2	6.1	3.2
U.S.	91.4	67.3	36.3	8.6	5.4

Note: Figures are percentages that cover the civilian noninstitutionalized population; (1) Figures cover the Lexington-Fayette, KY Metropolitan Statistical Area
Source: U.S. Census Bureau, 2019-2023 American Community Survey 5-Year Estimates

Number of Medical Professionals

Area	MDs[3]	DOs[3,4]	Dentists	Podiatrists	Chiropractors	Optometrists
County[1] (number)	2,704	213	479	26	83	94
County[1] (rate[2])	844.1	66.5	149.6	8.1	25.9	29.4
U.S. (rate[2])	302.5	29.2	74.6	6.4	29.5	18.0

Note: Data as of 2023 unless noted; (1) Data covers Fayette County; (2) Number of medical professionals per 100,000 population; (3) Data as of 2022 and includes all active, non-federal physicians; (4) Doctor of Osteopathic Medicine
Source: U.S. Department of Health and Human Services, Health Resources and Services Administration, Bureau of Health Professions, Area Resource File (ARF) 2023-2024

Best Hospitals

According to *U.S. News*, the Lexington-Fayette, KY metro area is home to two of the best hospitals in the U.S.: **University of Kentucky Albert B. Chandler Hospital** (3 adult specialties and 2 pediatric specialties); **University of Kentucky Markey Cancer Center** (3 adult specialties and 2 pediatric specialties). The hospitals listed were nationally ranked in at least one of 15 adult or 11 pediatric specialties. The number of specialties shown cover the parent hospital. Only 160 U.S. hospitals performed well enough to be nationally ranked in one or more specialties. Twenty hospitals in the U.S. made the Honor Roll. The Best Hospitals Honor Roll takes both the national rankings and the procedure and condition ratings into account. Hospitals received points if they were nationally ranked in one of the 15 adult specialties—the higher they ranked, the more points they got—and how many ratings of "high performing" they earned in the 20 procedures and conditions. *U.S. News Online, "America's Best Hospitals 2024-25"*

According to *U.S. News*, the Lexington-Fayette, KY metro area is home to one of the best children's hospitals in the U.S.: **Kentucky Children's Hospital** (2 pediatric specialties). The hospital listed was highly ranked in at least one of 11 pediatric specialties. One hundred five children's hospitals in the U.S. were nationally ranked in at least one specialty. Hospitals received points for being ranked in a specialty, and the 10 hospitals with the most points across the 11 specialties make up the Honor Roll. *U.S. News Online, "America's Best Children's Hospitals 2024-25"*

EDUCATION

Public School District Statistics

District Name	Schls	Pupils	Pupil/ Teacher Ratio	Minority Pupils[1] (%)	Total Rev. per Pupil ($)	Total Exp. per Pupil ($)
Fayette County	79	41,697	13.4	56.7	18,109	17,525

Note: Table includes school districts with 2,000 or more students; (1) Percentage of students that are not non-Hispanic white.
Source: U.S. Department of Education, National Center for Education Statistics, Common Core of Data, Local Education Agency (School District) Universe Survey: School Year 2023-2024; U.S. Department of Education, National Center for Education Statistics, Common Core of Data, School District Finance Survey (F-33): School Year 2021–22

Highest Level of Education

Area	Less than H.S.	H.S. Diploma	Some College, No Deg.	Associate Degree	Bachelor's Degree	Master's Degree	Prof. School Degree	Doctorate Degree
City	7.6	19.0	18.5	7.6	26.5	12.9	4.3	3.6
MSA[1]	8.1	23.5	19.2	8.1	23.4	11.4	3.5	2.8
U.S.	10.6	26.2	19.4	8.8	21.3	9.8	2.3	1.6

Note: Figures cover persons age 25 and over; (1) Figures cover the Lexington-Fayette, KY Metropolitan Statistical Area
Source: U.S. Census Bureau, 2019-2023 American Community Survey 5-Year Estimates

Educational Attainment by Race

Area	High School Graduate or Higher (%)					Bachelor's Degree or Higher (%)				
	Total	White	Black	Asian	Hisp.[2]	Total	White	Black	Asian	Hisp.[2]
City	92.4	95.3	90.4	89.9	65.1	47.3	51.9	27.1	72.2	25.3
MSA[1]	91.9	93.9	90.6	89.7	65.7	41.1	43.4	25.4	67.8	23.0
U.S.	89.4	92.9	88.1	88.0	72.5	35.0	37.7	24.7	57.0	19.9

Note: Figures shown cover persons 25 years old and over; (1) Figures cover the Lexington-Fayette, KY Metropolitan Statistical Area; (2) People of Hispanic origin can be of any race
Source: U.S. Census Bureau, 2019-2023 American Community Survey 5-Year Estimates

School Enrollment by Grade and Control

Area	Preschool (%)		Kindergarten (%)		Grades 1 - 4 (%)		Grades 5 - 8 (%)		Grades 9 - 12 (%)	
	Public	Private	Public	Private	Public	Private	Public	Private	Public	Private
City	29.5	70.5	81.0	19.0	82.3	17.7	85.7	14.3	85.4	14.6
MSA[1]	40.9	59.1	82.4	17.6	83.7	16.3	84.8	15.2	85.9	14.1
U.S.	58.7	41.3	85.2	14.8	87.2	12.8	87.9	12.1	89.0	11.0

Note: Figures shown cover persons 3 years old and over; (1) Figures cover the Lexington-Fayette, KY Metropolitan Statistical Area
Source: U.S. Census Bureau, 2019-2023 American Community Survey 5-Year Estimates

Higher Education

Four-Year Colleges			Two-Year Colleges			Medical Schools[1]	Law Schools[2]	Voc/ Tech[3]
Public	Private Non-profit	Private For-profit	Public	Private Non-profit	Private For-profit			
1	7	0	1	0	0	1	1	4

Note: Figures cover institutions located within the Lexington-Fayette, KY Metropolitan Statistical Area and include main campuses only; (1) includes schools accredited by the Liaison Committee on Medical Education and the American Osteopathic Association's Commission on Osteopathic College Accreditation; (2) includes ABA-accredited schools, schools with provisional ABA accreditation, and state accredited schools; (3) includes all schools with programs that are less than 2 years.
Source: National Center for Education Statistics, Integrated Postsecondary Education System (IPEDS), 2023-24; Wikipedia, List of Medical Schools in the United States, accessed May 2, 2025; Wikipedia, List of Law Schools in the United States, accessed May 2, 2025

According to *U.S. News & World Report,* the Lexington-Fayette, KY metro area is home to one of the top 200 national universities in the U.S.: **University of Kentucky** (#152 tie). The indicators used to capture academic quality fall into a number of categories: assessment by administrators at peer institutions; retention of students; faculty resources; student selectivity; financial resources; alumni giving; high school counselor ratings of colleges; and graduation rate. *U.S. News & World Report,* "America's Best Colleges 2025"

According to *U.S. News & World Report,* the Lexington-Fayette, KY metro area is home to one of the top 100 law schools in the U.S.: **University of Kentucky (Rosenberg)** (#68 tie). The rankings are based on a weighted average of 12 measures of quality: peer assessment score; assessment score by lawyers/judges; median LSAT scores; median undergrad GPA; acceptance rate; employment rates for graduates; placement success; bar passage rate; faculty resources; expenditures per student; student/faculty ratio; and library resources. *U.S. News & World Report,* "America's Best Graduate Schools, Law, 2025"

According to *U.S. News & World Report*, the Lexington-Fayette, KY metro area is home to one of the top 75 business schools in the U.S.: **University of Kentucky (Gatton)** (#61 tie). The rankings are based on a weighted average of the following nine measures: quality assessment; peer assessment; recruiter assessment; placement success; mean starting salary and bonus; student selectivity; mean GMAT and GRE scores; mean undergraduate GPA; and acceptance rate. *U.S. News & World Report*, "America's Best Graduate Schools, Business, 2025"

EMPLOYERS

Major Employers

Company Name	Industry
Amazon.com	Distribution
Baptist Health	Healthcare
Cardinal Hill Rehabilitation Hospital	Healthcare
Eastern Kentucky University	Education
Fayette County Public Schools	Education
Kentucky Health & Family Svcs Cabinet	Government
KentuckyOne Health	Healthcare
KY Dept for Workforce Inv	Government
Lexington-Fayette Urban County Govt	Government
Lexmark International	Enterprise software, hardware and services
Lockheed Martin	Manufacturing
Osram Sylvania	Manufacturing
Scott County Public Schools	Education
Tokico (USA) (Hitachi)	Manufacturing
Toyota Motor Manufacturing	Manufacturing
Transportation Cabinet of Kentucky	Government
University of Kentucky	Education
Veterans Medical Center	Healthcare
Wal-Mart Stores	Retail
Xerox	Outsourcing

Note: Companies shown are located within the Lexington-Fayette, KY Metropolitan Statistical Area.
Source: Chambers of Commerce; State Departments of Labor; Wikipedia

PUBLIC SAFETY

Crime Rate

Area	Total Crime Rate	Violent Crime Rate				Property Crime Rate		
		Murder	Rape	Robbery	Aggrav. Assault	Burglary	Larceny -Theft	Motor Vehicle Theft
City	3,004.7	4.4	56.6	76.9	115.9	337.8	2,022.9	390.3
U.S.	2,290.9	5.7	38.0	66.5	264.1	250.7	1,347.2	318.7

Note: Figures are crimes per 100,000 population.
Source: FBI, Table 8, Offenses Known to Law Enforcement, by State by City, 2023

Hate Crimes

Area	Number of Quarters Reported	Number of Incidents per Bias Motivation					
		Race/Ethnicity/ Ancestry	Religion	Sexual Orientation	Disability	Gender	Gender Identity
City[1]	4	8	2	4	0	0	3
U.S.	4	5,900	2,699	2,077	187	92	492

Note: (1) Figures include at least one incident reported with more than one bias motivation.
Source: Federal Bureau of Investigation, Hate Crime Statistics 2023

Identity Theft Consumer Reports

Area	Reports	Reports per 100,000 Population	Rank[2]
MSA[1]	960	186	187
U.S.	1,135,291	339	-

Note: (1) Figures cover the Lexington-Fayette, KY Metropolitan Statistical Area; (2) Rank ranges from 1 to 401 where 1 indicates greatest number of identity theft reports per 100,000 population
Source: Federal Trade Commission, Consumer Sentinel Network Data Book 2024

Fraud and Other Consumer Reports

Area	Reports	Reports per 100,000 Population	Rank[2]
MSA[1]	5,868	1,134	150
U.S.	5,360,641	1,601	-

Note: (1) Figures cover the Lexington-Fayette, KY Metropolitan Statistical Area; (2) Rank ranges from 1 to 401 where 1 indicates greatest number of fraud and other consumer reports per 100,000 population
Source: Federal Trade Commission, Consumer Sentinel Network Data Book 2024

POLITICS

2024 Presidential Election Results

Area	Trump (Rep.)	Harris (Dem.)	Stein (Green)	Kennedy (Ind.)	Oliver (Lib.)	Other
Fayette County	39.8	57.9	0.7	0.9	0.5	0.2
U.S.	49.7	48.2	0.6	0.5	0.4	0.6

Note: Results are percentages and may not add to 100% due to rounding
Source: Dave Leip's Atlas of U.S. Presidential Elections

SPORTS

Professional Sports Teams

Team Name	League	Year Established

No teams are located in the metro area
Source: Wikipedia, Major Professional Sports Teams of the United States and Canada, May 1, 2025

CLIMATE

Average and Extreme Temperatures

Temperature	Jan	Feb	Mar	Apr	May	Jun	Jul	Aug	Sep	Oct	Nov	Dec	Yr.
Extreme High (°F)	76	75	82	88	92	101	103	103	103	91	83	75	103
Average High (°F)	40	44	54	66	75	83	86	85	79	68	55	44	65
Average Temp. (°F)	32	36	45	55	64	73	76	75	69	57	46	36	55
Average Low (°F)	24	26	34	44	54	62	66	65	58	46	36	28	45
Extreme Low (°F)	-21	-15	-2	18	26	39	47	42	35	20	-3	-19	-21

Note: Figures cover the years 1948-1990
Source: National Climatic Data Center, International Station Meteorological Climate Summary, 9/96

Average Precipitation/Snowfall/Humidity

Precip./Humidity	Jan	Feb	Mar	Apr	May	Jun	Jul	Aug	Sep	Oct	Nov	Dec	Yr.
Avg. Precip. (in.)	3.6	3.4	4.4	3.9	4.3	4.0	4.8	3.7	3.0	2.4	3.5	3.9	45.1
Avg. Snowfall (in.)	6	5	3	Tr	Tr	0	0	0	0	Tr	1	3	17
Avg. Rel. Hum. 7am (%)	81	80	77	75	78	80	83	85	85	83	81	81	81
Avg. Rel. Hum. 4pm (%)	67	61	55	51	54	54	56	55	54	53	60	66	57

Note: Figures cover the years 1948-1990; Tr = Trace amounts (<0.05 in. of rain; <0.5 in. of snow)
Source: National Climatic Data Center, International Station Meteorological Climate Summary, 9/96

Weather Conditions

Temperature			Daytime Sky			Precipitation		
10°F & below	32°F & below	90°F & above	Clear	Partly cloudy	Cloudy	0.01 inch or more precip.	0.1 inch or more snow/ice	Thunder-storms
11	96	22	86	136	143	129	17	44

Note: Figures are average number of days per year and cover the years 1948-1990
Source: National Climatic Data Center, International Station Meteorological Climate Summary, 9/96

HAZARDOUS WASTE

Superfund Sites

The Lexington-Fayette, KY metro area has no sites on the EPA's Superfund Final National Priorities List (NPL) or Superfund Alternative Approach (SAA) list. The Superfund alternative approach uses the same investigation and cleanup process and standards that are used for sites listed on the National Priorities List. The SAA is an alternative to listing a site on the NPL; it is not an alternative to Superfund or the Superfund process. There are a total of 1,445 Superfund sites with a status of proposed or final on both lists in the United States. *U.S. Environmental Protection Agency, National Priorities List, May 1, 2025; U.S. Environmental Protection Agency, Superfund Alternative Approach Sites, May 1, 2025*

AIR QUALITY

Air Quality Trends: Ozone

	1990	1995	2000	2005	2010	2015	2020	2021	2022	2023
MSA[1]	0.078	0.088	0.077	0.078	0.070	0.069	0.060	0.064	0.065	0.070
U.S.	0.087	0.089	0.081	0.080	0.072	0.068	0.066	0.067	0.067	0.070

Note: (1) Data covers the Lexington-Fayette, KY Metropolitan Statistical Area. The values shown are the composite ozone concentration averages among trend sites based on the highest fourth daily maximum 8-hour concentration in parts per million. These trends are based on sites having an adequate record of monitoring data during the trend period. Data from exceptional events are included.
Source: U.S. Environmental Protection Agency, Air Quality Monitoring Information, "Air Quality Trends by City, 1990-2023"

Air Quality Index

Area	Percent of Days when Air Quality was...[2]					AQI Statistics[2]	
	Good	Moderate	Unhealthy for Sensitive Groups	Unhealthy	Very Unhealthy	Maximum	Median
MSA[1]	63.3	35.9	0.5	0.3	0.0	167	45

Note: (1) Data covers the Lexington-Fayette, KY Metropolitan Statistical Area; (2) Based on 365 days with AQI data in 2023. Air Quality Index (AQI) is an index for reporting daily air quality. EPA calculates the AQI for five major air pollutants regulated by the Clean Air Act: ground-level ozone, particle pollution (aka particulate matter), carbon monoxide, sulfur dioxide, and nitrogen dioxide. The AQI runs from 0 to 500. The higher the AQI value, the greater the level of air pollution and the greater the health concern. There are six AQI categories: "Good" AQI is between 0 and 50. Air quality is considered satisfactory; "Moderate" AQI is between 51 and 100. Air quality is acceptable; "Unhealthy for Sensitive Groups" When AQI values are between 101 and 150, members of sensitive groups may experience health effects; "Unhealthy" When AQI values are between 151 and 200 everyone may begin to experience health effects; "Very Unhealthy" AQI values between 201 and 300 trigger a health alert; "Hazardous" AQI values over 300 trigger warnings of emergency conditions (not shown).
Source: U.S. Environmental Protection Agency, Air Quality Index Report, 2023

Air Quality Index Pollutants

Area	Percent of Days when AQI Pollutant was...[2]					
	Carbon Monoxide	Nitrogen Dioxide	Ozone	Sulfur Dioxide	Particulate Matter 2.5	Particulate Matter 10
MSA[1]	0.0	1.1	40.0	(3)	58.9	0.0

Note: (1) Data covers the Lexington-Fayette, KY Metropolitan Statistical Area; (2) Based on 365 days with AQI data in 2023. The Air Quality Index (AQI) is an index for reporting daily air quality. EPA calculates the AQI for five major air pollutants regulated by the Clean Air Act: ground-level ozone, particle pollution (also known as particulate matter), carbon monoxide, sulfur dioxide, and nitrogen dioxide. The AQI runs from 0 to 500. The higher the AQI value, the greater the level of air pollution and the greater the health concern; (3) Sulfur dioxide is no longer included in this table because SO_2 concentrations tend to be very localized and not necessarily representative of broad geographical areas like counties and CBSAs.
Source: U.S. Environmental Protection Agency, Air Quality Index Report, 2023

Maximum Air Pollutant Concentrations: Particulate Matter, Ozone, CO and Lead

	Particulate Matter 10 (ug/m^3)	Particulate Matter 2.5 Wtd AM (ug/m^3)	Particulate Matter 2.5 24-Hr (ug/m^3)	Ozone (ppm)	Carbon Monoxide (ppm)	Lead (ug/m^3)
MSA[1] Level	28	8.3	27	0.07	n/a	n/a
NAAQS[2]	150	15	35	0.075	9	0.15
Met NAAQS[2]	Yes	Yes	Yes	Yes	n/a	n/a

Note: (1) Data covers the Lexington-Fayette, KY Metropolitan Statistical Area; Data from exceptional events are included; (2) National Ambient Air Quality Standards; ppm = parts per million; ug/m^3 = micrograms per cubic meter; n/a not available.
Concentrations: Particulate Matter 10 (coarse particulate)—highest second maximum 24-hour concentration; Particulate Matter 2.5 Wtd AM (fine particulate)—highest weighted annual mean concentration; Particulate Matter 2.5 24-Hour (fine particulate)—highest 98th percentile 24-hour concentration; Ozone—highest fourth daily maximum 8-hour concentration; Carbon Monoxide—highest second maximum non-overlapping 8-hour concentration; Lead—maximum running 3-month average
Source: U.S. Environmental Protection Agency, Air Quality Monitoring Information, "Air Quality Statistics by City, 2023"

Maximum Air Pollutant Concentrations: Nitrogen Dioxide and Sulfur Dioxide

	Nitrogen Dioxide AM (ppb)	Nitrogen Dioxide 1-Hr (ppb)	Sulfur Dioxide AM (ppb)	Sulfur Dioxide 1-Hr (ppb)	Sulfur Dioxide 24-Hr (ppb)
MSA[1] Level	6	39	n/a	7	n/a
NAAQS[2]	53	100	30	75	140
Met NAAQS[2]	Yes	Yes	n/a	Yes	n/a

Note: (1) Data covers the Lexington-Fayette, KY Metropolitan Statistical Area; Data from exceptional events are included; (2) National Ambient Air Quality Standards; ppm = parts per million; ug/m^3 = micrograms per cubic meter; n/a not available.
Concentrations: Nitrogen Dioxide AM—highest arithmetic mean concentration; Nitrogen Dioxide 1-Hr—highest 98th percentile 1-hour daily maximum concentration; Sulfur Dioxide AM—highest annual mean concentration; Sulfur Dioxide 1-Hr—highest 99th percentile 1-hour daily maximum concentration; Sulfur Dioxide 24-Hr—highest second maximum 24-hour concentration
Source: U.S. Environmental Protection Agency, Air Quality Monitoring Information, "Air Quality Statistics by City, 2023"

Louisville, Kentucky

Background

Louisville was founded in 1778, when George Rogers Clark, on his way to capture British Fort Vincennes, established a base on an island above the Falls of the Ohio River. Shortly thereafter a settlement grew on the south side of the river. Two years later the Virginia state legislature named the town Louisville to pay homage to King Louis XVI of France, who had allied his country with America during the American Revolution.

The Falls forced people traveling down the Ohio to use the portage of Louisville, which helped the town grow in the early nineteenth century. Kentucky incorporated the town as a city in 1828. Two years later, the Portland Canal opened, allowing boats to go around the rapids, thereby increasing river traffic and assisting the city's growth. In the next several years, the arrival of the railroad would link the town to much of the South. The cultivation of tobacco became important to the state in the 1830s, when Louisville became a prominent processing site.

The Civil War was an interesting period in the city's history, as adherents to both the North and the South walked the city's streets. Yet the North had the upper hand, and Louisville quickly became a supply center for Union armies marching south.

The postwar period saw boom times for Louisville, and by the end of the nineteenth century the population topped 200,000. In 1937, after the Ohio River flooded the city's environs, a floodwall was built to prevent such a catastrophe from recurring. World War II saw Louisville rebound as it became an important center for munitions production. After the war, the city desegregated its schools in a calm fashion, without the trouble seen in so many other areas.

The Kentucky Derby horserace—the annual Run for the Roses—has been held at Churchill Downs in Louisville since 1875, earning the city the nickname, "Derby Town." The fabled track now includes the Grandstand Terrace and Rooftop Garden and 165,000 seats. A stadium for the city's pro soccer team opened in 2020.

The city serves as an important corporate command post, and a number of major companies do business there, including the United Postal Service, Ford Motor Company, Humana, Walmart, Amazon, and Spectrum. Louisville also produces one third of all bourbon whiskey and has an official Bourbon District, home to several distilleries.

Louisville is a vital center of transportation, with two ports on the Ohio River and three interstate highways intersecting the city. The Louisville International Airport serves as the international hub for United Parcel Service. The Louisville metro area offers new businesses many incentives, including a foreign trade zone.

The "NuLu" District, formally called the East Market District, is hopping with shops, restaurants and breweries established in the old warehouse district. City attractions include the Kentucky Science Center with interactive exhibits and Science Education Wing, the Louisville Zoo, the Kentucky Derby Museum, Kentucky Kingdom and Hurricane Bay, the Louisville Slugger Museum & Factor (with the world's largest bat), and the Kentucky Exposition Center. The Speed Art Museum, the oldest (1927) and largest art museum in the state, reopened in 2016 with 220,000 of renovated space after a 3-year closure.

The city's climate is a typical continental one, with cool winters, warm summers, and thunderstorms with intense rainfall during spring and summer. Fall tends to be the driest, and snow can arrive anytime from November through March, although all precipitation varies from year to year.

Rankings

General Rankings

- To help military veterans find the best places in which to settle down, *WalletHub* compared the 100 largest U.S. cities across 19 key indicators of livability, affordability and veteran-friendliness. They range from the share of military skill-related jobs to veteran income growth to the availability of VA health facilities. Louisville ranked #57. *Wallethub.com, "Best & Worst Places for Veterans to Live (2025)," November 7, 2024*

- In their annual survey, Livability.com looked at data for more than 2,000 mid-sized U.S. cities to assign a "Livability Score"for each. The top 100 scoring cities make up Livability's "Top 100 Best Places to Live in the U.S." in 2025. Louisville was placed among the top 100 of the customizable list. Criteria: housing and economy; cost of living; environment; education; health care options; transportation; safety; and community amenities. *Livability.com, "Top 100 Best Places to Live in the U.S. in 2025" April 15, 2025*

Business/Finance Rankings

- Louisville was cited as one of America's top metros for total corporate facility investment projects in 2024. The area ranked #6 in the Tier 1 (large) metro area category (population over 1 million). *Site Selection, "Top Metros of 2024," March 2025*

- The Louisville metro area appeared on the Milken Institute "2025 Best Performing Cities" list. Rank: #114 out of 200 large metro areas (based on performance category). Criteria: job growth; wage growth; high-tech growth and impact; community resilience; housing affordability; household broadband access. *Milken Institute, "Best-Performing Cities 2025," January 14, 2025*

Education Rankings

- Personal finance website *WalletHub* analyzed the 150 largest U.S. metropolitan statistical areas to determine where the most educated Americans are putting their degrees to work. Criteria: education levels; percentage of workers with degrees; education quality and attainment gap; public school quality rankings; quality and enrollment of each metro area's universities. Louisville was ranked #90 (#1 = most educated city). *WalletHub.com, "Most & Least Educated Cities in America, 2025" July 2, 2024*

Environmental Rankings

- The U.S. Environmental Protection Agency (EPA) released its list of mid-size U.S. metropolitan areas with the most ENERGY STAR certified buildings in 2023. The Louisville metro area was ranked #3 out of 10. *U.S. Environmental Protection Agency, "2024 Energy Star Top Cities," May 22, 2024*

Health/Fitness Rankings

- For each of the 100 largest cities in the United States, the American Fitness Index®, compiled in partnership between the American College of Sports Medicine and the Elevance Health Foundation, evaluated community infrastructure and more than 30 health behaviors including preventive health, levels of chronic disease conditions, food insecurity, pedestrian safety, air quality, and community/environment resources that support physical activity. Louisville ranked #91 for "community fitness." *americanfitnessindex.org, "2024 ACSM American Fitness Index Summary Report," July 23, 2024*

- The Louisville metro area was identified as one of the worst cities for bed bugs in America by pest control company Orkin. The area ranked #49 out of 50 based on the number of bed bug treatments Orkin performed from December 2022 to November 2023. *Orkin, "Chicago Joins Paris In Global Bed Bug Spotlight Ranking As The Worst City On Orkin's U.S. Bed Bug Cities List," January 22, 2024*

- Louisville was identified as a "2025 Allergy Capital." The area ranked #69 out of the nation's 100 largest metropolitan areas. Three groups of factors were used to identify the most challenging cities for people with allergies: annual tree, grass, and weed pollen scores; over the counter allergy medicine use; number of board-certified allergy specialists. *Asthma and Allergy Foundation of America, "2025 Allergy Capitals: The Most Challenging Places to Live with Allergies," March 18, 2025*

- Louisville was identified as a "2024 Asthma Capital." The area ranked #40 out of the nation's 100 largest metropolitan areas. Criteria: estimated asthma prevalence; asthma-related mortality; and ER visits due to asthma. Risk factors analyzed but not factored in the rankings: annual air quality including pollution and ozone levels; public smoking laws; indoor air quality; access to asthma specialists; rescue and controller medication use; uninsured rate; pollen allergy; poverty rate. *Asthma and Allergy Foundation of America, "Asthma Capitals 2024: The Most Challenging Places to Live With Asthma," September 10, 2024*

Real Estate Rankings

- *WalletHub* compared the most populated U.S. cities to determine which had the best markets for real estate agents. Louisville ranked #142 where demand was high and pay was the best. Criteria: sales per agent; annual median wage for real-estate agents; monthly average starting salary for real estate agents; real estate job density and competition; unemployment rate; home turnover rate; housing-market health index; and other relevant metrics. *WalletHub.com, "2021 Best Places to Be a Real Estate Agent," May 12, 2021*

- Louisville was ranked #10 in the top 20 out of the 100 largest metro areas in terms of house price appreciation in 2024 (#1 = highest rate). *Federal Housing Finance Agency, "House Price Index, 4th Quarter 2024," February 25, 2025*

- Louisville was ranked #40 out of 176 metro areas in terms of cost of housing in 2024 by the National Association of Home Builders (#1 = most affordable). Criteria: the portion of an average family's income necessary to pay the mortgage on a median-priced home. *National Association of Home Builders®, NAHB-Wells Fargo Cost of Housing Index, 4th Quarter 2024*

Safety Rankings

- Allstate ranked the 100 most populous cities in America in terms of driver safety. Louisville ranked #22. Criteria based on anonymized driving behavior data from Allstate's mobile app powered by Arity: high speed driving (over 80 mph), phone handling, and hard braking. The report helps increase the importance of safety and awareness behind the wheel. *Allstate, "16th Allstate America's Best Drivers Report®" July 11, 2024*

- Louisville was identified as one of the most dangerous cities in America by NeighborhoodScout. The city ranked #82 out of 100 (#1 = most dangerous). Criteria: number of violent crimes per 1,000 residents. The editors evaluated cities with 25,000 or more residents. *NeighborhoodScout.com, "2023 Top 100 Most Dangerous Cities in the U.S.," January 12, 2023*

Women/Minorities Rankings

- Personal finance website *WalletHub* compared more than 180 U.S. cities across two key dimensions, "Hispanic Business-Friendliness" and "Hispanic Purchasing Power," to arrive at the most favorable conditions for Hispanic entrepreneurs. Louisville was ranked #98 out of 182. Criteria includes: share of Hispanic-Owned Businesses; average growth of Hispanic Business revenues; Small Business-Friendliness score; affordability; and number of Hispanics with at least a bachelor's degree. *WalletHub.com, "Best Cities for Hispanic Entrepreneurs," September 4, 2024*

Miscellaneous Rankings

- *WalletHub* compared 148 of the most populated U.S. cities to determine their operating efficiency. A "Quality of Services" score was constructed for each city and then measured against the total budget per capita to reveal which were managed the best. Louisville ranked #56. Criteria: financial stability; economy; education; safety; health; infrastructure and pollution. *WalletHub.com, "2025's Best- & Worst-Run Cities in America," June 18, 2024*

Business Environment

DEMOGRAPHICS

Population Growth

Area	1990 Census	2000 Census	2010 Census	2020 Census	2023 Estimate[2]	Population Growth 1990-2023 (%)
City	269,160	256,231	597,337	386,884	627,210	133.0
MSA[1]	1,055,973	1,161,975	1,283,566	1,285,439	1,361,847	29.0
U.S.	248,709,873	281,421,906	308,745,538	331,449,281	332,387,540	33.6

Note: (1) Figures cover the Louisville/Jefferson County, KY-IN Metropolitan Statistical Area; (2) 2019-2023 5-year ACS population estimate
Source: U.S. Census Bureau, 1990 Census, 2000 Census, 2010 Census, 2020 Census, 2019-2023 American Community Survey 5-Year Estimates

Race

Area	White Alone[2] (%)	Black Alone[2] (%)	Asian Alone[2] (%)	AIAN[3] Alone[2] (%)	NHOPI[4] Alone[2] (%)	Other Race Alone[2] (%)	Two or More Races (%)
City	63.1	23.7	2.6	0.1	0.0	2.1	8.4
MSA[1]	75.2	14.2	2.1	0.1	0.0	1.6	6.7
U.S.	63.4	12.4	5.8	0.9	0.2	6.6	10.7

Note: (1) Figures cover the Louisville/Jefferson County, KY-IN Metropolitan Statistical Area; (2) Alone is defined as not being in combination with one or more other races; (3) American Indian and Alaska Native; (4) Native Hawaiian and Other Pacific Islander
Source: U.S. Census Bureau, 2019-2023 American Community Survey 5-Year Estimates

Hispanic or Latino Origin

Area	Total (%)	Mexican (%)	Puerto Rican (%)	Cuban (%)	Other (%)
City	8.6	2.9	0.4	3.4	1.9
MSA[1]	6.5	2.7	0.5	1.8	1.5
U.S.	19.0	11.3	1.8	0.7	5.2

Note: Persons of Hispanic or Latino origin can be of any race; (1) Figures cover the Louisville/Jefferson County, KY-IN Metropolitan Statistical Area
Source: U.S. Census Bureau, 2019-2023 American Community Survey 5-Year Estimates

Age

Area	Percent of Population									Median Age
	Under Age 5	Age 5–19	Age 20–34	Age 35–44	Age 45–54	Age 55–64	Age 65–74	Age 75–84	Age 85+	
City	6.2	18.8	21.1	13.1	12.1	12.8	9.9	4.5	1.6	37.7
MSA[1]	5.9	18.8	19.6	13.1	12.6	13.4	10.3	4.7	1.7	39.3
U.S.	5.7	19.1	20.2	13.1	12.3	12.8	10.0	4.9	1.9	38.7

Note: (1) Figures cover the Louisville/Jefferson County, KY-IN Metropolitan Statistical Area
Source: U.S. Census Bureau, 2019-2023 American Community Survey 5-Year Estimates

Disability by Age

Area	All Ages	Under 18 Years Old	18 to 64 Years Old	65 Years and Over
City	14.7	5.3	13.3	34.1
MSA[1]	14.4	5.0	12.5	34.4
U.S.	13.0	4.7	10.7	32.9

Note: Figures show percent of the civilian noninstitutionalized population that reported having a disability. Disability status is determined from six types of difficulty: vision, hearing, cognitive, ambulatory, self-care, and independent living. For children under 5 years old, hearing and vision difficulty are used to determine disability status. For children between the ages of 5 and 14, disability status is determined from hearing, vision, cognitive, ambulatory, and self-care difficulties. For people aged 15 years and older, they are considered to have a disability if they have difficulty with any one of the six difficulty types; Note: (1) Figures cover the Louisville/Jefferson County, KY-IN Metropolitan Statistical Area
Source: U.S. Census Bureau, 2019-2023 American Community Survey 5-Year Estimates

Ancestry

Area	German	Irish	English	American	Italian	Polish	French[2]	European	Scottish
City	14.8	11.3	10.8	5.8	2.5	1.1	1.5	1.6	1.6
MSA[1]	16.6	12.4	12.6	7.6	2.6	1.1	1.7	1.7	1.9
U.S.	12.6	9.4	9.1	5.5	4.9	2.6	2.0	1.6	1.6

Note: Figures are the percentage of the total population reporting a particular ancestry. The nine most commonly reported ancestries in the U.S. are shown. Figures include multiple ancestries (e.g. if a person reported being Irish and Italian, they were included in both columns); (1) Figures cover the Louisville/Jefferson County, KY-IN Metropolitan Statistical Area; (2) Excludes Basque
Source: U.S. Census Bureau, 2019-2023 American Community Survey 5-Year Estimates

Foreign-born Population

Area	Any Foreign Country	Asia	Mexico	Europe	Caribbean	Central America[2]	South America	Africa	Canada
City	9.8	2.5	1.0	0.8	2.8	0.6	0.4	1.6	0.1
MSA[1]	6.7	1.9	0.9	0.6	1.5	0.4	0.3	1.0	0.1
U.S.	13.9	4.3	3.3	1.4	1.4	1.2	1.2	0.8	0.2

Note: (1) Figures cover the Louisville/Jefferson County, KY-IN Metropolitan Statistical Area; (2) Excludes Mexico.
Source: U.S. Census Bureau, 2019-2023 American Community Survey 5-Year Estimates

Household Size

Area	Persons in Household (%)							Average Household Size
	One	Two	Three	Four	Five	Six	Seven or More	
City	34.5	32.8	15.3	10.3	4.6	1.7	0.9	2.34
MSA[1]	30.6	34.4	15.5	11.8	5.1	1.8	0.9	2.43
U.S.	28.5	33.8	15.4	12.7	5.9	2.3	1.4	2.54

Note: (1) Figures cover the Louisville/Jefferson County, KY-IN Metropolitan Statistical Area
Source: U.S. Census Bureau, 2019-2023 American Community Survey 5-Year Estimates

Household Relationships

Area	House-holder	Opposite-sex Spouse	Same-sex Spouse	Opposite-sex Unmarried Partner	Same-sex Unmarried Partner	Child[2]	Grand-child	Other Relatives	Non-relatives
City	40.0	18.0	0.2	2.9	0.2	28.8	2.6	4.2	2.7
MSA[1]	40.5	17.7	0.2	2.8	0.2	27.6	2.5	3.6	2.9
U.S.	38.3	17.5	0.2	2.5	0.2	28.3	2.4	4.8	3.4

Note: Figures are percent of the total population; (1) Figures cover the Louisville/Jefferson County, KY-IN Metropolitan Statistical Area; (2) Includes biological, adopted, and stepchildren of the householder
Source: U.S. Census Bureau, 2020 Census

Gender

Area	Males	Females	Males per 100 Females
City	305,342	321,868	94.9
MSA[1]	669,908	691,939	96.8
U.S.	164,545,087	167,842,453	98.0

Note: (1) Figures cover the Louisville/Jefferson County, KY-IN Metropolitan Statistical Area
Source: U.S. Census Bureau, 2019-2023 American Community Survey 5-Year Estimates

Marital Status

Area	Never Married	Now Married[2]	Separated	Widowed	Divorced
City	37.2	41.9	2.0	6.1	12.8
MSA[1]	31.8	47.6	1.7	6.0	12.9
U.S.	34.1	47.9	1.7	5.6	10.7

Note: Figures are percentages and cover the population 15 years of age and older; (1) Figures cover the Louisville/Jefferson County, KY-IN Metropolitan Statistical Area; (2) Excludes separated
Source: U.S. Census Bureau, 2019-2023 American Community Survey 5-Year Estimates

Religious Groups by Family

Area	Catholic	Baptist	Methodist	LDS[2]	Pentecostal	Lutheran	Islam	Adventist	Other
MSA[1]	11.9	14.5	3.2	0.8	0.9	0.5	1.0	1.0	12.4
U.S.	18.7	7.3	3.0	2.0	1.8	1.7	1.3	1.3	11.6

Note: Figures are the number of adherents as a percentage of the total population and cover the eight largest religious groups in the U.S; (1) Figures cover the Louisville/Jefferson County, KY-IN Metropolitan Statistical Area; (2) Church of Jesus Christ of Latter-day Saints
Sources: 2020 U.S. Religion Census, Association of Statisticians of American Religious Bodies; The Association of Religion Data Archives (ARDA)

Religious Groups by Tradition

Area	Catholic	Evangelical Protestant	Mainline Protestant	Black Protestant	Islam	Judaism	Hinduism	Orthodox	Buddhism
MSA[1]	11.9	21.1	5.0	4.6	1.0	0.2	0.4	0.2	0.2
U.S.	18.7	16.5	5.2	2.3	1.3	0.6	0.4	0.4	0.3

Note: Figures are the number of adherents as a percentage of the total population; (1) Figures cover the Louisville/Jefferson County, KY-IN Metropolitan Statistical Area
Sources: 2020 U.S. Religion Census, Association of Statisticians of American Religious Bodies; The Association of Religion Data Archives (ARDA)

ECONOMY

Real Gross Domestic Product (GDP)

Area	2017	2018	2019	2020	2021	2022	2023	Rank[3]
MSA[1]	70.8	71.6	74.3	72.8	76.4	77.9	79.2	49
U.S.[2]	17,619.1	18,160.7	18,642.5	18,238.9	19,387.6	19,896.6	20,436.3	—

Note: Figures are in billions of chained 2017 dollars; (1) Figures cover the Louisville/Jefferson County, KY-IN Metropolitan Statistical Area; (2) Figures cover real GDP within metropolitan areas; (3) Rank is based on 2023 data and ranges from 1 to 384
Source: U.S. Bureau of Economic Analysis

Economic Growth

Area	2014	2015	2016	2017	2018	2019	2020	2021	2022	2023
MSA[1]	1.3	2.6	1.9	1.7	1.2	3.8	-2.0	4.9	2.0	1.6
U.S.[2]	2.6	3.2	2.0	2.7	3.1	2.7	-2.2	6.3	2.6	2.7

Note: Figures are real gross domestic product growth rates and represent percent change from preceding period; (1) Figures cover the Louisville/Jefferson County, KY-IN Metropolitan Statistical Area; (2) Figures are the average growth rates within metropolitan areas
Source: U.S. Bureau of Economic Analysis

Metropolitan Area Exports

Area	2018	2019	2020	2021	2022	2023	Rank[2]
MSA[1]	8,987.0	9,105.5	8,360.3	10,262.8	10,618.7	11,072.0	37
U.S.	1,664,056.1	1,645,173.7	1,431,406.6	1,753,941.4	2,062,937.4	2,019,160.5	—

Note: Figures are in millions of dollars; (1) Figures cover the Louisville/Jefferson County, KY-IN Metropolitan Statistical Area; (2) Rank is based on 2023 data and ranges from 1 to 386
Source: U.S. Department of Commerce, International Trade Administration, Office of Trade and Economic Analysis, Industry and Analysis, Exports by Metropolitan Area, data extracted April 2, 2025

Building Permits

Area	Single-Family			Multi-Family			Total		
	2023	2024	Pct. Chg.	2023	2024	Pct. Chg.	2023	2024	Pct. Chg.
City	1,014	1,168	15.2	2,686	1,690	-37.1	3,700	2,858	-22.8
MSA[1]	2,914	3,690	26.6	3,817	2,106	-44.8	6,731	5,796	-13.9
U.S.	920,000	981,900	6.7	591,100	496,100	-16.1	1,511,100	1,478,000	-2.2

Note: (1) Figures cover the Louisville/Jefferson County, KY-IN Metropolitan Statistical Area; Figures represent new, privately-owned housing units authorized (unadjusted data)
Source: U.S. Census Bureau, Building Permits Survey (BPS), 2023, 2024

Bankruptcy Filings

Area	Business Filings			Nonbusiness Filings		
	2023	2024	% Chg.	2023	2024	% Chg.
Jefferson County	28	35	25.0	2,280	2,258	-1.0
U.S.	18,926	23,107	22.1	434,064	494,201	13.9

Note: Business filings include Chapter 7, Chapter 9, Chapter 11, Chapter 12, Chapter 13, Chapter 15, and Section 304; Nonbusiness filings include Chapter 7, Chapter 11, and Chapter 13
Source: Administrative Office of the U.S. Courts, Business and Nonbusiness Bankruptcy, County Cases Commenced by Chapter of the Bankruptcy Code, During the 12-Month Period Ending December 31, 2023 and Business and Nonbusiness Bankruptcy, County Cases Commenced by Chapter of the Bankruptcy Code, During the 12-Month Period Ending December 31, 2024

Housing Vacancy Rates

Area	Gross Vacancy Rate[3] (%)			Year-Round Vacancy Rate[4] (%)			Rental Vacancy Rate[5] (%)			Homeowner Vacancy Rate[6] (%)		
	2022	2023	2024	2022	2023	2024	2022	2023	2024	2022	2023	2024
MSA[1]	5.7	6.3	6.7	5.7	6.2	6.5	5.3	3.6	7.1	0.5	0.4	1.2
U.S.[2]	9.1	9.0	9.1	7.5	7.5	7.6	5.7	6.5	6.8	0.8	0.8	1.0

Note: (1) Figures cover the Louisville/Jefferson County, KY-IN Metropolitan Statistical Area; (2) Figures cover the 75 largest Metropolitan Statistical Areas; (3) The percentage of the total housing inventory that is vacant; (4) The percentage of the housing inventory (excluding seasonal units) that is year-round vacant; (5) The percentage of rental inventory that is vacant for rent; (6) The percentage of homeowner inventory that is vacant for sale
Source: U.S. Census Bureau, Housing Vacancies and Homeownership Annual Statistics: 2022, 2023, 2024

INCOME

Income

Area	Per Capita ($)	Median Household ($)	Average Household ($)
City	38,890	64,731	91,264
MSA[1]	40,019	71,737	97,103
U.S.	43,289	78,538	110,491

Note: (1) Figures cover the Louisville/Jefferson County, KY-IN Metropolitan Statistical Area
Source: U.S. Census Bureau, 2019-2023 American Community Survey 5-Year Estimates

Household Income Distribution

Area	Percent of Households Earning							
	Under $15,000	$15,000 -$24,999	$25,000 -$34,999	$35,000 -$49,999	$50,000 -$74,999	$75,000 -$99,999	$100,000 -$149,999	$150,000 and up
City	10.6	7.6	8.2	12.7	17.2	12.8	15.9	15.0
MSA[1]	8.5	6.8	7.4	12.0	17.2	13.5	17.6	17.0
U.S.	8.5	6.6	6.8	10.4	15.7	12.7	17.4	21.9

Note: (1) Figures cover the Louisville/Jefferson County, KY-IN Metropolitan Statistical Area
Source: U.S. Census Bureau, 2019-2023 American Community Survey 5-Year Estimates

Poverty Rate

Area	All Ages	Under 18 Years Old	18 to 64 Years Old	65 Years and Over
City	16.1	23.2	14.9	10.8
MSA[1]	12.3	17.0	11.4	9.2
U.S.	12.4	16.3	11.6	10.4

Note: Figures are percentage of people whose income during the past 12 months was below the poverty level; (1) Figures cover the Louisville/Jefferson County, KY-IN Metropolitan Statistical Area
Source: U.S. Census Bureau, 2019-2023 American Community Survey 5-Year Estimates

EMPLOYMENT

Labor Force and Employment

Area	Civilian Labor Force			Workers Employed		
	Dec. 2023	Dec. 2024	% Chg.	Dec. 2023	Dec. 2024	% Chg.
City	394,849	401,525	1.7	379,511	382,789	0.9
MSA[1]	691,184	703,358	1.8	666,258	672,517	0.9
U.S.	166,661,000	167,746,000	0.7	160,754,000	161,294,000	0.3

Note: Data is not seasonally adjusted and covers workers 16 years of age and older; (1) Figures cover the Louisville/Jefferson County, KY-IN Metropolitan Statistical Area
Source: Bureau of Labor Statistics, Local Area Unemployment Statistics

Unemployment Rate

Area	2024											
	Jan.	Feb.	Mar.	Apr.	May	Jun.	Jul.	Aug.	Sep.	Oct.	Nov.	Dec.
City	4.5	4.9	4.7	4.2	4.3	4.9	5.9	4.9	4.6	4.7	4.7	4.7
MSA[1]	4.3	4.7	4.4	3.9	4.1	4.7	5.6	4.6	4.3	4.4	4.5	4.4
U.S.	4.1	4.2	3.9	3.5	3.7	4.3	4.5	4.4	3.9	3.9	4.0	3.8

Note: Data is not seasonally adjusted and covers workers 16 years of age and older; (1) Figures cover the Louisville/Jefferson County, KY-IN Metropolitan Statistical Area
Source: Bureau of Labor Statistics, Local Area Unemployment Statistics

Average Wages

Occupation	$/Hr.	Occupation	$/Hr.
Accountants and Auditors	39.40	Maintenance and Repair Workers	25.41
Automotive Mechanics	23.99	Marketing Managers	68.75
Bookkeepers	24.07	Network and Computer Systems Admin.	43.31
Carpenters	26.54	Nurses, Licensed Practical	29.46
Cashiers	14.14	Nurses, Registered	42.06
Computer Programmers	52.89	Nursing Assistants	19.38
Computer Systems Analysts	45.74	Office Clerks, General	18.96
Computer User Support Specialists	27.34	Physical Therapists	44.32
Construction Laborers	23.10	Physicians	137.23
Cooks, Restaurant	16.46	Plumbers, Pipefitters and Steamfitters	33.07
Customer Service Representatives	20.93	Police and Sheriff's Patrol Officers	31.32
Dentists	90.25	Postal Service Mail Carriers	28.87
Electricians	30.65	Real Estate Sales Agents	25.01
Engineers, Electrical	47.48	Retail Salespersons	16.47
Fast Food and Counter Workers	13.57	Sales Representatives, Technical/Scientific	51.44
Financial Managers	71.03	Secretaries, Exc. Legal/Medical/Executive	22.05
First-Line Supervisors of Office Workers	33.66	Security Guards	18.78
General and Operations Managers	51.34	Surgeons	n/a
Hairdressers/Cosmetologists	24.77	Teacher Assistants, Exc. Postsecondary[1]	16.51
Home Health and Personal Care Aides	17.39	Teachers, Secondary School, Exc. Sp. Ed.[1]	31.82
Janitors and Cleaners	16.81	Telemarketers	n/a
Landscaping/Groundskeeping Workers	18.54	Truck Drivers, Heavy/Tractor-Trailer	30.63
Lawyers	58.69	Truck Drivers, Light/Delivery Services	24.78
Maids and Housekeeping Cleaners	15.46	Waiters and Waitresses	14.86

Note: Wage data covers the Louisville/Jefferson County, KY-IN Metropolitan Statistical Area; (1) Hourly wages were calculated from annual wage data based on a 40 hour work week
Source: Bureau of Labor Statistics, Metro Area Occupational Employment & Wage Estimates, May 2024

Employment by Industry

Sector	MSA[1] Number of Employees	MSA[1] Percent of Total	U.S. Percent of Total
Construction, Mining, and Logging	37,100	5.1	5.5
Financial Activities	46,800	6.4	5.8
Government	77,100	10.6	14.9
Information	8,300	1.1	1.9
Leisure and Hospitality	69,500	9.6	10.4
Manufacturing	85,800	11.8	8.0
Other Services	27,500	3.8	3.7
Private Education and Health Services	112,100	15.4	16.9
Professional and Business Services	88,300	12.2	14.2
Retail Trade	69,000	9.5	10.0
Transportation, Warehousing, and Utilities	71,100	9.8	4.8
Wholesale Trade	33,900	4.7	3.9

Note: Figures are non-farm employment as of December 2024. Figures are not seasonally adjusted and include workers 16 years of age and older; (1) Figures cover the Louisville/Jefferson County, KY-IN Metropolitan Statistical Area
Source: Bureau of Labor Statistics, Current Employment Statistics, Employment, Hours, and Earnings

Employment by Occupation

Occupation Classification	City (%)	MSA[1] (%)	U.S. (%)
Management, Business, Science, and Arts	38.4	38.9	42.0
Natural Resources, Construction, and Maintenance	6.4	7.5	8.6
Production, Transportation, and Material Moving	19.8	18.8	13.0
Sales and Office	20.3	20.4	19.9
Service	15.0	14.4	16.5

Note: Figures cover employed civilians 16 years of age and older; (1) Figures cover the Louisville/Jefferson County, KY-IN Metropolitan Statistical Area
Source: U.S. Census Bureau, 2019-2023 American Community Survey 5-Year Estimates

Occupations with Greatest Projected Employment Growth: 2022 – 2032

Occupation[1]	2022 Employment	2032 Projected Employment	Numeric Employment Change	Percent Employment Change
Laborers and Freight, Stock, and Material Movers, Hand	57,770	64,360	6,590	11.4
Stockers and Order Fillers	50,640	56,760	6,120	12.1
Home Health and Personal Care Aides	24,650	30,540	5,890	23.9
Cooks, Restaurant	16,680	21,580	4,900	29.4
General and Operations Managers	51,300	54,500	3,200	6.2
Registered Nurses	47,300	50,400	3,100	6.6
Medical and Health Services Managers	9,660	12,440	2,780	28.8
Heavy and Tractor-Trailer Truck Drivers	31,110	33,340	2,230	7.2
Light Truck or Delivery Services Drivers	16,590	18,790	2,200	13.3
Nurse Practitioners	4,730	6,870	2,140	45.2

Note: Projections cover Kentucky; (1) Sorted by numeric employment change
Source: www.projectionscentral.org, State Occupational Projections, 2022–2032 Long-Term Projections

Fastest-Growing Occupations: 2022 – 2032

Occupation[1]	2022 Employment	2032 Projected Employment	Numeric Employment Change	Percent Employment Change
Nurse Practitioners	4,730	6,870	2,140	45.2
Information Security Analysts (SOC 2018)	1,230	1,600	370	30.1
Cooks, Restaurant	16,680	21,580	4,900	29.4
Medical and Health Services Managers	9,660	12,440	2,780	28.8
Taxi Drivers	1,250	1,590	340	27.2
Physician Assistants	1,220	1,550	330	27.0
Computer and Information Research Scientists (SOC 2018)	260	330	70	26.9
Computer Numerically Controlled Tool Programmers	240	300	60	25.0
Physical Therapist Assistants	2,280	2,840	560	24.6
Software Developers	6,650	8,260	1,610	24.2

Note: Projections cover Kentucky; (1) Sorted by percent employment change and excludes occupations with numeric employment change less than 50
Source: www.projectionscentral.org, State Occupational Projections, 2022–2032 Long-Term Projections

CITY FINANCES

City Government Finances

Component	2022 ($000)	2022 ($ per capita)
Total Revenues	2,045,259	2,665
Total Expenditures	2,681,116	3,494
Debt Outstanding	4,040,299	5,265

Source: U.S. Census Bureau, State & Local Government Finances 2022

City Government Revenue by Source

Source	2022 ($000)	2022 ($ per capita)	2022 (%)
General Revenue			
From Federal Government	438,901	572	21.5
From State Government	73,913	96	3.6
From Local Governments	144,874	189	7.1
Taxes			
Property	206,883	270	10.1
Sales and Gross Receipts	104,755	136	5.1
Personal Income	376,001	490	18.4
Corporate Income	116,790	152	5.7
Motor Vehicle License	637	1	0.0
Other Taxes	15,207	20	0.7
Current Charges	265,338	346	13.0
Liquor Store	0	0	0.0
Utility	235,697	307	11.5

Source: U.S. Census Bureau, State & Local Government Finances 2022

City Government Expenditures by Function

Function	2022 ($000)	2022 ($ per capita)	2022 (%)
General Direct Expenditures			
Air Transportation	128,619	167	4.8
Corrections	51,338	66	1.9
Education	81,412	106	3.0
Employment Security Administration	0	0	0.0
Financial Administration	59,733	77	2.2
Fire Protection	77,704	101	2.9
General Public Buildings	0	0	0.0
Governmental Administration, Other	41,080	53	1.5
Health	141,006	183	5.3
Highways	65,223	85	2.4
Hospitals	0	0	0.0
Housing and Community Development	76,532	99	2.9
Interest on General Debt	133,277	173	5.0
Judicial and Legal	11,877	15	0.4
Libraries	24,549	32	0.9
Parking	19,848	25	0.7
Parks and Recreation	21,288	27	0.8
Police Protection	207,627	270	7.7
Public Welfare	4,323	5	0.2
Sewerage	866,368	1,128	32.3
Solid Waste Management	29,410	38	1.1
Veterans' Services	0	0	0.0
Liquor Store	0	0	0.0
Utility	507,143	660	18.9

Source: U.S. Census Bureau, State & Local Government Finances 2022

TAXES

State Corporate Income Tax Rates

State	Tax Rate (%)	Income Brackets ($)	Num. of Brackets	Financial Institution Tax Rate (%)[a]	Federal Income Tax Ded.
Kentucky	5.0	Flat rate	1	5.0	No

Note: Tax rates for tax year 2024; (a) Rates listed are the corporate income tax rate applied to financial institutions or excise taxes based on income. Some states have other taxes based upon the value of deposits or shares.
Source: Federation of Tax Administrators, State Corporate Income Tax Rates, January 1, 2025

State Individual Income Tax Rates

State	Tax Rate (%)	Income Brackets ($)	Personal Exemptions ($)			Standard Ded. ($)	
			Single	Married	Depend.	Single	Married
Kentucky	4.0	Flat rate	None	None	None	3,160	6,320

Note: Tax rates for tax year 2024; Local- and county-level taxes are not included; Federal income tax is not deductible on state income tax returns
Source: Federation of Tax Administrators, State Individual Income Tax Rates, January 1, 2025

Various State Sales and Excise Tax Rates

State	State Sales Tax (%)	Gasoline[1] ($/gal.)	Cigarette[2] ($/pack)	Spirits[3] ($/gal.)	Wine[4] ($/gal.)	Beer[5] ($/gal.)	Recreational Marijuana (%)
Kentucky	6	0.28	1.10	9.56	3.82	0.89	Not legal

Note: All tax rates as of January 1, 2025; (1) The American Petroleum Institute has developed a methodology for determining the average tax rate on a gallon of fuel. Rates may include any of the following: excise taxes, environmental fees, storage tank fees, other fees or taxes, general sales tax, and local taxes; (2) The federal excise tax of $1.0066 per pack and local taxes are not included; (3) Rates are those applicable to off-premise sales of 40% alcohol by volume (a.b.v.) distilled spirits in 750ml containers. Local excise taxes are excluded; (4) Rates are those applicable to off-premise sales of 11% a.b.v. non-carbonated wine in 750ml containers; (5) Rates are those applicable to off-premise sales of 4.7% a.b.v. beer in 12 ounce containers.
Source: Tax Foundation, 2025 Facts & Figures: How Does Your State Compare?

State Tax Competitiveness Index

State	Overall Rank	Corporate Tax Rank	Individual Income Tax Rank	Sales Tax Rank	Property Tax Rank	Unemployment Insurance Tax Rank
Kentucky	22	18	23	18	27	34

Note: The Tax Foundation's State Tax Competitiveness Index enables policymakers, taxpayers, and business leaders to gauge how their states' tax systems compare. A rank of 1 is best, 50 is worst. Rankings do not average to the total. States without a tax rank equally as 1. DC's scores and rankings do not affect other states. The report shows tax systems as of July 1, 2024 (the beginning of Fiscal Year 2025).
Source: Tax Foundation, State Tax Competitiveness Index 2025

TRANSPORTATION

Means of Transportation to Work

Area	Car/Truck/Van		Public Transportation			Bicycle	Walked	Other Means	Worked at Home
	Drove Alone	Car-pooled	Bus	Subway	Railroad				
City	73.5	8.7	2.2	0.0	0.0	0.3	2.0	1.7	11.6
MSA[1]	76.0	8.4	1.1	0.0	0.0	0.2	1.5	1.2	11.6
U.S.	70.2	8.5	1.7	1.3	0.4	0.4	2.4	1.6	13.5

Note: Figures are percentages and cover workers 16 years of age and older; (1) Figures cover the Louisville/Jefferson County, KY-IN Metropolitan Statistical Area
Source: U.S. Census Bureau, 2019-2023 American Community Survey 5-Year Estimates

Travel Time to Work

Area	Less Than 10 Minutes	10 to 19 Minutes	20 to 29 Minutes	30 to 44 Minutes	45 to 59 Minutes	60 to 89 Minutes	90 Minutes or More
City	10.1	31.8	31.9	19.1	3.6	2.0	1.4
MSA[1]	10.6	29.6	28.4	20.9	6.1	2.9	1.5
U.S.	12.6	28.6	21.2	20.8	8.1	6.0	2.8

Note: Note: Figures are percentages and include workers 16 years old and over; (1) Figures cover the Louisville/Jefferson County, KY-IN Metropolitan Statistical Area
Source: U.S. Census Bureau, 2019-2023 American Community Survey 5-Year Estimates

Key Congestion Measures

Measure	2000	2010	2015	2020	2022
Annual Hours of Delay, Total (000)	17,140	24,266	28,088	13,886	33,204
Annual Hours of Delay, Per Auto Commuter	32	37	43	22	54
Annual Congestion Cost, Per Auto Commuter ($)	680	766	818	432	1,017

Note: Figures cover the Louisville-Jefferson County KY-IN urban area
Source: Texas A&M Transportation Institute, 2023 Urban Mobility Report

Freeway Travel Time Index

Measure	1985	1990	1995	2000	2005	2010	2015	2020	2022
Urban Area Index[1]	1.09	1.12	1.15	1.17	1.18	1.17	1.17	1.05	1.18
Urban Area Rank[1,2]	36	35	36	36	41	41	46	85	40

Note: Freeway Travel Time Index—the ratio of travel time in the peak period to the travel time at free-flow conditions. For example, a value of 1.30 indicates a 20-minute free-flow trip takes 26 minutes in the peak (20 minutes x 1.30 = 26 minutes); (1) Covers the Louisville-Jefferson County KY-IN urban area; (2) Rank is based on 101 larger urban areas (#1 = highest travel time index)
Source: Texas A&M Transportation Institute, 2023 Urban Mobility Report

Public Transportation

Agency Name / Mode of Transportation	Vehicles Operated in Maximum Service[1]	Annual Unlinked Passenger Trips[2] (in thous.)	Annual Passenger Miles[3] (in thous.)
Transit Authority of River City (TARC)			
Bus (directly operated)	159	5,882.9	19,354.6
Bus (purchased transportation)	1	3.9	11.0
Demand Response (purchased transportation)	77	211.6	1,878.0
Demand Response - Taxi	44	148.6	1,639.3

Note: (1) Number of revenue vehicles operated by the given mode and type of service to meet the annual maximum service requirement. This is the revenue vehicle count during the peak season of the year; on the week and day that maximum service is provided. Vehicles operated in maximum service (VOMS) exclude atypical days and one-time special events; (2) Number of passengers who boarded public transportation vehicles. Passengers are counted each time they board a vehicle no matter how many vehicles they use to travel from their origin to their destination. (3) Sum of the distances ridden by all passengers during the entire fiscal year.
Source: Federal Transit Administration, National Transit Database, 2023

Air Transportation

Airport Name and Code / Type of Service	Passenger Airlines[1]	Passenger Enplanements	Freight Carriers[2]	Freight (lbs)
Louisville International-Standiford Field (SDF)				
Domestic service (U.S. carriers only)	32	2,342,487	22	2,783,405,456
International service (U.S. carriers only)	1	1	4	284,309,481

Note: (1) Includes all U.S.-based major, minor and commuter airlines that carried at least one passenger during the year; (2) Includes all U.S.-based airlines and freight carriers that transported at least one pound of freight during the year.
Source: Bureau of Transportation Statistics, The Intermodal Transportation Database, Air Carriers: T-100 Domestic Market (U.S. carriers only), 2024; Bureau of Transportation Statistics, The Intermodal Transportation Database, Air Carriers: T-100 International Market (U.S. carriers only), 2024

BUSINESSES

Major Business Headquarters

Company Name	Industry	Rankings Fortune[1]	Forbes[2]
BrightSpring Health Services	Health care: pharmacy and other services	436	-
Humana	Health care: insurance and managed care	38	-

Note: (1) Companies that produce a 10-K are ranked 1 to 500 based on 2023 revenue; (2) All private companies with at least $2 billion in annual revenue through the end of their most current fiscal year are ranked 1 to 275; companies listed are headquartered in the city; dashes indicate no ranking
Source: Fortune, "Fortune 500," 2024; Forbes, "America's Largest Private Companies," 2024

Fastest-Growing Businesses

According to *Inc.*, Louisville is home to two of America's 500 fastest-growing private companies: **Cornbread Hemp** (#122); **OnPoint Warranty Solutions** (#338). Criteria: must be an independent, privately-held, for-profit, U.S. corporation, proprietorship or partnership as of December 31, 2023; revenues must be at least $100,000 in 2020 and $2 million in 2023; must have four-year operating/sales history. *Inc., "America's 500 Fastest-Growing Private Companies," 2024*

Living Environment

COST OF LIVING

Cost of Living Index

Composite Index	Groceries	Housing	Utilities	Transportation	Health Care	Misc. Goods/Services
94.1	99.1	80.1	83.2	96.7	114.9	102.4

Note: The Cost of Living Index measures regional differences in the cost of consumer goods and services, excluding taxes and non-consumer expenditures, for professional and managerial households in the top income quintile. It is based on more than 50,000 prices covering almost 60 different items for which prices are collected three times a year by chambers of commerce, economic development organizations or university applied economic centers in each participating urban area. The numbers shown should be read as a percentage above or below the national average of 100. For example, a value of 115.4 in the groceries column indicates that grocery prices are 15.4% higher than the national average. Small differences in the index numbers should not be interpreted as significant; Figures cover the Louisville KY urban area.
Source: The Council for Community and Economic Research, Cost of Living Index, 2024

Grocery Prices

Area[1]	T-Bone Steak ($/pound)	Frying Chicken ($/pound)	Whole Milk ($/half gal.)	Eggs ($/dozen)	Orange Juice ($/64 oz.)	Coffee ($/11.5 oz.)
City[2]	15.51	1.48	4.71	3.39	4.37	5.37
Avg.	15.42	1.55	4.69	3.25	4.41	5.46
Min.	14.50	1.16	4.43	2.75	4.00	4.85
Max.	17.56	2.89	5.49	4.78	5.54	7.89

Note: (1) Values for the local area are compared with the average, minimum and maximum values for all 276 areas in the Cost of Living Index; (2) Figures cover the Louisville KY urban area; **T-Bone Steak** (price per pound); **Frying Chicken** (price per pound, whole fryer); **Whole Milk** (half gallon carton); **Eggs** (price per dozen, Grade A, large); **Orange Juice** (64 oz. Tropicana or Florida Natural); **Coffee** (11.5 oz. can, vacuum-packed, Maxwell House, Hills Bros, or Folgers).
Source: The Council for Community and Economic Research, Cost of Living Index, 2024

Housing and Utility Costs

Area[1]	New Home Price ($)	Apartment Rent ($/month)	All Electric ($/month)	Part Electric ($/month)	Other Energy ($/month)	Telephone ($/month)
City[2]	388,161	1,369	-	82.51	72.69	188.14
Avg.	515,975	1,550	210.99	123.07	82.07	194.99
Min.	265,375	692	104.33	53.68	36.26	179.42
Max.	2,775,821	5,719	529.02	397.28	361.63	223.33

Note: (1) Values for the local area are compared with the average, minimum and maximum values for all 276 areas in the Cost of Living Index; (2) Figures cover the Louisville KY urban area; **New Home Price** (2,400 sf living area, 8,000 sf lot, in urban area with full utilities); **Apartment Rent** (950 sf 2 bedroom/1.5 or 2 bath, unfurnished, excluding all utilities except water); **All Electric** (average monthly cost for an all-electric home); **Part Electric** (average monthly cost for a part-electric home); **Other Energy** (average monthly cost for natural gas, fuel oil, coal, wood, and any other forms of energy except electricity); **Telephone** (price includes the base monthly rate plus taxes and fees for three lines of mobile phone service).
Source: The Council for Community and Economic Research, Cost of Living Index, 2024

Health Care, Transportation, and Other Costs

Area[1]	Doctor ($/visit)	Dentist ($/visit)	Optometrist ($/visit)	Gasoline ($/gallon)	Beauty Salon ($/visit)	Men's Shirt ($)
City[2]	152.10	159.00	107.05	3.21	43.89	48.00
Avg.	143.77	117.51	129.23	3.32	48.57	38.14
Min.	36.74	58.67	67.33	2.80	24.00	13.41
Max.	270.44	216.82	307.33	5.28	94.00	63.89

Note: (1) Values for the local area are compared with the average, minimum and maximum values for all 276 areas in the Cost of Living Index; (2) Figures cover the Louisville KY urban area; **Doctor** (general practitioners routine exam of an established patient); **Dentist** (adult teeth cleaning and periodic oral examination); **Optometrist** (full vision eye exam for established adult patient); **Gasoline** (one gallon regular unleaded, national brand, including all taxes, cash price at self-service pump if available); **Beauty Salon** (woman's shampoo, trim, and blow-dry); **Men's Shirt** (cotton/polyester dress shirt, pinpoint weave, long sleeves).
Source: The Council for Community and Economic Research, Cost of Living Index, 2024

HOUSING

Homeownership Rate

Area	2017 (%)	2018 (%)	2019 (%)	2020 (%)	2021 (%)	2022 (%)	2023 (%)	2024 (%)
MSA[1]	71.7	67.9	64.9	69.3	71.4	71.7	68.3	67.0
U.S.	63.9	64.4	64.6	66.6	65.5	65.8	65.9	65.6

Note: (1) Figures cover the Louisville/Jefferson County, KY-IN Metropolitan Statistical Area
Source: U.S. Census Bureau, Housing Vacancies and Homeownership Annual Statistics: 2017-2024

House Price Index (HPI)

Area	National Ranking[2]	Quarterly Change (%)	One-Year Change (%)	Five-Year Change (%)	Since 1991Q1 (%)
MSA[1]	81	0.59	6.45	50.59	291.73
U.S.[3]	–	1.43	4.51	57.13	327.82

Note: The HPI is a weighted repeat sales index. It measures average price changes in repeat sales or refinancings on the same properties. This information is obtained by reviewing repeat mortgage transactions on single-family properties whose mortgages have been purchased or securitized by Fannie Mae or Freddie Mac since January 1975; (1) Figures cover the Louisville/Jefferson County, KY-IN Metropolitan Statistical Area; (2) Rankings are based on annual percentage change for all metro areas containing at least 15,000 transactions over the last 10 years and ranges from 1 to 241; (3) figures based on a weighted average of Census Division estimates using a seasonally adjusted, purchase-only index; all figures are for the period ending December 31, 2024
Source: Federal Housing Finance Agency, Change in FHFA Metropolitan Area House Price Indexes, All Transactions Index, 2024Q4

Home Value

Area	Under $100,000	$100,000 -$199,999	$200,000 -$299,999	$300,000 -$399,999	$400,000 -$499,999	$500,000 -$999,999	$1,000,000 or more	Median ($)
City	11.8	32.0	25.5	13.2	7.6	8.4	1.5	221,500
MSA[1]	10.5	28.4	27.1	15.9	8.1	8.6	1.3	236,400
U.S.	12.1	17.8	19.5	14.4	10.5	19.1	6.5	303,400

Note: Figures are percentages except for median and cover owner-occupied housing units; (1) Figures cover the Louisville/Jefferson County, KY-IN Metropolitan Statistical Area
Source: U.S. Census Bureau, 2019-2023 American Community Survey 5-Year Estimates

Year Housing Structure Built

Area	2020 or Later	2010 -2019	2000 -2009	1990 -1999	1980 -1989	1970 -1979	1960 -1969	1950 -1959	1940 -1949	Before 1940	Median Year
City	0.8	7.7	11.8	10.4	6.9	13.0	12.7	14.2	6.6	15.9	1970
MSA[1]	1.1	8.4	13.5	13.4	9.3	14.8	11.1	11.7	5.1	11.6	1977
U.S.	1.2	8.9	13.6	12.8	13.0	14.4	10.0	9.7	4.5	11.9	1980

Note: Figures are percentages except for Median Year; Note: (1) Figures cover the Louisville/Jefferson County, KY-IN Metropolitan Statistical Area
Source: U.S. Census Bureau, 2019-2023 American Community Survey 5-Year Estimates

Gross Monthly Rent

Area	Under $500	$500 -$999	$1,000 -$1,499	$1,500 -$1,999	$2,000 -$2,499	$2,500 -$2,999	$3,000 and up	Median ($)
City	9.7	34.0	39.6	12.5	2.8	0.7	0.7	1,069
MSA[1]	9.1	34.6	40.1	12.2	2.6	0.7	0.8	1,064
U.S.	6.5	22.3	29.5	20.2	10.8	4.8	5.9	1,348

Note: Figures are percentages except for median; Gross rent is the contract rent plus the estimated average monthly cost of utilities (electricity, gas, and water and sewer) and fuels (oil, coal, kerosene, wood, etc.) if these are paid by the renter (or paid for the renter by someone else); (1) Figures cover the Louisville/Jefferson County, KY-IN Metropolitan Statistical Area
Source: U.S. Census Bureau, 2019-2023 American Community Survey 5-Year Estimates

HEALTH

Health Risk Factors

Category	MSA[1] (%)	U.S. (%)
Adults aged 18–64 who have any kind of health care coverage	n/a	90.8
Adults who reported being in good or better health	n/a	81.8
Adults who have been told they have high blood cholesterol	n/a	36.9
Adults who have been told they have high blood pressure	n/a	34.0
Adults who are current smokers	n/a	12.1
Adults who currently use e-cigarettes	n/a	7.7
Adults who currently use chewing tobacco, snuff, or snus	n/a	3.2
Adults who are heavy drinkers[2]	n/a	6.1
Adults who are binge drinkers[3]	n/a	15.2
Adults who are overweight (BMI 25.0 - 29.9)	n/a	34.4
Adults who are obese (BMI 30.0 - 99.8)	n/a	34.3
Adults who participated in any physical activities in the past month	n/a	75.8

Note: All figures are crude prevalence; (1) Figures for the Louisville/Jefferson County, KY-IN Metropolitan Statistical Area were not available.
(2) Heavy drinkers are classified as adult men having more than 14 drinks per week and adult women having more than 7 drinks per week; (3) Binge drinkers are classified as males having five or more drinks on one occasion or females having four or more drinks on one occasion
Source: Centers for Disease Control and Prevention, Behavioral Risk Factor Surveillance System, SMART: Selected Metropolitan Area Risk Trends, 2023

Acute and Chronic Health Conditions

Category	MSA[1] (%)	U.S. (%)
Adults who have ever been told they had a heart attack	n/a	4.2
Adults who have ever been told they have angina or coronary heart disease	n/a	4.0
Adults who have ever been told they had a stroke	n/a	3.3
Adults who have ever been told they have asthma	n/a	15.7
Adults who have ever been told they have arthritis	n/a	26.3
Adults who have ever been told they have diabetes[2]	n/a	11.5
Adults who have ever been told they had skin cancer	n/a	5.6
Adults who have ever been told they had any other types of cancer	n/a	8.4
Adults who have ever been told they have COPD	n/a	6.4
Adults who have ever been told they have kidney disease	n/a	3.7
Adults who have ever been told they have a form of depression	n/a	22.0

Note: All figures are crude prevalence; (1) Figures for the Louisville/Jefferson County, KY-IN Metropolitan Statistical Area were not available.
(2) Figures do not include pregnancy-related, borderline, or pre-diabetes
Source: Centers for Disease Control and Prevention, Behavioral Risk Factor Surveillance System, SMART: Selected Metropolitan Area Risk Trends, 2023

Health Screening and Vaccination Rates

Category	MSA[1] (%)	U.S. (%)
Adults who have ever been tested for HIV	n/a	37.5
Adults who have had their blood cholesterol checked within the last five years	n/a	87.0
Adults aged 65+ who have had flu shot within the past year	n/a	63.4
Adults aged 65+ who have ever had a pneumonia vaccination	n/a	71.9

Note: All figures are crude prevalence; (1) Figures for the Louisville/Jefferson County, KY-IN Metropolitan Statistical Area were not available.
Source: Centers for Disease Control and Prevention, Behavioral Risk Factor Surveillance System, SMART: Selected Metropolitan Area Risk Trends, 2023

Disability Status

Category	MSA[1] (%)	U.S. (%)
Adults who reported being deaf	n/a	7.4
Are you blind or have serious difficulty seeing, even when wearing glasses?	n/a	4.9
Do you have difficulty doing errands alone?	n/a	7.8
Do you have difficulty dressing or bathing?	n/a	3.6
Do you have serious difficulty concentrating/remembering/making decisions?	n/a	13.7
Do you have serious difficulty walking or climbing stairs?	n/a	13.2

Note: All figures are crude prevalence; (1) Figures for the Louisville/Jefferson County, KY-IN Metropolitan Statistical Area were not available.
Source: Centers for Disease Control and Prevention, Behavioral Risk Factor Surveillance System, SMART: Selected Metropolitan Area Risk Trends, 2023

Mortality Rates for the Top 10 Causes of Death in the U.S.

ICD-10[a] Sub-Chapter	ICD-10[a] Code	Crude Mortality Rate[2] per 100,000 population	
		County[3]	U.S.
Malignant neoplasms	C00-C97	206.8	182.7
Ischaemic heart diseases	I20-I25	77.3	109.6
Provisional assignment of new diseases of uncertain etiology[1]	U00-U49	67.6	65.3
Other forms of heart disease	I30-I51	84.1	65.1
Other degenerative diseases of the nervous system	G30-G31	49.0	52.4
Other external causes of accidental injury	W00-X59	92.6	52.3
Cerebrovascular diseases	I60-I69	43.0	49.1
Chronic lower respiratory diseases	J40-J47	50.5	43.5
Hypertensive diseases	I10-I15	72.9	38.9
Organic, including symptomatic, mental disorders	F01-F09	72.3	33.9

Note: (a) ICD-10 = International Classification of Diseases 10th Revision; (1) Includes COVID-19, adverse effects to COVID-19 vaccines, SARS, and vaping-related disorders; (2) Crude mortality rates are a three-year average covering 2021-2023; (3) Figures cover Jefferson County.
Source: Centers for Disease Control and Prevention, National Center for Health Statistics. National Vital Statistics System, Mortality 2018-2023 on CDC WONDER Online Database

Mortality Rates for Selected Causes of Death

Cause of Death	ICD-10[a] Code	Crude Mortality Rate[1] per 100,000 population	
		County[2]	U.S.
Accidental poisoning and exposure to noxious substances	X40-X49	68.1	30.5
Alzheimer disease	G30	21.8	35.4
Assault	X85-Y09	21.6	7.3
COVID-19	U07.1	67.6	65.3
Diabetes mellitus	E10-E14	30.0	30.0
Diseases of the liver	K70-K76	24.1	20.8
Human immunodeficiency virus (HIV) disease	B20-B24	2.2	1.5
Influenza and pneumonia	J09-J18	13.4	13.4
Intentional self-harm	X60-X84	17.9	14.7
Malnutrition	E40-E46	8.8	6.0
Obesity and other hyperalimentation	E65-E68	2.6	3.1
Renal failure	N17-N19	29.2	16.4
Transport accidents	V01-V99	17.1	14.4

Note: (a) ICD-10 = International Classification of Diseases 10th Revision; (1) Crude mortality rates are a three-year average covering 2021-2023; (2) Figures cover Jefferson County; Data are suppressed when the data meet the criteria for confidentiality constraints; Crude mortality rates are flagged as unreliable when the rate would be calculated with a numerator of 20 or less.
Source: Centers for Disease Control and Prevention, National Center for Health Statistics. National Vital Statistics System, Mortality 2018-2023 on CDC WONDER Online Database

Health Insurance Coverage

Area	With Health Insurance	With Private Health Insurance	With Public Health Insurance	Without Health Insurance	Population Under Age 19 Without Health Insurance
City	94.2	64.2	43.1	5.8	3.8
MSA[1]	94.7	69.5	38.9	5.3	3.6
U.S.	91.4	67.3	36.3	8.6	5.4

Note: Figures are percentages that cover the civilian noninstitutionalized population; (1) Figures cover the Louisville/Jefferson County, KY-IN Metropolitan Statistical Area
Source: U.S. Census Bureau, 2019-2023 American Community Survey 5-Year Estimates

Number of Medical Professionals

Area	MDs[3]	DOs[3,4]	Dentists	Podiatrists	Chiropractors	Optometrists
County[1] (number)	3,916	195	832	66	218	138
County[1] (rate[2])	506.3	25.2	107.8	8.5	28.2	17.9
U.S. (rate[2])	302.5	29.2	74.6	6.4	29.5	18.0

Note: Data as of 2023 unless noted; (1) Data covers Jefferson County; (2) Number of medical professionals per 100,000 population; (3) Data as of 2022 and includes all active, non-federal physicians; (4) Doctor of Osteopathic Medicine
Source: U.S. Department of Health and Human Services, Health Resources and Services Administration, Bureau of Health Professions, Area Resource File (ARF) 2023-2024

Best Hospitals

According to *U.S. News*, the Louisville/Jefferson County, KY-IN metro area is home to one of the best children's hospitals in the U.S.: **Norton Children's Hospital** (7 pediatric specialties). The hospital listed was highly ranked in at least one of 11 pediatric specialties. One hundred five children's hospitals in the U.S. were nationally ranked in at least one specialty. Hospitals received points for being ranked in a specialty, and the 10 hospitals with the most points across the 11 specialties make up the Honor Roll. *U.S. News Online, "America's Best Children's Hospitals 2024-25"*

EDUCATION

Public School District Statistics

District Name	Schls	Pupils	Pupil/ Teacher Ratio	Minority Pupils[1] (%)	Total Rev. per Pupil ($)	Total Exp. per Pupil ($)
Jefferson County	171	94,793	15.2	65.1	21,250	19,590

Note: Table includes school districts with 2,000 or more students; (1) Percentage of students that are not non-Hispanic white.
Source: U.S. Department of Education, National Center for Education Statistics, Common Core of Data, Local Education Agency (School District) Universe Survey: School Year 2023-2024; U.S. Department of Education, National Center for Education Statistics, Common Core of Data, School District Finance Survey (F-33): School Year 2021–22

Best High Schools

According to *U.S. News*, Louisville is home to three of the top 500 high schools in the U.S.: **Dupont Manual High School** (#87); **J. Graham Brown School** (#124); **Atherton High School** (#462). Nearly 25,000 public, magnet and charter schools were ranked based on their performance on state assessments and how well they prepare students for college. *U.S. News & World Report, "Best High Schools 2024"*

Highest Level of Education

Area	Less than H.S.	H.S. Diploma	Some College, No Deg.	Associate Degree	Bachelor's Degree	Master's Degree	Prof. School Degree	Doctorate Degree
City	9.5	27.7	21.0	8.4	19.9	9.6	2.4	1.5
MSA[1]	8.7	29.4	20.8	8.9	19.5	9.2	2.2	1.3
U.S.	10.6	26.2	19.4	8.8	21.3	9.8	2.3	1.6

Note: Figures cover persons age 25 and over; (1) Figures cover the Louisville/Jefferson County, KY-IN Metropolitan Statistical Area
Source: U.S. Census Bureau, 2019-2023 American Community Survey 5-Year Estimates

Educational Attainment by Race

Area	High School Graduate or Higher (%)					Bachelor's Degree or Higher (%)				
	Total	White	Black	Asian	Hisp.[2]	Total	White	Black	Asian	Hisp.[2]
City	90.5	92.9	87.6	83.3	78.7	33.4	37.4	20.2	56.1	27.5
MSA[1]	91.3	92.7	87.7	86.4	77.4	32.1	33.7	20.6	60.2	25.4
U.S.	89.4	92.9	88.1	88.0	72.5	35.0	37.7	24.7	57.0	19.9

Note: Figures shown cover persons 25 years old and over; (1) Figures cover the Louisville/Jefferson County, KY-IN Metropolitan Statistical Area; (2) People of Hispanic origin can be of any race
Source: U.S. Census Bureau, 2019-2023 American Community Survey 5-Year Estimates

School Enrollment by Grade and Control

Area	Preschool (%)		Kindergarten (%)		Grades 1 - 4 (%)		Grades 5 - 8 (%)		Grades 9 - 12 (%)	
	Public	Private	Public	Private	Public	Private	Public	Private	Public	Private
City	50.3	49.7	77.2	22.8	81.9	18.1	81.0	19.0	78.2	21.8
MSA[1]	53.0	47.0	79.7	20.3	81.8	18.2	82.4	17.6	81.0	19.0
U.S.	58.7	41.3	85.2	14.8	87.2	12.8	87.9	12.1	89.0	11.0

Note: Figures shown cover persons 3 years old and over; (1) Figures cover the Louisville/Jefferson County, KY-IN Metropolitan Statistical Area
Source: U.S. Census Bureau, 2019-2023 American Community Survey 5-Year Estimates

Higher Education

Four-Year Colleges			Two-Year Colleges			Medical Schools[1]	Law Schools[2]	Voc/ Tech[3]
Public	Private Non-profit	Private For-profit	Public	Private Non-profit	Private For-profit			
2	6	2	1	0	3	1	1	7

Note: Figures cover institutions located within the Louisville/Jefferson County, KY-IN Metropolitan Statistical Area and include main campuses only; (1) includes schools accredited by the Liaison Committee on Medical Education and the American Osteopathic Association's Commission on Osteopathic College Accreditation; (2) includes ABA-accredited schools, schools with provisional ABA accreditation, and state accredited schools; (3) includes all schools with programs that are less than 2 years.
Source: National Center for Education Statistics, Integrated Postsecondary Education System (IPEDS), 2023-24; Wikipedia, List of Medical Schools in the United States, accessed May 2, 2025; Wikipedia, List of Law Schools in the United States, accessed May 2, 2025

According to *U.S. News & World Report,* the Louisville/Jefferson County, KY-IN metro area is home to one of the top 200 national universities in the U.S.: **University of Louisville** (#179 tie). The indicators used to capture academic quality fall into a number of categories: assessment by administrators at peer institutions; retention of students; faculty resources; student selectivity; financial resources; alumni giving; high school counselor ratings of colleges; and graduation rate. *U.S. News & World Report, "America's Best Colleges 2025"*

EMPLOYERS

Major Employers

Company Name	Industry
Baptist Healthcare Systems	Healthcare
BF Cos./ERJ Dining	Restaurants
Catholic Archdiocese of Louisville	Schools/churches/related activities
Clark Memorial Hospital	Healthcare
Floyd Memorial Hospital & Health Services	Healthcare
Ford Motor Co.	Automotive manufacturer
GE Appliances & Lighting	Home appliance/lighting products
Horseshoe Southern Indiana	Entertainment
Humana	Health insurance
Jefferson County Public Schools	K-12 public education
Kentucky State Government	Government
KentuckyOne Health	Healthcare
Kindred Healthcare	Healthcare
LG&E and KU Energy	Utilities
Louisville/Jefferson County Metro Govt	Government
New Albany-Floyd County School Corp	K-12 public education
Norton Healthcare	Healthcare
Publishers Printing Co.	Printer
Robley Rex VA Medical Center	Healthcare
Securitas Security Services USA	Security services

Note: Companies shown are located within the Louisville/Jefferson County, KY-IN Metropolitan Statistical Area.
Source: Chambers of Commerce; State Departments of Labor; Wikipedia

Best Companies to Work For

Humana, headquartered in Louisville, is among "Best Workplaces in Health Care." To determine the Best Workplaces in Health Care list, Great Place To Work analyzed the survey responses of over 185,000 employees from Great Place To Work-Certified companies in the health care industry. Survey data analysis and company-provided datapoints are then factored into a combined score to compare and rank the companies that create the most consistently positive experience for all employees in this industry. *Fortune, "Best Workplaces in Health Care," 2024*

Norton Healthcare, headquartered in Louisville, is among the "Best Places to Work in IT." To qualify, companies had to have a minimum of 100 total employees and five IT employees. The best places to work were selected based on DEI (diversity, equity, and inclusion) practices; IT turnover, promotions, and growth; IT retention and engagement programs; remote/hybrid working; benefits and perks (such as elder care and child care, flextime, and reimbursement for college tuition); and training and career development opportunities. *Computerworld, "Best Places to Work in IT," 2025*

PUBLIC SAFETY

Crime Rate

Area	Total Crime Rate	Violent Crime Rate				Property Crime Rate		
		Murder	Rape	Robbery	Aggrav. Assault	Burglary	Larceny-Theft	Motor Vehicle Theft
City	4,385.4	22.9	32.7	148.2	561.8	498.8	2,104.4	1,016.8
U.S.	2,290.9	5.7	38.0	66.5	264.1	250.7	1,347.2	318.7

Note: Figures are crimes per 100,000 population.
Source: FBI, Table 8, Offenses Known to Law Enforcement, by State by City, 2023

Hate Crimes

Area	Number of Quarters Reported	Number of Incidents per Bias Motivation					
		Race/Ethnicity/Ancestry	Religion	Sexual Orientation	Disability	Gender	Gender Identity
City	4	16	4	7	0	0	2
U.S.	4	5,900	2,699	2,077	187	92	492

Source: Federal Bureau of Investigation, Hate Crime Statistics 2023

Identity Theft Consumer Reports

Area	Reports	Reports per 100,000 Population	Rank[2]
MSA[1]	2,653	195	168
U.S.	1,135,291	339	-

Note: (1) Figures cover the Louisville/Jefferson County, KY-IN Metropolitan Statistical Area; (2) Rank ranges from 1 to 401 where 1 indicates greatest number of identity theft reports per 100,000 population
Source: Federal Trade Commission, Consumer Sentinel Network Data Book 2024

Fraud and Other Consumer Reports

Area	Reports	Reports per 100,000 Population	Rank[2]
MSA[1]	14,501	1,065	180
U.S.	5,360,641	1,601	-

Note: (1) Figures cover the Louisville/Jefferson County, KY-IN Metropolitan Statistical Area; (2) Rank ranges from 1 to 401 where 1 indicates greatest number of fraud and other consumer reports per 100,000 population
Source: Federal Trade Commission, Consumer Sentinel Network Data Book 2024

POLITICS

2024 Presidential Election Results

Area	Trump (Rep.)	Harris (Dem.)	Stein (Green)	Kennedy (Ind.)	Oliver (Lib.)	Other
Jefferson County	40.6	57.1	0.6	0.7	0.3	0.6
U.S.	49.7	48.2	0.6	0.5	0.4	0.6

Note: Results are percentages and may not add to 100% due to rounding
Source: Dave Leip's Atlas of U.S. Presidential Elections

SPORTS

Professional Sports Teams

Team Name	League	Year Established

No teams are located in the metro area
Source: Wikipedia, Major Professional Sports Teams of the United States and Canada, May 1, 2025

CLIMATE

Average and Extreme Temperatures

Temperature	Jan	Feb	Mar	Apr	May	Jun	Jul	Aug	Sep	Oct	Nov	Dec	Yr.
Extreme High (°F)	77	77	86	91	95	102	105	101	104	92	84	76	105
Average High (°F)	41	46	56	68	77	85	88	87	80	69	56	45	67
Average Temp. (°F)	33	37	46	57	66	74	78	77	70	58	47	37	57
Average Low (°F)	25	27	36	46	55	64	68	66	59	47	37	29	46
Extreme Low (°F)	-20	-9	-1	22	31	42	50	46	33	23	-1	-15	-20

Note: Figures cover the years 1948-1990
Source: National Climatic Data Center, International Station Meteorological Climate Summary, 9/96

Average Precipitation/Snowfall/Humidity

Precip./Humidity	Jan	Feb	Mar	Apr	May	Jun	Jul	Aug	Sep	Oct	Nov	Dec	Yr.
Avg. Precip. (in.)	3.4	3.5	4.5	4.0	4.5	3.7	4.2	3.2	3.0	2.6	3.7	3.6	43.9
Avg. Snowfall (in.)	5	4	3	Tr	Tr	0	0	0	0	Tr	1	2	17
Avg. Rel. Hum. 7am (%)	78	78	75	75	79	80	82	85	86	84	79	78	80
Avg. Rel. Hum. 4pm (%)	62	58	52	49	52	53	55	53	53	51	57	62	55

Note: Figures cover the years 1948-1990; Tr = Trace amounts (<0.05 in. of rain; <0.5 in. of snow)
Source: National Climatic Data Center, International Station Meteorological Climate Summary, 9/96

Weather Conditions

Temperature			Daytime Sky			Precipitation		
10°F & below	32°F & below	90°F & above	Clear	Partly cloudy	Cloudy	0.01 inch or more precip.	0.1 inch or more snow/ice	Thunderstorms
8	90	35	82	143	140	125	15	45

Note: Figures are average number of days per year and cover the years 1948-1990
Source: National Climatic Data Center, International Station Meteorological Climate Summary, 9/96

HAZARDOUS WASTE

Superfund Sites

The Louisville/Jefferson County, KY-IN metro area is home to three sites on the EPA's Superfund National Priorities List (NPL) or Superfund Alternative Approach (SAA) list: **Distler Farm** (Final NPL); **Smith's Farm** (Final NPL); **Tri-city Disposal Co.** (Final NPL). The Superfund alternative approach uses the same investigation and cleanup process and standards that are used for sites listed on the National Priorities List. The SAA is an alternative to listing a site on the NPL; it is not an alternative to Superfund or the Superfund process. There are a total of 1,445 Superfund sites with a status of proposed or final on both lists in the United States. *U.S. Environmental Protection Agency, National Priorities List, May 1, 2025; U.S. Environmental Protection Agency, Superfund Alternative Approach Sites, May 1, 2025*

AIR QUALITY

Air Quality Trends: Ozone

	1990	1995	2000	2005	2010	2015	2020	2021	2022	2023
MSA[1]	0.082	0.091	0.087	0.083	0.076	0.071	0.063	0.064	0.063	0.072
U.S.	0.087	0.089	0.081	0.080	0.072	0.068	0.066	0.067	0.067	0.070

Note: (1) Data covers the Louisville/Jefferson County, KY-IN Metropolitan Statistical Area. The values shown are the composite ozone concentration averages among trend sites based on the highest fourth daily maximum 8-hour concentration in parts per million. These trends are based on sites having an adequate record of monitoring data during the trend period. Data from exceptional events are included.
Source: U.S. Environmental Protection Agency, Air Quality Monitoring Information, "Air Quality Trends by City, 1990-2023"

Air Quality Index

Area	Percent of Days when Air Quality was...[2]					AQI Statistics[2]	
	Good	Moderate	Unhealthy for Sensitive Groups	Unhealthy	Very Unhealthy	Maximum	Median
MSA[1]	32.1	62.2	5.5	0.3	0.0	182	55

Note: (1) Data covers the Louisville/Jefferson County, KY-IN Metropolitan Statistical Area; (2) Based on 365 days with AQI data in 2023. Air Quality Index (AQI) is an index for reporting daily air quality. EPA calculates the AQI for five major air pollutants regulated by the Clean Air Act: ground-level ozone, particle pollution (aka particulate matter), carbon monoxide, sulfur dioxide, and nitrogen dioxide. The AQI runs from 0 to 500. The higher the AQI value, the greater the level of air pollution and the greater the health concern. There are six AQI categories: "Good" AQI is between 0 and 50. Air quality is considered satisfactory; "Moderate" AQI is between 51 and 100. Air quality is acceptable; "Unhealthy for Sensitive Groups" When AQI values are between 101 and 150, members of sensitive groups may experience health effects; "Unhealthy" When AQI values are between 151 and 200 everyone may begin to experience health effects; "Very Unhealthy" AQI values between 201 and 300 trigger a health alert; "Hazardous" AQI values over 300 trigger warnings of emergency conditions (not shown).
Source: U.S. Environmental Protection Agency, Air Quality Index Report, 2023

Air Quality Index Pollutants

Area	Percent of Days when AQI Pollutant was...[2]					
	Carbon Monoxide	Nitrogen Dioxide	Ozone	Sulfur Dioxide	Particulate Matter 2.5	Particulate Matter 10
MSA[1]	0.0	0.5	28.2	(3)	71.2	0.0

Note: (1) Data covers the Louisville/Jefferson County, KY-IN Metropolitan Statistical Area; (2) Based on 365 days with AQI data in 2023. The Air Quality Index (AQI) is an index for reporting daily air quality. EPA calculates the AQI for five major air pollutants regulated by the Clean Air Act: ground-level ozone, particle pollution (also known as particulate matter), carbon monoxide, sulfur dioxide, and nitrogen dioxide. The AQI runs from 0 to 500. The higher the AQI value, the greater the level of air pollution and the greater the health concern; (3) Sulfur dioxide is no longer included in this table because SO_2 concentrations tend to be very localized and not necessarily representative of broad geographical areas like counties and CBSAs.
Source: U.S. Environmental Protection Agency, Air Quality Index Report, 2023

Maximum Air Pollutant Concentrations: Particulate Matter, Ozone, CO and Lead

	Particulate Matter 10 (ug/m^3)	Particulate Matter 2.5 Wtd AM (ug/m^3)	Particulate Matter 2.5 24-Hr (ug/m^3)	Ozone (ppm)	Carbon Monoxide (ppm)	Lead (ug/m^3)
MSA[1] Level	96	10.7	32	0.075	2	n/a
NAAQS[2]	150	15	35	0.075	9	0.15
Met NAAQS[2]	Yes	Yes	Yes	Yes	Yes	n/a

Note: (1) Data covers the Louisville/Jefferson County, KY-IN Metropolitan Statistical Area; Data from exceptional events are included; (2) National Ambient Air Quality Standards; ppm = parts per million; ug/m^3 = micrograms per cubic meter; n/a not available.
Concentrations: Particulate Matter 10 (coarse particulate)—highest second maximum 24-hour concentration; Particulate Matter 2.5 Wtd AM (fine particulate)—highest weighted annual mean concentration; Particulate Matter 2.5 24-Hour (fine particulate)—highest 98th percentile 24-hour concentration; Ozone—highest fourth daily maximum 8-hour concentration; Carbon Monoxide—highest second maximum non-overlapping 8-hour concentration; Lead—maximum running 3-month average
Source: U.S. Environmental Protection Agency, Air Quality Monitoring Information, "Air Quality Statistics by City, 2023"

Maximum Air Pollutant Concentrations: Nitrogen Dioxide and Sulfur Dioxide

	Nitrogen Dioxide AM (ppb)	Nitrogen Dioxide 1-Hr (ppb)	Sulfur Dioxide AM (ppb)	Sulfur Dioxide 1-Hr (ppb)	Sulfur Dioxide 24-Hr (ppb)
MSA[1] Level	13	47	n/a	13	n/a
NAAQS[2]	53	100	30	75	140
Met NAAQS[2]	Yes	Yes	n/a	Yes	n/a

Note: (1) Data covers the Louisville/Jefferson County, KY-IN Metropolitan Statistical Area; Data from exceptional events are included; (2) National Ambient Air Quality Standards; ppm = parts per million; ug/m^3 = micrograms per cubic meter; n/a not available.
Concentrations: Nitrogen Dioxide AM—highest arithmetic mean concentration; Nitrogen Dioxide 1-Hr—highest 98th percentile 1-hour daily maximum concentration; Sulfur Dioxide AM—highest annual mean concentration; Sulfur Dioxide 1-Hr—highest 99th percentile 1-hour daily maximum concentration; Sulfur Dioxide 24-Hr—highest second maximum 24-hour concentration
Source: U.S. Environmental Protection Agency, Air Quality Monitoring Information, "Air Quality Statistics by City, 2023"

Manchester, New Hampshire

Background

Manchester, the largest city in northern New England, lies along the Merrimack River in the southern part of the "Live Free or Die" state. Fifty-one miles northwest of Boston, Manchester is the region's major financial and manufacturing center and a main stop on the way to New Hampshire's many vacation resorts.

Amoskeag Falls, on the Merrimack, had been an important Penacook Indian fishing site for many years prior to the arrival of the first Europeans, who came in 1636 on instructions from Massachusetts Governor John Winthrop. A schoolhouse was built in 1650 by the missionary John Elliot, but for many years the European population was limited to a small number of hunters, trappers, and fishermen. The first permanent settlement was established in 1722 by a tiny group from the Massachusetts Bay Colony. The town was known by a variety of names, including Old Harrytown, Tyngstown, and Derryfield.

For many years "Derryfield's" fortunes depended on lumber and fishing, but in 1810, cotton mills relying on waterpower from the Merrimack River became an economic mainstay. Though the town's population was then only 615, a local resident, Judge Samuel Blodgett, predicted that it would eventually grow to become a mighty center of industry, like England's Manchester. The name change was a result of this unlikely prediction, and by 1846, the new American Manchester had grown to a population of more than 10,000.

Manchester's early industrial history is inextricably linked to the history of the Amoskeag Manufacturing Company, whose 64 mills lined the banks of the river with what was the world's largest cotton milling operation. As Amoskeag thrived, so did Manchester. By the 1920s, however, Amoskeag had lost its leading edge, with obsolete machinery and alternatives to cotton, like silk and rayon. It declared bankruptcy in 1935, paving the way for cheaper facilities, particularly in the Southern states, causing a decline in Manchester's jobs and population.

By the mid-1990s, Manchester recovered from its Depression-era difficulties to become the nation's fastest-growing city. A development company bought up the old mill buildings, restoring and adapting them to new commercial and residential uses. But the changes were not merely cosmetic; considering a lesson well-learned from its single-industry past, Manchester's economic renaissance was finely calibrated to fit in with regional and national trends.

The Neighborhood Initiative program has included streetscapes, infrastructure improvements and continued development of the Amoskeag Mill. The city's downtown includes the tallest buildings north of Cambridge, MA. In 2022, Manchester launched NAACP-Community Loan Fund initiative to offer assistance, training, and financing to support the city's minority-owned businesses.

The economic attractiveness of the city today, and its overall affordability, is enhanced by New Hampshire's unique reluctance to institute any sales or income tax. Manchester has been recognized as "tax friendly" and one of the best places in America to launch a business. The city is home to Segway, Inc., manufacturers of the two-wheeled, self-balancing electric vehicle, as well as headquarters for Bank of America and Citizens Bank.

The city is served by the Manchester-Boston Regional Airport, one of the nation's fastest-growing, serving 168,000 passengers in 2024. With its recent 74,000-square-foot addition, airport traffic continues to increase. In 2021, city leaders supported a downtown hybrid passenger rail station.

The cultural assets of Manchester include the Currier Museum of Art, and the New Hampshire Institute of Art. Another major attraction is the Manchester Historical Association's Millyard Museum founded in 1896. Institutions of higher education convenient to Manchester include St. Anselm College, Southern New Hampshire University, Franklin Pierce College, and the University of New Hampshire at Manchester, as well as a community college. SNHU's Arena is the centerpiece of the city's downtown, hosting concerts and other events.

Manchester has a four-season humid continental climate, with long, cold, snowy winters, and very warm and somewhat humid summers; spring and fall are crisp and relatively brief transitions. Precipitation is well-spread throughout the year, though winter is the driest season while early spring tends to be the wettest.

Rankings

General Rankings

- In their annual survey, Livability.com looked at data for more than 2,000 mid-sized U.S. cities to assign a "Livability Score"for each. The top 100 scoring cities make up Livability's "Top 100 Best Places to Live in the U.S." in 2025. Manchester was placed among the top 100 of the customizable list. Criteria: housing and economy; cost of living; environment; education; health care options; transportation; safety; and community amenities. *Livability.com, "Top 100 Best Places to Live in the U.S. in 2025" April 15, 2025*

Business/Finance Rankings

- The Manchester metro area appeared on the Milken Institute "2025 Best Performing Cities" list. Rank: #57 out of 200 large metro areas (based on performance category). Criteria: job growth; wage growth; high-tech growth and impact; community resilience; housing affordability; household broadband access. *Milken Institute, "Best-Performing Cities 2025," January 14, 2025*

Education Rankings

- Personal finance website *WalletHub* analyzed the 150 largest U.S. metropolitan statistical areas to determine where the most educated Americans are putting their degrees to work. Criteria: education levels; percentage of workers with degrees; education quality and attainment gap; public school quality rankings; quality and enrollment of each metro area's universities. Manchester was ranked #34 (#1 = most educated city). *WalletHub.com, "Most & Least Educated Cities in America, 2025" July 2, 2024*

Environmental Rankings

- *Niche* compiled a list of the nation's snowiest cities, based on the National Oceanic and Atmospheric Administration's 30-year average snowfall data. Among cities with a population of at least 50,000, Manchester ranked #23. *Niche.com, Top 25 Snowiest Cities in America, December 10, 2018*

Real Estate Rankings

- *WalletHub* compared the most populated U.S. cities to determine which had the best markets for real estate agents. Manchester ranked #31 where demand was high and pay was the best. Criteria: sales per agent; annual median wage for real-estate agents; monthly average starting salary for real estate agents; real estate job density and competition; unemployment rate; home turnover rate; housing-market health index; and other relevant metrics. *WalletHub.com, "2021 Best Places to Be a Real Estate Agent," May 12, 2021*

- The Manchester metro area was identified as one of the nations's 20 hottest housing markets in 2025. Criteria: unique listing views as an indicator of demand and number of days on the market as an indicator of pace. The area ranked #1. *Realtor.com, "January 2025 Top 20 Hottest Housing Markets," February 11, 2025*

- Manchester was ranked #139 out of 176 metro areas in terms of cost of housing in 2024 by the National Association of Home Builders (#1 = most affordable). Criteria: the portion of an average family's income necessary to pay the mortgage on a median-priced home. *National Association of Home Builders®, NAHB-Wells Fargo Cost of Housing Index, 4th Quarter 2024*

Women/Minorities Rankings

- Personal finance website *WalletHub* compared more than 180 U.S. cities across two key dimensions, "Hispanic Business-Friendliness" and "Hispanic Purchasing Power," to arrive at the most favorable conditions for Hispanic entrepreneurs. Manchester was ranked #153 out of 182. Criteria includes: share of Hispanic-Owned Businesses; average growth of Hispanic Business revenues; Small Business-Friendliness score; affordability; and number of Hispanics with at least a bachelor's degree. *WalletHub.com, "Best Cities for Hispanic Entrepreneurs," September 4, 2024*

Miscellaneous Rankings

- *WalletHub* compared 148 of the most populated U.S. cities to determine their operating efficiency. A "Quality of Services" score was constructed for each city and then measured against the total budget per capita to reveal which were managed the best. Manchester ranked #18. Criteria: financial stability; economy; education; safety; health; infrastructure and pollution. *WalletHub.com, "2025's Best- & Worst-Run Cities in America," June 18, 2024*

Business Environment

DEMOGRAPHICS

Population Growth

Area	1990 Census	2000 Census	2010 Census	2020 Census	2023 Estimate[2]	Population Growth 1990-2023 (%)
City	99,567	107,006	109,565	115,644	115,415	15.9
MSA[1]	336,073	380,841	400,721	422,937	424,732	26.4
U.S.	248,709,873	281,421,906	308,745,538	331,449,281	332,387,540	33.6

Note: (1) Figures cover the Manchester-Nashua, NH Metropolitan Statistical Area; (2) 2019-2023 5-year ACS population estimate
Source: U.S. Census Bureau, 1990 Census, 2000 Census, 2010 Census, 2020 Census, 2019-2023 American Community Survey 5-Year Estimates

Race

Area	White Alone[2] (%)	Black Alone[2] (%)	Asian Alone[2] (%)	AIAN[3] Alone[2] (%)	NHOPI[4] Alone[2] (%)	Other Race Alone[2] (%)	Two or More Races (%)
City	76.7	5.3	4.6	0.2	0.0	3.2	10.0
MSA[1]	83.3	2.6	4.2	0.1	0.0	2.1	7.7
U.S.	63.4	12.4	5.8	0.9	0.2	6.6	10.7

Note: (1) Figures cover the Manchester-Nashua, NH Metropolitan Statistical Area; (2) Alone is defined as not being in combination with one or more other races; (3) American Indian and Alaska Native; (4) Native Hawaiian and Other Pacific Islander
Source: U.S. Census Bureau, 2019-2023 American Community Survey 5-Year Estimates

Hispanic or Latino Origin

Area	Total (%)	Mexican (%)	Puerto Rican (%)	Cuban (%)	Other (%)
City	13.4	1.5	4.4	0.1	7.4
MSA[1]	8.3	1.2	2.6	0.2	4.2
U.S.	19.0	11.3	1.8	0.7	5.2

Note: Persons of Hispanic or Latino origin can be of any race; (1) Figures cover the Manchester-Nashua, NH Metropolitan Statistical Area
Source: U.S. Census Bureau, 2019-2023 American Community Survey 5-Year Estimates

Age

Area	Percent of Population									Median Age
	Under Age 5	Age 5–19	Age 20–34	Age 35–44	Age 45–54	Age 55–64	Age 65–74	Age 75–84	Age 85+	
City	4.9	15.1	25.7	13.8	11.6	13.7	8.7	4.6	2.0	37.9
MSA[1]	5.1	17.1	20.1	12.9	13.2	15.0	10.1	4.8	1.8	41.0
U.S.	5.7	19.1	20.2	13.1	12.3	12.8	10.0	4.9	1.9	38.7

Note: (1) Figures cover the Manchester-Nashua, NH Metropolitan Statistical Area
Source: U.S. Census Bureau, 2019-2023 American Community Survey 5-Year Estimates

Disability by Age

Area	All Ages	Under 18 Years Old	18 to 64 Years Old	65 Years and Over
City	13.6	7.4	11.5	31.1
MSA[1]	11.7	4.7	9.6	28.3
U.S.	13.0	4.7	10.7	32.9

Note: Figures show percent of the civilian noninstitutionalized population that reported having a disability. Disability status is determined from six types of difficulty: vision, hearing, cognitive, ambulatory, self-care, and independent living. For children under 5 years old, hearing and vision difficulty are used to determine disability status. For children between the ages of 5 and 14, disability status is determined from hearing, vision, cognitive, ambulatory, and self-care difficulties. For people aged 15 years and older, they are considered to have a disability if they have difficulty with any one of the six difficulty types; Note: (1) Figures cover the Manchester-Nashua, NH Metropolitan Statistical Area
Source: U.S. Census Bureau, 2019-2023 American Community Survey 5-Year Estimates

Ancestry

Area	German	Irish	English	American	Italian	Polish	French[2]	European	Scottish
City	6.5	18.5	10.0	3.0	8.7	3.6	10.5	0.8	2.3
MSA[1]	8.0	20.6	14.5	3.4	9.9	3.8	10.8	1.3	3.0
U.S.	12.6	9.4	9.1	5.5	4.9	2.6	2.0	1.6	1.6

Note: Figures are the percentage of the total population reporting a particular ancestry. The nine most commonly reported ancestries in the U.S. are shown. Figures include multiple ancestries (e.g. if a person reported being Irish and Italian, they were included in both columns); (1) Figures cover the Manchester-Nashua, NH Metropolitan Statistical Area; (2) Excludes Basque
Source: U.S. Census Bureau, 2019-2023 American Community Survey 5-Year Estimates

Foreign-born Population

Area	Percent of Population Born in								
	Any Foreign Country	Asia	Mexico	Europe	Caribbean	Central America[2]	South America	Africa	Canada
City	14.7	3.8	0.4	2.2	2.0	2.1	1.0	2.1	1.0
MSA[1]	10.4	3.4	0.4	1.7	1.4	0.8	0.9	0.9	0.8
U.S.	13.9	4.3	3.3	1.4	1.4	1.2	1.2	0.8	0.2

Note: (1) Figures cover the Manchester-Nashua, NH Metropolitan Statistical Area; (2) Excludes Mexico.
Source: U.S. Census Bureau, 2019-2023 American Community Survey 5-Year Estimates

Household Size

Area	Persons in Household (%)							Average Household Size
	One	Two	Three	Four	Five	Six	Seven or More	
City	34.5	34.2	14.7	10.7	3.7	1.7	0.5	2.27
MSA[1]	27.2	35.8	16.5	13.1	4.9	1.7	0.8	2.48
U.S.	28.5	33.8	15.4	12.7	5.9	2.3	1.4	2.54

Note: (1) Figures cover the Manchester-Nashua, NH Metropolitan Statistical Area
Source: U.S. Census Bureau, 2019-2023 American Community Survey 5-Year Estimates

Household Relationships

Area	Householder	Opposite-sex Spouse	Same-sex Spouse	Opposite-sex Unmarried Partner	Same-sex Unmarried Partner	Child[2]	Grandchild	Other Relatives	Non-relatives
City	42.5	14.9	0.3	4.3	0.2	24.3	1.6	4.3	4.7
MSA[1]	39.7	19.2	0.3	3.2	0.1	27.2	1.6	3.5	3.2
U.S.	38.3	17.5	0.2	2.5	0.2	28.3	2.4	4.8	3.4

Note: Figures are percent of the total population; (1) Figures cover the Manchester-Nashua, NH Metropolitan Statistical Area; (2) Includes biological, adopted, and stepchildren of the householder
Source: U.S. Census Bureau, 2020 Census

Gender

Area	Males	Females	Males per 100 Females
City	57,084	58,331	97.9
MSA[1]	212,913	211,819	100.5
U.S.	164,545,087	167,842,453	98.0

Note: (1) Figures cover the Manchester-Nashua, NH Metropolitan Statistical Area
Source: U.S. Census Bureau, 2019-2023 American Community Survey 5-Year Estimates

Marital Status

Area	Never Married	Now Married[2]	Separated	Widowed	Divorced
City	39.0	39.6	1.6	5.5	14.3
MSA[1]	32.0	49.8	1.1	5.2	11.8
U.S.	34.1	47.9	1.7	5.6	10.7

Note: Figures are percentages and cover the population 15 years of age and older; (1) Figures cover the Manchester-Nashua, NH Metropolitan Statistical Area; (2) Excludes separated
Source: U.S. Census Bureau, 2019-2023 American Community Survey 5-Year Estimates

Religious Groups by Family

Area	Catholic	Baptist	Methodist	LDS[2]	Pentecostal	Lutheran	Islam	Adventist	Other
MSA[1]	16.3	0.6	0.6	0.6	0.3	0.3	0.1	0.8	8.1
U.S.	18.7	7.3	3.0	2.0	1.8	1.7	1.3	1.3	11.6

Note: Figures are the number of adherents as a percentage of the total population and cover the eight largest religious groups in the U.S; (1) Figures cover the Manchester-Nashua, NH Metropolitan Statistical Area; (2) Church of Jesus Christ of Latter-day Saints
Sources: 2020 U.S. Religion Census, Association of Statisticians of American Religious Bodies; The Association of Religion Data Archives (ARDA)

Religious Groups by Tradition

Area	Catholic	Evangelical Protestant	Mainline Protestant	Black Protestant	Islam	Judaism	Hinduism	Orthodox	Buddhism
MSA[1]	16.3	5.8	2.7	n/a	0.1	0.3	<0.1	0.9	n/a
U.S.	18.7	16.5	5.2	2.3	1.3	0.6	0.4	0.4	0.3

Note: Figures are the number of adherents as a percentage of the total population; (1) Figures cover the Manchester-Nashua, NH Metropolitan Statistical Area
Sources: 2020 U.S. Religion Census, Association of Statisticians of American Religious Bodies; The Association of Religion Data Archives (ARDA)

ECONOMY

Real Gross Domestic Product (GDP)

Area	2017	2018	2019	2020	2021	2022	2023	Rank[3]
MSA[1]	26.0	26.5	27.2	27.0	29.5	30.0	30.5	108
U.S.[2]	17,619.1	18,160.7	18,642.5	18,238.9	19,387.6	19,896.6	20,436.3	—

Note: Figures are in billions of chained 2017 dollars; (1) Figures cover the Manchester-Nashua, NH Metropolitan Statistical Area; (2) Figures cover real GDP within metropolitan areas; (3) Rank is based on 2023 data and ranges from 1 to 384
Source: U.S. Bureau of Economic Analysis

Economic Growth

Area	2014	2015	2016	2017	2018	2019	2020	2021	2022	2023
MSA[1]	2.2	3.4	1.6	0.4	1.9	3.0	-0.9	9.3	1.7	1.6
U.S.[2]	2.6	3.2	2.0	2.7	3.1	2.7	-2.2	6.3	2.6	2.7

Note: Figures are real gross domestic product growth rates and represent percent change from preceding period; (1) Figures cover the Manchester-Nashua, NH Metropolitan Statistical Area; (2) Figures are the average growth rates within metropolitan areas
Source: U.S. Bureau of Economic Analysis

Metropolitan Area Exports

Area	2018	2019	2020	2021	2022	2023	Rank[2]
MSA[1]	1,651.4	1,587.1	1,704.9	2,077.6	2,349.8	2,416.7	101
U.S.	1,664,056.1	1,645,173.7	1,431,406.6	1,753,941.4	2,062,937.4	2,019,160.5	—

Note: Figures are in millions of dollars; (1) Figures cover the Manchester-Nashua, NH Metropolitan Statistical Area; (2) Rank is based on 2023 data and ranges from 1 to 386
Source: U.S. Department of Commerce, International Trade Administration, Office of Trade and Economic Analysis, Industry and Analysis, Exports by Metropolitan Area, data extracted April 2, 2025

Building Permits

Area	Single-Family			Multi-Family			Total		
	2023	2024	Pct. Chg.	2023	2024	Pct. Chg.	2023	2024	Pct. Chg.
City	99	26	-73.7	280	167	-40.4	379	193	-49.1
MSA[1]	532	427	-19.7	850	445	-47.6	1,382	872	-36.9
U.S.	920,000	981,900	6.7	591,100	496,100	-16.1	1,511,100	1,478,000	-2.2

Note: (1) Figures cover the Manchester-Nashua, NH Metropolitan Statistical Area; Figures represent new, privately-owned housing units authorized (unadjusted data)
Source: U.S. Census Bureau, Building Permits Survey (BPS), 2023, 2024

Bankruptcy Filings

Area	Business Filings			Nonbusiness Filings		
	2023	2024	% Chg.	2023	2024	% Chg.
Hillsborough County	8	21	162.5	235	298	26.8
U.S.	18,926	23,107	22.1	434,064	494,201	13.9

Note: Business filings include Chapter 7, Chapter 9, Chapter 11, Chapter 12, Chapter 13, Chapter 15, and Section 304; Nonbusiness filings include Chapter 7, Chapter 11, and Chapter 13
Source: Administrative Office of the U.S. Courts, Business and Nonbusiness Bankruptcy, County Cases Commenced by Chapter of the Bankruptcy Code, During the 12-Month Period Ending December 31, 2023 and Business and Nonbusiness Bankruptcy, County Cases Commenced by Chapter of the Bankruptcy Code, During the 12-Month Period Ending December 31, 2024

Housing Vacancy Rates

Area	Gross Vacancy Rate[3] (%)			Year-Round Vacancy Rate[4] (%)			Rental Vacancy Rate[5] (%)			Homeowner Vacancy Rate[6] (%)		
	2022	2023	2024	2022	2023	2024	2022	2023	2024	2022	2023	2024
MSA[1]	n/a	n/a	n/a	n/a	n/a	n/a	n/a	n/a	n/a	n/a	n/a	n/a
U.S.[2]	9.1	9.0	9.1	7.5	7.5	7.6	5.7	6.5	6.8	0.8	0.8	1.0

Note: (1) Figures cover the Manchester-Nashua, NH Metropolitan Statistical Area; (2) Figures cover the 75 largest Metropolitan Statistical Areas; (3) The percentage of the total housing inventory that is vacant; (4) The percentage of the housing inventory (excluding seasonal units) that is year-round vacant; (5) The percentage of rental inventory that is vacant for rent; (6) The percentage of homeowner inventory that is vacant for sale; n/a not available
Source: U.S. Census Bureau, Housing Vacancies and Homeownership Annual Statistics: 2022, 2023, 2024

INCOME

Income

Area	Per Capita ($)	Median Household ($)	Average Household ($)
City	44,220	77,415	100,102
MSA[1]	52,243	100,436	128,567
U.S.	43,289	78,538	110,491

Note: (1) Figures cover the Manchester-Nashua, NH Metropolitan Statistical Area
Source: U.S. Census Bureau, 2019-2023 American Community Survey 5-Year Estimates

Household Income Distribution

Area	Percent of Households Earning							
	Under $15,000	$15,000 -$24,999	$25,000 -$34,999	$35,000 -$49,999	$50,000 -$74,999	$75,000 -$99,999	$100,000 -$149,999	$150,000 and up
City	6.0	6.9	5.7	11.7	18.0	14.3	19.3	18.1
MSA[1]	4.5	4.5	4.6	8.8	14.6	12.8	19.9	30.3
U.S.	8.5	6.6	6.8	10.4	15.7	12.7	17.4	21.9

Note: (1) Figures cover the Manchester-Nashua, NH Metropolitan Statistical Area
Source: U.S. Census Bureau, 2019-2023 American Community Survey 5-Year Estimates

Poverty Rate

Area	All Ages	Under 18 Years Old	18 to 64 Years Old	65 Years and Over
City	10.7	17.2	9.3	9.5
MSA[1]	6.5	8.1	6.0	6.7
U.S.	12.4	16.3	11.6	10.4

Note: Figures are percentage of people whose income during the past 12 months was below the poverty level; (1) Figures cover the Manchester-Nashua, NH Metropolitan Statistical Area
Source: U.S. Census Bureau, 2019-2023 American Community Survey 5-Year Estimates

EMPLOYMENT

Labor Force and Employment

Area	Civilian Labor Force			Workers Employed		
	Dec. 2023	Dec. 2024	% Chg.	Dec. 2023	Dec. 2024	% Chg.
City	64,039	66,140	3.3	62,588	64,103	2.4
MSA[1]	238,986	245,151	2.6	233,791	237,759	1.7
U.S.	166,661,000	167,746,000	0.7	160,754,000	161,294,000	0.3

Note: Data is not seasonally adjusted and covers workers 16 years of age and older; (1) Figures cover the Manchester-Nashua, NH Metropolitan Statistical Area
Source: Bureau of Labor Statistics, Local Area Unemployment Statistics

Unemployment Rate

Area	2024											
	Jan.	Feb.	Mar.	Apr.	May	Jun.	Jul.	Aug.	Sep.	Oct.	Nov.	Dec.
City	2.8	3.1	2.9	2.5	2.4	2.7	3.0	2.9	2.5	2.6	3.2	3.1
MSA[1]	2.7	3.0	2.9	2.4	2.3	2.6	3.0	2.9	2.5	2.6	3.1	3.0
U.S.	4.1	4.2	3.9	3.5	3.7	4.3	4.5	4.4	3.9	3.9	4.0	3.8

Note: Data is not seasonally adjusted and covers workers 16 years of age and older; (1) Figures cover the Manchester-Nashua, NH Metropolitan Statistical Area
Source: Bureau of Labor Statistics, Local Area Unemployment Statistics

Average Wages

Occupation	$/Hr.	Occupation	$/Hr.
Accountants and Auditors	42.84	Maintenance and Repair Workers	26.41
Automotive Mechanics	28.99	Marketing Managers	79.04
Bookkeepers	25.41	Network and Computer Systems Admin.	50.29
Carpenters	28.98	Nurses, Licensed Practical	34.71
Cashiers	14.89	Nurses, Registered	44.26
Computer Programmers	41.19	Nursing Assistants	22.36
Computer Systems Analysts	52.98	Office Clerks, General	24.15
Computer User Support Specialists	34.06	Physical Therapists	44.89
Construction Laborers	22.66	Physicians	148.76
Cooks, Restaurant	18.60	Plumbers, Pipefitters and Steamfitters	31.71
Customer Service Representatives	23.92	Police and Sheriff's Patrol Officers	36.87
Dentists	77.22	Postal Service Mail Carriers	29.69
Electricians	30.59	Real Estate Sales Agents	25.56
Engineers, Electrical	70.89	Retail Salespersons	18.32
Fast Food and Counter Workers	14.45	Sales Representatives, Technical/Scientific	57.21
Financial Managers	76.66	Secretaries, Exc. Legal/Medical/Executive	22.59
First-Line Supervisors of Office Workers	37.63	Security Guards	22.02
General and Operations Managers	74.48	Surgeons	n/a
Hairdressers/Cosmetologists	18.36	Teacher Assistants, Exc. Postsecondary[1]	18.04
Home Health and Personal Care Aides	18.05	Teachers, Secondary School, Exc. Sp. Ed.[1]	34.04
Janitors and Cleaners	18.24	Telemarketers	15.89
Landscaping/Groundskeeping Workers	21.01	Truck Drivers, Heavy/Tractor-Trailer	27.49
Lawyers	90.60	Truck Drivers, Light/Delivery Services	22.94
Maids and Housekeeping Cleaners	16.93	Waiters and Waitresses	21.07

Note: Wage data covers the Manchester-Nashua, NH Metropolitan Statistical Area; (1) Hourly wages were calculated from annual wage data based on a 40 hour work week
Source: Bureau of Labor Statistics, Metro Area Occupational Employment & Wage Estimates, May 2024

Employment by Industry

Sector	MSA[1]		U.S.
	Number of Employees	Percent of Total	Percent of Total
Construction, Mining, and Logging	9,100	4.3	5.5
Financial Activities	11,700	5.6	5.8
Government	22,700	10.8	14.9
Information	5,000	2.4	1.9
Leisure and Hospitality	19,000	9.0	10.4
Manufacturing	25,200	12.0	8.0
Other Services	8,000	3.8	3.7
Private Education and Health Services	42,200	20.1	16.9
Professional and Business Services	29,700	14.1	14.2
Retail Trade	26,200	12.5	10.0
Transportation, Warehousing, and Utilities	5,000	2.4	4.8
Wholesale Trade	6,600	3.1	3.9

Note: Figures are non-farm employment as of December 2024. Figures are not seasonally adjusted and include workers 16 years of age and older; (1) Figures cover the Manchester-Nashua, NH Metropolitan Statistical Area
Source: Bureau of Labor Statistics, Current Employment Statistics, Employment, Hours, and Earnings

Employment by Occupation

Occupation Classification	City (%)	MSA[1] (%)	U.S. (%)
Management, Business, Science, and Arts	38.0	46.0	42.0
Natural Resources, Construction, and Maintenance	7.9	8.3	8.6
Production, Transportation, and Material Moving	15.5	12.5	13.0
Sales and Office	22.3	20.1	19.9
Service	16.3	13.1	16.5

Note: Figures cover employed civilians 16 years of age and older; (1) Figures cover the Manchester-Nashua, NH Metropolitan Statistical Area
Source: U.S. Census Bureau, 2019-2023 American Community Survey 5-Year Estimates

Occupations with Greatest Projected Employment Growth: 2022 – 2032

Occupation[1]	2022 Employment	2032 Projected Employment	Numeric Employment Change	Percent Employment Change
Software Developers	8,520	10,880	2,360	27.7
Home Health and Personal Care Aides	8,760	10,780	2,020	23.1
Cooks, Restaurant	6,380	8,150	1,770	27.7
Stockers and Order Fillers	14,480	15,980	1,500	10.4
General and Operations Managers	17,320	18,580	1,260	7.3
Fast Food and Counter Workers	13,650	14,560	910	6.7
Registered Nurses	13,690	14,600	910	6.6
Financial Managers	4,340	5,190	850	19.6
Light Truck or Delivery Services Drivers	5,610	6,380	770	13.7
Nurse Practitioners	1,520	2,290	770	50.7

Note: Projections cover New Hampshire; (1) Sorted by numeric employment change
Source: www.projectionscentral.org, State Occupational Projections, 2022–2032 Long-Term Projections

Fastest-Growing Occupations: 2022 – 2032

Occupation[1]	2022 Employment	2032 Projected Employment	Numeric Employment Change	Percent Employment Change
Nurse Practitioners	1,520	2,290	770	50.7
Data Scientists	640	900	260	40.6
Information Security Analysts (SOC 2018)	680	930	250	36.8
Physician Assistants	970	1,260	290	29.9
Physical Therapist Assistants	370	480	110	29.7
Cooks, Restaurant	6,380	8,150	1,770	27.7
Software Developers	8,520	10,880	2,360	27.7
Operations Research Analysts	470	590	120	25.5
Taxi Drivers	790	990	200	25.3
Software Quality Assurance Analysts and Testers	1,040	1,290	250	24.0

Note: Projections cover New Hampshire; (1) Sorted by percent employment change and excludes occupations with numeric employment change less than 50
Source: www.projectionscentral.org, State Occupational Projections, 2022–2032 Long-Term Projections

CITY FINANCES

City Government Finances

Component	2022 ($000)	2022 ($ per capita)
Total Revenues	384,553	3,417
Total Expenditures	522,089	4,639
Debt Outstanding	443,016	3,936

Source: U.S. Census Bureau, State & Local Government Finances 2022

City Government Revenue by Source

Source	2022 ($000)	2022 ($ per capita)	2022 (%)
General Revenue			
From Federal Government	19,638	174	5.1
From State Government	128,681	1,143	33.5
From Local Governments	1,502	13	0.4
Taxes			
Property	128,284	1,140	33.4
Sales and Gross Receipts	1,718	15	0.4
Personal Income	0	0	0.0
Corporate Income	0	0	0.0
Motor Vehicle License	0	0	0.0
Other Taxes	3,636	32	0.9
Current Charges	68,647	610	17.9
Liquor Store	0	0	0.0
Utility	24,841	221	6.5

Source: U.S. Census Bureau, State & Local Government Finances 2022

City Government Expenditures by Function

Function	2022 ($000)	2022 ($ per capita)	2022 (%)
General Direct Expenditures			
Air Transportation	32,185	286	6.2
Corrections	0	0	0.0
Education	207,660	1,845	39.8
Employment Security Administration	0	0	0.0
Financial Administration	2,683	23	0.5
Fire Protection	21,384	190	4.1
General Public Buildings	0	0	0.0
Governmental Administration, Other	7,785	69	1.5
Health	4,334	38	0.8
Highways	28,905	256	5.5
Hospitals	0	0	0.0
Housing and Community Development	4,147	36	0.8
Interest on General Debt	10,206	90	2.0
Judicial and Legal	0	0	0.0
Libraries	2,154	19	0.4
Parking	1,813	16	0.3
Parks and Recreation	13,666	121	2.6
Police Protection	27,991	248	5.4
Public Welfare	1,887	16	0.4
Sewerage	34,778	309	6.7
Solid Waste Management	0	0	0.0
Veterans' Services	0	0	0.0
Liquor Store	0	0	0.0
Utility	47,235	419	9.0

Source: U.S. Census Bureau, State & Local Government Finances 2022

TAXES

State Corporate Income Tax Rates

State	Tax Rate (%)	Income Brackets ($)	Num. of Brackets	Financial Institution Tax Rate (%)[a]	Federal Income Tax Ded.
New Hampshire	7.5 (n)	Flat rate	1	7.5 (n)	No

Note: Tax rates for tax year 2024; (a) Rates listed are the corporate income tax rate applied to financial institutions or excise taxes based on income. Some states have other taxes based upon the value of deposits or shares; (n) New Hampshire's 7.5% [for tax years ending on or before 12/31/23] Business Profits Tax is imposed on both corporations and unincorporated associations with gross income over $50,000. In addition, New Hampshire levies a Business Enterprise Tax of 0.55% on the enterprise base (total compensation, interest and dividends paid) for businesses with gross receipts over $281,000 from Jan 1 to Dec 31, 2024. $281,000 or enterprise base over $281,000 begining 1/1/2023, adjusted every biennium for CPI.
Source: Federation of Tax Administrators, State Corporate Income Tax Rates, January 1, 2025

State Individual Income Tax Rates

State	Tax Rate (%)	Income Brackets ($)	Personal Exemptions ($)			Standard Ded. ($)	
			Single	Married	Depend.	Single	Married
New Hampshire	– State income tax of 4% on dividends and interest income only –						

Note: Tax rates for tax year 2024; Local- and county-level taxes are not included; Federal income tax is not deductible on state income tax returns
Source: Federation of Tax Administrators, State Individual Income Tax Rates, January 1, 2025

Various State Sales and Excise Tax Rates

State	State Sales Tax (%)	Gasoline[1] ($/gal.)	Cigarette[2] ($/pack)	Spirits[3] ($/gal.)	Wine[4] ($/gal.)	Beer[5] ($/gal.)	Recreational Marijuana (%)
New Hampshire	None	0.24	1.78	0.00	0.00	0.30	Not legal

Note: All tax rates as of January 1, 2025; (1) The American Petroleum Institute has developed a methodology for determining the average tax rate on a gallon of fuel. Rates may include any of the following: excise taxes, environmental fees, storage tank fees, other fees or taxes, general sales tax, and local taxes; (2) The federal excise tax of $1.0066 per pack and local taxes are not included; (3) Rates are those applicable to off-premise sales of 40% alcohol by volume (a.b.v.) distilled spirits in 750ml containers. Local excise taxes are excluded; (4) Rates are those applicable to off-premise sales of 11% a.b.v. non-carbonated wine in 750ml containers; (5) Rates are those applicable to off-premise sales of 4.7% a.b.v. beer in 12 ounce containers.
Source: Tax Foundation, 2025 Facts & Figures: How Does Your State Compare?

State Tax Competitiveness Index

State	Overall Rank	Corporate Tax Rank	Individual Income Tax Rank	Sales Tax Rank	Property Tax Rank	Unemployment Insurance Tax Rank
New Hampshire	6	32	12	1	39	27

Note: The Tax Foundation's State Tax Competitiveness Index enables policymakers, taxpayers, and business leaders to gauge how their states' tax systems compare. A rank of 1 is best, 50 is worst. Rankings do not average to the total. States without a tax rank equally as 1. DC's scores and rankings do not affect other states. The report shows tax systems as of July 1, 2024 (the beginning of Fiscal Year 2025).
Source: Tax Foundation, State Tax Competitiveness Index 2025

TRANSPORTATION

Means of Transportation to Work

Area	Car/Truck/Van		Public Transportation			Bicycle	Walked	Other Means	Worked at Home
	Drove Alone	Car-pooled	Bus	Subway	Railroad				
City	74.2	9.1	0.4	0.1	0.0	0.3	2.4	1.5	12.1
MSA[1]	72.9	7.4	0.4	0.1	0.1	0.2	1.7	1.1	16.1
U.S.	70.2	8.5	1.7	1.3	0.4	0.4	2.4	1.6	13.5

Note: Figures are percentages and cover workers 16 years of age and older; (1) Figures cover the Manchester-Nashua, NH Metropolitan Statistical Area
Source: U.S. Census Bureau, 2019-2023 American Community Survey 5-Year Estimates

Travel Time to Work

Area	Less Than 10 Minutes	10 to 19 Minutes	20 to 29 Minutes	30 to 44 Minutes	45 to 59 Minutes	60 to 89 Minutes	90 Minutes or More
City	12.9	35.1	23.0	16.0	6.2	5.1	1.9
MSA[1]	11.5	29.3	21.6	19.8	8.2	6.9	2.8
U.S.	12.6	28.6	21.2	20.8	8.1	6.0	2.8

Note: Note: Figures are percentages and include workers 16 years old and over; (1) Figures cover the Manchester-Nashua, NH Metropolitan Statistical Area
Source: U.S. Census Bureau, 2019-2023 American Community Survey 5-Year Estimates

Key Congestion Measures

Measure	2000	2010	2015	2020	2022
Annual Hours of Delay, Total (000)	n/a	n/a	3,780	2,387	4,058
Annual Hours of Delay, Per Auto Commuter	n/a	n/a	22	13	22
Annual Congestion Cost, Per Auto Commuter ($)	n/a	n/a	511	338	535

Note: n/a not available
Source: Texas A&M Transportation Institute, 2023 Urban Mobility Report

Freeway Travel Time Index

Measure	1985	1990	1995	2000	2005	2010	2015	2020	2022
Urban Area Index[1]	n/a	n/a	n/a	n/a	n/a	n/a	1.07	1.05	1.09
Urban Area Rank[1,2]	n/a	n/a	n/a	n/a	n/a	n/a	n/a	n/a	n/a

Note: Freeway Travel Time Index—the ratio of travel time in the peak period to the travel time at free-flow conditions. For example, a value of 1.30 indicates a 20-minute free-flow trip takes 26 minutes in the peak (20 minutes x 1.30 = 26 minutes); (1) Covers the Manchester NH urban area; (2) Rank is based on 101 larger urban areas (#1 = highest travel time index); n/a not available
Source: Texas A&M Transportation Institute, 2023 Urban Mobility Report

Public Transportation

Agency Name / Mode of Transportation	Vehicles Operated in Maximum Service[1]	Annual Unlinked Passenger Trips[2] (in thous.)	Annual Passenger Miles[3] (in thous.)
Manchester Transit Authority (MTA)			
Bus (directly operated)	14	302.9	n/a
Demand Response (directly operated)	7	19.4	n/a

Note: (1) Number of revenue vehicles operated by the given mode and type of service to meet the annual maximum service requirement. This is the revenue vehicle count during the peak season of the year; on the week and day that maximum service is provided. Vehicles operated in maximum service (VOMS) exclude atypical days and one-time special events; (2) Number of passengers who boarded public transportation vehicles. Passengers are counted each time they board a vehicle no matter how many vehicles they use to travel from their origin to their destination. (3) Sum of the distances ridden by all passengers during the entire fiscal year.
Source: Federal Transit Administration, National Transit Database, 2023

Air Transportation

Airport Name and Code / Type of Service	Passenger Airlines[1]	Passenger Enplanements	Freight Carriers[2]	Freight (lbs)
Manchester Municipal (MHT)				
Domestic service (U.S. carriers only)	15	632,987	10	82,824,426
International service (U.S. carriers only)	0	0	0	0

Note: (1) Includes all U.S.-based major, minor and commuter airlines that carried at least one passenger during the year; (2) Includes all U.S.-based airlines and freight carriers that transported at least one pound of freight during the year.
Source: Bureau of Transportation Statistics, The Intermodal Transportation Database, Air Carriers: T-100 Domestic Market (U.S. carriers only), 2024; Bureau of Transportation Statistics, The Intermodal Transportation Database, Air Carriers: T-100 International Market (U.S. carriers only), 2024

BUSINESSES

Major Business Headquarters

Company Name	Industry	Rankings	
		Fortune[1]	Forbes[2]
No companies listed	-	-	-

Note: (1) Companies that produce a 10-K are ranked 1 to 500 based on 2023 revenue; (2) All private companies with at least $2 billion in annual revenue through the end of their most current fiscal year are ranked 1 to 275; companies listed are headquartered in the city; dashes indicate no ranking
Source: Fortune, "Fortune 500," 2024; Forbes, "America's Largest Private Companies," 2024

Fastest-Growing Businesses

According to *Initiative for a Competitive Inner City (ICIC)*, Manchester is home to one of America's 100 fastest-growing "inner city" companies: **Cookson Communications** (#36). To be eligible for the IC100, companies have to be independently operated, privately held, for-profit businesses with revenues of at least $50,000 in 2019 and $500,000 in 2023, and headquartered in an under-resourced community. Recognizing that concentrated poverty exists within metropolitan areas outside of big cities (and that poverty overall is suburbanizing), ICIC defines under-resourced communities as large low-income, high-poverty areas located in the urban and suburban parts of all but the smallest metropolitan areas. Companies were ranked overall by revenue growth over the five-year period between 2019 and 2023. *Initiative for a Competitive Inner City (ICIC), "Inner City 100 Companies," 2024*

According to Deloitte, Manchester is home to one of North America's 500 fastest-growing high-technology companies: **SpotOn GPS Fence** (#188). Companies are ranked by percentage growth in revenue over a four-year period. Criteria for inclusion: company must be headquartered within North America; must own proprietary intellectual property or technology that is sold to customers in products that contributes to a significant portion of the company's operating revenue; must have been in business for a minumum of four years with 2020 operating revenues of at least $50,000 USD/CD and 2023 operating revenues of at least $5 million USD/CD. *Deloitte, 2024 Technology Fast 500™*

Living Environment

COST OF LIVING

Cost of Living Index

Composite Index	Groceries	Housing	Utilities	Transportation	Health Care	Misc. Goods/Services
112.6	99.9	117.6	112.2	105.9	103.9	117.0

Note: The Cost of Living Index measures regional differences in the cost of consumer goods and services, excluding taxes and non-consumer expenditures, for professional and managerial households in the top income quintile. It is based on more than 50,000 prices covering almost 60 different items for which prices are collected three times a year by chambers of commerce, economic development organizations or university applied economic centers in each participating urban area. The numbers shown should be read as a percentage above or below the national average of 100. For example, a value of 115.4 in the groceries column indicates that grocery prices are 15.4% higher than the national average. Small differences in the index numbers should not be interpreted as significant; Figures cover the Manchester NH urban area.
Source: The Council for Community and Economic Research, Cost of Living Index, 2024

Grocery Prices

Area[1]	T-Bone Steak ($/pound)	Frying Chicken ($/pound)	Whole Milk ($/half gal.)	Eggs ($/dozen)	Orange Juice ($/64 oz.)	Coffee ($/11.5 oz.)
City[2]	15.51	1.42	4.71	2.98	4.42	5.31
Avg.	15.42	1.55	4.69	3.25	4.41	5.46
Min.	14.50	1.16	4.43	2.75	4.00	4.85
Max.	17.56	2.89	5.49	4.78	5.54	7.89

Note: (1) Values for the local area are compared with the average, minimum and maximum values for all 276 areas in the Cost of Living Index; (2) Figures cover the Manchester NH urban area; **T-Bone Steak** (price per pound); **Frying Chicken** (price per pound, whole fryer); **Whole Milk** (half gallon carton); **Eggs** (price per dozen, Grade A, large); **Orange Juice** (64 oz. Tropicana or Florida Natural); **Coffee** (11.5 oz. can, vacuum-packed, Maxwell House, Hills Bros, or Folgers).
Source: The Council for Community and Economic Research, Cost of Living Index, 2024

Housing and Utility Costs

Area[1]	New Home Price ($)	Apartment Rent ($/month)	All Electric ($/month)	Part Electric ($/month)	Other Energy ($/month)	Telephone ($/month)
City[2]	552,244	2,205	-	135.10	114.30	189.12
Avg.	515,975	1,550	210.99	123.07	82.07	194.99
Min.	265,375	692	104.33	53.68	36.26	179.42
Max.	2,775,821	5,719	529.02	397.28	361.63	223.33

Note: (1) Values for the local area are compared with the average, minimum and maximum values for all 276 areas in the Cost of Living Index; (2) Figures cover the Manchester NH urban area; **New Home Price** (2,400 sf living area, 8,000 sf lot, in urban area with full utilities); **Apartment Rent** (950 sf 2 bedroom/1.5 or 2 bath, unfurnished, excluding all utilities except water); **All Electric** (average monthly cost for an all-electric home); **Part Electric** (average monthly cost for a part-electric home); **Other Energy** (average monthly cost for natural gas, fuel oil, coal, wood, and any other forms of energy except electricity); **Telephone** (price includes the base monthly rate plus taxes and fees for three lines of mobile phone service).
Source: The Council for Community and Economic Research, Cost of Living Index, 2024

Health Care, Transportation, and Other Costs

Area[1]	Doctor ($/visit)	Dentist ($/visit)	Optometrist ($/visit)	Gasoline ($/gallon)	Beauty Salon ($/visit)	Men's Shirt ($)
City[2]	183.83	108.17	116.33	3.24	56.33	42.69
Avg.	143.77	117.51	129.23	3.32	48.57	38.14
Min.	36.74	58.67	67.33	2.80	24.00	13.41
Max.	270.44	216.82	307.33	5.28	94.00	63.89

Note: (1) Values for the local area are compared with the average, minimum and maximum values for all 276 areas in the Cost of Living Index; (2) Figures cover the Manchester NH urban area; **Doctor** (general practitioners routine exam of an established patient); **Dentist** (adult teeth cleaning and periodic oral examination); **Optometrist** (full vision eye exam for established adult patient); **Gasoline** (one gallon regular unleaded, national brand, including all taxes, cash price at self-service pump if available); **Beauty Salon** (woman's shampoo, trim, and blow-dry); **Men's Shirt** (cotton/polyester dress shirt, pinpoint weave, long sleeves).
Source: The Council for Community and Economic Research, Cost of Living Index, 2024

HOUSING

Homeownership Rate

Area	2017 (%)	2018 (%)	2019 (%)	2020 (%)	2021 (%)	2022 (%)	2023 (%)	2024 (%)
MSA[1]	n/a	n/a	n/a	n/a	n/a	n/a	n/a	n/a
U.S.	63.9	64.4	64.6	66.6	65.5	65.8	65.9	65.6

Note: (1) Figures cover the Manchester-Nashua, NH Metropolitan Statistical Area; n/a not available
Source: U.S. Census Bureau, Housing Vacancies and Homeownership Annual Statistics: 2017-2024

House Price Index (HPI)

Area	National Ranking[2]	Quarterly Change (%)	One-Year Change (%)	Five-Year Change (%)	Since 1991Q1 (%)
MSA[1]	25	-0.15	8.25	67.31	310.83
U.S.[3]	—	1.43	4.51	57.13	327.82

Note: The HPI is a weighted repeat sales index. It measures average price changes in repeat sales or refinancings on the same properties. This information is obtained by reviewing repeat mortgage transactions on single-family properties whose mortgages have been purchased or securitized by Fannie Mae or Freddie Mac since January 1975; (1) Figures cover the Manchester-Nashua, NH Metropolitan Statistical Area; (2) Rankings are based on annual percentage change for all metro areas containing at least 15,000 transactions over the last 10 years and ranges from 1 to 241; (3) figures based on a weighted average of Census Division estimates using a seasonally adjusted, purchase-only index; all figures are for the period ending December 31, 2024
Source: Federal Housing Finance Agency, Change in FHFA Metropolitan Area House Price Indexes, All Transactions Index, 2024Q4

Home Value

Area	Under $100,000	$100,000 -$199,999	$200,000 -$299,999	$300,000 -$399,999	$400,000 -$499,999	$500,000 -$999,999	$1,000,000 or more	Median ($)
City	3.9	10.2	24.0	32.7	19.8	8.6	0.7	336,300
MSA[1]	3.8	6.2	18.2	25.4	21.4	23.3	1.5	385,500
U.S.	12.1	17.8	19.5	14.4	10.5	19.1	6.5	303,400

Note: Figures are percentages except for median and cover owner-occupied housing units; (1) Figures cover the Manchester-Nashua, NH Metropolitan Statistical Area
Source: U.S. Census Bureau, 2019-2023 American Community Survey 5-Year Estimates

Year Housing Structure Built

Area	2020 or Later	2010 -2019	2000 -2009	1990 -1999	1980 -1989	1970 -1979	1960 -1969	1950 -1959	1940 -1949	Before 1940	Median Year
City	0.5	3.5	6.5	7.7	15.5	11.5	8.1	10.7	6.6	29.4	1964
MSA[1]	0.5	5.4	9.6	10.5	20.2	15.3	9.2	7.3	3.6	18.6	1977
U.S.	1.2	8.9	12.8	13.0	14.4	10.0	9.7	4.5	11.9		1980

Note: Figures are percentages except for Median Year; Note: (1) Figures cover the Manchester-Nashua, NH Metropolitan Statistical Area
Source: U.S. Census Bureau, 2019-2023 American Community Survey 5-Year Estimates

Gross Monthly Rent

Area	Under $500	$500 -$999	$1,000 -$1,499	$1,500 -$1,999	$2,000 -$2,499	$2,500 -$2,999	$3,000 and up	Median ($)
City	5.5	12.8	34.2	31.7	12.5	1.9	1.3	1,465
MSA[1]	5.5	11.2	31.2	31.7	14.5	3.8	2.0	1,532
U.S.	6.5	22.3	29.5	20.2	10.8	4.8	5.9	1,348

Note: Figures are percentages except for median; Gross rent is the contract rent plus the estimated average monthly cost of utilities (electricity, gas, and water and sewer) and fuels (oil, coal, kerosene, wood, etc.) if these are paid by the renter (or paid for the renter by someone else); (1) Figures cover the Manchester-Nashua, NH Metropolitan Statistical Area
Source: U.S. Census Bureau, 2019-2023 American Community Survey 5-Year Estimates

HEALTH

Health Risk Factors

Category	MSA[1] (%)	U.S. (%)
Adults aged 18–64 who have any kind of health care coverage	n/a	90.8
Adults who reported being in good or better health	n/a	81.8
Adults who have been told they have high blood cholesterol	n/a	36.9
Adults who have been told they have high blood pressure	n/a	34.0
Adults who are current smokers	n/a	12.1
Adults who currently use e-cigarettes	n/a	7.7
Adults who currently use chewing tobacco, snuff, or snus	n/a	3.2
Adults who are heavy drinkers[2]	n/a	6.1
Adults who are binge drinkers[3]	n/a	15.2
Adults who are overweight (BMI 25.0 - 29.9)	n/a	34.4
Adults who are obese (BMI 30.0 - 99.8)	n/a	34.3
Adults who participated in any physical activities in the past month	n/a	75.8

Note: All figures are crude prevalence; (1) Figures for the Manchester-Nashua, NH Metropolitan Statistical Area were not available.
(2) Heavy drinkers are classified as adult men having more than 14 drinks per week and adult women having more than 7 drinks per week; (3) Binge drinkers are classified as males having five or more drinks on one occasion or females having four or more drinks on one occasion
Source: Centers for Disease Control and Prevention, Behavioral Risk Factor Surveillance System, SMART: Selected Metropolitan Area Risk Trends, 2023

Acute and Chronic Health Conditions

Category	MSA[1] (%)	U.S. (%)
Adults who have ever been told they had a heart attack	n/a	4.2
Adults who have ever been told they have angina or coronary heart disease	n/a	4.0
Adults who have ever been told they had a stroke	n/a	3.3
Adults who have ever been told they have asthma	n/a	15.7
Adults who have ever been told they have arthritis	n/a	26.3
Adults who have ever been told they have diabetes[2]	n/a	11.5
Adults who have ever been told they had skin cancer	n/a	5.6
Adults who have ever been told they had any other types of cancer	n/a	8.4
Adults who have ever been told they have COPD	n/a	6.4
Adults who have ever been told they have kidney disease	n/a	3.7
Adults who have ever been told they have a form of depression	n/a	22.0

Note: All figures are crude prevalence; (1) Figures for the Manchester-Nashua, NH Metropolitan Statistical Area were not available.
(2) Figures do not include pregnancy-related, borderline, or pre-diabetes
Source: Centers for Disease Control and Prevention, Behavioral Risk Factor Surveillance System, SMART: Selected Metropolitan Area Risk Trends, 2023

Health Screening and Vaccination Rates

Category	MSA[1] (%)	U.S. (%)
Adults who have ever been tested for HIV	n/a	37.5
Adults who have had their blood cholesterol checked within the last five years	n/a	87.0
Adults aged 65+ who have had flu shot within the past year	n/a	63.4
Adults aged 65+ who have ever had a pneumonia vaccination	n/a	71.9

Note: All figures are crude prevalence; (1) Figures for the Manchester-Nashua, NH Metropolitan Statistical Area were not available.
Source: Centers for Disease Control and Prevention, Behavioral Risk Factor Surveillance System, SMART: Selected Metropolitan Area Risk Trends, 2023

Disability Status

Category	MSA[1] (%)	U.S. (%)
Adults who reported being deaf	n/a	7.4
Are you blind or have serious difficulty seeing, even when wearing glasses?	n/a	4.9
Do you have difficulty doing errands alone?	n/a	7.8
Do you have difficulty dressing or bathing?	n/a	3.6
Do you have serious difficulty concentrating/remembering/making decisions?	n/a	13.7
Do you have serious difficulty walking or climbing stairs?	n/a	13.2

Note: All figures are crude prevalence; (1) Figures for the Manchester-Nashua, NH Metropolitan Statistical Area were not available.
Source: Centers for Disease Control and Prevention, Behavioral Risk Factor Surveillance System, SMART: Selected Metropolitan Area Risk Trends, 2023

Mortality Rates for the Top 10 Causes of Death in the U.S.

ICD-10[a] Sub-Chapter	ICD-10[a] Code	Crude Mortality Rate[2] per 100,000 population	
		County[3]	U.S.
Malignant neoplasms	C00-C97	182.9	182.7
Ischaemic heart diseases	I20-I25	101.3	109.6
Provisional assignment of new diseases of uncertain etiology[1]	U00-U49	39.5	65.3
Other forms of heart disease	I30-I51	69.6	65.1
Other degenerative diseases of the nervous system	G30-G31	36.3	52.4
Other external causes of accidental injury	W00-X59	61.3	52.3
Cerebrovascular diseases	I60-I69	36.1	49.1
Chronic lower respiratory diseases	J40-J47	42.3	43.5
Hypertensive diseases	I10-I15	19.5	38.9
Organic, including symptomatic, mental disorders	F01-F09	58.1	33.9

Note: (a) ICD-10 = International Classification of Diseases 10th Revision; (1) Includes COVID-19, adverse effects to COVID-19 vaccines, SARS, and vaping-related disorders; (2) Crude mortality rates are a three-year average covering 2021-2023; (3) Figures cover Hillsborough County.
Source: Centers for Disease Control and Prevention, National Center for Health Statistics. National Vital Statistics System, Mortality 2018-2023 on CDC WONDER Online Database

Mortality Rates for Selected Causes of Death

Cause of Death	ICD-10[a] Code	Crude Mortality Rate[1] per 100,000 population	
		County[2]	U.S.
Accidental poisoning and exposure to noxious substances	X40-X49	37.9	30.5
Alzheimer disease	G30	29.7	35.4
Assault	X85-Y09	2.0	7.3
COVID-19	U07.1	39.5	65.3
Diabetes mellitus	E10-E14	27.8	30.0
Diseases of the liver	K70-K76	23.0	20.8
Human immunodeficiency virus (HIV) disease	B20-B24	Suppressed	1.5
Influenza and pneumonia	J09-J18	9.9	13.4
Intentional self-harm	X60-X84	17.2	14.7
Malnutrition	E40-E46	4.1	6.0
Obesity and other hyperalimentation	E65-E68	3.2	3.1
Renal failure	N17-N19	12.1	16.4
Transport accidents	V01-V99	9.5	14.4

Note: (a) ICD-10 = International Classification of Diseases 10th Revision; (1) Crude mortality rates are a three-year average covering 2021-2023; (2) Figures cover Hillsborough County; Data are suppressed when the data meet the criteria for confidentiality constraints; Crude mortality rates are flagged as unreliable when the rate would be calculated with a numerator of 20 or less.
Source: Centers for Disease Control and Prevention, National Center for Health Statistics. National Vital Statistics System, Mortality 2018-2023 on CDC WONDER Online Database

Health Insurance Coverage

Area	With Health Insurance	With Private Health Insurance	With Public Health Insurance	Without Health Insurance	Population Under Age 19 Without Health Insurance
City	91.2	66.6	35.0	8.8	4.9
MSA[1]	94.0	77.1	29.3	6.0	4.0
U.S.	91.4	67.3	36.3	8.6	5.4

Note: Figures are percentages that cover the civilian noninstitutionalized population; (1) Figures cover the Manchester-Nashua, NH Metropolitan Statistical Area
Source: U.S. Census Bureau, 2019-2023 American Community Survey 5-Year Estimates

Number of Medical Professionals

Area	MDs[3]	DOs[3,4]	Dentists	Podiatrists	Chiropractors	Optometrists
County[1] (number)	1,003	114	364	28	115	96
County[1] (rate[2])	235.1	26.7	85.2	6.6	26.9	22.5
U.S. (rate[2])	302.5	29.2	74.6	6.4	29.5	18.0

Note: Data as of 2023 unless noted; (1) Data covers Hillsborough County; (2) Number of medical professionals per 100,000 population; (3) Data as of 2022 and includes all active, non-federal physicians; (4) Doctor of Osteopathic Medicine
Source: U.S. Department of Health and Human Services, Health Resources and Services Administration, Bureau of Health Professions, Area Resource File (ARF) 2023-2024

EDUCATION

Public School District Statistics

District Name	Schls	Pupils	Pupil/Teacher Ratio	Minority Pupils[1] (%)	Total Rev. per Pupil ($)	Total Exp. per Pupil ($)
Manchester School District	21	11,980	11.6	51.2	17,666	16,662

Note: Table includes school districts with 2,000 or more students; (1) Percentage of students that are not non-Hispanic white.
Source: U.S. Department of Education, National Center for Education Statistics, Common Core of Data, Local Education Agency (School District) Universe Survey: School Year 2023-2024; U.S. Department of Education, National Center for Education Statistics, Common Core of Data, School District Finance Survey (F-33): School Year 2021–22

Highest Level of Education

Area	Less than H.S.	H.S. Diploma	Some College, No Deg.	Associate Degree	Bachelor's Degree	Master's Degree	Prof. School Degree	Doctorate Degree
City	11.3	29.1	18.1	8.0	22.5	8.8	1.3	0.9
MSA[1]	7.0	25.6	17.2	9.6	25.4	12.1	1.6	1.5
U.S.	10.6	26.2	19.4	8.8	21.3	9.8	2.3	1.6

Note: Figures cover persons age 25 and over; (1) Figures cover the Manchester-Nashua, NH Metropolitan Statistical Area
Source: U.S. Census Bureau, 2019-2023 American Community Survey 5-Year Estimates

Educational Attainment by Race

Area	High School Graduate or Higher (%)					Bachelor's Degree or Higher (%)				
	Total	White	Black	Asian	Hisp.[2]	Total	White	Black	Asian	Hisp.[2]
City	88.7	91.3	75.7	81.2	68.7	33.5	35.4	22.8	35.6	13.5
MSA[1]	93.0	94.3	83.0	90.5	74.3	40.6	41.1	26.8	60.6	20.1
U.S.	89.4	92.9	88.1	88.0	72.5	35.0	37.7	24.7	57.0	19.9

Note: Figures shown cover persons 25 years old and over; (1) Figures cover the Manchester-Nashua, NH Metropolitan Statistical Area; (2) People of Hispanic origin can be of any race
Source: U.S. Census Bureau, 2019-2023 American Community Survey 5-Year Estimates

School Enrollment by Grade and Control

Area	Preschool (%)		Kindergarten (%)		Grades 1 - 4 (%)		Grades 5 - 8 (%)		Grades 9 - 12 (%)	
	Public	Private	Public	Private	Public	Private	Public	Private	Public	Private
City	51.8	48.2	85.9	14.1	88.1	11.9	92.7	7.3	92.2	7.8
MSA[1]	45.6	54.4	81.4	18.6	85.2	14.8	87.5	12.5	89.8	10.2
U.S.	58.7	41.3	85.2	14.8	87.2	12.8	87.9	12.1	89.0	11.0

Note: Figures shown cover persons 3 years old and over; (1) Figures cover the Manchester-Nashua, NH Metropolitan Statistical Area
Source: U.S. Census Bureau, 2019-2023 American Community Survey 5-Year Estimates

Higher Education

Four-Year Colleges			Two-Year Colleges			Medical Schools[1]	Law Schools[2]	Voc/ Tech[3]
Public	Private Non-profit	Private For-profit	Public	Private Non-profit	Private For-profit			
2	3	0	2	1	0	0	0	2

Note: Figures cover institutions located within the Manchester-Nashua, NH Metropolitan Statistical Area and include main campuses only; (1) includes schools accredited by the Liaison Committee on Medical Education and the American Osteopathic Association's Commission on Osteopathic College Accreditation; (2) includes ABA-accredited schools, schools with provisional ABA accreditation, and state accredited schools; (3) includes all schools with programs that are less than 2 years.
Source: National Center for Education Statistics, Integrated Postsecondary Education System (IPEDS), 2023-24; Wikipedia, List of Medical Schools in the United States, accessed May 2, 2025; Wikipedia, List of Law Schools in the United States, accessed May 2, 2025

According to *U.S. News & World Report*, the Manchester-Nashua, NH metro area is home to one of the top 100 liberal arts colleges in the U.S.: **Saint Anselm College** (#90 tie). The indicators used to capture academic quality fall into a number of categories: assessment by administrators at peer institutions; retention of students; faculty resources; student selectivity; financial resources; alumni giving; high school counselor ratings of colleges; and graduation rate. *U.S. News & World Report*, "America's Best Colleges 2025"

EMPLOYERS

Major Employers

Company Name	Industry
C & S Wholesale Grocers Inc	Grocery stores
Concord Hospital	Healthcare
Dartmouth-Hitchcock Medical Center	Healthcare
Elliot Hospital	Healthcare
Fidelity Investments	Financial services
Freudenberg-Nok	Healthcare
Hypertherm	Technology
J Jill	Retailer
Liberty Life Assurance Co	Insurance companies/services
Southern New Hampshire Health	Healthcare
St. Joseph's Hospital	Healthcare
Sturm Ruger & Co. Inc	Firearms
Trustees of Dartmouth College	Education
UA Local 788 Marine Pipefitter	Union
United Physical Therapy	Healthcare
University of New Hampshire	Education
University System of NH	Education

Note: Companies shown are located within the Manchester-Nashua, NH Metropolitan Statistical Area.
Source: Chambers of Commerce; State Departments of Labor; Wikipedia

PUBLIC SAFETY

Crime Rate

Area	Total Crime Rate	Violent Crime Rate				Property Crime Rate		
		Murder	Rape	Robbery	Aggrav. Assault	Burglary	Larceny-Theft	Motor Vehicle Theft
City	2,061.5	7.0	59.1	87.9	229.6	147.9	1,342.2	187.9
U.S.	2,290.9	5.7	38.0	66.5	264.1	250.7	1,347.2	318.7

Note: Figures are crimes per 100,000 population.
Source: FBI, Table 8, Offenses Known to Law Enforcement, by State by City, 2023

Hate Crimes

Area	Number of Quarters Reported	Number of Incidents per Bias Motivation					
		Race/Ethnicity/Ancestry	Religion	Sexual Orientation	Disability	Gender	Gender Identity
City	4	1	1	1	0	0	0
U.S.	4	5,900	2,699	2,077	187	92	492

Source: Federal Bureau of Investigation, Hate Crime Statistics 2023

Identity Theft Consumer Reports

Area	Reports	Reports per 100,000 Population	Rank[2]
MSA[1]	709	167	226
U.S.	1,135,291	339	-

Note: (1) Figures cover the Manchester-Nashua, NH Metropolitan Statistical Area; (2) Rank ranges from 1 to 401 where 1 indicates greatest number of identity theft reports per 100,000 population
Source: Federal Trade Commission, Consumer Sentinel Network Data Book 2024

Fraud and Other Consumer Reports

Area	Reports	Reports per 100,000 Population	Rank[2]
MSA[1]	4,951	1,166	141
U.S.	5,360,641	1,601	-

Note: (1) Figures cover the Manchester-Nashua, NH Metropolitan Statistical Area; (2) Rank ranges from 1 to 401 where 1 indicates greatest number of fraud and other consumer reports per 100,000 population
Source: Federal Trade Commission, Consumer Sentinel Network Data Book 2024

POLITICS

2024 Presidential Election Results

Area	Trump (Rep.)	Harris (Dem.)	Stein (Green)	Kennedy (Ind.)	Oliver (Lib.)	Other
Hillsborough County	47.8	50.7	0.5	0.0	0.5	0.5
U.S.	49.7	48.2	0.6	0.5	0.4	0.6

Note: Results are percentages and may not add to 100% due to rounding
Source: Dave Leip's Atlas of U.S. Presidential Elections

SPORTS

Professional Sports Teams

Team Name	League	Year Established

No teams are located in the metro area
Source: Wikipedia, Major Professional Sports Teams of the United States and Canada, May 1, 2025

CLIMATE

Average and Extreme Temperatures

Temperature	Jan	Feb	Mar	Apr	May	Jun	Jul	Aug	Sep	Oct	Nov	Dec	Yr.
Extreme High (°F)	68	66	85	95	97	98	102	101	98	90	80	68	102
Average High (°F)	31	34	43	57	69	77	83	80	72	61	48	35	57
Average Temp. (°F)	20	23	33	44	56	65	70	68	59	48	38	25	46
Average Low (°F)	9	11	22	32	42	51	57	55	46	35	28	15	34
Extreme Low (°F)	-33	-27	-16	8	21	30	35	29	22	10	-5	-22	-33

Note: Figures cover the years 1948-1990
Source: National Climatic Data Center, International Station Meteorological Climate Summary, 9/96

Average Precipitation/Snowfall/Humidity

Precip./Humidity	Jan	Feb	Mar	Apr	May	Jun	Jul	Aug	Sep	Oct	Nov	Dec	Yr.
Avg. Precip. (in.)	2.8	2.5	2.9	3.1	3.2	3.1	3.1	3.3	2.9	3.1	3.8	3.2	36.9
Avg. Snowfall (in.)	18	15	11	2	Tr	0	0	0	0	Tr	4	14	63
Avg. Rel. Hum. 7am (%)	76	76	76	75	75	80	82	87	89	86	83	79	80
Avg. Rel. Hum. 4pm (%)	59	55	52	46	47	52	51	53	55	53	61	63	54

Note: Figures cover the years 1948-1990; Tr = Trace amounts (<0.05 in. of rain; <0.5 in. of snow)
Source: National Climatic Data Center, International Station Meteorological Climate Summary, 9/96

Weather Conditions

Temperature			Daytime Sky			Precipitation		
5°F & below	32°F & below	90°F & above	Clear	Partly cloudy	Cloudy	0.01 inch or more precip.	0.1 inch or more snow/ice	Thunderstorms
32	171	12	87	131	147	125	32	19

Note: Figures are average number of days per year and cover the years 1948-1990
Source: National Climatic Data Center, International Station Meteorological Climate Summary, 9/96

HAZARDOUS WASTE

Superfund Sites

The Manchester-Nashua, NH metro area is home to six sites on the EPA's Superfund National Priorities List (NPL) or Superfund Alternative Approach (SAA) list: **Fletcher's Paint Works & Storage** (Final NPL); **Mohawk Tannery** (Proposed NPL); **New Hampshire Plating Co.** (Final NPL); **Savage Municipal Water Supply** (Final NPL); **South Municipal Water Supply Well** (Final NPL); **Sylvester** (Final NPL). The Superfund alternative approach uses the same investigation and cleanup process and standards that are used for sites listed on the National Priorities List. The SAA is an alternative to listing a site on the NPL; it is not an alternative to Superfund or the Superfund process. There are a total of 1,445 Superfund sites with a status of proposed or final on both lists in the United States. *U.S. Environmental Protection Agency, National Priorities List, May 1, 2025; U.S. Environmental Protection Agency, Superfund Alternative Approach Sites, May 1, 2025*

AIR QUALITY

Air Quality Trends: Ozone

	1990	1995	2000	2005	2010	2015	2020	2021	2022	2023
MSA[1]	0.085	0.088	0.070	0.082	0.067	0.061	0.055	0.061	0.058	0.065
U.S.	0.087	0.089	0.081	0.080	0.072	0.068	0.066	0.067	0.067	0.070

Note: (1) Data covers the Manchester-Nashua, NH Metropolitan Statistical Area. The values shown are the composite ozone concentration averages among trend sites based on the highest fourth daily maximum 8-hour concentration in parts per million. These trends are based on sites having an adequate record of monitoring data during the trend period. Data from exceptional events are included.
Source: U.S. Environmental Protection Agency, Air Quality Monitoring Information, "Air Quality Trends by City, 1990-2023"

Air Quality Index

Area	Percent of Days when Air Quality was...[2]					AQI Statistics[2]	
	Good	Moderate	Unhealthy for Sensitive Groups	Unhealthy	Very Unhealthy	Maximum	Median
MSA[1]	83.6	15.1	1.4	0.0	0.0	119	39

Note: (1) Data covers the Manchester-Nashua, NH Metropolitan Statistical Area; (2) Based on 365 days with AQI data in 2023. Air Quality Index (AQI) is an index for reporting daily air quality. EPA calculates the AQI for five major air pollutants regulated by the Clean Air Act: ground-level ozone, particle pollution (aka particulate matter), carbon monoxide, sulfur dioxide, and nitrogen dioxide. The AQI runs from 0 to 500. The higher the AQI value, the greater the level of air pollution and the greater the health concern. There are six AQI categories: "Good" AQI is between 0 and 50. Air quality is considered satisfactory; "Moderate" AQI is between 51 and 100. Air quality is acceptable; "Unhealthy for Sensitive Groups" When AQI values are between 101 and 150, members of sensitive groups may experience health effects; "Unhealthy" When AQI values are between 151 and 200 everyone may begin to experience health effects; "Very Unhealthy" AQI values between 201 and 300 trigger a health alert; "Hazardous" AQI values over 300 trigger warnings of emergency conditions (not shown).
Source: U.S. Environmental Protection Agency, Air Quality Index Report, 2023

Air Quality Index Pollutants

Area	Percent of Days when AQI Pollutant was...[2]					
	Carbon Monoxide	Nitrogen Dioxide	Ozone	Sulfur Dioxide	Particulate Matter 2.5	Particulate Matter 10
MSA[1]	0.8	0.0	80.3	(3)	18.9	0.0

Note: (1) Data covers the Manchester-Nashua, NH Metropolitan Statistical Area; (2) Based on 365 days with AQI data in 2023. The Air Quality Index (AQI) is an index for reporting daily air quality. EPA calculates the AQI for five major air pollutants regulated by the Clean Air Act: ground-level ozone, particle pollution (also known as particulate matter), carbon monoxide, sulfur dioxide, and nitrogen dioxide. The AQI runs from 0 to 500. The higher the AQI value, the greater the level of air pollution and the greater the health concern; (3) Sulfur dioxide is no longer included in this table because SO_2 concentrations tend to be very localized and not necessarily representative of broad geographical areas like counties and CBSAs.
Source: U.S. Environmental Protection Agency, Air Quality Index Report, 2023

Maximum Air Pollutant Concentrations: Particulate Matter, Ozone, CO and Lead

	Particulate Matter 10 (ug/m^3)	Particulate Matter 2.5 Wtd AM (ug/m^3)	Particulate Matter 2.5 24-Hr (ug/m^3)	Ozone (ppm)	Carbon Monoxide (ppm)	Lead (ug/m^3)
MSA[1] Level	n/a	4.5	20	0.067	1	n/a
NAAQS[2]	150	15	35	0.075	9	0.15
Met NAAQS[2]	n/a	Yes	Yes	Yes	Yes	n/a

Note: (1) Data covers the Manchester-Nashua, NH Metropolitan Statistical Area; Data from exceptional events are included; (2) National Ambient Air Quality Standards; ppm = parts per million; ug/m³ = micrograms per cubic meter; n/a not available.
Concentrations: Particulate Matter 10 (coarse particulate)—highest second maximum 24-hour concentration; Particulate Matter 2.5 Wtd AM (fine particulate)—highest weighted annual mean concentration; Particulate Matter 2.5 24-Hour (fine particulate)—highest 98th percentile 24-hour concentration; Ozone—highest fourth daily maximum 8-hour concentration; Carbon Monoxide—highest second maximum non-overlapping 8-hour concentration; Lead—maximum running 3-month average
Source: U.S. Environmental Protection Agency, Air Quality Monitoring Information, "Air Quality Statistics by City, 2023"

Maximum Air Pollutant Concentrations: Nitrogen Dioxide and Sulfur Dioxide

	Nitrogen Dioxide AM (ppb)	Nitrogen Dioxide 1-Hr (ppb)	Sulfur Dioxide AM (ppb)	Sulfur Dioxide 1-Hr (ppb)	Sulfur Dioxide 24-Hr (ppb)
MSA[1] Level	n/a	n/a	n/a	1	n/a
NAAQS[2]	53	100	30	75	140
Met NAAQS[2]	n/a	n/a	n/a	Yes	n/a

Note: (1) Data covers the Manchester-Nashua, NH Metropolitan Statistical Area; Data from exceptional events are included; (2) National Ambient Air Quality Standards; ppm = parts per million; ug/m³ = micrograms per cubic meter; n/a not available.
Concentrations: Nitrogen Dioxide AM—highest arithmetic mean concentration; Nitrogen Dioxide 1-Hr—highest 98th percentile 1-hour daily maximum concentration; Sulfur Dioxide AM—highest annual mean concentration; Sulfur Dioxide 1-Hr—highest 99th percentile 1-hour daily maximum concentration; Sulfur Dioxide 24-Hr—highest second maximum 24-hour concentration
Source: U.S. Environmental Protection Agency, Air Quality Monitoring Information, "Air Quality Statistics by City, 2023"

New York, New York

Background

Few cities in the world can compare with New York. Known for its dramatic skyline, famous bridges, historic buildings, and world-class culture, the city is beautiful and mighty, and home to over 8 million people speaking 800 languages within its five boroughs—Bronx, Brooklyn, Queens, Manhattan, and Staten Island.

New York is the largest city in New York State, in the U.S., and one of the largest cities in the world. Located at the mouth of the Hudson River, the area was first explored by Giovanni da Verrazzano in 1524, and then by Henry Hudson in 1609. In 1625, it became New Amsterdam and, as the story goes, Peter Minuit purchased the island of Manhattan a year later from local Native Americans for the equivalent of $24.00.

The city offers the best in the arts—Metropolitan Museum of Art, Museum of Modern Art, Guggenheim Museum, among thousands of others; education—New York University and Columbia University; finance—the New York and the American stock exchanges; plus fashion, theaters, restaurants, political activism, and more. As a major cultural, financial and media center, it significantly influences commence, entertainment, research, technology, education, politics, tourism, dining, art, fashion, and sports and is the most photographed city in the world.

The city is home to the highest number of Fortune 500 companies (41) and to the highest number of billionaires (123) of any city in the world. As an international business capital, New York is abundant with entrepreneurial spirit, highly educated workers, first-rate transportation, telecommunications and infrastructure, and has the lowest crime rate of any big city in America.

New York is home to The Alvin Ailey American Dance Theater, American Ballet Theater, Brooklyn Academy of Music, Carnegie Hall, and Cunningham Dance Company, among many other world-famous artistic centers.

Professional sports abound in the New York metropolitan area, including New York Giants and Jets football teams, New York Rangers hockey team, New York Red Bulls soccer team, Knicks basketball team, and New York Yankees and Mets baseball teams. The Giants' MetLife Stadium hosted the Super Bowl in 2014, the first outdoor, cold-weather Super Bowl. In addition, Barclays Arena in Brooklyn is home to the New Jersey Nets basketball team, the New York Islanders hockey team, and hosts world-class entertainment.

On September 11, 2001, New York became the site of the deadliest terrorist attack ever to occur in the United States, destroying the complex of seven buildings at the World Trade Center and killing more than 3,500 people. Today, the 8-acre World Trade Center Complex consists of five new buildings with additional construction ongoing; Memorial and Museum with two pools in the footprints of the Twin Towers and the largest manmade waterfalls in the country; and The World Trade Center Transportation Hub.

The New York metropolitan area is home to a prominent LBGTQ+ community. More than 700,000 strong, it's the largest in the country. The annual New York City Pride March traverses southward down Fifth Avenue and ends at Greenwich Village in Lower Manhattan, attracting tens of thousands of participants and millions of sidewalk spectators each June.

The New York metro area is close to the path of most storm and frontal systems which move across the continent. The city can experience very high temperatures in summer and very low temperatures in winter, despite its coastal location. The passage of many weather systems helps to reduce the duration of both cold and warm spells, circulate the air, and reduce stagnation. The most recent major weather event occurred in 2012, as Hurricane Sandy flooded subways and tunnels, shut down hospitals and the New York Stock Exchange.

Rankings

General Rankings

- To help military veterans find the best places in which to settle down, *WalletHub* compared the 100 largest U.S. cities across 19 key indicators of livability, affordability and veteran-friendliness. They range from the share of military skill-related jobs to veteran income growth to the availability of VA health facilities. New York ranked #78. *Wallethub.com, "Best & Worst Places for Veterans to Live (2025)," November 7, 2024*

- The human resources consulting firm Mercer ranked 241 major cities worldwide in terms of overall quality of life. New York ranked #45. Criteria: political and personal safety, social, and economic factors; medical and health considerations; schools and education; public services and transportation; recreation; connectivity; housing and infrastructure; and climate. *Mercer, "Mercer 2024 Quality of Living Survey," December 2024*

- New York appeared on *Travel + Leisure's* list of "The 15 Best Cities in the United States." The city was ranked #8. Criteria: walkability; sights/landmarks; culture; food; friendliness; shopping; and overall value. *Travel + Leisure, "The World's Best Awards 2024" July 9, 2024*

- For its 37th annual "Readers' Choice Awards" survey, *Condé Nast Traveler* ranked its readers' favorite cities in the U.S. Whether it be a longed-for visit or the next big new thing, these are the places travelers loved best. The list was broken into large cities and cities under 250,000. New York ranked #8 in the big city category. *Condé Nast Traveler, Readers' Choice Awards 2024, "Best Big Cities in the U.S." October 1, 2024*

Business/Finance Rankings

- Payscale.com ranked the 32 largest metro areas in terms of wage growth. The New York metro area ranked #18. Criteria: quarterly changes in private industry employee and education professional wage growth from the previous year. *PayScale, "Wage Trends by Metro Area-4th Quarter," February 4, 2025*

- For its annual survey of the "Most Expensive U.S. Cities to Live In," Kiplinger applied Cost of Living Index statistics developed by the Council for Community and Economic Research to U.S. Census Bureau population and median household income data for 265 urban areas. New York ranked #7 among the most expensive in the country. *Kiplinger.com, "The 10 Most Expensive Cities to Live in the U.S.," February 3, 2025*

- The New York metro area appeared on the Milken Institute "2025 Best Performing Cities" list. Rank: #153 out of 200 large metro areas (based on performance category). Criteria: job growth; wage growth; high-tech growth and impact; community resilience; housing affordability; household broadband access. *Milken Institute, "Best-Performing Cities 2025," January 14, 2025*

- Mercer Human Resources Consulting ranked 226 cities worldwide in terms of cost-of-living. New York ranked #7 (the lower the ranking, the higher the cost-of-living). The survey measured the comparative cost of over 200 items (such as housing, food, clothing, domestic supplies, transportation, and recreation/entertainment) in each location. *Mercer, "2024 Cost of Living City Ranking," June 17, 2024*

Education Rankings

- Personal finance website *WalletHub* analyzed the 150 largest U.S. metropolitan statistical areas to determine where the most educated Americans are putting their degrees to work. Criteria: education levels; percentage of workers with degrees; education quality and attainment gap; public school quality rankings; quality and enrollment of each metro area's universities. New York was ranked #26 (#1 = most educated city). *WalletHub.com, "Most & Least Educated Cities in America, 2025" July 2, 2024*

Environmental Rankings

- The U.S. Environmental Protection Agency (EPA) released its list of U.S. metropolitan areas with the most ENERGY STAR certified buildings in 2023. The New York metro area was ranked #3 out of 25. *U.S. Environmental Protection Agency, "2024 Energy Star Top Cities," May 22, 2024*

- New York was highlighted as one of the 25 most ozone-polluted metro areas in the U.S. during 2021 through 2023. The area ranked #16. *American Lung Association, "State of the Air 2025," April 23, 2025*

Food/Drink Rankings

- New York was identified as one of the cities in America ordering the most vegan food options by GrubHub.com. The city ranked #2 out of 5. Criteria: percentage of vegan, vegetarian and plant-based food orders compared to the overall number of orders. *GrubHub.com, "State of the Plate Report 2021: Top Cities for Vegans," June 20, 2021*

- WalletHub compared the 100 largest U.S. cities across 17 key indicators of vegan- and vegetarian-friendliness. New York was ranked #11. Cities were selected based on metrics such as the cost of groceries for vegetarians, the share of restaurants serving meatless options and the number of salad shops per capita. *WalletHub.com, "Best Cities for Vegans & Vegetarians (2025)," September 24, 2024*

Health/Fitness Rankings

- For each of the 100 largest cities in the United States, the American Fitness Index®, compiled in partnership between the American College of Sports Medicine and the Elevance Health Foundation, evaluated community infrastructure and more than 30 health behaviors including preventive health, levels of chronic disease conditions, food insecurity, pedestrian safety, air quality, and community/environment resources that support physical activity. New York ranked #26 for "community fitness." *americanfitnessindex.org, "2024 ACSM American Fitness Index Summary Report," July 23, 2024*

- New York was identified as one of the 10 most walkable cities in the U.S. by Walk Score. The city ranked #1. Walk Score measures walkability by analyzing hundreds of walking routes to nearby amenities, and also measures pedestrian friendliness by analyzing population density and road metrics such as block length and intersection density. *WalkScore.com, April 13, 2021*

- The New York metro area was identified as one of the worst cities for bed bugs in America by pest control company Orkin. The area ranked #2 out of 50 based on the number of bed bug treatments Orkin performed from December 2022 to November 2023. *Orkin, "Chicago Joins Paris In Global Bed Bug Spotlight Ranking As The Worst City On Orkin's U.S. Bed Bug Cities List," January 22, 2024*

- New York was identified as a "2025 Allergy Capital." The area ranked #89 out of the nation's 100 largest metropolitan areas. Three groups of factors were used to identify the most challenging cities for people with allergies: annual tree, grass, and weed pollen scores; over the counter allergy medicine use; number of board-certified allergy specialists. *Asthma and Allergy Foundation of America, "2025 Allergy Capitals: The Most Challenging Places to Live with Allergies," March 18, 2025*

- New York was identified as a "2024 Asthma Capital." The area ranked #19 out of the nation's 100 largest metropolitan areas. Criteria: estimated asthma prevalence; asthma-related mortality; and ER visits due to asthma. Risk factors analyzed but not factored in the rankings: annual air quality including pollution and ozone levels; public smoking laws; indoor air quality; access to asthma specialists; rescue and controller medication use; uninsured rate; pollen allergy; poverty rate. *Asthma and Allergy Foundation of America, "Asthma Capitals 2024: The Most Challenging Places to Live With Asthma," September 10, 2024*

- The Sharecare Community Well-Being Index evaluates 10 individual and social health factors in order to measure what matters to Americans in the communities in which they live. The New York metro area ranked #7 in the top 10 across all 10 domains. Criteria: access to healthcare, food, and community resources; housing and transportation; economic security; feeling of purpose; and physical, financial, social, and community well-being. *Sharecare.com, "Community Well-Being Index: 2020 Metro Area & County Rankings Report," August 30, 2021*

Pet Rankings

- New York was selected by *Sniffspot.com* as one of the most dog-friendly cities in the U.S., ranking #48 out of 50. Criteria: dog parks; hiking; sniffspots; public parks; dog-friendly businesses; housing; dog waste cleanliness; leash laws; dog services; and overall cost. *Sniffspot.com, "The Top 50 Most Dog-Friendly Cities in the U.S.," September 30, 2024*

Real Estate Rankings

- *WalletHub* compared the most populated U.S. cities to determine which had the best markets for real estate agents. New York ranked #98 where demand was high and pay was the best. Criteria: sales per agent; annual median wage for real-estate agents; monthly average starting salary for real estate agents; real estate job density and competition; unemployment rate; home turnover rate; housing-market health index; and other relevant metrics. *WalletHub.com, "2021 Best Places to Be a Real Estate Agent," May 12, 2021*

- New York was ranked #13 in the top 20 out of the 100 largest metro areas in terms of house price appreciation in 2024 (#1 = highest rate). *Federal Housing Finance Agency, "House Price Index, 4th Quarter 2024," February 25, 2025*

- The New York metro area was identified as one of the 20 least affordable housing markets in the U.S. in 2024. The area ranked #211 out of 226 markets. Criteria: qualification for a mortgage loan with a 10 percent down payment on a typical home. *National Association of Realtors®, Qualifying Income Based on Sales Price of Existing Single-Family Homes for Metropolitan Areas, February 6, 2025*

- New York was ranked #169 out of 176 metro areas in terms of cost of housing in 2024 by the National Association of Home Builders (#1 = most affordable). Criteria: the portion of an average family's income necessary to pay the mortgage on a median-priced home. *National Association of Home Builders®, NAHB-Wells Fargo Cost of Housing Index, 4th Quarter 2024*

- The nation's largest metro areas were analyzed in terms of the percentage of households entering some stage of foreclosure in 2024. The New York metro area ranked #1 out of 5 (#1 = highest foreclosure rate). *ATTOM Data Solutions, "2024 Year-End U.S. Foreclosure Market Report™," January 15, 2025*

Safety Rankings

- Allstate ranked the 100 most populous cities in America in terms of driver safety. New York ranked #32. Criteria based on anonymized driving behavior data from Allstate's mobile app powered by Arity: high speed driving (over 80 mph), phone handling, and hard braking. The report helps increase the importance of safety and awareness behind the wheel. *Allstate, "16th Allstate America's Best Drivers Report®" July 11, 2024*

- The National Insurance Crime Bureau ranked the largest metro areas in the U.S. in terms of per capita rates of vehicle theft. The New York metro area ranked #6 out of the top 10 (#1 = highest rate). Criteria: number of vehicle theft offenses per 100,000 inhabitants in 2023. *National Insurance Crime Bureau, "Vehicle Thefts Surge Nationwide in 2023," April 9, 2024*

Transportation Rankings

- New York was identified as one of the most congested metro areas in the U.S. The area ranked #3 out of 10. Criteria: yearly delay per auto commuter in hours. *Texas A&M Transportation Institute, "2023 Urban Mobility Report," June 2024*

- According to the INRIX "2024 Global Traffic Scorecard," New York was identified as one of the most congested metro areas in the U.S. The area ranked #1 out of 10 in the country and among the top 25 most congested in the world. Criteria: average annual time spent in traffic and average cost of congestion per motorist. *Inrix.com, "Employees & Consumers Returned to Downtowns, Traffic Delays & Costs Grew," January 6, 2025*

Women/Minorities Rankings

- *Travel + Leisure* listed the best cities in and around the U.S. for a memorable and fun girls' trip, even on a budget. Whether it is for a special occasion, to make new memories or just to get away, New York is sure to have something for all the ladies in your tribe. *Travel + Leisure, "25 Affordable Girls Weekend Getaways That Won't Break the Bank," January 30, 2025*

- Personal finance website *WalletHub* compared more than 180 U.S. cities across two key dimensions, "Hispanic Business-Friendliness" and "Hispanic Purchasing Power," to arrive at the most favorable conditions for Hispanic entrepreneurs. New York was ranked #170 out of 182. Criteria includes: share of Hispanic-Owned Businesses; average growth of Hispanic Business revenues; Small Business-Friendliness score; affordability; and number of Hispanics with at least a bachelor's degree. *WalletHub.com, "Best Cities for Hispanic Entrepreneurs," September 4, 2024*

Miscellaneous Rankings

- In its roundup of St. Patrick's Day parades, *Gayot* listed the best festivals and parades of all things Irish. The festivities in New York as among the best in North America. *Gayot.com, "Best St. Patrick's Day Parades," March 2025*

- *WalletHub* compared 148 of the most populated U.S. cities to determine their operating efficiency. A "Quality of Services" score was constructed for each city and then measured against the total budget per capita to reveal which were managed the best. New York ranked #145. Criteria: financial stability; economy; education; safety; health; infrastructure and pollution. *WalletHub.com, "2025's Best- & Worst-Run Cities in America," June 18, 2024*

Business Environment

DEMOGRAPHICS

Population Growth

Area	1990 Census	2000 Census	2010 Census	2020 Census	2023 Estimate[2]	Population Growth 1990-2023 (%)
City	7,322,552	8,008,278	8,175,133	8,804,190	8,516,202	16.3
MSA[1]	16,845,992	18,323,002	18,897,109	20,140,470	19,756,722	17.3
U.S.	248,709,873	281,421,906	308,745,538	331,449,281	332,387,540	33.6

Note: (1) Figures cover the New York-Newark-Jersey City, NY-NJ Metropolitan Statistical Area; (2) 2019-2023 5-year ACS population estimate
Source: U.S. Census Bureau, 1990 Census, 2000 Census, 2010 Census, 2020 Census, 2019-2023 American Community Survey 5-Year Estimates

Race

Area	White Alone[2] (%)	Black Alone[2] (%)	Asian Alone[2] (%)	AIAN[3] Alone[2] (%)	NHOPI[4] Alone[2] (%)	Other Race Alone[2] (%)	Two or More Races (%)
City	35.9	22.7	14.6	0.7	0.1	15.5	10.5
MSA[1]	48.4	16.3	11.8	0.5	0.0	12.3	10.6
U.S.	63.4	12.4	5.8	0.9	0.2	6.6	10.7

Note: (1) Figures cover the New York-Newark-Jersey City, NY-NJ Metropolitan Statistical Area; (2) Alone is defined as not being in combination with one or more other races; (3) American Indian and Alaska Native; (4) Native Hawaiian and Other Pacific Islander
Source: U.S. Census Bureau, 2019-2023 American Community Survey 5-Year Estimates

Hispanic or Latino Origin

Area	Total (%)	Mexican (%)	Puerto Rican (%)	Cuban (%)	Other (%)
City	28.4	3.9	7.1	0.5	17.0
MSA[1]	25.4	3.0	5.6	0.8	16.0
U.S.	19.0	11.3	1.8	0.7	5.2

Note: Persons of Hispanic or Latino origin can be of any race; (1) Figures cover the New York-Newark-Jersey City, NY-NJ Metropolitan Statistical Area
Source: U.S. Census Bureau, 2019-2023 American Community Survey 5-Year Estimates

Age

Area	Under Age 5	Age 5–19	Age 20–34	Age 35–44	Age 45–54	Age 55–64	Age 65–74	Age 75–84	Age 85+	Median Age
City	5.9	16.7	22.9	13.9	12.4	12.2	9.2	4.8	2.0	38.0
MSA[1]	5.8	17.9	20.4	13.3	12.9	13.2	9.6	4.9	2.1	39.4
U.S.	5.7	19.1	20.2	13.1	12.3	12.8	10.0	4.9	1.9	38.7

Note: (1) Figures cover the New York-Newark-Jersey City, NY-NJ Metropolitan Statistical Area
Source: U.S. Census Bureau, 2019-2023 American Community Survey 5-Year Estimates

Disability by Age

Area	All Ages	Under 18 Years Old	18 to 64 Years Old	65 Years and Over
City	11.7	3.9	8.5	34.6
MSA[1]	10.6	3.5	7.7	30.9
U.S.	13.0	4.7	10.7	32.9

Note: Figures show percent of the civilian noninstitutionalized population that reported having a disability. Disability status is determined from six types of difficulty: vision, hearing, cognitive, ambulatory, self-care, and independent living. For children under 5 years old, hearing and vision difficulty are used to determine disability status. For children between the ages of 5 and 14, disability status is determined from hearing, vision, cognitive, ambulatory, and self-care difficulties. For people aged 15 years and older, they are considered to have a disability if they have difficulty with any one of the six difficulty types; Note: (1) Figures cover the New York-Newark-Jersey City, NY-NJ Metropolitan Statistical Area
Source: U.S. Census Bureau, 2019-2023 American Community Survey 5-Year Estimates

Ancestry

Area	German	Irish	English	American	Italian	Polish	French[2]	European	Scottish
City	2.9	4.4	2.1	3.7	5.8	2.1	0.8	0.9	0.5
MSA[1]	5.7	8.6	3.0	3.9	11.0	3.4	0.8	0.9	0.6
U.S.	12.6	9.4	9.1	5.5	4.9	2.6	2.0	1.6	1.6

Note: Figures are the percentage of the total population reporting a particular ancestry. The nine most commonly reported ancestries in the U.S. are shown. Figures include multiple ancestries (e.g. if a person reported being Irish and Italian, they were included in both columns); (1) Figures cover the New York-Newark-Jersey City, NY-NJ Metropolitan Statistical Area; (2) Excludes Basque
Source: U.S. Census Bureau, 2019-2023 American Community Survey 5-Year Estimates

Foreign-born Population

Area	Percent of Population Born in								
	Any Foreign Country	Asia	Mexico	Europe	Caribbean	Central America[2]	South America	Africa	Canada
City	36.5	11.0	1.8	5.1	9.7	1.4	5.1	1.9	0.3
MSA[1]	29.8	8.9	1.4	4.2	6.8	2.0	4.7	1.5	0.3
U.S.	13.9	4.3	3.3	1.4	1.4	1.2	1.2	0.8	0.2

Note: (1) Figures cover the New York-Newark-Jersey City, NY-NJ Metropolitan Statistical Area; (2) Excludes Mexico.
Source: U.S. Census Bureau, 2019-2023 American Community Survey 5-Year Estimates

Household Size

Area	Persons in Household (%)							Average Household Size
	One	Two	Three	Four	Five	Six	Seven or More	
City	33.4	28.8	16.1	11.7	5.6	2.5	1.9	2.51
MSA[1]	28.6	29.6	16.8	14.1	6.3	2.6	1.9	2.63
U.S.	28.5	33.8	15.4	12.7	5.9	2.3	1.4	2.54

Note: (1) Figures cover the New York-Newark-Jersey City, NY-NJ Metropolitan Statistical Area
Source: U.S. Census Bureau, 2019-2023 American Community Survey 5-Year Estimates

Household Relationships

Area	House-holder	Opposite-sex Spouse	Same-sex Spouse	Opposite-sex Unmarried Partner	Same-sex Unmarried Partner	Child[2]	Grand-child	Other Relatives	Non-relatives
City	38.3	12.7	0.3	2.2	0.2	27.6	2.5	8.3	5.3
MSA[1]	36.8	15.8	0.2	2.0	0.2	29.7	2.1	7.1	4.1
U.S.	38.3	17.5	0.2	2.5	0.2	28.3	2.4	4.8	3.4

Note: Figures are percent of the total population; (1) Figures cover the New York-Newark-Jersey City, NY-NJ Metropolitan Statistical Area; (2) Includes biological, adopted, and stepchildren of the householder
Source: U.S. Census Bureau, 2020 Census

Gender

Area	Males	Females	Males per 100 Females
City	4,088,026	4,428,176	92.3
MSA[1]	9,622,708	10,134,014	95.0
U.S.	164,545,087	167,842,453	98.0

Note: (1) Figures cover the New York-Newark-Jersey City, NY-NJ Metropolitan Statistical Area
Source: U.S. Census Bureau, 2019-2023 American Community Survey 5-Year Estimates

Marital Status

Area	Never Married	Now Married[2]	Separated	Widowed	Divorced
City	44.0	39.8	2.8	5.2	8.2
MSA[1]	38.3	46.0	2.1	5.4	8.1
U.S.	34.1	47.9	1.7	5.6	10.7

Note: Figures are percentages and cover the population 15 years of age and older; (1) Figures cover the New York-Newark-Jersey City, NY-NJ Metropolitan Statistical Area; (2) Excludes separated
Source: U.S. Census Bureau, 2019-2023 American Community Survey 5-Year Estimates

Religious Groups by Family

Area	Catholic	Baptist	Methodist	LDS[2]	Pentecostal	Lutheran	Islam	Adventist	Other
MSA[1]	32.5	1.7	1.2	0.3	0.9	0.5	4.5	1.4	10.6
U.S.	18.7	7.3	3.0	2.0	1.8	1.7	1.3	1.3	11.6

Note: Figures are the number of adherents as a percentage of the total population and cover the eight largest religious groups in the U.S; (1) Figures cover the New York-Newark-Jersey City, NY-NJ Metropolitan Statistical Area; (2) Church of Jesus Christ of Latter-day Saints
Sources: 2020 U.S. Religion Census, Association of Statisticians of American Religious Bodies; The Association of Religion Data Archives (ARDA)

Religious Groups by Tradition

Area	Catholic	Evangelical Protestant	Mainline Protestant	Black Protestant	Islam	Judaism	Hinduism	Orthodox	Buddhism
MSA[1]	32.5	4.4	3.0	1.5	4.5	4.4	1.0	0.8	0.3
U.S.	18.7	16.5	5.2	2.3	1.3	0.6	0.4	0.4	0.3

Note: Figures are the number of adherents as a percentage of the total population; (1) Figures cover the New York-Newark-Jersey City, NY-NJ Metropolitan Statistical Area
Sources: 2020 U.S. Religion Census, Association of Statisticians of American Religious Bodies; The Association of Religion Data Archives (ARDA)

ECONOMY

Real Gross Domestic Product (GDP)

Area	2017	2018	2019	2020	2021	2022	2023	Rank[3]
MSA[1]	1,714.1	1,766.3	1,801.1	1,744.7	1,834.5	1,875.1	1,905.2	1
U.S.[2]	17,619.1	18,160.7	18,642.5	18,238.9	19,387.6	19,896.6	20,436.3	—

Note: Figures are in billions of chained 2017 dollars; (1) Figures cover the New York-Newark-Jersey City, NY-NJ Metropolitan Statistical Area; (2) Figures cover real GDP within metropolitan areas; (3) Rank is based on 2023 data and ranges from 1 to 384
Source: U.S. Bureau of Economic Analysis

Economic Growth

Area	2014	2015	2016	2017	2018	2019	2020	2021	2022	2023
MSA[1]	1.9	2.2	1.7	2.0	3.0	2.0	-3.1	5.1	2.2	1.6
U.S.[2]	2.6	3.2	2.0	2.7	3.1	2.7	-2.2	6.3	2.6	2.7

Note: Figures are real gross domestic product growth rates and represent percent change from preceding period; (1) Figures cover the New York-Newark-Jersey City, NY-NJ Metropolitan Statistical Area; (2) Figures are the average growth rates within metropolitan areas
Source: U.S. Bureau of Economic Analysis

Metropolitan Area Exports

Area	2018	2019	2020	2021	2022	2023	Rank[2]
MSA[1]	97,692.4	87,365.7	75,745.4	103,930.9	120,643.7	106,209.0	2
U.S.	1,664,056.1	1,645,173.7	1,431,406.6	1,753,941.4	2,062,937.4	2,019,160.5	—

Note: Figures are in millions of dollars; (1) Figures cover the New York-Newark-Jersey City, NY-NJ Metropolitan Statistical Area; (2) Rank is based on 2023 data and ranges from 1 to 386
Source: U.S. Department of Commerce, International Trade Administration, Office of Trade and Economic Analysis, Industry and Analysis, Exports by Metropolitan Area, data extracted April 2, 2025

Building Permits

Area	Single-Family			Multi-Family			Total		
	2023	2024	Pct. Chg.	2023	2024	Pct. Chg.	2023	2024	Pct. Chg.
City	232	197	-15.1	31,733	27,044	-14.8	31,965	27,241	-14.8
MSA[1]	11,734	12,530	6.8	51,296	45,399	-11.5	63,030	57,929	-8.1
U.S.	920,000	981,900	6.7	591,100	496,100	-16.1	1,511,100	1,478,000	-2.2

Note: (1) Figures cover the New York-Newark-Jersey City, NY-NJ Metropolitan Statistical Area; Figures represent new, privately-owned housing units authorized (unadjusted data)
Source: U.S. Census Bureau, Building Permits Survey (BPS), 2023, 2024

Bankruptcy Filings

Area	Business Filings			Nonbusiness Filings		
	2023	2024	% Chg.	2023	2024	% Chg.
Bronx County	25	44	76.0	1,071	1,319	23.2
Kings County	394	457	16.0	1,781	2,036	14.3
New York County	750	361	-51.9	684	793	15.9
Queens County	215	209	-2.8	1,921	2,120	10.4
Richmond County	23	29	26.1	490	494	0.8
U.S.	18,926	23,107	22.1	434,064	494,201	13.9

Note: Business filings include Chapter 7, Chapter 9, Chapter 11, Chapter 12, Chapter 13, Chapter 15, and Section 304; Nonbusiness filings include Chapter 7, Chapter 11, and Chapter 13
Source: Administrative Office of the U.S. Courts, Business and Nonbusiness Bankruptcy, County Cases Commenced by Chapter of the Bankruptcy Code, During the 12-Month Period Ending December 31, 2023 and Business and Nonbusiness Bankruptcy, County Cases Commenced by Chapter of the Bankruptcy Code, During the 12-Month Period Ending December 31, 2024

Housing Vacancy Rates

Area	Gross Vacancy Rate[3] (%)			Year-Round Vacancy Rate[4] (%)			Rental Vacancy Rate[5] (%)			Homeowner Vacancy Rate[6] (%)		
	2022	2023	2024	2022	2023	2024	2022	2023	2024	2022	2023	2024
MSA[1]	8.2	7.8	8.3	7.0	6.7	7.4	3.5	3.9	4.7	1.0	0.9	1.0
U.S.[2]	9.1	9.0	9.1	7.5	7.5	7.6	5.7	6.5	6.8	0.8	0.8	1.0

Note: (1) Figures cover the New York-Newark-Jersey City, NY-NJ Metropolitan Statistical Area; (2) Figures cover the 75 largest Metropolitan Statistical Areas; (3) The percentage of the total housing inventory that is vacant; (4) The percentage of the housing inventory (excluding seasonal units) that is year-round vacant; (5) The percentage of rental inventory that is vacant for rent; (6) The percentage of homeowner inventory that is vacant for sale
Source: U.S. Census Bureau, Housing Vacancies and Homeownership Annual Statistics: 2022, 2023, 2024

INCOME

Income

Area	Per Capita ($)	Median Household ($)	Average Household ($)
City	50,776	79,713	127,894
MSA[1]	54,510	97,334	144,032
U.S.	43,289	78,538	110,491

Note: (1) Figures cover the New York-Newark-Jersey City, NY-NJ Metropolitan Statistical Area
Source: U.S. Census Bureau, 2019-2023 American Community Survey 5-Year Estimates

Household Income Distribution

Area	Percent of Households Earning							
	Under $15,000	$15,000 -$24,999	$25,000 -$34,999	$35,000 -$49,999	$50,000 -$74,999	$75,000 -$99,999	$100,000 -$149,999	$150,000 and up
City	12.3	7.0	6.3	8.9	13.3	10.8	15.3	26.1
MSA[1]	9.0	5.6	5.4	7.9	12.4	10.7	16.7	32.4
U.S.	8.5	6.6	6.8	10.4	15.7	12.7	17.4	21.9

Note: (1) Figures cover the New York-Newark-Jersey City, NY-NJ Metropolitan Statistical Area
Source: U.S. Census Bureau, 2019-2023 American Community Survey 5-Year Estimates

Poverty Rate

Area	All Ages	Under 18 Years Old	18 to 64 Years Old	65 Years and Over
City	17.4	23.2	15.1	18.9
MSA[1]	12.4	16.4	10.9	13.0
U.S.	12.4	16.3	11.6	10.4

Note: Figures are percentage of people whose income during the past 12 months was below the poverty level; (1) Figures cover the New York-Newark-Jersey City, NY-NJ Metropolitan Statistical Area
Source: U.S. Census Bureau, 2019-2023 American Community Survey 5-Year Estimates

EMPLOYMENT

Labor Force and Employment

Area	Civilian Labor Force			Workers Employed		
	Dec. 2023	Dec. 2024	% Chg.	Dec. 2023	Dec. 2024	% Chg.
City	4,197,201	4,289,830	2.2	4,004,371	4,065,287	1.5
MD[1]	6,077,969	6,169,474	1.5	5,813,964	5,874,694	1.0
U.S.	166,661,000	167,746,000	0.7	160,754,000	161,294,000	0.3

Note: Data is not seasonally adjusted and covers workers 16 years of age and older; (1) Figures cover the New York-Jersey City-White Plains, NY-NJ Metropolitan Division
Source: Bureau of Labor Statistics, Local Area Unemployment Statistics

Unemployment Rate

Area	2024											
	Jan.	Feb.	Mar.	Apr.	May	Jun.	Jul.	Aug.	Sep.	Oct.	Nov.	Dec.
City	4.8	5.1	4.8	4.6	4.9	5.4	6.1	6.1	5.3	5.5	5.5	5.2
MD[1]	4.6	4.9	4.6	4.3	4.6	5.1	5.7	5.6	4.8	5.0	5.0	4.8
U.S.	4.1	4.2	3.9	3.5	3.7	4.3	4.5	4.4	3.9	3.9	4.0	3.8

Note: Data is not seasonally adjusted and covers workers 16 years of age and older; (1) Figures cover the New York-Jersey City-White Plains, NY-NJ Metropolitan Division
Source: Bureau of Labor Statistics, Local Area Unemployment Statistics

Average Wages

Occupation	$/Hr.	Occupation	$/Hr.
Accountants and Auditors	58.64	Maintenance and Repair Workers	28.95
Automotive Mechanics	29.75	Marketing Managers	96.08
Bookkeepers	29.11	Network and Computer Systems Admin.	57.33
Carpenters	37.32	Nurses, Licensed Practical	34.69
Cashiers	17.91	Nurses, Registered	55.60
Computer Programmers	58.71	Nursing Assistants	23.60
Computer Systems Analysts	61.28	Office Clerks, General	24.07
Computer User Support Specialists	35.37	Physical Therapists	52.54
Construction Laborers	34.43	Physicians	125.08
Cooks, Restaurant	20.82	Plumbers, Pipefitters and Steamfitters	43.78
Customer Service Representatives	25.80	Police and Sheriff's Patrol Officers	44.53
Dentists	89.32	Postal Service Mail Carriers	28.97
Electricians	41.08	Real Estate Sales Agents	50.92
Engineers, Electrical	60.31	Retail Salespersons	21.03
Fast Food and Counter Workers	17.50	Sales Representatives, Technical/Scientific	71.17
Financial Managers	119.16	Secretaries, Exc. Legal/Medical/Executive	25.44
First-Line Supervisors of Office Workers	39.92	Security Guards	21.96
General and Operations Managers	89.97	Surgeons	153.50
Hairdressers/Cosmetologists	24.83	Teacher Assistants, Exc. Postsecondary[1]	19.26
Home Health and Personal Care Aides	19.02	Teachers, Secondary School, Exc. Sp. Ed.[1]	48.38
Janitors and Cleaners	21.61	Telemarketers	19.76
Landscaping/Groundskeeping Workers	21.91	Truck Drivers, Heavy/Tractor-Trailer	33.26
Lawyers	103.90	Truck Drivers, Light/Delivery Services	25.01
Maids and Housekeeping Cleaners	24.09	Waiters and Waitresses	25.65

Note: Wage data covers the New York-Newark-Jersey City, NY-NJ Metropolitan Statistical Area; (1) Hourly wages were calculated from annual wage data based on a 40 hour work week
Source: Bureau of Labor Statistics, Metro Area Occupational Employment & Wage Estimates, May 2024

Employment by Industry

Sector	MD[1] Number of Employees	MD[1] Percent of Total	U.S. Percent of Total
Construction, Mining, and Logging	212,600	3.3	5.5
Financial Activities	634,900	9.8	5.8
Government	810,100	12.5	14.9
Information	259,000	4.0	1.9
Leisure and Hospitality	587,700	9.0	10.4
Manufacturing	135,100	2.1	8.0
Other Services	249,600	3.8	3.7
Private Education and Health Services	1,642,300	25.2	16.9
Professional and Business Services	1,044,900	16.1	14.2
Retail Trade	473,400	7.3	10.0
Transportation, Warehousing, and Utilities	239,400	3.7	4.8
Wholesale Trade	215,500	3.3	3.9

Note: Figures are non-farm employment as of December 2024. Figures are not seasonally adjusted and include workers 16 years of age and older; (1) Figures cover the New York-Jersey City-White Plains, NY-NJ Metropolitan Division
Source: Bureau of Labor Statistics, Current Employment Statistics, Employment, Hours, and Earnings

Employment by Occupation

Occupation Classification	City (%)	MSA[1] (%)	U.S. (%)
Management, Business, Science, and Arts	45.9	47.2	42.0
Natural Resources, Construction, and Maintenance	5.5	6.4	8.6
Production, Transportation, and Material Moving	8.8	9.4	13.0
Sales and Office	18.1	19.2	19.9
Service	21.8	17.8	16.5

Note: Figures cover employed civilians 16 years of age and older; (1) Figures cover the New York-Newark-Jersey City, NY-NJ Metropolitan Statistical Area
Source: U.S. Census Bureau, 2019-2023 American Community Survey 5-Year Estimates

Occupations with Greatest Projected Employment Growth: 2022 – 2032

Occupation[1]	2022 Employment	2032 Projected Employment	Numeric Employment Change	Percent Employment Change
Home Health and Personal Care Aides	551,740	710,140	158,400	28.7
Registered Nurses	204,040	256,080	52,040	25.5
Fast Food and Counter Workers	201,110	237,100	35,990	17.9
Janitors and Cleaners, Except Maids and Housekeeping Cleaners	181,950	207,060	25,110	13.8
Teaching Assistants, Except Postsecondary	116,720	139,920	23,200	19.9
Nursing Assistants (SOC 2018)	92,350	114,280	21,930	23.7
Secretaries and Administrative Assistants, Except Legal, Medical, and Executive	177,980	197,740	19,760	11.1
Elementary School Teachers, Except Special Education	95,340	112,670	17,330	18.2
Maintenance and Repair Workers, General	144,750	161,950	17,200	11.9
General and Operations Managers	217,850	233,880	16,030	7.4

Note: Projections cover New York; (1) Sorted by numeric employment change
Source: www.projectionscentral.org, State Occupational Projections, 2022–2032 Long-Term Projections

Fastest-Growing Occupations: 2022 – 2032

Occupation[1]	2022 Employment	2032 Projected Employment	Numeric Employment Change	Percent Employment Change
Gaming Change Persons and Booth Cashiers	670	1,030	360	53.7
Gaming Dealers	2,910	4,230	1,320	45.4
Physical Therapist Aides	3,730	4,930	1,200	32.2
Lodging Managers	3,720	4,900	1,180	31.7
Physical Therapists	19,190	24,830	5,640	29.4
Podiatrists	1,190	1,540	350	29.4
Home Health and Personal Care Aides	551,740	710,140	158,400	28.7
Physical Therapist Assistants	4,260	5,470	1,210	28.4
Psychiatric Technicians	2,330	2,980	650	27.9
Radiation Therapists	1,220	1,560	340	27.9

Note: Projections cover New York; (1) Sorted by percent employment change and excludes occupations with numeric employment change less than 50
Source: www.projectionscentral.org, State Occupational Projections, 2022–2032 Long-Term Projections

CITY FINANCES

City Government Finances

Component	2022 ($000)	2022 ($ per capita)
Total Revenues	125,841,101	15,248
Total Expenditures	131,775,840	15,967
Debt Outstanding	127,818,519	15,487

Source: U.S. Census Bureau, State & Local Government Finances 2022

City Government Revenue by Source

Source	2022 ($000)	2022 ($ per capita)	2022 (%)
General Revenue			
From Federal Government	15,087,266	1,828	12.0
From State Government	14,429,369	1,748	11.5
From Local Governments	4,174,245	506	3.3
Taxes			
Property	29,507,123	3,575	23.4
Sales and Gross Receipts	10,477,820	1,270	8.3
Personal Income	17,084,016	2,070	13.6
Corporate Income	8,227,909	997	6.5
Motor Vehicle License	91,379	11	0.1
Other Taxes	3,953,411	479	3.1
Current Charges	11,152,981	1,351	8.9
Liquor Store	0	0	0.0
Utility	3,956,283	479	3.1

Source: U.S. Census Bureau, State & Local Government Finances 2022

City Government Expenditures by Function

Function	2022 ($000)	2022 ($ per capita)	2022 (%)
General Direct Expenditures			
Air Transportation	0	0	0.0
Corrections	1,595,558	193	1.2
Education	39,606,521	4,798	30.1
Employment Security Administration	0	0	0.0
Financial Administration	518,957	62	0.4
Fire Protection	2,572,675	311	2.0
General Public Buildings	678,832	82	0.5
Governmental Administration, Other	296,301	35	0.2
Health	2,132,606	258	1.6
Highways	1,102,684	133	0.8
Hospitals	10,989,070	1,331	8.3
Housing and Community Development	7,033,514	852	5.3
Interest on General Debt	6,380,821	773	4.8
Judicial and Legal	1,546,675	187	1.2
Libraries	542,892	65	0.4
Parking	50,303	6	0.0
Parks and Recreation	1,368,434	165	1.0
Police Protection	5,867,692	711	4.5
Public Welfare	10,017,325	1,213	7.6
Sewerage	2,700,182	327	2.0
Solid Waste Management	2,092,977	253	1.6
Veterans' Services	0	0	0.0
Liquor Store	0	0	0.0
Utility	12,948,108	1,568	9.8

Source: U.S. Census Bureau, State & Local Government Finances 2022

TAXES

State Corporate Income Tax Rates

State	Tax Rate (%)	Income Brackets ($)	Num. of Brackets	Financial Institution Tax Rate (%)[a]	Federal Income Tax Ded.
New York	7.25 (p)	Flat rate	1	7.25 (p)	No

Note: Tax rates for tax year 2024; (a) Rates listed are the corporate income tax rate applied to financial institutions or excise taxes based on income. Some states have other taxes based upon the value of deposits or shares; (p) Plus a Corporate Stocks Tax of 0.1875% for tax years 2022 - 2024. A top bracket of 7.25% is imposed on income over $5 million for 2022 - 2024. A minimum tax ranges from $25 to $200,000, depending on receipts ($250 minimum for banks). Certain qualified New York manufacturers pay 0%.
Source: Federation of Tax Administrators, State Corporate Income Tax Rates, January 1, 2025

State Individual Income Tax Rates

State	Tax Rate (%)	Income Brackets ($)	Personal Exemptions ($)			Standard Ded. ($)	
			Single	Married	Depend.	Single	Married
New York (a)	4.0 - 10.9	8,500 - 25 mil. (s)	0	0	1,000	8,000	16,050

Note: Tax rates for tax year 2024; Local- and county-level taxes are not included; Federal income tax is not deductible on state income tax returns; (a) 16 states have statutory provision for automatically adjusting to the rate of inflation the dollar values of the income tax brackets, standard deductions, and/or personal exemptions. Oregon does not index the income brackets for $125,000 and over See: INFL and SPEC above; (s) The income brackets reported for New York are for single individuals. For married couples filing jointly, the same tax rates apply to income brackets ranging from $17,150 to $25 million.
Source: Federation of Tax Administrators, State Individual Income Tax Rates, January 1, 2025

Various State Sales and Excise Tax Rates

State	State Sales Tax (%)	Gasoline[1] ($/gal.)	Cigarette[2] ($/pack)	Spirits[3] ($/gal.)	Wine[4] ($/gal.)	Beer[5] ($/gal.)	Recreational Marijuana (%)
New York	4	0.25	5.35	6.44	0.30	0.14	(r)

Note: All tax rates as of January 1, 2025; (1) The American Petroleum Institute has developed a methodology for determining the average tax rate on a gallon of fuel. Rates may include any of the following: excise taxes, environmental fees, storage tank fees, other fees or taxes, general sales tax, and local taxes; (2) The federal excise tax of $1.0066 per pack and local taxes are not included; (3) Rates are those applicable to off-premise sales of 40% alcohol by volume (a.b.v.) distilled spirits in 750ml containers. Local excise taxes are excluded; (4) Rates are those applicable to off-premise sales of 11% a.b.v. non-carbonated wine in 750ml containers; (5) Rates are those applicable to off-premise sales of 4.7% a.b.v. beer in 12 ounce containers; (r) 9% excise tax (wholesale price); 13% excise tax (retail price)
Source: Tax Foundation, 2025 Facts & Figures: How Does Your State Compare?

State Tax Competitiveness Index

State	Overall Rank	Corporate Tax Rank	Individual Income Tax Rank	Sales Tax Rank	Property Tax Rank	Unemployment Insurance Tax Rank
New York	50	28	50	42	47	37

Note: The Tax Foundation's State Tax Competitiveness Index enables policymakers, taxpayers, and business leaders to gauge how their states' tax systems compare. A rank of 1 is best, 50 is worst. Rankings do not average to the total. States without a tax rank equally as 1. DC's scores and rankings do not affect other states. The report shows tax systems as of July 1, 2024 (the beginning of Fiscal Year 2025).
Source: Tax Foundation, State Tax Competitiveness Index 2025

TRANSPORTATION

Means of Transportation to Work

Area	Car/Truck/Van Drove Alone	Car/Truck/Van Carpooled	Public Transportation Bus	Public Transportation Subway	Public Transportation Railroad	Bicycle	Walked	Other Means	Worked at Home
City	21.9	4.3	9.8	34.4	1.0	1.5	9.4	2.7	15.0
MSA[1]	45.5	6.1	6.4	15.6	2.6	0.8	5.4	2.7	14.9
U.S.	70.2	8.5	1.7	1.3	0.4	0.4	2.4	1.6	13.5

Note: Figures are percentages and cover workers 16 years of age and older; (1) Figures cover the New York-Newark-Jersey City, NY-NJ Metropolitan Statistical Area
Source: U.S. Census Bureau, 2019-2023 American Community Survey 5-Year Estimates

Travel Time to Work

Area	Less Than 10 Minutes	10 to 19 Minutes	20 to 29 Minutes	30 to 44 Minutes	45 to 59 Minutes	60 to 89 Minutes	90 Minutes or More
City	4.4	12.7	14.0	27.0	16.1	18.7	7.1
MSA[1]	7.3	19.0	16.6	23.9	12.6	14.2	6.4
U.S.	12.6	28.6	21.2	20.8	8.1	6.0	2.8

Note: Note: Figures are percentages and include workers 16 years old and over; (1) Figures cover the New York-Newark-Jersey City, NY-NJ Metropolitan Statistical Area
Source: U.S. Census Bureau, 2019-2023 American Community Survey 5-Year Estimates

Key Congestion Measures

Measure	2000	2010	2015	2020	2022
Annual Hours of Delay, Total (000)	480,809	688,933	778,986	494,268	781,553
Annual Hours of Delay, Per Auto Commuter	62	78	87	56	92
Annual Congestion Cost, Per Auto Commuter ($)	1,854	2,110	2,204	1,478	2,239

Note: Figures cover the New York-Newark NY-NJ-CT urban area
Source: Texas A&M Transportation Institute, 2023 Urban Mobility Report

Freeway Travel Time Index

Measure	1985	1990	1995	2000	2005	2010	2015	2020	2022
Urban Area Index[1]	1.16	1.20	1.24	1.29	1.33	1.33	1.35	1.17	1.32
Urban Area Rank[1,2]	10	9	7	6	6	7	7	1	8

Note: Freeway Travel Time Index—the ratio of travel time in the peak period to the travel time at free-flow conditions. For example, a value of 1.30 indicates a 20-minute free-flow trip takes 26 minutes in the peak (20 minutes x 1.30 = 26 minutes); (1) Covers the New York-Newark NY-NJ-CT urban area; (2) Rank is based on 101 larger urban areas (#1 = highest travel time index)
Source: Texas A&M Transportation Institute, 2023 Urban Mobility Report

Public Transportation

Agency Name / Mode of Transportation	Vehicles Operated in Maximum Service[1]	Annual Unlinked Passenger Trips[2] (in thous.)	Annual Passenger Miles[3] (in thous.)
MTA New York City Transit (NYCT)			
Bus (directly operated)	3,214	570,625.2	1,373,347.9
Bus Rapid Transit (directly operated)	123	31,784.2	55,443.5
Commuter Bus (directly operated)	443	8,995.4	135,709.7
Demand Response (purchased transportation)	876	2,716.6	24,803.0
Heavy Rail (directly operated)	5,384	2,017,881.7	8,001,949.4
MTA Metro-North Railroad (MTA-MNCR)			
Bus (purchased transportation)	9	181.1	139.3
Commuter Rail (directly operated)	1,132	66,366.3	1,150,348.9
Ferryboat (purchased transportation)	2	97.9	406.7
MTA Long Island Railroad (MTA-LIRR)			
Commuter Rail (directly operated)	1,109	83,835.7	2,033,685.8
MTA Staten Island Railway (SIRTOA)			
Heavy Rail (directly operated)	44	5,194.6	30,544.9
New York City Department of Transportation (NYCDOT)			
Ferryboat (directly operated)	4	14,715.4	76,519.9
Port Authority Trans-Hudson Corporation (PATH)			
Heavy Rail (directly operated)	288	55,108.9	268,404.8

Note: (1) Number of revenue vehicles operated by the given mode and type of service to meet the annual maximum service requirement. This is the revenue vehicle count during the peak season of the year; on the week and day that maximum service is provided. Vehicles operated in maximum service (VOMS) exclude atypical days and one-time special events; (2) Number of passengers who boarded public transportation vehicles. Passengers are counted each time they board a vehicle no matter how many vehicles they use to travel from their origin to their destination. (3) Sum of the distances ridden by all passengers during the entire fiscal year.
Source: Federal Transit Administration, National Transit Database, 2023

Air Transportation

Airport Name and Code / Type of Service	Passenger Airlines[1]	Passenger Enplanements	Freight Carriers[2]	Freight (lbs)
John F. Kennedy International (JFK)				
Domestic service (U.S. carriers only)	18	13,918,304	16	358,611,373
International service (U.S. carriers only)	8	7,731,158	6	111,951,655
La Guardia International (LGA)				
Domestic service (U.S. carriers only)	20	15,839,248	4	6,263,903
International service (U.S. carriers only)	7	429,147	0	0
Newark International (EWR)				
Domestic service (U.S. carriers only)	29	16,928,416	15	467,567,997
International service (U.S. carriers only)	10	5,069,183	5	94,420,610

Note: (1) Includes all U.S.-based major, minor and commuter airlines that carried at least one passenger during the year; (2) Includes all U.S.-based airlines and freight carriers that transported at least one pound of freight during the year.
Source: Bureau of Transportation Statistics, The Intermodal Transportation Database, Air Carriers: T-100 Domestic Market (U.S. carriers only), 2024; Bureau of Transportation Statistics, The Intermodal Transportation Database, Air Carriers: T-100 International Market (U.S. carriers only), 2024

BUSINESSES

Major Business Headquarters

Company Name	Industry	Fortune[1]	Forbes[2]
ABM Industries	Diversified outsourcing services	461	-
Altice USA	Telecommunications	424	-
AmTrust Financial Services	Insurance	-	101
American Express	Diversified financials	58	-
American International Group	Insurance: property and casualty (stock)	94	-
Apollo Global Management	Securities	136	-
Bank of New York Mellon	Commercial banks	130	-
BlackRock	Securities	231	-
Blackstone	Diversified financials	464	-
Bloomberg	Business services & supplies	-	33
Breakthru Beverage Group	Food, drink & tobacco	-	61
Citigroup	Commercial banks	21	-
Colgate-Palmolive	Household and personal products	207	-
Consolidated Edison	Utilities: gas and electric	289	-
Davis Polk & Wardwell	Services	-	270
Equitable Holdings	Insurance: life, health (stock)	381	-
Estée Lauder	Household and personal products	259	-

Foot Locker	Specialty retailers: apparel	458	-
Fox	Entertainment	277	-
Goldman Sachs Group	Commercial banks	35	-
Guardian Life Ins. Co. of America	Insurance: life, health (mutual)	252	-
Hearst	Media	-	39
Hess	Mining, crude-oil production	378	-
International Flavors & Fragrances	Chemicals	356	-
Interpublic Group	Advertising, marketing	372	-
J. Crew	Retailing	-	224
JPMorgan Chase	Commercial banks	12	-
Jefferies Financial Group	Diversified financials	480	-
JetBlue Airways	Airlines	413	-
KKR	Securities	188	-
Kyndryl Holdings	Information technology services	241	-
Latham & Watkins	Services	-	114
Loews	Insurance: property and casualty (stock)	260	-
Macy's	General merchandisers	172	-
Marsh & McLennan	Diversified financials	180	-
McKinsey & Company	Business services & supplies	-	25
MetLife	Insurance: life, health (stock)	60	-
Morgan Stanley	Commercial banks	41	-
New York Life Insurance	Insurance: life, health (mutual)	78	-
News Corp.	Publishing, printing	398	-
Omnicom Group	Advertising, marketing	287	-
PVH	Apparel	425	-
Paramount Global	Entertainment	142	-
Paul Weiss	Services	-	271
Pfizer	Pharmaceuticals	69	-
Red Apple Group	Oil & gas operations	-	74
Renco Group	Banking and financial services	-	137
S&P Global	Financial data services	329	-
STO Building Group	Construction	-	43
Simpson Thacher & Bartlett	Services	-	250
Skadden, Arps, Slate, Meagher & Flom	Services	-	186
Standard Industries	Multicompany	-	48
StoneX Group	Diversified financials	66	-
TIAA	Insurance: life, health (mutual)	96	-
Trammo	Trading companies	-	205
Travelers	Insurance: property and casualty (stock)	105	-
Verizon Communications	Telecommunications	31	-
Voya Financial	Diversified financials	487	-
Warner Bros. Discovery	Entertainment	106	-
White & Case	Services	-	214

Note: (1) Companies that produce a 10-K are ranked 1 to 500 based on 2023 revenue; (2) All private companies with at least $2 billion in annual revenue through the end of their most current fiscal year are ranked 1 to 275; companies listed are headquartered in the city; dashes indicate no ranking
Source: Fortune, "Fortune 500," 2024; Forbes, "America's Largest Private Companies," 2024

Fastest-Growing Businesses

According to *Inc.*, New York is home to 35 of America's 500 fastest-growing private companies: **Forest Media Group** (#31); **i80 Group** (#47); **Sharebite** (#56); **Canela Media** (#70); **Spring Health** (#91); **UPSTACK** (#101); **Transfr** (#106); **WorkBetterNow** (#114); **Resident Ventures** (#116); **Coterie** (#144); **Visit.org** (#179); **CookUnity** (#184); **Harness** (#192); **Mosaic** (#226); **Dossier** (#256); **Studs** (#281); **Authors On Mission** (#286); **DigitalZone** (#291); **EdSights** (#296); **Byzfunder** (#303); **Netsurit** (#305); **Horatio** (#354); **Curacity** (#394); **Glowbar** (#409); **Capital Rx** (#411); **UPKEEP** (#414); **The Law Firm of Moumita Rahman** (#418); **Thoropass** (#427); **Boost Insurance** (#429); **Raistone Capital** (#437); **Vesta Healthcare** (#448); **Lili** (#457); **Lengea Law** (#467); **Hexaview Technologies** (#469); **Vestwell** (#499). Criteria: must be an independent, privately-held, for-profit, U.S. corporation, proprietorship or partnership as of December 31, 2023; revenues must be at least $100,000 in 2020 and $2 million in 2023; must have four-year operating/sales history. *Inc., "America's 500 Fastest-Growing Private Companies," 2024*

According to *Initiative for a Competitive Inner City (ICIC)*, New York is home to four of America's 100 fastest-growing "inner city" companies: **Overwatch Services dba City Safe Partners Security** (#8); **MKJ Communications (Brooklyn)** (#40); **Creativebusinessinc.com (Brooklyn)** (#88); **Corkscrew Wines & Spirits (Brooklyn)** (#90). To be eligible for the IC100, companies have to be independently operated, privately held, for-profit businesses with revenues of at least $50,000 in 2019 and

$500,000 in 2023, and headquartered in an under-resourced community. Recognizing that concentrated poverty exists within metropolitan areas outside of big cities (and that poverty overall is suburbanizing), ICIC defines under-resourced communities as large low-income, high-poverty areas located in the urban and suburban parts of all but the smallest metropolitan areas. Companies were ranked overall by revenue growth over the five-year period between 2019 and 2023. *Initiative for a Competitive Inner City (ICIC), "Inner City 100 Companies," 2024*

According to Deloitte, New York is home to 54 of North America's 500 fastest-growing high-technology companies: **TG Therapeutics** (#1); **Talkiatry** (#6); **Odeko** (#12); **Trullion** (#14); **Crisp** (#21); **Interchecks Technologies** (#29); **Cyera** (#32); **Sharebite** (#35); **Spring Health** (#42); **Coro** (#51); **TailorMed Medical** (#58); **Intra-Cellular Therapies** (#70); **Kindbody** (#72); **Aidoc** (#86); **Datarails** (#92); **LeapXpert** (#113); **Lili** (#120); **Place Exchange** (#137); **Capital Rx** (#147); **Alloy** (#150); **Vic.ai** (#165); **Ethic** (#170); **Capitolis** (#173); **Click Therapeutics** (#182); **DailyPay** (#185); **Priori** (#191); **The Glimpse Group** (#197); **TheGuarantors** (#200); **Fubo** (#224); **ThetaRay** (#231); **Guesty** (#234); **Bubble Group** (#241); **Gloat** (#260); **BigID** (#273); **Overtime** (#278); **Wellthy** (#289); **Audigent** (#292); **Coursedog** (#299); **BlueVoyant** (#300); **Roc360** (#313); **Chainalysis** (#326); **Glia** (#333); **Litify** (#355); **Octane** (#366); **LifeMD** (#367); **Y-mAbs Therapeutics** (#368); **Claroty** (#378); **DriveWealth** (#403); **Braze** (#405); **Fi** (#422); **Datadog** (#428); **DataDome** (#463); **UiPath** (#482); **MongoDB** (#493). Companies are ranked by percentage growth in revenue over a four-year period. Criteria for inclusion: company must be headquartered within North America; must own proprietary intellectual property or technology that is sold to customers in products that contributes to a significant portion of the company's operating revenue; must have been in business for a minumum of four years with 2020 operating revenues of at least $50,000 USD/CD and 2023 operating revenues of at least $5 million USD/CD. *Deloitte, 2024 Technology Fast 500*^{TM}

Living Environment

COST OF LIVING

Cost of Living Index

Composite Index	Groceries	Housing	Utilities	Transportation	Health Care	Misc. Goods/Services
161.1	113.0	276.5	115.1	114.9	128.1	114.9

Note: The Cost of Living Index measures regional differences in the cost of consumer goods and services, excluding taxes and non-consumer expenditures, for professional and managerial households in the top income quintile. It is based on more than 50,000 prices covering almost 60 different items for which prices are collected three times a year by chambers of commerce, economic development organizations or university applied economic centers in each participating urban area. The numbers shown should be read as a percentage above or below the national average of 100. For example, a value of 115.4 in the groceries column indicates that grocery prices are 15.4% higher than the national average. Small differences in the index numbers should not be interpreted as significant; Figures cover the Brooklyn NY urban area.
Source: The Council for Community and Economic Research, Cost of Living Index, 2024

Grocery Prices

Area[1]	T-Bone Steak ($/pound)	Frying Chicken ($/pound)	Whole Milk ($/half gal.)	Eggs ($/dozen)	Orange Juice ($/64 oz.)	Coffee ($/11.5 oz.)
City[2]	15.52	1.56	5.14	3.63	4.79	5.93
Avg.	15.42	1.55	4.69	3.25	4.41	5.46
Min.	14.50	1.16	4.43	2.75	4.00	4.85
Max.	17.56	2.89	5.49	4.78	5.54	7.89

Note: (1) Values for the local area are compared with the average, minimum and maximum values for all 276 areas in the Cost of Living Index; (2) Figures cover the Brooklyn NY urban area; **T-Bone Steak** (price per pound); **Frying Chicken** (price per pound, whole fryer); **Whole Milk** (half gallon carton); **Eggs** (price per dozen, Grade A, large); **Orange Juice** (64 oz. Tropicana or Florida Natural); **Coffee** (11.5 oz. can, vacuum-packed, Maxwell House, Hills Bros, or Folgers).
Source: The Council for Community and Economic Research, Cost of Living Index, 2024

Housing and Utility Costs

Area[1]	New Home Price ($)	Apartment Rent ($/month)	All Electric ($/month)	Part Electric ($/month)	Other Energy ($/month)	Telephone ($/month)
City[2]	1,411,780	3,995	-	157.71	92.60	203.07
Avg.	515,975	1,550	210.99	123.07	82.07	194.99
Min.	265,375	692	104.33	53.68	36.26	179.42
Max.	2,775,821	5,719	529.02	397.28	361.63	223.33

Note: (1) Values for the local area are compared with the average, minimum and maximum values for all 276 areas in the Cost of Living Index; (2) Figures cover the Brooklyn NY urban area; **New Home Price** (2,400 sf living area, 8,000 sf lot, in urban area with full utilities); **Apartment Rent** (950 sf 2 bedroom/1.5 or 2 bath, unfurnished, excluding all utilities except water); **All Electric** (average monthly cost for an all-electric home); **Part Electric** (average monthly cost for a part-electric home); **Other Energy** (average monthly cost for natural gas, fuel oil, coal, wood, and any other forms of energy except electricity); **Telephone** (price includes the base monthly rate plus taxes and fees for three lines of mobile phone service).
Source: The Council for Community and Economic Research, Cost of Living Index, 2024

Health Care, Transportation, and Other Costs

Area[1]	Doctor ($/visit)	Dentist ($/visit)	Optometrist ($/visit)	Gasoline ($/gallon)	Beauty Salon ($/visit)	Men's Shirt ($)
City[2]	192.84	171.93	152.60	3.43	68.80	44.04
Avg.	143.77	117.51	129.23	3.32	48.57	38.14
Min.	36.74	58.67	67.33	2.80	24.00	13.41
Max.	270.44	216.82	307.33	5.28	94.00	63.89

Note: (1) Values for the local area are compared with the average, minimum and maximum values for all 276 areas in the Cost of Living Index; (2) Figures cover the Brooklyn NY urban area; **Doctor** (general practitioners routine exam of an established patient); **Dentist** (adult teeth cleaning and periodic oral examination); **Optometrist** (full vision eye exam for established adult patient); **Gasoline** (one gallon regular unleaded, national brand, including all taxes, cash price at self-service pump if available); **Beauty Salon** (woman's shampoo, trim, and blow-dry); **Men's Shirt** (cotton/polyester dress shirt, pinpoint weave, long sleeves).
Source: The Council for Community and Economic Research, Cost of Living Index, 2024

HOUSING

Homeownership Rate

Area	2017 (%)	2018 (%)	2019 (%)	2020 (%)	2021 (%)	2022 (%)	2023 (%)	2024 (%)
MSA[1]	49.9	49.7	50.4	50.9	50.7	50.5	50.2	49.4
U.S.	63.9	64.4	64.6	66.6	65.5	65.8	65.9	65.6

Note: (1) Figures cover the New York-Newark-Jersey City, NY-NJ Metropolitan Statistical Area
Source: U.S. Census Bureau, Housing Vacancies and Homeownership Annual Statistics: 2017-2024

House Price Index (HPI)

Area	National Ranking[2]	Quarterly Change (%)	One-Year Change (%)	Five-Year Change (%)	Since 1991Q1 (%)
MD[1]	34	0.62	7.86	43.82	309.75
U.S.[3]	—	1.43	4.51	57.13	327.82

Note: The HPI is a weighted repeat sales index. It measures average price changes in repeat sales or refinancings on the same properties. This information is obtained by reviewing repeat mortgage transactions on single-family properties whose mortgages have been purchased or securitized by Fannie Mae or Freddie Mac since January 1975; (1) Figures cover the New York-Jersey City-White Plains, NY-NJ Metropolitan Division; (2) Rankings are based on annual percentage change for all metro areas containing at least 15,000 transactions over the last 10 years and ranges from 1 to 241; (3) figures based on a weighted average of Census Division estimates using a seasonally adjusted, purchase-only index; all figures are for the period ending December 31, 2024
Source: Federal Housing Finance Agency, Change in FHFA Metropolitan Area House Price Indexes, All Transactions Index, 2024Q4

Home Value

Area	Under $100,000	$100,000 -$199,999	$200,000 -$299,999	$300,000 -$399,999	$400,000 -$499,999	$500,000 -$999,999	$1,000,000 or more	Median ($)
City	4.7	2.9	4.7	5.6	7.1	44.9	30.1	751,700
MSA[1]	3.6	3.3	7.3	11.1	14.3	44.4	16.0	587,400
U.S.	12.1	17.8	19.5	14.4	10.5	19.1	6.5	303,400

Note: Figures are percentages except for median and cover owner-occupied housing units; (1) Figures cover the New York-Newark-Jersey City, NY-NJ Metropolitan Statistical Area
Source: U.S. Census Bureau, 2019-2023 American Community Survey 5-Year Estimates

Year Housing Structure Built

Area	2020 or Later	2010 -2019	2000 -2009	1990 -1999	1980 -1989	1970 -1979	1960 -1969	1950 -1959	1940 -1949	Before 1940	Median Year
City	0.4	5.5	5.5	3.7	5.0	7.0	12.2	12.8	9.4	38.4	1952
MSA[1]	0.5	5.3	6.6	5.9	7.8	9.6	13.3	15.3	8.3	27.3	1959
U.S.	1.2	8.9	13.6	12.8	13.0	14.4	10.0	9.7	4.5	11.9	1980

Note: Figures are percentages except for Median Year; Note: (1) Figures cover the New York-Newark-Jersey City, NY-NJ Metropolitan Statistical Area
Source: U.S. Census Bureau, 2019-2023 American Community Survey 5-Year Estimates

Gross Monthly Rent

Area	Under $500	$500 -$999	$1,000 -$1,499	$1,500 -$1,999	$2,000 -$2,499	$2,500 -$2,999	$3,000 and up	Median ($)
City	8.3	10.0	19.2	22.4	16.2	8.5	15.4	1,779
MSA[1]	7.3	9.0	20.0	24.4	16.9	8.6	13.8	1,780
U.S.	6.5	22.3	29.5	20.2	10.8	4.8	5.9	1,348

Note: Figures are percentages except for median; Gross rent is the contract rent plus the estimated average monthly cost of utilities (electricity, gas, and water and sewer) and fuels (oil, coal, kerosene, wood, etc.) if these are paid by the renter (or paid for the renter by someone else); (1) Figures cover the New York-Newark-Jersey City, NY-NJ Metropolitan Statistical Area
Source: U.S. Census Bureau, 2019-2023 American Community Survey 5-Year Estimates

HEALTH

Health Risk Factors

Category	MD[1] (%)	U.S. (%)
Adults aged 18–64 who have any kind of health care coverage	90.0	90.8
Adults who reported being in good or better health	81.1	81.8
Adults who have been told they have high blood cholesterol	38.7	36.9
Adults who have been told they have high blood pressure	30.6	34.0
Adults who are current smokers	8.0	12.1
Adults who currently use e-cigarettes	5.3	7.7
Adults who currently use chewing tobacco, snuff, or snus	1.2	3.2
Adults who are heavy drinkers[2]	4.1	6.1
Adults who are binge drinkers[3]	15.0	15.2
Adults who are overweight (BMI 25.0 - 29.9)	35.8	34.4
Adults who are obese (BMI 30.0 - 99.8)	25.2	34.3
Adults who participated in any physical activities in the past month	72.6	75.8

Note: All figures are crude prevalence; (1) Figures cover the New York-Jersey City-White Plains, NY-NJ Metropolitan Division; (2) Heavy drinkers are classified as adult men having more than 14 drinks per week and adult women having more than 7 drinks per week; (3) Binge drinkers are classified as males having five or more drinks on one occasion or females having four or more drinks on one occasion
Source: Centers for Disease Control and Prevention, Behavioral Risk Factor Surveillance System, SMART: Selected Metropolitan Area Risk Trends, 2023

Acute and Chronic Health Conditions

Category	MD[1] (%)	U.S. (%)
Adults who have ever been told they had a heart attack	3.4	4.2
Adults who have ever been told they have angina or coronary heart disease	3.5	4.0
Adults who have ever been told they had a stroke	2.7	3.3
Adults who have ever been told they have asthma	13.4	15.7
Adults who have ever been told they have arthritis	19.5	26.3
Adults who have ever been told they have diabetes[2]	10.8	11.5
Adults who have ever been told they had skin cancer	2.8	5.6
Adults who have ever been told they had any other types of cancer	5.6	8.4
Adults who have ever been told they have COPD	4.0	6.4
Adults who have ever been told they have kidney disease	3.2	3.7
Adults who have ever been told they have a form of depression	14.2	22.0

Note: All figures are crude prevalence; (1) Figures cover the New York-Jersey City-White Plains, NY-NJ Metropolitan Division; (2) Figures do not include pregnancy-related, borderline, or pre-diabetes
Source: Centers for Disease Control and Prevention, Behaviorial Risk Factor Surveillance System, SMART: Selected Metropolitan Area Risk Trends, 2023

Health Screening and Vaccination Rates

Category	MD[1] (%)	U.S. (%)
Adults who have ever been tested for HIV	49.3	37.5
Adults who have had their blood cholesterol checked within the last five years	91.0	87.0
Adults aged 65+ who have had flu shot within the past year	64.2	63.4
Adults aged 65+ who have ever had a pneumonia vaccination	61.9	71.9

Note: All figures are crude prevalence; (1) Figures cover the New York-Jersey City-White Plains, NY-NJ Metropolitan Division.
Source: Centers for Disease Control and Prevention, Behaviorial Risk Factor Surveillance System, SMART: Selected Metropolitan Area Risk Trends, 2023

Disability Status

Category	MD[1] (%)	U.S. (%)
Adults who reported being deaf	3.7	7.4
Are you blind or have serious difficulty seeing, even when wearing glasses?	6.0	4.9
Do you have difficulty doing errands alone?	7.3	7.8
Do you have difficulty dressing or bathing?	4.4	3.6
Do you have serious difficulty concentrating/remembering/making decisions?	11.5	13.7
Do you have serious difficulty walking or climbing stairs?	13.9	13.2

Note: All figures are crude prevalence; (1) Figures cover the New York-Jersey City-White Plains, NY-NJ Metropolitan Division.
Source: Centers for Disease Control and Prevention, Behaviorial Risk Factor Surveillance System, SMART: Selected Metropolitan Area Risk Trends, 2023

Mortality Rates for the Top 10 Causes of Death in the U.S. (Bronx)

ICD-10[a] Sub-Chapter	ICD-10[a] Code	Crude Mortality Rate[2] per 100,000 population	
		County[3]	U.S.
Malignant neoplasms	C00-C97	129.2	182.7
Ischaemic heart diseases	I20-I25	141.3	109.6
Provisional assignment of new diseases of uncertain etiology[1]	U00-U49	55.8	65.3
Other forms of heart disease	I30-I51	24.9	65.1
Other degenerative diseases of the nervous system	G30-G31	16.1	52.4
Other external causes of accidental injury	W00-X59	72.9	52.3
Cerebrovascular diseases	I60-I69	31.8	49.1
Chronic lower respiratory diseases	J40-J47	21.8	43.5
Hypertensive diseases	I10-I15	54.2	38.9
Organic, including symptomatic, mental disorders	F01-F09	17.4	33.9

Note: (a) ICD-10 = International Classification of Diseases 10th Revision; (1) Includes COVID-19, adverse effects to COVID-19 vaccines, SARS, and vaping-related disorders; (2) Crude mortality rates are a three-year average covering 2021-2023; (3) Figures cover Bronx County
Source: Centers for Disease Control and Prevention, National Center for Health Statistics. National Vital Statistics System, Mortality 2018-2023 on CDC WONDER Online Database

Mortality Rates for the Top 10 Causes of Death in the U.S. (Brooklyn)

ICD-10[a] Sub-Chapter	ICD-10[a] Code	Crude Mortality Rate[2] per 100,000 population	
		County[3]	U.S.
Malignant neoplasms	C00-C97	121.3	182.7
Ischaemic heart diseases	I20-I25	139.7	109.6
Provisional assignment of new diseases of uncertain etiology[1]	U00-U49	57.1	65.3
Other forms of heart disease	I30-I51	23.1	65.1
Other degenerative diseases of the nervous system	G30-G31	13.8	52.4
Other external causes of accidental injury	W00-X59	36.5	52.3
Cerebrovascular diseases	I60-I69	23.2	49.1
Chronic lower respiratory diseases	J40-J47	13.9	43.5
Hypertensive diseases	I10-I15	42.3	38.9
Organic, including symptomatic, mental disorders	F01-F09	11.9	33.9

Note: (a) ICD-10 = International Classification of Diseases 10th Revision; (1) Includes COVID-19, adverse effects to COVID-19 vaccines, SARS, and vaping-related disorders; (2) Crude mortality rates are a three-year average covering 2021-2023; (3) Figures cover Kings County
Source: Centers for Disease Control and Prevention, National Center for Health Statistics. National Vital Statistics System, Mortality 2018-2023 on CDC WONDER Online Database

Mortality Rates for the Top 10 Causes of Death in the U.S. (Manhattan)

ICD-10[a] Sub-Chapter	ICD-10[a] Code	Crude Mortality Rate[2] per 100,000 population	
		County[3]	U.S.
Malignant neoplasms	C00-C97	135.2	182.7
Ischaemic heart diseases	I20-I25	110.3	109.6
Provisional assignment of new diseases of uncertain etiology[1]	U00-U49	41.2	65.3
Other forms of heart disease	I30-I51	26.2	65.1
Other degenerative diseases of the nervous system	G30-G31	27.1	52.4
Other external causes of accidental injury	W00-X59	44.5	52.3
Cerebrovascular diseases	I60-I69	27.5	49.1
Chronic lower respiratory diseases	J40-J47	17.0	43.5
Hypertensive diseases	I10-I15	40.6	38.9
Organic, including symptomatic, mental disorders	F01-F09	21.2	33.9

Note: (a) ICD-10 = International Classification of Diseases 10th Revision; (1) Includes COVID-19, adverse effects to COVID-19 vaccines, SARS, and vaping-related disorders; (2) Crude mortality rates are a three-year average covering 2021-2023; (3) Figures cover New York County
Source: Centers for Disease Control and Prevention, National Center for Health Statistics. National Vital Statistics System, Mortality 2018-2023 on CDC WONDER Online Database

Mortality Rates for the Top 10 Causes of Death in the U.S. (Queens)

ICD-10[a] Sub-Chapter	ICD-10[a] Code	Crude Mortality Rate[2] per 100,000 population	
		County[3]	U.S.
Malignant neoplasms	C00-C97	129.5	182.7
Ischaemic heart diseases	I20-I25	151.0	109.6
Provisional assignment of new diseases of uncertain etiology[1]	U00-U49	59.6	65.3
Other forms of heart disease	I30-I51	24.2	65.1
Other degenerative diseases of the nervous system	G30-G31	21.5	52.4
Other external causes of accidental injury	W00-X59	33.2	52.3
Cerebrovascular diseases	I60-I69	27.9	49.1
Chronic lower respiratory diseases	J40-J47	16.0	43.5
Hypertensive diseases	I10-I15	39.5	38.9
Organic, including symptomatic, mental disorders	F01-F09	13.4	33.9

Note: (a) ICD-10 = International Classification of Diseases 10th Revision; (1) Includes COVID-19, adverse effects to COVID-19 vaccines, SARS, and vaping-related disorders; (2) Crude mortality rates are a three-year average covering 2021-2023; (3) Figures cover Queens County
Source: Centers for Disease Control and Prevention, National Center for Health Statistics. National Vital Statistics System, Mortality 2018-2023 on CDC WONDER Online Database

Mortality Rates for the Top 10 Causes of Death in the U.S. (Staten Island)

ICD-10[a] Sub-Chapter	ICD-10[a] Code	Crude Mortality Rate[2] per 100,000 population	
		County[3]	U.S.
Malignant neoplasms	C00-C97	171.3	182.7
Ischaemic heart diseases	I20-I25	185.2	109.6
Provisional assignment of new diseases of uncertain etiology[1]	U00-U49	70.7	65.3
Other forms of heart disease	I30-I51	21.6	65.1
Other degenerative diseases of the nervous system	G30-G31	33.9	52.4
Other external causes of accidental injury	W00-X59	45.2	52.3
Cerebrovascular diseases	I60-I69	24.9	49.1
Chronic lower respiratory diseases	J40-J47	36.5	43.5
Hypertensive diseases	I10-I15	61.0	38.9
Organic, including symptomatic, mental disorders	F01-F09	11.7	33.9

Note: (a) ICD-10 = International Classification of Diseases 10th Revision; (1) Includes COVID-19, adverse effects to COVID-19 vaccines, SARS, and vaping-related disorders; (2) Crude mortality rates are a three-year average covering 2021-2023; (3) Figures cover Richmond County
Source: Centers for Disease Control and Prevention, National Center for Health Statistics. National Vital Statistics System, Mortality 2018-2023 on CDC WONDER Online Database

Mortality Rates for Selected Causes of Death (Bronx)

ICD-10[a] Sub-Chapter	ICD-10[a] Code	Crude Mortality Rate[1] per 100,000 population	
		County[2]	U.S.
Accidental poisoning and exposure to noxious substances	X40-X49	60.9	30.5
Alzheimer disease	G30	11.7	35.4
Assault	X85-Y09	9.6	7.3
COVID-19	U07.1	55.8	65.3
Diabetes mellitus	E10-E14	25.7	30.0
Diseases of the liver	K70-K76	11.7	20.8
Human immunodeficiency virus (HIV) disease	B20-B24	8.3	1.5
Influenza and pneumonia	J09-J18	22.9	13.4
Intentional self-harm	X60-X84	6.2	14.7
Malnutrition	E40-E46	Unreliable	6.0
Obesity and other hyperalimentation	E65-E68	2.2	3.1
Renal failure	N17-N19	9.1	16.4
Transport accidents	V01-V99	6.2	14.4

Note: (a) ICD-10 = International Classification of Diseases 10th Revision; (1) Crude mortality rates are a three-year average covering 2021-2023; (2) Figures cover Bronx County; Data are suppressed when the data meet the criteria for confidentiality constraints; Crude mortality rates are flagged as unreliable when the rate would be calculated with a numerator of 20 or less.
Source: Centers for Disease Control and Prevention, National Center for Health Statistics. National Vital Statistics System, Mortality 2018-2023 on CDC WONDER Online Database

Mortality Rates for Selected Causes of Death (Brooklyn)

ICD-10[a] Sub-Chapter	ICD-10[a] Code	Crude Mortality Rate[1] per 100,000 population	
		County[2]	U.S.
Accidental poisoning and exposure to noxious substances	X40-X49	26.6	30.5
Alzheimer disease	G30	8.8	35.4
Assault	X85-Y09	5.4	7.3
COVID-19	U07.1	57.1	65.3
Diabetes mellitus	E10-E14	20.6	30.0
Diseases of the liver	K70-K76	7.9	20.8
Human immunodeficiency virus (HIV) disease	B20-B24	3.1	1.5
Influenza and pneumonia	J09-J18	22.1	13.4
Intentional self-harm	X60-X84	6.0	14.7
Malnutrition	E40-E46	1.1	6.0
Obesity and other hyperalimentation	E65-E68	1.8	3.1
Renal failure	N17-N19	9.9	16.4
Transport accidents	V01-V99	4.7	14.4

Note: (a) ICD-10 = International Classification of Diseases 10th Revision; (1) Crude mortality rates are a three-year average covering 2021-2023; (2) Figures cover Kings County; Data are suppressed when the data meet the criteria for confidentiality constraints; Crude mortality rates are flagged as unreliable when the rate would be calculated with a numerator of 20 or less.
Source: Centers for Disease Control and Prevention, National Center for Health Statistics. National Vital Statistics System, Mortality 2018-2023 on CDC WONDER Online Database

Mortality Rates for Selected Causes of Death (Manhattan)

ICD-10[a] Sub-Chapter	ICD-10[a] Code	Crude Mortality Rate[1] per 100,000 population	
		County[2]	U.S.
Accidental poisoning and exposure to noxious substances	X40-X49	31.0	30.5
Alzheimer disease	G30	17.4	35.4
Assault	X85-Y09	4.1	7.3
COVID-19	U07.1	41.2	65.3
Diabetes mellitus	E10-E14	16.1	30.0
Diseases of the liver	K70-K76	7.1	20.8
Human immunodeficiency virus (HIV) disease	B20-B24	3.6	1.5
Influenza and pneumonia	J09-J18	13.3	13.4
Intentional self-harm	X60-X84	8.3	14.7
Malnutrition	E40-E46	2.4	6.0
Obesity and other hyperalimentation	E65-E68	1.8	3.1
Renal failure	N17-N19	8.7	16.4
Transport accidents	V01-V99	3.7	14.4

Note: (a) ICD-10 = International Classification of Diseases 10th Revision; (1) Crude mortality rates are a three-year average covering 2021-2023; (2) Figures cover New York County; Data are suppressed when the data meet the criteria for confidentiality constraints; Crude mortality rates are flagged as unreliable when the rate would be calculated with a numerator of 20 or less.
Source: Centers for Disease Control and Prevention, National Center for Health Statistics. National Vital Statistics System, Mortality 2018-2023 on CDC WONDER Online Database

Mortality Rates for Selected Causes of Death (Queens)

ICD-10[a] Sub-Chapter	ICD-10[a] Code	Crude Mortality Rate[1] per 100,000 population	
		County[2]	U.S.
Accidental poisoning and exposure to noxious substances	X40-X49	20.9	30.5
Alzheimer disease	G30	11.8	35.4
Assault	X85-Y09	3.3	7.3
COVID-19	U07.1	59.6	65.3
Diabetes mellitus	E10-E14	18.4	30.0
Diseases of the liver	K70-K76	9.3	20.8
Human immunodeficiency virus (HIV) disease	B20-B24	1.2	1.5
Influenza and pneumonia	J09-J18	18.0	13.4
Intentional self-harm	X60-X84	6.3	14.7
Malnutrition	E40-E46	0.9	6.0
Obesity and other hyperalimentation	E65-E68	1.6	3.1
Renal failure	N17-N19	8.2	16.4
Transport accidents	V01-V99	4.9	14.4

Note: (a) ICD-10 = International Classification of Diseases 10th Revision; (1) Crude mortality rates are a three-year average covering 2021-2023; (2) Figures cover Queens County; Data are suppressed when the data meet the criteria for confidentiality constraints; Crude mortality rates are flagged as unreliable when the rate would be calculated with a numerator of 20 or less.
Source: Centers for Disease Control and Prevention, National Center for Health Statistics. National Vital Statistics System, Mortality 2018-2023 on CDC WONDER Online Database

Mortality Rates for Selected Causes of Death (Staten Island)

ICD-10[a] Sub-Chapter	ICD-10[a] Code	Crude Mortality Rate[1] per 100,000 population	
		County[2]	U.S.
Accidental poisoning and exposure to noxious substances	X40-X49	32.7	30.5
Alzheimer disease	G30	15.3	35.4
Assault	X85-Y09	3.5	7.3
COVID-19	U07.1	70.7	65.3
Diabetes mellitus	E10-E14	35.6	30.0
Diseases of the liver	K70-K76	7.2	20.8
Human immunodeficiency virus (HIV) disease	B20-B24	Unreliable	1.5
Influenza and pneumonia	J09-J18	16.1	13.4
Intentional self-harm	X60-X84	6.8	14.7
Malnutrition	E40-E46	Unreliable	6.0
Obesity and other hyperalimentation	E65-E68	2.4	3.1
Renal failure	N17-N19	6.8	16.4
Transport accidents	V01-V99	4.6	14.4

Note: (a) ICD-10 = International Classification of Diseases 10th Revision; (1) Crude mortality rates are a three-year average covering 2021-2023; (2) Figures cover Richmond County; Data are suppressed when the data meet the criteria for confidentiality constraints; Crude mortality rates are flagged as unreliable when the rate would be calculated with a numerator of 20 or less.
Source: Centers for Disease Control and Prevention, National Center for Health Statistics. National Vital Statistics System, Mortality 2018-2023 on CDC WONDER Online Database

Health Insurance Coverage

Area	With Health Insurance	With Private Health Insurance	With Public Health Insurance	Without Health Insurance	Population Under Age 19 Without Health Insurance
City	93.6	58.2	45.3	6.4	2.3
MSA[1]	93.5	66.6	37.8	6.5	3.1
U.S.	91.4	67.3	36.3	8.6	5.4

Note: Figures are percentages that cover the civilian noninstitutionalized population; (1) Figures cover the New York-Newark-Jersey City, NY-NJ Metropolitan Statistical Area
Source: U.S. Census Bureau, 2019-2023 American Community Survey 5-Year Estimates

Number of Medical Professionals

Area	MDs[3]	DOs[3,4]	Dentists	Podiatrists	Chiropractors	Optometrists
City[1] (number)	45,469	2,027	7,504	1,139	1,386	1,636
City[1] (rate[2])	545.5	24.3	90.9	13.8	16.8	19.8
U.S. (rate[2])	302.5	29.2	74.6	6.4	29.5	18.0

Note: Data as of 2023 unless noted; (1) Data covers New York City; (2) Number of medical professionals per 100,000 population; (3) Data as of 2022 and includes all active, non-federal physicians; (4) Doctor of Osteopathic Medicine
Source: U.S. Department of Health and Human Services, Health Resources and Services Administration, Bureau of Health Professions, Area Resource File (ARF) 2023-2024

Best Hospitals

According to *U.S. News,* the New York-Newark-Jersey City, NY-NJ metro area is home to 30 of the best hospitals in the U.S.: **Burke Rehabilitation Hospital** (1 adult specialty); **Glen Cove Hospital at Northwell Health** (1 adult specialty); **Hackensack University Medical Center at Hackensack Meridian Health** (8 adult specialties and 3 pediatric specialties); **Hospital for Special Surgery** (2 adult specialties and 1 pediatric specialty); **Hospital for Special Surgery, New York-Presbyterian University Hospital of Columbia and Cornell** (2 adult specialties and 1 pediatric specialty); **Huntington Hospital at Northwell Health** (3 adult specialties); **JFK Johnson Rehabilitation Institute at Hackensack Meridian Health-Edison** (1 adult specialty); **Jersey Shore University Medical Center at Hackensack Meridian Health** (1 adult specialty and 3 pediatric specialties); **Kessler Institute for Rehabilitation** (1 adult specialty); **Lenox Hill Hospital at Northwell Health** (6 adult specialties); **Long Island Jewish Medical Center at Northwell Health** (9 adult specialties and 10 pediatric specialties); **Manhattan Eye, Ear & Throat Hospital** (6 adult specialties); **Memorial Sloan Kettering Cancer Center** (4 adult specialties and 1 pediatric specialty); **Montefiore Medical Center** (8 adult specialties and 3 pediatric specialties); **Morristown Medical Center Atlantic Health System** (4 adult specialties); **Mount Sinai Beth Israel Hospital** (1 adult specialty); **Mount Sinai Hospital** (Honor Roll/11 adult specialties and 3 pediatric specialties); **Mount Sinai Morningside and Mount Sinai West Hospitals** (5 adult specialties); **NYU Langone Hospitals** (Honor Roll/13 adult specialties and 4 pediatric specialties); **NYU Langone Orthopedic Hospital** (13 adult specialties and 4 pediatric specialties); **New York Eye and Ear Infirmary of Mount Sinai** (11 adult specialties and 3 pediatric specialties); **New York-Presbyterian Brooklyn Methodist Hospital** (4 adult specialties); **New York-Presbyterian Hospital-Columbia and Cornell** (Honor Roll/14 adult specialties and 11 pediatric specialties); **North Shore University Hospital at Northwell Health** (Honor Roll/9 adult specialties); **Northern Westchester Hospital at Northwell Health** (1 adult specialty); **Perlmutter Cancer Center at NYU Langone Hospitals** (13 adult specialties and 4 pediatric specialties); **Plainview Hospital at Northwell Health** (1 adult specialty); **Rusk Rehabilitation at NYU Langone Hospitals** (13 adult specialties and 4 pediatric specialties); **St. Francis Hospital and Heart Center** (8 adult specialties); **White Plains Hospital** (1 adult specialty). The hospitals listed were nationally ranked in at least one of 15 adult or 11 pediatric specialties. The number of specialties shown cover the parent hospital. Only 160 U.S. hospitals performed well enough to be nationally ranked in one or more specialties. Twenty hospitals in the U.S. made the Honor Roll. The Best Hospitals Honor Roll takes both the national rankings and the procedure and condition ratings into account. Hospitals received points if they were nationally ranked in one of the 15 adult specialties—the higher they ranked, the more points they got—and how many ratings of "high performing" they earned in the 20 procedures and conditions. *U.S. News Online, "America's Best Hospitals 2024-25"*

According to *U.S. News,* the New York-Newark-Jersey City, NY-NJ metro area is home to 10 of the best children's hospitals in the U.S.: **Children's Hospital at Montefiore** (3 pediatric specialties); **Cohen Children's Medical Center** (10 pediatric specialties); **Hackensack Meridian Health JM Sanzari and K Hovnanian Children's Hospitals** (3 pediatric specialties); **Hassenfeld Children's Hospital at NYU Langone** (4 pediatric specialties); **Lerner Children's Pavilion-Hospital for Special Surgery** (1 pediatric specialty); **MSK Kids at Memorial Sloan Kettering Cancer Center** (1 pediatric specialty); **Mount Sinai Kravis Children's Hospital** (3 pediatric specialties); **New York-Presbyterian Children's Hospital-Columbia and Cornell** (11 pediatric specialties); **RWJBarnabas Children's Health** (2 pediatric specialties); **The Bristol-Myers Squibb Children's Hospital at RWJ University Hospital** (2 pediatric specialties). The hospitals listed were highly ranked in at least one of 11 pediatric specialties. One hundred five children's hospitals in the U.S.

were nationally ranked in at least one specialty. Hospitals received points for being ranked in a specialty, and the 10 hospitals with the most points across the 11 specialties make up the Honor Roll.
U.S. News Online, "America's Best Children's Hospitals 2024-25"

EDUCATION

Public School District Statistics

District Name	Schls	Pupils	Pupil/Teacher Ratio	Minority Pupils[1] (%)	Total Rev. per Pupil ($)	Total Exp. per Pupil ($)
NYC Geo Dist #01 (Manhattan)	26	9,896	11.7	83.4	n/a	n/a
NYC Geo Dist #02 (Manhattan)	119	55,421	12.8	75.2	n/a	n/a
NYC Geo Dist #03 (Manhattan)	43	19,335	12.0	69.9	n/a	n/a
NYC Geo Dist #04 (Manhattan)	29	11,690	11.1	94.4	n/a	n/a
NYC Geo Dist #05 (Manhattan)	28	8,945	11.7	92.1	n/a	n/a
NYC Geo Dist #06 (Manhattan)	45	17,940	11.7	93.7	n/a	n/a
NYC Geo Dist #07 (Bronx)	41	15,146	11.1	98.4	n/a	n/a
NYC Geo Dist #08 (Bronx)	52	24,000	12.5	94.8	n/a	n/a
NYC Geo Dist #09 (Bronx)	69	26,766	11.6	98.6	n/a	n/a
NYC Geo Dist #10 (Bronx)	83	43,655	12.3	94.2	n/a	n/a
NYC Geo Dist #11 (Bronx)	62	32,583	12.9	90.8	n/a	n/a
NYC Geo Dist #12 (Bronx)	47	17,376	11.8	98.7	n/a	n/a
NYC Geo Dist #13 (Brooklyn)	41	19,232	13.5	80.4	n/a	n/a
NYC Geo Dist #14 (Brooklyn)	38	15,196	11.9	84.1	n/a	n/a
NYC Geo Dist #15 (Brooklyn)	49	26,808	12.1	70.7	n/a	n/a
NYC Geo Dist #16 (Brooklyn)	23	5,827	11.1	94.9	n/a	n/a
NYC Geo Dist #17 (Brooklyn)	49	17,805	12.4	95.1	n/a	n/a
NYC Geo Dist #18 (Brooklyn)	34	11,223	12.1	95.6	n/a	n/a
NYC Geo Dist #19 (Brooklyn)	52	19,963	12.6	98.0	n/a	n/a
NYC Geo Dist #20 (Brooklyn)	45	46,673	14.2	77.2	n/a	n/a
NYC Geo Dist #21 (Brooklyn)	40	34,525	13.8	66.5	n/a	n/a
NYC Geo Dist #22 (Brooklyn)	40	31,726	14.1	67.5	n/a	n/a
NYC Geo Dist #23 (Brooklyn)	28	8,334	12.6	98.3	n/a	n/a
NYC Geo Dist #24 (Corona)	57	50,843	13.5	88.8	n/a	n/a
NYC Geo Dist #25 (Flushing)	46	34,702	13.9	90.5	n/a	n/a
NYC Geo Dist #26 (Bayside)	34	29,442	14.7	88.2	n/a	n/a
NYC Geo Dist #27 (Ozone Park)	63	41,663	14.3	91.4	n/a	n/a
NYC Geo Dist #28 (Jamaica)	50	38,052	15.3	86.9	n/a	n/a
NYC Geo Dist #29 (Queens Village)	46	23,648	13.6	98.2	n/a	n/a
NYC Geo Dist #30 (Long Island City)	52	37,414	14.2	83.1	n/a	n/a
NYC Geo Dist #31 (Staten Island)	74	60,047	13.8	61.9	n/a	n/a
NYC Geo Dist #32 (Brooklyn)	27	9,633	11.2	97.1	n/a	n/a

Note: Table includes school districts with 2,000 or more students; (1) Percentage of students that are not non-Hispanic white.
Source: U.S. Department of Education, National Center for Education Statistics, Common Core of Data, Local Education Agency (School District) Universe Survey: School Year 2023-2024; U.S. Department of Education, National Center for Education Statistics, Common Core of Data, School District Finance Survey (F-33): School Year 2021–22

Best High Schools

According to *U.S. News,* New York is home to 29 of the top 500 high schools in the U.S.: **Queens High School for the Sciences at York College** (#25); **Stuyvesant High School** (#26); **High School Math Science and Engineering at CCNY** (#36); **Bronx High School of Science** (#37); **Staten Island Technical High School** (#50); **Brooklyn Latin School** (#54); **Brooklyn Technical High School** (#67); **High School of American Studies at Lehman College** (#76); **Townsend Harris High School** (#78); **Baccalaureate School for Global Education** (#106); **Success Academy Charter School-Harlem 1** (#116); **Eleanor Roosevelt High School** (#122); **Millennium Brooklyn High School** (#130); **Columbia Secondary School** (#137); **High School for Dual Language and Asian Studies** (#157); **New Explorations Into Science, Tech and Math High School** (#163); **Scholars' Academy** (#184); **KIPP Academy Charter School** (#216); **Manhattan/Hunter Science High School** (#223); **Baruch College Campus High School** (#251); **The Clinton School** (#271); **Manhattan Center for Science and Mathematics** (#287); **Millennium High School** (#292); **Special Music School** (#352); **Young Women's Leadership School of Queens** (#384); **Beacon High School** (#393); **Central Park East High School** (#411); **Leon M. Goldstein High School for the Sciences** (#433); **Harlem Village Academy West Charter School** (#483). Nearly 25,000 public, magnet and charter schools were ranked based on their performance on state assessments and how well they prepare students for college. *U.S. News & World Report, "Best High Schools 2024"*

Highest Level of Education

Area	Less than H.S.	H.S. Diploma	Some College, No Deg.	Associate Degree	Bachelor's Degree	Master's Degree	Prof. School Degree	Doctorate Degree
City	16.3	23.0	13.2	6.5	23.6	12.4	3.3	1.7
MSA[1]	12.4	23.2	14.0	6.8	24.9	13.3	3.5	1.8
U.S.	10.6	26.2	19.4	8.8	21.3	9.8	2.3	1.6

Note: Figures cover persons age 25 and over; (1) Figures cover the New York-Newark-Jersey City, NY-NJ Metropolitan Statistical Area
Source: U.S. Census Bureau, 2019-2023 American Community Survey 5-Year Estimates

Educational Attainment by Race

Area	High School Graduate or Higher (%)					Bachelor's Degree or Higher (%)				
	Total	White	Black	Asian	Hisp.[2]	Total	White	Black	Asian	Hisp.[2]
City	83.7	92.5	85.1	77.3	71.7	41.0	59.2	26.7	45.2	21.5
MSA[1]	87.6	93.7	86.9	84.4	74.1	43.5	52.7	28.4	57.0	22.8
U.S.	89.4	92.9	88.1	88.0	72.5	35.0	37.7	24.7	57.0	19.9

Note: Figures shown cover persons 25 years old and over; (1) Figures cover the New York-Newark-Jersey City, NY-NJ Metropolitan Statistical Area; (2) People of Hispanic origin can be of any race
Source: U.S. Census Bureau, 2019-2023 American Community Survey 5-Year Estimates

School Enrollment by Grade and Control

Area	Preschool (%)		Kindergarten (%)		Grades 1 - 4 (%)		Grades 5 - 8 (%)		Grades 9 - 12 (%)	
	Public	Private	Public	Private	Public	Private	Public	Private	Public	Private
City	67.6	32.4	78.2	21.8	80.9	19.1	80.6	19.4	80.3	19.7
MSA[1]	58.7	41.3	80.9	19.1	83.9	16.1	84.6	15.4	83.7	16.3
U.S.	58.7	41.3	85.2	14.8	87.2	12.8	87.9	12.1	89.0	11.0

Note: Figures shown cover persons 3 years old and over; (1) Figures cover the New York-Newark-Jersey City, NY-NJ Metropolitan Statistical Area
Source: U.S. Census Bureau, 2019-2023 American Community Survey 5-Year Estimates

Higher Education

Four-Year Colleges			Two-Year Colleges			Medical Schools[1]	Law Schools[2]	Voc/ Tech[3]
Public	Private Non-profit	Private For-profit	Public	Private Non-profit	Private For-profit			
30	153	18	23	20	33	16	13	85

Note: Figures cover institutions located within the New York-Newark-Jersey City, NY-NJ Metropolitan Statistical Area and include main campuses only; (1) includes schools accredited by the Liaison Committee on Medical Education and the American Osteopathic Association's Commission on Osteopathic College Accreditation; (2) includes ABA-accredited schools, schools with provisional ABA accreditation, and state accredited schools; (3) includes all schools with programs that are less than 2 years.
Source: National Center for Education Statistics, Integrated Postsecondary Education System (IPEDS), 2023-24; Wikipedia, List of Medical Schools in the United States, accessed May 2, 2025; Wikipedia, List of Law Schools in the United States, accessed May 2, 2025

According to *U.S. News & World Report,* the New York-Newark-Jersey City, NY-NJ metro area is home to 16 of the top 200 national universities in the U.S.: **Columbia University** (#13 tie); **New York University** (#30 tie); **Rutgers University—New Brunswick** (#41 tie); **Stony Brook University—SUNY** (#58 tie); **Stevens Institute of Technology** (#76 tie); **Rutgers University—Newark** (#80 tie); **New Jersey Institute of Technology** (#84 tie); **Fordham University** (#91 tie); **Yeshiva University** (#98 tie); **CUNY—City College** (#121 tie); **Montclair State University** (#152 tie); **St. John's University (NY)** (#152 tie); **Seton Hall University** (#165 tie); **Touro University** (#171 tie); **Adelphi University** (#189 tie); **Hofstra University** (#196 tie). The indicators used to capture academic quality fall into a number of categories: assessment by administrators at peer institutions; retention of students; faculty resources; student selectivity; financial resources; alumni giving; high school counselor ratings of colleges; and graduation rate. *U.S. News & World Report, "America's Best Colleges 2025"*

According to *U.S. News & World Report,* the New York-Newark-Jersey City, NY-NJ metro area is home to two of the top 100 liberal arts colleges in the U.S.: **Barnard College** (#14 tie); **Drew University** (#83 tie). The indicators used to capture academic quality fall into a number of categories: assessment by administrators at peer institutions; retention of students; faculty resources; student selectivity; financial resources; alumni giving; high school counselor ratings of colleges; and graduation rate. *U.S. News & World Report, "America's Best Colleges 2025"*

According to *U.S. News & World Report,* the New York-Newark-Jersey City, NY-NJ metro area is home to six of the top 100 law schools in the U.S.: **New York University 1** (#8 tie); **Columbia University 1** (#10 tie); **Fordham University** (#38 tie); **St. John's University** (#63 tie); **Yeshiva University (Cardozo)** (#63 tie); **Seton Hall University** (#71 tie). The rankings are based on a weighted average of 12 measures of quality: peer assessment score; assessment score by lawyers/judges; median LSAT scores; median undergrad GPA; acceptance rate; employment rates for graduates; placement success; bar passage rate; faculty resources; expenditures per student; student/faculty ratio; and library resources. *U.S. News & World Report, "America's Best Graduate Schools, Law, 2025"*

According to *U.S. News & World Report*, the New York-Newark-Jersey City, NY-NJ metro area is home to three of the top medical schools for research in the U.S.: **Hofstra University/Northwell Health (Zucker)** (Tier 1); **Rutgers Robert Wood Johnson Medical School—New Brunswick (Johnson)** (Tier 2); **Stony Brook University—SUNY (Renaissance)** (Tier 2). *U.S. News* placed medical and osteopathic schools into tiers based on their research productivity, faculty and admissions data. Each school's tier was derived from its overall score, calculated by summing the weighted normalized values generated across several factors of academic quality, outlined below. There are four tiers, with tier 1 medical schools as the highest-performing and tier 4 as the lowest-performing. Only tier 1 and 2 schools are shown. Because of the tier presentation, *U.S. News* calculated overall scores based on their percentile performance among all rated schools instead of dividing against the rescaled score of the No. 1-performing schools. Tier 1 included schools with overall scores of 85 to 99. The cutoffs for tiers 2 through 4 were schools scoring 50 to 84, 15 to 49 and 1 to 14, respectively. The rankings are based on a weighted average of the following measures of quality: total research activity; average research activity per faculty member; total NIH research grants at the medical school and its affiliated hospitals; average NIH research grants per faculty; median MCAT total score; median undergraduate GPA; acceptance rate; and faculty resources. *U.S. News & World Report, "America's Best Graduate Schools, Medical, 2025"*

According to *U.S. News & World Report*, the New York-Newark-Jersey City, NY-NJ metro area is home to six of the top 75 business schools in the U.S.: **New York University (Stern)** (#6 tie); **Columbia University** (#9); **Rutgers University—Newark and New Brunswick** (#53); **Fordham University (Gabelli)** (#58 tie); **CUNY Bernard M. Baruch College (Zicklin)** (#61 tie); **Stevens Institute of Technology** (#68 tie). The rankings are based on a weighted average of the following nine measures: quality assessment; peer assessment; recruiter assessment; placement success; mean starting salary and bonus; student selectivity; mean GMAT and GRE scores; mean undergraduate GPA; and acceptance rate. *U.S. News & World Report, "America's Best Graduate Schools, Business, 2025"*

EMPLOYERS

Major Employers

Company Name	Industry
City of Newark	Local government
Columbia University	Higher education
Hackensack University Medical Center	University
Merrill Lynch and Co	Security brokers & dealers
Metropolitan Transit Authority	Public transportation
Montefiore Health System	Healthcare system
Mount Sinai Hospital	General medical & surgical hospitals
Mount Sinai School of Medicine	Medical training services
New York City Hall	Government
New York Dept of Education	Education
New York Presbytrian Hospital	General medical & surgical hospitals
New York University	Higher education
Northwell Health	Healthcare system
NY State Government	State government
NYC Fire Dept	Firefighting
NYC Health + Hospitals	Healthcare system
Pfizer	Pharmaceutical
Rutgers University	Higher education
U.S. Government	Federal government
U.S. Postal Service	U.S. postal service

Note: Companies shown are located within the New York-Newark-Jersey City, NY-NJ Metropolitan Statistical Area.
Source: Chambers of Commerce; State Departments of Labor; Wikipedia

Best Companies to Work For

American Express; Deloitte; EY; KPMG; MetLife; PricewaterhouseCoopers, headquartered in New York, are among "The 100 Best Companies to Work For." To pick the best companies, *Fortune* partnered with the Great Place to Work Institute. Using their proprietary Trust Index™ survey, the core of what creates great a workplace is measured—key behaviors that drive trust in management, connection with colleagues, and loyalty to the company. To be eligible for the *Fortune* 100 Best Companies to Work For list, employers must have 1,000 or more employees in the U.S. and cannot be a government agency. *Fortune, "The 100 Best Companies to Work For," 2025*

American Express; Braze; Chainlink Labs; Deloitte; EY; FanDuel Group; Greenhouse; PricewaterhouseCoopers; Voya, headquartered in New York, are among "Fortune's Best Workplaces for Parents." To pick the best companies, *Fortune* partnered with the Great Place to Work Institute. To be considered for the list, companies must be Great Place To Work-Certified and have at least 50 responses from parents in the US. The survey enables employees to share confidential quantitative and qualitative feedback about their organization's culture by responding to 60 statements on a 5-point scale and answering two open-ended questions. Collectively, these statements describe a great employee experience, defined by high levels of trust, respect, credibility, fairness, pride, and camaraderie. In addition, companies provide organizational data like size, location, industry, demographics, roles, and levels; and provide information about parental leave, adoption, flexible schedule, childcare and dependent health care benefits. *Fortune, "Best Workplaces for Parents," 2024*

American Express; Boldly; Braze; CohnReznick; Deloitte; Greenhouse; MetLife; PricewaterhouseCoopers; Voya; W. P. Carey, headquartered in New York, are among "Fortune's Best Workplaces for Women." To pick the best companies, *Fortune* partnered with the Great Place to Work Institute. To be considered for the list, companies must be Great Place To Work-Certified. Companies must also employ at least 50 women, at least 20% of their non-executive managers must be female, and at least one executive must be female. To determine the Best Workplaces for Women, Great Place To Work measured the differences in women's survey responses to those of their peers and assesses the impact of demographics and roles on the quality and consistency of women's experiences. Great Place To Work also analyzed the gender balance of each workplace, how it compared to each company's industry, and patterns in representation as women rise from front-line positions to the board of directors. *Fortune, "Best Workplaces for Women," 2024*

EHE Health; Maven Clinic; MultiPlan; Progyny; Ro; Talkiatry; Unite Us; Zocdoc, headquartered in New York, are among "Best Workplaces in Health Care." To determine the Best Workplaces in Health Care list, Great Place To Work analyzed the survey responses of over 185,000 employees from Great Place To Work-Certified companies in the health care industry. Survey data analysis and company-provided datapoints are then factored into a combined score to compare and rank the companies that create the most consistently positive experience for all employees in this industry. *Fortune, "Best Workplaces in Health Care," 2024*

Empire State Realty; W. P. Carey, headquartered in New York, are among "Best Workplaces in Real Estate." To determine the Best Workplaces in Real Estate list, Great Place To Work analyzed the survey responses of over 29,000 employees from Great Place To Work-Certified companies in the real estate industry. Survey data analysis and company-provided datapoints are then factored into a combined score to compare and rank the companies that create the most consistently positive experience for all employees in this industry. *Fortune, "Best Workplaces in Real Estate," 2024*

A+E Television Networks; NewYork-Presbyterian Hospital, headquartered in New York, are among the "Best Places to Work in IT." To qualify, companies had to have a minimum of 100 total employees and five IT employees. The best places to work were selected based on DEI (diversity, equity, and inclusion) practices; IT turnover, promotions, and growth; IT retention and engagement programs; remote/hybrid working; benefits and perks (such as elder care and child care, flextime, and reimbursement for college tuition); and training and career development opportunities. *Computerworld, "Best Places to Work in IT," 2025*

PUBLIC SAFETY

Crime Rate

Area	Total Crime Rate	Violent Crime Rate				Property Crime Rate		
		Murder	Rape	Robbery	Aggrav. Assault	Burglary	Larceny-Theft	Motor Vehicle Theft
City	3,066.4	4.2	25.3	200.0	438.8	167.2	2,006.8	224.2
U.S.	2,290.9	5.7	38.0	66.5	264.1	250.7	1,347.2	318.7

Note: Figures are crimes per 100,000 population.
Source: FBI, Table 8, Offenses Known to Law Enforcement, by State by City, 2023

Hate Crimes

Area	Number of Quarters Reported	Number of Incidents per Bias Motivation					
		Race/Ethnicity/Ancestry	Religion	Sexual Orientation	Disability	Gender	Gender Identity
City[1]	4	153	361	94	0	2	20
U.S.	4	5,900	2,699	2,077	187	92	492

Note: (1) Figures include at least one incident reported with more than one bias motivation.
Source: Federal Bureau of Investigation, Hate Crime Statistics 2023

Identity Theft Consumer Reports

Area	Reports	Reports per 100,000 Population	Rank[2]
MSA[1]	67,819	343	39
U.S.	1,135,291	339	-

Note: (1) Figures cover the New York-Newark-Jersey City, NY-NJ Metropolitan Statistical Area; (2) Rank ranges from 1 to 401 where 1 indicates greatest number of identity theft reports per 100,000 population
Source: Federal Trade Commission, Consumer Sentinel Network Data Book 2024

Fraud and Other Consumer Reports

Area	Reports	Reports per 100,000 Population	Rank[2]
MSA[1]	309,066	1,564	49
U.S.	5,360,641	1,601	-

Note: (1) Figures cover the New York-Newark-Jersey City, NY-NJ Metropolitan Statistical Area; (2) Rank ranges from 1 to 401 where 1 indicates greatest number of fraud and other consumer reports per 100,000 population
Source: Federal Trade Commission, Consumer Sentinel Network Data Book 2024

POLITICS

2024 Presidential Election Results

Area	Trump (Rep.)	Harris (Dem.)	Stein (Green)	Kennedy (Ind.)	Oliver (Lib.)	Other
New York City	30.0	68.1	0.9	0.0	0.0	1.0
Bronx County	27.0	71.9	0.6	0.0	0.0	0.5
Kings County	27.4	70.4	1.1	0.0	0.0	1.1
New York County	17.2	80.8	0.7	0.0	0.0	1.3
Queens County	37.0	61.1	1.2	0.0	0.0	0.7
Richmond County	63.9	34.6	0.9	0.0	0.0	0.6
U.S.	49.7	48.2	0.6	0.5	0.4	0.6

Note: Results are percentages and may not add to 100% due to rounding
Source: Dave Leip's Atlas of U.S. Presidential Elections

SPORTS

Professional Sports Teams

Team Name	League	Year Established
Brooklyn Nets	National Basketball Association (NBA)	1967
New Jersey Devils	National Hockey League (NHL)	1982
New York City FC	Major League Soccer (MLS)	2015
New York Giants	National Football League (NFL)	1925
New York Islanders	National Hockey League (NHL)	1972
New York Jets	National Football League (NFL)	1960
New York Knicks	National Basketball Association (NBA)	1946
New York Mets	Major League Baseball (MLB)	1962
New York Rangers	National Hockey League (NHL)	1926
New York Red Bulls	Major League Soccer (MLS)	1996
New York Yankees	Major League Baseball (MLB)	1903

Note: Includes teams located in the New York-Newark-Jersey City, NY-NJ Metropolitan Statistical Area.
Source: Wikipedia, Major Professional Sports Teams of the United States and Canada, May 1, 2025

CLIMATE

Average and Extreme Temperatures

Temperature	Jan	Feb	Mar	Apr	May	Jun	Jul	Aug	Sep	Oct	Nov	Dec	Yr.
Extreme High (°F)	68	75	85	96	97	101	104	99	99	88	81	72	104
Average High (°F)	38	41	50	61	72	80	85	84	76	65	54	43	62
Average Temp. (°F)	32	34	43	53	63	72	77	76	68	58	48	37	55
Average Low (°F)	26	27	35	44	54	63	68	67	60	49	41	31	47
Extreme Low (°F)	-2	-2	8	21	36	46	53	50	40	29	17	-1	-2

Note: Figures cover the years 1962-1992
Source: National Climatic Data Center, International Station Meteorological Climate Summary, 9/96

Average Precipitation/Snowfall/Humidity

Precip./Humidity	Jan	Feb	Mar	Apr	May	Jun	Jul	Aug	Sep	Oct	Nov	Dec	Yr.
Avg. Precip. (in.)	3.5	3.1	4.0	3.9	4.5	3.8	4.5	4.1	4.1	3.3	4.5	3.8	47.0
Avg. Snowfall (in.)	7	8	4	Tr	Tr	0	0	0	0	Tr	Tr	3	23
Avg. Rel. Hum. 7am (%)	67	67	66	64	72	74	74	76	78	75	72	69	71
Avg. Rel. Hum. 4pm (%)	55	53	50	45	52	55	53	54	56	55	57	58	53

Note: Figures cover the years 1962-1992; Tr = Trace amounts (<0.05 in. of rain; <0.5 in. of snow)
Source: National Climatic Data Center, International Station Meteorological Climate Summary, 9/96

Weather Conditions

Temperature			Daytime Sky			Precipitation		
32°F & below	45°F & below	90°F & above	Clear	Partly cloudy	Cloudy	0.01 inch or more precip.	0.1 inch or more snow/ice	Thunder-storms
75	170	18	85	166	114	120	11	20

Note: Figures are average number of days per year and cover the years 1962-1992
Source: National Climatic Data Center, International Station Meteorological Climate Summary, 9/96

HAZARDOUS WASTE

Superfund Sites

The New York-Jersey City-White Plains, NY-NJ metro division is home to 22 sites on the EPA's Superfund National Priorities List (NPL) or Superfund Alternative Approach (SAA) list: **Arsenic Mine** (Final NPL); **Brewster Well Field** (Final NPL); **Curcio Scrap Metal, Inc.** (Final NPL); **Diamond Head Oil Refinery Division** (Final NPL); **Fair Lawn Well Field** (Final NPL); **Garfield Ground Water Contamination** (Final NPL); **Gowanus Canal** (Final NPL); **Lower Hackensack River** (Final NPL); **Magna Metals** (Final NPL); **Maywood Chemical Co.** (Final NPL); **Meeker Avenue Plume** (Final NPL); **Newtown Creek** (Final NPL); **PJP Landfill** (Final NPL); **Quanta Resources** (Final NPL); **Ramapo Landfill** (Final NPL); **Ringwood Mines/Landfill** (Final NPL); **Scientific Chemical Processing** (Final NPL); **Standard Chlorine** (Final NPL); **Syncon Resins** (Final NPL); **Universal Oil Products (Chemical Division)** (Final NPL); **Ventron/velsicol** (Final NPL); **Wolff-alport Chemical Company** (Final NPL). The Superfund alternative approach uses the same investigation and cleanup process and standards that are used for sites listed on the National Priorities List. The SAA is an alternative to listing a site on the NPL; it is not an alternative to Superfund or the Superfund process. There are a total of 1,445 Superfund sites with a status of proposed or final on both lists in the United States. *U.S. Environmental Protection Agency, National Priorities List, May 1, 2025; U.S. Environmental Protection Agency, Superfund Alternative Approach Sites, May 1, 2025*

AIR QUALITY

Air Quality Trends: Ozone

	1990	1995	2000	2005	2010	2015	2020	2021	2022	2023
MSA[1]	0.101	0.105	0.089	0.090	0.080	0.074	0.064	0.069	0.067	0.071
U.S.	0.087	0.089	0.081	0.080	0.072	0.068	0.066	0.067	0.067	0.070

Note: (1) Data covers the New York-Newark-Jersey City, NY-NJ Metropolitan Statistical Area. The values shown are the composite ozone concentration averages among trend sites based on the highest fourth daily maximum 8-hour concentration in parts per million. These trends are based on sites having an adequate record of monitoring data during the trend period. Data from exceptional events are included.
Source: U.S. Environmental Protection Agency, Air Quality Monitoring Information, "Air Quality Trends by City, 1990-2023"

Air Quality Index

Area	Percent of Days when Air Quality was...[2]					AQI Statistics[2]	
	Good	Moderate	Unhealthy for Sensitive Groups	Unhealthy	Very Unhealthy	Maximum	Median
MSA[1]	29.3	64.1	4.7	1.6	0.3	278	56

Note: (1) Data covers the New York-Newark-Jersey City, NY-NJ Metropolitan Statistical Area; (2) Based on 365 days with AQI data in 2023. Air Quality Index (AQI) is an index for reporting daily air quality. EPA calculates the AQI for five major air pollutants regulated by the Clean Air Act: ground-level ozone, particle pollution (aka particulate matter), carbon monoxide, sulfur dioxide, and nitrogen dioxide. The AQI runs from 0 to 500. The higher the AQI value, the greater the level of air pollution and the greater the health concern. There are six AQI categories: "Good" AQI is between 0 and 50. Air quality is considered satisfactory; "Moderate" AQI is between 51 and 100. Air quality is acceptable; "Unhealthy for Sensitive Groups" When AQI values are between 101 and 150, members of sensitive groups may experience health effects; "Unhealthy" When AQI values are between 151 and 200 everyone may begin to experience health effects; "Very Unhealthy" AQI values between 201 and 300 trigger a health alert; "Hazardous" AQI values over 300 trigger warnings of emergency conditions (not shown).
Source: U.S. Environmental Protection Agency, Air Quality Index Report, 2023

Air Quality Index Pollutants

Area	Percent of Days when AQI Pollutant was...[2]					
	Carbon Monoxide	Nitrogen Dioxide	Ozone	Sulfur Dioxide	Particulate Matter 2.5	Particulate Matter 10
MSA[1]	0.0	4.1	27.7	(3)	68.2	0.0

Note: (1) Data covers the New York-Newark-Jersey City, NY-NJ Metropolitan Statistical Area; (2) Based on 365 days with AQI data in 2023. The Air Quality Index (AQI) is an index for reporting daily air quality. EPA calculates the AQI for five major air pollutants regulated by the Clean Air Act: ground-level ozone, particle pollution (also known as particulate matter), carbon monoxide, sulfur dioxide, and nitrogen dioxide. The AQI runs from 0 to 500. The higher the AQI value, the greater the level of air pollution and the greater the health concern; (3) Sulfur dioxide is no longer included in this table because SO_2 concentrations tend to be very localized and not necessarily representative of broad geographical areas like counties and CBSAs.
Source: U.S. Environmental Protection Agency, Air Quality Index Report, 2023

Maximum Air Pollutant Concentrations: Particulate Matter, Ozone, CO and Lead

	Particulate Matter 10 (ug/m^3)	Particulate Matter 2.5 Wtd AM (ug/m^3)	Particulate Matter 2.5 24-Hr (ug/m^3)	Ozone (ppm)	Carbon Monoxide (ppm)	Lead (ug/m^3)
MSA[1] Level	41	10.5	40	0.076	2	n/a
NAAQS[2]	150	15	35	0.075	9	0.15
Met NAAQS[2]	Yes	Yes	No	No	Yes	n/a

Note: (1) Data covers the New York-Newark-Jersey City, NY-NJ Metropolitan Statistical Area; Data from exceptional events are included; (2) National Ambient Air Quality Standards; ppm = parts per million; ug/m^3 = micrograms per cubic meter; n/a not available.
Concentrations: Particulate Matter 10 (coarse particulate)—highest second maximum 24-hour concentration; Particulate Matter 2.5 Wtd AM (fine particulate)—highest weighted annual mean concentration; Particulate Matter 2.5 24-Hour (fine particulate)—highest 98th percentile 24-hour concentration; Ozone—highest fourth daily maximum 8-hour concentration; Carbon Monoxide—highest second maximum non-overlapping 8-hour concentration; Lead—maximum running 3-month average
Source: U.S. Environmental Protection Agency, Air Quality Monitoring Information, "Air Quality Statistics by City, 2023"

Maximum Air Pollutant Concentrations: Nitrogen Dioxide and Sulfur Dioxide

	Nitrogen Dioxide AM (ppb)	Nitrogen Dioxide 1-Hr (ppb)	Sulfur Dioxide AM (ppb)	Sulfur Dioxide 1-Hr (ppb)	Sulfur Dioxide 24-Hr (ppb)
MSA[1] Level	19	60	n/a	5	n/a
NAAQS[2]	53	100	30	75	140
Met NAAQS[2]	Yes	Yes	n/a	Yes	n/a

Note: (1) Data covers the New York-Newark-Jersey City, NY-NJ Metropolitan Statistical Area; Data from exceptional events are included; (2) National Ambient Air Quality Standards; ppm = parts per million; ug/m^3 = micrograms per cubic meter; n/a not available.
Concentrations: Nitrogen Dioxide AM—highest arithmetic mean concentration; Nitrogen Dioxide 1-Hr—highest 98th percentile 1-hour daily maximum concentration; Sulfur Dioxide AM—highest annual mean concentration; Sulfur Dioxide 1-Hr—highest 99th percentile 1-hour daily maximum concentration; Sulfur Dioxide 24-Hr—highest second maximum 24-hour concentration
Source: U.S. Environmental Protection Agency, Air Quality Monitoring Information, "Air Quality Statistics by City, 2023"

Philadelphia, Pennsylvania

Background

Philadelphia, the largest city in Pennsylvania, was settled by Swedes and Finns in 1638, in a settlement known as New Sweden, seized in 1655 by Peter Stuyvesant, director general of New Amsterdam for the Dutch crown. Inconsiderate of any previous claims by the Dutch, King Charles II of England conferred land between the Connecticut and Delaware rivers upon his brother, the duke of York causing the two countries to go to war. Thanks to a generous loan by Admiral Sir William Penn, the land fell permanently into English hands. To repay the loan, the king gave Sir William's son, also named William, sole proprietorship of the state of present-day Pennsylvania, ridding England of a subject heavily influenced by a dissenting religious sect known as the Society of Friends, or the Quakers.

Pennsylvania's landlord had the vision and the financial means to carry out a simple but radical experiment for the times, a city built upon religious tolerance, and this place of religious outcasts prospered. Thanks to forests abundant in natural resources, and ports busy with international trade, Philadelphia, in the state's southeast corner, was a bustling, ideal American city.

The service sector has emerged as the predominant economic force driving current and future growth in the city. Greater Philadelphia has one of the largest health care industries in the nation. It has become a major materials development and processing center, with more than 100,000 working in the manufacture of chemicals, advanced materials, glass, plastics, industrial gases, metals, composites, and textiles. Philadelphia is also a national leader in the biotech field. Its "knowledge industry," with over 80 colleges and universities helps to supply a skilled workforce for the growing technical and bio-industries. Because of Philadelphia's importance as a mecca for medical research, the region is a major center for the pharmaceutical industry.

The city claimed firsts in many cultural, educational, and political arenas. The Pennsylvania Academy of Fine Arts is the oldest museum and fine arts school in the country. The University of Pennsylvania, which Benjamin Franklin helped found, is the oldest university in the country. And on July 4, 1776, the United States was born when "longhaired radicals" such as Thomas Jefferson, George Washington, and John Hancock signed the Declaration of Independence in Philadelphia, breaking away from the mother country forever.

The city offers a thriving cultural scene with something for everyone, from chamber music to jazz, historic Society Hill to South Philadelphia, home of the open-air Italian Market and famous Philly cheesesteak. The waterfront district has many colonial-era homes and cobblestone streets, as well as the Liberty Bell, Independence Hall and Independence National Historic Park.

The Avenue of the Arts is home to several theaters. The Kimmel Center for the Performing Arts and the Academy of Music serve as home to a number of resident performing arts companies, including The Philadelphia Orchestra, Opera Company of Philadelphia, Pennsylvania Ballet, Chamber Orchestra of Philadelphia, American Theater Arts for Youth, PHILADANCO, Philadelphia Chamber Music Society, and Peter Nero and the Philly Pops. The Walnut Street Theater, a National Historical Landmark, and the oldest (1809) and most subscribed theater in the English-speaking world, completed a $39 million expansion and renovation to both public and nonpublic spaces in 2022.

The National Constitution Center Museum, devoted to exploring the role and meaning of the United States Constitution, is a glass, steel, and limestone building designed by Pei, Cobb Freed, and Partners, built in 2003. That same year, a new Liberty Bell Center, designed to enhance the viewing of the nation's iconic Liberty Bell, also opened.

Sports venues include Lincoln Financial Field for the Philadelphia Eagles NFL football team, who won Super Bowl LI in 2018 and 2025, and Citizens Bank Park for Major League Baseball's Philadelphia Phillies, who won the World Series in 2008. These replaced Veterans Stadium, which was razed in a sentimental farewell ceremony. The Wells Fargo Center along the Delaware River hosts the Philadelphia Flyers professional ice hockey team and the Philadelphia 76ers professional basketball team.

The Appalachian Mountains to the west and the Atlantic Ocean to the east have a moderating effect on the city's climate and temperatures. Summer brings humid days, owing to proximity to the ocean. Precipitation is evenly distributed throughout the year, but there are variations within the city. Summer rains and winter snows are sometimes heavier in suburbs to the north and west, with their higher elevations, than in the south and east.

Rankings

General Rankings

- To help military veterans find the best places in which to settle down, *WalletHub* compared the 100 largest U.S. cities across 19 key indicators of livability, affordability and veteran-friendliness. They range from the share of military skill-related jobs to veteran income growth to the availability of VA health facilities. Philadelphia ranked #61. *Wallethub.com, "Best & Worst Places for Veterans to Live (2025)," November 7, 2024*

- The human resources consulting firm Mercer ranked 241 major cities worldwide in terms of overall quality of life. Philadelphia ranked #69. Criteria: political and personal safety, social, and economic factors; medical and health considerations; schools and education; public services and transportation; recreation; connectivity; housing and infrastructure; and climate. *Mercer, "Mercer 2024 Quality of Living Survey," December 2024*

Business/Finance Rankings

- Mercer Human Resources Consulting ranked 226 cities worldwide in terms of cost-of-living. Philadelphia ranked #46 (the lower the ranking, the higher the cost-of-living). The survey measured the comparative cost of over 200 items (such as housing, food, clothing, domestic supplies, transportation, and recreation/entertainment) in each location. *Mercer, "2024 Cost of Living City Ranking," June 17, 2024*

Culture/Performing Arts Rankings

- Philadelphia was selected as one of the 25 best cities for moviemakers in North America. Great film cities are places where filmmaking dreams can come true, that offer more creative space, lower costs, and great outdoor locations. NYC & LA were intentionally excluded. Criteria: film industry presence and culture; tax incentives; affordability; and proximity of festivals and schools. The city was ranked #10. *MovieMaker Magazine, "Best Places to Live and Work as a Moviemaker, 2025," January 29, 2025*

Environmental Rankings

- The U.S. Environmental Protection Agency (EPA) released its list of U.S. metropolitan areas with the most ENERGY STAR certified buildings in 2023. The Philadelphia metro area was ranked #23 out of 25. *U.S. Environmental Protection Agency, "2024 Energy Star Top Cities," May 22, 2024*

Food/Drink Rankings

- Philadelphia was identified as one of the cities in America ordering the most vegan food options by GrubHub.com. The city ranked #5 out of 5. Criteria: percentage of vegan, vegetarian and plant-based food orders compared to the overall number of orders. *GrubHub.com, "State of the Plate Report 2021: Top Cities for Vegans," June 20, 2021*

Health/Fitness Rankings

- For each of the 100 largest cities in the United States, the American Fitness Index®, compiled in partnership between the American College of Sports Medicine and the Elevance Health Foundation, evaluated community infrastructure and more than 30 health behaviors including preventive health, levels of chronic disease conditions, food insecurity, pedestrian safety, air quality, and community/environment resources that support physical activity. Philadelphia ranked #55 for "community fitness." *americanfitnessindex.org, "2024 ACSM American Fitness Index Summary Report," July 23, 2024*

- Philadelphia was identified as one of the 10 most walkable cities in the U.S. by Walk Score. The city ranked #4. Walk Score measures walkability by analyzing hundreds of walking routes to nearby amenities, and also measures pedestrian friendliness by analyzing population density and road metrics such as block length and intersection density. *WalkScore.com, April 13, 2021*

- Philadelphia was identified as a "2025 Allergy Capital." The area ranked #77 out of the nation's 100 largest metropolitan areas. Three groups of factors were used to identify the most challenging cities for people with allergies: annual tree, grass, and weed pollen scores; over the counter allergy medicine use; number of board-certified allergy specialists. *Asthma and Allergy Foundation of America, "2025 Allergy Capitals: The Most Challenging Places to Live with Allergies," March 18, 2025*

- Philadelphia was identified as a "2024 Asthma Capital." The area ranked #5 out of the nation's 100 largest metropolitan areas. Criteria: estimated asthma prevalence; asthma-related mortality; and ER visits due to asthma. Risk factors analyzed but not factored in the rankings: annual air quality including pollution and ozone levels; public smoking laws; indoor air quality; access to asthma specialists; rescue and controller medication use; uninsured rate; pollen allergy; poverty rate. *Asthma and Allergy Foundation of America, "Asthma Capitals 2024: The Most Challenging Places to Live With Asthma," September 10, 2024*

Real Estate Rankings

- *WalletHub* compared the most populated U.S. cities to determine which had the best markets for real estate agents. Philadelphia ranked #144 where demand was high and pay was the best. Criteria: sales per agent; annual median wage for real-estate agents; monthly average starting salary for real estate agents; real estate job density and competition; unemployment rate; home turnover rate; housing-market health index; and other relevant metrics. *WalletHub.com, "2021 Best Places to Be a Real Estate Agent," May 12, 2021*

- Philadelphia was ranked #20 in the top 20 out of the 100 largest metro areas in terms of house price appreciation in 2024 (#1 = highest rate). *Federal Housing Finance Agency, "House Price Index, 4th Quarter 2024," February 25, 2025*

Safety Rankings

- Allstate ranked the 100 most populous cities in America in terms of driver safety. Philadelphia ranked #80. Criteria based on anonymized driving behavior data from Allstate's mobile app powered by Arity: high speed driving (over 80 mph), phone handling, and hard braking. The report helps increase the importance of safety and awareness behind the wheel. *Allstate, "16th Allstate America's Best Drivers Report®" July 11, 2024*

Seniors/Retirement Rankings

- *AARP the Magazine* selected Philadelphia as one of the great places in the United States for seniors, as well as younger generations, that represent "a place to call home." For the list, the magazine recognized the change in criteria due to the pandemic, and looked for cities with easy access to exercise/outdoors, quality healthcare, sense of community, relatively affordable housing costs, job markets that accommodate working from home, and reliable internet access. *AARP The Magazine, "Best Places to Live and Retire Now," November 29, 2021*

Transportation Rankings

- According to the INRIX "2024 Global Traffic Scorecard," Philadelphia was identified as one of the most congested metro areas in the U.S. The area ranked #5 out of 10 in the country and among the top 25 most congested in the world. Criteria: average annual time spent in traffic and average cost of congestion per motorist. *Inrix.com, "Employees & Consumers Returned to Downtowns, Traffic Delays & Costs Grew," January 6, 2025*

Women/Minorities Rankings

- Personal finance website *WalletHub* compared more than 180 U.S. cities across two key dimensions, "Hispanic Business-Friendliness" and "Hispanic Purchasing Power," to arrive at the most favorable conditions for Hispanic entrepreneurs. Philadelphia was ranked #164 out of 182. Criteria includes: share of Hispanic-Owned Businesses; average growth of Hispanic Business revenues; Small Business-Friendliness score; affordability; and number of Hispanics with at least a bachelor's degree. *WalletHub.com, "Best Cities for Hispanic Entrepreneurs," September 4, 2024*

Miscellaneous Rankings

- In its roundup of St. Patrick's Day parades, *Gayot* listed the best festivals and parades of all things Irish. The festivities in Philadelphia as among the best in North America. *Gayot.com, "Best St. Patrick's Day Parades," March 2025*

- *WalletHub* compared 148 of the most populated U.S. cities to determine their operating efficiency. A "Quality of Services" score was constructed for each city and then measured against the total budget per capita to reveal which were managed the best. Philadelphia ranked #138. Criteria: financial stability; economy; education; safety; health; infrastructure and pollution. *WalletHub.com, "2025's Best- & Worst-Run Cities in America," June 18, 2024*

Business Environment

DEMOGRAPHICS

Population Growth

Area	1990 Census	2000 Census	2010 Census	2020 Census	2023 Estimate[2]	Population Growth 1990-2023 (%)
City	1,585,577	1,517,550	1,526,006	1,603,797	1,582,432	-0.2
MSA[1]	5,435,470	5,687,147	5,965,343	6,245,051	6,241,882	14.8
U.S.	248,709,873	281,421,906	308,745,538	331,449,281	332,387,540	33.6

Note: (1) Figures cover the Philadelphia-Camden-Wilmington, PA-NJ-DE-MD Metropolitan Statistical Area; (2) 2019-2023 5-year ACS population estimate
Source: U.S. Census Bureau, 1990 Census, 2000 Census, 2010 Census, 2020 Census, 2019-2023 American Community Survey 5-Year Estimates

Race

Area	White Alone[2] (%)	Black Alone[2] (%)	Asian Alone[2] (%)	AIAN[3] Alone[2] (%)	NHOPI[4] Alone[2] (%)	Other Race Alone[2] (%)	Two or More Races (%)
City	36.1	39.9	7.8	0.4	0.1	8.4	7.3
MSA[1]	61.4	20.2	6.3	0.2	0.0	4.9	6.9
U.S.	63.4	12.4	5.8	0.9	0.2	6.6	10.7

Note: (1) Figures cover the Philadelphia-Camden-Wilmington, PA-NJ-DE-MD Metropolitan Statistical Area; (2) Alone is defined as not being in combination with one or more other races; (3) American Indian and Alaska Native; (4) Native Hawaiian and Other Pacific Islander
Source: U.S. Census Bureau, 2019-2023 American Community Survey 5-Year Estimates

Hispanic or Latino Origin

Area	Total (%)	Mexican (%)	Puerto Rican (%)	Cuban (%)	Other (%)
City	15.2	1.4	8.4	0.2	5.2
MSA[1]	10.4	2.0	4.6	0.3	3.6
U.S.	19.0	11.3	1.8	0.7	5.2

Note: Persons of Hispanic or Latino origin can be of any race; (1) Figures cover the Philadelphia-Camden-Wilmington, PA-NJ-DE-MD Metropolitan Statistical Area
Source: U.S. Census Bureau, 2019-2023 American Community Survey 5-Year Estimates

Age

Area	Under Age 5	Age 5–19	Age 20–34	Age 35–44	Age 45–54	Age 55–64	Age 65–74	Age 75–84	Age 85+	Median Age
City	6.1	18.4	25.5	13.4	10.9	11.6	8.6	4.1	1.6	35.1
MSA[1]	5.5	18.6	20.2	13.1	12.3	13.4	10.0	4.8	2.0	39.1
U.S.	5.7	19.1	20.2	13.1	12.3	12.8	10.0	4.9	1.9	38.7

Note: (1) Figures cover the Philadelphia-Camden-Wilmington, PA-NJ-DE-MD Metropolitan Statistical Area
Source: U.S. Census Bureau, 2019-2023 American Community Survey 5-Year Estimates

Disability by Age

Area	All Ages	Under 18 Years Old	18 to 64 Years Old	65 Years and Over
City	17.4	7.7	15.6	40.8
MSA[1]	13.2	5.5	11.0	31.5
U.S.	13.0	4.7	10.7	32.9

Note: Figures show percent of the civilian noninstitutionalized population that reported having a disability. Disability status is determined from six types of difficulty: vision, hearing, cognitive, ambulatory, self-care, and independent living. For children under 5 years old, hearing and vision difficulty are used to determine disability status. For children between the ages of 5 and 14, disability status is determined from hearing, vision, cognitive, ambulatory, and self-care difficulties. For people aged 15 years and older, they are considered to have a disability if they have difficulty with any one of the six difficulty types; Note: (1) Figures cover the Philadelphia-Camden-Wilmington, PA-NJ-DE-MD Metropolitan Statistical Area
Source: U.S. Census Bureau, 2019-2023 American Community Survey 5-Year Estimates

Ancestry

Area	German	Irish	English	American	Italian	Polish	French[2]	European	Scottish
City	7.0	9.6	3.2	2.2	6.7	3.0	0.7	0.7	0.7
MSA[1]	13.7	16.9	7.8	3.2	12.2	4.6	1.2	1.0	1.2
U.S.	12.6	9.4	9.1	5.5	4.9	2.6	2.0	1.6	1.6

Note: Figures are the percentage of the total population reporting a particular ancestry. The nine most commonly reported ancestries in the U.S. are shown. Figures include multiple ancestries (e.g. if a person reported being Irish and Italian, they were included in both columns); (1) Figures cover the Philadelphia-Camden-Wilmington, PA-NJ-DE-MD Metropolitan Statistical Area; (2) Excludes Basque
Source: U.S. Census Bureau, 2019-2023 American Community Survey 5-Year Estimates

Foreign-born Population

Area	Any Foreign Country	Percent of Population Born in							
		Asia	Mexico	Europe	Caribbean	Central America[2]	South America	Africa	Canada
City	14.6	5.6	0.5	2.2	2.8	0.7	1.0	1.7	0.1
MSA[1]	11.5	4.7	0.8	1.8	1.5	0.5	0.8	1.2	0.2
U.S.	13.9	4.3	3.3	1.4	1.4	1.2	1.2	0.8	0.2

Note: (1) Figures cover the Philadelphia-Camden-Wilmington, PA-NJ-DE-MD Metropolitan Statistical Area; (2) Excludes Mexico.
Source: U.S. Census Bureau, 2019-2023 American Community Survey 5-Year Estimates

Household Size

Area	Persons in Household (%)							Average Household Size
	One	Two	Three	Four	Five	Six	Seven or More	
City	37.6	29.9	14.9	9.6	4.8	1.7	1.4	2.29
MSA[1]	29.7	32.3	16.0	13.2	5.7	1.9	1.1	2.49
U.S.	28.5	33.8	15.4	12.7	5.9	2.3	1.4	2.54

Note: (1) Figures cover the Philadelphia-Camden-Wilmington, PA-NJ-DE-MD Metropolitan Statistical Area
Source: U.S. Census Bureau, 2019-2023 American Community Survey 5-Year Estimates

Household Relationships

Area	House-holder	Opposite-sex Spouse	Same-sex Spouse	Opposite-sex Unmarried Partner	Same-sex Unmarried Partner	Child[2]	Grand-child	Other Relatives	Non-relatives
City	41.0	10.9	0.3	3.1	0.3	26.8	3.6	5.9	5.2
MSA[1]	38.7	16.9	0.2	2.5	0.2	29.2	2.5	4.4	3.0
U.S.	38.3	17.5	0.2	2.5	0.2	28.3	2.4	4.8	3.4

Note: Figures are percent of the total population; (1) Figures cover the Philadelphia-Camden-Wilmington, PA-NJ-DE-MD Metropolitan Statistical Area; (2) Includes biological, adopted, and stepchildren of the householder
Source: U.S. Census Bureau, 2020 Census

Gender

Area	Males	Females	Males per 100 Females
City	749,410	833,022	90.0
MSA[1]	3,031,854	3,210,028	94.4
U.S.	164,545,087	167,842,453	98.0

Note: (1) Figures cover the Philadelphia-Camden-Wilmington, PA-NJ-DE-MD Metropolitan Statistical Area
Source: U.S. Census Bureau, 2019-2023 American Community Survey 5-Year Estimates

Marital Status

Area	Never Married	Now Married[2]	Separated	Widowed	Divorced
City	50.7	31.9	2.8	5.5	9.1
MSA[1]	37.7	45.7	1.8	5.6	9.1
U.S.	34.1	47.9	1.7	5.6	10.7

Note: Figures are percentages and cover the population 15 years of age and older; (1) Figures cover the Philadelphia-Camden-Wilmington, PA-NJ-DE-MD Metropolitan Statistical Area; (2) Excludes separated
Source: U.S. Census Bureau, 2019-2023 American Community Survey 5-Year Estimates

Religious Groups by Family

Area	Catholic	Baptist	Methodist	LDS[2]	Pentecostal	Lutheran	Islam	Adventist	Other
MSA[1]	26.8	3.3	2.4	0.3	1.0	1.2	2.6	1.0	10.5
U.S.	18.7	7.3	3.0	2.0	1.8	1.7	1.3	1.3	11.6

Note: Figures are the number of adherents as a percentage of the total population and cover the eight largest religious groups in the U.S; (1) Figures cover the Philadelphia-Camden-Wilmington, PA-NJ-DE-MD Metropolitan Statistical Area; (2) Church of Jesus Christ of Latter-day Saints
Sources: 2020 U.S. Religion Census, Association of Statisticians of American Religious Bodies; The Association of Religion Data Archives (ARDA)

Religious Groups by Tradition

Area	Catholic	Evangelical Protestant	Mainline Protestant	Black Protestant	Islam	Judaism	Hinduism	Orthodox	Buddhism
MSA[1]	26.8	7.3	6.6	2.2	2.6	1.1	0.6	0.4	0.4
U.S.	18.7	16.5	5.2	2.3	1.3	0.6	0.4	0.4	0.3

Note: Figures are the number of adherents as a percentage of the total population; (1) Figures cover the Philadelphia-Camden-Wilmington, PA-NJ-DE-MD Metropolitan Statistical Area
Sources: 2020 U.S. Religion Census, Association of Statisticians of American Religious Bodies; The Association of Religion Data Archives (ARDA)

ECONOMY

Real Gross Domestic Product (GDP)

Area	2017	2018	2019	2020	2021	2022	2023	Rank[3]
MSA[1]	425.4	432.3	437.0	420.4	438.8	450.2	459.5	11
U.S.[2]	17,619.1	18,160.7	18,642.5	18,238.9	19,387.6	19,896.6	20,436.3	—

Note: Figures are in billions of chained 2017 dollars; (1) Figures cover the Philadelphia-Camden-Wilmington, PA-NJ-DE-MD Metropolitan Statistical Area; (2) Figures cover real GDP within metropolitan areas; (3) Rank is based on 2023 data and ranges from 1 to 384
Source: U.S. Bureau of Economic Analysis

Economic Growth

Area	2014	2015	2016	2017	2018	2019	2020	2021	2022	2023
MSA[1]	2.5	1.7	1.4	-0.3	1.6	1.1	-3.8	4.4	2.6	2.1
U.S.[2]	2.6	3.2	2.0	2.7	3.1	2.7	-2.2	6.3	2.6	2.7

Note: Figures are real gross domestic product growth rates and represent percent change from preceding period; (1) Figures cover the Philadelphia-Camden-Wilmington, PA-NJ-DE-MD Metropolitan Statistical Area; (2) Figures are the average growth rates within metropolitan areas
Source: U.S. Bureau of Economic Analysis

Metropolitan Area Exports

Area	2018	2019	2020	2021	2022	2023	Rank[2]
MSA[1]	23,663.2	24,721.3	23,022.1	28,724.4	29,352.1	28,760.2	16
U.S.	1,664,056.1	1,645,173.7	1,431,406.6	1,753,941.4	2,062,937.4	2,019,160.5	—

Note: Figures are in millions of dollars; (1) Figures cover the Philadelphia-Camden-Wilmington, PA-NJ-DE-MD Metropolitan Statistical Area; (2) Rank is based on 2023 data and ranges from 1 to 386
Source: U.S. Department of Commerce, International Trade Administration, Office of Trade and Economic Analysis, Industry and Analysis, Exports by Metropolitan Area, data extracted April 2, 2025

Building Permits

Area	Single-Family			Multi-Family			Total		
	2023	2024	Pct. Chg.	2023	2024	Pct. Chg.	2023	2024	Pct. Chg.
City	405	539	33.1	3,458	2,423	-29.9	3,863	2,962	-23.3
MSA[1]	6,255	8,324	33.1	5,764	5,890	2.2	12,019	14,214	18.3
U.S.	920,000	981,900	6.7	591,100	496,100	-16.1	1,511,100	1,478,000	-2.2

Note: (1) Figures cover the Philadelphia-Camden-Wilmington, PA-NJ-DE-MD Metropolitan Statistical Area; Figures represent new, privately-owned housing units authorized (unadjusted data)
Source: U.S. Census Bureau, Building Permits Survey (BPS), 2023, 2024

Bankruptcy Filings

Area	Business Filings			Nonbusiness Filings		
	2023	2024	% Chg.	2023	2024	% Chg.
Philadelphia County	227	131	-42.3	940	1,094	16.4
U.S.	18,926	23,107	22.1	434,064	494,201	13.9

Note: Business filings include Chapter 7, Chapter 9, Chapter 11, Chapter 12, Chapter 13, Chapter 15, and Section 304; Nonbusiness filings include Chapter 7, Chapter 11, and Chapter 13
Source: Administrative Office of the U.S. Courts, Business and Nonbusiness Bankruptcy, County Cases Commenced by Chapter of the Bankruptcy Code, During the 12-Month Period Ending December 31, 2023 and Business and Nonbusiness Bankruptcy, County Cases Commenced by Chapter of the Bankruptcy Code, During the 12-Month Period Ending December 31, 2024

Housing Vacancy Rates

Area	Gross Vacancy Rate[3] (%)			Year-Round Vacancy Rate[4] (%)			Rental Vacancy Rate[5] (%)			Homeowner Vacancy Rate[6] (%)		
	2022	2023	2024	2022	2023	2024	2022	2023	2024	2022	2023	2024
MSA[1]	5.5	5.3	5.3	5.4	5.2	5.2	4.2	5.2	6.3	1.0	0.9	0.5
U.S.[2]	9.1	9.0	9.1	7.5	7.5	7.6	5.7	6.5	6.8	0.8	0.8	1.0

Note: (1) Figures cover the Philadelphia-Camden-Wilmington, PA-NJ-DE-MD Metropolitan Statistical Area; (2) Figures cover the 75 largest Metropolitan Statistical Areas; (3) The percentage of the total housing inventory that is vacant; (4) The percentage of the housing inventory (excluding seasonal units) that is year-round vacant; (5) The percentage of rental inventory that is vacant for rent; (6) The percentage of homeowner inventory that is vacant for sale
Source: U.S. Census Bureau, Housing Vacancies and Homeownership Annual Statistics: 2022, 2023, 2024

INCOME

Income

Area	Per Capita ($)	Median Household ($)	Average Household ($)
City	37,669	60,698	88,307
MSA[1]	49,178	89,273	123,454
U.S.	43,289	78,538	110,491

Note: (1) Figures cover the Philadelphia-Camden-Wilmington, PA-NJ-DE-MD Metropolitan Statistical Area
Source: U.S. Census Bureau, 2019-2023 American Community Survey 5-Year Estimates

Household Income Distribution

Area	Percent of Households Earning							
	Under $15,000	$15,000 -$24,999	$25,000 -$34,999	$35,000 -$49,999	$50,000 -$74,999	$75,000 -$99,999	$100,000 -$149,999	$150,000 and up
City	15.1	8.7	8.2	11.0	15.8	11.8	14.0	15.3
MSA[1]	8.4	5.8	6.0	8.9	14.0	11.9	17.9	27.1
U.S.	8.5	6.6	6.8	10.4	15.7	12.7	17.4	21.9

Note: (1) Figures cover the Philadelphia-Camden-Wilmington, PA-NJ-DE-MD Metropolitan Statistical Area
Source: U.S. Census Bureau, 2019-2023 American Community Survey 5-Year Estimates

Poverty Rate

Area	All Ages	Under 18 Years Old	18 to 64 Years Old	65 Years and Over
City	22.0	30.1	19.5	21.1
MSA[1]	11.7	15.7	10.6	10.3
U.S.	12.4	16.3	11.6	10.4

Note: Figures are percentage of people whose income during the past 12 months was below the poverty level;
(1) Figures cover the Philadelphia-Camden-Wilmington, PA-NJ-DE-MD Metropolitan Statistical Area
Source: U.S. Census Bureau, 2019-2023 American Community Survey 5-Year Estimates

EMPLOYMENT

Labor Force and Employment

Area	Civilian Labor Force			Workers Employed		
	Dec. 2023	Dec. 2024	% Chg.	Dec. 2023	Dec. 2024	% Chg.
City	750,976	745,485	-0.7	719,837	713,546	-0.9
MD[1]	1,055,097	1,047,116	-0.8	1,014,794	1,006,018	-0.9
U.S.	166,661,000	167,746,000	0.7	160,754,000	161,294,000	0.3

Note: Data is not seasonally adjusted and covers workers 16 years of age and older; (1) Figures cover the Philadelphia, PA Metropolitan Division
Source: Bureau of Labor Statistics, Local Area Unemployment Statistics

Unemployment Rate

Area	2024											
	Jan.	Feb.	Mar.	Apr.	May	Jun.	Jul.	Aug.	Sep.	Oct.	Nov.	Dec.
City	4.7	4.9	4.4	4.0	4.4	4.9	5.5	5.7	4.4	4.6	4.5	4.3
MD[1]	4.3	4.6	4.1	3.7	4.1	4.5	5.1	5.3	4.1	4.2	4.0	3.9
U.S.	4.1	4.2	3.9	3.5	3.7	4.3	4.5	4.4	3.9	3.9	4.0	3.8

Note: Data is not seasonally adjusted and covers workers 16 years of age and older; (1) Figures cover the Philadelphia, PA Metropolitan Division
Source: Bureau of Labor Statistics, Local Area Unemployment Statistics

Average Wages

Occupation	$/Hr.	Occupation	$/Hr.
Accountants and Auditors	46.34	Maintenance and Repair Workers	26.00
Automotive Mechanics	27.57	Marketing Managers	81.62
Bookkeepers	26.12	Network and Computer Systems Admin.	49.02
Carpenters	32.62	Nurses, Licensed Practical	32.87
Cashiers	15.31	Nurses, Registered	46.88
Computer Programmers	46.77	Nursing Assistants	20.72
Computer Systems Analysts	51.52	Office Clerks, General	22.87
Computer User Support Specialists	31.66	Physical Therapists	50.29
Construction Laborers	28.19	Physicians	103.98
Cooks, Restaurant	17.84	Plumbers, Pipefitters and Steamfitters	38.73
Customer Service Representatives	23.03	Police and Sheriff's Patrol Officers	41.45
Dentists	87.74	Postal Service Mail Carriers	28.61
Electricians	38.14	Real Estate Sales Agents	31.43
Engineers, Electrical	61.83	Retail Salespersons	17.58
Fast Food and Counter Workers	15.05	Sales Representatives, Technical/Scientific	57.13
Financial Managers	85.35	Secretaries, Exc. Legal/Medical/Executive	23.47
First-Line Supervisors of Office Workers	35.52	Security Guards	20.88
General and Operations Managers	66.76	Surgeons	n/a
Hairdressers/Cosmetologists	19.65	Teacher Assistants, Exc. Postsecondary[1]	16.42
Home Health and Personal Care Aides	15.40	Teachers, Secondary School, Exc. Sp. Ed.[1]	37.57
Janitors and Cleaners	18.54	Telemarketers	18.66
Landscaping/Groundskeeping Workers	19.86	Truck Drivers, Heavy/Tractor-Trailer	29.70
Lawyers	82.76	Truck Drivers, Light/Delivery Services	23.32
Maids and Housekeeping Cleaners	16.94	Waiters and Waitresses	19.57

Note: Wage data covers the Philadelphia-Camden-Wilmington, PA-NJ-DE-MD Metropolitan Statistical Area;
(1) Hourly wages were calculated from annual wage data based on a 40 hour work week
Source: Bureau of Labor Statistics, Metro Area Occupational Employment & Wage Estimates, May 2024

Employment by Industry

Sector	MD[1] Number of Employees	MD[1] Percent of Total	U.S. Percent of Total
Construction, Mining, and Logging	25,000	2.4	5.5
Financial Activities	62,900	6.1	5.8
Government	133,400	13.0	14.9
Information	18,500	1.8	1.9
Leisure and Hospitality	95,500	9.3	10.4
Manufacturing	31,800	3.1	8.0
Other Services	42,700	4.2	3.7
Private Education and Health Services	338,100	32.9	16.9
Professional and Business Services	147,700	14.4	14.2
Retail Trade	69,100	6.7	10.0
Transportation, Warehousing, and Utilities	39,900	3.9	4.8
Wholesale Trade	23,100	2.2	3.9

Note: Figures are non-farm employment as of December 2024. Figures are not seasonally adjusted and include workers 16 years of age and older; (1) Figures cover the Philadelphia, PA Metropolitan Division
Source: Bureau of Labor Statistics, Current Employment Statistics, Employment, Hours, and Earnings

Employment by Occupation

Occupation Classification	City (%)	MSA[1] (%)	U.S. (%)
Management, Business, Science, and Arts	43.9	47.8	42.0
Natural Resources, Construction, and Maintenance	4.9	6.4	8.6
Production, Transportation, and Material Moving	11.3	10.6	13.0
Sales and Office	18.2	19.6	19.9
Service	21.7	15.7	16.5

Note: Figures cover employed civilians 16 years of age and older; (1) Figures cover the Philadelphia-Camden-Wilmington, PA-NJ-DE-MD Metropolitan Statistical Area
Source: U.S. Census Bureau, 2019-2023 American Community Survey 5-Year Estimates

Occupations with Greatest Projected Employment Growth: 2022 – 2032

Occupation[1]	2022 Employment	2032 Projected Employment	Numeric Employment Change	Percent Employment Change
Home Health and Personal Care Aides	188,340	217,220	28,880	15.3
Cooks, Restaurant	47,000	56,390	9,390	20.0
Software Developers	44,860	53,670	8,810	19.6
Stockers and Order Fillers	101,890	109,260	7,370	7.2
Registered Nurses	148,790	155,810	7,020	4.7
Laborers and Freight, Stock, and Material Movers, Hand	150,410	156,080	5,670	3.8
General and Operations Managers	128,890	134,210	5,320	4.1
Medical and Health Services Managers	17,770	22,610	4,840	27.2
Financial Managers	25,890	29,980	4,090	15.8
Medical Assistants	27,920	31,740	3,820	13.7

Note: Projections cover Pennsylvania; (1) Sorted by numeric employment change
Source: www.projectionscentral.org, State Occupational Projections, 2022–2032 Long-Term Projections

Fastest-Growing Occupations: 2022 – 2032

Occupation[1]	2022 Employment	2032 Projected Employment	Numeric Employment Change	Percent Employment Change
Nurse Practitioners	8,010	11,430	3,420	42.7
Data Scientists	3,810	5,060	1,250	32.8
Wind Turbine Service Technicians	160	210	50	31.3
Statisticians	2,590	3,380	790	30.5
Physician Assistants	7,240	9,290	2,050	28.3
Information Security Analysts (SOC 2018)	4,470	5,720	1,250	28.0
Medical and Health Services Managers	17,770	22,610	4,840	27.2
Physical Therapist Assistants	4,990	6,280	1,290	25.9
Occupational Therapy Assistants	2,180	2,700	520	23.9
Operations Research Analysts	3,110	3,800	690	22.2

Note: Projections cover Pennsylvania; (1) Sorted by percent employment change and excludes occupations with numeric employment change less than 50
Source: www.projectionscentral.org, State Occupational Projections, 2022–2032 Long-Term Projections

CITY FINANCES

City Government Finances

Component	2022 ($000)	2022 ($ per capita)
Total Revenues	9,910,935	6,279
Total Expenditures	9,649,672	6,113
Debt Outstanding	5,558,849	3,522

Source: U.S. Census Bureau, State & Local Government Finances 2022

City Government Revenue by Source

Source	2022 ($000)	2022 ($ per capita)	2022 (%)
General Revenue			
From Federal Government	757,147	480	7.6
From State Government	2,199,819	1,394	22.2
From Local Governments	26,612	17	0.3
Taxes			
Property	723,321	458	7.3
Sales and Gross Receipts	720,843	457	7.3
Personal Income	1,981,407	1,255	20.0
Corporate Income	746,171	473	7.5
Motor Vehicle License	0	0	0.0
Other Taxes	381,173	241	3.8
Current Charges	1,168,780	740	11.8
Liquor Store	0	0	0.0
Utility	1,063,519	674	10.7

Source: U.S. Census Bureau, State & Local Government Finances 2022

City Government Expenditures by Function

Function	2022 ($000)	2022 ($ per capita)	2022 (%)
General Direct Expenditures			
Air Transportation	402,161	254	4.2
Corrections	324,299	205	3.4
Education	0	0	0.0
Employment Security Administration	0	0	0.0
Financial Administration	86,593	54	0.9
Fire Protection	344,950	218	3.6
General Public Buildings	249,115	157	2.6
Governmental Administration, Other	413,833	262	4.3
Health	2,206,934	1,398	22.9
Highways	251,516	159	2.6
Hospitals	0	0	0.0
Housing and Community Development	479,892	304	5.0
Interest on General Debt	210,092	133	2.2
Judicial and Legal	374,734	237	3.9
Libraries	47,265	29	0.5
Parking	0	0	0.0
Parks and Recreation	106,037	67	1.1
Police Protection	783,933	496	8.1
Public Welfare	251,104	159	2.6
Sewerage	365,958	231	3.8
Solid Waste Management	194,784	123	2.0
Veterans' Services	0	0	0.0
Liquor Store	0	0	0.0
Utility	926,320	586	9.6

Source: U.S. Census Bureau, State & Local Government Finances 2022

TAXES

State Corporate Income Tax Rates

State	Tax Rate (%)	Income Brackets ($)	Num. of Brackets	Financial Institution Tax Rate (%)[a]	Federal Income Tax Ded.
Pennsylvania	8.49	Flat rate	1	(a)	No

Note: Tax rates for tax year 2024; (a) Rates listed are the corporate income tax rate applied to financial institutions or excise taxes based on income. Some states have other taxes based upon the value of deposits or shares.
Source: Federation of Tax Administrators, State Corporate Income Tax Rates, January 1, 2025

State Individual Income Tax Rates

State	Tax Rate (%)	Income Brackets ($)	Personal Exemptions ($)			Standard Ded. ($)	
			Single	Married	Depend.	Single	Married
Pennsylvania	3.07	Flat rate	None	None	None	–	–

Note: Tax rates for tax year 2024; Local- and county-level taxes are not included; Federal income tax is not deductible on state income tax returns
Source: Federation of Tax Administrators, State Individual Income Tax Rates, January 1, 2025

Various State Sales and Excise Tax Rates

State	State Sales Tax (%)	Gasoline[1] ($/gal.)	Cigarette[2] ($/pack)	Spirits[3] ($/gal.)	Wine[4] ($/gal.)	Beer[5] ($/gal.)	Recreational Marijuana (%)
Pennsylvania	6	0.59	2.60	7.48	0.00	0.08	Not legal

Note: All tax rates as of January 1, 2025; (1) The American Petroleum Institute has developed a methodology for determining the average tax rate on a gallon of fuel. Rates may include any of the following: excise taxes, environmental fees, storage tank fees, other fees or taxes, general sales tax, and local taxes; (2) The federal excise tax of $1.0066 per pack and local taxes are not included; (3) Rates are those applicable to off-premise sales of 40% alcohol by volume (a.b.v.) distilled spirits in 750ml containers. Local excise taxes are excluded; (4) Rates are those applicable to off-premise sales of 11% a.b.v. non-carbonated wine in 750ml containers; (5) Rates are those applicable to off-premise sales of 4.7% a.b.v. beer in 12 ounce containers.
Source: Tax Foundation, 2025 Facts & Figures: How Does Your State Compare?

State Tax Competitiveness Index

State	Overall Rank	Corporate Tax Rank	Individual Income Tax Rank	Sales Tax Rank	Property Tax Rank	Unemployment Insurance Tax Rank
Pennsylvania	34	38	38	22	9	36

Note: The Tax Foundation's State Tax Competitiveness Index enables policymakers, taxpayers, and business leaders to gauge how their states' tax systems compare. A rank of 1 is best, 50 is worst. Rankings do not average to the total. States without a tax rank equally as 1. DC's scores and rankings do not affect other states. The report shows tax systems as of July 1, 2024 (the beginning of Fiscal Year 2025).
Source: Tax Foundation, State Tax Competitiveness Index 2025

TRANSPORTATION

Means of Transportation to Work

Area	Car/Truck/Van		Public Transportation			Bicycle	Walked	Other Means	Worked at Home
	Drove Alone	Car-pooled	Bus	Subway	Railroad				
City	46.7	7.6	10.9	4.7	1.6	1.9	7.5	2.8	16.4
MSA[1]	64.4	7.0	3.4	1.5	1.3	0.6	3.2	1.7	16.8
U.S.	70.2	8.5	1.7	1.3	0.4	0.4	2.4	1.6	13.5

Note: Figures are percentages and cover workers 16 years of age and older; (1) Figures cover the Philadelphia-Camden-Wilmington, PA-NJ-DE-MD Metropolitan Statistical Area
Source: U.S. Census Bureau, 2019-2023 American Community Survey 5-Year Estimates

Travel Time to Work

Area	Less Than 10 Minutes	10 to 19 Minutes	20 to 29 Minutes	30 to 44 Minutes	45 to 59 Minutes	60 to 89 Minutes	90 Minutes or More
City	6.7	19.7	20.8	28.1	12.0	9.2	3.5
MSA[1]	10.0	24.4	20.8	24.1	10.6	7.3	2.8
U.S.	12.6	28.6	21.2	20.8	8.1	6.0	2.8

Note: Note: Figures are percentages and include workers 16 years old and over; (1) Figures cover the Philadelphia-Camden-Wilmington, PA-NJ-DE-MD Metropolitan Statistical Area
Source: U.S. Census Bureau, 2019-2023 American Community Survey 5-Year Estimates

Key Congestion Measures

Measure	2000	2010	2015	2020	2022
Annual Hours of Delay, Total (000)	111,501	149,593	163,314	100,726	176,742
Annual Hours of Delay, Per Auto Commuter	41	50	58	37	68
Annual Congestion Cost, Per Auto Commuter ($)	1,263	1,346	1,358	882	1,528

Note: Figures cover the Philadelphia PA-NJ-DE-MD urban area
Source: Texas A&M Transportation Institute, 2023 Urban Mobility Report

Freeway Travel Time Index

Measure	1985	1990	1995	2000	2005	2010	2015	2020	2022
Urban Area Index[1]	1.12	1.15	1.18	1.21	1.25	1.24	1.24	1.12	1.23
Urban Area Rank[1,2]	21	22	26	27	25	24	26	10	24

Note: Freeway Travel Time Index—the ratio of travel time in the peak period to the travel time at free-flow conditions. For example, a value of 1.30 indicates a 20-minute free-flow trip takes 26 minutes in the peak (20 minutes x 1.30 = 26 minutes); (1) Covers the Philadelphia PA-NJ-DE-MD urban area; (2) Rank is based on 101 larger urban areas (#1 = highest travel time index)
Source: Texas A&M Transportation Institute, 2023 Urban Mobility Report

Public Transportation

Agency Name / Mode of Transportation	Vehicles Operated in Maximum Service[1]	Annual Unlinked Passenger Trips[2] (in thous.)	Annual Passenger Miles[3] (in thous.)
Southeastern Pennsylvania Transportation Authority (SEPTA)			
Bus (directly operated)	1,046	101,419.1	280,491.0
Bus (purchased transportation)	3	38.4	242.3
Commuter Rail (directly operated)	306	19,103.6	260,671.1
Demand Response (purchased transportation)	240	856.7	5,713.3
Heavy Rail (directly operated)	238	57,976.4	242,101.1
Streetcar Rail (directly operated)	91	14,431.4	38,627.6
Trolleybus (directly operated)	28	3,439.3	6,963.1

Note: (1) Number of revenue vehicles operated by the given mode and type of service to meet the annual maximum service requirement. This is the revenue vehicle count during the peak season of the year; on the week and day that maximum service is provided. Vehicles operated in maximum service (VOMS) exclude atypical days and one-time special events; (2) Number of passengers who boarded public transportation vehicles. Passengers are counted each time they board a vehicle no matter how many vehicles they use to travel from their origin to their destination. (3) Sum of the distances ridden by all passengers during the entire fiscal year.
Source: Federal Transit Administration, National Transit Database, 2023

Air Transportation

Airport Name and Code / Type of Service	Passenger Airlines[1]	Passenger Enplanements	Freight Carriers[2]	Freight (lbs)
Philadelphia International (PHL)				
Domestic service (U.S. carriers only)	31	13,195,311	16	329,733,866
International service (U.S. carriers only)	12	1,639,721	4	80,721,151

Note: (1) Includes all U.S.-based major, minor and commuter airlines that carried at least one passenger during the year; (2) Includes all U.S.-based airlines and freight carriers that transported at least one pound of freight during the year.
Source: Bureau of Transportation Statistics, The Intermodal Transportation Database, Air Carriers: T-100 Domestic Market (U.S. carriers only), 2024; Bureau of Transportation Statistics, The Intermodal Transportation Database, Air Carriers: T-100 International Market (U.S. carriers only), 2024

BUSINESSES

Major Business Headquarters

Company Name	Industry	Rankings	
		Fortune[1]	Forbes[2]
Aramark	Diversified outsourcing services	220	-
Comcast	Telecommunications	33	-
Day & Zimmermann	Construction	-	238
Morgan Lewis & Bockius	Services	-	217
Rite Aid	Food & drug stores	171	-

Note: (1) Companies that produce a 10-K are ranked 1 to 500 based on 2023 revenue; (2) All private companies with at least $2 billion in annual revenue through the end of their most current fiscal year are ranked 1 to 275; companies listed are headquartered in the city; dashes indicate no ranking
Source: Fortune, "Fortune 500," 2024; Forbes, "America's Largest Private Companies," 2024

Fastest-Growing Businesses

According to *Inc.*, Philadelphia is home to three of America's 500 fastest-growing private companies: **Mainfactor** (#58); **UMortgage** (#88); **rockITdata** (#339). Criteria: must be an independent, privately-held, for-profit, U.S. corporation, proprietorship or partnership as of December 31, 2023; revenues must be at least $100,000 in 2020 and $2 million in 2023; must have four-year operating/sales history. *Inc., "America's 500 Fastest-Growing Private Companies," 2024*

According to *Initiative for a Competitive Inner City (ICIC)*, Philadelphia is home to five of America's 100 fastest-growing "inner city" companies: **Printfresh** (#2); **Sarah Car Care** (#28); **Bennett Compost** (#34); **The Tactile Group** (#51); **Seer Interactive** (#99). To be eligible for the IC100, companies have to be independently operated, privately held, for-profit businesses with revenues of at least $50,000 in 2019 and $500,000 in 2023, and headquartered in an under-resourced community. Recognizing that concentrated poverty exists within metropolitan areas outside of big cities (and that poverty overall is suburbanizing), ICIC defines under-resourced communities as large low-income, high-poverty areas located in the urban and suburban parts of all but the smallest metropolitan areas. Companies were ranked overall by revenue growth over the five-year period between 2019 and 2023. *Initiative for a Competitive Inner City (ICIC), "Inner City 100 Companies," 2024*

According to Deloitte, Philadelphia is home to two of North America's 500 fastest-growing high-technology companies: **dbt Labs** (#77); **GLOBO** (#455). Companies are ranked by percentage growth in revenue over a four-year period. Criteria for inclusion: company must be headquartered within North America; must own proprietary intellectual property or technology that is sold to customers in products that contributes to a significant portion of the company's operating revenue; must have been in business for a minumum of four years with 2020 operating revenues of at least $50,000 USD/CD and 2023 operating revenues of at least $5 million USD/CD. *Deloitte, 2024 Technology Fast 500*™

Living Environment

COST OF LIVING

Cost of Living Index

Composite Index	Groceries	Housing	Utilities	Transportation	Health Care	Misc. Goods/Services
103.2	104.1	99.2	105.5	105.3	96.2	106.0

Note: The Cost of Living Index measures regional differences in the cost of consumer goods and services, excluding taxes and non-consumer expenditures, for professional and managerial households in the top income quintile. It is based on more than 50,000 prices covering almost 60 different items for which prices are collected three times a year by chambers of commerce, economic development organizations or university applied economic centers in each participating urban area. The numbers shown should be read as a percentage above or below the national average of 100. For example, a value of 115.4 in the groceries column indicates that grocery prices are 15.4% higher than the national average. Small differences in the index numbers should not be interpreted as significant; Figures cover the Philadelphia PA urban area.
Source: The Council for Community and Economic Research, Cost of Living Index, 2024

Grocery Prices

Area[1]	T-Bone Steak ($/pound)	Frying Chicken ($/pound)	Whole Milk ($/half gal.)	Eggs ($/dozen)	Orange Juice ($/64 oz.)	Coffee ($/11.5 oz.)
City[2]	15.46	1.52	4.70	3.48	4.41	5.43
Avg.	15.42	1.55	4.69	3.25	4.41	5.46
Min.	14.50	1.16	4.43	2.75	4.00	4.85
Max.	17.56	2.89	5.49	4.78	5.54	7.89

Note: (1) Values for the local area are compared with the average, minimum and maximum values for all 276 areas in the Cost of Living Index; (2) Figures cover the Philadelphia PA urban area; **T-Bone Steak** (price per pound); **Frying Chicken** (price per pound, whole fryer); **Whole Milk** (half gallon carton); **Eggs** (price per dozen, Grade A, large); **Orange Juice** (64 oz. Tropicana or Florida Natural); **Coffee** (11.5 oz. can, vacuum-packed, Maxwell House, Hills Bros, or Folgers).
Source: The Council for Community and Economic Research, Cost of Living Index, 2024

Housing and Utility Costs

Area[1]	New Home Price ($)	Apartment Rent ($/month)	All Electric ($/month)	Part Electric ($/month)	Other Energy ($/month)	Telephone ($/month)
City[2]	470,985	1,851	-	138.01	81.94	201.51
Avg.	515,975	1,550	210.99	123.07	82.07	194.99
Min.	265,375	692	104.33	53.68	36.26	179.42
Max.	2,775,821	5,719	529.02	397.28	361.63	223.33

Note: (1) Values for the local area are compared with the average, minimum and maximum values for all 276 areas in the Cost of Living Index; (2) Figures cover the Philadelphia PA urban area; **New Home Price** (2,400 sf living area, 8,000 sf lot, in urban area with full utilities); **Apartment Rent** (950 sf 2 bedroom/1.5 or 2 bath, unfurnished, excluding all utilities except water); **All Electric** (average monthly cost for an all-electric home); **Part Electric** (average monthly cost for a part-electric home); **Other Energy** (average monthly cost for natural gas, fuel oil, coal, wood, and any other forms of energy except electricity); **Telephone** (price includes the base monthly rate plus taxes and fees for three lines of mobile phone service).
Source: The Council for Community and Economic Research, Cost of Living Index, 2024

Health Care, Transportation, and Other Costs

Area[1]	Doctor ($/visit)	Dentist ($/visit)	Optometrist ($/visit)	Gasoline ($/gallon)	Beauty Salon ($/visit)	Men's Shirt ($)
City[2]	148.84	111.61	125.00	3.33	67.25	36.90
Avg.	143.77	117.51	129.23	3.32	48.57	38.14
Min.	36.74	58.67	67.33	2.80	24.00	13.41
Max.	270.44	216.82	307.33	5.28	94.00	63.89

Note: (1) Values for the local area are compared with the average, minimum and maximum values for all 276 areas in the Cost of Living Index; (2) Figures cover the Philadelphia PA urban area; **Doctor** (general practitioners routine exam of an established patient); **Dentist** (adult teeth cleaning and periodic oral examination); **Optometrist** (full vision eye exam for established adult patient); **Gasoline** (one gallon regular unleaded, national brand, including all taxes, cash price at self-service pump if available); **Beauty Salon** (woman's shampoo, trim, and blow-dry); **Men's Shirt** (cotton/polyester dress shirt, pinpoint weave, long sleeves).
Source: The Council for Community and Economic Research, Cost of Living Index, 2024

HOUSING

Homeownership Rate

Area	2017 (%)	2018 (%)	2019 (%)	2020 (%)	2021 (%)	2022 (%)	2023 (%)	2024 (%)
MSA[1]	65.6	67.4	67.4	69.2	69.8	68.2	67.4	69.6
U.S.	63.9	64.4	64.6	66.6	65.5	65.8	65.9	65.6

Note: (1) Figures cover the Philadelphia-Camden-Wilmington, PA-NJ-DE-MD Metropolitan Statistical Area
Source: U.S. Census Bureau, Housing Vacancies and Homeownership Annual Statistics: 2017-2024

House Price Index (HPI)

Area	National Ranking[2]	Quarterly Change (%)	One-Year Change (%)	Five-Year Change (%)	Since 1991Q1 (%)
MD[1]	110	0.84	5.64	41.74	286.32
U.S.[3]	—	1.43	4.51	57.13	327.82

Note: The HPI is a weighted repeat sales index. It measures average price changes in repeat sales or refinancings on the same properties. This information is obtained by reviewing repeat mortgage transactions on single-family properties whose mortgages have been purchased or securitized by Fannie Mae or Freddie Mac since January 1975; (1) Figures cover the Philadelphia, PA Metropolitan Division; (2) Rankings are based on annual percentage change for all metro areas containing at least 15,000 transactions over the last 10 years and ranges from 1 to 241; (3) figures based on a weighted average of Census Division estimates using a seasonally adjusted, purchase-only index; all figures are for the period ending December 31, 2024
Source: Federal Housing Finance Agency, Change in FHFA Metropolitan Area House Price Indexes, All Transactions Index, 2024Q4

Home Value

Area	Under $100,000	$100,000 -$199,999	$200,000 -$299,999	$300,000 -$399,999	$400,000 -$499,999	$500,000 -$999,999	$1,000,000 or more	Median ($)
City	14.0	26.4	26.8	14.6	6.6	9.5	2.0	232,400
MSA[1]	7.1	14.6	23.2	19.2	13.4	19.5	3.0	326,700
U.S.	12.1	17.8	19.5	14.4	10.5	19.1	6.5	303,400

Note: Figures are percentages except for median and cover owner-occupied housing units; (1) Figures cover the Philadelphia-Camden-Wilmington, PA-NJ-DE-MD Metropolitan Statistical Area
Source: U.S. Census Bureau, 2019-2023 American Community Survey 5-Year Estimates

Year Housing Structure Built

Area	2020 or Later	2010 -2019	2000 -2009	1990 -1999	1980 -1989	1970 -1979	1960 -1969	1950 -1959	1940 -1949	Before 1940	Median Year
City	0.6	4.8	3.2	2.7	4.5	7.8	10.9	15.0	10.7	39.9	1949
MSA[1]	0.7	5.3	7.9	8.9	9.9	12.2	11.7	14.9	7.0	21.5	1966
U.S.	1.2	8.9	13.6	12.8	13.0	14.4	10.0	9.7	4.5	11.9	1980

Note: Figures are percentages except for Median Year; Note: (1) Figures cover the Philadelphia-Camden-Wilmington, PA-NJ-DE-MD Metropolitan Statistical Area
Source: U.S. Census Bureau, 2019-2023 American Community Survey 5-Year Estimates

Gross Monthly Rent

Area	Under $500	$500 -$999	$1,000 -$1,499	$1,500 -$1,999	$2,000 -$2,499	$2,500 -$2,999	$3,000 and up	Median ($)
City	8.5	18.1	35.8	22.6	8.7	3.1	3.2	1,323
MSA[1]	6.4	14.6	35.3	25.2	11.2	3.7	3.7	1,413
U.S.	6.5	22.3	29.5	20.2	10.8	4.8	5.9	1,348

Note: Figures are percentages except for median; Gross rent is the contract rent plus the estimated average monthly cost of utilities (electricity, gas, and water and sewer) and fuels (oil, coal, kerosene, wood, etc.) if these are paid by the renter (or paid for the renter by someone else); (1) Figures cover the Philadelphia-Camden-Wilmington, PA-NJ-DE-MD Metropolitan Statistical Area
Source: U.S. Census Bureau, 2019-2023 American Community Survey 5-Year Estimates

HEALTH

Health Risk Factors

Category	MSA[1] (%)	U.S. (%)
Adults aged 18–64 who have any kind of health care coverage	n/a	90.8
Adults who reported being in good or better health	n/a	81.8
Adults who have been told they have high blood cholesterol	n/a	36.9
Adults who have been told they have high blood pressure	n/a	34.0
Adults who are current smokers	n/a	12.1
Adults who currently use e-cigarettes	n/a	7.7
Adults who currently use chewing tobacco, snuff, or snus	n/a	3.2
Adults who are heavy drinkers[2]	n/a	6.1
Adults who are binge drinkers[3]	n/a	15.2
Adults who are overweight (BMI 25.0 - 29.9)	n/a	34.4
Adults who are obese (BMI 30.0 - 99.8)	n/a	34.3
Adults who participated in any physical activities in the past month	n/a	75.8

Note: All figures are crude prevalence; (1) Figures for the Philadelphia-Camden-Wilmington, PA-NJ-DE-MD Metropolitan Statistical Area were not available.
(2) Heavy drinkers are classified as adult men having more than 14 drinks per week and adult women having more than 7 drinks per week; (3) Binge drinkers are classified as males having five or more drinks on one occasion or females having four or more drinks on one occasion
Source: Centers for Disease Control and Prevention, Behavioral Risk Factor Surveillance System, SMART: Selected Metropolitan Area Risk Trends, 2023

Acute and Chronic Health Conditions

Category	MSA[1] (%)	U.S. (%)
Adults who have ever been told they had a heart attack	n/a	4.2
Adults who have ever been told they have angina or coronary heart disease	n/a	4.0
Adults who have ever been told they had a stroke	n/a	3.3
Adults who have ever been told they have asthma	n/a	15.7
Adults who have ever been told they have arthritis	n/a	26.3
Adults who have ever been told they have diabetes[2]	n/a	11.5
Adults who have ever been told they had skin cancer	n/a	5.6
Adults who have ever been told they had any other types of cancer	n/a	8.4
Adults who have ever been told they have COPD	n/a	6.4
Adults who have ever been told they have kidney disease	n/a	3.7
Adults who have ever been told they have a form of depression	n/a	22.0

Note: All figures are crude prevalence; (1) Figures for the Philadelphia-Camden-Wilmington, PA-NJ-DE-MD Metropolitan Statistical Area were not available.
(2) Figures do not include pregnancy-related, borderline, or pre-diabetes
Source: Centers for Disease Control and Prevention, Behavioral Risk Factor Surveillance System, SMART: Selected Metropolitan Area Risk Trends, 2023

Health Screening and Vaccination Rates

Category	MSA[1] (%)	U.S. (%)
Adults who have ever been tested for HIV	n/a	37.5
Adults who have had their blood cholesterol checked within the last five years	n/a	87.0
Adults aged 65+ who have had flu shot within the past year	n/a	63.4
Adults aged 65+ who have ever had a pneumonia vaccination	n/a	71.9

Note: All figures are crude prevalence; (1) Figures for the Philadelphia-Camden-Wilmington, PA-NJ-DE-MD Metropolitan Statistical Area were not available.
Source: Centers for Disease Control and Prevention, Behavioral Risk Factor Surveillance System, SMART: Selected Metropolitan Area Risk Trends, 2023

Disability Status

Category	MSA[1] (%)	U.S. (%)
Adults who reported being deaf	n/a	7.4
Are you blind or have serious difficulty seeing, even when wearing glasses?	n/a	4.9
Do you have difficulty doing errands alone?	n/a	7.8
Do you have difficulty dressing or bathing?	n/a	3.6
Do you have serious difficulty concentrating/remembering/making decisions?	n/a	13.7
Do you have serious difficulty walking or climbing stairs?	n/a	13.2

Note: All figures are crude prevalence; (1) Figures for the Philadelphia-Camden-Wilmington, PA-NJ-DE-MD Metropolitan Statistical Area were not available.
Source: Centers for Disease Control and Prevention, Behavioral Risk Factor Surveillance System, SMART: Selected Metropolitan Area Risk Trends, 2023

Mortality Rates for the Top 10 Causes of Death in the U.S.

ICD-10[a] Sub-Chapter	ICD-10[a] Code	Crude Mortality Rate[2] per 100,000 population	
		County[3]	U.S.
Malignant neoplasms	C00-C97	174.5	182.7
Ischaemic heart diseases	I20-I25	115.3	109.6
Provisional assignment of new diseases of uncertain etiology[1]	U00-U49	55.7	65.3
Other forms of heart disease	I30-I51	66.3	65.1
Other degenerative diseases of the nervous system	G30-G31	21.8	52.4
Other external causes of accidental injury	W00-X59	94.5	52.3
Cerebrovascular diseases	I60-I69	44.7	49.1
Chronic lower respiratory diseases	J40-J47	29.8	43.5
Hypertensive diseases	I10-I15	39.9	38.9
Organic, including symptomatic, mental disorders	F01-F09	27.5	33.9

Note: (a) ICD-10 = International Classification of Diseases 10th Revision; (1) Includes COVID-19, adverse effects to COVID-19 vaccines, SARS, and vaping-related disorders; (2) Crude mortality rates are a three-year average covering 2021-2023; (3) Figures cover Philadelphia County.
Source: Centers for Disease Control and Prevention, National Center for Health Statistics. National Vital Statistics System, Mortality 2018-2023 on CDC WONDER Online Database

Mortality Rates for Selected Causes of Death

Cause of Death	ICD-10[a] Code	Crude Mortality Rate[1] per 100,000 population	
		County[2]	U.S.
Accidental poisoning and exposure to noxious substances	X40-X49	76.0	30.5
Alzheimer disease	G30	14.8	35.4
Assault	X85-Y09	31.2	7.3
COVID-19	U07.1	55.7	65.3
Diabetes mellitus	E10-E14	26.1	30.0
Diseases of the liver	K70-K76	14.1	20.8
Human immunodeficiency virus (HIV) disease	B20-B24	3.1	1.5
Influenza and pneumonia	J09-J18	14.8	13.4
Intentional self-harm	X60-X84	11.7	14.7
Malnutrition	E40-E46	4.7	6.0
Obesity and other hyperalimentation	E65-E68	3.4	3.1
Renal failure	N17-N19	21.0	16.4
Transport accidents	V01-V99	10.9	14.4

Note: (a) ICD-10 = International Classification of Diseases 10th Revision; (1) Crude mortality rates are a three-year average covering 2021-2023; (2) Figures cover Philadelphia County; Data are suppressed when the data meet the criteria for confidentiality constraints; Crude mortality rates are flagged as unreliable when the rate would be calculated with a numerator of 20 or less.
Source: Centers for Disease Control and Prevention, National Center for Health Statistics. National Vital Statistics System, Mortality 2018-2023 on CDC WONDER Online Database

Health Insurance Coverage

Area	With Health Insurance	With Private Health Insurance	With Public Health Insurance	Without Health Insurance	Population Under Age 19 Without Health Insurance
City	92.8	58.8	45.9	7.2	4.5
MSA[1]	94.7	72.5	35.5	5.3	3.4
U.S.	91.4	67.3	36.3	8.6	5.4

Note: Figures are percentages that cover the civilian noninstitutionalized population; (1) Figures cover the Philadelphia-Camden-Wilmington, PA-NJ-DE-MD Metropolitan Statistical Area
Source: U.S. Census Bureau, 2019-2023 American Community Survey 5-Year Estimates

Number of Medical Professionals

Area	MDs[3]	DOs[3,4]	Dentists	Podiatrists	Chiropractors	Optometrists
County[1] (number)	10,394	1,049	1,340	252	242	323
County[1] (rate[2])	663.2	66.9	86.4	16.3	15.6	20.8
U.S. (rate[2])	302.5	29.2	74.6	6.4	29.5	18.0

Note: Data as of 2023 unless noted; (1) Data covers Philadelphia County; (2) Number of medical professionals per 100,000 population; (3) Data as of 2022 and includes all active, non-federal physicians; (4) Doctor of Osteopathic Medicine
Source: U.S. Department of Health and Human Services, Health Resources and Services Administration, Bureau of Health Professions, Area Resource File (ARF) 2023-2024

Best Hospitals

According to *U.S. News,* the Philadelphia-Camden-Wilmington, PA-NJ-DE-MD metro area is home to 10 of the best hospitals in the U.S.: **Fox Chase Cancer Center** (2 adult specialties); **Hospitals of the University of Pennsylvania-Penn Presbyterian** (Honor Roll/11 adult specialties); **MossRehab-Jefferson Health** (1 adult specialty); **Pennsylvania Hospital** (1 adult specialty); **Rothman Orthopaedics at Thomas Jefferson University Hospitals-Jefferson Health** (7 adult specialties); **Scheie Eye Institute, Hospitals of the University of Pennsylvania-Penn Presbyterian** (11 adult specialties); **Thomas Jefferson University Hospitals-Jane and Leonard Korman Respiratory Institute-Jefferson Health** (7 adult specialties); **Thomas Jefferson University Hospitals-Jefferson Health** (7 adult specialties); **Thomas Jefferson University Hospitals-Vickie and Jack Farber Institute for Neuroscience-Jefferson He** (7 adult specialties); **Wills Eye Hospital, Thomas Jefferson University Hospitals** (1 adult specialty). The hospitals listed were nationally ranked in at least one of 15 adult or 11 pediatric specialties. The number of specialties shown cover the parent hospital. Only 160 U.S. hospitals performed well enough to be nationally ranked in one or more specialties. Twenty hospitals in the U.S. made the Honor Roll. The Best Hospitals Honor Roll takes both the national rankings and the procedure and condition ratings into account. Hospitals received points if they were nationally ranked in one of the 15 adult specialties—the higher they ranked, the more points they got—and how many ratings of "high performing" they earned in the 20 procedures and conditions. *U.S. News Online, "America's Best Hospitals 2024-25"*

According to *U.S. News,* the Philadelphia-Camden-Wilmington, PA-NJ-DE-MD metro area is home to two of the best children's hospitals in the U.S.: **Children's Hospital of Philadelphia** (Honor Roll/11 pediatric specialties); **Nemours Children's Hospital-Delaware** (9 pediatric specialties). The hospitals listed were highly ranked in at least one of 11 pediatric specialties. One hundred five children's hospitals in the U.S. were nationally ranked in at least one specialty. Hospitals received points for being ranked in a specialty, and the 10 hospitals with the most points across the 11 specialties make up the Honor Roll. *U.S. News Online, "America's Best Children's Hospitals 2024-25"*

EDUCATION

Public School District Statistics

District Name	Schls	Pupils	Pupil/ Teacher Ratio	Minority Pupils[1] (%)	Total Rev. per Pupil ($)	Total Exp. per Pupil ($)
Philadelphia City SD	221	117,907	13.7	85.4	38,034	36,791
Philadelphia Performing Arts CS	1	2,638	14.6	69.3	19,021	17,686

Note: Table includes school districts with 2,000 or more students; (1) Percentage of students that are not non-Hispanic white.
Source: U.S. Department of Education, National Center for Education Statistics, Common Core of Data, Local Education Agency (School District) Universe Survey: School Year 2023-2024; U.S. Department of Education, National Center for Education Statistics, Common Core of Data, School District Finance Survey (F-33): School Year 2021–22

Best High Schools

According to *U.S. News,* Philadelphia is home to two of the top 500 high schools in the U.S.: **Julia R. Masterman Secondary School** (#4); **Central High School** (#222). Nearly 25,000 public, magnet and charter schools were ranked based on their performance on state assessments and how well they prepare students for college. *U.S. News & World Report, "Best High Schools 2024"*

Highest Level of Education

Area	Less than H.S.	H.S. Diploma	Some College, No Deg.	Associate Degree	Bachelor's Degree	Master's Degree	Prof. School Degree	Doctorate Degree
City	12.6	29.8	16.4	6.5	19.4	10.2	3.0	2.1
MSA[1]	7.9	27.0	16.1	7.5	24.1	12.2	3.0	2.2
U.S.	10.6	26.2	19.4	8.8	21.3	9.8	2.3	1.6

Note: Figures cover persons age 25 and over; (1) Figures cover the Philadelphia-Camden-Wilmington, PA-NJ-DE-MD Metropolitan Statistical Area
Source: U.S. Census Bureau, 2019-2023 American Community Survey 5-Year Estimates

Educational Attainment by Race

Area	High School Graduate or Higher (%)					Bachelor's Degree or Higher (%)				
	Total	White	Black	Asian	Hisp.[2]	Total	White	Black	Asian	Hisp.[2]
City	87.4	93.5	88.1	74.3	72.6	34.6	51.0	20.4	42.0	19.5
MSA[1]	92.1	95.3	89.7	85.5	74.5	41.5	46.8	24.3	59.2	22.5
U.S.	89.4	92.9	88.1	88.0	72.5	35.0	37.7	24.7	57.0	19.9

Note: Figures shown cover persons 25 years old and over; (1) Figures cover the Philadelphia-Camden-Wilmington, PA-NJ-DE-MD Metropolitan Statistical Area; (2) People of Hispanic origin can be of any race
Source: U.S. Census Bureau, 2019-2023 American Community Survey 5-Year Estimates

School Enrollment by Grade and Control

Area	Preschool (%)		Kindergarten (%)		Grades 1 - 4 (%)		Grades 5 - 8 (%)		Grades 9 - 12 (%)	
	Public	Private	Public	Private	Public	Private	Public	Private	Public	Private
City	54.5	45.5	78.0	22.0	79.4	20.6	79.1	20.9	77.6	22.4
MSA[1]	47.4	52.6	81.4	18.6	85.0	15.0	84.4	15.6	83.6	16.4
U.S.	58.7	41.3	85.2	14.8	87.2	12.8	87.9	12.1	89.0	11.0

Note: Figures shown cover persons 3 years old and over; (1) Figures cover the Philadelphia-Camden-Wilmington, PA-NJ-DE-MD Metropolitan Statistical Area
Source: U.S. Census Bureau, 2019-2023 American Community Survey 5-Year Estimates

Higher Education

Four-Year Colleges			Two-Year Colleges			Medical Schools[1]	Law Schools[2]	Voc/ Tech[3]
Public	Private Non-profit	Private For-profit	Public	Private Non-profit	Private For-profit			
10	45	3	9	6	12	7	6	33

Note: Figures cover institutions located within the Philadelphia-Camden-Wilmington, PA-NJ-DE-MD Metropolitan Statistical Area and include main campuses only; (1) includes schools accredited by the Liaison Committee on Medical Education and the American Osteopathic Association's Commission on Osteopathic College Accreditation; (2) includes ABA-accredited schools, schools with provisional ABA accreditation, and state accredited schools; (3) includes all schools with programs that are less than 2 years.
Source: National Center for Education Statistics, Integrated Postsecondary Education System (IPEDS), 2023-24; Wikipedia, List of Medical Schools in the United States, accessed May 2, 2025; Wikipedia, List of Law Schools in the United States, accessed May 2, 2025

According to *U.S. News & World Report,* the Philadelphia-Camden-Wilmington, PA-NJ-DE-MD metro area is home to eight of the top 200 national universities in the U.S.: **University of Pennsylvania** (#10); **Villanova University** (#58 tie); **Drexel University** (#86 tie); **University of Delaware**

(#86 tie); **Rutgers University—Camden** (#98 tie); **Temple University** (#98 tie); **Thomas Jefferson University** (#136 tie); **Rowan University** (#171 tie). The indicators used to capture academic quality fall into a number of categories: assessment by administrators at peer institutions; retention of students; faculty resources; student selectivity; financial resources; alumni giving; high school counselor ratings of colleges; and graduation rate. *U.S. News & World Report, "America's Best Colleges 2025"*

According to *U.S. News & World Report,* the Philadelphia-Camden-Wilmington, PA-NJ-DE-MD metro area is home to four of the top 100 liberal arts colleges in the U.S.: **Swarthmore College** (#3); **Haverford College** (#24); **Bryn Mawr College** (#29 tie); **Ursinus College** (#83 tie). The indicators used to capture academic quality fall into a number of categories: assessment by administrators at peer institutions; retention of students; faculty resources; student selectivity; financial resources; alumni giving; high school counselor ratings of colleges; and graduation rate. *U.S. News & World Report, "America's Best Colleges 2025"*

According to *U.S. News & World Report,* the Philadelphia-Camden-Wilmington, PA-NJ-DE-MD metro area is home to four of the top 100 law schools in the U.S.: **University of Pennsylvania (Carey)** 1 (#5); **Villanova University (Widger)** (#48 tie); **Temple University (Beasley)** (#50 tie); **Drexel University (Kline)** (#79 tie). The rankings are based on a weighted average of 12 measures of quality: peer assessment score; assessment score by lawyers/judges; median LSAT scores; median undergrad GPA; acceptance rate; employment rates for graduates; placement success; bar passage rate; faculty resources; expenditures per student; student/faculty ratio; and library resources. *U.S. News & World Report, "America's Best Graduate Schools, Law, 2025"*

According to *U.S. News & World Report,* the Philadelphia-Camden-Wilmington, PA-NJ-DE-MD metro area is home to two of the top medical schools for research in the U.S.: **Temple University (Katz)** (Tier 2); **Thomas Jefferson University (Kimmel)** (Tier 2). *U.S. News* placed medical and osteopathic schools into tiers based on their research productivity, faculty and admissions data. Each school's tier was derived from its overall score, calculated by summing the weighted normalized values generated across several factors of academic quality, outlined below. There are four tiers, with tier 1 medical schools as the highest-performing and tier 4 as the lowest-performing. Only tier 1 and 2 schools are shown. Because of the tier presentation, *U.S. News* calculated overall scores based on their percentile performance among all rated schools instead of dividing against the rescaled score of the No. 1-performing schools. Tier 1 included schools with overall scores of 85 to 99. The cutoffs for tiers 2 through 4 were schools scoring 50 to 84, 15 to 49 and 1 to 14, respectively. The rankings are based on a weighted average of the following measures of quality: total research activity; average research activity per faculty member; total NIH research grants at the medical school and its affiliated hospitals; average NIH research grants per faculty; median MCAT total score; median undergraduate GPA; acceptance rate; and faculty resources. *U.S. News & World Report, "America's Best Graduate Schools, Medical, 2025"*

According to *U.S. News & World Report,* the Philadelphia-Camden-Wilmington, PA-NJ-DE-MD metro area is home to two of the top medical schools for primary care in the U.S.: **Cooper Medical School of Rowan University** (Tier 2); **Drexel University** (Tier 2). *U.S. News* placed medical and osteopathic schools into tiers based on their research productivity, faculty and admissions data. Each school's tier was derived from its overall score, calculated by summing the weighted normalized values generated across several factors of academic quality, outlined below. There are four tiers, with tier 1 medical schools as the highest-performing and tier 4 as the lowest-performing. Only tier 1 and 2 schools are shown. Because of the tier presentation, *U.S. News* calculated overall scores based on their percentile performance among all rated schools instead of dividing against the rescaled score of the No. 1-performing schools. Tier 1 included schools with overall scores of 85 to 99. The cutoffs for tiers 2 through 4 were schools scoring 50 to 84, 15 to 49 and 1 to 14, respectively. The rankings are based on a weighted average of the following measures of quality: graduates practicing in primary care specialties; graduates entering primary care residencies; median MCAT total score; median undergraduate GPA; acceptance rate; and faculty resources. *U.S. News & World Report, "America's Best Graduate Schools, Medical, 2025"*

According to *U.S. News & World Report,* the Philadelphia-Camden-Wilmington, PA-NJ-DE-MD metro area is home to one of the top 75 business schools in the U.S.: **University of Pennsylvania (Wharton)** (#1). The rankings are based on a weighted average of the following nine measures: quality assessment; peer assessment; recruiter assessment; placement success; mean starting salary and bonus; student selectivity; mean GMAT and GRE scores; mean undergraduate GPA; and acceptance rate. *U.S. News & World Report, "America's Best Graduate Schools, Business, 2025"*

EMPLOYERS

Major Employers

Company Name	Industry
Abington Memorial Hospital	General medical & surgical hospitals
AstraZeneca Pharmaceuticals	Pharmaceutical preparations
City of Philadelphia	Municipal government
Comcast Holdings Corporation	Cable & other pay television services
Cooper Health Care	Hospital management
E.I. du Pont de Nemours and Company	Agricultural chemicals
Einstein Community Health Associates	Offices & clinics of medical doctors
Glaxosmithkline	Commerical physical research
Lockheed Martin Corporation	Defense systems & equipment
Mercy Health System of SE Pennsylvania	General medical & surgical hospitals
On Time Staffing	Employment agencies
Richlieu Associates	Apartment building operators
Temple University	General medical & surgical hospitals
The University of Pennsylvania	Colleges & universities
The Vanguard Group	Management, investment, open-end
Thomas Jefferson University Hospital	General medical & surgical hospitals
Trustees of the University of Penn	General medical & surgical hospitals
U.S. Navy	U.S. military
Unisys Corporation	Computer integrated systems design
University of Delaware	Colleges & universities

Note: Companies shown are located within the Philadelphia-Camden-Wilmington, PA-NJ-DE-MD Metropolitan Statistical Area.
Source: Chambers of Commerce; State Departments of Labor; Wikipedia

Best Companies to Work For

Indevets, headquartered in Philadelphia, is among "Fortune's Best Workplaces for Women." To pick the best companies, *Fortune* partnered with the Great Place to Work Institute. To be considered for the list, companies must be Great Place To Work-Certified. Companies must also employ at least 50 women, at least 20% of their non-executive managers must be female, and at least one executive must be female. To determine the Best Workplaces for Women, Great Place To Work measured the differences in women's survey responses to those of their peers and assesses the impact of demographics and roles on the quality and consistency of women's experiences. Great Place To Work also analyzed the gender balance of each workplace, how it compared to each company's industry, and patterns in representation as women rise from front-line positions to the board of directors. *Fortune, "Best Workplaces for Women," 2024*

Indevets, headquartered in Philadelphia, is among "Best Workplaces in Health Care." To determine the Best Workplaces in Health Care list, Great Place To Work analyzed the survey responses of over 185,000 employees from Great Place To Work-Certified companies in the health care industry. Survey data analysis and company-provided datapoints are then factored into a combined score to compare and rank the companies that create the most consistently positive experience for all employees in this industry. *Fortune, "Best Workplaces in Health Care," 2024*

Children's Hospital of Philadelphia (CHOP); Janney Montgomery Scott, headquartered in Philadelphia, are among the "Best Places to Work in IT." To qualify, companies had to have a minimum of 100 total employees and five IT employees. The best places to work were selected based on DEI (diversity, equity, and inclusion) practices; IT turnover, promotions, and growth; IT retention and engagement programs; remote/hybrid working; benefits and perks (such as elder care and child care, flextime, and reimbursement for college tuition); and training and career development opportunities. *Computerworld, "Best Places to Work in IT," 2025*

PUBLIC SAFETY

Crime Rate

Area	Total Crime Rate	Violent Crime Rate				Property Crime Rate		
		Murder	Rape	Robbery	Aggrav. Assault	Burglary	Larceny-Theft	Motor Vehicle Theft
City	6,039.7	26.0	46.6	336.1	574.4	363.9	3,161.8	1,530.9
U.S.	2,290.9	5.7	38.0	66.5	264.1	250.7	1,347.2	318.7

Note: Figures are crimes per 100,000 population.
Source: FBI, Table 8, Offenses Known to Law Enforcement, by State by City, 2023

Hate Crimes

Area	Number of Quarters Reported	Number of Incidents per Bias Motivation					
		Race/Ethnicity/Ancestry	Religion	Sexual Orientation	Disability	Gender	Gender Identity
City[1]	4	67	39	17	1	0	3
U.S.	4	5,900	2,699	2,077	187	92	492

Note: (1) Figures include at least one incident reported with more than one bias motivation.
Source: Federal Bureau of Investigation, Hate Crime Statistics 2023

Identity Theft Consumer Reports

Area	Reports	Reports per 100,000 Population	Rank[2]
MSA[1]	28,438	456	13
U.S.	1,135,291	339	-

Note: (1) Figures cover the Philadelphia-Camden-Wilmington, PA-NJ-DE-MD Metropolitan Statistical Area; (2) Rank ranges from 1 to 401 where 1 indicates greatest number of identity theft reports per 100,000 population
Source: Federal Trade Commission, Consumer Sentinel Network Data Book 2024

Fraud and Other Consumer Reports

Area	Reports	Reports per 100,000 Population	Rank[2]
MSA[1]	121,966	1,954	14
U.S.	5,360,641	1,601	-

Note: (1) Figures cover the Philadelphia-Camden-Wilmington, PA-NJ-DE-MD Metropolitan Statistical Area; (2) Rank ranges from 1 to 401 where 1 indicates greatest number of fraud and other consumer reports per 100,000 population
Source: Federal Trade Commission, Consumer Sentinel Network Data Book 2024

POLITICS

2024 Presidential Election Results

Area	Trump (Rep.)	Harris (Dem.)	Stein (Green)	Kennedy (Ind.)	Oliver (Lib.)	Other
Philadelphia County	19.9	78.6	0.9	0.0	0.3	0.3
U.S.	49.7	48.2	0.6	0.5	0.4	0.6

Note: Results are percentages and may not add to 100% due to rounding
Source: Dave Leip's Atlas of U.S. Presidential Elections

SPORTS

Professional Sports Teams

Team Name	League	Year Established
Philadelphia 76ers	National Basketball Association (NBA)	1963
Philadelphia Eagles	National Football League (NFL)	1933
Philadelphia Flyers	National Hockey League (NHL)	1967
Philadelphia Phillies	Major League Baseball (MLB)	1883
Philadelphia Union	Major League Soccer (MLS)	2010

Note: Includes teams located in the Philadelphia-Camden-Wilmington, PA-NJ-DE-MD Metropolitan Statistical Area.
Source: Wikipedia, Major Professional Sports Teams of the United States and Canada, May 1, 2025

CLIMATE

Average and Extreme Temperatures

Temperature	Jan	Feb	Mar	Apr	May	Jun	Jul	Aug	Sep	Oct	Nov	Dec	Yr.
Extreme High (°F)	74	74	85	94	96	100	104	101	100	89	84	72	104
Average High (°F)	39	42	51	63	73	82	86	85	78	67	55	43	64
Average Temp. (°F)	32	34	42	53	63	72	77	76	68	57	47	36	55
Average Low (°F)	24	26	33	43	53	62	67	66	59	47	38	28	45
Extreme Low (°F)	-7	-4	7	19	28	44	51	44	35	25	15	1	-7

Note: Figures cover the years 1948-1990
Source: National Climatic Data Center, International Station Meteorological Climate Summary, 9/96

Average Precipitation/Snowfall/Humidity

Precip./Humidity	Jan	Feb	Mar	Apr	May	Jun	Jul	Aug	Sep	Oct	Nov	Dec	Yr.
Avg. Precip. (in.)	3.2	2.8	3.7	3.5	3.7	3.6	4.1	4.0	3.3	2.7	3.4	3.3	41.4
Avg. Snowfall (in.)	7	7	4	Tr	Tr	0	0	0	0	Tr	1	4	22
Avg. Rel. Hum. 7am (%)	74	73	73	72	75	77	80	82	84	83	79	75	77
Avg. Rel. Hum. 4pm (%)	60	55	51	48	51	52	54	55	55	54	57	60	54

Note: Figures cover the years 1948-1990; Tr = Trace amounts (<0.05 in. of rain; <0.5 in. of snow)
Source: National Climatic Data Center, International Station Meteorological Climate Summary, 9/96

Weather Conditions

Temperature			Daytime Sky			Precipitation		
10°F & below	32°F & below	90°F & above	Clear	Partly cloudy	Cloudy	0.01 inch or more precip.	0.1 inch or more snow/ice	Thunder-storms
5	94	23	81	146	138	117	14	27

Note: Figures are average number of days per year and cover the years 1948-1990
Source: National Climatic Data Center, International Station Meteorological Climate Summary, 9/96

HAZARDOUS WASTE

Superfund Sites

The Philadelphia, PA metro division is home to five sites on the EPA's Superfund National Priorities List (NPL) or Superfund Alternative Approach (SAA) list: **Franklin Slag Pile (MDC)** (Final NPL); **Havertown Pcp** (Final NPL); **Lower Darby Creek Area** (Final NPL); **Metal Bank** (Final NPL); **Metro Container Corporation** (Final NPL). The Superfund alternative approach uses the same investigation and cleanup process and standards that are used for sites listed on the National Priorities List. The SAA is an alternative to listing a site on the NPL; it is not an alternative to Superfund or the Superfund process. There are a total of 1,445 Superfund sites with a status of proposed or final on both lists in the United States. *U.S. Environmental Protection Agency, National Priorities List, May 1, 2025; U.S. Environmental Protection Agency, Superfund Alternative Approach Sites, May 1, 2025*

AIR QUALITY

Air Quality Trends: Ozone

	1990	1995	2000	2005	2010	2015	2020	2021	2022	2023
MSA[1]	0.102	0.109	0.099	0.091	0.083	0.074	0.065	0.069	0.067	0.071
U.S.	0.087	0.089	0.081	0.080	0.072	0.068	0.066	0.067	0.067	0.070

Note: (1) Data covers the Philadelphia-Camden-Wilmington, PA-NJ-DE-MD Metropolitan Statistical Area. The values shown are the composite ozone concentration averages among trend sites based on the highest fourth daily maximum 8-hour concentration in parts per million. These trends are based on sites having an adequate record of monitoring data during the trend period. Data from exceptional events are included.
Source: U.S. Environmental Protection Agency, Air Quality Monitoring Information, "Air Quality Trends by City, 1990-2023"

Air Quality Index

Area	Percent of Days when Air Quality was...[2]					AQI Statistics[2]	
	Good	Moderate	Unhealthy for Sensitive Groups	Unhealthy	Very Unhealthy	Maximum	Median
MSA[1]	17.8	75.3	5.2	1.1	0.3	331	59

Note: (1) Data covers the Philadelphia-Camden-Wilmington, PA-NJ-DE-MD Metropolitan Statistical Area; (2) Based on 365 days with AQI data in 2023. Air Quality Index (AQI) is an index for reporting daily air quality. EPA calculates the AQI for five major air pollutants regulated by the Clean Air Act: ground-level ozone, particle pollution (aka particulate matter), carbon monoxide, sulfur dioxide, and nitrogen dioxide. The AQI runs from 0 to 500. The higher the AQI value, the greater the level of air pollution and the greater the health concern. There are six AQI categories: "Good" AQI is between 0 and 50. Air quality is considered satisfactory; "Moderate" AQI is between 51 and 100. Air quality is acceptable; "Unhealthy for Sensitive Groups" When AQI values are between 101 and 150, members of sensitive groups may experience health effects; "Unhealthy" When AQI values are between 151 and 200 everyone may begin to experience health effects; "Very Unhealthy" AQI values between 201 and 300 trigger a health alert; "Hazardous" AQI values over 300 trigger warnings of emergency conditions (not shown).
Source: U.S. Environmental Protection Agency, Air Quality Index Report, 2023

Air Quality Index Pollutants

Area	Percent of Days when AQI Pollutant was...[2]					
	Carbon Monoxide	Nitrogen Dioxide	Ozone	Sulfur Dioxide	Particulate Matter 2.5	Particulate Matter 10
MSA[1]	0.0	0.3	22.5	(3)	77.3	0.0

Note: (1) Data covers the Philadelphia-Camden-Wilmington, PA-NJ-DE-MD Metropolitan Statistical Area; (2) Based on 365 days with AQI data in 2023. The Air Quality Index (AQI) is an index for reporting daily air quality. EPA calculates the AQI for five major air pollutants regulated by the Clean Air Act: ground-level ozone, particle pollution (also known as particulate matter), carbon monoxide, sulfur dioxide, and nitrogen dioxide. The AQI runs from 0 to 500. The higher the AQI value, the greater the level of air pollution and the greater the health concern; (3) Sulfur dioxide is no longer included in this table because SO_2 concentrations tend to be very localized and not necessarily representative of broad geographical areas like counties and CBSAs.
Source: U.S. Environmental Protection Agency, Air Quality Index Report, 2023

Maximum Air Pollutant Concentrations: Particulate Matter, Ozone, CO and Lead

	Particulate Matter 10 (ug/m^3)	Particulate Matter 2.5 Wtd AM (ug/m^3)	Particulate Matter 2.5 24-Hr (ug/m^3)	Ozone (ppm)	Carbon Monoxide (ppm)	Lead (ug/m^3)
MSA[1] Level	174	13.3	37	0.074	1	0
NAAQS[2]	150	15	35	0.075	9	0.15
Met NAAQS[2]	No	Yes	No	Yes	Yes	Yes

Note: (1) Data covers the Philadelphia-Camden-Wilmington, PA-NJ-DE-MD Metropolitan Statistical Area; Data from exceptional events are included; (2) National Ambient Air Quality Standards; ppm = parts per million; ug/m^3 = micrograms per cubic meter; n/a not available.
Concentrations: Particulate Matter 10 (coarse particulate)—highest second maximum 24-hour concentration; Particulate Matter 2.5 Wtd AM (fine particulate)—highest weighted annual mean concentration; Particulate Matter 2.5 24-Hour (fine particulate)—highest 98th percentile 24-hour concentration; Ozone—highest fourth daily maximum 8-hour concentration; Carbon Monoxide—highest second maximum non-overlapping 8-hour concentration; Lead—maximum running 3-month average
Source: U.S. Environmental Protection Agency, Air Quality Monitoring Information, "Air Quality Statistics by City, 2023"

Maximum Air Pollutant Concentrations: Nitrogen Dioxide and Sulfur Dioxide

	Nitrogen Dioxide AM (ppb)	Nitrogen Dioxide 1-Hr (ppb)	Sulfur Dioxide AM (ppb)	Sulfur Dioxide 1-Hr (ppb)	Sulfur Dioxide 24-Hr (ppb)
MSA[1] Level	15	48	n/a	5	n/a
NAAQS[2]	53	100	30	75	140
Met NAAQS[2]	Yes	Yes	n/a	Yes	n/a

Note: (1) Data covers the Philadelphia-Camden-Wilmington, PA-NJ-DE-MD Metropolitan Statistical Area; Data from exceptional events are included; (2) National Ambient Air Quality Standards; ppm = parts per million; ug/m^3 = micrograms per cubic meter; n/a not available.
Concentrations: Nitrogen Dioxide AM—highest arithmetic mean concentration; Nitrogen Dioxide 1-Hr—highest 98th percentile 1-hour daily maximum concentration; Sulfur Dioxide AM—highest annual mean concentration; Sulfur Dioxide 1-Hr—highest 99th percentile 1-hour daily maximum concentration; Sulfur Dioxide 24-Hr—highest second maximum 24-hour concentration
Source: U.S. Environmental Protection Agency, Air Quality Monitoring Information, "Air Quality Statistics by City, 2023"

Pittsburgh, Pennsylvania

Background

Pittsburgh, once the creaking, croaking, belching giant of heavy industry, the city forged a prosperous economy based on steel, glass, rubber, petroleum, and machinery. Unregulated spews of soot into the air by these factories earned Pittsburgh the title of "Smoky City," prompting concerned citizens and politicians to pass smoke-control laws. Today, Pittsburgh's renaissance is a result of its citizens' unflagging faith.

In the eighteenth century, the area in and around the Ohio Valley and the Allegheny River, where present-day Pittsburgh lies, was claimed by both the British and the French. After being lobbed back and forth, the land finally fell into British hands and named Pittsborough, for the British prime minister at the time, William Pitt.

Almost immediately, the city showed signs of what it was to become. In 1792, the first blast furnace was built by George Anschulz. In 1797, the first glass factory was opened, and in 1804, the first cotton factory. Irish, Scottish, and a smattering of English immigrants provided the labor pool for these factories. During the Civil War, a wave of German immigrant workers swept in. During the late nineteenth century, Poles, Czechs, Slovaks, Italians, Russians, and Hungarians completed the picture in the colorful quilt of Pittsburgh's workforce. The last wave particularly contributed their sweat and toil to the fortunes of captains of industry such as Andrew Carnegie, Henry Clay Frick, and Charles M. Schwab.

Fortunately for Pittsburgh, these industrialists gave back to the city in the form of their cultural and educational patronage. The Carnegie Museum of Natural History has an extensive dinosaur collection and ancient Egypt wing. The Frick Art & Historical Center holds a noted private collection featuring such artists as Rubens, Tintoretto, Fragonard, and Boucher. Other educational and cultural attractions include the Pittsburgh Ballet Theatre, Pittsburgh Opera, Pittsburgh Civic Light Opera, Pittsburgh Symphony Orchestra, Pittsburgh Broadway Across America series, Carnegie Science Center, Phipps Conservatory and Botanical Gardens, Pittsburgh Zoo and PPG Aquarium, Children's Museum of Pittsburgh, Johnstown Flood Museum, Rachel Carson Homestead, and the Andy Warhol Museum.

By the late 1990s, Pittsburgh was showing tremendous growth. Technology and health care services, their manufacturing counterparts, and financial institutions were dominant forces behind a steadily diversifying economy. Today, the city's economy depends on services, medicine, higher education, tourism, banking, and technology. Although the city has no steel mills within its limits, Pittsburgh-based companies US Steel, Ampco Pittsburgh, and Allegheny Technologies own working mills in the Pittsburgh metro area. The city was the site of the 2009 G-20 summit as its transformation is an example of a 21st century economy, and is home to ten Fortune 500 companies.

An incredible amount of downtown building has occurred in recent years. Two downtown stadiums were opened in 2001: PNC Park for the Pittsburgh Pirates baseball team, and Acrisure Stadium for the Steelers football team, 2009 Superbowl XLII champions. PNC Park is built along the lines of traditional two-tier ballparks, providing spectators intimate contact with the game.

Acrisure Stadium is an open, natural-turf field with stands in a horseshoe shape, the open-end affording visitors a magnificent view of the Pittsburgh skyline.

In September 2003, the city inaugurated its handsome riverfront David L. Lawrence Convention Center, the first and largest certified "green" convention center, which provides 330,000 square feet of exhibition space, meeting rooms, two lecture halls, and a 35,000 square-foot ballroom.

Pittsburgh has ranked high in several "Most Livable City" lists for nearly 40 years, with criteria including cost of living, crime, and cultural opportunities. Pittsburgh has a low cost of living compared to other northeastern U.S. cities. Pittsburgh has 146 parks and birding enthusiasts love to visit the Clayton Hill area of Frick Park, where well over 100 species of birds have been recorded

Pittsburgh is a little over 100 miles southeast of Lake Erie. Its nearness to the Great Lakes and to the Atlantic Seaboard helps to modify its humid, continental climate. Winter is influenced primarily by Canadian air masses. During the summer, Gulf air brings warm, humid weather. Once every four years, the Monongahela and Ohio rivers combine, causing the Ohio River to reach flood stage.

Rankings

General Rankings

- To help military veterans find the best places in which to settle down, *WalletHub* compared the 100 largest U.S. cities across 19 key indicators of livability, affordability and veteran-friendliness. They range from the share of military skill-related jobs to veteran income growth to the availability of VA health facilities. Pittsburgh ranked #14. *Wallethub.com, "Best & Worst Places for Veterans to Live (2025)," November 7, 2024*

- The human resources consulting firm Mercer ranked 241 major cities worldwide in terms of overall quality of life. Pittsburgh ranked #61. Criteria: political and personal safety, social, and economic factors; medical and health considerations; schools and education; public services and transportation; recreation; connectivity; housing and infrastructure; and climate. *Mercer, "Mercer 2024 Quality of Living Survey," December 2024*

- In their annual survey, Livability.com looked at data for more than 2,000 mid-sized U.S. cities to assign a "Livability Score"for each. The top 100 scoring cities make up Livability's "Top 100 Best Places to Live in the U.S." in 2025. Pittsburgh was placed among the top 100 of the customizable list. Criteria: housing and economy; cost of living; environment; education; health care options; transportation; safety; and community amenities. *Livability.com, "Top 100 Best Places to Live in the U.S. in 2025" April 15, 2025*

Business/Finance Rankings

- Payscale.com ranked the 32 largest metro areas in terms of wage growth. The Pittsburgh metro area ranked #7. Criteria: quarterly changes in private industry employee and education professional wage growth from the previous year. *PayScale, "Wage Trends by Metro Area-4th Quarter," February 4, 2025*

- The Pittsburgh metro area appeared on the Milken Institute "2025 Best Performing Cities" list. Rank: #145 out of 200 large metro areas (based on performance category). Criteria: job growth; wage growth; high-tech growth and impact; community resilience; housing affordability; household broadband access. *Milken Institute, "Best-Performing Cities 2025," January 14, 2025*

- Mercer Human Resources Consulting ranked 226 cities worldwide in terms of cost-of-living. Pittsburgh ranked #62 (the lower the ranking, the higher the cost-of-living). The survey measured the comparative cost of over 200 items (such as housing, food, clothing, domestic supplies, transportation, and recreation/entertainment) in each location. *Mercer, "2024 Cost of Living City Ranking," June 17, 2024*

Culture/Performing Arts Rankings

- Pittsburgh was selected as one of the 25 best cities for moviemakers in North America. Great film cities are places where filmmaking dreams can come true, that offer more creative space, lower costs, and great outdoor locations. NYC & LA were intentionally excluded. Criteria: film industry presence and culture; tax incentives; affordability; and proximity of festivals and schools. The city was ranked #17. *MovieMaker Magazine, "Best Places to Live and Work as a Moviemaker, 2025," January 29, 2025*

Education Rankings

- Personal finance website *WalletHub* analyzed the 150 largest U.S. metropolitan statistical areas to determine where the most educated Americans are putting their degrees to work. Criteria: education levels; percentage of workers with degrees; education quality and attainment gap; public school quality rankings; quality and enrollment of each metro area's universities. Pittsburgh was ranked #33 (#1 = most educated city). *WalletHub.com, "Most & Least Educated Cities in America, 2025" July 2, 2024*

Environmental Rankings

- Pittsburgh was highlighted as one of the 25 metro areas most polluted by year-round particle pollution (Annual PM 2.5) in the U.S. during 2021 through 2023. The area ranked #12. *American Lung Association, "State of the Air 2025," April 23, 2025*

- Pittsburgh was highlighted as one of the 25 metro areas most polluted by short-term particle pollution (24-hour PM 2.5) in the U.S. during 2021 through 2023. The area ranked #16. *American Lung Association, "State of the Air 2025," April 23, 2025*

Health/Fitness Rankings

- For each of the 100 largest cities in the United States, the American Fitness Index®, compiled in partnership between the American College of Sports Medicine and the Elevance Health Foundation, evaluated community infrastructure and more than 30 health behaviors including preventive health, levels of chronic disease conditions, food insecurity, pedestrian safety, air quality, and community/environment resources that support physical activity. Pittsburgh ranked #17 for "community fitness." *americanfitnessindex.org, "2024 ACSM American Fitness Index Summary Report," July 23, 2024*

- The Pittsburgh metro area was identified as one of the worst cities for bed bugs in America by pest control company Orkin. The area ranked #21 out of 50 based on the number of bed bug treatments Orkin performed from December 2022 to November 2023. *Orkin, "Chicago Joins Paris In Global Bed Bug Spotlight Ranking As The Worst City On Orkin's U.S. Bed Bug Cities List," January 22, 2024*

- Pittsburgh was identified as a "2025 Allergy Capital." The area ranked #63 out of the nation's 100 largest metropolitan areas. Three groups of factors were used to identify the most challenging cities for people with allergies: annual tree, grass, and weed pollen scores; over the counter allergy medicine use; number of board-certified allergy specialists. *Asthma and Allergy Foundation of America, "2025 Allergy Capitals: The Most Challenging Places to Live with Allergies," March 18, 2025*

- Pittsburgh was identified as a "2024 Asthma Capital." The area ranked #45 out of the nation's 100 largest metropolitan areas. Criteria: estimated asthma prevalence; asthma-related mortality; and ER visits due to asthma. Risk factors analyzed but not factored in the rankings: annual air quality including pollution and ozone levels; public smoking laws; indoor air quality; access to asthma specialists; rescue and controller medication use; uninsured rate; pollen allergy; poverty rate. *Asthma and Allergy Foundation of America, "Asthma Capitals 2024: The Most Challenging Places to Live With Asthma," September 10, 2024*

Pet Rankings

- Pittsburgh was selected by *Sniffspot.com* as one of the most dog-friendly cities in the U.S., ranking #21 out of 50. Criteria: dog parks; hiking; sniffspots; public parks; dog-friendly businesses; housing; dog waste cleanliness; leash laws; dog services; and overall cost. *Sniffspot.com, "The Top 50 Most Dog-Friendly Cities in the U.S.," September 30, 2024*

Real Estate Rankings

- *WalletHub* compared the most populated U.S. cities to determine which had the best markets for real estate agents. Pittsburgh ranked #112 where demand was high and pay was the best. Criteria: sales per agent; annual median wage for real-estate agents; monthly average starting salary for real estate agents; real estate job density and competition; unemployment rate; home turnover rate; housing-market health index; and other relevant metrics. *WalletHub.com, "2021 Best Places to Be a Real Estate Agent," May 12, 2021*

Safety Rankings

- Allstate ranked the 100 most populous cities in America in terms of driver safety. Pittsburgh ranked #50. Criteria based on anonymized driving behavior data from Allstate's mobile app powered by Arity: high speed driving (over 80 mph), phone handling, and hard braking. The report helps increase the importance of safety and awareness behind the wheel. *Allstate, "16th Allstate America's Best Drivers Report®" July 11, 2024*

Seniors/Retirement Rankings

- Pittsburgh made the 2024 *Forbes* list of "25 Best Places to Retire." Criteria, focused on overall affordability as well as quality of life indicators, include: housing/living costs compared to the national average and taxes; air quality; crime rates; median home prices; risk associated with climate-change/natural hazards; availability of medical care; bikeability; walkability; healthy living. *Forbes.com, "The Best Places to Retire in 2024: Las Cruces and Other Unexpected Hot Spots," May 10, 2024*

Sports/Recreation Rankings

- Pittsburgh was chosen as a bicycle friendly community by the League of American Bicyclists. A "Bicycle Friendly Community" welcomes cyclists by providing safe and supportive accommodation for cycling and encouraging people to bike for transportation and recreation. There are four award levels: Platinum; Gold; Silver; and Bronze. The community achieved an award level of Silver. *League of American Bicyclists, "2024 Awards-New & Renewing Bicycle Friendly Communities List," January 28, 2025*

Women/Minorities Rankings

- Pittsburgh was listed as one of the most LGBTQ-friendly cities in America by *The Advocate*, as compiled by the real estate data site *Clever*. The city ranked #13 out of 15. Criteria, among many: Pride events; gay bars; LGBTQ-affirming healthcare options; state and local laws; number of PFLAG chapters; LGBTQ+ population. *The Advocate, "These Are the 15 Most LGBTQ-Friendly Cities in the U.S." November 1, 2023*

- Personal finance website *WalletHub* compared more than 180 U.S. cities across two key dimensions, "Hispanic Business-Friendliness" and "Hispanic Purchasing Power," to arrive at the most favorable conditions for Hispanic entrepreneurs. Pittsburgh was ranked #130 out of 182. Criteria includes: share of Hispanic-Owned Businesses; average growth of Hispanic Business revenues; Small Business-Friendliness score; affordability; and number of Hispanics with at least a bachelor's degree. *WalletHub.com, "Best Cities for Hispanic Entrepreneurs," September 4, 2024*

Miscellaneous Rankings

- *MoveHub* ranked 446 hipster cities across 20 countries, using its new and improved alternative Hipster Index and Pittsburgh came out as #18 among the top 50. Criteria: population over 150,000; number of vintage boutiques; density of tattoo parlors; vegan places to eat; coffee shops; and density of vinyl record stores. *MoveHub.com, "The Hipster Index: Brighton Pips Portland to Global Top Spot," July 28, 2021*

- *WalletHub* compared 148 of the most populated U.S. cities to determine their operating efficiency. A "Quality of Services" score was constructed for each city and then measured against the total budget per capita to reveal which were managed the best. Pittsburgh ranked #114. Criteria: financial stability; economy; education; safety; health; infrastructure and pollution. *WalletHub.com, "2025's Best- & Worst-Run Cities in America," June 18, 2024*

Business Environment

DEMOGRAPHICS

Population Growth

Area	1990 Census	2000 Census	2010 Census	2020 Census	2023 Estimate[2]	Population Growth 1990-2023 (%)
City	369,785	334,563	305,704	302,971	303,620	-17.9
MSA[1]	2,468,289	2,431,087	2,356,285	2,370,930	2,443,921	-1.0
U.S.	248,709,873	281,421,906	308,745,538	331,449,281	332,387,540	33.6

Note: (1) Figures cover the Pittsburgh, PA Metropolitan Statistical Area; (2) 2019-2023 5-year ACS population estimate
Source: U.S. Census Bureau, 1990 Census, 2000 Census, 2010 Census, 2020 Census, 2019-2023 American Community Survey 5-Year Estimates

Race

Area	White Alone[2] (%)	Black Alone[2] (%)	Asian Alone[2] (%)	AIAN[3] Alone[2] (%)	NHOPI[4] Alone[2] (%)	Other Race Alone[2] (%)	Two or More Races (%)
City	63.7	22.5	5.8	0.2	0.0	1.6	6.2
MSA[1]	84.1	7.9	2.5	0.1	0.0	0.8	4.6
U.S.	63.4	12.4	5.8	0.9	0.2	6.6	10.7

Note: (1) Figures cover the Pittsburgh, PA Metropolitan Statistical Area; (2) Alone is defined as not being in combination with one or more other races; (3) American Indian and Alaska Native; (4) Native Hawaiian and Other Pacific Islander
Source: U.S. Census Bureau, 2019-2023 American Community Survey 5-Year Estimates

Hispanic or Latino Origin

Area	Total (%)	Mexican (%)	Puerto Rican (%)	Cuban (%)	Other (%)
City	4.2	1.4	0.8	0.1	2.0
MSA[1]	2.3	0.8	0.5	0.1	0.9
U.S.	19.0	11.3	1.8	0.7	5.2

Note: Persons of Hispanic or Latino origin can be of any race; (1) Figures cover the Pittsburgh, PA Metropolitan Statistical Area
Source: U.S. Census Bureau, 2019-2023 American Community Survey 5-Year Estimates

Age

Area	Under Age 5	Age 5–19	Age 20–34	Age 35–44	Age 45–54	Age 55–64	Age 65–74	Age 75–84	Age 85+	Median Age
City	4.4	16.1	32.1	12.5	9.0	10.8	9.0	4.0	2.0	33.5
MSA[1]	4.9	16.6	18.7	12.4	12.0	14.5	12.4	5.9	2.8	42.8
U.S.	5.7	19.1	20.2	13.1	12.3	12.8	10.0	4.9	1.9	38.7

Note: (1) Figures cover the Pittsburgh, PA Metropolitan Statistical Area
Source: U.S. Census Bureau, 2019-2023 American Community Survey 5-Year Estimates

Disability by Age

Area	All Ages	Under 18 Years Old	18 to 64 Years Old	65 Years and Over
City	14.2	7.4	11.5	34.3
MSA[1]	14.7	5.7	11.7	31.9
U.S.	13.0	4.7	10.7	32.9

Note: Figures show percent of the civilian noninstitutionalized population that reported having a disability. Disability status is determined from six types of difficulty: vision, hearing, cognitive, ambulatory, self-care, and independent living. For children under 5 years old, hearing and vision difficulty are used to determine disability status. For children between the ages of 5 and 14, disability status is determined from hearing, vision, cognitive, ambulatory, and self-care difficulties. For people aged 15 years and older, they are considered to have a disability if they have difficulty with any one of the six difficulty types; Note: (1) Figures cover the Pittsburgh, PA Metropolitan Statistical Area
Source: U.S. Census Bureau, 2019-2023 American Community Survey 5-Year Estimates

Ancestry

Area	German	Irish	English	American	Italian	Polish	French[2]	European	Scottish
City	17.1	13.2	6.1	2.7	11.4	6.6	1.2	1.2	1.4
MSA[1]	24.5	16.9	9.2	3.3	15.1	7.8	1.4	1.1	1.8
U.S.	12.6	9.4	9.1	5.5	4.9	2.6	2.0	1.6	1.6

Note: Figures are the percentage of the total population reporting a particular ancestry. The nine most commonly reported ancestries in the U.S. are shown. Figures include multiple ancestries (e.g. if a person reported being Irish and Italian, they were included in both columns); (1) Figures cover the Pittsburgh, PA Metropolitan Statistical Area; (2) Excludes Basque
Source: U.S. Census Bureau, 2019-2023 American Community Survey 5-Year Estimates

Foreign-born Population

Area	Percent of Population Born in								
	Any Foreign Country	Asia	Mexico	Europe	Caribbean	Central America[2]	South America	Africa	Canada
City	9.3	4.5	0.3	1.8	0.4	0.2	0.6	1.0	0.3
MSA[1]	4.1	2.0	0.2	0.9	0.2	0.1	0.2	0.4	0.1
U.S.	13.9	4.3	3.3	1.4	1.4	1.2	1.2	0.8	0.2

Note: (1) Figures cover the Pittsburgh, PA Metropolitan Statistical Area; (2) Excludes Mexico.
Source: U.S. Census Bureau, 2019-2023 American Community Survey 5-Year Estimates

Household Size

Area	Persons in Household (%)							Average Household Size
	One	Two	Three	Four	Five	Six	Seven or More	
City	43.9	33.0	11.6	7.1	2.9	0.8	0.7	2.03
MSA[1]	34.1	35.8	13.7	10.6	4.1	1.2	0.6	2.25
U.S.	28.5	33.8	15.4	12.7	5.9	2.3	1.4	2.54

Note: (1) Figures cover the Pittsburgh, PA Metropolitan Statistical Area
Source: U.S. Census Bureau, 2019-2023 American Community Survey 5-Year Estimates

Household Relationships

Area	Householder	Opposite-sex Spouse	Same-sex Spouse	Opposite-sex Unmarried Partner	Same-sex Unmarried Partner	Child[2]	Grandchild	Other Relatives	Non-relatives
City	46.1	11.5	0.3	3.6	0.4	19.3	1.7	3.1	6.7
MSA[1]	43.2	19.0	0.2	2.8	0.2	25.6	1.6	2.6	2.4
U.S.	38.3	17.5	0.2	2.5	0.2	28.3	2.4	4.8	3.4

Note: Figures are percent of the total population; (1) Figures cover the Pittsburgh, PA Metropolitan Statistical Area; (2) Includes biological, adopted, and stepchildren of the householder
Source: U.S. Census Bureau, 2020 Census

Gender

Area	Males	Females	Males per 100 Females
City	149,240	154,380	96.7
MSA[1]	1,200,522	1,243,399	96.6
U.S.	164,545,087	167,842,453	98.0

Note: (1) Figures cover the Pittsburgh, PA Metropolitan Statistical Area
Source: U.S. Census Bureau, 2019-2023 American Community Survey 5-Year Estimates

Marital Status

Area	Never Married	Now Married[2]	Separated	Widowed	Divorced
City	54.4	30.6	1.7	5.0	8.3
MSA[1]	33.1	48.4	1.5	7.0	10.0
U.S.	34.1	47.9	1.7	5.6	10.7

Note: Figures are percentages and cover the population 15 years of age and older; (1) Figures cover the Pittsburgh, PA Metropolitan Statistical Area; (2) Excludes separated
Source: U.S. Census Bureau, 2019-2023 American Community Survey 5-Year Estimates

Religious Groups by Family

Area	Catholic	Baptist	Methodist	LDS[2]	Pentecostal	Lutheran	Islam	Adventist	Other
MSA[1]	30.6	1.9	4.3	0.4	1.3	2.5	0.6	0.6	12.5
U.S.	18.7	7.3	3.0	2.0	1.8	1.7	1.3	1.3	11.6

Note: Figures are the number of adherents as a percentage of the total population and cover the eight largest religious groups in the U.S; (1) Figures cover the Pittsburgh, PA Metropolitan Statistical Area; (2) Church of Jesus Christ of Latter-day Saints
Sources: 2020 U.S. Religion Census, Association of Statisticians of American Religious Bodies; The Association of Religion Data Archives (ARDA)

Religious Groups by Tradition

Area	Catholic	Evangelical Protestant	Mainline Protestant	Black Protestant	Islam	Judaism	Hinduism	Orthodox	Buddhism
MSA[1]	30.6	8.8	10.1	1.3	0.6	0.6	1.2	0.6	0.1
U.S.	18.7	16.5	5.2	2.3	1.3	0.6	0.4	0.4	0.3

Note: Figures are the number of adherents as a percentage of the total population; (1) Figures cover the Pittsburgh, PA Metropolitan Statistical Area
Sources: 2020 U.S. Religion Census, Association of Statisticians of American Religious Bodies; The Association of Religion Data Archives (ARDA)

ECONOMY

Real Gross Domestic Product (GDP)

Area	2017	2018	2019	2020	2021	2022	2023	Rank[3]
MSA[1]	150.7	154.3	155.9	147.7	153.2	155.0	159.6	30
U.S.[2]	17,619.1	18,160.7	18,642.5	18,238.9	19,387.6	19,896.6	20,436.3	—

Note: Figures are in billions of chained 2017 dollars; (1) Figures cover the Pittsburgh, PA Metropolitan Statistical Area; (2) Figures cover real GDP within metropolitan areas; (3) Rank is based on 2023 data and ranges from 1 to 384
Source: U.S. Bureau of Economic Analysis

Economic Growth

Area	2014	2015	2016	2017	2018	2019	2020	2021	2022	2023
MSA[1]	1.8	3.1	0.2	4.4	2.4	1.0	-5.3	3.7	1.2	2.9
U.S.[2]	2.6	3.2	2.0	2.7	3.1	2.7	-2.2	6.3	2.6	2.7

Note: Figures are real gross domestic product growth rates and represent percent change from preceding period; (1) Figures cover the Pittsburgh, PA Metropolitan Statistical Area; (2) Figures are the average growth rates within metropolitan areas
Source: U.S. Bureau of Economic Analysis

Metropolitan Area Exports

Area	2018	2019	2020	2021	2022	2023	Rank[2]
MSA[1]	9,824.2	9,672.9	7,545.1	9,469.6	11,188.3	11,538.4	33
U.S.	1,664,056.1	1,645,173.7	1,431,406.6	1,753,941.4	2,062,937.4	2,019,160.5	—

Note: Figures are in millions of dollars; (1) Figures cover the Pittsburgh, PA Metropolitan Statistical Area; (2) Rank is based on 2023 data and ranges from 1 to 386
Source: U.S. Department of Commerce, International Trade Administration, Office of Trade and Economic Analysis, Industry and Analysis, Exports by Metropolitan Area, data extracted April 2, 2025

Building Permits

Area	Single-Family			Multi-Family			Total		
	2023	2024	Pct. Chg.	2023	2024	Pct. Chg.	2023	2024	Pct. Chg.
City	229	229	0.0	2,283	1,435	-37.1	2,512	1,664	-33.8
MSA[1]	3,332	3,530	5.9	2,962	1,882	-36.5	6,294	5,412	-14.0
U.S.	920,000	981,900	6.7	591,100	496,100	-16.1	1,511,100	1,478,000	-2.2

Note: (1) Figures cover the Pittsburgh, PA Metropolitan Statistical Area; Figures represent new, privately-owned housing units authorized (unadjusted data)
Source: U.S. Census Bureau, Building Permits Survey (BPS), 2023, 2024

Bankruptcy Filings

Area	Business Filings			Nonbusiness Filings		
	2023	2024	% Chg.	2023	2024	% Chg.
Allegheny County	59	111	88.1	1,217	1,424	17.0
U.S.	18,926	23,107	22.1	434,064	494,201	13.9

Note: Business filings include Chapter 7, Chapter 9, Chapter 11, Chapter 12, Chapter 13, Chapter 15, and Section 304; Nonbusiness filings include Chapter 7, Chapter 11, and Chapter 13
Source: Administrative Office of the U.S. Courts, Business and Nonbusiness Bankruptcy, County Cases Commenced by Chapter of the Bankruptcy Code, During the 12-Month Period Ending December 31, 2023 and Business and Nonbusiness Bankruptcy, County Cases Commenced by Chapter of the Bankruptcy Code, During the 12-Month Period Ending December 31, 2024

Housing Vacancy Rates

Area	Gross Vacancy Rate[3] (%)			Year-Round Vacancy Rate[4] (%)			Rental Vacancy Rate[5] (%)			Homeowner Vacancy Rate[6] (%)		
	2022	2023	2024	2022	2023	2024	2022	2023	2024	2022	2023	2024
MSA[1]	11.5	10.0	10.5	11.0	9.2	9.7	8.3	6.3	8.9	0.7	0.9	0.8
U.S.[2]	9.1	9.0	9.1	7.5	7.5	7.6	5.7	6.5	6.8	0.8	0.8	1.0

Note: (1) Figures cover the Pittsburgh, PA Metropolitan Statistical Area; (2) Figures cover the 75 largest Metropolitan Statistical Areas; (3) The percentage of the total housing inventory that is vacant; (4) The percentage of the housing inventory (excluding seasonal units) that is year-round vacant; (5) The percentage of rental inventory that is vacant for rent; (6) The percentage of homeowner inventory that is vacant for sale
Source: U.S. Census Bureau, Housing Vacancies and Homeownership Annual Statistics: 2022, 2023, 2024

INCOME

Income

Area	Per Capita ($)	Median Household ($)	Average Household ($)
City	43,590	64,137	93,301
MSA[1]	44,726	73,942	101,289
U.S.	43,289	78,538	110,491

Note: (1) Figures cover the Pittsburgh, PA Metropolitan Statistical Area
Source: U.S. Census Bureau, 2019-2023 American Community Survey 5-Year Estimates

Household Income Distribution

Area	Percent of Households Earning							
	Under $15,000	$15,000 -$24,999	$25,000 -$34,999	$35,000 -$49,999	$50,000 -$74,999	$75,000 -$99,999	$100,000 -$149,999	$150,000 and up
City	14.2	8.1	7.4	11.0	16.6	11.4	14.6	16.8
MSA[1]	8.8	7.3	7.3	10.9	16.2	12.9	17.2	19.3
U.S.	8.5	6.6	6.8	10.4	15.7	12.7	17.4	21.9

Note: (1) Figures cover the Pittsburgh, PA Metropolitan Statistical Area
Source: U.S. Census Bureau, 2019-2023 American Community Survey 5-Year Estimates

Poverty Rate

Area	All Ages	Under 18 Years Old	18 to 64 Years Old	65 Years and Over
City	19.5	29.5	18.4	14.1
MSA[1]	10.9	14.4	10.5	8.9
U.S.	12.4	16.3	11.6	10.4

Note: Figures are percentage of people whose income during the past 12 months was below the poverty level; (1) Figures cover the Pittsburgh, PA Metropolitan Statistical Area
Source: U.S. Census Bureau, 2019-2023 American Community Survey 5-Year Estimates

EMPLOYMENT

Labor Force and Employment

Area	Civilian Labor Force			Workers Employed		
	Dec. 2023	Dec. 2024	% Chg.	Dec. 2023	Dec. 2024	% Chg.
City	152,654	151,757	-0.6	148,435	147,774	-0.4
MSA[1]	1,218,768	1,213,214	-0.5	1,179,001	1,172,526	-0.5
U.S.	166,661,000	167,746,000	0.7	160,754,000	161,294,000	0.3

Note: Data is not seasonally adjusted and covers workers 16 years of age and older; (1) Figures cover the Pittsburgh, PA Metropolitan Statistical Area
Source: Bureau of Labor Statistics, Local Area Unemployment Statistics

Unemployment Rate

Area	2024											
	Jan.	Feb.	Mar.	Apr.	May	Jun.	Jul.	Aug.	Sep.	Oct.	Nov.	Dec.
City	3.2	3.2	3.1	2.5	3.0	3.5	3.7	4.0	2.8	3.0	2.9	2.6
MSA[1]	3.9	4.1	3.6	3.1	3.3	3.9	4.2	4.4	3.1	3.4	3.3	3.4
U.S.	4.1	4.2	3.9	3.5	3.7	4.3	4.5	4.4	3.9	3.9	4.0	3.8

Note: Data is not seasonally adjusted and covers workers 16 years of age and older; (1) Figures cover the Pittsburgh, PA Metropolitan Statistical Area
Source: Bureau of Labor Statistics, Local Area Unemployment Statistics

Average Wages

Occupation	$/Hr.	Occupation	$/Hr.
Accountants and Auditors	39.21	Maintenance and Repair Workers	24.30
Automotive Mechanics	24.59	Marketing Managers	63.96
Bookkeepers	23.05	Network and Computer Systems Admin.	44.03
Carpenters	31.17	Nurses, Licensed Practical	28.96
Cashiers	14.11	Nurses, Registered	41.36
Computer Programmers	42.07	Nursing Assistants	19.62
Computer Systems Analysts	47.00	Office Clerks, General	21.43
Computer User Support Specialists	29.05	Physical Therapists	45.46
Construction Laborers	25.52	Physicians	106.62
Cooks, Restaurant	15.76	Plumbers, Pipefitters and Steamfitters	34.88
Customer Service Representatives	21.46	Police and Sheriff's Patrol Officers	39.89
Dentists	78.26	Postal Service Mail Carriers	28.52
Electricians	34.21	Real Estate Sales Agents	31.38
Engineers, Electrical	53.62	Retail Salespersons	16.07
Fast Food and Counter Workers	13.48	Sales Representatives, Technical/Scientific	51.43
Financial Managers	73.83	Secretaries, Exc. Legal/Medical/Executive	20.70
First-Line Supervisors of Office Workers	32.42	Security Guards	18.83
General and Operations Managers	57.41	Surgeons	n/a
Hairdressers/Cosmetologists	17.44	Teacher Assistants, Exc. Postsecondary[1]	15.48
Home Health and Personal Care Aides	14.92	Teachers, Secondary School, Exc. Sp. Ed.[1]	37.69
Janitors and Cleaners	17.29	Telemarketers	18.78
Landscaping/Groundskeeping Workers	18.69	Truck Drivers, Heavy/Tractor-Trailer	27.85
Lawyers	72.59	Truck Drivers, Light/Delivery Services	20.24
Maids and Housekeeping Cleaners	15.75	Waiters and Waitresses	16.99

Note: Wage data covers the Pittsburgh, PA Metropolitan Statistical Area; (1) Hourly wages were calculated from annual wage data based on a 40 hour work week
Source: Bureau of Labor Statistics, Metro Area Occupational Employment & Wage Estimates, May 2024

Employment by Industry

Sector	MSA[1] Number of Employees	MSA[1] Percent of Total	U.S. Percent of Total
Construction	56,400	4.7	5.1
Financial Activities	78,700	6.5	5.8
Government	119,600	9.9	14.9
Information	20,800	1.7	1.9
Leisure and Hospitality	118,500	9.8	10.4
Manufacturing	86,300	7.1	8.0
Mining and Logging	8,000	0.7	0.4
Other Services	50,200	4.1	3.7
Private Education and Health Services	269,500	22.2	16.9
Professional and Business Services	186,400	15.4	14.2
Retail Trade	121,300	10.0	10.0
Transportation, Warehousing, and Utilities	54,500	4.5	4.8
Wholesale Trade	42,100	3.5	3.9

Note: Figures are non-farm employment as of December 2024. Figures are not seasonally adjusted and include workers 16 years of age and older; (1) Figures cover the Pittsburgh, PA Metropolitan Statistical Area
Source: Bureau of Labor Statistics, Current Employment Statistics, Employment, Hours, and Earnings

Employment by Occupation

Occupation Classification	City (%)	MSA[1] (%)	U.S. (%)
Management, Business, Science, and Arts	54.9	45.2	42.0
Natural Resources, Construction, and Maintenance	3.8	7.7	8.6
Production, Transportation, and Material Moving	7.4	11.7	13.0
Sales and Office	17.1	19.8	19.9
Service	16.9	15.5	16.5

Note: Figures cover employed civilians 16 years of age and older; (1) Figures cover the Pittsburgh, PA Metropolitan Statistical Area
Source: U.S. Census Bureau, 2019-2023 American Community Survey 5-Year Estimates

Occupations with Greatest Projected Employment Growth: 2022 – 2032

Occupation[1]	2022 Employment	2032 Projected Employment	Numeric Employment Change	Percent Employment Change
Home Health and Personal Care Aides	188,340	217,220	28,880	15.3
Cooks, Restaurant	47,000	56,390	9,390	20.0
Software Developers	44,860	53,670	8,810	19.6
Stockers and Order Fillers	101,890	109,260	7,370	7.2
Registered Nurses	148,790	155,810	7,020	4.7
Laborers and Freight, Stock, and Material Movers, Hand	150,410	156,080	5,670	3.8
General and Operations Managers	128,890	134,210	5,320	4.1
Medical and Health Services Managers	17,770	22,610	4,840	27.2
Financial Managers	25,890	29,980	4,090	15.8
Medical Assistants	27,920	31,740	3,820	13.7

Note: Projections cover Pennsylvania; (1) Sorted by numeric employment change
Source: www.projectionscentral.org, State Occupational Projections, 2022–2032 Long-Term Projections

Fastest-Growing Occupations: 2022 – 2032

Occupation[1]	2022 Employment	2032 Projected Employment	Numeric Employment Change	Percent Employment Change
Nurse Practitioners	8,010	11,430	3,420	42.7
Data Scientists	3,810	5,060	1,250	32.8
Wind Turbine Service Technicians	160	210	50	31.3
Statisticians	2,590	3,380	790	30.5
Physician Assistants	7,240	9,290	2,050	28.3
Information Security Analysts (SOC 2018)	4,470	5,720	1,250	28.0
Medical and Health Services Managers	17,770	22,610	4,840	27.2
Physical Therapist Assistants	4,990	6,280	1,290	25.9
Occupational Therapy Assistants	2,180	2,700	520	23.9
Operations Research Analysts	3,110	3,800	690	22.2

Note: Projections cover Pennsylvania; (1) Sorted by percent employment change and excludes occupations with numeric employment change less than 50
Source: www.projectionscentral.org, State Occupational Projections, 2022–2032 Long-Term Projections

CITY FINANCES

City Government Finances

Component	2022 ($000)	2022 ($ per capita)
Total Revenues	687,878	2,299
Total Expenditures	761,746	2,546
Debt Outstanding	472,711	1,580

Source: U.S. Census Bureau, State & Local Government Finances 2022

City Government Revenue by Source

Source	2022 ($000)	2022 ($ per capita)	2022 (%)
General Revenue			
From Federal Government	84,809	283	12.3
From State Government	60,301	202	8.8
From Local Governments	4,875	16	0.7
Taxes			
Property	164,635	550	23.9
Sales and Gross Receipts	108,647	363	15.8
Personal Income	114,444	382	16.6
Corporate Income	0	0	0.0
Motor Vehicle License	0	0	0.0
Other Taxes	95,086	318	13.8
Current Charges	37,523	125	5.5
Liquor Store	0	0	0.0
Utility	0	0	0.0

Source: U.S. Census Bureau, State & Local Government Finances 2022

City Government Expenditures by Function

Function	2022 ($000)	2022 ($ per capita)	2022 (%)
General Direct Expenditures			
Air Transportation	0	0	0.0
Corrections	0	0	0.0
Education	0	0	0.0
Employment Security Administration	0	0	0.0
Financial Administration	20,109	67	2.6
Fire Protection	90,470	302	11.9
General Public Buildings	14,227	47	1.9
Governmental Administration, Other	60,864	203	8.0
Health	31,842	106	4.2
Highways	133,287	445	17.5
Hospitals	0	0	0.0
Housing and Community Development	8,887	29	1.2
Interest on General Debt	17,334	57	2.3
Judicial and Legal	589	2	0.1
Libraries	0	0	0.0
Parking	0	0	0.0
Parks and Recreation	11,924	39	1.6
Police Protection	130,559	436	17.1
Public Welfare	0	0	0.0
Sewerage	0	0	0.0
Solid Waste Management	20,794	69	2.7
Veterans' Services	0	0	0.0
Liquor Store	0	0	0.0
Utility	0	0	0.0

Source: U.S. Census Bureau, State & Local Government Finances 2022

TAXES

State Corporate Income Tax Rates

State	Tax Rate (%)	Income Brackets ($)	Num. of Brackets	Financial Institution Tax Rate (%)[a]	Federal Income Tax Ded.
Pennsylvania	8.49	Flat rate	1	(a)	No

Note: Tax rates for tax year 2024; (a) Rates listed are the corporate income tax rate applied to financial institutions or excise taxes based on income. Some states have other taxes based upon the value of deposits or shares.
Source: Federation of Tax Administrators, State Corporate Income Tax Rates, January 1, 2025

State Individual Income Tax Rates

State	Tax Rate (%)	Income Brackets ($)	Personal Exemptions ($)			Standard Ded. ($)	
			Single	Married	Depend.	Single	Married
Pennsylvania	3.07	Flat rate	None	None	None	–	–

Note: Tax rates for tax year 2024; Local- and county-level taxes are not included; Federal income tax is not deductible on state income tax returns
Source: Federation of Tax Administrators, State Individual Income Tax Rates, January 1, 2025

Various State Sales and Excise Tax Rates

State	State Sales Tax (%)	Gasoline[1] ($/gal.)	Cigarette[2] ($/pack)	Spirits[3] ($/gal.)	Wine[4] ($/gal.)	Beer[5] ($/gal.)	Recreational Marijuana (%)
Pennsylvania	6	0.59	2.60	7.48	0.00	0.08	Not legal

Note: All tax rates as of January 1, 2025; (1) The American Petroleum Institute has developed a methodology for determining the average tax rate on a gallon of fuel. Rates may include any of the following: excise taxes, environmental fees, storage tank fees, other fees or taxes, general sales tax, and local taxes; (2) The federal excise tax of $1.0066 per pack and local taxes are not included; (3) Rates are those applicable to off-premise sales of 40% alcohol by volume (a.b.v.) distilled spirits in 750ml containers. Local excise taxes are excluded; (4) Rates are those applicable to off-premise sales of 11% a.b.v. non-carbonated wine in 750ml containers; (5) Rates are those applicable to off-premise sales of 4.7% a.b.v. beer in 12 ounce containers.
Source: Tax Foundation, 2025 Facts & Figures: How Does Your State Compare?

State Tax Competitiveness Index

State	Overall Rank	Corporate Tax Rank	Individual Income Tax Rank	Sales Tax Rank	Property Tax Rank	Unemployment Insurance Tax Rank
Pennsylvania	34	38	38	22	9	36

Note: The Tax Foundation's State Tax Competitiveness Index enables policymakers, taxpayers, and business leaders to gauge how their states' tax systems compare. A rank of 1 is best, 50 is worst. Rankings do not average to the total. States without a tax rank equally as 1. DC's scores and rankings do not affect other states. The report shows tax systems as of July 1, 2024 (the beginning of Fiscal Year 2025).
Source: Tax Foundation, State Tax Competitiveness Index 2025

TRANSPORTATION

Means of Transportation to Work

Area	Car/Truck/Van		Public Transportation			Bicycle	Walked	Other Means	Worked at Home
	Drove Alone	Carpooled	Bus	Subway	Railroad				
City	48.2	6.2	11.6	0.3	0.0	1.1	9.8	2.3	20.4
MSA[1]	69.9	6.9	3.2	0.2	0.0	0.2	2.9	1.4	15.4
U.S.	70.2	8.5	1.7	1.3	0.4	0.4	2.4	1.6	13.5

Note: Figures are percentages and cover workers 16 years of age and older; (1) Figures cover the Pittsburgh, PA Metropolitan Statistical Area
Source: U.S. Census Bureau, 2019-2023 American Community Survey 5-Year Estimates

Travel Time to Work

Area	Less Than 10 Minutes	10 to 19 Minutes	20 to 29 Minutes	30 to 44 Minutes	45 to 59 Minutes	60 to 89 Minutes	90 Minutes or More
City	10.3	34.0	26.0	20.5	4.6	3.2	1.5
MSA[1]	12.3	27.5	21.7	22.5	8.7	5.3	2.0
U.S.	12.6	28.6	21.2	20.8	8.1	6.0	2.8

Note: Note: Figures are percentages and include workers 16 years old and over; (1) Figures cover the Pittsburgh, PA Metropolitan Statistical Area
Source: U.S. Census Bureau, 2019-2023 American Community Survey 5-Year Estimates

Key Congestion Measures

Measure	2000	2010	2015	2020	2022
Annual Hours of Delay, Total (000)	30,888	37,291	43,037	24,743	43,830
Annual Hours of Delay, Per Auto Commuter	33	39	45	25	47
Annual Congestion Cost, Per Auto Commuter ($)	995	954	1,017	617	1,082

Note: Figures cover the Pittsburgh PA urban area
Source: Texas A&M Transportation Institute, 2023 Urban Mobility Report

Freeway Travel Time Index

Measure	1985	1990	1995	2000	2005	2010	2015	2020	2022
Urban Area Index[1]	1.08	1.13	1.15	1.16	1.18	1.17	1.19	1.08	1.16
Urban Area Rank[1,2]	40	34	36	43	41	41	38	44	50

Note: Freeway Travel Time Index—the ratio of travel time in the peak period to the travel time at free-flow conditions. For example, a value of 1.30 indicates a 20-minute free-flow trip takes 26 minutes in the peak (20 minutes x 1.30 = 26 minutes); (1) Covers the Pittsburgh PA urban area; (2) Rank is based on 101 larger urban areas (#1 = highest travel time index)
Source: Texas A&M Transportation Institute, 2023 Urban Mobility Report

Public Transportation

Agency Name / Mode of Transportation	Vehicles Operated in Maximum Service[1]	Annual Unlinked Passenger Trips[2] (in thous.)	Annual Passenger Miles[3] (in thous.)
Port Authority of Allegheny County			
Bus (directly operated)	524	33,573.0	135,291.3
Demand Response (purchased transportation)	207	926.8	7,281.9
Inclined Plane (directly operated)	2	165.0	19.3
Light Rail (directly operated)	47	3,243.8	12,527.1

Note: (1) Number of revenue vehicles operated by the given mode and type of service to meet the annual maximum service requirement. This is the revenue vehicle count during the peak season of the year; on the week and day that maximum service is provided. Vehicles operated in maximum service (VOMS) exclude atypical days and one-time special events; (2) Number of passengers who boarded public transportation vehicles. Passengers are counted each time they board a vehicle no matter how many vehicles they use to travel from their origin to their destination. (3) Sum of the distances ridden by all passengers during the entire fiscal year.
Source: Federal Transit Administration, National Transit Database, 2023

Air Transportation

Airport Name and Code / Type of Service	Passenger Airlines[1]	Passenger Enplanements	Freight Carriers[2]	Freight (lbs)
Pittsburgh International Airport (PIT)				
Domestic service (U.S. carriers only)	32	4,742,054	13	80,429,874
International service (U.S. carriers only)	8	21,985	1	134,506

Note: (1) Includes all U.S.-based major, minor and commuter airlines that carried at least one passenger during the year; (2) Includes all U.S.-based airlines and freight carriers that transported at least one pound of freight during the year.
Source: Bureau of Transportation Statistics, The Intermodal Transportation Database, Air Carriers: T-100 Domestic Market (U.S. carriers only), 2024; Bureau of Transportation Statistics, The Intermodal Transportation Database, Air Carriers: T-100 International Market (U.S. carriers only), 2024

BUSINESSES

Major Business Headquarters

Company Name	Industry	Fortune[1]	Forbes[2]
Alcoa	Metals	380	-
Arconic	Materials	-	77
Armada Sunset Holdings	Business services & supplies	-	111
Giant Eagle	Food markets	-	42
PNC Financial Services Group	Commercial banks	139	-
PPG Industries	Chemicals	226	-
United States Steel	Metals	227	-
WESCO International	Wholesalers: diversified	183	-
Westinghouse Air Brake Technologies	Industrial machinery	407	-

Note: (1) Companies that produce a 10-K are ranked 1 to 500 based on 2023 revenue; (2) All private companies with at least $2 billion in annual revenue through the end of their most current fiscal year are ranked 1 to 275; companies listed are headquartered in the city; dashes indicate no ranking
Source: Fortune, "Fortune 500," 2024; Forbes, "America's Largest Private Companies," 2024

Fastest-Growing Businesses

According to *Inc.*, Pittsburgh is home to one of America's 500 fastest-growing private companies: **Wolfe** (#486). Criteria: must be an independent, privately-held, for-profit, U.S. corporation, proprietorship or partnership as of December 31, 2023; revenues must be at least $100,000 in 2020 and $2 million in 2023; must have four-year operating/sales history. *Inc., "America's 500 Fastest-Growing Private Companies," 2024*

Living Environment

COST OF LIVING

Cost of Living Index

Composite Index	Groceries	Housing	Utilities	Transportation	Health Care	Misc. Goods/Services
98.1	97.8	94.9	119.9	107.2	99.2	93.2

Note: The Cost of Living Index measures regional differences in the cost of consumer goods and services, excluding taxes and non-consumer expenditures, for professional and managerial households in the top income quintile. It is based on more than 50,000 prices covering almost 60 different items for which prices are collected three times a year by chambers of commerce, economic development organizations or university applied economic centers in each participating urban area. The numbers shown should be read as a percentage above or below the national average of 100. For example, a value of 115.4 in the groceries column indicates that grocery prices are 15.4% higher than the national average. Small differences in the index numbers should not be interpreted as significant; Figures cover the Pittsburgh PA urban area.
Source: The Council for Community and Economic Research, Cost of Living Index, 2024

Grocery Prices

Area[1]	T-Bone Steak ($/pound)	Frying Chicken ($/pound)	Whole Milk ($/half gal.)	Eggs ($/dozen)	Orange Juice ($/64 oz.)	Coffee ($/11.5 oz.)
City[2]	15.52	1.43	4.52	3.27	4.44	5.15
Avg.	15.42	1.55	4.69	3.25	4.41	5.46
Min.	14.50	1.16	4.43	2.75	4.00	4.85
Max.	17.56	2.89	5.49	4.78	5.54	7.89

Note: (1) Values for the local area are compared with the average, minimum and maximum values for all 276 areas in the Cost of Living Index; (2) Figures cover the Pittsburgh PA urban area; **T-Bone Steak** (price per pound); **Frying Chicken** (price per pound, whole fryer); **Whole Milk** (half gallon carton); **Eggs** (price per dozen, Grade A, large); **Orange Juice** (64 oz. Tropicana or Florida Natural); **Coffee** (11.5 oz. can, vacuum-packed, Maxwell House, Hills Bros, or Folgers).
Source: The Council for Community and Economic Research, Cost of Living Index, 2024

Housing and Utility Costs

Area[1]	New Home Price ($)	Apartment Rent ($/month)	All Electric ($/month)	Part Electric ($/month)	Other Energy ($/month)	Telephone ($/month)
City[2]	478,461	1,602	-	137.23	130.44	200.01
Avg.	515,975	1,550	210.99	123.07	82.07	194.99
Min.	265,375	692	104.33	53.68	36.26	179.42
Max.	2,775,821	5,719	529.02	397.28	361.63	223.33

Note: (1) Values for the local area are compared with the average, minimum and maximum values for all 276 areas in the Cost of Living Index; (2) Figures cover the Pittsburgh PA urban area; **New Home Price** (2,400 sf living area, 8,000 sf lot, in urban area with full utilities); **Apartment Rent** (950 sf 2 bedroom/1.5 or 2 bath, unfurnished, excluding all utilities except water); **All Electric** (average monthly cost for an all-electric home); **Part Electric** (average monthly cost for a part-electric home); **Other Energy** (average monthly cost for natural gas, fuel oil, coal, wood, and any other forms of energy except electricity); **Telephone** (price includes the base monthly rate plus taxes and fees for three lines of mobile phone service).
Source: The Council for Community and Economic Research, Cost of Living Index, 2024

Health Care, Transportation, and Other Costs

Area[1]	Doctor ($/visit)	Dentist ($/visit)	Optometrist ($/visit)	Gasoline ($/gallon)	Beauty Salon ($/visit)	Men's Shirt ($)
City[2]	96.56	128.63	105.71	3.67	44.32	28.77
Avg.	143.77	117.51	129.23	3.32	48.57	38.14
Min.	36.74	58.67	67.33	2.80	24.00	13.41
Max.	270.44	216.82	307.33	5.28	94.00	63.89

Note: (1) Values for the local area are compared with the average, minimum and maximum values for all 276 areas in the Cost of Living Index; (2) Figures cover the Pittsburgh PA urban area; **Doctor** (general practitioners routine exam of an established patient); **Dentist** (adult teeth cleaning and periodic oral examination); **Optometrist** (full vision eye exam for established adult patient); **Gasoline** (one gallon regular unleaded, national brand, including all taxes, cash price at self-service pump if available); **Beauty Salon** (woman's shampoo, trim, and blow-dry); **Men's Shirt** (cotton/polyester dress shirt, pinpoint weave, long sleeves).
Source: The Council for Community and Economic Research, Cost of Living Index, 2024

HOUSING

Homeownership Rate

Area	2017 (%)	2018 (%)	2019 (%)	2020 (%)	2021 (%)	2022 (%)	2023 (%)	2024 (%)
MSA[1]	72.7	71.7	71.5	69.8	69.1	72.7	72.4	71.7
U.S.	63.9	64.4	64.6	66.6	65.5	65.8	65.9	65.6

Note: (1) Figures cover the Pittsburgh, PA Metropolitan Statistical Area
Source: U.S. Census Bureau, Housing Vacancies and Homeownership Annual Statistics: 2017-2024

House Price Index (HPI)

Area	National Ranking[2]	Quarterly Change (%)	One-Year Change (%)	Five-Year Change (%)	Since 1991Q1 (%)
MSA[1]	104	0.17	5.87	45.46	262.85
U.S.[3]	—	1.43	4.51	57.13	327.82

Note: The HPI is a weighted repeat sales index. It measures average price changes in repeat sales or refinancings on the same properties. This information is obtained by reviewing repeat mortgage transactions on single-family properties whose mortgages have been purchased or securitized by Fannie Mae or Freddie Mac since January 1975; (1) Figures cover the Pittsburgh, PA Metropolitan Statistical Area; (2) Rankings are based on annual percentage change for all metro areas containing at least 15,000 transactions over the last 10 years and ranges from 1 to 241; (3) figures based on a weighted average of Census Division estimates using a seasonally adjusted, purchase-only index; all figures are for the period ending December 31, 2024
Source: Federal Housing Finance Agency, Change in FHFA Metropolitan Area House Price Indexes, All Transactions Index, 2024Q4

Home Value

Area	Under $100,000	$100,000 -$199,999	$200,000 -$299,999	$300,000 -$399,999	$400,000 -$499,999	$500,000 -$999,999	$1,000,000 or more	Median ($)
City	22.7	29.2	19.5	10.3	5.6	10.3	2.2	193,200
MSA[1]	19.2	29.5	23.7	12.0	6.6	7.6	1.3	204,500
U.S.	12.1	17.8	19.5	14.4	10.5	19.1	6.5	303,400

Note: Figures are percentages except for median and cover owner-occupied housing units; (1) Figures cover the Pittsburgh, PA Metropolitan Statistical Area
Source: U.S. Census Bureau, 2019-2023 American Community Survey 5-Year Estimates

Year Housing Structure Built

Area	2020 or Later	2010 -2019	2000 -2009	1990 -1999	1980 -1989	1970 -1979	1960 -1969	1950 -1959	1940 -1949	Before 1940	Median Year
City	0.5	4.8	3.7	3.4	4.2	6.5	7.9	13.0	7.6	48.4	1942
MSA[1]	0.6	4.6	6.4	7.3	7.7	11.8	11.3	16.3	8.2	25.8	1960
U.S.	1.2	8.9	13.6	12.8	13.0	14.4	10.0	9.7	4.5	11.9	1980

Note: Figures are percentages except for Median Year; Note: (1) Figures cover the Pittsburgh, PA Metropolitan Statistical Area
Source: U.S. Census Bureau, 2019-2023 American Community Survey 5-Year Estimates

Gross Monthly Rent

Area	Under $500	$500 -$999	$1,000 -$1,499	$1,500 -$1,999	$2,000 -$2,499	$2,500 -$2,999	$3,000 and up	Median ($)
City	10.6	21.9	35.1	18.4	8.3	3.3	2.4	1,221
MSA[1]	11.8	37.3	32.0	11.5	4.4	1.5	1.6	1,011
U.S.	6.5	22.3	29.5	20.2	10.8	4.8	5.9	1,348

Note: Figures are percentages except for median; Gross rent is the contract rent plus the estimated average monthly cost of utilities (electricity, gas, and water and sewer) and fuels (oil, coal, kerosene, wood, etc.) if these are paid by the renter (or paid for the renter by someone else); (1) Figures cover the Pittsburgh, PA Metropolitan Statistical Area
Source: U.S. Census Bureau, 2019-2023 American Community Survey 5-Year Estimates

HEALTH

Health Risk Factors

Category	MSA[1] (%)	U.S. (%)
Adults aged 18–64 who have any kind of health care coverage	n/a	90.8
Adults who reported being in good or better health	n/a	81.8
Adults who have been told they have high blood cholesterol	n/a	36.9
Adults who have been told they have high blood pressure	n/a	34.0
Adults who are current smokers	n/a	12.1
Adults who currently use e-cigarettes	n/a	7.7
Adults who currently use chewing tobacco, snuff, or snus	n/a	3.2
Adults who are heavy drinkers[2]	n/a	6.1
Adults who are binge drinkers[3]	n/a	15.2
Adults who are overweight (BMI 25.0 - 29.9)	n/a	34.4
Adults who are obese (BMI 30.0 - 99.8)	n/a	34.3
Adults who participated in any physical activities in the past month	n/a	75.8

Note: All figures are crude prevalence; (1) Figures for the Pittsburgh, PA Metropolitan Statistical Area were not available.
(2) Heavy drinkers are classified as adult men having more than 14 drinks per week and adult women having more than 7 drinks per week; (3) Binge drinkers are classified as males having five or more drinks on one occasion or females having four or more drinks on one occasion
Source: Centers for Disease Control and Prevention, Behavioral Risk Factor Surveillance System, SMART: Selected Metropolitan Area Risk Trends, 2023

Acute and Chronic Health Conditions

Category	MSA[1] (%)	U.S. (%)
Adults who have ever been told they had a heart attack	n/a	4.2
Adults who have ever been told they have angina or coronary heart disease	n/a	4.0
Adults who have ever been told they had a stroke	n/a	3.3
Adults who have ever been told they have asthma	n/a	15.7
Adults who have ever been told they have arthritis	n/a	26.3
Adults who have ever been told they have diabetes[2]	n/a	11.5
Adults who have ever been told they had skin cancer	n/a	5.6
Adults who have ever been told they had any other types of cancer	n/a	8.4
Adults who have ever been told they have COPD	n/a	6.4
Adults who have ever been told they have kidney disease	n/a	3.7
Adults who have ever been told they have a form of depression	n/a	22.0

Note: All figures are crude prevalence; (1) Figures for the Pittsburgh, PA Metropolitan Statistical Area were not available.
(2) Figures do not include pregnancy-related, borderline, or pre-diabetes
Source: Centers for Disease Control and Prevention, Behaviorial Risk Factor Surveillance System, SMART: Selected Metropolitan Area Risk Trends, 2023

Health Screening and Vaccination Rates

Category	MSA[1] (%)	U.S. (%)
Adults who have ever been tested for HIV	n/a	37.5
Adults who have had their blood cholesterol checked within the last five years	n/a	87.0
Adults aged 65+ who have had flu shot within the past year	n/a	63.4
Adults aged 65+ who have ever had a pneumonia vaccination	n/a	71.9

Note: All figures are crude prevalence; (1) Figures for the Pittsburgh, PA Metropolitan Statistical Area were not available.
Source: Centers for Disease Control and Prevention, Behaviorial Risk Factor Surveillance System, SMART: Selected Metropolitan Area Risk Trends, 2023

Disability Status

Category	MSA[1] (%)	U.S. (%)
Adults who reported being deaf	n/a	7.4
Are you blind or have serious difficulty seeing, even when wearing glasses?	n/a	4.9
Do you have difficulty doing errands alone?	n/a	7.8
Do you have difficulty dressing or bathing?	n/a	3.6
Do you have serious difficulty concentrating/remembering/making decisions?	n/a	13.7
Do you have serious difficulty walking or climbing stairs?	n/a	13.2

Note: All figures are crude prevalence; (1) Figures for the Pittsburgh, PA Metropolitan Statistical Area were not available.
Source: Centers for Disease Control and Prevention, Behaviorial Risk Factor Surveillance System, SMART: Selected Metropolitan Area Risk Trends, 2023

Mortality Rates for the Top 10 Causes of Death in the U.S.

ICD-10[a] Sub-Chapter	ICD-10[a] Code	Crude Mortality Rate[2] per 100,000 population	
		County[3]	U.S.
Malignant neoplasms	C00-C97	221.0	182.7
Ischaemic heart diseases	I20-I25	154.9	109.6
Provisional assignment of new diseases of uncertain etiology[1]	U00-U49	62.5	65.3
Other forms of heart disease	I30-I51	92.4	65.1
Other degenerative diseases of the nervous system	G30-G31	47.9	52.4
Other external causes of accidental injury	W00-X59	82.7	52.3
Cerebrovascular diseases	I60-I69	51.1	49.1
Chronic lower respiratory diseases	J40-J47	47.0	43.5
Hypertensive diseases	I10-I15	32.5	38.9
Organic, including symptomatic, mental disorders	F01-F09	54.4	33.9

Note: (a) ICD-10 = International Classification of Diseases 10th Revision; (1) Includes COVID-19, adverse effects to COVID-19 vaccines, SARS, and vaping-related disorders; (2) Crude mortality rates are a three-year average covering 2021-2023; (3) Figures cover Allegheny County.
Source: Centers for Disease Control and Prevention, National Center for Health Statistics. National Vital Statistics System, Mortality 2018-2023 on CDC WONDER Online Database

Mortality Rates for Selected Causes of Death

Cause of Death	ICD-10[a] Code	Crude Mortality Rate[1] per 100,000 population	
		County[2]	U.S.
Accidental poisoning and exposure to noxious substances	X40-X49	50.4	30.5
Alzheimer disease	G30	35.2	35.4
Assault	X85-Y09	9.0	7.3
COVID-19	U07.1	62.5	65.3
Diabetes mellitus	E10-E14	27.3	30.0
Diseases of the liver	K70-K76	20.8	20.8
Human immunodeficiency virus (HIV) disease	B20-B24	0.6	1.5
Influenza and pneumonia	J09-J18	13.5	13.4
Intentional self-harm	X60-X84	13.7	14.7
Malnutrition	E40-E46	11.2	6.0
Obesity and other hyperalimentation	E65-E68	3.2	3.1
Renal failure	N17-N19	22.0	16.4
Transport accidents	V01-V99	7.5	14.4

Note: (a) ICD-10 = International Classification of Diseases 10th Revision; (1) Crude mortality rates are a three-year average covering 2021-2023; (2) Figures cover Allegheny County; Data are suppressed when the data meet the criteria for confidentiality constraints; Crude mortality rates are flagged as unreliable when the rate would be calculated with a numerator of 20 or less.
Source: Centers for Disease Control and Prevention, National Center for Health Statistics. National Vital Statistics System, Mortality 2018-2023 on CDC WONDER Online Database

Health Insurance Coverage

Area	With Health Insurance	With Private Health Insurance	With Public Health Insurance	Without Health Insurance	Population Under Age 19 Without Health Insurance
City	94.8	72.9	33.5	5.2	3.8
MSA[1]	96.2	74.5	37.9	3.8	2.4
U.S.	91.4	67.3	36.3	8.6	5.4

Note: Figures are percentages that cover the civilian noninstitutionalized population; (1) Figures cover the Pittsburgh, PA Metropolitan Statistical Area
Source: U.S. Census Bureau, 2019-2023 American Community Survey 5-Year Estimates

Number of Medical Professionals

Area	MDs[3]	DOs[3,4]	Dentists	Podiatrists	Chiropractors	Optometrists
County[1] (number)	8,358	733	1,219	114	550	259
County[1] (rate[2])	677.7	59.4	99.5	9.3	44.9	21.1
U.S. (rate[2])	302.5	29.2	74.6	6.4	29.5	18.0

Note: Data as of 2023 unless noted; (1) Data covers Allegheny County; (2) Number of medical professionals per 100,000 population; (3) Data as of 2022 and includes all active, non-federal physicians; (4) Doctor of Osteopathic Medicine
Source: U.S. Department of Health and Human Services, Health Resources and Services Administration, Bureau of Health Professions, Area Resource File (ARF) 2023-2024

Best Hospitals

According to *U.S. News,* the Pittsburgh, PA metro area is home to five of the best hospitals in the U.S.: **AHN West Penn Hospital** (1 adult specialty); **UPMC Magee-Womens Hospital** (1 adult specialty); **UPMC Mercy** (1 adult specialty); **UPMC Presbyterian Shadyside** (7 adult specialties); **UPMC Western Psychiatric Hospital** (7 adult specialties). The hospitals listed were nationally ranked in at least one of 15 adult or 11 pediatric specialties. The number of specialties shown cover the parent hospital. Only 160 U.S. hospitals performed well enough to be nationally ranked in one or more specialties. Twenty hospitals in the U.S. made the Honor Roll. The Best Hospitals Honor Roll takes both the national rankings and the procedure and condition ratings into account. Hospitals received points if they were nationally ranked in one of the 15 adult specialties—the higher they ranked, the more points they got—and how many ratings of "high performing" they earned in the 20 procedures and conditions. *U.S. News Online, "America's Best Hospitals 2024-25"*

According to *U.S. News,* the Pittsburgh, PA metro area is home to two of the best children's hospitals in the U.S.: **UPMC Children's Hospital of Pittsburgh** (11 pediatric specialties); **UPMC Children's Hospital of Pittsburgh-Shriners Hospitals for Children Erie** (11 pediatric specialties). The hospitals listed were highly ranked in at least one of 11 pediatric specialties. One hundred five children's hospitals in the U.S. were nationally ranked in at least one specialty. Hospitals received points for being ranked in a specialty, and the 10 hospitals with the most points across the 11 specialties make up the Honor Roll. *U.S. News Online, "America's Best Children's Hospitals 2024-25"*

EDUCATION

Public School District Statistics

District Name	Schls	Pupils	Pupil/Teacher Ratio	Minority Pupils[1] (%)	Total Rev. per Pupil ($)	Total Exp. per Pupil ($)
Baldwin-Whitehall SD	4	4,484	16.6	36.9	18,838	18,807
Chartiers Valley SD	4	3,522	15.4	24.3	22,264	22,278
Fox Chapel Area SD	6	4,181	12.8	21.7	26,807	24,861
Mount Lebanon SD	10	5,492	13.8	18.6	21,058	19,806
North Allegheny SD	11	8,554	13.9	29.5	22,145	20,851
North Hills SD	6	4,648	13.6	18.9	20,125	19,209
Penn Hills SD	3	3,016	15.2	78.9	33,106	30,034
Pittsburgh SD	56	19,769	11.4	70.6	38,882	37,128
Upper Saint Clair SD	6	3,967	14.2	21.2	24,198	24,170

Note: Table includes school districts with 2,000 or more students; (1) Percentage of students that are not non-Hispanic white.
Source: U.S. Department of Education, National Center for Education Statistics, Common Core of Data, Local Education Agency (School District) Universe Survey: School Year 2023-2024; U.S. Department of Education, National Center for Education Statistics, Common Core of Data, School District Finance Survey (F-33): School Year 2021–22

Best High Schools

According to *U.S. News*, Pittsburgh is home to two of the top 500 high schools in the U.S.: **Pittsburgh CAPA 6-12** (#413); **Upper Saint Clair High School** (#426). Nearly 25,000 public, magnet and charter schools were ranked based on their performance on state assessments and how well they prepare students for college. *U.S. News & World Report, "Best High Schools 2024"*

Highest Level of Education

Area	Less than H.S.	H.S. Diploma	Some College, No Deg.	Associate Degree	Bachelor's Degree	Master's Degree	Prof. School Degree	Doctorate Degree
City	5.7	23.7	14.7	8.0	24.6	14.1	4.5	4.6
MSA[1]	5.1	31.4	15.5	10.6	22.6	10.6	2.3	1.9
U.S.	10.6	26.2	19.4	8.8	21.3	9.8	2.3	1.6

Note: Figures cover persons age 25 and over; (1) Figures cover the Pittsburgh, PA Metropolitan Statistical Area
Source: U.S. Census Bureau, 2019-2023 American Community Survey 5-Year Estimates

Educational Attainment by Race

Area	High School Graduate or Higher (%)					Bachelor's Degree or Higher (%)				
	Total	White	Black	Asian	Hisp.[2]	Total	White	Black	Asian	Hisp.[2]
City	94.3	95.7	90.6	92.3	87.4	47.8	53.2	20.3	82.0	55.8
MSA[1]	94.9	95.4	91.7	87.5	86.9	37.4	37.8	21.5	69.8	39.9
U.S.	89.4	92.9	88.1	88.0	72.5	35.0	37.7	24.7	57.0	19.9

Note: Figures shown cover persons 25 years old and over; (1) Figures cover the Pittsburgh, PA Metropolitan Statistical Area; (2) People of Hispanic origin can be of any race
Source: U.S. Census Bureau, 2019-2023 American Community Survey 5-Year Estimates

School Enrollment by Grade and Control

Area	Preschool (%)		Kindergarten (%)		Grades 1 - 4 (%)		Grades 5 - 8 (%)		Grades 9 - 12 (%)	
	Public	Private	Public	Private	Public	Private	Public	Private	Public	Private
City	53.9	46.1	71.0	29.0	75.1	24.9	79.8	20.2	79.1	20.9
MSA[1]	52.6	47.4	81.9	18.1	87.4	12.6	89.1	10.9	89.6	10.4
U.S.	58.7	41.3	85.2	14.8	87.2	12.8	87.9	12.1	89.0	11.0

Note: Figures shown cover persons 3 years old and over; (1) Figures cover the Pittsburgh, PA Metropolitan Statistical Area
Source: U.S. Census Bureau, 2019-2023 American Community Survey 5-Year Estimates

Higher Education

Four-Year Colleges			Two-Year Colleges			Medical Schools[1]	Law Schools[2]	Voc/Tech[3]
Public	Private Non-profit	Private For-profit	Public	Private Non-profit	Private For-profit			
8	17	0	4	10	10	1	2	17

Note: Figures cover institutions located within the Pittsburgh, PA Metropolitan Statistical Area and include main campuses only; (1) includes schools accredited by the Liaison Committee on Medical Education and the American Osteopathic Association's Commission on Osteopathic College Accreditation; (2) includes ABA-accredited schools, schools with provisional ABA accreditation, and state accredited schools; (3) includes all schools with programs that are less than 2 years.
Source: National Center for Education Statistics, Integrated Postsecondary Education System (IPEDS), 2023-24; Wikipedia, List of Medical Schools in the United States, accessed May 2, 2025; Wikipedia, List of Law Schools in the United States, accessed May 2, 2025

According to *U.S. News & World Report,* the Pittsburgh, PA metro area is home to three of the top 200 national universities in the U.S.: **Carnegie Mellon University** (#21 tie); **University of Pittsburgh** (#70 tie); **Duquesne University** (#165 tie). The indicators used to capture academic quality fall into a number of categories: assessment by administrators at peer institutions; retention of students; faculty resources; student selectivity; financial resources; alumni giving; high school counselor ratings of colleges; and graduation rate. *U.S. News & World Report,* "America's Best Colleges 2025"

According to *U.S. News & World Report,* the Pittsburgh, PA metro area is home to one of the top 100 liberal arts colleges in the U.S.: **Washington & Jefferson College** (#90 tie). The indicators used to capture academic quality fall into a number of categories: assessment by administrators at peer institutions; retention of students; faculty resources; student selectivity; financial resources; alumni giving; high school counselor ratings of colleges; and graduation rate. *U.S. News & World Report,* "America's Best Colleges 2025"

According to *U.S. News & World Report,* the Pittsburgh, PA metro area is home to two of the top 100 law schools in the U.S.: **University of Pittsburgh 1** (#79 tie); **Duquesne University (Kline)** (#92 tie). The rankings are based on a weighted average of 12 measures of quality: peer assessment score; assessment score by lawyers/judges; median LSAT scores; median undergrad GPA; acceptance rate; employment rates for graduates; placement success; bar passage rate; faculty resources; expenditures per student; student/faculty ratio; and library resources. *U.S. News & World Report,* "America's Best Graduate Schools, Law, 2025"

According to *U.S. News & World Report,* the Pittsburgh, PA metro area is home to one of the top medical schools for research in the U.S.: **University of Pittsburgh** (Tier 1). *U.S. News* placed medical and osteopathic schools into tiers based on their research productivity, faculty and admissions data. Each school's tier was derived from its overall score, calculated by summing the weighted normalized values generated across several factors of academic quality, outlined below. There are four tiers, with tier 1 medical schools as the highest-performing and tier 4 as the lowest-performing. Only tier 1 and 2 schools are shown. Because of the tier presentation, *U.S. News* calculated overall scores based on their percentile performance among all rated schools instead of dividing against the rescaled score of the No. 1-performing schools. Tier 1 included schools with overall scores of 85 to 99. The cutoffs for tiers 2 through 4 were schools scoring 50 to 84, 15 to 49 and 1 to 14, respectively. The rankings are based on a weighted average of the following measures of quality: total research activity; average research activity per faculty member; total NIH research grants at the medical school and its affiliated hospitals; average NIH research grants per faculty; median MCAT total score; median undergraduate GPA; acceptance rate; and faculty resources. *U.S. News & World Report,* "America's Best Graduate Schools, Medical, 2025"

According to *U.S. News & World Report,* the Pittsburgh, PA metro area is home to one of the top medical schools for primary care in the U.S.: **University of Pittsburgh** (Tier 2). *U.S. News* placed medical and osteopathic schools into tiers based on their research productivity, faculty and admissions data. Each school's tier was derived from its overall score, calculated by summing the weighted normalized values generated across several factors of academic quality, outlined below. There are four tiers, with tier 1 medical schools as the highest-performing and tier 4 as the lowest-performing. Only tier 1 and 2 schools are shown. Because of the tier presentation, *U.S. News* calculated overall scores based on their percentile performance among all rated schools instead of dividing against the rescaled score of the No. 1-performing schools. Tier 1 included schools with overall scores of 85 to 99. The cutoffs for tiers 2 through 4 were schools scoring 50 to 84, 15 to 49 and 1 to 14, respectively. The rankings are based on a weighted average of the following measures of quality: graduates practicing in primary care specialties; graduates entering primary care residencies; median MCAT total score; median undergraduate GPA; acceptance rate; and faculty resources. *U.S. News & World Report,* "America's Best Graduate Schools, Medical, 2025"

According to *U.S. News & World Report,* the Pittsburgh, PA metro area is home to two of the top 75 business schools in the U.S.: **Carnegie Mellon University (Tepper)** (#18 tie); **University of Pittsburgh (Katz)** (#46 tie). The rankings are based on a weighted average of the following nine measures: quality assessment; peer assessment; recruiter assessment; placement success; mean starting salary and bonus; student selectivity; mean GMAT and GRE scores; mean undergraduate GPA; and acceptance rate. *U.S. News & World Report,* "America's Best Graduate Schools, Business, 2025"

EMPLOYERS

Major Employers

Company Name	Industry
Allegheny General Hospital	Extended care facility
Associated Cleaning Consultants	Janitorial service, contract basis
Bayer Corporation	Pharmaceutical preparations
Children's Hospital of Pittsburgh	Specialty hospitals, except psychiatric
City of Pittsburgh	Local government
Duquesne University of the Holy Spirit	Colleges & universities
Highmark	Hospital & medical services plans
Jefferson Regional Medical Center	General medical & surgical hospitals
Magee-Womens Hospital of UPMC	Hospital, affiliated with ama residency
Mercy Life Center Corporation	Mental health clinic, outpatient
PNC Bank	National trust companies with deposits, commercial
U.S. Dept of Energy	Noncommercial research organizations
United States Steel Corporation	Blast furnaces & steel mills
United States Steel International	Steel
University of Pittsburgh	Colleges & universities
UPMC Mercy	General medical & surgical hospitals
UPMC Shadyside	General medical & surgical hospitals
Veterans Health Administration	Administration of veterans' affairs
West Penn Allegheny Health System	Management services

Note: Companies shown are located within the Pittsburgh, PA Metropolitan Statistical Area.
Source: Chambers of Commerce; State Departments of Labor; Wikipedia

Best Companies to Work For

PPG, headquartered in Pittsburgh, is among the "Best Places to Work in IT." To qualify, companies had to have a minimum of 100 total employees and five IT employees. The best places to work were selected based on DEI (diversity, equity, and inclusion) practices; IT turnover, promotions, and growth; IT retention and engagement programs; remote/hybrid working; benefits and perks (such as elder care and child care, flextime, and reimbursement for college tuition); and training and career development opportunities. *Computerworld, "Best Places to Work in IT," 2025*

PUBLIC SAFETY

Crime Rate

Area	Total Crime Rate	Violent Crime Rate				Property Crime Rate		
		Murder	Rape	Robbery	Aggrav. Assault	Burglary	Larceny-Theft	Motor Vehicle Theft
City	n/a	n/a	n/a	n/a	n/a	n/a	n/a	n/a
U.S.	2,290.9	5.7	38.0	66.5	264.1	250.7	1,347.2	318.7

Note: Figures are crimes per 100,000 population; n/a not available.
Source: FBI, Table 8, Offenses Known to Law Enforcement, by State by City, 2023

Hate Crimes

Area	Number of Quarters Reported	Number of Incidents per Bias Motivation					
		Race/Ethnicity/Ancestry	Religion	Sexual Orientation	Disability	Gender	Gender Identity
City	3	9	1	0	0	0	0
U.S.	4	5,900	2,699	2,077	187	92	492

Source: Federal Bureau of Investigation, Hate Crime Statistics 2023

Identity Theft Consumer Reports

Area	Reports	Reports per 100,000 Population	Rank[2]
MSA[1]	4,571	187	184
U.S.	1,135,291	339	-

Note: (1) Figures cover the Pittsburgh, PA Metropolitan Statistical Area; (2) Rank ranges from 1 to 401 where 1 indicates greatest number of identity theft reports per 100,000 population
Source: Federal Trade Commission, Consumer Sentinel Network Data Book 2024

Fraud and Other Consumer Reports

Area	Reports	Reports per 100,000 Population	Rank[2]
MSA[1]	30,335	1,241	115
U.S.	5,360,641	1,601	-

Note: (1) Figures cover the Pittsburgh, PA Metropolitan Statistical Area; (2) Rank ranges from 1 to 401 where 1 indicates greatest number of fraud and other consumer reports per 100,000 population
Source: Federal Trade Commission, Consumer Sentinel Network Data Book 2024

POLITICS

2024 Presidential Election Results

Area	Trump (Rep.)	Harris (Dem.)	Stein (Green)	Kennedy (Ind.)	Oliver (Lib.)	Other
Allegheny County	39.2	59.4	0.5	0.0	0.5	0.5
U.S.	49.7	48.2	0.6	0.5	0.4	0.6

Note: Results are percentages and may not add to 100% due to rounding
Source: Dave Leip's Atlas of U.S. Presidential Elections

SPORTS

Professional Sports Teams

Team Name	League	Year Established
Pittsburgh Penguins	National Hockey League (NHL)	1967
Pittsburgh Pirates	Major League Baseball (MLB)	1882
Pittsburgh Steelers	National Football League (NFL)	1933

Note: Includes teams located in the Pittsburgh, PA Metropolitan Statistical Area.
Source: Wikipedia, Major Professional Sports Teams of the United States and Canada, May 1, 2025

CLIMATE

Average and Extreme Temperatures

Temperature	Jan	Feb	Mar	Apr	May	Jun	Jul	Aug	Sep	Oct	Nov	Dec	Yr.
Extreme High (°F)	75	69	83	89	91	98	103	100	97	89	82	74	103
Average High (°F)	35	38	48	61	71	79	83	81	75	63	50	39	60
Average Temp. (°F)	28	30	39	50	60	68	73	71	64	53	42	32	51
Average Low (°F)	20	22	29	39	49	57	62	61	54	43	34	25	41
Extreme Low (°F)	-18	-12	-1	14	26	34	42	39	31	16	-1	-12	-18

Note: Figures cover the years 1948-1990
Source: National Climatic Data Center, International Station Meteorological Climate Summary, 9/96

Average Precipitation/Snowfall/Humidity

Precip./Humidity	Jan	Feb	Mar	Apr	May	Jun	Jul	Aug	Sep	Oct	Nov	Dec	Yr.
Avg. Precip. (in.)	2.8	2.4	3.4	3.3	3.6	3.9	3.8	3.2	2.8	2.4	2.7	2.8	37.1
Avg. Snowfall (in.)	11	9	8	2	Tr	0	0	0	0	Tr	4	8	43
Avg. Rel. Hum. 7am (%)	76	75	75	73	76	79	82	86	85	81	78	77	79
Avg. Rel. Hum. 4pm (%)	64	60	54	49	50	51	53	54	55	53	60	66	56

Note: Figures cover the years 1948-1990; Tr = Trace amounts (<0.05 in. of rain; <0.5 in. of snow)
Source: National Climatic Data Center, International Station Meteorological Climate Summary, 9/96

Weather Conditions

Temperature			Daytime Sky			Precipitation		
5°F & below	32°F & below	90°F & above	Clear	Partly cloudy	Cloudy	0.01 inch or more precip.	0.1 inch or more snow/ice	Thunder-storms
9	121	8	62	137	166	154	42	35

Note: Figures are average number of days per year and cover the years 1948-1990
Source: National Climatic Data Center, International Station Meteorological Climate Summary, 9/96

HAZARDOUS WASTE

Superfund Sites

The Pittsburgh, PA metro area is home to three sites on the EPA's Superfund National Priorities List (NPL) or Superfund Alternative Approach (SAA) list: **Breslube-Penn, Inc.** (Final NPL); **Lindane Dump** (Final NPL); **Ohio River Park** (Final NPL). The Superfund alternative approach uses the same investigation and cleanup process and standards that are used for sites listed on the National Priorities List. The SAA is an alternative to listing a site on the NPL; it is not an alternative to Superfund or the Superfund process. There are a total of 1,445 Superfund sites with a status of proposed or final on both lists in the United States. *U.S. Environmental Protection Agency, National Priorities List, May 1, 2025; U.S. Environmental Protection Agency, Superfund Alternative Approach Sites, May 1, 2025*

AIR QUALITY

Air Quality Trends: Ozone

	1990	1995	2000	2005	2010	2015	2020	2021	2022	2023
MSA[1]	0.080	0.100	0.084	0.083	0.077	0.070	0.066	0.066	0.064	0.067
U.S.	0.087	0.089	0.081	0.080	0.072	0.068	0.066	0.067	0.067	0.070

Note: (1) Data covers the Pittsburgh, PA Metropolitan Statistical Area. The values shown are the composite ozone concentration averages among trend sites based on the highest fourth daily maximum 8-hour concentration in parts per million. These trends are based on sites having an adequate record of monitoring data during the trend period. Data from exceptional events are included.
Source: U.S. Environmental Protection Agency, Air Quality Monitoring Information, "Air Quality Trends by City, 1990-2023"

Air Quality Index

Area	Percent of Days when Air Quality was...[2]					AQI Statistics[2]	
	Good	Moderate	Unhealthy for Sensitive Groups	Unhealthy	Very Unhealthy	Maximum	Median
MSA[1]	26.8	66.6	5.5	0.5	0.5	237	58

Note: (1) Data covers the Pittsburgh, PA Metropolitan Statistical Area; (2) Based on 365 days with AQI data in 2023. Air Quality Index (AQI) is an index for reporting daily air quality. EPA calculates the AQI for five major air pollutants regulated by the Clean Air Act: ground-level ozone, particle pollution (aka particulate matter), carbon monoxide, sulfur dioxide, and nitrogen dioxide. The AQI runs from 0 to 500. The higher the AQI value, the greater the level of air pollution and the greater the health concern. There are six AQI categories: "Good" AQI is between 0 and 50. Air quality is considered satisfactory; "Moderate" AQI is between 51 and 100. Air quality is acceptable; "Unhealthy for Sensitive Groups" When AQI values are between 101 and 150, members of sensitive groups may experience health effects; "Unhealthy" When AQI values are between 151 and 200 everyone may begin to experience health effects; "Very Unhealthy" AQI values between 201 and 300 trigger a health alert; "Hazardous" AQI values over 300 trigger warnings of emergency conditions (not shown).
Source: U.S. Environmental Protection Agency, Air Quality Index Report, 2023

Air Quality Index Pollutants

Area	Percent of Days when AQI Pollutant was...[2]					
	Carbon Monoxide	Nitrogen Dioxide	Ozone	Sulfur Dioxide	Particulate Matter 2.5	Particulate Matter 10
MSA[1]	0.0	0.0	19.7	(3)	80.3	0.0

Note: (1) Data covers the Pittsburgh, PA Metropolitan Statistical Area; (2) Based on 365 days with AQI data in 2023. The Air Quality Index (AQI) is an index for reporting daily air quality. EPA calculates the AQI for five major air pollutants regulated by the Clean Air Act: ground-level ozone, particle pollution (also known as particulate matter), carbon monoxide, sulfur dioxide, and nitrogen dioxide. The AQI runs from 0 to 500. The higher the AQI value, the greater the level of air pollution and the greater the health concern; (3) Sulfur dioxide is no longer included in this table because SO_2 concentrations tend to be very localized and not necessarily representative of broad geographical areas like counties and CBSAs.
Source: U.S. Environmental Protection Agency, Air Quality Index Report, 2023

Maximum Air Pollutant Concentrations: Particulate Matter, Ozone, CO and Lead

	Particulate Matter 10 (ug/m³)	Particulate Matter 2.5 Wtd AM (ug/m³)	Particulate Matter 2.5 24-Hr (ug/m³)	Ozone (ppm)	Carbon Monoxide (ppm)	Lead (ug/m³)
MSA[1] Level	168	12	36	0.071	3	0
NAAQS[2]	150	15	35	0.075	9	0.15
Met NAAQS[2]	No	Yes	No	Yes	Yes	Yes

Note: (1) Data covers the Pittsburgh, PA Metropolitan Statistical Area; Data from exceptional events are included; (2) National Ambient Air Quality Standards; ppm = parts per million; ug/m³ = micrograms per cubic meter; n/a not available.
Concentrations: Particulate Matter 10 (coarse particulate)—highest second maximum 24-hour concentration; Particulate Matter 2.5 Wtd AM (fine particulate)—highest weighted annual mean concentration; Particulate Matter 2.5 24-Hour (fine particulate)—highest 98th percentile 24-hour concentration; Ozone—highest fourth daily maximum 8-hour concentration; Carbon Monoxide—highest second maximum non-overlapping 8-hour concentration; Lead—maximum running 3-month average
Source: U.S. Environmental Protection Agency, Air Quality Monitoring Information, "Air Quality Statistics by City, 2023"

Maximum Air Pollutant Concentrations: Nitrogen Dioxide and Sulfur Dioxide

	Nitrogen Dioxide AM (ppb)	Nitrogen Dioxide 1-Hr (ppb)	Sulfur Dioxide AM (ppb)	Sulfur Dioxide 1-Hr (ppb)	Sulfur Dioxide 24-Hr (ppb)
MSA[1] Level	9	38	n/a	65	n/a
NAAQS[2]	53	100	30	75	140
Met NAAQS[2]	Yes	Yes	n/a	Yes	n/a

Note: (1) Data covers the Pittsburgh, PA Metropolitan Statistical Area; Data from exceptional events are included; (2) National Ambient Air Quality Standards; ppm = parts per million; ug/m³ = micrograms per cubic meter; n/a not available.
Concentrations: Nitrogen Dioxide AM—highest arithmetic mean concentration; Nitrogen Dioxide 1-Hr—highest 98th percentile 1-hour daily maximum concentration; Sulfur Dioxide AM—highest annual mean concentration; Sulfur Dioxide 1-Hr—highest 99th percentile 1-hour daily maximum concentration; Sulfur Dioxide 24-Hr—highest second maximum 24-hour concentration
Source: U.S. Environmental Protection Agency, Air Quality Monitoring Information, "Air Quality Statistics by City, 2023"

Providence, Rhode Island

Background

Providence, the capital of Rhode Island, sits at the head of Narragansett Bay. It's one of the nation's most historic and inviting cities, known for having big city qualities on a small city scale.

Providence was founded in 1636 by Roger Williams, the Massachusetts preacher exiled by the Puritans for his radical religious ideas. In a reversal of the usual procedure, Williams first obtained title to the land directly from the Narragansett Native American tribe, and then in 1644 he received a Royal Charter from London for the settlement.

Though the economy originally depended on agriculture, trade soon dominated. Whaling was an important activity not only to Providence but to all of Rhode Island's ports. During this trade, several Rhode Islanders amassed considerable wealth and endowed many of Providence's enduring public and cultural institutions, including Brown University, one of the nation's oldest.

After the Revolution, Providence industrialized and became a major center for the textile, silver, and jewelry trades. Plating base metal with gold or silver was an innovation born from Providence workshops. By the time of the Civil War, the economy had shifted from mercantile shipping to fully industrial, making the city a major economic resource to the Union during the Civil War.

By the mid-twentieth century, Providence's population had declined and government mismanagement, along with the national decline of heavy industry, combined for a negative effect on the city. Since the 1980s, however, reforms and improvements have brought to Providence a renaissance of jobs, city services, downtown revitalization, and cultural assets. The city is now regarded, particularly by younger professionals, as one of the most desirable urban locations on the East Coast. Educational and cultural assets include museums, theaters, an award-winning zoo, highly acclaimed restaurants, and renowned venues for arts and entertainment. Providence and the surrounding areas have been a backdrop for several movies and television series and the city continues to lure filmmakers by offering a tax credit to motion picture companies.

A living testament to Providence's renaissance is WaterFire, a fire sculpture installation by Barnaby Evans which burns anew each spring on downtown Providence's three rivers. Waterplace Park and Riverwalk was perhaps the most important revitalization project to happen in Providence for many years. Parts of the river that had long been paved over were reopened, and park areas were created along the banks. The picturesque river is now used routinely for boating and sculling and by the Brown University rowing crews.

Downtown Providence offers the Providence Place Mall, a state-of-the-art emporium that mirrors the historically mercantile character of the city, and the famous 1922 Biltmore Hotel. A favorite Providence neighborhood, College Hill, connects the campuses of Brown University and the Rhode Island School of Design with cafes, restaurants, shops, and street vendors.

Providence is home to 120 parks that cover 1,600 acres. In addition to Waterplace Park and the Riverwalk, the city boasts Roger Williams Park, Roger Williams National Memorial, and Prospect Terrace Park with expansive views of the downtown area, as well as a 15-foot tall granite statue of Roger Williams. As one of the first cities in America, Providence contains many historic buildings, while the East Side neighborhood in particular includes the largest contiguous area of buildings listed on the National Register of Historic Places in the U.S., with many pre-revolutionary houses.

Getting around Providence is getting easier. In 2020, Providence's public transit system expanded service in the city, and Transit Master Plan 2050 sees improvements or expansions to all aspects of public transportation, including the recent construction of 60 miles of bike paths, bike lanes, and greenways.

The city is considered one of the most active gay and lesbian communities in the Northeast. Former mayor David Cicilline ran as openly gay, and former Mayor Cianci instituted the position of Mayor's Liaison to the Gay and Lesbian community in the 1990s.

Providence enjoys variable southern New England weather with temperatures slightly moderated by the city's proximity to Narragansett Bay and the Atlantic Ocean. The weather is changeable, due to the convergence of weather systems from the west, the Gulf of Mexico, and the North Atlantic. Precipitation is evenly distributed throughout the year.

Rankings

Business/Finance Rankings

- The Providence metro area appeared on the Milken Institute "2025 Best Performing Cities" list. Rank: #182 out of 200 large metro areas (based on performance category). Criteria: job growth; wage growth; high-tech growth and impact; community resilience; housing affordability; household broadband access. *Milken Institute, "Best-Performing Cities 2025," January 14, 2025*

Culture/Performing Arts Rankings

- Providence was selected as one of the ten best small North American cities and towns for moviemakers. Of cities with smaller populations, the area ranked #4. As with the 2025 list for bigger cities, film community and culture were highly factored in. Other criteria: access to equipment and facilities; affordability; tax incentives; and quality of life. *MovieMaker Magazine, "Best Places to Live and Work as a Moviemaker, 2025," January 29, 2025*

Education Rankings

- Personal finance website *WalletHub* analyzed the 150 largest U.S. metropolitan statistical areas to determine where the most educated Americans are putting their degrees to work. Criteria: education levels; percentage of workers with degrees; education quality and attainment gap; public school quality rankings; quality and enrollment of each metro area's universities. Providence was ranked #97 (#1 = most educated city). *WalletHub.com, "Most & Least Educated Cities in America, 2025" July 2, 2024*

Environmental Rankings

- Sperling's *BestPlaces* assessed the 50 largest metropolitan areas of the United States for the likelihood of dangerously extreme weather events or earthquakes. In general the Southeast and South-Central regions have the highest risk of weather extremes and earthquakes, while the Pacific Northwest enjoys the lowest risk. Of the least risky metropolitan areas, the Providence metro area was ranked #9. *Bestplaces.net, "Avoid Natural Disasters: BestPlaces Reveals The Top 10 Safest Places to Live," October 25, 2017*

Health/Fitness Rankings

- Providence was identified as a "2025 Allergy Capital." The area ranked #78 out of the nation's 100 largest metropolitan areas. Three groups of factors were used to identify the most challenging cities for people with allergies: annual tree, grass, and weed pollen scores; over the counter allergy medicine use; number of board-certified allergy specialists. *Asthma and Allergy Foundation of America, "2025 Allergy Capitals: The Most Challenging Places to Live with Allergies," March 18, 2025*

- Providence was identified as a "2024 Asthma Capital." The area ranked #10 out of the nation's 100 largest metropolitan areas. Criteria: estimated asthma prevalence; asthma-related mortality; and ER visits due to asthma. Risk factors analyzed but not factored in the rankings: annual air quality including pollution and ozone levels; public smoking laws; indoor air quality; access to asthma specialists; rescue and controller medication use; uninsured rate; pollen allergy; poverty rate. *Asthma and Allergy Foundation of America, "Asthma Capitals 2024: The Most Challenging Places to Live With Asthma," September 10, 2024*

Real Estate Rankings

- *WalletHub* compared the most populated U.S. cities to determine which had the best markets for real estate agents. Providence ranked #152 where demand was high and pay was the best. Criteria: sales per agent; annual median wage for real-estate agents; monthly average starting salary for real estate agents; real estate job density and competition; unemployment rate; home turnover rate; housing-market health index; and other relevant metrics. *WalletHub.com, "2021 Best Places to Be a Real Estate Agent," May 12, 2021*

- The Providence metro area was identified as one of the nations's 20 hottest housing markets in 2025. Criteria: unique listing views as an indicator of demand and number of days on the market as an indicator of pace. The area ranked #9. *Realtor.com, "January 2025 Top 20 Hottest Housing Markets," February 11, 2025*

- Providence was ranked #19 in the top 20 out of the 100 largest metro areas in terms of house price appreciation in 2024 (#1 = highest rate). *Federal Housing Finance Agency, "House Price Index, 4th Quarter 2024," February 25, 2025*

- The Providence metro area was identified as one of the 10 best condo markets in the U.S. in 2024. The area ranked #4 out of 63 markets. Criteria: year-over-year change of median sales price of existing apartment condo-coop homes between the 4th quarter of 2023 and the 4th quarter of 2024. *National Association of Realtors®, Median Sales Price of Existing Apartment Condo-Coops Homes for Metropolitan Areas, 4th Quarter 2024*
- Providence was ranked #139 out of 176 metro areas in terms of cost of housing in 2024 by the National Association of Home Builders (#1 = most affordable). Criteria: the portion of an average family's income necessary to pay the mortgage on a median-priced home. *National Association of Home Builders®, NAHB-Wells Fargo Cost of Housing Index, 4th Quarter 2024*

Safety Rankings

- Allstate ranked the 100 most populous cities in America in terms of driver safety. Providence ranked #35. Criteria based on anonymized driving behavior data from Allstate's mobile app powered by Arity: high speed driving (over 80 mph), phone handling, and hard braking. The report helps increase the importance of safety and awareness behind the wheel. *Allstate, "16th Allstate America's Best Drivers Report®" July 11, 2024*

Women/Minorities Rankings

- Personal finance website *WalletHub* compared more than 180 U.S. cities across two key dimensions, "Hispanic Business-Friendliness" and "Hispanic Purchasing Power," to arrive at the most favorable conditions for Hispanic entrepreneurs. Providence was ranked #178 out of 182. Criteria includes: share of Hispanic-Owned Businesses; average growth of Hispanic Business revenues; Small Business-Friendliness score; affordability; and number of Hispanics with at least a bachelor's degree. *WalletHub.com, "Best Cities for Hispanic Entrepreneurs," September 4, 2024*

Miscellaneous Rankings

- *MoveHub* ranked 446 hipster cities across 20 countries, using its new and improved alternative Hipster Index and Providence came out as #33 among the top 50. Criteria: population over 150,000; number of vintage boutiques; density of tattoo parlors; vegan places to eat; coffee shops; and density of vinyl record stores. *MoveHub.com, "The Hipster Index: Brighton Pips Portland to Global Top Spot," July 28, 2021*
- *WalletHub* compared 148 of the most populated U.S. cities to determine their operating efficiency. A "Quality of Services" score was constructed for each city and then measured against the total budget per capita to reveal which were managed the best. Providence ranked #60. Criteria: financial stability; economy; education; safety; health; infrastructure and pollution. *WalletHub.com, "2025's Best- & Worst-Run Cities in America," June 18, 2024*

Business Environment

DEMOGRAPHICS

Population Growth

Area	1990 Census	2000 Census	2010 Census	2020 Census	2023 Estimate[2]	Population Growth 1990-2023 (%)
City	160,734	173,618	178,042	190,934	190,214	18.3
MSA[1]	1,509,789	1,582,997	1,600,852	1,676,579	1,673,807	10.9
U.S.	248,709,873	281,421,906	308,745,538	331,449,281	332,387,540	33.6

Note: (1) Figures cover the Providence-Warwick, RI-MA Metropolitan Statistical Area; (2) 2019-2023 5-year ACS population estimate
Source: U.S. Census Bureau, 1990 Census, 2000 Census, 2010 Census, 2020 Census, 2019-2023 American Community Survey 5-Year Estimates

Race

Area	White Alone[2] (%)	Black Alone[2] (%)	Asian Alone[2] (%)	AIAN[3] Alone[2] (%)	NHOPI[4] Alone[2] (%)	Other Race Alone[2] (%)	Two or More Races (%)
City	40.7	13.3	5.9	1.0	0.1	20.4	18.7
MSA[1]	74.5	5.3	3.1	0.4	0.1	6.6	10.0
U.S.	63.4	12.4	5.8	0.9	0.2	6.6	10.7

Note: (1) Figures cover the Providence-Warwick, RI-MA Metropolitan Statistical Area; (2) Alone is defined as not being in combination with one or more other races; (3) American Indian and Alaska Native; (4) Native Hawaiian and Other Pacific Islander
Source: U.S. Census Bureau, 2019-2023 American Community Survey 5-Year Estimates

Hispanic or Latino Origin

Area	Total (%)	Mexican (%)	Puerto Rican (%)	Cuban (%)	Other (%)
City	44.3	1.6	6.8	0.3	35.6
MSA[1]	14.6	1.0	4.3	0.2	9.1
U.S.	19.0	11.3	1.8	0.7	5.2

Note: Persons of Hispanic or Latino origin can be of any race; (1) Figures cover the Providence-Warwick, RI-MA Metropolitan Statistical Area
Source: U.S. Census Bureau, 2019-2023 American Community Survey 5-Year Estimates

Age

Area	Under Age 5	Age 5–19	Age 20–34	Age 35–44	Age 45–54	Age 55–64	Age 65–74	Age 75–84	Age 85+	Median Age
City	5.4	20.3	28.3	12.6	11.9	10.0	6.8	3.3	1.5	32.9
MSA[1]	5.0	17.6	20.1	12.6	12.6	14.2	10.6	5.2	2.2	40.6
U.S.	5.7	19.1	20.2	13.1	12.3	12.8	10.0	4.9	1.9	38.7

Note: (1) Figures cover the Providence-Warwick, RI-MA Metropolitan Statistical Area
Source: U.S. Census Bureau, 2019-2023 American Community Survey 5-Year Estimates

Disability by Age

Area	All Ages	Under 18 Years Old	18 to 64 Years Old	65 Years and Over
City	13.7	6.0	12.4	37.3
MSA[1]	13.9	5.6	11.7	31.4
U.S.	13.0	4.7	10.7	32.9

Note: Figures show percent of the civilian noninstitutionalized population that reported having a disability. Disability status is determined from six types of difficulty: vision, hearing, cognitive, ambulatory, self-care, and independent living. For children under 5 years old, hearing and vision difficulty are used to determine disability status. For children between the ages of 5 and 14, disability status is determined from hearing, vision, cognitive, ambulatory, and self-care difficulties. For people aged 15 years and older, they are considered to have a disability if they have difficulty with any one of the six difficulty types; Note: (1) Figures cover the Providence-Warwick, RI-MA Metropolitan Statistical Area
Source: U.S. Census Bureau, 2019-2023 American Community Survey 5-Year Estimates

Ancestry

Area	German	Irish	English	American	Italian	Polish	French[2]	European	Scottish
City	3.3	8.1	4.4	2.4	6.9	1.7	2.7	0.7	0.9
MSA[1]	4.5	16.5	10.8	3.4	12.8	3.2	7.9	0.7	1.5
U.S.	12.6	9.4	9.1	5.5	4.9	2.6	2.0	1.6	1.6

Note: Figures are the percentage of the total population reporting a particular ancestry. The nine most commonly reported ancestries in the U.S. are shown. Figures include multiple ancestries (e.g. if a person reported being Irish and Italian, they were included in both columns); (1) Figures cover the Providence-Warwick, RI-MA Metropolitan Statistical Area; (2) Excludes Basque
Source: U.S. Census Bureau, 2019-2023 American Community Survey 5-Year Estimates

Foreign-born Population

Area	Percent of Population Born in								
	Any Foreign Country	Asia	Mexico	Europe	Caribbean	Central America[2]	South America	Africa	Canada
City	32.8	3.9	0.5	2.2	15.3	5.9	1.2	3.4	0.3
MSA[1]	14.4	2.3	0.3	3.8	2.9	1.7	1.3	1.7	0.2
U.S.	13.9	4.3	3.3	1.4	1.4	1.2	1.2	0.8	0.2

Note: (1) Figures cover the Providence-Warwick, RI-MA Metropolitan Statistical Area; (2) Excludes Mexico.
Source: U.S. Census Bureau, 2019-2023 American Community Survey 5-Year Estimates

Household Size

Area	Persons in Household (%)							Average Household Size
	One	Two	Three	Four	Five	Six	Seven or More	
City	33.8	28.4	15.4	11.7	7.0	2.3	1.4	2.48
MSA[1]	29.5	33.7	16.3	12.9	5.1	1.6	0.9	2.41
U.S.	28.5	33.8	15.4	12.7	5.9	2.3	1.4	2.54

Note: (1) Figures cover the Providence-Warwick, RI-MA Metropolitan Statistical Area
Source: U.S. Census Bureau, 2019-2023 American Community Survey 5-Year Estimates

Household Relationships

Area	House-holder	Opposite-sex Spouse	Same-sex Spouse	Opposite-sex Unmarried Partner	Same-sex Unmarried Partner	Child[2]	Grand-child	Other Relatives	Non-relatives
City	36.5	10.5	0.3	2.9	0.3	27.3	1.9	5.7	6.1
MSA[1]	40.0	16.9	0.2	3.0	0.2	27.2	1.9	4.1	3.0
U.S.	38.3	17.5	0.2	2.5	0.2	28.3	2.4	4.8	3.4

Note: Figures are percent of the total population; (1) Figures cover the Providence-Warwick, RI-MA Metropolitan Statistical Area; (2) Includes biological, adopted, and stepchildren of the householder
Source: U.S. Census Bureau, 2020 Census

Gender

Area	Males	Females	Males per 100 Females
City	93,138	97,076	95.9
MSA[1]	819,607	854,200	96.0
U.S.	164,545,087	167,842,453	98.0

Note: (1) Figures cover the Providence-Warwick, RI-MA Metropolitan Statistical Area
Source: U.S. Census Bureau, 2019-2023 American Community Survey 5-Year Estimates

Marital Status

Area	Never Married	Now Married[2]	Separated	Widowed	Divorced
City	53.4	32.1	2.0	4.1	8.5
MSA[1]	36.7	45.0	1.5	5.8	11.0
U.S.	34.1	47.9	1.7	5.6	10.7

Note: Figures are percentages and cover the population 15 years of age and older; (1) Figures cover the Providence-Warwick, RI-MA Metropolitan Statistical Area; (2) Excludes separated
Source: U.S. Census Bureau, 2019-2023 American Community Survey 5-Year Estimates

Religious Groups by Family

Area	Catholic	Baptist	Methodist	LDS[2]	Pentecostal	Lutheran	Islam	Adventist	Other
MSA[1]	37.9	0.9	0.6	0.3	0.6	0.3	0.5	0.9	6.1
U.S.	18.7	7.3	3.0	2.0	1.8	1.7	1.3	1.3	11.6

Note: Figures are the number of adherents as a percentage of the total population and cover the eight largest religious groups in the U.S; (1) Figures cover the Providence-Warwick, RI-MA Metropolitan Statistical Area; (2) Church of Jesus Christ of Latter-day Saints
Sources: 2020 U.S. Religion Census, Association of Statisticians of American Religious Bodies; The Association of Religion Data Archives (ARDA)

Religious Groups by Tradition

Area	Catholic	Evangelical Protestant	Mainline Protestant	Black Protestant	Islam	Judaism	Hinduism	Orthodox	Buddhism
MSA[1]	37.9	4.0	3.2	0.1	0.5	0.6	0.1	0.5	0.2
U.S.	18.7	16.5	5.2	2.3	1.3	0.6	0.4	0.4	0.3

Note: Figures are the number of adherents as a percentage of the total population; (1) Figures cover the Providence-Warwick, RI-MA Metropolitan Statistical Area
Sources: 2020 U.S. Religion Census, Association of Statisticians of American Religious Bodies; The Association of Religion Data Archives (ARDA)

ECONOMY

Real Gross Domestic Product (GDP)

Area	2017	2018	2019	2020	2021	2022	2023	Rank[3]
MSA[1]	84.6	84.7	86.8	84.2	88.5	89.3	90.4	45
U.S.[2]	17,619.1	18,160.7	18,642.5	18,238.9	19,387.6	19,896.6	20,436.3	—

Note: Figures are in billions of chained 2017 dollars; (1) Figures cover the Providence-Warwick, RI-MA Metropolitan Statistical Area; (2) Figures cover real GDP within metropolitan areas; (3) Rank is based on 2023 data and ranges from 1 to 384
Source: U.S. Bureau of Economic Analysis

Economic Growth

Area	2014	2015	2016	2017	2018	2019	2020	2021	2022	2023
MSA[1]	1.6	2.5	0.2	0.5	0.1	2.4	-3.0	5.1	0.9	1.2
U.S.[2]	2.6	3.2	2.0	2.7	3.1	2.7	-2.2	6.3	2.6	2.7

Note: Figures are real gross domestic product growth rates and represent percent change from preceding period; (1) Figures cover the Providence-Warwick, RI-MA Metropolitan Statistical Area; (2) Figures are the average growth rates within metropolitan areas
Source: U.S. Bureau of Economic Analysis

Metropolitan Area Exports

Area	2018	2019	2020	2021	2022	2023	Rank[2]
MSA[1]	6,236.6	7,424.8	6,685.2	6,708.2	7,179.7	6,517.8	53
U.S.	1,664,056.1	1,645,173.7	1,431,406.6	1,753,941.4	2,062,937.4	2,019,160.5	—

Note: Figures are in millions of dollars; (1) Figures cover the Providence-Warwick, RI-MA Metropolitan Statistical Area; (2) Rank is based on 2023 data and ranges from 1 to 386
Source: U.S. Department of Commerce, International Trade Administration, Office of Trade and Economic Analysis, Industry and Analysis, Exports by Metropolitan Area, data extracted April 2, 2025

Building Permits

Area	Single-Family			Multi-Family			Total		
	2023	2024	Pct. Chg.	2023	2024	Pct. Chg.	2023	2024	Pct. Chg.
City	0	31	—	5	238	4,660.0	5	269	5,280.0
MSA[1]	1,255	1,339	6.7	675	1,281	89.8	1,930	2,620	35.8
U.S.	920,000	981,900	6.7	591,100	496,100	-16.1	1,511,100	1,478,000	-2.2

Note: (1) Figures cover the Providence-Warwick, RI-MA Metropolitan Statistical Area; Figures represent new, privately-owned housing units authorized (unadjusted data)
Source: U.S. Census Bureau, Building Permits Survey (BPS), 2023, 2024

Bankruptcy Filings

Area	Business Filings			Nonbusiness Filings		
	2023	2024	% Chg.	2023	2024	% Chg.
Providence County	13	22	69.2	520	581	11.7
U.S.	18,926	23,107	22.1	434,064	494,201	13.9

Note: Business filings include Chapter 7, Chapter 9, Chapter 11, Chapter 12, Chapter 13, Chapter 15, and Section 304; Nonbusiness filings include Chapter 7, Chapter 11, and Chapter 13
Source: Administrative Office of the U.S. Courts, Business and Nonbusiness Bankruptcy, County Cases Commenced by Chapter of the Bankruptcy Code, During the 12-Month Period Ending December 31, 2023 and Business and Nonbusiness Bankruptcy, County Cases Commenced by Chapter of the Bankruptcy Code, During the 12-Month Period Ending December 31, 2024

Housing Vacancy Rates

Area	Gross Vacancy Rate[3] (%)			Year-Round Vacancy Rate[4] (%)			Rental Vacancy Rate[5] (%)			Homeowner Vacancy Rate[6] (%)		
	2022	2023	2024	2022	2023	2024	2022	2023	2024	2022	2023	2024
MSA[1]	9.5	9.4	8.5	7.6	7.6	6.8	4.5	3.7	3.2	0.4	0.3	0.4
U.S.[2]	9.1	9.0	9.1	7.5	7.5	7.6	5.7	6.5	6.8	0.8	0.8	1.0

Note: (1) Figures cover the Providence-Warwick, RI-MA Metropolitan Statistical Area; (2) Figures cover the 75 largest Metropolitan Statistical Areas; (3) The percentage of the total housing inventory that is vacant; (4) The percentage of the housing inventory (excluding seasonal units) that is year-round vacant; (5) The percentage of rental inventory that is vacant for rent; (6) The percentage of homeowner inventory that is vacant for sale
Source: U.S. Census Bureau, Housing Vacancies and Homeownership Annual Statistics: 2022, 2023, 2024

INCOME

Income

Area	Per Capita ($)	Median Household ($)	Average Household ($)
City	36,694	66,772	95,112
MSA[1]	45,170	85,646	111,377
U.S.	43,289	78,538	110,491

Note: (1) Figures cover the Providence-Warwick, RI-MA Metropolitan Statistical Area
Source: U.S. Census Bureau, 2019-2023 American Community Survey 5-Year Estimates

Household Income Distribution

Area	Percent of Households Earning							
	Under $15,000	$15,000 -$24,999	$25,000 -$34,999	$35,000 -$49,999	$50,000 -$74,999	$75,000 -$99,999	$100,000 -$149,999	$150,000 and up
City	13.7	8.4	6.6	10.7	16.0	11.7	15.8	17.1
MSA[1]	8.7	6.7	6.0	9.1	14.0	12.6	19.0	23.8
U.S.	8.5	6.6	6.8	10.4	15.7	12.7	17.4	21.9

Note: (1) Figures cover the Providence-Warwick, RI-MA Metropolitan Statistical Area
Source: U.S. Census Bureau, 2019-2023 American Community Survey 5-Year Estimates

Poverty Rate

Area	All Ages	Under 18 Years Old	18 to 64 Years Old	65 Years and Over
City	20.1	26.0	18.2	19.9
MSA[1]	11.2	14.2	10.3	10.6
U.S.	12.4	16.3	11.6	10.4

Note: Figures are percentage of people whose income during the past 12 months was below the poverty level;
(1) Figures cover the Providence-Warwick, RI-MA Metropolitan Statistical Area
Source: U.S. Census Bureau, 2019-2023 American Community Survey 5-Year Estimates

EMPLOYMENT

Labor Force and Employment

Area	Civilian Labor Force			Workers Employed		
	Dec. 2023	Dec. 2024	% Chg.	Dec. 2023	Dec. 2024	% Chg.
City	90,820	92,307	1.6	86,757	87,271	0.6
MSA[1]	887,464	901,729	1.6	854,672	862,458	0.9
U.S.	166,661,000	167,746,000	0.7	160,754,000	161,294,000	0.3

Note: Data is not seasonally adjusted and covers workers 16 years of age and older; (1) Figures cover the Providence-Warwick, RI-MA Metropolitan Statistical Area
Source: Bureau of Labor Statistics, Local Area Unemployment Statistics

Unemployment Rate

Area	2024											
	Jan.	Feb.	Mar.	Apr.	May	Jun.	Jul.	Aug.	Sep.	Oct.	Nov.	Dec.
City	5.7	6.4	5.6	4.7	5.4	5.4	6.3	6.7	5.2	5.3	5.8	5.5
MSA[1]	4.8	5.2	4.5	3.8	4.1	4.3	4.9	5.0	4.0	4.2	4.4	4.4
U.S.	4.1	4.2	3.9	3.5	3.7	4.3	4.5	4.4	3.9	3.9	4.0	3.8

Note: Data is not seasonally adjusted and covers workers 16 years of age and older; (1) Figures cover the Providence-Warwick, RI-MA Metropolitan Statistical Area
Source: Bureau of Labor Statistics, Local Area Unemployment Statistics

Average Wages

Occupation	$/Hr.	Occupation	$/Hr.
Accountants and Auditors	46.37	Maintenance and Repair Workers	25.96
Automotive Mechanics	26.05	Marketing Managers	82.62
Bookkeepers	26.20	Network and Computer Systems Admin.	50.61
Carpenters	32.98	Nurses, Licensed Practical	35.27
Cashiers	16.12	Nurses, Registered	47.85
Computer Programmers	49.33	Nursing Assistants	20.93
Computer Systems Analysts	57.45	Office Clerks, General	23.21
Computer User Support Specialists	30.62	Physical Therapists	47.81
Construction Laborers	30.51	Physicians	115.77
Cooks, Restaurant	19.97	Plumbers, Pipefitters and Steamfitters	36.48
Customer Service Representatives	22.77	Police and Sheriff's Patrol Officers	37.31
Dentists	n/a	Postal Service Mail Carriers	29.03
Electricians	34.24	Real Estate Sales Agents	31.86
Engineers, Electrical	54.44	Retail Salespersons	18.21
Fast Food and Counter Workers	15.96	Sales Representatives, Technical/Scientific	51.21
Financial Managers	82.12	Secretaries, Exc. Legal/Medical/Executive	24.94
First-Line Supervisors of Office Workers	36.46	Security Guards	19.43
General and Operations Managers	63.72	Surgeons	n/a
Hairdressers/Cosmetologists	19.74	Teacher Assistants, Exc. Postsecondary[1]	17.96
Home Health and Personal Care Aides	19.36	Teachers, Secondary School, Exc. Sp. Ed.[1]	39.10
Janitors and Cleaners	19.58	Telemarketers	18.03
Landscaping/Groundskeeping Workers	21.36	Truck Drivers, Heavy/Tractor-Trailer	28.07
Lawyers	73.53	Truck Drivers, Light/Delivery Services	23.04
Maids and Housekeeping Cleaners	17.71	Waiters and Waitresses	20.77

Note: Wage data covers the Providence-Warwick, RI-MA Metropolitan Statistical Area; (1) Hourly wages were calculated from annual wage data based on a 40 hour work week
Source: Bureau of Labor Statistics, Metro Area Occupational Employment & Wage Estimates, May 2024

Employment by Industry

Sector	MSA[1]		U.S.
	Number of Employees	Percent of Total	Percent of Total
Construction	33,400	4.5	5.1
Financial Activities	40,900	5.5	5.8
Government	98,400	13.3	14.9
Information	7,700	1.0	1.9
Leisure and Hospitality	79,400	10.7	10.4
Manufacturing	63,300	8.5	8.0
Mining and Logging	200	<0.1	0.4
Other Services	31,400	4.2	3.7
Private Education and Health Services	160,100	21.6	16.9
Professional and Business Services	89,900	12.1	14.2
Retail Trade	81,400	11.0	10.0
Transportation, Warehousing, and Utilities	26,800	3.6	4.8
Wholesale Trade	28,500	3.8	3.9

Note: Figures are non-farm employment as of December 2024. Figures are not seasonally adjusted and include workers 16 years of age and older; (1) Figures cover the Providence-Warwick, RI-MA Metropolitan Statistical Area
Source: Bureau of Labor Statistics, Current Employment Statistics, Employment, Hours, and Earnings

Employment by Occupation

Occupation Classification	City (%)	MSA[1] (%)	U.S. (%)
Management, Business, Science, and Arts	41.6	42.3	42.0
Natural Resources, Construction, and Maintenance	6.0	8.3	8.6
Production, Transportation, and Material Moving	16.0	12.3	13.0
Sales and Office	16.2	20.0	19.9
Service	20.2	17.2	16.5

Note: Figures cover employed civilians 16 years of age and older; (1) Figures cover the Providence-Warwick, RI-MA Metropolitan Statistical Area
Source: U.S. Census Bureau, 2019-2023 American Community Survey 5-Year Estimates

Occupations with Greatest Projected Employment Growth: 2022 – 2032

Occupation[1]	2022 Employment	2032 Projected Employment	Numeric Employment Change	Percent Employment Change
Home Health and Personal Care Aides	8,070	10,000	1,930	23.9
Cooks, Restaurant	7,110	8,760	1,650	23.2
Stockers and Order Fillers	6,530	7,510	980	15.0
Nursing Assistants (SOC 2018)	9,060	10,010	950	10.5
Registered Nurses	11,920	12,700	780	6.5
Retail Salespersons	12,370	13,100	730	5.9
Nurse Practitioners	1,440	2,090	650	45.1
Laborers and Freight, Stock, and Material Movers, Hand	7,390	8,030	640	8.7
Market Research Analysts and Marketing Specialists	3,750	4,350	600	16.0
General and Operations Managers	6,930	7,500	570	8.2

Note: Projections cover Rhode Island; (1) Sorted by numeric employment change
Source: www.projectionscentral.org, State Occupational Projections, 2022–2032 Long-Term Projections

Fastest-Growing Occupations: 2022 – 2032

Occupation[1]	2022 Employment	2032 Projected Employment	Numeric Employment Change	Percent Employment Change
Nurse Practitioners	1,440	2,090	650	45.1
Data Scientists	570	750	180	31.6
Reservation and Transportation Ticket Agents and Travel Clerks	210	270	60	28.6
Industrial Machinery Mechanics	810	1,040	230	28.4
Information Security Analysts (SOC 2018)	500	640	140	28.0
Occupational Therapy Assistants	430	550	120	27.9
Medical and Health Services Managers	1,670	2,120	450	26.9
Physical Therapist Assistants	380	480	100	26.3
Medical Equipment Repairers	280	350	70	25.0
Home Health and Personal Care Aides	8,070	10,000	1,930	23.9

Note: Projections cover Rhode Island; (1) Sorted by percent employment change and excludes occupations with numeric employment change less than 50
Source: www.projectionscentral.org, State Occupational Projections, 2022–2032 Long-Term Projections

CITY FINANCES

City Government Finances

Component	2022 ($000)	2022 ($ per capita)
Total Revenues	1,124,873	6,275
Total Expenditures	1,024,544	5,715
Debt Outstanding	733,600	4,092

Source: U.S. Census Bureau, State & Local Government Finances 2022

City Government Revenue by Source

Source	2022 ($000)	2022 ($ per capita)	2022 (%)
General Revenue			
From Federal Government	27,941	156	2.5
From State Government	399,820	2,230	35.5
From Local Governments	80,103	447	7.1
Taxes			
Property	359,936	2,008	32.0
Sales and Gross Receipts	8,698	49	0.8
Personal Income	0	0	0.0
Corporate Income	0	0	0.0
Motor Vehicle License	0	0	0.0
Other Taxes	6,830	38	0.6
Current Charges	118,688	662	10.6
Liquor Store	0	0	0.0
Utility	88,825	495	7.9

Source: U.S. Census Bureau, State & Local Government Finances 2022

City Government Expenditures by Function

Function	2022 ($000)	2022 ($ per capita)	2022 (%)
General Direct Expenditures			
Air Transportation	0	0	0.0
Corrections	0	0	0.0
Education	527,884	2,944	51.5
Employment Security Administration	0	0	0.0
Financial Administration	7,658	42	0.7
Fire Protection	85,446	476	8.3
General Public Buildings	24,365	135	2.4
Governmental Administration, Other	7,739	43	0.8
Health	0	0	0.0
Highways	8,108	45	0.8
Hospitals	0	0	0.0
Housing and Community Development	10,300	57	1.0
Interest on General Debt	40,196	224	3.9
Judicial and Legal	14,827	82	1.4
Libraries	3,995	22	0.4
Parking	594	3	0.1
Parks and Recreation	10,348	57	1.0
Police Protection	90,777	506	8.9
Public Welfare	1,176	6	0.1
Sewerage	971	5	0.1
Solid Waste Management	13,686	76	1.3
Veterans' Services	0	0	0.0
Liquor Store	0	0	0.0
Utility	85,644	477	8.4

Source: U.S. Census Bureau, State & Local Government Finances 2022

TAXES

State Corporate Income Tax Rates

State	Tax Rate (%)	Income Brackets ($)	Num. of Brackets	Financial Institution Tax Rate (%)[a]	Federal Income Tax Ded.
Rhode Island	7.0 (b)	Flat rate	1	9.0 (b)	No

Note: Tax rates for tax year 2024; (a) Rates listed are the corporate income tax rate applied to financial institutions or excise taxes based on income. Some states have other taxes based upon the value of deposits or shares; (b) Minimum tax is $800 in California, $250 in District of Columbia, $50 in Arizona and North Dakota (banks), $400 ($100 banks) in Rhode Island, $200 per location in South Dakota (banks), $100 in Utah, in Vermont, simplified entity business tax for residents only at $250, otherwise minimum tax ($100 - $100,000) is based upon gross receipts.
Source: Federation of Tax Administrators, State Corporate Income Tax Rates, January 1, 2025

State Individual Income Tax Rates

State	Tax Rate (%)	Income Brackets ($)	Personal Exemptions ($)			Standard Ded. ($)	
			Single	Married	Depend.	Single	Married
Rhode Island (a)	3.75 - 5.99	77,450 - 176,050	4,950	9,900	4,950	10,500	21,150 (z)

Note: Tax rates for tax year 2024; Local- and county-level taxes are not included; Federal income tax is not deductible on state income tax returns; (a) 16 states have statutory provision for automatically adjusting to the rate of inflation the dollar values of the income tax brackets, standard deductions, and/or personal exemptions. Oregon does not index the income brackets for $125,000 and over See: INFL and SPEC above; (z) Alabama standard deduction is phased out for incomes over $25,500 after 2017 (MFJ, HOH and Single); $12,750 for MFS. Rhode Island exemptions & standard deductions phased out for incomes over $274,650; Wisconsin standard deduciton phases out for income over $124,500.
Source: Federation of Tax Administrators, State Individual Income Tax Rates, January 1, 2025

Various State Sales and Excise Tax Rates

State	State Sales Tax (%)	Gasoline[1] ($/gal.)	Cigarette[2] ($/pack)	Spirits[3] ($/gal.)	Wine[4] ($/gal.)	Beer[5] ($/gal.)	Recreational Marijuana (%)
Rhode Island	7	0.38	4.25	5.40	1.40	0.12	(u)

Note: All tax rates as of January 1, 2025; (1) The American Petroleum Institute has developed a methodology for determining the average tax rate on a gallon of fuel. Rates may include any of the following: excise taxes, environmental fees, storage tank fees, other fees or taxes, general sales tax, and local taxes; (2) The federal excise tax of $1.0066 per pack and local taxes are not included; (3) Rates are those applicable to off-premise sales of 40% alcohol by volume (a.b.v.) distilled spirits in 750ml containers. Local excise taxes are excluded; (4) Rates are those applicable to off-premise sales of 11% a.b.v. non-carbonated wine in 750ml containers; (5) Rates are those applicable to off-premise sales of 4.7% a.b.v. beer in 12 ounce containers; (u) 13% excise tax (retail price)
Source: Tax Foundation, 2025 Facts & Figures: How Does Your State Compare?

State Tax Competitiveness Index

State	Overall Rank	Corporate Tax Rank	Individual Income Tax Rank	Sales Tax Rank	Property Tax Rank	Unemployment Insurance Tax Rank
Rhode Island	39	35	30	26	37	48

Note: The Tax Foundation's State Tax Competitiveness Index enables policymakers, taxpayers, and business leaders to gauge how their states' tax systems compare. A rank of 1 is best, 50 is worst. Rankings do not average to the total. States without a tax rank equally as 1. DC's scores and rankings do not affect other states. The report shows tax systems as of July 1, 2024 (the beginning of Fiscal Year 2025).
Source: Tax Foundation, State Tax Competitiveness Index 2025

TRANSPORTATION

Means of Transportation to Work

Area	Car/Truck/Van		Public Transportation			Bicycle	Walked	Other Means	Worked at Home
	Drove Alone	Carpooled	Bus	Subway	Railroad				
City	62.6	9.8	3.1	0.0	1.1	0.8	7.3	2.6	12.7
MSA[1]	74.9	8.1	1.1	0.1	0.7	0.3	2.6	1.5	10.9
U.S.	70.2	8.5	1.7	1.3	0.4	0.4	2.4	1.6	13.5

Note: Figures are percentages and cover workers 16 years of age and older; (1) Figures cover the Providence-Warwick, RI-MA Metropolitan Statistical Area
Source: U.S. Census Bureau, 2019-2023 American Community Survey 5-Year Estimates

Travel Time to Work

Area	Less Than 10 Minutes	10 to 19 Minutes	20 to 29 Minutes	30 to 44 Minutes	45 to 59 Minutes	60 to 89 Minutes	90 Minutes or More
City	11.0	36.1	20.6	16.8	6.7	6.1	2.7
MSA[1]	11.7	30.0	21.3	20.3	7.9	6.1	2.9
U.S.	12.6	28.6	21.2	20.8	8.1	6.0	2.8

Note: Note: Figures are percentages and include workers 16 years old and over; (1) Figures cover the Providence-Warwick, RI-MA Metropolitan Statistical Area
Source: U.S. Census Bureau, 2019-2023 American Community Survey 5-Year Estimates

Key Congestion Measures

Measure	2000	2010	2015	2020	2022
Annual Hours of Delay, Total (000)	24,093	31,473	36,249	26,373	34,831
Annual Hours of Delay, Per Auto Commuter	36	41	46	33	45
Annual Congestion Cost, Per Auto Commuter ($)	839	870	925	704	883

Note: Figures cover the Providence RI-MA urban area
Source: Texas A&M Transportation Institute, 2023 Urban Mobility Report

Freeway Travel Time Index

Measure	1985	1990	1995	2000	2005	2010	2015	2020	2022
Urban Area Index[1]	1.04	1.08	1.12	1.16	1.19	1.17	1.17	1.13	1.15
Urban Area Rank[1,2]	81	62	57	43	38	41	46	6	54

Note: Freeway Travel Time Index—the ratio of travel time in the peak period to the travel time at free-flow conditions. For example, a value of 1.30 indicates a 20-minute free-flow trip takes 26 minutes in the peak (20 minutes x 1.30 = 26 minutes); (1) Covers the Providence RI-MA urban area; (2) Rank is based on 101 larger urban areas (#1 = highest travel time index)
Source: Texas A&M Transportation Institute, 2023 Urban Mobility Report

Public Transportation

Agency Name / Mode of Transportation	Vehicles Operated in Maximum Service[1]	Annual Unlinked Passenger Trips[2] (in thous.)	Annual Passenger Miles[3] (in thous.)
Rhode Island Public Transit Authority (RIPTA)			
Bus (directly operated)	192	11,040.1	46,337.5
Demand Response (directly operated)	74	249.7	3,521.4
Demand Response - Taxi	9	44.8	1,180.5
Vanpool (purchased transportation)	28	77.9	3,264.0

Note: (1) Number of revenue vehicles operated by the given mode and type of service to meet the annual maximum service requirement. This is the revenue vehicle count during the peak season of the year; on the week and day that maximum service is provided. Vehicles operated in maximum service (VOMS) exclude atypical days and one-time special events; (2) Number of passengers who boarded public transportation vehicles. Passengers are counted each time they board a vehicle no matter how many vehicles they use to travel from their origin to their destination. (3) Sum of the distances ridden by all passengers during the entire fiscal year.
Source: Federal Transit Administration, National Transit Database, 2023

Air Transportation

Airport Name and Code / Type of Service	Passenger Airlines[1]	Passenger Enplanements	Freight Carriers[2]	Freight (lbs)
Theodore Francis Green State Airport (PVD)				
Domestic service (U.S. carriers only)	28	1,984,163	9	11,474,532
International service (U.S. carriers only)	4	312	0	0

Note: (1) Includes all U.S.-based major, minor and commuter airlines that carried at least one passenger during the year; (2) Includes all U.S.-based airlines and freight carriers that transported at least one pound of freight during the year.
Source: Bureau of Transportation Statistics, The Intermodal Transportation Database, Air Carriers: T-100 Domestic Market (U.S. carriers only), 2024; Bureau of Transportation Statistics, The Intermodal Transportation Database, Air Carriers: T-100 International Market (U.S. carriers only), 2024

BUSINESSES

Major Business Headquarters

Company Name	Industry	Rankings	
		Fortune[1]	Forbes[2]
Citizens Financial Group	Commercial banks	337	-
Gilbane	Construction	-	82
Textron	Aerospace & defense	308	-
United Natural Foods	Wholesalers: food and grocery	144	-

Note: (1) Companies that produce a 10-K are ranked 1 to 500 based on 2023 revenue; (2) All private companies with at least $2 billion in annual revenue through the end of their most current fiscal year are ranked 1 to 275; companies listed are headquartered in the city; dashes indicate no ranking
Source: Fortune, "Fortune 500," 2024; Forbes, "America's Largest Private Companies," 2024

Living Environment

COST OF LIVING

Cost of Living Index

Composite Index	Groceries	Housing	Utilities	Transportation	Health Care	Misc. Goods/Services
112.2	102.0	113.4	139.7	96.5	104.4	114.1

Note: The Cost of Living Index measures regional differences in the cost of consumer goods and services, excluding taxes and non-consumer expenditures, for professional and managerial households in the top income quintile. It is based on more than 50,000 prices covering almost 60 different items for which prices are collected three times a year by chambers of commerce, economic development organizations or university applied economic centers in each participating urban area. The numbers shown should be read as a percentage above or below the national average of 100. For example, a value of 115.4 in the groceries column indicates that grocery prices are 15.4% higher than the national average. Small differences in the index numbers should not be interpreted as significant; Figures cover the Providence RI urban area.
Source: The Council for Community and Economic Research, Cost of Living Index, 2024

Grocery Prices

Area[1]	T-Bone Steak ($/pound)	Frying Chicken ($/pound)	Whole Milk ($/half gal.)	Eggs ($/dozen)	Orange Juice ($/64 oz.)	Coffee ($/11.5 oz.)
City[2]	15.51	1.68	4.70	3.55	4.43	4.91
Avg.	15.42	1.55	4.69	3.25	4.41	5.46
Min.	14.50	1.16	4.43	2.75	4.00	4.85
Max.	17.56	2.89	5.49	4.78	5.54	7.89

Note: (1) Values for the local area are compared with the average, minimum and maximum values for all 276 areas in the Cost of Living Index; (2) Figures cover the Providence RI urban area; **T-Bone Steak** (price per pound); **Frying Chicken** (price per pound, whole fryer); **Whole Milk** (half gallon carton); **Eggs** (price per dozen, Grade A, large); **Orange Juice** (64 oz. Tropicana or Florida Natural); **Coffee** (11.5 oz. can, vacuum-packed, Maxwell House, Hills Bros, or Folgers).
Source: The Council for Community and Economic Research, Cost of Living Index, 2024

Housing and Utility Costs

Area[1]	New Home Price ($)	Apartment Rent ($/month)	All Electric ($/month)	Part Electric ($/month)	Other Energy ($/month)	Telephone ($/month)
City[2]	474,141	2,453	-	171.99	161.54	198.12
Avg.	515,975	1,550	210.99	123.07	82.07	194.99
Min.	265,375	692	104.33	53.68	36.26	179.42
Max.	2,775,821	5,719	529.02	397.28	361.63	223.33

Note: (1) Values for the local area are compared with the average, minimum and maximum values for all 276 areas in the Cost of Living Index; (2) Figures cover the Providence RI urban area; **New Home Price** (2,400 sf living area, 8,000 sf lot, in urban area with full utilities); **Apartment Rent** (950 sf 2 bedroom/1.5 or 2 bath, unfurnished, excluding all utilities except water); **All Electric** (average monthly cost for an all-electric home); **Part Electric** (average monthly cost for a part-electric home); **Other Energy** (average monthly cost for natural gas, fuel oil, coal, wood, and any other forms of energy except electricity); **Telephone** (price includes the base monthly rate plus taxes and fees for three lines of mobile phone service).
Source: The Council for Community and Economic Research, Cost of Living Index, 2024

Health Care, Transportation, and Other Costs

Area[1]	Doctor ($/visit)	Dentist ($/visit)	Optometrist ($/visit)	Gasoline ($/gallon)	Beauty Salon ($/visit)	Men's Shirt ($)
City[2]	168.33	117.58	111.08	3.28	50.22	31.37
Avg.	143.77	117.51	129.23	3.32	48.57	38.14
Min.	36.74	58.67	67.33	2.80	24.00	13.41
Max.	270.44	216.82	307.33	5.28	94.00	63.89

Note: (1) Values for the local area are compared with the average, minimum and maximum values for all 276 areas in the Cost of Living Index; (2) Figures cover the Providence RI urban area; **Doctor** (general practitioners routine exam of an established patient); **Dentist** (adult teeth cleaning and periodic oral examination); **Optometrist** (full vision eye exam for established adult patient); **Gasoline** (one gallon regular unleaded, national brand, including all taxes, cash price at self-service pump if available); **Beauty Salon** (woman's shampoo, trim, and blow-dry); **Men's Shirt** (cotton/polyester dress shirt, pinpoint weave, long sleeves).
Source: The Council for Community and Economic Research, Cost of Living Index, 2024

HOUSING

Homeownership Rate

Area	2017 (%)	2018 (%)	2019 (%)	2020 (%)	2021 (%)	2022 (%)	2023 (%)	2024 (%)
MSA[1]	58.6	61.3	63.5	64.8	64.1	66.3	65.4	63.2
U.S.	63.9	64.4	64.6	66.6	65.5	65.8	65.9	65.6

Note: (1) Figures cover the Providence-Warwick, RI-MA Metropolitan Statistical Area
Source: U.S. Census Bureau, Housing Vacancies and Homeownership Annual Statistics: 2017-2024

House Price Index (HPI)

Area	National Ranking[2]	Quarterly Change (%)	One-Year Change (%)	Five-Year Change (%)	Since 1991Q1 (%)
MSA[1]	41	0.25	7.70	64.34	289.70
U.S.[3]	–	1.43	4.51	57.13	327.82

Note: The HPI is a weighted repeat sales index. It measures average price changes in repeat sales or refinancings on the same properties. This information is obtained by reviewing repeat mortgage transactions on single-family properties whose mortgages have been purchased or securitized by Fannie Mae or Freddie Mac since January 1975; (1) Figures cover the Providence-Warwick, RI-MA Metropolitan Statistical Area; (2) Rankings are based on annual percentage change for all metro areas containing at least 15,000 transactions over the last 10 years and ranges from 1 to 241; (3) figures based on a weighted average of Census Division estimates using a seasonally adjusted, purchase-only index; all figures are for the period ending December 31, 2024
Source: Federal Housing Finance Agency, Change in FHFA Metropolitan Area House Price Indexes, All Transactions Index, 2024Q4

Home Value

Area	Under $100,000	$100,000 -$199,999	$200,000 -$299,999	$300,000 -$399,999	$400,000 -$499,999	$500,000 -$999,999	$1,000,000 or more	Median ($)
City	4.1	9.3	30.8	25.2	11.6	14.5	4.4	322,800
MSA[1]	3.3	4.7	20.9	24.5	18.9	24.2	3.4	385,900
U.S.	12.1	17.8	19.5	14.4	10.5	19.1	6.5	303,400

Note: Figures are percentages except for median and cover owner-occupied housing units; (1) Figures cover the Providence-Warwick, RI-MA Metropolitan Statistical Area
Source: U.S. Census Bureau, 2019-2023 American Community Survey 5-Year Estimates

Year Housing Structure Built

Area	2020 or Later	2010 -2019	2000 -2009	1990 -1999	1980 -1989	1970 -1979	1960 -1969	1950 -1959	1940 -1949	Before 1940	Median Year
City	0.4	2.2	4.9	4.5	5.6	7.8	5.4	7.5	6.3	55.6	1938
MSA[1]	0.4	3.6	6.3	7.6	11.6	11.9	10.3	11.6	5.9	30.8	1962
U.S.	1.2	8.9	13.6	12.8	13.0	14.4	10.0	9.7	4.5	11.9	1980

Note: Figures are percentages except for Median Year; Note: (1) Figures cover the Providence-Warwick, RI-MA Metropolitan Statistical Area
Source: U.S. Census Bureau, 2019-2023 American Community Survey 5-Year Estimates

Gross Monthly Rent

Area	Under $500	$500 -$999	$1,000 -$1,499	$1,500 -$1,999	$2,000 -$2,499	$2,500 -$2,999	$3,000 and up	Median ($)
City	16.9	11.3	33.2	22.3	10.5	3.4	2.4	1,333
MSA[1]	12.9	18.9	35.1	20.9	7.8	2.5	1.9	1,236
U.S.	6.5	22.3	29.5	20.2	10.8	4.8	5.9	1,348

Note: Figures are percentages except for median; Gross rent is the contract rent plus the estimated average monthly cost of utilities (electricity, gas, and water and sewer) and fuels (oil, coal, kerosene, wood, etc.) if these are paid by the renter (or paid for the renter by someone else); (1) Figures cover the Providence-Warwick, RI-MA Metropolitan Statistical Area
Source: U.S. Census Bureau, 2019-2023 American Community Survey 5-Year Estimates

HEALTH

Health Risk Factors

Category	MSA[1] (%)	U.S. (%)
Adults aged 18–64 who have any kind of health care coverage	94.3	90.8
Adults who reported being in good or better health	82.1	81.8
Adults who have been told they have high blood cholesterol	35.0	36.9
Adults who have been told they have high blood pressure	33.5	34.0
Adults who are current smokers	11.7	12.1
Adults who currently use e-cigarettes	7.4	7.7
Adults who currently use chewing tobacco, snuff, or snus	1.1	3.2
Adults who are heavy drinkers[2]	5.8	6.1
Adults who are binge drinkers[3]	17.1	15.2
Adults who are overweight (BMI 25.0 - 29.9)	34.8	34.4
Adults who are obese (BMI 30.0 - 99.8)	32.4	34.3
Adults who participated in any physical activities in the past month	73.2	75.8

Note: All figures are crude prevalence; (1) Figures cover the Providence-Warwick, RI-MA Metropolitan Statistical Area; (2) Heavy drinkers are classified as adult men having more than 14 drinks per week and adult women having more than 7 drinks per week; (3) Binge drinkers are classified as males having five or more drinks on one occasion or females having four or more drinks on one occasion
Source: Centers for Disease Control and Prevention, Behaviorial Risk Factor Surveillance System, SMART: Selected Metropolitan Area Risk Trends, 2023

Acute and Chronic Health Conditions

Category	MSA[1] (%)	U.S. (%)
Adults who have ever been told they had a heart attack	4.5	4.2
Adults who have ever been told they have angina or coronary heart disease	4.6	4.0
Adults who have ever been told they had a stroke	3.0	3.3
Adults who have ever been told they have asthma	17.3	15.7
Adults who have ever been told they have arthritis	27.7	26.3
Adults who have ever been told they have diabetes[2]	11.5	11.5
Adults who have ever been told they had skin cancer	6.5	5.6
Adults who have ever been told they had any other types of cancer	8.1	8.4
Adults who have ever been told they have COPD	7.1	6.4
Adults who have ever been told they have kidney disease	3.4	3.7
Adults who have ever been told they have a form of depression	21.6	22.0

Note: All figures are crude prevalence; (1) Figures cover the Providence-Warwick, RI-MA Metropolitan Statistical Area; (2) Figures do not include pregnancy-related, borderline, or pre-diabetes
Source: Centers for Disease Control and Prevention, Behaviorial Risk Factor Surveillance System, SMART: Selected Metropolitan Area Risk Trends, 2023

Health Screening and Vaccination Rates

Category	MSA[1] (%)	U.S. (%)
Adults who have ever been tested for HIV	37.6	37.5
Adults who have had their blood cholesterol checked within the last five years	91.6	87.0
Adults aged 65+ who have had flu shot within the past year	71.5	63.4
Adults aged 65+ who have ever had a pneumonia vaccination	74.6	71.9

Note: All figures are crude prevalence; (1) Figures cover the Providence-Warwick, RI-MA Metropolitan Statistical Area.
Source: Centers for Disease Control and Prevention, Behaviorial Risk Factor Surveillance System, SMART: Selected Metropolitan Area Risk Trends, 2023

Disability Status

Category	MSA[1] (%)	U.S. (%)
Adults who reported being deaf	6.9	7.4
Are you blind or have serious difficulty seeing, even when wearing glasses?	5.2	4.9
Do you have difficulty doing errands alone?	9.2	7.8
Do you have difficulty dressing or bathing?	3.7	3.6
Do you have serious difficulty concentrating/remembering/making decisions?	13.7	13.7
Do you have serious difficulty walking or climbing stairs?	13.0	13.2

Note: All figures are crude prevalence; (1) Figures cover the Providence-Warwick, RI-MA Metropolitan Statistical Area.
Source: Centers for Disease Control and Prevention, Behaviorial Risk Factor Surveillance System, SMART: Selected Metropolitan Area Risk Trends, 2023

Mortality Rates for the Top 10 Causes of Death in the U.S.

ICD-10[a] Sub-Chapter	ICD-10[a] Code	Crude Mortality Rate[2] per 100,000 population	
		County[3]	U.S.
Malignant neoplasms	C00-C97	171.8	182.7
Ischaemic heart diseases	I20-I25	130.2	109.6
Provisional assignment of new diseases of uncertain etiology[1]	U00-U49	52.6	65.3
Other forms of heart disease	I30-I51	51.1	65.1
Other degenerative diseases of the nervous system	G30-G31	49.4	52.4
Other external causes of accidental injury	W00-X59	71.5	52.3
Cerebrovascular diseases	I60-I69	35.9	49.1
Chronic lower respiratory diseases	J40-J47	36.6	43.5
Hypertensive diseases	I10-I15	31.3	38.9
Organic, including symptomatic, mental disorders	F01-F09	38.8	33.9

Note: (a) ICD-10 = International Classification of Diseases 10th Revision; (1) Includes COVID-19, adverse effects to COVID-19 vaccines, SARS, and vaping-related disorders; (2) Crude mortality rates are a three-year average covering 2021-2023; (3) Figures cover Providence County.
Source: Centers for Disease Control and Prevention, National Center for Health Statistics. National Vital Statistics System, Mortality 2018-2023 on CDC WONDER Online Database

Mortality Rates for Selected Causes of Death

Cause of Death	ICD-10[a] Code	Crude Mortality Rate[1] per 100,000 population	
		County[2]	U.S.
Accidental poisoning and exposure to noxious substances	X40-X49	43.8	30.5
Alzheimer disease	G30	42.6	35.4
Assault	X85-Y09	3.5	7.3
COVID-19	U07.1	52.6	65.3
Diabetes mellitus	E10-E14	27.5	30.0
Diseases of the liver	K70-K76	21.4	20.8
Human immunodeficiency virus (HIV) disease	B20-B24	Unreliable	1.5
Influenza and pneumonia	J09-J18	9.1	13.4
Intentional self-harm	X60-X84	10.0	14.7
Malnutrition	E40-E46	2.5	6.0
Obesity and other hyperalimentation	E65-E68	3.8	3.1
Renal failure	N17-N19	11.8	16.4
Transport accidents	V01-V99	7.7	14.4

Note: (a) ICD-10 = International Classification of Diseases 10th Revision; (1) Crude mortality rates are a three-year average covering 2021-2023; (2) Figures cover Providence County; Data are suppressed when the data meet the criteria for confidentiality constraints; Crude mortality rates are flagged as unreliable when the rate would be calculated with a numerator of 20 or less.
Source: Centers for Disease Control and Prevention, National Center for Health Statistics. National Vital Statistics System, Mortality 2018-2023 on CDC WONDER Online Database

Health Insurance Coverage

Area	With Health Insurance	With Private Health Insurance	With Public Health Insurance	Without Health Insurance	Population Under Age 19 Without Health Insurance
City	92.6	57.0	44.1	7.4	5.1
MSA[1]	96.1	70.1	39.7	3.9	2.4
U.S.	91.4	67.3	36.3	8.6	5.4

Note: Figures are percentages that cover the civilian noninstitutionalized population; (1) Figures cover the Providence-Warwick, RI-MA Metropolitan Statistical Area
Source: U.S. Census Bureau, 2019-2023 American Community Survey 5-Year Estimates

Number of Medical Professionals

Area	MDs[3]	DOs[3,4]	Dentists	Podiatrists	Chiropractors	Optometrists
County[1] (number)	3,460	128	395	67	140	148
County[1] (rate[2])	526.4	19.5	59.8	10.1	21.2	22.4
U.S. (rate[2])	302.5	29.2	74.6	6.4	29.5	18.0

Note: Data as of 2023 unless noted; (1) Data covers Providence County; (2) Number of medical professionals per 100,000 population; (3) Data as of 2022 and includes all active, non-federal physicians; (4) Doctor of Osteopathic Medicine
Source: U.S. Department of Health and Human Services, Health Resources and Services Administration, Bureau of Health Professions, Area Resource File (ARF) 2023-2024

EDUCATION

Public School District Statistics

District Name	Schls	Pupils	Pupil/Teacher Ratio	Minority Pupils[1] (%)	Total Rev. per Pupil ($)	Total Exp. per Pupil ($)
Achievement First Rhode Island	7	2,846	14.8	96.3	19,895	18,724
Providence	39	19,856	13.7	92.4	26,566	25,933

Note: Table includes school districts with 2,000 or more students; (1) Percentage of students that are not non-Hispanic white.
Source: U.S. Department of Education, National Center for Education Statistics, Common Core of Data, Local Education Agency (School District) Universe Survey: School Year 2023-2024; U.S. Department of Education, National Center for Education Statistics, Common Core of Data, School District Finance Survey (F-33): School Year 2021–22

Best High Schools

According to *U.S. News*, Providence is home to one of the top 500 high schools in the U.S.: **Classical High School** (#202). Nearly 25,000 public, magnet and charter schools were ranked based on their performance on state assessments and how well they prepare students for college. *U.S. News & World Report, "Best High Schools 2024"*

Highest Level of Education

Area	Less than H.S.	H.S. Diploma	Some College, No Deg.	Associate Degree	Bachelor's Degree	Master's Degree	Prof. School Degree	Doctorate Degree
City	18.1	27.5	14.8	4.9	18.3	9.7	3.5	3.3
MSA[1]	11.6	27.8	17.2	8.4	21.3	9.9	2.1	1.7
U.S.	10.6	26.2	19.4	8.8	21.3	9.8	2.3	1.6

Note: Figures cover persons age 25 and over; (1) Figures cover the Providence-Warwick, RI-MA Metropolitan Statistical Area
Source: U.S. Census Bureau, 2019-2023 American Community Survey 5-Year Estimates

Educational Attainment by Race

Area	High School Graduate or Higher (%)					Bachelor's Degree or Higher (%)				
	Total	White	Black	Asian	Hisp.[2]	Total	White	Black	Asian	Hisp.[2]
City	81.9	89.9	87.0	87.7	69.5	34.7	51.7	23.6	58.3	12.9
MSA[1]	88.4	90.8	85.6	88.6	72.1	35.0	37.5	25.4	56.3	16.8
U.S.	89.4	92.9	88.1	88.0	72.5	35.0	37.7	24.7	57.0	19.9

Note: Figures shown cover persons 25 years old and over; (1) Figures cover the Providence-Warwick, RI-MA Metropolitan Statistical Area; (2) People of Hispanic origin can be of any race
Source: U.S. Census Bureau, 2019-2023 American Community Survey 5-Year Estimates

School Enrollment by Grade and Control

Area	Preschool (%)		Kindergarten (%)		Grades 1 - 4 (%)		Grades 5 - 8 (%)		Grades 9 - 12 (%)	
	Public	Private	Public	Private	Public	Private	Public	Private	Public	Private
City	58.9	41.1	80.8	19.2	89.3	10.7	86.2	13.8	90.1	9.9
MSA[1]	57.9	42.1	85.5	14.5	89.4	10.6	88.9	11.1	88.7	11.3
U.S.	58.7	41.3	85.2	14.8	87.2	12.8	87.9	12.1	89.0	11.0

Note: Figures shown cover persons 3 years old and over; (1) Figures cover the Providence-Warwick, RI-MA Metropolitan Statistical Area
Source: U.S. Census Bureau, 2019-2023 American Community Survey 5-Year Estimates

Higher Education

Four-Year Colleges			Two-Year Colleges			Medical Schools[1]	Law Schools[2]	Voc/ Tech[3]
Public	Private Non-profit	Private For-profit	Public	Private Non-profit	Private For-profit			
3	13	0	2	1	0	1	2	12

Note: Figures cover institutions located within the Providence-Warwick, RI-MA Metropolitan Statistical Area and include main campuses only; (1) includes schools accredited by the Liaison Committee on Medical Education and the American Osteopathic Association's Commission on Osteopathic College Accreditation; (2) includes ABA-accredited schools, schools with provisional ABA accreditation, and state accredited schools; (3) includes all schools with programs that are less than 2 years.
Source: National Center for Education Statistics, Integrated Postsecondary Education System (IPEDS), 2023-24; Wikipedia, List of Medical Schools in the United States, accessed May 2, 2025; Wikipedia, List of Law Schools in the United States, accessed May 2, 2025

According to *U.S. News & World Report*, the Providence-Warwick, RI-MA metro area is home to two of the top 200 national universities in the U.S.: **Brown University** (#13 tie); **University of Rhode Island** (#152 tie). The indicators used to capture academic quality fall into a number of categories: assessment by administrators at peer institutions; retention of students; faculty resources; student selectivity; financial resources; alumni giving; high school counselor ratings of colleges; and graduation rate. *U.S. News & World Report*, "America's Best Colleges 2025"

According to *U.S. News & World Report*, the Providence-Warwick, RI-MA metro area is home to two of the top 100 liberal arts colleges in the U.S.: **Wheaton College (MA)** (#74 tie); **Stonehill College** (#83 tie). The indicators used to capture academic quality fall into a number of categories: assessment by administrators at peer institutions; retention of students; faculty resources; student selectivity; financial resources; alumni giving; high school counselor ratings of colleges; and graduation rate. *U.S. News & World Report*, "America's Best Colleges 2025"

EMPLOYERS

Major Employers

Company Name	Industry
AAA Southern New England Inc	Road service, travel insurance
Broadcast Media Partners Holdings, Inc.	Entertainment holding company
Brown University	Higher education
Care New England Health System	Healthcare
Citizens Financial Group	Banking
City of Providence	Government
Cookson America	Material science
CVS Pharmacy	Drug stores
Hasbro	Family entertainment
IGT	Gaming
JCG Holdings	Holding company
Johnson & Wales University	Higher education
Roger Williams Medical Center	Healthcare
State of Rhode Island	Government
Sterling Parent Inc	Securities
Textron	Aerospace industries, mfg
U.S. Navy	U.S. military
United Natural Foods	Grocery
University of Rhode Island	Higher education
Women & Infants Hospital of Rhode Island	Specialty outpatient clinics

Note: Companies shown are located within the Providence-Warwick, RI-MA Metropolitan Statistical Area.
Source: Chambers of Commerce; State Departments of Labor; Wikipedia

PUBLIC SAFETY

Crime Rate

Area	Total Crime Rate	Violent Crime Rate				Property Crime Rate		
		Murder	Rape	Robbery	Aggrav. Assault	Burglary	Larceny-Theft	Motor Vehicle Theft
City	2,215.3	5.8	34.3	59.6	209.9	157.2	1,482.7	265.8
U.S.	2,290.9	5.7	38.0	66.5	264.1	250.7	1,347.2	318.7

Note: Figures are crimes per 100,000 population.
Source: FBI, Table 8, Offenses Known to Law Enforcement, by State by City, 2023

Hate Crimes

Area	Number of Quarters Reported	Number of Incidents per Bias Motivation					
		Race/Ethnicity/Ancestry	Religion	Sexual Orientation	Disability	Gender	Gender Identity
City	4	0	2	0	0	0	0
U.S.	4	5,900	2,699	2,077	187	92	492

Source: Federal Bureau of Investigation, Hate Crime Statistics 2023

Identity Theft Consumer Reports

Area	Reports	Reports per 100,000 Population	Rank[2]
MSA[1]	5,422	324	52
U.S.	1,135,291	339	-

Note: (1) Figures cover the Providence-Warwick, RI-MA Metropolitan Statistical Area; (2) Rank ranges from 1 to 401 where 1 indicates greatest number of identity theft reports per 100,000 population
Source: Federal Trade Commission, Consumer Sentinel Network Data Book 2024

Fraud and Other Consumer Reports

Area	Reports	Reports per 100,000 Population	Rank[2]
MSA[1]	17,440	1,042	188
U.S.	5,360,641	1,601	-

Note: (1) Figures cover the Providence-Warwick, RI-MA Metropolitan Statistical Area; (2) Rank ranges from 1 to 401 where 1 indicates greatest number of fraud and other consumer reports per 100,000 population
Source: Federal Trade Commission, Consumer Sentinel Network Data Book 2024

POLITICS

2024 Presidential Election Results

Area	Trump (Rep.)	Harris (Dem.)	Stein (Green)	Kennedy (Ind.)	Oliver (Lib.)	Other
Providence County	41.7	55.7	0.6	0.9	0.3	0.8
U.S.	49.7	48.2	0.6	0.5	0.4	0.6

Note: Results are percentages and may not add to 100% due to rounding
Source: Dave Leip's Atlas of U.S. Presidential Elections

SPORTS

Professional Sports Teams

Team Name	League	Year Established
No teams are located in the metro area		

Source: Wikipedia, Major Professional Sports Teams of the United States and Canada, May 1, 2025

CLIMATE

Average and Extreme Temperatures

Temperature	Jan	Feb	Mar	Apr	May	Jun	Jul	Aug	Sep	Oct	Nov	Dec	Yr.
Extreme High (°F)	66	72	80	98	94	97	102	104	100	88	81	70	104
Average High (°F)	37	39	46	58	68	77	82	80	73	63	52	41	60
Average Temp. (°F)	29	30	38	48	58	67	73	71	64	54	44	33	51
Average Low (°F)	20	22	29	39	48	57	63	62	54	43	35	25	42
Extreme Low (°F)	-13	-7	1	14	29	41	48	40	32	20	6	-10	-13

Note: Figures cover the years 1948-1992
Source: National Climatic Data Center, International Station Meteorological Climate Summary, 9/96

Average Precipitation/Snowfall/Humidity

Precip./Humidity	Jan	Feb	Mar	Apr	May	Jun	Jul	Aug	Sep	Oct	Nov	Dec	Yr.
Avg. Precip. (in.)	3.9	3.6	4.2	4.1	3.7	2.9	3.2	4.0	3.5	3.6	4.5	4.3	45.3
Avg. Snowfall (in.)	10	10	7	1	Tr	0	0	0	0	Tr	1	7	35
Avg. Rel. Hum. 7am (%)	71	71	71	70	73	75	78	81	83	81	78	74	75
Avg. Rel. Hum. 4pm (%)	58	56	54	51	55	58	58	60	60	58	60	60	57

Note: Figures cover the years 1948-1992; Tr = Trace amounts (<0.05 in. of rain; <0.5 in. of snow)
Source: National Climatic Data Center, International Station Meteorological Climate Summary, 9/96

Weather Conditions

Temperature			Daytime Sky			Precipitation		
5°F & below	32°F & below	90°F & above	Clear	Partly cloudy	Cloudy	0.01 inch or more precip.	0.1 inch or more snow/ice	Thunder-storms
6	117	9	85	134	146	123	21	21

Note: Figures are average number of days per year and cover the years 1948-1992
Source: National Climatic Data Center, International Station Meteorological Climate Summary, 9/96

HAZARDOUS WASTE

Superfund Sites

The Providence-Warwick, RI-MA metro area is home to 17 sites on the EPA's Superfund National Priorities List (NPL) or Superfund Alternative Approach (SAA) list: **Atlas Tack Corp.** (Final NPL); **Central Landfill** (Final NPL); **Centredale Manor Restoration Project** (Final NPL); **Davis Liquid Waste** (Final NPL); **Davisville Naval Construction Battalion Center** (Final NPL); **Landfill & Resource Recovery, Inc. (L&RR)** (Final NPL); **New Bedford** (Final NPL); **Newport Naval Education & Training Center** (Final NPL); **Peterson/Puritan, Inc.** (Final NPL); **Picillo Farm** (Final NPL); **Re-Solve, Inc.** (Final NPL); **Rose Hill Regional Landfill** (Final NPL); **Stamina Mills** (Final NPL); **Sullivan's Ledge** (Final NPL); **Walton & Lonsbury Inc.** (Final NPL); **West Kingston Town Dump/URI Disposal Area** (Final NPL); **Western Sand & Gravel** (Final NPL). The Superfund alternative approach uses the same investigation and cleanup process and standards that are used for sites listed on the National Priorities List. The SAA is an alternative to listing a site on the NPL; it is not an alternative to Superfund or the Superfund process. There are a total of 1,445 Superfund sites with a status of proposed or final on both lists in the United States. *U.S. Environmental Protection Agency, National Priorities List, May 1, 2025; U.S. Environmental Protection Agency, Superfund Alternative Approach Sites, May 1, 2025*

AIR QUALITY

Air Quality Trends: Ozone

	1990	1995	2000	2005	2010	2015	2020	2021	2022	2023
MSA[1]	0.106	0.107	0.087	0.090	0.072	0.070	0.065	0.067	0.060	0.066
U.S.	0.087	0.089	0.081	0.080	0.072	0.068	0.066	0.067	0.067	0.070

Note: (1) Data covers the Providence-Warwick, RI-MA Metropolitan Statistical Area. The values shown are the composite ozone concentration averages among trend sites based on the highest fourth daily maximum 8-hour concentration in parts per million. These trends are based on sites having an adequate record of monitoring data during the trend period. Data from exceptional events are included.
Source: U.S. Environmental Protection Agency, Air Quality Monitoring Information, "Air Quality Trends by City, 1990-2023"

Air Quality Index

Area	Percent of Days when Air Quality was...[2]					AQI Statistics[2]	
	Good	Moderate	Unhealthy for Sensitive Groups	Unhealthy	Very Unhealthy	Maximum	Median
MSA[1]	54.8	42.2	3.0	0.0	0.0	140	48

Note: (1) Data covers the Providence-Warwick, RI-MA Metropolitan Statistical Area; (2) Based on 365 days with AQI data in 2023. Air Quality Index (AQI) is an index for reporting daily air quality. EPA calculates the AQI for five major air pollutants regulated by the Clean Air Act: ground-level ozone, particle pollution (aka particulate matter), carbon monoxide, sulfur dioxide, and nitrogen dioxide. The AQI runs from 0 to 500. The higher the AQI value, the greater the level of air pollution and the greater the health concern. There are six AQI categories: "Good" AQI is between 0 and 50. Air quality is considered satisfactory; "Moderate" AQI is between 51 and 100. Air quality is acceptable; "Unhealthy for Sensitive Groups" When AQI values are between 101 and 150, members of sensitive groups may experience health effects; "Unhealthy" When AQI values are between 151 and 200 everyone may begin to experience health effects; "Very Unhealthy" AQI values between 201 and 300 trigger a health alert; "Hazardous" AQI values over 300 trigger warnings of emergency conditions (not shown).
Source: U.S. Environmental Protection Agency, Air Quality Index Report, 2023

Air Quality Index Pollutants

Area	Percent of Days when AQI Pollutant was...[2]					
	Carbon Monoxide	Nitrogen Dioxide	Ozone	Sulfur Dioxide	Particulate Matter 2.5	Particulate Matter 10
MSA[1]	0.0	0.3	41.9	(3)	57.8	0.0

Note: (1) Data covers the Providence-Warwick, RI-MA Metropolitan Statistical Area; (2) Based on 365 days with AQI data in 2023. The Air Quality Index (AQI) is an index for reporting daily air quality. EPA calculates the AQI for five major air pollutants regulated by the Clean Air Act: ground-level ozone, particle pollution (also known as particulate matter), carbon monoxide, sulfur dioxide, and nitrogen dioxide. The AQI runs from 0 to 500. The higher the AQI value, the greater the level of air pollution and the greater the health concern; (3) Sulfur dioxide is no longer included in this table because SO_2 concentrations tend to be very localized and not necessarily representative of broad geographical areas like counties and CBSAs.
Source: U.S. Environmental Protection Agency, Air Quality Index Report, 2023

Maximum Air Pollutant Concentrations: Particulate Matter, Ozone, CO and Lead

	Particulate Matter 10 (ug/m^3)	Particulate Matter 2.5 Wtd AM (ug/m^3)	Particulate Matter 2.5 24-Hr (ug/m^3)	Ozone (ppm)	Carbon Monoxide (ppm)	Lead (ug/m^3)
MSA[1] Level	29	8.2	29	0.075	2	n/a
NAAQS[2]	150	15	35	0.075	9	0.15
Met NAAQS[2]	Yes	Yes	Yes	Yes	Yes	n/a

Note: (1) Data covers the Providence-Warwick, RI-MA Metropolitan Statistical Area; Data from exceptional events are included; (2) National Ambient Air Quality Standards; ppm = parts per million; ug/m^3 = micrograms per cubic meter; n/a not available.
Concentrations: Particulate Matter 10 (coarse particulate)—highest second maximum 24-hour concentration; Particulate Matter 2.5 Wtd AM (fine particulate)—highest weighted annual mean concentration; Particulate Matter 2.5 24-Hour (fine particulate)—highest 98th percentile 24-hour concentration; Ozone—highest fourth daily maximum 8-hour concentration; Carbon Monoxide—highest second maximum non-overlapping 8-hour concentration; Lead—maximum running 3-month average
Source: U.S. Environmental Protection Agency, Air Quality Monitoring Information, "Air Quality Statistics by City, 2023"

Maximum Air Pollutant Concentrations: Nitrogen Dioxide and Sulfur Dioxide

	Nitrogen Dioxide AM (ppb)	Nitrogen Dioxide 1-Hr (ppb)	Sulfur Dioxide AM (ppb)	Sulfur Dioxide 1-Hr (ppb)	Sulfur Dioxide 24-Hr (ppb)
MSA[1] Level	13	35	n/a	3	n/a
NAAQS[2]	53	100	30	75	140
Met NAAQS[2]	Yes	Yes	n/a	Yes	n/a

Note: (1) Data covers the Providence-Warwick, RI-MA Metropolitan Statistical Area; Data from exceptional events are included; (2) National Ambient Air Quality Standards; ppm = parts per million; ug/m^3 = micrograms per cubic meter; n/a not available.
Concentrations: Nitrogen Dioxide AM—highest arithmetic mean concentration; Nitrogen Dioxide 1-Hr—highest 98th percentile 1-hour daily maximum concentration; Sulfur Dioxide AM—highest annual mean concentration; Sulfur Dioxide 1-Hr—highest 99th percentile 1-hour daily maximum concentration; Sulfur Dioxide 24-Hr—highest second maximum 24-hour concentration
Source: U.S. Environmental Protection Agency, Air Quality Monitoring Information, "Air Quality Statistics by City, 2023"

Raleigh, North Carolina

Background

Raleigh, 120 miles west of the Atlantic Ocean, is named for Queen Elizabeth I's swashbuckling favorite, Sir Walter Raleigh. In her name, he plundered Spanish ships for gold in the New World and founded the first English settlement along the North Carolina coast. His excessive piracy led to his execution in 1618.

Raleigh is the capital of North Carolina, and its cultural and educational center. It's the retail and wholesale center of eastern North Carolina. Its top industries are manufacturing, trade, information, finance, professional services, education and health services, and government. The city boasts first-rate universities such as North Carolina State, Duke University, and the University of North Carolina. The Research Triangle Park—one of the largest university-affiliated research parks in the world, comprising Raleigh, Durham, and Chapel Hill—continues to pump money into the local economy.

The region has a high business startup rate, a low unemployment rate, and average wages above the state level. North Carolina State University's Centennial Campus has also encouraged major corporations to relocate, bringing with them thousands of jobs. Top employers in Raleigh include IBM, Red Hat Software, and Duke and North Carolina universities.

Called the "City of Oaks," for its tree-lined streets, architecture in Raleigh ranges from the modern architecture of the North Carolina Museum of Art, designed by Edward Durrell Stone (architect of Washington DC's John F. Kennedy Center), to the antebellum structures such as the Greek Revival Capitol Building. The city's street grid simplifies exploration of Raleigh's downtown, which continues to prosper and develop. In 2009, Raleigh became one of three United States cities participating in Project Get Ready—a non-profit program led by the Rocky Mountain Institute (RMI) to advance Electric Vehicle policies. Today, Raleigh operates a diverse fleet of nearly 1,000 electric vehicles. The city's climate action goal is an 80 percent reduction in greenhouse gases by 2050.

Cultural attractions include the North Carolina Symphony, the Opera Company of North Carolina, and the Carolina Ballet, all of which perform at the Progress Energy Center for the Performing Arts. There are numerous other musical, dance and theater groups in the city and the City of Raleigh Arts Commission actively supports the arts. Children enjoy the Marbles Kids Museum & Wachovia IMAX® Theatre.

The Coastal Credit Union Music Park at Walnut Creek hosts major international touring acts. The Downtown Raleigh Amphitheater (aka the Red Hat Amphitheater) hosts numerous concerts in the summer months. An additional amphitheater sits on the grounds of the North Carolina Museum of Art, which hosts summer concerts and outdoor movies.

Because it is centrally located between the mountains on the west and the coast on the south and east, the Raleigh area enjoys a pleasant climate. The mountains form a partial barrier to cold air masses moving from the west. As a result, there are few seriously cold winter days. In the summer, tropical air is present over the eastern and central sections of North Carolina, bringing warm temperatures and high humidity to the area. Raleigh usually is not dangerously affected by coastal storms. In April 2011, a devastating tornado hit the city, killing 24 people. While snow and sleet usually occur each year, excessive accumulations of snow are rare.

Rankings

General Rankings

- To help military veterans find the best places in which to settle down, *WalletHub* compared the 100 largest U.S. cities across 19 key indicators of livability, affordability and veteran-friendliness. They range from the share of military skill-related jobs to veteran income growth to the availability of VA health facilities. Raleigh ranked #3. *Wallethub.com, "Best & Worst Places for Veterans to Live (2025)," November 7, 2024*

- *US News & World Report* conducted a survey of more than 3,500 people and analyzed the 150 largest metropolitan areas to determine what matters most when selecting the next place to live. Raleigh ranked #6 out of the top 25 as having the best combination of desirable factors. Criteria: cost of living; quality of life and education; climate; job market; desirability; and other factors. *realestate.usnews.com, "Best Places to Live in the U.S. in 2024-2025," May 21, 2024*

- In their annual survey, Livability.com looked at data for more than 2,000 mid-sized U.S. cities to assign a "Livability Score" for each. The top 100 scoring cities make up Livability's "Top 100 Best Places to Live in the U.S." in 2025. Raleigh was placed among the top 100 of the customizable list. Criteria: housing and economy; cost of living; environment; education; health care options; transportation; safety; and community amenities. *Livability.com, "Top 100 Best Places to Live in the U.S. in 2025" April 15, 2025*

Business/Finance Rankings

- According to *Business Insider*, the Raleigh metro area is a prime place to run a startup or move an existing business to. The area ranked #16. More than 300 metro areas were analyzed for factors that were of top concern to new business owners. Data was based on the 2019 U.S. Census Bureau American Community Survey, statistics from the CDC, and University of Chicago analysis. Criteria: business formations; percentage of vaccinated population; percentage of households with internet subscriptions; median household income; and share of work that can be done from home. *BusinessInsider.com, "The 20 Best Cities for Starting a Business in 2022 Include Denver, Raleigh, and Olympia," June 7, 2022*

- Payscale.com ranked the 32 largest metro areas in terms of wage growth. The Raleigh metro area ranked #27. Criteria: quarterly changes in private industry employee and education professional wage growth from the previous year. *PayScale, "Wage Trends by Metro Area-4th Quarter," February 4, 2025*

- The Raleigh metro area appeared on the Milken Institute "2025 Best Performing Cities" list. Rank: #1 out of 200 large metro areas (based on performance category). Criteria: job growth; wage growth; high-tech growth and impact; community resilience; housing affordability; household broadband access. *Milken Institute, "Best-Performing Cities 2025," January 14, 2025*

Education Rankings

- Personal finance website *WalletHub* analyzed the 150 largest U.S. metropolitan statistical areas to determine where the most educated Americans are putting their degrees to work. Criteria: education levels; percentage of workers with degrees; education quality and attainment gap; public school quality rankings; quality and enrollment of each metro area's universities. Raleigh was ranked #7 (#1 = most educated city). *WalletHub.com, "Most & Least Educated Cities in America, 2025" July 2, 2024*

Environmental Rankings

- The U.S. Environmental Protection Agency (EPA) released its list of U.S. metropolitan areas with the most ENERGY STAR certified buildings in 2023. The Raleigh metro area was ranked #25 out of 25. *U.S. Environmental Protection Agency, "2024 Energy Star Top Cities," May 22, 2024*

- The U.S. Environmental Protection Agency (EPA) released its list of mid-size U.S. metropolitan areas with the most ENERGY STAR certified buildings in 2023. The Raleigh metro area was ranked #2 out of 10. *U.S. Environmental Protection Agency, "2024 Energy Star Top Cities," May 22, 2024*

Health/Fitness Rankings

- For each of the 100 largest cities in the United States, the American Fitness Index®, compiled in partnership between the American College of Sports Medicine and the Elevance Health Foundation, evaluated community infrastructure and more than 30 health behaviors including preventive health, levels of chronic disease conditions, food insecurity, pedestrian safety, air quality, and community/environment resources that support physical activity. Raleigh ranked #24 for "community fitness." *americanfitnessindex.org, "2024 ACSM American Fitness Index Summary Report," July 23, 2024*

- The Raleigh metro area was identified as one of the worst cities for bed bugs in America by pest control company Orkin. The area ranked #24 out of 50 based on the number of bed bug treatments Orkin performed from December 2022 to November 2023. *Orkin, "Chicago Joins Paris In Global Bed Bug Spotlight Ranking As The Worst City On Orkin's U.S. Bed Bug Cities List," January 22, 2024*

- Raleigh was identified as a "2025 Allergy Capital." The area ranked #7 out of the nation's 100 largest metropolitan areas. Three groups of factors were used to identify the most challenging cities for people with allergies: annual tree, grass, and weed pollen scores; over the counter allergy medicine use; number of board-certified allergy specialists. *Asthma and Allergy Foundation of America, "2025 Allergy Capitals: The Most Challenging Places to Live with Allergies," March 18, 2025*

- Raleigh was identified as a "2024 Asthma Capital." The area ranked #62 out of the nation's 100 largest metropolitan areas. Criteria: estimated asthma prevalence; asthma-related mortality; and ER visits due to asthma. Risk factors analyzed but not factored in the rankings: annual air quality including pollution and ozone levels; public smoking laws; indoor air quality; access to asthma specialists; rescue and controller medication use; uninsured rate; pollen allergy; poverty rate. *Asthma and Allergy Foundation of America, "Asthma Capitals 2024: The Most Challenging Places to Live With Asthma," September 10, 2024*

Pet Rankings

- Raleigh was selected by *Sniffspot.com* as one of the most dog-friendly cities in the U.S., ranking #14 out of 50. Criteria: dog parks; hiking; sniffspots; public parks; dog-friendly businesses; housing; dog waste cleanliness; leash laws; dog services; and overall cost. *Sniffspot.com, "The Top 50 Most Dog-Friendly Cities in the U.S.," September 30, 2024*

Real Estate Rankings

- *WalletHub* compared the most populated U.S. cities to determine which had the best markets for real estate agents. Raleigh ranked #54 where demand was high and pay was the best. Criteria: sales per agent; annual median wage for real-estate agents; monthly average starting salary for real estate agents; real estate job density and competition; unemployment rate; home turnover rate; housing-market health index; and other relevant metrics. *WalletHub.com, "2021 Best Places to Be a Real Estate Agent," May 12, 2021*

- Raleigh was ranked #89 out of 176 metro areas in terms of cost of housing in 2024 by the National Association of Home Builders (#1 = most affordable). Criteria: the portion of an average family's income necessary to pay the mortgage on a median-priced home. *National Association of Home Builders®, NAHB-Wells Fargo Cost of Housing Index, 4th Quarter 2024*

Safety Rankings

- Allstate ranked the 100 most populous cities in America in terms of driver safety. Raleigh ranked #68. Criteria based on anonymized driving behavior data from Allstate's mobile app powered by Arity: high speed driving (over 80 mph), phone handling, and hard braking. The report helps increase the importance of safety and awareness behind the wheel. *Allstate, "16th Allstate America's Best Drivers Report®," July 11, 2024*

Women/Minorities Rankings

- Personal finance website *WalletHub* compared more than 180 U.S. cities across two key dimensions, "Hispanic Business-Friendliness" and "Hispanic Purchasing Power," to arrive at the most favorable conditions for Hispanic entrepreneurs. Raleigh was ranked #114 out of 182. Criteria includes: share of Hispanic-Owned Businesses; average growth of Hispanic Business revenues; Small Business-Friendliness score; affordability; and number of Hispanics with at least a bachelor's degree. *WalletHub.com, "Best Cities for Hispanic Entrepreneurs," September 4, 2024*

Miscellaneous Rankings

- *WalletHub* compared 148 of the most populated U.S. cities to determine their operating efficiency. A "Quality of Services" score was constructed for each city and then measured against the total budget per capita to reveal which were managed the best. Raleigh ranked #11. Criteria: financial stability; economy; education; safety; health; infrastructure and pollution. *WalletHub.com, "2025's Best- & Worst-Run Cities in America," June 18, 2024*

Raleigh, North Carolina

Business Environment

DEMOGRAPHICS

Population Growth

Area	1990 Census	2000 Census	2010 Census	2020 Census	2023 Estimate[2]	Population Growth 1990-2023 (%)
City	226,841	276,093	403,892	467,665	470,763	107.5
MSA[1]	541,081	797,071	1,130,490	1,413,982	1,449,594	167.9
U.S.	248,709,873	281,421,906	308,745,538	331,449,281	332,387,540	33.6

Note: (1) Figures cover the Raleigh-Cary, NC Metropolitan Statistical Area; (2) 2019-2023 5-year ACS population estimate
Source: U.S. Census Bureau, 1990 Census, 2000 Census, 2010 Census, 2020 Census, 2019-2023 American Community Survey 5-Year Estimates

Race

Area	White Alone[2] (%)	Black Alone[2] (%)	Asian Alone[2] (%)	AIAN[3] Alone[2] (%)	NHOPI[4] Alone[2] (%)	Other Race Alone[2] (%)	Two or More Races (%)
City	53.8	27.5	4.7	0.4	0.0	5.5	8.0
MSA[1]	60.7	19.1	6.6	0.4	0.0	5.4	7.8
U.S.	63.4	12.4	5.8	0.9	0.2	6.6	10.7

Note: (1) Figures cover the Raleigh-Cary, NC Metropolitan Statistical Area; (2) Alone is defined as not being in combination with one or more other races; (3) American Indian and Alaska Native; (4) Native Hawaiian and Other Pacific Islander
Source: U.S. Census Bureau, 2019-2023 American Community Survey 5-Year Estimates

Hispanic or Latino Origin

Area	Total (%)	Mexican (%)	Puerto Rican (%)	Cuban (%)	Other (%)
City	12.7	5.0	1.4	0.4	5.9
MSA[1]	12.1	6.0	1.4	0.4	4.4
U.S.	19.0	11.3	1.8	0.7	5.2

Note: Persons of Hispanic or Latino origin can be of any race; (1) Figures cover the Raleigh-Cary, NC Metropolitan Statistical Area
Source: U.S. Census Bureau, 2019-2023 American Community Survey 5-Year Estimates

Age

Area	Under Age 5	Age 5–19	Age 20–34	Age 35–44	Age 45–54	Age 55–64	Age 65–74	Age 75–84	Age 85+	Median Age
City	5.7	17.8	27.0	14.4	13.0	10.4	7.1	3.3	1.3	34.7
MSA[1]	5.9	20.4	20.2	14.8	14.1	11.9	8.0	3.6	1.3	37.5
U.S.	5.7	19.1	20.2	13.1	12.3	12.8	10.0	4.9	1.9	38.7

Note: (1) Figures cover the Raleigh-Cary, NC Metropolitan Statistical Area
Source: U.S. Census Bureau, 2019-2023 American Community Survey 5-Year Estimates

Disability by Age

Area	All Ages	Under 18 Years Old	18 to 64 Years Old	65 Years and Over
City	9.6	4.4	7.9	29.1
MSA[1]	10.0	3.9	8.3	30.1
U.S.	13.0	4.7	10.7	32.9

Note: Figures show percent of the civilian noninstitutionalized population that reported having a disability. Disability status is determined from six types of difficulty: vision, hearing, cognitive, ambulatory, self-care, and independent living. For children under 5 years old, hearing and vision difficulty are used to determine disability status. For children between the ages of 5 and 14, disability status is determined from hearing, vision, cognitive, ambulatory, and self-care difficulties. For people aged 15 years and older, they are considered to have a disability if they have difficulty with any one of the six difficulty types; Note: (1) Figures cover the Raleigh-Cary, NC Metropolitan Statistical Area
Source: U.S. Census Bureau, 2019-2023 American Community Survey 5-Year Estimates

Ancestry

Area	German	Irish	English	American	Italian	Polish	French[2]	European	Scottish
City	9.2	8.5	11.8	5.7	3.8	1.9	1.7	1.6	2.2
MSA[1]	9.7	8.8	12.8	6.8	4.6	2.0	1.8	2.0	2.3
U.S.	12.6	9.4	9.1	5.5	4.9	2.6	2.0	1.6	1.6

Note: Figures are the percentage of the total population reporting a particular ancestry. The nine most commonly reported ancestries in the U.S. are shown. Figures include multiple ancestries (e.g. if a person reported being Irish and Italian, they were included in both columns); (1) Figures cover the Raleigh-Cary, NC Metropolitan Statistical Area; (2) Excludes Basque
Source: U.S. Census Bureau, 2019-2023 American Community Survey 5-Year Estimates

Foreign-born Population

Area	Any Foreign Country	Percent of Population Born in							
		Asia	Mexico	Europe	Caribbean	Central America[2]	South America	Africa	Canada
City	13.6	3.8	2.4	1.3	1.1	1.4	1.1	2.2	0.2
MSA[1]	13.1	5.0	2.5	1.3	0.8	1.0	0.8	1.3	0.3
U.S.	13.9	4.3	3.3	1.4	1.4	1.2	1.2	0.8	0.2

Note: (1) Figures cover the Raleigh-Cary, NC Metropolitan Statistical Area; (2) Excludes Mexico.
Source: U.S. Census Bureau, 2019-2023 American Community Survey 5-Year Estimates

Household Size

Area	Persons in Household (%)							Average Household Size
	One	Two	Three	Four	Five	Six	Seven or More	
City	35.3	33.7	13.8	11.4	4.2	1.1	0.5	2.30
MSA[1]	25.9	34.7	16.1	14.5	6.0	1.9	0.9	2.57
U.S.	28.5	33.8	15.4	12.7	5.9	2.3	1.4	2.54

Note: (1) Figures cover the Raleigh-Cary, NC Metropolitan Statistical Area
Source: U.S. Census Bureau, 2019-2023 American Community Survey 5-Year Estimates

Household Relationships

Area	Householder	Opposite-sex Spouse	Same-sex Spouse	Opposite-sex Unmarried Partner	Same-sex Unmarried Partner	Child[2]	Grandchild	Other Relatives	Non-relatives
City	41.8	15.1	0.2	2.9	0.2	25.5	1.4	3.9	5.0
MSA[1]	38.4	19.2	0.2	2.2	0.2	30.0	1.5	3.7	3.0
U.S.	38.3	17.5	0.2	2.5	0.2	28.3	2.4	4.8	3.4

Note: Figures are percent of the total population; (1) Figures cover the Raleigh-Cary, NC Metropolitan Statistical Area; (2) Includes biological, adopted, and stepchildren of the householder
Source: U.S. Census Bureau, 2020 Census

Gender

Area	Males	Females	Males per 100 Females
City	228,452	242,311	94.3
MSA[1]	711,279	738,315	96.3
U.S.	164,545,087	167,842,453	98.0

Note: (1) Figures cover the Raleigh-Cary, NC Metropolitan Statistical Area
Source: U.S. Census Bureau, 2019-2023 American Community Survey 5-Year Estimates

Marital Status

Area	Never Married	Now Married[2]	Separated	Widowed	Divorced
City	43.1	40.5	1.9	3.9	10.6
MSA[1]	32.4	52.4	1.8	4.2	9.3
U.S.	34.1	47.9	1.7	5.6	10.7

Note: Figures are percentages and cover the population 15 years of age and older; (1) Figures cover the Raleigh-Cary, NC Metropolitan Statistical Area; (2) Excludes separated
Source: U.S. Census Bureau, 2019-2023 American Community Survey 5-Year Estimates

Religious Groups by Family

Area	Catholic	Baptist	Methodist	LDS[2]	Pentecostal	Lutheran	Islam	Adventist	Other
MSA[1]	12.4	9.8	5.4	1.2	1.9	0.7	3.2	1.5	12.8
U.S.	18.7	7.3	3.0	2.0	1.8	1.7	1.3	1.3	11.6

Note: Figures are the number of adherents as a percentage of the total population and cover the eight largest religious groups in the U.S; (1) Figures cover the Raleigh-Cary, NC Metropolitan Statistical Area; (2) Church of Jesus Christ of Latter-day Saints
Sources: 2020 U.S. Religion Census, Association of Statisticians of American Religious Bodies; The Association of Religion Data Archives (ARDA)

Religious Groups by Tradition

Area	Catholic	Evangelical Protestant	Mainline Protestant	Black Protestant	Islam	Judaism	Hinduism	Orthodox	Buddhism
MSA[1]	12.4	19.3	7.4	2.8	3.2	0.2	0.4	0.3	0.4
U.S.	18.7	16.5	5.2	2.3	1.3	0.6	0.4	0.4	0.3

Note: Figures are the number of adherents as a percentage of the total population; (1) Figures cover the Raleigh-Cary, NC Metropolitan Statistical Area
Sources: 2020 U.S. Religion Census, Association of Statisticians of American Religious Bodies; The Association of Religion Data Archives (ARDA)

ECONOMY

Real Gross Domestic Product (GDP)

Area[1]	2017	2018	2019	2020	2021	2022	2023	Rank[3]
MSA[1]	84.9	89.5	92.3	92.4	101.0	105.8	110.6	38
U.S.[2]	17,619.1	18,160.7	18,642.5	18,238.9	19,387.6	19,896.6	20,436.3	—

Note: Figures are in billions of chained 2017 dollars; (1) Figures cover the Raleigh-Cary, NC Metropolitan Statistical Area; (2) Figures cover real GDP within metropolitan areas; (3) Rank is based on 2023 data and ranges from 1 to 384
Source: U.S. Bureau of Economic Analysis

Economic Growth

Area	2014	2015	2016	2017	2018	2019	2020	2021	2022	2023
MSA[1]	6.1	7.4	6.5	4.6	5.4	3.1	0.2	9.3	4.7	4.6
U.S.[2]	2.6	3.2	2.0	2.7	3.1	2.7	-2.2	6.3	2.6	2.7

Note: Figures are real gross domestic product growth rates and represent percent change from preceding period; (1) Figures cover the Raleigh-Cary, NC Metropolitan Statistical Area; (2) Figures are the average growth rates within metropolitan areas
Source: U.S. Bureau of Economic Analysis

Metropolitan Area Exports

Area	2018	2019	2020	2021	2022	2023	Rank[2]
MSA[1]	3,193.2	3,546.8	3,372.0	3,962.7	4,714.1	5,965.8	58
U.S.	1,664,056.1	1,645,173.7	1,431,406.6	1,753,941.4	2,062,937.4	2,019,160.5	—

Note: Figures are in millions of dollars; (1) Figures cover the Raleigh-Cary, NC Metropolitan Statistical Area; (2) Rank is based on 2023 data and ranges from 1 to 386
Source: U.S. Department of Commerce, International Trade Administration, Office of Trade and Economic Analysis, Industry and Analysis, Exports by Metropolitan Area, data extracted April 2, 2025

Building Permits

Area	Single-Family			Multi-Family			Total		
	2023	2024	Pct. Chg.	2023	2024	Pct. Chg.	2023	2024	Pct. Chg.
City	1,762	1,653	-6.2	4,626	3,391	-26.7	6,388	5,044	-21.0
MSA[1]	12,147	13,343	9.8	8,472	5,636	-33.5	20,619	18,979	-8.0
U.S.	920,000	981,900	6.7	591,100	496,100	-16.1	1,511,100	1,478,000	-2.2

Note: (1) Figures cover the Raleigh-Cary, NC Metropolitan Statistical Area; Figures represent new, privately-owned housing units authorized (unadjusted data)
Source: U.S. Census Bureau, Building Permits Survey (BPS), 2023, 2024

Bankruptcy Filings

Area	Business Filings			Nonbusiness Filings		
	2023	2024	% Chg.	2023	2024	% Chg.
Wake County	51	76	49.0	653	830	27.1
U.S.	18,926	23,107	22.1	434,064	494,201	13.9

Note: Business filings include Chapter 7, Chapter 9, Chapter 11, Chapter 12, Chapter 13, Chapter 15, and Section 304; Nonbusiness filings include Chapter 7, Chapter 11, and Chapter 13
Source: Administrative Office of the U.S. Courts, Business and Nonbusiness Bankruptcy, County Cases Commenced by Chapter of the Bankruptcy Code, During the 12-Month Period Ending December 31, 2023 and Business and Nonbusiness Bankruptcy, County Cases Commenced by Chapter of the Bankruptcy Code, During the 12-Month Period Ending December 31, 2024

Housing Vacancy Rates

Area	Gross Vacancy Rate[3] (%)			Year-Round Vacancy Rate[4] (%)			Rental Vacancy Rate[5] (%)			Homeowner Vacancy Rate[6] (%)		
	2022	2023	2024	2022	2023	2024	2022	2023	2024	2022	2023	2024
MSA[1]	7.4	6.7	6.3	7.3	6.6	6.2	7.1	8.8	8.8	0.5	0.5	0.7
U.S.[2]	9.1	9.0	9.1	7.5	7.5	7.6	5.7	6.5	6.8	0.8	0.8	1.0

Note: (1) Figures cover the Raleigh-Cary, NC Metropolitan Statistical Area; (2) Figures cover the 75 largest Metropolitan Statistical Areas; (3) The percentage of the total housing inventory that is vacant; (4) The percentage of the housing inventory (excluding seasonal units) that is year-round vacant; (5) The percentage of rental inventory that is vacant for rent; (6) The percentage of homeowner inventory that is vacant for sale
Source: U.S. Census Bureau, Housing Vacancies and Homeownership Annual Statistics: 2022, 2023, 2024

INCOME

Income

Area	Per Capita ($)	Median Household ($)	Average Household ($)
City	49,948	82,424	116,724
MSA[1]	49,462	96,066	126,566
U.S.	43,289	78,538	110,491

Note: (1) Figures cover the Raleigh-Cary, NC Metropolitan Statistical Area
Source: U.S. Census Bureau, 2019-2023 American Community Survey 5-Year Estimates

Household Income Distribution

Area	Percent of Households Earning							
	Under $15,000	$15,000 -$24,999	$25,000 -$34,999	$35,000 -$49,999	$50,000 -$74,999	$75,000 -$99,999	$100,000 -$149,999	$150,000 and up
City	7.0	5.6	6.0	11.2	15.9	13.0	17.2	24.1
MSA[1]	5.6	4.9	5.4	9.0	14.6	12.1	19.5	28.8
U.S.	8.5	6.6	6.8	10.4	15.7	12.7	17.4	21.9

Note: (1) Figures cover the Raleigh-Cary, NC Metropolitan Statistical Area
Source: U.S. Census Bureau, 2019-2023 American Community Survey 5-Year Estimates

Poverty Rate

Area	All Ages	Under 18 Years Old	18 to 64 Years Old	65 Years and Over
City	11.4	14.6	10.9	9.1
MSA[1]	8.6	10.3	8.0	7.9
U.S.	12.4	16.3	11.6	10.4

Note: Figures are percentage of people whose income during the past 12 months was below the poverty level; (1) Figures cover the Raleigh-Cary, NC Metropolitan Statistical Area
Source: U.S. Census Bureau, 2019-2023 American Community Survey 5-Year Estimates

EMPLOYMENT

Labor Force and Employment

Area	Civilian Labor Force			Workers Employed		
	Dec. 2023	Dec. 2024	% Chg.	Dec. 2023	Dec. 2024	% Chg.
City	276,576	277,882	0.5	267,801	269,378	0.6
MSA[1]	799,354	803,302	0.5	775,484	780,100	0.6
U.S.	166,661,000	167,746,000	0.7	160,754,000	161,294,000	0.3

Note: Data is not seasonally adjusted and covers workers 16 years of age and older; (1) Figures cover the Raleigh-Cary, NC Metropolitan Statistical Area
Source: Bureau of Labor Statistics, Local Area Unemployment Statistics

Unemployment Rate

Area	2024											
	Jan.	Feb.	Mar.	Apr.	May	Jun.	Jul.	Aug.	Sep.	Oct.	Nov.	Dec.
City	3.5	3.6	3.5	3.0	3.2	3.6	3.8	3.6	3.0	3.0	3.3	3.1
MSA[1]	3.3	3.4	3.2	2.9	3.1	3.4	3.6	3.5	2.9	2.9	3.1	2.9
U.S.	4.1	4.2	3.9	3.5	3.7	4.3	4.5	4.4	3.9	3.9	4.0	3.8

Note: Data is not seasonally adjusted and covers workers 16 years of age and older; (1) Figures cover the Raleigh-Cary, NC Metropolitan Statistical Area
Source: Bureau of Labor Statistics, Local Area Unemployment Statistics

Average Wages

Occupation	$/Hr.	Occupation	$/Hr.
Accountants and Auditors	44.26	Maintenance and Repair Workers	24.47
Automotive Mechanics	26.71	Marketing Managers	81.03
Bookkeepers	24.19	Network and Computer Systems Admin.	50.43
Carpenters	23.43	Nurses, Licensed Practical	30.60
Cashiers	13.98	Nurses, Registered	43.18
Computer Programmers	41.74	Nursing Assistants	18.76
Computer Systems Analysts	52.76	Office Clerks, General	20.44
Computer User Support Specialists	29.83	Physical Therapists	45.60
Construction Laborers	22.02	Physicians	140.88
Cooks, Restaurant	17.14	Plumbers, Pipefitters and Steamfitters	27.06
Customer Service Representatives	21.36	Police and Sheriff's Patrol Officers	31.94
Dentists	104.78	Postal Service Mail Carriers	29.38
Electricians	26.83	Real Estate Sales Agents	33.92
Engineers, Electrical	65.68	Retail Salespersons	16.98
Fast Food and Counter Workers	14.64	Sales Representatives, Technical/Scientific	55.52
Financial Managers	85.21	Secretaries, Exc. Legal/Medical/Executive	22.71
First-Line Supervisors of Office Workers	31.78	Security Guards	20.01
General and Operations Managers	66.79	Surgeons	n/a
Hairdressers/Cosmetologists	22.26	Teacher Assistants, Exc. Postsecondary[1]	15.69
Home Health and Personal Care Aides	15.48	Teachers, Secondary School, Exc. Sp. Ed.[1]	26.95
Janitors and Cleaners	16.07	Telemarketers	n/a
Landscaping/Groundskeeping Workers	19.00	Truck Drivers, Heavy/Tractor-Trailer	26.45
Lawyers	71.98	Truck Drivers, Light/Delivery Services	20.95
Maids and Housekeeping Cleaners	15.98	Waiters and Waitresses	16.07

Note: Wage data covers the Raleigh-Cary, NC Metropolitan Statistical Area; (1) Hourly wages were calculated from annual wage data based on a 40 hour work week
Source: Bureau of Labor Statistics, Metro Area Occupational Employment & Wage Estimates, May 2024

Employment by Industry

Sector	MSA[1]		U.S.
	Number of Employees	Percent of Total	Percent of Total
Construction, Mining, and Logging	53,000	7.0	5.5
Financial Activities	41,400	5.5	5.8
Government	108,800	14.4	14.9
Information	25,200	3.3	1.9
Leisure and Hospitality	79,600	10.5	10.4
Manufacturing	34,200	4.5	8.0
Other Services	33,100	4.4	3.7
Private Education and Health Services	104,600	13.8	16.9
Professional and Business Services	146,800	19.4	14.2
Retail Trade	76,600	10.1	10.0
Transportation, Warehousing, and Utilities	26,300	3.5	4.8
Wholesale Trade	28,500	3.8	3.9

Note: Figures are non-farm employment as of December 2024. Figures are not seasonally adjusted and include workers 16 years of age and older; (1) Figures cover the Raleigh-Cary, NC Metropolitan Statistical Area
Source: Bureau of Labor Statistics, Current Employment Statistics, Employment, Hours, and Earnings

Employment by Occupation

Occupation Classification	City (%)	MSA[1] (%)	U.S. (%)
Management, Business, Science, and Arts	52.5	53.1	42.0
Natural Resources, Construction, and Maintenance	5.5	6.9	8.6
Production, Transportation, and Material Moving	8.5	8.8	13.0
Sales and Office	19.9	18.8	19.9
Service	13.6	12.5	16.5

Note: Figures cover employed civilians 16 years of age and older; (1) Figures cover the Raleigh-Cary, NC Metropolitan Statistical Area
Source: U.S. Census Bureau, 2019-2023 American Community Survey 5-Year Estimates

Occupations with Greatest Projected Employment Growth: 2022 – 2032

Occupation[1]	2022 Employment	2032 Projected Employment	Numeric Employment Change	Percent Employment Change
Software Developers	57,190	75,660	18,470	32.3
Cooks, Restaurant	47,710	66,050	18,340	38.4
Registered Nurses	106,190	123,650	17,460	16.4
Home Health and Personal Care Aides	62,750	77,390	14,640	23.3
Stockers and Order Fillers	92,790	105,710	12,920	13.9
Laborers and Freight, Stock, and Material Movers, Hand	121,680	133,850	12,170	10.0
General and Operations Managers	94,010	105,400	11,390	12.1
Fast Food and Counter Workers	65,320	75,130	9,810	15.0
First-Line Supervisors of Food Preparation and Serving Workers	41,690	49,690	8,000	19.2
Waiters and Waitresses	71,300	79,060	7,760	10.9

Note: Projections cover North Carolina; (1) Sorted by numeric employment change
Source: www.projectionscentral.org, State Occupational Projections, 2022–2032 Long-Term Projections

Fastest-Growing Occupations: 2022 – 2032

Occupation[1]	2022 Employment	2032 Projected Employment	Numeric Employment Change	Percent Employment Change
Nurse Practitioners	8,200	12,750	4,550	55.5
Solar Photovoltaic Installers	950	1,400	450	47.4
Statisticians	1,580	2,270	690	43.7
Data Scientists	5,430	7,720	2,290	42.2
Medical and Health Services Managers	12,880	17,860	4,980	38.7
Cooks, Restaurant	47,710	66,050	18,340	38.4
Physician Assistants	7,440	10,170	2,730	36.7
Information Security Analysts (SOC 2018)	5,920	8,070	2,150	36.3
Occupational Therapy Assistants	1,310	1,780	470	35.9
Wind Turbine Service Technicians	140	190	50	35.7

Note: Projections cover North Carolina; (1) Sorted by percent employment change and excludes occupations with numeric employment change less than 50
Source: www.projectionscentral.org, State Occupational Projections, 2022–2032 Long-Term Projections

CITY FINANCES

City Government Finances

Component	2022 ($000)	2022 ($ per capita)
Total Revenues	1,102,444	2,324
Total Expenditures	1,060,557	2,236
Debt Outstanding	1,393,773	2,938

Source: U.S. Census Bureau, State & Local Government Finances 2022

City Government Revenue by Source

Source	2022 ($000)	2022 ($ per capita)	2022 (%)
General Revenue			
From Federal Government	62,951	133	5.7
From State Government	51,612	109	4.7
From Local Governments	80,439	170	7.3
Taxes			
Property	291,708	615	26.5
Sales and Gross Receipts	140,212	296	12.7
Personal Income	0	0	0.0
Corporate Income	0	0	0.0
Motor Vehicle License	11,164	24	1.0
Other Taxes	31,325	66	2.8
Current Charges	299,575	631	27.2
Liquor Store	0	0	0.0
Utility	119,382	252	10.8

Source: U.S. Census Bureau, State & Local Government Finances 2022

City Government Expenditures by Function

Function	2022 ($000)	2022 ($ per capita)	2022 (%)
General Direct Expenditures			
Air Transportation	0	0	0.0
Corrections	0	0	0.0
Education	0	0	0.0
Employment Security Administration	0	0	0.0
Financial Administration	12,812	27	1.2
Fire Protection	76,676	161	7.2
General Public Buildings	24,257	51	2.3
Governmental Administration, Other	9,549	20	0.9
Health	0	0	0.0
Highways	65,557	138	6.2
Hospitals	0	0	0.0
Housing and Community Development	28,587	60	2.7
Interest on General Debt	35,535	74	3.4
Judicial and Legal	4,491	9	0.4
Libraries	0	0	0.0
Parking	8,050	17	0.8
Parks and Recreation	114,751	241	10.8
Police Protection	119,431	251	11.3
Public Welfare	0	0	0.0
Sewerage	248,173	523	23.4
Solid Waste Management	38,128	80	3.6
Veterans' Services	0	0	0.0
Liquor Store	0	0	0.0
Utility	196,365	413	18.5

Source: U.S. Census Bureau, State & Local Government Finances 2022

TAXES

State Corporate Income Tax Rates

State	Tax Rate (%)	Income Brackets ($)	Num. of Brackets	Financial Institution Tax Rate (%)[a]	Federal Income Tax Ded.
North Carolina	2.5	Flat rate	1	2.5	No

Note: Tax rates for tax year 2024; (a) Rates listed are the corporate income tax rate applied to financial institutions or excise taxes based on income. Some states have other taxes based upon the value of deposits or shares.
Source: Federation of Tax Administrators, State Corporate Income Tax Rates, January 1, 2025

State Individual Income Tax Rates

State	Tax Rate (%)	Income Brackets ($)	Personal Exemptions ($)			Standard Ded. ($)	
			Single	Married	Depend.	Single	Married
North Carolina	4.5	Flat rate	None	None	None	12,750	25,500

Note: Tax rates for tax year 2024; Local- and county-level taxes are not included; Federal income tax is not deductible on state income tax returns
Source: Federation of Tax Administrators, State Individual Income Tax Rates, January 1, 2025

Various State Sales and Excise Tax Rates

State	State Sales Tax (%)	Gasoline[1] ($/gal.)	Cigarette[2] ($/pack)	Spirits[3] ($/gal.)	Wine[4] ($/gal.)	Beer[5] ($/gal.)	Recreational Marijuana (%)
North Carolina	4.75	0.41	0.45	18.23	1.00	0.62	Not legal

Note: All tax rates as of January 1, 2025; (1) The American Petroleum Institute has developed a methodology for determining the average tax rate on a gallon of fuel. Rates may include any of the following: excise taxes, environmental fees, storage tank fees, other fees or taxes, general sales tax, and local taxes; (2) The federal excise tax of $1.0066 per pack and local taxes are not included; (3) Rates are those applicable to off-premise sales of 40% alcohol by volume (a.b.v.) distilled spirits in 750ml containers. Local excise taxes are excluded; (4) Rates are those applicable to off-premise sales of 11% a.b.v. non-carbonated wine in 750ml containers; (5) Rates are those applicable to off-premise sales of 4.7% a.b.v. beer in 12 ounce containers.
Source: Tax Foundation, 2025 Facts & Figures: How Does Your State Compare?

State Tax Competitiveness Index

State	Overall Rank	Corporate Tax Rank	Individual Income Tax Rank	Sales Tax Rank	Property Tax Rank	Unemployment Insurance Tax Rank
North Carolina	12	3	21	16	20	7

Note: The Tax Foundation's State Tax Competitiveness Index enables policymakers, taxpayers, and business leaders to gauge how their states' tax systems compare. A rank of 1 is best, 50 is worst. Rankings do not average to the total. States without a tax rank equally as 1. DC's scores and rankings do not affect other states. The report shows tax systems as of July 1, 2024 (the beginning of Fiscal Year 2025).
Source: Tax Foundation, State Tax Competitiveness Index 2025

TRANSPORTATION

Means of Transportation to Work

Area	Car/Truck/Van		Public Transportation			Bicycle	Walked	Other Means	Worked at Home
	Drove Alone	Car-pooled	Bus	Subway	Railroad				
City	65.1	6.6	1.3	0.0	0.0	0.4	1.6	1.6	23.4
MSA[1]	67.0	6.5	0.5	0.0	0.0	0.2	1.1	1.3	23.4
U.S.	70.2	8.5	1.7	1.3	0.4	0.4	2.4	1.6	13.5

Note: Figures are percentages and cover workers 16 years of age and older; (1) Figures cover the Raleigh-Cary, NC Metropolitan Statistical Area
Source: U.S. Census Bureau, 2019-2023 American Community Survey 5-Year Estimates

Travel Time to Work

Area	Less Than 10 Minutes	10 to 19 Minutes	20 to 29 Minutes	30 to 44 Minutes	45 to 59 Minutes	60 to 89 Minutes	90 Minutes or More
City	10.3	33.4	26.8	19.9	5.4	2.5	1.7
MSA[1]	9.0	26.8	23.5	24.3	9.6	5.0	1.8
U.S.	12.6	28.6	21.2	20.8	8.1	6.0	2.8

Note: Note: Figures are percentages and include workers 16 years old and over; (1) Figures cover the Raleigh-Cary, NC Metropolitan Statistical Area
Source: U.S. Census Bureau, 2019-2023 American Community Survey 5-Year Estimates

Key Congestion Measures

Measure	2000	2010	2015	2020	2022
Annual Hours of Delay, Total (000)	13,776	21,618	25,692	11,144	22,473
Annual Hours of Delay, Per Auto Commuter	28	34	39	17	37
Annual Congestion Cost, Per Auto Commuter ($)	645	807	885	404	818

Note: Figures cover the Raleigh NC urban area
Source: Texas A&M Transportation Institute, 2023 Urban Mobility Report

Freeway Travel Time Index

Measure	1985	1990	1995	2000	2005	2010	2015	2020	2022
Urban Area Index[1]	1.06	1.10	1.12	1.14	1.16	1.16	1.17	1.05	1.13
Urban Area Rank[1,2]	53	47	57	62	57	54	46	85	71

Note: Freeway Travel Time Index—the ratio of travel time in the peak period to the travel time at free-flow conditions. For example, a value of 1.30 indicates a 20-minute free-flow trip takes 26 minutes in the peak (20 minutes x 1.30 = 26 minutes); (1) Covers the Raleigh NC urban area; (2) Rank is based on 101 larger urban areas (#1 = highest travel time index)
Source: Texas A&M Transportation Institute, 2023 Urban Mobility Report

Public Transportation

Agency Name / Mode of Transportation	Vehicles Operated in Maximum Service[1]	Annual Unlinked Passenger Trips[2] (in thous.)	Annual Passenger Miles[3] (in thous.)
Capital Area Transit (CAT)			
Bus (purchased transportation)	84	4,518.7	19,610.1
Demand Response - Taxi	178	819.4	4,880.0

Note: (1) Number of revenue vehicles operated by the given mode and type of service to meet the annual maximum service requirement. This is the revenue vehicle count during the peak season of the year; on the week and day that maximum service is provided. Vehicles operated in maximum service (VOMS) exclude atypical days and one-time special events; (2) Number of passengers who boarded public transportation vehicles. Passengers are counted each time they board a vehicle no matter how many vehicles they use to travel from their origin to their destination. (3) Sum of the distances ridden by all passengers during the entire fiscal year.
Source: Federal Transit Administration, National Transit Database, 2023

Air Transportation

Airport Name and Code / Type of Service	Passenger Airlines[1]	Passenger Enplanements	Freight Carriers[2]	Freight (lbs)
Raleigh-Durham International (RDU)				
Domestic service (U.S. carriers only)	29	7,285,042	10	69,157,417
International service (U.S. carriers only)	9	86,141	1	1,274,372

Note: (1) Includes all U.S.-based major, minor and commuter airlines that carried at least one passenger during the year; (2) Includes all U.S.-based airlines and freight carriers that transported at least one pound of freight during the year.
Source: Bureau of Transportation Statistics, The Intermodal Transportation Database, Air Carriers: T-100 Domestic Market (U.S. carriers only), 2024; Bureau of Transportation Statistics, The Intermodal Transportation Database, Air Carriers: T-100 International Market (U.S. carriers only), 2024

BUSINESSES

Major Business Headquarters

Company Name	Industry	Rankings Fortune[1]	Rankings Forbes[2]
Advance Auto Parts	Specialty retailers: other	358	-
First Citizens BancShares	Commercial banks	182	-

Note: (1) Companies that produce a 10-K are ranked 1 to 500 based on 2023 revenue; (2) All private companies with at least $2 billion in annual revenue through the end of their most current fiscal year are ranked 1 to 275; companies listed are headquartered in the city; dashes indicate no ranking
Source: Fortune, "Fortune 500," 2024; Forbes, "America's Largest Private Companies," 2024

Fastest-Growing Businesses

According to *Inc.*, Raleigh is home to one of America's 500 fastest-growing private companies: **BaseMonkeys** (#216). Criteria: must be an independent, privately-held, for-profit, U.S. corporation, proprietorship or partnership as of December 31, 2023; revenues must be at least $100,000 in 2020 and $2 million in 2023; must have four-year operating/sales history. *Inc., "America's 500 Fastest-Growing Private Companies," 2024*

According to Deloitte, Raleigh is home to three of North America's 500 fastest-growing high-technology companies: **Levitate** (#195); **Relay** (#222); **Element451** (#400). Companies are ranked by percentage growth in revenue over a four-year period. Criteria for inclusion: company must be headquartered within North America; must own proprietary intellectual property or technology that is sold to customers in products that contributes to a significant portion of the company's operating revenue; must have been in business for a minumum of four years with 2020 operating revenues of at least $50,000 USD/CD and 2023 operating revenues of at least $5 million USD/CD. *Deloitte, 2024 Technology Fast 500™*

Living Environment

COST OF LIVING

Cost of Living Index

Composite Index	Groceries	Housing	Utilities	Transportation	Health Care	Misc. Goods/Services
97.2	100.6	91.9	89.8	92.1	112.2	101.0

Note: The Cost of Living Index measures regional differences in the cost of consumer goods and services, excluding taxes and non-consumer expenditures, for professional and managerial households in the top income quintile. It is based on more than 50,000 prices covering almost 60 different items for which prices are collected three times a year by chambers of commerce, economic development organizations or university applied economic centers in each participating urban area. The numbers shown should be read as a percentage above or below the national average of 100. For example, a value of 115.4 in the groceries column indicates that grocery prices are 15.4% higher than the national average. Small differences in the index numbers should not be interpreted as significant; Figures cover the Raleigh NC urban area.
Source: The Council for Community and Economic Research, Cost of Living Index, 2024

Grocery Prices

Area[1]	T-Bone Steak ($/pound)	Frying Chicken ($/pound)	Whole Milk ($/half gal.)	Eggs ($/dozen)	Orange Juice ($/64 oz.)	Coffee ($/11.5 oz.)
City[2]	15.51	1.45	4.58	3.33	4.31	5.44
Avg.	15.42	1.55	4.69	3.25	4.41	5.46
Min.	14.50	1.16	4.43	2.75	4.00	4.85
Max.	17.56	2.89	5.49	4.78	5.54	7.89

Note: (1) Values for the local area are compared with the average, minimum and maximum values for all 276 areas in the Cost of Living Index; (2) Figures cover the Raleigh NC urban area; **T-Bone Steak** (price per pound); **Frying Chicken** (price per pound, whole fryer); **Whole Milk** (half gallon carton); **Eggs** (price per dozen, Grade A, large); **Orange Juice** (64 oz. Tropicana or Florida Natural); **Coffee** (11.5 oz. can, vacuum-packed, Maxwell House, Hills Bros, or Folgers).
Source: The Council for Community and Economic Research, Cost of Living Index, 2024

Housing and Utility Costs

Area[1]	New Home Price ($)	Apartment Rent ($/month)	All Electric ($/month)	Part Electric ($/month)	Other Energy ($/month)	Telephone ($/month)
City[2]	466,683	1,514	-	107.05	69.13	189.30
Avg.	515,975	1,550	210.99	123.07	82.07	194.99
Min.	265,375	692	104.33	53.68	36.26	179.42
Max.	2,775,821	5,719	529.02	397.28	361.63	223.33

Note: (1) Values for the local area are compared with the average, minimum and maximum values for all 276 areas in the Cost of Living Index; (2) Figures cover the Raleigh NC urban area; **New Home Price** (2,400 sf living area, 8,000 sf lot, in urban area with full utilities); **Apartment Rent** (950 sf 2 bedroom/1.5 or 2 bath, unfurnished, excluding all utilities except water); **All Electric** (average monthly cost for an all-electric home); **Part Electric** (average monthly cost for a part-electric home); **Other Energy** (average monthly cost for natural gas, fuel oil, coal, wood, and any other forms of energy except electricity); **Telephone** (price includes the base monthly rate plus taxes and fees for three lines of mobile phone service).
Source: The Council for Community and Economic Research, Cost of Living Index, 2024

Health Care, Transportation, and Other Costs

Area[1]	Doctor ($/visit)	Dentist ($/visit)	Optometrist ($/visit)	Gasoline ($/gallon)	Beauty Salon ($/visit)	Men's Shirt ($)
City[2]	146.67	153.61	109.33	3.23	55.17	32.17
Avg.	143.77	117.51	129.23	3.32	48.57	38.14
Min.	36.74	58.67	67.33	2.80	24.00	13.41
Max.	270.44	216.82	307.33	5.28	94.00	63.89

Note: (1) Values for the local area are compared with the average, minimum and maximum values for all 276 areas in the Cost of Living Index; (2) Figures cover the Raleigh NC urban area; **Doctor** (general practitioners routine exam of an established patient); **Dentist** (adult teeth cleaning and periodic oral examination); **Optometrist** (full vision eye exam for established adult patient); **Gasoline** (one gallon regular unleaded, national brand, including all taxes, cash price at self-service pump if available); **Beauty Salon** (woman's shampoo, trim, and blow-dry); **Men's Shirt** (cotton/polyester dress shirt, pinpoint weave, long sleeves).
Source: The Council for Community and Economic Research, Cost of Living Index, 2024

HOUSING

Homeownership Rate

Area	2017 (%)	2018 (%)	2019 (%)	2020 (%)	2021 (%)	2022 (%)	2023 (%)	2024 (%)
MSA[1]	68.2	64.9	63.0	68.2	62.7	65.1	68.8	65.0
U.S.	63.9	64.4	64.6	66.6	65.5	65.8	65.9	65.6

Note: (1) Figures cover the Raleigh-Cary, NC Metropolitan Statistical Area
Source: U.S. Census Bureau, Housing Vacancies and Homeownership Annual Statistics: 2017-2024

House Price Index (HPI)

Area	National Ranking[2]	Quarterly Change (%)	One-Year Change (%)	Five-Year Change (%)	Since 1991Q1 (%)
MSA[1]	185	0.14	3.78	65.05	335.12
U.S.[3]	—	1.43	4.51	57.13	327.82

Note: The HPI is a weighted repeat sales index. It measures average price changes in repeat sales or refinancings on the same properties. This information is obtained by reviewing repeat mortgage transactions on single-family properties whose mortgages have been purchased or securitized by Fannie Mae or Freddie Mac since January 1975; (1) Figures cover the Raleigh, NC Metropolitan Statistical Area; (2) Rankings are based on annual percentage change for all metro areas containing at least 15,000 transactions over the last 10 years and ranges from 1 to 241; (3) figures based on a weighted average of Census Division estimates using a seasonally adjusted, purchase-only index; all figures are for the period ending December 31, 2024
Source: Federal Housing Finance Agency, Change in FHFA Metropolitan Area House Price Indexes, All Transactions Index, 2024Q4

Home Value

Area	Under $100,000	$100,000 -$199,999	$200,000 -$299,999	$300,000 -$399,999	$400,000 -$499,999	$500,000 -$999,999	$1,000,000 or more	Median ($)
City	3.1	7.7	22.7	21.2	15.2	24.4	5.7	377,800
MSA[1]	5.3	9.2	19.3	20.0	16.2	26.2	3.9	381,000
U.S.	12.1	17.8	19.5	14.4	10.5	19.1	6.5	303,400

Note: Figures are percentages except for median and cover owner-occupied housing units; (1) Figures cover the Raleigh-Cary, NC Metropolitan Statistical Area
Source: U.S. Census Bureau, 2019-2023 American Community Survey 5-Year Estimates

Year Housing Structure Built

Area	2020 or Later	2010 -2019	2000 -2009	1990 -1999	1980 -1989	1970 -1979	1960 -1969	1950 -1959	1940 -1949	Before 1940	Median Year
City	1.6	17.5	23.5	17.1	16.0	9.6	6.8	3.7	1.3	2.9	1996
MSA[1]	2.9	20.7	23.7	19.4	13.7	8.2	4.8	3.0	1.2	2.5	1999
U.S.	1.2	8.9	13.6	12.8	13.0	14.4	10.0	9.7	4.5	11.9	1980

Note: Figures are percentages except for Median Year; Note: (1) Figures cover the Raleigh-Cary, NC Metropolitan Statistical Area
Source: U.S. Census Bureau, 2019-2023 American Community Survey 5-Year Estimates

Gross Monthly Rent

Area	Under $500	$500 -$999	$1,000 -$1,499	$1,500 -$1,999	$2,000 -$2,499	$2,500 -$2,999	$3,000 and up	Median ($)
City	2.5	9.3	41.1	33.8	8.8	2.7	1.8	1,468
MSA[1]	3.4	13.4	36.5	31.2	10.0	3.4	2.1	1,459
U.S.	6.5	22.3	29.5	20.2	10.8	4.8	5.9	1,348

Note: Figures are percentages except for median; Gross rent is the contract rent plus the estimated average monthly cost of utilities (electricity, gas, and water and sewer) and fuels (oil, coal, kerosene, wood, etc.) if these are paid by the renter (or paid for the renter by someone else); (1) Figures cover the Raleigh-Cary, NC Metropolitan Statistical Area
Source: U.S. Census Bureau, 2019-2023 American Community Survey 5-Year Estimates

HEALTH

Health Risk Factors

Category	MSA[1] (%)	U.S. (%)
Adults aged 18–64 who have any kind of health care coverage	91.4	90.8
Adults who reported being in good or better health	85.5	81.8
Adults who have been told they have high blood cholesterol	36.4	36.9
Adults who have been told they have high blood pressure	33.9	34.0
Adults who are current smokers	9.9	12.1
Adults who currently use e-cigarettes	6.0	7.7
Adults who currently use chewing tobacco, snuff, or snus	1.9	3.2
Adults who are heavy drinkers[2]	3.1	6.1
Adults who are binge drinkers[3]	14.0	15.2
Adults who are overweight (BMI 25.0 - 29.9)	34.8	34.4
Adults who are obese (BMI 30.0 - 99.8)	29.2	34.3
Adults who participated in any physical activities in the past month	85.3	75.8

Note: All figures are crude prevalence; (1) Figures cover the Raleigh, NC Metropolitan Statistical Area; (2) Heavy drinkers are classified as adult men having more than 14 drinks per week and adult women having more than 7 drinks per week; (3) Binge drinkers are classified as males having five or more drinks on one occasion or females having four or more drinks on one occasion
Source: Centers for Disease Control and Prevention, Behaviorial Risk Factor Surveillance System, SMART: Selected Metropolitan Area Risk Trends, 2023

Acute and Chronic Health Conditions

Category	MSA[1] (%)	U.S. (%)
Adults who have ever been told they had a heart attack	n/a	4.2
Adults who have ever been told they have angina or coronary heart disease	2.6	4.0
Adults who have ever been told they had a stroke	n/a	3.3
Adults who have ever been told they have asthma	15.5	15.7
Adults who have ever been told they have arthritis	20.2	26.3
Adults who have ever been told they have diabetes[2]	12.4	11.5
Adults who have ever been told they had skin cancer	6.5	5.6
Adults who have ever been told they had any other types of cancer	4.9	8.4
Adults who have ever been told they have COPD	3.6	6.4
Adults who have ever been told they have kidney disease	n/a	3.7
Adults who have ever been told they have a form of depression	22.4	22.0

Note: All figures are crude prevalence; (1) Figures cover the Raleigh, NC Metropolitan Statistical Area; (2) Figures do not include pregnancy-related, borderline, or pre-diabetes
Source: Centers for Disease Control and Prevention, Behavioral Risk Factor Surveillance System, SMART: Selected Metropolitan Area Risk Trends, 2023

Health Screening and Vaccination Rates

Category	MSA[1] (%)	U.S. (%)
Adults who have ever been tested for HIV	39.5	37.5
Adults who have had their blood cholesterol checked within the last five years	93.7	87.0
Adults aged 65+ who have had flu shot within the past year	78.4	63.4
Adults aged 65+ who have ever had a pneumonia vaccination	80.2	71.9

Note: All figures are crude prevalence; (1) Figures cover the Raleigh, NC Metropolitan Statistical Area.
Source: Centers for Disease Control and Prevention, Behavioral Risk Factor Surveillance System, SMART: Selected Metropolitan Area Risk Trends, 2023

Disability Status

Category	MSA[1] (%)	U.S. (%)
Adults who reported being deaf	6.7	7.4
Are you blind or have serious difficulty seeing, even when wearing glasses?	4.1	4.9
Do you have difficulty doing errands alone?	3.6	7.8
Do you have difficulty dressing or bathing?	n/a	3.6
Do you have serious difficulty concentrating/remembering/making decisions?	13.1	13.7
Do you have serious difficulty walking or climbing stairs?	8.9	13.2

Note: All figures are crude prevalence; (1) Figures cover the Raleigh, NC Metropolitan Statistical Area.
Source: Centers for Disease Control and Prevention, Behavioral Risk Factor Surveillance System, SMART: Selected Metropolitan Area Risk Trends, 2023

Mortality Rates for the Top 10 Causes of Death in the U.S.

ICD-10[a] Sub-Chapter	ICD-10[a] Code	Crude Mortality Rate[2] per 100,000 population	
		County[3]	U.S.
Malignant neoplasms	C00-C97	116.1	182.7
Ischaemic heart diseases	I20-I25	51.6	109.6
Provisional assignment of new diseases of uncertain etiology[1]	U00-U49	24.7	65.3
Other forms of heart disease	I30-I51	39.7	65.1
Other degenerative diseases of the nervous system	G30-G31	29.8	52.4
Other external causes of accidental injury	W00-X59	36.6	52.3
Cerebrovascular diseases	I60-I69	50.3	49.1
Chronic lower respiratory diseases	J40-J47	18.1	43.5
Hypertensive diseases	I10-I15	15.7	38.9
Organic, including symptomatic, mental disorders	F01-F09	27.0	33.9

Note: (a) ICD-10 = International Classification of Diseases 10th Revision; (1) Includes COVID-19, adverse effects to COVID-19 vaccines, SARS, and vaping-related disorders; (2) Crude mortality rates are a three-year average covering 2021-2023; (3) Figures cover Wake County.
Source: Centers for Disease Control and Prevention, National Center for Health Statistics. National Vital Statistics System, Mortality 2018-2023 on CDC WONDER Online Database

Mortality Rates for Selected Causes of Death

Cause of Death	ICD-10[a] Code	Crude Mortality Rate[1] per 100,000 population	
		County[2]	U.S.
Accidental poisoning and exposure to noxious substances	X40-X49	18.0	30.5
Alzheimer disease	G30	21.2	35.4
Assault	X85-Y09	4.3	7.3
COVID-19	U07.1	24.7	65.3
Diabetes mellitus	E10-E14	17.7	30.0
Diseases of the liver	K70-K76	11.0	20.8
Human immunodeficiency virus (HIV) disease	B20-B24	0.8	1.5
Influenza and pneumonia	J09-J18	5.1	13.4
Intentional self-harm	X60-X84	10.1	14.7
Malnutrition	E40-E46	3.3	6.0
Obesity and other hyperalimentation	E65-E68	2.6	3.1
Renal failure	N17-N19	11.8	16.4
Transport accidents	V01-V99	9.8	14.4

Note: (a) ICD-10 = International Classification of Diseases 10th Revision; (1) Crude mortality rates are a three-year average covering 2021-2023; (2) Figures cover Wake County; Data are suppressed when the data meet the criteria for confidentiality constraints; Crude mortality rates are flagged as unreliable when the rate would be calculated with a numerator of 20 or less.
Source: Centers for Disease Control and Prevention, National Center for Health Statistics. National Vital Statistics System, Mortality 2018-2023 on CDC WONDER Online Database

Health Insurance Coverage

Area	With Health Insurance	With Private Health Insurance	With Public Health Insurance	Without Health Insurance	Population Under Age 19 Without Health Insurance
City	89.9	73.5	26.0	10.1	6.0
MSA[1]	91.3	76.0	25.6	8.7	5.0
U.S.	91.4	67.3	36.3	8.6	5.4

Note: Figures are percentages that cover the civilian noninstitutionalized population; (1) Figures cover the Raleigh-Cary, NC Metropolitan Statistical Area
Source: U.S. Census Bureau, 2019-2023 American Community Survey 5-Year Estimates

Number of Medical Professionals

Area	MDs[3]	DOs[3,4]	Dentists	Podiatrists	Chiropractors	Optometrists
County[1] (number)	3,443	186	902	45	354	198
County[1] (rate[2])	293.0	15.8	75.8	3.8	29.7	16.6
U.S. (rate[2])	302.5	29.2	74.6	6.4	29.5	18.0

Note: Data as of 2023 unless noted; (1) Data covers Wake County; (2) Number of medical professionals per 100,000 population; (3) Data as of 2022 and includes all active, non-federal physicians; (4) Doctor of Osteopathic Medicine
Source: U.S. Department of Health and Human Services, Health Resources and Services Administration, Bureau of Health Professions, Area Resource File (ARF) 2023-2024

Best Hospitals

According to *U.S. News*, the Raleigh-Cary, NC metro area is home to one of the best hospitals in the U.S.: **WakeMed Raleigh Campus** (1 adult specialty). The hospital listed was nationally ranked in at least one of 15 adult or 11 pediatric specialties. The number of specialties shown cover the parent hospital. Only 160 U.S. hospitals performed well enough to be nationally ranked in one or more specialties. Twenty hospitals in the U.S. made the Honor Roll. The Best Hospitals Honor Roll takes both the national rankings and the procedure and condition ratings into account. Hospitals received points if they were nationally ranked in one of the 15 adult specialties—the higher they ranked, the more points they got—and how many ratings of "high performing" they earned in the 20 procedures and conditions. *U.S. News Online, "America's Best Hospitals 2024-25"*

EDUCATION

Public School District Statistics

District Name	Schls	Pupils	Pupil/ Teacher Ratio	Minority Pupils[1] (%)	Total Rev. per Pupil ($)	Total Exp. per Pupil ($)
Wake County Schools	198	161,481	15.0	58.2	12,435	14,074

Note: Table includes school districts with 2,000 or more students; (1) Percentage of students that are not non-Hispanic white.
Source: U.S. Department of Education, National Center for Education Statistics, Common Core of Data, Local Education Agency (School District) Universe Survey: School Year 2023-2024; U.S. Department of Education, National Center for Education Statistics, Common Core of Data, School District Finance Survey (F-33): School Year 2021–22

Best High Schools

According to *U.S. News,* Raleigh is home to one of the top 500 high schools in the U.S.: **Raleigh Charter High School** (#156). Nearly 25,000 public, magnet and charter schools were ranked based on their performance on state assessments and how well they prepare students for college. *U.S. News & World Report, "Best High Schools 2024"*

Highest Level of Education

Area	Less than H.S.	H.S. Diploma	Some College, No Deg.	Associate Degree	Bachelor's Degree	Master's Degree	Prof. School Degree	Doctorate Degree
City	7.5	15.9	16.2	7.4	32.5	14.3	3.5	2.6
MSA[1]	7.1	17.3	16.6	8.8	30.8	14.4	2.6	2.4
U.S.	10.6	26.2	19.4	8.8	21.3	9.8	2.3	1.6

Note: Figures cover persons age 25 and over; (1) Figures cover the Raleigh-Cary, NC Metropolitan Statistical Area
Source: U.S. Census Bureau, 2019-2023 American Community Survey 5-Year Estimates

Educational Attainment by Race

Area	High School Graduate or Higher (%)					Bachelor's Degree or Higher (%)				
	Total	White	Black	Asian	Hisp.[2]	Total	White	Black	Asian	Hisp.[2]
City	92.5	96.8	92.0	90.0	67.3	52.9	66.4	32.5	62.5	23.7
MSA[1]	92.9	96.0	92.2	93.3	69.1	50.2	55.5	33.9	76.2	22.7
U.S.	89.4	92.9	88.1	88.0	72.5	35.0	37.7	24.7	57.0	19.9

Note: Figures shown cover persons 25 years old and over; (1) Figures cover the Raleigh-Cary, NC Metropolitan Statistical Area; (2) People of Hispanic origin can be of any race
Source: U.S. Census Bureau, 2019-2023 American Community Survey 5-Year Estimates

School Enrollment by Grade and Control

Area	Preschool (%)		Kindergarten (%)		Grades 1 - 4 (%)		Grades 5 - 8 (%)		Grades 9 - 12 (%)	
	Public	Private	Public	Private	Public	Private	Public	Private	Public	Private
City	33.6	66.4	86.9	13.1	85.2	14.8	87.2	12.8	86.8	13.2
MSA[1]	33.6	66.4	82.6	17.4	85.2	14.8	85.7	14.3	87.6	12.4
U.S.	58.7	41.3	85.2	14.8	87.2	12.8	87.9	12.1	89.0	11.0

Note: Figures shown cover persons 3 years old and over; (1) Figures cover the Raleigh-Cary, NC Metropolitan Statistical Area
Source: U.S. Census Bureau, 2019-2023 American Community Survey 5-Year Estimates

Higher Education

Four-Year Colleges			Two-Year Colleges			Medical Schools[1]	Law Schools[2]	Voc/ Tech[3]
Public	Private Non-profit	Private For-profit	Public	Private Non-profit	Private For-profit			
1	7	0	2	1	2	0	1	3

Note: Figures cover institutions located within the Raleigh-Cary, NC Metropolitan Statistical Area and include main campuses only; (1) includes schools accredited by the Liaison Committee on Medical Education and the American Osteopathic Association's Commission on Osteopathic College Accreditation; (2) includes ABA-accredited schools, schools with provisional ABA accreditation, and state accredited schools; (3) includes all schools with programs that are less than 2 years.
Source: National Center for Education Statistics, Integrated Postsecondary Education System (IPEDS), 2023-24; Wikipedia, List of Medical Schools in the United States, accessed May 2, 2025; Wikipedia, List of Law Schools in the United States, accessed May 2, 2025

According to *U.S. News & World Report,* the Raleigh-Cary, NC metro area is home to one of the top 200 national universities in the U.S.: **North Carolina State University** (#58 tie). The indicators used to capture academic quality fall into a number of categories: assessment by administrators at peer institutions; retention of students; faculty resources; student selectivity; financial resources; alumni giving; high school counselor ratings of colleges; and graduation rate. *U.S. News & World Report, "America's Best Colleges 2025"*

EMPLOYERS

Major Employers

Company Name	Industry
Cisco Systems	Software
City of Raleigh	Municipal government
Duke Energy	Electric services
Fidelity Investments	Financial services
GlaxoSmithKline	Healthcare
IBM	Technology
Lenovo	Technology
N.C. DHHS	Government
North Carolina State University	Education
Rex Healthcare	Healthcare
RTI International	Research & development
SAS Institute	Data management
State of North Carolina	State government
Wake County Government	Government
Wake County Public School System	Education
Wake Technical Community College	Education
WakeMed Health & Hospitals	Education
Wells Fargo	Financial services

Note: Companies shown are located within the Raleigh-Cary, NC Metropolitan Statistical Area.
Source: Chambers of Commerce; State Departments of Labor; Wikipedia

Best Companies to Work For

Kimley-Horn, headquartered in Raleigh, is among "The 100 Best Companies to Work For." To pick the best companies, *Fortune* partnered with the Great Place to Work Institute. Using their proprietary Trust Index™ survey, the core of what creates great a workplace is measured—key behaviors that drive trust in management, connection with colleagues, and loyalty to the company. To be eligible for the *Fortune* 100 Best Companies to Work For list, employers must have 1,000 or more employees in the U.S. and cannot be a government agency. *Fortune, "The 100 Best Companies to Work For," 2025*

IAT Insurance Group; Kimley-Horn, headquartered in Raleigh, are among "Fortune's Best Workplaces for Women." To pick the best companies, *Fortune* partnered with the Great Place to Work Institute. To be considered for the list, companies must be Great Place To Work-Certified. Companies must also employ at least 50 women, at least 20% of their non-executive managers must be female, and at least one executive must be female. To determine the Best Workplaces for Women, Great Place To Work measured the differences in women's survey responses to those of their peers and assesses the impact of demographics and roles on the quality and consistency of women's experiences. Great Place To Work also analyzed the gender balance of each workplace, how it compared to each company's industry, and patterns in representation as women rise from front-line positions to the board of directors. *Fortune, "Best Workplaces for Women," 2024*

Merz Aesthetics, headquartered in Raleigh, is among "Best Workplaces in Health Care." To determine the Best Workplaces in Health Care list, Great Place To Work analyzed the survey responses of over 185,000 employees from Great Place To Work-Certified companies in the health care industry. Survey data analysis and company-provided datapoints are then factored into a combined score to compare and rank the companies that create the most consistently positive experience for all employees in this industry. *Fortune, "Best Workplaces in Health Care," 2024*

PUBLIC SAFETY

Crime Rate

Area	Total Crime Rate	Violent Crime Rate				Property Crime Rate		
		Murder	Rape	Robbery	Aggrav. Assault	Burglary	Larceny-Theft	Motor Vehicle Theft
City	3,117.6	5.4	32.1	87.2	403.4	306.3	1,891.3	391.8
U.S.	2,290.9	5.7	38.0	66.5	264.1	250.7	1,347.2	318.7

Note: Figures are crimes per 100,000 population.
Source: FBI, Table 8, Offenses Known to Law Enforcement, by State by City, 2023

Hate Crimes

Area	Number of Quarters Reported	Number of Incidents per Bias Motivation					
		Race/Ethnicity/Ancestry	Religion	Sexual Orientation	Disability	Gender	Gender Identity
City	4	17	3	7	0	0	0
U.S.	4	5,900	2,699	2,077	187	92	492

Source: Federal Bureau of Investigation, Hate Crime Statistics 2023

Identity Theft Consumer Reports

Area	Reports	Reports per 100,000 Population	Rank[2]
MSA[1]	4,150	286	76
U.S.	1,135,291	339	-

Note: (1) Figures cover the Raleigh-Cary, NC Metropolitan Statistical Area; (2) Rank ranges from 1 to 401 where 1 indicates greatest number of identity theft reports per 100,000 population
Source: Federal Trade Commission, Consumer Sentinel Network Data Book 2024

Fraud and Other Consumer Reports

Area	Reports	Reports per 100,000 Population	Rank[2]
MSA[1]	21,651	1,494	59
U.S.	5,360,641	1,601	-

Note: (1) Figures cover the Raleigh-Cary, NC Metropolitan Statistical Area; (2) Rank ranges from 1 to 401 where 1 indicates greatest number of fraud and other consumer reports per 100,000 population
Source: Federal Trade Commission, Consumer Sentinel Network Data Book 2024

POLITICS

2024 Presidential Election Results

Area	Trump (Rep.)	Harris (Dem.)	Stein (Green)	Kennedy (Ind.)	Oliver (Lib.)	Other
Wake County	36.2	61.7	0.8	0.0	0.5	0.8
U.S.	49.7	48.2	0.6	0.5	0.4	0.6

Note: Results are percentages and may not add to 100% due to rounding
Source: Dave Leip's Atlas of U.S. Presidential Elections

SPORTS

Professional Sports Teams

Team Name	League	Year Established
Carolina Hurricanes	National Hockey League (NHL)	1997

Note: Includes teams located in the Raleigh-Cary, NC Metropolitan Statistical Area.
Source: Wikipedia, Major Professional Sports Teams of the United States and Canada, May 1, 2025

CLIMATE

Average and Extreme Temperatures

Temperature	Jan	Feb	Mar	Apr	May	Jun	Jul	Aug	Sep	Oct	Nov	Dec	Yr.
Extreme High (°F)	79	84	90	95	97	104	105	105	104	98	88	79	105
Average High (°F)	50	53	61	72	79	86	89	87	81	72	62	53	71
Average Temp. (°F)	40	43	50	59	67	75	78	77	71	60	51	42	60
Average Low (°F)	29	31	38	46	55	63	68	67	60	48	39	32	48
Extreme Low (°F)	-9	5	11	23	29	38	48	46	37	19	11	4	-9

Note: Figures cover the years 1948-1990
Source: National Climatic Data Center, International Station Meteorological Climate Summary, 9/96

Average Precipitation/Snowfall/Humidity

Precip./Humidity	Jan	Feb	Mar	Apr	May	Jun	Jul	Aug	Sep	Oct	Nov	Dec	Yr.
Avg. Precip. (in.)	3.4	3.6	3.6	2.9	3.9	3.6	4.4	4.4	3.2	2.9	3.0	3.1	42.0
Avg. Snowfall (in.)	2	3	1	Tr	0	0	0	0	0	0	Tr	1	8
Avg. Rel. Hum. 7am (%)	79	79	79	80	84	86	88	91	91	90	84	81	84
Avg. Rel. Hum. 4pm (%)	53	49	46	43	51	54	57	59	57	53	51	53	52

Note: Figures cover the years 1948-1990; Tr = Trace amounts (<0.05 in. of rain; <0.5 in. of snow)
Source: National Climatic Data Center, International Station Meteorological Climate Summary, 9/96

Weather Conditions

Temperature			Daytime Sky			Precipitation		
32°F & below	45°F & below	90°F & above	Clear	Partly cloudy	Cloudy	0.01 inch or more precip.	0.1 inch or more snow/ice	Thunder-storms
77	160	39	98	143	124	110	3	42

Note: Figures are average number of days per year and cover the years 1948-1990
Source: National Climatic Data Center, International Station Meteorological Climate Summary, 9/96

HAZARDOUS WASTE

Superfund Sites

The Raleigh-Cary, NC metro area is home to four sites on the EPA's Superfund National Priorities List (NPL) or Superfund Alternative Approach (SAA) list: **Gurley Pesticide Burial** (SAA); **Koppers Co., Inc. (Morrisville Plant)** (Final NPL); **North Carolina State University (Lot 86, Farm Unit #1)** (Final NPL); **Ward Transformer** (Final NPL). The Superfund alternative approach uses the same investigation and cleanup process and standards that are used for sites listed on the National Priorities List. The SAA is an alternative to listing a site on the NPL; it is not an alternative to Superfund or the Superfund process. There are a total of 1,445 Superfund sites with a status of proposed or final on both lists in the United States. *U.S. Environmental Protection Agency, National Priorities List, May 1, 2025; U.S. Environmental Protection Agency, Superfund Alternative Approach Sites, May 1, 2025*

AIR QUALITY

Air Quality Trends: Ozone

	1990	1995	2000	2005	2010	2015	2020	2021	2022	2023
MSA[1]	0.093	0.081	0.087	0.082	0.071	0.065	0.054	0.062	0.064	0.064
U.S.	0.087	0.089	0.081	0.080	0.072	0.068	0.066	0.067	0.067	0.070

Note: (1) Data covers the Raleigh-Cary, NC Metropolitan Statistical Area. The values shown are the composite ozone concentration averages among trend sites based on the highest fourth daily maximum 8-hour concentration in parts per million. These trends are based on sites having an adequate record of monitoring data during the trend period. Data from exceptional events are included.
Source: U.S. Environmental Protection Agency, Air Quality Monitoring Information, "Air Quality Trends by City, 1990-2023"

Air Quality Index

Area	Percent of Days when Air Quality was...[2]					AQI Statistics[2]	
	Good	Moderate	Unhealthy for Sensitive Groups	Unhealthy	Very Unhealthy	Maximum	Median
MSA[1]	50.4	48.2	1.4	0.0	0.0	130	50

Note: (1) Data covers the Raleigh-Cary, NC Metropolitan Statistical Area; (2) Based on 365 days with AQI data in 2023. Air Quality Index (AQI) is an index for reporting daily air quality. EPA calculates the AQI for five major air pollutants regulated by the Clean Air Act: ground-level ozone, particle pollution (aka particulate matter), carbon monoxide, sulfur dioxide, and nitrogen dioxide. The AQI runs from 0 to 500. The higher the AQI value, the greater the level of air pollution and the greater the health concern. There are six AQI categories: "Good" AQI is between 0 and 50. Air quality is considered satisfactory; "Moderate" AQI is between 51 and 100. Air quality is acceptable; "Unhealthy for Sensitive Groups" When AQI values are between 101 and 150, members of sensitive groups may experience health effects; "Unhealthy" When AQI values are between 151 and 200 everyone may begin to experience health effects; "Very Unhealthy" AQI values between 201 and 300 trigger a health alert; "Hazardous" AQI values over 300 trigger warnings of emergency conditions (not shown).
Source: U.S. Environmental Protection Agency, Air Quality Index Report, 2023

Air Quality Index Pollutants

Area	Percent of Days when AQI Pollutant was...[2]					
	Carbon Monoxide	Nitrogen Dioxide	Ozone	Sulfur Dioxide	Particulate Matter 2.5	Particulate Matter 10
MSA[1]	0.0	0.3	32.1	(3)	67.7	0.0

Note: (1) Data covers the Raleigh-Cary, NC Metropolitan Statistical Area; (2) Based on 365 days with AQI data in 2023. The Air Quality Index (AQI) is an index for reporting daily air quality. EPA calculates the AQI for five major air pollutants regulated by the Clean Air Act: ground-level ozone, particle pollution (also known as particulate matter), carbon monoxide, sulfur dioxide, and nitrogen dioxide. The AQI runs from 0 to 500. The higher the AQI value, the greater the level of air pollution and the greater the health concern; (3) Sulfur dioxide is no longer included in this table because SO_2 concentrations tend to be very localized and not necessarily representative of broad geographical areas like counties and CBSAs.
Source: U.S. Environmental Protection Agency, Air Quality Index Report, 2023

Maximum Air Pollutant Concentrations: Particulate Matter, Ozone, CO and Lead

	Particulate Matter 10 (ug/m^3)	Particulate Matter 2.5 Wtd AM (ug/m^3)	Particulate Matter 2.5 24-Hr (ug/m^3)	Ozone (ppm)	Carbon Monoxide (ppm)	Lead (ug/m^3)
MSA[1] Level	60	9.2	31	0.064	1	n/a
NAAQS[2]	150	15	35	0.075	9	0.15
Met NAAQS[2]	Yes	Yes	Yes	Yes	Yes	n/a

Note: (1) Data covers the Raleigh-Cary, NC Metropolitan Statistical Area; Data from exceptional events are included; (2) National Ambient Air Quality Standards; ppm = parts per million; ug/m^3 = micrograms per cubic meter; n/a not available.
Concentrations: Particulate Matter 10 (coarse particulate)—highest second maximum 24-hour concentration; Particulate Matter 2.5 Wtd AM (fine particulate)—highest weighted annual mean concentration; Particulate Matter 2.5 24-Hour (fine particulate)—highest 98th percentile 24-hour concentration; Ozone—highest fourth daily maximum 8-hour concentration; Carbon Monoxide—highest second maximum non-overlapping 8-hour concentration; Lead—maximum running 3-month average
Source: U.S. Environmental Protection Agency, Air Quality Monitoring Information, "Air Quality Statistics by City, 2023"

Maximum Air Pollutant Concentrations: Nitrogen Dioxide and Sulfur Dioxide

	Nitrogen Dioxide AM (ppb)	Nitrogen Dioxide 1-Hr (ppb)	Sulfur Dioxide AM (ppb)	Sulfur Dioxide 1-Hr (ppb)	Sulfur Dioxide 24-Hr (ppb)
MSA[1] Level	9	36	n/a	2	n/a
NAAQS[2]	53	100	30	75	140
Met NAAQS[2]	Yes	Yes	n/a	Yes	n/a

Note: (1) Data covers the Raleigh-Cary, NC Metropolitan Statistical Area; Data from exceptional events are included; (2) National Ambient Air Quality Standards; ppm = parts per million; ug/m^3 = micrograms per cubic meter; n/a not available.
Concentrations: Nitrogen Dioxide AM—highest arithmetic mean concentration; Nitrogen Dioxide 1-Hr—highest 98th percentile 1-hour daily maximum concentration; Sulfur Dioxide AM—highest annual mean concentration; Sulfur Dioxide 1-Hr—highest 99th percentile 1-hour daily maximum concentration; Sulfur Dioxide 24-Hr—highest second maximum 24-hour concentration
Source: U.S. Environmental Protection Agency, Air Quality Monitoring Information, "Air Quality Statistics by City, 2023"

Richmond, Virginia

Background

Richmond, the capital of Virginia, sits on the James River in east central Virginia and played a central role in both U.S. and Confederate histories.

John Smith and Christopher Newport first claimed Richmond in 1607 as English territory. In 1679, the area was granted to William Byrd I, with the understanding that he establish a settlement. His son, William Byrd II, continued his father's work and along with William Mayo surveyed lots for what was to be named Richmond. During the Revolutionary War, Richmond played host to two Virginia Conventions, which gathered founding fathers George Washington, Thomas Jefferson, and Patrick Henry in the same room, and ratified the Constitution as the law of the land for the emerging nation. In 1775, Patrick Henry delivered his famous "Give me Liberty or Give me Death" speech in the city's St. John's Church.

Not long after the United States congealed as a nation, dissension caused fragmentation and Richmond became the Confederate States' capital. From its Roman temple-inspired capitol designed by Thomas Jefferson, Jefferson Davis presided over the Confederacy.

Today Richmond is home to authoritative repositories of both Southern and Virginia history, which include the Virginia State Library, the Museum of the Confederacy, and the Virginia Historical Society. Government and higher education are economic mainstays for the city, with Virginia Commonwealth University (VCU), the Medical College of Virginia, the University of Richmond, and Virginia Union University all located within the city limits. The Virginia BioTechnology Research Park houses nearly 70 life sciences organizations, from young companies to international bioscience organizations, in 1.3 million square feet of research and office space adjacent to the VCU Medical Center. Banking and telecommunications sectors are also well represented in the city's economy. Major employers include VCU and VCU Health, Capital One, Bon Secours Richmond, Dominion Energy, and Truist.

The city's James River waterfront, with a multimillion-dollar flood wall to protect it from the frequent rising waters of the river, is now home to much of Richmond's entertainment, dining, and nightlife, bolstered by the creation of a Canal Walk along the city's former industrial canals. In 2018, the city's first rapid transit system began operating.

Richmond's cultural offerings include the Richmond Symphony, Richmond Ballet, and the Virginia Museum of Fine Arts, known for its travelling Faberge collection. A variety of murals from internationally recognized street artists have appeared throughout the city as a result of the efforts of Art Whino and *RVA Magazine* with The Richmond Mural Project and the RVA Street Art Festival. After some controversy, a bronze statue of African American Richmond native and tennis star Arthur Ashe was completed on the city's Monument Avenue.

Richmond's Northside is home to several historic districts, including Chestnut Hill-Plateau and Barton Heights. The affluent West End is home to the University of Richmond and the Country Club of Virginia.

Richmond's climate is modified continental with warm summers and humid, mild winters. Snow remains on the ground for only a day or so. Ice storms are not uncommon but usually do not cause considerable damage. Hurricanes and tropical storms, when they occur, are responsible for flooding during the summer and early fall months. Tornadoes are infrequent, but some notable occurrences have been observed in the vicinity.

Rankings

General Rankings

- Richmond was selected as one of the best places to live in the United States by *Money* magazine. The city placed among the top 50. This year's list focused on cities built around community spirit, thoughtful policy and civic engagement. Instead of relying on a predetermined dataset, the cities and towns were grouped according to their strengths and chosen due their affordability, good schools and strong job markets. *Money, "The 50 Best Places to Live in the U.S., 2024" April 8, 2024*

- In their annual survey, Livability.com looked at data for more than 2,000 mid-sized U.S. cities to assign a "Livability Score"for each. The top 100 scoring cities make up Livability's "Top 100 Best Places to Live in the U.S." in 2025. Richmond was placed among the top 100 of the customizable list. Criteria: housing and economy; cost of living; environment; education; health care options; transportation; safety; and community amenities. *Livability.com, "Top 100 Best Places to Live in the U.S. in 2025" April 15, 2025*

Business/Finance Rankings

- The Richmond metro area appeared on the Milken Institute "2025 Best Performing Cities" list. Rank: #51 out of 200 large metro areas (based on performance category). Criteria: job growth; wage growth; high-tech growth and impact; community resilience; housing affordability; household broadband access. *Milken Institute, "Best-Performing Cities 2025," January 14, 2025*

Education Rankings

- Personal finance website *WalletHub* analyzed the 150 largest U.S. metropolitan statistical areas to determine where the most educated Americans are putting their degrees to work. Criteria: education levels; percentage of workers with degrees; education quality and attainment gap; public school quality rankings; quality and enrollment of each metro area's universities. Richmond was ranked #32 (#1 = most educated city). *WalletHub.com, "Most & Least Educated Cities in America, 2025" July 2, 2024*

Environmental Rankings

- Sperling's *BestPlaces* assessed the 50 largest metropolitan areas of the United States for the likelihood of dangerously extreme weather events or earthquakes. In general the Southeast and South-Central regions have the highest risk of weather extremes and earthquakes, while the Pacific Northwest enjoys the lowest risk. Of the least risky metropolitan areas, the Richmond metro area was ranked #8. *Bestplaces.net, "Avoid Natural Disasters: BestPlaces Reveals The Top 10 Safest Places to Live," October 25, 2017*

Health/Fitness Rankings

- For each of the 100 largest cities in the United States, the American Fitness Index®, compiled in partnership between the American College of Sports Medicine and the Elevance Health Foundation, evaluated community infrastructure and more than 30 health behaviors including preventive health, levels of chronic disease conditions, food insecurity, pedestrian safety, air quality, and community/environment resources that support physical activity. Richmond ranked #28 for "community fitness." *americanfitnessindex.org, "2024 ACSM American Fitness Index Summary Report," July 23, 2024*

- The Richmond metro area was identified as one of the worst cities for bed bugs in America by pest control company Orkin. The area ranked #17 out of 50 based on the number of bed bug treatments Orkin performed from December 2022 to November 2023. *Orkin, "Chicago Joins Paris In Global Bed Bug Spotlight Ranking As The Worst City On Orkin's U.S. Bed Bug Cities List," January 22, 2024*

- Richmond was identified as a "2025 Allergy Capital." The area ranked #8 out of the nation's 100 largest metropolitan areas. Three groups of factors were used to identify the most challenging cities for people with allergies: annual tree, grass, and weed pollen scores; over the counter allergy medicine use; number of board-certified allergy specialists. *Asthma and Allergy Foundation of America, "2025 Allergy Capitals: The Most Challenging Places to Live with Allergies," March 18, 2025*

- Richmond was identified as a "2024 Asthma Capital." The area ranked #12 out of the nation's 100 largest metropolitan areas. Criteria: estimated asthma prevalence; asthma-related mortality; and ER visits due to asthma. Risk factors analyzed but not factored in the rankings: annual air quality including pollution and ozone levels; public smoking laws; indoor air quality; access to asthma specialists; rescue and controller medication use; uninsured rate; pollen allergy; poverty rate. *Asthma and Allergy Foundation of America, "Asthma Capitals 2024: The Most Challenging Places to Live With Asthma," September 10, 2024*

Pet Rankings

- Richmond was selected by *Sniffspot.com* as one of the most dog-friendly cities in the U.S., ranking #18 out of 50. Criteria: dog parks; hiking; sniffspots; public parks; dog-friendly businesses; housing; dog waste cleanliness; leash laws; dog services; and overall cost. *Sniffspot.com, "The Top 50 Most Dog-Friendly Cities in the U.S.," September 30, 2024*

Real Estate Rankings

- *WalletHub* compared the most populated U.S. cities to determine which had the best markets for real estate agents. Richmond ranked #77 where demand was high and pay was the best. Criteria: sales per agent; annual median wage for real-estate agents; monthly average starting salary for real estate agents; real estate job density and competition; unemployment rate; home turnover rate; housing-market health index; and other relevant metrics. *WalletHub.com, "2021 Best Places to Be a Real Estate Agent," May 12, 2021*

- The Richmond metro area appeared on Realtor.com's list of hot housing markets to watch in 2025. The area ranked #5. Criteria: forecasted home price and sales growth; overall economy; population trends. *Realtor.com®, "Top 10 Housing Markets Positioned for Growth in 2025," December 10, 2024*

- The Richmond metro area was identified as one of the top 16 housing markets to invest in for 2025 by *Forbes*. Criteria: stable local economies with good population growth and increase in jobs providing good support for home prices and rents. *Forbes.com, "Best Local Markets For Real Estate Investing In 2025," November 6, 2024*

- Richmond was ranked #111 out of 176 metro areas in terms of cost of housing in 2024 by the National Association of Home Builders (#1 = most affordable). Criteria: the portion of an average family's income necessary to pay the mortgage on a median-priced home. *National Association of Home Builders®, NAHB-Wells Fargo Cost of Housing Index, 4th Quarter 2024*

Safety Rankings

- Allstate ranked the 100 most populous cities in America in terms of driver safety. Richmond ranked #6. Criteria based on anonymized driving behavior data from Allstate's mobile app powered by Arity: high speed driving (over 80 mph), phone handling, and hard braking. The report helps increase the importance of safety and awareness behind the wheel. *Allstate, "16th Allstate America's Best Drivers Report®" July 11, 2024*

Women/Minorities Rankings

- Richmond was listed as one of the most LGBTQ-friendly cities in America by *The Advocate*, as compiled by the real estate data site *Clever*. The city ranked #12 out of 15. Criteria, among many: Pride events; gay bars; LGBTQ-affirming healthcare options; state and local laws; number of PFLAG chapters; LGBTQ+ population. *The Advocate, "These Are the 15 Most LGBTQ-Friendly Cities in the U.S." November 1, 2023*

- Personal finance website *WalletHub* compared more than 180 U.S. cities across two key dimensions, "Hispanic Business-Friendliness" and "Hispanic Purchasing Power," to arrive at the most favorable conditions for Hispanic entrepreneurs. Richmond was ranked #104 out of 182. Criteria includes: share of Hispanic-Owned Businesses; average growth of Hispanic Business revenues; Small Business-Friendliness score; affordability; and number of Hispanics with at least a bachelor's degree. *WalletHub.com, "Best Cities for Hispanic Entrepreneurs," September 4, 2024*

Miscellaneous Rankings

- *MoveHub* ranked 446 hipster cities across 20 countries, using its new and improved alternative Hipster Index and Richmond came out as #20 among the top 50. Criteria: population over 150,000; number of vintage boutiques; density of tattoo parlors; vegan places to eat; coffee shops; and density of vinyl record stores. *MoveHub.com, "The Hipster Index: Brighton Pips Portland to Global Top Spot," July 28, 2021*

- *WalletHub* compared 148 of the most populated U.S. cities to determine their operating efficiency. A "Quality of Services" score was constructed for each city and then measured against the total budget per capita to reveal which were managed the best. Richmond ranked #95. Criteria: financial stability; economy; education; safety; health; infrastructure and pollution. *WalletHub.com, "2025's Best- & Worst-Run Cities in America," June 18, 2024*

Business Environment

DEMOGRAPHICS

Population Growth

Area	1990 Census	2000 Census	2010 Census	2020 Census	2023 Estimate[2]	Population Growth 1990-2023 (%)
City	202,783	197,790	204,214	226,610	227,595	12.2
MSA[1]	949,244	1,096,957	1,258,251	1,314,434	1,327,321	39.8
U.S.	248,709,873	281,421,906	308,745,538	331,449,281	332,387,540	33.6

Note: (1) Figures cover the Richmond, VA Metropolitan Statistical Area; (2) 2019-2023 5-year ACS population estimate
Source: U.S. Census Bureau, 1990 Census, 2000 Census, 2010 Census, 2020 Census, 2019-2023 American Community Survey 5-Year Estimates

Race

Area	White Alone[2] (%)	Black Alone[2] (%)	Asian Alone[2] (%)	AIAN[3] Alone[2] (%)	NHOPI[4] Alone[2] (%)	Other Race Alone[2] (%)	Two or More Races (%)
City	43.2	42.0	2.1	0.2	0.0	5.3	7.1
MSA[1]	56.8	28.5	4.1	0.3	0.1	4.0	6.2
U.S.	63.4	12.4	5.8	0.9	0.2	6.6	10.7

Note: (1) Figures cover the Richmond, VA Metropolitan Statistical Area; (2) Alone is defined as not being in combination with one or more other races; (3) American Indian and Alaska Native; (4) Native Hawaiian and Other Pacific Islander
Source: U.S. Census Bureau, 2019-2023 American Community Survey 5-Year Estimates

Hispanic or Latino Origin

Area	Total (%)	Mexican (%)	Puerto Rican (%)	Cuban (%)	Other (%)
City	10.3	2.1	1.1	0.3	6.8
MSA[1]	8.1	1.9	1.2	0.3	4.7
U.S.	19.0	11.3	1.8	0.7	5.2

Note: Persons of Hispanic or Latino origin can be of any race; (1) Figures cover the Richmond, VA Metropolitan Statistical Area
Source: U.S. Census Bureau, 2019-2023 American Community Survey 5-Year Estimates

Age

Area	Under Age 5	Age 5–19	Age 20–34	Age 35–44	Age 45–54	Age 55–64	Age 65–74	Age 75–84	Age 85+	Median Age
City	5.9	15.4	29.6	13.5	10.1	11.9	8.7	3.5	1.4	34.5
MSA[1]	5.7	18.4	20.5	13.5	12.4	13.1	10.0	4.6	1.7	38.7
U.S.	5.7	19.1	20.2	13.1	12.3	12.8	10.0	4.9	1.9	38.7

Note: (1) Figures cover the Richmond, VA Metropolitan Statistical Area
Source: U.S. Census Bureau, 2019-2023 American Community Survey 5-Year Estimates

Disability by Age

Area	All Ages	Under 18 Years Old	18 to 64 Years Old	65 Years and Over
City	14.0	7.0	12.0	33.1
MSA[1]	12.8	5.3	10.7	30.4
U.S.	13.0	4.7	10.7	32.9

Note: Figures show percent of the civilian noninstitutionalized population that reported having a disability. Disability status is determined from six types of difficulty: vision, hearing, cognitive, ambulatory, self-care, and independent living. For children under 5 years old, hearing and vision difficulty are used to determine disability status. For children between the ages of 5 and 14, disability status is determined from hearing, vision, cognitive, ambulatory, and self-care difficulties. For people aged 15 years and older, they are considered to have a disability if they have difficulty with any one of the six difficulty types; Note: (1) Figures cover the Richmond, VA Metropolitan Statistical Area
Source: U.S. Census Bureau, 2019-2023 American Community Survey 5-Year Estimates

Ancestry

Area	German	Irish	English	American	Italian	Polish	French[2]	European	Scottish
City	8.2	7.9	9.9	3.9	3.8	1.4	1.5	1.3	1.8
MSA[1]	9.1	8.2	12.7	6.6	3.7	1.5	1.4	1.7	1.8
U.S.	12.6	9.4	9.1	5.5	4.9	2.6	2.0	1.6	1.6

Note: Figures are the percentage of the total population reporting a particular ancestry. The nine most commonly reported ancestries in the U.S. are shown. Figures include multiple ancestries (e.g. if a person reported being Irish and Italian, they were included in both columns); (1) Figures cover the Richmond, VA Metropolitan Statistical Area; (2) Excludes Basque
Source: U.S. Census Bureau, 2019-2023 American Community Survey 5-Year Estimates

Foreign-born Population

Area	Percent of Population Born in								
	Any Foreign Country	Asia	Mexico	Europe	Caribbean	Central America[2]	South America	Africa	Canada
City	8.6	1.5	0.9	0.8	0.7	3.5	0.4	0.6	0.1
MSA[1]	8.7	3.2	0.7	1.0	0.5	1.8	0.7	0.8	0.1
U.S.	13.9	4.3	3.3	1.4	1.4	1.2	1.2	0.8	0.2

Note: (1) Figures cover the Richmond, VA Metropolitan Statistical Area; (2) Excludes Mexico.
Source: U.S. Census Bureau, 2019-2023 American Community Survey 5-Year Estimates

Household Size

Area	Persons in Household (%)							Average Household Size
	One	Two	Three	Four	Five	Six	Seven or More	
City	42.9	32.7	12.2	7.7	2.6	1.2	0.6	2.13
MSA[1]	29.5	34.7	15.8	12.2	5.1	1.8	1.0	2.47
U.S.	28.5	33.8	15.4	12.7	5.9	2.3	1.4	2.54

Note: (1) Figures cover the Richmond, VA Metropolitan Statistical Area
Source: U.S. Census Bureau, 2019-2023 American Community Survey 5-Year Estimates

Household Relationships

Area	Householder	Opposite-sex Spouse	Same-sex Spouse	Opposite-sex Unmarried Partner	Same-sex Unmarried Partner	Child[2]	Grandchild	Other Relatives	Non-relatives
City	45.2	10.4	0.4	4.0	0.4	20.8	2.1	4.3	7.4
MSA[1]	39.5	17.3	0.2	2.5	0.2	27.7	2.4	4.0	3.3
U.S.	38.3	17.5	0.2	2.5	0.2	28.3	2.4	4.8	3.4

Note: Figures are percent of the total population; (1) Figures cover the Richmond, VA Metropolitan Statistical Area; (2) Includes biological, adopted, and stepchildren of the householder
Source: U.S. Census Bureau, 2020 Census

Gender

Area	Males	Females	Males per 100 Females
City	108,090	119,505	90.4
MSA[1]	645,193	682,128	94.6
U.S.	164,545,087	167,842,453	98.0

Note: (1) Figures cover the Richmond, VA Metropolitan Statistical Area
Source: U.S. Census Bureau, 2019-2023 American Community Survey 5-Year Estimates

Marital Status

Area	Never Married	Now Married[2]	Separated	Widowed	Divorced
City	51.4	30.0	2.7	4.6	11.2
MSA[1]	35.0	47.0	2.0	5.5	10.4
U.S.	34.1	47.9	1.7	5.6	10.7

Note: Figures are percentages and cover the population 15 years of age and older; (1) Figures cover the Richmond, VA Metropolitan Statistical Area; (2) Excludes separated
Source: U.S. Census Bureau, 2019-2023 American Community Survey 5-Year Estimates

Religious Groups by Family

Area	Catholic	Baptist	Methodist	LDS[2]	Pentecostal	Lutheran	Islam	Adventist	Other
MSA[1]	12.3	14.2	4.8	0.9	3.2	0.5	2.1	1.2	14.8
U.S.	18.7	7.3	3.0	2.0	1.8	1.7	1.3	1.3	11.6

Note: Figures are the number of adherents as a percentage of the total population and cover the eight largest religious groups in the U.S; (1) Figures cover the Richmond, VA Metropolitan Statistical Area; (2) Church of Jesus Christ of Latter-day Saints
Sources: 2020 U.S. Religion Census, Association of Statisticians of American Religious Bodies; The Association of Religion Data Archives (ARDA)

Religious Groups by Tradition

Area	Catholic	Evangelical Protestant	Mainline Protestant	Black Protestant	Islam	Judaism	Hinduism	Orthodox	Buddhism
MSA[1]	12.3	23.1	9.3	3.1	2.1	0.3	1.3	0.4	0.2
U.S.	18.7	16.5	5.2	2.3	1.3	0.6	0.4	0.4	0.3

Note: Figures are the number of adherents as a percentage of the total population; (1) Figures cover the Richmond, VA Metropolitan Statistical Area
Sources: 2020 U.S. Religion Census, Association of Statisticians of American Religious Bodies; The Association of Religion Data Archives (ARDA)

Richmond, Virginia

ECONOMY

Real Gross Domestic Product (GDP)

Area	2017	2018	2019	2020	2021	2022	2023	Rank[3]
MSA[1]	84.5	86.5	88.6	87.2	91.8	93.9	94.8	44
U.S.[2]	17,619.1	18,160.7	18,642.5	18,238.9	19,387.6	19,896.6	20,436.3	—

Note: Figures are in billions of chained 2017 dollars; (1) Figures cover the Richmond, VA Metropolitan Statistical Area; (2) Figures cover real GDP within metropolitan areas; (3) Rank is based on 2023 data and ranges from 1 to 384
Source: U.S. Bureau of Economic Analysis

Economic Growth

Area	2014	2015	2016	2017	2018	2019	2020	2021	2022	2023
MSA[1]	1.2	3.9	1.5	1.8	2.4	2.4	-1.6	5.3	2.3	1.0
U.S.[2]	2.6	3.2	2.0	2.7	3.1	2.7	-2.2	6.3	2.6	2.7

Note: Figures are real gross domestic product growth rates and represent percent change from preceding period; (1) Figures cover the Richmond, VA Metropolitan Statistical Area; (2) Figures are the average growth rates within metropolitan areas
Source: U.S. Bureau of Economic Analysis

Metropolitan Area Exports

Area	2018	2019	2020	2021	2022	2023	Rank[2]
MSA[1]	3,535.0	3,203.2	2,719.1	3,010.7	3,283.5	2,579.8	95
U.S.	1,664,056.1	1,645,173.7	1,431,406.6	1,753,941.4	2,062,937.4	2,019,160.5	—

Note: Figures are in millions of dollars; (1) Figures cover the Richmond, VA Metropolitan Statistical Area; (2) Rank is based on 2023 data and ranges from 1 to 386
Source: U.S. Department of Commerce, International Trade Administration, Office of Trade and Economic Analysis, Industry and Analysis, Exports by Metropolitan Area, data extracted April 2, 2025

Building Permits

Area	Single-Family			Multi-Family			Total		
	2023	2024	Pct. Chg.	2023	2024	Pct. Chg.	2023	2024	Pct. Chg.
City	387	380	-1.8	1,896	2,160	13.9	2,283	2,540	11.3
MSA[1]	4,590	5,023	9.4	5,383	3,619	-32.8	9,973	8,642	-13.3
U.S.	920,000	981,900	6.7	591,100	496,100	-16.1	1,511,100	1,478,000	-2.2

Note: (1) Figures cover the Richmond, VA Metropolitan Statistical Area; Figures represent new, privately-owned housing units authorized (unadjusted data)
Source: U.S. Census Bureau, Building Permits Survey (BPS), 2023, 2024

Bankruptcy Filings

Area	Business Filings			Nonbusiness Filings		
	2023	2024	% Chg.	2023	2024	% Chg.
Richmond city	2	14	600.0	620	678	9.4
U.S.	18,926	23,107	22.1	434,064	494,201	13.9

Note: Business filings include Chapter 7, Chapter 9, Chapter 11, Chapter 12, Chapter 13, Chapter 15, and Section 304; Nonbusiness filings include Chapter 7, Chapter 11, and Chapter 13
Source: Administrative Office of the U.S. Courts, Business and Nonbusiness Bankruptcy, County Cases Commenced by Chapter of the Bankruptcy Code, During the 12-Month Period Ending December 31, 2023 and Business and Nonbusiness Bankruptcy, County Cases Commenced by Chapter of the Bankruptcy Code, During the 12-Month Period Ending December 31, 2024

Housing Vacancy Rates

Area	Gross Vacancy Rate[3] (%)			Year-Round Vacancy Rate[4] (%)			Rental Vacancy Rate[5] (%)			Homeowner Vacancy Rate[6] (%)		
	2022	2023	2024	2022	2023	2024	2022	2023	2024	2022	2023	2024
MSA[1]	6.1	5.9	7.7	6.1	5.9	7.7	3.0	5.2	7.9	0.7	0.2	0.7
U.S.[2]	9.1	9.0	9.1	7.5	7.5	7.6	5.7	6.5	6.8	0.8	0.8	1.0

Note: (1) Figures cover the Richmond, VA Metropolitan Statistical Area; (2) Figures cover the 75 largest Metropolitan Statistical Areas; (3) The percentage of the total housing inventory that is vacant; (4) The percentage of the housing inventory (excluding seasonal units) that is year-round vacant; (5) The percentage of rental inventory that is vacant for rent; (6) The percentage of homeowner inventory that is vacant for sale
Source: U.S. Census Bureau, Housing Vacancies and Homeownership Annual Statistics: 2022, 2023, 2024

INCOME

Income

Area	Per Capita ($)	Median Household ($)	Average Household ($)
City	44,249	62,671	94,647
MSA[1]	46,237	84,405	114,424
U.S.	43,289	78,538	110,491

Note: (1) Figures cover the Richmond, VA Metropolitan Statistical Area
Source: U.S. Census Bureau, 2019-2023 American Community Survey 5-Year Estimates

Household Income Distribution

Area	Percent of Households Earning							
	Under $15,000	$15,000 -$24,999	$25,000 -$34,999	$35,000 -$49,999	$50,000 -$74,999	$75,000 -$99,999	$100,000 -$149,999	$150,000 and up
City	13.0	8.4	7.7	12.7	16.6	12.0	12.4	17.1
MSA[1]	7.2	5.6	5.9	10.0	16.3	12.7	18.9	23.4
U.S.	8.5	6.6	6.8	10.4	15.7	12.7	17.4	21.9

Note: (1) Figures cover the Richmond, VA Metropolitan Statistical Area
Source: U.S. Census Bureau, 2019-2023 American Community Survey 5-Year Estimates

Poverty Rate

Area	All Ages	Under 18 Years Old	18 to 64 Years Old	65 Years and Over
City	18.8	28.3	17.2	14.6
MSA[1]	10.0	13.4	9.3	8.0
U.S.	12.4	16.3	11.6	10.4

Note: Figures are percentage of people whose income during the past 12 months was below the poverty level; (1) Figures cover the Richmond, VA Metropolitan Statistical Area
Source: U.S. Census Bureau, 2019-2023 American Community Survey 5-Year Estimates

EMPLOYMENT

Labor Force and Employment

Area	Civilian Labor Force			Workers Employed		
	Dec. 2023	Dec. 2024	% Chg.	Dec. 2023	Dec. 2024	% Chg.
City	123,724	126,447	2.2	120,027	122,541	2.1
MSA[1]	703,806	718,292	2.1	685,441	699,371	2.0
U.S.	166,661,000	167,746,000	0.7	160,754,000	161,294,000	0.3

Note: Data is not seasonally adjusted and covers workers 16 years of age and older; (1) Figures cover the Richmond, VA Metropolitan Statistical Area
Source: Bureau of Labor Statistics, Local Area Unemployment Statistics

Unemployment Rate

Area	2024											
	Jan.	Feb.	Mar.	Apr.	May	Jun.	Jul.	Aug.	Sep.	Oct.	Nov.	Dec.
City	3.4	3.4	3.4	3.0	3.4	3.6	3.8	3.9	3.5	3.4	3.4	3.1
MSA[1]	3.0	3.0	2.9	2.6	2.9	3.2	3.3	3.4	3.0	2.9	3.0	2.6
U.S.	4.1	4.2	3.9	3.5	3.7	4.3	4.5	4.4	3.9	3.9	4.0	3.8

Note: Data is not seasonally adjusted and covers workers 16 years of age and older; (1) Figures cover the Richmond, VA Metropolitan Statistical Area
Source: Bureau of Labor Statistics, Local Area Unemployment Statistics

Average Wages

Occupation	$/Hr.	Occupation	$/Hr.
Accountants and Auditors	42.37	Maintenance and Repair Workers	25.46
Automotive Mechanics	27.70	Marketing Managers	84.07
Bookkeepers	24.33	Network and Computer Systems Admin.	49.36
Carpenters	24.90	Nurses, Licensed Practical	30.78
Cashiers	15.01	Nurses, Registered	43.52
Computer Programmers	46.29	Nursing Assistants	19.49
Computer Systems Analysts	51.27	Office Clerks, General	22.18
Computer User Support Specialists	29.64	Physical Therapists	49.10
Construction Laborers	19.84	Physicians	124.83
Cooks, Restaurant	17.56	Plumbers, Pipefitters and Steamfitters	28.27
Customer Service Representatives	20.92	Police and Sheriff's Patrol Officers	33.25
Dentists	103.90	Postal Service Mail Carriers	29.19
Electricians	29.24	Real Estate Sales Agents	34.95
Engineers, Electrical	56.26	Retail Salespersons	17.09
Fast Food and Counter Workers	14.48	Sales Representatives, Technical/Scientific	54.94
Financial Managers	88.63	Secretaries, Exc. Legal/Medical/Executive	22.38
First-Line Supervisors of Office Workers	33.36	Security Guards	21.69
General and Operations Managers	63.23	Surgeons	n/a
Hairdressers/Cosmetologists	25.31	Teacher Assistants, Exc. Postsecondary[1]	16.87
Home Health and Personal Care Aides	14.98	Teachers, Secondary School, Exc. Sp. Ed.[1]	30.92
Janitors and Cleaners	16.42	Telemarketers	n/a
Landscaping/Groundskeeping Workers	18.50	Truck Drivers, Heavy/Tractor-Trailer	29.88
Lawyers	80.01	Truck Drivers, Light/Delivery Services	21.77
Maids and Housekeeping Cleaners	15.53	Waiters and Waitresses	19.74

Note: Wage data covers the Richmond, VA Metropolitan Statistical Area; (1) Hourly wages were calculated from annual wage data based on a 40 hour work week
Source: Bureau of Labor Statistics, Metro Area Occupational Employment & Wage Estimates, May 2024

Employment by Industry

Sector	MSA[1] Number of Employees	MSA[1] Percent of Total	U.S. Percent of Total
Construction, Mining, and Logging	42,900	5.9	5.5
Financial Activities	57,500	7.9	5.8
Government	114,100	15.7	14.9
Information	6,400	0.9	1.9
Leisure and Hospitality	67,600	9.3	10.4
Manufacturing	32,100	4.4	8.0
Other Services	33,300	4.6	3.7
Private Education and Health Services	111,500	15.3	16.9
Professional and Business Services	123,700	17.0	14.2
Retail Trade	67,100	9.2	10.0
Transportation, Warehousing, and Utilities	43,500	6.0	4.8
Wholesale Trade	27,500	3.8	3.9

Note: Figures are non-farm employment as of December 2024. Figures are not seasonally adjusted and include workers 16 years of age and older; (1) Figures cover the Richmond, VA Metropolitan Statistical Area
Source: Bureau of Labor Statistics, Current Employment Statistics, Employment, Hours, and Earnings

Employment by Occupation

Occupation Classification	City (%)	MSA[1] (%)	U.S. (%)
Management, Business, Science, and Arts	47.4	45.9	42.0
Natural Resources, Construction, and Maintenance	5.9	7.7	8.6
Production, Transportation, and Material Moving	10.1	10.9	13.0
Sales and Office	19.4	20.3	19.9
Service	17.2	15.1	16.5

Note: Figures cover employed civilians 16 years of age and older; (1) Figures cover the Richmond, VA Metropolitan Statistical Area
Source: U.S. Census Bureau, 2019-2023 American Community Survey 5-Year Estimates

Occupations with Greatest Projected Employment Growth: 2022 – 2032

Occupation[1]	2022 Employment	2032 Projected Employment	Numeric Employment Change	Percent Employment Change
Home Health and Personal Care Aides	60,230	81,100	20,870	34.7
Software Developers	86,610	105,120	18,510	21.4
Management Analysts	78,250	86,170	7,920	10.1
Stockers and Order Fillers	78,610	85,530	6,920	8.8
Cooks, Restaurant	35,850	42,650	6,800	19.0
Information Security Analysts (SOC 2018)	18,390	24,060	5,670	30.8
General and Operations Managers	91,700	96,880	5,180	5.6
Nursing Assistants (SOC 2018)	37,640	41,750	4,110	10.9
Nurse Practitioners	7,170	11,160	3,990	55.6
Laborers and Freight, Stock, and Material Movers, Hand	52,200	56,090	3,890	7.5

Note: Projections cover Virginia; (1) Sorted by numeric employment change
Source: www.projectionscentral.org, State Occupational Projections, 2022–2032 Long-Term Projections

Fastest-Growing Occupations: 2022 – 2032

Occupation[1]	2022 Employment	2032 Projected Employment	Numeric Employment Change	Percent Employment Change
Nurse Practitioners	7,170	11,160	3,990	55.6
Solar Photovoltaic Installers	150	210	60	40.0
Physician Assistants	4,390	5,920	1,530	34.9
Data Scientists	4,650	6,270	1,620	34.8
Home Health and Personal Care Aides	60,230	81,100	20,870	34.7
Statisticians	1,010	1,360	350	34.7
Epidemiologists	270	360	90	33.3
Medical and Health Services Managers	9,620	12,670	3,050	31.7
Information Security Analysts (SOC 2018)	18,390	24,060	5,670	30.8
Physical Therapist Assistants	2,770	3,560	790	28.5

Note: Projections cover Virginia; (1) Sorted by percent employment change and excludes occupations with numeric employment change less than 50
Source: www.projectionscentral.org, State Occupational Projections, 2022–2032 Long-Term Projections

CITY FINANCES

City Government Finances

Component	2022 ($000)	2022 ($ per capita)
Total Revenues	1,717,042	7,394
Total Expenditures	1,813,262	7,808
Debt Outstanding	1,791,985	7,717

Source: U.S. Census Bureau, State & Local Government Finances 2022

City Government Revenue by Source

Source	2022 ($000)	2022 ($ per capita)	2022 (%)
General Revenue			
From Federal Government	207,991	896	12.1
From State Government	281,302	1,211	16.4
From Local Governments	20,004	86	1.2
Taxes			
Property	450,892	1,942	26.3
Sales and Gross Receipts	133,434	575	7.8
Personal Income	0	0	0.0
Corporate Income	0	0	0.0
Motor Vehicle License	6,337	27	0.4
Other Taxes	44,367	191	2.6
Current Charges	200,735	864	11.7
Liquor Store	0	0	0.0
Utility	296,196	1,275	17.3

Source: U.S. Census Bureau, State & Local Government Finances 2022

City Government Expenditures by Function

Function	2022 ($000)	2022 ($ per capita)	2022 (%)
General Direct Expenditures			
Air Transportation	0	0	0.0
Corrections	46,553	200	2.6
Education	482,836	2,079	26.6
Employment Security Administration	0	0	0.0
Financial Administration	25,600	110	1.4
Fire Protection	85,640	368	4.7
General Public Buildings	23,076	99	1.3
Governmental Administration, Other	21,035	90	1.2
Health	104,798	451	5.8
Highways	74,157	319	4.1
Hospitals	0	0	0.0
Housing and Community Development	95,854	412	5.3
Interest on General Debt	35,016	150	1.9
Judicial and Legal	25,297	108	1.4
Libraries	6,834	29	0.4
Parking	10,197	43	0.6
Parks and Recreation	27,763	119	1.5
Police Protection	117,876	507	6.5
Public Welfare	65,144	280	3.6
Sewerage	102,440	441	5.6
Solid Waste Management	28,128	121	1.6
Veterans' Services	0	0	0.0
Liquor Store	0	0	0.0
Utility	360,915	1,554	19.9

Source: U.S. Census Bureau, State & Local Government Finances 2022

TAXES

State Corporate Income Tax Rates

State	Tax Rate (%)	Income Brackets ($)	Num. of Brackets	Financial Institution Tax Rate (%)[a]	Federal Income Tax Ded.
Virginia	6.0	Flat rate	1	6.0	No

Note: Tax rates for tax year 2024; (a) Rates listed are the corporate income tax rate applied to financial institutions or excise taxes based on income. Some states have other taxes based upon the value of deposits or shares.
Source: Federation of Tax Administrators, State Corporate Income Tax Rates, January 1, 2025

State Individual Income Tax Rates

State	Tax Rate (%)	Income Brackets ($)	Personal Exemptions ($)			Standard Ded. ($)	
			Single	Married	Depend.	Single	Married
Virginia	2.0 - 5.75	3,000 - 17,001	930	1,860	930	8,000	16,000

Note: Tax rates for tax year 2024; Local- and county-level taxes are not included; Federal income tax is not deductible on state income tax returns
Source: Federation of Tax Administrators, State Individual Income Tax Rates, January 1, 2025

Various State Sales and Excise Tax Rates

State	State Sales Tax (%)	Gasoline[1] ($/gal.)	Cigarette[2] ($/pack)	Spirits[3] ($/gal.)	Wine[4] ($/gal.)	Beer[5] ($/gal.)	Recreational Marijuana (%)
Virginia	5.3	0.40	0.60	23.47	1.51	0.26	(w)

Note: All tax rates as of January 1, 2025; (1) The American Petroleum Institute has developed a methodology for determining the average tax rate on a gallon of fuel. Rates may include any of the following: excise taxes, environmental fees, storage tank fees, other fees or taxes, general sales tax, and local taxes; (2) The federal excise tax of $1.0066 per pack and local taxes are not included; (3) Rates are those applicable to off-premise sales of 40% alcohol by volume (a.b.v.) distilled spirits in 750ml containers. Local excise taxes are excluded; (4) Rates are those applicable to off-premise sales of 11% a.b.v. non-carbonated wine in 750ml containers; (5) Rates are those applicable to off-premise sales of 4.7% a.b.v. beer in 12 ounce containers; (w) The House and the Senate passed a bill to allow legal recreational sales to commence on May 1, 2025 with a tax rate of 11.625%; Governor Youngkin vetoed the bill on March 28, 2024
Source: Tax Foundation, 2025 Facts & Figures: How Does Your State Compare?

State Tax Competitiveness Index

State	Overall Rank	Corporate Tax Rank	Individual Income Tax Rank	Sales Tax Rank	Property Tax Rank	Unemployment Insurance Tax Rank
Virginia	28	24	36	10	22	38

Note: The Tax Foundation's State Tax Competitiveness Index enables policymakers, taxpayers, and business leaders to gauge how their states' tax systems compare. A rank of 1 is best, 50 is worst. Rankings do not average to the total. States without a tax rank equally as 1. DC's scores and rankings do not affect other states. The report shows tax systems as of July 1, 2024 (the beginning of Fiscal Year 2025).
Source: Tax Foundation, State Tax Competitiveness Index 2025

TRANSPORTATION

Means of Transportation to Work

Area	Car/Truck/Van		Public Transportation			Bicycle	Walked	Other Means	Worked at Home
	Drove Alone	Car-pooled	Bus	Subway	Railroad				
City	64.9	7.8	3.6	0.0	0.0	1.1	4.2	1.5	16.9
MSA[1]	71.6	7.3	1.0	0.0	0.1	0.3	1.7	1.2	16.7
U.S.	70.2	8.5	1.7	1.3	0.4	0.4	2.4	1.6	13.5

Note: Figures are percentages and cover workers 16 years of age and older; (1) Figures cover the Richmond, VA Metropolitan Statistical Area
Source: U.S. Census Bureau, 2019-2023 American Community Survey 5-Year Estimates

Travel Time to Work

Area	Less Than 10 Minutes	10 to 19 Minutes	20 to 29 Minutes	30 to 44 Minutes	45 to 59 Minutes	60 to 89 Minutes	90 Minutes or More
City	11.4	37.4	27.0	16.8	2.9	2.8	1.7
MSA[1]	9.7	28.3	26.8	23.2	6.5	3.2	2.2
U.S.	12.6	28.6	21.2	20.8	8.1	6.0	2.8

Note: Note: Figures are percentages and include workers 16 years old and over; (1) Figures cover the Richmond, VA Metropolitan Statistical Area
Source: U.S. Census Bureau, 2019-2023 American Community Survey 5-Year Estimates

Key Congestion Measures

Measure	2000	2010	2015	2020	2022
Annual Hours of Delay, Total (000)	10,256	20,216	23,120	15,862	22,642
Annual Hours of Delay, Per Auto Commuter	23	28	31	24	35
Annual Congestion Cost, Per Auto Commuter ($)	430	679	713	539	746

Note: Figures cover the Richmond VA urban area
Source: Texas A&M Transportation Institute, 2023 Urban Mobility Report

Freeway Travel Time Index

Measure	1985	1990	1995	2000	2005	2010	2015	2020	2022
Urban Area Index[1]	1.04	1.06	1.09	1.09	1.11	1.12	1.12	1.07	1.10
Urban Area Rank[1,2]	81	85	77	92	92	89	92	57	89

Note: Freeway Travel Time Index—the ratio of travel time in the peak period to the travel time at free-flow conditions. For example, a value of 1.30 indicates a 20-minute free-flow trip takes 26 minutes in the peak (20 minutes x 1.30 = 26 minutes); (1) Covers the Richmond VA urban area; (2) Rank is based on 101 larger urban areas (#1 = highest travel time index)
Source: Texas A&M Transportation Institute, 2023 Urban Mobility Report

Public Transportation

Agency Name / Mode of Transportation	Vehicles Operated in Maximum Service[1]	Annual Unlinked Passenger Trips[2] (in thous.)	Annual Passenger Miles[3] (in thous.)
Greater Richmond Transit Company (GRTC)			
Bus (directly operated)	84	7,624.7	31,246.5
Bus Rapid Transit (directly operated)	9	1,707.0	4,706.1
Demand Response (purchased transportation)	37	242.0	2,319.9
Vanpool (purchased transportation)	66	150.0	10,138.1

Note: (1) Number of revenue vehicles operated by the given mode and type of service to meet the annual maximum service requirement. This is the revenue vehicle count during the peak season of the year; on the week and day that maximum service is provided. Vehicles operated in maximum service (VOMS) exclude atypical days and one-time special events; (2) Number of passengers who boarded public transportation vehicles. Passengers are counted each time they board a vehicle no matter how many vehicles they use to travel from their origin to their destination. (3) Sum of the distances ridden by all passengers during the entire fiscal year.
Source: Federal Transit Administration, National Transit Database, 2023

Air Transportation

Airport Name and Code / Type of Service	Passenger Airlines[1]	Passenger Enplanements	Freight Carriers[2]	Freight (lbs)
Richmond International (RIC)				
Domestic service (U.S. carriers only)	28	2,455,831	14	84,713,970
International service (U.S. carriers only)	1	164	0	0

Note: (1) Includes all U.S.-based major, minor and commuter airlines that carried at least one passenger during the year; (2) Includes all U.S.-based airlines and freight carriers that transported at least one pound of freight during the year.
Source: Bureau of Transportation Statistics, The Intermodal Transportation Database, Air Carriers: T-100 Domestic Market (U.S. carriers only), 2024; Bureau of Transportation Statistics, The Intermodal Transportation Database, Air Carriers: T-100 International Market (U.S. carriers only), 2024

BUSINESSES

Major Business Headquarters

Company Name	Industry	Rankings	
		Fortune[1]	Forbes[2]
ARKO	Specialty retailers: other	453	-
Altria Group	Tobacco	196	-
CarMax	Automotive retailing, services	141	-
Dominion Energy	Utilities: gas and electric	230	-
Estes Express Lines	Transportation	-	130
Genworth Financial	Insurance: life, health (stock)	477	-
Performance Food Group	Wholesalers: food and grocery	84	-

Note: (1) Companies that produce a 10-K are ranked 1 to 500 based on 2023 revenue; (2) All private companies with at least $2 billion in annual revenue through the end of their most current fiscal year are ranked 1 to 275; companies listed are headquartered in the city; dashes indicate no ranking
Source: Fortune, "Fortune 500," 2024; Forbes, "America's Largest Private Companies," 2024

Fastest-Growing Businesses

According to *Inc.*, Richmond is home to one of America's 500 fastest-growing private companies: **Servos** (#99). Criteria: must be an independent, privately-held, for-profit, U.S. corporation, proprietorship or partnership as of December 31, 2023; revenues must be at least $100,000 in 2020 and $2 million in 2023; must have four-year operating/sales history. *Inc., "America's 500 Fastest-Growing Private Companies," 2024*

According to *Initiative for a Competitive Inner City (ICIC)*, Richmond is home to one of America's 100 fastest-growing "inner city" companies: **Astyra Corporation** (#71). To be eligible for the IC100, companies have to be independently operated, privately held, for-profit businesses with revenues of at least $50,000 in 2019 and $500,000 in 2023, and headquartered in an under-resourced community. Recognizing that concentrated poverty exists within metropolitan areas outside of big cities (and that poverty overall is suburbanizing), ICIC defines under-resourced communities as large low-income, high-poverty areas located in the urban and suburban parts of all but the smallest metropolitan areas. Companies were ranked overall by revenue growth over the five-year period between 2019 and 2023. *Initiative for a Competitive Inner City (ICIC), "Inner City 100 Companies," 2024*

Living Environment

COST OF LIVING

Cost of Living Index

Composite Index	Groceries	Housing	Utilities	Transportation	Health Care	Misc. Goods/Services
94.2	99.9	84.6	96.2	95.3	91.1	99.2

Note: The Cost of Living Index measures regional differences in the cost of consumer goods and services, excluding taxes and non-consumer expenditures, for professional and managerial households in the top income quintile. It is based on more than 50,000 prices covering almost 60 different items for which prices are collected three times a year by chambers of commerce, economic development organizations or university applied economic centers in each participating urban area. The numbers shown should be read as a percentage above or below the national average of 100. For example, a value of 115.4 in the groceries column indicates that grocery prices are 15.4% higher than the national average. Small differences in the index numbers should not be interpreted as significant; Figures cover the Richmond VA urban area.
Source: The Council for Community and Economic Research, Cost of Living Index, 2024

Grocery Prices

Area[1]	T-Bone Steak ($/pound)	Frying Chicken ($/pound)	Whole Milk ($/half gal.)	Eggs ($/dozen)	Orange Juice ($/64 oz.)	Coffee ($/11.5 oz.)
City[2]	15.51	1.43	4.65	3.38	4.37	5.55
Avg.	15.42	1.55	4.69	3.25	4.41	5.46
Min.	14.50	1.16	4.43	2.75	4.00	4.85
Max.	17.56	2.89	5.49	4.78	5.54	7.89

Note: (1) Values for the local area are compared with the average, minimum and maximum values for all 276 areas in the Cost of Living Index; (2) Figures cover the Richmond VA urban area; **T-Bone Steak** (price per pound); **Frying Chicken** (price per pound, whole fryer); **Whole Milk** (half gallon carton); **Eggs** (price per dozen, Grade A, large); **Orange Juice** (64 oz. Tropicana or Florida Natural); **Coffee** (11.5 oz. can, vacuum-packed, Maxwell House, Hills Bros, or Folgers).
Source: The Council for Community and Economic Research, Cost of Living Index, 2024

Housing and Utility Costs

Area[1]	New Home Price ($)	Apartment Rent ($/month)	All Electric ($/month)	Part Electric ($/month)	Other Energy ($/month)	Telephone ($/month)
City[2]	418,775	1,466	-	117.64	80.21	187.77
Avg.	515,975	1,550	210.99	123.07	82.07	194.99
Min.	265,375	692	104.33	53.68	36.26	179.42
Max.	2,775,821	5,719	529.02	397.28	361.63	223.33

Note: (1) Values for the local area are compared with the average, minimum and maximum values for all 276 areas in the Cost of Living Index; (2) Figures cover the Richmond VA urban area; **New Home Price** (2,400 sf living area, 8,000 sf lot, in urban area with full utilities); **Apartment Rent** (950 sf 2 bedroom/1.5 or 2 bath, unfurnished, excluding all utilities except water); **All Electric** (average monthly cost for an all-electric home); **Part Electric** (average monthly cost for a part-electric home); **Other Energy** (average monthly cost for natural gas, fuel oil, coal, wood, and any other forms of energy except electricity); **Telephone** (price includes the base monthly rate plus taxes and fees for three lines of mobile phone service).
Source: The Council for Community and Economic Research, Cost of Living Index, 2024

Health Care, Transportation, and Other Costs

Area[1]	Doctor ($/visit)	Dentist ($/visit)	Optometrist ($/visit)	Gasoline ($/gallon)	Beauty Salon ($/visit)	Men's Shirt ($)
City[2]	120.19	104.13	133.02	3.24	48.38	20.26
Avg.	143.77	117.51	129.23	3.32	48.57	38.14
Min.	36.74	58.67	67.33	2.80	24.00	13.41
Max.	270.44	216.82	307.33	5.28	94.00	63.89

Note: (1) Values for the local area are compared with the average, minimum and maximum values for all 276 areas in the Cost of Living Index; (2) Figures cover the Richmond VA urban area; **Doctor** (general practitioners routine exam of an established patient); **Dentist** (adult teeth cleaning and periodic oral examination); **Optometrist** (full vision eye exam for established adult patient); **Gasoline** (one gallon regular unleaded, national brand, including all taxes, cash price at self-service pump if available); **Beauty Salon** (woman's shampoo, trim, and blow-dry); **Men's Shirt** (cotton/polyester dress shirt, pinpoint weave, long sleeves).
Source: The Council for Community and Economic Research, Cost of Living Index, 2024

HOUSING

Homeownership Rate

Area	2017 (%)	2018 (%)	2019 (%)	2020 (%)	2021 (%)	2022 (%)	2023 (%)	2024 (%)
MSA[1]	63.1	62.9	66.4	66.5	64.9	66.3	64.9	65.4
U.S.	63.9	64.4	64.6	66.6	65.5	65.8	65.9	65.6

Note: (1) Figures cover the Richmond, VA Metropolitan Statistical Area
Source: U.S. Census Bureau, Housing Vacancies and Homeownership Annual Statistics: 2017-2024

House Price Index (HPI)

Area	National Ranking[2]	Quarterly Change (%)	One-Year Change (%)	Five-Year Change (%)	Since 1991Q1 (%)
MSA[1]	98	0.07	5.98	59.60	306.38
U.S.[3]	—	1.43	4.51	57.13	327.82

Note: The HPI is a weighted repeat sales index. It measures average price changes in repeat sales or refinancings on the same properties. This information is obtained by reviewing repeat mortgage transactions on single-family properties whose mortgages have been purchased or securitized by Fannie Mae or Freddie Mac since January 1975; (1) Figures cover the Richmond, VA Metropolitan Statistical Area; (2) Rankings are based on annual percentage change for all metro areas containing at least 15,000 transactions over the last 10 years and ranges from 1 to 241; (3) figures based on a weighted average of Census Division estimates using a seasonally adjusted, purchase-only index; all figures are for the period ending December 31, 2024
Source: Federal Housing Finance Agency, Change in FHFA Metropolitan Area House Price Indexes, All Transactions Index, 2024Q4

Home Value

Area	Under $100,000	$100,000 -$199,999	$200,000 -$299,999	$300,000 -$399,999	$400,000 -$499,999	$500,000 -$999,999	$1,000,000 or more	Median ($)
City	4.9	17.9	22.4	17.1	13.0	19.0	5.7	328,100
MSA[1]	4.9	12.5	26.9	22.4	13.5	17.3	2.6	325,800
U.S.	12.1	17.8	19.5	14.4	10.5	19.1	6.5	303,400

Note: Figures are percentages except for median and cover owner-occupied housing units; (1) Figures cover the Richmond, VA Metropolitan Statistical Area
Source: U.S. Census Bureau, 2019-2023 American Community Survey 5-Year Estimates

Year Housing Structure Built

Area	2020 or Later	2010 -2019	2000 -2009	1990 -1999	1980 -1989	1970 -1979	1960 -1969	1950 -1959	1940 -1949	Before 1940	Median Year
City	1.1	8.6	5.9	5.7	7.3	8.7	11.1	14.1	9.0	28.6	1959
MSA[1]	1.3	10.3	14.2	14.3	15.3	13.7	9.3	8.5	4.2	8.8	1984
U.S.	1.2	8.9	13.6	12.8	13.0	14.4	10.0	9.7	4.5	11.9	1980

Note: Figures are percentages except for Median Year; Note: (1) Figures cover the Richmond, VA Metropolitan Statistical Area
Source: U.S. Census Bureau, 2019-2023 American Community Survey 5-Year Estimates

Gross Monthly Rent

Area	Under $500	$500 -$999	$1,000 -$1,499	$1,500 -$1,999	$2,000 -$2,499	$2,500 -$2,999	$3,000 and up	Median ($)
City	9.4	14.9	41.0	24.1	7.9	1.9	0.8	1,314
MSA[1]	5.5	14.0	39.6	27.9	9.1	1.8	2.0	1,388
U.S.	6.5	22.3	29.5	20.2	10.8	4.8	5.9	1,348

Note: Figures are percentages except for median; Gross rent is the contract rent plus the estimated average monthly cost of utilities (electricity, gas, and water and sewer) and fuels (oil, coal, kerosene, wood, etc.) if these are paid by the renter (or paid for the renter by someone else); (1) Figures cover the Richmond, VA Metropolitan Statistical Area
Source: U.S. Census Bureau, 2019-2023 American Community Survey 5-Year Estimates

HEALTH

Health Risk Factors

Category	MSA[1] (%)	U.S. (%)
Adults aged 18–64 who have any kind of health care coverage	91.8	90.8
Adults who reported being in good or better health	83.9	81.8
Adults who have been told they have high blood cholesterol	39.1	36.9
Adults who have been told they have high blood pressure	39.4	34.0
Adults who are current smokers	14.9	12.1
Adults who currently use e-cigarettes	8.1	7.7
Adults who currently use chewing tobacco, snuff, or snus	2.5	3.2
Adults who are heavy drinkers[2]	6.4	6.1
Adults who are binge drinkers[3]	15.2	15.2
Adults who are overweight (BMI 25.0 - 29.9)	32.4	34.4
Adults who are obese (BMI 30.0 - 99.8)	36.7	34.3
Adults who participated in any physical activities in the past month	81.6	75.8

Note: All figures are crude prevalence; (1) Figures cover the Richmond, VA Metropolitan Statistical Area; (2) Heavy drinkers are classified as adult men having more than 14 drinks per week and adult women having more than 7 drinks per week; (3) Binge drinkers are classified as males having five or more drinks on one occasion or females having four or more drinks on one occasion
Source: Centers for Disease Control and Prevention, Behavioral Risk Factor Surveillance System, SMART: Selected Metropolitan Area Risk Trends, 2023

Acute and Chronic Health Conditions

Category	MSA[1] (%)	U.S. (%)
Adults who have ever been told they had a heart attack	3.3	4.2
Adults who have ever been told they have angina or coronary heart disease	3.9	4.0
Adults who have ever been told they had a stroke	5.1	3.3
Adults who have ever been told they have asthma	16.4	15.7
Adults who have ever been told they have arthritis	28.1	26.3
Adults who have ever been told they have diabetes[2]	11.8	11.5
Adults who have ever been told they had skin cancer	5.7	5.6
Adults who have ever been told they had any other types of cancer	7.7	8.4
Adults who have ever been told they have COPD	6.6	6.4
Adults who have ever been told they have kidney disease	3.5	3.7
Adults who have ever been told they have a form of depression	17.4	22.0

Note: All figures are crude prevalence; (1) Figures cover the Richmond, VA Metropolitan Statistical Area; (2) Figures do not include pregnancy-related, borderline, or pre-diabetes
Source: Centers for Disease Control and Prevention, Behavioral Risk Factor Surveillance System, SMART: Selected Metropolitan Area Risk Trends, 2023

Health Screening and Vaccination Rates

Category	MSA[1] (%)	U.S. (%)
Adults who have ever been tested for HIV	41.7	37.5
Adults who have had their blood cholesterol checked within the last five years	87.6	87.0
Adults aged 65+ who have had flu shot within the past year	69.1	63.4
Adults aged 65+ who have ever had a pneumonia vaccination	71.2	71.9

Note: All figures are crude prevalence; (1) Figures cover the Richmond, VA Metropolitan Statistical Area.
Source: Centers for Disease Control and Prevention, Behavioral Risk Factor Surveillance System, SMART: Selected Metropolitan Area Risk Trends, 2023

Disability Status

Category	MSA[1] (%)	U.S. (%)
Adults who reported being deaf	6.7	7.4
Are you blind or have serious difficulty seeing, even when wearing glasses?	6.0	4.9
Do you have difficulty doing errands alone?	7.8	7.8
Do you have difficulty dressing or bathing?	3.1	3.6
Do you have serious difficulty concentrating/remembering/making decisions?	16.1	13.7
Do you have serious difficulty walking or climbing stairs?	13.2	13.2

Note: All figures are crude prevalence; (1) Figures cover the Richmond, VA Metropolitan Statistical Area.
Source: Centers for Disease Control and Prevention, Behavioral Risk Factor Surveillance System, SMART: Selected Metropolitan Area Risk Trends, 2023

Mortality Rates for the Top 10 Causes of Death in the U.S.

ICD-10[a] Sub-Chapter	ICD-10[a] Code	Crude Mortality Rate[2] per 100,000 population	
		County[3]	U.S.
Malignant neoplasms	C00-C97	156.9	182.7
Ischaemic heart diseases	I20-I25	86.7	109.6
Provisional assignment of new diseases of uncertain etiology[1]	U00-U49	54.0	65.3
Other forms of heart disease	I30-I51	75.0	65.1
Other degenerative diseases of the nervous system	G30-G31	38.8	52.4
Other external causes of accidental injury	W00-X59	110.9	52.3
Cerebrovascular diseases	I60-I69	50.5	49.1
Chronic lower respiratory diseases	J40-J47	34.9	43.5
Hypertensive diseases	I10-I15	31.5	38.9
Organic, including symptomatic, mental disorders	F01-F09	31.7	33.9

Note: (a) ICD-10 = International Classification of Diseases 10th Revision; (1) Includes COVID-19, adverse effects to COVID-19 vaccines, SARS, and vaping-related disorders; (2) Crude mortality rates are a three-year average covering 2021-2023; (3) Figures cover Richmond city.
Source: Centers for Disease Control and Prevention, National Center for Health Statistics. National Vital Statistics System, Mortality 2018-2023 on CDC WONDER Online Database

Mortality Rates for Selected Causes of Death

Cause of Death	ICD-10[a] Code	Crude Mortality Rate[1] per 100,000 population	
		County[2]	U.S.
Accidental poisoning and exposure to noxious substances	X40-X49	93.5	30.5
Alzheimer disease	G30	14.7	35.4
Assault	X85-Y09	26.6	7.3
COVID-19	U07.1	54.0	65.3
Diabetes mellitus	E10-E14	32.0	30.0
Diseases of the liver	K70-K76	13.1	20.8
Human immunodeficiency virus (HIV) disease	B20-B24	5.3	1.5
Influenza and pneumonia	J09-J18	8.0	13.4
Intentional self-harm	X60-X84	13.6	14.7
Malnutrition	E40-E46	Unreliable	6.0
Obesity and other hyperalimentation	E65-E68	Unreliable	3.1
Renal failure	N17-N19	21.2	16.4
Transport accidents	V01-V99	14.9	14.4

Note: (a) ICD-10 = International Classification of Diseases 10th Revision; (1) Crude mortality rates are a three-year average covering 2021-2023; (2) Figures cover Richmond city; Data are suppressed when the data meet the criteria for confidentiality constraints; Crude mortality rates are flagged as unreliable when the rate would be calculated with a numerator of 20 or less.
Source: Centers for Disease Control and Prevention, National Center for Health Statistics. National Vital Statistics System, Mortality 2018-2023 on CDC WONDER Online Database

Health Insurance Coverage

Area	With Health Insurance	With Private Health Insurance	With Public Health Insurance	Without Health Insurance	Population Under Age 19 Without Health Insurance
City	90.2	63.3	36.9	9.8	7.2
MSA[1]	93.2	73.3	33.5	6.8	5.0
U.S.	91.4	67.3	36.3	8.6	5.4

Note: Figures are percentages that cover the civilian noninstitutionalized population; (1) Figures cover the Richmond, VA Metropolitan Statistical Area
Source: U.S. Census Bureau, 2019-2023 American Community Survey 5-Year Estimates

Number of Medical Professionals

Area	MDs[3]	DOs[3,4]	Dentists	Podiatrists	Chiropractors	Optometrists
City[1] (number)	1,887	146	357	31	17	36
City[1] (rate[2])	822.6	63.6	155.7	13.5	7.4	15.7
U.S. (rate[2])	302.5	29.2	74.6	6.4	29.5	18.0

Note: Data as of 2023 unless noted; (1) Data covers the city of Richmond; (2) Number of medical professionals per 100,000 population; (3) Data as of 2022 and includes all active, non-federal physicians; (4) Doctor of Osteopathic Medicine
Source: U.S. Department of Health and Human Services, Health Resources and Services Administration, Bureau of Health Professions, Area Resource File (ARF) 2023-2024

Best Hospitals

According to *U.S. News,* the Richmond, VA metro area is home to two of the best hospitals in the U.S.: **Sheltering Arms Institute** (1 adult specialty); **VCU Medical Center** (3 adult specialties and 2 pediatric specialties). The hospitals listed were nationally ranked in at least one of 15 adult or 11 pediatric specialties. The number of specialties shown cover the parent hospital. Only 160 U.S. hospitals performed well enough to be nationally ranked in one or more specialties. Twenty hospitals in the U.S. made the Honor Roll. The Best Hospitals Honor Roll takes both the national rankings and the procedure and condition ratings into account. Hospitals received points if they were nationally ranked in one of the 15 adult specialties—the higher they ranked, the more points they got—and how many ratings of "high performing" they earned in the 20 procedures and conditions. *U.S. News Online,* "America's Best Hospitals 2024-25"

According to *U.S. News,* the Richmond, VA metro area is home to one of the best children's hospitals in the U.S.: **Children's Hospital of Richmond at VCU** (2 pediatric specialties). The hospital listed was highly ranked in at least one of 11 pediatric specialties. One hundred five children's hospitals in the U.S. were nationally ranked in at least one specialty. Hospitals received points for being ranked in a specialty, and the 10 hospitals with the most points across the 11 specialties make up the Honor Roll. *U.S. News Online,* "America's Best Children's Hospitals 2024-25"

EDUCATION

Public School District Statistics

District Name	Schls	Pupils	Pupil/Teacher Ratio	Minority Pupils[1] (%)	Total Rev. per Pupil ($)	Total Exp. per Pupil ($)
Richmond City Public Schools	54	20,819	15.0	88.4	22,805	22,807

Note: Table includes school districts with 2,000 or more students; (1) Percentage of students that are not non-Hispanic white.
Source: U.S. Department of Education, National Center for Education Statistics, Common Core of Data, Local Education Agency (School District) Universe Survey: School Year 2023-2024; U.S. Department of Education, National Center for Education Statistics, Common Core of Data, School District Finance Survey (F-33): School Year 2021–22

Best High Schools

According to *U.S. News,* Richmond is home to two of the top 500 high schools in the U.S.: **Open High School** (#161); **Richmond Community High School** (#254). Nearly 25,000 public, magnet and charter schools were ranked based on their performance on state assessments and how well they prepare students for college. *U.S. News & World Report, "Best High Schools 2024"*

Highest Level of Education

Area	Less than H.S.	H.S. Diploma	Some College, No Deg.	Associate Degree	Bachelor's Degree	Master's Degree	Prof. School Degree	Doctorate Degree
City	10.7	21.2	18.8	5.3	26.0	12.3	3.5	2.2
MSA[1]	8.1	24.4	19.5	7.8	24.4	11.7	2.5	1.7
U.S.	10.6	26.2	19.4	8.8	21.3	9.8	2.3	1.6

Note: Figures cover persons age 25 and over; (1) Figures cover the Richmond, VA Metropolitan Statistical Area
Source: U.S. Census Bureau, 2019-2023 American Community Survey 5-Year Estimates

Educational Attainment by Race

Area	High School Graduate or Higher (%)					Bachelor's Degree or Higher (%)				
	Total	White	Black	Asian	Hisp.[2]	Total	White	Black	Asian	Hisp.[2]
City	89.3	96.6	85.0	90.3	61.4	44.1	70.1	16.1	64.9	25.2
MSA[1]	91.9	95.0	89.7	90.1	71.2	40.2	47.4	24.6	63.9	22.8
U.S.	89.4	92.9	88.1	88.0	72.5	35.0	37.7	24.7	57.0	19.9

Note: Figures shown cover persons 25 years old and over; (1) Figures cover the Richmond, VA Metropolitan Statistical Area; (2) People of Hispanic origin can be of any race
Source: U.S. Census Bureau, 2019-2023 American Community Survey 5-Year Estimates

School Enrollment by Grade and Control

Area	Preschool (%)		Kindergarten (%)		Grades 1 - 4 (%)		Grades 5 - 8 (%)		Grades 9 - 12 (%)	
	Public	Private	Public	Private	Public	Private	Public	Private	Public	Private
City	53.2	46.8	90.2	9.8	87.7	12.3	84.7	15.3	82.7	17.3
MSA[1]	44.4	55.6	86.4	13.6	87.5	12.5	89.1	10.9	90.0	10.0
U.S.	58.7	41.3	85.2	14.8	87.2	12.8	87.9	12.1	89.0	11.0

Note: Figures shown cover persons 3 years old and over; (1) Figures cover the Richmond, VA Metropolitan Statistical Area
Source: U.S. Census Bureau, 2019-2023 American Community Survey 5-Year Estimates

Higher Education

Four-Year Colleges			Two-Year Colleges			Medical Schools[1]	Law Schools[2]	Voc/Tech[3]
Public	Private Non-profit	Private For-profit	Public	Private Non-profit	Private For-profit			
2	5	2	3	2	3	1	1	7

Note: Figures cover institutions located within the Richmond, VA Metropolitan Statistical Area and include main campuses only; (1) includes schools accredited by the Liaison Committee on Medical Education and the American Osteopathic Association's Commission on Osteopathic College Accreditation; (2) includes ABA-accredited schools, schools with provisional ABA accreditation, and state accredited schools; (3) includes all schools with programs that are less than 2 years.
Source: National Center for Education Statistics, Integrated Postsecondary Education System (IPEDS), 2023-24; Wikipedia, List of Medical Schools in the United States, accessed May 2, 2025; Wikipedia, List of Law Schools in the United States, accessed May 2, 2025

According to *U.S. News & World Report,* the Richmond, VA metro area is home to one of the top 200 national universities in the U.S.: **Virginia Commonwealth University** (#136 tie). The indicators used to capture academic quality fall into a number of categories: assessment by administrators at peer institutions; retention of students; faculty resources; student selectivity; financial resources; alumni giving; high school counselor ratings of colleges; and graduation rate. *U.S. News & World Report, "America's Best Colleges 2025"*

According to *U.S. News & World Report*, the Richmond, VA metro area is home to one of the top 100 liberal arts colleges in the U.S.: **University of Richmond** (#22 tie). The indicators used to capture academic quality fall into a number of categories: assessment by administrators at peer institutions; retention of students; faculty resources; student selectivity; financial resources; alumni giving; high school counselor ratings of colleges; and graduation rate. *U.S. News & World Report, "America's Best Colleges 2025"*

According to *U.S. News & World Report*, the Richmond, VA metro area is home to one of the top 100 law schools in the U.S.: **University of Richmond** (#71 tie). The rankings are based on a weighted average of 12 measures of quality: peer assessment score; assessment score by lawyers/judges; median LSAT scores; median undergrad GPA; acceptance rate; employment rates for graduates; placement success; bar passage rate; faculty resources; expenditures per student; student/faculty ratio; and library resources. *U.S. News & World Report, "America's Best Graduate Schools, Law, 2025"*

According to *U.S. News & World Report*, the Richmond, VA metro area is home to one of the top medical schools for research in the U.S.: **Virginia Commonwealth University** (Tier 2). *U.S. News* placed medical and osteopathic schools into tiers based on their research productivity, faculty and admissions data. Each school's tier was derived from its overall score, calculated by summing the weighted normalized values generated across several factors of academic quality, outlined below. There are four tiers, with tier 1 medical schools as the highest-performing and tier 4 as the lowest-performing. Only tier 1 and 2 schools are shown. Because of the tier presentation, *U.S. News* calculated overall scores based on their percentile performance among all rated schools instead of dividing against the rescaled score of the No. 1-performing schools. Tier 1 included schools with overall scores of 85 to 99. The cutoffs for tiers 2 through 4 were schools scoring 50 to 84, 15 to 49 and 1 to 14, respectively. The rankings are based on a weighted average of the following measures of quality: total research activity; average research activity per faculty member; total NIH research grants at the medical school and its affiliated hospitals; average NIH research grants per faculty; median MCAT total score; median undergraduate GPA; acceptance rate; and faculty resources. *U.S. News & World Report, "America's Best Graduate Schools, Medical, 2025"*

According to *U.S. News & World Report*, the Richmond, VA metro area is home to one of the top medical schools for primary care in the U.S.: **Virginia Commonwealth University** (Tier 2). *U.S. News* placed medical and osteopathic schools into tiers based on their research productivity, faculty and admissions data. Each school's tier was derived from its overall score, calculated by summing the weighted normalized values generated across several factors of academic quality, outlined below. There are four tiers, with tier 1 medical schools as the highest-performing and tier 4 as the lowest-performing. Only tier 1 and 2 schools are shown. Because of the tier presentation, *U.S. News* calculated overall scores based on their percentile performance among all rated schools instead of dividing against the rescaled score of the No. 1-performing schools. Tier 1 included schools with overall scores of 85 to 99. The cutoffs for tiers 2 through 4 were schools scoring 50 to 84, 15 to 49 and 1 to 14, respectively. The rankings are based on a weighted average of the following measures of quality: graduates practicing in primary care specialties; graduates entering primary care residencies; median MCAT total score; median undergraduate GPA; acceptance rate; and faculty resources. *U.S. News & World Report, "America's Best Graduate Schools, Medical, 2025"*

EMPLOYERS

Major Employers

Company Name	Industry
Altria Group	Cigarettes
Amazon.com	Retail
Anthem Blue Cross and Blue Shield	Insurance
Bank of America	Financial services
Bon Secours Richmond	Healthcare
Capital One Financial Corp.	Financial services
Dominion Resources	Power & energy
DuPont	Conglomerate
Federal Reserve Bank of Richmond	Financial services
Food Lion	Grocery stores
HCA	General medical & surgical hospitals
Markel Corporation	Specialty insurance products
SunTrust Banks	Financial services
The Kroger Co.	Grocery stores
United Parcel Service	Package delivery services
University of Richmond	Education
VCU Health System	Healthcare
Verizon Communications	Communications
Wal-Mart Stores	Retail
Wells Fargo	Financial services

Note: Companies shown are located within the Richmond, VA Metropolitan Statistical Area.
Source: Chambers of Commerce; State Departments of Labor; Wikipedia

Best Companies to Work For

CarMax, headquartered in Richmond, is among "The 100 Best Companies to Work For." To pick the best companies, *Fortune* partnered with the Great Place to Work Institute. Using their proprietary Trust Index™ survey, the core of what creates great a workplace is measured—key behaviors that drive trust in management, connection with colleagues, and loyalty to the company. To be eligible for the *Fortune* 100 Best Companies to Work For list, employers must have 1,000 or more employees in the U.S. and cannot be a government agency. *Fortune*, "The 100 Best Companies to Work For," 2025

PUBLIC SAFETY

Crime Rate

Area	Total Crime Rate	Violent Crime Rate				Property Crime Rate		
		Murder	Rape	Robbery	Aggrav. Assault	Burglary	Larceny-Theft	Motor Vehicle Theft
City	4,078.2	26.9	29.5	97.1	204.1	287.3	2,899.2	534.3
U.S.	2,290.9	5.7	38.0	66.5	264.1	250.7	1,347.2	318.7

Note: Figures are crimes per 100,000 population.
Source: FBI, Table 8, Offenses Known to Law Enforcement, by State by City, 2023

Hate Crimes

Area	Number of Quarters Reported	Number of Incidents per Bias Motivation					
		Race/Ethnicity/Ancestry	Religion	Sexual Orientation	Disability	Gender	Gender Identity
City	4	0	0	1	0	0	0
U.S.	4	5,900	2,699	2,077	187	92	492

Source: Federal Bureau of Investigation, Hate Crime Statistics 2023

Identity Theft Consumer Reports

Area	Reports	Reports per 100,000 Population	Rank[2]
MSA[1]	3,637	274	86
U.S.	1,135,291	339	-

Note: (1) Figures cover the Richmond, VA Metropolitan Statistical Area; (2) Rank ranges from 1 to 401 where 1 indicates greatest number of identity theft reports per 100,000 population
Source: Federal Trade Commission, Consumer Sentinel Network Data Book 2024

Fraud and Other Consumer Reports

Area	Reports	Reports per 100,000 Population	Rank[2]
MSA[1]	20,145	1,518	53
U.S.	5,360,641	1,601	-

Note: (1) Figures cover the Richmond, VA Metropolitan Statistical Area; (2) Rank ranges from 1 to 401 where 1 indicates greatest number of fraud and other consumer reports per 100,000 population
Source: Federal Trade Commission, Consumer Sentinel Network Data Book 2024

POLITICS

2024 Presidential Election Results

Area	Trump (Rep.)	Harris (Dem.)	Stein (Green)	Kennedy (Ind.)	Oliver (Lib.)	Other
Richmond City	64.7	34.5	0.2	0.0	0.2	0.3
U.S.	49.7	48.2	0.6	0.5	0.4	0.6

Note: Results are percentages and may not add to 100% due to rounding
Source: Dave Leip's Atlas of U.S. Presidential Elections

SPORTS

Professional Sports Teams

Team Name	League	Year Established

No teams are located in the metro area
Source: Wikipedia, Major Professional Sports Teams of the United States and Canada, May 1, 2025

CLIMATE

Average and Extreme Temperatures

Temperature	Jan	Feb	Mar	Apr	May	Jun	Jul	Aug	Sep	Oct	Nov	Dec	Yr.
Extreme High (°F)	80	82	91	96	98	104	105	103	103	99	86	80	105
Average High (°F)	47	50	59	69	78	85	88	86	81	71	60	50	69
Average Temp. (°F)	38	40	48	58	66	75	78	77	71	60	50	41	58
Average Low (°F)	28	30	37	45	55	63	68	67	60	48	38	31	48
Extreme Low (°F)	-6	-8	11	19	31	40	51	47	35	21	14	1	-8

Note: Figures cover the years 1921-1990
Source: National Climatic Data Center, International Station Meteorological Climate Summary, 9/96

Average Precipitation/Snowfall/Humidity

Precip./Humidity	Jan	Feb	Mar	Apr	May	Jun	Jul	Aug	Sep	Oct	Nov	Dec	Yr.
Avg. Precip. (in.)	3.3	3.0	3.5	3.1	3.7	3.7	5.2	4.9	3.3	3.1	2.9	3.1	43.0
Avg. Snowfall (in.)	5	4	2	Tr	0	0	0	0	0	Tr	1	2	13
Avg. Rel. Hum. 7am (%)	79	79	78	76	81	82	85	89	90	89	84	80	83
Avg. Rel. Hum. 4pm (%)	54	51	46	43	51	53	56	58	57	53	51	55	52

Note: Figures cover the years 1921-1990; Tr = Trace amounts (<0.05 in. of rain; <0.5 in. of snow)
Source: National Climatic Data Center, International Station Meteorological Climate Summary, 9/96

Weather Conditions

Temperature			Daytime Sky			Precipitation		
10°F & below	32°F & below	90°F & above	Clear	Partly cloudy	Cloudy	0.01 inch or more precip.	0.1 inch or more snow/ice	Thunder-storms
3	79	41	90	147	128	115	7	43

Note: Figures are average number of days per year and cover the years 1921-1990
Source: National Climatic Data Center, International Station Meteorological Climate Summary, 9/96

HAZARDOUS WASTE

Superfund Sites

The Richmond, VA metro area is home to three sites on the EPA's Superfund National Priorities List (NPL) or Superfund Alternative Approach (SAA) list: **Defense General Supply Center (DLA)** (Final NPL); **H & H Inc., Burn Pit** (Final NPL); **Rentokil, Inc. (Virginia Wood Preserving Division)** (Final NPL). The Superfund alternative approach uses the same investigation and cleanup process and standards that are used for sites listed on the National Priorities List. The SAA is an alternative to listing a site on the NPL; it is not an alternative to Superfund or the Superfund process. There are a total of 1,445 Superfund sites with a status of proposed or final on both lists in the United States. *U.S. Environmental Protection Agency, National Priorities List, May 1, 2025; U.S. Environmental Protection Agency, Superfund Alternative Approach Sites, May 1, 2025*

AIR QUALITY

Air Quality Trends: Ozone

	1990	1995	2000	2005	2010	2015	2020	2021	2022	2023
MSA[1]	0.083	0.089	0.080	0.082	0.079	0.062	0.054	0.061	0.060	0.063
U.S.	0.087	0.089	0.081	0.080	0.072	0.068	0.066	0.067	0.067	0.070

Note: (1) Data covers the Richmond, VA Metropolitan Statistical Area. The values shown are the composite ozone concentration averages among trend sites based on the highest fourth daily maximum 8-hour concentration in parts per million. These trends are based on sites having an adequate record of monitoring data during the trend period. Data from exceptional events are included.
Source: U.S. Environmental Protection Agency, Air Quality Monitoring Information, "Air Quality Trends by City, 1990-2023"

Air Quality Index

Area	Percent of Days when Air Quality was...[2]					AQI Statistics[2]	
	Good	Moderate	Unhealthy for Sensitive Groups	Unhealthy	Very Unhealthy	Maximum	Median
MSA[1]	55.9	42.7	0.5	0.8	0.0	159	48

Note: (1) Data covers the Richmond, VA Metropolitan Statistical Area; (2) Based on 365 days with AQI data in 2023. Air Quality Index (AQI) is an index for reporting daily air quality. EPA calculates the AQI for five major air pollutants regulated by the Clean Air Act: ground-level ozone, particle pollution (aka particulate matter), carbon monoxide, sulfur dioxide, and nitrogen dioxide. The AQI runs from 0 to 500. The higher the AQI value, the greater the level of air pollution and the greater the health concern. There are six AQI categories: "Good" AQI is between 0 and 50. Air quality is considered satisfactory; "Moderate" AQI is between 51 and 100. Air quality is acceptable; "Unhealthy for Sensitive Groups" When AQI values are between 101 and 150, members of sensitive groups may experience health effects; "Unhealthy" When AQI values are between 151 and 200 everyone may begin to experience health effects; "Very Unhealthy" AQI values between 201 and 300 trigger a health alert; "Hazardous" AQI values over 300 trigger warnings of emergency conditions (not shown).
Source: U.S. Environmental Protection Agency, Air Quality Index Report, 2023

Air Quality Index Pollutants

Area	Percent of Days when AQI Pollutant was...[2]					
	Carbon Monoxide	Nitrogen Dioxide	Ozone	Sulfur Dioxide	Particulate Matter 2.5	Particulate Matter 10
MSA[1]	0.0	4.4	34.8	(3)	60.8	0.0

Note: (1) Data covers the Richmond, VA Metropolitan Statistical Area; (2) Based on 365 days with AQI data in 2023. The Air Quality Index (AQI) is an index for reporting daily air quality. EPA calculates the AQI for five major air pollutants regulated by the Clean Air Act: ground-level ozone, particle pollution (also known as particulate matter), carbon monoxide, sulfur dioxide, and nitrogen dioxide. The AQI runs from 0 to 500. The higher the AQI value, the greater the level of air pollution and the greater the health concern; (3) Sulfur dioxide is no longer included in this table because SO_2 concentrations tend to be very localized and not necessarily representative of broad geographical areas like counties and CBSAs.
Source: U.S. Environmental Protection Agency, Air Quality Index Report, 2023

Maximum Air Pollutant Concentrations: Particulate Matter, Ozone, CO and Lead

	Particulate Matter 10 (ug/m^3)	Particulate Matter 2.5 Wtd AM (ug/m^3)	Particulate Matter 2.5 24-Hr (ug/m^3)	Ozone (ppm)	Carbon Monoxide (ppm)	Lead (ug/m^3)
MSA[1] Level	65	8.7	28	0.067	1	n/a
NAAQS[2]	150	15	35	0.075	9	0.15
Met NAAQS[2]	Yes	Yes	Yes	Yes	Yes	n/a

Note: (1) Data covers the Richmond, VA Metropolitan Statistical Area; Data from exceptional events are included; (2) National Ambient Air Quality Standards; ppm = parts per million; ug/m³ = micrograms per cubic meter; n/a not available.
Concentrations: Particulate Matter 10 (coarse particulate)—highest second maximum 24-hour concentration; Particulate Matter 2.5 Wtd AM (fine particulate)—highest weighted annual mean concentration; Particulate Matter 2.5 24-Hour (fine particulate)—highest 98th percentile 24-hour concentration; Ozone—highest fourth daily maximum 8-hour concentration; Carbon Monoxide—highest second maximum non-overlapping 8-hour concentration; Lead—maximum running 3-month average
Source: U.S. Environmental Protection Agency, Air Quality Monitoring Information, "Air Quality Statistics by City, 2023"

Maximum Air Pollutant Concentrations: Nitrogen Dioxide and Sulfur Dioxide

	Nitrogen Dioxide AM (ppb)	Nitrogen Dioxide 1-Hr (ppb)	Sulfur Dioxide AM (ppb)	Sulfur Dioxide 1-Hr (ppb)	Sulfur Dioxide 24-Hr (ppb)
MSA[1] Level	13	47	n/a	3	n/a
NAAQS[2]	53	100	30	75	140
Met NAAQS[2]	Yes	Yes	n/a	Yes	n/a

Note: (1) Data covers the Richmond, VA Metropolitan Statistical Area; Data from exceptional events are included; (2) National Ambient Air Quality Standards; ppm = parts per million; ug/m³ = micrograms per cubic meter; n/a not available.
Concentrations: Nitrogen Dioxide AM—highest arithmetic mean concentration; Nitrogen Dioxide 1-Hr—highest 98th percentile 1-hour daily maximum concentration; Sulfur Dioxide AM—highest annual mean concentration; Sulfur Dioxide 1-Hr—highest 99th percentile 1-hour daily maximum concentration; Sulfur Dioxide 24-Hr—highest second maximum 24-hour concentration
Source: U.S. Environmental Protection Agency, Air Quality Monitoring Information, "Air Quality Statistics by City, 2023"

Virginia Beach, Virginia

Background

Virginia Beach is located in southeastern Virginia, on the shores of the Chesapeake Bay and the Atlantic Ocean. With 38 miles of waterfront, it's a paradise for beach lovers.

The history of Virginia Beach began in 1607 when English settlers led by Captain John Smith reached Virginia's shore at Cape Henry aboard the *Susan Constant*, the *Godspeed*, and the *Discovery*. The 100 colonists, sent by the Virginia Company to investigate trade possibilities, shortly moved up the James River to found the first permanent English settlement in America at Jamestown. The first settlement within the Virginia Beach city limits was at Lynnhaven Bay in 1621. It was at Cape Henry that the French Admiral Comte de Grassein came to the aid of American patriots during the Revolutionary War by blockading the British fleet during the Battle of Yorktown. To this day, the area is home to strategically important military bases.

With the connection of a railway to Norfolk in the late nineteenth century, Virginia Beach became a popular shore resort. It was incorporated as a town in 1906, and a city in 1952. In 1963, all neighboring Princess Ann County merged with the city, and today's Virginia Beach covers a territory of 310 square miles with 38 miles of shoreline, making tourism the economic mainstay. It hosts the East Coast Surfing Championship and the North American Sand Soccer Championship every year.

Virginia Beach is listed in the *Guinness Book of World Records* as having the longest pleasure beach in the world and is located at the southern end of the Chesapeake Bay Bridge Tunnel—which was the longest bridge-tunnel in the world until 2018, when it was surpassed by a tunnel in China.

The city naturally enjoys a lifestyle focused to the water, with 28 miles of public beaches and 79 miles of scenic waterways, and plentiful sailing and fishing opportunities. With three state and regional parks, three national wildlife refuges, and 293 city parks, Virginia Beach offers a unique mix of urban, natural, and ecotourist attractions.

Virginia Beach has a large agribusiness sector which produces $190 million for the city economy, supported by hundreds of farms exist in Virginia Beach, mostly below the Green Line in the southern portion of the city where development is severely restricted. Farmers sell their goods and products at dozens of farmers markets.

Virginia Beach is home to several United States Military bases. These include the United States Navy's NAS Oceana and Training Support Center Hampton Roads, and the Joint Expeditionary Base East located at Cape Henry. Additionally, NAB Little Creek is located mostly within the city of Virginia Beach but carries a Norfolk address. Both NAS Oceana and Training Support Center Hampton Roads are considered to be the largest of their respective kind in the world. The central hub of the United States Navy's Atlantic Fleet, Norfolk Navy Base is located in nearby Norfolk.

Virginia Beach is located alongside the Port of Hampton Roads, one of the world's finest harbors. Rail service and nearby Norfolk International Airport serves major industrial centers and cities. Nearly 200 foreign firms have a presence in the city and major employers include Advanced Manufacturing, the Christian Broadcasting Network, Adecco Staffing, and Avmac. Amazon opened a Virginia Beach delivery facility in 2024, and a fulfillment center will open in late 2025.

Institutions of higher learning in and around Virginia Beach include the Virginia Beach Higher Education Center, College of William and Mary, Old Dominion University, Norfolk State University, Virginia Wesleyan College, Eastern Virginia Medical School, and Tidewater Community College.

There are hundreds of art and cultural organizations based in the city, including the Virginia Museum of Contemporary Art, the Virginia Aquarium & Marine Science Center, and the Military Aviation Museum. Performing arts are offered at the Veterans United Home Loans Amphitheater at Virginia Beach, the Sandler Center, and the Virginia Beach Town Center.

The city's many historical sites include the Adam Thoroughgood House, the Francis Land House, the Cape Henry Lights and Light Station, DeWitt Cottage and Adam Keeling House.

The climate of Virginia Beach is classified as humid subtropical, and much of the year is mild to warm. The long summer season from late May through late September is often hot and humid, with frequent, brief late day thundershowers. Winters are cool with little frozen precipitation, and snowfall is light.

Rankings

General Rankings

- To help military veterans find the best places in which to settle down, *WalletHub* compared the 100 largest U.S. cities across 19 key indicators of livability, affordability and veteran-friendliness. They range from the share of military skill-related jobs to veteran income growth to the availability of VA health facilities. Virginia Beach ranked #5. *Wallethub.com, "Best & Worst Places for Veterans to Live (2025)," November 7, 2024*

- *US News & World Report* conducted a survey of more than 3,500 people and analyzed the 150 largest metropolitan areas to determine what matters most when selecting the next place to live. Virginia Beach ranked #8 out of the top 25 as having the best combination of desirable factors. Criteria: cost of living; quality of life and education; climate; job market; desirability; and other factors. *realestate.usnews.com, "Best Places to Live in the U.S. in 2024-2025," May 21, 2024*

- *Insider* listed 23 places in the U.S. that travel industry trends reveal would be popular destinations in 2023. This year the list trends towards cultural and historical happenings, sports events, wellness experiences and invigorating outdoor escapes. According to the website insider.com Virginia Beach is a place to visit in 2023. *Insider, "23 of the Best Places You Should Travel to in the U.S. in 2023," December 17, 2022*

- In their annual survey, Livability.com looked at data for more than 2,000 mid-sized U.S. cities to assign a "Livability Score"for each. The top 100 scoring cities make up Livability's "Top 100 Best Places to Live in the U.S." in 2025. Virginia Beach was placed among the top 100 of the customizable list. Criteria: housing and economy; cost of living; environment; education; health care options; transportation; safety; and community amenities. *Livability.com, "Top 100 Best Places to Live in the U.S. in 2025" April 15, 2025*

Business/Finance Rankings

- The Virginia Beach metro area appeared on the Milken Institute "2025 Best Performing Cities" list. Rank: #90 out of 200 large metro areas (based on performance category). Criteria: job growth; wage growth; high-tech growth and impact; community resilience; housing affordability; household broadband access. *Milken Institute, "Best-Performing Cities 2025," January 14, 2025*

Education Rankings

- Personal finance website *WalletHub* analyzed the 150 largest U.S. metropolitan statistical areas to determine where the most educated Americans are putting their degrees to work. Criteria: education levels; percentage of workers with degrees; education quality and attainment gap; public school quality rankings; quality and enrollment of each metro area's universities. Virginia Beach was ranked #41 (#1 = most educated city). *WalletHub.com, "Most & Least Educated Cities in America, 2025" July 2, 2024*

Health/Fitness Rankings

- For each of the 100 largest cities in the United States, the American Fitness Index®, compiled in partnership between the American College of Sports Medicine and the Elevance Health Foundation, evaluated community infrastructure and more than 30 health behaviors including preventive health, levels of chronic disease conditions, food insecurity, pedestrian safety, air quality, and community/environment resources that support physical activity. Virginia Beach ranked #44 for "community fitness." *americanfitnessindex.org, "2024 ACSM American Fitness Index Summary Report," July 23, 2024*

- Virginia Beach was identified as a "2025 Allergy Capital." The area ranked #11 out of the nation's 100 largest metropolitan areas. Three groups of factors were used to identify the most challenging cities for people with allergies: annual tree, grass, and weed pollen scores; over the counter allergy medicine use; number of board-certified allergy specialists. *Asthma and Allergy Foundation of America, "2025 Allergy Capitals: The Most Challenging Places to Live with Allergies," March 18, 2025*

- Virginia Beach was identified as a "2024 Asthma Capital." The area ranked #31 out of the nation's 100 largest metropolitan areas. Criteria: estimated asthma prevalence; asthma-related mortality; and ER visits due to asthma. Risk factors analyzed but not factored in the rankings: annual air quality including pollution and ozone levels; public smoking laws; indoor air quality; access to asthma specialists; rescue and controller medication use; uninsured rate; pollen allergy; poverty rate. *Asthma and Allergy Foundation of America, "Asthma Capitals 2024: The Most Challenging Places to Live With Asthma," September 10, 2024*

Real Estate Rankings

- *WalletHub* compared the most populated U.S. cities to determine which had the best markets for real estate agents. Virginia Beach ranked #29 where demand was high and pay was the best. Criteria: sales per agent; annual median wage for real-estate agents; monthly average starting salary for real estate agents; real estate job density and competition; unemployment rate; home turnover rate; housing-market health index; and other relevant metrics. *WalletHub.com, "2021 Best Places to Be a Real Estate Agent," May 12, 2021*

- The Virginia Beach metro area appeared on Realtor.com's list of hot housing markets to watch in 2025. The area ranked #3. Criteria: forecasted home price and sales growth; overall economy; population trends. *Realtor.com®, "Top 10 Housing Markets Positioned for Growth in 2025," December 10, 2024*

- Virginia Beach was ranked #16 in the top 20 out of the 100 largest metro areas in terms of house price appreciation in 2024 (#1 = highest rate). *Federal Housing Finance Agency, "House Price Index, 4th Quarter 2024," February 25, 2025*

- Virginia Beach was ranked #82 out of 176 metro areas in terms of cost of housing in 2024 by the National Association of Home Builders (#1 = most affordable). Criteria: the portion of an average family's income necessary to pay the mortgage on a median-priced home. *National Association of Home Builders®, NAHB-Wells Fargo Cost of Housing Index, 4th Quarter 2024*

Safety Rankings

- Allstate ranked the 100 most populous cities in America in terms of driver safety. Virginia Beach ranked #5. Criteria based on anonymized driving behavior data from Allstate's mobile app powered by Arity: high speed driving (over 80 mph), phone handling, and hard braking. The report helps increase the importance of safety and awareness behind the wheel. *Allstate, "16th Allstate America's Best Drivers Report®" July 11, 2024*

Seniors/Retirement Rankings

- Virginia Beach made the 2024 *Forbes* list of "25 Best Places to Retire." Criteria, focused on overall affordability as well as quality of life indicators, include: housing/living costs compared to the national average and taxes; air quality; crime rates; median home prices; risk associated with climate-change/natural hazards; availability of medical care; bikeability; walkability; healthy living. *Forbes.com, "The Best Places to Retire in 2024: Las Cruces and Other Unexpected Hot Spots," May 10, 2024*

Women/Minorities Rankings

- Personal finance website *WalletHub* compared more than 180 U.S. cities across two key dimensions, "Hispanic Business-Friendliness" and "Hispanic Purchasing Power," to arrive at the most favorable conditions for Hispanic entrepreneurs. Virginia Beach was ranked #73 out of 182. Criteria includes: share of Hispanic-Owned Businesses; average growth of Hispanic Business revenues; Small Business-Friendliness score; affordability; and number of Hispanics with at least a bachelor's degree. *WalletHub.com, "Best Cities for Hispanic Entrepreneurs," September 4, 2024*

Miscellaneous Rankings

- Virginia Beach was selected as a 2024 Digital Cities Survey winner. The city ranked #3 in the large city (250,000 to 499,999 population) category. The survey examined and assessed how city governments are utilizing new technology and modernized applications to provide residents an array of contactless services and conveniences. Survey questions focused on ten initiatives: cybersecurity; citizen experience; disaster recovery; business intelligence; IT personnel retention; data governance; business automation; AI/machine learning; application modernization; and IT collaboration. *Center for Digital Government, "2024 Digital Cities Survey," November 5, 2024*

- The financial planning site *SmartAsset* has compiled its annual study on the best places for Halloween in the U.S. for 2022. 146 cities were compared to determine that Virginia Beach ranked #15 out of 35 for still being able to enjoy the festivities despite COVID-19. Metrics included: safety, family-friendliness, percentage of children in the population, concentration of candy and costume shops, weather and COVID infection rates. *SmartAsset.com, "2022 Edition-Best Places to Celebrate Halloween," October 19, 2022*

- *WalletHub* compared 148 of the most populated U.S. cities to determine their operating efficiency. A "Quality of Services" score was constructed for each city and then measured against the total budget per capita to reveal which were managed the best. Virginia Beach ranked #22. Criteria: financial stability; economy; education; safety; health; infrastructure and pollution. *WalletHub.com, "2025's Best- & Worst-Run Cities in America," June 18, 2024*

Business Environment

DEMOGRAPHICS

Population Growth

Area	1990 Census	2000 Census	2010 Census	2020 Census	2023 Estimate[2]	Population Growth 1990-2023 (%)
City	393,069	425,257	437,994	459,470	457,066	16.3
MSA[1]	1,449,389	1,576,370	1,671,683	1,799,674	1,782,590	23.0
U.S.	248,709,873	281,421,906	308,745,538	331,449,281	332,387,540	33.6

Note: (1) Figures cover the Virginia Beach-Chesapeake-Norfolk, VA-NC Metropolitan Statistical Area; (2) 2019-2023 5-year ACS population estimate
Source: U.S. Census Bureau, 1990 Census, 2000 Census, 2010 Census, 2020 Census, 2019-2023 American Community Survey 5-Year Estimates

Race

Area	White Alone[2] (%)	Black Alone[2] (%)	Asian Alone[2] (%)	AIAN[3] Alone[2] (%)	NHOPI[4] Alone[2] (%)	Other Race Alone[2] (%)	Two or More Races (%)
City	61.6	18.9	7.3	0.2	0.2	2.4	9.4
MSA[1]	55.0	29.7	4.1	0.3	0.1	2.4	8.4
U.S.	63.4	12.4	5.8	0.9	0.2	6.6	10.7

Note: (1) Figures cover the Virginia Beach-Chesapeake-Norfolk, VA-NC Metropolitan Statistical Area; (2) Alone is defined as not being in combination with one or more other races; (3) American Indian and Alaska Native; (4) Native Hawaiian and Other Pacific Islander
Source: U.S. Census Bureau, 2019-2023 American Community Survey 5-Year Estimates

Hispanic or Latino Origin

Area	Total (%)	Mexican (%)	Puerto Rican (%)	Cuban (%)	Other (%)
City	8.9	2.8	2.5	0.3	3.3
MSA[1]	7.8	2.6	2.2	0.3	2.8
U.S.	19.0	11.3	1.8	0.7	5.2

Note: Persons of Hispanic or Latino origin can be of any race; (1) Figures cover the Virginia Beach-Chesapeake-Norfolk, VA-NC Metropolitan Statistical Area
Source: U.S. Census Bureau, 2019-2023 American Community Survey 5-Year Estimates

Age

Area	Under Age 5	Age 5–19	Age 20–34	Age 35–44	Age 45–54	Age 55–64	Age 65–74	Age 75–84	Age 85+	Median Age
City	6.0	18.3	22.1	14.1	11.7	12.6	9.2	4.5	1.6	37.4
MSA[1]	6.0	18.8	22.1	13.3	11.3	12.8	9.4	4.6	1.6	37.2
U.S.	5.7	19.1	20.2	13.1	12.3	12.8	10.0	4.9	1.9	38.7

Note: (1) Figures cover the Virginia Beach-Chesapeake-Norfolk, VA-NC Metropolitan Statistical Area
Source: U.S. Census Bureau, 2019-2023 American Community Survey 5-Year Estimates

Disability by Age

Area	All Ages	Under 18 Years Old	18 to 64 Years Old	65 Years and Over
City	11.7	4.4	10.1	28.7
MSA[1]	13.6	5.4	11.6	32.5
U.S.	13.0	4.7	10.7	32.9

Note: Figures show percent of the civilian noninstitutionalized population that reported having a disability. Disability status is determined from six types of difficulty: vision, hearing, cognitive, ambulatory, self-care, and independent living. For children under 5 years old, hearing and vision difficulty are used to determine disability status. For children between the ages of 5 and 14, disability status is determined from hearing, vision, cognitive, ambulatory, and self-care difficulties. For people aged 15 years and older, they are considered to have a disability if they have difficulty with any one of the six difficulty types; Note: (1) Figures cover the Virginia Beach-Chesapeake-Norfolk, VA-NC Metropolitan Statistical Area
Source: U.S. Census Bureau, 2019-2023 American Community Survey 5-Year Estimates

Ancestry

Area	German	Irish	English	American	Italian	Polish	French[2]	European	Scottish
City	11.2	10.5	11.3	7.5	5.5	2.3	1.9	1.6	2.2
MSA[1]	9.4	8.6	10.8	8.0	4.1	1.7	1.7	1.6	1.8
U.S.	12.6	9.4	9.1	5.5	4.9	2.6	2.0	1.6	1.6

Note: Figures are the percentage of the total population reporting a particular ancestry. The nine most commonly reported ancestries in the U.S. are shown. Figures include multiple ancestries (e.g. if a person reported being Irish and Italian, they were included in both columns); (1) Figures cover the Virginia Beach-Chesapeake-Norfolk, VA-NC Metropolitan Statistical Area; (2) Excludes Basque
Source: U.S. Census Bureau, 2019-2023 American Community Survey 5-Year Estimates

Foreign-born Population

Area	Any Foreign Country	Asia	Mexico	Europe	Caribbean	Central America[2]	South America	Africa	Canada
City	9.1	5.0	0.3	1.4	0.5	0.4	0.8	0.5	0.2
MSA[1]	6.8	2.9	0.4	1.1	0.6	0.6	0.4	0.5	0.2
U.S.	13.9	4.3	3.3	1.4	1.4	1.2	1.2	0.8	0.2

Note: (1) Figures cover the Virginia Beach-Chesapeake-Norfolk, VA-NC Metropolitan Statistical Area; (2) Excludes Mexico.
Source: U.S. Census Bureau, 2019-2023 American Community Survey 5-Year Estimates

Household Size

Area	One	Two	Three	Four	Five	Six	Seven or More	Average Household Size
City	26.1	35.6	17.3	12.7	5.9	1.7	0.8	2.50
MSA[1]	28.6	34.6	16.5	12.2	5.5	1.9	0.9	2.46
U.S.	28.5	33.8	15.4	12.7	5.9	2.3	1.4	2.54

Note: (1) Figures cover the Virginia Beach-Chesapeake-Norfolk, VA-NC Metropolitan Statistical Area
Source: U.S. Census Bureau, 2019-2023 American Community Survey 5-Year Estimates

Household Relationships

Area	Householder	Opposite-sex Spouse	Same-sex Spouse	Opposite-sex Unmarried Partner	Same-sex Unmarried Partner	Child[2]	Grandchild	Other Relatives	Non-relatives
City	38.8	18.6	0.2	2.4	0.1	28.7	2.2	4.0	3.5
MSA[1]	39.0	17.4	0.2	2.3	0.1	27.7	2.5	4.0	3.3
U.S.	38.3	17.5	0.2	2.5	0.2	28.3	2.4	4.8	3.4

Note: Figures are percent of the total population; (1) Figures cover the Virginia Beach-Chesapeake-Norfolk, VA-NC Metropolitan Statistical Area; (2) Includes biological, adopted, and stepchildren of the householder
Source: U.S. Census Bureau, 2020 Census

Gender

Area	Males	Females	Males per 100 Females
City	224,463	232,603	96.5
MSA[1]	875,910	906,680	96.6
U.S.	164,545,087	167,842,453	98.0

Note: (1) Figures cover the Virginia Beach-Chesapeake-Norfolk, VA-NC Metropolitan Statistical Area
Source: U.S. Census Bureau, 2019-2023 American Community Survey 5-Year Estimates

Marital Status

Area	Never Married	Now Married[2]	Separated	Widowed	Divorced
City	31.2	50.6	2.0	5.0	11.2
MSA[1]	33.7	47.7	2.2	5.5	10.8
U.S.	34.1	47.9	1.7	5.6	10.7

Note: Figures are percentages and cover the population 15 years of age and older; (1) Figures cover the Virginia Beach-Chesapeake-Norfolk, VA-NC Metropolitan Statistical Area; (2) Excludes separated
Source: U.S. Census Bureau, 2019-2023 American Community Survey 5-Year Estimates

Religious Groups by Family

Area	Catholic	Baptist	Methodist	LDS[2]	Pentecostal	Lutheran	Islam	Adventist	Other
MSA[1]	8.3	9.5	4.8	0.7	2.0	0.5	1.0	0.9	16.1
U.S.	18.7	7.3	3.0	2.0	1.8	1.7	1.3	1.3	11.6

Note: Figures are the number of adherents as a percentage of the total population and cover the eight largest religious groups in the U.S; (1) Figures cover the Virginia Beach-Chesapeake-Norfolk, VA-NC Metropolitan Statistical Area; (2) Church of Jesus Christ of Latter-day Saints
Sources: 2020 U.S. Religion Census, Association of Statisticians of American Religious Bodies; The Association of Religion Data Archives (ARDA)

Religious Groups by Tradition

Area	Catholic	Evangelical Protestant	Mainline Protestant	Black Protestant	Islam	Judaism	Hinduism	Orthodox	Buddhism
MSA[1]	8.3	21.3	6.9	3.7	1.0	0.3	0.2	0.3	0.3
U.S.	18.7	16.5	5.2	2.3	1.3	0.6	0.4	0.4	0.3

Note: Figures are the number of adherents as a percentage of the total population; (1) Figures cover the Virginia Beach-Chesapeake-Norfolk, VA-NC Metropolitan Statistical Area
Sources: 2020 U.S. Religion Census, Association of Statisticians of American Religious Bodies; The Association of Religion Data Archives (ARDA)

ECONOMY

Real Gross Domestic Product (GDP)

Area	2017	2018	2019	2020	2021	2022	2023	Rank[3]
MSA[1]	94.9	93.9	94.9	94.3	99.0	100.9	104.0	41
U.S.[2]	17,619.1	18,160.7	18,642.5	18,238.9	19,387.6	19,896.6	20,436.3	—

Note: Figures are in billions of chained 2017 dollars; (1) Figures cover the Virginia Beach-Chesapeake-Norfolk, VA-NC Metropolitan Statistical Area; (2) Figures cover real GDP within metropolitan areas; (3) Rank is based on 2023 data and ranges from 1 to 384
Source: U.S. Bureau of Economic Analysis

Economic Growth

Area	2014	2015	2016	2017	2018	2019	2020	2021	2022	2023
MSA[1]	-1.0	1.7	1.1	0.7	-1.2	1.2	-0.7	5.0	1.9	3.2
U.S.[2]	2.6	3.2	2.0	2.7	3.1	2.7	-2.2	6.3	2.6	2.7

Note: Figures are real gross domestic product growth rates and represent percent change from preceding period; (1) Figures cover the Virginia Beach-Chesapeake-Norfolk, VA-NC Metropolitan Statistical Area; (2) Figures are the average growth rates within metropolitan areas
Source: U.S. Bureau of Economic Analysis

Metropolitan Area Exports

Area	2018	2019	2020	2021	2022	2023	Rank[2]
MSA[1]	3,950.6	3,642.4	4,284.3	4,566.3	5,750.1	6,338.3	54
U.S.	1,664,056.1	1,645,173.7	1,431,406.6	1,753,941.4	2,062,937.4	2,019,160.5	—

Note: Figures are in millions of dollars; (1) Figures cover the Virginia Beach-Chesapeake-Norfolk, VA-NC Metropolitan Statistical Area; (2) Rank is based on 2023 data and ranges from 1 to 386
Source: U.S. Department of Commerce, International Trade Administration, Office of Trade and Economic Analysis, Industry and Analysis, Exports by Metropolitan Area, data extracted April 2, 2025

Building Permits

Area	Single-Family 2023	Single-Family 2024	Pct. Chg.	Multi-Family 2023	Multi-Family 2024	Pct. Chg.	Total 2023	Total 2024	Pct. Chg.
City	201	319	58.7	341	347	1.8	542	666	22.9
MSA[1]	3,393	3,544	4.5	2,721	862	-68.3	6,114	4,406	-27.9
U.S.	920,000	981,900	6.7	591,100	496,100	-16.1	1,511,100	1,478,000	-2.2

Note: (1) Figures cover the Virginia Beach-Chesapeake-Norfolk, VA-NC Metropolitan Statistical Area; Figures represent new, privately-owned housing units authorized (unadjusted data)
Source: U.S. Census Bureau, Building Permits Survey (BPS), 2023, 2024

Bankruptcy Filings

Area	Business Filings 2023	Business Filings 2024	% Chg.	Nonbusiness Filings 2023	Nonbusiness Filings 2024	% Chg.
Virginia Beach city	10	20	100.0	822	966	17.5
U.S.	18,926	23,107	22.1	434,064	494,201	13.9

Note: Business filings include Chapter 7, Chapter 9, Chapter 11, Chapter 12, Chapter 13, Chapter 15, and Section 304; Nonbusiness filings include Chapter 7, Chapter 11, and Chapter 13
Source: Administrative Office of the U.S. Courts, Business and Nonbusiness Bankruptcy, County Cases Commenced by Chapter of the Bankruptcy Code, During the 12-Month Period Ending December 31, 2023 and Business and Nonbusiness Bankruptcy, County Cases Commenced by Chapter of the Bankruptcy Code, During the 12-Month Period Ending December 31, 2024

Housing Vacancy Rates

Area	Gross Vacancy Rate[3] (%) 2022	2023	2024	Year-Round Vacancy Rate[4] (%) 2022	2023	2024	Rental Vacancy Rate[5] (%) 2022	2023	2024	Homeowner Vacancy Rate[6] (%) 2022	2023	2024
MSA[1]	8.1	5.9	9.2	7.3	5.4	8.5	6.3	5.1	9.1	1.0	0.5	1.4
U.S.[2]	9.1	9.0	9.1	7.5	7.5	7.6	5.7	6.5	6.8	0.8	0.8	1.0

Note: (1) Figures cover the Virginia Beach-Chesapeake-Norfolk, VA-NC Metropolitan Statistical Area; (2) Figures cover the 75 largest Metropolitan Statistical Areas; (3) The percentage of the total housing inventory that is vacant; (4) The percentage of the housing inventory (excluding seasonal units) that is year-round vacant; (5) The percentage of rental inventory that is vacant for rent; (6) The percentage of homeowner inventory that is vacant for sale
Source: U.S. Census Bureau, Housing Vacancies and Homeownership Annual Statistics: 2022, 2023, 2024

INCOME

Income

Area	Per Capita ($)	Median Household ($)	Average Household ($)
City	47,372	90,685	118,081
MSA[1]	42,791	80,533	105,690
U.S.	43,289	78,538	110,491

Note: (1) Figures cover the Virginia Beach-Chesapeake-Norfolk, VA-NC Metropolitan Statistical Area
Source: U.S. Census Bureau, 2019-2023 American Community Survey 5-Year Estimates

Household Income Distribution

Area	Percent of Households Earning							
	Under $15,000	$15,000 -$24,999	$25,000 -$34,999	$35,000 -$49,999	$50,000 -$74,999	$75,000 -$99,999	$100,000 -$149,999	$150,000 and up
City	5.7	3.9	5.1	8.5	18.1	13.7	20.8	24.2
MSA[1]	7.5	5.5	6.6	10.0	17.3	13.3	19.2	20.7
U.S.	8.5	6.6	6.8	10.4	15.7	12.7	17.4	21.9

Note: (1) Figures cover the Virginia Beach-Chesapeake-Norfolk, VA-NC Metropolitan Statistical Area
Source: U.S. Census Bureau, 2019-2023 American Community Survey 5-Year Estimates

Poverty Rate

Area	All Ages	Under 18 Years Old	18 to 64 Years Old	65 Years and Over
City	8.4	11.2	8.0	5.9
MSA[1]	10.9	15.4	9.9	8.4
U.S.	12.4	16.3	11.6	10.4

Note: Figures are percentage of people whose income during the past 12 months was below the poverty level; (1) Figures cover the Virginia Beach-Chesapeake-Norfolk, VA-NC Metropolitan Statistical Area
Source: U.S. Census Bureau, 2019-2023 American Community Survey 5-Year Estimates

EMPLOYMENT

Labor Force and Employment

Area	Civilian Labor Force			Workers Employed		
	Dec. 2023	Dec. 2024	% Chg.	Dec. 2023	Dec. 2024	% Chg.
City	237,550	239,534	0.8	231,972	233,678	0.7
MSA[1]	883,468	890,934	0.8	860,628	866,842	0.7
U.S.	166,661,000	167,746,000	0.7	160,754,000	161,294,000	0.3

Note: Data is not seasonally adjusted and covers workers 16 years of age and older; (1) Figures cover the Virginia Beach-Chesapeake-Norfolk, VA-NC Metropolitan Statistical Area
Source: Bureau of Labor Statistics, Local Area Unemployment Statistics

Unemployment Rate

Area	2024											
	Jan.	Feb.	Mar.	Apr.	May	Jun.	Jul.	Aug.	Sep.	Oct.	Nov.	Dec.
City	2.6	2.7	2.5	2.3	2.7	2.9	3.0	3.1	2.8	2.7	2.8	2.4
MSA[1]	3.0	3.0	2.9	2.6	3.0	3.2	3.4	3.4	3.1	3.0	3.1	2.7
U.S.	4.1	4.2	3.9	3.5	3.7	4.3	4.5	4.4	3.9	3.9	4.0	3.8

Note: Data is not seasonally adjusted and covers workers 16 years of age and older; (1) Figures cover the Virginia Beach-Chesapeake-Norfolk, VA-NC Metropolitan Statistical Area
Source: Bureau of Labor Statistics, Local Area Unemployment Statistics

Average Wages

Occupation	$/Hr.	Occupation	$/Hr.
Accountants and Auditors	41.24	Maintenance and Repair Workers	24.23
Automotive Mechanics	26.43	Marketing Managers	77.38
Bookkeepers	23.13	Network and Computer Systems Admin.	47.60
Carpenters	24.88	Nurses, Licensed Practical	29.68
Cashiers	14.28	Nurses, Registered	42.13
Computer Programmers	50.07	Nursing Assistants	18.43
Computer Systems Analysts	50.99	Office Clerks, General	21.17
Computer User Support Specialists	29.01	Physical Therapists	48.12
Construction Laborers	19.76	Physicians	125.27
Cooks, Restaurant	17.15	Plumbers, Pipefitters and Steamfitters	27.83
Customer Service Representatives	19.47	Police and Sheriff's Patrol Officers	32.02
Dentists	87.77	Postal Service Mail Carriers	28.31
Electricians	29.26	Real Estate Sales Agents	31.93
Engineers, Electrical	53.55	Retail Salespersons	16.44
Fast Food and Counter Workers	14.30	Sales Representatives, Technical/Scientific	52.97
Financial Managers	78.26	Secretaries, Exc. Legal/Medical/Executive	21.87
First-Line Supervisors of Office Workers	32.80	Security Guards	20.46
General and Operations Managers	57.87	Surgeons	n/a
Hairdressers/Cosmetologists	23.44	Teacher Assistants, Exc. Postsecondary[1]	18.39
Home Health and Personal Care Aides	14.33	Teachers, Secondary School, Exc. Sp. Ed.[1]	34.95
Janitors and Cleaners	16.05	Telemarketers	20.17
Landscaping/Groundskeeping Workers	17.88	Truck Drivers, Heavy/Tractor-Trailer	24.69
Lawyers	71.39	Truck Drivers, Light/Delivery Services	20.85
Maids and Housekeeping Cleaners	15.26	Waiters and Waitresses	19.88

Note: Wage data covers the Virginia Beach-Chesapeake-Norfolk, VA-NC Metropolitan Statistical Area; (1) Hourly wages were calculated from annual wage data based on a 40 hour work week
Source: Bureau of Labor Statistics, Metro Area Occupational Employment & Wage Estimates, May 2024

Employment by Industry

Sector	MSA[1] Number of Employees	MSA[1] Percent of Total	U.S. Percent of Total
Construction, Mining, and Logging	41,500	5.0	5.5
Financial Activities	40,800	4.9	5.8
Government	166,700	20.1	14.9
Information	8,100	1.0	1.9
Leisure and Hospitality	91,600	11.1	10.4
Manufacturing	58,100	7.0	8.0
Other Services	35,600	4.3	3.7
Private Education and Health Services	127,300	15.4	16.9
Professional and Business Services	122,900	14.8	14.2
Retail Trade	82,700	10.0	10.0
Transportation, Warehousing, and Utilities	32,700	3.9	4.8
Wholesale Trade	20,000	2.4	3.9

Note: Figures are non-farm employment as of December 2024. Figures are not seasonally adjusted and include workers 16 years of age and older; (1) Figures cover the Virginia Beach-Chesapeake-Norfolk, VA-NC Metropolitan Statistical Area
Source: Bureau of Labor Statistics, Current Employment Statistics, Employment, Hours, and Earnings

Employment by Occupation

Occupation Classification	City (%)	MSA[1] (%)	U.S. (%)
Management, Business, Science, and Arts	46.4	42.4	42.0
Natural Resources, Construction, and Maintenance	6.5	8.4	8.6
Production, Transportation, and Material Moving	9.7	11.5	13.0
Sales and Office	20.5	20.4	19.9
Service	17.0	17.3	16.5

Note: Figures cover employed civilians 16 years of age and older; (1) Figures cover the Virginia Beach-Chesapeake-Norfolk, VA-NC Metropolitan Statistical Area
Source: U.S. Census Bureau, 2019-2023 American Community Survey 5-Year Estimates

Occupations with Greatest Projected Employment Growth: 2022 – 2032

Occupation[1]	2022 Employment	2032 Projected Employment	Numeric Employment Change	Percent Employment Change
Home Health and Personal Care Aides	60,230	81,100	20,870	34.7
Software Developers	86,610	105,120	18,510	21.4
Management Analysts	78,250	86,170	7,920	10.1
Stockers and Order Fillers	78,610	85,530	6,920	8.8
Cooks, Restaurant	35,850	42,650	6,800	19.0
Information Security Analysts (SOC 2018)	18,390	24,060	5,670	30.8
General and Operations Managers	91,700	96,880	5,180	5.6
Nursing Assistants (SOC 2018)	37,640	41,750	4,110	10.9
Nurse Practitioners	7,170	11,160	3,990	55.6
Laborers and Freight, Stock, and Material Movers, Hand	52,200	56,090	3,890	7.5

Note: Projections cover Virginia; (1) Sorted by numeric employment change
Source: www.projectionscentral.org, State Occupational Projections, 2022–2032 Long-Term Projections

Fastest-Growing Occupations: 2022 – 2032

Occupation[1]	2022 Employment	2032 Projected Employment	Numeric Employment Change	Percent Employment Change
Nurse Practitioners	7,170	11,160	3,990	55.6
Solar Photovoltaic Installers	150	210	60	40.0
Physician Assistants	4,390	5,920	1,530	34.9
Data Scientists	4,650	6,270	1,620	34.8
Home Health and Personal Care Aides	60,230	81,100	20,870	34.7
Statisticians	1,010	1,360	350	34.7
Epidemiologists	270	360	90	33.3
Medical and Health Services Managers	9,620	12,670	3,050	31.7
Information Security Analysts (SOC 2018)	18,390	24,060	5,670	30.8
Physical Therapist Assistants	2,770	3,560	790	28.5

Note: Projections cover Virginia; (1) Sorted by percent employment change and excludes occupations with numeric employment change less than 50
Source: www.projectionscentral.org, State Occupational Projections, 2022–2032 Long-Term Projections

CITY FINANCES

City Government Finances

Component	2022 ($000)	2022 ($ per capita)
Total Revenues	2,143,952	4,751
Total Expenditures	2,205,464	4,888
Debt Outstanding	1,455,061	3,225

Source: U.S. Census Bureau, State & Local Government Finances 2022

City Government Revenue by Source

Source	2022 ($000)	2022 ($ per capita)	2022 (%)
General Revenue			
From Federal Government	108,672	241	5.1
From State Government	538,548	1,194	25.1
From Local Governments	22,601	50	1.1
Taxes			
Property	774,069	1,715	36.1
Sales and Gross Receipts	284,971	632	13.3
Personal Income	0	0	0.0
Corporate Income	0	0	0.0
Motor Vehicle License	10,475	23	0.5
Other Taxes	74,043	164	3.5
Current Charges	217,615	482	10.2
Liquor Store	0	0	0.0
Utility	65,509	145	3.1

Source: U.S. Census Bureau, State & Local Government Finances 2022

City Government Expenditures by Function

Function	2022 ($000)	2022 ($ per capita)	2022 (%)
General Direct Expenditures			
Air Transportation	0	0	0.0
Corrections	49,543	109	2.2
Education	974,257	2,159	44.2
Employment Security Administration	0	0	0.0
Financial Administration	22,979	50	1.0
Fire Protection	84,383	187	3.8
General Public Buildings	58,249	129	2.6
Governmental Administration, Other	34,208	75	1.6
Health	86,996	192	3.9
Highways	113,633	251	5.2
Hospitals	0	0	0.0
Housing and Community Development	41,441	91	1.9
Interest on General Debt	41,992	93	1.9
Judicial and Legal	21,891	48	1.0
Libraries	17,976	39	0.8
Parking	6,294	13	0.3
Parks and Recreation	86,379	191	3.9
Police Protection	115,978	257	5.3
Public Welfare	64,606	143	2.9
Sewerage	115,108	255	5.2
Solid Waste Management	38,683	85	1.8
Veterans' Services	0	0	0.0
Liquor Store	0	0	0.0
Utility	54,864	121	2.5

Source: U.S. Census Bureau, State & Local Government Finances 2022

TAXES

State Corporate Income Tax Rates

State	Tax Rate (%)	Income Brackets ($)	Num. of Brackets	Financial Institution Tax Rate (%)[a]	Federal Income Tax Ded.
Virginia	6.0	Flat rate	1	6.0	No

Note: Tax rates for tax year 2024; (a) Rates listed are the corporate income tax rate applied to financial institutions or excise taxes based on income. Some states have other taxes based upon the value of deposits or shares.
Source: Federation of Tax Administrators, State Corporate Income Tax Rates, January 1, 2025

State Individual Income Tax Rates

State	Tax Rate (%)	Income Brackets ($)	Personal Exemptions ($)			Standard Ded. ($)	
			Single	Married	Depend.	Single	Married
Virginia	2.0 - 5.75	3,000 - 17,001	930	1,860	930	8,000	16,000

Note: Tax rates for tax year 2024; Local- and county-level taxes are not included; Federal income tax is not deductible on state income tax returns
Source: Federation of Tax Administrators, State Individual Income Tax Rates, January 1, 2025

Various State Sales and Excise Tax Rates

State	State Sales Tax (%)	Gasoline[1] ($/gal.)	Cigarette[2] ($/pack)	Spirits[3] ($/gal.)	Wine[4] ($/gal.)	Beer[5] ($/gal.)	Recreational Marijuana (%)
Virginia	5.3	0.40	0.60	23.47	1.51	0.26	(w)

Note: All tax rates as of January 1, 2025; (1) The American Petroleum Institute has developed a methodology for determining the average tax rate on a gallon of fuel. Rates may include any of the following: excise taxes, environmental fees, storage tank fees, other fees or taxes, general sales tax, and local taxes; (2) The federal excise tax of $1.0066 per pack and local taxes are not included; (3) Rates are those applicable to off-premise sales of 40% alcohol by volume (a.b.v.) distilled spirits in 750ml containers. Local excise taxes are excluded; (4) Rates are those applicable to off-premise sales of 11% a.b.v. non-carbonated wine in 750ml containers; (5) Rates are those applicable to off-premise sales of 4.7% a.b.v. beer in 12 ounce containers; (w) The House and the Senate passed a bill to allow legal recreational sales to commence on May 1, 2025 with a tax rate of 11.625%; Governor Youngkin vetoed the bill on March 28, 2024
Source: Tax Foundation, 2025 Facts & Figures: How Does Your State Compare?

State Tax Competitiveness Index

State	Overall Rank	Corporate Tax Rank	Individual Income Tax Rank	Sales Tax Rank	Property Tax Rank	Unemployment Insurance Tax Rank
Virginia	28	24	36	10	22	38

Note: The Tax Foundation's State Tax Competitiveness Index enables policymakers, taxpayers, and business leaders to gauge how their states' tax systems compare. A rank of 1 is best, 50 is worst. Rankings do not average to the total. States without a tax rank equally as 1. DC's scores and rankings do not affect other states. The report shows tax systems as of July 1, 2024 (the beginning of Fiscal Year 2025).
Source: Tax Foundation, State Tax Competitiveness Index 2025

TRANSPORTATION

Means of Transportation to Work

Area	Car/Truck/Van		Public Transportation			Bicycle	Walked	Other Means	Worked at Home
	Drove Alone	Car-pooled	Bus	Subway	Railroad				
City	75.3	7.5	0.8	0.0	0.0	0.4	1.8	1.6	12.7
MSA[1]	75.8	8.2	1.0	0.0	0.0	0.3	2.4	1.6	10.7
U.S.	70.2	8.5	1.7	1.3	0.4	0.4	2.4	1.6	13.5

Note: Figures are percentages and cover workers 16 years of age and older; (1) Figures cover the Virginia Beach-Chesapeake-Norfolk, VA-NC Metropolitan Statistical Area
Source: U.S. Census Bureau, 2019-2023 American Community Survey 5-Year Estimates

Travel Time to Work

Area	Less Than 10 Minutes	10 to 19 Minutes	20 to 29 Minutes	30 to 44 Minutes	45 to 59 Minutes	60 to 89 Minutes	90 Minutes or More
City	10.2	31.3	27.8	21.8	5.4	2.1	1.4
MSA[1]	10.5	31.2	24.1	21.7	6.9	3.9	1.8
U.S.	12.6	28.6	21.2	20.8	8.1	6.0	2.8

Note: Note: Figures are percentages and include workers 16 years old and over; (1) Figures cover the Virginia Beach-Chesapeake-Norfolk, VA-NC Metropolitan Statistical Area
Source: U.S. Census Bureau, 2019-2023 American Community Survey 5-Year Estimates

Key Congestion Measures

Measure	2000	2010	2015	2020	2022
Annual Hours of Delay, Total (000)	29,281	36,000	39,492	19,220	36,300
Annual Hours of Delay, Per Auto Commuter	39	38	44	22	42
Annual Congestion Cost, Per Auto Commuter ($)	881	862	873	446	798

Note: Figures cover the Virginia Beach VA urban area
Source: Texas A&M Transportation Institute, 2023 Urban Mobility Report

Freeway Travel Time Index

Measure	1985	1990	1995	2000	2005	2010	2015	2020	2022
Urban Area Index[1]	1.08	1.10	1.14	1.17	1.18	1.17	1.17	1.06	1.14
Urban Area Rank[1,2]	40	47	41	36	41	41	46	75	64

Note: Freeway Travel Time Index—the ratio of travel time in the peak period to the travel time at free-flow conditions. For example, a value of 1.30 indicates a 20-minute free-flow trip takes 26 minutes in the peak (20 minutes x 1.30 = 26 minutes); (1) Covers the Virginia Beach VA urban area; (2) Rank is based on 101 larger urban areas (#1 = highest travel time index)
Source: Texas A&M Transportation Institute, 2023 Urban Mobility Report

Public Transportation

Agency Name / Mode of Transportation	Vehicles Operated in Maximum Service[1]	Annual Unlinked Passenger Trips[2] (in thous.)	Annual Passenger Miles[3] (in thous.)
Hampton Roads Transit (HRT)			
Bus (directly operated)	225	5,814.5	28,852.1
Demand Response (purchased transportation)	65	262.4	2,507.8
Demand Response - Taxi	2	11.4	161.6
Demand Response - Transportation Network Company	32	84.1	787.8
Ferryboat (purchased transportation)	3	227.2	167.8
Light Rail (directly operated)	5	728.4	2,523.4
Vanpool (purchased transportation)	17	39.2	1,796.6

Note: (1) Number of revenue vehicles operated by the given mode and type of service to meet the annual maximum service requirement. This is the revenue vehicle count during the peak season of the year; on the week and day that maximum service is provided. Vehicles operated in maximum service (VOMS) exclude atypical days and one-time special events; (2) Number of passengers who boarded public transportation vehicles. Passengers are counted each time they board a vehicle no matter how many vehicles they use to travel from their origin to their destination. (3) Sum of the distances ridden by all passengers during the entire fiscal year.
Source: Federal Transit Administration, National Transit Database, 2023

Air Transportation

Airport Name and Code / Type of Service	Passenger Airlines[1]	Passenger Enplanements	Freight Carriers[2]	Freight (lbs)
Norfolk International (ORF)				
Domestic service (U.S. carriers only)	25	2,444,479	11	17,320,717
International service (U.S. carriers only)	3	297	1	22,222

Note: (1) Includes all U.S.-based major, minor and commuter airlines that carried at least one passenger during the year; (2) Includes all U.S.-based airlines and freight carriers that transported at least one pound of freight during the year.
Source: Bureau of Transportation Statistics, The Intermodal Transportation Database, Air Carriers: T-100 Domestic Market (U.S. carriers only), 2024; Bureau of Transportation Statistics, The Intermodal Transportation Database, Air Carriers: T-100 International Market (U.S. carriers only), 2024

BUSINESSES

Major Business Headquarters

Company Name	Industry	Rankings	
		Fortune[1]	Forbes[2]
No companies listed	-	-	-

Note: (1) Companies that produce a 10-K are ranked 1 to 500 based on 2023 revenue; (2) All private companies with at least $2 billion in annual revenue through the end of their most current fiscal year are ranked 1 to 275; companies listed are headquartered in the city; dashes indicate no ranking
Source: Fortune, "Fortune 500," 2024; Forbes, "America's Largest Private Companies," 2024

Living Environment

COST OF LIVING

Cost of Living Index

Composite Index	Groceries	Housing	Utilities	Trans-portation	Health Care	Misc. Goods/Services
94.0	98.5	82.4	104.2	96.0	110.6	96.4

Note: The Cost of Living Index measures regional differences in the cost of consumer goods and services, excluding taxes and non-consumer expenditures, for professional and managerial households in the top income quintile. It is based on more than 50,000 prices covering almost 60 different items for which prices are collected three times a year by chambers of commerce, economic development organizations or university applied economic centers in each participating urban area. The numbers shown should be read as a percentage above or below the national average of 100. For example, a value of 115.4 in the groceries column indicates that grocery prices are 15.4% higher than the national average. Small differences in the index numbers should not be interpreted as significant; Figures cover the Hampton Roads-SE Virginia VA urban area.
Source: The Council for Community and Economic Research, Cost of Living Index, 2024

Grocery Prices

Area[1]	T-Bone Steak ($/pound)	Frying Chicken ($/pound)	Whole Milk ($/half gal.)	Eggs ($/dozen)	Orange Juice ($/64 oz.)	Coffee ($/11.5 oz.)
City[2]	15.52	1.46	4.58	3.35	4.34	5.34
Avg.	15.42	1.55	4.69	3.25	4.41	5.46
Min.	14.50	1.16	4.43	2.75	4.00	4.85
Max.	17.56	2.89	5.49	4.78	5.54	7.89

*Note: (1) Values for the local area are compared with the average, minimum and maximum values for all 276 areas in the Cost of Living Index; (2) Figures cover the Hampton Roads-SE Virginia VA urban area; **T-Bone Steak** (price per pound); **Frying Chicken** (price per pound, whole fryer); **Whole Milk** (half gallon carton); **Eggs** (price per dozen, Grade A, large); **Orange Juice** (64 oz. Tropicana or Florida Natural); **Coffee** (11.5 oz. can, vacuum-packed, Maxwell House, Hills Bros, or Folgers).*
Source: The Council for Community and Economic Research, Cost of Living Index, 2024

Housing and Utility Costs

Area[1]	New Home Price ($)	Apartment Rent ($/month)	All Electric ($/month)	Part Electric ($/month)	Other Energy ($/month)	Telephone ($/month)
City[2]	389,841	1,484	-	120.02	103.90	187.93
Avg.	515,975	1,550	210.99	123.07	82.07	194.99
Min.	265,375	692	104.33	53.68	36.26	179.42
Max.	2,775,821	5,719	529.02	397.28	361.63	223.33

*Note: (1) Values for the local area are compared with the average, minimum and maximum values for all 276 areas in the Cost of Living Index; (2) Figures cover the Hampton Roads-SE Virginia VA urban area; **New Home Price** (2,400 sf living area, 8,000 sf lot, in urban area with full utilities); **Apartment Rent** (950 sf 2 bedroom/1.5 or 2 bath, unfurnished, excluding all utilities except water); **All Electric** (average monthly cost for an all-electric home); **Part Electric** (average monthly cost for a part-electric home); **Other Energy** (average monthly cost for natural gas, fuel oil, coal, wood, and any other forms of energy except electricity); **Telephone** (price includes the base monthly rate plus taxes and fees for three lines of mobile phone service).*
Source: The Council for Community and Economic Research, Cost of Living Index, 2024

Health Care, Transportation, and Other Costs

Area[1]	Doctor ($/visit)	Dentist ($/visit)	Optometrist ($/visit)	Gasoline ($/gallon)	Beauty Salon ($/visit)	Men's Shirt ($)
City[2]	144.92	148.93	69.03	3.20	42.70	32.71
Avg.	143.77	117.51	129.23	3.32	48.57	38.14
Min.	36.74	58.67	67.33	2.80	24.00	13.41
Max.	270.44	216.82	307.33	5.28	94.00	63.89

*Note: (1) Values for the local area are compared with the average, minimum and maximum values for all 276 areas in the Cost of Living Index; (2) Figures cover the Hampton Roads-SE Virginia VA urban area; **Doctor** (general practitioners routine exam of an established patient); **Dentist** (adult teeth cleaning and periodic oral examination); **Optometrist** (full vision eye exam for established adult patient); **Gasoline** (one gallon regular unleaded, national brand, including all taxes, cash price at self-service pump if available); **Beauty Salon** (woman's shampoo, trim, and blow-dry); **Men's Shirt** (cotton/polyester dress shirt, pinpoint weave, long sleeves).*
Source: The Council for Community and Economic Research, Cost of Living Index, 2024

HOUSING

Homeownership Rate

Area	2017 (%)	2018 (%)	2019 (%)	2020 (%)	2021 (%)	2022 (%)	2023 (%)	2024 (%)
MSA[1]	65.3	62.8	63.0	65.8	64.4	61.4	67.8	69.8
U.S.	63.9	64.4	64.6	66.6	65.5	65.8	65.9	65.6

Note: (1) Figures cover the Virginia Beach-Chesapeake-Norfolk, VA-NC Metropolitan Statistical Area
Source: U.S. Census Bureau, Housing Vacancies and Homeownership Annual Statistics: 2017-2024

House Price Index (HPI)

Area	National Ranking[2]	Quarterly Change (%)	One-Year Change (%)	Five-Year Change (%)	Since 1991Q1 (%)
MSA[1]	64	1.54	6.94	53.57	289.47
U.S.[3]	–	1.43	4.51	57.13	327.82

Note: The HPI is a weighted repeat sales index. It measures average price changes in repeat sales or refinancings on the same properties. This information is obtained by reviewing repeat mortgage transactions on single-family properties whose mortgages have been purchased or securitized by Fannie Mae or Freddie Mac since January 1975; (1) Figures cover the Virginia Beach-Norfolk-Newport News, VA-NC Metropolitan Statistical Area; (2) Rankings are based on annual percentage change for all metro areas containing at least 15,000 transactions over the last 10 years and ranges from 1 to 241; (3) figures based on a weighted average of Census Division estimates using a seasonally adjusted, purchase-only index; all figures are for the period ending December 31, 2024
Source: Federal Housing Finance Agency, Change in FHFA Metropolitan Area House Price Indexes, All Transactions Index, 2024Q4

Home Value

Area	Under $100,000	$100,000 -$199,999	$200,000 -$299,999	$300,000 -$399,999	$400,000 -$499,999	$500,000 -$999,999	$1,000,000 or more	Median ($)
City	3.1	7.5	23.9	23.4	16.1	21.5	4.5	366,300
MSA[1]	5.2	13.4	27.6	21.5	14.3	15.6	2.5	318,000
U.S.	12.1	17.8	19.5	14.4	10.5	19.1	6.5	303,400

Note: Figures are percentages except for median and cover owner-occupied housing units; (1) Figures cover the Virginia Beach-Chesapeake-Norfolk, VA-NC Metropolitan Statistical Area
Source: U.S. Census Bureau, 2019-2023 American Community Survey 5-Year Estimates

Year Housing Structure Built

Area	2020 or Later	2010 -2019	2000 -2009	1990 -1999	1980 -1989	1970 -1979	1960 -1969	1950 -1959	1940 -1949	Before 1940	Median Year
City	0.4	8.2	10.9	13.1	27.2	19.7	12.3	5.7	1.3	1.1	1984
MSA[1]	1.0	9.6	12.6	14.0	18.1	14.3	11.5	9.1	4.2	5.6	1983
U.S.	1.2	8.9	13.6	12.8	13.0	14.4	10.0	9.7	4.5	11.9	1980

Note: Figures are percentages except for Median Year; Note: (1) Figures cover the Virginia Beach-Chesapeake-Norfolk, VA-NC Metropolitan Statistical Area
Source: U.S. Census Bureau, 2019-2023 American Community Survey 5-Year Estimates

Gross Monthly Rent

Area	Under $500	$500 -$999	$1,000 -$1,499	$1,500 -$1,999	$2,000 -$2,499	$2,500 -$2,999	$3,000 and up	Median ($)
City	1.9	5.3	31.3	38.7	14.9	3.9	4.0	1,649
MSA[1]	5.0	13.8	37.7	28.0	10.3	2.6	2.7	1,416
U.S.	6.5	22.3	29.5	20.2	10.8	4.8	5.9	1,348

Note: Figures are percentages except for median; Gross rent is the contract rent plus the estimated average monthly cost of utilities (electricity, gas, and water and sewer) and fuels (oil, coal, kerosene, wood, etc.) if these are paid by the renter (or paid for the renter by someone else); (1) Figures cover the Virginia Beach-Chesapeake-Norfolk, VA-NC Metropolitan Statistical Area
Source: U.S. Census Bureau, 2019-2023 American Community Survey 5-Year Estimates

HEALTH

Health Risk Factors

Category	MSA[1] (%)	U.S. (%)
Adults aged 18–64 who have any kind of health care coverage	92.4	90.8
Adults who reported being in good or better health	82.3	81.8
Adults who have been told they have high blood cholesterol	38.3	36.9
Adults who have been told they have high blood pressure	37.3	34.0
Adults who are current smokers	10.1	12.1
Adults who currently use e-cigarettes	6.9	7.7
Adults who currently use chewing tobacco, snuff, or snus	2.4	3.2
Adults who are heavy drinkers[2]	5.7	6.1
Adults who are binge drinkers[3]	13.5	15.2
Adults who are overweight (BMI 25.0 - 29.9)	33.9	34.4
Adults who are obese (BMI 30.0 - 99.8)	37.5	34.3
Adults who participated in any physical activities in the past month	79.7	75.8

Note: All figures are crude prevalence; (1) Figures cover the Virginia Beach-Norfolk-Newport News, VA-NC Metropolitan Statistical Area; (2) Heavy drinkers are classified as adult men having more than 14 drinks per week and adult women having more than 7 drinks per week; (3) Binge drinkers are classified as males having five or more drinks on one occasion or females having four or more drinks on one occasion
Source: Centers for Disease Control and Prevention, Behavioral Risk Factor Surveillance System, SMART: Selected Metropolitan Area Risk Trends, 2023

Acute and Chronic Health Conditions

Category	MSA[1] (%)	U.S. (%)
Adults who have ever been told they had a heart attack	4.4	4.2
Adults who have ever been told they have angina or coronary heart disease	4.7	4.0
Adults who have ever been told they had a stroke	2.9	3.3
Adults who have ever been told they have asthma	16.8	15.7
Adults who have ever been told they have arthritis	30.3	26.3
Adults who have ever been told they have diabetes[2]	13.7	11.5
Adults who have ever been told they had skin cancer	5.1	5.6
Adults who have ever been told they had any other types of cancer	8.6	8.4
Adults who have ever been told they have COPD	7.5	6.4
Adults who have ever been told they have kidney disease	5.3	3.7
Adults who have ever been told they have a form of depression	20.8	22.0

Note: All figures are crude prevalence; (1) Figures cover the Virginia Beach-Norfolk-Newport News, VA-NC Metropolitan Statistical Area; (2) Figures do not include pregnancy-related, borderline, or pre-diabetes
Source: Centers for Disease Control and Prevention, Behavioral Risk Factor Surveillance System, SMART: Selected Metropolitan Area Risk Trends, 2023

Health Screening and Vaccination Rates

Category	MSA[1] (%)	U.S. (%)
Adults who have ever been tested for HIV	49.7	37.5
Adults who have had their blood cholesterol checked within the last five years	89.7	87.0
Adults aged 65+ who have had flu shot within the past year	68.2	63.4
Adults aged 65+ who have ever had a pneumonia vaccination	76.0	71.9

Note: All figures are crude prevalence; (1) Figures cover the Virginia Beach-Norfolk-Newport News, VA-NC Metropolitan Statistical Area.
Source: Centers for Disease Control and Prevention, Behavioral Risk Factor Surveillance System, SMART: Selected Metropolitan Area Risk Trends, 2023

Disability Status

Category	MSA[1] (%)	U.S. (%)
Adults who reported being deaf	6.3	7.4
Are you blind or have serious difficulty seeing, even when wearing glasses?	5.4	4.9
Do you have difficulty doing errands alone?	7.3	7.8
Do you have difficulty dressing or bathing?	2.7	3.6
Do you have serious difficulty concentrating/remembering/making decisions?	13.8	13.7
Do you have serious difficulty walking or climbing stairs?	15.4	13.2

Note: All figures are crude prevalence; (1) Figures cover the Virginia Beach-Norfolk-Newport News, VA-NC Metropolitan Statistical Area.
Source: Centers for Disease Control and Prevention, Behavioral Risk Factor Surveillance System, SMART: Selected Metropolitan Area Risk Trends, 2023

Mortality Rates for the Top 10 Causes of Death in the U.S.

ICD-10[a] Sub-Chapter	ICD-10[a] Code	Crude Mortality Rate[2] per 100,000 population	
		County[3]	U.S.
Malignant neoplasms	C00-C97	169.2	182.7
Ischaemic heart diseases	I20-I25	85.1	109.6
Provisional assignment of new diseases of uncertain etiology[1]	U00-U49	49.2	65.3
Other forms of heart disease	I30-I51	73.5	65.1
Other degenerative diseases of the nervous system	G30-G31	43.7	52.4
Other external causes of accidental injury	W00-X59	41.6	52.3
Cerebrovascular diseases	I60-I69	57.4	49.1
Chronic lower respiratory diseases	J40-J47	30.6	43.5
Hypertensive diseases	I10-I15	20.9	38.9
Organic, including symptomatic, mental disorders	F01-F09	40.7	33.9

Note: (a) ICD-10 = International Classification of Diseases 10th Revision; (1) Includes COVID-19, adverse effects to COVID-19 vaccines, SARS, and vaping-related disorders; (2) Crude mortality rates are a three-year average covering 2021-2023; (3) Figures cover Virginia Beach city.
Source: Centers for Disease Control and Prevention, National Center for Health Statistics. National Vital Statistics System, Mortality 2018-2023 on CDC WONDER Online Database

Mortality Rates for Selected Causes of Death

Cause of Death	ICD-10[a] Code	Crude Mortality Rate[1] per 100,000 population	
		County[2]	U.S.
Accidental poisoning and exposure to noxious substances	X40-X49	25.5	30.5
Alzheimer disease	G30	24.9	35.4
Assault	X85-Y09	6.1	7.3
COVID-19	U07.1	49.2	65.3
Diabetes mellitus	E10-E14	24.4	30.0
Diseases of the liver	K70-K76	16.5	20.8
Human immunodeficiency virus (HIV) disease	B20-B24	Unreliable	1.5
Influenza and pneumonia	J09-J18	8.3	13.4
Intentional self-harm	X60-X84	15.1	14.7
Malnutrition	E40-E46	3.1	6.0
Obesity and other hyperalimentation	E65-E68	2.7	3.1
Renal failure	N17-N19	17.3	16.4
Transport accidents	V01-V99	8.1	14.4

Note: (a) ICD-10 = International Classification of Diseases 10th Revision; (1) Crude mortality rates are a three-year average covering 2021-2023; (2) Figures cover Virginia Beach city; Data are suppressed when the data meet the criteria for confidentiality constraints; Crude mortality rates are flagged as unreliable when the rate would be calculated with a numerator of 20 or less.
Source: Centers for Disease Control and Prevention, National Center for Health Statistics. National Vital Statistics System, Mortality 2018-2023 on CDC WONDER Online Database

Health Insurance Coverage

Area	With Health Insurance	With Private Health Insurance	With Public Health Insurance	Without Health Insurance	Population Under Age 19 Without Health Insurance
City	93.5	78.0	30.8	6.5	3.8
MSA[1]	93.3	73.2	35.8	6.7	4.0
U.S.	91.4	67.3	36.3	8.6	5.4

Note: Figures are percentages that cover the civilian noninstitutionalized population; (1) Figures cover the Virginia Beach-Chesapeake-Norfolk, VA-NC Metropolitan Statistical Area
Source: U.S. Census Bureau, 2019-2023 American Community Survey 5-Year Estimates

Number of Medical Professionals

Area	MDs[3]	DOs[3,4]	Dentists	Podiatrists	Chiropractors	Optometrists
City[1] (number)	1,200	68	372	34	121	74
City[1] (rate[2])	263.4	14.9	82.0	7.5	26.7	16.3
U.S. (rate[2])	302.5	29.2	74.6	6.4	29.5	18.0

Note: Data as of 2023 unless noted; (1) Data covers the city of Virginia Beach; (2) Number of medical professionals per 100,000 population; (3) Data as of 2022 and includes all active, non-federal physicians; (4) Doctor of Osteopathic Medicine
Source: U.S. Department of Health and Human Services, Health Resources and Services Administration, Bureau of Health Professions, Area Resource File (ARF) 2023-2024

EDUCATION

Public School District Statistics

District Name	Schls	Pupils	Pupil/ Teacher Ratio	Minority Pupils[1] (%)	Total Rev. per Pupil ($)	Total Exp. per Pupil ($)
Virginia Beach City Pblc Schs	88	64,986	14.3	54.9	15,914	15,459

Note: Table includes school districts with 2,000 or more students; (1) Percentage of students that are not non-Hispanic white.
Source: U.S. Department of Education, National Center for Education Statistics, Common Core of Data, Local Education Agency (School District) Universe Survey: School Year 2023-2024; U.S. Department of Education, National Center for Education Statistics, Common Core of Data, School District Finance Survey (F-33): School Year 2021–22

Highest Level of Education

Area	Less than H.S.	H.S. Diploma	Some College, No Deg.	Associate Degree	Bachelor's Degree	Master's Degree	Prof. School Degree	Doctorate Degree
City	5.3	21.3	22.4	10.5	25.0	11.4	2.3	1.8
MSA[1]	7.2	25.1	22.8	9.8	21.2	10.4	1.9	1.6
U.S.	10.6	26.2	19.4	8.8	21.3	9.8	2.3	1.6

Note: Figures cover persons age 25 and over; (1) Figures cover the Virginia Beach-Chesapeake-Norfolk, VA-NC Metropolitan Statistical Area
Source: U.S. Census Bureau, 2019-2023 American Community Survey 5-Year Estimates

Educational Attainment by Race

Area	High School Graduate or Higher (%)					Bachelor's Degree or Higher (%)				
	Total	White	Black	Asian	Hisp.[2]	Total	White	Black	Asian	Hisp.[2]
City	94.7	96.4	92.7	89.4	89.9	40.4	44.2	27.9	46.6	32.5
MSA[1]	92.8	95.3	89.6	88.9	86.0	35.1	39.9	24.9	47.4	29.2
U.S.	89.4	92.9	88.1	88.0	72.5	35.0	37.7	24.7	57.0	19.9

Note: Figures shown cover persons 25 years old and over; (1) Figures cover the Virginia Beach-Chesapeake-Norfolk, VA-NC Metropolitan Statistical Area; (2) People of Hispanic origin can be of any race
Source: U.S. Census Bureau, 2019-2023 American Community Survey 5-Year Estimates

School Enrollment by Grade and Control

Area	Preschool (%)		Kindergarten (%)		Grades 1 - 4 (%)		Grades 5 - 8 (%)		Grades 9 - 12 (%)	
	Public	Private	Public	Private	Public	Private	Public	Private	Public	Private
City	39.5	60.5	77.6	22.4	88.8	11.2	88.5	11.5	91.2	8.8
MSA[1]	50.5	49.5	80.8	19.2	87.9	12.1	88.8	11.2	89.9	10.1
U.S.	58.7	41.3	85.2	14.8	87.2	12.8	87.9	12.1	89.0	11.0

Note: Figures shown cover persons 3 years old and over; (1) Figures cover the Virginia Beach-Chesapeake-Norfolk, VA-NC Metropolitan Statistical Area
Source: U.S. Census Bureau, 2019-2023 American Community Survey 5-Year Estimates

Higher Education

Four-Year Colleges			Two-Year Colleges			Medical Schools[1]	Law Schools[2]	Voc/ Tech[3]
Public	Private Non-profit	Private For-profit	Public	Private Non-profit	Private For-profit			
5	7	3	3	0	5	1	2	12

Note: Figures cover institutions located within the Virginia Beach-Chesapeake-Norfolk, VA-NC Metropolitan Statistical Area and include main campuses only; (1) includes schools accredited by the Liaison Committee on Medical Education and the American Osteopathic Association's Commission on Osteopathic College Accreditation; (2) includes ABA-accredited schools, schools with provisional ABA accreditation, and state accredited schools; (3) includes all schools with programs that are less than 2 years.
Source: National Center for Education Statistics, Integrated Postsecondary Education System (IPEDS), 2023-24; Wikipedia, List of Medical Schools in the United States, accessed May 2, 2025; Wikipedia, List of Law Schools in the United States, accessed May 2, 2025

According to *U.S. News & World Report,* the Virginia Beach-Chesapeake-Norfolk, VA-NC metro area is home to one of the top 200 national universities in the U.S.: **William & Mary** (#54 tie). The indicators used to capture academic quality fall into a number of categories: assessment by administrators at peer institutions; retention of students; faculty resources; student selectivity; financial resources; alumni giving; high school counselor ratings of colleges; and graduation rate. *U.S. News & World Report, "America's Best Colleges 2025"*

According to *U.S. News & World Report,* the Virginia Beach-Chesapeake-Norfolk, VA-NC metro area is home to two of the top 100 law schools in the U.S.: **William & Mary Law School** (#31 tie); **Regent University** (#94 tie). The rankings are based on a weighted average of 12 measures of quality: peer assessment score; assessment score by lawyers/judges; median LSAT scores; median undergrad GPA; acceptance rate; employment rates for graduates; placement success; bar passage rate; faculty resources; expenditures per student; student/faculty ratio; and library resources. *U.S. News & World Report, "America's Best Graduate Schools, Law, 2025"*

According to *U.S. News & World Report,* the Virginia Beach-Chesapeake-Norfolk, VA-NC metro area is home to one of the top 75 business schools in the U.S.: **William & Mary (Mason)** (#61 tie). The rankings are based on a weighted average of the following nine measures: quality assessment; peer assessment; recruiter assessment; placement success; mean starting salary and bonus; student selectivity; mean GMAT and GRE scores; mean undergraduate GPA; and acceptance rate. *U.S. News & World Report, "America's Best Graduate Schools, Business, 2025"*

EMPLOYERS

Major Employers

Company Name	Industry
Bank of America, National Association	National commerical banks
Canon	Chemical manufacturing
Chesapeake Hospital Authority	General medical & surgical hospitals
Children's Health System	Specialty hospitals, except psychiatric
City Line Apts.	Apartment building operators
City of Newport News	Municipal government
City of Virginia Beach	Municipal government
Cox Communications Hampton Roads	Cable & other pay television services
Ford Motor Company	Truck & tractor truck assembly
Gwaltney of Smithfield	Meat packing plants
Hampton Training School for Nurses	General medical & surgical hospitals
Northrop Grumman Systems Corporation	Systems integration services
Old Dominion University	University
Riverside Hospital	General medical & surgical hospitals
STIHL Incorporated	Power-driven handtools
The College of William & Mary	Colleges & universities
The Colonial Williamsburg Foundation	Management consulting services
The Smithfield Packing Company	Hams & picnics, from meat slaughtered on site
U.S. Navy	Offices & clinics of medical doctors
Williamsburg James City Co. Pub Schls	Schools & educational services

Note: Companies shown are located within the Virginia Beach-Chesapeake-Norfolk, VA-NC Metropolitan Statistical Area.
Source: Chambers of Commerce; State Departments of Labor; Wikipedia

PUBLIC SAFETY

Crime Rate

Area	Total Crime Rate	Violent Crime Rate				Property Crime Rate		
		Murder	Rape	Robbery	Aggrav. Assault	Burglary	Larceny -Theft	Motor Vehicle Theft
City	1,751.8	3.7	22.0	29.5	40.1	86.6	1,431.3	138.5
U.S.	2,290.9	5.7	38.0	66.5	264.1	250.7	1,347.2	318.7

Note: Figures are crimes per 100,000 population.
Source: FBI, Table 8, Offenses Known to Law Enforcement, by State by City, 2023

Hate Crimes

Area	Number of Quarters Reported	Number of Incidents per Bias Motivation					
		Race/Ethnicity/ Ancestry	Religion	Sexual Orientation	Disability	Gender	Gender Identity
City	4	3	1	2	1	0	0
U.S.	4	5,900	2,699	2,077	187	92	492

Source: Federal Bureau of Investigation, Hate Crime Statistics 2023

Identity Theft Consumer Reports

Area	Reports	Reports per 100,000 Population	Rank[2]
MSA[1]	4,689	263	94
U.S.	1,135,291	339	-

Note: (1) Figures cover the Virginia Beach-Chesapeake-Norfolk, VA-NC Metropolitan Statistical Area; (2) Rank ranges from 1 to 401 where 1 indicates greatest number of identity theft reports per 100,000 population
Source: Federal Trade Commission, Consumer Sentinel Network Data Book 2024

Fraud and Other Consumer Reports

Area	Reports	Reports per 100,000 Population	Rank[2]
MSA[1]	28,077	1,575	48
U.S.	5,360,641	1,601	-

Note: (1) Figures cover the Virginia Beach-Chesapeake-Norfolk, VA-NC Metropolitan Statistical Area; (2) Rank ranges from 1 to 401 where 1 indicates greatest number of fraud and other consumer reports per 100,000 population
Source: Federal Trade Commission, Consumer Sentinel Network Data Book 2024

POLITICS

2024 Presidential Election Results

Area	Trump (Rep.)	Harris (Dem.)	Stein (Green)	Kennedy (Ind.)	Oliver (Lib.)	Other
Virginia Beach City	47.8	50.4	0.4	0.0	0.5	0.9
U.S.	49.7	48.2	0.6	0.5	0.4	0.6

Note: Results are percentages and may not add to 100% due to rounding
Source: Dave Leip's Atlas of U.S. Presidential Elections

SPORTS

Professional Sports Teams

Team Name	League	Year Established

No teams are located in the metro area
Source: Wikipedia, Major Professional Sports Teams of the United States and Canada, May 1, 2025

CLIMATE

Average and Extreme Temperatures

Temperature	Jan	Feb	Mar	Apr	May	Jun	Jul	Aug	Sep	Oct	Nov	Dec	Yr.
Extreme High (°F)	78	81	88	97	100	101	103	104	99	95	86	80	104
Average High (°F)	48	51	58	68	76	84	88	86	80	70	61	52	69
Average Temp. (°F)	41	42	49	58	67	75	79	78	72	62	53	44	60
Average Low (°F)	32	33	40	48	57	66	71	70	64	53	44	35	51
Extreme Low (°F)	-3	8	18	28	36	45	54	49	45	27	20	7	-3

Note: Figures cover the years 1948-1995
Source: National Climatic Data Center, International Station Meteorological Climate Summary, 9/96

Average Precipitation/Snowfall/Humidity

Precip./Humidity	Jan	Feb	Mar	Apr	May	Jun	Jul	Aug	Sep	Oct	Nov	Dec	Yr.
Avg. Precip. (in.)	3.6	3.3	3.8	3.0	3.7	3.5	5.2	5.3	3.9	3.3	3.0	3.1	44.8
Avg. Snowfall (in.)	3	3	1	Tr	0	0	0	0	0	0	Tr	1	8
Avg. Rel. Hum. 7am (%)	74	74	74	73	77	79	81	84	83	82	79	75	78
Avg. Rel. Hum. 4pm (%)	59	56	53	50	56	57	60	63	62	60	58	59	58

Note: Figures cover the years 1948-1995; Tr = Trace amounts (<0.05 in. of rain; <0.5 in. of snow)
Source: National Climatic Data Center, International Station Meteorological Climate Summary, 9/96

Weather Conditions

Temperature			Daytime Sky			Precipitation		
10°F & below	32°F & below	90°F & above	Clear	Partly cloudy	Cloudy	0.01 inch or more precip.	0.1 inch or more snow/ice	Thunder-storms
< 1	53	33	89	149	127	115	5	38

Note: Figures are average number of days per year and cover the years 1948-1995
Source: National Climatic Data Center, International Station Meteorological Climate Summary, 9/96

HAZARDOUS WASTE

Superfund Sites

The Virginia Beach-Chesapeake-Norfolk, VA-NC metro area is home to 14 sites on the EPA's Superfund National Priorities List (NPL) or Superfund Alternative Approach (SAA) list: **Abex Corp.** (Final NPL); **Atlantic Wood Industries, Inc.** (Final NPL); **Chisman Creek** (Final NPL); **Former Nansemond Ordnance Depot** (Final NPL); **Fort Eustis (USARMY)** (Final NPL); **Langley Air Force Base/Nasa Langley Research Center** (Final NPL); **Naval Amphibious Base Little Creek** (Final NPL); **Naval Weapons Station - Yorktown** (Final NPL); **Norfolk Naval Base (Sewells Point Naval Complex)** (Final NPL); **Norfolk Naval Shipyard** (Final NPL); **NWS Yorktown - Cheatham Annex** (Final NPL); **Peck Iron and Metal** (Final NPL); **Saunders Supply Co.** (Final NPL); **St. Juliens Creek Annex (U.S. Navy)** (Final NPL). The Superfund alternative approach uses the same investigation and cleanup process and standards that are used for sites listed on the National Priorities List. The SAA is an alternative to listing a site on the NPL; it is not an alternative to Superfund or the Superfund process. There are a total of 1,445 Superfund sites with a status of proposed or final on both lists in the United States. *U.S. Environmental Protection Agency, National Priorities List, May 1, 2025; U.S. Environmental Protection Agency, Superfund Alternative Approach Sites, May 1, 2025*

AIR QUALITY

Air Quality Trends: Ozone

	1990	1995	2000	2005	2010	2015	2020	2021	2022	2023
MSA[1]	0.085	0.084	0.083	0.078	0.074	0.061	0.053	0.057	0.057	0.059
U.S.	0.087	0.089	0.081	0.080	0.072	0.068	0.066	0.067	0.067	0.070

Note: (1) Data covers the Virginia Beach-Chesapeake-Norfolk, VA-NC Metropolitan Statistical Area. The values shown are the composite ozone concentration averages among trend sites based on the highest fourth daily maximum 8-hour concentration in parts per million. These trends are based on sites having an adequate record of monitoring data during the trend period. Data from exceptional events are included.
Source: U.S. Environmental Protection Agency, Air Quality Monitoring Information, "Air Quality Trends by City, 1990-2023"

Air Quality Index

Area	Percent of Days when Air Quality was...[2]					AQI Statistics[2]	
	Good	Moderate	Unhealthy for Sensitive Groups	Unhealthy	Very Unhealthy	Maximum	Median
MSA[1]	62.7	36.4	0.5	0.3	0.0	174	44

Note: (1) Data covers the Virginia Beach-Chesapeake-Norfolk, VA-NC Metropolitan Statistical Area; (2) Based on 365 days with AQI data in 2023. Air Quality Index (AQI) is an index for reporting daily air quality. EPA calculates the AQI for five major air pollutants regulated by the Clean Air Act: ground-level ozone, particle pollution (aka particulate matter), carbon monoxide, sulfur dioxide, and nitrogen dioxide. The AQI runs from 0 to 500. The higher the AQI value, the greater the level of air pollution and the greater the health concern. There are six AQI categories: "Good" AQI is between 0 and 50. Air quality is considered satisfactory; "Moderate" AQI is between 51 and 100. Air quality is acceptable; "Unhealthy for Sensitive Groups" When AQI values are between 101 and 150, members of sensitive groups may experience health effects; "Unhealthy" When AQI values are between 151 and 200 everyone may begin to experience health effects; "Very Unhealthy" AQI values between 201 and 300 trigger a health alert; "Hazardous" AQI values over 300 trigger warnings of emergency conditions (not shown).
Source: U.S. Environmental Protection Agency, Air Quality Index Report, 2023

Air Quality Index Pollutants

Area	Percent of Days when AQI Pollutant was...[2]					
	Carbon Monoxide	Nitrogen Dioxide	Ozone	Sulfur Dioxide	Particulate Matter 2.5	Particulate Matter 10
MSA[1]	0.0	1.6	33.7	(3)	64.7	0.0

Note: (1) Data covers the Virginia Beach-Chesapeake-Norfolk, VA-NC Metropolitan Statistical Area; (2) Based on 365 days with AQI data in 2023. The Air Quality Index (AQI) is an index for reporting daily air quality. EPA calculates the AQI for five major air pollutants regulated by the Clean Air Act: ground-level ozone, particle pollution (also known as particulate matter), carbon monoxide, sulfur dioxide, and nitrogen dioxide. The AQI runs from 0 to 500. The higher the AQI value, the greater the level of air pollution and the greater the health concern; (3) Sulfur dioxide is no longer included in this table because SO_2 concentrations tend to be very localized and not necessarily representative of broad geographical areas like counties and CBSAs.
Source: U.S. Environmental Protection Agency, Air Quality Index Report, 2023

Maximum Air Pollutant Concentrations: Particulate Matter, Ozone, CO and Lead

	Particulate Matter 10 (ug/m³)	Particulate Matter 2.5 Wtd AM (ug/m³)	Particulate Matter 2.5 24-Hr (ug/m³)	Ozone (ppm)	Carbon Monoxide (ppm)	Lead (ug/m³)
MSA[1] Level	62	8.1	28	0.066	1	n/a
NAAQS[2]	150	15	35	0.075	9	0.15
Met NAAQS[2]	Yes	Yes	Yes	Yes	Yes	n/a

Note: (1) Data covers the Virginia Beach-Chesapeake-Norfolk, VA-NC Metropolitan Statistical Area; Data from exceptional events are included; (2) National Ambient Air Quality Standards; ppm = parts per million; ug/m³ = micrograms per cubic meter; n/a not available.
Concentrations: Particulate Matter 10 (coarse particulate)—highest second maximum 24-hour concentration; Particulate Matter 2.5 Wtd AM (fine particulate)—highest weighted annual mean concentration; Particulate Matter 2.5 24-Hour (fine particulate)—highest 98th percentile 24-hour concentration; Ozone—highest fourth daily maximum 8-hour concentration; Carbon Monoxide—highest second maximum non-overlapping 8-hour concentration; Lead—maximum running 3-month average
Source: U.S. Environmental Protection Agency, Air Quality Monitoring Information, "Air Quality Statistics by City, 2023"

Maximum Air Pollutant Concentrations: Nitrogen Dioxide and Sulfur Dioxide

	Nitrogen Dioxide AM (ppb)	Nitrogen Dioxide 1-Hr (ppb)	Sulfur Dioxide AM (ppb)	Sulfur Dioxide 1-Hr (ppb)	Sulfur Dioxide 24-Hr (ppb)
MSA[1] Level	8	37	n/a	3	n/a
NAAQS[2]	53	100	30	75	140
Met NAAQS[2]	Yes	Yes	n/a	Yes	n/a

Note: (1) Data covers the Virginia Beach-Chesapeake-Norfolk, VA-NC Metropolitan Statistical Area; Data from exceptional events are included; (2) National Ambient Air Quality Standards; ppm = parts per million; ug/m³ = micrograms per cubic meter; n/a not available.
Concentrations: Nitrogen Dioxide AM—highest arithmetic mean concentration; Nitrogen Dioxide 1-Hr—highest 98th percentile 1-hour daily maximum concentration; Sulfur Dioxide AM—highest annual mean concentration; Sulfur Dioxide 1-Hr—highest 99th percentile 1-hour daily maximum concentration; Sulfur Dioxide 24-Hr—highest second maximum 24-hour concentration
Source: U.S. Environmental Protection Agency, Air Quality Monitoring Information, "Air Quality Statistics by City, 2023"

Washington, D.C.

Background

The capital city and federal district of the United States, Washington, D.C. is on the Potomac River across from Virginia and shares a land border with Maryland. It hosts 177 foreign embassies, and is among the country's top tourist destinations.

In 1793, the first cornerstone of the White House was laid. In 1800, the north wing was completed, a drifting Congress found its home, and President John Adams was the first president to reside at the White House. The building was burned down by the British in 1814 during the War of 1812, and its final reconstruction was completed in 1891.

In addition to its importance as an important world political capital, D.C. is renowned for its brilliant annual springtime display of cherry blossoms, and a breathtaking collection of architectural styles, including Greek Revival, Federal, Victorian, and Baroque. Some of the city's monuments and well-known sites include the Washington Monument, Lincoln Memorial, the White House, Jefferson Memorial, Vietnam Veterans Memorial, and Arlington National Cemetery.

As the political machine of the country and a leading center for national and international research organization, especially think tanks engaged in public policy, the main industry is government. Other major industries include tourism, education, finance, public policy, and scientific research, and top employers include Capital One, Booz Allen Hamilton, Lockheed Martin, and Fannie Mae. Public universities include the University of the District of Columbia (UDC), American, Gallaudet, Georgetown, George Washington, and Howard. Private institutions are Catholic University of America, Johns Hopkins University Paul H. Nitze School of Advanced International Studies and Trinity Washington University.

On September 11, 2001, the city suffered an attack orchestrated by Saudi terrorist Osama bin Laden as part of a wider assault on the U.S. that included the World Trade Center in New York on the same day. Both these major incidents led to tightening of security in the district itself.

D.C. continues to be in an urban renaissance, home to DC Streetcar system, Capital Bikeshare, and 683 parks and greenspaces.

The Walter E. Washington Convention Center hosts hundreds of events annually. City Museum sits across the street from the Convention Center at the old Carnegie Library. A few blocks south, restaurants fill the vicinity of the International Spy Museum and the Verizon Center, home to the NBA Wizards, WNBA Mystics, and the NHL Capitals. The Washington Nationals major league baseball teams plays at Nationals Park, a state-of-the-art, 41,000-seat facility, and won the 2019 World Series.

The Smithsonian Institution's National Air and Space Museum has expanded into a second museum near the Washington Dulles International Airport in Virginia, the Steven F. Udvar-Hazy Center. Other museums in the city include the National Gallery of Art, U.S. Holocaust Memorial Museum, Corcoran Gallery, Phillips Collection, Hirshhorn Museum and Sculpture Garden, and the many other Smithsonian museums. The National Museum of the American Indian is housed in a dramatic building on the National Mall, with a mission to explore and celebrate the histories and cultures of Native Americans from North, Central, and South America.

Washington is a global media center with bureaus of all worldwide major news outlets. It is home to C-SPAN, National Public Radio, and the Washington Post Company.

Washington's climate is humid subtropical. Winters are cool to cold with some snow of varying intensity, while summers are hot and humid. The combination of heat and humidity in the summer brings very frequent thunderstorms, some of which occasionally produce tornadoes in the area. Blizzards affect Washington once every four to six years on average. The most violent storms, known as nor'easters, often impact large regions of the East Coast. Hurricanes or their remnants occasionally impact the area in late summer and early fall, often weakened by the time they reach Washington.

Rankings

General Rankings

- To help military veterans find the best places in which to settle down, *WalletHub* compared the 100 largest U.S. cities across 19 key indicators of livability, affordability and veteran-friendliness. They range from the share of military skill-related jobs to veteran income growth to the availability of VA health facilities. Washington ranked #66. *Wallethub.com, "Best & Worst Places for Veterans to Live (2025)," November 7, 2024*

- The human resources consulting firm Mercer ranked 241 major cities worldwide in terms of overall quality of life. Washington ranked #49. Criteria: political and personal safety, social, and economic factors; medical and health considerations; schools and education; public services and transportation; recreation; connectivity; housing and infrastructure; and climate. *Mercer, "Mercer 2024 Quality of Living Survey," December 2024*

- For its 37th annual "Readers' Choice Awards" survey, *Condé Nast Traveler* ranked its readers' favorite cities in the U.S. Whether it be a longed-for visit or the next big new thing, these are the places travelers loved best. The list was broken into large cities and cities under 250,000. Washington ranked #5 in the big city category. *Condé Nast Traveler, Readers' Choice Awards 2024, "Best Big Cities in the U.S." October 1, 2024*

Business/Finance Rankings

- According to *Business Insider*, the Washington metro area is a prime place to run a startup or move an existing business to. The area ranked #3. More than 300 metro areas were analyzed for factors that were of top concern to new business owners. Data was based on the 2019 U.S. Census Bureau American Community Survey, statistics from the CDC, and University of Chicago analysis. Criteria: business formations; percentage of vaccinated population; percentage of households with internet subscriptions; median household income; and share of work that can be done from home. *BusinessInsider.com, "The 20 Best Cities for Starting a Business in 2022 Include Denver, Raleigh, and Olympia," June 7, 2022*

- Payscale.com ranked the 32 largest metro areas in terms of wage growth. The Washington metro area ranked #11. Criteria: quarterly changes in private industry employee and education professional wage growth from the previous year. *PayScale, "Wage Trends by Metro Area-4th Quarter," February 4, 2025*

- The Washington metro area appeared on the Milken Institute "2025 Best Performing Cities" list. Rank: #62 out of 200 large metro areas (based on performance category). Criteria: job growth; wage growth; high-tech growth and impact; community resilience; housing affordability; household broadband access. *Milken Institute, "Best-Performing Cities 2025," January 14, 2025*

- Mercer Human Resources Consulting ranked 226 cities worldwide in terms of cost-of-living. Washington ranked #22 (the lower the ranking, the higher the cost-of-living). The survey measured the comparative cost of over 200 items (such as housing, food, clothing, domestic supplies, transportation, and recreation/entertainment) in each location. *Mercer, "2024 Cost of Living City Ranking," June 17, 2024*

Dating/Romance Rankings

- *Apartment List* conducted its Annual Renter Satisfaction Survey and asked renters "how satisfied are you with opportunities for dating in your current city." The cities were ranked from highest to lowest based on their satisfaction scores. Washington ranked #7 out of 10 cities. *Apartment List, "Best Cities for Dating 2022 with Local Dating Insights from Bumble," February 7, 2022*

Education Rankings

- Personal finance website *WalletHub* analyzed the 150 largest U.S. metropolitan statistical areas to determine where the most educated Americans are putting their degrees to work. Criteria: education levels; percentage of workers with degrees; education quality and attainment gap; public school quality rankings; quality and enrollment of each metro area's universities. Washington was ranked #3 (#1 = most educated city). *WalletHub.com, "Most & Least Educated Cities in America, 2025" July 2, 2024*

Environmental Rankings

- The U.S. Environmental Protection Agency (EPA) released its list of U.S. metropolitan areas with the most ENERGY STAR certified buildings in 2023. The Washington metro area was ranked #2 out of 25. *U.S. Environmental Protection Agency, "2024 Energy Star Top Cities," May 22, 2024*

Food/Drink Rankings

- WalletHub compared the 100 largest U.S. cities across 17 key indicators of vegan- and vegetarian-friendliness. Washington was ranked #12. Cities were selected based on metrics such as the cost of groceries for vegetarians, the share of restaurants serving meatless options and the number of salad shops per capita. *WalletHub.com, "Best Cities for Vegans & Vegetarians (2025)," September 24, 2024*

Health/Fitness Rankings

- For each of the 100 largest cities in the United States, the American Fitness Index®, compiled in partnership between the American College of Sports Medicine and the Elevance Health Foundation, evaluated community infrastructure and more than 30 health behaviors including preventive health, levels of chronic disease conditions, food insecurity, pedestrian safety, air quality, and community/environment resources that support physical activity. Washington ranked #2 for "community fitness." *americanfitnessindex.org, "2024 ACSM American Fitness Index Summary Report," July 23, 2024*

- Washington was identified as one of the 10 most walkable cities in the U.S. by Walk Score. The city ranked #7. Walk Score measures walkability by analyzing hundreds of walking routes to nearby amenities, and also measures pedestrian friendliness by analyzing population density and road metrics such as block length and intersection density. *WalkScore.com, April 13, 2021*

- The Washington metro area was identified as one of the worst cities for bed bugs in America by pest control company Orkin. The area ranked #7 out of 50 based on the number of bed bug treatments Orkin performed from December 2022 to November 2023. *Orkin, "Chicago Joins Paris In Global Bed Bug Spotlight Ranking As The Worst City On Orkin's U.S. Bed Bug Cities List," January 22, 2024*

- Washington was identified as a "2025 Allergy Capital." The area ranked #70 out of the nation's 100 largest metropolitan areas. Three groups of factors were used to identify the most challenging cities for people with allergies: annual tree, grass, and weed pollen scores; over the counter allergy medicine use; number of board-certified allergy specialists. *Asthma and Allergy Foundation of America, "2025 Allergy Capitals: The Most Challenging Places to Live with Allergies," March 18, 2025*

- Washington was identified as a "2024 Asthma Capital." The area ranked #24 out of the nation's 100 largest metropolitan areas. Criteria: estimated asthma prevalence; asthma-related mortality; and ER visits due to asthma. Risk factors analyzed but not factored in the rankings: annual air quality including pollution and ozone levels; public smoking laws; indoor air quality; access to asthma specialists; rescue and controller medication use; uninsured rate; pollen allergy; poverty rate. *Asthma and Allergy Foundation of America, "Asthma Capitals 2024: The Most Challenging Places to Live With Asthma," September 10, 2024*

- The Sharecare Community Well-Being Index evaluates 10 individual and social health factors in order to measure what matters to Americans in the communities in which they live. The Washington metro area ranked #3 in the top 10 across all 10 domains. Criteria: access to healthcare, food, and community resources; housing and transportation; economic security; feeling of purpose; and physical, financial, social, and community well-being. *Sharecare.com, "Community Well-Being Index: 2020 Metro Area & County Rankings Report," August 30, 2021*

Real Estate Rankings

- *WalletHub* compared the most populated U.S. cities to determine which had the best markets for real estate agents. Washington ranked #7 where demand was high and pay was the best. Criteria: sales per agent; annual median wage for real-estate agents; monthly average starting salary for real estate agents; real estate job density and competition; unemployment rate; home turnover rate; housing-market health index; and other relevant metrics. *WalletHub.com, "2021 Best Places to Be a Real Estate Agent," May 12, 2021*

- Washington was ranked #111 out of 176 metro areas in terms of cost of housing in 2024 by the National Association of Home Builders (#1 = most affordable). Criteria: the portion of an average family's income necessary to pay the mortgage on a median-priced home. *National Association of Home Builders®, NAHB-Wells Fargo Cost of Housing Index, 4th Quarter 2024*

Safety Rankings

- Allstate ranked the 100 most populous cities in America in terms of driver safety. Washington ranked #8. Criteria based on anonymized driving behavior data from Allstate's mobile app powered by Arity: high speed driving (over 80 mph), phone handling, and hard braking. The report helps increase the importance of safety and awareness behind the wheel. *Allstate, "16th Allstate America's Best Drivers Report®" July 11, 2024*

- Washington was identified as one of the most dangerous cities in America by NeighborhoodScout. The city ranked #80 out of 100 (#1 = most dangerous). Criteria: number of violent crimes per 1,000 residents. The editors evaluated cities with 25,000 or more residents. *NeighborhoodScout.com, "2023 Top 100 Most Dangerous Cities in the U.S.," January 12, 2023*

- The National Insurance Crime Bureau ranked the largest metro areas in the U.S. in terms of per capita rates of vehicle theft. The Washington metro area ranked #9 out of the top 10 (#1 = highest rate). Criteria: number of vehicle theft offenses per 100,000 inhabitants in 2023. *National Insurance Crime Bureau, "Vehicle Thefts Surge Nationwide in 2023," April 9, 2024*

Transportation Rankings

- Washington was identified as one of the most congested metro areas in the U.S. The area ranked #4 out of 10. Criteria: yearly delay per auto commuter in hours. *Texas A&M Transportation Institute, "2023 Urban Mobility Report," June 2024*

- According to the INRIX "2024 Global Traffic Scorecard," Washington was identified as one of the most congested metro areas in the U.S. The area ranked #9 out of 10 in the country and among the top 25 most congested in the world. Criteria: average annual time spent in traffic and average cost of congestion per motorist. *Inrix.com, "Employees & Consumers Returned to Downtowns, Traffic Delays & Costs Grew," January 6, 2025*

Women/Minorities Rankings

- Personal finance website *WalletHub* compared more than 180 U.S. cities across two key dimensions, "Hispanic Business-Friendliness" and "Hispanic Purchasing Power," to arrive at the most favorable conditions for Hispanic entrepreneurs. Washington was ranked #117 out of 182. Criteria includes: share of Hispanic-Owned Businesses; average growth of Hispanic Business revenues; Small Business-Friendliness score; affordability; and number of Hispanics with at least a bachelor's degree. *WalletHub.com, "Best Cities for Hispanic Entrepreneurs," September 4, 2024*

Business Environment

DEMOGRAPHICS

Population Growth

Area	1990 Census	2000 Census	2010 Census	2020 Census	2023 Estimate[2]	Population Growth 1990-2023 (%)
City	606,900	572,059	601,723	689,545	672,079	10.7
MSA[1]	4,122,914	4,796,183	5,582,170	6,385,162	6,263,796	51.9
U.S.	248,709,873	281,421,906	308,745,538	331,449,281	332,387,540	33.6

Note: (1) Figures cover the Washington-Arlington-Alexandria, DC-VA-MD-WV Metropolitan Statistical Area; (2) 2019-2023 5-year ACS population estimate
Source: U.S. Census Bureau, 1990 Census, 2000 Census, 2010 Census, 2020 Census, 2019-2023 American Community Survey 5-Year Estimates

Race

Area	White Alone[2] (%)	Black Alone[2] (%)	Asian Alone[2] (%)	AIAN[3] Alone[2] (%)	NHOPI[4] Alone[2] (%)	Other Race Alone[2] (%)	Two or More Races (%)
City	39.1	43.3	4.1	0.3	0.1	4.8	8.4
MSA[1]	45.5	24.9	10.7	0.5	0.0	8.3	10.1
U.S.	63.4	12.4	5.8	0.9	0.2	6.6	10.7

Note: (1) Figures cover the Washington-Arlington-Alexandria, DC-VA-MD-WV Metropolitan Statistical Area; (2) Alone is defined as not being in combination with one or more other races; (3) American Indian and Alaska Native; (4) Native Hawaiian and Other Pacific Islander
Source: U.S. Census Bureau, 2019-2023 American Community Survey 5-Year Estimates

Hispanic or Latino Origin

Area	Total (%)	Mexican (%)	Puerto Rican (%)	Cuban (%)	Other (%)
City	11.6	2.1	0.8	0.4	8.2
MSA[1]	17.6	2.5	1.2	0.3	13.6
U.S.	19.0	11.3	1.8	0.7	5.2

Note: Persons of Hispanic or Latino origin can be of any race; (1) Figures cover the Washington-Arlington-Alexandria, DC-VA-MD-WV Metropolitan Statistical Area
Source: U.S. Census Bureau, 2019-2023 American Community Survey 5-Year Estimates

Age

Area	Under Age 5	Age 5–19	Age 20–34	Age 35–44	Age 45–54	Age 55–64	Age 65–74	Age 75–84	Age 85+	Median Age
City	6.1	15.2	29.0	16.4	10.7	9.8	7.4	3.8	1.5	34.9
MSA[1]	6.1	19.2	20.3	14.8	13.4	12.3	8.3	4.0	1.5	37.9
U.S.	5.7	19.1	20.2	13.1	12.3	12.8	10.0	4.9	1.9	38.7

Note: (1) Figures cover the Washington-Arlington-Alexandria, DC-VA-MD-WV Metropolitan Statistical Area
Source: U.S. Census Bureau, 2019-2023 American Community Survey 5-Year Estimates

Disability by Age

Area	All Ages	Under 18 Years Old	18 to 64 Years Old	65 Years and Over
City	11.0	4.5	8.8	32.3
MSA[1]	9.1	3.5	7.0	27.9
U.S.	13.0	4.7	10.7	32.9

Note: Figures show percent of the civilian noninstitutionalized population that reported having a disability. Disability status is determined from six types of difficulty: vision, hearing, cognitive, ambulatory, self-care, and independent living. For children under 5 years old, hearing and vision difficulty are used to determine disability status. For children between the ages of 5 and 14, disability status is determined from hearing, vision, cognitive, ambulatory, and self-care difficulties. For people aged 15 years and older, they are considered to have a disability if they have difficulty with any one of the six difficulty types; Note: (1) Figures cover the Washington-Arlington-Alexandria, DC-VA-MD-WV Metropolitan Statistical Area
Source: U.S. Census Bureau, 2019-2023 American Community Survey 5-Year Estimates

Ancestry

Area	German	Irish	English	American	Italian	Polish	French[2]	European	Scottish
City	7.7	7.8	6.8	2.8	4.5	2.2	1.7	1.7	1.4
MSA[1]	8.8	8.1	8.0	3.7	4.1	2.1	1.4	1.8	1.5
U.S.	12.6	9.4	9.1	5.5	4.9	2.6	2.0	1.6	1.6

Note: Figures are the percentage of the total population reporting a particular ancestry. The nine most commonly reported ancestries in the U.S. are shown. Figures include multiple ancestries (e.g. if a person reported being Irish and Italian, they were included in both columns); (1) Figures cover the Washington-Arlington-Alexandria, DC-VA-MD-WV Metropolitan Statistical Area; (2) Excludes Basque
Source: U.S. Census Bureau, 2019-2023 American Community Survey 5-Year Estimates

Foreign-born Population

Area	Any Foreign Country	Percent of Population Born in							
		Asia	Mexico	Europe	Caribbean	Central America[2]	South America	Africa	Canada
City	13.3	2.8	0.6	2.3	1.2	2.2	1.7	2.2	0.3
MSA[1]	24.0	8.4	0.9	1.8	1.1	5.2	2.5	3.8	0.2
U.S.	13.9	4.3	3.3	1.4	1.4	1.2	1.2	0.8	0.2

Note: (1) Figures cover the Washington-Arlington-Alexandria, DC-VA-MD-WV Metropolitan Statistical Area; (2) Excludes Mexico.
Source: U.S. Census Bureau, 2019-2023 American Community Survey 5-Year Estimates

Household Size

Area	Persons in Household (%)							Average Household Size
	One	Two	Three	Four	Five	Six	Seven or More	
City	46.7	30.2	11.1	7.4	2.8	1.2	0.7	1.99
MSA[1]	28.6	30.4	15.9	14.3	6.5	2.6	1.7	2.62
U.S.	28.5	33.8	15.4	12.7	5.9	2.3	1.4	2.54

Note: (1) Figures cover the Washington-Arlington-Alexandria, DC-VA-MD-WV Metropolitan Statistical Area
Source: U.S. Census Bureau, 2019-2023 American Community Survey 5-Year Estimates

Household Relationships

Area	House-holder	Opposite-sex Spouse	Same-sex Spouse	Opposite-sex Unmarried Partner	Same-sex Unmarried Partner	Child[2]	Grand-child	Other Relatives	Non-relatives
City	45.3	10.3	0.6	3.1	0.5	20.4	2.4	4.2	7.1
MSA[1]	37.0	17.3	0.3	2.0	0.2	29.3	2.0	5.9	4.4
U.S.	38.3	17.5	0.2	2.5	0.2	28.3	2.4	4.8	3.4

Note: Figures are percent of the total population; (1) Figures cover the Washington-Arlington-Alexandria, DC-VA-MD-WV Metropolitan Statistical Area; (2) Includes biological, adopted, and stepchildren of the householder
Source: U.S. Census Bureau, 2020 Census

Gender

Area	Males	Females	Males per 100 Females
City	320,001	352,078	90.9
MSA[1]	3,081,518	3,182,278	96.8
U.S.	164,545,087	167,842,453	98.0

Note: (1) Figures cover the Washington-Arlington-Alexandria, DC-VA-MD-WV Metropolitan Statistical Area
Source: U.S. Census Bureau, 2019-2023 American Community Survey 5-Year Estimates

Marital Status

Area	Never Married	Now Married[2]	Separated	Widowed	Divorced
City	55.2	31.5	1.4	3.4	8.5
MSA[1]	36.7	48.8	1.6	4.2	8.7
U.S.	34.1	47.9	1.7	5.6	10.7

Note: Figures are percentages and cover the population 15 years of age and older; (1) Figures cover the Washington-Arlington-Alexandria, DC-VA-MD-WV Metropolitan Statistical Area; (2) Excludes separated
Source: U.S. Census Bureau, 2019-2023 American Community Survey 5-Year Estimates

Religious Groups by Family

Area	Catholic	Baptist	Methodist	LDS[2]	Pentecostal	Lutheran	Islam	Adventist	Other
MSA[1]	16.1	6.0	4.1	1.1	1.3	0.8	3.3	1.5	12.6
U.S.	18.7	7.3	3.0	2.0	1.8	1.7	1.3	1.3	11.6

Note: Figures are the number of adherents as a percentage of the total population and cover the eight largest religious groups in the U.S; (1) Figures cover the Washington-Arlington-Alexandria, DC-VA-MD-WV Metropolitan Statistical Area; (2) Church of Jesus Christ of Latter-day Saints
Sources: 2020 U.S. Religion Census, Association of Statisticians of American Religious Bodies; The Association of Religion Data Archives (ARDA)

Religious Groups by Tradition

Area	Catholic	Evangelical Protestant	Mainline Protestant	Black Protestant	Islam	Judaism	Hinduism	Orthodox	Buddhism
MSA[1]	16.1	12.3	6.5	3.3	3.3	1.0	0.9	0.9	0.5
U.S.	18.7	16.5	5.2	2.3	1.3	0.6	0.4	0.4	0.3

Note: Figures are the number of adherents as a percentage of the total population; (1) Figures cover the Washington-Arlington-Alexandria, DC-VA-MD-WV Metropolitan Statistical Area
Sources: 2020 U.S. Religion Census, Association of Statisticians of American Religious Bodies; The Association of Religion Data Archives (ARDA)

ECONOMY

Real Gross Domestic Product (GDP)

Area	2017	2018	2019	2020	2021	2022	2023	Rank[3]
MSA[1]	528.9	542.4	551.9	543.4	571.1	584.2	600.2	6
U.S.[2]	17,619.1	18,160.7	18,642.5	18,238.9	19,387.6	19,896.6	20,436.3	—

Note: Figures are in billions of chained 2017 dollars; (1) Figures cover the Washington-Arlington-Alexandria, DC-VA-MD-WV Metropolitan Statistical Area; (2) Figures cover real GDP within metropolitan areas; (3) Rank is based on 2023 data and ranges from 1 to 384
Source: U.S. Bureau of Economic Analysis

Economic Growth

Area	2014	2015	2016	2017	2018	2019	2020	2021	2022	2023
MSA[1]	1.2	2.1	2.5	2.4	2.5	1.8	-1.6	5.1	2.3	2.7
U.S.[2]	2.6	3.2	2.0	2.7	3.1	2.7	-2.2	6.3	2.6	2.7

Note: Figures are real gross domestic product growth rates and represent percent change from preceding period; (1) Figures cover the Washington-Arlington-Alexandria, DC-VA-MD-WV Metropolitan Statistical Area; (2) Figures are the average growth rates within metropolitan areas
Source: U.S. Bureau of Economic Analysis

Metropolitan Area Exports

Area	2018	2019	2020	2021	2022	2023	Rank[2]
MSA[1]	13,602.7	14,563.8	13,537.3	12,210.8	14,001.9	14,758.9	29
U.S.	1,664,056.1	1,645,173.7	1,431,406.6	1,753,941.4	2,062,937.4	2,019,160.5	—

Note: Figures are in millions of dollars; (1) Figures cover the Washington-Arlington-Alexandria, DC-VA-MD-WV Metropolitan Statistical Area; (2) Rank is based on 2023 data and ranges from 1 to 386
Source: U.S. Department of Commerce, International Trade Administration, Office of Trade and Economic Analysis, Industry and Analysis, Exports by Metropolitan Area, data extracted April 2, 2025

Building Permits

Area	Single-Family			Multi-Family			Total		
	2023	2024	Pct. Chg.	2023	2024	Pct. Chg.	2023	2024	Pct. Chg.
City	166	146	-12.0	2,854	1,591	-44.3	3,020	1,737	-42.5
MSA[1]	10,936	11,743	7.4	12,557	9,744	-22.4	23,493	21,487	-8.5
U.S.	920,000	981,900	6.7	591,100	496,100	-16.1	1,511,100	1,478,000	-2.2

Note: (1) Figures cover the Washington-Arlington-Alexandria, DC-VA-MD-WV Metropolitan Statistical Area; Figures represent new, privately-owned housing units authorized (unadjusted data)
Source: U.S. Census Bureau, Building Permits Survey (BPS), 2023, 2024

Bankruptcy Filings

Area	Business Filings			Nonbusiness Filings		
	2023	2024	% Chg.	2023	2024	% Chg.
District of Columbia	78	81	3.8	293	347	18.4
U.S.	18,926	23,107	22.1	434,064	494,201	13.9

Note: Business filings include Chapter 7, Chapter 9, Chapter 11, Chapter 12, Chapter 13, Chapter 15, and Section 304; Nonbusiness filings include Chapter 7, Chapter 11, and Chapter 13
Source: Administrative Office of the U.S. Courts, Business and Nonbusiness Bankruptcy, County Cases Commenced by Chapter of the Bankruptcy Code, During the 12-Month Period Ending December 31, 2023 and Business and Nonbusiness Bankruptcy, County Cases Commenced by Chapter of the Bankruptcy Code, During the 12-Month Period Ending December 31, 2024

Housing Vacancy Rates

Area	Gross Vacancy Rate[3] (%)			Year-Round Vacancy Rate[4] (%)			Rental Vacancy Rate[5] (%)			Homeowner Vacancy Rate[6] (%)		
	2022	2023	2024	2022	2023	2024	2022	2023	2024	2022	2023	2024
MSA[1]	5.2	5.1	5.5	5.0	5.0	5.4	5.3	5.5	4.7	0.6	0.3	0.4
U.S.[2]	9.1	9.0	9.1	7.5	7.5	7.6	5.7	6.5	6.8	0.8	0.8	1.0

Note: (1) Figures cover the Washington-Arlington-Alexandria, DC-VA-MD-WV Metropolitan Statistical Area; (2) Figures cover the 75 largest Metropolitan Statistical Areas; (3) The percentage of the total housing inventory that is vacant; (4) The percentage of the housing inventory (excluding seasonal units) that is year-round vacant; (5) The percentage of rental inventory that is vacant for rent; (6) The percentage of homeowner inventory that is vacant for sale
Source: U.S. Census Bureau, Housing Vacancies and Homeownership Annual Statistics: 2022, 2023, 2024

INCOME

Income

Area	Per Capita ($)	Median Household ($)	Average Household ($)
City	75,253	106,287	157,604
MSA[1]	62,026	123,896	162,905
U.S.	43,289	78,538	110,491

Note: (1) Figures cover the Washington-Arlington-Alexandria, DC-VA-MD-WV Metropolitan Statistical Area
Source: U.S. Census Bureau, 2019-2023 American Community Survey 5-Year Estimates

Household Income Distribution

Area	Percent of Households Earning							
	Under $15,000	$15,000 -$24,999	$25,000 -$34,999	$35,000 -$49,999	$50,000 -$74,999	$75,000 -$99,999	$100,000 -$149,999	$150,000 and up
City	10.5	4.6	3.8	6.8	11.4	10.4	15.7	36.9
MSA[1]	5.4	3.2	3.5	5.9	11.0	11.0	18.9	41.0
U.S.	8.5	6.6	6.8	10.4	15.7	12.7	17.4	21.9

Note: (1) Figures cover the Washington-Arlington-Alexandria, DC-VA-MD-WV Metropolitan Statistical Area
Source: U.S. Census Bureau, 2019-2023 American Community Survey 5-Year Estimates

Poverty Rate

Area	All Ages	Under 18 Years Old	18 to 64 Years Old	65 Years and Over
City	14.5	20.4	12.9	14.6
MSA[1]	7.9	9.8	7.2	7.6
U.S.	12.4	16.3	11.6	10.4

Note: Figures are percentage of people whose income during the past 12 months was below the poverty level;
(1) Figures cover the Washington-Arlington-Alexandria, DC-VA-MD-WV Metropolitan Statistical Area
Source: U.S. Census Bureau, 2019-2023 American Community Survey 5-Year Estimates

EMPLOYMENT

Labor Force and Employment

Area	Civilian Labor Force			Workers Employed		
	Dec. 2023	Dec. 2024	% Chg.	Dec. 2023	Dec. 2024	% Chg.
City	411,135	417,094	1.4	391,912	396,492	1.2
MD[1]	1,000,003	1,013,650	1.4	966,020	974,957	0.9
U.S.	166,661,000	167,746,000	0.7	160,754,000	161,294,000	0.3

Note: Data is not seasonally adjusted and covers workers 16 years of age and older; (1) Figures cover the Washington, DC-MD Metropolitan Division
Source: Bureau of Labor Statistics, Local Area Unemployment Statistics

Unemployment Rate

Area	2024											
	Jan.	Feb.	Mar.	Apr.	May	Jun.	Jul.	Aug.	Sep.	Oct.	Nov.	Dec.
City	5.1	5.3	5.0	4.5	5.0	5.7	6.0	6.0	5.2	5.2	5.0	4.9
MD[1]	3.9	4.1	3.9	3.4	3.7	4.4	4.6	4.7	4.0	4.1	4.1	3.8
U.S.	4.1	4.2	3.9	3.5	3.7	4.3	4.5	4.4	3.9	3.9	4.0	3.8

Note: Data is not seasonally adjusted and covers workers 16 years of age and older; (1) Figures cover the Washington, DC-MD Metropolitan Division
Source: Bureau of Labor Statistics, Local Area Unemployment Statistics

Average Wages

Occupation	$/Hr.	Occupation	$/Hr.
Accountants and Auditors	52.24	Maintenance and Repair Workers	27.76
Automotive Mechanics	31.94	Marketing Managers	91.27
Bookkeepers	28.25	Network and Computer Systems Admin.	60.06
Carpenters	30.71	Nurses, Licensed Practical	34.17
Cashiers	17.17	Nurses, Registered	49.29
Computer Programmers	54.17	Nursing Assistants	20.85
Computer Systems Analysts	62.36	Office Clerks, General	26.37
Computer User Support Specialists	38.26	Physical Therapists	53.25
Construction Laborers	23.15	Physicians	100.51
Cooks, Restaurant	20.33	Plumbers, Pipefitters and Steamfitters	34.13
Customer Service Representatives	23.55	Police and Sheriff's Patrol Officers	41.76
Dentists	109.72	Postal Service Mail Carriers	29.66
Electricians	37.78	Real Estate Sales Agents	34.90
Engineers, Electrical	67.24	Retail Salespersons	18.96
Fast Food and Counter Workers	16.65	Sales Representatives, Technical/Scientific	54.33
Financial Managers	93.22	Secretaries, Exc. Legal/Medical/Executive	26.32
First-Line Supervisors of Office Workers	38.57	Security Guards	26.46
General and Operations Managers	77.26	Surgeons	178.95
Hairdressers/Cosmetologists	25.20	Teacher Assistants, Exc. Postsecondary[1]	20.42
Home Health and Personal Care Aides	18.26	Teachers, Secondary School, Exc. Sp. Ed.[1]	38.87
Janitors and Cleaners	18.52	Telemarketers	19.03
Landscaping/Groundskeeping Workers	20.84	Truck Drivers, Heavy/Tractor-Trailer	29.14
Lawyers	105.48	Truck Drivers, Light/Delivery Services	24.85
Maids and Housekeeping Cleaners	18.53	Waiters and Waitresses	22.84

Note: Wage data covers the Washington-Arlington-Alexandria, DC-VA-MD-WV Metropolitan Statistical Area;
(1) Hourly wages were calculated from annual wage data based on a 40 hour work week
Source: Bureau of Labor Statistics, Metro Area Occupational Employment & Wage Estimates, May 2024

Employment by Industry

Sector	MD[1] Number of Employees	MD[1] Percent of Total	U.S. Percent of Total
Construction, Mining, and Logging	48,900	4.2	5.5
Financial Activities	38,800	3.3	5.8
Government	352,300	30.2	14.9
Information	21,300	1.8	1.9
Leisure and Hospitality	115,800	9.9	10.4
Manufacturing	9,100	0.8	8.0
Other Services	78,300	6.7	3.7
Private Education and Health Services	172,300	14.8	16.9
Professional and Business Services	226,000	19.4	14.2
Retail Trade	65,600	5.6	10.0
Transportation, Warehousing, and Utilities	22,700	1.9	4.8
Wholesale Trade	16,500	1.4	3.9

Note: Figures are non-farm employment as of December 2024. Figures are not seasonally adjusted and include workers 16 years of age and older; (1) Figures cover the Washington, DC-MD Metropolitan Division
Source: Bureau of Labor Statistics, Current Employment Statistics, Employment, Hours, and Earnings

Employment by Occupation

Occupation Classification	City (%)	MSA[1] (%)	U.S. (%)
Management, Business, Science, and Arts	71.1	56.9	42.0
Natural Resources, Construction, and Maintenance	2.0	6.4	8.6
Production, Transportation, and Material Moving	3.2	6.5	13.0
Sales and Office	12.2	15.6	19.9
Service	11.4	14.5	16.5

Note: Figures cover employed civilians 16 years of age and older; (1) Figures cover the Washington-Arlington-Alexandria, DC-VA-MD-WV Metropolitan Statistical Area
Source: U.S. Census Bureau, 2019-2023 American Community Survey 5-Year Estimates

Occupations with Greatest Projected Employment Growth: 2022 – 2032

Occupation[1]	2022 Employment	2032 Projected Employment	Numeric Employment Change	Percent Employment Change
Cooks, Restaurant	6,430	9,500	3,070	47.7
Management Analysts	24,060	26,930	2,870	11.9
Home Health and Personal Care Aides	11,530	13,630	2,100	18.2
Waiters and Waitresses	10,770	12,820	2,050	19.0
Fast Food and Counter Workers	7,840	9,770	1,930	24.6
Computer Occupations, All Other (SOC 2018)	20,050	21,920	1,870	9.3
Janitors and Cleaners, Except Maids and Housekeeping Cleaners	15,250	16,950	1,700	11.1
Software Developers	8,460	10,120	1,660	19.6
General and Operations Managers	38,290	39,880	1,590	4.2
Lawyers	42,430	43,920	1,490	3.5

Note: Projections cover District of Columbia; (1) Sorted by numeric employment change
Source: www.projectionscentral.org, State Occupational Projections, 2022–2032 Long-Term Projections

Fastest-Growing Occupations: 2022 – 2032

Occupation[1]	2022 Employment	2032 Projected Employment	Numeric Employment Change	Percent Employment Change
Animal Trainers	230	370	140	60.9
Massage Therapists	140	210	70	50.0
Cooks, Restaurant	6,430	9,500	3,070	47.7
Nurse Practitioners	600	850	250	41.7
Entertainers and Performers, Sports and Related Workers, All Other	670	920	250	37.3
Driver/Sales Workers	810	1,090	280	34.6
Hairdressers, Hairstylists, and Cosmetologists	1,080	1,440	360	33.3
Data Scientists	3,130	4,140	1,010	32.3
Physician Assistants	450	590	140	31.1
First-Line Supervisors of Food Preparation and Serving Workers	3,150	4,120	970	30.8

Note: Projections cover District of Columbia; (1) Sorted by percent employment change and excludes occupations with numeric employment change less than 50
Source: www.projectionscentral.org, State Occupational Projections, 2022–2032 Long-Term Projections

CITY FINANCES

City Government Finances

Component	2022 ($000)	2022 ($ per capita)
Total Revenues	19,440,804	27,273
Total Expenditures	20,553,329	28,834
Debt Outstanding	18,139,708	25,448

Source: U.S. Census Bureau, State & Local Government Finances 2022

City Government Revenue by Source

Source	2022 ($000)	2022 ($ per capita)	2022 (%)
General Revenue			
From Federal Government	6,386,642	8,960	32.9
From State Government	195,094	274	1.0
From Local Governments	408,340	573	2.1
Taxes			
Property	2,908,139	4,080	15.0
Sales and Gross Receipts	2,121,928	2,977	10.9
Personal Income	3,116,991	4,373	16.0
Corporate Income	991,322	1,391	5.1
Motor Vehicle License	59,002	83	0.3
Other Taxes	880,183	1,235	4.5
Current Charges	960,035	1,347	4.9
Liquor Store	0	0	0.0
Utility	255,977	359	1.3

Source: U.S. Census Bureau, State & Local Government Finances 2022

City Government Expenditures by Function

Function	2022 ($000)	2022 ($ per capita)	2022 (%)
General Direct Expenditures			
Air Transportation	0	0	0.0
Corrections	280,618	393	1.4
Education	3,822,354	5,362	18.6
Employment Security Administration	35,947	50	0.2
Financial Administration	868,293	1,218	4.2
Fire Protection	379,189	532	1.8
General Public Buildings	179,953	252	0.9
Governmental Administration, Other	312,395	438	1.5
Health	999,819	1,402	4.9
Highways	657,215	922	3.2
Hospitals	281,660	395	1.4
Housing and Community Development	1,260,252	1,768	6.1
Interest on General Debt	664,292	931	3.2
Judicial and Legal	278,005	390	1.4
Libraries	89,794	126	0.4
Parking	35,891	50	0.2
Parks and Recreation	280,886	394	1.4
Police Protection	672,157	943	3.3
Public Welfare	5,314,100	7,455	25.9
Sewerage	384,087	538	1.9
Solid Waste Management	191,493	268	0.9
Veterans' Services	0	0	0.0
Liquor Store	0	0	0.0
Utility	412,412	578	2.0

Source: U.S. Census Bureau, State & Local Government Finances 2022

TAXES

State Corporate Income Tax Rates

State	Tax Rate (%)	Income Brackets ($)	Num. of Brackets	Financial Institution Tax Rate (%)[a]	Federal Income Tax Ded.
D.C.	8.25 (b)	Flat rate	1	8.25 (b)	No

Note: Tax rates for tax year 2024; (a) Rates listed are the corporate income tax rate applied to financial institutions or excise taxes based on income. Some states have other taxes based upon the value of deposits or shares; (b) Minimum tax is $800 in California, $250 in District of Columbia, $50 in Arizona and North Dakota (banks), $400 ($100 banks) in Rhode Island, $200 per location in South Dakota (banks), $100 in Utah, in Vermont, simplified entity business tax for residents only at $250, otherwise minimum tax ($100 - $100,000) is based upon gross receipts.
Source: Federation of Tax Administrators, State Corporate Income Tax Rates, January 1, 2025

State Individual Income Tax Rates

State	Tax Rate (%)	Income Brackets ($)	Personal Exemptions ($)			Standard Ded. ($)	
			Single	Married	Depend.	Single	Married
D.C.	4.0 - 10.75	10,000 - 1 million	(d)	(d)	(d)	14,600	29,200 (d)

Note: Tax rates for tax year 2024; Local- and county-level taxes are not included; Federal income tax is not deductible on state income tax returns; (d) These states use the personal exemption/standard deduction amounts provided in the federal Internal Revenue Code. Montana personal exemption subject to repeal under Section 15-30-2114.
Source: Federation of Tax Administrators, State Individual Income Tax Rates, January 1, 2025

Various State Sales and Excise Tax Rates

State	State Sales Tax (%)	Gasoline[1] ($/gal.)	Cigarette[2] ($/pack)	Spirits[3] ($/gal.)	Wine[4] ($/gal.)	Beer[5] ($/gal.)	Recreational Marijuana (%)
D.C.	6	0.35	5.03	6.68	2.07	0.79	(y)

Note: All tax rates as of January 1, 2025; (1) The American Petroleum Institute has developed a methodology for determining the average tax rate on a gallon of fuel. Rates may include any of the following: excise taxes, environmental fees, storage tank fees, other fees or taxes, general sales tax, and local taxes; (2) The federal excise tax of $1.0066 per pack and local taxes are not included; (3) Rates are those applicable to off-premise sales of 40% alcohol by volume (a.b.v.) distilled spirits in 750ml containers. Local excise taxes are excluded; (4) Rates are those applicable to off-premise sales of 11% a.b.v. non-carbonated wine in 750ml containers; (5) Rates are those applicable to off-premise sales of 4.7% a.b.v. beer in 12 ounce containers; (y) District of Columbia voters approved legalization and purchase of marijuana in 2014 but federal law prohibits any action to implement it
Source: Tax Foundation, 2025 Facts & Figures: How Does Your State Compare?

State Tax Competitiveness Index

State	Overall Rank	Corporate Tax Rank	Individual Income Tax Rank	Sales Tax Rank	Property Tax Rank	Unemployment Insurance Tax Rank
District of Columbia	48	32	47	41	48	25

Note: The Tax Foundation's State Tax Competitiveness Index enables policymakers, taxpayers, and business leaders to gauge how their states' tax systems compare. A rank of 1 is best, 50 is worst. Rankings do not average to the total. States without a tax rank equally as 1. DC's scores and rankings do not affect other states. The report shows tax systems as of July 1, 2024 (the beginning of Fiscal Year 2025).
Source: Tax Foundation, State Tax Competitiveness Index 2025

TRANSPORTATION

Means of Transportation to Work

Area	Car/Truck/Van		Public Transportation			Bicycle	Walked	Other Means	Worked at Home
	Drove Alone	Car-pooled	Bus	Subway	Railroad				
City	28.2	4.3	8.1	13.8	0.3	3.3	10.0	2.7	29.4
MSA[1]	56.4	8.0	2.9	4.4	0.4	0.7	2.7	1.9	22.6
U.S.	70.2	8.5	1.7	1.3	0.4	0.4	2.4	1.6	13.5

Note: Figures are percentages and cover workers 16 years of age and older; (1) Figures cover the Washington-Arlington-Alexandria, DC-VA-MD-WV Metropolitan Statistical Area
Source: U.S. Census Bureau, 2019-2023 American Community Survey 5-Year Estimates

Travel Time to Work

Area	Less Than 10 Minutes	10 to 19 Minutes	20 to 29 Minutes	30 to 44 Minutes	45 to 59 Minutes	60 to 89 Minutes	90 Minutes or More
City	5.2	19.2	22.5	33.1	11.8	6.3	1.9
MSA[1]	6.5	20.1	19.2	26.3	13.2	11.0	3.6
U.S.	12.6	28.6	21.2	20.8	8.1	6.0	2.8

Note: Note: Figures are percentages and include workers 16 years old and over; (1) Figures cover the Washington-Arlington-Alexandria, DC-VA-MD-WV Metropolitan Statistical Area
Source: U.S. Census Bureau, 2019-2023 American Community Survey 5-Year Estimates

Key Congestion Measures

Measure	2000	2010	2015	2020	2022
Annual Hours of Delay, Total (000)	137,652	211,442	234,531	101,775	188,563
Annual Hours of Delay, Per Auto Commuter	70	90	96	42	85
Annual Congestion Cost, Per Auto Commuter ($)	1,800	2,197	2,253	1,012	1,903

Note: Figures cover the Washington DC-VA-MD urban area
Source: Texas A&M Transportation Institute, 2023 Urban Mobility Report

Freeway Travel Time Index

Measure	1985	1990	1995	2000	2005	2010	2015	2020	2022
Urban Area Index[1]	1.19	1.22	1.27	1.29	1.34	1.35	1.35	1.12	1.25
Urban Area Rank[1,2]	6	5	5	6	5	5	7	10	19

Note: Freeway Travel Time Index—the ratio of travel time in the peak period to the travel time at free-flow conditions. For example, a value of 1.30 indicates a 20-minute free-flow trip takes 26 minutes in the peak (20 minutes x 1.30 = 26 minutes); (1) Covers the Washington DC-VA-MD urban area; (2) Rank is based on 101 larger urban areas (#1 = highest travel time index)
Source: Texas A&M Transportation Institute, 2023 Urban Mobility Report

Public Transportation

Agency Name / Mode of Transportation	Vehicles Operated in Maximum Service[1]	Annual Unlinked Passenger Trips[2] (in thous.)	Annual Passenger Miles[3] (in thous.)
Washington Metropolitan Area Transit Authority (WMATA)			
Bus (directly operated)	1,148	102,855.9	307,224.1
Demand Response (purchased transportation)	675	1,394.1	16,059.7
Heavy Rail (directly operated)	904	126,773.7	589,321.1

Note: (1) Number of revenue vehicles operated by the given mode and type of service to meet the annual maximum service requirement. This is the revenue vehicle count during the peak season of the year; on the week and day that maximum service is provided. Vehicles operated in maximum service (VOMS) exclude atypical days and one-time special events; (2) Number of passengers who boarded public transportation vehicles. Passengers are counted each time they board a vehicle no matter how many vehicles they use to travel from their origin to their destination. (3) Sum of the distances ridden by all passengers during the entire fiscal year.
Source: Federal Transit Administration, National Transit Database, 2023

Air Transportation

Airport Name and Code / Type of Service	Passenger Airlines[1]	Passenger Enplanements	Freight Carriers[2]	Freight (lbs)
Ronald Reagan Washington National (DCA)				
Domestic service (U.S. carriers only)	18	12,500,236	6	1,159,121
International service (U.S. carriers only)	4	97,221	1	1
Dulles International (IAD)				
Domestic service (U.S. carriers only)	32	8,041,768	9	88,691,038
International service (U.S. carriers only)	12	2,088,249	6	51,331,205

Note: (1) Includes all U.S.-based major, minor and commuter airlines that carried at least one passenger during the year; (2) Includes all U.S.-based airlines and freight carriers that transported at least one pound of freight during the year.
Source: Bureau of Transportation Statistics, The Intermodal Transportation Database, Air Carriers: T-100 Domestic Market (U.S. carriers only), 2024; Bureau of Transportation Statistics, The Intermodal Transportation Database, Air Carriers: T-100 International Market (U.S. carriers only), 2024

BUSINESSES

Major Business Headquarters

Company Name	Industry	Rankings	
		Fortune[1]	Forbes[2]
Danaher	Medical products and equipment	153	-
Fannie Mae	Diversified financials	27	-
Hogan Lovells	Services	-	228
Xylem	Industrial machinery	486	-

Note: (1) Companies that produce a 10-K are ranked 1 to 500 based on 2023 revenue; (2) All private companies with at least $2 billion in annual revenue through the end of their most current fiscal year are ranked 1 to 275; companies listed are headquartered in the city; dashes indicate no ranking
Source: Fortune, "Fortune 500," 2024; Forbes, "America's Largest Private Companies," 2024

Fastest-Growing Businesses

According to *Inc.*, Washington is home to three of America's 500 fastest-growing private companies: **CaryHealth** (#82); **Veltrust** (#261); **Totem** (#283). Criteria: must be an independent, privately-held, for-profit, U.S. corporation, proprietorship or partnership as of December 31, 2023; revenues must be at least $100,000 in 2020 and $2 million in 2023; must have four-year operating/sales history. *Inc.*, "America's 500 Fastest-Growing Private Companies," 2024

According to *Initiative for a Competitive Inner City (ICIC)*, Washington is home to five of America's 100 fastest-growing "inner city" companies: **Northern Real Estate Urban Ventures** (#6); **MDM Enterprises dba Equus Striping** (#13); **Lalini Enterprises dba LE Global** (#16); **MW Consulting** (#31); **TCG** (#85). To be eligible for the IC100, companies have to be independently operated, privately held, for-profit businesses with revenues of at least $50,000 in 2019 and $500,000 in 2023, and headquartered in an under-resourced community. Recognizing that concentrated poverty exists within metropolitan areas outside of big cities (and that poverty overall is suburbanizing), ICIC defines under-resourced communities as large low-income, high-poverty areas located in the urban and suburban parts of all but the smallest metropolitan areas. Companies were ranked overall by revenue growth over the five-year period between 2019 and 2023. *Initiative for a Competitive Inner City (ICIC), "Inner City 100 Companies," 2024*

According to Deloitte, Washington is home to four of North America's 500 fastest-growing high-technology companies: **Adlumin** (#157); **Sayari Labs** (#258); **MPOWER Financing** (#275); **Fundrise** (#356). Companies are ranked by percentage growth in revenue over a four-year period. Criteria for inclusion: company must be headquartered within North America; must own proprietary intellectual property or technology that is sold to customers in products that contributes to a significant portion of the company's operating revenue; must have been in business for a minumum of four years with 2020 operating revenues of at least $50,000 USD/CD and 2023 operating revenues of at least $5 million USD/CD. *Deloitte, 2024 Technology Fast 500™*

Living Environment

COST OF LIVING

Cost of Living Index

Composite Index	Groceries	Housing	Utilities	Transportation	Health Care	Misc. Goods/Services
141.9	105.9	222.4	102.4	107.9	117.0	113.2

Note: The Cost of Living Index measures regional differences in the cost of consumer goods and services, excluding taxes and non-consumer expenditures, for professional and managerial households in the top income quintile. It is based on more than 50,000 prices covering almost 60 different items for which prices are collected three times a year by chambers of commerce, economic development organizations or university applied economic centers in each participating urban area. The numbers shown should be read as a percentage above or below the national average of 100. For example, a value of 115.4 in the groceries column indicates that grocery prices are 15.4% higher than the national average. Small differences in the index numbers should not be interpreted as significant; Figures cover the Washington DC urban area.
Source: The Council for Community and Economic Research, Cost of Living Index, 2024

Grocery Prices

Area[1]	T-Bone Steak ($/pound)	Frying Chicken ($/pound)	Whole Milk ($/half gal.)	Eggs ($/dozen)	Orange Juice ($/64 oz.)	Coffee ($/11.5 oz.)
City[2]	15.51	1.42	4.62	3.47	4.44	5.77
Avg.	15.42	1.55	4.69	3.25	4.41	5.46
Min.	14.50	1.16	4.43	2.75	4.00	4.85
Max.	17.56	2.89	5.49	4.78	5.54	7.89

Note: (1) Values for the local area are compared with the average, minimum and maximum values for all 276 areas in the Cost of Living Index; (2) Figures cover the Washington DC urban area; **T-Bone Steak** (price per pound); **Frying Chicken** (price per pound, whole fryer); **Whole Milk** (half gallon carton); **Eggs** (price per dozen, Grade A, large); **Orange Juice** (64 oz. Tropicana or Florida Natural); **Coffee** (11.5 oz. can, vacuum-packed, Maxwell House, Hills Bros, or Folgers).
Source: The Council for Community and Economic Research, Cost of Living Index, 2024

Housing and Utility Costs

Area[1]	New Home Price ($)	Apartment Rent ($/month)	All Electric ($/month)	Part Electric ($/month)	Other Energy ($/month)	Telephone ($/month)
City[2]	1,149,206	3,212	-	122.00	92.52	193.65
Avg.	515,975	1,550	210.99	123.07	82.07	194.99
Min.	265,375	692	104.33	53.68	36.26	179.42
Max.	2,775,821	5,719	529.02	397.28	361.63	223.33

Note: (1) Values for the local area are compared with the average, minimum and maximum values for all 276 areas in the Cost of Living Index; (2) Figures cover the Washington DC urban area; **New Home Price** (2,400 sf living area, 8,000 sf lot, in urban area with full utilities); **Apartment Rent** (950 sf 2 bedroom/1.5 or 2 bath, unfurnished, excluding all utilities except water); **All Electric** (average monthly cost for an all-electric home); **Part Electric** (average monthly cost for a part-electric home); **Other Energy** (average monthly cost for natural gas, fuel oil, coal, wood, and any other forms of energy except electricity); **Telephone** (price includes the base monthly rate plus taxes and fees for three lines of mobile phone service).
Source: The Council for Community and Economic Research, Cost of Living Index, 2024

Health Care, Transportation, and Other Costs

Area[1]	Doctor ($/visit)	Dentist ($/visit)	Optometrist ($/visit)	Gasoline ($/gallon)	Beauty Salon ($/visit)	Men's Shirt ($)
City[2]	177.67	151.33	125.50	3.36	78.76	37.95
Avg.	143.77	117.51	129.23	3.32	48.57	38.14
Min.	36.74	58.67	67.33	2.80	24.00	13.41
Max.	270.44	216.82	307.33	5.28	94.00	63.89

Note: (1) Values for the local area are compared with the average, minimum and maximum values for all 276 areas in the Cost of Living Index; (2) Figures cover the Washington DC urban area; **Doctor** (general practitioners routine exam of an established patient); **Dentist** (adult teeth cleaning and periodic oral examination); **Optometrist** (full vision eye exam for established adult patient); **Gasoline** (one gallon regular unleaded, national brand, including all taxes, cash price at self-service pump if available); **Beauty Salon** (woman's shampoo, trim, and blow-dry); **Men's Shirt** (cotton/polyester dress shirt, pinpoint weave, long sleeves).
Source: The Council for Community and Economic Research, Cost of Living Index, 2024

HOUSING

Homeownership Rate

Area	2017 (%)	2018 (%)	2019 (%)	2020 (%)	2021 (%)	2022 (%)	2023 (%)	2024 (%)
MSA[1]	63.3	62.9	64.7	67.9	65.8	66.2	65.1	64.0
U.S.	63.9	64.4	64.6	66.6	65.5	65.8	65.9	65.6

Note: (1) Figures cover the Washington-Arlington-Alexandria, DC-VA-MD-WV Metropolitan Statistical Area
Source: U.S. Census Bureau, Housing Vacancies and Homeownership Annual Statistics: 2017-2024

House Price Index (HPI)

Area	National Ranking[2]	Quarterly Change (%)	One-Year Change (%)	Five-Year Change (%)	Since 1991Q1 (%)
MD[1]	106	-0.50	5.79	38.73	288.38
U.S.[3]	–	1.43	4.51	57.13	327.82

Note: The HPI is a weighted repeat sales index. It measures average price changes in repeat sales or refinancings on the same properties. This information is obtained by reviewing repeat mortgage transactions on single-family properties whose mortgages have been purchased or securitized by Fannie Mae or Freddie Mac since January 1975; (1) Figures cover the Washington-Arlington-Alexandria, DC-VA-MD-WV Metropolitan Division; (2) Rankings are based on annual percentage change for all metro areas containing at least 15,000 transactions over the last 10 years and ranges from 1 to 241; (3) figures based on a weighted average of Census Division estimates using a seasonally adjusted, purchase-only index; all figures are for the period ending December 31, 2024
Source: Federal Housing Finance Agency, Change in FHFA Metropolitan Area House Price Indexes, All Transactions Index, 2024Q4

Home Value

Area	Under $100,000	$100,000 -$199,999	$200,000 -$299,999	$300,000 -$399,999	$400,000 -$499,999	$500,000 -$999,999	$1,000,000 or more	Median ($)
City	1.4	1.8	4.6	9.1	11.2	41.8	30.1	724,600
MSA[1]	2.5	2.4	8.4	14.5	16.2	42.5	13.4	553,000
U.S.	12.1	17.8	19.5	14.4	10.5	19.1	6.5	303,400

Note: Figures are percentages except for median and cover owner-occupied housing units; (1) Figures cover the Washington-Arlington-Alexandria, DC-VA-MD-WV Metropolitan Statistical Area
Source: U.S. Census Bureau, 2019-2023 American Community Survey 5-Year Estimates

Year Housing Structure Built

Area	2020 or Later	2010 -2019	2000 -2009	1990 -1999	1980 -1989	1970 -1979	1960 -1969	1950 -1959	1940 -1949	Before 1940	Median Year
City	1.7	12.5	7.7	3.0	4.7	6.7	9.9	11.6	10.3	31.7	1957
MSA[1]	1.2	10.7	14.1	12.9	15.2	13.0	11.5	8.7	4.7	8.1	1983
U.S.	1.2	8.9	12.8	13.0	14.4	10.0	9.7	4.5	11.9		1980

Note: Figures are percentages except for Median Year; Note: (1) Figures cover the Washington-Arlington-Alexandria, DC-VA-MD-WV Metropolitan Statistical Area
Source: U.S. Census Bureau, 2019-2023 American Community Survey 5-Year Estimates

Gross Monthly Rent

Area	Under $500	$500 -$999	$1,000 -$1,499	$1,500 -$1,999	$2,000 -$2,499	$2,500 -$2,999	$3,000 and up	Median ($)
City	7.4	7.8	17.8	21.2	16.8	11.4	17.6	1,900
MSA[1]	3.7	4.7	14.3	28.7	23.5	12.3	12.9	1,975
U.S.	6.5	22.3	29.5	20.2	10.8	4.8	5.9	1,348

Note: Figures are percentages except for median; Gross rent is the contract rent plus the estimated average monthly cost of utilities (electricity, gas, and water and sewer) and fuels (oil, coal, kerosene, wood, etc.) if these are paid by the renter (or paid for the renter by someone else); (1) Figures cover the Washington-Arlington-Alexandria, DC-VA-MD-WV Metropolitan Statistical Area
Source: U.S. Census Bureau, 2019-2023 American Community Survey 5-Year Estimates

HEALTH

Health Risk Factors

Category	MD[1] (%)	U.S. (%)
Adults aged 18–64 who have any kind of health care coverage	89.0	90.8
Adults who reported being in good or better health	84.4	81.8
Adults who have been told they have high blood cholesterol	37.5	36.9
Adults who have been told they have high blood pressure	30.7	34.0
Adults who are current smokers	8.2	12.1
Adults who currently use e-cigarettes	4.9	7.7
Adults who currently use chewing tobacco, snuff, or snus	1.5	3.2
Adults who are heavy drinkers[2]	5.1	6.1
Adults who are binge drinkers[3]	14.2	15.2
Adults who are overweight (BMI 25.0 - 29.9)	37.1	34.4
Adults who are obese (BMI 30.0 - 99.8)	29.0	34.3
Adults who participated in any physical activities in the past month	79.7	75.8

Note: All figures are crude prevalence; (1) Figures cover the Washington, DC-MD Metropolitan Division; (2) Heavy drinkers are classified as adult men having more than 14 drinks per week and adult women having more than 7 drinks per week; (3) Binge drinkers are classified as males having five or more drinks on one occasion or females having four or more drinks on one occasion
Source: Centers for Disease Control and Prevention, Behavioral Risk Factor Surveillance System, SMART: Selected Metropolitan Area Risk Trends, 2023

Acute and Chronic Health Conditions

Category	MD[1] (%)	U.S. (%)
Adults who have ever been told they had a heart attack	3.0	4.2
Adults who have ever been told they have angina or coronary heart disease	3.2	4.0
Adults who have ever been told they had a stroke	2.9	3.3
Adults who have ever been told they have asthma	15.4	15.7
Adults who have ever been told they have arthritis	20.5	26.3
Adults who have ever been told they have diabetes[2]	9.2	11.5
Adults who have ever been told they had skin cancer	3.6	5.6
Adults who have ever been told they had any other types of cancer	6.4	8.4
Adults who have ever been told they have COPD	4.7	6.4
Adults who have ever been told they have kidney disease	3.1	3.7
Adults who have ever been told they have a form of depression	17.0	22.0

Note: All figures are crude prevalence; (1) Figures cover the Washington, DC-MD Metropolitan Division; (2) Figures do not include pregnancy-related, borderline, or pre-diabetes
Source: Centers for Disease Control and Prevention, Behavioral Risk Factor Surveillance System, SMART: Selected Metropolitan Area Risk Trends, 2023

Health Screening and Vaccination Rates

Category	MD[1] (%)	U.S. (%)
Adults who have ever been tested for HIV	47.0	37.5
Adults who have had their blood cholesterol checked within the last five years	90.6	87.0
Adults aged 65+ who have had flu shot within the past year	69.3	63.4
Adults aged 65+ who have ever had a pneumonia vaccination	70.2	71.9

Note: All figures are crude prevalence; (1) Figures cover the Washington, DC-MD Metropolitan Division.
Source: Centers for Disease Control and Prevention, Behavioral Risk Factor Surveillance System, SMART: Selected Metropolitan Area Risk Trends, 2023

Disability Status

Category	MD[1] (%)	U.S. (%)
Adults who reported being deaf	4.8	7.4
Are you blind or have serious difficulty seeing, even when wearing glasses?	3.8	4.9
Do you have difficulty doing errands alone?	5.5	7.8
Do you have difficulty dressing or bathing?	2.5	3.6
Do you have serious difficulty concentrating/remembering/making decisions?	11.4	13.7
Do you have serious difficulty walking or climbing stairs?	10.2	13.2

Note: All figures are crude prevalence; (1) Figures cover the Washington, DC-MD Metropolitan Division.
Source: Centers for Disease Control and Prevention, Behavioral Risk Factor Surveillance System, SMART: Selected Metropolitan Area Risk Trends, 2023

Mortality Rates for the Top 10 Causes of Death in the U.S.

ICD-10[a] Sub-Chapter	ICD-10[a] Code	Crude Mortality Rate[2] per 100,000 population	
		County[3]	U.S.
Malignant neoplasms	C00-C97	140.9	182.7
Ischaemic heart diseases	I20-I25	98.7	109.6
Provisional assignment of new diseases of uncertain etiology[1]	U00-U49	37.2	65.3
Other forms of heart disease	I30-I51	35.9	65.1
Other degenerative diseases of the nervous system	G30-G31	15.2	52.4
Other external causes of accidental injury	W00-X59	82.9	52.3
Cerebrovascular diseases	I60-I69	41.6	49.1
Chronic lower respiratory diseases	J40-J47	17.3	43.5
Hypertensive diseases	I10-I15	47.1	38.9
Organic, including symptomatic, mental disorders	F01-F09	39.8	33.9

Note: (a) ICD-10 = International Classification of Diseases 10th Revision; (1) Includes COVID-19, adverse effects to COVID-19 vaccines, SARS, and vaping-related disorders; (2) Crude mortality rates are a three-year average covering 2021-2023; (3) Figures cover District of Columbia.
Source: Centers for Disease Control and Prevention, National Center for Health Statistics. National Vital Statistics System, Mortality 2018-2023 on CDC WONDER Online Database

Mortality Rates for Selected Causes of Death

Cause of Death	ICD-10[a] Code	Crude Mortality Rate[1] per 100,000 population	
		County[2]	U.S.
Accidental poisoning and exposure to noxious substances	X40-X49	64.3	30.5
Alzheimer disease	G30	9.3	35.4
Assault	X85-Y09	30.6	7.3
COVID-19	U07.1	37.2	65.3
Diabetes mellitus	E10-E14	20.8	30.0
Diseases of the liver	K70-K76	11.0	20.8
Human immunodeficiency virus (HIV) disease	B20-B24	7.0	1.5
Influenza and pneumonia	J09-J18	8.8	13.4
Intentional self-harm	X60-X84	6.4	14.7
Malnutrition	E40-E46	1.2	6.0
Obesity and other hyperalimentation	E65-E68	2.3	3.1
Renal failure	N17-N19	7.9	16.4
Transport accidents	V01-V99	9.1	14.4

Note: (a) ICD-10 = International Classification of Diseases 10th Revision; (1) Crude mortality rates are a three-year average covering 2021-2023; (2) Figures cover District of Columbia; Data are suppressed when the data meet the criteria for confidentiality constraints; Crude mortality rates are flagged as unreliable when the rate would be calculated with a numerator of 20 or less.
Source: Centers for Disease Control and Prevention, National Center for Health Statistics. National Vital Statistics System, Mortality 2018-2023 on CDC WONDER Online Database

Health Insurance Coverage

Area	With Health Insurance	With Private Health Insurance	With Public Health Insurance	Without Health Insurance	Population Under Age 19 Without Health Insurance
City	96.6	72.4	34.2	3.4	2.7
MSA[1]	92.6	76.7	27.8	7.4	4.9
U.S.	91.4	67.3	36.3	8.6	5.4

Note: Figures are percentages that cover the civilian noninstitutionalized population; (1) Figures cover the Washington-Arlington-Alexandria, DC-VA-MD-WV Metropolitan Statistical Area
Source: U.S. Census Bureau, 2019-2023 American Community Survey 5-Year Estimates

Number of Medical Professionals

Area	MDs[3]	DOs[3,4]	Dentists	Podiatrists	Chiropractors	Optometrists
DC[1] (number)	6,237	196	886	63	76	103
DC[1] (rate[2])	928.4	29.2	130.5	9.3	11.2	15.2
U.S. (rate[2])	302.5	29.2	74.6	6.4	29.5	18.0

Note: Data as of 2023 unless noted; (1) Data covers the District of Columbia; (2) Number of medical professionals per 100,000 population; (3) Data as of 2022 and includes all active, non-federal physicians; (4) Doctor of Osteopathic Medicine
Source: U.S. Department of Health and Human Services, Health Resources and Services Administration, Bureau of Health Professions, Area Resource File (ARF) 2023-2024

Best Hospitals

According to *U.S. News,* the Washington-Arlington-Alexandria, DC-VA-MD-WV metro area is home to five of the best hospitals in the U.S.: **Inova Fairfax Hospital** (1 adult specialty and 1 pediatric specialty); **MedStar Georgetown University Hospital** (1 adult specialty); **MedStar Heart & Vascular Institute at MedStar Washington Hospital Center** (2 adult specialties); **MedStar National Rehabilitation Hospital** (1 adult specialty); **MedStar Washington Hospital Center** (2 adult specialties). The hospitals listed were nationally ranked in at least one of 15 adult or 11 pediatric specialties. The number of specialties shown cover the parent hospital. Only 160 U.S. hospitals performed well enough to be nationally ranked in one or more specialties. Twenty hospitals in the U.S. made the Honor Roll. The Best Hospitals Honor Roll takes both the national rankings and the procedure and condition ratings into account. Hospitals received points if they were nationally ranked in one of the 15 adult specialties—the higher they ranked, the more points they got—and how many ratings of "high performing" they earned in the 20 procedures and conditions. *U.S. News Online, "America's Best Hospitals 2024-25"*

According to *U.S. News,* the Washington-Arlington-Alexandria, DC-VA-MD-WV metro area is home to two of the best children's hospitals in the U.S.: **Children's National Hospital** (Honor Roll/11 pediatric specialties); **Inova L.J. Murphy Children's Hospital** (1 pediatric specialty). The hospitals listed were highly ranked in at least one of 11 pediatric specialties. One hundred five children's hospitals in the U.S. were nationally ranked in at least one specialty. Hospitals received points for being ranked in a specialty, and the 10 hospitals with the most points across the 11 specialties make up the Honor Roll. *U.S. News Online, "America's Best Children's Hospitals 2024-25"*

EDUCATION

Public School District Statistics

District Name	Schls	Pupils	Pupil/Teacher Ratio	Minority Pupils[1] (%)	Total Rev. per Pupil ($)	Total Exp. per Pupil ($)
DC Prep PCS	6	2,144	11.2	99.8	25,838	22,411
District of Columbia Public Schls	117	50,839	11.1	82.5	32,846	36,134
Friendship PCS	15	4,511	10.5	99.7	30,782	22,668
Kipp DC PCS	20	7,323	12.6	99.8	30,801	32,978

Note: Table includes school districts with 2,000 or more students; (1) Percentage of students that are not non-Hispanic white.
Source: U.S. Department of Education, National Center for Education Statistics, Common Core of Data, Local Education Agency (School District) Universe Survey: School Year 2023-2024; U.S. Department of Education, National Center for Education Statistics, Common Core of Data, School District Finance Survey (F-33): School Year 2021–22

Best High Schools

According to *U.S. News,* Washington is home to three of the top 500 high schools in the U.S.: **School Without Walls High School** (#68); **Benjamin Banneker Academy High School** (#96); **BASIS DC** (#400). Nearly 25,000 public, magnet and charter schools were ranked based on their performance on state assessments and how well they prepare students for college. *U.S. News & World Report, "Best High Schools 2024"*

Highest Level of Education

Area	Less than H.S.	H.S. Diploma	Some College, No Deg.	Associate Degree	Bachelor's Degree	Master's Degree	Prof. School Degree	Doctorate Degree
City	7.2	14.5	11.8	2.9	26.1	22.7	10.3	4.6
MSA[1]	8.5	17.3	14.6	5.8	27.0	18.7	4.7	3.4
U.S.	10.6	26.2	19.4	8.8	21.3	9.8	2.3	1.6

Note: Figures cover persons age 25 and over; (1) Figures cover the Washington-Arlington-Alexandria, DC-VA-MD-WV Metropolitan Statistical Area
Source: U.S. Census Bureau, 2019-2023 American Community Survey 5-Year Estimates

Educational Attainment by Race

Area	High School Graduate or Higher (%)					Bachelor's Degree or Higher (%)				
	Total	White	Black	Asian	Hisp.[2]	Total	White	Black	Asian	Hisp.[2]
City	92.8	99.1	88.5	95.8	81.3	63.6	92.0	33.3	84.7	56.7
MSA[1]	91.5	96.2	92.8	91.8	70.7	53.8	64.4	39.1	67.2	29.3
U.S.	89.4	92.9	88.1	88.0	72.5	35.0	37.7	24.7	57.0	19.9

Note: Figures shown cover persons 25 years old and over; (1) Figures cover the Washington-Arlington-Alexandria, DC-VA-MD-WV Metropolitan Statistical Area; (2) People of Hispanic origin can be of any race
Source: U.S. Census Bureau, 2019-2023 American Community Survey 5-Year Estimates

School Enrollment by Grade and Control

Area	Preschool (%)		Kindergarten (%)		Grades 1 - 4 (%)		Grades 5 - 8 (%)		Grades 9 - 12 (%)	
	Public	Private	Public	Private	Public	Private	Public	Private	Public	Private
City	74.8	25.2	90.5	9.5	85.6	14.4	83.0	17.0	79.9	20.1
MSA[1]	45.5	54.5	82.8	17.2	86.8	13.2	87.5	12.5	88.2	11.8
U.S.	58.7	41.3	85.2	14.8	87.2	12.8	87.9	12.1	89.0	11.0

Note: Figures shown cover persons 3 years old and over; (1) Figures cover the Washington-Arlington-Alexandria, DC-VA-MD-WV Metropolitan Statistical Area
Source: U.S. Census Bureau, 2019-2023 American Community Survey 5-Year Estimates

Higher Education

Four-Year Colleges			Two-Year Colleges			Medical Schools[1]	Law Schools[2]	Voc/Tech[3]
Public	Private Non-profit	Private For-profit	Public	Private Non-profit	Private For-profit			
7	26	13	5	1	7	4	7	18

Note: Figures cover institutions located within the Washington-Arlington-Alexandria, DC-VA-MD-WV Metropolitan Statistical Area and include main campuses only; (1) includes schools accredited by the Liaison Committee on Medical Education and the American Osteopathic Association's Commission on Osteopathic College Accreditation; (2) includes ABA-accredited schools, schools with provisional ABA accreditation, and state accredited schools; (3) includes all schools with programs that are less than 2 years.
Source: National Center for Education Statistics, Integrated Postsecondary Education System (IPEDS), 2023-24; Wikipedia, List of Medical Schools in the United States, accessed May 2, 2025; Wikipedia, List of Law Schools in the United States, accessed May 2, 2025

According to *U.S. News & World Report,* the Washington-Arlington-Alexandria, DC-VA-MD-WV metro area is home to seven of the top 200 national universities in the U.S.: **Georgetown University** (#24 tie); **University of Maryland, College Park** (#44 tie); **George Washington University** (#63 tie); **Howard University** (#86 tie); **American University** (#91 tie); **George Mason University** (#109 tie); **The Catholic University of America** (#171 tie). The indicators used to capture academic quality fall into a number of categories: assessment by administrators at peer institutions; retention of students; faculty resources; student selectivity; financial resources; alumni giving; high school counselor ratings of colleges; and graduation rate. *U.S. News & World Report, "America's Best Colleges 2025"*

According to *U.S. News & World Report*, the Washington-Arlington-Alexandria, DC-VA-MD-WV metro area is home to four of the top 100 law schools in the U.S.: **Georgetown University 1** (#14 tie); **George Mason University (Scalia)** (#31 tie); **George Washington University** (#31 tie); **The Catholic University of America** (#71 tie). The rankings are based on a weighted average of 12 measures of quality: peer assessment score; assessment score by lawyers/judges; median LSAT scores; median undergrad GPA; acceptance rate; employment rates for graduates; placement success; bar passage rate; faculty resources; expenditures per student; student/faculty ratio; and library resources. *U.S. News & World Report, "America's Best Graduate Schools, Law, 2025"*

According to *U.S. News & World Report*, the Washington-Arlington-Alexandria, DC-VA-MD-WV metro area is home to four of the top 75 business schools in the U.S.: **Georgetown University (McDonough)** (#24 tie); **University of Maryland—College Park (Smith)** (#52); **American University (Kogod)** (#58 tie); **George Washington University** (#61 tie). The rankings are based on a weighted average of the following nine measures: quality assessment; peer assessment; recruiter assessment; placement success; mean starting salary and bonus; student selectivity; mean GMAT and GRE scores; mean undergraduate GPA; and acceptance rate. *U.S. News & World Report, "America's Best Graduate Schools, Business, 2025"*

EMPLOYERS

Major Employers

Company Name	Industry
Adventist HealthCare	General medical & surgical hospitals
Bechtel National	Engineering services
Computer Sciences Corporation	Computer related consulting services
Federal Aviation Administration	Air traffic control operations, government
Federal Bureau of Investigation	Police protection
Howard University	Colleges & universities
HR Solutions	Human resource consulting services
Internal Revenue Service	Finance, taxation, and monetary policy
Intl Bank for Recons. & Dev.	Foreign trade & international banks
Natl Inst of Standards & Technology	Administration of general economic programs
Office of the Secretary of Defense	National security
U.S. Department of Agriculture	Regulation of agricultural marketing
U.S. Department of Commerce	Regulation, miscellaneous commercial sectors
U.S. Department of Labor	Administration of social & manpower programs
U.S. Department of the Army	National security
U.S. Department of the Navy	National security
U.S. Department of Transportation	Regulation, administration of transportation
U.S. Environmental Protection Agency	Land, mineral, & wildlife conservation
U.S. Fish and Wildlife Service	Fish & wildlife conservation agency, government
Washington Hospital Center Corporation	General medical & surgical hospitals

Note: Companies shown are located within the Washington-Arlington-Alexandria, DC-VA-MD-WV Metropolitan Statistical Area.
Source: Chambers of Commerce; State Departments of Labor; Wikipedia

Best Companies to Work For

Fannie Mae, headquartered in Washington, is among "The 100 Best Companies to Work For." To pick the best companies, *Fortune* partnered with the Great Place to Work Institute. Using their proprietary Trust Index™ survey, the core of what creates great a workplace is measured—key behaviors that drive trust in management, connection with colleagues, and loyalty to the company. To be eligible for the *Fortune* 100 Best Companies to Work For list, employers must have 1,000 or more employees in the U.S. and cannot be a government agency. *Fortune, "The 100 Best Companies to Work For," 2025*

Fannie Mae, headquartered in Washington, is among "Fortune's Best Workplaces for Parents." To pick the best companies, *Fortune* partnered with the Great Place to Work Institute. To be considered for the list, companies must be Great Place To Work-Certified and have at least 50 responses from parents in the US. The survey enables employees to share confidential quantitative and qualitative feedback about their organization's culture by responding to 60 statements on a 5-point scale and answering two open-ended questions. Collectively, these statements describe a great employee experience, defined by high levels of trust, respect, credibility, fairness, pride, and camaraderie. In addition, companies provide organizational data like size, location, industry, demographics, roles, and levels; and provide information about parental leave, adoption, flexible schedule, childcare and dependent health care benefits. *Fortune, "Best Workplaces for Parents," 2024*

Fannie Mae, headquartered in Washington, is among "Fortune's Best Workplaces for Women." To pick the best companies, *Fortune* partnered with the Great Place to Work Institute. To be considered for the list, companies must be Great Place To Work-Certified. Companies must also employ at least 50 women, at least 20% of their non-executive managers must be female, and at least one executive must be female. To determine the Best Workplaces for Women, Great Place To Work measured the differences in women's survey responses to those of their peers and assesses the impact of demographics and roles on the quality and consistency of women's experiences. Great Place To Work also analyzed the gender balance of each workplace, how it compared to each company's industry, and patterns in representation as women rise from front-line positions to the board of directors. *Fortune, "Best Workplaces for Women," 2024*

Fannie Mae; FINRA; U.S. Department of Veterans Affairs, Office of Information and Technology, headquartered in Washington, are among the "Best Places to Work in IT." To qualify, companies had to have a minimum of 100 total employees and five IT employees. The best places to work were selected based on DEI (diversity, equity, and inclusion) practices; IT turnover, promotions, and growth; IT retention and engagement programs; remote/hybrid working; benefits and perks (such as elder care and child care, flextime, and reimbursement for college tuition); and training and career development opportunities. *Computerworld, "Best Places to Work in IT," 2025*

PUBLIC SAFETY

Crime Rate

Area	Total Crime Rate	Violent Crime Rate				Property Crime Rate		
		Murder	Rape	Robbery	Aggrav. Assault	Burglary	Larceny-Theft	Motor Vehicle Theft
City	5,205.1	38.9	38.4	558.0	412.1	245.1	2,905.0	1,007.6
U.S.	2,290.9	5.7	38.0	66.5	264.1	250.7	1,347.2	318.7

Note: Figures are crimes per 100,000 population.
Source: FBI, Table 8, Offenses Known to Law Enforcement, by State by City, 2023

Hate Crimes

Area	Number of Quarters Reported	Number of Incidents per Bias Motivation					
		Race/Ethnicity/Ancestry	Religion	Sexual Orientation	Disability	Gender	Gender Identity
City	4	73	13	45	2	1	15
U.S.	4	5,900	2,699	2,077	187	92	492

Source: Federal Bureau of Investigation, Hate Crime Statistics 2023

Identity Theft Consumer Reports

Area	Reports	Reports per 100,000 Population	Rank[2]
MSA[1]	19,689	314	59
U.S.	1,135,291	339	-

Note: (1) Figures cover the Washington-Arlington-Alexandria, DC-VA-MD-WV Metropolitan Statistical Area; (2) Rank ranges from 1 to 401 where 1 indicates greatest number of identity theft reports per 100,000 population
Source: Federal Trade Commission, Consumer Sentinel Network Data Book 2024

Fraud and Other Consumer Reports

Area	Reports	Reports per 100,000 Population	Rank[2]
MSA[1]	109,978	1,756	27
U.S.	5,360,641	1,601	-

Note: (1) Figures cover the Washington-Arlington-Alexandria, DC-VA-MD-WV Metropolitan Statistical Area; (2) Rank ranges from 1 to 401 where 1 indicates greatest number of fraud and other consumer reports per 100,000 population
Source: Federal Trade Commission, Consumer Sentinel Network Data Book 2024

POLITICS

2024 Presidential Election Results

Area	Trump (Rep.)	Harris (Dem.)	Stein (Green)	Kennedy (Ind.)	Oliver (Lib.)	Other
District of Columbia	6.5	90.3	0.0	0.9	0.0	2.4
U.S.	49.7	48.2	0.6	0.5	0.4	0.6

Note: Results are percentages and may not add to 100% due to rounding
Source: Dave Leip's Atlas of U.S. Presidential Elections

SPORTS

Professional Sports Teams

Team Name	League	Year Established
D.C. United	Major League Soccer (MLS)	1996
Washington Capitals	National Hockey League (NHL)	1974
Washington Nationals	Major League Baseball (MLB)	2005
Washington Redskins	National Football League (NFL)	1937
Washington Wizards	National Basketball Association (NBA)	1973

Note: Includes teams located in the Washington-Arlington-Alexandria, DC-VA-MD-WV Metropolitan Statistical Area.
Source: Wikipedia, Major Professional Sports Teams of the United States and Canada, May 1, 2025

CLIMATE

Average and Extreme Temperatures

Temperature	Jan	Feb	Mar	Apr	May	Jun	Jul	Aug	Sep	Oct	Nov	Dec	Yr.
Extreme High (°F)	79	82	89	95	97	101	104	103	101	94	86	75	104
Average High (°F)	43	46	55	67	76	84	88	86	80	69	58	47	67
Average Temp. (°F)	36	38	46	57	66	75	79	78	71	60	49	39	58
Average Low (°F)	28	30	37	46	56	65	70	69	62	50	40	31	49
Extreme Low (°F)	-5	4	14	24	34	47	54	49	39	29	16	3	-5

Note: Figures cover the years 1945-1990
Source: National Climatic Data Center, International Station Meteorological Climate Summary, 9/96

Average Precipitation/Snowfall/Humidity

Precip./Humidity	Jan	Feb	Mar	Apr	May	Jun	Jul	Aug	Sep	Oct	Nov	Dec	Yr.
Avg. Precip. (in.)	2.8	2.6	3.3	2.9	4.0	3.4	4.1	4.2	3.3	2.9	3.0	3.1	39.5
Avg. Snowfall (in.)	6	6	2	Tr	0	0	0	0	0	Tr	1	3	18
Avg. Rel. Hum. 7am (%)	71	70	70	70	74	75	77	80	82	80	76	72	75
Avg. Rel. Hum. 4pm (%)	54	50	46	45	51	52	53	54	54	53	53	55	52

Note: Figures cover the years 1945-1990; Tr = Trace amounts (<0.05 in. of rain; <0.5 in. of snow)
Source: National Climatic Data Center, International Station Meteorological Climate Summary, 9/96

Weather Conditions

Temperature			Daytime Sky			Precipitation		
10°F & below	32°F & below	90°F & above	Clear	Partly cloudy	Cloudy	0.01 inch or more precip.	0.1 inch or more snow/ice	Thunderstorms
2	71	34	84	143	138	112	9	30

Note: Figures are average number of days per year and cover the years 1945-1990
Source: National Climatic Data Center, International Station Meteorological Climate Summary, 9/96

HAZARDOUS WASTE

Superfund Sites

The Washington, DC-MD metro division is home to five sites on the EPA's Superfund National Priorities List (NPL) or Superfund Alternative Approach (SAA) list: **Andrews Air Force Base** (Final NPL); **Beltsville Agricultural Research Center (USDA)** (Final NPL); **Brandywine Drmo** (Final NPL); **Indian Head Naval Surface Warfare Center** (Final NPL); **Washington Navy Yard** (Final NPL). The Superfund alternative approach uses the same investigation and cleanup process and standards that are used for sites listed on the National Priorities List. The SAA is an alternative to listing a site on the NPL; it is not an alternative to Superfund or the Superfund process. There are a total of 1,445 Superfund sites with a status of proposed or final on both lists in the United States. *U.S. Environmental Protection Agency, National Priorities List, May 1, 2025; U.S. Environmental Protection Agency, Superfund Alternative Approach Sites, May 1, 2025*

AIR QUALITY

Air Quality Trends: Ozone

	1990	1995	2000	2005	2010	2015	2020	2021	2022	2023
MSA[1]	0.075	0.083	0.073	0.069	0.069	0.067	0.057	0.066	0.061	0.069
U.S.	0.087	0.089	0.081	0.080	0.072	0.068	0.066	0.067	0.067	0.070

Note: (1) Data covers the Washington-Arlington-Alexandria, DC-VA-MD-WV Metropolitan Statistical Area. The values shown are the composite ozone concentration averages among trend sites based on the highest fourth daily maximum 8-hour concentration in parts per million. These trends are based on sites having an adequate record of monitoring data during the trend period. Data from exceptional events are included.
Source: U.S. Environmental Protection Agency, Air Quality Monitoring Information, "Air Quality Trends by City, 1990-2023"

Air Quality Index

Area	Percent of Days when Air Quality was...[2]					AQI Statistics[2]	
	Good	Moderate	Unhealthy for Sensitive Groups	Unhealthy	Very Unhealthy	Maximum	Median
MSA[1]	43.3	51.2	4.4	0.8	0.3	222	52

Note: (1) Data covers the Washington-Arlington-Alexandria, DC-VA-MD-WV Metropolitan Statistical Area; (2) Based on 365 days with AQI data in 2023. Air Quality Index (AQI) is an index for reporting daily air quality. EPA calculates the AQI for five major air pollutants regulated by the Clean Air Act: ground-level ozone, particle pollution (aka particulate matter), carbon monoxide, sulfur dioxide, and nitrogen dioxide. The AQI runs from 0 to 500. The higher the AQI value, the greater the level of air pollution and the greater the health concern. There are six AQI categories: "Good" AQI is between 0 and 50. Air quality is considered satisfactory; "Moderate" AQI is between 51 and 100. Air quality is acceptable; "Unhealthy for Sensitive Groups" When AQI values are between 101 and 150, members of sensitive groups may experience health effects; "Unhealthy" When AQI values are between 151 and 200 everyone may begin to experience health effects; "Very Unhealthy" AQI values between 201 and 300 trigger a health alert; "Hazardous" AQI values over 300 trigger warnings of emergency conditions (not shown).
Source: U.S. Environmental Protection Agency, Air Quality Index Report, 2023

Air Quality Index Pollutants

Area	Percent of Days when AQI Pollutant was...[2]					
	Carbon Monoxide	Nitrogen Dioxide	Ozone	Sulfur Dioxide	Particulate Matter 2.5	Particulate Matter 10
MSA[1]	0.0	1.4	44.1	(3)	54.2	0.3

Note: (1) Data covers the Washington-Arlington-Alexandria, DC-VA-MD-WV Metropolitan Statistical Area; (2) Based on 365 days with AQI data in 2023. The Air Quality Index (AQI) is an index for reporting daily air quality. EPA calculates the AQI for five major air pollutants regulated by the Clean Air Act: ground-level ozone, particle pollution (also known as particulate matter), carbon monoxide, sulfur dioxide, and nitrogen dioxide. The AQI runs from 0 to 500. The higher the AQI value, the greater the level of air pollution and the greater the health concern; (3) Sulfur dioxide is no longer included in this table because SO_2 concentrations tend to be very localized and not necessarily representative of broad geographical areas like counties and CBSAs.
Source: U.S. Environmental Protection Agency, Air Quality Index Report, 2023

Maximum Air Pollutant Concentrations: Particulate Matter, Ozone, CO and Lead

	Particulate Matter 10 (ug/m³)	Particulate Matter 2.5 Wtd AM (ug/m³)	Particulate Matter 2.5 24-Hr (ug/m³)	Ozone (ppm)	Carbon Monoxide (ppm)	Lead (ug/m³)
MSA[1] Level	142	9.7	33	0.076	2	n/a
NAAQS[2]	150	15	35	0.075	9	0.15
Met NAAQS[2]	Yes	Yes	Yes	No	Yes	n/a

Note: (1) Data covers the Washington-Arlington-Alexandria, DC-VA-MD-WV Metropolitan Statistical Area; Data from exceptional events are included; (2) National Ambient Air Quality Standards; ppm = parts per million; ug/m³ = micrograms per cubic meter; n/a not available.
Concentrations: Particulate Matter 10 (coarse particulate)—highest second maximum 24-hour concentration; Particulate Matter 2.5 Wtd AM (fine particulate)—highest weighted annual mean concentration; Particulate Matter 2.5 24-Hour (fine particulate)—highest 98th percentile 24-hour concentration; Ozone—highest fourth daily maximum 8-hour concentration; Carbon Monoxide—highest second maximum non-overlapping 8-hour concentration; Lead—maximum running 3-month average
Source: U.S. Environmental Protection Agency, Air Quality Monitoring Information, "Air Quality Statistics by City, 2023"

Maximum Air Pollutant Concentrations: Nitrogen Dioxide and Sulfur Dioxide

	Nitrogen Dioxide AM (ppb)	Nitrogen Dioxide 1-Hr (ppb)	Sulfur Dioxide AM (ppb)	Sulfur Dioxide 1-Hr (ppb)	Sulfur Dioxide 24-Hr (ppb)
MSA[1] Level	16	47	n/a	3	n/a
NAAQS[2]	53	100	30	75	140
Met NAAQS[2]	Yes	Yes	n/a	Yes	n/a

Note: (1) Data covers the Washington-Arlington-Alexandria, DC-VA-MD-WV Metropolitan Statistical Area; Data from exceptional events are included; (2) National Ambient Air Quality Standards; ppm = parts per million; ug/m³ = micrograms per cubic meter; n/a not available.
Concentrations: Nitrogen Dioxide AM—highest arithmetic mean concentration; Nitrogen Dioxide 1-Hr—highest 98th percentile 1-hour daily maximum concentration; Sulfur Dioxide AM—highest annual mean concentration; Sulfur Dioxide 1-Hr—highest 99th percentile 1-hour daily maximum concentration; Sulfur Dioxide 24-Hr—highest second maximum 24-hour concentration
Source: U.S. Environmental Protection Agency, Air Quality Monitoring Information, "Air Quality Statistics by City, 2023"

Wilmington, North Carolina

Background

Wilmington sits in southeastern North Carolina between the Cape Fear River and the Atlantic Ocean, about 15 miles from the coast. In pre-revolutionary times, Wilmington's importance as a port city was slow to be realized. Lack of good roads amid bogs and swamps hindered its role in the American Revolution. Its boggy landscape would later be a boon to the city's growing economy, providing it with natural resources for shipbuilding (tar, pitch, rosin, turpentine) for the navy. Improved navigational tools for sailing and invention of the steam-powered engine helped Wilmington become North Carolina's largest city by 1840, and a major port for U.S. exports of peanuts, rice, flax, and cotton.

The city was the site of one of the first rebellions in the United States' revolt against British rule, specifically The Stamp Act, which required that colonists only use paper produced and stamped in London. In 1765, about 500 Wilmington citizens burned an effigy of their stamp collector, Lord Bute, and forced him to resign.

By the time of the Civil War, Wilmington had become a major port for the eastern seaboard, but wartime brought Wilmington's normal export industry to an abrupt end. The city turned its attention to importing supplies for the Confederate armies and was considered the "lifeline of the Confederacy." By late 1864, Wilmington was the only port not captured by Union forces.

Following the Civil War and the Emancipation Proclamation, Wilmington became home to large numbers of freed slaves, and free people of color, who sought employment in the city, where about two thirds of the population was black. A large black middle-class grew, holding important positions in the community and local government. Wilmington produced the first black attorney, George Mabson (1871), and the nation's first black architect, Robert R. Taylor, who graduated from Massachusetts Institute of Technology.

In response, white supremacists overtook the legitimate, bi-racial government and instituted the first Jim Crow laws in North Carolina. In one year, 1,400 black residents left Wilmington. Those who stayed were disenfranchised, unable to vote when the new leadership adopted new literacy requirements.

In 1961, Wilmington became the permanent home of the USS *North Carolina*. Considered to be the greatest U. S. sea weapon in 1941, it is now a museum—and a major draw in Wilmington's vibrant tourism industry. Adding to its tourist appeal is the city's one-mile Riverwalk, and its location between beach and river, with several popular beach communities, including Ford Fisher, Wrightsville Beach, Carolina Beach, and Kure Beach.

Wilmington hosts many popular annual festivals, including the 3-day North Carolina Jazz Festival and the Azalea Festival.

In the late 70s, Wilmington began aggressive revitalization and restoration efforts, creating a revolving loan fund to draw in new small businesses. More recently, abandoned warehouses on the downtown's northern end have been demolished and the area has been reinvented as a center for pharmaceutical product development among other uses. Project Grace redevelopment project promises a new library in late 2025 and the Cape Fear Museum in 2026.

Cinespace Wilmington, one of the largest sound stage and facilities operators in the world, operates in the city, supporting Wilmington's prominent place in cinema. Recent filming activity in Wilmington include the film *Iron Man 3* and television series *The Summer I Turned Pretty* and *The Waterfront*.

Wilmington boasts a large historic district. Twenty locations within the city are on the National Register of Historic Places, including Market Street Mansion District, Moores Creek National Battlefield, and USS *North Carolina* Historic National Landmark.

Wilmington's sub-tropical climate creates very hot summers and occasional hurricanes, the most recent are Florence in 2018 and Dorian in 2019. Winters in the city are moderate, and spring and fall offer clear skies, less mugginess, and temperatures in the upper 60s low 70s.

Rankings

General Rankings

- In their annual survey, Livability.com looked at data for more than 2,000 mid-sized U.S. cities to assign a "Livability Score"for each. The top 100 scoring cities make up Livability's "Top 100 Best Places to Live in the U.S." in 2025. Wilmington was placed among the top 100 of the customizable list. Criteria: housing and economy; cost of living; environment; education; health care options; transportation; safety; and community amenities. *Livability.com, "Top 100 Best Places to Live in the U.S. in 2025" April 15, 2025*

Business/Finance Rankings

- The Wilmington metro area appeared on the Milken Institute "2025 Best Performing Cities" list. Rank: #13 out of 200 large metro areas (based on performance category). Criteria: job growth; wage growth; high-tech growth and impact; community resilience; housing affordability; household broadband access. *Milken Institute, "Best-Performing Cities 2025," January 14, 2025*

Culture/Performing Arts Rankings

- Wilmington was selected as one of the ten best small North American cities and towns for moviemakers. Of cities with smaller populations, the area ranked #3. As with the 2025 list for bigger cities, film community and culture were highly factored in. Other criteria: access to equipment and facilities; affordability; tax incentives; and quality of life. *MovieMaker Magazine, "Best Places to Live and Work as a Moviemaker, 2025," January 29, 2025*

Environmental Rankings

- Wilmington was highlighted as one of the cleanest metro areas for ozone air pollution in the U.S. during 2021 through 2023. The list represents cities with no monitored ozone air pollution in unhealthful ranges. *American Lung Association, "State of the Air 2025," April 23, 2025*

- Wilmington was highlighted as one of the top 25 cleanest metro areas for year-round particle pollution (Annual PM 2.5) in the U.S. during 2021 through 2023. The area ranked #11. *American Lung Association, "State of the Air 2025," April 23, 2025*

Real Estate Rankings

- The Wilmington metro area was identified as one of the 10 best condo markets in the U.S. in 2024. The area ranked #8 out of 63 markets. Criteria: year-over-year change of median sales price of existing apartment condo-coop homes between the 4th quarter of 2023 and the 4th quarter of 2024. *National Association of Realtors®, Median Sales Price of Existing Apartment Condo-Coops Homes for Metropolitan Areas, 4th Quarter 2024*

- Wilmington was ranked #145 out of 176 metro areas in terms of cost of housing in 2024 by the National Association of Home Builders (#1 = most affordable). Criteria: the portion of an average family's income necessary to pay the mortgage on a median-priced home. *National Association of Home Builders®, NAHB-Wells Fargo Cost of Housing Index, 4th Quarter 2024*

Sports/Recreation Rankings

- Wilmington was chosen as a bicycle friendly community by the League of American Bicyclists. A "Bicycle Friendly Community" welcomes cyclists by providing safe and supportive accommodation for cycling and encouraging people to bike for transportation and recreation. There are four award levels: Platinum; Gold; Silver; and Bronze. The community achieved an award level of Bronze. *League of American Bicyclists, "2024 Awards-New & Renewing Bicycle Friendly Communities List," January 28, 2025*

Business Environment

DEMOGRAPHICS

Population Growth

Area	1990 Census	2000 Census	2010 Census	2020 Census	2023 Estimate[2]	Population Growth 1990-2023 (%)
City	64,609	75,838	106,476	115,451	118,578	83.5
MSA[1]	200,124	274,532	362,315	285,905	440,578	120.2
U.S.	248,709,873	281,421,906	308,745,538	331,449,281	332,387,540	33.6

Note: (1) Figures cover the Wilmington, NC Metropolitan Statistical Area; (2) 2019-2023 5-year ACS population estimate
Source: U.S. Census Bureau, 1990 Census, 2000 Census, 2010 Census, 2020 Census, 2019-2023 American Community Survey 5-Year Estimates

Race

Area	White Alone[2] (%)	Black Alone[2] (%)	Asian Alone[2] (%)	AIAN[3] Alone[2] (%)	NHOPI[4] Alone[2] (%)	Other Race Alone[2] (%)	Two or More Races (%)
City	72.9	14.9	1.3	0.3	0.0	4.8	5.9
MSA[1]	78.8	10.4	1.0	0.3	0.0	3.5	5.9
U.S.	63.4	12.4	5.8	0.9	0.2	6.6	10.7

Note: (1) Figures cover the Wilmington, NC Metropolitan Statistical Area; (2) Alone is defined as not being in combination with one or more other races; (3) American Indian and Alaska Native; (4) Native Hawaiian and Other Pacific Islander
Source: U.S. Census Bureau, 2019-2023 American Community Survey 5-Year Estimates

Hispanic or Latino Origin

Area	Total (%)	Mexican (%)	Puerto Rican (%)	Cuban (%)	Other (%)
City	8.9	3.6	1.4	0.4	3.5
MSA[1]	7.1	3.4	0.9	0.3	2.5
U.S.	19.0	11.3	1.8	0.7	5.2

Note: Persons of Hispanic or Latino origin can be of any race; (1) Figures cover the Wilmington, NC Metropolitan Statistical Area
Source: U.S. Census Bureau, 2019-2023 American Community Survey 5-Year Estimates

Age

Area	Percent of Population									Median Age
	Under Age 5	Age 5–19	Age 20–34	Age 35–44	Age 45–54	Age 55–64	Age 65–74	Age 75–84	Age 85+	
City	4.3	17.0	25.9	11.7	10.8	12.6	10.2	5.3	2.3	37.5
MSA[1]	4.5	15.5	18.1	11.8	11.8	14.9	14.8	6.6	2.0	45.1
U.S.	5.7	19.1	20.2	13.1	12.3	12.8	10.0	4.9	1.9	38.7

Note: (1) Figures cover the Wilmington, NC Metropolitan Statistical Area
Source: U.S. Census Bureau, 2019-2023 American Community Survey 5-Year Estimates

Disability by Age

Area	All Ages	Under 18 Years Old	18 to 64 Years Old	65 Years and Over
City	12.9	3.7	10.4	31.1
MSA[1]	13.5	5.5	10.7	26.6
U.S.	13.0	4.7	10.7	32.9

Note: Figures show percent of the civilian noninstitutionalized population that reported having a disability. Disability status is determined from six types of difficulty: vision, hearing, cognitive, ambulatory, self-care, and independent living. For children under 5 years old, hearing and vision difficulty are used to determine disability status. For children between the ages of 5 and 14, disability status is determined from hearing, vision, cognitive, ambulatory, and self-care difficulties. For people aged 15 years and older, they are considered to have a disability if they have difficulty with any one of the six difficulty types; Note: (1) Figures cover the Wilmington, NC Metropolitan Statistical Area
Source: U.S. Census Bureau, 2019-2023 American Community Survey 5-Year Estimates

Ancestry

Area	German	Irish	English	American	Italian	Polish	French[2]	European	Scottish
City	10.8	10.8	13.8	4.7	5.6	2.2	2.1	2.3	2.7
MSA[1]	12.2	12.4	14.8	5.9	5.9	2.4	2.1	1.8	2.8
U.S.	12.6	9.4	9.1	5.5	4.9	2.6	2.0	1.6	1.6

Note: Figures are the percentage of the total population reporting a particular ancestry. The nine most commonly reported ancestries in the U.S. are shown. Figures include multiple ancestries (e.g. if a person reported being Irish and Italian, they were included in both columns); (1) Figures cover the Wilmington, NC Metropolitan Statistical Area; (2) Excludes Basque
Source: U.S. Census Bureau, 2019-2023 American Community Survey 5-Year Estimates

Foreign-born Population

| Area | Percent of Population Born in |||||||||
	Any Foreign Country	Asia	Mexico	Europe	Caribbean	Central America[2]	South America	Africa	Canada
City	5.7	1.2	1.5	1.0	0.2	0.8	0.7	0.2	0.1
MSA[1]	4.9	0.9	1.2	1.0	0.1	0.7	0.7	0.2	0.2
U.S.	13.9	4.3	3.3	1.4	1.4	1.2	1.2	0.8	0.2

Note: (1) Figures cover the Wilmington, NC Metropolitan Statistical Area; (2) Excludes Mexico.
Source: U.S. Census Bureau, 2019-2023 American Community Survey 5-Year Estimates

Household Size

| Area | Persons in Household (%) ||||||| Average Household Size |
	One	Two	Three	Four	Five	Six	Seven or More	
City	38.5	38.5	12.3	6.8	2.8	0.8	0.3	2.06
MSA[1]	29.9	42.0	14.0	8.9	3.6	1.2	0.4	2.26
U.S.	28.5	33.8	15.4	12.7	5.9	2.3	1.4	2.54

Note: (1) Figures cover the Wilmington, NC Metropolitan Statistical Area
Source: U.S. Census Bureau, 2019-2023 American Community Survey 5-Year Estimates

Household Relationships

Area	House-holder	Opposite-sex Spouse	Same-sex Spouse	Opposite-sex Unmarried Partner	Same-sex Unmarried Partner	Child[2]	Grand-child	Other Relatives	Non-relatives
City	45.7	14.9	0.3	3.4	0.3	21.2	1.5	3.0	5.9
MSA[1]	42.3	18.7	0.2	2.9	0.2	24.4	1.9	3.1	3.9
U.S.	38.3	17.5	0.2	2.5	0.2	28.3	2.4	4.8	3.4

Note: Figures are percent of the total population; (1) Figures cover the Wilmington, NC Metropolitan Statistical Area; (2) Includes biological, adopted, and stepchildren of the householder
Source: U.S. Census Bureau, 2020 Census

Gender

Area	Males	Females	Males per 100 Females
City	55,595	62,983	88.3
MSA[1]	212,689	227,889	93.3
U.S.	164,545,087	167,842,453	98.0

Note: (1) Figures cover the Wilmington, NC Metropolitan Statistical Area
Source: U.S. Census Bureau, 2019-2023 American Community Survey 5-Year Estimates

Marital Status

Area	Never Married	Now Married[2]	Separated	Widowed	Divorced
City	42.2	38.8	2.3	5.3	11.4
MSA[1]	28.5	52.5	1.9	6.2	10.9
U.S.	34.1	47.9	1.7	5.6	10.7

Note: Figures are percentages and cover the population 15 years of age and older; (1) Figures cover the Wilmington, NC Metropolitan Statistical Area; (2) Excludes separated
Source: U.S. Census Bureau, 2019-2023 American Community Survey 5-Year Estimates

Religious Groups by Family

Area	Catholic	Baptist	Methodist	LDS[2]	Pentecostal	Lutheran	Islam	Adventist	Other
MSA[1]	13.2	9.9	8.1	1.0	1.0	0.7	0.7	1.4	12.6
U.S.	18.7	7.3	3.0	2.0	1.8	1.7	1.3	1.3	11.6

Note: Figures are the number of adherents as a percentage of the total population and cover the eight largest religious groups in the U.S; (1) Figures cover the Wilmington, NC Metropolitan Statistical Area; (2) Church of Jesus Christ of Latter-day Saints
Sources: 2020 U.S. Religion Census, Association of Statisticians of American Religious Bodies; The Association of Religion Data Archives (ARDA)

Religious Groups by Tradition

Area	Catholic	Evangelical Protestant	Mainline Protestant	Black Protestant	Islam	Judaism	Hinduism	Orthodox	Buddhism
MSA[1]	13.2	17.9	9.3	4.6	0.7	0.3	0.1	0.3	n/a
U.S.	18.7	16.5	5.2	2.3	1.3	0.6	0.4	0.4	0.3

Note: Figures are the number of adherents as a percentage of the total population; (1) Figures cover the Wilmington, NC Metropolitan Statistical Area
Sources: 2020 U.S. Religion Census, Association of Statisticians of American Religious Bodies; The Association of Religion Data Archives (ARDA)

ECONOMY

Real Gross Domestic Product (GDP)

Area	2017	2018	2019	2020	2021	2022	2023	Rank[3]
MSA[1]	14.1	14.5	15.1	15.1	16.5	17.1	17.7	160
U.S.[2]	17,619.1	18,160.7	18,642.5	18,238.9	19,387.6	19,896.6	20,436.3	—

Note: Figures are in billions of chained 2017 dollars; (1) Figures cover the Wilmington, NC Metropolitan Statistical Area; (2) Figures cover real GDP within metropolitan areas; (3) Rank is based on 2023 data and ranges from 1 to 384
Source: U.S. Bureau of Economic Analysis

Economic Growth

Area	2014	2015	2016	2017	2018	2019	2020	2021	2022	2023
MSA[1]	4.1	1.5	5.1	0.6	3.0	4.2	0.1	9.2	3.6	3.5
U.S.[2]	2.6	3.2	2.0	2.7	3.1	2.7	-2.2	6.3	2.6	2.7

Note: Figures are real gross domestic product growth rates and represent percent change from preceding period; (1) Figures cover the Wilmington, NC Metropolitan Statistical Area; (2) Figures are the average growth rates within metropolitan areas
Source: U.S. Bureau of Economic Analysis

Metropolitan Area Exports

Area	2018	2019	2020	2021	2022	2023	Rank[2]
MSA[1]	634.4	526.4	553.6	497.8	593.6	671.5	206
U.S.	1,664,056.1	1,645,173.7	1,431,406.6	1,753,941.4	2,062,937.4	2,019,160.5	—

Note: Figures are in millions of dollars; (1) Figures cover the Wilmington, NC Metropolitan Statistical Area; (2) Rank is based on 2023 data and ranges from 1 to 386
Source: U.S. Department of Commerce, International Trade Administration, Office of Trade and Economic Analysis, Industry and Analysis, Exports by Metropolitan Area, data extracted April 2, 2025

Building Permits

Area	Single-Family			Multi-Family			Total		
	2023	2024	Pct. Chg.	2023	2024	Pct. Chg.	2023	2024	Pct. Chg.
City	n/a	n/a	n/a	n/a	n/a	n/a	n/a	n/a	n/a
MSA[1]	2,228	7,263	226.0	1,737	2,355	35.6	3,965	9,618	142.6
U.S.	920,000	981,900	6.7	591,100	496,100	-16.1	1,511,100	1,478,000	-2.2

Note: (1) Figures cover the Wilmington, NC Metropolitan Statistical Area; Figures represent new, privately-owned housing units authorized (unadjusted data)
Source: U.S. Census Bureau, Building Permits Survey (BPS), 2023, 2024

Bankruptcy Filings

Area	Business Filings			Nonbusiness Filings		
	2023	2024	% Chg.	2023	2024	% Chg.
New Hanover County	29	19	-34.5	145	183	26.2
U.S.	18,926	23,107	22.1	434,064	494,201	13.9

Note: Business filings include Chapter 7, Chapter 9, Chapter 11, Chapter 12, Chapter 13, Chapter 15, and Section 304; Nonbusiness filings include Chapter 7, Chapter 11, and Chapter 13
Source: Administrative Office of the U.S. Courts, Business and Nonbusiness Bankruptcy, County Cases Commenced by Chapter of the Bankruptcy Code, During the 12-Month Period Ending December 31, 2023 and Business and Nonbusiness Bankruptcy, County Cases Commenced by Chapter of the Bankruptcy Code, During the 12-Month Period Ending December 31, 2024

Housing Vacancy Rates

Area	Gross Vacancy Rate[3] (%)			Year-Round Vacancy Rate[4] (%)			Rental Vacancy Rate[5] (%)			Homeowner Vacancy Rate[6] (%)		
	2022	2023	2024	2022	2023	2024	2022	2023	2024	2022	2023	2024
MSA[1]	n/a	n/a	n/a	n/a	n/a	n/a	n/a	n/a	n/a	n/a	n/a	n/a
U.S.[2]	9.1	9.0	9.1	7.5	7.5	7.6	5.7	6.5	6.8	0.8	0.8	1.0

Note: (1) Figures cover the Wilmington, NC Metropolitan Statistical Area; (2) Figures cover the 75 largest Metropolitan Statistical Areas; (3) The percentage of the total housing inventory that is vacant; (4) The percentage of the housing inventory (excluding seasonal units) that is year-round vacant; (5) The percentage of rental inventory that is vacant for rent; (6) The percentage of homeowner inventory that is vacant for sale; n/a not available
Source: U.S. Census Bureau, Housing Vacancies and Homeownership Annual Statistics: 2022, 2023, 2024

INCOME

Income

Area	Per Capita ($)	Median Household ($)	Average Household ($)
City	46,062	63,900	98,401
MSA[1]	44,459	73,687	100,847
U.S.	43,289	78,538	110,491

Note: (1) Figures cover the Wilmington, NC Metropolitan Statistical Area
Source: U.S. Census Bureau, 2019-2023 American Community Survey 5-Year Estimates

Household Income Distribution

Area	Percent of Households Earning							
	Under $15,000	$15,000 -$24,999	$25,000 -$34,999	$35,000 -$49,999	$50,000 -$74,999	$75,000 -$99,999	$100,000 -$149,999	$150,000 and up
City	11.3	6.8	8.3	13.0	17.6	11.9	14.2	16.8
MSA[1]	8.2	6.4	6.8	11.5	18.0	13.4	17.6	18.0
U.S.	8.5	6.6	6.8	10.4	15.7	12.7	17.4	21.9

Note: (1) Figures cover the Wilmington, NC Metropolitan Statistical Area
Source: U.S. Census Bureau, 2019-2023 American Community Survey 5-Year Estimates

Poverty Rate

Area	All Ages	Under 18 Years Old	18 to 64 Years Old	65 Years and Over
City	16.3	18.1	17.3	11.0
MSA[1]	11.1	13.9	11.9	7.0
U.S.	12.4	16.3	11.6	10.4

Note: Figures are percentage of people whose income during the past 12 months was below the poverty level; (1) Figures cover the Wilmington, NC Metropolitan Statistical Area
Source: U.S. Census Bureau, 2019-2023 American Community Survey 5-Year Estimates

EMPLOYMENT

Labor Force and Employment

Area	Civilian Labor Force			Workers Employed		
	Dec. 2023	Dec. 2024	% Chg.	Dec. 2023	Dec. 2024	% Chg.
City	69,827	69,943	0.2	67,604	67,846	0.4
MSA[1]	222,997	222,642	-0.2	215,630	215,604	0.0
U.S.	166,661,000	167,746,000	0.7	160,754,000	161,294,000	0.3

Note: Data is not seasonally adjusted and covers workers 16 years of age and older; (1) Figures cover the Wilmington, NC Metropolitan Statistical Area
Source: Bureau of Labor Statistics, Local Area Unemployment Statistics

Unemployment Rate

Area	2024											
	Jan.	Feb.	Mar.	Apr.	May	Jun.	Jul.	Aug.	Sep.	Oct.	Nov.	Dec.
City	3.6	3.5	3.3	2.8	3.1	3.5	3.7	3.5	2.9	2.9	3.2	3.0
MSA[1]	3.8	3.8	3.4	3.0	3.3	3.6	3.7	3.7	3.1	3.2	3.4	3.2
U.S.	4.1	4.2	3.9	3.5	3.7	4.3	4.5	4.4	3.9	3.9	4.0	3.8

Note: Data is not seasonally adjusted and covers workers 16 years of age and older; (1) Figures cover the Wilmington, NC Metropolitan Statistical Area
Source: Bureau of Labor Statistics, Local Area Unemployment Statistics

Average Wages

Occupation	$/Hr.	Occupation	$/Hr.
Accountants and Auditors	37.67	Maintenance and Repair Workers	22.36
Automotive Mechanics	23.96	Marketing Managers	72.18
Bookkeepers	22.76	Network and Computer Systems Admin.	42.11
Carpenters	24.06	Nurses, Licensed Practical	29.97
Cashiers	13.23	Nurses, Registered	39.17
Computer Programmers	37.74	Nursing Assistants	18.20
Computer Systems Analysts	46.73	Office Clerks, General	18.96
Computer User Support Specialists	28.36	Physical Therapists	41.99
Construction Laborers	21.81	Physicians	129.60
Cooks, Restaurant	16.50	Plumbers, Pipefitters and Steamfitters	25.08
Customer Service Representatives	19.57	Police and Sheriff's Patrol Officers	26.40
Dentists	104.98	Postal Service Mail Carriers	29.33
Electricians	26.12	Real Estate Sales Agents	24.73
Engineers, Electrical	54.21	Retail Salespersons	16.08
Fast Food and Counter Workers	13.68	Sales Representatives, Technical/Scientific	51.06
Financial Managers	73.03	Secretaries, Exc. Legal/Medical/Executive	21.11
First-Line Supervisors of Office Workers	29.78	Security Guards	21.00
General and Operations Managers	55.43	Surgeons	n/a
Hairdressers/Cosmetologists	19.37	Teacher Assistants, Exc. Postsecondary[1]	14.70
Home Health and Personal Care Aides	14.82	Teachers, Secondary School, Exc. Sp. Ed.[1]	25.61
Janitors and Cleaners	16.04	Telemarketers	16.58
Landscaping/Groundskeeping Workers	17.61	Truck Drivers, Heavy/Tractor-Trailer	24.77
Lawyers	60.44	Truck Drivers, Light/Delivery Services	19.92
Maids and Housekeeping Cleaners	14.71	Waiters and Waitresses	14.23

Note: Wage data covers the Wilmington, NC Metropolitan Statistical Area; (1) Hourly wages were calculated from annual wage data based on a 40 hour work week
Source: Bureau of Labor Statistics, Metro Area Occupational Employment & Wage Estimates, May 2024

Employment by Industry

Sector	MSA[1] Number of Employees	MSA[1] Percent of Total	U.S. Percent of Total
Construction, Mining, and Logging	14,100	7.3	5.5
Financial Activities	9,400	4.9	5.8
Government	24,800	12.9	14.9
Information	3,000	1.6	1.9
Leisure and Hospitality	29,900	15.5	10.4
Manufacturing	8,600	4.5	8.0
Other Services	8,800	4.6	3.7
Private Education and Health Services	32,500	16.9	16.9
Professional and Business Services	23,500	12.2	14.2
Retail Trade	25,600	13.3	10.0
Transportation, Warehousing, and Utilities	6,900	3.6	4.8
Wholesale Trade	5,400	2.8	3.9

Note: Figures are non-farm employment as of December 2024. Figures are not seasonally adjusted and include workers 16 years of age and older; (1) Figures cover the Wilmington, NC Metropolitan Statistical Area
Source: Bureau of Labor Statistics, Current Employment Statistics, Employment, Hours, and Earnings

Employment by Occupation

Occupation Classification	City (%)	MSA[1] (%)	U.S. (%)
Management, Business, Science, and Arts	46.8	42.5	42.0
Natural Resources, Construction, and Maintenance	7.2	9.8	8.6
Production, Transportation, and Material Moving	8.1	9.6	13.0
Sales and Office	19.0	20.9	19.9
Service	18.8	17.2	16.5

Note: Figures cover employed civilians 16 years of age and older; (1) Figures cover the Wilmington, NC Metropolitan Statistical Area
Source: U.S. Census Bureau, 2019-2023 American Community Survey 5-Year Estimates

Occupations with Greatest Projected Employment Growth: 2022 – 2032

Occupation[1]	2022 Employment	2032 Projected Employment	Numeric Employment Change	Percent Employment Change
Software Developers	57,190	75,660	18,470	32.3
Cooks, Restaurant	47,710	66,050	18,340	38.4
Registered Nurses	106,190	123,650	17,460	16.4
Home Health and Personal Care Aides	62,750	77,390	14,640	23.3
Stockers and Order Fillers	92,790	105,710	12,920	13.9
Laborers and Freight, Stock, and Material Movers, Hand	121,680	133,850	12,170	10.0
General and Operations Managers	94,010	105,400	11,390	12.1
Fast Food and Counter Workers	65,320	75,130	9,810	15.0
First-Line Supervisors of Food Preparation and Serving Workers	41,690	49,690	8,000	19.2
Waiters and Waitresses	71,300	79,060	7,760	10.9

Note: Projections cover North Carolina; (1) Sorted by numeric employment change
Source: www.projectionscentral.org, State Occupational Projections, 2022–2032 Long-Term Projections

Fastest-Growing Occupations: 2022 – 2032

Occupation[1]	2022 Employment	2032 Projected Employment	Numeric Employment Change	Percent Employment Change
Nurse Practitioners	8,200	12,750	4,550	55.5
Solar Photovoltaic Installers	950	1,400	450	47.4
Statisticians	1,580	2,270	690	43.7
Data Scientists	5,430	7,720	2,290	42.2
Medical and Health Services Managers	12,880	17,860	4,980	38.7
Cooks, Restaurant	47,710	66,050	18,340	38.4
Physician Assistants	7,440	10,170	2,730	36.7
Information Security Analysts (SOC 2018)	5,920	8,070	2,150	36.3
Occupational Therapy Assistants	1,310	1,780	470	35.9
Wind Turbine Service Technicians	140	190	50	35.7

Note: Projections cover North Carolina; (1) Sorted by percent employment change and excludes occupations with numeric employment change less than 50
Source: www.projectionscentral.org, State Occupational Projections, 2022–2032 Long-Term Projections

Wilmington, North Carolina

CITY FINANCES

City Government Finances

Component	2022 ($000)	2022 ($ per capita)
Total Revenues	201,965	1,618
Total Expenditures	193,194	1,548
Debt Outstanding	262,035	2,100

Source: U.S. Census Bureau, State & Local Government Finances 2022

City Government Revenue by Source

Source	2022 ($000)	2022 ($ per capita)	2022 (%)
General Revenue			
From Federal Government	11,110	89	5.5
From State Government	17,055	137	8.4
From Local Governments	671	5	0.3
Taxes			
Property	82,974	665	41.1
Sales and Gross Receipts	44,845	359	22.2
Personal Income	0	0	0.0
Corporate Income	0	0	0.0
Motor Vehicle License	886	7	0.4
Other Taxes	307	2	0.2
Current Charges	37,085	297	18.4
Liquor Store	0	0	0.0
Utility	0	0	0.0

Source: U.S. Census Bureau, State & Local Government Finances 2022

City Government Expenditures by Function

Function	2022 ($000)	2022 ($ per capita)	2022 (%)
General Direct Expenditures			
Air Transportation	0	0	0.0
Corrections	0	0	0.0
Education	0	0	0.0
Employment Security Administration	0	0	0.0
Financial Administration	3,114	25	1.6
Fire Protection	19,955	159	10.3
General Public Buildings	17,027	136	8.8
Governmental Administration, Other	9,052	72	4.7
Health	0	0	0.0
Highways	12,009	96	6.2
Hospitals	0	0	0.0
Housing and Community Development	9,693	77	5.0
Interest on General Debt	10,009	80	5.2
Judicial and Legal	1,310	10	0.7
Libraries	0	0	0.0
Parking	4,091	32	2.1
Parks and Recreation	16,406	131	8.5
Police Protection	37,537	300	19.4
Public Welfare	1,046	8	0.5
Sewerage	9,819	78	5.1
Solid Waste Management	12,823	102	6.6
Veterans' Services	0	0	0.0
Liquor Store	0	0	0.0
Utility	3,785	30	2.0

Source: U.S. Census Bureau, State & Local Government Finances 2022

TAXES

State Corporate Income Tax Rates

State	Tax Rate (%)	Income Brackets ($)	Num. of Brackets	Financial Institution Tax Rate (%)[a]	Federal Income Tax Ded.
North Carolina	2.5	Flat rate	1	2.5	No

Note: Tax rates for tax year 2024; (a) Rates listed are the corporate income tax rate applied to financial institutions or excise taxes based on income. Some states have other taxes based upon the value of deposits or shares.
Source: Federation of Tax Administrators, State Corporate Income Tax Rates, January 1, 2025

State Individual Income Tax Rates

State	Tax Rate (%)	Income Brackets ($)	Personal Exemptions ($)			Standard Ded. ($)	
			Single	Married	Depend.	Single	Married
North Carolina	4.5	Flat rate	None	None	None	12,750	25,500

Note: Tax rates for tax year 2024; Local- and county-level taxes are not included; Federal income tax is not deductible on state income tax returns
Source: Federation of Tax Administrators, State Individual Income Tax Rates, January 1, 2025

Various State Sales and Excise Tax Rates

State	State Sales Tax (%)	Gasoline[1] ($/gal.)	Cigarette[2] ($/pack)	Spirits[3] ($/gal.)	Wine[4] ($/gal.)	Beer[5] ($/gal.)	Recreational Marijuana (%)
North Carolina	4.75	0.41	0.45	18.23	1.00	0.62	Not legal

Note: All tax rates as of January 1, 2025; (1) The American Petroleum Institute has developed a methodology for determining the average tax rate on a gallon of fuel. Rates may include any of the following: excise taxes, environmental fees, storage tank fees, other fees or taxes, general sales tax, and local taxes; (2) The federal excise tax of $1.0066 per pack and local taxes are not included; (3) Rates are those applicable to off-premise sales of 40% alcohol by volume (a.b.v.) distilled spirits in 750ml containers. Local excise taxes are excluded; (4) Rates are those applicable to off-premise sales of 11% a.b.v. non-carbonated wine in 750ml containers; (5) Rates are those applicable to off-premise sales of 4.7% a.b.v. beer in 12 ounce containers.
Source: Tax Foundation, 2025 Facts & Figures: How Does Your State Compare?

State Tax Competitiveness Index

State	Overall Rank	Corporate Tax Rank	Individual Income Tax Rank	Sales Tax Rank	Property Tax Rank	Unemployment Insurance Tax Rank
North Carolina	12	3	21	16	20	7

Note: The Tax Foundation's State Tax Competitiveness Index enables policymakers, taxpayers, and business leaders to gauge how their states' tax systems compare. A rank of 1 is best, 50 is worst. Rankings do not average to the total. States without a tax rank equally as 1. DC's scores and rankings do not affect other states. The report shows tax systems as of July 1, 2024 (the beginning of Fiscal Year 2025).
Source: Tax Foundation, State Tax Competitiveness Index 2025

TRANSPORTATION

Means of Transportation to Work

Area	Car/Truck/Van		Public Transportation			Bicycle	Walked	Other Means	Worked at Home
	Drove Alone	Car-pooled	Bus	Subway	Railroad				
City	70.9	7.0	0.4	0.0	0.0	0.8	2.2	1.0	17.7
MSA[1]	73.9	7.8	0.2	0.0	0.0	0.3	1.2	1.1	15.5
U.S.	70.2	8.5	1.7	1.3	0.4	0.4	2.4	1.6	13.5

Note: Figures are percentages and cover workers 16 years of age and older; (1) Figures cover the Wilmington, NC Metropolitan Statistical Area
Source: U.S. Census Bureau, 2019-2023 American Community Survey 5-Year Estimates

Travel Time to Work

Area	Less Than 10 Minutes	10 to 19 Minutes	20 to 29 Minutes	30 to 44 Minutes	45 to 59 Minutes	60 to 89 Minutes	90 Minutes or More
City	16.7	46.7	20.7	10.2	2.9	1.2	1.6
MSA[1]	12.4	35.0	23.4	18.2	5.8	3.0	2.3
U.S.	12.6	28.6	21.2	20.8	8.1	6.0	2.8

Note: Note: Figures are percentages and include workers 16 years old and over; (1) Figures cover the Wilmington, NC Metropolitan Statistical Area
Source: U.S. Census Bureau, 2019-2023 American Community Survey 5-Year Estimates

Key Congestion Measures

Measure	2000	2010	2015	2020	2022
Annual Hours of Delay, Total (000)	n/a	n/a	6,466	3,223	6,843
Annual Hours of Delay, Per Auto Commuter	n/a	n/a	27	13	28
Annual Congestion Cost, Per Auto Commuter ($)	n/a	n/a	603	303	613

Note: n/a not available
Source: Texas A&M Transportation Institute, 2023 Urban Mobility Report

Freeway Travel Time Index

Measure	1985	1990	1995	2000	2005	2010	2015	2020	2022
Urban Area Index[1]	n/a	n/a	n/a	n/a	n/a	n/a	1.13	1.07	1.13
Urban Area Rank[1,2]	n/a	n/a	n/a	n/a	n/a	n/a	n/a	n/a	n/a

Note: Freeway Travel Time Index—the ratio of travel time in the peak period to the travel time at free-flow conditions. For example, a value of 1.30 indicates a 20-minute free-flow trip takes 26 minutes in the peak (20 minutes x 1.30 = 26 minutes); (1) Covers the Wilmington NC urban area; (2) Rank is based on 101 larger urban areas (#1 = highest travel time index); n/a not available
Source: Texas A&M Transportation Institute, 2023 Urban Mobility Report

Public Transportation

Agency Name / Mode of Transportation	Vehicles Operated in Maximum Service[1]	Annual Unlinked Passenger Trips[2] (in thous.)	Annual Passenger Miles[3] (in thous.)
Cape Fear Public Transportation Authority (Wave Transit)			
Bus (purchased transportation)	25	668.5	1,883.7
Demand Response (directly operated)	18	52.8	268.7

Note: (1) Number of revenue vehicles operated by the given mode and type of service to meet the annual maximum service requirement. This is the revenue vehicle count during the peak season of the year; on the week and day that maximum service is provided. Vehicles operated in maximum service (VOMS) exclude atypical days and one-time special events; (2) Number of passengers who boarded public transportation vehicles. Passengers are counted each time they board a vehicle no matter how many vehicles they use to travel from their origin to their destination. (3) Sum of the distances ridden by all passengers during the entire fiscal year.
Source: Federal Transit Administration, National Transit Database, 2023

Air Transportation

Airport Name and Code / Type of Service	Passenger Airlines[1]	Passenger Enplanements	Freight Carriers[2]	Freight (lbs)
Wilmington International Airport (ILM)				
Domestic service (U.S. carriers only)	15	736,506	6	1,332,283
International service (U.S. carriers only)	0	0	0	0

Note: (1) Includes all U.S.-based major, minor and commuter airlines that carried at least one passenger during the year; (2) Includes all U.S.-based airlines and freight carriers that transported at least one pound of freight during the year.
Source: Bureau of Transportation Statistics, The Intermodal Transportation Database, Air Carriers: T-100 Domestic Market (U.S. carriers only), 2024; Bureau of Transportation Statistics, The Intermodal Transportation Database, Air Carriers: T-100 International Market (U.S. carriers only), 2024

BUSINESSES

Major Business Headquarters

Company Name	Industry	Rankings	
		Fortune[1]	Forbes[2]
No companies listed	-	-	-

Note: (1) Companies that produce a 10-K are ranked 1 to 500 based on 2023 revenue; (2) All private companies with at least $2 billion in annual revenue through the end of their most current fiscal year are ranked 1 to 275; companies listed are headquartered in the city; dashes indicate no ranking
Source: Fortune, "Fortune 500," 2024; Forbes, "America's Largest Private Companies," 2024

Living Environment

COST OF LIVING

Cost of Living Index

Composite Index	Groceries	Housing	Utilities	Transportation	Health Care	Misc. Goods/Services
n/a	n/a	n/a	n/a	n/a	n/a	n/a

Note: The Cost of Living Index measures regional differences in the cost of consumer goods and services, excluding taxes and non-consumer expenditures, for professional and managerial households in the top income quintile. It is based on more than 50,000 prices covering almost 60 different items for which prices are collected three times a year by chambers of commerce, economic development organizations or university applied economic centers in each participating urban area. The numbers shown should be read as a percentage above or below the national average of 100. For example, a value of 115.4 in the groceries column indicates that grocery prices are 15.4% higher than the national average. Small differences in the index numbers should not be interpreted as significant; n/a not available.
Source: The Council for Community and Economic Research, Cost of Living Index, 2024

Grocery Prices

Area[1]	T-Bone Steak ($/pound)	Frying Chicken ($/pound)	Whole Milk ($/half gal.)	Eggs ($/dozen)	Orange Juice ($/64 oz.)	Coffee ($/11.5 oz.)
City[2]	n/a	n/a	n/a	n/a	n/a	n/a
Avg.	15.42	1.55	4.69	3.25	4.41	5.46
Min.	14.50	1.16	4.43	2.75	4.00	4.85
Max.	17.56	2.89	5.49	4.78	5.54	7.89

Note: (1) Values for the local area are compared with the average, minimum and maximum values for all 276 areas in the Cost of Living Index; (2) Figures cover the Wilmington NC urban area; n/a not available; **T-Bone Steak** (price per pound); **Frying Chicken** (price per pound, whole fryer); **Whole Milk** (half gallon carton); **Eggs** (price per dozen, Grade A, large); **Orange Juice** (64 oz. Tropicana or Florida Natural); **Coffee** (11.5 oz. can, vacuum-packed, Maxwell House, Hills Bros, or Folgers).
Source: The Council for Community and Economic Research, Cost of Living Index, 2024

Housing and Utility Costs

Area[1]	New Home Price ($)	Apartment Rent ($/month)	All Electric ($/month)	Part Electric ($/month)	Other Energy ($/month)	Telephone ($/month)
City[2]	n/a	n/a	n/a	n/a	n/a	n/a
Avg.	515,975	1,550	210.99	123.07	82.07	194.99
Min.	265,375	692	104.33	53.68	36.26	179.42
Max.	2,775,821	5,719	529.02	397.28	361.63	223.33

Note: (1) Values for the local area are compared with the average, minimum and maximum values for all 276 areas in the Cost of Living Index; (2) Figures cover the Wilmington NC urban area; n/a not available; **New Home Price** (2,400 sf living area, 8,000 sf lot, in urban area with full utilities); **Apartment Rent** (950 sf 2 bedroom/1.5 or 2 bath, unfurnished, excluding all utilities except water); **All Electric** (average monthly cost for an all-electric home); **Part Electric** (average monthly cost for a part-electric home); **Other Energy** (average monthly cost for natural gas, fuel oil, coal, wood, and any other forms of energy except electricity); **Telephone** (price includes the base monthly rate plus taxes and fees for three lines of mobile phone service).
Source: The Council for Community and Economic Research, Cost of Living Index, 2024

Health Care, Transportation, and Other Costs

Area[1]	Doctor ($/visit)	Dentist ($/visit)	Optometrist ($/visit)	Gasoline ($/gallon)	Beauty Salon ($/visit)	Men's Shirt ($)
City[2]	n/a	n/a	n/a	n/a	n/a	n/a
Avg.	143.77	117.51	129.23	3.32	48.57	38.14
Min.	36.74	58.67	67.33	2.80	24.00	13.41
Max.	270.44	216.82	307.33	5.28	94.00	63.89

Note: (1) Values for the local area are compared with the average, minimum and maximum values for all 276 areas in the Cost of Living Index; (2) Figures cover the Wilmington NC urban area; n/a not available; **Doctor** (general practitioners routine exam of an established patient); **Dentist** (adult teeth cleaning and periodic oral examination); **Optometrist** (full vision eye exam for established adult patient); **Gasoline** (one gallon regular unleaded, national brand, including all taxes, cash price at self-service pump if available); **Beauty Salon** (woman's shampoo, trim, and blow-dry); **Men's Shirt** (cotton/polyester dress shirt, pinpoint weave, long sleeves).
Source: The Council for Community and Economic Research, Cost of Living Index, 2024

HOUSING

Homeownership Rate

Area	2017 (%)	2018 (%)	2019 (%)	2020 (%)	2021 (%)	2022 (%)	2023 (%)	2024 (%)
MSA[1]	n/a	n/a	n/a	n/a	n/a	n/a	n/a	n/a
U.S.	63.9	64.4	64.6	66.6	65.5	65.8	65.9	65.6

Note: (1) Figures cover the Wilmington, NC Metropolitan Statistical Area; n/a not available
Source: U.S. Census Bureau, Housing Vacancies and Homeownership Annual Statistics: 2017-2024

House Price Index (HPI)

Area	National Ranking[2]	Quarterly Change (%)	One-Year Change (%)	Five-Year Change (%)	Since 1991Q1 (%)
MSA[1]	137	0.32	4.98	74.07	421.24
U.S.[3]	–	1.43	4.51	57.13	327.82

Note: The HPI is a weighted repeat sales index. It measures average price changes in repeat sales or refinancings on the same properties. This information is obtained by reviewing repeat mortgage transactions on single-family properties whose mortgages have been purchased or securitized by Fannie Mae or Freddie Mac since January 1975; (1) Figures cover the Wilmington, NC Metropolitan Statistical Area; (2) Rankings are based on annual percentage change for all metro areas containing at least 15,000 transactions over the last 10 years and ranges from 1 to 241; (3) figures based on a weighted average of Census Division estimates using a seasonally adjusted, purchase-only index; all figures are for the period ending December 31, 2024
Source: Federal Housing Finance Agency, Change in FHFA Metropolitan Area House Price Indexes, All Transactions Index, 2024Q4

Home Value

Area	Under $100,000	$100,000 -$199,999	$200,000 -$299,999	$300,000 -$399,999	$400,000 -$499,999	$500,000 -$999,999	$1,000,000 or more	Median ($)
City	3.3	13.2	23.0	21.1	14.2	19.1	6.2	350,300
MSA[1]	7.5	14.3	22.8	19.4	13.3	19.0	3.8	328,000
U.S.	12.1	17.8	19.5	14.4	10.5	19.1	6.5	303,400

Note: Figures are percentages except for median and cover owner-occupied housing units; (1) Figures cover the Wilmington, NC Metropolitan Statistical Area
Source: U.S. Census Bureau, 2019-2023 American Community Survey 5-Year Estimates

Year Housing Structure Built

Area	2020 or Later	2010 -2019	2000 -2009	1990 -1999	1980 -1989	1970 -1979	1960 -1969	1950 -1959	1940 -1949	Before 1940	Median Year
City	2.3	13.1	14.9	16.2	15.2	11.1	6.2	6.3	5.7	9.1	1988
MSA[1]	2.7	17.1	23.5	18.8	14.4	9.9	4.4	3.2	2.4	3.6	1996
U.S.	1.2	8.9	13.6	12.8	13.0	14.4	10.0	9.7	4.5	11.9	1980

Note: Figures are percentages except for Median Year; Note: (1) Figures cover the Wilmington, NC Metropolitan Statistical Area
Source: U.S. Census Bureau, 2019-2023 American Community Survey 5-Year Estimates

Gross Monthly Rent

Area	Under $500	$500 -$999	$1,000 -$1,499	$1,500 -$1,999	$2,000 -$2,499	$2,500 -$2,999	$3,000 and up	Median ($)
City	6.3	17.3	40.7	25.1	7.1	1.9	1.5	1,311
MSA[1]	5.1	19.5	40.4	23.1	7.7	2.0	2.3	1,313
U.S.	6.5	22.3	29.5	20.2	10.8	4.8	5.9	1,348

Note: Figures are percentages except for median; Gross rent is the contract rent plus the estimated average monthly cost of utilities (electricity, gas, and water and sewer) and fuels (oil, coal, kerosene, wood, etc.) if these are paid by the renter (or paid for the renter by someone else); (1) Figures cover the Wilmington, NC Metropolitan Statistical Area
Source: U.S. Census Bureau, 2019-2023 American Community Survey 5-Year Estimates

HEALTH

Health Risk Factors

Category	MSA[1] (%)	U.S. (%)
Adults aged 18–64 who have any kind of health care coverage	n/a	90.8
Adults who reported being in good or better health	n/a	81.8
Adults who have been told they have high blood cholesterol	n/a	36.9
Adults who have been told they have high blood pressure	n/a	34.0
Adults who are current smokers	n/a	12.1
Adults who currently use e-cigarettes	n/a	7.7
Adults who currently use chewing tobacco, snuff, or snus	n/a	3.2
Adults who are heavy drinkers[2]	n/a	6.1
Adults who are binge drinkers[3]	n/a	15.2
Adults who are overweight (BMI 25.0 - 29.9)	n/a	34.4
Adults who are obese (BMI 30.0 - 99.8)	n/a	34.3
Adults who participated in any physical activities in the past month	n/a	75.8

Note: All figures are crude prevalence; (1) Figures for the Wilmington, NC Metropolitan Statistical Area were not available.
(2) Heavy drinkers are classified as adult men having more than 14 drinks per week and adult women having more than 7 drinks per week; (3) Binge drinkers are classified as males having five or more drinks on one occasion or females having four or more drinks on one occasion
Source: Centers for Disease Control and Prevention, Behavioral Risk Factor Surveillance System, SMART: Selected Metropolitan Area Risk Trends, 2023

Acute and Chronic Health Conditions

Category	MSA[1] (%)	U.S. (%)
Adults who have ever been told they had a heart attack	n/a	4.2
Adults who have ever been told they have angina or coronary heart disease	n/a	4.0
Adults who have ever been told they had a stroke	n/a	3.3
Adults who have ever been told they have asthma	n/a	15.7
Adults who have ever been told they have arthritis	n/a	26.3
Adults who have ever been told they have diabetes[2]	n/a	11.5
Adults who have ever been told they had skin cancer	n/a	5.6
Adults who have ever been told they had any other types of cancer	n/a	8.4
Adults who have ever been told they have COPD	n/a	6.4
Adults who have ever been told they have kidney disease	n/a	3.7
Adults who have ever been told they have a form of depression	n/a	22.0

Note: All figures are crude prevalence; (1) Figures for the Wilmington, NC Metropolitan Statistical Area were not available.
(2) Figures do not include pregnancy-related, borderline, or pre-diabetes
Source: Centers for Disease Control and Prevention, Behavioral Risk Factor Surveillance System, SMART: Selected Metropolitan Area Risk Trends, 2023

Health Screening and Vaccination Rates

Category	MSA[1] (%)	U.S. (%)
Adults who have ever been tested for HIV	n/a	37.5
Adults who have had their blood cholesterol checked within the last five years	n/a	87.0
Adults aged 65+ who have had flu shot within the past year	n/a	63.4
Adults aged 65+ who have ever had a pneumonia vaccination	n/a	71.9

Note: All figures are crude prevalence; (1) Figures for the Wilmington, NC Metropolitan Statistical Area were not available.
Source: Centers for Disease Control and Prevention, Behavioral Risk Factor Surveillance System, SMART: Selected Metropolitan Area Risk Trends, 2023

Disability Status

Category	MSA[1] (%)	U.S. (%)
Adults who reported being deaf	n/a	7.4
Are you blind or have serious difficulty seeing, even when wearing glasses?	n/a	4.9
Do you have difficulty doing errands alone?	n/a	7.8
Do you have difficulty dressing or bathing?	n/a	3.6
Do you have serious difficulty concentrating/remembering/making decisions?	n/a	13.7
Do you have serious difficulty walking or climbing stairs?	n/a	13.2

Note: All figures are crude prevalence; (1) Figures for the Wilmington, NC Metropolitan Statistical Area were not available.
Source: Centers for Disease Control and Prevention, Behavioral Risk Factor Surveillance System, SMART: Selected Metropolitan Area Risk Trends, 2023

Mortality Rates for the Top 10 Causes of Death in the U.S.

ICD-10[a] Sub-Chapter	ICD-10[a] Code	Crude Mortality Rate[2] per 100,000 population	
		County[3]	U.S.
Malignant neoplasms	C00-C97	198.4	182.7
Ischaemic heart diseases	I20-I25	86.2	109.6
Provisional assignment of new diseases of uncertain etiology[1]	U00-U49	52.1	65.3
Other forms of heart disease	I30-I51	64.7	65.1
Other degenerative diseases of the nervous system	G30-G31	57.3	52.4
Other external causes of accidental injury	W00-X59	62.6	52.3
Cerebrovascular diseases	I60-I69	59.5	49.1
Chronic lower respiratory diseases	J40-J47	38.7	43.5
Hypertensive diseases	I10-I15	20.6	38.9
Organic, including symptomatic, mental disorders	F01-F09	58.2	33.9

Note: (a) ICD-10 = International Classification of Diseases 10th Revision; (1) Includes COVID-19, adverse effects to COVID-19 vaccines, SARS, and vaping-related disorders; (2) Crude mortality rates are a three-year average covering 2021-2023; (3) Figures cover New Hanover County.
Source: Centers for Disease Control and Prevention, National Center for Health Statistics. National Vital Statistics System, Mortality 2018-2023 on CDC WONDER Online Database

Mortality Rates for Selected Causes of Death

Cause of Death	ICD-10[a] Code	Crude Mortality Rate[1] per 100,000 population	
		County[2]	U.S.
Accidental poisoning and exposure to noxious substances	X40-X49	37.3	30.5
Alzheimer disease	G30	33.7	35.4
Assault	X85-Y09	6.3	7.3
COVID-19	U07.1	51.9	65.3
Diabetes mellitus	E10-E14	22.9	30.0
Diseases of the liver	K70-K76	23.8	20.8
Human immunodeficiency virus (HIV) disease	B20-B24	Unreliable	1.5
Influenza and pneumonia	J09-J18	13.8	13.4
Intentional self-harm	X60-X84	15.4	14.7
Malnutrition	E40-E46	11.8	6.0
Obesity and other hyperalimentation	E65-E68	3.3	3.1
Renal failure	N17-N19	17.9	16.4
Transport accidents	V01-V99	13.9	14.4

Note: (a) ICD-10 = International Classification of Diseases 10th Revision; (1) Crude mortality rates are a three-year average covering 2021-2023; (2) Figures cover New Hanover County; Data are suppressed when the data meet the criteria for confidentiality constraints; Crude mortality rates are flagged as unreliable when the rate would be calculated with a numerator of 20 or less.
Source: Centers for Disease Control and Prevention, National Center for Health Statistics. National Vital Statistics System, Mortality 2018-2023 on CDC WONDER Online Database

Health Insurance Coverage

Area	With Health Insurance	With Private Health Insurance	With Public Health Insurance	Without Health Insurance	Population Under Age 19 Without Health Insurance
City	88.4	69.5	32.5	11.6	8.0
MSA[1]	90.4	71.3	38.0	9.6	6.8
U.S.	91.4	67.3	36.3	8.6	5.4

Note: Figures are percentages that cover the civilian noninstitutionalized population; (1) Figures cover the Wilmington, NC Metropolitan Statistical Area
Source: U.S. Census Bureau, 2019-2023 American Community Survey 5-Year Estimates

Number of Medical Professionals

Area	MDs[3]	DOs[3,4]	Dentists	Podiatrists	Chiropractors	Optometrists
County[1] (number)	864	89	198	20	86	58
County[1] (rate[2])	367.8	37.9	82.9	8.4	36.0	24.3
U.S. (rate[2])	302.5	29.2	74.6	6.4	29.5	18.0

Note: Data as of 2023 unless noted; (1) Data covers New Hanover County; (2) Number of medical professionals per 100,000 population; (3) Data as of 2022 and includes all active, non-federal physicians; (4) Doctor of Osteopathic Medicine
Source: U.S. Department of Health and Human Services, Health Resources and Services Administration, Bureau of Health Professions, Area Resource File (ARF) 2023-2024

EDUCATION

Public School District Statistics

District Name	Schls	Pupils	Pupil/ Teacher Ratio	Minority Pupils[1] (%)	Total Rev. per Pupil ($)	Total Exp. per Pupil ($)
New Hanover County Schools	42	25,028	14.4	42.8	14,533	14,481

Note: Table includes school districts with 2,000 or more students; (1) Percentage of students that are not non-Hispanic white.
Source: U.S. Department of Education, National Center for Education Statistics, Common Core of Data, Local Education Agency (School District) Universe Survey: School Year 2023-2024; U.S. Department of Education, National Center for Education Statistics, Common Core of Data, School District Finance Survey (F-33): School Year 2021–22

Highest Level of Education

Area	Less than H.S.	H.S. Diploma	Some College, No Deg.	Associate Degree	Bachelor's Degree	Master's Degree	Prof. School Degree	Doctorate Degree
City	6.5	18.0	18.9	10.8	29.2	11.1	3.3	2.3
MSA[1]	6.9	22.3	20.8	11.4	24.9	9.7	2.5	1.4
U.S.	10.6	26.2	19.4	8.8	21.3	9.8	2.3	1.6

Note: Figures cover persons age 25 and over; (1) Figures cover the Wilmington, NC Metropolitan Statistical Area
Source: U.S. Census Bureau, 2019-2023 American Community Survey 5-Year Estimates

Educational Attainment by Race

Area	High School Graduate or Higher (%)					Bachelor's Degree or Higher (%)				
	Total	White	Black	Asian	Hisp.[2]	Total	White	Black	Asian	Hisp.[2]
City	93.5	96.4	84.9	87.8	77.5	45.8	51.7	23.0	61.8	30.2
MSA[1]	93.1	95.0	86.8	85.4	75.6	38.5	41.1	23.8	56.4	25.1
U.S.	89.4	92.9	88.1	88.0	72.5	35.0	37.7	24.7	57.0	19.9

Note: Figures shown cover persons 25 years old and over; (1) Figures cover the Wilmington, NC Metropolitan Statistical Area; (2) People of Hispanic origin can be of any race
Source: U.S. Census Bureau, 2019-2023 American Community Survey 5-Year Estimates

School Enrollment by Grade and Control

Area	Preschool (%)		Kindergarten (%)		Grades 1 - 4 (%)		Grades 5 - 8 (%)		Grades 9 - 12 (%)	
	Public	Private	Public	Private	Public	Private	Public	Private	Public	Private
City	55.8	44.2	84.8	15.2	79.3	20.7	75.6	24.4	87.1	12.9
MSA[1]	52.1	47.9	83.4	16.6	83.8	16.2	84.3	15.7	88.3	11.7
U.S.	58.7	41.3	85.2	14.8	87.2	12.8	87.9	12.1	89.0	11.0

Note: Figures shown cover persons 3 years old and over; (1) Figures cover the Wilmington, NC Metropolitan Statistical Area
Source: U.S. Census Bureau, 2019-2023 American Community Survey 5-Year Estimates

Higher Education

Four-Year Colleges			Two-Year Colleges			Medical Schools[1]	Law Schools[2]	Voc/Tech[3]
Public	Private Non-profit	Private For-profit	Public	Private Non-profit	Private For-profit			
1	0	1	2	0	0	0	0	1

Note: Figures cover institutions located within the Wilmington, NC Metropolitan Statistical Area and include main campuses only; (1) includes schools accredited by the Liaison Committee on Medical Education and the American Osteopathic Association's Commission on Osteopathic College Accreditation; (2) includes ABA-accredited schools, schools with provisional ABA accreditation, and state accredited schools; (3) includes all schools with programs that are less than 2 years.
Source: National Center for Education Statistics, Integrated Postsecondary Education System (IPEDS), 2023-24; Wikipedia, List of Medical Schools in the United States, accessed May 2, 2025; Wikipedia, List of Law Schools in the United States, accessed May 2, 2025

According to *U.S. News & World Report*, the Wilmington, NC metro area is home to one of the top 200 national universities in the U.S.: **University of North Carolina—Wilmington** (#196 tie). The indicators used to capture academic quality fall into a number of categories: assessment by administrators at peer institutions; retention of students; faculty resources; student selectivity; financial resources; alumni giving; high school counselor ratings of colleges; and graduation rate. *U.S. News & World Report*, "America's Best Colleges 2025"

EMPLOYERS

Major Employers

Company Name	Industry
Brunswick County Schools	Education
Cape Fear Community College	Education
City of Wilmington	Municipal government
Corning	Optical fiber
Duke Energy	Utilities
GE Wilmington	Electronics & aviation
Mastec Services	Engineering services
New Hanover County	Government
New Hanover County Schools	Education
New Hanover Reg Med Ctr/Cape Fear Hosp	Healthcare
Novant Medical/Brunswick Community Hosp	Healthcare
PPD	Discovery & development services to pharma/biotech
University of NC Wilmington	Education
Verizon Wireless	Communications
Wal-Mart Stores	Retail

Note: Companies shown are located within the Wilmington, NC Metropolitan Statistical Area.
Source: Chambers of Commerce; State Departments of Labor; Wikipedia

PUBLIC SAFETY

Crime Rate

Area	Total Crime Rate	Violent Crime Rate				Property Crime Rate		
		Murder	Rape	Robbery	Aggrav. Assault	Burglary	Larceny-Theft	Motor Vehicle Theft
City	3,995.9	8.2	31.0	99.4	348.9	455.7	2,763.4	289.4
U.S.	2,290.9	5.7	38.0	66.5	264.1	250.7	1,347.2	318.7

Note: Figures are crimes per 100,000 population.
Source: FBI, Table 8, Offenses Known to Law Enforcement, by State by City, 2023

Hate Crimes

Area	Number of Quarters Reported	Number of Incidents per Bias Motivation					
		Race/Ethnicity/Ancestry	Religion	Sexual Orientation	Disability	Gender	Gender Identity
City[1]	4	3	2	1	0	0	0
U.S.	4	5,900	2,699	2,077	187	92	492

Note: (1) Figures include at least one incident reported with more than one bias motivation.
Source: Federal Bureau of Investigation, Hate Crime Statistics 2023

Identity Theft Consumer Reports

Area	Reports	Reports per 100,000 Population	Rank[2]
MSA[1]	855	194	171
U.S.	1,135,291	339	-

Note: (1) Figures cover the Wilmington, NC Metropolitan Statistical Area; (2) Rank ranges from 1 to 401 where 1 indicates greatest number of identity theft reports per 100,000 population
Source: Federal Trade Commission, Consumer Sentinel Network Data Book 2024

Fraud and Other Consumer Reports

Area	Reports	Reports per 100,000 Population	Rank[2]
MSA[1]	5,300	1,203	127
U.S.	5,360,641	1,601	-

Note: (1) Figures cover the Wilmington, NC Metropolitan Statistical Area; (2) Rank ranges from 1 to 401 where 1 indicates greatest number of fraud and other consumer reports per 100,000 population
Source: Federal Trade Commission, Consumer Sentinel Network Data Book 2024

POLITICS

2024 Presidential Election Results

Area	Trump (Rep.)	Harris (Dem.)	Stein (Green)	Kennedy (Ind.)	Oliver (Lib.)	Other
New Hanover County	49.0	49.6	0.4	0.0	0.4	0.6
U.S.	49.7	48.2	0.6	0.5	0.4	0.6

Note: Results are percentages and may not add to 100% due to rounding
Source: Dave Leip's Atlas of U.S. Presidential Elections

SPORTS

Professional Sports Teams

Team Name	League	Year Established

No teams are located in the metro area
Source: Wikipedia, Major Professional Sports Teams of the United States and Canada, May 1, 2025

CLIMATE

Average and Extreme Temperatures

Temperature	Jan	Feb	Mar	Apr	May	Jun	Jul	Aug	Sep	Oct	Nov	Dec	Yr.
Extreme High (°F)	82	85	89	95	98	104	102	102	98	95	87	81	104
Average High (°F)	56	59	65	74	81	86	90	88	84	75	67	59	74
Average Temp. (°F)	46	48	55	63	71	77	81	80	75	65	56	49	64
Average Low (°F)	36	37	43	51	60	67	72	71	65	54	45	37	53
Extreme Low (°F)	5	11	9	30	35	48	55	55	44	27	16	0	0

Note: Figures cover the years 1948-1995
Source: National Climatic Data Center, International Station Meteorological Climate Summary, 9/96

Average Precipitation/Snowfall/Humidity

Precip./Humidity	Jan	Feb	Mar	Apr	May	Jun	Jul	Aug	Sep	Oct	Nov	Dec	Yr.
Avg. Precip. (in.)	3.9	3.5	4.3	2.9	4.3	5.4	7.9	7.0	5.6	3.3	3.3	3.5	55.0
Avg. Snowfall (in.)	Tr	1	Tr	Tr	0	0	0	0	0	0	Tr	1	2
Avg. Rel. Hum. 7am (%)	82	80	82	81	84	85	87	90	90	89	86	82	85
Avg. Rel. Hum. 4pm (%)	58	55	54	51	58	62	66	67	66	60	58	58	59

Note: Figures cover the years 1948-1995; Tr = Trace amounts (<0.05 in. of rain; <0.5 in. of snow)
Source: National Climatic Data Center, International Station Meteorological Climate Summary, 9/96

Weather Conditions

Temperature			Daytime Sky			Precipitation		
10°F & below	32°F & below	90°F & above	Clear	Partly cloudy	Cloudy	0.01 inch or more precip.	0.1 inch or more snow/ice	Thunderstorms
< 1	42	46	96	150	119	115	1	47

Note: Figures are average number of days per year and cover the years 1948-1995
Source: National Climatic Data Center, International Station Meteorological Climate Summary, 9/96

HAZARDOUS WASTE

Superfund Sites

The Wilmington, NC metro area is home to three sites on the EPA's Superfund National Priorities List (NPL) or Superfund Alternative Approach (SAA) list: **Horton Iron and Metal** (Final NPL); **Kerr-Mcgee Chemical Corp - Navassa** (Final NPL); **Potter's Septic Tank Service Pits** (Final NPL). The Superfund alternative approach uses the same investigation and cleanup process and standards that are used for sites listed on the National Priorities List. The SAA is an alternative to listing a site on the NPL; it is not an alternative to Superfund or the Superfund process. There are a total of 1,445 Superfund sites with a status of proposed or final on both lists in the United States. *U.S. Environmental Protection Agency, National Priorities List, May 1, 2025; U.S. Environmental Protection Agency, Superfund Alternative Approach Sites, May 1, 2025*

AIR QUALITY

Air Quality Trends: Ozone

	1990	1995	2000	2005	2010	2015	2020	2021	2022	2023
MSA[1]	0.082	0.079	0.080	0.075	0.062	0.057	0.054	0.062	0.058	0.067
U.S.	0.087	0.089	0.081	0.080	0.072	0.068	0.066	0.067	0.067	0.070

Note: (1) Data covers the Wilmington, NC Metropolitan Statistical Area. The values shown are the composite ozone concentration averages among trend sites based on the highest fourth daily maximum 8-hour concentration in parts per million. These trends are based on sites having an adequate record of monitoring data during the trend period. Data from exceptional events are included.
Source: U.S. Environmental Protection Agency, Air Quality Monitoring Information, "Air Quality Trends by City, 1990-2023"

Air Quality Index

Area	Percent of Days when Air Quality was...[2]					AQI Statistics[2]	
	Good	Moderate	Unhealthy for Sensitive Groups	Unhealthy	Very Unhealthy	Maximum	Median
MSA[1]	65.5	34.3	0.3	0.0	0.0	142	44

Note: (1) Data covers the Wilmington, NC Metropolitan Statistical Area; (2) Based on 362 days with AQI data in 2023. Air Quality Index (AQI) is an index for reporting daily air quality. EPA calculates the AQI for five major air pollutants regulated by the Clean Air Act: ground-level ozone, particle pollution (aka particulate matter), carbon monoxide, sulfur dioxide, and nitrogen dioxide. The AQI runs from 0 to 500. The higher the AQI value, the greater the level of air pollution and the greater the health concern. There are six AQI categories: "Good" AQI is between 0 and 50. Air quality is considered satisfactory; "Moderate" AQI is between 51 and 100. Air quality is acceptable; "Unhealthy for Sensitive Groups" When AQI values are between 101 and 150, members of sensitive groups may experience health effects; "Unhealthy" When AQI values are between 151 and 200 everyone may begin to experience health effects; "Very Unhealthy" AQI values between 201 and 300 trigger a health alert; "Hazardous" AQI values over 300 trigger warnings of emergency conditions (not shown).
Source: U.S. Environmental Protection Agency, Air Quality Index Report, 2023

Air Quality Index Pollutants

Area	Percent of Days when AQI Pollutant was...[2]					
	Carbon Monoxide	Nitrogen Dioxide	Ozone	Sulfur Dioxide	Particulate Matter 2.5	Particulate Matter 10
MSA[1]	0.0	0.0	25.1	(3)	74.9	0.0

Note: (1) Data covers the Wilmington, NC Metropolitan Statistical Area; (2) Based on 362 days with AQI data in 2023. The Air Quality Index (AQI) is an index for reporting daily air quality. EPA calculates the AQI for five major air pollutants regulated by the Clean Air Act: ground-level ozone, particle pollution (also known as particulate matter), carbon monoxide, sulfur dioxide, and nitrogen dioxide. The AQI runs from 0 to 500. The higher the AQI value, the greater the level of air pollution and the greater the health concern; (3) Sulfur dioxide is no longer included in this table because SO_2 concentrations tend to be very localized and not necessarily representative of broad geographical areas like counties and CBSAs.
Source: U.S. Environmental Protection Agency, Air Quality Index Report, 2023

Maximum Air Pollutant Concentrations: Particulate Matter, Ozone, CO and Lead

	Particulate Matter 10 (ug/m^3)	Particulate Matter 2.5 Wtd AM (ug/m^3)	Particulate Matter 2.5 24-Hr (ug/m^3)	Ozone (ppm)	Carbon Monoxide (ppm)	Lead (ug/m^3)
MSA[1] Level	45	6.8	19	0.067	n/a	n/a
NAAQS[2]	150	15	35	0.075	9	0.15
Met NAAQS[2]	Yes	Yes	Yes	Yes	n/a	n/a

Note: (1) Data covers the Wilmington, NC Metropolitan Statistical Area; Data from exceptional events are included; (2) National Ambient Air Quality Standards; ppm = parts per million; ug/m^3 = micrograms per cubic meter; n/a not available.
Concentrations: Particulate Matter 10 (coarse particulate)—highest second maximum 24-hour concentration; Particulate Matter 2.5 Wtd AM (fine particulate)—highest weighted annual mean concentration; Particulate Matter 2.5 24-Hour (fine particulate)—highest 98th percentile 24-hour concentration; Ozone—highest fourth daily maximum 8-hour concentration; Carbon Monoxide—highest second maximum non-overlapping 8-hour concentration; Lead—maximum running 3-month average
Source: U.S. Environmental Protection Agency, Air Quality Monitoring Information, "Air Quality Statistics by City, 2023"

Maximum Air Pollutant Concentrations: Nitrogen Dioxide and Sulfur Dioxide

	Nitrogen Dioxide AM (ppb)	Nitrogen Dioxide 1-Hr (ppb)	Sulfur Dioxide AM (ppb)	Sulfur Dioxide 1-Hr (ppb)	Sulfur Dioxide 24-Hr (ppb)
MSA[1] Level	n/a	n/a	n/a	n/a	n/a
NAAQS[2]	53	100	30	75	140
Met NAAQS[2]	n/a	n/a	n/a	n/a	n/a

Note: (1) Data covers the Wilmington, NC Metropolitan Statistical Area; Data from exceptional events are included; (2) National Ambient Air Quality Standards; ppm = parts per million; ug/m^3 = micrograms per cubic meter; n/a not available.
Concentrations: Nitrogen Dioxide AM—highest arithmetic mean concentration; Nitrogen Dioxide 1-Hr—highest 98th percentile 1-hour daily maximum concentration; Sulfur Dioxide AM—highest annual mean concentration; Sulfur Dioxide 1-Hr—highest 99th percentile 1-hour daily maximum concentration; Sulfur Dioxide 24-Hr—highest second maximum 24-hour concentration
Source: U.S. Environmental Protection Agency, Air Quality Monitoring Information, "Air Quality Statistics by City, 2023"

Winston-Salem, North Carolina

Background

The "Twin City" of Winston-Salem officially came to be in 1913 when the towns of Winston and Salem joined forces.

Salem dates to January of 1753 when the Moravain Church purchased approximately 100,000 acres in North Carolina. The eastern European based church settled in the Wachovia Tract and was known as Bethabara. It was renamed Salem, from the Hebrew word for peace, in 1766. The community was established around a town square with all the property owned by the church and all the town's residents members of the church. The Moravains were known for their craftsmanship and artistry and soon established the town as an economic trade center. In 1856 Salem was officially incorporated in what is now Forsyth County.

Winston was established in 1849 when Forsyth County purchased land from the Moravain congregation of Salem. Situated to the north of Salem, Winston was officially named in 1851 after local politician and Revolutionary War hero Mayor John Winston. At the end of the Civil War in 1865, Winston became a major industrial center, and Winston and Salem connected to the North Carolina Railroad. In 1868, Winston's first tobacco factories were built and in 1875, Richard Joshua Reynolds joined the party. By the mid-1880s Winston had nearly 40 tobacco factories and when Reynolds bought out Hanes, the last of the smaller companies, the reign of giant R.J. Reynolds Tobacco Company began. Pleasant Henderson Hanes reinvested his proceeds and founded the P.H. Hanes Knitting Company in Winston-Salem.

The tobacco and textile industries fueled the city's economy. In 1917, 180 houses, known as Reynoldstown, were built by the Reynold's Company for their employees, as well as the 21-story Reynold's Building in 1929, one of the tallest buildings in the United States at the time, and the prototype to the Empire State Building.

The surging economy brought about the merger of Wachovia National Bank and Wachovia Loan and Trust (both established in Winston-Salem in 1879) to form the Wachovia Bank and Trust in 1911. In 2001 the bank became Wachovia and, in 2009, Wells Fargo. Today, Winston-Salem is headquarters to many thriving companies including Branch Banking and Trust Company (BB&T), Hanesbands, Novant Health, Inmar, Reynolds American, Primo Water and Krispy Kreme Doughnuts.

Winston-Salem continues to transform itself from a leader in the textile and tobacco industries to one in the nanotech, high-tech and biotech fields. Medical research is a fast-growing local industry, and Atrium Health Wake Forest Baptist Medical Center is the city's largest employer.

The city's downtown's Wake-Forest Innovation Quarter features businesses, education in biomedical research and engineering, information technology and digital media, as well as public gathering spaces and residences. In 2023, the Center for Healthcare Innovation joined the program, looking for ways to reduce the time it takes for research discovery to reach the bedside.

Popular attractions in the city include Reynolds Gardens, Wake Forest University Museum of Anthropology, children's museums Kaleideum North and Kaleideum Downtown, and New Winston Museum.

Truist Stadium is a minor-league stadium primarily used for baseball, with a seating capacity of 5,500. It's located near downtown Winston-Salem and home to the Winston-Salem Dash minor league baseball team.

Winston-Salem's climate is temperate, characterized by cold, occasionally snowy winters and hot, humid summers. Spring and fall offer pleasant transitional weather, and it is partly cloudy year-round. Temperatures range from 32 degrees to 87 degrees and rainfall is significant.

Rankings

General Rankings

- To help military veterans find the best places in which to settle down, *WalletHub* compared the 100 largest U.S. cities across 19 key indicators of livability, affordability and veteran-friendliness. They range from the share of military skill-related jobs to veteran income growth to the availability of VA health facilities. Winston-Salem ranked #60. *Wallethub.com, "Best & Worst Places for Veterans to Live (2025)," November 7, 2024*

- In their annual survey, Livability.com looked at data for more than 2,000 mid-sized U.S. cities to assign a "Livability Score" for each. The top 100 scoring cities make up Livability's "Top 100 Best Places to Live in the U.S." in 2025. Winston-Salem was placed among the top 100 of the customizable list. Criteria: housing and economy; cost of living; environment; education; health care options; transportation; safety; and community amenities. *Livability.com, "Top 100 Best Places to Live in the U.S. in 2025" April 15, 2025*

Business/Finance Rankings

- The Winston-Salem metro area appeared on the Milken Institute "2025 Best Performing Cities" list. Rank: #179 out of 200 large metro areas (based on performance category). Criteria: job growth; wage growth; high-tech growth and impact; community resilience; housing affordability; household broadband access. *Milken Institute, "Best-Performing Cities 2025," January 14, 2025*

Education Rankings

- Personal finance website *WalletHub* analyzed the 150 largest U.S. metropolitan statistical areas to determine where the most educated Americans are putting their degrees to work. Criteria: education levels; percentage of workers with degrees; education quality and attainment gap; public school quality rankings; quality and enrollment of each metro area's universities. Winston-Salem was ranked #113 (#1 = most educated city). *WalletHub.com, "Most & Least Educated Cities in America, 2025" July 2, 2024*

Health/Fitness Rankings

- For each of the 100 largest cities in the United States, the American Fitness Index®, compiled in partnership between the American College of Sports Medicine and the Elevance Health Foundation, evaluated community infrastructure and more than 30 health behaviors including preventive health, levels of chronic disease conditions, food insecurity, pedestrian safety, air quality, and community/environment resources that support physical activity. Winston-Salem ranked #76 for "community fitness." *americanfitnessindex.org, "2024 ACSM American Fitness Index Summary Report," July 23, 2024*

- Winston-Salem was identified as a "2025 Allergy Capital." The area ranked #15 out of the nation's 100 largest metropolitan areas. Three groups of factors were used to identify the most challenging cities for people with allergies: annual tree, grass, and weed pollen scores; over the counter allergy medicine use; number of board-certified allergy specialists. *Asthma and Allergy Foundation of America, "2025 Allergy Capitals: The Most Challenging Places to Live with Allergies," March 18, 2025*

- Winston-Salem was identified as a "2024 Asthma Capital." The area ranked #98 out of the nation's 100 largest metropolitan areas. Criteria: estimated asthma prevalence; asthma-related mortality; and ER visits due to asthma. Risk factors analyzed but not factored in the rankings: annual air quality including pollution and ozone levels; public smoking laws; indoor air quality; access to asthma specialists; rescue and controller medication use; uninsured rate; pollen allergy; poverty rate. *Asthma and Allergy Foundation of America, "Asthma Capitals 2024: The Most Challenging Places to Live With Asthma," September 10, 2024*

Real Estate Rankings

- *WalletHub* compared the most populated U.S. cities to determine which had the best markets for real estate agents. Winston-Salem ranked #56 where demand was high and pay was the best. Criteria: sales per agent; annual median wage for real-estate agents; monthly average starting salary for real estate agents; real estate job density and competition; unemployment rate; home turnover rate; housing-market health index; and other relevant metrics. *WalletHub.com, "2021 Best Places to Be a Real Estate Agent," May 12, 2021*

- Winston-Salem was ranked #9 in the top 20 out of the 100 largest metro areas in terms of house price appreciation in 2024 (#1 = highest rate). *Federal Housing Finance Agency, "House Price Index, 4th Quarter 2024," February 25, 2025*

- Winston-Salem was ranked #96 out of 176 metro areas in terms of cost of housing in 2024 by the National Association of Home Builders (#1 = most affordable). Criteria: the portion of an average family's income necessary to pay the mortgage on a median-priced home. *National Association of Home Builders®, NAHB-Wells Fargo Cost of Housing Index, 4th Quarter 2024*

Safety Rankings

- Allstate ranked the 100 most populous cities in America in terms of driver safety. Winston-Salem ranked #41. Criteria based on anonymized driving behavior data from Allstate's mobile app powered by Arity: high speed driving (over 80 mph), phone handling, and hard braking. The report helps increase the importance of safety and awareness behind the wheel. *Allstate, "16th Allstate America's Best Drivers Report®" July 11, 2024*

- Winston-Salem was identified as one of the most dangerous cities in America by NeighborhoodScout. The city ranked #58 out of 100 (#1 = most dangerous). Criteria: number of violent crimes per 1,000 residents. The editors evaluated cities with 25,000 or more residents. *NeighborhoodScout.com, "2023 Top 100 Most Dangerous Cities in the U.S.," January 12, 2023*

Women/Minorities Rankings

- Personal finance website *WalletHub* compared more than 180 U.S. cities across two key dimensions, "Hispanic Business-Friendliness" and "Hispanic Purchasing Power," to arrive at the most favorable conditions for Hispanic entrepreneurs. Winston-Salem was ranked #162 out of 182. Criteria includes: share of Hispanic-Owned Businesses; average growth of Hispanic Business revenues; Small Business-Friendliness score; affordability; and number of Hispanics with at least a bachelor's degree. *WalletHub.com, "Best Cities for Hispanic Entrepreneurs," September 4, 2024*

Business Environment

DEMOGRAPHICS

Population Growth

Area	1990 Census	2000 Census	2010 Census	2020 Census	2023 Estimate[2]	Population Growth 1990-2023 (%)
City	168,139	185,776	229,617	249,545	250,887	49.2
MSA[1]	361,091	421,961	477,717	675,966	683,637	89.3
U.S.	248,709,873	281,421,906	308,745,538	331,449,281	332,387,540	33.6

Note: (1) Figures cover the Winston-Salem, NC Metropolitan Statistical Area; (2) 2019-2023 5-year ACS population estimate
Source: U.S. Census Bureau, 1990 Census, 2000 Census, 2010 Census, 2020 Census, 2019-2023 American Community Survey 5-Year Estimates

Race

Area	White Alone[2] (%)	Black Alone[2] (%)	Asian Alone[2] (%)	AIAN[3] Alone[2] (%)	NHOPI[4] Alone[2] (%)	Other Race Alone[2] (%)	Two or More Races (%)
City	48.7	32.4	2.3	0.5	0.0	7.3	8.8
MSA[1]	68.8	17.4	1.8	0.3	0.0	4.4	7.3
U.S.	63.4	12.4	5.8	0.9	0.2	6.6	10.7

Note: (1) Figures cover the Winston-Salem, NC Metropolitan Statistical Area; (2) Alone is defined as not being in combination with one or more other races; (3) American Indian and Alaska Native; (4) Native Hawaiian and Other Pacific Islander
Source: U.S. Census Bureau, 2019-2023 American Community Survey 5-Year Estimates

Hispanic or Latino Origin

Area	Total (%)	Mexican (%)	Puerto Rican (%)	Cuban (%)	Other (%)
City	17.9	10.1	1.7	0.3	5.8
MSA[1]	11.8	7.0	1.1	0.3	3.4
U.S.	19.0	11.3	1.8	0.7	5.2

Note: Persons of Hispanic or Latino origin can be of any race; (1) Figures cover the Winston-Salem, NC Metropolitan Statistical Area
Source: U.S. Census Bureau, 2019-2023 American Community Survey 5-Year Estimates

Age

Area	Percent of Population									Median Age
	Under Age 5	Age 5–19	Age 20–34	Age 35–44	Age 45–54	Age 55–64	Age 65–74	Age 75–84	Age 85+	
City	5.9	21.7	21.6	12.1	11.9	12.0	8.5	4.3	1.9	35.6
MSA[1]	5.5	19.2	18.7	11.8	13.0	13.8	10.7	5.4	2.0	40.6
U.S.	5.7	19.1	20.2	13.1	12.3	12.8	10.0	4.9	1.9	38.7

Note: (1) Figures cover the Winston-Salem, NC Metropolitan Statistical Area
Source: U.S. Census Bureau, 2019-2023 American Community Survey 5-Year Estimates

Disability by Age

Area	All Ages	Under 18 Years Old	18 to 64 Years Old	65 Years and Over
City	12.6	4.7	10.9	32.8
MSA[1]	14.2	4.9	12.0	33.1
U.S.	13.0	4.7	10.7	32.9

Note: Figures show percent of the civilian noninstitutionalized population that reported having a disability. Disability status is determined from six types of difficulty: vision, hearing, cognitive, ambulatory, self-care, and independent living. For children under 5 years old, hearing and vision difficulty are used to determine disability status. For children between the ages of 5 and 14, disability status is determined from hearing, vision, cognitive, ambulatory, and self-care difficulties. For people aged 15 years and older, they are considered to have a disability if they have difficulty with any one of the six difficulty types; Note: (1) Figures cover the Winston-Salem, NC Metropolitan Statistical Area
Source: U.S. Census Bureau, 2019-2023 American Community Survey 5-Year Estimates

Ancestry

Area	German	Irish	English	American	Italian	Polish	French[2]	European	Scottish
City	7.9	6.3	9.5	5.3	2.5	0.8	1.0	1.7	1.9
MSA[1]	10.9	8.3	13.1	7.8	2.6	1.0	1.1	1.7	2.1
U.S.	12.6	9.4	9.1	5.5	4.9	2.6	2.0	1.6	1.6

Note: Figures are the percentage of the total population reporting a particular ancestry. The nine most commonly reported ancestries in the U.S. are shown. Figures include multiple ancestries (e.g. if a person reported being Irish and Italian, they were included in both columns); (1) Figures cover the Winston-Salem, NC Metropolitan Statistical Area; (2) Excludes Basque
Source: U.S. Census Bureau, 2019-2023 American Community Survey 5-Year Estimates

Foreign-born Population

Area	Percent of Population Born in								
	Any Foreign Country	Asia	Mexico	Europe	Caribbean	Central America[2]	South America	Africa	Canada
City	10.7	2.0	4.1	0.6	0.6	1.7	1.0	0.6	0.1
MSA[1]	7.3	1.4	2.8	0.7	0.3	1.0	0.7	0.3	0.1
U.S.	13.9	4.3	3.3	1.4	1.4	1.2	1.2	0.8	0.2

Note: (1) Figures cover the Winston-Salem, NC Metropolitan Statistical Area; (2) Excludes Mexico.
Source: U.S. Census Bureau, 2019-2023 American Community Survey 5-Year Estimates

Household Size

Area	Persons in Household (%)							Average Household Size
	One	Two	Three	Four	Five	Six	Seven or More	
City	35.2	32.7	14.2	9.8	4.8	2.3	1.0	2.40
MSA[1]	30.3	35.6	15.4	11.1	4.7	2.0	0.9	2.43
U.S.	28.5	33.8	15.4	12.7	5.9	2.3	1.4	2.54

Note: (1) Figures cover the Winston-Salem, NC Metropolitan Statistical Area
Source: U.S. Census Bureau, 2019-2023 American Community Survey 5-Year Estimates

Household Relationships

Area	Householder	Opposite-sex Spouse	Same-sex Spouse	Opposite-sex Unmarried Partner	Same-sex Unmarried Partner	Child[2]	Grandchild	Other Relatives	Non-relatives
City	40.9	14.6	0.2	2.5	0.2	28.1	2.4	4.3	2.7
MSA[1]	40.9	18.6	0.2	2.3	0.1	27.5	2.4	3.7	2.2
U.S.	38.3	17.5	0.2	2.5	0.2	28.3	2.4	4.8	3.4

Note: Figures are percent of the total population; (1) Figures cover the Winston-Salem, NC Metropolitan Statistical Area; (2) Includes biological, adopted, and stepchildren of the householder
Source: U.S. Census Bureau, 2020 Census

Gender

Area	Males	Females	Males per 100 Females
City	116,981	133,906	87.4
MSA[1]	330,177	353,460	93.4
U.S.	164,545,087	167,842,453	98.0

Note: (1) Figures cover the Winston-Salem, NC Metropolitan Statistical Area
Source: U.S. Census Bureau, 2019-2023 American Community Survey 5-Year Estimates

Marital Status

Area	Never Married	Now Married[2]	Separated	Widowed	Divorced
City	42.5	39.6	2.4	5.2	10.3
MSA[1]	31.7	48.8	2.2	6.3	11.1
U.S.	34.1	47.9	1.7	5.6	10.7

Note: Figures are percentages and cover the population 15 years of age and older; (1) Figures cover the Winston-Salem, NC Metropolitan Statistical Area; (2) Excludes separated
Source: U.S. Census Bureau, 2019-2023 American Community Survey 5-Year Estimates

Religious Groups by Family

Area	Catholic	Baptist	Methodist	LDS[2]	Pentecostal	Lutheran	Islam	Adventist	Other
MSA[1]	9.3	12.8	11.4	0.5	1.0	0.6	0.8	1.4	22.5
U.S.	18.7	7.3	3.0	2.0	1.8	1.7	1.3	1.3	11.6

Note: Figures are the number of adherents as a percentage of the total population and cover the eight largest religious groups in the U.S; (1) Figures cover the Winston-Salem, NC Metropolitan Statistical Area; (2) Church of Jesus Christ of Latter-day Saints
Sources: 2020 U.S. Religion Census, Association of Statisticians of American Religious Bodies; The Association of Religion Data Archives (ARDA)

Religious Groups by Tradition

Area	Catholic	Evangelical Protestant	Mainline Protestant	Black Protestant	Islam	Judaism	Hinduism	Orthodox	Buddhism
MSA[1]	9.3	31.4	13.6	3.4	0.8	n/a	<0.1	0.3	0.1
U.S.	18.7	16.5	5.2	2.3	1.3	0.6	0.4	0.4	0.3

Note: Figures are the number of adherents as a percentage of the total population; (1) Figures cover the Winston-Salem, NC Metropolitan Statistical Area
Sources: 2020 U.S. Religion Census, Association of Statisticians of American Religious Bodies; The Association of Religion Data Archives (ARDA)

ECONOMY

Real Gross Domestic Product (GDP)

Area	2017	2018	2019	2020	2021	2022	2023	Rank[3]
MSA[1]	34.9	34.2	34.7	32.6	34.8	35.7	36.1	91
U.S.[2]	17,619.1	18,160.7	18,642.5	18,238.9	19,387.6	19,896.6	20,436.3	–

Note: Figures are in billions of chained 2017 dollars; (1) Figures cover the Winston-Salem, NC Metropolitan Statistical Area; (2) Figures cover real GDP within metropolitan areas; (3) Rank is based on 2023 data and ranges from 1 to 384
Source: U.S. Bureau of Economic Analysis

Economic Growth

Area	2014	2015	2016	2017	2018	2019	2020	2021	2022	2023
MSA[1]	2.6	1.0	1.4	2.6	-2.1	1.4	-6.0	6.9	2.5	1.3
U.S.[2]	2.6	3.2	2.0	2.7	3.1	2.7	-2.2	6.3	2.6	2.7

Note: Figures are real gross domestic product growth rates and represent percent change from preceding period; (1) Figures cover the Winston-Salem, NC Metropolitan Statistical Area; (2) Figures are the average growth rates within metropolitan areas
Source: U.S. Bureau of Economic Analysis

Metropolitan Area Exports

Area	2018	2019	2020	2021	2022	2023	Rank[2]
MSA[1]	1,107.5	1,209.1	913.1	918.2	1,012.1	1,071.1	166
U.S.	1,664,056.1	1,645,173.7	1,431,406.6	1,753,941.4	2,062,937.4	2,019,160.5	–

Note: Figures are in millions of dollars; (1) Figures cover the Winston-Salem, NC Metropolitan Statistical Area; (2) Rank is based on 2023 data and ranges from 1 to 386
Source: U.S. Department of Commerce, International Trade Administration, Office of Trade and Economic Analysis, Industry and Analysis, Exports by Metropolitan Area, data extracted April 2, 2025

Building Permits

Area	Single-Family			Multi-Family			Total		
	2023	2024	Pct. Chg.	2023	2024	Pct. Chg.	2023	2024	Pct. Chg.
City	860	1,168	35.8	1,281	966	-24.6	2,141	2,134	-0.3
MSA[1]	3,567	4,010	12.4	1,507	1,446	-4.0	5,074	5,456	7.5
U.S.	920,000	981,900	6.7	591,100	496,100	-16.1	1,511,100	1,478,000	-2.2

Note: (1) Figures cover the Winston-Salem, NC Metropolitan Statistical Area; Figures represent new, privately-owned housing units authorized (unadjusted data)
Source: U.S. Census Bureau, Building Permits Survey (BPS), 2023, 2024

Bankruptcy Filings

Area	Business Filings			Nonbusiness Filings		
	2023	2024	% Chg.	2023	2024	% Chg.
Forsyth County	7	18	157.1	263	330	25.5
U.S.	18,926	23,107	22.1	434,064	494,201	13.9

Note: Business filings include Chapter 7, Chapter 9, Chapter 11, Chapter 12, Chapter 13, Chapter 15, and Section 304; Nonbusiness filings include Chapter 7, Chapter 11, and Chapter 13
Source: Administrative Office of the U.S. Courts, Business and Nonbusiness Bankruptcy, County Cases Commenced by Chapter of the Bankruptcy Code, During the 12-Month Period Ending December 31, 2023 and Business and Nonbusiness Bankruptcy, County Cases Commenced by Chapter of the Bankruptcy Code, During the 12-Month Period Ending December 31, 2024

Housing Vacancy Rates

Area	Gross Vacancy Rate[3] (%)			Year-Round Vacancy Rate[4] (%)			Rental Vacancy Rate[5] (%)			Homeowner Vacancy Rate[6] (%)		
	2022	2023	2024	2022	2023	2024	2022	2023	2024	2022	2023	2024
MSA[1]	n/a	n/a	n/a	n/a	n/a	n/a	n/a	n/a	n/a	n/a	n/a	n/a
U.S.[2]	9.1	9.0	9.1	7.5	7.5	7.6	5.7	6.5	6.8	0.8	0.8	1.0

Note: (1) Figures cover the Winston-Salem, NC Metropolitan Statistical Area; (2) Figures cover the 75 largest Metropolitan Statistical Areas; (3) The percentage of the total housing inventory that is vacant; (4) The percentage of the housing inventory (excluding seasonal units) that is year-round vacant; (5) The percentage of rental inventory that is vacant for rent; (6) The percentage of homeowner inventory that is vacant for sale; n/a not available
Source: U.S. Census Bureau, Housing Vacancies and Homeownership Annual Statistics: 2022, 2023, 2024

INCOME

Income

Area	Per Capita ($)	Median Household ($)	Average Household ($)
City	35,074	57,673	85,278
MSA[1]	35,829	64,282	87,020
U.S.	43,289	78,538	110,491

Note: (1) Figures cover the Winston-Salem, NC Metropolitan Statistical Area
Source: U.S. Census Bureau, 2019-2023 American Community Survey 5-Year Estimates

Household Income Distribution

Area	Percent of Households Earning							
	Under $15,000	$15,000 -$24,999	$25,000 -$34,999	$35,000 -$49,999	$50,000 -$74,999	$75,000 -$99,999	$100,000 -$149,999	$150,000 and up
City	11.3	8.9	10.0	13.2	17.2	12.5	13.8	13.0
MSA[1]	9.2	8.1	9.0	12.8	18.0	13.7	15.4	13.9
U.S.	8.5	6.6	6.8	10.4	15.7	12.7	17.4	21.9

Note: (1) Figures cover the Winston-Salem, NC Metropolitan Statistical Area
Source: U.S. Census Bureau, 2019-2023 American Community Survey 5-Year Estimates

Poverty Rate

Area	All Ages	Under 18 Years Old	18 to 64 Years Old	65 Years and Over
City	17.9	27.1	16.0	10.7
MSA[1]	13.9	21.2	12.5	9.7
U.S.	12.4	16.3	11.6	10.4

Note: Figures are percentage of people whose income during the past 12 months was below the poverty level; (1) Figures cover the Winston-Salem, NC Metropolitan Statistical Area
Source: U.S. Census Bureau, 2019-2023 American Community Survey 5-Year Estimates

EMPLOYMENT

Labor Force and Employment

Area	Civilian Labor Force			Workers Employed		
	Dec. 2023	Dec. 2024	% Chg.	Dec. 2023	Dec. 2024	% Chg.
City	118,508	118,217	-0.2	114,267	114,055	-0.2
MSA[1]	329,205	328,631	-0.2	318,577	317,977	-0.2
U.S.	166,661,000	167,746,000	0.7	160,754,000	161,294,000	0.3

Note: Data is not seasonally adjusted and covers workers 16 years of age and older; (1) Figures cover the Winston-Salem, NC Metropolitan Statistical Area
Source: Bureau of Labor Statistics, Local Area Unemployment Statistics

Unemployment Rate

Area	2024											
	Jan.	Feb.	Mar.	Apr.	May	Jun.	Jul.	Aug.	Sep.	Oct.	Nov.	Dec.
City	4.0	4.0	4.0	3.4	3.8	4.3	4.6	4.4	3.5	3.6	3.8	3.5
MSA[1]	3.6	3.7	3.6	3.1	3.4	3.9	4.1	4.0	3.3	3.3	3.6	3.2
U.S.	4.1	4.2	3.9	3.5	3.7	4.3	4.5	4.4	3.9	3.9	4.0	3.8

Note: Data is not seasonally adjusted and covers workers 16 years of age and older; (1) Figures cover the Winston-Salem, NC Metropolitan Statistical Area
Source: Bureau of Labor Statistics, Local Area Unemployment Statistics

Average Wages

Occupation	$/Hr.	Occupation	$/Hr.
Accountants and Auditors	40.27	Maintenance and Repair Workers	24.06
Automotive Mechanics	25.20	Marketing Managers	74.45
Bookkeepers	22.66	Network and Computer Systems Admin.	43.84
Carpenters	23.60	Nurses, Licensed Practical	28.98
Cashiers	13.15	Nurses, Registered	42.11
Computer Programmers	44.83	Nursing Assistants	18.13
Computer Systems Analysts	50.74	Office Clerks, General	19.25
Computer User Support Specialists	27.29	Physical Therapists	47.50
Construction Laborers	21.31	Physicians	n/a
Cooks, Restaurant	15.89	Plumbers, Pipefitters and Steamfitters	25.08
Customer Service Representatives	19.29	Police and Sheriff's Patrol Officers	27.78
Dentists	77.83	Postal Service Mail Carriers	28.87
Electricians	26.05	Real Estate Sales Agents	23.59
Engineers, Electrical	42.46	Retail Salespersons	15.88
Fast Food and Counter Workers	13.91	Sales Representatives, Technical/Scientific	51.83
Financial Managers	77.03	Secretaries, Exc. Legal/Medical/Executive	21.50
First-Line Supervisors of Office Workers	30.59	Security Guards	20.24
General and Operations Managers	59.42	Surgeons	n/a
Hairdressers/Cosmetologists	18.68	Teacher Assistants, Exc. Postsecondary[1]	13.12
Home Health and Personal Care Aides	14.44	Teachers, Secondary School, Exc. Sp. Ed.[1]	26.41
Janitors and Cleaners	15.37	Telemarketers	n/a
Landscaping/Groundskeeping Workers	17.78	Truck Drivers, Heavy/Tractor-Trailer	25.99
Lawyers	83.92	Truck Drivers, Light/Delivery Services	20.43
Maids and Housekeeping Cleaners	15.70	Waiters and Waitresses	14.25

Note: Wage data covers the Winston-Salem, NC Metropolitan Statistical Area; (1) Hourly wages were calculated from annual wage data based on a 40 hour work week
Source: Bureau of Labor Statistics, Metro Area Occupational Employment & Wage Estimates, May 2024

Employment by Industry

Sector	MSA[1] Number of Employees	MSA[1] Percent of Total	U.S. Percent of Total
Construction, Mining, and Logging	13,500	4.7	5.5
Financial Activities	12,700	4.5	5.8
Government	34,900	12.3	14.9
Information	1,900	0.7	1.9
Leisure and Hospitality	30,500	10.7	10.4
Manufacturing	33,300	11.7	8.0
Other Services	11,000	3.9	3.7
Private Education and Health Services	61,300	21.5	16.9
Professional and Business Services	33,800	11.9	14.2
Retail Trade	32,400	11.4	10.0
Transportation, Warehousing, and Utilities	10,300	3.6	4.8
Wholesale Trade	9,100	3.2	3.9

Note: Figures are non-farm employment as of December 2024. Figures are not seasonally adjusted and include workers 16 years of age and older; (1) Figures cover the Winston-Salem, NC Metropolitan Statistical Area
Source: Bureau of Labor Statistics, Current Employment Statistics, Employment, Hours, and Earnings

Employment by Occupation

Occupation Classification	City (%)	MSA[1] (%)	U.S. (%)
Management, Business, Science, and Arts	40.9	38.0	42.0
Natural Resources, Construction, and Maintenance	7.7	9.5	8.6
Production, Transportation, and Material Moving	14.0	16.1	13.0
Sales and Office	20.0	20.5	19.9
Service	17.4	15.8	16.5

Note: Figures cover employed civilians 16 years of age and older; (1) Figures cover the Winston-Salem, NC Metropolitan Statistical Area
Source: U.S. Census Bureau, 2019-2023 American Community Survey 5-Year Estimates

Occupations with Greatest Projected Employment Growth: 2022 – 2032

Occupation[1]	2022 Employment	2032 Projected Employment	Numeric Employment Change	Percent Employment Change
Software Developers	57,190	75,660	18,470	32.3
Cooks, Restaurant	47,710	66,050	18,340	38.4
Registered Nurses	106,190	123,650	17,460	16.4
Home Health and Personal Care Aides	62,750	77,390	14,640	23.3
Stockers and Order Fillers	92,790	105,710	12,920	13.9
Laborers and Freight, Stock, and Material Movers, Hand	121,680	133,850	12,170	10.0
General and Operations Managers	94,010	105,400	11,390	12.1
Fast Food and Counter Workers	65,320	75,130	9,810	15.0
First-Line Supervisors of Food Preparation and Serving Workers	41,690	49,690	8,000	19.2
Waiters and Waitresses	71,300	79,060	7,760	10.9

Note: Projections cover North Carolina; (1) Sorted by numeric employment change
Source: www.projectionscentral.org, State Occupational Projections, 2022–2032 Long-Term Projections

Fastest-Growing Occupations: 2022 – 2032

Occupation[1]	2022 Employment	2032 Projected Employment	Numeric Employment Change	Percent Employment Change
Nurse Practitioners	8,200	12,750	4,550	55.5
Solar Photovoltaic Installers	950	1,400	450	47.4
Statisticians	1,580	2,270	690	43.7
Data Scientists	5,430	7,720	2,290	42.2
Medical and Health Services Managers	12,880	17,860	4,980	38.7
Cooks, Restaurant	47,710	66,050	18,340	38.4
Physician Assistants	7,440	10,170	2,730	36.7
Information Security Analysts (SOC 2018)	5,920	8,070	2,150	36.3
Occupational Therapy Assistants	1,310	1,780	470	35.9
Wind Turbine Service Technicians	140	190	50	35.7

Note: Projections cover North Carolina; (1) Sorted by percent employment change and excludes occupations with numeric employment change less than 50
Source: www.projectionscentral.org, State Occupational Projections, 2022–2032 Long-Term Projections

CITY FINANCES

City Government Finances

Component	2022 ($000)	2022 ($ per capita)
Total Revenues	505,506	2,037
Total Expenditures	393,944	1,588
Debt Outstanding	824,844	3,324

Source: U.S. Census Bureau, State & Local Government Finances 2022

City Government Revenue by Source

Source	2022 ($000)	2022 ($ per capita)	2022 (%)
General Revenue			
From Federal Government	62,490	252	12.4
From State Government	29,390	118	5.8
From Local Governments	1,133	5	0.2
Taxes			
Property	162,247	654	32.1
Sales and Gross Receipts	63,951	258	12.7
Personal Income	0	0	0.0
Corporate Income	0	0	0.0
Motor Vehicle License	2,329	9	0.5
Other Taxes	2,167	9	0.4
Current Charges	102,239	412	20.2
Liquor Store	0	0	0.0
Utility	65,371	263	12.9

Source: U.S. Census Bureau, State & Local Government Finances 2022

City Government Expenditures by Function

Function	2022 ($000)	2022 ($ per capita)	2022 (%)
General Direct Expenditures			
Air Transportation	0	0	0.0
Corrections	0	0	0.0
Education	0	0	0.0
Employment Security Administration	0	0	0.0
Financial Administration	3,676	14	0.9
Fire Protection	39,853	160	10.1
General Public Buildings	11,762	47	3.0
Governmental Administration, Other	17,709	71	4.5
Health	0	0	0.0
Highways	25,517	102	6.5
Hospitals	0	0	0.0
Housing and Community Development	33,997	137	8.6
Interest on General Debt	22,413	90	5.7
Judicial and Legal	1,665	6	0.4
Libraries	0	0	0.0
Parking	1,253	5	0.3
Parks and Recreation	38,140	153	9.7
Police Protection	80,717	325	20.5
Public Welfare	0	0	0.0
Sewerage	23,668	95	6.0
Solid Waste Management	29,288	118	7.4
Veterans' Services	0	0	0.0
Liquor Store	0	0	0.0
Utility	56,952	229	14.5

Source: U.S. Census Bureau, State & Local Government Finances 2022

TAXES

State Corporate Income Tax Rates

State	Tax Rate (%)	Income Brackets ($)	Num. of Brackets	Financial Institution Tax Rate (%)[a]	Federal Income Tax Ded.
North Carolina	2.5	Flat rate	1	2.5	No

Note: Tax rates for tax year 2024; (a) Rates listed are the corporate income tax rate applied to financial institutions or excise taxes based on income. Some states have other taxes based upon the value of deposits or shares.
Source: Federation of Tax Administrators, State Corporate Income Tax Rates, January 1, 2025

State Individual Income Tax Rates

State	Tax Rate (%)	Income Brackets ($)	Personal Exemptions ($)			Standard Ded. ($)	
			Single	Married	Depend.	Single	Married
North Carolina	4.5	Flat rate	None	None	None	12,750	25,500

Note: Tax rates for tax year 2024; Local- and county-level taxes are not included; Federal income tax is not deductible on state income tax returns
Source: Federation of Tax Administrators, State Individual Income Tax Rates, January 1, 2025

Various State Sales and Excise Tax Rates

State	State Sales Tax (%)	Gasoline[1] ($/gal.)	Cigarette[2] ($/pack)	Spirits[3] ($/gal.)	Wine[4] ($/gal.)	Beer[5] ($/gal.)	Recreational Marijuana (%)
North Carolina	4.75	0.41	0.45	18.23	1.00	0.62	Not legal

Note: All tax rates as of January 1, 2025; (1) The American Petroleum Institute has developed a methodology for determining the average tax rate on a gallon of fuel. Rates may include any of the following: excise taxes, environmental fees, storage tank fees, other fees or taxes, general sales tax, and local taxes; (2) The federal excise tax of $1.0066 per pack and local taxes are not included; (3) Rates are those applicable to off-premise sales of 40% alcohol by volume (a.b.v.) distilled spirits in 750ml containers. Local excise taxes are excluded; (4) Rates are those applicable to off-premise sales of 11% a.b.v. non-carbonated wine in 750ml containers; (5) Rates are those applicable to off-premise sales of 4.7% a.b.v. beer in 12 ounce containers.
Source: Tax Foundation, 2025 Facts & Figures: How Does Your State Compare?

State Tax Competitiveness Index

State	Overall Rank	Corporate Tax Rank	Individual Income Tax Rank	Sales Tax Rank	Property Tax Rank	Unemployment Insurance Tax Rank
North Carolina	12	3	21	16	20	7

Note: The Tax Foundation's State Tax Competitiveness Index enables policymakers, taxpayers, and business leaders to gauge how their states' tax systems compare. A rank of 1 is best, 50 is worst. Rankings do not average to the total. States without a tax rank equally as 1. DC's scores and rankings do not affect other states. The report shows tax systems as of July 1, 2024 (the beginning of Fiscal Year 2025).
Source: Tax Foundation, State Tax Competitiveness Index 2025

TRANSPORTATION

Means of Transportation to Work

Area	Car/Truck/Van		Public Transportation			Bicycle	Walked	Other Means	Worked at Home
	Drove Alone	Car-pooled	Bus	Subway	Railroad				
City	73.2	9.5	1.1	0.0	0.0	0.3	2.0	1.6	12.3
MSA[1]	77.9	8.7	0.5	0.0	0.0	0.1	1.2	1.1	10.6
U.S.	70.2	8.5	1.7	1.3	0.4	0.4	2.4	1.6	13.5

Note: Figures are percentages and cover workers 16 years of age and older; (1) Figures cover the Winston-Salem, NC Metropolitan Statistical Area
Source: U.S. Census Bureau, 2019-2023 American Community Survey 5-Year Estimates

Travel Time to Work

Area	Less Than 10 Minutes	10 to 19 Minutes	20 to 29 Minutes	30 to 44 Minutes	45 to 59 Minutes	60 to 89 Minutes	90 Minutes or More
City	14.4	39.6	23.0	14.0	4.1	2.9	2.0
MSA[1]	12.5	32.1	24.5	19.3	5.8	3.5	2.2
U.S.	12.6	28.6	21.2	20.8	8.1	6.0	2.8

Note: Note: Figures are percentages and include workers 16 years old and over; (1) Figures cover the Winston-Salem, NC Metropolitan Statistical Area
Source: U.S. Census Bureau, 2019-2023 American Community Survey 5-Year Estimates

Key Congestion Measures

Measure	2000	2010	2015	2020	2022
Annual Hours of Delay, Total (000)	4,032	6,414	7,278	4,455	7,202
Annual Hours of Delay, Per Auto Commuter	17	20	24	15	25
Annual Congestion Cost, Per Auto Commuter ($)	399	502	530	339	523

Note: Figures cover the Winston-Salem NC urban area
Source: Texas A&M Transportation Institute, 2023 Urban Mobility Report

Freeway Travel Time Index

Measure	1985	1990	1995	2000	2005	2010	2015	2020	2022
Urban Area Index[1]	1.05	1.05	1.06	1.10	1.12	1.12	1.11	1.04	1.07
Urban Area Rank[1,2]	64	89	93	85	86	89	96	101	101

Note: Freeway Travel Time Index—the ratio of travel time in the peak period to the travel time at free-flow conditions. For example, a value of 1.30 indicates a 20-minute free-flow trip takes 26 minutes in the peak (20 minutes x 1.30 = 26 minutes); (1) Covers the Winston-Salem NC urban area; (2) Rank is based on 101 larger urban areas (#1 = highest travel time index)
Source: Texas A&M Transportation Institute, 2023 Urban Mobility Report

Public Transportation

Agency Name / Mode of Transportation	Vehicles Operated in Maximum Service[1]	Annual Unlinked Passenger Trips[2] (in thous.)	Annual Passenger Miles[3] (in thous.)
Winston-Salem Transit Authority (WSTA)			
Bus (directly operated)	30	1,552.5	4,308.6
Demand Response (directly operated)	27	163.1	1,580.1

Note: (1) Number of revenue vehicles operated by the given mode and type of service to meet the annual maximum service requirement. This is the revenue vehicle count during the peak season of the year; on the week and day that maximum service is provided. Vehicles operated in maximum service (VOMS) exclude atypical days and one-time special events; (2) Number of passengers who boarded public transportation vehicles. Passengers are counted each time they board a vehicle no matter how many vehicles they use to travel from their origin to their destination. (3) Sum of the distances ridden by all passengers during the entire fiscal year.
Source: Federal Transit Administration, National Transit Database, 2023

Air Transportation

Airport Name and Code / Type of Service	Passenger Airlines[1]	Passenger Enplanements	Freight Carriers[2]	Freight (lbs)
Piedmont Triad International Airport (23 miles) (GSO)				
Domestic service (U.S. carriers only)	22	985,423	13	76,702,652
International service (U.S. carriers only)	0	0	1	3,906

Note: (1) Includes all U.S.-based major, minor and commuter airlines that carried at least one passenger during the year; (2) Includes all U.S.-based airlines and freight carriers that transported at least one pound of freight during the year.
Source: Bureau of Transportation Statistics, The Intermodal Transportation Database, Air Carriers: T-100 Domestic Market (U.S. carriers only), 2024; Bureau of Transportation Statistics, The Intermodal Transportation Database, Air Carriers: T-100 International Market (U.S. carriers only), 2024

BUSINESSES

Major Business Headquarters

Company Name	Industry	Rankings	
		Fortune[1]	Forbes[2]
No companies listed	-	-	-

Note: (1) Companies that produce a 10-K are ranked 1 to 500 based on 2023 revenue; (2) All private companies with at least $2 billion in annual revenue through the end of their most current fiscal year are ranked 1 to 275; companies listed are headquartered in the city; dashes indicate no ranking
Source: Fortune, "Fortune 500," 2024; Forbes, "America's Largest Private Companies," 2024

Fastest-Growing Businesses

According to *Inc.*, Winston-Salem is home to one of America's 500 fastest-growing private companies: **Accelerated Brands** (#491). Criteria: must be an independent, privately-held, for-profit, U.S. corporation, proprietorship or partnership as of December 31, 2023; revenues must be at least $100,000 in 2020 and $2 million in 2023; must have four-year operating/sales history. *Inc.*, "America's 500 Fastest-Growing Private Companies," 2024

Living Environment

COST OF LIVING

Cost of Living Index

Composite Index	Groceries	Housing	Utilities	Transportation	Health Care	Misc. Goods/Services
93.4	97.0	77.5	101.7	92.1	105.8	101.5

Note: The Cost of Living Index measures regional differences in the cost of consumer goods and services, excluding taxes and non-consumer expenditures, for professional and managerial households in the top income quintile. It is based on more than 50,000 prices covering almost 60 different items for which prices are collected three times a year by chambers of commerce, economic development organizations or university applied economic centers in each participating urban area. The numbers shown should be read as a percentage above or below the national average of 100. For example, a value of 115.4 in the groceries column indicates that grocery prices are 15.4% higher than the national average. Small differences in the index numbers should not be interpreted as significant; Figures cover the Winston-Salem NC urban area.
Source: The Council for Community and Economic Research, Cost of Living Index, 2024

Grocery Prices

Area[1]	T-Bone Steak ($/pound)	Frying Chicken ($/pound)	Whole Milk ($/half gal.)	Eggs ($/dozen)	Orange Juice ($/64 oz.)	Coffee ($/11.5 oz.)
City[2]	15.51	1.46	4.60	3.19	4.30	5.15
Avg.	15.42	1.55	4.69	3.25	4.41	5.46
Min.	14.50	1.16	4.43	2.75	4.00	4.85
Max.	17.56	2.89	5.49	4.78	5.54	7.89

Note: (1) Values for the local area are compared with the average, minimum and maximum values for all 276 areas in the Cost of Living Index; (2) Figures cover the Winston-Salem NC urban area; **T-Bone Steak** (price per pound); **Frying Chicken** (price per pound, whole fryer); **Whole Milk** (half gallon carton); **Eggs** (price per dozen, Grade A, large); **Orange Juice** (64 oz. Tropicana or Florida Natural); **Coffee** (11.5 oz. can, vacuum-packed, Maxwell House, Hills Bros, or Folgers).
Source: The Council for Community and Economic Research, Cost of Living Index, 2024

Housing and Utility Costs

Area[1]	New Home Price ($)	Apartment Rent ($/month)	All Electric ($/month)	Part Electric ($/month)	Other Energy ($/month)	Telephone ($/month)
City[2]	383,928	1,301	214.90	-	-	189.30
Avg.	515,975	1,550	210.99	123.07	82.07	194.99
Min.	265,375	692	104.33	53.68	36.26	179.42
Max.	2,775,821	5,719	529.02	397.28	361.63	223.33

Note: (1) Values for the local area are compared with the average, minimum and maximum values for all 276 areas in the Cost of Living Index; (2) Figures cover the Winston-Salem NC urban area; **New Home Price** (2,400 sf living area, 8,000 sf lot, in urban area with full utilities); **Apartment Rent** (950 sf 2 bedroom/1.5 or 2 bath, unfurnished, excluding all utilities except water); **All Electric** (average monthly cost for an all-electric home); **Part Electric** (average monthly cost for a part-electric home); **Other Energy** (average monthly cost for natural gas, fuel oil, coal, wood, and any other forms of energy except electricity); **Telephone** (price includes the base monthly rate plus taxes and fees for three lines of mobile phone service).
Source: The Council for Community and Economic Research, Cost of Living Index, 2024

Health Care, Transportation, and Other Costs

Area[1]	Doctor ($/visit)	Dentist ($/visit)	Optometrist ($/visit)	Gasoline ($/gallon)	Beauty Salon ($/visit)	Men's Shirt ($)
City[2]	152.89	120.67	145.61	3.15	50.94	38.49
Avg.	143.77	117.51	129.23	3.32	48.57	38.14
Min.	36.74	58.67	67.33	2.80	24.00	13.41
Max.	270.44	216.82	307.33	5.28	94.00	63.89

Note: (1) Values for the local area are compared with the average, minimum and maximum values for all 276 areas in the Cost of Living Index; (2) Figures cover the Winston-Salem NC urban area; **Doctor** (general practitioners routine exam of an established patient); **Dentist** (adult teeth cleaning and periodic oral examination); **Optometrist** (full vision eye exam for established adult patient); **Gasoline** (one gallon regular unleaded, national brand, including all taxes, cash price at self-service pump if available); **Beauty Salon** (woman's shampoo, trim, and blow-dry); **Men's Shirt** (cotton/polyester dress shirt, pinpoint weave, long sleeves).
Source: The Council for Community and Economic Research, Cost of Living Index, 2024

HOUSING

Homeownership Rate

Area	2017 (%)	2018 (%)	2019 (%)	2020 (%)	2021 (%)	2022 (%)	2023 (%)	2024 (%)
MSA[1]	n/a	n/a	n/a	n/a	n/a	n/a	n/a	n/a
U.S.	63.9	64.4	64.6	66.6	65.5	65.8	65.9	65.6

Note: (1) Figures cover the Winston-Salem, NC Metropolitan Statistical Area; n/a not available
Source: U.S. Census Bureau, Housing Vacancies and Homeownership Annual Statistics: 2017-2024

House Price Index (HPI)

Area	National Ranking[2]	Quarterly Change (%)	One-Year Change (%)	Five-Year Change (%)	Since 1991Q1 (%)
MSA[1]	33	1.41	7.91	70.24	245.21
U.S.[3]	–	1.43	4.51	57.13	327.82

Note: The HPI is a weighted repeat sales index. It measures average price changes in repeat sales or refinancings on the same properties. This information is obtained by reviewing repeat mortgage transactions on single-family properties whose mortgages have been purchased or securitized by Fannie Mae or Freddie Mac since January 1975; (1) Figures cover the Winston-Salem, NC Metropolitan Statistical Area; (2) Rankings are based on annual percentage change for all metro areas containing at least 15,000 transactions over the last 10 years and ranges from 1 to 241; (3) figures based on a weighted average of Census Division estimates using a seasonally adjusted, purchase-only index; all figures are for the period ending December 31, 2024
Source: Federal Housing Finance Agency, Change in FHFA Metropolitan Area House Price Indexes, All Transactions Index, 2024Q4

Home Value

Area	Under $100,000	$100,000 -$199,999	$200,000 -$299,999	$300,000 -$399,999	$400,000 -$499,999	$500,000 -$999,999	$1,000,000 or more	Median ($)
City	12.9	34.6	25.9	12.1	4.6	8.3	1.7	208,200
MSA[1]	14.0	32.0	26.0	13.0	6.5	7.3	1.2	213,300
U.S.	12.1	17.8	19.5	14.4	10.5	19.1	6.5	303,400

Note: Figures are percentages except for median and cover owner-occupied housing units; (1) Figures cover the Winston-Salem, NC Metropolitan Statistical Area
Source: U.S. Census Bureau, 2019-2023 American Community Survey 5-Year Estimates

Year Housing Structure Built

Area	2020 or Later	2010 -2019	2000 -2009	1990 -1999	1980 -1989	1970 -1979	1960 -1969	1950 -1959	1940 -1949	Before 1940	Median Year
City	1.1	8.6	13.2	12.5	15.0	14.4	11.0	12.2	4.1	7.7	1980
MSA[1]	1.0	8.7	15.6	15.9	14.5	15.5	10.1	9.0	3.7	6.1	1984
U.S.	1.2	8.9	13.6	12.8	13.0	14.4	10.0	9.7	4.5	11.9	1980

Note: Figures are percentages except for Median Year; Note: (1) Figures cover the Winston-Salem, NC Metropolitan Statistical Area
Source: U.S. Census Bureau, 2019-2023 American Community Survey 5-Year Estimates

Gross Monthly Rent

Area	Under $500	$500 -$999	$1,000 -$1,499	$1,500 -$1,999	$2,000 -$2,499	$2,500 -$2,999	$3,000 and up	Median ($)
City	6.7	40.1	36.5	11.4	3.5	0.8	1.0	1,033
MSA[1]	7.6	45.5	32.7	10.3	2.5	0.7	0.6	973
U.S.	6.5	22.3	29.5	20.2	10.8	4.8	5.9	1,348

Note: Figures are percentages except for median; Gross rent is the contract rent plus the estimated average monthly cost of utilities (electricity, gas, and water and sewer) and fuels (oil, coal, kerosene, wood, etc.) if these are paid by the renter (or paid for the renter by someone else); (1) Figures cover the Winston-Salem, NC Metropolitan Statistical Area
Source: U.S. Census Bureau, 2019-2023 American Community Survey 5-Year Estimates

HEALTH

Health Risk Factors

Category	MSA[1] (%)	U.S. (%)
Adults aged 18–64 who have any kind of health care coverage	n/a	90.8
Adults who reported being in good or better health	n/a	81.8
Adults who have been told they have high blood cholesterol	n/a	36.9
Adults who have been told they have high blood pressure	n/a	34.0
Adults who are current smokers	n/a	12.1
Adults who currently use e-cigarettes	n/a	7.7
Adults who currently use chewing tobacco, snuff, or snus	n/a	3.2
Adults who are heavy drinkers[2]	n/a	6.1
Adults who are binge drinkers[3]	n/a	15.2
Adults who are overweight (BMI 25.0 - 29.9)	n/a	34.4
Adults who are obese (BMI 30.0 - 99.8)	n/a	34.3
Adults who participated in any physical activities in the past month	n/a	75.8

Note: All figures are crude prevalence; (1) Figures for the Winston-Salem, NC Metropolitan Statistical Area were not available.
(2) Heavy drinkers are classified as adult men having more than 14 drinks per week and adult women having more than 7 drinks per week; (3) Binge drinkers are classified as males having five or more drinks on one occasion or females having four or more drinks on one occasion
Source: Centers for Disease Control and Prevention, Behavioral Risk Factor Surveillance System, SMART: Selected Metropolitan Area Risk Trends, 2023

Acute and Chronic Health Conditions

Category	MSA[1] (%)	U.S. (%)
Adults who have ever been told they had a heart attack	n/a	4.2
Adults who have ever been told they have angina or coronary heart disease	n/a	4.0
Adults who have ever been told they had a stroke	n/a	3.3
Adults who have ever been told they have asthma	n/a	15.7
Adults who have ever been told they have arthritis	n/a	26.3
Adults who have ever been told they have diabetes[2]	n/a	11.5
Adults who have ever been told they had skin cancer	n/a	5.6
Adults who have ever been told they had any other types of cancer	n/a	8.4
Adults who have ever been told they have COPD	n/a	6.4
Adults who have ever been told they have kidney disease	n/a	3.7
Adults who have ever been told they have a form of depression	n/a	22.0

Note: All figures are crude prevalence; (1) Figures for the Winston-Salem, NC Metropolitan Statistical Area were not available.
(2) Figures do not include pregnancy-related, borderline, or pre-diabetes
Source: Centers for Disease Control and Prevention, Behavioral Risk Factor Surveillance System, SMART: Selected Metropolitan Area Risk Trends, 2023

Health Screening and Vaccination Rates

Category	MSA[1] (%)	U.S. (%)
Adults who have ever been tested for HIV	n/a	37.5
Adults who have had their blood cholesterol checked within the last five years	n/a	87.0
Adults aged 65+ who have had flu shot within the past year	n/a	63.4
Adults aged 65+ who have ever had a pneumonia vaccination	n/a	71.9

Note: All figures are crude prevalence; (1) Figures for the Winston-Salem, NC Metropolitan Statistical Area were not available.
Source: Centers for Disease Control and Prevention, Behavioral Risk Factor Surveillance System, SMART: Selected Metropolitan Area Risk Trends, 2023

Disability Status

Category	MSA[1] (%)	U.S. (%)
Adults who reported being deaf	n/a	7.4
Are you blind or have serious difficulty seeing, even when wearing glasses?	n/a	4.9
Do you have difficulty doing errands alone?	n/a	7.8
Do you have difficulty dressing or bathing?	n/a	3.6
Do you have serious difficulty concentrating/remembering/making decisions?	n/a	13.7
Do you have serious difficulty walking or climbing stairs?	n/a	13.2

Note: All figures are crude prevalence; (1) Figures for the Winston-Salem, NC Metropolitan Statistical Area were not available.
Source: Centers for Disease Control and Prevention, Behavioral Risk Factor Surveillance System, SMART: Selected Metropolitan Area Risk Trends, 2023

Mortality Rates for the Top 10 Causes of Death in the U.S.

ICD-10[a] Sub-Chapter	ICD-10[a] Code	Crude Mortality Rate[2] per 100,000 population	
		County[3]	U.S.
Malignant neoplasms	C00-C97	197.5	182.7
Ischaemic heart diseases	I20-I25	93.9	109.6
Provisional assignment of new diseases of uncertain etiology[1]	U00-U49	59.6	65.3
Other forms of heart disease	I30-I51	67.1	65.1
Other degenerative diseases of the nervous system	G30-G31	56.0	52.4
Other external causes of accidental injury	W00-X59	69.0	52.3
Cerebrovascular diseases	I60-I69	56.5	49.1
Chronic lower respiratory diseases	J40-J47	52.3	43.5
Hypertensive diseases	I10-I15	27.9	38.9
Organic, including symptomatic, mental disorders	F01-F09	52.4	33.9

Note: (a) ICD-10 = International Classification of Diseases 10th Revision; (1) Includes COVID-19, adverse effects to COVID-19 vaccines, SARS, and vaping-related disorders; (2) Crude mortality rates are a three-year average covering 2021-2023; (3) Figures cover Forsyth County.
Source: Centers for Disease Control and Prevention, National Center for Health Statistics. National Vital Statistics System, Mortality 2018-2023 on CDC WONDER Online Database

Mortality Rates for Selected Causes of Death

Cause of Death	ICD-10[a] Code	Crude Mortality Rate[1] per 100,000 population	
		County[2]	U.S.
Accidental poisoning and exposure to noxious substances	X40-X49	40.5	30.5
Alzheimer disease	G30	43.9	35.4
Assault	X85-Y09	12.2	7.3
COVID-19	U07.1	59.6	65.3
Diabetes mellitus	E10-E14	34.8	30.0
Diseases of the liver	K70-K76	21.4	20.8
Human immunodeficiency virus (HIV) disease	B20-B24	2.8	1.5
Influenza and pneumonia	J09-J18	14.7	13.4
Intentional self-harm	X60-X84	13.4	14.7
Malnutrition	E40-E46	5.8	6.0
Obesity and other hyperalimentation	E65-E68	4.8	3.1
Renal failure	N17-N19	22.9	16.4
Transport accidents	V01-V99	14.1	14.4

Note: (a) ICD-10 = International Classification of Diseases 10th Revision; (1) Crude mortality rates are a three-year average covering 2021-2023; (2) Figures cover Forsyth County; Data are suppressed when the data meet the criteria for confidentiality constraints; Crude mortality rates are flagged as unreliable when the rate would be calculated with a numerator of 20 or less.
Source: Centers for Disease Control and Prevention, National Center for Health Statistics. National Vital Statistics System, Mortality 2018-2023 on CDC WONDER Online Database

Health Insurance Coverage

Area	With Health Insurance	With Private Health Insurance	With Public Health Insurance	Without Health Insurance	Population Under Age 19 Without Health Insurance
City	88.1	61.8	37.5	11.9	4.7
MSA[1]	89.6	64.5	37.6	10.4	4.6
U.S.	91.4	67.3	36.3	8.6	5.4

Note: Figures are percentages that cover the civilian noninstitutionalized population; (1) Figures cover the Winston-Salem, NC Metropolitan Statistical Area
Source: U.S. Census Bureau, 2019-2023 American Community Survey 5-Year Estimates

Number of Medical Professionals

Area	MDs[3]	DOs[3,4]	Dentists	Podiatrists	Chiropractors	Optometrists
County[1] (number)	2,787	160	255	27	75	73
County[1] (rate[2])	716.2	41.1	64.9	6.9	19.1	18.6
U.S. (rate[2])	302.5	29.2	74.6	6.4	29.5	18.0

Note: Data as of 2023 unless noted; (1) Data covers Forsyth County; (2) Number of medical professionals per 100,000 population; (3) Data as of 2022 and includes all active, non-federal physicians; (4) Doctor of Osteopathic Medicine
Source: U.S. Department of Health and Human Services, Health Resources and Services Administration, Bureau of Health Professions, Area Resource File (ARF) 2023-2024

EDUCATION

Public School District Statistics

District Name	Schls	Pupils	Pupil/ Teacher Ratio	Minority Pupils[1] (%)	Total Rev. per Pupil ($)	Total Exp. per Pupil ($)
Winston Salem/Forsyth Co. Schls	81	52,157	14.3	67.8	13,739	14,195

Note: Table includes school districts with 2,000 or more students; (1) Percentage of students that are not non-Hispanic white.
Source: U.S. Department of Education, National Center for Education Statistics, Common Core of Data, Local Education Agency (School District) Universe Survey: School Year 2023-2024; U.S. Department of Education, National Center for Education Statistics, Common Core of Data, School District Finance Survey (F-33): School Year 2021–22

Highest Level of Education

Area	Less than H.S.	H.S. Diploma	Some College, No Deg.	Associate Degree	Bachelor's Degree	Master's Degree	Prof. School Degree	Doctorate Degree
City	11.6	23.7	19.5	7.9	21.6	10.2	2.8	2.6
MSA[1]	10.8	28.4	21.4	9.8	18.9	7.3	1.9	1.5
U.S.	10.6	26.2	19.4	8.8	21.3	9.8	2.3	1.6

Note: Figures cover persons age 25 and over; (1) Figures cover the Winston-Salem, NC Metropolitan Statistical Area
Source: U.S. Census Bureau, 2019-2023 American Community Survey 5-Year Estimates

Educational Attainment by Race

Area	High School Graduate or Higher (%)					Bachelor's Degree or Higher (%)				
	Total	White	Black	Asian	Hisp.[2]	Total	White	Black	Asian	Hisp.[2]
City	88.4	91.9	89.4	96.1	61.1	37.2	47.5	24.1	70.3	16.3
MSA[1]	89.2	91.0	90.0	88.5	63.8	29.6	31.4	24.6	54.1	14.7
U.S.	89.4	92.9	88.1	88.0	72.5	35.0	37.7	24.7	57.0	19.9

Note: Figures shown cover persons 25 years old and over; (1) Figures cover the Winston-Salem, NC Metropolitan Statistical Area; (2) People of Hispanic origin can be of any race
Source: U.S. Census Bureau, 2019-2023 American Community Survey 5-Year Estimates

School Enrollment by Grade and Control

Area	Preschool (%)		Kindergarten (%)		Grades 1 - 4 (%)		Grades 5 - 8 (%)		Grades 9 - 12 (%)	
	Public	Private	Public	Private	Public	Private	Public	Private	Public	Private
City	60.4	39.6	88.7	11.3	88.2	11.8	90.5	9.5	90.4	9.6
MSA[1]	48.5	51.5	85.5	14.5	87.3	12.7	89.0	11.0	86.7	13.3
U.S.	58.7	41.3	85.2	14.8	87.2	12.8	87.9	12.1	89.0	11.0

Note: Figures shown cover persons 3 years old and over; (1) Figures cover the Winston-Salem, NC Metropolitan Statistical Area
Source: U.S. Census Bureau, 2019-2023 American Community Survey 5-Year Estimates

Higher Education

Four-Year Colleges			Two-Year Colleges			Medical Schools[1]	Law Schools[2]	Voc/Tech[3]
Public	Private Non-profit	Private For-profit	Public	Private Non-profit	Private For-profit			
2	4	0	2	0	0	1	1	2

Note: Figures cover institutions located within the Winston-Salem, NC Metropolitan Statistical Area and include main campuses only; (1) includes schools accredited by the Liaison Committee on Medical Education and the American Osteopathic Association's Commission on Osteopathic College Accreditation; (2) includes ABA-accredited schools, schools with provisional ABA accreditation, and state accredited schools; (3) includes all schools with programs that are less than 2 years.
Source: National Center for Education Statistics, Integrated Postsecondary Education System (IPEDS), 2023-24; Wikipedia, List of Medical Schools in the United States, accessed May 2, 2025; Wikipedia, List of Law Schools in the United States, accessed May 2, 2025

According to *U.S. News & World Report,* the Winston-Salem, NC metro area is home to one of the top 200 national universities in the U.S.: **Wake Forest University** (#46 tie). The indicators used to capture academic quality fall into a number of categories: assessment by administrators at peer institutions; retention of students; faculty resources; student selectivity; financial resources; alumni giving; high school counselor ratings of colleges; and graduation rate. *U.S. News & World Report, "America's Best Colleges 2025"*

According to *U.S. News & World Report,* the Winston-Salem, NC metro area is home to one of the top 100 law schools in the U.S.: **Wake Forest University** (#26 tie). The rankings are based on a weighted average of 12 measures of quality: peer assessment score; assessment score by lawyers/judges; median LSAT scores; median undergrad GPA; acceptance rate; employment rates for graduates; placement success; bar passage rate; faculty resources; expenditures per student; student/faculty ratio; and library resources. *U.S. News & World Report, "America's Best Graduate Schools, Law, 2025"*

EMPLOYERS

Major Employers

Company Name	Industry
AT&T	Telecommunications
Atrium Health Wake Forest Baptist	Healthcare
City of Winston-Salem	Government
Collins Aerospace Interiors	Aerospace interiors
Forsyth County	Government
Forsyth Technical College	Education
Hanesbrands	Clothing
Hayward Industries	Pumps and pool equipment
Herbalife	Healthcare supplements
Inmar Inc.	Insurance
Lowes Food Stores	Grocery
National General Insurance	Insurance
Novant Health	Healthcare
Reynolds American	Tobacco manufacturing
Truist	Financial services
Wake Forest University	Higher education
Wells Fargo	Financial services
Winston Salem/Forsyth County Schools	Public education
Winston-Salem State University	Higher education
YMCA of NWNC	Non-profit

Note: Companies shown are located within the Winston-Salem, NC Metropolitan Statistical Area.
Source: Chambers of Commerce; State Departments of Labor; Wikipedia

PUBLIC SAFETY

Crime Rate

Area	Total Crime Rate	Violent Crime Rate				Property Crime Rate		
		Murder	Rape	Robbery	Aggrav. Assault	Burglary	Larceny-Theft	Motor Vehicle Theft
City	3,897.6	16.7	34.9	97.2	737.7	629.4	1,994.6	387.1
U.S.	2,290.9	5.7	38.0	66.5	264.1	250.7	1,347.2	318.7

Note: Figures are crimes per 100,000 population.
Source: FBI, Table 8, Offenses Known to Law Enforcement, by State by City, 2023

Hate Crimes

Area	Number of Quarters Reported	Number of Incidents per Bias Motivation					
		Race/Ethnicity/Ancestry	Religion	Sexual Orientation	Disability	Gender	Gender Identity
City[1]	4	2	2	0	0	0	0
U.S.	4	5,900	2,699	2,077	187	92	492

Note: (1) Figures include at least one incident reported with more than one bias motivation.
Source: Federal Bureau of Investigation, Hate Crime Statistics 2023

Identity Theft Consumer Reports

Area	Reports	Reports per 100,000 Population	Rank[2]
MSA[1]	1,279	187	183
U.S.	1,135,291	339	-

Note: (1) Figures cover the Winston-Salem, NC Metropolitan Statistical Area; (2) Rank ranges from 1 to 401 where 1 indicates greatest number of identity theft reports per 100,000 population
Source: Federal Trade Commission, Consumer Sentinel Network Data Book 2024

Fraud and Other Consumer Reports

Area	Reports	Reports per 100,000 Population	Rank[2]
MSA[1]	7,415	1,085	168
U.S.	5,360,641	1,601	-

Note: (1) Figures cover the Winston-Salem, NC Metropolitan Statistical Area; (2) Rank ranges from 1 to 401 where 1 indicates greatest number of fraud and other consumer reports per 100,000 population
Source: Federal Trade Commission, Consumer Sentinel Network Data Book 2024

POLITICS

2024 Presidential Election Results

Area	Trump (Rep.)	Harris (Dem.)	Stein (Green)	Kennedy (Ind.)	Oliver (Lib.)	Other
Forsyth County	42.6	55.8	0.4	0.0	0.4	0.8
U.S.	49.7	48.2	0.6	0.5	0.4	0.6

Note: Results are percentages and may not add to 100% due to rounding
Source: Dave Leip's Atlas of U.S. Presidential Elections

SPORTS

Professional Sports Teams

Team Name	League	Year Established
No teams are located in the metro area		

Source: Wikipedia, Major Professional Sports Teams of the United States and Canada, May 1, 2025

CLIMATE

Average and Extreme Temperatures

Temperature	Jan	Feb	Mar	Apr	May	Jun	Jul	Aug	Sep	Oct	Nov	Dec	Yr.
Extreme High (°F)	78	81	89	91	96	102	102	103	100	95	85	78	103
Average High (°F)	48	51	60	70	78	84	87	86	80	70	60	50	69
Average Temp. (°F)	38	41	49	58	67	74	78	76	70	59	49	40	58
Average Low (°F)	28	30	37	46	55	63	67	66	59	47	37	30	47
Extreme Low (°F)	-8	-1	5	23	32	42	49	45	37	20	10	0	-8

Note: Figures cover the years 1948-1990
Source: National Climatic Data Center, International Station Meteorological Climate Summary, 9/96

Average Precipitation/Snowfall/Humidity

Precip./Humidity	Jan	Feb	Mar	Apr	May	Jun	Jul	Aug	Sep	Oct	Nov	Dec	Yr.
Avg. Precip. (in.)	3.2	3.4	3.7	3.1	3.7	3.8	4.5	4.2	3.4	3.4	2.9	3.3	42.5
Avg. Snowfall (in.)	4	3	2	Tr	0	0	0	0	0	0	Tr	1	10
Avg. Rel. Hum. 7am (%)	80	78	78	77	82	84	87	90	90	88	83	80	83
Avg. Rel. Hum. 4pm (%)	53	50	47	44	51	54	57	58	56	51	51	54	52

Note: Figures cover the years 1948-1990; Tr = Trace amounts (<0.05 in. of rain; <0.5 in. of snow)
Source: National Climatic Data Center, International Station Meteorological Climate Summary, 9/96

Weather Conditions

Temperature			Daytime Sky			Precipitation		
10°F & below	32°F & below	90°F & above	Clear	Partly cloudy	Cloudy	0.01 inch or more precip.	0.1 inch or more snow/ice	Thunderstorms
3	85	32	94	143	128	113	5	43

Note: Figures are average number of days per year and cover the years 1948-1990
Source: National Climatic Data Center, International Station Meteorological Climate Summary, 9/96

HAZARDOUS WASTE

Superfund Sites

The Winston-Salem, NC metro area is home to one site on the EPA's Superfund National Priorities List (NPL) or Superfund Alternative Approach (SAA) list: **Holcomb Creosote Co** (Final NPL). The Superfund alternative approach uses the same investigation and cleanup process and standards that are used for sites listed on the National Priorities List. The SAA is an alternative to listing a site on the NPL; it is not an alternative to Superfund or the Superfund process. There are a total of 1,445 Superfund sites with a status of proposed or final on both lists in the United States. *U.S. Environmental Protection Agency, National Priorities List, May 1, 2025; U.S. Environmental Protection Agency, Superfund Alternative Approach Sites, May 1, 2025*

AIR QUALITY

Air Quality Trends: Ozone

	1990	1995	2000	2005	2010	2015	2020	2021	2022	2023
MSA[1]	0.084	0.086	0.089	0.080	0.078	0.065	0.058	0.062	0.057	0.066
U.S.	0.087	0.089	0.081	0.080	0.072	0.068	0.066	0.067	0.067	0.070

Note: (1) Data covers the Winston-Salem, NC Metropolitan Statistical Area. The values shown are the composite ozone concentration averages among trend sites based on the highest fourth daily maximum 8-hour concentration in parts per million. These trends are based on sites having an adequate record of monitoring data during the trend period. Data from exceptional events are included.
Source: U.S. Environmental Protection Agency, Air Quality Monitoring Information, "Air Quality Trends by City, 1990-2023"

Air Quality Index

Area	Percent of Days when Air Quality was...[2]					AQI Statistics[2]	
	Good	Moderate	Unhealthy for Sensitive Groups	Unhealthy	Very Unhealthy	Maximum	Median
MSA[1]	40.3	57.8	1.6	0.3	0.0	154	53

Note: (1) Data covers the Winston-Salem, NC Metropolitan Statistical Area; (2) Based on 365 days with AQI data in 2023. Air Quality Index (AQI) is an index for reporting daily air quality. EPA calculates the AQI for five major air pollutants regulated by the Clean Air Act: ground-level ozone, particle pollution (aka particulate matter), carbon monoxide, sulfur dioxide, and nitrogen dioxide. The AQI runs from 0 to 500. The higher the AQI value, the greater the level of air pollution and the greater the health concern. There are six AQI categories: "Good" AQI is between 0 and 50. Air quality is considered satisfactory; "Moderate" AQI is between 51 and 100. Air quality is acceptable; "Unhealthy for Sensitive Groups" When AQI values are between 101 and 150, members of sensitive groups may experience health effects; "Unhealthy" When AQI values are between 151 and 200 everyone may begin to experience health effects; "Very Unhealthy" AQI values between 201 and 300 trigger a health alert; "Hazardous" AQI values over 300 trigger warnings of emergency conditions (not shown).
Source: U.S. Environmental Protection Agency, Air Quality Index Report, 2023

Air Quality Index Pollutants

Area	Percent of Days when AQI Pollutant was...[2]					
	Carbon Monoxide	Nitrogen Dioxide	Ozone	Sulfur Dioxide	Particulate Matter 2.5	Particulate Matter 10
MSA[1]	0.0	0.0	27.7	(3)	72.3	0.0

Note: (1) Data covers the Winston-Salem, NC Metropolitan Statistical Area; (2) Based on 365 days with AQI data in 2023. The Air Quality Index (AQI) is an index for reporting daily air quality. EPA calculates the AQI for five major air pollutants regulated by the Clean Air Act: ground-level ozone, particle pollution (also known as particulate matter), carbon monoxide, sulfur dioxide, and nitrogen dioxide. The AQI runs from 0 to 500. The higher the AQI value, the greater the level of air pollution and the greater the health concern; (3) Sulfur dioxide is no longer included in this table because SO_2 concentrations tend to be very localized and not necessarily representative of broad geographical areas like counties and CBSAs.
Source: U.S. Environmental Protection Agency, Air Quality Index Report, 2023

Maximum Air Pollutant Concentrations: Particulate Matter, Ozone, CO and Lead

	Particulate Matter 10 (ug/m^3)	Particulate Matter 2.5 Wtd AM (ug/m^3)	Particulate Matter 2.5 24-Hr (ug/m^3)	Ozone (ppm)	Carbon Monoxide (ppm)	Lead (ug/m^3)
MSA[1] Level	72	9.5	31	0.069	n/a	n/a
NAAQS[2]	150	15	35	0.075	9	0.15
Met NAAQS[2]	Yes	Yes	Yes	Yes	n/a	n/a

Note: (1) Data covers the Winston-Salem, NC Metropolitan Statistical Area; Data from exceptional events are included; (2) National Ambient Air Quality Standards; ppm = parts per million; ug/m^3 = micrograms per cubic meter; n/a not available.
Concentrations: Particulate Matter 10 (coarse particulate)—highest second maximum 24-hour concentration; Particulate Matter 2.5 Wtd AM (fine particulate)—highest weighted annual mean concentration; Particulate Matter 2.5 24-Hour (fine particulate)—highest 98th percentile 24-hour concentration; Ozone—highest fourth daily maximum 8-hour concentration; Carbon Monoxide—highest second maximum non-overlapping 8-hour concentration; Lead—maximum running 3-month average
Source: U.S. Environmental Protection Agency, Air Quality Monitoring Information, "Air Quality Statistics by City, 2023"

Maximum Air Pollutant Concentrations: Nitrogen Dioxide and Sulfur Dioxide

	Nitrogen Dioxide AM (ppb)	Nitrogen Dioxide 1-Hr (ppb)	Sulfur Dioxide AM (ppb)	Sulfur Dioxide 1-Hr (ppb)	Sulfur Dioxide 24-Hr (ppb)
MSA[1] Level	7	40	n/a	2	n/a
NAAQS[2]	53	100	30	75	140
Met NAAQS[2]	Yes	Yes	n/a	Yes	n/a

Note: (1) Data covers the Winston-Salem, NC Metropolitan Statistical Area; Data from exceptional events are included; (2) National Ambient Air Quality Standards; ppm = parts per million; ug/m^3 = micrograms per cubic meter; n/a not available.
Concentrations: Nitrogen Dioxide AM—highest arithmetic mean concentration; Nitrogen Dioxide 1-Hr—highest 98th percentile 1-hour daily maximum concentration; Sulfur Dioxide AM—highest annual mean concentration; Sulfur Dioxide 1-Hr—highest 99th percentile 1-hour daily maximum concentration; Sulfur Dioxide 24-Hr—highest second maximum 24-hour concentration
Source: U.S. Environmental Protection Agency, Air Quality Monitoring Information, "Air Quality Statistics by City, 2023"

Appendixes

Appendices

Appendix A: Comparative Statistics

Table of Contents

Demographics
- Population Growth: City A-4
- Population Growth: Metro Area A-6
- Male/Female Ratio: City A-8
- Male/Female Ratio: Metro Area A-10
- Race: City A-12
- Race: Metro Area A-14
- Hispanic Origin: City A-16
- Hispanic Origin: Metro Area A-18
- Household Size: City A-20
- Household Size: Metro Area A-22
- Household Relationships: City A-24
- Household Relationships: Metro Area A-26
- Age: City A-28
- Age: Metro Area A-30
- Ancestry: City A-32
- Ancestry: Metro Area A-34
- Foreign-born Population: City A-36
- Foreign-born Population: Metro Area A-38
- Marital Status: City A-40
- Marital Status: Metro Area A-42
- Disability by Age: City A-44
- Disability by Age: Metro Area A-46
- Religious Groups by Family A-48
- Religious Groups by Tradition A-50

Economy
- Gross Metropolitan Product A-52
- Economic Growth A-54
- Metropolitan Area Exports A-56
- Building Permits: City A-58
- Building Permits: Metro Area A-60
- Housing Vacancy Rates A-62
- Bankruptcy Filings A-64

Income and Poverty
- Income: City A-66
- Income: Metro Area A-68
- Household Income Distribution: City A-70
- Household Income Distribution: Metro Area A-72
- Poverty Rate: City A-74
- Poverty Rate: Metro Area A-76

Employment and Earnings
- Employment by Industry A-78
- Labor Force, Employment and Job Growth: City A-80
- Labor Force, Employment and Job Growth: Metro Area . A-82
- Unemployment Rate: City A-84
- Unemployment Rate: Metro Area A-86
- Average Hourly Wages: Occupations A - C A-88
- Average Hourly Wages: Occupations C - E A-90
- Average Hourly Wages: Occupations F - J A-92
- Average Hourly Wages: Occupations L - N A-94
- Average Hourly Wages: Occupations N - P A-96
- Average Hourly Wages: Occupations P - S A-98
- Average Hourly Wages: Occupations T - W A-100
- Means of Transportation to Work: City A-102
- Means of Transportation to Work: Metro Area A-104
- Travel Time to Work: City A-106
- Travel Time to Work: Metro Area A-108

Election Results
- 2020 Presidential Election Results A-110

Housing
- House Price Index (HPI) A-112
- Home Value: City A-114
- Home Value: Metro Area A-116
- Homeownership Rate A-118
- Year Housing Structure Built: City A-120
- Year Housing Structure Built: Metro Area A-122
- Gross Monthly Rent: City A-124
- Gross Monthly Rent: Metro Area A-126

Education
- Highest Level of Education: City A-128
- Highest Level of Education: Metro Area A-130
- School Enrollment by Grade and Control: City A-132
- School Enrollment by Grade and Control: Metro Area A-134
- Educational Attainment by Race: City A-136
- Educational Attainment by Race: Metro Area A-138

Cost of Living
- Cost of Living Index A-140
- Grocery Prices A-142
- Housing and Utility Costs A-144
- Health Care, Transportation, and Other Costs A-146

Health Care
- Number of Medical Professionals A-148
- Health Insurance Coverage: City A-150
- Health Insurance Coverage: Metro Area A-152

Public Safety
- Crime Rate A-154

Climate
- Temperature & Precipitation: Yearly Averages and Extremes A-156
- Weather Conditions A-158

Air Quality
- Air Quality Index A-160
- Air Quality Index Pollutants A-162
- Air Quality Trends: Ozone A-164
- Maximum Air Pollutant Concentrations: Particulate Matter, Ozone, CO and Lead A-166
- Maximum Air Pollutant Concentrations: Nitrogen Dioxide and Sulfur Dioxide A-168

Appendix A: Comparative Statistics

Population Growth: City

City	1990 Census	2000 Census	2010 Census	2020 Census	Current Estimate[1]	Population Growth 1990-2023 (%)
Albuquerque, NM	388,375	448,607	545,852	564,559	562,488	44.8
Anchorage, AK	226,338	260,283	291,826	291,247	289,069	27.7
Ann Arbor, MI	111,018	114,024	113,934	123,851	121,179	9.2
Athens, GA	86,561	100,266	115,452	127,315	126,987	46.7
Atlanta, GA	394,092	416,474	420,003	498,715	499,287	26.7
Austin, TX	499,053	656,562	790,390	961,855	967,862	93.9
Baltimore, MD	736,014	651,154	620,961	585,708	577,193	-21.6
Billings, MT	81,812	89,847	104,170	117,116	118,321	44.6
Boise City, ID	144,317	185,787	205,671	235,684	235,701	63.3
Boston, MA	574,283	589,141	617,594	675,647	663,972	15.6
Boulder, CO	87,737	94,673	97,385	108,250	106,274	21.1
Cape Coral, FL	75,507	102,286	154,305	194,016	206,387	173.3
Cedar Rapids, IA	110,829	120,758	126,326	137,710	136,859	23.5
Charleston, SC	96,102	96,650	120,083	150,227	152,014	58.2
Charlotte, NC	428,283	540,828	731,424	874,579	886,283	106.9
Chicago, IL	2,783,726	2,896,016	2,695,598	2,746,388	2,707,648	-2.7
Cincinnati, OH	363,974	331,285	296,943	309,317	309,595	-14.9
Clarksville, TN	78,569	103,455	132,929	166,722	171,897	118.8
Cleveland, OH	505,333	478,403	396,815	372,624	367,523	-27.3
College Station, TX	53,318	67,890	93,857	120,511	122,280	129.3
Colorado Springs, CO	283,798	360,890	416,427	478,961	483,099	70.2
Columbia, MO	71,069	84,531	108,500	126,254	127,200	79.0
Columbia, SC	115,475	116,278	129,272	136,632	138,019	19.5
Columbus, OH	648,656	711,470	787,033	905,748	906,480	39.7
Dallas, TX	1,006,971	1,188,580	1,197,816	1,304,379	1,299,553	29.1
Davenport, IA	95,705	98,359	99,685	101,724	101,083	5.6
Denver, CO	467,153	554,636	600,158	715,522	713,734	52.8
Des Moines, IA	193,569	198,682	203,433	214,133	212,464	9.8
Detroit, MI	1,027,974	951,270	713,777	639,111	636,644	-38.1
Durham, NC	151,737	187,035	228,330	283,506	288,465	90.1
El Paso, TX	515,541	563,662	649,121	678,815	678,147	31.5
Eugene, OR	118,073	137,893	156,185	176,654	177,520	50.3
Fargo, ND	74,372	90,599	105,549	125,990	129,064	73.5
Fort Collins, CO	89,555	118,652	143,986	169,810	169,705	89.5
Fort Wayne, IN	205,671	205,727	253,691	263,886	266,235	29.4
Fort Worth, TX	448,311	534,694	741,206	918,915	941,311	110.0
Gainesville, FL	90,519	95,447	124,354	141,085	143,611	58.7
Green Bay, WI	96,466	102,313	104,057	107,395	106,585	10.5
Greensboro, NC	193,389	223,891	269,666	299,035	298,564	54.4
Honolulu, HI	376,465	371,657	337,256	350,964	346,323	-8.0
Houston, TX	1,697,610	1,953,631	2,099,451	2,304,580	2,300,419	35.5
Huntsville, AL	161,842	158,216	180,105	215,006	218,814	35.2
Indianapolis, IN	730,993	781,870	820,445	887,642	882,043	20.7
Jacksonville, FL	635,221	735,617	821,784	949,611	961,739	51.4
Kansas City, MO	434,967	441,545	459,787	508,090	508,233	16.8
Lafayette, LA	104,735	110,257	120,623	121,374	121,537	16.0
Las Vegas, NV	261,374	478,434	583,756	641,903	650,873	149.0
Lexington, KY	225,366	260,512	295,803	322,570	321,122	42.5
Lincoln, NE	193,629	225,581	258,379	291,082	291,932	50.8
Little Rock, AR	177,519	183,133	193,524	202,591	202,739	14.2
Los Angeles, CA	3,487,671	3,694,820	3,792,621	3,898,747	3,857,897	10.6
Louisville, KY	269,160	256,231	597,337	386,884	627,210	133.0
Madison, WI	193,451	208,054	233,209	269,840	275,568	42.4
Manchester, NH	99,567	107,006	109,565	115,644	115,415	15.9
McAllen, TX	86,145	106,414	129,877	142,210	143,789	66.9

Table continued on following page.

City	1990 Census	2000 Census	2010 Census	2020 Census	Current Estimate[1]	Population Growth 1990-2023 (%)
Memphis, TN	660,536	650,100	646,889	633,104	629,063	-4.8
Miami, FL	358,843	362,470	399,457	442,241	446,663	24.5
Midland, TX	89,358	94,996	111,147	132,524	133,998	50.0
Milwaukee, WI	628,095	596,974	594,833	577,222	569,756	-9.3
Minneapolis, MN	368,383	382,618	382,578	429,954	426,845	15.9
Nashville, TN	488,364	545,524	601,222	689,447	684,298	40.1
New Orleans, LA	496,938	484,674	343,829	383,997	376,035	-24.3
New York, NY	7,322,552	8,008,278	8,175,133	8,804,190	8,516,202	16.3
Oklahoma City, OK	445,065	506,132	579,999	681,054	688,693	54.7
Omaha, NE	371,972	390,007	408,958	486,051	488,197	31.2
Orlando, FL	161,172	185,951	238,300	307,573	311,732	93.4
Philadelphia, PA	1,585,577	1,517,550	1,526,006	1,603,797	1,582,432	-0.2
Phoenix, AZ	989,873	1,321,045	1,445,632	1,608,139	1,624,832	64.1
Pittsburgh, PA	369,785	334,563	305,704	302,971	303,620	-17.9
Portland, OR	485,833	529,121	583,776	652,503	642,715	32.3
Providence, RI	160,734	173,618	178,042	190,934	190,214	18.3
Provo, UT	87,148	105,166	112,488	115,162	114,303	31.2
Raleigh, NC	226,841	276,093	403,892	467,665	470,763	107.5
Reno, NV	139,950	180,480	225,221	264,165	268,959	92.2
Richmond, VA	202,783	197,790	204,214	226,610	227,595	12.2
Rochester, MN	74,151	85,806	106,769	121,395	121,638	64.0
Sacramento, CA	368,923	407,018	466,488	524,943	524,802	42.3
Saint Louis, MO	396,685	348,189	319,294	301,578	293,109	-26.1
Saint Paul, MN	272,235	287,151	285,068	311,527	307,762	13.1
Salem, OR	112,046	136,924	154,637	175,535	176,666	57.7
Salt Lake City, UT	159,796	181,743	186,440	199,723	203,888	27.6
San Antonio, TX	997,258	1,144,646	1,327,407	1,434,625	1,458,954	46.3
San Diego, CA	1,111,048	1,223,400	1,307,402	1,386,932	1,385,061	24.7
San Francisco, CA	723,959	776,733	805,235	873,965	836,321	15.5
San Jose, CA	784,324	894,943	945,942	1,013,240	990,054	26.2
Santa Rosa, CA	123,297	147,595	167,815	178,127	177,216	43.7
Savannah, GA	138,038	131,510	136,286	147,780	147,546	6.9
Seattle, WA	516,262	563,374	608,660	737,015	741,440	43.6
Sioux Falls, SD	102,262	123,975	153,888	192,517	197,642	93.3
Tampa, FL	279,960	303,447	335,709	384,959	393,389	40.5
Tucson, AZ	417,942	486,699	520,116	542,629	543,348	30.0
Tulsa, OK	367,241	393,049	391,906	413,066	412,322	12.3
Virginia Beach, VA	393,069	425,257	437,994	459,470	457,066	16.3
Washington, DC	606,900	572,059	601,723	689,545	672,079	10.7
Wichita, KS	313,693	344,284	382,368	397,532	396,488	26.4
Wilmington, NC	64,609	75,838	106,476	115,451	118,578	83.5
Winston-Salem, NC	168,139	185,776	229,617	249,545	250,887	49.2
U.S.	248,709,873	281,421,906	308,745,538	331,449,281	332,387,540	33.6

Note: (1) 2019-2023 5-year estimated population
Source: U.S. Census Bureau: 1990 Census, Census 2000, Census 2010, Census 2020, 2019-2023 American Community Survey 5-Year Estimates

Appendix A: Comparative Statistics

Population Growth: Metro Area

Metro Area	1990 Census	2000 Census	2010 Census	2020 Census	Current Estimate[1]	Population Growth 1990-2023 (%)
Albuquerque, NM	599,416	729,649	887,077	916,528	918,567	53.2
Anchorage, AK	266,021	319,605	380,821	398,328	399,746	50.3
Ann Arbor, MI	282,937	322,895	344,791	372,258	368,394	30.2
Athens, GA	136,025	166,079	192,541	215,415	218,190	60.4
Atlanta, GA	3,069,411	4,247,981	5,268,860	6,089,815	6,176,937	101.2
Austin, TX	846,217	1,249,763	1,716,289	2,283,371	2,357,497	178.6
Baltimore, MD	2,382,172	2,552,994	2,710,489	2,844,510	2,839,409	19.2
Billings, MT	121,499	138,904	158,050	184,167	187,269	54.1
Boise City, ID	319,596	464,840	616,561	764,718	790,640	147.4
Boston, MA	4,133,895	4,391,344	4,552,402	4,941,632	4,917,661	19.0
Boulder, CO	208,898	269,758	294,567	330,758	328,317	57.2
Cape Coral, FL	335,113	440,888	618,754	760,822	792,692	136.5
Cedar Rapids, IA	210,640	237,230	257,940	276,520	275,960	31.0
Charleston, SC	506,875	549,033	664,607	799,636	817,756	61.3
Charlotte, NC	1,024,331	1,330,448	1,758,038	2,660,329	2,712,818	164.8
Chicago, IL	8,182,076	9,098,316	9,461,105	9,618,502	9,359,555	14.4
Cincinnati, OH	1,844,917	2,009,632	2,130,151	2,256,884	2,255,257	22.2
Clarksville, TN	189,277	232,000	273,949	320,535	328,626	73.6
Cleveland, OH	2,102,219	2,148,143	2,077,240	2,088,251	2,171,978	3.3
College Station, TX	150,998	184,885	228,660	268,248	273,280	81.0
Colorado Springs, CO	409,482	537,484	645,613	755,105	760,782	85.8
Columbia, MO	122,010	145,666	172,786	210,864	212,850	74.5
Columbia, SC	548,325	647,158	767,598	829,470	839,868	53.2
Columbus, OH	1,405,176	1,612,694	1,836,536	2,138,926	2,151,847	53.1
Dallas, TX	3,989,294	5,161,544	6,371,773	7,637,387	7,807,555	95.7
Davenport, IA	368,151	376,019	379,690	384,324	381,864	3.7
Denver, CO	1,666,935	2,179,296	2,543,482	2,963,821	2,977,085	78.6
Des Moines, IA	416,346	481,394	569,633	709,466	720,331	73.0
Detroit, MI	4,248,699	4,452,557	4,296,250	4,392,041	4,367,620	2.8
Durham, NC	344,646	426,493	504,357	649,903	594,291	72.4
El Paso, TX	591,610	679,622	800,647	868,859	869,606	47.0
Eugene, OR	282,912	322,959	351,715	382,971	382,628	35.2
Fargo, ND	153,296	174,367	208,777	249,843	254,914	66.3
Fort Collins, CO	186,136	251,494	299,630	359,066	363,561	95.3
Fort Wayne, IN	354,435	390,156	416,257	419,601	451,440	27.4
Fort Worth, TX	3,989,294	5,161,544	6,371,773	7,637,387	7,807,555	95.7
Gainesville, FL	191,263	232,392	264,275	339,247	344,521	80.1
Green Bay, WI	243,698	282,599	306,241	328,268	329,375	35.2
Greensboro, NC	540,257	643,430	723,801	776,566	779,894	44.4
Honolulu, HI	836,231	876,156	953,207	1,016,508	1,003,666	20.0
Houston, TX	3,767,335	4,715,407	5,946,800	7,122,240	7,274,714	93.1
Huntsville, AL	293,047	342,376	417,593	491,723	504,712	72.2
Indianapolis, IN	1,294,217	1,525,104	1,756,241	2,111,040	2,106,327	62.7
Jacksonville, FL	925,213	1,122,750	1,345,596	1,605,848	1,645,707	77.9
Kansas City, MO	1,636,528	1,836,038	2,035,334	2,192,035	2,202,006	34.6
Lafayette, LA	208,740	239,086	273,738	478,384	410,883	96.8
Las Vegas, NV	741,459	1,375,765	1,951,269	2,265,461	2,293,764	209.4
Lexington, KY	348,428	408,326	472,099	516,811	517,378	48.5
Lincoln, NE	229,091	266,787	302,157	340,217	341,309	49.0
Little Rock, AR	535,034	610,518	699,757	748,031	753,605	40.9
Los Angeles, CA	11,273,720	12,365,627	12,828,837	13,200,998	13,012,469	15.4
Louisville, KY	1,055,973	1,161,975	1,283,566	1,285,439	1,361,847	29.0
Madison, WI	432,323	501,774	568,593	680,796	683,967	58.2
Manchester, NH	336,073	380,841	400,721	422,937	424,732	26.4
McAllen, TX	383,545	569,463	774,769	870,781	880,921	129.7

Table continued on following page.

Metro Area	1990 Census	2000 Census	2010 Census	2020 Census	Current Estimate[1]	Population Growth 1990-2023 (%)
Memphis, TN	1,067,263	1,205,204	1,316,100	1,337,779	1,341,606	25.7
Miami, FL	4,056,100	5,007,564	5,564,635	6,138,333	6,138,876	51.3
Midland, TX	106,611	116,009	136,872	175,220	176,726	65.8
Milwaukee, WI	1,432,149	1,500,741	1,555,908	1,574,731	1,566,361	9.4
Minneapolis, MN	2,538,834	2,968,806	3,279,833	3,690,261	3,693,351	45.5
Nashville, TN	1,048,218	1,311,789	1,589,934	1,989,519	2,043,713	95.0
New Orleans, LA	1,264,391	1,316,510	1,167,764	1,271,845	988,763	-21.8
New York, NY	16,845,992	18,323,002	18,897,109	20,140,470	19,756,722	17.3
Oklahoma City, OK	971,042	1,095,421	1,252,987	1,425,695	1,445,122	48.8
Omaha, NE	685,797	767,041	865,350	967,604	972,840	41.9
Orlando, FL	1,224,852	1,644,561	2,134,411	2,673,376	2,721,022	122.2
Philadelphia, PA	5,435,470	5,687,147	5,965,343	6,245,051	6,241,882	14.8
Phoenix, AZ	2,238,480	3,251,876	4,192,887	4,845,832	4,941,206	120.7
Pittsburgh, PA	2,468,289	2,431,087	2,356,285	2,370,930	2,443,921	-1.0
Portland, OR	1,523,741	1,927,881	2,226,009	2,512,859	2,510,529	64.8
Providence, RI	1,509,789	1,582,997	1,600,852	1,676,579	1,673,807	10.9
Provo, UT	269,407	376,774	526,810	671,185	695,895	158.3
Raleigh, NC	541,081	797,071	1,130,490	1,413,982	1,449,594	167.9
Reno, NV	257,193	342,885	425,417	490,596	556,539	116.4
Richmond, VA	949,244	1,096,957	1,258,251	1,314,434	1,327,321	39.8
Rochester, MN	141,945	163,618	186,011	226,329	227,252	60.1
Sacramento, CA	1,481,126	1,796,857	2,149,127	2,397,382	2,406,563	62.5
Saint Louis, MO	2,580,897	2,698,687	2,812,896	2,820,253	2,809,414	8.9
Saint Paul, MN	2,538,834	2,968,806	3,279,833	3,690,261	3,693,351	45.5
Salem, OR	278,024	347,214	390,738	433,353	435,085	56.5
Salt Lake City, UT	768,075	968,858	1,124,197	1,257,936	1,261,337	64.2
San Antonio, TX	1,407,745	1,711,703	2,142,508	2,558,143	2,612,802	85.6
San Diego, CA	2,498,016	2,813,833	3,095,313	3,298,634	3,282,782	31.4
San Francisco, CA	3,686,592	4,123,740	4,335,391	4,749,008	4,653,593	26.2
San Jose, CA	1,534,280	1,735,819	1,836,911	2,000,468	1,969,353	28.4
Santa Rosa, CA	388,222	458,614	483,878	488,863	485,642	25.1
Savannah, GA	258,060	293,000	347,611	404,798	412,089	59.7
Seattle, WA	2,559,164	3,043,878	3,439,809	4,018,762	4,021,467	57.1
Sioux Falls, SD	153,500	187,093	228,261	276,730	293,107	90.9
Tampa, FL	2,067,959	2,395,997	2,783,243	3,175,275	3,240,469	56.7
Tucson, AZ	666,880	843,746	980,263	1,043,433	1,049,947	57.4
Tulsa, OK	761,019	859,532	937,478	1,015,331	1,026,209	34.8
Virginia Beach, VA	1,449,389	1,576,370	1,671,683	1,799,674	1,782,590	23.0
Washington, DC	4,122,914	4,796,183	5,582,170	6,385,162	6,263,796	51.9
Wichita, KS	511,111	571,166	623,061	647,610	648,935	27.0
Wilmington, NC	200,124	274,532	362,315	285,905	440,578	120.2
Winston-Salem, NC	361,091	421,961	477,717	675,966	683,637	89.3
U.S.	248,709,873	281,421,906	308,745,538	331,449,281	332,387,540	33.6

Note: (1) 2019-2023 5-year estimated population; Figures cover the Metropolitan Statistical Area (MSA)
Source: U.S. Census Bureau: 1990 Census, Census 2000, Census 2010, Census 2020, 2019-2023 American Community Survey 5-Year Estimates

Male/Female Ratio: City

City	Males	Females	Males per 100 Females
Albuquerque, NM	275,413	287,075	95.9
Anchorage, AK	147,620	141,449	104.4
Ann Arbor, MI	60,397	60,782	99.4
Athens, GA	60,237	66,750	90.2
Atlanta, GA	242,994	256,293	94.8
Austin, TX	495,563	472,299	104.9
Baltimore, MD	268,932	308,261	87.2
Billings, MT	58,615	59,706	98.2
Boise City, ID	118,294	117,407	100.8
Boston, MA	319,182	344,790	92.6
Boulder, CO	55,022	51,252	107.4
Cape Coral, FL	103,313	103,074	100.2
Cedar Rapids, IA	67,551	69,308	97.5
Charleston, SC	72,280	79,734	90.7
Charlotte, NC	427,869	458,414	93.3
Chicago, IL	1,314,256	1,393,392	94.3
Cincinnati, OH	148,944	160,651	92.7
Clarksville, TN	86,129	85,768	100.4
Cleveland, OH	177,863	189,660	93.8
College Station, TX	62,870	59,410	105.8
Colorado Springs, CO	241,781	241,318	100.2
Columbia, MO	61,139	66,061	92.5
Columbia, SC	68,245	69,774	97.8
Columbus, OH	445,564	460,916	96.7
Dallas, TX	647,372	652,181	99.3
Davenport, IA	50,102	50,981	98.3
Denver, CO	359,969	353,765	101.8
Des Moines, IA	105,131	107,333	97.9
Detroit, MI	302,503	334,141	90.5
Durham, NC	136,368	152,097	89.7
El Paso, TX	333,802	344,345	96.9
Eugene, OR	87,095	90,425	96.3
Fargo, ND	65,129	63,935	101.9
Fort Collins, CO	84,686	85,019	99.6
Fort Wayne, IN	129,959	136,276	95.4
Fort Worth, TX	461,317	479,994	96.1
Gainesville, FL	68,593	75,018	91.4
Green Bay, WI	52,829	53,756	98.3
Greensboro, NC	138,079	160,485	86.0
Honolulu, HI	173,028	173,295	99.8
Houston, TX	1,138,504	1,161,915	98.0
Huntsville, AL	107,036	111,778	95.8
Indianapolis, IN	428,660	453,383	94.5
Jacksonville, FL	466,421	495,318	94.2
Kansas City, MO	245,780	262,453	93.6
Lafayette, LA	58,993	62,544	94.3
Las Vegas, NV	325,629	325,244	100.1
Lexington, KY	158,152	162,970	97.0
Lincoln, NE	146,855	145,077	101.2
Little Rock, AR	95,597	107,142	89.2
Los Angeles, CA	1,921,735	1,936,162	99.3
Louisville, KY	305,342	321,868	94.9
Madison, WI	137,655	137,913	99.8
Manchester, NH	57,084	58,331	97.9
McAllen, TX	71,212	72,577	98.1

Table continued on following page.

City	Males	Females	Males per 100 Females
Memphis, TN	298,855	330,208	90.5
Miami, FL	226,349	220,314	102.7
Midland, TX	68,527	65,471	104.7
Milwaukee, WI	275,637	294,119	93.7
Minneapolis, MN	218,753	208,092	105.1
Nashville, TN	331,646	352,652	94.0
New Orleans, LA	177,299	198,736	89.2
New York, NY	4,088,026	4,428,176	92.3
Oklahoma City, OK	340,327	348,366	97.7
Omaha, NE	242,508	245,689	98.7
Orlando, FL	153,714	158,018	97.3
Philadelphia, PA	749,410	833,022	90.0
Phoenix, AZ	815,308	809,524	100.7
Pittsburgh, PA	149,240	154,380	96.7
Portland, OR	319,454	323,261	98.8
Providence, RI	93,138	97,076	95.9
Provo, UT	56,107	58,196	96.4
Raleigh, NC	228,452	242,311	94.3
Reno, NV	136,341	132,618	102.8
Richmond, VA	108,090	119,505	90.4
Rochester, MN	59,099	62,539	94.5
Sacramento, CA	260,163	264,639	98.3
Saint Louis, MO	142,190	150,919	94.2
Saint Paul, MN	151,659	156,103	97.2
Salem, OR	89,295	87,371	102.2
Salt Lake City, UT	105,049	98,839	106.3
San Antonio, TX	722,875	736,079	98.2
San Diego, CA	703,091	681,970	103.1
San Francisco, CA	429,837	406,484	105.7
San Jose, CA	504,179	485,875	103.8
Santa Rosa, CA	86,188	91,028	94.7
Savannah, GA	69,345	78,201	88.7
Seattle, WA	378,278	363,162	104.2
Sioux Falls, SD	99,791	97,851	102.0
Tampa, FL	197,565	195,824	100.9
Tucson, AZ	270,198	273,150	98.9
Tulsa, OK	201,524	210,798	95.6
Virginia Beach, VA	224,463	232,603	96.5
Washington, DC	320,001	352,078	90.9
Wichita, KS	197,295	199,193	99.0
Wilmington, NC	55,595	62,983	88.3
Winston-Salem, NC	116,981	133,906	87.4
U.S.	164,545,087	167,842,453	98.0

Source: U.S. Census Bureau, 2019-2023 American Community Survey 5-Year Estimates

Male/Female Ratio: Metro Area

Metro Area	Males	Females	Males per 100 Females
Albuquerque, NM	452,929	465,638	97.3
Anchorage, AK	205,511	194,235	105.8
Ann Arbor, MI	183,761	184,633	99.5
Athens, GA	105,119	113,071	93.0
Atlanta, GA	2,998,312	3,178,625	94.3
Austin, TX	1,190,277	1,167,220	102.0
Baltimore, MD	1,371,348	1,468,061	93.4
Billings, MT	92,957	94,312	98.6
Boise City, ID	397,370	393,270	101.0
Boston, MA	2,405,154	2,512,507	95.7
Boulder, CO	165,677	162,640	101.9
Cape Coral, FL	389,853	402,839	96.8
Cedar Rapids, IA	137,287	138,673	99.0
Charleston, SC	400,382	417,374	95.9
Charlotte, NC	1,323,612	1,389,206	95.3
Chicago, IL	4,607,366	4,752,189	97.0
Cincinnati, OH	1,113,237	1,142,020	97.5
Clarksville, TN	165,784	162,842	101.8
Cleveland, OH	1,057,990	1,113,988	95.0
College Station, TX	137,218	136,062	100.8
Colorado Springs, CO	386,799	373,983	103.4
Columbia, MO	103,590	109,260	94.8
Columbia, SC	407,291	432,577	94.2
Columbus, OH	1,066,090	1,085,757	98.2
Dallas, TX	3,864,152	3,943,403	98.0
Davenport, IA	189,025	192,839	98.0
Denver, CO	1,499,649	1,477,436	101.5
Des Moines, IA	359,219	361,112	99.5
Detroit, MI	2,140,962	2,226,658	96.2
Durham, NC	285,396	308,895	92.4
El Paso, TX	432,470	437,136	98.9
Eugene, OR	189,067	193,561	97.7
Fargo, ND	128,561	126,353	101.7
Fort Collins, CO	181,725	181,836	99.9
Fort Wayne, IN	222,504	228,936	97.2
Fort Worth, TX	3,864,152	3,943,403	98.0
Gainesville, FL	166,988	177,533	94.1
Green Bay, WI	165,274	164,101	100.7
Greensboro, NC	374,844	405,050	92.5
Honolulu, HI	507,355	496,311	102.2
Houston, TX	3,616,570	3,658,144	98.9
Huntsville, AL	249,354	255,358	97.6
Indianapolis, IN	1,034,791	1,071,536	96.6
Jacksonville, FL	804,019	841,688	95.5
Kansas City, MO	1,087,932	1,114,074	97.7
Lafayette, LA	200,575	210,308	95.4
Las Vegas, NV	1,148,112	1,145,652	100.2
Lexington, KY	254,019	263,359	96.5
Lincoln, NE	172,052	169,257	101.7
Little Rock, AR	365,071	388,534	94.0
Los Angeles, CA	6,447,486	6,564,983	98.2
Louisville, KY	669,908	691,939	96.8
Madison, WI	343,409	340,558	100.8
Manchester, NH	212,913	211,819	100.5
McAllen, TX	434,784	446,137	97.5

Table continued on following page.

Metro Area	Males	Females	Males per 100 Females
Memphis, TN	642,599	699,007	91.9
Miami, FL	3,005,200	3,133,676	95.9
Midland, TX	90,328	86,398	104.5
Milwaukee, WI	768,160	798,201	96.2
Minneapolis, MN	1,842,197	1,851,154	99.5
Nashville, TN	1,004,473	1,039,240	96.7
New Orleans, LA	476,985	511,778	93.2
New York, NY	9,622,708	10,134,014	95.0
Oklahoma City, OK	714,932	730,190	97.9
Omaha, NE	485,489	487,351	99.6
Orlando, FL	1,336,264	1,384,758	96.5
Philadelphia, PA	3,031,854	3,210,028	94.4
Phoenix, AZ	2,466,995	2,474,211	99.7
Pittsburgh, PA	1,200,522	1,243,399	96.6
Portland, OR	1,251,055	1,259,474	99.3
Providence, RI	819,607	854,200	96.0
Provo, UT	353,303	342,592	103.1
Raleigh, NC	711,279	738,315	96.3
Reno, NV	283,387	273,152	103.7
Richmond, VA	645,193	682,128	94.6
Rochester, MN	112,416	114,836	97.9
Sacramento, CA	1,184,908	1,221,655	97.0
Saint Louis, MO	1,370,976	1,438,438	95.3
Saint Paul, MN	1,842,197	1,851,154	99.5
Salem, OR	217,233	217,852	99.7
Salt Lake City, UT	637,671	623,666	102.2
San Antonio, TX	1,298,427	1,314,375	98.8
San Diego, CA	1,660,156	1,622,626	102.3
San Francisco, CA	2,318,841	2,334,752	99.3
San Jose, CA	1,003,282	966,071	103.9
Santa Rosa, CA	238,817	246,825	96.8
Savannah, GA	200,060	212,029	94.4
Seattle, WA	2,031,168	1,990,299	102.1
Sioux Falls, SD	148,246	144,861	102.3
Tampa, FL	1,583,138	1,657,331	95.5
Tucson, AZ	518,998	530,949	97.7
Tulsa, OK	506,779	519,430	97.6
Virginia Beach, VA	875,910	906,680	96.6
Washington, DC	3,081,518	3,182,278	96.8
Wichita, KS	323,191	325,744	99.2
Wilmington, NC	212,689	227,889	93.3
Winston-Salem, NC	330,177	353,460	93.4
U.S.	164,545,087	167,842,453	98.0

Note: Figures cover the Metropolitan Statistical Area (MSA)
Source: U.S. Census Bureau, 2019-2023 American Community Survey 5-Year Estimates

Race: City

City	White Alone[1] (%)	Black Alone[1] (%)	Asian Alone[1] (%)	AIAN[2] Alone[1] (%)	NHOPI[3] Alone[1] (%)	Other Race Alone[1] (%)	Two or More Races (%)
Albuquerque, NM	55.3	3.3	3.3	5.0	0.1	11.1	21.9
Anchorage, AK	58.3	5.3	9.8	7.3	3.1	3.1	13.1
Ann Arbor, MI	68.8	7.2	15.2	0.3	0.0	1.2	7.3
Athens, GA	57.6	26.2	4.3	0.4	0.0	3.4	8.1
Atlanta, GA	39.9	46.9	5.0	0.3	0.1	2.1	5.8
Austin, TX	59.9	7.5	8.6	0.7	0.1	7.7	15.5
Baltimore, MD	27.4	60.0	2.5	0.4	0.0	4.4	5.2
Billings, MT	86.3	1.0	0.9	4.4	0.1	1.4	6.1
Boise City, ID	83.6	1.4	3.3	0.7	0.3	3.0	7.6
Boston, MA	47.8	21.5	10.0	0.3	0.1	7.1	13.2
Boulder, CO	81.8	1.1	5.8	0.3	0.1	1.8	9.2
Cape Coral, FL	72.9	4.5	1.5	0.1	0.0	4.1	16.9
Cedar Rapids, IA	79.7	8.5	2.6	0.2	0.0	1.4	7.6
Charleston, SC	72.9	17.4	2.2	0.6	0.2	1.9	5.0
Charlotte, NC	41.5	34.1	6.4	0.4	0.0	8.8	8.9
Chicago, IL	39.0	28.4	7.1	0.9	0.1	12.4	12.0
Cincinnati, OH	49.4	38.7	2.8	0.1	0.0	2.0	7.0
Clarksville, TN	59.4	23.0	2.5	0.4	0.3	2.8	11.7
Cleveland, OH	36.7	46.8	2.3	0.4	0.0	4.6	9.2
College Station, TX	67.0	8.8	9.6	0.3	0.1	3.3	10.9
Colorado Springs, CO	72.3	5.8	3.0	1.0	0.2	4.9	12.8
Columbia, MO	74.3	12.1	6.1	0.1	0.1	1.2	6.1
Columbia, SC	49.9	39.5	2.7	0.2	0.2	1.7	5.9
Columbus, OH	53.3	29.0	5.8	0.3	0.0	3.4	8.2
Dallas, TX	41.9	23.7	3.7	0.8	0.1	12.5	17.3
Davenport, IA	75.9	11.2	2.0	0.3	0.1	2.1	8.5
Denver, CO	62.9	8.8	3.6	0.9	0.1	8.2	15.5
Des Moines, IA	66.9	12.0	6.2	0.5	0.0	5.2	9.1
Detroit, MI	11.7	76.8	1.6	0.4	0.0	4.6	4.8
Durham, NC	43.9	34.4	5.6	0.5	0.1	6.8	8.6
El Paso, TX	39.3	3.6	1.5	0.9	0.2	16.0	38.6
Eugene, OR	78.9	1.8	3.9	0.8	0.4	3.8	10.5
Fargo, ND	80.8	8.3	3.9	1.0	0.0	1.1	5.0
Fort Collins, CO	81.7	1.4	3.3	0.8	0.1	2.2	10.5
Fort Wayne, IN	66.4	14.6	5.8	0.4	0.0	4.3	8.4
Fort Worth, TX	47.7	19.5	5.2	0.6	0.1	10.4	16.4
Gainesville, FL	59.2	21.6	6.2	0.2	0.1	3.0	9.7
Green Bay, WI	69.9	3.8	4.1	3.3	0.0	7.1	11.8
Greensboro, NC	40.4	42.2	5.0	0.5	0.0	4.5	7.5
Honolulu, HI	17.0	1.8	52.9	0.2	8.5	1.2	18.4
Houston, TX	35.5	22.9	6.9	0.9	0.1	14.6	19.2
Huntsville, AL	58.4	29.7	2.0	0.6	0.1	2.9	6.2
Indianapolis, IN	53.6	28.1	4.1	0.5	0.0	5.7	8.0
Jacksonville, FL	51.2	30.1	4.9	0.2	0.1	3.9	9.6
Kansas City, MO	57.8	25.8	2.7	0.4	0.3	4.5	8.6
Lafayette, LA	59.1	28.6	2.1	0.1	0.1	1.2	8.8
Las Vegas, NV	49.2	11.9	6.9	1.1	0.8	13.9	16.2
Lexington, KY	69.9	14.4	4.2	0.2	0.0	3.5	7.8
Lincoln, NE	80.9	4.2	4.5	0.7	0.1	2.3	7.4
Little Rock, AR	46.3	39.4	3.0	0.3	0.1	4.2	6.6
Los Angeles, CA	37.3	8.5	12.0	1.2	0.1	25.1	15.7
Louisville, KY	63.1	23.7	2.6	0.1	0.0	2.1	8.4
Madison, WI	73.0	7.1	8.0	0.4	0.0	2.1	9.4
Manchester, NH	76.7	5.3	4.6	0.2	0.0	3.2	10.0

Table continued on following page.

City	White Alone[1] (%)	Black Alone[1] (%)	Asian Alone[1] (%)	AIAN[2] Alone[1] (%)	NHOPI[3] Alone[1] (%)	Other Race Alone[1] (%)	Two or More Races (%)
McAllen, TX	43.1	0.9	2.9	0.6	0.0	17.5	35.1
Memphis, TN	25.0	62.9	1.7	0.5	0.1	5.1	4.6
Miami, FL	34.2	13.7	1.6	0.4	0.0	7.5	42.6
Midland, TX	58.8	8.6	2.1	0.7	0.0	12.0	17.9
Milwaukee, WI	36.5	38.6	4.8	0.7	0.0	6.9	12.4
Minneapolis, MN	61.6	18.3	5.2	1.1	0.1	4.9	8.9
Nashville, TN	56.5	25.5	3.5	0.3	0.1	4.9	9.2
New Orleans, LA	31.6	55.2	2.8	0.3	0.0	2.8	7.3
New York, NY	35.9	22.7	14.6	0.7	0.1	15.5	10.5
Oklahoma City, OK	58.4	13.4	4.5	3.4	0.1	5.8	14.4
Omaha, NE	68.8	11.8	4.0	0.8	0.0	5.0	9.7
Orlando, FL	43.2	22.9	4.4	0.1	0.1	8.4	21.0
Philadelphia, PA	36.1	39.9	7.8	0.4	0.1	8.4	7.3
Phoenix, AZ	53.7	7.8	3.9	2.3	0.2	11.4	20.8
Pittsburgh, PA	63.7	22.5	5.8	0.2	0.0	1.6	6.2
Portland, OR	70.1	5.8	8.1	0.8	0.5	3.3	11.3
Providence, RI	40.7	13.3	5.9	1.0	0.1	20.4	18.7
Provo, UT	78.6	1.1	2.2	1.0	1.4	5.4	10.2
Raleigh, NC	53.8	27.5	4.7	0.4	0.0	5.5	8.0
Reno, NV	63.5	3.2	7.0	1.0	0.7	11.1	13.5
Richmond, VA	43.2	42.0	2.1	0.2	0.0	5.3	7.1
Rochester, MN	74.3	9.4	8.0	0.2	0.1	2.1	5.9
Sacramento, CA	36.8	12.4	19.7	1.0	1.7	13.4	15.0
Saint Louis, MO	45.7	43.1	3.4	0.2	0.0	1.6	5.9
Saint Paul, MN	53.2	16.2	17.9	0.7	0.0	3.5	8.4
Salem, OR	69.8	1.6	3.5	1.2	1.6	8.2	14.1
Salt Lake City, UT	70.5	2.7	5.4	1.2	1.4	9.2	9.6
San Antonio, TX	48.3	6.9	3.1	1.1	0.1	10.9	29.6
San Diego, CA	50.4	5.7	17.6	0.7	0.5	9.5	15.6
San Francisco, CA	40.5	5.1	35.0	0.7	0.4	7.7	10.7
San Jose, CA	29.0	2.9	38.6	1.0	0.5	13.6	14.4
Santa Rosa, CA	56.2	1.9	6.5	1.4	0.6	20.0	13.4
Savannah, GA	37.2	52.2	2.9	0.2	0.2	2.0	5.4
Seattle, WA	61.8	6.6	17.2	0.6	0.3	3.0	10.5
Sioux Falls, SD	79.9	7.0	2.3	1.9	0.0	2.0	7.0
Tampa, FL	51.8	21.3	4.8	0.3	0.1	4.8	17.0
Tucson, AZ	58.2	5.0	3.1	2.7	0.2	11.6	19.1
Tulsa, OK	57.0	14.2	3.5	4.3	0.2	5.9	14.9
Virginia Beach, VA	61.6	18.9	7.3	0.2	0.2	2.4	9.4
Washington, DC	39.1	43.3	4.1	0.3	0.1	4.8	8.4
Wichita, KS	66.6	9.7	4.9	0.9	0.0	5.5	12.4
Wilmington, NC	72.9	14.9	1.3	0.3	0.0	4.8	5.9
Winston-Salem, NC	48.7	32.4	2.3	0.5	0.0	7.3	8.8
U.S.	63.4	12.4	5.8	0.9	0.2	6.6	10.7

Note: (1) Alone is defined as not being in combination with one or more other races; (2) American Indian and Alaska Native; (3) Native Hawaiian and Other Pacific Islander
Source: U.S. Census Bureau, 2019-2023 American Community Survey 5-Year Estimates

Race: Metro Area

Metro Area	White Alone[1] (%)	Black Alone[1] (%)	Asian Alone[1] (%)	AIAN[2] Alone[1] (%)	NHOPI[3] Alone[1] (%)	Other Race Alone[1] (%)	Two or More Races (%)
Albuquerque, NM	55.2	2.7	2.5	6.2	0.1	10.9	22.3
Anchorage, AK	63.8	4.2	7.6	6.9	2.4	2.7	12.5
Ann Arbor, MI	69.9	11.6	8.9	0.3	0.0	1.6	7.7
Athens, GA	67.1	18.6	3.7	0.4	0.2	3.0	7.1
Atlanta, GA	46.3	34.0	6.4	0.4	0.1	4.9	7.9
Austin, TX	61.4	7.2	6.9	0.7	0.1	7.3	16.5
Baltimore, MD	54.8	29.0	5.8	0.3	0.0	3.6	6.4
Billings, MT	87.5	0.8	0.8	3.6	0.0	1.6	5.7
Boise City, ID	81.5	1.0	1.9	0.8	0.2	5.6	9.0
Boston, MA	69.2	7.5	8.5	0.2	0.0	5.5	9.1
Boulder, CO	80.7	0.8	4.7	0.3	0.1	2.9	10.6
Cape Coral, FL	70.5	8.0	1.7	0.6	0.0	4.3	15.0
Cedar Rapids, IA	86.2	5.0	2.0	0.3	0.0	1.1	5.5
Charleston, SC	64.6	23.9	2.0	0.4	0.2	3.3	5.7
Charlotte, NC	60.2	22.2	4.2	0.4	0.0	5.5	7.5
Chicago, IL	55.7	16.2	7.1	0.6	0.0	9.5	10.8
Cincinnati, OH	78.0	11.9	2.9	0.1	0.1	1.7	5.5
Clarksville, TN	67.3	18.5	2.1	0.3	0.3	2.2	9.5
Cleveland, OH	70.5	18.6	2.3	0.2	0.0	1.9	6.4
College Station, TX	66.6	11.4	5.1	0.6	0.1	4.4	11.8
Colorado Springs, CO	73.1	5.8	2.8	0.9	0.3	4.3	12.8
Columbia, MO	79.2	9.0	4.1	0.2	0.1	1.3	6.1
Columbia, SC	55.4	33.3	2.3	0.2	0.1	2.7	5.9
Columbus, OH	70.3	15.8	4.8	0.2	0.0	2.2	6.7
Dallas, TX	52.7	16.2	7.8	0.6	0.1	8.0	14.5
Davenport, IA	79.4	7.7	2.4	0.2	0.1	2.8	7.5
Denver, CO	69.1	5.6	4.3	0.9	0.2	6.4	13.6
Des Moines, IA	81.5	5.7	4.2	0.3	0.0	2.5	5.8
Detroit, MI	65.6	21.5	4.8	0.2	0.0	1.9	5.9
Durham, NC	56.6	24.0	5.1	0.5	0.0	5.9	7.8
El Paso, TX	39.2	3.3	1.3	0.9	0.2	16.3	38.9
Eugene, OR	82.0	1.2	2.6	1.0	0.2	3.6	9.5
Fargo, ND	84.2	6.1	2.7	0.9	0.1	0.9	5.1
Fort Collins, CO	84.1	1.0	2.1	0.6	0.1	2.6	9.5
Fort Wayne, IN	75.6	9.5	4.3	0.3	0.0	3.2	7.1
Fort Worth, TX	52.7	16.2	7.8	0.6	0.1	8.0	14.5
Gainesville, FL	66.6	17.1	4.9	0.2	0.0	2.5	8.7
Green Bay, WI	82.9	2.2	2.7	1.7	0.0	3.3	7.1
Greensboro, NC	57.7	26.9	3.8	0.4	0.0	4.3	6.9
Honolulu, HI	18.8	2.4	42.6	0.2	9.9	1.6	24.4
Houston, TX	45.3	17.3	8.2	0.7	0.1	10.7	17.8
Huntsville, AL	66.6	21.8	2.4	0.7	0.1	2.2	6.2
Indianapolis, IN	70.8	15.1	3.8	0.3	0.0	3.4	6.5
Jacksonville, FL	62.8	20.7	4.0	0.2	0.1	3.2	9.0
Kansas City, MO	73.0	11.9	2.9	0.4	0.2	3.7	7.8
Lafayette, LA	68.0	22.7	1.5	0.2	0.1	1.1	6.4
Las Vegas, NV	47.1	12.1	10.5	1.1	0.8	12.9	15.5
Lexington, KY	76.6	10.6	2.9	0.2	0.0	2.9	6.7
Lincoln, NE	83.0	3.6	3.9	0.7	0.1	2.0	6.8
Little Rock, AR	65.9	23.5	1.6	0.3	0.0	2.8	5.8
Los Angeles, CA	38.1	6.3	16.7	1.1	0.2	21.2	16.2
Louisville, KY	75.2	14.2	2.1	0.1	0.0	1.6	6.7
Madison, WI	81.4	4.5	5.0	0.3	0.1	1.7	7.1
Manchester, NH	83.3	2.6	4.2	0.1	0.0	2.1	7.7

Table continued on following page.

Metro Area	White Alone[1] (%)	Black Alone[1] (%)	Asian Alone[1] (%)	AIAN[2] Alone[1] (%)	NHOPI[3] Alone[1] (%)	Other Race Alone[1] (%)	Two or More Races (%)
McAllen, TX	39.5	0.7	1.0	0.4	0.0	10.8	47.6
Memphis, TN	42.5	46.8	2.2	0.3	0.1	3.4	4.7
Miami, FL	43.7	20.3	2.6	0.2	0.0	6.6	26.6
Midland, TX	60.4	7.1	2.1	0.6	0.0	12.8	17.1
Milwaukee, WI	67.4	16.1	4.0	0.4	0.0	3.8	8.3
Minneapolis, MN	73.8	8.9	6.9	0.5	0.0	3.0	6.8
Nashville, TN	71.6	14.3	2.9	0.2	0.1	3.4	7.6
New Orleans, LA	45.0	38.5	3.2	0.6	0.0	4.4	8.4
New York, NY	48.4	16.3	11.8	0.5	0.0	12.3	10.6
Oklahoma City, OK	66.5	9.8	3.3	3.6	0.1	3.9	12.8
Omaha, NE	77.1	7.4	3.2	0.6	0.1	3.7	7.9
Orlando, FL	52.5	16.0	4.5	0.3	0.1	9.5	17.2
Philadelphia, PA	61.4	20.2	6.3	0.2	0.0	4.9	6.9
Phoenix, AZ	63.2	5.7	4.1	2.2	0.2	8.4	16.1
Pittsburgh, PA	84.1	7.9	2.5	0.1	0.0	0.8	4.6
Portland, OR	73.0	3.0	7.0	0.8	0.5	4.5	11.2
Providence, RI	74.5	5.3	3.1	0.4	0.1	6.6	10.0
Provo, UT	83.9	0.7	1.4	0.6	0.8	4.0	8.6
Raleigh, NC	60.7	19.1	6.6	0.4	0.0	5.4	7.8
Reno, NV	66.9	2.3	5.1	1.4	0.6	10.0	13.7
Richmond, VA	56.8	28.5	4.1	0.3	0.1	4.0	6.2
Rochester, MN	83.0	5.4	4.7	0.2	0.1	1.7	4.9
Sacramento, CA	54.8	6.9	14.8	0.8	0.8	8.7	13.2
Saint Louis, MO	72.1	17.5	2.8	0.1	0.0	1.3	6.1
Saint Paul, MN	73.8	8.9	6.9	0.5	0.0	3.0	6.8
Salem, OR	71.3	1.1	2.0	1.4	1.0	9.3	14.0
Salt Lake City, UT	73.6	1.7	3.9	0.9	1.5	8.7	9.6
San Antonio, TX	53.5	7.0	2.8	0.9	0.1	9.5	26.2
San Diego, CA	53.0	4.7	12.2	0.9	0.4	10.6	18.1
San Francisco, CA	39.9	7.0	27.6	0.9	0.6	11.8	12.2
San Jose, CA	33.6	2.3	38.3	0.8	0.4	10.7	13.9
Santa Rosa, CA	64.5	1.6	4.4	1.3	0.4	14.1	13.7
Savannah, GA	55.2	32.4	2.5	0.2	0.1	3.1	6.5
Seattle, WA	60.9	6.1	15.4	0.8	0.9	4.6	11.4
Sioux Falls, SD	84.2	5.1	1.6	1.5	0.0	1.6	6.0
Tampa, FL	66.0	11.8	3.8	0.3	0.1	4.8	13.2
Tucson, AZ	63.2	3.6	3.0	3.1	0.2	9.9	17.0
Tulsa, OK	65.3	7.6	2.8	7.2	0.1	3.5	13.4
Virginia Beach, VA	55.0	29.7	4.1	0.3	0.1	2.4	8.4
Washington, DC	45.5	24.9	10.7	0.5	0.0	8.3	10.1
Wichita, KS	74.4	6.7	3.7	0.8	0.1	4.3	10.1
Wilmington, NC	78.8	10.4	1.0	0.3	0.0	3.5	5.9
Winston-Salem, NC	68.8	17.4	1.8	0.3	0.0	4.4	7.3
U.S.	63.4	12.4	5.8	0.9	0.2	6.6	10.7

Note: Figures cover the Metropolitan Statistical Area (MSA); (1) Alone is defined as not being in combination with one or more other races; (2) American Indian and Alaska Native; (3) Native Hawaiian & Other Pacific Islander
Source: U.S. Census Bureau, 2019-2023 American Community Survey 5-Year Estimates

Hispanic Origin: City

City	Hispanic or Latino (%)	Mexican (%)	Puerto Rican (%)	Cuban (%)	Other Hispanic or Latino (%)
Albuquerque, NM	47.9	28.9	0.7	0.5	17.9
Anchorage, AK	9.3	4.2	1.4	0.5	3.1
Ann Arbor, MI	5.4	2.3	0.7	0.2	2.3
Athens, GA	11.5	6.1	0.4	0.7	4.2
Atlanta, GA	6.3	2.0	0.9	0.3	3.0
Austin, TX	32.2	23.7	1.0	0.9	6.7
Baltimore, MD	7.9	1.6	1.0	0.4	4.8
Billings, MT	7.2	5.0	0.3	0.2	1.8
Boise City, ID	9.5	7.0	0.4	0.1	2.1
Boston, MA	18.9	1.2	4.4	0.4	13.0
Boulder, CO	11.2	6.6	0.3	0.5	3.8
Cape Coral, FL	25.0	1.9	4.9	10.7	7.5
Cedar Rapids, IA	5.1	3.5	0.4	0.1	1.2
Charleston, SC	5.9	2.6	0.7	0.2	2.4
Charlotte, NC	17.0	6.0	1.2	0.5	9.3
Chicago, IL	29.6	21.6	3.5	0.4	4.2
Cincinnati, OH	5.4	1.6	0.9	0.2	2.6
Clarksville, TN	12.5	6.0	3.0	0.3	3.2
Cleveland, OH	12.8	1.7	8.8	0.2	2.2
College Station, TX	18.4	12.9	0.7	0.5	4.3
Colorado Springs, CO	18.7	12.0	1.2	0.2	5.3
Columbia, MO	4.3	2.5	0.2	0.2	1.3
Columbia, SC	5.7	2.0	1.3	0.2	2.2
Columbus, OH	7.9	3.7	1.1	0.1	3.0
Dallas, TX	41.9	33.6	0.6	0.4	7.4
Davenport, IA	9.1	8.0	0.4	0.1	0.6
Denver, CO	27.9	20.9	0.7	0.3	6.1
Des Moines, IA	16.0	11.4	0.6	0.3	3.8
Detroit, MI	8.0	5.5	0.9	0.2	1.3
Durham, NC	14.7	6.6	0.9	0.5	6.7
El Paso, TX	81.3	76.1	1.1	0.2	3.9
Eugene, OR	11.4	8.0	0.4	0.2	2.8
Fargo, ND	3.7	2.2	0.6	0.0	0.8
Fort Collins, CO	12.3	8.2	0.7	0.2	3.3
Fort Wayne, IN	10.5	7.7	0.7	0.1	2.2
Fort Worth, TX	34.6	28.7	1.3	0.4	4.2
Gainesville, FL	13.4	1.3	2.9	2.9	6.3
Green Bay, WI	18.1	13.8	2.3	0.1	1.9
Greensboro, NC	10.5	4.5	1.7	0.2	4.1
Honolulu, HI	6.6	2.3	1.8	0.1	2.4
Houston, TX	44.1	28.5	0.8	0.8	14.0
Huntsville, AL	8.1	4.3	1.0	0.2	2.5
Indianapolis, IN	13.3	8.7	0.8	0.3	3.5
Jacksonville, FL	12.0	2.0	3.9	1.8	4.3
Kansas City, MO	12.3	8.3	0.6	0.4	3.0
Lafayette, LA	7.6	1.9	0.4	0.5	4.8
Las Vegas, NV	34.1	24.7	1.2	1.6	6.6
Lexington, KY	9.2	5.9	0.7	0.3	2.4
Lincoln, NE	8.8	5.7	0.4	0.2	2.5
Little Rock, AR	10.4	6.8	0.2	0.1	3.3
Los Angeles, CA	47.2	30.0	0.5	0.4	16.3
Louisville, KY	8.6	2.9	0.4	3.4	1.9
Madison, WI	9.3	5.7	0.7	0.2	2.8
Manchester, NH	13.4	1.5	4.4	0.1	7.4
McAllen, TX	86.5	81.1	0.5	0.1	4.8

Table continued on following page.

City	Hispanic or Latino (%)	Mexican (%)	Puerto Rican (%)	Cuban (%)	Other Hispanic or Latino (%)
Memphis, TN	10.2	5.7	0.3	0.2	3.9
Miami, FL	71.2	2.2	3.3	31.0	34.8
Midland, TX	44.3	38.1	0.6	1.3	4.3
Milwaukee, WI	20.7	13.7	4.9	0.1	1.9
Minneapolis, MN	10.5	5.9	0.4	0.2	4.0
Nashville, TN	13.8	6.8	0.7	0.6	5.7
New Orleans, LA	7.9	1.5	0.4	0.8	5.3
New York, NY	28.4	3.9	7.1	0.5	17.0
Oklahoma City, OK	21.7	17.3	0.5	0.1	3.8
Omaha, NE	15.6	11.4	0.5	0.2	3.5
Orlando, FL	35.6	2.0	15.2	2.6	15.8
Philadelphia, PA	15.2	1.4	8.4	0.2	5.2
Phoenix, AZ	41.8	36.7	0.7	0.4	4.0
Pittsburgh, PA	4.2	1.4	0.8	0.1	2.0
Portland, OR	11.3	7.6	0.5	0.4	2.8
Providence, RI	44.3	1.6	6.8	0.3	35.6
Provo, UT	18.9	11.4	0.7	0.2	6.6
Raleigh, NC	12.7	5.0	1.4	0.4	5.9
Reno, NV	24.6	17.9	0.7	0.3	5.7
Richmond, VA	10.3	2.1	1.1	0.3	6.8
Rochester, MN	6.2	3.9	0.4	0.1	1.8
Sacramento, CA	29.5	24.1	0.9	0.1	4.4
Saint Louis, MO	5.1	3.1	0.3	0.3	1.4
Saint Paul, MN	9.1	5.9	0.4	0.2	2.7
Salem, OR	23.4	20.0	0.4	0.1	2.9
Salt Lake City, UT	20.8	15.2	0.5	0.3	4.8
San Antonio, TX	64.4	54.1	1.4	0.4	8.6
San Diego, CA	29.6	24.9	0.8	0.3	3.6
San Francisco, CA	15.9	7.8	0.7	0.2	7.2
San Jose, CA	31.0	25.4	0.5	0.2	4.9
Santa Rosa, CA	35.8	30.3	0.5	0.1	4.9
Savannah, GA	7.1	2.2	2.0	0.5	2.4
Seattle, WA	8.2	4.8	0.4	0.2	2.8
Sioux Falls, SD	6.4	2.7	0.3	0.1	3.3
Tampa, FL	26.2	3.2	6.1	7.8	9.1
Tucson, AZ	42.7	38.1	0.8	0.3	3.5
Tulsa, OK	19.2	14.5	0.7	0.1	4.0
Virginia Beach, VA	8.9	2.8	2.5	0.3	3.3
Washington, DC	11.6	2.1	0.8	0.4	8.2
Wichita, KS	18.4	15.1	0.8	0.1	2.5
Wilmington, NC	8.9	3.6	1.4	0.4	3.5
Winston-Salem, NC	17.9	10.1	1.7	0.3	5.8
U.S.	19.0	11.3	1.8	0.7	5.2

Note: Persons of Hispanic or Latino origin can be of any race
Source: U.S. Census Bureau, 2019-2023 American Community Survey 5-Year Estimates

Hispanic Origin: Metro Area

Metro Area	Hispanic or Latino (%)	Mexican (%)	Puerto Rican (%)	Cuban (%)	Other Hispanic or Latino (%)
Albuquerque, NM	48.3	28.5	0.7	0.4	18.6
Anchorage, AK	8.2	3.8	1.2	0.4	2.8
Ann Arbor, MI	5.6	2.8	0.6	0.2	2.1
Athens, GA	9.3	5.1	0.4	0.5	3.3
Atlanta, GA	12.1	5.7	1.2	0.4	4.7
Austin, TX	32.0	24.8	1.0	0.6	5.6
Baltimore, MD	7.8	1.6	1.2	0.3	4.7
Billings, MT	6.1	4.4	0.2	0.1	1.3
Boise City, ID	14.7	11.8	0.4	0.1	2.4
Boston, MA	12.0	0.8	2.7	0.3	8.3
Boulder, CO	14.6	9.8	0.5	0.3	3.9
Cape Coral, FL	23.6	4.7	4.5	6.7	7.8
Cedar Rapids, IA	3.7	2.6	0.2	0.0	0.8
Charleston, SC	7.5	3.5	1.1	0.3	2.7
Charlotte, NC	12.0	4.9	1.1	0.4	5.6
Chicago, IL	23.8	18.3	2.3	0.3	2.9
Cincinnati, OH	4.3	1.8	0.5	0.2	1.9
Clarksville, TN	9.7	5.0	2.3	0.2	2.2
Cleveland, OH	6.5	1.5	3.6	0.1	1.3
College Station, TX	26.4	21.9	0.5	0.5	3.6
Colorado Springs, CO	18.0	10.8	1.5	0.3	5.3
Columbia, MO	4.1	2.7	0.2	0.1	1.0
Columbia, SC	6.8	3.2	1.1	0.3	2.3
Columbus, OH	5.3	2.5	0.8	0.1	2.0
Dallas, TX	29.4	23.1	0.9	0.4	5.1
Davenport, IA	9.5	8.3	0.4	0.1	0.8
Denver, CO	23.6	17.5	0.7	0.2	5.3
Des Moines, IA	8.4	5.7	0.4	0.1	2.2
Detroit, MI	5.1	3.4	0.6	0.1	1.0
Durham, NC	13.2	6.3	0.8	0.4	5.8
El Paso, TX	82.6	77.5	1.0	0.2	4.0
Eugene, OR	10.2	7.3	0.4	0.2	2.3
Fargo, ND	3.8	2.5	0.4	0.0	0.8
Fort Collins, CO	12.7	9.0	0.5	0.2	3.0
Fort Wayne, IN	8.0	5.7	0.6	0.1	1.7
Fort Worth, TX	29.4	23.1	0.9	0.4	5.1
Gainesville, FL	11.6	1.8	2.8	2.1	4.9
Green Bay, WI	8.7	6.2	1.0	0.1	1.3
Greensboro, NC	10.2	5.9	1.2	0.2	2.8
Honolulu, HI	9.3	3.1	3.1	0.2	3.0
Houston, TX	37.8	26.1	0.8	0.8	10.1
Huntsville, AL	6.7	3.6	0.9	0.2	1.9
Indianapolis, IN	8.6	5.4	0.6	0.2	2.4
Jacksonville, FL	10.6	1.8	3.3	1.5	4.0
Kansas City, MO	10.6	7.5	0.5	0.3	2.3
Lafayette, LA	5.3	1.9	0.2	0.2	3.0
Las Vegas, NV	31.4	22.7	1.1	1.5	6.1
Lexington, KY	7.8	4.9	0.5	0.3	2.0
Lincoln, NE	8.0	5.2	0.4	0.2	2.2
Little Rock, AR	7.1	4.6	0.3	0.1	2.1
Los Angeles, CA	44.8	33.8	0.5	0.4	10.2
Louisville, KY	6.5	2.7	0.5	1.8	1.5
Madison, WI	6.9	4.2	0.6	0.1	1.9
Manchester, NH	8.3	1.2	2.6	0.2	4.2
McAllen, TX	91.9	87.6	0.3	0.1	3.9

Table continued on following page.

Metro Area	Hispanic or Latino (%)	Mexican (%)	Puerto Rican (%)	Cuban (%)	Other Hispanic or Latino (%)
Memphis, TN	7.2	4.2	0.3	0.2	2.5
Miami, FL	46.0	2.5	3.7	18.4	21.5
Midland, TX	44.8	39.3	0.6	1.2	3.8
Milwaukee, WI	11.8	7.7	2.6	0.1	1.4
Minneapolis, MN	6.7	4.1	0.3	0.1	2.1
Nashville, TN	9.7	5.1	0.7	0.4	3.5
New Orleans, LA	12.6	2.0	0.7	0.9	9.1
New York, NY	25.4	3.0	5.6	0.8	16.0
Oklahoma City, OK	15.3	11.9	0.5	0.1	2.8
Omaha, NE	11.9	8.7	0.4	0.2	2.6
Orlando, FL	32.5	2.7	14.3	2.6	12.9
Philadelphia, PA	10.4	2.0	4.6	0.3	3.6
Phoenix, AZ	30.8	26.2	0.7	0.3	3.6
Pittsburgh, PA	2.3	0.8	0.5	0.1	0.9
Portland, OR	13.5	10.2	0.4	0.2	2.6
Providence, RI	14.6	1.0	4.3	0.2	9.1
Provo, UT	13.7	8.1	0.4	0.1	5.1
Raleigh, NC	12.1	6.0	1.4	0.4	4.4
Reno, NV	24.7	18.9	0.6	0.3	5.0
Richmond, VA	8.1	1.9	1.2	0.3	4.7
Rochester, MN	5.1	3.2	0.3	0.1	1.5
Sacramento, CA	22.6	17.9	0.7	0.2	3.8
Saint Louis, MO	3.8	2.3	0.3	0.1	1.1
Saint Paul, MN	6.7	4.1	0.3	0.1	2.1
Salem, OR	25.6	22.2	0.3	0.2	3.0
Salt Lake City, UT	19.6	13.7	0.4	0.1	5.3
San Antonio, TX	54.5	45.5	1.5	0.3	7.2
San Diego, CA	34.3	29.6	0.8	0.2	3.6
San Francisco, CA	23.0	14.5	0.7	0.2	7.6
San Jose, CA	26.3	21.2	0.4	0.2	4.5
Santa Rosa, CA	29.4	23.7	0.4	0.2	5.1
Savannah, GA	7.7	2.9	1.9	0.5	2.4
Seattle, WA	11.4	7.7	0.6	0.2	2.9
Sioux Falls, SD	5.3	2.4	0.2	0.1	2.6
Tampa, FL	21.1	3.7	6.0	4.5	6.9
Tucson, AZ	36.1	32.1	0.9	0.2	3.0
Tulsa, OK	12.0	8.9	0.5	0.1	2.5
Virginia Beach, VA	7.8	2.6	2.2	0.3	2.8
Washington, DC	17.6	2.5	1.2	0.3	13.6
Wichita, KS	14.5	11.8	0.6	0.1	2.0
Wilmington, NC	7.1	3.4	0.9	0.3	2.5
Winston-Salem, NC	11.8	7.0	1.1	0.3	3.4
U.S.	19.0	11.3	1.8	0.7	5.2

Note: Persons of Hispanic or Latino origin can be of any race; Figures cover the Metropolitan Statistical Area (MSA)
Source: U.S. Census Bureau, 2019-2023 American Community Survey 5-Year Estimates

Household Size: City

City	Persons in Household (%)							Average Household Size
	One	Two	Three	Four	Five	Six	Seven or More	
Albuquerque, NM	37.3	32.4	13.7	9.8	4.6	1.4	0.8	2.29
Anchorage, AK	28.5	33.7	14.8	13.5	5.4	2.3	1.8	2.61
Ann Arbor, MI	34.0	35.9	14.5	9.9	3.2	1.8	0.7	2.19
Athens, GA	33.6	35.1	15.3	10.6	4.0	0.9	0.6	2.18
Atlanta, GA	47.0	32.0	10.6	6.5	2.3	1.0	0.6	2.01
Austin, TX	36.9	34.0	13.4	10.0	3.4	1.5	0.7	2.14
Baltimore, MD	43.4	29.6	13.4	7.7	3.7	1.3	1.0	2.22
Billings, MT	34.0	35.0	13.2	10.8	4.7	1.2	1.1	2.29
Boise City, ID	30.1	37.7	15.0	10.9	4.2	1.5	0.7	2.30
Boston, MA	36.9	33.2	14.6	8.9	4.0	1.5	0.9	2.22
Boulder, CO	34.9	36.6	13.9	10.9	2.5	0.6	0.7	2.16
Cape Coral, FL	24.2	44.1	13.7	10.3	5.5	1.3	0.8	2.59
Cedar Rapids, IA	34.4	35.4	13.5	9.4	5.0	1.1	1.3	2.27
Charleston, SC	34.5	40.1	12.4	8.7	3.2	0.8	0.3	2.20
Charlotte, NC	35.1	31.7	14.8	11.2	4.7	1.5	1.0	2.42
Chicago, IL	39.2	29.4	13.1	9.9	4.8	2.1	1.5	2.32
Cincinnati, OH	44.9	30.5	10.7	8.5	3.0	1.4	1.0	2.07
Clarksville, TN	25.7	33.0	18.0	13.6	5.5	2.5	1.6	2.59
Cleveland, OH	46.4	28.4	11.9	7.4	3.4	1.7	0.9	2.11
College Station, TX	31.1	32.3	15.1	15.1	3.5	2.4	0.6	2.42
Colorado Springs, CO	28.2	36.1	15.4	11.8	5.3	2.2	1.0	2.39
Columbia, MO	34.5	33.8	13.4	12.2	4.6	1.0	0.5	2.29
Columbia, SC	39.3	33.0	14.2	8.3	3.7	1.2	0.3	2.16
Columbus, OH	36.5	32.2	13.4	9.7	4.9	2.0	1.3	2.29
Dallas, TX	37.1	29.7	12.7	10.1	6.1	2.6	1.6	2.43
Davenport, IA	34.9	35.3	13.1	9.5	5.1	1.4	0.7	2.25
Denver, CO	40.0	33.5	11.4	9.0	3.7	1.5	1.0	2.12
Des Moines, IA	37.1	30.7	13.2	10.3	4.8	2.1	1.8	2.30
Detroit, MI	42.5	25.3	13.8	8.9	4.8	2.7	1.9	2.47
Durham, NC	36.1	34.1	13.9	9.9	4.0	1.4	0.6	2.25
El Paso, TX	25.8	28.2	18.0	15.5	8.0	2.8	1.7	2.77
Eugene, OR	34.3	35.7	13.6	10.6	4.0	1.2	0.5	2.23
Fargo, ND	41.1	33.0	11.6	9.3	3.4	1.1	0.5	2.10
Fort Collins, CO	26.6	37.8	17.6	12.5	4.1	1.0	0.4	2.27
Fort Wayne, IN	33.5	33.1	13.3	10.7	5.4	2.5	1.4	2.39
Fort Worth, TX	27.7	29.8	15.6	14.1	7.6	3.1	2.0	2.76
Gainesville, FL	39.2	33.2	14.6	8.8	3.1	0.5	0.6	2.17
Green Bay, WI	35.7	32.4	12.0	11.7	4.8	2.0	1.3	2.35
Greensboro, NC	36.4	30.7	15.3	9.8	4.8	1.5	1.5	2.33
Honolulu, HI	35.0	31.1	14.6	9.7	4.5	2.1	3.0	2.47
Houston, TX	34.1	29.2	15.6	11.6	5.7	2.3	1.5	2.47
Huntsville, AL	36.9	35.6	13.6	8.6	3.8	1.2	0.4	2.21
Indianapolis, IN	36.6	31.9	13.1	9.8	5.4	1.9	1.3	2.41
Jacksonville, FL	32.2	33.3	16.2	10.6	5.0	1.8	0.9	2.44
Kansas City, MO	37.7	31.3	12.3	10.8	4.7	2.1	1.0	2.28
Lafayette, LA	33.8	36.5	13.4	9.1	5.0	1.4	0.9	2.25
Las Vegas, NV	30.3	31.2	15.8	11.9	6.3	2.7	1.9	2.63
Lexington, KY	34.8	33.4	14.3	10.8	4.0	1.7	0.9	2.24
Lincoln, NE	32.7	34.1	13.7	11.0	4.9	2.5	1.0	2.31
Little Rock, AR	39.4	31.1	13.5	9.1	4.3	1.4	1.1	2.28
Los Angeles, CA	31.5	28.9	15.5	12.5	6.4	2.6	2.5	2.64
Louisville, KY	34.5	32.8	15.3	10.3	4.6	1.7	0.9	2.34
Madison, WI	39.0	35.2	12.0	9.1	3.3	0.8	0.7	2.09
Manchester, NH	34.5	34.2	14.7	10.7	3.7	1.7	0.5	2.27

Table continued on following page.

City	Persons in Household (%)							Average Household Size
	One	Two	Three	Four	Five	Six	Seven or More	
McAllen, TX	21.4	28.2	18.3	16.3	10.9	2.4	2.5	2.96
Memphis, TN	38.9	29.6	14.5	9.4	4.3	1.8	1.5	2.42
Miami, FL	36.5	32.1	15.8	9.5	3.8	1.1	1.2	2.30
Midland, TX	29.9	27.2	15.3	16.3	7.6	2.6	1.1	2.51
Milwaukee, WI	38.7	29.0	13.7	9.4	5.6	2.1	1.6	2.40
Minneapolis, MN	42.0	30.8	11.5	9.2	3.5	1.5	1.4	2.16
Nashville, TN	36.9	33.0	13.6	9.2	4.6	1.5	1.2	2.19
New Orleans, LA	44.7	29.3	13.2	8.0	3.3	1.0	0.5	2.34
New York, NY	33.4	28.8	16.1	11.7	5.6	2.5	1.9	2.51
Oklahoma City, OK	31.6	31.7	15.5	11.5	6.3	2.3	1.1	2.46
Omaha, NE	34.5	31.5	13.1	10.7	6.0	2.5	1.7	2.39
Orlando, FL	32.4	33.5	15.9	11.2	4.5	1.4	1.1	2.44
Philadelphia, PA	37.6	29.9	14.9	9.6	4.8	1.7	1.4	2.29
Phoenix, AZ	28.3	30.6	15.2	12.8	7.3	3.3	2.5	2.66
Pittsburgh, PA	43.9	33.0	11.6	7.1	2.9	0.8	0.7	2.03
Portland, OR	36.4	34.8	13.8	9.9	3.2	1.1	0.7	2.18
Providence, RI	33.8	28.4	15.4	11.7	7.0	2.3	1.4	2.48
Provo, UT	14.0	36.9	17.7	14.4	7.6	6.5	3.0	2.98
Raleigh, NC	35.3	33.7	13.8	11.4	4.2	1.1	0.5	2.30
Reno, NV	31.9	34.1	14.9	12.1	4.5	1.3	1.2	2.35
Richmond, VA	42.9	32.7	12.2	7.7	2.6	1.2	0.6	2.13
Rochester, MN	31.6	34.6	13.4	12.5	5.0	1.8	1.1	2.35
Sacramento, CA	31.7	29.8	14.4	12.4	6.6	2.6	2.5	2.58
Saint Louis, MO	47.9	30.1	10.3	6.9	3.0	1.0	0.8	1.96
Saint Paul, MN	37.1	29.8	12.5	9.6	5.1	2.9	3.1	2.42
Salem, OR	29.2	33.2	15.5	11.5	5.8	3.0	1.8	2.51
Salt Lake City, UT	39.3	34.1	11.6	8.2	3.8	1.8	1.3	2.19
San Antonio, TX	31.3	29.4	15.5	12.5	6.7	2.8	1.8	2.62
San Diego, CA	28.8	34.2	15.5	12.8	5.4	2.0	1.4	2.55
San Francisco, CA	38.0	32.3	13.4	9.9	3.5	1.6	1.2	2.24
San Jose, CA	20.7	29.4	18.8	17.6	7.6	3.0	2.9	2.98
Santa Rosa, CA	28.0	33.1	16.1	13.7	5.7	2.2	1.2	2.54
Savannah, GA	35.4	34.5	14.8	9.4	3.7	1.1	1.1	2.35
Seattle, WA	41.3	35.4	11.2	8.5	2.5	0.7	0.5	2.03
Sioux Falls, SD	33.9	33.0	12.9	10.3	6.9	1.8	1.2	2.32
Tampa, FL	35.7	32.1	15.4	10.9	4.1	1.4	0.5	2.35
Tucson, AZ	36.3	31.0	13.7	10.7	5.2	2.0	1.1	2.30
Tulsa, OK	35.9	31.9	13.4	10.3	4.9	2.4	1.3	2.36
Virginia Beach, VA	26.1	35.6	17.3	12.7	5.9	1.7	0.8	2.50
Washington, DC	46.7	30.2	11.1	7.4	2.8	1.2	0.7	1.99
Wichita, KS	33.2	32.6	13.2	10.8	5.7	2.7	1.7	2.47
Wilmington, NC	38.5	38.5	12.3	6.8	2.8	0.8	0.3	2.06
Winston-Salem, NC	35.2	32.7	14.2	9.8	4.8	2.3	1.0	2.40
U.S.	28.5	33.8	15.4	12.7	5.9	2.3	1.4	2.54

U.S. Census Bureau, 2019-2023 American Community Survey 5-Year Estimates

Household Size: Metro Area

Metro Area	Persons in Household (%)							Average Household Size
	One	Two	Three	Four	Five	Six	Seven or More	
Albuquerque, NM	33.0	33.6	14.6	10.8	5.0	1.9	1.2	2.44
Anchorage, AK	27.2	33.9	14.5	13.6	6.1	2.7	2.1	2.64
Ann Arbor, MI	30.6	36.1	14.9	11.5	4.2	1.9	0.9	2.34
Athens, GA	28.1	35.1	16.5	12.8	5.1	1.7	0.7	2.43
Atlanta, GA	27.1	32.0	17.0	13.7	6.2	2.4	1.5	2.67
Austin, TX	28.7	33.8	15.6	13.2	5.3	2.3	1.1	2.44
Baltimore, MD	30.0	32.8	15.7	13.0	5.3	2.1	1.2	2.51
Billings, MT	31.0	36.9	13.2	11.3	4.8	1.5	1.3	2.36
Boise City, ID	23.2	36.6	15.4	13.4	6.5	3.3	1.7	2.62
Boston, MA	28.0	33.2	16.7	14.0	5.5	1.7	0.9	2.47
Boulder, CO	29.8	37.0	14.5	12.6	4.2	1.3	0.6	2.33
Cape Coral, FL	28.3	44.7	11.6	8.8	4.4	1.5	0.7	2.44
Cedar Rapids, IA	29.8	37.2	13.8	11.3	5.4	1.4	1.1	2.38
Charleston, SC	29.3	36.3	15.3	11.8	5.0	1.6	0.7	2.45
Charlotte, NC	28.0	34.2	15.9	13.2	5.6	1.9	1.1	2.55
Chicago, IL	29.9	31.0	15.4	13.5	6.4	2.3	1.5	2.55
Cincinnati, OH	29.7	34.2	14.5	12.8	5.6	2.1	1.2	2.46
Clarksville, TN	26.0	33.6	17.5	12.8	5.8	2.4	1.9	2.63
Cleveland, OH	35.3	33.7	13.6	10.5	4.4	1.6	0.9	2.29
College Station, TX	30.3	32.8	14.7	13.5	5.3	2.3	1.1	2.48
Colorado Springs, CO	24.8	36.1	16.2	13.0	6.1	2.4	1.4	2.51
Columbia, MO	31.1	36.1	13.7	12.2	5.0	1.2	0.8	2.37
Columbia, SC	30.6	34.0	15.5	11.9	5.2	1.9	0.9	2.42
Columbus, OH	29.4	33.6	15.1	12.7	5.8	2.2	1.2	2.46
Dallas, TX	25.9	30.9	16.4	14.7	7.5	2.9	1.7	2.73
Davenport, IA	31.5	35.8	13.6	11.3	5.3	1.8	0.8	2.32
Denver, CO	29.2	34.9	14.8	12.7	5.0	2.2	1.2	2.45
Des Moines, IA	29.6	33.9	14.0	12.8	6.4	2.1	1.1	2.44
Detroit, MI	31.9	32.8	15.0	11.9	5.3	1.9	1.2	2.46
Durham, NC	31.7	35.8	14.8	10.9	4.6	1.5	0.6	2.33
El Paso, TX	23.9	27.3	18.2	16.3	9.0	3.5	1.8	2.88
Eugene, OR	29.5	38.4	14.1	10.8	4.8	1.5	0.9	2.34
Fargo, ND	35.2	33.4	13.1	11.0	5.0	1.5	0.8	2.28
Fort Collins, CO	25.5	39.2	16.4	12.1	4.5	1.4	0.9	2.33
Fort Wayne, IN	29.7	34.7	13.4	11.7	6.1	2.7	1.6	2.48
Fort Worth, TX	25.9	30.9	16.4	14.7	7.5	2.9	1.7	2.73
Gainesville, FL	32.9	35.5	15.3	10.3	3.9	1.2	0.9	2.36
Green Bay, WI	29.3	37.6	13.1	12.1	5.2	1.8	0.8	2.38
Greensboro, NC	31.0	33.8	15.5	11.4	5.2	2.0	1.1	2.42
Honolulu, HI	24.9	30.8	16.7	13.1	6.8	3.5	4.1	2.88
Houston, TX	24.8	29.9	17.2	15.3	8.0	3.0	1.8	2.76
Huntsville, AL	29.4	36.4	15.1	12.1	4.8	1.5	0.6	2.42
Indianapolis, IN	29.6	33.8	14.7	12.7	6.1	1.9	1.1	2.50
Jacksonville, FL	27.8	35.6	16.4	11.8	5.5	1.9	1.0	2.51
Kansas City, MO	29.8	34.3	14.1	12.6	5.8	2.3	1.2	2.46
Lafayette, LA	29.1	33.5	16.1	12.4	5.4	2.1	1.2	2.49
Las Vegas, NV	28.0	32.7	15.8	12.3	6.8	2.8	1.8	2.68
Lexington, KY	31.6	34.5	15.2	11.6	4.3	1.9	0.9	2.35
Lincoln, NE	30.8	35.3	13.6	11.4	5.2	2.5	1.1	2.35
Little Rock, AR	31.7	34.1	15.2	11.0	5.3	1.7	1.0	2.41
Los Angeles, CA	25.1	29.0	17.0	15.1	7.7	3.2	2.8	2.86
Louisville, KY	30.6	34.4	15.5	11.8	5.1	1.8	0.9	2.43
Madison, WI	32.9	36.5	13.2	11.1	4.3	1.4	0.7	2.25
Manchester, NH	27.2	35.8	16.5	13.1	4.9	1.7	0.8	2.48

Table continued on following page.

Metro Area	Persons in Household (%)							Average Household Size
	One	Two	Three	Four	Five	Six	Seven or More	
McAllen, TX	18.5	25.1	16.9	17.1	12.2	5.6	4.5	3.30
Memphis, TN	31.2	31.7	16.4	11.7	5.5	2.0	1.5	2.55
Miami, FL	27.9	32.2	17.3	13.3	6.0	2.1	1.3	2.62
Midland, TX	28.9	27.1	15.8	16.0	8.2	2.7	1.4	2.53
Milwaukee, WI	33.0	34.4	13.7	11.3	5.1	1.7	0.9	2.37
Minneapolis, MN	28.9	34.2	14.3	13.3	5.8	2.1	1.4	2.49
Nashville, TN	28.0	34.5	16.1	12.7	5.7	1.9	1.1	2.49
New Orleans, LA	36.4	30.5	15.4	10.8	4.4	1.6	0.9	2.44
New York, NY	28.6	29.6	16.8	14.1	6.3	2.6	1.9	2.63
Oklahoma City, OK	29.0	33.1	15.7	12.4	6.3	2.3	1.2	2.51
Omaha, NE	29.6	33.1	14.3	12.3	6.6	2.5	1.5	2.49
Orlando, FL	24.5	34.1	17.0	14.3	6.5	2.2	1.3	2.71
Philadelphia, PA	29.7	32.3	16.0	13.2	5.7	1.9	1.1	2.49
Phoenix, AZ	26.0	34.8	14.8	12.6	6.7	3.0	2.1	2.62
Pittsburgh, PA	34.1	35.8	13.7	10.6	4.1	1.2	0.6	2.25
Portland, OR	27.6	35.7	15.6	12.8	5.2	1.9	1.2	2.47
Providence, RI	29.5	33.7	16.3	12.9	5.1	1.6	0.9	2.41
Provo, UT	12.3	29.0	16.2	16.6	12.5	8.1	5.3	3.40
Raleigh, NC	25.9	34.7	16.1	14.5	6.0	1.9	0.9	2.57
Reno, NV	27.5	35.2	15.5	12.9	5.6	2.1	1.3	2.49
Richmond, VA	29.5	34.7	15.8	12.2	5.1	1.8	1.0	2.47
Rochester, MN	27.9	36.9	13.2	13.3	5.9	1.8	1.1	2.42
Sacramento, CA	25.1	32.7	16.0	14.5	7.1	2.7	2.0	2.70
Saint Louis, MO	31.3	34.4	14.6	11.9	5.2	1.6	0.9	2.38
Saint Paul, MN	28.9	34.2	14.3	13.3	5.8	2.1	1.4	2.49
Salem, OR	25.5	33.8	15.8	12.5	6.7	3.3	2.3	2.67
Salt Lake City, UT	24.0	31.1	15.7	13.9	7.9	4.4	3.0	2.83
San Antonio, TX	26.8	31.1	16.3	13.8	7.3	2.8	1.9	2.71
San Diego, CA	24.5	33.0	16.7	14.6	6.7	2.6	1.8	2.74
San Francisco, CA	27.2	31.8	16.7	14.5	5.9	2.3	1.6	2.63
San Jose, CA	21.4	31.1	18.8	17.2	6.9	2.6	2.1	2.86
Santa Rosa, CA	27.5	35.1	15.1	13.5	5.5	2.0	1.2	2.50
Savannah, GA	28.1	36.4	15.7	12.1	5.2	1.5	1.1	2.52
Seattle, WA	28.0	34.0	15.8	13.6	5.4	1.9	1.3	2.49
Sioux Falls, SD	30.0	34.4	13.6	11.4	7.3	2.1	1.2	2.41
Tampa, FL	30.8	36.3	15.0	10.9	4.6	1.6	0.8	2.44
Tucson, AZ	31.8	35.4	13.2	11.1	5.1	2.3	1.2	2.37
Tulsa, OK	29.2	33.6	15.2	12.3	5.9	2.5	1.4	2.53
Virginia Beach, VA	28.6	34.6	16.5	12.2	5.5	1.9	0.9	2.46
Washington, DC	28.6	30.4	15.9	14.3	6.5	2.6	1.7	2.62
Wichita, KS	30.1	33.6	14.0	11.7	6.2	2.8	1.7	2.52
Wilmington, NC	29.9	42.0	14.0	8.9	3.6	1.2	0.4	2.26
Winston-Salem, NC	30.3	35.6	15.4	11.1	4.7	2.0	0.9	2.43
U.S.	28.5	33.8	15.4	12.7	5.9	2.3	1.4	2.54

Note: Figures cover the Metropolitan Statistical Area (MSA)
Source: U.S. Census Bureau, 2019-2023 American Community Survey 5-Year Estimates

Household Relationships: City

City	House-holder	Opposite-sex Spouse	Same-sex Spouse	Opposite-sex Unmarried Partner	Same-sex Unmarried Partner	Child[1]	Grand-child	Other Relatives	Non-relatives
Albuquerque, NM	42.1	15.1	0.3	3.4	0.3	27.0	2.5	4.6	3.2
Anchorage, AK	37.5	17.0	0.2	3.0	0.2	28.3	1.9	4.6	4.2
Ann Arbor, MI	40.3	13.3	0.3	2.4	0.2	17.1	0.5	1.6	11.5
Athens, GA	40.1	11.6	0.2	2.7	0.2	20.8	2.0	3.7	10.7
Atlanta, GA	45.7	10.4	0.5	3.1	0.6	20.7	2.1	3.9	5.9
Austin, TX	42.7	14.5	0.4	3.6	0.4	23.2	1.5	4.1	6.4
Baltimore, MD	42.9	9.6	0.3	3.3	0.3	24.9	3.7	5.8	6.1
Billings, MT	42.2	17.7	0.2	3.1	0.1	26.0	1.7	2.5	3.5
Boise City, ID	41.4	17.8	0.2	3.2	0.2	24.7	1.3	2.9	5.4
Boston, MA	41.4	10.4	0.5	3.1	0.4	20.6	1.7	5.3	9.7
Boulder, CO	40.2	13.0	0.3	3.1	0.2	16.4	0.3	1.6	12.3
Cape Coral, FL	39.5	21.2	0.3	3.2	0.1	25.5	2.1	4.8	2.8
Cedar Rapids, IA	42.2	16.7	0.2	3.5	0.2	26.8	1.3	2.9	3.4
Charleston, SC	45.0	17.0	0.3	3.1	0.2	21.8	1.4	2.7	5.3
Charlotte, NC	40.6	15.2	0.2	2.8	0.2	28.0	2.1	4.9	4.2
Chicago, IL	41.6	12.2	0.3	3.0	0.3	26.6	3.0	6.4	4.8
Cincinnati, OH	45.1	10.2	0.3	3.4	0.3	24.6	2.2	3.4	5.3
Clarksville, TN	36.6	16.9	0.2	2.5	0.1	31.2	2.4	3.9	3.5
Cleveland, OH	45.0	8.5	0.2	3.5	0.3	27.0	3.3	5.0	3.8
College Station, TX	35.2	11.2	0.2	1.8	0.1	19.7	0.7	2.7	13.7
Colorado Springs, CO	39.7	18.3	0.3	2.6	0.2	27.5	1.9	3.6	4.3
Columbia, MO	40.5	14.1	0.2	2.8	0.2	22.4	1.0	2.5	7.8
Columbia, SC	39.2	10.5	0.2	2.1	0.2	19.5	1.6	2.8	5.8
Columbus, OH	42.2	12.9	0.3	3.6	0.3	26.2	2.1	4.4	5.2
Dallas, TX	40.1	13.4	0.4	2.6	0.3	28.6	3.2	6.2	4.0
Davenport, IA	41.9	15.9	0.2	3.7	0.2	27.0	2.0	3.0	3.2
Denver, CO	44.4	14.0	0.5	4.1	0.4	22.3	1.9	4.4	5.9
Des Moines, IA	41.1	14.2	0.3	3.5	0.2	27.9	2.0	4.4	3.9
Detroit, MI	39.8	7.3	0.1	2.9	0.2	32.0	4.8	7.3	3.9
Durham, NC	42.0	14.8	0.4	2.9	0.3	24.6	1.8	4.4	4.6
El Paso, TX	35.9	15.8	0.2	1.8	0.1	32.7	3.9	6.4	2.0
Eugene, OR	41.6	14.7	0.3	3.8	0.3	20.7	1.1	2.7	8.3
Fargo, ND	44.5	15.5	0.1	3.6	0.2	23.5	0.7	2.5	5.0
Fort Collins, CO	39.9	16.0	0.2	3.3	0.2	22.1	0.9	2.4	9.0
Fort Wayne, IN	40.7	15.6	0.2	3.1	0.2	29.7	2.0	3.4	3.0
Fort Worth, TX	35.2	15.8	0.2	2.1	0.1	33.0	3.1	5.6	3.0
Gainesville, FL	41.0	9.4	0.3	3.0	0.3	17.0	1.5	3.4	12.5
Green Bay, WI	40.7	15.2	0.2	4.0	0.2	28.6	1.6	3.4	3.0
Greensboro, NC	40.9	13.6	0.2	2.6	0.2	26.4	2.0	4.1	3.6
Honolulu, HI	39.1	15.0	0.3	2.4	0.2	22.2	3.1	9.1	5.6
Houston, TX	38.9	14.0	0.3	2.4	0.2	29.5	2.9	6.5	3.6
Huntsville, AL	42.8	16.5	0.2	2.2	0.2	25.1	2.1	3.5	3.1
Indianapolis, IN	40.7	14.0	0.3	3.4	0.3	28.6	2.5	4.5	3.9
Jacksonville, FL	39.9	15.6	0.2	2.8	0.2	27.7	2.8	4.9	3.6
Kansas City, MO	42.6	14.5	0.3	3.3	0.3	27.2	2.3	4.0	3.8
Lafayette, LA	43.0	15.3	0.2	2.8	0.2	27.0	2.3	3.5	3.8
Las Vegas, NV	37.5	15.2	0.3	2.9	0.2	29.3	2.7	6.7	4.3
Lexington, KY	41.7	16.0	0.3	2.9	0.3	25.3	1.6	3.4	4.4
Lincoln, NE	40.1	16.9	0.2	2.8	0.1	26.6	1.1	2.7	4.6
Little Rock, AR	43.5	14.5	0.3	2.4	0.3	27.1	2.3	3.9	3.1
Los Angeles, CA	36.2	13.1	0.3	2.8	0.3	26.5	2.8	9.0	6.3
Louisville, KY	40.0	18.0	0.2	2.9	0.2	28.8	2.6	4.2	2.7
Madison, WI	44.8	14.5	0.4	3.8	0.3	19.7	0.7	2.4	8.2
Manchester, NH	42.5	14.9	0.3	4.3	0.2	24.3	1.6	4.3	4.7
McAllen, TX	34.3	16.0	0.1	1.7	0.1	34.6	3.5	6.8	2.0

Table continued on following page.

City	House-holder	Opposite-sex Spouse	Same-sex Spouse	Opposite-sex Unmarried Partner	Same-sex Unmarried Partner	Child[1]	Grand-child	Other Relatives	Non-relatives
Memphis, TN	40.4	10.9	0.2	2.7	0.2	29.7	4.3	6.1	3.7
Miami, FL	42.4	12.6	0.5	3.3	0.3	22.5	2.4	8.7	5.8
Midland, TX	36.4	18.5	0.1	2.1	0.1	31.9	3.0	4.2	2.5
Milwaukee, WI	40.8	10.2	0.2	3.6	0.2	30.2	2.7	4.9	4.4
Minneapolis, MN	43.7	12.0	0.6	3.9	0.5	22.1	1.1	3.5	8.0
Nashville, TN	42.1	14.3	0.3	3.0	0.3	24.0	1.9	4.7	5.7
New Orleans, LA	43.0	11.0	0.3	3.1	0.4	26.1	3.2	4.6	4.3
New York, NY	38.3	12.7	0.3	2.2	0.2	27.6	2.5	8.3	5.3
Oklahoma City, OK	39.4	16.6	0.2	2.6	0.2	29.4	2.3	4.3	3.1
Omaha, NE	39.8	16.0	0.2	2.8	0.2	29.6	1.8	3.7	3.6
Orlando, FL	41.7	13.7	0.5	3.5	0.4	26.1	2.0	5.9	5.0
Philadelphia, PA	41.0	10.9	0.3	3.1	0.3	26.8	3.6	5.9	5.2
Phoenix, AZ	36.3	14.4	0.3	3.1	0.3	30.2	2.9	6.6	4.2
Pittsburgh, PA	46.1	11.5	0.3	3.6	0.4	19.3	1.7	3.1	6.7
Portland, OR	43.2	14.9	0.7	4.4	0.6	21.2	1.1	3.7	7.2
Providence, RI	36.5	10.5	0.3	2.9	0.3	27.3	1.9	5.7	6.1
Provo, UT	29.6	15.9	0.1	0.6	0.0	25.7	1.6	4.0	12.7
Raleigh, NC	41.8	15.1	0.2	2.9	0.2	25.5	1.4	3.9	5.0
Reno, NV	41.1	15.2	0.3	3.8	0.2	24.8	1.7	4.7	5.7
Richmond, VA	45.2	10.4	0.4	4.0	0.4	20.8	2.1	4.3	7.4
Rochester, MN	41.1	18.5	0.2	2.8	0.1	27.8	0.9	2.8	3.3
Sacramento, CA	36.7	13.5	0.4	3.0	0.3	28.0	2.6	7.5	4.7
Saint Louis, MO	48.0	10.3	0.4	3.7	0.4	22.5	2.6	4.0	4.3
Saint Paul, MN	38.7	12.7	0.4	3.3	0.3	28.8	1.7	5.6	4.8
Salem, OR	36.6	16.0	0.2	3.1	0.2	28.1	1.9	4.6	4.2
Salt Lake City, UT	42.3	13.9	0.5	3.4	0.4	22.1	1.7	4.2	7.6
San Antonio, TX	37.5	14.7	0.3	2.7	0.2	30.3	3.8	5.5	3.2
San Diego, CA	37.2	15.7	0.4	2.6	0.3	25.0	2.0	6.2	6.1
San Francisco, CA	42.6	13.6	0.8	3.3	0.6	17.6	1.3	6.8	10.3
San Jose, CA	32.4	17.1	0.2	1.9	0.1	28.6	2.3	9.8	6.1
Santa Rosa, CA	37.6	16.2	0.4	3.0	0.2	27.3	1.8	6.2	5.5
Savannah, GA	39.9	11.2	0.3	2.7	0.3	24.9	3.2	4.4	5.0
Seattle, WA	46.9	15.2	0.8	4.3	0.6	17.5	0.7	2.8	7.3
Sioux Falls, SD	40.7	18.0	0.1	3.2	0.1	28.4	1.1	2.7	3.1
Tampa, FL	40.9	13.8	0.3	3.2	0.3	25.8	2.3	4.9	4.5
Tucson, AZ	41.1	13.3	0.3	3.3	0.3	25.4	2.8	4.8	4.5
Tulsa, OK	41.6	14.8	0.2	2.9	0.2	27.8	2.3	4.3	3.4
Virginia Beach, VA	38.8	18.6	0.2	2.4	0.1	28.7	2.2	4.0	3.5
Washington, DC	45.3	10.3	0.6	3.1	0.5	20.4	2.4	4.2	7.1
Wichita, KS	40.0	16.4	0.2	2.7	0.2	29.1	2.2	3.7	3.1
Wilmington, NC	45.7	14.9	0.3	3.4	0.3	21.2	1.5	3.0	5.9
Winston-Salem, NC	40.9	14.6	0.2	2.5	0.2	28.1	2.4	4.3	2.7
U.S.	38.3	17.5	0.2	2.5	0.2	28.3	2.4	4.8	3.4

Note: Figures are percent of the total population; (1) Includes biological, adopted, and stepchildren of the householder
Source: U.S. Census Bureau, 2020 Census

Household Relationships: Metro Area

Metro Area	House-holder	Opposite-sex Spouse	Same-sex Spouse	Opposite-sex Unmarried Partner	Same-sex Unmarried Partner	Child[1]	Grand-child	Other Relatives	Non-relatives
Albuquerque, NM	40.1	16.3	0.3	3.1	0.3	27.7	3.1	4.6	2.9
Anchorage, AK	37.1	17.6	0.2	2.9	0.1	29.1	1.9	4.2	4.0
Ann Arbor, MI	39.7	17.0	0.3	2.4	0.2	24.3	1.3	2.5	5.8
Athens, GA	38.6	15.6	0.2	2.3	0.2	25.1	2.3	3.7	7.3
Atlanta, GA	37.1	16.7	0.2	2.1	0.2	30.4	2.7	5.7	3.5
Austin, TX	38.6	17.3	0.3	2.7	0.3	27.8	1.9	4.4	4.6
Baltimore, MD	38.7	16.8	0.2	2.4	0.2	28.7	2.5	4.8	3.5
Billings, MT	41.3	19.5	0.1	2.8	0.1	26.5	1.8	2.5	3.1
Boise City, ID	36.6	19.5	0.2	2.5	0.1	29.7	1.9	3.5	3.8
Boston, MA	38.7	17.4	0.3	2.5	0.2	27.1	1.6	4.5	4.4
Boulder, CO	40.1	18.0	0.3	2.8	0.2	23.8	1.0	2.6	6.8
Cape Coral, FL	41.8	20.9	0.3	3.0	0.2	22.4	1.8	4.4	3.3
Cedar Rapids, IA	40.9	19.3	0.1	3.0	0.1	27.9	1.2	2.3	2.5
Charleston, SC	39.9	18.1	0.2	2.4	0.1	27.3	2.6	3.8	3.5
Charlotte, NC	38.9	18.3	0.2	2.4	0.2	29.2	2.4	4.2	2.8
Chicago, IL	38.2	17.1	0.2	2.3	0.1	30.3	2.4	5.1	2.8
Cincinnati, OH	39.5	18.1	0.2	2.7	0.1	28.9	2.3	3.2	2.9
Clarksville, TN	36.7	18.2	0.2	2.2	0.1	30.5	2.5	3.6	3.0
Cleveland, OH	42.5	17.1	0.1	2.7	0.1	27.7	2.1	3.3	2.3
College Station, TX	36.9	14.6	0.1	2.0	0.1	24.7	1.9	3.5	8.3
Colorado Springs, CO	37.5	19.3	0.2	2.2	0.1	28.5	2.0	3.6	3.8
Columbia, MO	39.8	16.5	0.2	2.8	0.2	24.9	1.4	2.5	5.7
Columbia, SC	39.9	17.0	0.2	2.1	0.2	27.5	2.7	3.8	3.0
Columbus, OH	39.4	17.4	0.2	2.9	0.2	28.5	2.0	3.5	3.3
Dallas, TX	36.2	17.6	0.2	2.0	0.2	31.7	2.7	5.5	2.9
Davenport, IA	41.4	18.8	0.2	2.9	0.1	27.9	1.8	2.5	2.2
Denver, CO	39.4	17.9	0.3	2.9	0.2	27.4	1.9	4.4	4.3
Des Moines, IA	39.6	19.2	0.2	2.7	0.1	29.6	1.3	2.8	2.6
Detroit, MI	40.1	17.2	0.1	2.5	0.1	30.1	2.3	4.2	2.4
Durham, NC	40.3	17.2	0.3	2.5	0.2	25.1	1.9	3.8	3.9
El Paso, TX	34.2	15.8	0.2	1.7	0.1	33.5	4.2	6.5	1.8
Eugene, OR	40.9	17.0	0.3	3.7	0.2	22.7	1.8	3.5	6.6
Fargo, ND	41.5	17.7	0.1	3.2	0.1	27.0	0.7	2.2	3.9
Fort Collins, CO	40.2	19.4	0.2	2.8	0.2	24.0	1.2	2.7	6.0
Fort Wayne, IN	39.5	18.0	0.2	2.7	0.1	30.5	1.9	2.9	2.5
Fort Worth, TX	36.2	17.6	0.2	2.0	0.2	31.7	2.7	5.5	2.9
Gainesville, FL	40.4	14.9	0.2	2.8	0.2	22.9	2.2	3.9	6.9
Green Bay, WI	40.5	19.8	0.1	3.3	0.1	28.1	1.2	2.2	2.2
Greensboro, NC	40.2	17.1	0.2	2.4	0.2	27.4	2.3	3.9	2.6
Honolulu, HI	33.1	16.3	0.2	1.9	0.1	26.2	4.5	9.2	4.9
Houston, TX	35.2	17.1	0.2	2.0	0.1	32.7	2.8	6.1	2.6
Huntsville, AL	40.1	19.3	0.1	1.9	0.1	27.8	2.3	3.4	2.3
Indianapolis, IN	39.2	17.9	0.2	2.8	0.2	29.6	2.1	3.5	2.8
Jacksonville, FL	39.1	17.9	0.2	2.6	0.2	28.0	2.6	4.3	3.2
Kansas City, MO	39.6	18.4	0.2	2.6	0.2	29.4	2.0	3.3	2.7
Lafayette, LA	39.5	17.1	0.2	2.7	0.2	30.4	2.9	3.5	2.5
Las Vegas, NV	37.3	15.5	0.3	3.0	0.2	28.7	2.6	7.0	4.4
Lexington, KY	40.5	17.4	0.2	2.8	0.2	26.5	2.0	3.4	3.7
Lincoln, NE	39.5	17.9	0.2	2.6	0.1	27.2	1.1	2.6	4.1
Little Rock, AR	40.8	17.7	0.2	2.3	0.2	27.9	2.6	3.6	2.7
Los Angeles, CA	34.0	15.2	0.2	2.3	0.2	29.0	3.0	9.1	5.1
Louisville, KY	40.5	17.7	0.2	2.8	0.2	27.6	2.5	3.6	2.9
Madison, WI	42.2	18.6	0.3	3.3	0.2	25.0	0.8	2.1	4.5
Manchester, NH	39.7	19.2	0.3	3.2	0.1	27.2	1.6	3.5	3.2
McAllen, TX	29.7	15.0	0.1	1.6	0.1	38.3	5.2	7.5	1.6

Table continued on following page.

Metro Area	House-holder	Opposite-sex Spouse	Same-sex Spouse	Opposite-sex Unmarried Partner	Same-sex Unmarried Partner	Child[1]	Grand-child	Other Relatives	Non-relatives
Memphis, TN	38.6	15.1	0.1	2.2	0.1	30.4	3.9	5.2	2.7
Miami, FL	38.0	16.0	0.3	2.6	0.2	27.6	2.5	7.8	3.7
Midland, TX	35.8	18.6	0.1	2.0	0.1	32.3	3.2	4.4	2.6
Milwaukee, WI	41.3	17.5	0.2	2.9	0.2	28.7	1.6	3.1	2.7
Minneapolis, MN	38.9	18.7	0.2	2.8	0.2	29.4	1.2	3.3	3.3
Nashville, TN	38.8	18.2	0.2	2.4	0.2	28.1	2.2	4.1	3.8
New Orleans, LA	40.3	15.3	0.2	2.7	0.2	28.8	3.1	4.6	2.9
New York, NY	36.8	15.8	0.2	2.0	0.2	29.7	2.1	7.1	4.1
Oklahoma City, OK	38.8	17.7	0.2	2.4	0.2	29.0	2.3	3.8	3.1
Omaha, NE	38.8	18.4	0.2	2.6	0.1	30.6	1.6	3.1	2.8
Orlando, FL	37.0	17.0	0.3	2.7	0.2	28.4	2.4	6.0	4.2
Philadelphia, PA	38.7	16.9	0.2	2.5	0.2	29.2	2.5	4.4	3.0
Phoenix, AZ	36.9	17.2	0.2	2.8	0.2	29.0	2.5	5.4	3.7
Pittsburgh, PA	43.2	19.0	0.2	2.8	0.2	25.6	1.6	2.6	2.4
Portland, OR	39.0	18.1	0.4	3.2	0.3	26.7	1.6	4.2	4.9
Providence, RI	40.0	16.9	0.2	3.0	0.2	27.2	1.9	4.1	3.0
Provo, UT	28.0	18.8	0.1	0.7	0.0	39.0	2.1	4.0	4.8
Raleigh, NC	38.4	19.2	0.2	2.2	0.2	30.0	1.5	3.7	3.0
Reno, NV	39.5	17.2	0.2	3.4	0.2	26.1	2.1	5.0	4.9
Richmond, VA	39.5	17.3	0.2	2.5	0.2	27.7	2.4	4.0	3.3
Rochester, MN	40.1	20.5	0.1	2.7	0.1	28.9	1.0	2.2	2.5
Sacramento, CA	36.2	17.1	0.3	2.4	0.2	29.4	2.2	6.0	4.2
Saint Louis, MO	40.8	18.2	0.2	2.6	0.2	28.5	2.2	3.0	2.4
Saint Paul, MN	38.9	18.7	0.2	2.8	0.2	29.4	1.2	3.3	3.3
Salem, OR	35.7	17.6	0.2	2.7	0.1	29.3	2.3	5.0	4.1
Salt Lake City, UT	34.0	17.4	0.3	2.1	0.2	32.4	2.5	5.3	4.4
San Antonio, TX	36.2	16.9	0.2	2.3	0.2	31.0	3.5	5.1	2.8
San Diego, CA	35.1	16.9	0.3	2.3	0.2	27.8	2.3	6.6	5.1
San Francisco, CA	36.7	17.0	0.4	2.3	0.3	26.3	1.8	6.9	5.9
San Jose, CA	33.8	18.4	0.2	1.8	0.1	28.3	1.9	7.9	5.6
Santa Rosa, CA	38.4	17.6	0.4	2.9	0.2	26.1	1.9	5.2	5.5
Savannah, GA	38.7	16.6	0.2	2.4	0.2	28.0	2.8	4.1	3.4
Seattle, WA	38.9	18.3	0.3	2.9	0.2	26.7	1.5	4.6	4.7
Sioux Falls, SD	39.5	19.4	0.1	2.9	0.1	29.8	1.1	2.3	2.6
Tampa, FL	41.2	17.6	0.3	3.1	0.2	25.5	2.2	4.6	3.4
Tucson, AZ	40.9	17.2	0.3	2.9	0.2	25.5	2.6	4.4	3.4
Tulsa, OK	39.1	18.2	0.2	2.4	0.1	29.0	2.6	3.9	2.7
Virginia Beach, VA	39.0	17.4	0.2	2.3	0.1	27.7	2.5	4.0	3.3
Washington, DC	37.0	17.3	0.3	2.0	0.2	29.3	2.0	5.9	4.4
Wichita, KS	39.0	18.2	0.1	2.4	0.1	29.8	2.1	3.2	2.6
Wilmington, NC	42.3	18.7	0.2	2.9	0.2	24.4	1.9	3.1	3.9
Winston-Salem, NC	40.9	18.6	0.2	2.3	0.1	27.5	2.4	3.7	2.2
U.S.	38.3	17.5	0.2	2.5	0.2	28.3	2.4	4.8	3.4

Note: Figures are percent of the total population; Figures cover the Metropolitan Statistical Area (MSA); (1) Includes biological, adopted, and stepchildren of the householder
Source: U.S. Census Bureau, 2020 Census

Age: City

City	Percent of Population									Median Age
	Under Age 5	Age 5–19	Age 20–34	Age 35–44	Age 45–54	Age 55–64	Age 65–74	Age 75–84	Age 85+	
Albuquerque, NM	5.1	18.0	21.5	13.9	11.7	12.5	10.4	4.7	2.1	38.7
Anchorage, AK	6.5	19.6	24.0	14.2	11.6	11.6	8.2	3.4	0.9	34.9
Ann Arbor, MI	3.8	18.7	38.6	10.1	8.2	7.9	7.3	4.0	1.4	27.7
Athens, GA	4.8	19.9	33.9	11.5	9.1	8.9	7.4	3.5	1.1	29.2
Atlanta, GA	5.1	15.7	31.0	14.7	11.4	9.8	7.5	3.5	1.3	34.0
Austin, TX	5.4	15.7	29.9	17.3	12.0	9.6	6.4	2.6	1.1	34.5
Baltimore, MD	6.1	17.5	24.5	13.7	10.7	12.5	9.3	4.0	1.6	36.1
Billings, MT	5.9	18.9	21.1	14.0	10.2	11.6	10.3	5.4	2.6	38.1
Boise City, ID	4.4	17.8	23.2	14.2	12.6	12.5	9.2	4.6	1.6	38.2
Boston, MA	4.6	15.3	33.4	13.3	10.2	10.5	7.6	3.4	1.7	33.2
Boulder, CO	2.0	20.2	36.8	10.3	10.0	8.4	7.4	3.2	1.8	28.8
Cape Coral, FL	4.5	14.5	15.7	10.8	13.4	15.9	14.6	7.9	2.5	48.7
Cedar Rapids, IA	5.7	18.7	22.7	13.5	11.4	11.8	9.3	4.7	2.3	36.9
Charleston, SC	5.1	15.6	27.7	14.1	10.2	11.3	9.5	4.5	2.1	36.1
Charlotte, NC	6.5	19.1	25.5	14.8	12.8	10.7	6.7	2.8	1.2	34.4
Chicago, IL	5.6	16.6	26.7	14.6	11.8	11.2	8.1	3.9	1.7	35.7
Cincinnati, OH	6.3	18.7	28.1	12.5	10.0	11.1	8.2	3.4	1.7	33.0
Clarksville, TN	8.5	21.0	29.2	14.0	9.6	9.0	5.8	2.3	0.7	30.4
Cleveland, OH	5.6	18.2	24.4	12.2	11.2	13.4	9.3	4.1	1.6	36.3
College Station, TX	4.8	25.3	40.0	10.3	6.8	6.2	4.2	1.9	0.6	22.9
Colorado Springs, CO	5.9	18.5	24.7	13.7	11.2	11.2	8.7	4.3	1.7	35.6
Columbia, MO	5.4	20.7	32.4	12.5	8.9	8.8	6.4	3.3	1.6	29.2
Columbia, SC	5.4	21.9	32.9	10.9	9.5	8.4	6.8	3.2	1.0	28.7
Columbus, OH	6.7	18.6	28.6	13.8	10.9	10.5	6.9	2.9	1.2	33.0
Dallas, TX	7.0	19.5	26.0	13.8	11.6	10.7	7.0	3.1	1.3	33.4
Davenport, IA	6.1	17.9	22.1	13.4	11.1	12.9	9.8	4.6	2.2	37.8
Denver, CO	5.5	14.8	29.4	16.9	11.7	9.5	7.6	3.3	1.4	35.2
Des Moines, IA	6.8	19.2	24.7	13.0	11.8	11.9	7.7	3.3	1.5	34.6
Detroit, MI	6.8	20.8	22.2	11.8	11.8	11.8	9.0	4.1	1.7	35.1
Durham, NC	6.1	17.6	26.8	14.3	11.5	10.7	8.1	3.5	1.4	34.8
El Paso, TX	6.5	21.6	23.2	12.5	11.5	10.8	8.1	4.1	1.8	34.1
Eugene, OR	3.9	17.1	28.5	12.4	10.4	10.1	10.4	5.2	2.1	35.4
Fargo, ND	6.0	18.4	30.1	12.8	9.0	10.1	7.9	3.9	1.8	32.2
Fort Collins, CO	3.9	18.9	33.6	12.6	9.4	9.4	7.3	3.3	1.6	30.6
Fort Wayne, IN	7.0	20.0	22.9	12.5	11.4	11.3	8.8	4.1	2.0	35.0
Fort Worth, TX	7.3	22.1	23.3	14.4	12.0	10.3	6.5	2.9	1.0	33.4
Gainesville, FL	3.7	19.7	40.6	9.6	7.3	7.3	6.7	3.3	1.7	26.5
Green Bay, WI	6.5	20.5	21.8	13.5	11.6	12.2	8.3	3.7	1.7	35.7
Greensboro, NC	5.7	21.4	24.2	12.4	11.6	10.8	8.2	3.9	1.9	34.1
Honolulu, HI	4.5	13.9	20.6	13.8	12.8	12.7	11.5	6.5	3.6	42.9
Houston, TX	6.7	19.4	25.1	14.5	11.7	10.6	7.3	3.4	1.3	34.3
Huntsville, AL	5.6	17.5	24.7	12.3	10.9	12.5	9.2	5.2	2.1	36.4
Indianapolis, IN	7.0	20.5	23.8	13.2	11.2	11.4	8.1	3.3	1.5	34.1
Jacksonville, FL	6.5	18.7	22.6	13.4	11.8	12.5	9.0	4.1	1.6	36.4
Kansas City, MO	6.2	18.7	24.1	13.7	11.4	11.8	8.8	3.6	1.7	35.7
Lafayette, LA	6.1	18.0	22.9	12.8	10.2	12.9	10.9	4.5	1.8	37.1
Las Vegas, NV	5.8	19.1	20.4	13.7	13.0	12.4	9.3	4.8	1.5	38.5
Lexington, KY	5.7	18.8	25.1	13.1	11.6	11.2	8.8	4.2	1.4	35.2
Lincoln, NE	5.9	20.0	26.1	12.8	10.4	10.4	8.8	4.0	1.7	33.4
Little Rock, AR	6.7	19.9	21.8	13.4	12.1	11.0	9.2	4.0	2.0	36.4
Los Angeles, CA	5.2	16.8	24.8	14.8	13.0	11.6	8.1	3.8	1.9	36.9
Louisville, KY	6.2	18.8	21.1	13.1	12.1	12.8	9.9	4.5	1.6	37.7
Madison, WI	4.8	16.9	33.7	12.8	9.6	9.5	7.7	3.6	1.4	31.8
Manchester, NH	4.9	15.1	25.7	13.8	11.6	13.7	8.7	4.6	2.0	37.9

Table continued on following page.

City	Percent of Population									Median Age
	Under Age 5	Age 5–19	Age 20–34	Age 35–44	Age 45–54	Age 55–64	Age 65–74	Age 75–84	Age 85+	
McAllen, TX	7.0	23.3	21.2	13.3	12.4	9.4	8.1	3.8	1.5	34.0
Memphis, TN	7.2	20.2	23.7	12.1	11.1	11.6	8.9	3.9	1.3	34.3
Miami, FL	5.3	12.8	23.8	15.4	13.5	12.8	8.5	5.2	2.6	39.7
Midland, TX	8.8	22.6	24.9	14.7	9.6	8.9	6.0	2.9	1.6	31.6
Milwaukee, WI	6.9	22.2	25.1	13.0	10.6	10.4	7.4	3.0	1.4	32.2
Minneapolis, MN	5.7	17.1	30.9	14.9	10.7	9.9	7.0	2.7	1.1	33.0
Nashville, TN	6.6	16.9	27.6	14.5	11.2	10.8	7.9	3.4	1.2	34.4
New Orleans, LA	5.5	16.9	22.0	14.9	11.5	12.7	10.4	4.3	1.7	38.4
New York, NY	5.9	16.7	22.9	13.9	12.4	12.2	9.2	4.8	2.0	38.0
Oklahoma City, OK	6.8	20.5	22.6	14.2	11.4	11.1	8.3	3.8	1.2	35.0
Omaha, NE	6.8	20.5	22.4	13.6	11.2	11.4	8.7	3.9	1.5	35.3
Orlando, FL	6.2	16.8	26.7	16.5	12.4	10.2	6.6	3.2	1.3	35.1
Philadelphia, PA	6.1	18.4	25.5	13.4	10.9	11.6	8.6	4.1	1.6	35.1
Phoenix, AZ	6.1	20.7	23.4	14.1	12.5	11.2	7.4	3.2	1.2	34.8
Pittsburgh, PA	4.4	16.1	32.1	12.5	9.0	10.8	9.0	4.0	2.0	33.5
Portland, OR	4.3	14.5	24.5	18.0	13.8	10.7	8.8	3.9	1.5	38.6
Providence, RI	5.4	20.3	28.3	12.6	11.9	10.0	6.8	3.3	1.5	32.9
Provo, UT	5.8	20.1	48.3	8.2	5.7	5.3	3.7	1.9	0.9	23.7
Raleigh, NC	5.7	17.8	27.0	14.4	13.0	10.4	7.1	3.3	1.3	34.7
Reno, NV	5.3	17.2	23.9	13.8	11.0	12.3	10.1	4.6	1.6	37.3
Richmond, VA	5.9	15.4	29.6	13.5	10.1	11.9	8.7	3.5	1.4	34.5
Rochester, MN	6.8	18.9	22.4	14.1	10.3	11.5	8.8	4.9	2.3	36.4
Sacramento, CA	5.9	18.4	24.4	14.7	11.6	11.0	8.5	3.8	1.7	35.7
Saint Louis, MO	5.8	15.0	26.2	14.2	11.1	12.6	9.6	3.7	1.6	36.6
Saint Paul, MN	6.3	20.3	25.8	13.9	10.7	10.7	7.9	3.0	1.3	33.5
Salem, OR	5.9	20.2	22.9	13.6	11.4	10.8	8.9	4.7	1.7	35.7
Salt Lake City, UT	4.9	15.8	32.5	14.0	10.9	9.6	7.5	3.3	1.3	33.0
San Antonio, TX	6.3	20.5	23.7	13.8	11.8	10.7	7.9	3.7	1.6	34.6
San Diego, CA	5.3	16.6	26.4	14.7	12.0	10.9	8.2	4.3	1.7	36.0
San Francisco, CA	4.2	11.0	26.1	16.3	13.2	12.0	9.8	4.8	2.6	39.7
San Jose, CA	5.2	18.3	21.9	14.6	13.8	12.1	8.2	4.1	1.8	38.1
Santa Rosa, CA	4.9	17.9	19.3	14.1	12.9	12.1	11.2	5.1	2.4	40.5
Savannah, GA	6.1	18.1	28.1	11.9	10.3	11.4	8.1	4.5	1.4	33.7
Seattle, WA	4.2	12.2	32.7	16.3	12.2	9.7	7.7	3.4	1.6	35.5
Sioux Falls, SD	7.0	20.0	22.8	14.4	10.8	11.4	8.8	3.4	1.4	35.1
Tampa, FL	5.8	18.5	24.6	14.2	12.5	11.2	7.8	4.1	1.3	35.6
Tucson, AZ	5.3	18.5	26.7	12.2	10.4	11.0	9.0	4.8	2.0	34.6
Tulsa, OK	6.7	20.3	22.3	13.2	11.2	11.3	9.1	4.2	1.7	35.5
Virginia Beach, VA	6.0	18.3	22.1	14.1	11.7	12.6	9.2	4.5	1.6	37.4
Washington, DC	6.1	15.2	29.0	16.4	10.7	9.8	7.4	3.8	1.5	34.9
Wichita, KS	6.3	20.7	22.0	12.9	11.0	11.7	9.4	4.1	1.9	35.7
Wilmington, NC	4.3	17.0	25.9	11.7	10.8	12.6	10.2	5.3	2.3	37.5
Winston-Salem, NC	5.9	21.7	21.6	12.1	11.9	12.0	8.5	4.3	1.9	35.6
U.S.	5.7	19.1	20.2	13.1	12.3	12.8	10.0	4.9	1.9	38.7

Source: U.S. Census Bureau, 2019-2023 American Community Survey 5-Year Estimates

Age: Metro Area

Metro Area	Percent of Population									Median Age
	Under Age 5	Age 5–19	Age 20–34	Age 35–44	Age 45–54	Age 55–64	Age 65–74	Age 75–84	Age 85+	
Albuquerque, NM	5.0	18.5	20.0	13.4	11.8	12.9	11.1	5.1	2.0	39.6
Anchorage, AK	6.5	20.2	22.8	14.2	11.7	11.9	8.5	3.3	0.9	35.4
Ann Arbor, MI	4.6	19.1	26.4	11.9	11.3	11.3	9.2	4.5	1.5	34.8
Athens, GA	5.0	20.7	26.4	12.2	11.0	10.6	8.8	4.1	1.3	33.2
Atlanta, GA	5.9	20.6	20.5	13.9	13.7	12.2	8.2	3.7	1.2	37.0
Austin, TX	5.8	19.0	23.8	16.3	13.0	10.5	7.5	3.1	1.1	35.9
Baltimore, MD	5.8	18.8	19.8	13.5	12.3	13.4	9.7	4.7	1.9	38.9
Billings, MT	5.5	19.3	18.9	13.2	11.4	12.9	11.3	5.2	2.2	39.7
Boise City, ID	5.7	20.8	19.9	13.9	12.2	11.8	9.6	4.6	1.4	37.4
Boston, MA	5.1	17.2	21.6	13.2	12.6	13.5	9.8	4.7	2.1	39.3
Boulder, CO	4.0	19.1	23.8	12.6	12.6	12.2	9.8	4.2	1.8	37.5
Cape Coral, FL	4.5	14.9	15.7	10.6	11.3	14.2	15.4	10.2	3.3	49.3
Cedar Rapids, IA	5.8	19.3	19.1	13.2	12.1	13.1	10.1	5.1	2.2	39.3
Charleston, SC	5.9	18.2	21.0	14.1	12.0	12.6	10.0	4.5	1.6	38.1
Charlotte, NC	5.9	19.9	20.1	13.9	13.7	12.2	8.7	4.1	1.4	37.9
Chicago, IL	5.6	19.2	20.4	13.6	12.8	12.7	9.3	4.4	1.8	38.4
Cincinnati, OH	6.0	20.0	19.7	12.8	12.1	13.1	9.9	4.5	1.8	38.2
Clarksville, TN	8.1	21.2	25.9	13.1	10.3	10.0	7.1	3.3	1.1	31.9
Cleveland, OH	5.3	17.9	18.9	12.1	12.2	14.2	11.5	5.6	2.4	41.6
College Station, TX	5.6	22.3	30.9	11.6	9.2	9.0	6.9	3.0	1.4	28.4
Colorado Springs, CO	6.1	19.7	23.6	13.5	11.3	11.7	8.7	3.9	1.4	35.4
Columbia, MO	5.5	20.2	26.9	12.3	10.3	10.9	8.5	3.9	1.5	33.1
Columbia, SC	5.6	20.1	21.2	12.8	12.1	12.5	9.8	4.5	1.5	37.5
Columbus, OH	6.3	19.8	21.6	14.0	12.4	11.9	8.7	3.9	1.5	36.6
Dallas, TX	6.4	21.6	21.3	14.4	13.0	11.4	7.4	3.3	1.1	35.5
Davenport, IA	5.7	19.6	17.9	12.9	11.8	13.2	11.1	5.6	2.3	40.2
Denver, CO	5.5	18.2	22.7	15.4	12.8	11.6	8.6	3.8	1.4	37.2
Des Moines, IA	6.5	20.7	20.4	14.4	12.1	11.7	8.6	4.0	1.7	36.7
Detroit, MI	5.6	18.4	19.6	12.2	12.9	14.0	10.5	4.8	2.0	40.2
Durham, NC	5.3	18.5	22.6	13.0	12.2	12.1	10.0	4.7	1.7	37.6
El Paso, TX	6.8	22.6	23.1	12.8	11.4	10.4	7.6	3.7	1.6	33.3
Eugene, OR	4.4	16.8	22.2	12.5	11.2	12.5	12.5	5.8	2.2	40.2
Fargo, ND	6.5	20.6	26.1	13.8	10.0	9.9	7.7	3.6	1.7	33.0
Fort Collins, CO	4.5	18.2	24.9	12.9	11.0	11.7	10.5	4.5	1.8	36.6
Fort Wayne, IN	6.7	21.0	20.2	12.6	11.7	12.1	9.5	4.3	1.9	36.8
Fort Worth, TX	6.4	21.6	21.3	14.4	13.0	11.4	7.4	3.3	1.1	35.5
Gainesville, FL	4.9	18.6	27.4	11.4	10.1	11.2	9.9	4.7	2.0	34.3
Green Bay, WI	5.7	19.6	18.8	12.9	12.1	13.9	10.4	4.8	1.7	39.2
Greensboro, NC	5.6	20.1	19.7	12.0	12.9	13.0	9.9	4.8	1.9	38.9
Honolulu, HI	5.8	17.0	21.0	13.3	11.8	12.0	10.3	5.8	3.0	39.4
Houston, TX	6.7	22.0	20.8	14.5	12.8	11.1	7.7	3.3	1.1	35.3
Huntsville, AL	5.6	18.9	20.4	13.1	12.5	14.0	9.2	4.7	1.5	38.8
Indianapolis, IN	6.3	20.6	20.5	13.7	12.4	12.2	8.8	3.9	1.6	36.7
Jacksonville, FL	5.8	18.7	19.8	13.3	12.4	13.2	10.2	4.8	1.7	39.1
Kansas City, MO	6.1	20.1	19.9	13.7	12.2	12.6	9.4	4.4	1.8	37.8
Lafayette, LA	6.6	20.1	20.1	13.6	11.7	12.8	9.5	4.2	1.4	37.2
Las Vegas, NV	5.8	19.0	20.5	14.1	13.0	12.1	9.5	4.7	1.3	38.3
Lexington, KY	5.8	19.3	22.7	12.9	12.1	11.9	9.2	4.4	1.5	36.6
Lincoln, NE	5.9	20.6	24.1	12.8	10.7	10.9	9.3	4.0	1.7	34.4
Little Rock, AR	6.1	19.8	20.8	13.3	11.9	12.2	9.7	4.6	1.7	37.4
Los Angeles, CA	5.3	18.2	21.9	13.8	13.3	12.6	8.7	4.3	2.0	38.2
Louisville, KY	5.9	18.8	19.6	13.1	12.6	13.4	10.3	4.7	1.7	39.3
Madison, WI	5.2	18.3	23.8	13.6	11.6	12.0	9.6	4.2	1.7	36.9
Manchester, NH	5.1	17.1	20.1	12.9	13.2	15.0	10.1	4.8	1.8	41.0

Table continued on following page.

Metro Area	Percent of Population									Median Age
	Under Age 5	Age 5–19	Age 20–34	Age 35–44	Age 45–54	Age 55–64	Age 65–74	Age 75–84	Age 85+	
McAllen, TX	8.0	26.8	21.3	12.3	11.4	8.6	6.5	3.8	1.2	30.3
Memphis, TN	6.5	20.8	20.4	12.9	12.2	12.4	9.3	4.1	1.4	36.7
Miami, FL	5.4	16.9	18.5	13.2	13.6	13.4	10.2	6.1	2.7	41.9
Midland, TX	8.3	23.1	22.7	15.3	10.2	9.9	6.5	2.7	1.4	32.7
Milwaukee, WI	5.9	19.3	19.8	13.1	11.9	13.2	10.0	4.5	2.1	38.5
Minneapolis, MN	6.1	19.7	20.0	14.1	12.2	12.8	9.1	4.2	1.7	37.8
Nashville, TN	6.1	19.3	21.9	14.2	12.6	12.1	8.6	4.0	1.2	36.8
New Orleans, LA	5.9	18.1	20.2	13.9	11.8	13.3	10.5	4.5	1.9	38.9
New York, NY	5.8	17.9	20.4	13.3	12.9	13.2	9.6	4.9	2.1	39.4
Oklahoma City, OK	6.3	21.0	21.7	13.7	11.4	11.5	8.9	4.2	1.4	35.8
Omaha, NE	6.6	21.3	20.0	13.9	11.7	12.0	8.9	4.0	1.6	36.5
Orlando, FL	5.5	18.5	21.4	14.2	12.9	12.0	9.1	4.7	1.8	38.3
Philadelphia, PA	5.5	18.6	20.2	13.1	12.3	13.4	10.0	4.8	2.0	39.1
Phoenix, AZ	5.7	19.6	20.9	13.3	12.3	11.8	9.5	5.2	1.8	37.7
Pittsburgh, PA	4.9	16.6	18.7	12.4	12.0	14.5	12.4	5.9	2.8	42.8
Portland, OR	5.1	17.7	20.9	15.2	13.2	12.0	9.8	4.4	1.7	39.1
Providence, RI	5.0	17.6	20.1	12.6	12.6	14.2	10.6	5.2	2.2	40.6
Provo, UT	8.7	27.7	27.3	12.5	9.2	6.7	4.8	2.3	0.8	25.6
Raleigh, NC	5.9	20.4	20.2	14.8	14.1	11.9	8.0	3.6	1.3	37.5
Reno, NV	5.4	17.8	20.9	13.0	11.8	13.1	11.3	5.1	1.6	39.4
Richmond, VA	5.7	18.4	20.5	13.5	12.4	13.1	10.0	4.6	1.7	38.7
Rochester, MN	6.2	20.1	18.7	13.6	11.1	12.9	9.8	5.2	2.3	38.8
Sacramento, CA	5.6	19.3	20.3	13.8	12.2	12.3	9.7	4.6	2.0	38.3
Saint Louis, MO	5.6	18.8	19.2	13.2	12.0	13.8	10.5	4.9	2.0	39.8
Saint Paul, MN	6.1	19.7	20.0	14.1	12.2	12.8	9.1	4.2	1.7	37.8
Salem, OR	5.9	20.5	20.5	13.0	11.6	11.6	10.1	4.9	1.9	37.3
Salt Lake City, UT	6.6	22.3	23.3	14.9	11.7	9.9	7.2	3.1	1.2	33.7
San Antonio, TX	6.3	21.1	21.5	14.1	12.2	11.2	8.3	3.8	1.5	35.7
San Diego, CA	5.7	18.2	23.0	14.1	12.1	11.8	8.9	4.4	1.8	37.1
San Francisco, CA	5.1	16.5	20.6	15.0	13.5	12.7	9.6	4.8	2.1	40.0
San Jose, CA	5.4	18.3	22.1	14.4	13.4	12.1	8.1	4.3	2.0	37.8
Santa Rosa, CA	4.7	17.1	17.8	13.2	12.4	14.0	12.8	5.8	2.4	42.7
Savannah, GA	6.1	19.5	22.0	13.8	11.7	11.8	9.2	4.4	1.5	36.7
Seattle, WA	5.7	17.5	22.8	15.4	12.7	11.9	8.6	3.8	1.6	37.4
Sioux Falls, SD	6.9	21.1	20.4	14.3	11.2	11.8	9.1	3.7	1.5	36.1
Tampa, FL	5.0	16.7	18.7	12.9	12.8	13.7	11.4	6.4	2.4	42.2
Tucson, AZ	5.0	18.0	21.4	11.6	10.8	12.2	12.0	6.8	2.4	39.7
Tulsa, OK	6.3	20.7	19.9	13.1	11.9	12.2	9.6	4.7	1.7	37.3
Virginia Beach, VA	6.0	18.8	22.1	13.3	11.3	12.8	9.4	4.6	1.6	37.2
Washington, DC	6.1	19.2	20.3	14.8	13.4	12.3	8.3	4.0	1.5	37.9
Wichita, KS	6.3	21.5	20.2	12.8	11.2	12.3	9.6	4.3	2.0	36.6
Wilmington, NC	4.5	15.5	18.1	11.8	11.8	14.9	14.8	6.6	2.0	45.1
Winston-Salem, NC	5.5	19.2	18.7	11.8	13.0	13.8	10.7	5.4	2.0	40.6
U.S.	5.7	19.1	20.2	13.1	12.3	12.8	10.0	4.9	1.9	38.7

Note: Figures cover the Metropolitan Statistical Area (MSA)
Source: U.S. Census Bureau, 2019-2023 American Community Survey 5-Year Estimates

Ancestry: City

City	German	Irish	English	American	Italian	Polish	French[1]	European	Scottish
Albuquerque, NM	9.8	7.9	9.1	3.1	3.4	1.4	1.8	1.6	1.5
Anchorage, AK	13.5	9.0	9.9	3.6	3.1	1.9	1.9	2.1	1.8
Ann Arbor, MI	16.5	10.7	9.7	2.1	4.5	6.2	2.2	2.7	2.3
Athens, GA	9.0	8.9	12.2	3.9	3.1	1.8	1.6	2.7	2.7
Atlanta, GA	7.1	6.4	9.3	3.8	2.9	1.4	1.7	1.7	1.4
Austin, TX	11.5	8.7	10.2	2.8	3.2	1.9	2.4	2.4	2.2
Baltimore, MD	5.8	5.7	3.7	2.7	2.9	2.0	0.9	0.7	0.7
Billings, MT	27.7	13.2	13.3	3.7	3.1	1.7	2.6	2.0	2.8
Boise City, ID	18.2	11.5	17.8	3.9	4.2	1.7	2.4	3.7	3.1
Boston, MA	4.8	13.2	5.4	2.2	7.3	2.2	1.7	1.1	1.1
Boulder, CO	16.0	11.3	11.4	2.6	5.2	3.4	2.4	4.2	3.2
Cape Coral, FL	13.4	11.5	8.5	10.4	9.2	3.3	2.2	1.5	1.3
Cedar Rapids, IA	26.8	13.3	10.4	3.3	1.7	1.4	1.8	1.5	1.6
Charleston, SC	11.7	11.0	13.6	13.0	4.8	2.4	2.8	1.9	2.4
Charlotte, NC	7.4	6.7	7.7	4.7	3.5	1.5	1.2	1.1	1.6
Chicago, IL	7.4	7.2	3.2	2.0	3.8	5.0	0.9	0.9	0.7
Cincinnati, OH	17.5	9.8	6.9	3.0	3.7	1.4	1.2	1.2	1.0
Clarksville, TN	12.5	8.8	8.3	6.0	3.6	1.0	1.6	3.7	1.5
Cleveland, OH	9.4	8.4	3.5	2.5	4.4	3.7	0.8	0.5	0.7
College Station, TX	14.8	8.0	9.8	3.2	3.3	2.3	1.9	1.8	1.6
Colorado Springs, CO	17.8	11.4	12.8	4.2	4.7	2.6	2.4	2.9	2.6
Columbia, MO	24.0	12.1	13.5	5.1	3.4	1.6	1.9	2.2	2.3
Columbia, SC	9.0	7.2	8.8	5.3	3.0	1.1	1.7	1.9	2.0
Columbus, OH	14.9	10.0	8.0	3.4	4.6	2.1	1.3	1.5	1.6
Dallas, TX	5.4	4.4	6.0	3.8	1.7	0.8	1.2	1.2	1.1
Davenport, IA	28.1	14.7	8.7	3.0	2.6	1.9	1.3	1.1	1.8
Denver, CO	14.0	10.9	10.4	3.0	5.5	2.8	2.1	2.5	2.0
Des Moines, IA	19.1	12.4	9.2	3.1	3.5	1.0	1.4	1.5	1.3
Detroit, MI	1.8	1.6	1.1	4.4	0.8	1.1	0.5	0.2	0.3
Durham, NC	8.2	6.7	10.0	3.8	3.4	1.8	1.5	1.7	1.8
El Paso, TX	3.8	2.4	2.2	2.2	1.3	0.5	0.6	0.5	0.4
Eugene, OR	18.4	12.9	14.5	3.1	5.2	1.9	3.1	3.8	3.9
Fargo, ND	32.9	8.1	5.2	2.9	1.3	2.2	3.4	0.8	1.4
Fort Collins, CO	23.1	12.3	14.9	3.2	5.6	3.4	3.1	3.6	3.5
Fort Wayne, IN	22.5	9.0	9.2	5.0	2.1	1.9	2.4	2.3	1.9
Fort Worth, TX	7.1	6.0	7.4	3.7	1.8	0.8	1.3	1.4	1.5
Gainesville, FL	10.6	8.9	10.5	3.4	5.1	2.5	1.6	1.3	2.6
Green Bay, WI	26.6	8.2	4.6	3.6	2.0	7.2	3.0	1.6	1.0
Greensboro, NC	6.5	5.3	9.4	4.5	2.4	0.8	1.2	1.6	1.7
Honolulu, HI	4.5	3.4	3.6	1.4	1.3	0.9	1.0	0.5	0.7
Houston, TX	5.0	3.6	5.0	3.1	1.6	0.9	1.4	1.0	0.9
Huntsville, AL	9.2	8.5	13.0	10.2	2.4	1.3	1.8	2.2	2.1
Indianapolis, IN	12.8	7.9	8.0	4.5	2.0	1.4	1.4	1.4	1.5
Jacksonville, FL	7.8	7.7	7.6	6.3	3.6	1.4	1.4	2.2	1.6
Kansas City, MO	15.2	10.0	9.5	4.1	3.7	1.6	1.5	2.3	1.4
Lafayette, LA	9.2	5.6	6.7	5.2	3.8	0.5	16.7	0.7	1.1
Las Vegas, NV	8.0	7.2	7.2	2.9	4.9	1.8	1.5	1.6	1.3
Lexington, KY	12.7	10.8	13.8	7.7	2.7	1.4	1.6	2.4	2.4
Lincoln, NE	30.2	11.0	9.3	3.4	1.9	2.2	1.7	1.8	1.4
Little Rock, AR	7.5	6.5	10.4	4.6	1.2	0.7	1.3	1.7	1.7
Los Angeles, CA	3.9	3.7	3.5	3.8	2.7	1.3	1.1	1.3	0.7
Louisville, KY	14.8	11.3	10.8	5.8	2.5	1.1	1.5	1.6	1.6
Madison, WI	28.4	12.2	9.2	1.9	4.0	5.5	2.0	2.0	1.9
Manchester, NH	6.5	18.5	10.0	3.0	8.7	3.6	10.5	0.8	2.3
McAllen, TX	2.6	1.6	1.9	3.1	0.9	0.4	1.0	0.3	0.2
Memphis, TN	3.3	3.6	4.9	3.3	1.5	0.5	0.7	1.6	0.9

Table continued on following page.

City	German	Irish	English	American	Italian	Polish	French[1]	European	Scottish
Miami, FL	1.9	1.3	1.3	2.6	3.0	0.7	0.9	0.6	0.2
Midland, TX	6.6	6.1	7.8	4.6	0.9	0.4	1.3	1.1	1.5
Milwaukee, WI	15.1	5.4	2.2	1.4	2.4	5.5	1.2	1.0	0.5
Minneapolis, MN	21.0	10.7	7.4	1.7	2.6	3.9	2.7	2.0	1.4
Nashville, TN	8.7	7.9	10.2	5.9	2.7	1.4	1.5	1.7	1.9
New Orleans, LA	6.4	6.0	5.3	2.3	4.0	0.9	5.4	1.2	1.1
New York, NY	2.9	4.4	2.1	3.7	5.8	2.1	0.8	0.9	0.5
Oklahoma City, OK	10.1	7.8	9.5	5.3	1.5	0.7	1.2	1.9	1.7
Omaha, NE	24.8	12.8	8.4	2.7	3.7	3.3	1.9	1.6	1.8
Orlando, FL	6.4	5.4	5.9	6.1	4.5	1.6	1.5	0.8	0.9
Philadelphia, PA	7.0	9.6	3.2	2.2	6.7	3.0	0.7	0.7	0.7
Phoenix, AZ	9.6	7.4	6.8	2.7	3.9	1.8	1.4	1.5	1.3
Pittsburgh, PA	17.1	13.2	6.1	2.7	11.4	6.6	1.2	1.2	1.4
Portland, OR	15.2	11.6	12.9	4.3	4.5	2.4	2.6	4.4	3.1
Providence, RI	3.3	8.1	4.4	2.4	6.9	1.7	2.7	0.7	0.9
Provo, UT	10.4	4.9	28.2	2.2	2.2	0.7	1.3	4.0	3.6
Raleigh, NC	9.2	8.5	11.8	5.7	3.8	1.9	1.7	1.6	2.2
Reno, NV	12.3	11.0	11.1	4.4	5.9	1.6	2.2	2.6	2.0
Richmond, VA	8.2	7.9	9.9	3.9	3.8	1.4	1.5	1.3	1.8
Rochester, MN	28.8	9.8	7.1	2.6	1.8	2.6	1.8	1.6	1.4
Sacramento, CA	6.5	5.8	6.0	2.3	3.4	1.0	1.4	1.4	1.0
Saint Louis, MO	15.9	9.7	6.4	6.3	4.0	1.7	2.5	1.2	1.3
Saint Paul, MN	19.5	9.9	5.6	1.9	2.5	2.6	2.6	1.5	1.2
Salem, OR	16.3	8.2	12.7	4.1	2.9	1.2	2.3	4.2	2.5
Salt Lake City, UT	11.5	7.7	19.4	3.1	4.0	1.4	2.1	3.0	3.4
San Antonio, TX	7.2	4.6	4.7	3.4	2.0	0.9	1.2	0.8	0.9
San Diego, CA	8.7	7.3	7.0	2.3	4.2	1.8	1.7	1.7	1.3
San Francisco, CA	7.1	7.5	6.0	2.1	4.5	1.8	2.2	2.1	1.3
San Jose, CA	4.4	4.0	4.0	1.5	3.2	0.8	1.0	1.2	0.7
Santa Rosa, CA	11.1	10.1	10.4	2.2	6.3	1.6	2.4	2.4	1.9
Savannah, GA	6.6	7.3	6.3	3.8	3.2	1.1	1.3	0.8	1.4
Seattle, WA	14.0	10.8	12.2	2.4	4.7	2.6	2.8	3.9	2.7
Sioux Falls, SD	31.7	10.1	7.4	4.3	1.5	1.4	1.6	1.3	0.8
Tampa, FL	8.8	7.6	7.6	6.2	6.2	2.0	1.6	1.1	1.4
Tucson, AZ	11.5	8.4	8.0	2.9	3.7	1.9	1.8	1.5	1.7
Tulsa, OK	10.4	8.5	10.6	6.0	2.0	0.9	1.6	1.6	2.1
Virginia Beach, VA	11.2	10.5	11.3	7.5	5.5	2.3	1.9	1.6	2.2
Washington, DC	7.7	7.8	6.8	2.8	4.5	2.2	1.7	1.7	1.4
Wichita, KS	19.2	9.8	10.4	4.8	1.7	0.9	1.8	1.6	1.6
Wilmington, NC	10.8	10.8	13.8	4.7	5.6	2.2	2.1	2.3	2.7
Winston-Salem, NC	7.9	6.3	9.5	5.3	2.5	0.8	1.0	1.7	1.9
U.S.	12.6	9.4	9.1	5.5	4.9	2.6	2.0	1.6	1.6

Note: Figures are the percentage of the total population reporting a particular ancestry. The nine most commonly reported ancestries in the U.S. are shown. Figures include multiple ancestries (e.g. if a person reported being Irish and Italian, they were included in both columns); (1) Excludes Basque
Source: U.S. Census Bureau, 2019-2023 American Community Survey 5-Year Estimates

Ancestry: Metro Area

Metro Area	German	Irish	English	American	Italian	Polish	French[1]	European	Scottish
Albuquerque, NM	9.7	7.6	8.9	3.7	3.3	1.4	1.8	1.6	1.7
Anchorage, AK	14.5	9.7	10.1	4.2	2.9	1.9	1.9	2.1	1.9
Ann Arbor, MI	17.8	10.2	11.1	5.1	4.5	6.2	2.5	2.3	2.8
Athens, GA	8.8	10.4	13.5	6.1	2.8	1.4	1.5	2.4	2.5
Atlanta, GA	6.3	6.3	9.1	6.8	2.5	1.2	1.2	1.5	1.6
Austin, TX	12.4	8.3	10.4	3.6	2.9	1.7	2.3	2.4	2.2
Baltimore, MD	13.7	10.9	8.6	4.4	5.5	3.6	1.3	1.4	1.4
Billings, MT	29.0	13.1	12.6	4.2	3.2	1.5	2.6	2.1	2.6
Boise City, ID	17.0	10.2	18.2	4.8	3.5	1.4	2.4	3.1	3.1
Boston, MA	5.7	19.8	10.0	3.2	12.0	3.0	3.9	1.3	2.0
Boulder, CO	18.0	12.1	14.5	3.0	5.1	3.0	2.8	3.2	2.9
Cape Coral, FL	13.1	10.6	9.0	10.2	7.9	3.1	2.0	1.4	1.6
Cedar Rapids, IA	31.4	14.1	10.6	4.0	1.6	1.2	1.8	1.7	1.8
Charleston, SC	10.5	9.6	12.6	8.7	4.1	1.8	2.1	1.8	2.2
Charlotte, NC	10.2	8.4	10.3	8.3	3.9	1.7	1.4	1.5	2.0
Chicago, IL	12.9	10.2	4.8	2.5	6.1	8.0	1.2	1.2	0.9
Cincinnati, OH	25.7	12.9	11.4	5.6	3.9	1.6	1.6	1.6	1.8
Clarksville, TN	11.5	8.6	9.9	7.4	2.8	1.0	1.5	3.5	1.7
Cleveland, OH	18.5	13.3	8.6	4.1	9.1	6.9	1.4	1.1	1.5
College Station, TX	13.5	7.5	9.3	3.8	2.6	2.0	2.1	1.5	1.6
Colorado Springs, CO	17.6	11.0	12.3	4.5	4.5	2.4	2.3	3.0	2.7
Columbia, MO	24.4	11.8	13.9	6.4	2.8	1.4	1.9	2.2	2.1
Columbia, SC	9.5	7.3	9.5	6.5	2.5	1.3	1.5	1.6	1.9
Columbus, OH	20.0	12.4	11.1	5.3	5.1	2.2	1.6	1.8	2.1
Dallas, TX	8.1	6.4	8.7	5.3	2.2	1.0	1.4	1.4	1.5
Davenport, IA	25.2	13.0	9.4	3.8	2.5	1.9	1.5	1.5	1.5
Denver, CO	16.9	11.0	11.7	3.3	5.2	2.5	2.2	2.6	2.2
Des Moines, IA	25.8	13.5	11.3	3.8	3.1	1.2	1.6	2.3	1.7
Detroit, MI	14.3	9.1	7.9	4.0	5.8	8.9	2.8	1.5	2.0
Durham, NC	9.3	8.2	12.5	5.0	3.7	1.9	1.7	1.9	2.3
El Paso, TX	3.5	2.2	2.0	2.3	1.2	0.4	0.5	0.5	0.3
Eugene, OR	18.3	13.1	14.6	3.9	4.4	1.6	3.3	3.4	3.3
Fargo, ND	33.8	7.6	5.1	2.5	1.4	2.2	3.2	0.9	1.3
Fort Collins, CO	24.4	12.6	16.0	4.2	5.1	2.9	3.2	3.5	3.5
Fort Wayne, IN	26.1	9.0	9.8	5.8	2.2	2.0	2.8	2.6	1.8
Fort Worth, TX	8.1	6.4	8.7	5.3	2.2	1.0	1.4	1.4	1.5
Gainesville, FL	11.6	10.3	12.1	4.6	4.5	2.1	2.0	1.7	2.9
Green Bay, WI	33.7	9.3	4.9	4.0	2.2	9.4	3.5	1.6	0.7
Greensboro, NC	8.4	6.9	11.0	7.4	2.4	1.0	1.3	1.8	2.1
Honolulu, HI	5.2	4.0	4.1	1.3	1.8	0.8	1.0	0.6	0.7
Houston, TX	7.1	5.0	6.6	3.6	2.0	1.1	1.8	1.2	1.1
Huntsville, AL	9.4	9.3	13.8	11.4	2.3	1.2	1.5	2.2	2.1
Indianapolis, IN	16.6	9.4	10.9	7.3	2.5	1.7	1.5	1.7	1.8
Jacksonville, FL	9.6	9.6	10.2	7.5	4.5	1.8	1.8	2.1	2.0
Kansas City, MO	19.5	11.8	12.5	4.6	3.0	1.5	1.9	3.4	1.8
Lafayette, LA	7.1	4.5	5.3	6.2	3.0	0.6	17.1	0.7	0.7
Las Vegas, NV	7.9	6.8	7.0	2.9	4.7	1.7	1.4	1.3	1.2
Lexington, KY	12.3	11.3	14.6	10.4	2.5	1.3	1.5	2.3	2.3
Lincoln, NE	32.0	10.9	9.3	3.6	1.8	2.1	1.6	1.7	1.3
Little Rock, AR	8.5	8.4	11.7	6.6	1.4	0.8	1.4	1.6	1.8
Los Angeles, CA	5.1	4.3	4.5	3.5	2.8	1.1	1.1	1.2	0.8
Louisville, KY	16.6	12.4	12.6	7.6	2.6	1.1	1.7	1.7	1.9
Madison, WI	34.3	12.8	9.8	2.6	3.5	5.0	2.3	1.9	1.7
Manchester, NH	8.0	20.6	14.5	3.4	9.9	3.8	10.8	1.3	3.0
McAllen, TX	1.7	1.0	1.1	2.1	0.4	0.2	0.4	0.2	0.2
Memphis, TN	5.1	5.9	7.7	6.6	2.0	0.7	1.0	1.6	1.2

Table continued on following page.

Metro Area	German	Irish	English	American	Italian	Polish	French[1]	European	Scottish
Miami, FL	4.2	4.1	3.1	5.6	4.9	1.8	1.1	0.9	0.6
Midland, TX	7.0	5.8	7.6	5.2	0.9	0.3	1.3	1.0	1.4
Milwaukee, WI	31.6	9.3	5.0	2.4	4.3	9.8	2.1	1.4	0.9
Minneapolis, MN	27.4	10.7	6.9	3.1	2.5	4.0	2.9	2.0	1.2
Nashville, TN	9.6	8.9	12.9	10.5	2.6	1.2	1.6	2.3	2.2
New Orleans, LA	8.2	6.6	5.2	3.8	6.7	0.6	9.1	0.9	0.8
New York, NY	5.7	8.6	3.0	3.9	11.0	3.4	0.8	0.9	0.6
Oklahoma City, OK	11.8	9.0	11.2	6.2	1.7	0.8	1.5	2.0	1.9
Omaha, NE	27.8	12.9	9.7	3.5	3.7	3.5	1.8	1.7	1.6
Orlando, FL	8.2	7.2	7.1	9.1	5.0	1.7	1.6	1.1	1.2
Philadelphia, PA	13.7	16.9	7.8	3.2	12.2	4.6	1.2	1.0	1.2
Phoenix, AZ	12.6	8.7	9.5	4.2	4.5	2.2	1.8	1.8	1.6
Pittsburgh, PA	24.5	16.9	9.2	3.3	15.1	7.8	1.4	1.1	1.8
Portland, OR	16.0	10.5	12.8	4.4	3.5	1.7	2.4	3.8	2.8
Providence, RI	4.5	16.5	10.8	3.4	12.8	3.2	7.9	0.7	1.5
Provo, UT	10.0	4.9	32.1	4.1	2.1	0.5	1.4	4.8	4.1
Raleigh, NC	9.7	8.8	12.8	6.8	4.6	2.0	1.8	2.0	2.3
Reno, NV	12.7	10.9	11.6	4.0	6.0	1.6	2.3	3.5	2.0
Richmond, VA	9.1	8.2	12.7	6.6	3.7	1.5	1.4	1.7	1.8
Rochester, MN	32.8	10.3	7.3	3.6	1.5	2.5	1.7	1.8	1.3
Sacramento, CA	10.1	8.0	9.4	2.6	4.5	1.2	1.8	2.4	1.7
Saint Louis, MO	25.5	12.6	9.6	5.5	4.5	2.3	2.8	1.6	1.5
Saint Paul, MN	27.4	10.7	6.9	3.1	2.5	4.0	2.9	2.0	1.2
Salem, OR	16.6	8.4	12.1	3.9	2.6	1.4	2.3	3.6	2.6
Salt Lake City, UT	9.9	6.1	23.6	3.8	3.0	0.9	1.7	3.3	3.6
San Antonio, TX	10.0	5.8	6.6	3.8	2.2	1.4	1.5	1.1	1.3
San Diego, CA	9.0	7.5	7.6	2.6	4.1	1.6	1.8	1.9	1.5
San Francisco, CA	7.1	6.8	6.6	2.2	4.2	1.4	1.7	2.0	1.3
San Jose, CA	5.6	4.6	4.9	1.8	3.5	1.0	1.2	1.6	0.9
Santa Rosa, CA	12.4	12.2	11.8	2.4	7.9	1.8	2.9	3.7	2.5
Savannah, GA	9.4	9.4	10.2	6.8	3.7	1.2	1.5	1.2	1.8
Seattle, WA	13.2	9.0	10.9	2.9	3.4	1.7	2.4	3.2	2.3
Sioux Falls, SD	33.6	9.6	6.6	5.0	1.4	1.3	1.5	1.3	0.8
Tampa, FL	11.3	9.8	9.2	8.6	7.2	2.8	2.1	1.3	1.6
Tucson, AZ	13.2	9.0	10.1	3.5	4.1	2.2	2.1	1.7	2.0
Tulsa, OK	12.4	10.2	11.7	5.6	1.9	0.9	1.7	1.7	2.1
Virginia Beach, VA	9.4	8.6	10.8	8.0	4.1	1.7	1.7	1.6	1.8
Washington, DC	8.8	8.1	8.0	3.7	4.1	2.1	1.4	1.8	1.5
Wichita, KS	21.4	9.8	11.1	5.5	1.8	0.9	1.8	1.9	1.8
Wilmington, NC	12.2	12.4	14.8	5.9	5.9	2.4	2.1	1.8	2.8
Winston-Salem, NC	10.9	8.3	13.1	7.8	2.6	1.0	1.1	1.7	2.1
U.S.	12.6	9.4	9.1	5.5	4.9	2.6	2.0	1.6	1.6

Note: Figures are the percentage of the total population reporting a particular ancestry. The nine most commonly reported ancestries in the U.S. are shown. Figures include multiple ancestries (e.g. if a person reported being Irish and Italian, they were included in both columns); Figures cover the Metropolitan Statistical Area (MSA); (1) Excludes Basque
Source: U.S. Census Bureau, 2019-2023 American Community Survey 5-Year Estimates

Foreign-born Population: City

City	Percent of Population Born in							
	Any Foreign Country	Asia	Mexico	Europe	Caribbean	Central America[1]	South America	Africa	Canada
Albuquerque, NM	10.4	2.7	5.0	1.0	0.4	0.2	0.5	0.4	0.1
Anchorage, AK	10.9	6.0	0.6	1.2	0.5	0.2	0.6	0.5	0.4
Ann Arbor, MI	18.7	11.8	0.5	2.9	0.1	0.3	0.6	1.6	0.7
Athens, GA	9.8	3.2	2.3	0.9	0.4	1.3	0.8	0.7	0.2
Atlanta, GA	8.6	3.1	0.7	1.3	0.9	0.3	0.9	1.1	0.3
Austin, TX	18.1	6.2	5.2	1.6	0.8	2.0	0.9	1.0	0.3
Baltimore, MD	8.8	2.1	0.4	0.9	1.3	1.6	0.6	1.7	0.1
Billings, MT	2.0	0.7	0.2	0.6	0.0	0.0	0.1	0.0	0.3
Boise City, ID	7.2	3.0	1.3	1.3	0.1	0.1	0.3	0.6	0.5
Boston, MA	27.5	7.8	0.4	3.0	8.1	2.3	2.3	3.0	0.4
Boulder, CO	10.2	4.2	1.0	3.0	0.2	0.4	0.6	0.3	0.6
Cape Coral, FL	17.9	1.3	0.4	2.2	9.2	1.2	2.8	0.1	0.7
Cedar Rapids, IA	7.1	2.6	0.7	0.5	0.1	0.3	0.2	2.5	0.1
Charleston, SC	5.4	1.6	0.6	1.2	0.3	0.3	0.8	0.3	0.2
Charlotte, NC	18.1	4.9	2.7	1.5	1.2	3.8	1.7	2.1	0.2
Chicago, IL	20.7	5.2	8.2	3.3	0.4	0.9	1.4	1.1	0.2
Cincinnati, OH	7.1	2.1	0.3	0.7	0.2	1.0	0.3	2.2	0.1
Clarksville, TN	6.8	1.9	1.2	1.0	0.6	0.6	0.6	0.6	0.2
Cleveland, OH	6.1	2.3	0.4	1.1	0.5	0.5	0.3	0.9	0.1
College Station, TX	12.3	7.1	1.5	0.9	0.1	1.0	1.0	0.5	0.1
Colorado Springs, CO	7.4	2.0	1.7	1.5	0.2	0.6	0.4	0.5	0.3
Columbia, MO	8.1	4.9	0.6	0.4	0.3	0.2	0.5	1.1	0.0
Columbia, SC	5.1	2.0	0.2	0.7	0.8	0.3	0.5	0.4	0.1
Columbus, OH	14.4	4.7	1.3	0.8	0.7	0.9	0.7	5.1	0.1
Dallas, TX	23.4	2.9	12.8	0.8	0.4	3.3	1.0	2.0	0.1
Davenport, IA	4.6	1.5	1.5	0.5	0.0	0.1	0.0	0.6	0.2
Denver, CO	13.8	2.7	5.8	1.5	0.3	0.5	1.2	1.5	0.3
Des Moines, IA	14.0	4.4	3.6	0.8	0.2	1.6	0.1	3.2	0.1
Detroit, MI	6.0	2.4	1.7	0.2	0.3	0.5	0.1	0.5	0.2
Durham, NC	15.3	4.1	2.8	1.4	0.8	3.4	0.8	1.7	0.3
El Paso, TX	22.3	1.0	19.5	0.6	0.2	0.3	0.2	0.3	0.1
Eugene, OR	6.8	2.7	1.5	1.2	0.1	0.4	0.2	0.4	0.3
Fargo, ND	9.7	3.2	0.1	0.6	0.1	0.0	0.1	4.9	0.4
Fort Collins, CO	6.6	2.5	1.2	1.3	0.1	0.3	0.6	0.3	0.2
Fort Wayne, IN	9.0	4.4	2.1	0.5	0.2	1.0	0.2	0.5	0.2
Fort Worth, TX	17.0	4.1	8.9	0.5	0.3	0.8	0.6	1.6	0.1
Gainesville, FL	12.1	4.6	0.2	1.7	1.7	0.4	2.3	0.8	0.4
Green Bay, WI	8.8	2.1	4.5	0.4	0.2	0.5	0.3	0.6	0.2
Greensboro, NC	12.7	4.0	1.9	1.0	0.6	0.9	0.8	3.4	0.2
Honolulu, HI	27.8	22.9	0.2	1.0	0.1	0.1	0.3	0.2	0.2
Houston, TX	28.8	5.7	9.9	1.2	1.0	6.8	1.9	2.0	0.2
Huntsville, AL	6.6	1.7	1.6	0.8	0.7	0.5	0.3	0.5	0.2
Indianapolis, IN	11.6	3.1	3.2	0.5	0.7	1.3	0.6	2.2	0.1
Jacksonville, FL	12.2	4.1	0.5	1.7	2.5	0.8	1.7	0.8	0.1
Kansas City, MO	8.5	2.2	2.2	0.6	0.5	0.9	0.4	1.5	0.1
Lafayette, LA	6.6	2.1	0.5	0.4	0.2	1.8	0.8	0.4	0.1
Las Vegas, NV	20.9	5.3	8.5	1.6	1.3	2.2	1.0	0.4	0.4
Lexington, KY	11.0	3.8	2.3	1.0	0.4	0.8	0.5	2.0	0.2
Lincoln, NE	9.2	4.9	1.3	0.9	0.4	0.6	0.3	0.8	0.1
Little Rock, AR	7.9	2.7	2.1	0.6	0.1	1.6	0.3	0.4	0.1
Los Angeles, CA	35.8	11.2	11.2	2.4	0.3	8.3	1.2	0.7	0.4
Louisville, KY	9.8	2.5	1.0	0.8	2.8	0.6	0.4	1.6	0.1
Madison, WI	11.6	5.5	1.9	1.4	0.2	0.2	1.1	1.0	0.2
Manchester, NH	14.7	3.8	0.4	2.2	2.0	2.1	1.0	2.1	1.0

Table continued on following page.

City	Any Foreign Country	Asia	Mexico	Europe	Caribbean	Central America[1]	South America	Africa	Canada
McAllen, TX	25.7	2.2	22.0	0.2	0.3	0.5	0.4	0.1	0.0
Memphis, TN	7.4	1.3	2.3	0.3	0.3	1.9	0.5	0.7	0.1
Miami, FL	57.7	1.5	1.2	2.2	28.5	11.8	11.9	0.4	0.2
Midland, TX	13.7	2.0	7.1	0.4	1.0	0.5	1.1	1.0	0.6
Milwaukee, WI	10.8	2.8	5.1	0.6	0.3	0.4	0.3	1.0	0.1
Minneapolis, MN	14.1	3.2	1.8	1.0	0.2	0.3	1.5	5.7	0.3
Nashville, TN	15.1	3.6	3.1	0.8	0.6	3.1	0.6	2.9	0.3
New Orleans, LA	6.6	2.0	0.4	0.6	0.6	1.9	0.5	0.3	0.2
New York, NY	36.5	11.0	1.8	5.1	9.7	1.4	5.1	1.9	0.3
Oklahoma City, OK	12.0	3.1	5.4	0.5	0.2	1.3	0.5	0.7	0.2
Omaha, NE	11.0	3.3	3.4	0.6	0.2	1.5	0.3	1.5	0.2
Orlando, FL	24.1	3.0	0.8	1.8	6.5	1.2	10.1	0.5	0.2
Philadelphia, PA	14.6	5.6	0.5	2.2	2.8	0.7	1.0	1.7	0.1
Phoenix, AZ	19.0	3.1	11.3	1.3	0.4	0.9	0.4	1.1	0.3
Pittsburgh, PA	9.3	4.5	0.3	1.8	0.4	0.2	0.6	1.0	0.3
Portland, OR	12.4	5.5	2.0	2.3	0.2	0.4	0.3	0.8	0.5
Providence, RI	32.8	3.9	0.5	2.2	15.3	5.9	1.2	3.4	0.3
Provo, UT	12.2	1.6	3.8	0.7	0.4	1.0	3.3	0.5	0.4
Raleigh, NC	13.6	3.8	2.4	1.3	1.1	1.4	1.1	2.2	0.2
Reno, NV	16.1	5.4	5.3	1.4	0.3	2.2	0.4	0.5	0.3
Richmond, VA	8.6	1.5	0.9	0.8	0.7	3.5	0.4	0.6	0.1
Rochester, MN	14.1	5.9	1.0	1.2	0.1	0.3	0.4	4.9	0.2
Sacramento, CA	21.3	10.6	5.5	1.6	0.1	0.9	0.4	0.6	0.2
Saint Louis, MO	6.6	2.7	0.8	1.0	0.3	0.3	0.3	0.9	0.1
Saint Paul, MN	18.7	9.3	1.8	0.7	0.2	0.9	0.4	4.9	0.3
Salem, OR	12.2	2.5	6.2	1.0	0.0	0.8	0.2	0.4	0.2
Salt Lake City, UT	15.4	4.2	5.1	1.8	0.2	0.7	1.4	1.0	0.3
San Antonio, TX	14.3	2.6	8.8	0.6	0.3	1.0	0.6	0.4	0.1
San Diego, CA	24.8	11.8	7.5	2.3	0.2	0.5	0.9	1.0	0.4
San Francisco, CA	34.2	21.9	2.4	4.4	0.1	2.4	1.3	0.6	0.7
San Jose, CA	41.6	27.3	8.4	2.2	0.1	1.3	1.0	0.7	0.3
Santa Rosa, CA	20.8	4.7	11.5	1.5	0.1	1.4	0.3	0.6	0.3
Savannah, GA	6.7	2.6	0.8	0.8	0.9	0.7	0.5	0.4	0.2
Seattle, WA	19.9	11.4	1.4	2.5	0.2	0.4	0.7	2.1	1.1
Sioux Falls, SD	9.0	2.0	0.6	1.1	0.1	1.7	0.2	3.2	0.1
Tampa, FL	19.0	4.0	1.1	1.8	7.4	1.3	2.4	0.6	0.3
Tucson, AZ	13.7	2.4	8.3	1.0	0.1	0.4	0.3	0.8	0.2
Tulsa, OK	12.0	2.6	5.5	0.7	0.3	1.3	0.7	0.6	0.1
Virginia Beach, VA	9.1	5.0	0.3	1.4	0.5	0.4	0.8	0.5	0.2
Washington, DC	13.3	2.8	0.6	2.3	1.2	2.2	1.7	2.2	0.3
Wichita, KS	10.0	3.5	4.4	0.5	0.1	0.5	0.4	0.6	0.1
Wilmington, NC	5.7	1.2	1.5	1.0	0.2	0.8	0.7	0.2	0.1
Winston-Salem, NC	10.7	2.0	4.1	0.6	0.6	1.7	1.0	0.6	0.1
U.S.	13.9	4.3	3.3	1.4	1.4	1.2	1.2	0.8	0.2

Note: (1) Excludes Mexico
Source: U.S. Census Bureau, 2019-2023 American Community Survey 5-Year Estimates

Foreign-born Population: Metro Area

Metro Area	Any Foreign Country	Asia	Mexico	Europe	Caribbean	Central America[1]	South America	Africa	Canada
Albuquerque, NM	9.2	2.0	4.9	0.8	0.3	0.2	0.4	0.4	0.1
Anchorage, AK	8.7	4.6	0.5	1.2	0.4	0.2	0.5	0.4	0.3
Ann Arbor, MI	12.8	7.3	0.7	2.2	0.1	0.5	0.4	0.9	0.5
Athens, GA	8.0	2.7	1.7	0.7	0.2	1.1	0.5	0.7	0.2
Atlanta, GA	14.8	4.8	2.3	1.1	1.7	1.4	1.4	1.8	0.2
Austin, TX	15.5	5.1	5.1	1.3	0.5	1.4	0.8	0.8	0.3
Baltimore, MD	11.2	4.4	0.4	1.2	0.8	1.5	0.7	2.1	0.1
Billings, MT	1.8	0.5	0.2	0.5	0.0	0.0	0.1	0.1	0.2
Boise City, ID	6.6	1.5	2.6	1.1	0.0	0.3	0.3	0.3	0.3
Boston, MA	19.7	6.4	0.2	3.1	3.5	1.7	2.5	1.8	0.4
Boulder, CO	10.0	3.4	2.0	2.5	0.1	0.4	0.7	0.3	0.5
Cape Coral, FL	17.9	1.4	1.7	1.9	7.0	2.4	2.2	0.2	1.0
Cedar Rapids, IA	4.5	1.8	0.5	0.4	0.1	0.2	0.1	1.3	0.1
Charleston, SC	6.3	1.5	1.1	1.1	0.4	0.7	1.0	0.3	0.2
Charlotte, NC	11.4	3.2	2.0	1.2	0.7	1.8	1.2	1.0	0.2
Chicago, IL	18.3	5.4	6.5	3.7	0.3	0.6	0.8	0.7	0.2
Cincinnati, OH	5.7	2.3	0.5	0.7	0.2	0.6	0.2	0.9	0.2
Clarksville, TN	5.4	1.6	0.9	0.8	0.4	0.4	0.4	0.6	0.2
Cleveland, OH	5.8	2.2	0.3	2.0	0.2	0.2	0.3	0.5	0.2
College Station, TX	11.7	3.8	4.9	0.7	0.2	0.9	0.7	0.4	0.1
Colorado Springs, CO	6.7	1.8	1.5	1.4	0.3	0.5	0.4	0.4	0.3
Columbia, MO	5.8	3.4	0.6	0.4	0.2	0.1	0.3	0.7	0.0
Columbia, SC	5.6	1.8	1.0	0.7	0.5	0.7	0.5	0.3	0.1
Columbus, OH	9.5	3.8	0.8	0.7	0.4	0.5	0.4	2.7	0.1
Dallas, TX	19.0	6.0	7.4	0.8	0.3	1.7	0.8	1.7	0.2
Davenport, IA	5.4	1.8	1.7	0.4	0.1	0.1	0.1	1.1	0.1
Denver, CO	12.1	3.1	4.5	1.4	0.2	0.5	0.8	1.2	0.3
Des Moines, IA	8.6	3.1	1.6	1.0	0.1	0.8	0.3	1.6	0.1
Detroit, MI	10.3	6.0	0.8	1.9	0.2	0.2	0.2	0.4	0.5
Durham, NC	13.2	3.7	2.7	1.6	0.5	2.4	0.8	1.1	0.2
El Paso, TX	23.1	0.9	20.6	0.5	0.2	0.4	0.2	0.3	0.1
Eugene, OR	5.4	1.7	1.6	0.8	0.1	0.2	0.1	0.3	0.4
Fargo, ND	6.9	2.4	0.2	0.5	0.1	0.0	0.1	3.2	0.3
Fort Collins, CO	5.4	1.6	1.4	1.1	0.1	0.3	0.4	0.2	0.2
Fort Wayne, IN	6.9	3.3	1.4	0.5	0.1	0.7	0.2	0.4	0.2
Fort Worth, TX	19.0	6.0	7.4	0.8	0.3	1.7	0.8	1.7	0.2
Gainesville, FL	10.2	3.7	0.5	1.5	1.3	0.6	1.7	0.5	0.4
Green Bay, WI	4.8	1.5	1.9	0.5	0.1	0.3	0.2	0.2	0.1
Greensboro, NC	9.5	2.9	2.3	0.7	0.4	0.7	0.5	1.7	0.1
Honolulu, HI	19.6	15.7	0.2	0.7	0.1	0.1	0.2	0.1	0.3
Houston, TX	23.8	6.2	8.0	1.0	1.0	3.9	1.8	1.6	0.3
Huntsville, AL	5.4	1.8	1.1	0.8	0.4	0.4	0.3	0.3	0.2
Indianapolis, IN	8.4	2.8	1.8	0.6	0.4	0.7	0.5	1.5	0.1
Jacksonville, FL	10.0	3.2	0.5	1.7	1.8	0.6	1.4	0.5	0.2
Kansas City, MO	7.2	2.2	2.0	0.6	0.3	0.8	0.3	0.8	0.1
Lafayette, LA	3.8	1.2	0.5	0.2	0.2	1.0	0.4	0.1	0.0
Las Vegas, NV	21.7	7.4	7.3	1.6	1.3	1.8	0.9	0.9	0.4
Lexington, KY	8.2	2.6	1.8	0.9	0.3	0.7	0.4	1.3	0.2
Lincoln, NE	8.1	4.3	1.1	0.8	0.3	0.5	0.3	0.7	0.1
Little Rock, AR	4.6	1.3	1.4	0.4	0.1	0.9	0.2	0.2	0.1
Los Angeles, CA	32.5	13.0	11.1	1.7	0.3	4.3	1.0	0.6	0.3
Louisville, KY	6.7	1.9	0.9	0.6	1.5	0.4	0.3	1.0	0.1
Madison, WI	7.6	3.3	1.3	1.0	0.1	0.2	0.8	0.6	0.2
Manchester, NH	10.4	3.4	0.4	1.7	1.4	0.8	0.9	0.9	0.8

Table continued on following page.

Metro Area	Percent of Population Born in								
	Any Foreign Country	Asia	Mexico	Europe	Caribbean	Central America[1]	South America	Africa	Canada
McAllen, TX	26.0	0.8	24.1	0.1	0.1	0.5	0.2	0.1	0.1
Memphis, TN	6.1	1.7	1.6	0.4	0.2	1.0	0.4	0.6	0.1
Miami, FL	41.9	2.2	1.1	2.4	20.6	4.3	10.2	0.4	0.5
Midland, TX	13.0	1.9	7.2	0.3	0.9	0.4	0.9	0.8	0.5
Milwaukee, WI	7.6	2.7	2.4	1.1	0.2	0.2	0.3	0.6	0.1
Minneapolis, MN	10.7	4.0	1.2	1.0	0.2	0.4	0.6	3.1	0.2
Nashville, TN	9.4	2.4	2.1	0.7	0.4	1.6	0.5	1.4	0.3
New Orleans, LA	9.5	2.4	0.6	0.5	1.1	3.9	0.5	0.4	0.1
New York, NY	29.8	8.9	1.4	4.2	6.8	2.0	4.7	1.5	0.3
Oklahoma City, OK	8.2	2.3	3.4	0.5	0.1	0.8	0.4	0.5	0.2
Omaha, NE	7.9	2.6	2.4	0.6	0.2	0.9	0.3	1.0	0.1
Orlando, FL	20.3	3.1	0.9	1.6	5.9	1.2	6.8	0.6	0.3
Philadelphia, PA	11.5	4.7	0.8	1.8	1.5	0.5	0.8	1.2	0.2
Phoenix, AZ	13.9	3.3	6.6	1.3	0.3	0.6	0.4	0.7	0.6
Pittsburgh, PA	4.1	2.0	0.2	0.9	0.2	0.1	0.2	0.4	0.1
Portland, OR	12.5	5.0	3.0	2.3	0.2	0.5	0.4	0.6	0.4
Providence, RI	14.4	2.3	0.3	3.8	2.9	1.7	1.3	1.7	0.2
Provo, UT	7.7	1.0	2.5	0.5	0.2	0.6	2.0	0.3	0.3
Raleigh, NC	13.1	5.0	2.5	1.3	0.8	1.0	0.8	1.3	0.3
Reno, NV	13.4	3.6	5.5	1.1	0.2	1.6	0.4	0.3	0.3
Richmond, VA	8.7	3.2	0.7	1.0	0.5	1.8	0.7	0.8	0.1
Rochester, MN	8.8	3.5	0.8	0.9	0.1	0.2	0.4	2.7	0.2
Sacramento, CA	18.9	9.4	4.2	2.8	0.1	0.7	0.4	0.5	0.3
Saint Louis, MO	5.0	2.3	0.5	1.0	0.1	0.3	0.2	0.5	0.1
Saint Paul, MN	10.7	4.0	1.2	1.0	0.2	0.4	0.6	3.1	0.2
Salem, OR	12.0	1.5	7.4	1.0	0.1	0.8	0.2	0.3	0.2
Salt Lake City, UT	12.4	3.0	4.2	1.2	0.1	0.6	1.9	0.6	0.2
San Antonio, TX	11.8	2.2	6.8	0.6	0.3	0.8	0.5	0.4	0.1
San Diego, CA	22.5	8.9	9.1	1.9	0.2	0.6	0.7	0.6	0.4
San Francisco, CA	31.6	18.0	4.9	2.8	0.2	2.7	1.2	0.9	0.5
San Jose, CA	40.3	27.1	6.5	3.0	0.1	1.0	1.1	0.7	0.5
Santa Rosa, CA	16.6	3.1	9.1	1.8	0.1	1.0	0.5	0.4	0.4
Savannah, GA	6.9	2.1	1.1	0.9	0.8	0.6	0.7	0.5	0.2
Seattle, WA	20.4	11.0	2.4	2.8	0.2	0.6	0.7	1.7	0.7
Sioux Falls, SD	6.7	1.5	0.5	0.9	0.1	1.2	0.1	2.2	0.1
Tampa, FL	15.0	2.9	1.2	2.2	4.3	0.8	2.4	0.5	0.6
Tucson, AZ	11.9	2.3	6.6	1.3	0.2	0.3	0.3	0.6	0.3
Tulsa, OK	7.2	2.0	2.9	0.6	0.2	0.7	0.4	0.4	0.1
Virginia Beach, VA	6.8	2.9	0.4	1.1	0.6	0.6	0.4	0.5	0.2
Washington, DC	24.0	8.4	0.9	1.8	1.1	5.2	2.5	3.8	0.2
Wichita, KS	7.4	2.6	3.1	0.5	0.1	0.4	0.3	0.4	0.1
Wilmington, NC	4.9	0.9	1.2	1.0	0.1	0.7	0.7	0.2	0.2
Winston-Salem, NC	7.3	1.4	2.8	0.7	0.3	1.0	0.7	0.3	0.1
U.S.	13.9	4.3	3.3	1.4	1.4	1.2	1.2	0.8	0.2

Note: Figures cover the Metropolitan Statistical Area (MSA); (1) Excludes Mexico
Source: U.S. Census Bureau, 2019-2023 American Community Survey 5-Year Estimates

Marital Status: City

City	Never Married	Now Married[1]	Separated	Widowed	Divorced
Albuquerque, NM	38.6	39.4	1.5	5.5	15.1
Anchorage, AK	34.6	47.7	1.9	3.5	12.2
Ann Arbor, MI	55.4	35.4	0.6	2.3	6.3
Athens, GA	53.9	31.2	1.3	4.3	9.3
Atlanta, GA	55.0	28.9	1.5	4.1	10.5
Austin, TX	44.0	41.7	1.3	3.0	9.9
Baltimore, MD	52.7	27.1	2.9	5.9	11.4
Billings, MT	31.9	47.2	1.0	5.6	14.3
Boise City, ID	35.2	46.8	1.0	4.3	12.7
Boston, MA	55.7	31.0	2.2	3.8	7.4
Boulder, CO	57.8	30.4	0.5	2.2	9.0
Cape Coral, FL	24.7	52.6	1.5	7.8	13.4
Cedar Rapids, IA	36.8	44.3	1.5	5.0	12.3
Charleston, SC	39.4	44.3	1.6	4.8	10.0
Charlotte, NC	42.9	41.1	2.1	3.8	10.1
Chicago, IL	49.1	35.6	2.2	5.0	8.1
Cincinnati, OH	53.4	29.8	1.8	4.5	10.6
Clarksville, TN	30.0	50.9	2.2	4.2	12.7
Cleveland, OH	53.7	23.7	2.8	6.1	13.7
College Station, TX	60.3	31.2	1.2	2.4	5.0
Colorado Springs, CO	30.7	50.8	1.5	4.5	12.5
Columbia, MO	49.8	37.9	1.0	3.4	8.0
Columbia, SC	55.8	29.7	2.0	3.9	8.6
Columbus, OH	45.8	36.3	2.0	4.2	11.7
Dallas, TX	43.0	40.2	2.5	4.0	10.2
Davenport, IA	37.3	44.0	1.0	5.6	12.0
Denver, CO	44.4	39.3	1.3	3.4	11.5
Des Moines, IA	40.8	38.8	2.3	5.7	12.5
Detroit, MI	57.0	22.0	2.9	6.3	11.9
Durham, NC	44.1	40.5	1.8	3.7	9.8
El Paso, TX	35.5	44.8	3.3	5.6	10.9
Eugene, OR	44.6	37.5	1.3	4.2	12.4
Fargo, ND	44.3	41.2	1.0	3.8	9.6
Fort Collins, CO	46.5	41.1	0.7	3.0	8.8
Fort Wayne, IN	37.2	42.9	1.5	5.9	12.5
Fort Worth, TX	35.8	46.5	2.2	4.6	10.7
Gainesville, FL	62.8	24.3	1.3	2.9	8.8
Green Bay, WI	39.4	41.0	1.1	4.9	13.5
Greensboro, NC	45.1	36.4	2.4	5.8	10.3
Honolulu, HI	38.0	44.0	1.2	6.6	10.1
Houston, TX	42.2	40.5	2.8	4.4	10.0
Huntsville, AL	37.9	42.7	1.9	6.0	11.6
Indianapolis, IN	41.1	40.4	1.7	4.8	12.0
Jacksonville, FL	36.2	42.5	2.1	5.5	13.6
Kansas City, MO	39.5	40.6	1.9	4.8	13.2
Lafayette, LA	40.0	42.8	2.2	5.1	9.9
Las Vegas, NV	36.4	42.8	1.8	5.3	13.5
Lexington, KY	38.8	43.1	1.4	4.6	12.0
Lincoln, NE	39.6	45.4	0.8	4.2	10.0
Little Rock, AR	38.6	41.0	1.5	5.5	13.4
Los Angeles, CA	46.5	38.6	2.3	4.5	8.0
Louisville, KY	37.2	41.9	2.0	6.1	12.8
Madison, WI	50.7	37.5	0.8	3.0	8.0
Manchester, NH	39.0	39.6	1.6	5.5	14.3
McAllen, TX	35.1	48.8	2.1	5.6	8.4
Memphis, TN	48.1	30.9	3.3	5.9	11.7

Table continued on following page.

City	Never Married	Now Married[1]	Separated	Widowed	Divorced
Miami, FL	40.4	37.0	3.3	5.7	13.5
Midland, TX	29.3	54.5	1.9	4.8	9.6
Milwaukee, WI	54.7	29.2	1.9	4.3	9.9
Minneapolis, MN	52.0	33.9	1.2	2.9	9.9
Nashville, TN	41.6	41.4	1.7	4.3	11.0
New Orleans, LA	49.2	30.8	2.3	5.2	12.5
New York, NY	44.0	39.8	2.8	5.2	8.2
Oklahoma City, OK	34.2	46.4	2.1	5.2	12.2
Omaha, NE	37.9	45.3	1.2	4.7	11.0
Orlando, FL	42.9	38.6	2.4	3.7	12.5
Philadelphia, PA	50.7	31.9	2.8	5.5	9.1
Phoenix, AZ	40.2	42.0	1.9	4.0	11.9
Pittsburgh, PA	54.4	30.6	1.7	5.0	8.3
Portland, OR	42.9	39.8	1.3	3.5	12.6
Providence, RI	53.4	32.1	2.0	4.1	8.5
Provo, UT	49.3	43.5	0.7	2.2	4.3
Raleigh, NC	43.1	40.5	1.9	3.9	10.6
Reno, NV	37.7	41.7	1.5	4.9	14.2
Richmond, VA	51.4	30.0	2.7	4.6	11.2
Rochester, MN	34.2	51.3	0.9	4.8	8.8
Sacramento, CA	41.5	40.8	2.3	4.7	10.7
Saint Louis, MO	49.7	30.2	2.7	5.3	12.2
Saint Paul, MN	46.4	37.8	1.5	3.6	10.6
Salem, OR	35.6	44.6	1.4	5.3	13.1
Salt Lake City, UT	45.4	39.1	1.6	2.9	10.9
San Antonio, TX	39.1	40.8	2.9	5.3	12.0
San Diego, CA	40.5	44.7	1.6	3.9	9.2
San Francisco, CA	45.6	40.7	1.4	4.5	7.8
San Jose, CA	37.2	49.3	1.6	4.4	7.5
Santa Rosa, CA	34.6	45.9	2.0	5.6	12.0
Savannah, GA	48.6	31.4	2.6	5.4	12.0
Seattle, WA	46.1	40.3	1.1	3.0	9.5
Sioux Falls, SD	34.5	48.4	1.4	4.3	11.4
Tampa, FL	43.1	38.1	2.2	4.7	11.8
Tucson, AZ	42.9	36.0	1.8	5.2	14.1
Tulsa, OK	36.5	41.7	2.4	5.5	14.0
Virginia Beach, VA	31.2	50.6	2.0	5.0	11.2
Washington, DC	55.2	31.5	1.4	3.4	8.5
Wichita, KS	35.0	45.2	1.8	5.2	12.8
Wilmington, NC	42.2	38.8	2.3	5.3	11.4
Winston-Salem, NC	42.5	39.6	2.4	5.2	10.3
U.S.	34.1	47.9	1.7	5.6	10.7

Note: Figures are percentages and cover the population 15 years of age and older; (1) Excludes separated
Source: U.S. Census Bureau, 2019-2023 American Community Survey 5-Year Estimates

Marital Status: Metro Area

Metro Area	Never Married	Now Married[1]	Separated	Widowed	Divorced
Albuquerque, NM	36.1	43.1	1.4	5.4	13.9
Anchorage, AK	33.3	49.3	1.8	3.7	11.9
Ann Arbor, MI	42.3	44.6	0.9	3.8	8.4
Athens, GA	43.0	41.4	1.3	4.7	9.5
Atlanta, GA	36.2	47.1	1.7	4.4	10.6
Austin, TX	35.9	49.4	1.3	3.5	9.8
Baltimore, MD	36.4	46.2	1.8	5.7	9.9
Billings, MT	28.7	51.5	1.0	5.5	13.3
Boise City, ID	28.9	54.0	1.0	4.4	11.8
Boston, MA	37.5	47.6	1.5	4.9	8.6
Boulder, CO	39.2	45.4	0.7	3.7	11.1
Cape Coral, FL	26.5	51.8	1.5	7.8	12.3
Cedar Rapids, IA	30.9	51.1	1.3	5.2	11.5
Charleston, SC	33.2	48.9	2.0	5.4	10.5
Charlotte, NC	33.6	49.4	2.0	4.9	10.0
Chicago, IL	37.6	46.7	1.6	5.3	8.8
Cincinnati, OH	33.2	49.0	1.3	5.5	11.0
Clarksville, TN	29.2	51.6	1.9	5.2	12.0
Cleveland, OH	35.7	44.2	1.5	6.4	12.1
College Station, TX	46.7	39.5	1.6	4.3	7.9
Colorado Springs, CO	29.4	53.8	1.3	4.1	11.5
Columbia, MO	41.1	44.4	1.1	4.3	9.2
Columbia, SC	36.0	45.7	2.3	5.7	10.2
Columbus, OH	35.0	47.4	1.6	4.8	11.2
Dallas, TX	33.4	50.6	1.7	4.2	10.0
Davenport, IA	31.1	50.1	1.2	6.2	11.5
Denver, CO	34.5	49.4	1.3	3.7	11.0
Des Moines, IA	31.7	51.3	1.3	5.0	10.7
Detroit, MI	35.9	45.7	1.2	6.0	11.2
Durham, NC	38.3	46.2	1.7	4.5	9.3
El Paso, TX	35.5	45.7	3.2	5.4	10.2
Eugene, OR	35.8	44.3	1.3	5.4	13.2
Fargo, ND	38.8	47.3	0.9	3.9	9.1
Fort Collins, CO	35.3	50.3	0.8	3.9	9.7
Fort Wayne, IN	31.8	49.9	1.3	5.5	11.5
Fort Worth, TX	33.4	50.6	1.7	4.2	10.0
Gainesville, FL	43.5	39.6	1.3	5.1	10.4
Green Bay, WI	31.8	51.2	0.6	5.2	11.1
Greensboro, NC	35.2	45.3	2.3	6.2	11.0
Honolulu, HI	34.6	49.5	1.1	6.0	8.7
Houston, TX	34.3	50.1	2.1	4.3	9.2
Huntsville, AL	30.6	51.3	1.4	5.5	11.2
Indianapolis, IN	32.7	49.7	1.2	4.9	11.5
Jacksonville, FL	31.4	48.4	1.8	5.6	12.7
Kansas City, MO	31.3	50.3	1.5	5.1	11.8
Lafayette, LA	33.9	47.8	2.0	5.4	10.9
Las Vegas, NV	35.6	44.3	2.0	5.1	13.1
Lexington, KY	34.4	46.7	1.5	5.1	12.3
Lincoln, NE	37.2	48.2	0.8	4.2	9.6
Little Rock, AR	31.5	48.0	1.7	5.9	12.9
Los Angeles, CA	40.7	44.3	2.0	4.7	8.3
Louisville, KY	31.8	47.6	1.7	6.0	12.9
Madison, WI	37.6	48.1	0.7	4.1	9.5
Manchester, NH	32.0	49.8	1.1	5.2	11.8
McAllen, TX	36.7	47.8	3.0	4.9	7.6
Memphis, TN	38.5	42.0	2.5	5.9	11.1

Table continued on following page.

Metro Area	Never Married	Now Married[1]	Separated	Widowed	Divorced
Miami, FL	34.0	44.7	2.4	6.1	12.8
Midland, TX	28.6	55.2	1.6	4.9	9.8
Milwaukee, WI	37.7	45.9	1.2	5.1	10.1
Minneapolis, MN	34.1	50.7	0.9	4.3	10.0
Nashville, TN	32.8	50.3	1.4	4.9	10.6
New Orleans, LA	40.3	38.9	2.3	6.0	12.4
New York, NY	38.3	46.0	2.1	5.4	8.1
Oklahoma City, OK	32.3	48.6	1.8	5.5	11.9
Omaha, NE	32.4	51.2	1.1	4.6	10.8
Orlando, FL	35.1	47.0	1.8	4.9	11.2
Philadelphia, PA	37.7	45.7	1.8	5.6	9.1
Phoenix, AZ	34.3	47.9	1.4	4.9	11.5
Pittsburgh, PA	33.1	48.4	1.5	7.0	10.0
Portland, OR	33.7	48.9	1.3	4.3	11.8
Providence, RI	36.7	45.0	1.5	5.8	11.0
Provo, UT	33.4	57.7	0.8	2.6	5.5
Raleigh, NC	32.4	52.4	1.8	4.2	9.3
Reno, NV	32.6	47.1	1.4	5.1	13.8
Richmond, VA	35.0	47.0	2.0	5.5	10.4
Rochester, MN	29.3	55.9	0.7	4.9	9.1
Sacramento, CA	34.2	48.5	1.8	4.9	10.5
Saint Louis, MO	32.9	48.4	1.6	5.8	11.2
Saint Paul, MN	34.1	50.7	0.9	4.3	10.0
Salem, OR	32.4	48.5	1.6	5.4	12.1
Salt Lake City, UT	33.6	51.2	1.5	3.6	10.2
San Antonio, TX	34.3	47.2	2.3	5.1	11.1
San Diego, CA	36.3	48.1	1.6	4.4	9.6
San Francisco, CA	36.8	48.8	1.4	4.6	8.4
San Jose, CA	35.5	51.7	1.4	4.2	7.1
Santa Rosa, CA	32.7	48.5	1.4	5.2	12.2
Savannah, GA	35.8	45.9	2.1	5.1	11.2
Seattle, WA	33.8	50.4	1.3	4.0	10.5
Sioux Falls, SD	30.7	53.1	1.1	4.3	10.8
Tampa, FL	32.1	46.3	1.8	6.8	13.1
Tucson, AZ	35.1	44.8	1.5	5.8	12.9
Tulsa, OK	29.9	49.5	1.8	6.1	12.7
Virginia Beach, VA	33.7	47.7	2.2	5.5	10.8
Washington, DC	36.7	48.8	1.6	4.2	8.7
Wichita, KS	31.2	50.0	1.4	5.4	12.0
Wilmington, NC	28.5	52.5	1.9	6.2	10.9
Winston-Salem, NC	31.7	48.8	2.2	6.3	11.1
U.S.	34.1	47.9	1.7	5.6	10.7

Note: Figures are percentages and cover the population 15 years of age and older; Figures cover the Metropolitan Statistical Area (MSA); (1) Excludes separated
Source: U.S. Census Bureau, 2019-2023 American Community Survey 5-Year Estimates

Disability by Age: City

City	All Ages	Under 18 Years Old	18 to 64 Years Old	65 Years and Over
Albuquerque, NM	15.2	4.8	13.2	35.2
Anchorage, AK	12.2	4.9	10.7	33.7
Ann Arbor, MI	8.1	4.7	6.1	23.8
Athens, GA	12.2	5.9	10.1	34.0
Atlanta, GA	11.6	5.4	9.6	32.3
Austin, TX	9.5	3.8	8.4	28.3
Baltimore, MD	16.5	5.7	14.6	40.0
Billings, MT	14.5	4.4	11.8	36.3
Boise City, ID	12.1	5.3	10.2	29.4
Boston, MA	12.1	5.8	9.1	37.2
Boulder, CO	7.5	2.9	6.1	20.9
Cape Coral, FL	14.0	3.8	10.0	30.5
Cedar Rapids, IA	11.6	4.9	10.0	27.3
Charleston, SC	9.7	3.2	6.7	29.6
Charlotte, NC	8.3	2.8	7.0	28.3
Chicago, IL	11.9	3.8	9.6	35.4
Cincinnati, OH	13.6	6.0	12.6	31.7
Clarksville, TN	14.8	5.7	15.1	41.8
Cleveland, OH	19.9	9.8	18.5	40.7
College Station, TX	8.2	6.2	6.8	29.3
Colorado Springs, CO	13.2	5.7	11.9	30.1
Columbia, MO	11.9	5.4	10.5	32.2
Columbia, SC	12.7	3.9	10.7	38.0
Columbus, OH	12.2	5.3	10.9	34.7
Dallas, TX	11.4	4.7	9.8	34.9
Davenport, IA	13.9	5.5	11.8	33.3
Denver, CO	10.1	3.3	8.3	30.7
Des Moines, IA	14.3	5.8	13.4	35.2
Detroit, MI	19.6	6.0	19.7	42.6
Durham, NC	9.9	3.6	8.0	29.6
El Paso, TX	14.3	5.5	12.0	40.2
Eugene, OR	15.1	4.8	13.2	31.7
Fargo, ND	11.4	5.4	9.0	32.6
Fort Collins, CO	8.9	3.0	7.7	24.0
Fort Wayne, IN	13.6	5.3	12.5	32.5
Fort Worth, TX	10.2	3.7	9.0	34.4
Gainesville, FL	10.5	3.9	8.3	33.6
Green Bay, WI	15.0	7.1	13.9	34.3
Greensboro, NC	11.8	5.4	9.9	31.4
Honolulu, HI	12.5	3.9	7.9	32.1
Houston, TX	11.0	4.7	8.9	35.1
Huntsville, AL	14.3	5.4	11.8	34.8
Indianapolis, IN	13.5	5.1	12.6	34.6
Jacksonville, FL	13.5	5.0	11.8	34.1
Kansas City, MO	12.8	3.7	11.6	33.3
Lafayette, LA	12.9	3.5	10.3	33.9
Las Vegas, NV	13.3	4.5	11.3	34.2
Lexington, KY	12.8	4.9	11.0	32.4
Lincoln, NE	12.0	4.8	10.6	29.5
Little Rock, AR	13.9	6.8	12.0	33.8
Los Angeles, CA	11.1	3.5	8.3	36.3
Louisville, KY	14.7	5.3	13.3	34.1
Madison, WI	9.1	4.1	7.5	24.6
Manchester, NH	13.6	7.4	11.5	31.1
McAllen, TX	13.0	6.1	9.4	43.8

Table continued on following page.

City	All Ages	Under 18 Years Old	18 to 64 Years Old	65 Years and Over
Memphis, TN	13.6	4.6	12.5	34.6
Miami, FL	11.5	3.7	7.0	38.2
Midland, TX	10.4	3.4	8.7	40.3
Milwaukee, WI	13.2	4.8	12.5	35.3
Minneapolis, MN	11.6	4.8	10.7	30.5
Nashville, TN	11.0	4.5	8.8	33.8
New Orleans, LA	14.1	5.7	11.6	34.2
New York, NY	11.7	3.9	8.5	34.6
Oklahoma City, OK	13.9	5.6	12.5	36.6
Omaha, NE	11.1	3.8	9.8	30.2
Orlando, FL	10.3	5.2	8.3	33.4
Philadelphia, PA	17.4	7.7	15.6	40.8
Phoenix, AZ	11.5	4.6	10.2	32.5
Pittsburgh, PA	14.2	7.4	11.5	34.3
Portland, OR	13.2	4.9	10.9	34.3
Providence, RI	13.7	6.0	12.4	37.3
Provo, UT	10.2	4.2	8.9	42.2
Raleigh, NC	9.6	4.4	7.9	29.1
Reno, NV	12.1	4.0	9.8	31.2
Richmond, VA	14.0	7.0	12.0	33.1
Rochester, MN	10.1	3.8	7.8	28.9
Sacramento, CA	12.4	4.0	10.1	35.8
Saint Louis, MO	16.6	6.5	14.4	39.0
Saint Paul, MN	12.5	4.7	11.9	31.3
Salem, OR	15.4	5.9	13.7	36.8
Salt Lake City, UT	12.1	5.0	9.9	34.9
San Antonio, TX	15.5	6.7	13.5	41.8
San Diego, CA	10.0	3.4	7.3	31.2
San Francisco, CA	11.2	2.7	7.3	34.1
San Jose, CA	9.6	3.6	6.3	34.3
Santa Rosa, CA	12.7	4.3	10.3	30.0
Savannah, GA	15.9	7.0	13.5	40.7
Seattle, WA	10.0	2.8	8.0	30.3
Sioux Falls, SD	10.0	3.4	8.7	28.4
Tampa, FL	11.9	4.1	9.3	38.0
Tucson, AZ	15.5	6.1	13.2	36.8
Tulsa, OK	14.4	5.3	13.3	34.2
Virginia Beach, VA	11.7	4.4	10.1	28.7
Washington, DC	11.0	4.5	8.8	32.3
Wichita, KS	14.9	5.9	13.6	34.7
Wilmington, NC	12.9	3.7	10.4	31.1
Winston-Salem, NC	12.6	4.7	10.9	32.8
U.S.	13.0	4.7	10.7	32.9

Note: Figures show percent of the civilian noninstitutionalized population that reported having a disability. Disability status is determined from from six types of difficulty: vision, hearing, cognitive, ambulatory, self-care, and independent living. For children under 5 years old, hearing and vision difficulty are used to determine disability status. For children between the ages of 5 and 14, disability status is determined from hearing, vision, cognitive, ambulatory, and self-care difficulties. For people aged 15 years and older, they are considered to have a disability if they have difficulty with any one of the six difficulty types.
Source: U.S. Census Bureau, 2019-2023 American Community Survey 5-Year Estimates

Disability by Age: Metro Area

Metro Area	All Ages	Under 18 Years Old	18 to 64 Years Old	65 Years and Over
Albuquerque, NM	16.1	4.7	14.1	36.3
Anchorage, AK	12.6	4.8	11.3	34.0
Ann Arbor, MI	10.3	4.1	8.3	26.9
Athens, GA	12.8	4.9	11.0	32.7
Atlanta, GA	10.8	4.5	9.0	31.3
Austin, TX	10.0	4.3	8.5	29.1
Baltimore, MD	12.0	4.5	9.8	30.7
Billings, MT	14.3	4.4	11.6	35.1
Boise City, ID	12.7	4.9	11.0	31.0
Boston, MA	10.9	4.5	8.2	29.6
Boulder, CO	8.8	2.9	6.9	23.8
Cape Coral, FL	13.7	4.0	9.6	27.1
Cedar Rapids, IA	11.5	5.0	9.5	27.3
Charleston, SC	12.1	4.5	9.8	31.5
Charlotte, NC	10.6	3.4	8.7	31.0
Chicago, IL	10.7	3.6	8.4	30.2
Cincinnati, OH	12.7	5.1	10.8	31.5
Clarksville, TN	16.4	6.5	16.1	41.9
Cleveland, OH	14.6	5.6	12.2	32.1
College Station, TX	10.9	5.5	8.8	33.8
Colorado Springs, CO	12.5	5.4	11.3	29.7
Columbia, MO	13.0	5.3	11.5	31.9
Columbia, SC	14.3	5.1	12.3	35.3
Columbus, OH	12.1	5.0	10.4	32.3
Dallas, TX	10.1	4.0	8.5	32.0
Davenport, IA	13.5	5.7	10.9	30.9
Denver, CO	10.2	3.7	8.4	29.1
Des Moines, IA	10.8	3.8	9.3	29.8
Detroit, MI	14.0	4.6	11.9	33.5
Durham, NC	10.4	3.7	8.1	28.1
El Paso, TX	13.9	5.5	11.7	41.5
Eugene, OR	17.1	6.2	15.0	33.4
Fargo, ND	11.0	4.1	9.3	32.1
Fort Collins, CO	10.3	3.3	8.2	26.6
Fort Wayne, IN	12.4	4.7	11.1	30.4
Fort Worth, TX	10.1	4.0	8.5	32.0
Gainesville, FL	13.3	5.4	10.2	34.6
Green Bay, WI	12.0	4.4	10.6	27.3
Greensboro, NC	13.4	4.9	11.2	32.9
Honolulu, HI	12.2	3.6	8.5	32.8
Houston, TX	10.4	4.3	8.6	32.8
Huntsville, AL	13.5	4.5	11.5	34.9
Indianapolis, IN	12.4	5.0	10.9	32.1
Jacksonville, FL	13.1	4.8	11.1	31.8
Kansas City, MO	12.0	4.4	10.3	31.1
Lafayette, LA	14.5	4.7	12.9	37.2
Las Vegas, NV	13.0	4.4	10.7	34.3
Lexington, KY	13.9	5.4	12.2	33.8
Lincoln, NE	11.8	4.5	10.2	29.6
Little Rock, AR	15.5	5.7	13.6	37.4
Los Angeles, CA	10.5	3.5	7.7	32.8
Louisville, KY	14.4	5.0	12.5	34.4
Madison, WI	9.4	3.8	7.6	24.3
Manchester, NH	11.7	4.7	9.6	28.3
McAllen, TX	12.5	5.5	9.7	45.5

Table continued on following page.

Metro Area	All Ages	Under 18 Years Old	18 to 64 Years Old	65 Years and Over
Memphis, TN	13.5	5.0	12.1	34.6
Miami, FL	11.0	4.0	7.2	30.9
Midland, TX	10.9	3.5	9.3	40.7
Milwaukee, WI	11.3	4.0	9.4	28.9
Minneapolis, MN	10.4	4.0	8.6	27.9
Nashville, TN	11.4	4.2	9.4	32.9
New Orleans, LA	15.3	6.1	12.9	36.3
New York, NY	10.6	3.5	7.7	30.9
Oklahoma City, OK	14.7	5.2	13.0	38.3
Omaha, NE	11.2	3.8	9.7	31.0
Orlando, FL	12.3	5.6	9.5	33.1
Philadelphia, PA	13.2	5.5	11.0	31.5
Phoenix, AZ	12.3	4.9	10.1	31.1
Pittsburgh, PA	14.7	5.7	11.7	31.9
Portland, OR	12.9	4.5	10.8	32.6
Providence, RI	13.9	5.6	11.7	31.4
Provo, UT	8.7	3.9	8.3	31.3
Raleigh, NC	10.0	3.9	8.3	30.1
Reno, NV	13.0	4.7	10.4	31.7
Richmond, VA	12.8	5.3	10.7	30.4
Rochester, MN	10.1	3.6	7.8	27.2
Sacramento, CA	12.3	4.0	9.6	33.8
Saint Louis, MO	13.3	4.7	11.2	32.1
Saint Paul, MN	10.4	4.0	8.6	27.9
Salem, OR	15.8	5.8	13.8	36.9
Salt Lake City, UT	10.2	4.4	9.1	29.8
San Antonio, TX	14.6	6.3	12.6	39.1
San Diego, CA	10.7	3.6	8.2	31.3
San Francisco, CA	10.3	3.2	7.3	30.4
San Jose, CA	8.8	3.1	5.7	31.3
Santa Rosa, CA	12.1	4.0	9.1	28.2
Savannah, GA	14.5	5.3	12.8	35.7
Seattle, WA	11.4	4.2	9.2	32.6
Sioux Falls, SD	9.9	3.3	8.5	28.5
Tampa, FL	14.4	5.3	11.1	33.5
Tucson, AZ	15.1	5.6	12.2	32.3
Tulsa, OK	15.0	5.2	13.4	37.0
Virginia Beach, VA	13.6	5.4	11.6	32.5
Washington, DC	9.1	3.5	7.0	27.9
Wichita, KS	14.6	5.6	13.0	35.1
Wilmington, NC	13.5	5.5	10.7	26.6
Winston-Salem, NC	14.2	4.9	12.0	33.1
U.S.	13.0	4.7	10.7	32.9

Note: Figures show percent of the civilian noninstitutionalized population that reported having a disability. Disability status is determined from from six types of difficulty: vision, hearing, cognitive, ambulatory, self-care, and independent living. For children under 5 years old, hearing and vision difficulty are used to determine disability status. For children between the ages of 5 and 14, disability status is determined from hearing, vision, cognitive, ambulatory, and self-care difficulties. For people aged 15 years and older, they are considered to have a disability if they have difficulty with any one of the six difficulty types; Figures cover the Metropolitan Statistical Area (MSA)
Source: U.S. Census Bureau, 2019-2023 American Community Survey 5-Year Estimates

Religious Groups by Family

Metro Area	Catholic	Baptist	Methodist	LDS[1]	Pentecostal	Lutheran	Islam	Adventist	Other
Albuquerque, NM	32.6	3.2	0.9	2.7	1.7	0.4	0.7	1.5	10.8
Anchorage, AK	4.9	3.4	1.0	5.1	1.7	1.5	0.1	1.7	16.3
Ann Arbor, MI	9.7	2.0	2.4	0.8	1.5	2.3	2.2	0.9	10.0
Athens, GA	6.4	12.8	5.7	1.0	2.4	0.3	0.2	1.3	7.9
Atlanta, GA	10.7	14.7	6.7	0.8	2.0	0.4	1.9	1.9	12.4
Austin, TX	18.8	6.5	2.2	1.3	0.7	1.1	1.0	1.0	9.9
Baltimore, MD	12.4	3.2	4.4	0.6	1.2	1.4	3.3	1.2	11.7
Billings, MT	7.4	1.9	1.1	5.2	3.6	4.9	n/a	1.2	7.8
Boise City, ID	13.0	0.8	2.5	15.0	1.6	0.8	0.3	1.7	10.0
Boston, MA	37.0	1.0	0.7	0.5	0.7	0.2	2.2	0.9	7.1
Boulder, CO	16.0	0.3	0.7	0.7	0.5	1.7	0.4	0.9	15.2
Cape Coral, FL	18.8	2.5	1.7	0.6	3.0	0.7	0.2	2.0	12.2
Cedar Rapids, IA	16.8	1.0	5.3	1.0	1.3	8.1	1.3	0.6	9.6
Charleston, SC	11.5	7.7	8.0	0.8	1.9	0.7	0.2	1.0	12.8
Charlotte, NC	12.1	13.9	7.0	0.7	2.2	1.1	1.7	1.4	15.9
Chicago, IL	28.6	3.4	1.4	0.3	1.5	2.1	4.7	1.1	9.2
Cincinnati, OH	17.0	5.7	2.3	0.6	1.5	0.8	1.1	0.7	21.8
Clarksville, TN	4.6	23.2	4.4	1.4	3.2	0.5	0.1	0.8	12.4
Cleveland, OH	26.1	4.3	2.3	0.4	1.5	1.8	1.1	1.3	16.8
College Station, TX	17.2	10.6	4.3	1.7	0.5	1.1	0.6	0.5	6.8
Colorado Springs, CO	16.4	2.6	1.3	3.0	1.0	1.2	0.1	1.0	16.2
Columbia, MO	7.1	9.0	3.5	1.7	1.1	1.6	1.4	1.2	12.4
Columbia, SC	6.6	15.1	8.5	1.2	3.8	2.3	0.3	1.3	15.4
Columbus, OH	11.7	3.4	3.0	0.8	1.9	1.7	2.1	0.9	17.5
Dallas, TX	14.2	14.3	4.7	1.4	2.2	0.5	1.8	1.3	13.8
Davenport, IA	13.2	3.2	3.6	0.8	1.5	6.6	0.7	0.8	6.7
Denver, CO	16.1	1.5	1.0	2.1	0.6	1.4	0.3	1.1	10.4
Des Moines, IA	12.1	1.8	4.0	0.9	2.5	6.6	1.6	0.8	8.7
Detroit, MI	18.6	4.8	1.7	0.3	2.1	2.2	4.5	1.0	8.5
Durham, NC	8.5	12.3	6.5	0.9	1.3	0.3	1.5	1.1	13.7
El Paso, TX	47.9	2.5	0.4	1.2	1.1	0.2	0.1	2.1	6.9
Eugene, OR	5.6	0.7	0.5	2.8	2.5	0.8	<0.1	2.0	9.0
Fargo, ND	14.2	0.2	1.0	0.6	1.3	24.0	<0.1	0.6	8.1
Fort Collins, CO	9.9	1.2	1.3	4.0	2.7	2.5	<0.1	1.2	12.1
Fort Wayne, IN	13.1	8.1	3.9	0.4	1.1	7.1	1.0	0.9	17.6
Fort Worth, TX	14.2	14.3	4.7	1.4	2.2	0.5	1.8	1.3	13.8
Gainesville, FL	8.5	10.6	4.8	1.4	3.2	0.3	0.4	1.3	14.5
Green Bay, WI	31.8	0.3	1.4	0.5	1.1	10.8	0.4	0.9	7.0
Greensboro, NC	7.9	10.0	8.0	0.7	2.8	0.4	1.5	1.4	17.8
Honolulu, HI	18.0	1.4	0.5	4.1	2.6	0.2	<0.1	1.9	9.8
Houston, TX	18.3	13.1	3.7	1.2	1.6	0.7	1.7	1.5	13.1
Huntsville, AL	7.5	23.6	6.6	1.4	1.2	0.4	0.8	2.7	17.5
Indianapolis, IN	11.5	6.2	3.3	0.7	1.3	1.1	1.1	1.0	17.4
Jacksonville, FL	13.0	14.5	3.0	1.0	1.4	0.4	0.6	1.3	20.5
Kansas City, MO	11.3	9.1	5.0	1.6	2.7	1.7	1.0	1.0	12.1
Lafayette, LA	44.3	9.3	2.0	0.4	1.8	0.1	0.1	0.8	7.0
Las Vegas, NV	26.2	1.9	0.3	5.8	1.5	0.6	0.3	1.3	5.5
Lexington, KY	5.8	14.9	5.5	1.2	1.6	0.3	0.5	1.2	16.6
Lincoln, NE	13.2	1.0	5.7	1.2	3.1	9.1	0.1	1.8	10.0
Little Rock, AR	4.9	23.5	6.2	0.8	3.7	0.4	0.4	1.0	13.6
Los Angeles, CA	31.1	2.6	0.8	1.5	2.4	0.4	1.4	1.5	9.1
Louisville, KY	11.9	14.5	3.2	0.8	0.9	0.5	1.0	1.0	12.4
Madison, WI	14.4	0.5	2.0	0.7	0.2	9.2	1.2	0.7	8.4
Manchester, NH	16.3	0.6	0.6	0.6	0.3	0.3	0.1	0.8	8.1
McAllen, TX	46.6	2.2	0.8	1.2	1.0	0.3	0.2	3.2	6.0
Memphis, TN	4.8	26.6	6.0	0.7	5.1	0.3	1.3	1.3	18.4

Table continued on following page.

Metro Area	Catholic	Baptist	Methodist	LDS[1]	Pentecostal	Lutheran	Islam	Adventist	Other
Miami, FL	23.8	5.1	0.9	0.5	1.3	0.3	0.8	2.4	11.1
Midland, TX	15.4	25.5	2.5	2.0	1.2	0.3	0.4	1.3	16.5
Milwaukee, WI	24.5	3.0	1.0	0.4	2.8	9.1	2.8	0.9	10.7
Minneapolis, MN	19.8	0.8	1.4	0.5	2.5	10.7	2.9	0.7	7.4
Nashville, TN	6.2	16.4	4.8	0.9	1.6	0.4	0.8	1.3	19.4
New Orleans, LA	42.1	9.3	2.5	0.5	2.1	0.5	1.4	1.0	8.0
New York, NY	32.5	1.7	1.2	0.3	0.9	0.5	4.5	1.4	10.6
Oklahoma City, OK	10.0	16.6	6.2	1.3	3.9	0.6	0.6	0.9	21.4
Omaha, NE	19.9	2.8	2.8	1.6	1.0	6.1	0.2	1.0	9.0
Orlando, FL	17.6	5.7	2.1	0.9	2.7	0.6	1.3	2.8	14.6
Philadelphia, PA	26.8	3.3	2.4	0.3	1.0	1.2	2.6	1.0	10.5
Phoenix, AZ	22.9	1.7	0.6	6.2	1.5	1.0	1.9	1.5	9.3
Pittsburgh, PA	30.6	1.9	4.3	0.4	1.3	2.5	0.6	0.6	12.5
Portland, OR	11.8	0.8	0.6	3.3	1.4	1.1	0.2	2.0	14.4
Providence, RI	37.9	0.9	0.6	0.3	0.6	0.3	0.5	0.9	6.1
Provo, UT	4.9	0.1	<0.1	82.6	0.1	<0.1	0.3	0.3	0.4
Raleigh, NC	12.4	9.8	5.4	1.2	1.9	0.7	3.2	1.5	12.8
Reno, NV	24.4	1.4	0.5	4.0	0.9	0.5	0.3	1.4	5.3
Richmond, VA	12.3	14.2	4.8	0.9	3.2	0.5	2.1	1.2	14.8
Rochester, MN	15.6	0.4	2.8	1.5	1.9	19.3	1.0	0.7	10.1
Sacramento, CA	17.1	1.9	1.1	3.1	2.2	0.6	1.9	1.9	8.2
Saint Louis, MO	21.2	8.6	2.9	0.7	1.4	3.2	1.3	0.8	11.1
Saint Paul, MN	19.8	0.8	1.4	0.5	2.5	10.7	2.9	0.7	7.4
Salem, OR	19.5	0.5	0.6	3.8	2.9	1.2	n/a	2.5	10.7
Salt Lake City, UT	9.0	0.6	0.2	52.0	0.7	0.2	1.6	0.7	2.6
San Antonio, TX	27.3	6.4	2.1	1.4	1.6	1.1	0.5	1.5	11.0
San Diego, CA	22.9	1.5	0.6	2.1	1.0	0.6	1.5	1.9	9.4
San Francisco, CA	21.5	2.2	0.9	1.5	1.4	0.4	2.0	1.0	7.7
San Jose, CA	27.2	1.2	0.6	1.4	0.9	0.4	2.0	1.3	11.4
Santa Rosa, CA	23.5	1.1	0.5	1.4	0.5	0.5	0.2	1.8	6.9
Savannah, GA	5.5	11.9	4.8	0.8	1.5	1.1	0.2	1.4	12.3
Seattle, WA	11.0	1.0	0.7	2.6	2.8	1.2	0.6	1.4	19.8
Sioux Falls, SD	13.1	0.7	2.9	0.7	1.7	16.4	0.1	0.6	20.3
Tampa, FL	23.1	6.3	2.9	0.5	1.9	0.6	0.7	1.8	12.1
Tucson, AZ	18.9	1.9	0.6	2.8	1.3	1.1	1.0	1.4	9.7
Tulsa, OK	5.6	15.5	7.7	1.2	2.5	0.5	0.5	1.2	22.2
Virginia Beach, VA	8.3	9.5	4.8	0.7	2.0	0.5	1.0	0.9	16.1
Washington, DC	16.1	6.0	4.1	1.1	1.3	0.8	3.3	1.5	12.6
Wichita, KS	12.7	23.5	4.5	1.5	1.4	1.3	0.1	1.1	15.0
Wilmington, NC	13.2	9.9	8.1	1.0	1.0	0.7	0.7	1.4	12.6
Winston-Salem, NC	9.3	12.8	11.4	0.5	1.0	0.6	0.8	1.4	22.5
U.S.	18.7	7.3	3.0	2.0	1.8	1.7	1.3	1.3	11.6

Note: Figures are the number of adherents as a percentage of the total population; Figures cover the Metropolitan Statistical Area (MSA);
(1) Church of Jesus Christ of Latter-day Saints
Source: 2020 U.S. Religion Census, Association of Statisticians of American Religious Bodies; The Association of Religion Data Archives

Religious Groups by Tradition

Metro Area	Catholic	Evangelical Protestant	Mainline Protestant	Black Protestant	Islam	Judaism	Hinduism	Orthodox	Buddhism
Albuquerque, NM	32.6	13.4	2.2	0.5	0.7	0.2	0.2	0.1	0.6
Anchorage, AK	4.9	19.2	2.4	0.9	0.1	0.1	0.1	0.5	1.3
Ann Arbor, MI	9.7	8.1	5.6	2.5	2.2	0.8	0.5	0.4	0.3
Athens, GA	6.4	19.1	7.2	2.6	0.2	0.2	0.2	0.1	<0.1
Atlanta, GA	10.7	22.3	7.4	5.3	1.9	0.5	0.7	0.3	0.2
Austin, TX	18.8	13.5	4.0	1.7	1.0	0.2	0.6	0.2	0.3
Baltimore, MD	12.4	10.6	5.9	3.3	3.3	1.7	0.1	0.5	0.1
Billings, MT	7.4	13.9	5.2	0.1	n/a	n/a	n/a	0.1	n/a
Boise City, ID	13.0	11.9	3.9	<0.1	0.3	0.1	0.2	0.1	0.1
Boston, MA	37.0	3.4	3.2	0.3	2.2	1.1	0.3	0.9	0.4
Boulder, CO	16.0	12.7	3.4	n/a	0.4	0.7	0.5	0.2	1.0
Cape Coral, FL	18.8	16.4	3.0	0.6	0.2	0.2	0.2	0.1	0.1
Cedar Rapids, IA	16.8	11.9	12.2	0.4	1.3	0.1	0.7	0.1	<0.1
Charleston, SC	11.5	17.1	6.8	6.6	0.2	0.4	<0.1	0.2	n/a
Charlotte, NC	12.1	26.4	9.5	3.4	1.7	0.2	0.2	0.4	0.1
Chicago, IL	28.6	8.2	3.7	3.6	4.7	0.7	0.4	0.7	0.4
Cincinnati, OH	17.0	24.9	4.1	2.0	1.1	0.4	0.3	0.3	0.1
Clarksville, TN	4.6	35.7	4.8	3.4	0.1	n/a	n/a	0.1	n/a
Cleveland, OH	26.1	15.1	5.6	3.5	1.1	1.3	0.3	0.8	0.2
College Station, TX	17.2	16.1	5.3	1.8	0.6	n/a	0.1	0.1	n/a
Colorado Springs, CO	16.4	18.3	2.9	0.9	0.1	<0.1	<0.1	0.1	0.3
Columbia, MO	7.1	19.4	6.3	1.9	1.4	0.2	0.1	0.1	<0.1
Columbia, SC	6.6	27.9	10.7	5.6	0.3	0.2	0.4	0.1	0.3
Columbus, OH	11.7	18.1	6.8	1.5	2.1	0.4	0.4	0.5	0.2
Dallas, TX	14.2	25.4	5.9	3.3	1.8	0.3	0.5	0.3	0.2
Davenport, IA	13.2	8.5	10.6	1.9	0.7	0.1	0.2	0.1	n/a
Denver, CO	16.1	9.6	2.8	0.6	0.3	0.4	0.5	0.4	0.5
Des Moines, IA	12.1	10.3	12.2	1.0	1.6	<0.1	0.2	0.1	0.1
Detroit, MI	18.6	9.1	3.3	5.1	4.5	0.8	0.3	0.8	0.2
Durham, NC	8.5	20.0	8.8	4.3	1.5	0.5	0.1	0.3	0.1
El Paso, TX	47.9	9.9	0.6	0.4	0.1	0.2	<0.1	<0.1	0.2
Eugene, OR	5.6	10.3	2.3	0.1	<0.1	0.4	0.3	0.1	0.5
Fargo, ND	14.2	11.1	23.4	n/a	<0.1	<0.1	n/a	0.1	n/a
Fort Collins, CO	9.9	15.6	3.3	0.4	<0.1	n/a	0.1	0.1	0.1
Fort Wayne, IN	13.1	24.7	6.1	6.5	1.0	0.1	0.1	0.2	0.4
Fort Worth, TX	14.2	25.4	5.9	3.3	1.8	0.3	0.5	0.3	0.2
Gainesville, FL	8.5	25.3	5.4	2.0	0.4	0.3	0.3	<0.1	0.3
Green Bay, WI	31.8	14.6	6.2	<0.1	0.4	n/a	n/a	<0.1	<0.1
Greensboro, NC	7.9	24.9	10.1	3.5	1.5	0.3	0.3	0.1	0.1
Honolulu, HI	18.0	8.1	2.3	0.2	<0.1	0.1	0.2	<0.1	4.0
Houston, TX	18.3	23.8	4.7	2.3	1.7	0.3	0.7	0.3	0.3
Huntsville, AL	7.5	34.8	8.2	7.2	0.8	0.1	0.9	0.1	0.1
Indianapolis, IN	11.5	16.8	7.6	4.2	1.1	0.4	0.2	0.3	0.1
Jacksonville, FL	13.0	29.8	3.5	5.6	0.6	0.3	0.3	0.3	0.2
Kansas City, MO	11.3	19.1	7.1	3.6	1.0	0.3	0.4	0.1	0.2
Lafayette, LA	44.3	12.6	2.4	5.0	0.1	n/a	<0.1	<0.1	0.1
Las Vegas, NV	26.2	6.6	1.0	0.5	0.3	0.3	0.2	0.6	0.7
Lexington, KY	5.8	26.9	8.1	3.5	0.5	0.3	0.1	0.2	<0.1
Lincoln, NE	13.2	16.6	12.9	0.3	0.1	0.1	0.1	0.1	0.1
Little Rock, AR	4.9	32.1	6.6	8.5	0.4	0.1	<0.1	0.1	0.1
Los Angeles, CA	31.1	9.3	1.5	1.7	1.4	0.8	0.4	0.9	0.9
Louisville, KY	11.9	21.1	5.0	4.6	1.0	0.2	0.4	0.2	0.2
Madison, WI	14.4	8.0	10.6	0.2	1.2	0.4	0.1	0.1	0.9
Manchester, NH	16.3	5.8	2.7	n/a	0.1	0.3	<0.1	0.9	n/a
McAllen, TX	46.6	10.0	1.1	0.1	0.2	<0.1	<0.1	<0.1	n/a

Table continued on following page.

Metro Area	Catholic	Evangelical Protestant	Mainline Protestant	Black Protestant	Islam	Judaism	Hinduism	Orthodox	Buddhism
Memphis, TN	4.8	32.4	5.8	17.2	1.3	0.6	0.4	0.1	0.1
Miami, FL	23.8	13.7	1.6	2.2	0.8	1.2	0.3	0.2	0.3
Midland, TX	15.4	35.5	3.0	7.6	0.4	n/a	0.2	n/a	n/a
Milwaukee, WI	24.5	16.3	5.4	3.3	2.8	0.4	0.4	0.5	0.4
Minneapolis, MN	19.8	10.6	10.3	0.5	2.9	0.6	0.2	0.3	0.3
Nashville, TN	6.2	30.1	6.0	5.2	0.8	0.2	0.4	1.1	0.2
New Orleans, LA	42.1	13.5	3.0	4.9	1.4	0.4	0.3	0.1	0.3
New York, NY	32.5	4.4	3.0	1.5	4.5	4.4	1.0	0.8	0.3
Oklahoma City, OK	10.0	38.7	7.1	2.2	0.6	0.1	0.4	0.1	0.4
Omaha, NE	19.9	10.8	7.9	1.5	0.2	0.3	1.0	0.2	0.2
Orlando, FL	17.6	20.6	2.5	2.7	1.3	0.2	0.5	0.3	0.3
Philadelphia, PA	26.8	7.3	6.6	2.2	2.6	1.1	0.6	0.4	0.4
Phoenix, AZ	22.9	11.0	1.6	0.3	1.9	0.3	0.5	0.4	0.2
Pittsburgh, PA	30.6	8.8	10.1	1.3	0.6	0.6	1.2	0.6	0.1
Portland, OR	11.8	14.6	2.3	0.4	0.2	0.3	0.7	0.3	0.4
Providence, RI	37.9	4.0	3.2	0.1	0.5	0.6	0.1	0.5	0.2
Provo, UT	4.9	0.4	<0.1	n/a	0.3	n/a	0.1	n/a	n/a
Raleigh, NC	12.4	19.3	7.4	2.8	3.2	0.2	0.4	0.3	0.4
Reno, NV	24.4	6.8	1.3	0.2	0.3	0.1	0.1	0.1	0.2
Richmond, VA	12.3	23.1	9.3	3.1	2.1	0.3	1.3	0.4	0.2
Rochester, MN	15.6	15.0	19.1	n/a	1.0	0.1	0.1	0.2	0.2
Sacramento, CA	17.1	10.4	1.4	1.1	1.9	0.2	0.4	0.3	0.5
Saint Louis, MO	21.2	16.1	5.7	3.9	1.3	0.6	0.2	0.2	0.3
Saint Paul, MN	19.8	10.6	10.3	0.5	2.9	0.6	0.2	0.3	0.3
Salem, OR	19.5	14.4	2.0	0.2	n/a	0.1	<0.1	<0.1	<0.1
Salt Lake City, UT	9.0	2.4	0.7	0.1	1.6	0.1	0.3	0.4	0.3
San Antonio, TX	27.3	17.7	3.1	0.8	0.5	0.2	0.1	0.1	0.3
San Diego, CA	22.9	9.5	1.5	0.6	1.5	0.4	0.3	0.4	0.7
San Francisco, CA	21.5	5.2	2.2	1.8	2.0	0.7	1.1	0.7	1.1
San Jose, CA	27.2	8.4	1.4	0.3	2.0	0.6	2.4	0.6	1.2
Santa Rosa, CA	23.5	5.3	1.5	<0.1	0.2	0.4	0.3	0.4	1.7
Savannah, GA	5.5	19.0	5.7	5.9	0.2	0.7	0.5	0.1	n/a
Seattle, WA	11.0	19.5	2.7	0.6	0.6	0.4	0.4	0.6	1.6
Sioux Falls, SD	13.1	21.0	20.2	0.1	0.1	n/a	n/a	0.8	<0.1
Tampa, FL	23.1	16.9	3.8	1.7	0.7	0.4	0.3	0.8	0.4
Tucson, AZ	18.9	10.4	2.4	0.6	1.0	0.4	0.4	0.2	0.3
Tulsa, OK	5.6	37.8	8.6	1.7	0.5	0.2	0.1	0.1	<0.1
Virginia Beach, VA	8.3	21.3	6.9	3.7	1.0	0.3	0.2	0.3	0.3
Washington, DC	16.1	12.3	6.5	3.3	3.3	1.0	0.9	0.9	0.5
Wichita, KS	12.7	19.4	23.2	2.6	0.1	<0.1	0.1	0.2	0.5
Wilmington, NC	13.2	17.9	9.3	4.6	0.7	0.3	0.1	0.3	n/a
Winston-Salem, NC	9.3	31.4	13.6	3.4	0.8	n/a	<0.1	0.3	0.1
U.S.	18.7	16.5	5.2	2.3	1.3	0.6	0.4	0.4	0.3

Note: Figures are the number of adherents as a percentage of the total population; Figures cover the Metropolitan Statistical Area (MSA)
Source: 2020 U.S. Religion Census, Association of Statisticians of American Religious Bodies; The Association of Religion Data Archives

Real Gross Domestic Product (GDP)

Metro Area	2017	2018	2019	2020	2021	2022	2023	Rank[1]
Albuquerque, NM	41.9	42.7	43.9	43.3	45.7	47.4	48.6	70
Anchorage, AK	25.8	26.0	26.0	25.3	25.9	26.3	27.3	116
Ann Arbor, MI	24.0	24.6	25.6	25.0	26.3	27.0	27.8	114
Athens, GA	10.0	10.3	10.3	9.8	10.4	10.8	11.0	211
Atlanta, GA	398.2	413.0	429.7	416.6	444.7	462.0	471.7	10
Austin, TX	141.1	149.3	159.1	163.6	181.1	198.5	207.5	20
Baltimore, MD	198.3	200.4	201.6	194.8	204.8	210.2	213.5	19
Billings, MT	10.2	10.3	10.0	9.8	10.5	10.5	10.9	215
Boise City, ID	32.3	34.8	36.4	37.0	40.4	43.4	44.6	76
Boston, MA	433.8	451.3	467.4	463.3	495.9	507.8	515.4	8
Boulder, CO	26.3	27.2	29.7	29.1	31.3	31.9	32.9	100
Cape Coral, FL	31.3	32.6	33.3	33.2	36.0	38.8	40.4	84
Cedar Rapids, IA	18.3	18.7	18.3	18.0	19.2	19.0	18.8	155
Charleston, SC	41.7	43.4	45.5	44.2	46.6	49.6	52.1	65
Charlotte, NC	168.1	171.6	177.5	179.1	190.5	197.3	206.5	21
Chicago, IL	674.6	691.2	697.5	659.6	698.0	715.6	725.7	3
Cincinnati, OH	145.2	145.3	152.3	149.5	155.9	157.4	160.1	29
Clarksville, TN	12.3	12.4	12.7	12.9	13.6	13.9	14.2	189
Cleveland, OH	128.6	130.6	134.0	129.2	136.3	139.1	139.9	36
College Station, TX	12.5	13.0	13.6	13.5	14.2	14.7	15.8	171
Colorado Springs, CO	35.1	36.2	37.7	38.8	41.1	41.8	43.6	79
Columbia, MO	10.0	10.0	10.4	10.1	10.6	10.7	11.0	213
Columbia, SC	41.0	41.7	42.7	42.2	44.6	45.5	47.0	73
Columbus, OH	129.9	131.5	135.7	134.2	143.6	145.5	148.0	34
Dallas, TX	483.7	506.2	526.2	520.2	562.1	594.5	613.4	5
Davenport, IA	21.6	21.4	21.6	21.0	21.6	22.0	22.4	136
Denver, CO	202.2	211.2	222.5	222.8	239.1	250.3	259.0	18
Des Moines, IA	51.8	51.9	54.2	55.6	60.7	59.8	60.4	57
Detroit, MI	256.2	261.5	262.7	249.7	263.7	271.7	276.5	16
Durham, NC	46.4	48.7	50.1	51.5	55.1	57.0	59.0	58
El Paso, TX	30.4	31.4	33.1	32.9	35.3	35.9	38.1	87
Eugene, OR	15.9	16.3	16.4	16.3	17.4	17.7	18.1	157
Fargo, ND	15.0	15.1	15.4	14.9	15.7	15.8	16.3	167
Fort Collins, CO	18.6	19.5	20.3	20.2	21.3	21.7	22.0	139
Fort Wayne, IN	22.4	23.3	23.5	21.8	23.4	24.3	24.7	120
Fort Worth, TX	483.7	506.2	526.2	520.2	562.1	594.5	613.4	5
Gainesville, FL	14.5	15.0	15.4	15.4	16.4	17.0	17.7	159
Green Bay, WI	20.0	20.6	20.7	20.1	20.5	20.8	21.1	144
Greensboro, NC	41.2	41.4	41.0	39.5	41.1	42.2	42.5	80
Honolulu, HI	65.8	66.0	65.6	60.1	62.8	64.5	66.0	55
Houston, TX	470.7	491.2	486.9	478.0	501.2	522.6	550.8	7
Huntsville, AL	27.5	28.6	30.2	30.7	32.6	34.1	36.1	92
Indianapolis, IN	135.9	140.7	143.8	142.8	152.5	158.8	161.8	28
Jacksonville, FL	80.3	83.0	86.5	87.7	94.4	100.4	104.7	40
Kansas City, MO	133.8	136.4	139.5	136.8	141.7	148.9	152.8	32
Lafayette, LA	21.1	22.0	21.8	20.8	21.8	21.8	22.6	132
Las Vegas, NV	116.3	122.7	128.2	117.3	130.1	138.5	142.8	35
Lexington, KY	28.7	29.5	30.0	28.7	29.6	30.6	31.4	105
Lincoln, NE	19.6	19.9	20.3	20.2	21.1	22.1	22.8	130
Little Rock, AR	36.5	37.1	37.4	37.7	39.4	39.9	41.3	82
Los Angeles, CA	965.3	991.3	1,026.5	982.0	1,041.7	1,065.3	1,075.1	2
Louisville, KY	70.8	71.6	74.3	72.8	76.4	77.9	79.2	49
Madison, WI	47.4	49.3	50.6	49.4	52.3	53.4	55.1	59
Manchester, NH	26.0	26.5	27.2	27.0	29.5	30.0	30.5	108
McAllen, TX	20.7	21.2	22.0	21.5	22.7	23.1	24.0	124
Memphis, TN	75.3	76.0	76.6	75.7	79.9	79.7	81.2	47

Table continued on following page.

Metro Area	2017	2018	2019	2020	2021	2022	2023	Rank[1]
Miami, FL	347.0	359.9	367.6	353.8	391.4	415.2	431.9	12
Midland, TX	21.9	27.6	33.1	31.1	31.7	31.0	44.2	78
Milwaukee, WI	99.3	100.8	102.3	98.2	102.4	105.2	106.6	39
Minneapolis, MN	257.8	265.7	270.1	260.6	275.7	281.3	286.7	15
Nashville, TN	130.5	134.6	139.3	138.4	154.0	163.2	168.2	27
New Orleans, LA	78.2	78.1	79.8	73.4	76.8	75.7	79.6	48
New York, NY	1,714.1	1,766.3	1,801.1	1,744.7	1,834.5	1,875.1	1,905.2	1
Oklahoma City, OK	74.4	77.0	78.4	76.1	76.7	76.3	81.6	46
Omaha, NE	64.3	65.7	66.4	65.2	68.9	73.7	75.3	50
Orlando, FL	136.2	141.2	146.8	140.3	156.9	167.8	175.3	26
Philadelphia, PA	425.4	432.3	437.0	420.4	438.8	450.2	459.5	11
Phoenix, AZ	246.1	257.4	269.4	274.6	299.1	313.6	322.8	14
Pittsburgh, PA	150.7	154.3	155.9	147.7	153.2	155.0	159.6	30
Portland, OR	155.8	162.7	166.7	164.9	174.8	178.8	182.0	25
Providence, RI	84.6	84.7	86.8	84.2	88.5	89.3	90.4	45
Provo, UT	25.5	27.6	30.1	31.5	34.1	35.8	37.4	90
Raleigh, NC	84.9	89.5	92.3	92.4	101.0	105.8	110.6	38
Reno, NV	29.4	28.8	29.9	30.1	33.2	33.6	34.1	96
Richmond, VA	84.5	86.5	88.6	87.2	91.8	93.9	94.8	44
Rochester, MN	13.1	13.6	13.8	13.6	14.1	14.4	14.9	182
Sacramento, CA	131.2	136.9	141.9	138.9	147.4	150.4	153.8	31
Saint Louis, MO	164.4	166.6	169.5	165.7	175.8	180.2	184.8	24
Saint Paul, MN	257.8	265.7	270.1	260.6	275.7	281.3	286.7	15
Salem, OR	17.1	18.0	18.6	18.6	19.8	20.1	20.6	147
Salt Lake City, UT	92.0	97.2	103.0	102.5	111.3	114.3	118.0	37
San Antonio, TX	118.9	124.5	129.0	127.4	134.2	143.7	150.3	33
San Diego, CA	224.8	230.5	236.6	233.3	250.4	258.0	261.7	17
San Francisco, CA	526.6	560.6	594.3	596.5	662.4	659.3	681.9	4
San Jose, CA	282.7	304.6	319.4	339.4	381.6	379.7	392.5	13
Santa Rosa, CA	28.9	30.2	30.5	29.6	31.7	31.0	31.0	106
Savannah, GA	21.2	21.5	22.3	22.2	23.9	24.5	25.7	118
Seattle, WA	368.2	395.7	417.4	418.4	449.5	459.5	487.8	9
Sioux Falls, SD	22.2	21.9	22.8	22.0	23.2	22.8	23.2	128
Tampa, FL	152.7	158.0	163.9	165.5	180.0	190.7	198.9	23
Tucson, AZ	42.3	43.9	45.4	45.3	47.9	48.6	50.8	68
Tulsa, OK	51.6	53.1	52.0	49.2	51.1	51.6	53.9	61
Virginia Beach, VA	94.9	93.9	94.9	94.3	99.0	100.9	104.0	41
Washington, DC	528.9	542.4	551.9	543.4	571.1	584.2	600.2	6
Wichita, KS	35.9	35.8	35.8	34.7	35.7	36.7	37.7	89
Wilmington, NC	14.1	14.5	15.1	15.1	16.5	17.1	17.7	160
Winston-Salem, NC	34.9	34.2	34.7	32.6	34.8	35.7	36.1	91
U.S.[2]	17,619.1	18,160.7	18,642.5	18,238.9	19,387.6	19,896.6	20,436.3	—

Note: Figures are in billions of chained 2017 dollars; Figures cover the Metropolitan Statistical Area (MSA); (1) Rank is based on 2023 data and ranges from 1 to 384; (2) Figures cover real GDP within metropolitan areas
Source: U.S. Bureau of Economic Analysis

Economic Growth

Metro Area	2014	2015	2016	2017	2018	2019	2020	2021	2022	2023
Albuquerque, NM	2.0	1.2	1.7	0.4	1.9	2.9	-1.3	5.4	3.9	2.4
Anchorage, AK	0.3	4.3	1.2	-1.5	0.7	-0.3	-2.6	2.6	1.4	3.7
Ann Arbor, MI	1.7	3.7	2.2	3.3	2.5	4.0	-2.5	5.2	2.6	2.9
Athens, GA	2.4	4.3	2.2	5.7	3.5	-0.7	-4.3	5.7	4.5	1.5
Atlanta, GA	4.6	5.3	5.3	4.8	3.7	4.0	-3.0	6.7	3.9	2.1
Austin, TX	5.7	7.7	4.2	4.5	5.8	6.5	2.8	10.7	9.6	4.5
Baltimore, MD	1.6	2.0	3.4	2.1	1.0	0.6	-3.4	5.1	2.6	1.6
Billings, MT	5.4	4.6	-5.8	7.2	0.6	-2.4	-2.3	7.3	0.1	3.5
Boise City, ID	4.5	1.6	4.2	5.5	7.8	4.7	1.6	9.1	7.5	2.9
Boston, MA	2.1	4.0	1.7	2.3	4.0	3.6	-0.9	7.0	2.4	1.5
Boulder, CO	3.3	3.9	3.5	4.9	3.7	9.0	-1.9	7.5	1.9	3.4
Cape Coral, FL	5.0	6.1	7.5	0.6	4.1	2.4	-0.5	8.5	7.8	4.2
Cedar Rapids, IA	4.4	4.0	3.1	0.1	1.8	-1.9	-1.8	6.7	-1.0	-0.9
Charleston, SC	2.8	4.7	5.6	2.0	4.0	4.8	-2.7	5.4	6.4	5.2
Charlotte, NC	3.3	4.2	3.0	3.7	2.1	3.4	0.9	6.4	3.6	4.7
Chicago, IL	2.3	2.4	0.8	1.4	2.5	0.9	-5.4	5.8	2.5	1.4
Cincinnati, OH	3.6	2.9	3.7	3.1	0.0	4.8	-1.8	4.3	1.0	1.7
Clarksville, TN	-1.2	0.5	-1.0	0.0	1.1	2.0	1.4	5.9	2.1	1.9
Cleveland, OH	2.3	0.8	0.1	2.4	1.6	2.6	-3.6	5.5	2.1	0.6
College Station, TX	6.3	6.2	-0.3	1.7	4.3	4.5	-0.2	4.6	4.0	7.4
Colorado Springs, CO	0.9	1.1	2.0	4.2	3.3	4.2	2.9	5.8	1.7	4.4
Columbia, MO	0.4	2.1	0.4	2.4	0.6	4.0	-2.9	5.1	0.5	2.8
Columbia, SC	3.6	2.9	2.9	0.3	1.6	2.4	-1.0	5.6	2.0	3.4
Columbus, OH	3.6	2.1	2.1	4.4	1.2	3.2	-1.1	7.0	1.3	1.8
Dallas, TX	3.8	4.8	2.3	3.6	4.6	3.9	-1.1	8.1	5.8	3.2
Davenport, IA	0.4	-1.4	-0.7	1.0	-0.7	0.8	-2.4	2.8	1.6	2.1
Denver, CO	4.5	5.3	2.2	3.8	4.4	5.3	0.1	7.3	4.7	3.5
Des Moines, IA	12.6	8.5	3.8	-1.3	0.2	4.3	2.6	9.3	-1.5	1.0
Detroit, MI	1.4	1.7	1.9	0.9	2.1	0.4	-4.9	5.6	3.0	1.8
Durham, NC	-1.9	-1.7	-0.7	-0.5	4.9	2.8	2.8	7.0	3.4	3.5
El Paso, TX	-1.5	1.5	0.9	2.1	3.1	5.4	-0.5	7.2	1.9	6.1
Eugene, OR	1.5	5.0	3.0	3.8	2.7	0.4	-0.7	7.0	1.9	2.3
Fargo, ND	7.0	3.5	-0.3	3.3	0.7	2.5	-3.4	5.3	0.4	3.6
Fort Collins, CO	5.3	4.6	4.0	7.7	4.8	4.4	-0.9	5.8	1.9	1.3
Fort Wayne, IN	7.7	4.3	3.2	3.8	3.8	0.7	-7.1	7.2	4.2	1.4
Fort Worth, TX	3.8	4.8	2.3	3.6	4.6	3.9	-1.1	8.1	5.8	3.2
Gainesville, FL	3.2	1.9	2.1	3.8	3.3	2.9	0.1	6.5	3.4	4.5
Green Bay, WI	6.3	2.8	1.0	-0.2	3.2	0.4	-2.8	1.9	1.4	1.3
Greensboro, NC	-0.4	2.5	-1.1	0.5	0.5	-1.1	-3.6	4.0	2.8	0.5
Honolulu, HI	0.9	2.7	1.9	2.1	0.4	-0.6	-8.5	4.5	2.6	2.4
Houston, TX	1.7	5.5	-2.1	0.7	4.4	-0.9	-1.8	4.8	4.3	5.4
Huntsville, AL	0.3	1.8	3.1	3.8	3.9	5.7	1.6	6.0	4.6	6.0
Indianapolis, IN	2.1	-2.5	2.4	2.4	3.6	2.2	-0.7	6.8	4.1	1.9
Jacksonville, FL	2.4	4.2	3.8	4.5	3.3	4.3	1.3	7.7	6.3	4.3
Kansas City, MO	2.7	3.8	0.5	3.3	2.0	2.3	-1.9	3.6	5.0	2.7
Lafayette, LA	1.4	-7.6	-9.3	0.0	4.4	-1.0	-4.5	4.6	0.1	3.8
Las Vegas, NV	1.5	4.4	3.2	3.6	5.5	4.5	-8.5	10.9	6.4	3.2
Lexington, KY	2.6	3.9	2.2	1.2	2.8	1.9	-4.5	3.1	3.6	2.7
Lincoln, NE	4.9	3.5	1.7	5.3	2.0	1.9	-0.7	4.5	4.6	3.3
Little Rock, AR	1.1	1.4	1.1	-0.8	1.5	0.8	0.8	4.6	1.1	3.5
Los Angeles, CA	2.7	4.3	1.8	3.7	2.7	3.6	-4.3	6.1	2.3	0.9
Louisville, KY	1.3	2.6	1.9	1.7	1.2	3.8	-2.0	4.9	2.0	1.6
Madison, WI	5.0	3.7	3.3	1.5	3.9	2.7	-2.4	5.9	2.2	3.2
Manchester, NH	2.2	3.4	1.6	0.4	1.9	3.0	-0.9	9.3	1.7	1.6
McAllen, TX	1.7	1.1	-0.4	0.5	2.2	3.8	-2.1	5.4	1.9	3.8
Memphis, TN	-0.2	2.0	1.3	1.8	0.8	0.9	-1.2	5.5	-0.2	1.9

Table continued on following page.

Metro Area	2014	2015	2016	2017	2018	2019	2020	2021	2022	2023
Miami, FL	3.4	4.4	3.1	4.5	3.7	2.1	-3.7	10.6	6.1	4.0
Midland, TX	9.0	9.5	-1.7	14.0	25.9	20.3	-6.1	1.8	-2.3	42.9
Milwaukee, WI	0.6	1.2	0.5	1.5	1.6	1.5	-4.0	4.3	2.7	1.4
Minneapolis, MN	3.8	2.2	1.6	1.9	3.1	1.6	-3.5	5.8	2.0	2.0
Nashville, TN	4.6	6.7	3.7	4.6	3.1	3.6	-0.7	11.3	6.0	3.1
New Orleans, LA	1.2	0.3	0.8	5.8	-0.1	2.1	-8.0	4.6	-1.3	5.0
New York, NY	1.9	2.2	1.7	2.0	3.0	2.0	-3.1	5.1	2.2	1.6
Oklahoma City, OK	6.4	4.2	0.3	3.1	3.5	1.7	-2.8	0.7	-0.5	6.9
Omaha, NE	6.2	3.3	0.5	4.6	2.1	1.1	-1.8	5.6	7.0	2.2
Orlando, FL	3.8	5.5	3.8	5.5	3.7	4.0	-4.4	11.9	6.9	4.5
Philadelphia, PA	2.5	1.7	1.4	-0.3	1.6	1.1	-3.8	4.4	2.6	2.1
Phoenix, AZ	1.6	3.1	3.6	4.6	4.6	4.7	1.9	8.9	4.8	2.9
Pittsburgh, PA	1.8	3.1	0.2	4.4	2.4	1.0	-5.3	3.7	1.2	2.9
Portland, OR	3.4	5.7	4.7	5.7	4.4	2.5	-1.1	6.0	2.3	1.8
Providence, RI	1.6	2.5	0.2	0.5	0.1	2.4	-3.0	5.1	0.9	1.2
Provo, UT	4.7	8.2	7.0	6.8	8.3	9.1	4.6	8.3	4.9	4.4
Raleigh, NC	6.1	7.4	6.5	4.6	5.4	3.1	0.2	9.3	4.7	4.6
Reno, NV	0.4	7.7	4.1	7.1	-2.0	3.9	0.8	10.2	1.4	1.4
Richmond, VA	1.2	3.9	1.5	1.8	2.4	2.4	-1.6	5.3	2.3	1.0
Rochester, MN	1.6	2.9	1.4	3.6	3.5	2.0	-1.6	3.9	2.0	3.2
Sacramento, CA	2.8	4.3	2.1	2.9	4.4	3.6	-2.1	6.1	2.1	2.2
Saint Louis, MO	1.4	0.8	0.1	-0.4	1.3	1.7	-2.2	6.1	2.5	2.5
Saint Paul, MN	3.8	2.2	1.6	1.9	3.1	1.6	-3.5	5.8	2.0	2.0
Salem, OR	3.4	5.4	5.1	4.5	5.6	3.2	-0.3	6.4	1.7	2.6
Salt Lake City, UT	3.2	3.4	4.7	5.2	5.7	6.0	-0.5	8.6	2.7	3.2
San Antonio, TX	5.3	5.7	0.9	0.3	4.7	3.6	-1.3	5.4	7.1	4.6
San Diego, CA	3.1	3.3	1.3	3.7	2.6	2.7	-1.4	7.3	3.1	1.4
San Francisco, CA	6.1	6.0	5.7	9.3	6.5	6.0	0.4	11.0	-0.5	3.4
San Jose, CA	7.2	8.9	6.1	4.9	7.8	4.8	6.3	12.4	-0.5	3.4
Santa Rosa, CA	4.1	4.8	2.5	1.6	4.7	0.9	-3.0	7.0	-2.2	0.2
Savannah, GA	4.3	3.0	3.9	2.5	1.4	4.0	-0.5	7.7	2.6	4.9
Seattle, WA	4.9	4.6	4.1	8.2	7.5	5.5	0.2	7.4	2.2	6.2
Sioux Falls, SD	5.5	1.3	1.4	1.5	-1.2	4.3	-3.5	5.4	-2.0	2.0
Tampa, FL	2.0	4.2	3.3	2.1	3.5	3.7	1.0	8.8	5.9	4.3
Tucson, AZ	0.2	-0.5	3.4	3.5	3.7	3.5	-0.3	5.7	1.4	4.6
Tulsa, OK	5.4	1.7	-5.9	3.5	2.9	-2.1	-5.4	3.9	1.0	4.4
Virginia Beach, VA	-1.0	1.7	1.1	0.7	-1.2	1.2	-0.7	5.0	1.9	3.2
Washington, DC	1.2	2.1	2.5	2.4	2.5	1.8	-1.6	5.1	2.3	2.7
Wichita, KS	6.2	5.6	8.2	0.4	-0.1	-0.2	-2.9	2.8	2.9	2.8
Wilmington, NC	4.1	1.5	5.1	0.6	3.0	4.2	0.1	9.2	3.6	3.5
Winston-Salem, NC	2.6	1.0	1.4	2.6	-2.1	1.4	-6.0	6.9	2.5	1.3
U.S.[1]	2.6	3.2	2.0	2.7	3.1	2.7	-2.2	6.3	2.6	2.7

Note: Figures are real gross domestic product growth rates and represent percent change from preceding period; Figures cover the Metropolitan Statistical Area (MSA); (1) Figures are the average growth rates within metropolitan areas
Source: U.S. Bureau of Economic Analysis

Metropolitan Area Exports

Metro Area	2018	2019	2020	2021	2022	2023	Rank[1]
Albuquerque, NM	771.5	1,629.7	1,265.3	2,215.0	939.7	789.4	195
Anchorage, AK	1,510.8	1,348.0	990.9	n/a	n/a	n/a	n/a
Ann Arbor, MI	1,538.7	1,432.7	1,183.1	1,230.7	1,334.2	1,196.2	156
Athens, GA	378.1	442.1	338.7	448.1	489.9	533.9	217
Atlanta, GA	24,091.6	25,800.8	25,791.0	28,116.4	30,833.1	32,336.4	13
Austin, TX	12,929.9	12,509.0	13,041.5	15,621.9	17,290.7	17,251.5	27
Baltimore, MD	6,039.2	7,081.8	6,084.6	8,200.6	7,820.0	10,196.2	43
Billings, MT	114.3	141.9	116.0	173.8	156.0	119.2	349
Boise City, ID	2,771.7	2,062.8	1,632.9	1,937.1	2,156.7	1,922.6	121
Boston, MA	24,450.1	23,505.8	23,233.8	32,084.2	33,101.8	34,519.4	12
Boulder, CO	1,044.1	1,014.9	1,110.4	1,078.0	1,201.9	1,213.1	153
Cape Coral, FL	668.0	694.9	654.8	797.5	886.9	935.4	177
Cedar Rapids, IA	1,025.0	1,028.4	832.0	980.0	1,018.7	1,175.4	159
Charleston, SC	10,943.2	16,337.9	6,110.5	3,381.6	4,256.0	9,497.6	44
Charlotte, NC	14,083.2	13,892.4	8,225.6	10,554.3	12,223.1	11,470.3	34
Chicago, IL	47,287.8	42,438.8	41,279.4	54,498.1	63,374.6	56,656.6	5
Cincinnati, OH	27,396.3	28,778.3	21,002.2	23,198.7	29,285.0	31,216.2	14
Clarksville, TN	435.5	341.8	246.8	288.7	376.7	445.6	236
Cleveland, OH	9,382.9	8,829.9	7,415.8	8,560.4	9,561.2	10,206.2	42
College Station, TX	153.0	160.5	114.9	110.3	136.2	180.0	323
Colorado Springs, CO	850.6	864.2	979.2	866.9	1,209.5	1,425.7	137
Columbia, MO	238.6	291.4	256.2	335.4	368.7	474.1	230
Columbia, SC	2,083.8	2,184.6	2,058.8	2,100.2	2,351.3	2,160.3	112
Columbus, OH	7,529.5	7,296.6	6,304.8	6,557.9	7,597.3	8,418.9	47
Dallas, TX	36,260.9	39,474.0	35,642.0	43,189.0	50,632.9	51,863.7	6
Davenport, IA	6,761.9	6,066.3	5,097.5	6,341.0	8,173.6	6,050.0	57
Denver, CO	4,544.3	4,555.6	4,604.4	4,670.8	5,761.7	5,724.2	59
Des Moines, IA	1,293.7	1,437.8	1,414.0	1,706.6	1,706.8	2,175.7	110
Detroit, MI	44,131.4	41,070.4	30,715.1	35,433.2	40,395.3	45,591.4	7
Durham, NC	3,945.8	4,452.9	3,359.3	3,326.4	4,071.8	4,898.7	65
El Paso, TX	30,052.0	32,749.6	27,154.4	32,397.9	36,488.3	35,223.0	11
Eugene, OR	400.1	360.0	340.6	426.7	434.9	415.2	241
Fargo, ND	553.5	515.0	438.3	539.4	518.7	880.1	185
Fort Collins, CO	1,021.8	1,060.0	1,092.5	1,132.5	1,178.8	1,180.5	157
Fort Wayne, IN	1,593.3	1,438.5	1,144.6	1,592.7	1,787.5	2,032.1	115
Fort Worth, TX	36,260.9	39,474.0	35,642.0	43,189.0	50,632.9	51,863.7	6
Gainesville, FL	370.2	297.2	260.9	320.7	307.2	306.6	274
Green Bay, WI	1,044.3	928.2	736.4	765.6	855.1	835.1	190
Greensboro, NC	3,053.5	2,561.8	2,007.3	2,356.2	2,375.6	2,239.4	108
Honolulu, HI	438.9	308.6	169.0	164.3	258.8	450.6	234
Houston, TX	120,714.3	129,656.0	104,538.2	140,750.4	191,846.9	175,470.1	1
Huntsville, AL	1,608.7	1,534.2	1,263.0	1,579.5	1,558.7	1,762.1	125
Indianapolis, IN	11,069.9	11,148.7	11,100.4	12,740.4	14,671.5	23,080.6	20
Jacksonville, FL	2,406.7	2,975.5	2,473.3	2,683.7	3,007.8	2,730.8	92
Kansas City, MO	7,316.9	7,652.6	7,862.7	9,177.6	9,623.5	10,627.2	40
Lafayette, LA	1,001.7	1,086.2	946.2	895.7	911.8	836.2	189
Las Vegas, NV	2,240.6	2,430.8	1,705.9	1,866.2	2,116.3	2,762.3	91
Lexington, KY	2,148.0	2,093.8	1,586.3	1,880.0	2,677.2	3,343.3	81
Lincoln, NE	885.6	807.0	726.3	872.6	1,161.3	1,082.2	165
Little Rock, AR	1,607.4	1,642.5	n/a	1,370.6	1,373.7	1,464.0	134
Los Angeles, CA	64,814.6	61,041.1	50,185.4	58,588.4	60,979.7	59,561.6	4
Louisville, KY	8,987.0	9,105.5	8,360.3	10,262.8	10,618.7	11,072.0	37
Madison, WI	2,460.2	2,337.6	2,450.5	2,756.3	2,893.8	2,822.9	90
Manchester, NH	1,651.4	1,587.1	1,704.9	2,077.6	2,349.8	2,416.7	101
McAllen, TX	6,627.9	5,234.1	4,087.6	5,164.6	5,677.1	7,072.4	51
Memphis, TN	12,695.4	13,751.7	13,350.3	16,761.5	17,835.3	17,853.5	25

Table continued on following page.

Metro Area	2018	2019	2020	2021	2022	2023	Rank[1]
Miami, FL	35,650.2	35,498.9	29,112.1	36,011.3	41,517.8	44,256.4	8
Midland, TX	63.6	63.7	57.7	49.9	76.2	72.4	365
Milwaukee, WI	7,337.6	6,896.3	6,624.0	7,282.8	8,742.5	9,352.5	45
Minneapolis, MN	20,016.2	18,633.0	17,109.5	21,098.8	21,964.3	22,209.4	23
Nashville, TN	8,723.7	7,940.7	6,569.9	8,256.1	9,347.5	10,385.4	41
New Orleans, LA	36,570.4	34,109.6	31,088.4	35,773.5	52,912.9	38,978.6	9
New York, NY	97,692.4	87,365.7	75,745.4	103,930.9	120,643.7	106,209.0	2
Oklahoma City, OK	1,489.4	1,434.5	1,326.6	1,773.2	2,019.1	2,277.7	107
Omaha, NE	4,371.6	3,725.7	3,852.5	4,595.1	4,585.5	3,411.0	80
Orlando, FL	3,131.7	3,363.9	2,849.8	3,313.6	4,096.9	4,443.5	71
Philadelphia, PA	23,663.2	24,721.3	23,022.1	28,724.4	29,352.1	28,760.2	16
Phoenix, AZ	13,614.9	15,136.6	11,073.9	14,165.1	16,658.8	17,553.6	26
Pittsburgh, PA	9,824.2	9,672.9	7,545.1	9,469.6	11,188.3	11,538.4	33
Portland, OR	21,442.9	23,761.9	27,824.7	33,787.5	34,368.0	26,973.2	18
Providence, RI	6,236.6	7,424.8	6,685.2	6,708.2	7,179.7	6,517.8	53
Provo, UT	1,788.1	1,783.7	1,888.5	2,053.8	1,318.4	1,416.7	140
Raleigh, NC	3,193.2	3,546.8	3,372.0	3,962.7	4,714.1	5,965.8	58
Reno, NV	2,631.7	2,598.3	4,553.3	4,503.0	3,864.0	3,434.1	78
Richmond, VA	3,535.0	3,203.2	2,719.1	3,010.7	3,283.5	2,579.8	95
Rochester, MN	537.6	390.1	194.0	224.9	215.9	258.7	293
Sacramento, CA	6,222.8	5,449.2	4,980.9	5,682.3	5,716.7	7,586.6	50
Saint Louis, MO	10,866.8	10,711.1	9,089.4	10,486.1	14,215.6	13,817.0	30
Saint Paul, MN	20,016.2	18,633.0	17,109.5	21,098.8	21,964.3	22,209.4	23
Salem, OR	410.2	405.7	350.5	372.0	422.3	404.8	244
Salt Lake City, UT	9,748.6	13,273.9	13,565.5	13,469.1	12,340.1	12,775.2	32
San Antonio, TX	11,678.1	11,668.0	10,987.9	13,086.4	13,173.6	12,821.8	31
San Diego, CA	20,156.8	19,774.1	18,999.7	23,687.8	24,657.9	22,975.3	22
San Francisco, CA	27,417.0	28,003.8	23,864.5	29,972.0	30,649.0	24,253.0	19
San Jose, CA	22,224.2	20,909.4	19,534.5	22,293.6	24,342.2	22,985.4	21
Santa Rosa, CA	1,231.7	1,234.5	1,131.4	1,301.8	1,297.3	1,121.8	161
Savannah, GA	5,407.8	4,925.5	4,557.0	5,520.5	6,171.2	6,206.1	56
Seattle, WA	59,742.9	41,249.0	23,851.0	28,866.7	34,159.9	36,267.3	10
Sioux Falls, SD	400.0	431.5	524.9	547.3	371.3	510.9	224
Tampa, FL	4,966.7	6,219.7	5,082.2	5,754.7	9,588.2	7,923.6	49
Tucson, AZ	2,824.8	2,943.7	2,640.7	2,846.1	3,779.4	4,503.0	68
Tulsa, OK	3,351.7	3,399.2	2,567.8	3,064.8	3,379.2	3,234.5	84
Virginia Beach, VA	3,950.6	3,642.4	4,284.3	4,566.3	5,750.1	6,338.3	54
Washington, DC	13,602.7	14,563.8	13,537.3	12,210.8	14,001.9	14,758.9	29
Wichita, KS	3,817.0	3,494.7	2,882.1	3,615.3	4,550.4	4,475.1	69
Wilmington, NC	634.4	526.4	553.6	497.8	593.6	671.5	206
Winston-Salem, NC	1,107.5	1,209.1	913.1	918.2	1,012.1	1,071.1	166
U.S.	1,664,056.1	1,645,173.7	1,431,406.6	1,753,941.4	2,062,937.4	2,019,160.5	—

Note: Figures are in millions of dollars; Figures cover the Metropolitan Statistical Area (MSA); (1) Rank is based on 2023 data and ranges from 1 to 386
Source: U.S. Department of Commerce, International Trade Administration, Office of Trade and Economic Analysis, Industry and Analysis, Exports by Metropolitan Area, data extracted April 2, 2025

Building Permits: City

City	Single-Family			Multi-Family			Total		
	2023	2024	Pct. Chg.	2023	2024	Pct. Chg.	2023	2024	Pct. Chg.
Albuquerque, NM	587	525	-10.6	512	574	12.1	1,099	1,099	0.0
Anchorage, AK	271	161	-40.6	28	180	542.9	299	341	14.0
Ann Arbor, MI	161	28	-82.6	61	266	336.1	222	294	32.4
Athens, GA	168	212	26.2	238	960	303.4	406	1,172	188.7
Atlanta, GA	1,139	791	-30.6	6,482	7,318	12.9	7,621	8,109	6.4
Austin, TX	1,799	1,946	8.2	11,885	7,498	-36.9	13,684	9,444	-31.0
Baltimore, MD	92	165	79.3	1,751	1,108	-36.7	1,843	1,273	-30.9
Billings, MT	259	327	26.3	0	328	—	259	655	152.9
Boise City, ID	447	468	4.7	1,450	273	-81.2	1,897	741	-60.9
Boston, MA	108	72	-33.3	1,943	1,717	-11.6	2,051	1,789	-12.8
Boulder, CO	30	35	16.7	225	371	64.9	255	406	59.2
Cape Coral, FL	2,023	2,671	32.0	1,972	726	-63.2	3,995	3,397	-15.0
Cedar Rapids, IA	145	143	-1.4	229	465	103.1	374	608	62.6
Charleston, SC	891	878	-1.5	363	266	-26.7	1,254	1,144	-8.8
Charlotte, NC	n/a	n/a	n/a	n/a	n/a	n/a	n/a	n/a	n/a
Chicago, IL	290	325	12.1	3,326	4,046	21.6	3,616	4,371	20.9
Cincinnati, OH	117	110	-6.0	514	114	-77.8	631	224	-64.5
Clarksville, TN	805	1,366	69.7	1,455	703	-51.7	2,260	2,069	-8.5
Cleveland, OH	161	234	45.3	644	662	2.8	805	896	11.3
College Station, TX	448	650	45.1	293	462	57.7	741	1,112	50.1
Colorado Springs, CO	n/a	n/a	n/a	n/a	n/a	n/a	n/a	n/a	n/a
Columbia, MO	314	461	46.8	56	549	880.4	370	1,010	173.0
Columbia, SC	883	833	-5.7	718	1,315	83.1	1,601	2,148	34.2
Columbus, OH	943	828	-12.2	4,340	5,256	21.1	5,283	6,084	15.2
Dallas, TX	1,995	1,957	-1.9	4,429	4,081	-7.9	6,424	6,038	-6.0
Davenport, IA	94	149	58.5	121	162	33.9	215	311	44.7
Denver, CO	1,174	872	-25.7	4,551	3,122	-31.4	5,725	3,994	-30.2
Des Moines, IA	248	218	-12.1	321	400	24.6	569	618	8.6
Detroit, MI	397	483	21.7	828	1,436	73.4	1,225	1,919	56.7
Durham, NC	1,687	1,822	8.0	2,678	971	-63.7	4,365	2,793	-36.0
El Paso, TX	1,572	1,644	4.6	280	243	-13.2	1,852	1,887	1.9
Eugene, OR	171	309	80.7	422	693	64.2	593	1,002	69.0
Fargo, ND	292	241	-17.5	980	410	-58.2	1,272	651	-48.8
Fort Collins, CO	372	371	-0.3	631	314	-50.2	1,003	685	-31.7
Fort Wayne, IN	n/a	n/a	n/a	n/a	n/a	n/a	n/a	n/a	n/a
Fort Worth, TX	6,631	6,257	-5.6	3,429	6,891	101.0	10,060	13,148	30.7
Gainesville, FL	236	296	25.4	544	922	69.5	780	1,218	56.2
Green Bay, WI	37	42	13.5	0	434	—	37	476	1,186.5
Greensboro, NC	704	618	-12.2	1,063	1,336	25.7	1,767	1,954	10.6
Honolulu, HI	n/a	n/a	n/a	n/a	n/a	n/a	n/a	n/a	n/a
Houston, TX	6,609	6,808	3.0	9,821	5,090	-48.2	16,430	11,898	-27.6
Huntsville, AL	1,403	1,245	-11.3	1,197	240	-79.9	2,600	1,485	-42.9
Indianapolis, IN	896	1,170	30.6	1,517	653	-57.0	2,413	1,823	-24.5
Jacksonville, FL	4,223	5,037	19.3	5,485	1,361	-75.2	9,708	6,398	-34.1
Kansas City, MO	776	429	-44.7	458	2,449	434.7	1,234	2,878	133.2
Lafayette, LA	n/a	n/a	n/a	n/a	n/a	n/a	n/a	n/a	n/a
Las Vegas, NV	2,590	2,655	2.5	1,026	935	-8.9	3,616	3,590	-0.7
Lexington, KY	624	492	-21.2	774	544	-29.7	1,398	1,036	-25.9
Lincoln, NE	699	937	34.0	1,282	793	-38.1	1,981	1,730	-12.7
Little Rock, AR	703	468	-33.4	230	18	-92.2	933	486	-47.9
Los Angeles, CA	2,918	3,041	4.2	10,236	7,447	-27.2	13,154	10,488	-20.3
Louisville, KY	1,014	1,168	15.2	2,686	1,690	-37.1	3,700	2,858	-22.8
Madison, WI	332	250	-24.7	2,288	2,562	12.0	2,620	2,812	7.3
Manchester, NH	99	26	-73.7	280	167	-40.4	379	193	-49.1

Table continued on following page.

	Single-Family			Multi-Family			Total		
City	2023	2024	Pct. Chg.	2023	2024	Pct. Chg.	2023	2024	Pct. Chg.
McAllen, TX	428	669	56.3	753	1,053	39.8	1,181	1,722	45.8
Memphis, TN	n/a	n/a	n/a	n/a	n/a	n/a	n/a	n/a	n/a
Miami, FL	113	145	28.3	5,307	5,878	10.8	5,420	6,023	11.1
Midland, TX	805	1,504	86.8	0	0	0.0	805	1,504	86.8
Milwaukee, WI	61	72	18.0	36	164	355.6	97	236	143.3
Minneapolis, MN	70	65	-7.1	1,458	387	-73.5	1,528	452	-70.4
Nashville, TN	3,106	2,662	-14.3	8,052	4,137	-48.6	11,158	6,799	-39.1
New Orleans, LA	249	202	-18.9	818	508	-37.9	1,067	710	-33.5
New York, NY	232	197	-15.1	31,733	27,044	-14.8	31,965	27,241	-14.8
Oklahoma City, OK	3,339	3,460	3.6	805	938	16.5	4,144	4,398	6.1
Omaha, NE	1,294	1,692	30.8	1,756	2,668	51.9	3,050	4,360	43.0
Orlando, FL	887	914	3.0	1,514	1,056	-30.3	2,401	1,970	-18.0
Philadelphia, PA	405	539	33.1	3,458	2,423	-29.9	3,863	2,962	-23.3
Phoenix, AZ	4,200	4,062	-3.3	10,268	4,935	-51.9	14,468	8,997	-37.8
Pittsburgh, PA	229	229	0.0	2,283	1,435	-37.1	2,512	1,664	-33.8
Portland, OR	877	815	-7.1	2,212	885	-60.0	3,089	1,700	-45.0
Providence, RI	0	31	—	5	238	4,660.0	5	269	5,280.0
Provo, UT	147	133	-9.5	80	153	91.3	227	286	26.0
Raleigh, NC	1,762	1,653	-6.2	4,626	3,391	-26.7	6,388	5,044	-21.0
Reno, NV	1,059	1,087	2.6	2,176	1,636	-24.8	3,235	2,723	-15.8
Richmond, VA	387	380	-1.8	1,896	2,160	13.9	2,283	2,540	11.3
Rochester, MN	241	193	-19.9	551	925	67.9	792	1,118	41.2
Sacramento, CA	653	708	8.4	1,864	1,335	-28.4	2,517	2,043	-18.8
Saint Louis, MO	51	56	9.8	227	238	4.8	278	294	5.8
Saint Paul, MN	48	75	56.3	1,156	329	-71.5	1,204	404	-66.4
Salem, OR	360	392	8.9	326	513	57.4	686	905	31.9
Salt Lake City, UT	243	397	63.4	2,929	886	-69.8	3,172	1,283	-59.6
San Antonio, TX	4,299	5,000	16.3	4,860	1,258	-74.1	9,159	6,258	-31.7
San Diego, CA	516	775	50.2	5,249	5,840	11.3	5,765	6,615	14.7
San Francisco, CA	29	27	-6.9	1,107	743	-32.9	1,136	770	-32.2
San Jose, CA	581	642	10.5	2,069	1,356	-34.5	2,650	1,998	-24.6
Santa Rosa, CA	441	292	-33.8	905	0	-100.0	1,346	292	-78.3
Savannah, GA	589	565	-4.1	12	14	16.7	601	579	-3.7
Seattle, WA	473	405	-14.4	4,826	5,490	13.8	5,299	5,895	11.2
Sioux Falls, SD	750	880	17.3	1,986	1,239	-37.6	2,736	2,119	-22.6
Tampa, FL	738	912	23.6	2,415	1,634	-32.3	3,153	2,546	-19.3
Tucson, AZ	839	923	10.0	829	582	-29.8	1,668	1,505	-9.8
Tulsa, OK	524	424	-19.1	352	299	-15.1	876	723	-17.5
Virginia Beach, VA	201	319	58.7	341	347	1.8	542	666	22.9
Washington, DC	166	146	-12.0	2,854	1,591	-44.3	3,020	1,737	-42.5
Wichita, KS	605	558	-7.8	1,173	742	-36.7	1,778	1,300	-26.9
Wilmington, NC	n/a	n/a	n/a	n/a	n/a	n/a	n/a	n/a	n/a
Winston-Salem, NC	860	1,168	35.8	1,281	966	-24.6	2,141	2,134	-0.3
U.S.	920,000	981,900	6.7	591,100	496,100	-16.1	1,511,100	1,478,000	-2.2

Note: Figures represent new, privately-owned housing units authorized (unadjusted data)
Source: U.S. Census Bureau, Building Permits Survey (BPS), 2023, 2024

Building Permits: Metro Area

Metro Area	Single-Family			Multi-Family			Total		
	2023	2024	Pct. Chg.	2023	2024	Pct. Chg.	2023	2024	Pct. Chg.
Albuquerque, NM	2,057	2,064	0.3	777	812	4.5	2,834	2,876	1.5
Anchorage, AK	338	198	-41.4	119	228	91.6	457	426	-6.8
Ann Arbor, MI	485	557	14.8	1,112	636	-42.8	1,597	1,193	-25.3
Athens, GA	776	863	11.2	250	972	288.8	1,026	1,835	78.8
Atlanta, GA	24,022	25,773	7.3	14,617	14,914	2.0	38,639	40,687	5.3
Austin, TX	16,532	16,435	-0.6	22,241	15,859	-28.7	38,773	32,294	-16.7
Baltimore, MD	3,798	3,849	1.3	3,741	2,435	-34.9	7,539	6,284	-16.6
Billings, MT	343	896	161.2	6	629	10,383.3	349	1,525	337.0
Boise City, ID	6,508	8,252	26.8	3,383	811	-76.0	9,891	9,063	-8.4
Boston, MA	3,396	3,734	10.0	7,426	7,501	1.0	10,822	11,235	3.8
Boulder, CO	791	441	-44.2	851	1,239	45.6	1,642	1,680	2.3
Cape Coral, FL	8,654	10,554	22.0	4,902	4,857	-0.9	13,556	15,411	13.7
Cedar Rapids, IA	467	494	5.8	301	593	97.0	768	1,087	41.5
Charleston, SC	6,184	6,817	10.2	2,389	1,697	-29.0	8,573	8,514	-0.7
Charlotte, NC	19,146	18,954	-1.0	10,273	6,981	-32.0	29,419	25,935	-11.8
Chicago, IL	8,452	9,509	12.5	6,576	8,555	30.1	15,028	18,064	20.2
Cincinnati, OH	3,714	4,025	8.4	2,527	3,064	21.3	6,241	7,089	13.6
Clarksville, TN	1,385	1,975	42.6	1,554	823	-47.0	2,939	2,798	-4.8
Cleveland, OH	2,500	2,980	19.2	991	1,309	32.1	3,491	4,289	22.9
College Station, TX	1,155	1,482	28.3	307	839	173.3	1,462	2,321	58.8
Colorado Springs, CO	2,670	2,878	7.8	2,607	1,116	-57.2	5,277	3,994	-24.3
Columbia, MO	609	763	25.3	72	568	688.9	681	1,331	95.4
Columbia, SC	4,634	4,469	-3.6	831	1,423	71.2	5,465	5,892	7.8
Columbus, OH	5,364	6,094	13.6	6,076	7,868	29.5	11,440	13,962	22.0
Dallas, TX	44,366	46,440	4.7	23,663	25,348	7.1	68,029	71,788	5.5
Davenport, IA	366	401	9.6	248	564	127.4	614	965	57.2
Denver, CO	9,012	9,012	0.0	11,638	6,558	-43.7	20,650	15,570	-24.6
Des Moines, IA	3,689	3,717	0.8	1,311	1,347	2.7	5,000	5,064	1.3
Detroit, MI	4,541	4,878	7.4	2,193	2,826	28.9	6,734	7,704	14.4
Durham, NC	3,127	2,815	-10.0	4,083	1,043	-74.5	7,210	3,858	-46.5
El Paso, TX	1,967	2,077	5.6	280	243	-13.2	2,247	2,320	3.2
Eugene, OR	732	799	9.2	507	1,015	100.2	1,239	1,814	46.4
Fargo, ND	885	832	-6.0	1,204	660	-45.2	2,089	1,492	-28.6
Fort Collins, CO	1,289	1,370	6.3	1,397	416	-70.2	2,686	1,786	-33.5
Fort Wayne, IN	1,680	1,409	-16.1	756	625	-17.3	2,436	2,034	-16.5
Fort Worth, TX	44,366	46,440	4.7	23,663	25,348	7.1	68,029	71,788	5.5
Gainesville, FL	1,247	1,115	-10.6	698	928	33.0	1,945	2,043	5.0
Green Bay, WI	578	717	24.0	415	1,108	167.0	993	1,825	83.8
Greensboro, NC	2,368	2,337	-1.3	1,139	2,639	131.7	3,507	4,976	41.9
Honolulu, HI	657	706	7.5	1,194	932	-21.9	1,851	1,638	-11.5
Houston, TX	50,444	52,703	4.5	18,311	13,044	-28.8	68,755	65,747	-4.4
Huntsville, AL	3,908	3,972	1.6	2,032	1,234	-39.3	5,940	5,206	-12.4
Indianapolis, IN	7,252	9,168	26.4	5,302	2,620	-50.6	12,554	11,788	-6.1
Jacksonville, FL	12,479	12,936	3.7	7,847	2,066	-73.7	20,326	15,002	-26.2
Kansas City, MO	4,299	4,875	13.4	3,215	4,273	32.9	7,514	9,148	21.7
Lafayette, LA	2,008	2,001	-0.3	378	18	-95.2	2,386	2,019	-15.4
Las Vegas, NV	10,087	12,277	21.7	2,986	2,477	-17.0	13,073	14,754	12.9
Lexington, KY	1,319	1,392	5.5	1,123	809	-28.0	2,442	2,201	-9.9
Lincoln, NE	849	1,077	26.9	1,288	959	-25.5	2,137	2,036	-4.7
Little Rock, AR	1,932	2,055	6.4	732	551	-24.7	2,664	2,606	-2.2
Los Angeles, CA	12,035	11,777	-2.1	18,732	15,004	-19.9	30,767	26,781	-13.0
Louisville, KY	2,914	3,690	26.6	3,817	2,106	-44.8	6,731	5,796	-13.9
Madison, WI	1,534	1,679	9.5	3,827	4,159	8.7	5,361	5,838	8.9
Manchester, NH	532	427	-19.7	850	445	-47.6	1,382	872	-36.9

Table continued on following page.

Metro Area	Single-Family			Multi-Family			Total		
	2023	2024	Pct. Chg.	2023	2024	Pct. Chg.	2023	2024	Pct. Chg.
McAllen, TX	4,143	4,336	4.7	2,756	2,956	7.3	6,899	7,292	5.7
Memphis, TN	3,062	2,773	-9.4	996	1,467	47.3	4,058	4,240	4.5
Miami, FL	5,512	5,825	5.7	15,808	10,527	-33.4	21,320	16,352	-23.3
Midland, TX	810	1,505	85.8	8	4	-50.0	818	1,509	84.5
Milwaukee, WI	1,408	1,712	21.6	1,436	2,346	63.4	2,844	4,058	42.7
Minneapolis, MN	8,245	9,300	12.8	10,388	4,722	-54.5	18,633	14,022	-24.7
Nashville, TN	13,842	14,465	4.5	9,716	5,573	-42.6	23,558	20,038	-14.9
New Orleans, LA	1,865	1,007	-46.0	1,207	604	-50.0	3,072	1,611	-47.6
New York, NY	11,734	12,530	6.8	51,296	45,399	-11.5	63,030	57,929	-8.1
Oklahoma City, OK	5,573	6,014	7.9	1,163	1,693	45.6	6,736	7,707	14.4
Omaha, NE	2,763	3,505	26.9	1,956	3,692	88.8	4,719	7,197	52.5
Orlando, FL	17,049	15,364	-9.9	8,366	8,771	4.8	25,415	24,135	-5.0
Philadelphia, PA	6,255	8,324	33.1	5,764	5,890	2.2	12,019	14,214	18.3
Phoenix, AZ	24,708	30,277	22.5	20,908	15,607	-25.4	45,616	45,884	0.6
Pittsburgh, PA	3,332	3,530	5.9	2,962	1,882	-36.5	6,294	5,412	-14.0
Portland, OR	6,326	6,345	0.3	5,056	3,108	-38.5	11,382	9,453	-16.9
Providence, RI	1,255	1,339	6.7	675	1,281	89.8	1,930	2,620	35.8
Provo, UT	4,663	5,246	12.5	1,518	1,182	-22.1	6,181	6,428	4.0
Raleigh, NC	12,147	13,343	9.8	8,472	5,636	-33.5	20,619	18,979	-8.0
Reno, NV	1,992	2,474	24.2	2,279	1,917	-15.9	4,271	4,391	2.8
Richmond, VA	4,590	5,023	9.4	5,383	3,619	-32.8	9,973	8,642	-13.3
Rochester, MN	604	491	-18.7	570	993	74.2	1,174	1,484	26.4
Sacramento, CA	7,931	8,579	8.2	4,010	3,034	-24.3	11,941	11,613	-2.7
Saint Louis, MO	4,599	4,653	1.2	2,508	2,364	-5.7	7,107	7,017	-1.3
Saint Paul, MN	8,245	9,300	12.8	10,388	4,722	-54.5	18,633	14,022	-24.7
Salem, OR	826	994	20.3	1,140	865	-24.1	1,966	1,859	-5.4
Salt Lake City, UT	3,163	3,525	11.4	6,072	1,922	-68.3	9,235	5,447	-41.0
San Antonio, TX	8,718	10,999	26.2	7,767	3,858	-50.3	16,485	14,857	-9.9
San Diego, CA	3,049	3,377	10.8	8,420	8,195	-2.7	11,469	11,572	0.9
San Francisco, CA	3,015	2,776	-7.9	4,515	3,138	-30.5	7,530	5,914	-21.5
San Jose, CA	2,037	2,207	8.3	4,190	1,908	-54.5	6,227	4,115	-33.9
Santa Rosa, CA	1,020	832	-18.4	1,333	180	-86.5	2,353	1,012	-57.0
Savannah, GA	2,620	2,936	12.1	768	1,101	43.4	3,388	4,037	19.2
Seattle, WA	6,296	6,489	3.1	10,927	11,431	4.6	17,223	17,920	4.0
Sioux Falls, SD	1,155	1,270	10.0	2,284	1,532	-32.9	3,439	2,802	-18.5
Tampa, FL	14,852	13,205	-11.1	10,534	7,745	-26.5	25,386	20,950	-17.5
Tucson, AZ	3,688	4,150	12.5	1,567	1,100	-29.8	5,255	5,250	-0.1
Tulsa, OK	3,393	3,602	6.2	1,616	709	-56.1	5,009	4,311	-13.9
Virginia Beach, VA	3,393	3,544	4.5	2,721	862	-68.3	6,114	4,406	-27.9
Washington, DC	10,936	11,743	7.4	12,557	9,744	-22.4	23,493	21,487	-8.5
Wichita, KS	1,470	1,479	0.6	2,063	1,560	-24.4	3,533	3,039	-14.0
Wilmington, NC	2,228	7,263	226.0	1,737	2,355	35.6	3,965	9,618	142.6
Winston-Salem, NC	3,567	4,010	12.4	1,507	1,446	-4.0	5,074	5,456	7.5
U.S.	920,000	981,900	6.7	591,100	496,100	-16.1	1,511,100	1,478,000	-2.2

Note: Figures cover the Metropolitan Statistical Area (MSA); Figures represent new, privately-owned housing units authorized (unadjusted data)
Source: U.S. Census Bureau, Building Permits Survey (BPS), 2023, 2024

Housing Vacancy Rates

Metro Area	Gross Vacancy Rate[1] (%)			Year-Round Vacancy Rate[2] (%)			Rental Vacancy Rate[3] (%)			Homeowner Vacancy Rate[4] (%)		
	2022	2023	2024	2022	2023	2024	2022	2023	2024	2022	2023	2024
Albuquerque, NM	5.3	5.6	6.4	5.1	5.4	6.1	5.5	6.1	6.7	1.0	0.7	1.6
Anchorage, AK	n/a	n/a	n/a	n/a	n/a	n/a	n/a	n/a	n/a	n/a	n/a	n/a
Ann Arbor, MI	n/a	n/a	n/a	n/a	n/a	n/a	n/a	n/a	n/a	n/a	n/a	n/a
Athens, GA	n/a	n/a	n/a	n/a	n/a	n/a	n/a	n/a	n/a	n/a	n/a	n/a
Atlanta, GA	5.9	6.6	6.8	5.7	6.4	6.6	6.7	8.7	9.3	0.8	1.2	0.9
Austin, TX	5.5	8.5	8.6	4.9	8.2	8.3	5.6	9.0	8.2	0.6	1.3	1.7
Baltimore, MD	5.9	6.6	7.0	5.7	6.5	6.5	5.3	9.4	6.1	0.5	0.6	0.9
Billings, MT	n/a	n/a	n/a	n/a	n/a	n/a	n/a	n/a	n/a	n/a	n/a	n/a
Boise City, ID	n/a	n/a	n/a	n/a	n/a	n/a	n/a	n/a	n/a	n/a	n/a	n/a
Boston, MA	6.2	6.1	5.7	5.4	5.3	4.8	2.5	2.5	3.0	0.7	0.6	0.6
Boulder, CO	n/a	n/a	n/a	n/a	n/a	n/a	n/a	n/a	n/a	n/a	n/a	n/a
Cape Coral, FL	38.2	38.7	34.1	16.9	16.1	14.7	11.6	15.3	10.1	3.9	2.3	3.0
Cedar Rapids, IA	n/a	n/a	n/a	n/a	n/a	n/a	n/a	n/a	n/a	n/a	n/a	n/a
Charleston, SC	10.6	12.6	11.9	7.5	10.2	9.8	8.8	12.0	12.8	0.4	0.5	0.9
Charlotte, NC	7.4	7.6	8.1	7.0	7.4	7.7	5.9	6.6	6.7	0.7	0.4	0.9
Chicago, IL	7.3	6.0	5.8	7.1	5.8	5.6	6.1	5.6	5.1	1.1	0.5	0.6
Cincinnati, OH	6.8	5.4	5.8	6.3	5.2	5.5	6.3	7.2	6.1	0.3	0.2	0.8
Clarksville, TN	n/a	n/a	n/a	n/a	n/a	n/a	n/a	n/a	n/a	n/a	n/a	n/a
Cleveland, OH	7.0	7.6	7.5	6.8	7.2	7.4	3.2	4.7	5.8	1.0	0.5	0.4
College Station, TX	n/a	n/a	n/a	n/a	n/a	n/a	n/a	n/a	n/a	n/a	n/a	n/a
Colorado Springs, CO	n/a	n/a	n/a	n/a	n/a	n/a	n/a	n/a	n/a	n/a	n/a	n/a
Columbia, MO	n/a	n/a	n/a	n/a	n/a	n/a	n/a	n/a	n/a	n/a	n/a	n/a
Columbia, SC	12.0	12.7	8.8	12.0	12.6	8.8	6.1	8.5	6.8	0.6	1.0	0.5
Columbus, OH	5.6	6.6	7.4	5.4	6.5	7.3	3.8	5.8	7.3	0.8	0.8	0.3
Dallas, TX	6.6	7.6	7.9	6.3	7.2	7.6	6.8	8.4	8.9	0.7	0.8	1.3
Davenport, IA	n/a	n/a	n/a	n/a	n/a	n/a	n/a	n/a	n/a	n/a	n/a	n/a
Denver, CO	5.8	6.0	4.9	5.2	5.5	4.4	5.1	5.3	4.7	0.3	0.7	0.7
Des Moines, IA	n/a	n/a	n/a	n/a	n/a	n/a	n/a	n/a	n/a	n/a	n/a	n/a
Detroit, MI	7.1	9.0	9.4	6.6	8.7	9.3	4.5	9.3	8.7	0.9	1.0	1.1
Durham, NC	n/a	n/a	n/a	n/a	n/a	n/a	n/a	n/a	n/a	n/a	n/a	n/a
El Paso, TX	n/a	n/a	n/a	n/a	n/a	n/a	n/a	n/a	n/a	n/a	n/a	n/a
Eugene, OR	n/a	n/a	n/a	n/a	n/a	n/a	n/a	n/a	n/a	n/a	n/a	n/a
Fargo, ND	n/a	n/a	n/a	n/a	n/a	n/a	n/a	n/a	n/a	n/a	n/a	n/a
Fort Collins, CO	n/a	n/a	n/a	n/a	n/a	n/a	n/a	n/a	n/a	n/a	n/a	n/a
Fort Wayne, IN	n/a	n/a	n/a	n/a	n/a	n/a	n/a	n/a	n/a	n/a	n/a	n/a
Fort Worth, TX	6.6	7.6	7.9	6.3	7.2	7.6	6.8	8.4	8.9	0.7	0.8	1.3
Gainesville, FL	n/a	n/a	n/a	n/a	n/a	n/a	n/a	n/a	n/a	n/a	n/a	n/a
Green Bay, WI	n/a	n/a	n/a	n/a	n/a	n/a	n/a	n/a	n/a	n/a	n/a	n/a
Greensboro, NC	8.7	6.1	7.8	8.7	5.7	6.0	10.2	5.7	5.5	0.7	0.1	0.5
Honolulu, HI	10.6	11.5	11.9	10.0	10.7	11.1	5.7	6.8	6.2	0.6	0.5	0.9
Houston, TX	6.9	7.9	7.8	6.3	7.3	7.2	8.9	10.9	9.8	0.6	1.4	1.2
Huntsville, AL	n/a	n/a	n/a	n/a	n/a	n/a	n/a	n/a	n/a	n/a	n/a	n/a
Indianapolis, IN	7.7	6.2	6.7	7.2	5.6	5.8	11.0	8.8	9.2	1.0	0.8	0.8
Jacksonville, FL	8.9	8.6	9.2	7.7	7.8	8.5	6.2	9.4	8.8	1.7	0.7	1.0
Kansas City, MO	7.1	7.0	6.9	7.1	6.6	6.3	7.8	7.6	8.9	0.6	1.2	0.9
Lafayette, LA	n/a	n/a	n/a	n/a	n/a	n/a	n/a	n/a	n/a	n/a	n/a	n/a
Las Vegas, NV	9.2	9.6	9.7	8.3	8.8	9.3	5.7	7.2	8.3	0.9	1.1	1.1
Lexington, KY	n/a	n/a	n/a	n/a	n/a	n/a	n/a	n/a	n/a	n/a	n/a	n/a
Lincoln, NE	n/a	n/a	n/a	n/a	n/a	n/a	n/a	n/a	n/a	n/a	n/a	n/a
Little Rock, AR	9.4	10.1	10.7	9.2	9.8	9.9	11.4	10.8	11.7	0.7	0.9	0.6
Los Angeles, CA	5.9	5.8	6.2	5.5	5.7	6.1	4.1	4.0	4.8	0.5	0.6	0.7
Louisville, KY	5.7	6.3	6.7	5.7	6.2	6.5	5.3	3.6	7.1	0.5	0.4	1.2
Madison, WI	n/a	n/a	n/a	n/a	n/a	n/a	n/a	n/a	n/a	n/a	n/a	n/a
Manchester, NH	n/a	n/a	n/a	n/a	n/a	n/a	n/a	n/a	n/a	n/a	n/a	n/a

Table continued on following page.

Metro Area	Gross Vacancy Rate[1] (%)			Year-Round Vacancy Rate[2] (%)			Rental Vacancy Rate[3] (%)			Homeowner Vacancy Rate[4] (%)		
	2022	2023	2024	2022	2023	2024	2022	2023	2024	2022	2023	2024
McAllen, TX	n/a	n/a	n/a	n/a	n/a	n/a	n/a	n/a	n/a	n/a	n/a	n/a
Memphis, TN	6.2	7.0	7.4	6.1	6.9	7.2	6.4	11.4	12.0	0.4	0.4	0.9
Miami, FL	12.6	14.7	14.8	7.5	8.9	9.3	6.3	8.4	9.5	1.1	0.9	1.4
Midland, TX	n/a	n/a	n/a	n/a	n/a	n/a	n/a	n/a	n/a	n/a	n/a	n/a
Milwaukee, WI	5.2	6.7	5.6	5.1	6.6	5.1	5.9	4.1	4.8	0.1	0.8	0.4
Minneapolis, MN	4.8	5.5	4.9	4.5	5.3	4.6	6.7	8.1	5.2	0.8	0.5	0.4
Nashville, TN	7.6	7.5	7.0	7.1	7.0	6.4	6.4	9.3	8.6	0.9	0.9	1.5
New Orleans, LA	13.4	10.9	11.9	11.5	9.8	10.8	6.6	9.2	9.1	1.6	1.6	1.4
New York, NY	8.2	7.8	8.3	7.0	6.7	7.4	3.5	3.9	4.7	1.0	0.9	1.0
Oklahoma City, OK	8.6	7.8	7.0	8.5	7.6	6.7	10.6	10.6	9.0	0.9	1.6	1.2
Omaha, NE	5.4	5.4	5.1	5.0	5.1	5.1	4.2	4.3	5.3	0.8	0.9	0.3
Orlando, FL	9.6	9.5	9.8	7.4	7.6	8.4	6.5	7.0	9.4	1.4	1.1	1.5
Philadelphia, PA	5.5	5.3	5.3	5.4	5.2	5.2	4.2	5.2	6.3	1.0	0.9	0.5
Phoenix, AZ	10.9	11.0	12.6	6.7	7.2	7.9	6.4	8.0	7.9	0.9	0.7	1.0
Pittsburgh, PA	11.5	10.0	10.5	11.0	9.2	9.7	8.3	6.3	8.9	0.7	0.9	0.8
Portland, OR	5.4	5.4	5.7	5.1	5.1	5.5	4.0	6.8	5.7	1.2	0.8	1.0
Providence, RI	9.5	9.4	8.5	7.6	7.6	6.8	4.5	3.7	3.2	0.4	0.3	0.4
Provo, UT	n/a	n/a	n/a	n/a	n/a	n/a	n/a	n/a	n/a	n/a	n/a	n/a
Raleigh, NC	7.4	6.7	6.3	7.3	6.6	6.2	7.1	8.8	8.8	0.5	0.5	0.7
Reno, NV	n/a	n/a	n/a	n/a	n/a	n/a	n/a	n/a	n/a	n/a	n/a	n/a
Richmond, VA	6.1	5.9	7.7	6.1	5.9	7.7	3.0	5.2	7.9	0.7	0.2	0.7
Rochester, MN	n/a	n/a	n/a	n/a	n/a	n/a	n/a	n/a	n/a	n/a	n/a	n/a
Sacramento, CA	6.3	6.4	8.0	6.1	6.2	7.6	2.3	4.2	3.9	0.6	0.6	0.9
Saint Louis, MO	7.2	7.4	7.7	7.1	7.3	7.6	6.8	7.8	7.9	1.4	0.6	0.9
Saint Paul, MN	4.8	5.5	4.9	4.5	5.3	4.6	6.7	8.1	5.2	0.8	0.5	0.4
Salem, OR	n/a	n/a	n/a	n/a	n/a	n/a	n/a	n/a	n/a	n/a	n/a	n/a
Salt Lake City, UT	5.1	6.1	10.1	4.5	5.0	5.8	4.6	6.2	6.1	0.6	0.6	0.7
San Antonio, TX	7.5	7.4	9.9	7.1	6.9	7.9	8.1	8.8	10.0	0.9	1.3	1.9
San Diego, CA	6.9	6.8	6.4	6.6	6.2	6.0	3.6	4.1	5.2	0.6	0.2	0.5
San Francisco, CA	7.9	8.1	8.3	7.7	8.0	8.1	5.4	6.6	6.3	1.3	0.5	0.7
San Jose, CA	5.8	4.5	4.7	5.8	4.5	4.7	4.7	3.3	3.3	0.4	0.3	1.0
Santa Rosa, CA	n/a	n/a	n/a	n/a	n/a	n/a	n/a	n/a	n/a	n/a	n/a	n/a
Savannah, GA	n/a	n/a	n/a	n/a	n/a	n/a	n/a	n/a	n/a	n/a	n/a	n/a
Seattle, WA	5.7	5.1	6.2	5.2	4.7	5.9	4.9	4.0	6.5	0.7	0.6	1.1
Sioux Falls, SD	n/a	n/a	n/a	n/a	n/a	n/a	n/a	n/a	n/a	n/a	n/a	n/a
Tampa, FL	13.3	13.3	14.2	9.9	9.1	10.9	8.1	8.5	8.7	1.2	1.0	2.0
Tucson, AZ	13.5	14.2	10.1	10.3	11.2	8.7	8.0	10.2	9.3	1.4	1.3	1.1
Tulsa, OK	8.9	8.3	7.5	8.5	7.9	6.8	5.6	6.7	7.2	0.7	0.8	0.7
Virginia Beach, VA	8.1	5.9	9.2	7.3	5.4	8.5	6.3	5.1	9.1	1.0	0.5	1.4
Washington, DC	5.2	5.1	5.5	5.0	5.0	5.4	5.3	5.5	4.7	0.6	0.3	0.4
Wichita, KS	n/a	n/a	n/a	n/a	n/a	n/a	n/a	n/a	n/a	n/a	n/a	n/a
Wilmington, NC	n/a	n/a	n/a	n/a	n/a	n/a	n/a	n/a	n/a	n/a	n/a	n/a
Winston-Salem, NC	n/a	n/a	n/a	n/a	n/a	n/a	n/a	n/a	n/a	n/a	n/a	n/a
U.S.[5]	9.1	9.0	9.1	7.5	7.5	7.6	5.7	6.5	6.8	0.8	0.8	1.0

Note: Figures cover the Metropolitan Statistical Area (MSA); (1) The percentage of the total housing inventory that is vacant; (2) The percentage of the housing inventory (excluding seasonal units) that is year-round vacant; (3) The percentage of rental inventory that is vacant for rent; (4) The percentage of homeowner inventory that is vacant for sale; (5) Figures cover the 75 largest Metropolitan Statistical Areas; n/a not available
Source: U.S. Census Bureau, Housing Vacancies and Homeownership Annual Statistics: 2022, 2023, 2024

Bankruptcy Filings

City	Area Covered	Business Filings			Nonbusiness Filings		
		2023	2024	% Chg.	2023	2024	% Chg.
Albuquerque, NM	Bernalillo County	24	33	37.5	373	454	21.7
Anchorage, AK	Anchorage Borough	9	7	-22.2	113	90	-20.4
Ann Arbor, MI	Washtenaw County	7	8	14.3	396	404	2.0
Athens, GA	Clarke County	2	5	150.0	176	189	7.4
Atlanta, GA	Fulton County	318	251	-21.1	2,723	2,846	4.5
Austin, TX	Travis County	133	121	-9.0	408	619	51.7
Baltimore, MD	Baltimore City	35	43	22.9	1,502	1,656	10.3
Billings, MT	Yellowstone County	5	9	80.0	111	153	37.8
Boise City, ID	Ada County	18	26	44.4	350	466	33.1
Boston, MA	Suffolk County	53	63	18.9	233	316	35.6
Boulder, CO	Boulder County	25	35	40.0	228	247	8.3
Cape Coral, FL	Lee County	97	64	-34.0	860	1,216	41.4
Cedar Rapids, IA	Linn County	9	7	-22.2	224	278	24.1
Charleston, SC	Charleston County	7	13	85.7	195	215	10.3
Charlotte, NC	Mecklenburg County	69	60	-13.0	577	689	19.4
Chicago, IL	Cook County	361	479	32.7	12,419	13,840	11.4
Cincinnati, OH	Hamilton County	32	42	31.3	1,286	1,619	25.9
Clarksville, TN	Montgomery County	4	11	175.0	475	513	8.0
Cleveland, OH	Cuyahoga County	37	60	62.2	3,437	4,054	18.0
College Station, TX	Brazos County	5	7	40.0	65	80	23.1
Colorado Springs, CO	El Paso County	23	50	117.4	784	973	24.1
Columbia, MO	Boone County	3	5	66.7	191	201	5.2
Columbia, SC	Richland County	7	10	42.9	453	584	28.9
Columbus, OH	Franklin County	43	81	88.4	2,330	2,671	14.6
Dallas, TX	Dallas County	296	496	67.6	2,363	3,025	28.0
Davenport, IA	Scott County	9	4	-55.6	157	158	0.6
Denver, CO	Denver County	61	79	29.5	669	854	27.7
Des Moines, IA	Polk County	15	13	-13.3	566	594	4.9
Detroit, MI	Wayne County	43	58	34.9	6,087	6,501	6.8
Durham, NC	Durham County	14	42	200.0	162	195	20.4
El Paso, TX	El Paso County	65	72	10.8	1,351	1,512	11.9
Eugene, OR	Lane County	12	18	50.0	535	707	32.1
Fargo, ND	Cass County	5	14	180.0	129	132	2.3
Fort Collins, CO	Larimer County	21	28	33.3	347	417	20.2
Fort Wayne, IN	Allen County	17	17	0.0	924	959	3.8
Fort Worth, TX	Tarrant County	200	198	-1.0	2,934	3,513	19.7
Gainesville, FL	Alachua County	11	30	172.7	153	177	15.7
Green Bay, WI	Brown County	5	10	100.0	320	408	27.5
Greensboro, NC	Guilford County	11	16	45.5	375	473	26.1
Honolulu, HI	Honolulu County	36	38	5.6	757	840	11.0
Houston, TX	Harris County	356	426	19.7	3,285	3,853	17.3
Huntsville, AL	Madison County	20	35	75.0	902	946	4.9
Indianapolis, IN	Marion County	45	43	-4.4	2,601	3,166	21.7
Jacksonville, FL	Duval County	73	83	13.7	1,514	1,784	17.8
Kansas City, MO	Jackson County	22	27	22.7	1,186	1,166	-1.7
Lafayette, LA	Lafayette Parish	19	44	131.6	335	410	22.4
Las Vegas, NV	Clark County	194	178	-8.2	5,622	6,690	19.0
Lexington, KY	Fayette County	13	14	7.7	468	540	15.4
Lincoln, NE	Lancaster County	11	15	36.4	367	405	10.4
Little Rock, AR	Pulaski County	17	29	70.6	1,436	1,390	-3.2
Los Angeles, CA	Los Angeles County	815	977	19.9	10,059	12,169	21.0
Louisville, KY	Jefferson County	28	35	25.0	2,280	2,258	-1.0
Madison, WI	Dane County	25	21	-16.0	437	494	13.0
Manchester, NH	Hillsborough County	8	21	162.5	235	298	26.8
McAllen, TX	Hidalgo County	13	11	-15.4	263	274	4.2

Table continued on following page.

Appendix A: Comparative Statistics A-65

City	Area Covered	Business Filings 2023	2024	% Chg.	Nonbusiness Filings 2023	2024	% Chg.
Memphis, TN	Shelby County	48	45	-6.3	5,959	6,030	1.2
Miami, FL	Miami-Dade County	242	413	70.7	5,320	6,779	27.4
Midland, TX	Midland County	14	17	21.4	66	93	40.9
Milwaukee, WI	Milwaukee County	24	40	66.7	2,881	3,306	14.8
Minneapolis, MN	Hennepin County	64	77	20.3	1,473	1,952	32.5
Nashville, TN	Davidson County	303	123	-59.4	1,109	1,195	7.8
New Orleans, LA	Orleans Parish	28	35	25.0	388	446	14.9
New York, NY	Bronx County	25	44	76.0	1,071	1,319	23.2
New York, NY	Kings County	394	457	16.0	1,781	2,036	14.3
New York, NY	New York County	750	361	-51.9	684	793	15.9
New York, NY	Queens County	215	209	-2.8	1,921	2,120	10.4
New York, NY	Richmond County	23	29	26.1	490	494	0.8
Oklahoma City, OK	Oklahoma County	46	54	17.4	1,374	1,526	11.1
Omaha, NE	Douglas County	21	26	23.8	687	802	16.7
Orlando, FL	Orange County	152	231	52.0	1,832	2,279	24.4
Philadelphia, PA	Philadelphia County	227	131	-42.3	940	1,094	16.4
Phoenix, AZ	Maricopa County	252	355	40.9	6,085	7,026	15.5
Pittsburgh, PA	Allegheny County	59	111	88.1	1,217	1,424	17.0
Portland, OR	Multnomah County	35	61	74.3	938	1,078	14.9
Providence, RI	Providence County	13	22	69.2	520	581	11.7
Provo, UT	Utah County	33	36	9.1	925	1,070	15.7
Raleigh, NC	Wake County	51	76	49.0	653	830	27.1
Reno, NV	Washoe County	35	59	68.6	610	860	41.0
Richmond, VA	Richmond city	2	14	600.0	620	678	9.4
Rochester, MN	Olmsted County	8	6	-25.0	137	161	17.5
Sacramento, CA	Sacramento County	96	163	69.8	1,675	2,259	34.9
Saint Louis, MO	Saint Louis City	12	23	91.7	1,497	1,311	-12.4
Saint Paul, MN	Ramsey County	20	19	-5.0	694	840	21.0
Salem, OR	Marion County	10	11	10.0	599	674	12.5
Salt Lake City, UT	Salt Lake County	58	58	0.0	2,508	2,763	10.2
San Antonio, TX	Bexar County	126	169	34.1	1,270	1,813	42.8
San Diego, CA	San Diego County	214	267	24.8	3,866	4,558	17.9
San Francisco, CA	San Francisco County	68	140	105.9	348	417	19.8
San Jose, CA	Santa Clara County	86	105	22.1	782	1,008	28.9
Santa Rosa, CA	Sonoma County	17	56	229.4	338	378	11.8
Savannah, GA	Chatham County	8	3	-62.5	732	695	-5.1
Seattle, WA	King County	92	113	22.8	1,134	1,459	28.7
Sioux Falls, SD	Minnehaha County	10	8	-20.0	220	220	0.0
Tampa, FL	Hillsborough County	121	158	30.6	1,822	2,440	33.9
Tucson, AZ	Pima County	28	27	-3.6	1,402	1,638	16.8
Tulsa, OK	Tulsa County	46	44	-4.3	867	1,065	22.8
Virginia Beach, VA	Virginia Beach City	10	20	100.0	822	966	17.5
Washington, DC	District of Columbia	78	81	3.8	293	347	18.4
Wichita, KS	Sedgwick County	24	27	12.5	757	777	2.6
Wilmington, NC	New Hanover County	29	19	-34.5	145	183	26.2
Winston-Salem, NC	Forsyth County	7	18	157.1	263	330	25.5
U.S.	U.S.	18,926	23,107	22.1	434,064	494,201	13.9

Note: Business filings include Chapter 7, Chapter 9, Chapter 11, Chapter 12, Chapter 13, Chapter 15, and Section 304; Nonbusiness filings include Chapter 7, Chapter 11, and Chapter 13
Source: Administrative Office of the U.S. Courts, Business and Nonbusiness Bankruptcy, County Cases Commenced by Chapter of the Bankruptcy Code, During the 12-Month Period Ending December 31, 2023 and Business and Nonbusiness Bankruptcy, County Cases Commenced by Chapter of the Bankruptcy Code, During the 12-Month Period Ending December 31, 2024

Income: City

City	Per Capita ($)	Median Household ($)	Average Household ($)
Albuquerque, NM	39,117	65,604	88,262
Anchorage, AK	49,338	98,152	127,598
Ann Arbor, MI	54,604	81,089	121,561
Athens, GA	31,836	51,655	76,375
Atlanta, GA	64,063	81,938	135,218
Austin, TX	59,427	91,461	130,163
Baltimore, MD	39,195	59,623	87,339
Billings, MT	42,639	71,855	98,655
Boise City, ID	48,274	81,308	112,482
Boston, MA	60,001	94,755	140,807
Boulder, CO	59,450	85,364	140,662
Cape Coral, FL	39,603	76,062	97,070
Cedar Rapids, IA	39,824	67,859	91,040
Charleston, SC	58,583	90,038	129,666
Charlotte, NC	49,991	78,438	119,473
Chicago, IL	48,148	75,134	112,443
Cincinnati, OH	38,878	51,707	83,146
Clarksville, TN	31,266	66,786	79,769
Cleveland, OH	27,078	39,187	56,900
College Station, TX	32,123	51,776	84,849
Colorado Springs, CO	44,893	83,198	108,459
Columbia, MO	37,359	64,488	91,425
Columbia, SC	38,087	55,653	90,935
Columbus, OH	37,189	65,327	85,919
Dallas, TX	44,138	67,760	106,979
Davenport, IA	36,583	64,497	83,699
Denver, CO	61,202	91,681	131,349
Des Moines, IA	36,459	63,966	83,728
Detroit, MI	24,029	39,575	56,528
Durham, NC	47,246	79,234	108,538
El Paso, TX	28,942	58,734	78,842
Eugene, OR	41,035	63,836	94,063
Fargo, ND	42,212	66,029	91,129
Fort Collins, CO	46,341	83,598	110,629
Fort Wayne, IN	32,884	60,293	78,764
Fort Worth, TX	37,157	76,602	101,838
Gainesville, FL	30,282	45,611	71,640
Green Bay, WI	34,514	62,546	81,363
Greensboro, NC	35,858	58,884	85,861
Honolulu, HI	48,465	85,428	120,718
Houston, TX	41,142	62,894	101,848
Huntsville, AL	44,733	70,778	101,671
Indianapolis, IN	36,194	62,995	86,913
Jacksonville, FL	37,269	66,981	90,429
Kansas City, MO	40,112	67,449	91,703
Lafayette, LA	39,861	61,454	91,871
Las Vegas, NV	38,421	70,723	98,664
Lexington, KY	42,272	67,631	98,429
Lincoln, NE	39,187	69,991	94,181
Little Rock, AR	43,242	60,583	98,728
Los Angeles, CA	46,270	80,366	122,610
Louisville, KY	38,890	64,731	91,264
Madison, WI	48,557	76,983	104,969
Manchester, NH	44,220	77,415	100,102
McAllen, TX	29,406	60,165	86,175
Memphis, TN	32,314	51,211	77,102

Table continued on following page.

City	Per Capita ($)	Median Household ($)	Average Household ($)
Miami, FL	42,528	59,390	97,643
Midland, TX	49,327	91,169	126,317
Milwaukee, WI	29,679	51,888	70,559
Minneapolis, MN	50,605	80,269	112,607
Nashville, TN	46,820	75,197	106,483
New Orleans, LA	39,698	55,339	89,943
New York, NY	50,776	79,713	127,894
Oklahoma City, OK	37,109	66,702	91,131
Omaha, NE	42,515	72,708	103,010
Orlando, FL	41,985	69,268	100,135
Philadelphia, PA	37,669	60,698	88,307
Phoenix, AZ	40,309	77,041	106,845
Pittsburgh, PA	43,590	64,137	93,301
Portland, OR	55,312	88,792	122,267
Providence, RI	36,694	66,772	95,112
Provo, UT	26,755	62,800	86,072
Raleigh, NC	49,948	82,424	116,724
Reno, NV	45,180	78,448	107,386
Richmond, VA	44,249	62,671	94,647
Rochester, MN	49,727	87,767	119,510
Sacramento, CA	42,300	83,753	108,939
Saint Louis, MO	38,947	55,279	78,097
Saint Paul, MN	41,594	73,055	102,197
Salem, OR	36,477	71,900	94,087
Salt Lake City, UT	49,642	74,925	111,189
San Antonio, TX	32,983	62,917	85,107
San Diego, CA	54,678	104,321	139,707
San Francisco, CA	90,285	141,446	204,625
San Jose, CA	63,253	141,565	187,711
Santa Rosa, CA	50,520	97,410	129,680
Savannah, GA	32,004	56,782	77,786
Seattle, WA	82,508	121,984	170,038
Sioux Falls, SD	43,231	74,714	102,058
Tampa, FL	49,513	71,302	117,408
Tucson, AZ	31,152	54,546	73,528
Tulsa, OK	37,533	58,407	88,998
Virginia Beach, VA	47,372	90,685	118,081
Washington, DC	75,253	106,287	157,604
Wichita, KS	35,958	63,072	87,820
Wilmington, NC	46,062	63,900	98,401
Winston-Salem, NC	35,074	57,673	85,278
U.S.	43,289	78,538	110,491

Source: U.S. Census Bureau, 2019-2023 American Community Survey 5-Year Estimates

Income: Metro Area

Metro Area	Per Capita ($)	Median Household ($)	Average Household ($)
Albuquerque, NM	38,300	67,995	91,376
Anchorage, AK	47,015	95,918	123,232
Ann Arbor, MI	51,746	87,156	122,847
Athens, GA	36,105	62,897	91,841
Atlanta, GA	44,798	86,338	118,625
Austin, TX	53,550	97,638	132,189
Baltimore, MD	51,146	97,300	128,719
Billings, MT	43,176	74,599	102,275
Boise City, ID	41,793	82,694	110,044
Boston, MA	61,389	112,484	155,005
Boulder, CO	60,272	102,772	144,869
Cape Coral, FL	43,365	73,099	102,290
Cedar Rapids, IA	41,820	77,084	100,451
Charleston, SC	46,863	82,272	114,464
Charlotte, NC	44,995	80,201	113,387
Chicago, IL	48,107	88,850	122,980
Cincinnati, OH	43,371	79,490	107,457
Clarksville, TN	31,813	66,210	82,303
Cleveland, OH	41,791	68,507	96,273
College Station, TX	34,136	59,691	88,300
Colorado Springs, CO	44,315	87,180	112,662
Columbia, MO	37,799	69,463	93,435
Columbia, SC	37,159	66,146	90,520
Columbus, OH	43,665	79,847	108,257
Dallas, TX	44,447	87,155	120,397
Davenport, IA	39,357	71,925	93,006
Denver, CO	55,529	102,339	135,703
Des Moines, IA	44,796	84,209	109,864
Detroit, MI	42,145	75,123	102,705
Durham, NC	48,827	81,017	116,697
El Paso, TX	27,509	58,800	77,734
Eugene, OR	38,563	69,311	91,348
Fargo, ND	43,099	75,523	100,645
Fort Collins, CO	49,323	91,364	118,812
Fort Wayne, IN	36,444	69,378	90,705
Fort Worth, TX	44,447	87,155	120,397
Gainesville, FL	36,810	58,946	89,302
Green Bay, WI	40,606	77,459	98,052
Greensboro, NC	35,569	63,083	87,043
Honolulu, HI	46,361	104,264	133,753
Houston, TX	41,559	80,458	115,043
Huntsville, AL	45,250	83,529	110,607
Indianapolis, IN	42,522	77,065	106,219
Jacksonville, FL	41,987	77,013	104,828
Kansas City, MO	44,205	81,927	108,186
Lafayette, LA	34,845	60,910	86,057
Las Vegas, NV	38,654	73,845	101,010
Lexington, KY	41,230	70,717	99,405
Lincoln, NE	40,527	73,095	99,081
Little Rock, AR	37,678	65,309	90,691
Los Angeles, CA	46,385	93,525	132,022
Louisville, KY	40,019	71,737	97,103
Madison, WI	49,799	86,827	113,809
Manchester, NH	52,243	100,436	128,567
McAllen, TX	22,005	52,281	71,722
Memphis, TN	36,519	64,743	92,389

Table continued on following page.

Metro Area	Per Capita ($)	Median Household ($)	Average Household ($)
Miami, FL	42,369	73,481	109,356
Midland, TX	48,843	93,442	126,152
Milwaukee, WI	44,476	76,404	104,403
Minneapolis, MN	51,500	98,180	128,647
Nashville, TN	45,266	82,499	113,441
New Orleans, LA	37,547	62,271	90,627
New York, NY	54,510	97,334	144,032
Oklahoma City, OK	38,240	70,499	95,891
Omaha, NE	44,338	83,023	111,142
Orlando, FL	38,776	75,611	103,312
Philadelphia, PA	49,178	89,273	123,454
Phoenix, AZ	43,395	84,703	113,623
Pittsburgh, PA	44,726	73,942	101,289
Portland, OR	50,158	94,573	124,372
Providence, RI	45,170	85,646	111,377
Provo, UT	35,045	96,745	121,112
Raleigh, NC	49,462	96,066	126,566
Reno, NV	45,849	84,684	114,037
Richmond, VA	46,237	84,405	114,424
Rochester, MN	48,977	89,675	120,598
Sacramento, CA	45,964	93,986	123,767
Saint Louis, MO	44,689	78,225	107,013
Saint Paul, MN	51,500	98,180	128,647
Salem, OR	36,260	76,010	97,771
Salt Lake City, UT	43,026	95,045	121,478
San Antonio, TX	37,425	74,297	100,400
San Diego, CA	49,891	102,285	136,236
San Francisco, CA	72,306	133,780	190,258
San Jose, CA	75,895	157,444	217,226
Santa Rosa, CA	54,941	102,840	138,572
Savannah, GA	39,158	74,632	99,643
Seattle, WA	61,286	112,594	152,753
Sioux Falls, SD	43,434	81,418	106,253
Tampa, FL	42,023	71,254	100,901
Tucson, AZ	38,564	67,929	92,561
Tulsa, OK	37,865	67,823	94,114
Virginia Beach, VA	42,791	80,533	105,690
Washington, DC	62,026	123,896	162,905
Wichita, KS	36,529	68,930	91,559
Wilmington, NC	44,459	73,687	100,847
Winston-Salem, NC	35,829	64,282	87,020
U.S.	43,289	78,538	110,491

Note: Figures cover the Metropolitan Statistical Area (MSA)
Source: U.S. Census Bureau, 2019-2023 American Community Survey 5-Year Estimates

Household Income Distribution: City

City	Percent of Households Earning							
	Under $15,000	$15,000 -$24,999	$25,000 -$34,999	$35,000 -$49,999	$50,000 -$74,999	$75,000 -$99,999	$100,000 -$149,999	$150,000 and up
Albuquerque, NM	10.9	8.5	7.9	11.5	17.5	12.6	16.0	15.2
Anchorage, AK	5.2	4.6	4.4	8.3	14.6	13.7	19.5	29.7
Ann Arbor, MI	12.8	5.7	5.8	8.8	14.4	10.6	15.2	26.8
Athens, GA	15.5	10.4	10.3	12.4	16.1	10.9	12.9	11.6
Atlanta, GA	13.2	6.7	6.1	8.2	12.8	11.5	15.0	26.5
Austin, TX	7.8	4.6	4.9	9.3	15.1	12.4	17.2	28.7
Baltimore, MD	15.7	8.4	7.4	11.4	16.6	11.3	13.5	15.7
Billings, MT	7.2	7.0	7.4	12.6	18.1	13.0	17.9	16.9
Boise City, ID	5.7	6.0	6.3	11.2	16.6	15.1	17.4	21.6
Boston, MA	12.9	6.5	5.1	7.1	10.6	9.9	15.5	32.5
Boulder, CO	12.4	6.7	7.3	7.7	11.5	9.5	14.0	30.9
Cape Coral, FL	6.2	5.0	7.7	10.6	19.9	15.6	19.3	15.7
Cedar Rapids, IA	7.3	6.6	8.9	14.1	18.3	14.2	16.0	14.8
Charleston, SC	7.7	6.1	4.3	9.6	14.7	12.7	18.6	26.4
Charlotte, NC	7.0	5.6	6.2	11.6	17.6	12.7	16.9	22.5
Chicago, IL	12.1	7.2	6.9	9.8	14.0	11.7	16.0	22.4
Cincinnati, OH	16.9	10.2	8.7	12.9	15.0	10.3	11.8	14.2
Clarksville, TN	7.7	5.7	7.7	13.4	21.0	16.7	17.8	10.0
Cleveland, OH	22.1	12.6	10.7	14.2	16.0	9.2	8.9	6.4
College Station, TX	18.3	8.3	9.5	12.9	12.2	11.0	12.2	15.6
Colorado Springs, CO	6.2	5.3	5.8	10.4	17.7	13.6	19.8	21.3
Columbia, MO	12.4	8.3	8.5	10.8	17.1	11.8	14.3	17.0
Columbia, SC	16.5	8.6	8.2	11.7	16.7	10.7	11.7	15.8
Columbus, OH	10.0	7.1	7.4	13.3	18.5	13.5	16.6	13.5
Dallas, TX	10.2	6.8	7.7	12.3	17.9	12.5	13.7	18.8
Davenport, IA	10.8	7.0	8.8	11.5	19.0	13.5	17.4	12.0
Denver, CO	7.8	5.2	5.1	8.6	14.4	12.6	17.9	28.4
Des Moines, IA	8.8	7.7	7.2	14.3	19.3	15.4	15.2	12.1
Detroit, MI	22.8	12.2	10.2	15.2	15.1	9.5	9.2	5.8
Durham, NC	7.7	5.8	6.4	10.6	16.9	12.9	17.9	21.7
El Paso, TX	12.9	9.1	8.9	12.8	18.2	12.6	14.2	11.5
Eugene, OR	11.3	7.8	7.6	13.2	15.5	12.5	15.8	16.3
Fargo, ND	8.5	7.3	9.2	12.9	18.1	13.8	15.2	15.0
Fort Collins, CO	9.5	5.7	5.5	10.0	14.9	12.5	18.4	23.5
Fort Wayne, IN	9.3	7.9	9.6	14.5	19.5	14.1	15.2	9.9
Fort Worth, TX	7.4	5.9	6.9	11.1	17.3	13.7	18.1	19.4
Gainesville, FL	18.0	10.4	11.2	14.8	14.8	10.2	10.4	10.2
Green Bay, WI	9.5	8.6	7.4	13.6	19.7	14.6	16.2	10.4
Greensboro, NC	11.7	8.0	9.0	13.8	17.8	12.2	15.0	12.6
Honolulu, HI	8.8	5.7	5.1	9.4	15.2	12.7	17.4	25.7
Houston, TX	10.9	8.2	8.5	12.6	17.4	11.6	13.1	17.7
Huntsville, AL	9.2	8.0	8.7	11.3	15.0	12.6	15.6	19.6
Indianapolis, IN	10.7	7.5	8.2	13.5	18.7	12.5	15.0	13.8
Jacksonville, FL	10.0	7.3	7.5	12.7	17.9	13.3	16.9	14.5
Kansas City, MO	10.3	7.2	7.5	12.5	17.2	12.6	16.9	15.7
Lafayette, LA	13.8	8.8	8.0	11.5	14.6	12.8	14.9	15.6
Las Vegas, NV	10.0	6.7	7.5	11.4	17.3	12.9	16.8	17.4
Lexington, KY	9.8	7.2	8.6	11.9	16.8	11.9	15.7	18.1
Lincoln, NE	8.1	6.4	8.2	12.5	18.3	14.0	17.1	15.6
Little Rock, AR	10.7	8.2	9.9	13.9	15.6	11.3	13.1	17.2
Los Angeles, CA	10.8	6.7	6.5	9.4	14.0	11.5	16.0	25.1
Louisville, KY	10.6	7.6	8.2	12.7	17.2	12.8	15.9	15.0
Madison, WI	9.4	6.2	7.2	10.3	15.5	12.8	17.6	20.9
Manchester, NH	6.0	6.9	5.7	11.7	18.0	14.3	19.3	18.1

Table continued on following page.

City	Percent of Households Earning							
	Under $15,000	$15,000 -$24,999	$25,000 -$34,999	$35,000 -$49,999	$50,000 -$74,999	$75,000 -$99,999	$100,000 -$149,999	$150,000 and up
McAllen, TX	11.9	10.2	9.3	11.4	16.1	11.7	15.7	13.7
Memphis, TN	14.7	9.9	10.1	14.4	17.9	10.9	11.6	10.5
Miami, FL	14.4	9.3	8.1	11.9	15.7	10.2	13.1	17.4
Midland, TX	9.1	4.8	5.8	9.2	14.3	10.1	18.0	28.6
Milwaukee, WI	14.5	9.7	10.4	13.8	18.0	12.0	12.7	8.9
Minneapolis, MN	9.5	6.6	6.2	9.7	15.2	12.3	17.3	23.1
Nashville, TN	8.5	5.6	6.6	11.8	17.4	13.6	17.2	19.3
New Orleans, LA	18.7	9.7	7.7	10.8	14.8	9.6	12.8	15.8
New York, NY	12.3	7.0	6.3	8.9	13.3	10.8	15.3	26.1
Oklahoma City, OK	10.0	7.0	7.9	12.4	18.1	13.3	15.9	15.4
Omaha, NE	8.8	6.5	7.2	11.4	17.6	13.1	17.1	18.2
Orlando, FL	9.5	7.0	8.7	11.7	17.1	12.5	16.3	17.2
Philadelphia, PA	15.1	8.7	8.2	11.0	15.8	11.8	14.0	15.3
Phoenix, AZ	7.7	5.6	6.7	11.5	17.3	13.7	17.4	20.1
Pittsburgh, PA	14.2	8.1	7.4	11.0	16.6	11.4	14.6	16.8
Portland, OR	8.8	5.3	5.6	9.2	14.2	11.9	17.6	27.3
Providence, RI	13.7	8.4	6.6	10.7	16.0	11.7	15.8	17.1
Provo, UT	9.4	8.2	9.2	13.5	17.7	13.6	14.5	13.8
Raleigh, NC	7.0	5.6	6.0	11.2	15.9	13.0	17.2	24.1
Reno, NV	7.9	6.4	6.9	10.2	16.6	13.2	18.7	19.9
Richmond, VA	13.0	8.4	7.7	12.7	16.6	12.0	12.4	17.1
Rochester, MN	5.2	5.8	5.7	9.1	16.3	13.5	19.9	24.5
Sacramento, CA	9.1	6.1	5.2	9.5	15.1	13.6	18.7	22.7
Saint Louis, MO	15.5	8.8	9.1	12.5	17.5	11.3	13.1	12.4
Saint Paul, MN	9.0	6.6	6.9	10.4	18.4	13.2	16.1	19.4
Salem, OR	9.0	6.5	7.5	11.2	17.5	12.6	19.0	16.5
Salt Lake City, UT	9.0	6.7	6.5	11.1	16.8	13.5	15.9	20.5
San Antonio, TX	10.3	7.9	9.2	12.4	18.6	13.4	15.0	13.4
San Diego, CA	6.7	4.4	4.8	7.3	12.5	12.4	19.4	32.5
San Francisco, CA	8.5	4.8	3.9	5.2	8.1	8.4	13.4	47.7
San Jose, CA	4.9	3.6	3.5	5.5	9.2	9.3	16.6	47.3
Santa Rosa, CA	6.3	4.1	4.4	7.7	15.6	13.4	19.5	29.1
Savannah, GA	13.4	8.3	9.8	13.0	18.8	11.7	13.9	11.2
Seattle, WA	7.3	3.9	4.0	6.5	11.4	9.5	16.3	41.1
Sioux Falls, SD	6.0	5.5	7.5	12.3	18.8	14.3	18.6	16.9
Tampa, FL	11.1	7.2	7.2	11.2	15.6	11.2	14.4	22.1
Tucson, AZ	12.0	9.6	10.2	14.6	17.5	12.7	14.1	9.5
Tulsa, OK	11.9	7.6	10.1	13.5	17.8	11.5	13.4	14.2
Virginia Beach, VA	5.7	3.9	5.1	8.5	18.1	13.7	20.8	24.2
Washington, DC	10.5	4.6	3.8	6.8	11.4	10.4	15.7	36.9
Wichita, KS	9.5	7.6	9.6	13.0	18.1	13.3	15.6	13.3
Wilmington, NC	11.3	6.8	8.3	13.0	17.6	11.9	14.2	16.8
Winston-Salem, NC	11.3	8.9	10.0	13.2	17.2	12.5	13.8	13.0
U.S.	8.5	6.6	6.8	10.4	15.7	12.7	17.4	21.9

Source: U.S. Census Bureau, 2019-2023 American Community Survey 5-Year Estimates

Household Income Distribution: Metro Area

Metro Area	Percent of Households Earning							
	Under $15,000	$15,000 -$24,999	$25,000 -$34,999	$35,000 -$49,999	$50,000 -$74,999	$75,000 -$99,999	$100,000 -$149,999	$150,000 and up
Albuquerque, NM	10.3	7.9	7.6	11.2	17.5	12.8	16.6	16.0
Anchorage, AK	5.4	4.9	4.7	8.5	14.6	13.8	19.8	28.2
Ann Arbor, MI	8.8	5.3	5.8	9.3	14.9	11.8	17.5	26.6
Athens, GA	12.6	8.5	9.0	11.3	15.5	12.1	14.8	16.2
Atlanta, GA	6.9	5.4	6.0	9.8	15.4	13.4	18.3	24.8
Austin, TX	6.3	4.1	4.8	8.6	14.8	12.4	19.2	29.9
Baltimore, MD	7.6	4.9	5.0	8.3	13.3	12.0	18.8	30.1
Billings, MT	6.6	6.8	7.6	11.5	17.6	13.4	18.1	18.2
Boise City, ID	5.3	5.3	5.6	10.5	18.4	15.3	19.7	19.8
Boston, MA	7.2	4.9	4.5	6.7	11.2	10.5	17.7	37.2
Boulder, CO	7.5	5.3	5.2	7.4	12.4	11.1	17.3	33.9
Cape Coral, FL	7.9	6.2	7.5	11.7	18.0	14.2	17.3	17.2
Cedar Rapids, IA	6.1	6.2	7.2	12.0	17.3	14.5	18.2	18.5
Charleston, SC	7.2	6.1	6.1	10.0	16.8	13.0	19.2	21.6
Charlotte, NC	6.8	6.1	6.5	10.9	16.7	13.0	17.7	22.2
Chicago, IL	8.1	5.6	5.9	9.0	14.2	12.5	18.4	26.4
Cincinnati, OH	8.4	6.5	6.7	10.4	15.5	13.0	18.7	20.9
Clarksville, TN	9.1	6.6	8.1	12.3	20.0	15.2	17.1	11.5
Cleveland, OH	10.1	7.6	7.8	11.6	16.9	12.5	16.0	17.3
College Station, TX	14.7	7.7	8.7	12.5	14.6	12.2	14.2	15.4
Colorado Springs, CO	5.7	4.8	5.6	9.8	16.9	13.7	20.3	23.3
Columbia, MO	10.3	7.4	7.6	11.1	17.3	13.3	16.6	16.2
Columbia, SC	10.1	7.3	8.1	12.5	17.5	13.0	15.8	15.7
Columbus, OH	7.6	5.8	6.4	11.0	16.6	12.9	18.2	21.5
Dallas, TX	6.3	4.9	5.8	10.0	16.1	13.1	18.5	25.2
Davenport, IA	9.0	6.9	7.5	11.5	17.0	13.6	18.6	16.0
Denver, CO	5.7	4.1	4.5	7.9	14.0	12.8	19.7	31.4
Des Moines, IA	5.6	5.4	6.1	11.0	16.5	14.0	19.1	22.4
Detroit, MI	9.3	6.7	7.0	11.1	15.7	12.8	17.0	20.2
Durham, NC	7.8	6.2	6.4	10.3	16.0	12.0	17.3	23.9
El Paso, TX	12.8	8.9	8.9	12.8	18.6	12.6	14.4	11.1
Eugene, OR	10.0	7.3	7.5	12.5	16.2	14.2	17.8	14.6
Fargo, ND	7.8	6.5	7.5	11.4	16.5	13.8	18.0	18.5
Fort Collins, CO	7.2	5.1	5.3	8.9	14.9	13.5	19.9	25.2
Fort Wayne, IN	7.2	6.9	7.9	12.8	18.9	15.0	17.0	14.1
Fort Worth, TX	6.3	4.9	5.8	10.0	16.1	13.1	18.5	25.2
Gainesville, FL	13.2	8.5	9.1	12.6	16.2	11.1	14.0	15.2
Green Bay, WI	6.7	5.6	7.0	11.1	17.9	14.8	20.8	16.1
Greensboro, NC	10.1	8.0	8.3	13.7	17.6	12.6	16.3	13.5
Honolulu, HI	6.3	4.2	4.2	7.9	12.9	12.6	20.4	31.6
Houston, TX	7.7	6.2	6.7	10.5	15.9	12.5	16.9	23.6
Huntsville, AL	7.3	6.6	6.8	10.1	15.1	12.5	18.2	23.4
Indianapolis, IN	7.7	6.0	6.6	11.2	17.3	13.2	17.5	20.5
Jacksonville, FL	8.0	6.1	6.7	11.1	16.9	13.3	18.3	19.7
Kansas City, MO	6.9	5.7	6.4	10.4	16.6	13.3	19.1	21.3
Lafayette, LA	13.1	9.6	8.3	12.0	14.7	12.2	15.8	14.3
Las Vegas, NV	8.6	6.4	7.2	11.3	17.2	13.6	17.4	18.2
Lexington, KY	9.1	6.8	8.1	11.7	17.0	12.5	17.0	17.6
Lincoln, NE	7.4	6.1	7.7	12.0	17.9	13.8	18.0	17.1
Little Rock, AR	9.9	7.9	8.8	12.9	17.0	12.7	16.1	14.8
Los Angeles, CA	8.3	5.4	5.6	8.5	13.4	11.7	17.9	29.3
Louisville, KY	8.5	6.8	7.4	12.0	17.2	13.5	17.6	17.0
Madison, WI	6.5	5.2	6.1	9.4	16.1	13.5	19.4	23.8
Manchester, NH	4.5	4.5	4.6	8.8	14.6	12.8	19.9	30.3

Table continued on following page.

Metro Area	Percent of Households Earning							
	Under $15,000	$15,000 -$24,999	$25,000 -$34,999	$35,000 -$49,999	$50,000 -$74,999	$75,000 -$99,999	$100,000 -$149,999	$150,000 and up
McAllen, TX	14.0	11.7	10.0	12.6	16.7	11.7	13.8	9.5
Memphis, TN	10.9	8.0	8.2	12.2	16.7	12.1	16.0	15.9
Miami, FL	9.3	7.1	7.4	10.9	16.1	12.6	16.3	20.1
Midland, TX	8.0	4.3	5.9	9.4	13.7	11.6	18.6	28.4
Milwaukee, WI	8.5	6.5	7.4	10.4	16.3	13.1	17.8	20.0
Minneapolis, MN	5.5	4.5	4.9	8.5	14.5	13.0	20.3	28.9
Nashville, TN	6.6	5.5	5.8	10.7	16.8	13.9	19.0	21.7
New Orleans, LA	13.6	8.8	8.5	11.2	15.6	11.7	14.6	15.9
New York, NY	9.0	5.6	5.4	7.9	12.4	10.7	16.7	32.4
Oklahoma City, OK	8.9	6.7	7.8	11.9	17.6	13.5	17.0	16.6
Omaha, NE	6.9	5.6	6.3	10.1	16.6	13.2	19.6	21.7
Orlando, FL	7.3	6.3	7.3	11.1	17.7	13.5	18.0	18.9
Philadelphia, PA	8.4	5.8	6.0	8.9	14.0	11.9	17.9	27.1
Phoenix, AZ	6.6	5.0	5.9	10.1	16.6	13.9	19.3	22.5
Pittsburgh, PA	8.8	7.3	7.3	10.9	16.2	12.9	17.2	19.3
Portland, OR	6.4	4.7	5.1	8.8	14.6	13.1	19.7	27.6
Providence, RI	8.7	6.7	6.0	9.1	14.0	12.6	19.0	23.8
Provo, UT	4.4	4.1	4.6	8.5	15.1	15.0	22.7	25.6
Raleigh, NC	5.6	4.9	5.4	9.0	14.6	12.1	19.5	28.8
Reno, NV	6.9	5.4	6.0	9.9	16.4	13.4	20.5	21.6
Richmond, VA	7.2	5.6	5.9	10.0	16.3	12.7	18.9	23.4
Rochester, MN	5.2	5.4	5.6	9.0	16.3	13.4	20.4	24.7
Sacramento, CA	7.3	5.2	5.3	8.5	13.9	12.7	19.3	27.9
Saint Louis, MO	7.6	6.2	6.8	11.1	16.4	13.1	18.1	20.7
Saint Paul, MN	5.5	4.5	4.9	8.5	14.5	13.0	20.3	28.9
Salem, OR	7.7	6.4	6.9	11.0	17.3	13.4	19.7	17.5
Salt Lake City, UT	5.3	4.0	4.7	8.8	15.3	14.6	21.5	25.8
San Antonio, TX	8.2	6.5	7.5	10.9	17.2	13.3	17.4	18.9
San Diego, CA	6.3	4.7	5.0	7.8	13.1	12.1	19.1	31.9
San Francisco, CA	6.3	3.8	3.8	5.9	9.6	9.3	15.9	45.4
San Jose, CA	4.6	3.0	3.1	4.8	8.4	8.5	15.5	52.0
Santa Rosa, CA	5.9	4.1	4.7	7.8	13.4	12.7	19.3	32.2
Savannah, GA	8.5	6.0	7.5	11.0	17.3	13.8	18.5	17.4
Seattle, WA	5.6	3.8	4.2	7.0	12.6	11.5	19.2	36.1
Sioux Falls, SD	5.4	5.2	6.6	11.6	17.7	14.7	20.0	18.9
Tampa, FL	8.6	6.9	7.6	11.6	17.6	12.8	16.6	18.3
Tucson, AZ	9.3	7.6	8.5	12.3	16.7	12.8	16.7	16.0
Tulsa, OK	8.9	7.1	8.4	12.3	17.8	12.9	16.9	15.8
Virginia Beach, VA	7.5	5.5	6.6	10.0	17.3	13.3	19.2	20.7
Washington, DC	5.4	3.2	3.5	5.9	11.0	11.0	18.9	41.0
Wichita, KS	8.3	6.6	8.7	12.2	18.3	13.9	17.0	14.8
Wilmington, NC	8.2	6.4	6.8	11.5	18.0	13.4	17.6	18.0
Winston-Salem, NC	9.2	8.1	9.0	12.8	18.0	13.7	15.4	13.9
U.S.	8.5	6.6	6.8	10.4	15.7	12.7	17.4	21.9

Note: Figures cover the Metropolitan Statistical Area (MSA)
Source: U.S. Census Bureau, 2019-2023 American Community Survey 5-Year Estimates

Poverty Rate: City

City	All Ages	Under 18 Years Old	18 to 64 Years Old	65 Years and Over
Albuquerque, NM	16.0	20.8	15.3	12.6
Anchorage, AK	9.3	11.3	8.8	7.8
Ann Arbor, MI	23.0	13.5	27.9	6.0
Athens, GA	26.3	24.3	29.5	11.7
Atlanta, GA	17.9	25.9	15.6	18.7
Austin, TX	12.3	15.7	11.6	10.9
Baltimore, MD	20.1	26.4	17.8	20.9
Billings, MT	10.6	13.0	10.2	8.9
Boise City, ID	10.6	12.7	10.8	7.3
Boston, MA	16.9	21.8	15.0	21.0
Boulder, CO	21.8	9.7	26.8	6.2
Cape Coral, FL	9.8	13.1	9.1	9.2
Cedar Rapids, IA	11.8	14.3	11.9	7.8
Charleston, SC	12.0	15.4	12.2	7.3
Charlotte, NC	11.7	16.9	10.1	10.4
Chicago, IL	16.8	24.0	14.6	17.1
Cincinnati, OH	24.5	34.2	22.8	17.1
Clarksville, TN	12.8	16.8	11.8	7.7
Cleveland, OH	30.8	45.3	27.4	24.5
College Station, TX	28.6	14.8	34.5	5.8
Colorado Springs, CO	9.3	10.8	9.2	7.7
Columbia, MO	20.0	13.4	23.5	10.7
Columbia, SC	23.3	29.4	22.6	17.2
Columbus, OH	17.8	25.9	16.1	12.1
Dallas, TX	17.2	25.7	14.3	15.0
Davenport, IA	15.6	20.7	15.0	11.3
Denver, CO	11.2	14.9	10.2	11.5
Des Moines, IA	14.9	22.1	13.1	10.8
Detroit, MI	31.5	44.2	28.8	20.9
Durham, NC	12.2	16.9	11.5	8.2
El Paso, TX	18.4	24.8	15.4	20.0
Eugene, OR	18.2	15.1	21.4	9.4
Fargo, ND	12.8	14.6	13.7	6.0
Fort Collins, CO	16.0	9.2	19.1	8.0
Fort Wayne, IN	15.6	22.5	14.3	9.1
Fort Worth, TX	12.9	18.0	11.1	10.2
Gainesville, FL	28.0	18.0	32.8	11.4
Green Bay, WI	16.5	23.4	15.0	11.0
Greensboro, NC	18.4	26.0	16.5	14.2
Honolulu, HI	11.9	15.0	11.1	11.7
Houston, TX	19.7	29.9	16.6	16.0
Huntsville, AL	13.8	19.5	13.3	8.9
Indianapolis, IN	15.7	21.2	14.3	11.5
Jacksonville, FL	15.0	20.9	13.1	14.2
Kansas City, MO	14.6	20.5	12.9	12.4
Lafayette, LA	19.1	28.3	17.1	14.8
Las Vegas, NV	14.2	18.8	13.2	11.7
Lexington, KY	15.7	19.3	16.3	7.7
Lincoln, NE	12.6	13.0	13.6	8.0
Little Rock, AR	16.4	25.1	15.1	7.8
Los Angeles, CA	16.5	22.1	14.8	16.9
Louisville, KY	16.1	23.2	14.9	10.8
Madison, WI	16.2	13.1	18.7	7.0
Manchester, NH	10.7	17.2	9.3	9.5
McAllen, TX	20.2	27.2	17.6	17.0

Table continued on following page.

City	All Ages	Under 18 Years Old	18 to 64 Years Old	65 Years and Over
Memphis, TN	22.5	34.7	18.9	16.4
Miami, FL	19.2	23.4	15.3	31.4
Midland, TX	11.7	14.0	10.6	11.5
Milwaukee, WI	23.3	32.5	20.7	16.7
Minneapolis, MN	16.4	19.8	15.7	14.2
Nashville, TN	14.1	21.2	12.5	11.2
New Orleans, LA	22.6	32.2	20.1	20.7
New York, NY	17.4	23.2	15.1	18.9
Oklahoma City, OK	15.2	20.6	14.2	9.4
Omaha, NE	12.8	15.9	12.3	9.3
Orlando, FL	15.5	23.0	12.9	16.8
Philadelphia, PA	22.0	30.1	19.5	21.1
Phoenix, AZ	14.3	20.3	12.5	11.7
Pittsburgh, PA	19.5	29.5	18.4	14.1
Portland, OR	12.8	14.5	12.5	11.8
Providence, RI	20.1	26.0	18.2	19.9
Provo, UT	22.3	12.8	26.3	9.4
Raleigh, NC	11.4	14.6	10.9	9.1
Reno, NV	12.5	13.9	12.2	11.8
Richmond, VA	18.8	28.3	17.2	14.6
Rochester, MN	9.1	9.0	9.4	7.6
Sacramento, CA	14.4	17.9	13.5	12.8
Saint Louis, MO	19.8	26.9	18.2	17.8
Saint Paul, MN	15.7	22.9	13.8	11.7
Salem, OR	14.7	17.2	14.4	11.8
Salt Lake City, UT	13.4	12.3	14.1	11.0
San Antonio, TX	17.1	24.8	14.8	14.2
San Diego, CA	11.1	12.3	11.0	10.2
San Francisco, CA	10.6	8.2	9.6	16.4
San Jose, CA	7.8	7.6	7.4	10.5
Santa Rosa, CA	9.5	10.8	9.1	9.5
Savannah, GA	19.5	28.9	17.6	14.0
Seattle, WA	9.9	8.6	9.7	12.3
Sioux Falls, SD	9.6	12.3	9.1	7.1
Tampa, FL	15.9	20.3	13.5	21.2
Tucson, AZ	18.8	24.3	18.7	12.5
Tulsa, OK	18.6	27.0	17.3	10.4
Virginia Beach, VA	8.4	11.2	8.0	5.9
Washington, DC	14.5	20.4	12.9	14.6
Wichita, KS	15.9	21.6	15.0	10.3
Wilmington, NC	16.3	18.1	17.3	11.0
Winston-Salem, NC	17.9	27.1	16.0	10.7
U.S.	12.4	16.3	11.6	10.4

Note: Figures are percentage of people whose income during the past 12 months was below the poverty level
Source: U.S. Census Bureau, 2019-2023 American Community Survey 5-Year Estimates

Poverty Rate: Metro Area

Metro Area	All Ages	Under 18 Years Old	18 to 64 Years Old	65 Years and Over
Albuquerque, NM	15.1	19.6	14.5	12.0
Anchorage, AK	9.6	11.6	9.1	7.9
Ann Arbor, MI	13.8	12.5	16.2	5.9
Athens, GA	19.7	19.0	22.1	10.1
Atlanta, GA	11.0	15.0	9.7	9.3
Austin, TX	9.9	11.5	9.6	8.7
Baltimore, MD	9.9	12.0	9.0	10.2
Billings, MT	10.0	12.0	9.9	8.2
Boise City, ID	9.1	10.7	8.9	7.7
Boston, MA	8.9	9.7	8.3	10.3
Boulder, CO	11.4	7.5	13.7	7.1
Cape Coral, FL	11.7	17.1	11.2	9.5
Cedar Rapids, IA	9.7	11.5	9.7	7.5
Charleston, SC	11.2	15.6	10.3	9.0
Charlotte, NC	10.5	14.2	9.4	9.3
Chicago, IL	11.1	14.8	10.0	10.2
Cincinnati, OH	11.6	14.7	11.1	9.2
Clarksville, TN	13.2	16.4	12.3	10.5
Cleveland, OH	13.6	19.3	12.6	10.6
College Station, TX	22.6	19.9	26.0	8.5
Colorado Springs, CO	8.5	10.2	8.2	6.9
Columbia, MO	16.5	14.6	18.8	9.0
Columbia, SC	14.7	19.8	13.9	10.6
Columbus, OH	12.2	16.5	11.4	8.7
Dallas, TX	10.5	14.5	9.2	9.3
Davenport, IA	12.4	16.9	12.0	8.3
Denver, CO	8.2	10.3	7.6	7.6
Des Moines, IA	8.9	11.0	8.5	7.1
Detroit, MI	13.2	19.1	12.0	10.2
Durham, NC	12.3	16.2	12.2	7.9
El Paso, TX	18.9	25.1	15.8	20.6
Eugene, OR	15.3	14.3	17.4	9.7
Fargo, ND	11.4	11.8	12.2	6.7
Fort Collins, CO	11.1	8.5	12.9	7.1
Fort Wayne, IN	11.8	16.1	11.1	7.3
Fort Worth, TX	10.5	14.5	9.2	9.3
Gainesville, FL	18.9	16.3	21.8	10.7
Green Bay, WI	9.5	11.6	9.3	7.5
Greensboro, NC	15.3	21.4	14.1	11.6
Honolulu, HI	9.1	11.4	8.5	8.7
Houston, TX	13.6	19.1	11.7	11.3
Huntsville, AL	10.4	13.1	9.8	9.1
Indianapolis, IN	10.5	13.6	9.8	8.3
Jacksonville, FL	12.1	16.9	10.9	10.2
Kansas City, MO	10.0	13.2	9.2	8.5
Lafayette, LA	18.5	25.0	16.8	14.8
Las Vegas, NV	13.2	18.1	12.1	10.6
Lexington, KY	14.0	17.4	14.1	8.6
Lincoln, NE	11.4	11.3	12.5	7.6
Little Rock, AR	14.2	19.7	13.5	8.7
Los Angeles, CA	12.6	16.0	11.4	13.1
Louisville, KY	12.3	17.0	11.4	9.2
Madison, WI	10.0	8.5	11.4	6.1
Manchester, NH	6.5	8.1	6.0	6.7
McAllen, TX	27.2	37.1	22.6	22.9

Table continued on following page.

Metro Area	All Ages	Under 18 Years Old	18 to 64 Years Old	65 Years and Over
Memphis, TN	16.3	24.2	14.0	12.2
Miami, FL	13.1	16.9	11.0	15.9
Midland, TX	10.6	12.7	9.3	11.6
Milwaukee, WI	12.4	17.0	11.2	10.3
Minneapolis, MN	8.2	9.6	7.7	7.7
Nashville, TN	10.4	13.6	9.5	8.9
New Orleans, LA	18.3	25.6	16.5	14.9
New York, NY	12.4	16.4	10.9	13.0
Oklahoma City, OK	13.9	18.3	13.3	8.8
Omaha, NE	9.5	11.2	9.1	8.1
Orlando, FL	11.8	15.0	11.0	10.5
Philadelphia, PA	11.7	15.7	10.6	10.3
Phoenix, AZ	11.2	15.1	10.3	9.2
Pittsburgh, PA	10.9	14.4	10.5	8.9
Portland, OR	9.5	10.5	9.4	9.0
Providence, RI	11.2	14.2	10.3	10.6
Provo, UT	8.7	7.2	10.0	5.5
Raleigh, NC	8.6	10.3	8.0	7.9
Reno, NV	10.7	12.1	10.3	10.3
Richmond, VA	10.0	13.4	9.3	8.0
Rochester, MN	7.8	8.3	7.8	7.1
Sacramento, CA	11.6	13.6	11.4	9.3
Saint Louis, MO	10.3	13.3	9.7	8.7
Saint Paul, MN	8.2	9.6	7.7	7.7
Salem, OR	12.9	16.0	12.5	10.2
Salt Lake City, UT	8.1	8.8	8.0	7.5
San Antonio, TX	13.4	18.5	11.9	11.4
San Diego, CA	10.4	12.0	10.0	9.4
San Francisco, CA	8.7	8.8	8.2	10.4
San Jose, CA	6.9	6.6	6.5	9.0
Santa Rosa, CA	8.6	9.3	8.4	8.4
Savannah, GA	12.4	16.6	11.4	9.9
Seattle, WA	8.4	9.5	7.9	8.8
Sioux Falls, SD	8.1	9.7	7.7	6.8
Tampa, FL	12.2	15.5	11.3	11.9
Tucson, AZ	14.4	18.7	14.9	8.9
Tulsa, OK	13.7	18.9	12.9	8.9
Virginia Beach, VA	10.9	15.4	9.9	8.4
Washington, DC	7.9	9.8	7.2	7.6
Wichita, KS	13.1	17.4	12.4	8.8
Wilmington, NC	11.1	13.9	11.9	7.0
Winston-Salem, NC	13.9	21.2	12.5	9.7
U.S.	12.4	16.3	11.6	10.4

Note: Figures are percentage of people whose income during the past 12 months was below the poverty level; Figures cover the Metropolitan Statistical Area (MSA)
Source: U.S. Census Bureau, 2019-2023 American Community Survey 5-Year Estimates

Employment by Industry

Metro Area	(A)	(B)	(C)	(D)	(E)	(F)	(G)	(H)	(I)	(J)	(K)	(L)	(M)	(N)
Albuquerque, NM	6.6	n/a	4.6	19.8	1.3	10.4	4.0	n/a	3.1	17.3	16.0	10.3	3.9	2.7
Anchorage, AK	7.3	6.2	4.0	19.3	1.7	10.9	1.3	1.1	3.7	19.1	11.0	10.9	8.0	2.8
Ann Arbor, MI	2.2	n/a	2.9	37.3	2.5	7.1	5.1	n/a	2.8	15.0	12.4	7.3	2.2	3.1
Athens, GA	3.9	n/a	3.3	28.7	0.7	11.4	6.7	n/a	3.6	16.0	8.8	11.1	1.8	4.0
Atlanta, GA[1]	4.2	4.1	7.0	11.9	3.8	9.7	5.3	0.1	3.6	14.6	18.3	9.4	7.1	5.1
Austin, TX	6.5	n/a	6.5	15.3	3.6	10.7	5.3	n/a	3.9	12.0	20.5	9.0	2.7	4.1
Baltimore, MD	5.4	n/a	5.3	16.6	1.1	8.4	3.9	n/a	3.7	20.0	17.5	9.0	5.3	3.7
Billings, MT	8.0	n/a	5.4	11.1	0.9	14.6	4.3	n/a	4.2	18.0	9.8	12.6	5.0	6.0
Boise City, ID	9.1	n/a	5.8	13.3	1.1	10.0	7.6	n/a	3.5	15.4	14.6	10.0	4.6	4.7
Boston, MA[1]	4.1	n/a	9.6	12.2	2.6	10.5	2.8	n/a	3.6	24.6	16.3	7.8	3.4	2.5
Boulder, CO	2.7	n/a	3.3	19.7	4.0	9.6	10.0	n/a	4.3	13.2	20.1	8.2	1.1	3.7
Cape Coral, FL	13.6	n/a	4.9	15.3	1.1	13.0	2.6	n/a	4.0	11.5	14.2	14.3	2.5	3.0
Cedar Rapids, IA	6.3	n/a	6.6	11.9	2.0	8.4	14.2	n/a	3.6	16.3	11.1	10.4	5.1	4.1
Charleston, SC	5.7	n/a	5.1	16.7	1.8	12.4	8.1	n/a	3.9	11.9	15.8	10.9	4.7	3.0
Charlotte, NC	5.9	n/a	8.8	12.9	1.9	10.9	7.7	n/a	4.0	11.1	16.2	10.0	6.1	4.7
Chicago, IL[1]	3.4	3.4	7.2	11.2	1.8	9.8	7.3	<0.1	4.1	17.0	18.0	8.7	6.5	4.9
Cincinnati, OH	4.6	n/a	6.8	11.6	1.1	10.6	10.4	n/a	3.6	15.9	15.3	9.0	5.8	5.3
Clarksville, TN	4.5	n/a	3.8	20.6	1.3	12.1	12.9	n/a	3.3	13.1	8.4	13.2	4.5	2.3
Cleveland, OH	3.7	n/a	6.5	12.5	1.3	9.5	11.6	n/a	3.5	19.7	13.9	9.1	3.8	4.9
College Station, TX	5.3	n/a	3.3	35.1	1.1	14.4	4.2	n/a	2.8	10.9	9.8	9.1	1.9	2.2
Colorado Springs, CO	5.4	n/a	5.8	17.9	1.5	12.4	3.6	n/a	7.0	14.6	16.0	10.2	3.8	2.0
Columbia, MO	3.6	3.5	7.6	31.5	1.1	10.6	4.7	0.1	2.8	13.9	9.1	10.1	2.6	2.5
Columbia, SC	4.3	n/a	8.3	19.4	1.1	9.4	7.4	n/a	4.2	13.9	13.6	10.5	4.2	3.7
Columbus, OH	4.5	n/a	6.9	16.6	1.5	9.1	6.5	n/a	3.8	15.5	16.3	9.2	6.7	3.6
Dallas, TX[1]	5.4	n/a	10.0	11.3	2.5	9.4	6.6	n/a	3.1	11.5	20.2	9.0	5.4	5.6
Davenport, IA	5.7	n/a	4.1	14.4	0.8	9.7	12.8	n/a	3.7	15.0	11.3	11.7	4.2	6.5
Denver, CO	6.9	n/a	7.1	13.7	3.0	10.4	4.0	n/a	4.2	12.9	19.4	8.5	5.3	4.7
Des Moines, IA	5.9	n/a	13.6	12.8	1.5	8.8	5.4	n/a	3.3	15.2	13.4	10.6	4.8	4.8
Detroit, MI[1]	4.0	n/a	6.2	9.6	1.4	9.1	12.1	n/a	3.8	16.2	18.4	9.9	5.2	4.1
Durham, NC	3.1	n/a	4.8	19.3	1.6	7.8	7.9	n/a	3.7	21.8	17.8	6.9	2.4	2.8
El Paso, TX	4.5	n/a	4.1	20.8	1.8	11.6	4.8	n/a	2.8	15.5	12.6	11.4	6.0	4.0
Eugene, OR	5.0	4.4	5.2	19.8	1.2	10.1	8.5	0.6	3.1	18.6	10.9	11.7	2.3	3.5
Fargo, ND	6.0	n/a	7.1	14.0	1.5	9.6	8.0	n/a	3.3	19.6	9.5	10.3	5.2	5.9
Fort Collins, CO	6.0	n/a	3.8	26.3	1.3	12.1	8.0	n/a	3.6	11.3	11.6	10.5	2.5	3.2
Fort Wayne, IN	5.5	n/a	5.1	9.6	0.8	8.8	15.8	n/a	5.6	19.2	9.6	10.4	5.0	4.6
Fort Worth, TX[1]	7.1	n/a	6.4	11.7	1.0	11.1	8.9	n/a	3.5	12.9	12.8	10.9	8.7	5.0
Gainesville, FL	4.3	n/a	4.0	28.7	1.2	10.5	3.1	n/a	3.0	19.7	10.7	10.0	2.8	2.1
Green Bay, WI	4.8	n/a	4.7	11.8	0.9	9.8	18.1	n/a	4.4	15.8	10.5	9.5	4.8	4.9
Greensboro, NC	5.3	n/a	4.3	12.6	1.0	9.9	12.8	n/a	3.7	14.9	12.6	11.3	5.7	5.8
Honolulu, HI	6.0	n/a	4.5	21.0	1.5	15.8	2.1	n/a	4.4	14.9	12.1	9.3	5.5	2.9
Houston, TX	9.0	6.7	5.2	13.4	0.9	10.4	6.9	2.3	3.9	13.3	16.4	9.6	5.8	5.2
Huntsville, AL	4.0	n/a	3.1	20.8	1.0	8.4	12.4	n/a	3.3	9.0	23.6	9.9	2.2	2.5
Indianapolis, IN	5.5	5.5	6.3	12.6	1.0	9.1	8.1	0.1	4.1	15.8	15.7	8.8	8.3	4.7
Jacksonville, FL	6.6	6.6	9.0	10.1	1.8	11.3	4.5	<0.1	3.6	16.3	14.9	11.0	7.3	3.7
Kansas City, MO	5.3	5.2	6.9	13.4	1.5	9.6	7.9	0.1	3.7	15.3	16.0	9.9	6.0	4.6
Lafayette, LA	9.6	5.5	4.7	12.6	0.8	11.1	7.7	4.1	3.6	18.3	11.3	12.6	3.3	4.4
Las Vegas, NV	6.8	6.8	5.3	10.7	1.3	25.8	2.6	<0.1	3.0	11.4	14.3	9.8	6.7	2.3
Lexington, KY	4.9	n/a	4.0	19.6	1.0	10.7	10.5	n/a	4.8	13.2	13.5	9.6	4.2	3.9
Lincoln, NE	5.4	n/a	5.4	21.8	2.0	9.7	7.4	n/a	4.3	17.0	10.3	9.3	5.3	2.2
Little Rock, AR	5.4	n/a	7.1	17.8	1.3	8.5	5.4	n/a	4.8	16.9	12.4	10.0	6.0	4.6
Los Angeles, CA[1]	3.2	3.2	4.5	12.9	4.1	11.6	6.5	<0.1	3.4	21.4	14.4	8.9	4.9	4.2
Louisville, KY	5.1	n/a	6.4	10.6	1.1	9.6	11.8	n/a	3.8	15.4	12.2	9.5	9.8	4.7
Madison, WI	4.6	n/a	5.5	22.4	5.0	8.4	8.7	n/a	5.0	13.1	12.2	9.1	2.5	3.6
Manchester, NH	4.3	n/a	5.6	10.8	2.4	9.0	12.0	n/a	3.8	20.1	14.1	12.5	2.4	3.1
McAllen, TX	3.0	n/a	3.3	20.3	1.0	9.8	2.3	n/a	2.2	30.1	8.9	12.7	3.3	3.1
Memphis, TN	3.8	n/a	4.5	13.2	0.8	9.3	6.1	n/a	4.2	15.2	13.5	9.4	14.1	5.8

Table continued on following page.

Appendix A: Comparative Statistics

Metro Area	(A)	(B)	(C)	(D)	(E)	(F)	(G)	(H)	(I)	(J)	(K)	(L)	(M)	(N)
Miami, FL[1]	4.5	4.5	7.1	10.6	1.7	11.4	3.5	<0.1	3.7	16.6	15.7	11.2	7.8	6.2
Midland, TX	33.1	n/a	5.0	8.7	0.8	9.2	3.7	n/a	3.4	7.7	9.5	7.9	5.2	5.8
Milwaukee, WI	4.3	4.2	5.5	9.6	1.3	9.2	12.8	0.1	5.1	20.8	14.0	9.0	4.0	4.5
Minneapolis, MN	4.3	n/a	7.2	13.2	1.4	8.9	10.0	n/a	3.9	19.0	14.4	9.2	4.4	4.2
Nashville, TN	5.5	n/a	6.8	11.2	2.7	11.2	7.4	n/a	4.2	15.1	16.1	9.2	6.4	4.2
New Orleans, LA	6.0	5.6	5.0	11.6	1.4	14.5	5.5	0.4	4.3	20.3	12.9	9.3	5.6	3.6
New York, NY[1]	3.3	n/a	9.8	12.5	4.0	9.0	2.1	n/a	3.8	25.2	16.1	7.3	3.7	3.3
Oklahoma City, OK	6.5	5.0	5.2	19.0	0.9	11.4	4.9	1.4	4.3	16.7	12.7	10.2	4.7	3.5
Omaha, NE	6.2	n/a	7.7	13.5	1.7	10.7	6.9	n/a	3.5	17.6	13.6	10.2	5.2	3.2
Orlando, FL	6.3	6.3	6.1	8.9	1.8	19.2	3.5	<0.1	3.7	12.9	19.1	10.5	4.5	3.5
Philadelphia, PA[1]	2.4	n/a	6.1	13.0	1.8	9.3	3.1	n/a	4.2	32.9	14.4	6.7	3.9	2.2
Phoenix, AZ	7.3	7.2	8.5	10.5	1.6	10.7	6.0	0.1	3.2	16.9	15.6	10.3	5.3	4.1
Pittsburgh, PA	5.3	4.7	6.5	9.9	1.7	9.8	7.1	0.7	4.1	22.2	15.4	10.0	4.5	3.5
Portland, OR	6.4	6.3	5.8	12.9	2.1	9.4	9.6	0.1	3.5	16.6	15.5	9.3	4.3	4.6
Providence, RI	4.5	4.5	5.5	13.3	1.0	10.7	8.5	<0.1	4.2	21.6	12.1	11.0	3.6	3.8
Provo, UT	9.5	n/a	4.0	11.9	3.9	9.1	7.8	n/a	2.3	22.1	14.4	10.8	2.0	2.2
Raleigh, NC	7.0	n/a	5.5	14.4	3.3	10.5	4.5	n/a	4.4	13.8	19.4	10.1	3.5	3.8
Reno, NV	8.8	8.5	4.2	12.8	1.4	14.2	10.6	0.3	2.7	11.6	12.1	9.4	8.8	3.5
Richmond, VA	5.9	n/a	7.9	15.7	0.9	9.3	4.4	n/a	4.6	15.3	17.0	9.2	6.0	3.8
Rochester, MN	4.1	n/a	2.2	10.5	0.8	8.2	6.9	n/a	3.0	45.2	5.3	9.6	2.1	2.1
Sacramento, CA	6.9	6.8	4.2	24.0	0.9	10.1	3.6	<0.1	3.5	18.7	12.2	9.2	4.0	2.6
Saint Louis, MO	5.4	n/a	6.7	11.2	2.0	9.7	8.2	n/a	3.6	19.5	14.9	9.6	4.8	4.6
Saint Paul, MN	4.3	n/a	7.2	13.2	1.4	8.9	10.0	n/a	3.9	19.0	14.4	9.2	4.4	4.2
Salem, OR	7.4	7.1	3.2	24.5	1.0	8.5	6.2	0.3	3.0	19.9	10.0	10.1	3.9	2.2
Salt Lake City, UT	7.2	n/a	7.7	14.3	2.8	8.3	7.7	n/a	2.7	12.2	17.1	9.2	6.0	4.9
San Antonio, TX	6.3	5.7	8.5	16.1	1.6	12.2	5.2	0.6	3.5	15.2	13.3	10.7	4.0	3.2
San Diego, CA	5.8	5.7	4.5	16.6	1.3	12.9	7.0	<0.1	3.6	16.6	17.0	9.1	2.9	2.7
San Francisco, CA[1]	3.4	3.3	6.7	12.4	9.7	10.6	2.6	<0.1	3.3	14.3	25.1	5.5	4.4	2.0
San Jose, CA	4.6	4.5	3.1	8.8	8.1	9.0	10.6	<0.1	2.4	18.4	24.6	6.5	1.5	2.5
Santa Rosa, CA	8.0	7.9	3.3	13.9	1.3	12.4	10.5	0.1	3.8	18.6	11.5	11.2	2.3	3.2
Savannah, GA	4.8	n/a	3.7	12.3	0.7	13.1	11.0	n/a	4.1	14.2	11.2	11.5	9.8	3.7
Seattle, WA[1]	4.8	4.8	4.9	12.8	8.7	9.3	6.2	<0.1	3.2	13.7	20.9	7.2	4.5	4.0
Sioux Falls, SD	6.8	n/a	8.2	9.5	1.5	9.1	8.7	n/a	3.7	21.6	9.7	11.4	4.6	5.2
Tampa, FL[1]	n/a	6.6	10.2	10.4	1.8	10.3	3.7	n/a	3.3	16.0	18.1	10.9	4.3	4.3
Tucson, AZ	5.7	5.0	4.3	19.9	1.3	11.2	7.0	0.6	3.7	17.9	11.1	10.9	5.1	2.0
Tulsa, OK	6.4	5.7	5.1	13.2	1.0	9.9	11.1	0.7	4.5	17.0	13.2	10.3	4.6	3.7
Virginia Beach, VA	5.0	n/a	4.9	20.1	1.0	11.1	7.0	n/a	4.3	15.4	14.8	10.0	3.9	2.4
Washington, DC[1]	4.2	n/a	3.3	30.2	1.8	9.9	0.8	n/a	6.7	14.8	19.4	5.6	1.9	1.4
Wichita, KS	5.5	n/a	4.1	14.0	1.1	10.2	16.7	n/a	4.0	15.9	10.8	10.1	4.4	3.2
Wilmington, NC	7.3	n/a	4.9	12.9	1.6	15.5	4.5	n/a	4.6	16.9	12.2	13.3	3.6	2.8
Winston-Salem, NC	4.7	n/a	4.5	12.3	0.7	10.7	11.7	n/a	3.9	21.5	11.9	11.4	3.6	3.2
U.S.	5.5	5.1	5.8	14.9	1.9	10.4	8.0	0.4	3.7	16.9	14.2	10.0	4.8	3.9

Note: All figures are percentages covering non-farm employment as of December 2024 and are not seasonally adjusted; Figures cover the Metropolitan Statistical Area (MSA) except where noted; (1) Metropolitan Division; (A) Construction, Mining, and Logging (some areas report Construction separate from Mining and Logging); (B) Construction; (C) Financial Activities; (D) Government; (E) Information; (F) Leisure and Hospitality; (G) Manufacturing; (H) Mining and Logging; (I) Other Services; (J) Private Education and Health Services; (K) Professional and Business Services; (L) Retail Trade; (M) Transportation and Utilities; (N) Wholesale Trade; n/a not available
Source: Bureau of Labor Statistics, Current Employment Statistics, Employment, Hours, and Earnings, December 2024

Labor Force, Employment and Job Growth: City

City	Civilian Labor Force			Workers Employed		
	Dec. 2023	Dec. 2024	% Chg.	Dec. 2023	Dec. 2024	% Chg.
Albuquerque, NM	295,286	297,348	0.7	286,112	286,738	0.2
Anchorage, AK	153,020	155,068	1.3	147,538	149,604	1.4
Ann Arbor, MI	66,518	68,304	2.6	64,986	66,059	1.6
Athens, GA	61,309	61,837	0.8	59,338	59,852	0.8
Atlanta, GA	278,364	279,245	0.3	268,161	267,879	-0.1
Austin, TX	692,732	711,010	2.6	671,863	690,459	2.7
Baltimore, MD	276,136	279,771	1.3	267,011	268,805	0.6
Billings, MT	59,483	58,785	-1.1	57,662	57,121	-0.9
Boise City, ID	146,113	151,831	3.9	142,029	147,110	3.5
Boston, MA	403,771	411,958	2.0	390,365	395,765	1.3
Boulder, CO	68,299	68,728	0.6	66,297	66,171	-0.1
Cape Coral, FL	100,486	101,752	1.2	97,397	98,477	1.1
Cedar Rapids, IA	70,086	70,636	0.7	67,783	68,276	0.7
Charleston, SC	81,443	83,687	2.7	79,209	80,914	2.1
Charlotte, NC	531,420	537,158	1.0	513,465	519,577	1.1
Chicago, IL	1,391,216	1,432,019	2.9	1,330,946	1,363,159	2.4
Cincinnati, OH	150,446	153,060	1.7	145,104	146,196	0.7
Clarksville, TN	65,211	66,900	2.5	62,910	64,067	1.8
Cleveland, OH	154,882	158,055	2.0	148,680	151,454	1.8
College Station, TX	70,826	73,610	3.9	68,915	71,605	3.9
Colorado Springs, CO	254,636	258,951	1.6	245,377	247,188	0.7
Columbia, MO	69,206	70,699	2.1	67,566	68,998	2.1
Columbia, SC	59,838	60,914	1.8	57,599	58,055	0.7
Columbus, OH	490,638	493,589	0.6	474,627	473,223	-0.3
Dallas, TX	753,950	773,828	2.6	727,021	746,370	2.6
Davenport, IA	49,490	49,873	0.7	47,766	47,656	-0.2
Denver, CO	439,297	444,521	1.1	421,359	422,120	0.1
Des Moines, IA	113,506	113,721	0.1	109,944	109,495	-0.4
Detroit, MI	252,407	254,935	1.0	235,064	230,371	-2.0
Durham, NC	161,695	163,549	1.1	156,943	158,778	1.1
El Paso, TX	321,869	330,289	2.6	309,686	317,905	2.6
Eugene, OR	86,438	87,547	1.2	82,952	83,877	1.1
Fargo, ND	75,385	76,672	1.7	73,971	74,762	1.0
Fort Collins, CO	104,877	106,076	1.1	101,643	102,156	0.5
Fort Wayne, IN	130,643	133,106	1.8	126,751	127,554	0.6
Fort Worth, TX	492,810	506,338	2.7	474,900	487,778	2.7
Gainesville, FL	71,265	72,407	1.6	68,797	69,722	1.3
Green Bay, WI	53,842	54,171	0.6	52,558	52,661	0.2
Greensboro, NC	145,300	143,645	-1.1	139,667	137,971	-1.2
Honolulu, HI	458,516	467,102	1.8	447,781	454,669	1.5
Houston, TX	1,221,575	1,251,524	2.4	1,168,408	1,201,001	2.7
Huntsville, AL	110,121	113,202	2.8	107,585	109,886	2.1
Indianapolis, IN	468,727	483,276	3.1	453,754	464,036	2.2
Jacksonville, FL	491,737	495,209	0.7	476,373	479,227	0.6
Kansas City, MO	261,274	264,629	1.2	252,452	255,316	1.1
Lafayette, LA	59,760	59,993	0.3	57,644	57,720	0.1
Las Vegas, NV	330,736	337,672	2.1	312,658	317,296	1.4
Lexington, KY	178,351	182,353	2.2	172,195	175,041	1.6
Lincoln, NE	164,857	168,647	2.3	161,204	164,571	2.0
Little Rock, AR	100,778	102,786	1.9	97,463	99,326	1.9
Los Angeles, CA	2,074,549	2,094,633	0.9	1,964,638	1,972,226	0.3
Louisville, KY	394,849	401,525	1.6	379,511	382,789	0.8
Madison, WI	167,700	168,775	0.6	164,752	165,214	0.2
Manchester, NH	64,039	66,140	3.2	62,588	64,103	2.4
McAllen, TX	72,499	74,052	2.1	69,572	71,063	2.1

Table continued on following page.

City	Civilian Labor Force			Workers Employed		
	Dec. 2023	Dec. 2024	% Chg.	Dec. 2023	Dec. 2024	% Chg.
Memphis, TN	283,933	286,196	0.8	271,779	271,426	-0.1
Miami, FL	247,114	249,197	0.8	242,276	243,343	0.4
Midland, TX	93,937	96,111	2.3	91,915	93,872	2.1
Milwaukee, WI	273,443	274,723	0.4	264,071	263,797	-0.1
Minneapolis, MN	244,672	245,657	0.4	238,965	239,886	0.3
Nashville, TN	421,198	426,189	1.1	411,304	413,569	0.5
New Orleans, LA	173,294	173,800	0.2	165,506	165,809	0.1
New York, NY	4,197,201	4,289,830	2.2	4,004,371	4,065,287	1.5
Oklahoma City, OK	352,331	357,109	1.3	341,478	346,634	1.5
Omaha, NE	251,851	256,156	1.7	245,154	248,481	1.3
Orlando, FL	181,418	181,948	0.2	176,377	176,719	0.1
Philadelphia, PA	750,976	745,485	-0.7	719,837	713,546	-0.8
Phoenix, AZ	913,817	927,572	1.5	887,451	898,365	1.2
Pittsburgh, PA	152,654	151,757	-0.5	148,435	147,774	-0.4
Portland, OR	386,871	388,825	0.5	372,067	372,849	0.2
Providence, RI	90,820	92,307	1.6	86,757	87,271	0.5
Provo, UT	73,763	74,411	0.8	72,156	72,484	0.4
Raleigh, NC	276,576	277,882	0.4	267,801	269,378	0.5
Reno, NV	144,664	147,939	2.2	138,887	141,134	1.6
Richmond, VA	123,724	126,447	2.2	120,027	122,541	2.0
Rochester, MN	68,874	73,886	7.2	67,640	72,557	7.2
Sacramento, CA	246,247	248,837	1.0	234,662	236,718	0.8
Saint Louis, MO	150,472	152,715	1.4	144,679	146,505	1.2
Saint Paul, MN	156,382	157,144	0.4	152,569	153,219	0.4
Salem, OR	86,857	88,580	1.9	83,316	84,776	1.7
Salt Lake City, UT	128,957	131,406	1.9	125,261	127,540	1.8
San Antonio, TX	780,314	813,666	4.2	753,069	786,995	4.5
San Diego, CA	730,171	734,863	0.6	701,246	703,991	0.3
San Francisco, CA	564,822	561,032	-0.6	545,573	541,446	-0.7
San Jose, CA	550,266	551,509	0.2	528,718	529,659	0.1
Santa Rosa, CA	87,410	88,152	0.8	84,056	84,516	0.5
Savannah, GA	69,925	69,887	0.0	67,803	67,610	-0.2
Seattle, WA	511,941	526,448	2.8	495,245	511,570	3.3
Sioux Falls, SD	113,602	115,243	1.4	111,615	112,947	1.1
Tampa, FL	222,684	223,321	0.2	215,665	215,892	0.1
Tucson, AZ	263,211	266,440	1.2	254,477	256,864	0.9
Tulsa, OK	206,897	209,496	1.2	199,811	203,133	1.6
Virginia Beach, VA	237,550	239,534	0.8	231,972	233,678	0.7
Washington, DC	411,135	417,094	1.4	391,912	396,492	1.1
Wichita, KS	194,170	197,795	1.8	188,497	190,038	0.8
Wilmington, NC	69,827	69,943	0.1	67,604	67,846	0.3
Winston-Salem, NC	118,508	118,217	-0.2	114,267	114,055	-0.1
U.S.	166,661,000	167,746,000	0.7	160,754,000	161,294,000	0.3

Note: Data is not seasonally adjusted and covers workers 16 years of age and older
Source: Bureau of Labor Statistics, Local Area Unemployment Statistics

Labor Force, Employment and Job Growth: Metro Area

Metro Area	Civilian Labor Force			Workers Employed		
	Dec. 2023	Dec. 2024	% Chg.	Dec. 2023	Dec. 2024	% Chg.
Albuquerque, NM	459,168	462,519	0.7	444,472	445,570	0.2
Anchorage, AK	203,512	206,186	1.3	195,498	198,110	1.3
Ann Arbor, MI	201,644	207,512	2.9	195,986	199,223	1.6
Athens, GA	103,836	104,775	0.9	100,776	101,698	0.9
Atlanta, GA[1]	2,520,105	2,525,607	0.2	2,441,223	2,439,016	0.0
Austin, TX	1,480,563	1,521,172	2.7	1,434,717	1,474,387	2.7
Baltimore, MD	1,496,175	1,509,109	0.8	1,460,563	1,468,370	0.5
Billings, MT	99,307	98,165	-1.1	96,370	95,349	-1.0
Boise City, ID	432,273	448,781	3.8	418,731	433,330	3.4
Boston, MA[1]	1,158,650	1,182,153	2.0	1,119,472	1,135,105	1.4
Boulder, CO	204,348	205,677	0.6	197,756	197,382	-0.1
Cape Coral, FL	376,769	381,593	1.2	365,271	369,323	1.1
Cedar Rapids, IA	141,248	142,473	0.8	136,873	137,885	0.7
Charleston, SC	433,190	445,523	2.8	421,406	430,483	2.1
Charlotte, NC	1,472,294	1,492,625	1.3	1,424,686	1,443,425	1.3
Chicago, IL[1]	3,780,647	3,890,015	2.8	3,630,697	3,719,159	2.4
Cincinnati, OH	1,154,630	1,170,746	1.4	1,116,229	1,123,236	0.6
Clarksville, TN	126,537	129,924	2.6	121,844	124,244	1.9
Cleveland, OH	1,067,052	1,088,179	1.9	1,033,451	1,051,761	1.7
College Station, TX	154,708	160,796	3.9	150,546	156,418	3.9
Colorado Springs, CO	380,947	387,217	1.6	366,679	369,336	0.7
Columbia, MO	113,118	115,648	2.2	110,484	112,817	2.1
Columbia, SC	419,770	426,736	1.6	406,945	410,354	0.8
Columbus, OH	1,134,646	1,141,335	0.5	1,099,340	1,096,249	-0.2
Dallas, TX[1]	3,019,102	3,099,037	2.6	2,914,521	2,992,023	2.6
Davenport, IA	184,725	184,714	0.0	177,254	176,542	-0.4
Denver, CO	1,731,722	1,751,255	1.1	1,667,215	1,670,077	0.1
Des Moines, IA	394,185	394,876	0.1	384,347	382,847	-0.3
Detroit, MI[1]	816,930	814,679	-0.2	784,713	769,048	-2.0
Durham, NC	323,131	326,577	1.0	313,852	317,268	1.0
El Paso, TX	388,422	398,643	2.6	372,959	382,859	2.6
Eugene, OR	184,890	187,239	1.2	177,117	179,091	1.1
Fargo, ND	149,293	152,175	1.9	146,516	148,732	1.5
Fort Collins, CO	216,529	219,305	1.2	209,634	210,691	0.5
Fort Wayne, IN	220,472	224,223	1.7	214,223	215,591	0.6
Fort Worth, TX[1]	1,397,596	1,435,889	2.7	1,349,809	1,386,446	2.7
Gainesville, FL	168,667	171,235	1.5	163,355	165,582	1.3
Green Bay, WI	174,722	175,808	0.6	170,734	171,226	0.2
Greensboro, NC	366,503	362,230	-1.1	353,122	348,882	-1.2
Honolulu, HI	458,516	467,102	1.8	447,781	454,669	1.5
Houston, TX	3,704,314	3,811,882	2.9	3,557,779	3,657,192	2.7
Huntsville, AL	257,532	264,722	2.7	252,062	257,486	2.1
Indianapolis, IN	1,114,296	1,147,341	2.9	1,082,623	1,106,085	2.1
Jacksonville, FL	845,904	852,367	0.7	820,842	825,781	0.6
Kansas City, MO	1,160,004	1,182,211	1.9	1,127,092	1,144,249	1.5
Lafayette, LA	185,004	185,747	0.4	178,352	178,532	0.1
Las Vegas, NV	1,199,294	1,224,775	2.1	1,135,389	1,152,230	1.4
Lexington, KY	278,181	284,384	2.2	268,513	272,804	1.6
Lincoln, NE	191,591	195,942	2.2	187,422	191,304	2.0
Little Rock, AR	371,026	378,813	2.1	359,838	366,941	1.9
Los Angeles, CA[1]	5,037,643	5,091,130	1.0	4,782,176	4,800,645	0.3
Louisville, KY	691,184	703,358	1.7	666,258	672,517	0.9
Madison, WI	410,987	413,894	0.7	403,502	404,881	0.3
Manchester, NH	238,986	245,151	2.5	233,791	237,759	1.7
McAllen, TX	385,693	394,540	2.2	362,243	370,007	2.1

Table continued on following page.

Metro Area	Civilian Labor Force			Workers Employed		
	Dec. 2023	Dec. 2024	% Chg.	Dec. 2023	Dec. 2024	% Chg.
Memphis, TN	620,716	627,549	1.1	598,585	600,246	0.2
Miami, FL[1]	1,433,283	1,445,779	0.8	1,404,765	1,410,954	0.4
Midland, TX	116,721	119,415	2.3	114,162	116,595	2.1
Milwaukee, WI	822,104	825,110	0.3	800,656	800,116	0.0
Minneapolis, MN	2,005,284	2,015,070	0.4	1,956,084	1,964,999	0.4
Nashville, TN	1,150,386	1,163,681	1.1	1,123,659	1,129,538	0.5
New Orleans, LA	461,088	463,007	0.4	442,552	443,450	0.2
New York, NY[1]	6,077,969	6,169,474	1.5	5,813,964	5,874,694	1.0
Oklahoma City, OK	752,168	762,662	1.4	729,908	740,966	1.5
Omaha, NE	505,378	514,350	1.7	492,693	499,953	1.4
Orlando, FL	1,476,354	1,481,986	0.3	1,432,973	1,435,926	0.2
Philadelphia, PA[1]	1,055,097	1,047,116	-0.7	1,014,794	1,006,018	-0.8
Phoenix, AZ	2,660,126	2,699,326	1.4	2,583,768	2,614,930	1.2
Pittsburgh, PA	1,218,768	1,213,214	-0.4	1,179,001	1,172,526	-0.5
Portland, OR	1,358,801	1,358,994	0.0	1,305,393	1,301,850	-0.2
Providence, RI	887,464	901,729	1.6	854,672	862,458	0.9
Provo, UT	363,569	366,874	0.9	354,453	356,068	0.4
Raleigh, NC	799,354	803,302	0.4	775,484	780,100	0.6
Reno, NV	291,520	298,309	2.3	279,599	284,384	1.7
Richmond, VA	703,806	718,292	2.0	685,441	699,371	2.0
Rochester, MN	128,702	138,168	7.3	126,091	135,339	7.3
Sacramento, CA	1,144,784	1,156,797	1.0	1,094,502	1,103,633	0.8
Saint Louis, MO	1,476,468	1,495,860	1.3	1,428,392	1,447,762	1.3
Saint Paul, MN	2,005,284	2,015,070	0.4	1,956,084	1,964,999	0.4
Salem, OR	215,316	219,611	1.9	206,688	210,311	1.7
Salt Lake City, UT	738,638	754,401	2.1	719,094	732,202	1.8
San Antonio, TX	1,308,187	1,349,973	3.1	1,265,057	1,304,101	3.0
San Diego, CA	1,608,713	1,619,332	0.6	1,543,490	1,549,532	0.3
San Francisco, CA[1]	1,011,370	1,004,815	-0.6	978,032	970,469	-0.7
San Jose, CA	1,075,900	1,078,520	0.2	1,034,963	1,036,708	0.1
Santa Rosa, CA	249,694	251,825	0.8	240,531	241,848	0.5
Savannah, GA	202,550	202,333	-0.1	197,273	196,748	-0.2
Seattle, WA[1]	1,366,721	1,405,582	2.8	1,318,947	1,362,424	3.3
Sioux Falls, SD	171,226	173,604	1.3	168,466	170,431	1.1
Tampa, FL[1]	1,167,354	1,171,736	0.3	1,130,613	1,132,522	0.1
Tucson, AZ	493,139	499,226	1.2	477,781	482,263	0.9
Tulsa, OK	510,676	517,614	1.3	494,038	502,372	1.6
Virginia Beach, VA	883,468	890,934	0.8	860,628	866,842	0.7
Washington, DC[1]	1,000,003	1,013,650	1.3	966,020	974,957	0.9
Wichita, KS	320,952	326,697	1.7	311,687	314,280	0.8
Wilmington, NC	222,997	222,642	-0.1	215,630	215,604	0.0
Winston-Salem, NC	329,205	328,631	-0.1	318,577	317,977	-0.1
U.S.	166,661,000	167,746,000	0.7	160,754,000	161,294,000	0.3

Note: Data is not seasonally adjusted and covers workers 16 years of age and older; Figures cover the Metropolitan Statistical Area (MSA) except where noted; (1) Metropolitan Division
Source: Bureau of Labor Statistics, Local Area Unemployment Statistics

Unemployment Rate: City

City	2024											
	Jan.	Feb.	Mar.	Apr.	May	Jun.	Jul.	Aug.	Sep.	Oct.	Nov.	Dec.
Albuquerque, NM	3.5	3.4	3.1	3.1	3.5	4.4	4.9	4.3	3.8	3.9	3.9	3.6
Anchorage, AK	4.0	4.2	3.8	3.7	3.6	4.2	3.8	3.5	3.5	3.6	3.8	3.5
Ann Arbor, MI	2.5	2.7	2.8	2.6	3.2	3.8	4.2	3.7	3.2	3.1	3.2	3.3
Athens, GA	3.7	3.5	3.6	2.8	3.7	4.6	4.5	4.5	3.8	4.0	3.3	3.2
Atlanta, GA	3.9	3.9	3.8	3.6	4.0	4.5	4.5	4.6	4.1	4.2	4.2	4.1
Austin, TX	3.3	3.5	3.2	2.9	3.1	3.5	3.5	3.5	3.3	3.2	3.2	2.9
Baltimore, MD	4.2	4.2	4.0	3.6	3.8	4.5	4.8	4.8	4.0	4.3	4.2	3.9
Billings, MT	3.5	3.3	3.0	2.6	2.6	3.2	3.1	3.0	2.5	2.5	2.6	2.8
Boise City, ID	3.3	3.4	3.3	2.9	3.0	3.3	3.5	3.3	3.1	3.1	3.3	3.1
Boston, MA	3.7	3.7	3.5	3.2	3.8	4.3	4.6	4.4	3.8	3.9	3.9	3.9
Boulder, CO	3.3	3.5	3.4	3.2	4.0	4.5	4.5	4.5	4.1	4.1	4.4	3.7
Cape Coral, FL	3.4	3.2	3.2	3.0	3.2	3.8	3.9	3.9	3.6	3.5	3.6	3.2
Cedar Rapids, IA	3.9	4.3	3.2	2.7	3.6	4.5	4.2	4.0	3.3	3.5	3.6	3.3
Charleston, SC	3.0	3.3	3.0	2.7	3.2	3.9	4.0	4.1	3.5	3.7	3.6	3.3
Charlotte, NC	3.8	3.9	3.6	3.2	3.4	3.8	4.1	3.9	3.2	3.3	3.5	3.3
Chicago, IL	5.0	5.5	5.1	5.1	5.6	6.9	6.7	6.4	5.8	5.8	5.4	4.8
Cincinnati, OH	4.3	4.4	4.3	4.1	4.5	5.2	5.3	5.0	4.6	4.3	4.6	4.5
Clarksville, TN	4.0	3.7	3.8	3.3	3.5	4.6	4.6	4.4	4.2	4.2	4.3	4.2
Cleveland, OH	5.0	5.8	5.2	4.7	5.0	5.5	5.5	4.7	4.1	3.8	4.0	4.2
College Station, TX	3.4	3.6	3.0	2.5	3.0	3.7	3.8	3.7	3.3	3.2	3.1	2.7
Colorado Springs, CO	4.1	4.2	3.8	3.7	3.9	4.4	4.7	4.6	4.3	4.4	4.7	4.5
Columbia, MO	3.1	2.9	3.2	2.7	3.3	3.6	3.8	3.4	2.4	2.7	2.8	2.4
Columbia, SC	4.1	4.4	4.1	3.8	5.0	5.8	6.1	5.8	4.9	5.7	5.3	4.7
Columbus, OH	4.0	4.0	4.0	3.8	4.0	4.5	4.5	4.3	4.2	3.9	4.2	4.1
Dallas, TX	4.0	4.1	3.9	3.5	3.7	4.3	4.3	4.3	4.0	4.0	4.0	3.5
Davenport, IA	4.2	3.6	3.5	3.0	3.8	4.5	4.8	4.9	5.1	4.9	4.9	4.4
Denver, CO	4.5	4.5	4.0	4.1	4.1	4.5	4.9	4.9	4.6	4.8	5.0	5.0
Des Moines, IA	4.3	3.8	3.5	2.6	3.1	3.6	4.1	4.4	3.5	3.7	3.9	3.7
Detroit, MI	8.3	8.3	8.1	7.4	8.6	10.0	12.7	9.7	9.6	10.8	10.6	9.6
Durham, NC	3.3	3.3	3.2	2.8	3.1	3.4	3.6	3.5	2.9	2.9	3.1	2.9
El Paso, TX	4.3	4.5	4.1	3.7	3.9	4.5	4.5	4.5	4.2	4.2	4.2	3.7
Eugene, OR	4.6	4.5	4.2	3.6	3.6	4.1	4.5	4.4	4.0	3.9	3.8	4.2
Fargo, ND	2.5	2.6	2.7	2.3	2.0	2.5	2.2	2.3	1.9	1.9	2.2	2.5
Fort Collins, CO	3.5	3.6	3.3	3.1	3.5	3.9	4.1	4.1	3.8	3.7	4.1	3.7
Fort Wayne, IN	3.9	4.3	4.1	3.4	3.9	4.4	6.0	4.4	4.0	4.1	4.4	4.2
Fort Worth, TX	4.1	4.3	4.1	3.6	3.9	4.6	4.6	4.4	4.1	4.1	4.1	3.7
Gainesville, FL	3.8	3.6	4.0	3.4	3.8	4.6	4.4	4.6	3.9	4.2	4.4	3.7
Green Bay, WI	2.7	3.2	3.3	2.8	2.8	3.3	3.1	2.8	2.5	2.5	2.6	2.8
Greensboro, NC	4.4	4.4	4.3	3.7	4.0	4.8	5.2	4.9	4.0	3.9	4.2	4.0
Honolulu, HI	2.5	2.5	2.4	2.4	2.3	3.2	3.0	3.1	3.1	2.9	3.0	2.7
Houston, TX	4.4	4.4	4.2	3.8	4.0	4.7	5.1	4.9	4.5	4.4	4.5	4.0
Huntsville, AL	2.8	2.8	2.6	2.1	2.1	2.9	3.1	3.1	2.7	2.8	2.9	2.9
Indianapolis, IN	3.9	4.3	4.2	3.6	4.0	4.4	4.7	4.5	4.1	4.0	4.2	4.0
Jacksonville, FL	3.5	3.4	3.3	3.1	3.3	3.9	4.1	4.0	3.6	3.6	3.5	3.2
Kansas City, MO	3.9	4.1	4.1	3.5	4.0	4.1	4.6	4.2	3.3	3.6	3.6	3.5
Lafayette, LA	4.0	3.9	3.8	3.4	3.6	4.5	4.4	4.4	4.3	4.3	4.1	3.8
Las Vegas, NV	5.7	5.8	5.7	5.5	5.6	6.2	6.5	6.3	5.9	6.0	6.1	6.0
Lexington, KY	3.9	4.3	4.2	3.5	3.9	4.5	4.7	4.4	4.1	4.0	4.1	4.0
Lincoln, NE	2.5	2.7	2.5	2.2	2.5	3.0	2.7	2.8	2.4	2.6	2.6	2.4
Little Rock, AR	3.8	3.8	3.6	3.3	3.4	3.8	4.0	3.6	3.3	3.3	3.4	3.4
Los Angeles, CA	5.8	5.5	5.4	5.1	5.5	6.2	6.8	6.8	6.1	6.1	6.1	5.8
Louisville, KY	4.5	4.9	4.7	4.2	4.3	4.9	5.9	4.9	4.6	4.7	4.7	4.7
Madison, WI	1.9	2.2	2.4	2.2	2.3	2.8	2.6	2.3	2.2	2.1	2.1	2.1
Manchester, NH	2.8	3.1	2.9	2.5	2.4	2.7	3.0	2.9	2.5	2.6	3.2	3.1
McAllen, TX	4.5	4.6	4.3	4.0	4.2	4.9	4.9	4.8	4.3	4.2	4.3	4.0

Table continued on following page.

City	2024											
	Jan.	Feb.	Mar.	Apr.	May	Jun.	Jul.	Aug.	Sep.	Oct.	Nov.	Dec.
Memphis, TN	4.9	4.5	4.7	4.2	4.4	5.8	6.2	5.8	5.3	5.4	5.3	5.2
Miami, FL	1.8	2.0	2.2	2.2	2.2	2.4	2.8	2.8	2.4	2.4	2.3	2.3
Midland, TX	2.6	2.8	2.4	2.2	2.4	2.8	2.8	2.9	2.6	2.7	2.7	2.3
Milwaukee, WI	3.9	4.5	4.6	4.2	4.0	4.9	4.9	4.8	3.8	3.9	4.1	4.0
Minneapolis, MN	2.8	3.0	2.8	2.6	2.5	3.3	3.4	3.4	2.9	2.7	2.5	2.3
Nashville, TN	2.6	2.5	2.6	2.4	2.5	3.1	3.2	3.1	2.9	3.0	3.1	3.0
New Orleans, LA	5.3	4.8	4.7	4.3	4.4	5.7	5.8	5.5	5.2	5.3	4.9	4.6
New York, NY	4.8	5.1	4.8	4.6	4.9	5.4	6.1	6.1	5.3	5.5	5.5	5.2
Oklahoma City, OK	3.4	3.4	3.1	2.7	3.2	3.4	3.4	3.3	3.1	3.1	3.1	2.9
Omaha, NE	3.2	3.5	3.2	3.1	3.1	3.5	3.6	3.3	3.0	3.2	3.0	3.0
Orlando, FL	3.0	2.8	2.7	2.7	2.9	3.3	3.5	3.5	3.2	3.1	3.1	2.9
Philadelphia, PA	4.7	4.9	4.4	4.0	4.4	4.9	5.5	5.7	4.4	4.6	4.5	4.3
Phoenix, AZ	3.0	3.0	2.7	2.5	2.9	3.5	3.8	3.7	3.4	3.4	3.4	3.1
Pittsburgh, PA	3.2	3.2	3.1	2.5	3.0	3.5	3.7	4.0	2.8	3.0	2.9	2.6
Portland, OR	4.5	4.4	4.3	3.6	3.6	4.0	4.4	4.3	3.9	3.9	4.0	4.1
Providence, RI	5.7	6.4	5.6	4.7	5.4	5.4	6.3	6.7	5.2	5.3	5.8	5.5
Provo, UT	2.6	2.6	2.4	2.4	3.2	3.8	3.2	3.4	2.9	2.6	2.8	2.6
Raleigh, NC	3.5	3.6	3.5	3.0	3.2	3.6	3.8	3.6	3.0	3.0	3.3	3.1
Reno, NV	4.5	4.6	4.6	4.4	4.6	4.9	5.1	4.9	4.4	4.6	4.5	4.6
Richmond, VA	3.4	3.4	3.4	3.0	3.4	3.6	3.8	3.9	3.5	3.4	3.4	3.1
Rochester, MN	2.2	2.5	2.1	2.0	1.9	2.6	2.6	2.5	2.0	1.9	1.9	1.8
Sacramento, CA	5.2	5.2	4.9	4.5	4.3	5.1	5.5	5.6	5.0	5.1	5.2	4.9
Saint Louis, MO	4.4	4.8	4.6	3.9	4.3	4.6	4.9	4.8	3.8	4.0	4.0	4.1
Saint Paul, MN	3.0	3.3	3.1	2.8	2.7	3.6	3.7	3.7	3.1	2.8	2.6	2.5
Salem, OR	4.7	4.6	4.5	3.8	3.7	4.2	4.6	4.5	4.0	4.0	4.1	4.3
Salt Lake City, UT	3.0	3.4	3.2	3.0	3.0	3.3	3.5	3.5	3.0	3.1	3.1	2.9
San Antonio, TX	3.9	4.1	3.6	3.4	3.4	4.5	4.3	4.2	3.8	3.8	4.0	3.3
San Diego, CA	4.4	4.4	4.2	3.8	3.7	4.4	4.8	4.9	4.3	4.4	4.5	4.2
San Francisco, CA	3.8	3.6	3.5	3.3	3.1	3.7	4.0	4.1	3.6	3.7	3.7	3.5
San Jose, CA	4.3	4.2	4.1	3.8	3.6	4.4	4.7	4.7	4.2	4.3	4.3	4.0
Santa Rosa, CA	4.5	4.3	4.2	3.8	3.6	4.3	4.7	4.7	4.1	4.3	4.4	4.1
Savannah, GA	3.5	3.5	3.5	3.0	3.6	4.1	4.0	4.2	3.5	3.6	3.4	3.3
Seattle, WA	4.0	3.6	3.5	3.5	3.7	4.5	4.2	4.1	3.9	3.7	3.4	2.8
Sioux Falls, SD	1.9	2.2	1.7	1.7	1.6	1.8	1.6	1.8	1.4	1.6	1.6	2.0
Tampa, FL	3.5	3.3	3.4	3.1	3.3	3.8	3.9	4.0	3.6	3.7	3.8	3.3
Tucson, AZ	3.5	3.4	3.1	2.9	3.4	4.2	4.4	4.3	3.9	3.8	3.9	3.6
Tulsa, OK	4.0	4.0	3.3	3.0	3.5	3.7	3.7	3.6	3.2	3.3	3.3	3.0
Virginia Beach, VA	2.6	2.7	2.5	2.3	2.7	2.9	3.0	3.1	2.8	2.7	2.8	2.4
Washington, DC	5.1	5.3	5.0	4.5	5.0	5.7	6.0	6.0	5.2	5.2	5.0	4.9
Wichita, KS	3.7	4.1	3.9	3.5	3.9	4.4	5.1	4.7	3.9	4.4	4.5	3.9
Wilmington, NC	3.6	3.5	3.3	2.8	3.1	3.5	3.7	3.5	2.9	2.9	3.2	3.0
Winston-Salem, NC	4.0	4.0	4.0	3.4	3.8	4.3	4.6	4.4	3.5	3.6	3.8	3.5
U.S.	4.1	4.2	3.9	3.5	3.7	4.3	4.5	4.4	3.9	3.9	4.0	3.8

Note: Data is not seasonally adjusted and covers workers 16 years of age and older; All figures are percentages
Source: Bureau of Labor Statistics, Local Area Unemployment Statistics

Unemployment Rate: Metro Area

Metro Area	2024											
	Jan.	Feb.	Mar.	Apr.	May	Jun.	Jul.	Aug.	Sep.	Oct.	Nov.	Dec.
Albuquerque, NM	3.6	3.5	3.2	3.3	3.6	4.6	5.1	4.4	3.9	4.0	4.1	3.7
Anchorage, AK	4.4	4.6	4.2	4.0	3.9	4.5	4.1	3.7	3.7	3.9	4.2	3.9
Ann Arbor, MI	3.1	3.3	3.4	3.2	3.9	4.6	5.1	4.5	3.9	3.8	3.8	4.0
Athens, GA	3.4	3.2	3.3	2.6	3.4	4.1	4.0	4.1	3.4	3.6	3.1	2.9
Atlanta, GA[1]	3.4	3.4	3.4	3.1	3.5	4.0	3.9	4.0	3.5	3.6	3.6	3.4
Austin, TX	3.5	3.6	3.4	3.0	3.2	3.7	3.7	3.7	3.5	3.4	3.4	3.1
Baltimore, MD	3.0	3.1	2.9	2.5	2.7	3.4	3.5	3.5	2.9	3.1	3.0	2.7
Billings, MT	3.3	3.3	2.9	2.6	2.5	3.1	3.0	2.9	2.4	2.3	2.4	2.9
Boise City, ID	3.8	3.9	3.7	3.2	3.3	3.6	3.8	3.7	3.3	3.4	3.6	3.4
Boston, MA[1]	3.9	4.0	3.7	3.2	3.8	4.2	4.5	4.3	3.7	3.9	3.9	4.0
Boulder, CO	3.6	3.7	3.4	3.3	3.7	4.2	4.4	4.3	4.0	4.1	4.3	4.0
Cape Coral, FL	3.4	3.3	3.2	3.0	3.2	3.7	4.0	3.9	3.7	3.6	3.6	3.2
Cedar Rapids, IA	3.9	4.0	3.2	2.5	3.2	3.8	3.8	3.7	3.0	3.3	3.4	3.2
Charleston, SC	3.1	3.4	3.1	2.7	3.3	4.0	4.2	4.3	3.6	3.8	3.6	3.4
Charlotte, NC	3.6	3.8	3.5	3.1	3.4	3.8	4.0	3.9	3.3	3.4	3.5	3.3
Chicago, IL[1]	4.7	5.2	4.8	4.6	5.1	6.2	6.0	5.7	5.1	5.1	4.8	4.4
Cincinnati, OH	4.1	4.2	4.2	3.8	4.0	4.6	4.6	4.3	4.1	3.9	4.1	4.1
Clarksville, TN	4.2	4.1	4.1	3.6	3.8	4.8	4.9	4.6	4.4	4.4	4.5	4.4
Cleveland, OH	4.0	4.7	4.2	3.6	3.9	4.4	4.4	3.7	3.3	3.0	3.2	3.3
College Station, TX	3.3	3.4	3.0	2.6	3.0	3.6	3.7	3.6	3.2	3.1	3.1	2.7
Colorado Springs, CO	4.2	4.3	3.9	3.8	4.0	4.5	4.8	4.8	4.4	4.5	4.8	4.6
Columbia, MO	3.2	3.0	3.2	2.7	3.2	3.5	3.7	3.3	2.4	2.7	2.7	2.4
Columbia, SC	3.5	3.7	3.5	3.1	3.8	4.5	4.7	4.8	4.1	4.3	4.1	3.8
Columbus, OH	3.9	3.9	3.9	3.6	3.8	4.3	4.3	4.1	4.0	3.7	4.0	4.0
Dallas, TX[1]	3.9	4.0	3.8	3.4	3.6	4.2	4.2	4.2	3.9	3.8	3.8	3.5
Davenport, IA	5.2	4.8	4.5	4.0	4.2	4.7	4.8	4.9	5.2	5.0	4.8	4.4
Denver, CO	4.1	4.2	3.8	3.8	3.9	4.4	4.6	4.7	4.3	4.5	4.7	4.6
Des Moines, IA	3.3	2.9	2.7	2.1	2.6	3.1	3.5	3.6	3.0	3.1	3.2	3.0
Detroit, MI[1]	4.8	4.8	4.7	4.3	5.0	5.8	7.5	5.6	5.6	6.3	6.2	5.6
Durham, NC	3.2	3.2	3.2	2.8	3.0	3.4	3.6	3.4	2.8	2.9	3.1	2.9
El Paso, TX	4.5	4.7	4.3	3.9	4.1	4.8	4.8	4.7	4.4	4.4	4.4	4.0
Eugene, OR	4.9	4.7	4.4	3.8	3.8	4.2	4.7	4.6	4.1	4.1	4.1	4.4
Fargo, ND	2.5	2.7	2.7	2.2	2.0	2.6	2.3	2.3	1.8	1.8	2.0	2.3
Fort Collins, CO	3.6	3.8	3.4	3.3	3.5	3.9	4.1	4.2	3.8	3.9	4.2	3.9
Fort Wayne, IN	3.8	4.1	3.9	3.2	3.7	4.2	5.8	4.1	3.7	3.8	4.1	3.8
Fort Worth, TX[1]	3.9	4.1	3.8	3.4	3.6	4.2	4.3	4.2	3.9	3.9	3.9	3.4
Gainesville, FL	3.5	3.3	3.5	3.1	3.4	4.0	4.0	4.0	3.5	3.7	3.8	3.3
Green Bay, WI	2.6	3.1	3.1	2.6	2.6	3.0	2.9	2.6	2.3	2.3	2.4	2.6
Greensboro, NC	4.2	4.2	4.0	3.5	3.9	4.5	4.8	4.5	3.7	3.7	4.0	3.7
Honolulu, HI	2.5	2.5	2.4	2.4	2.3	3.2	3.0	3.1	3.1	2.9	3.0	2.7
Houston, TX	4.4	4.5	4.1	3.8	4.0	4.7	5.0	4.8	4.5	4.4	4.4	4.1
Huntsville, AL	2.6	2.7	2.4	2.0	2.0	2.7	2.9	3.0	2.6	2.7	2.8	2.7
Indianapolis, IN	3.6	3.9	3.9	3.2	3.6	4.0	4.3	4.0	3.6	3.6	3.9	3.6
Jacksonville, FL	3.3	3.2	3.2	2.9	3.1	3.7	3.9	3.8	3.4	3.4	3.5	3.1
Kansas City, MO	3.5	3.8	3.8	3.2	3.6	3.8	4.2	3.9	3.2	3.5	3.3	3.2
Lafayette, LA	4.1	4.0	3.8	3.4	3.6	4.5	4.4	4.4	4.3	4.3	4.2	3.9
Las Vegas, NV	5.6	5.6	5.5	5.4	5.5	6.1	6.4	6.2	5.8	5.9	6.0	5.9
Lexington, KY	4.0	4.4	4.2	3.5	3.9	4.6	4.7	4.5	4.1	4.1	4.2	4.1
Lincoln, NE	2.4	2.6	2.4	2.2	2.5	3.0	2.6	2.7	2.4	2.6	2.5	2.4
Little Rock, AR	3.5	3.5	3.2	2.9	3.1	3.5	3.7	3.3	3.0	2.9	3.0	3.1
Los Angeles, CA[1]	5.6	5.3	5.3	5.0	5.4	6.1	6.7	6.7	6.0	6.0	6.0	5.7
Louisville, KY	4.3	4.7	4.4	3.9	4.1	4.7	5.6	4.6	4.3	4.4	4.5	4.4
Madison, WI	2.1	2.5	2.5	2.2	2.3	2.7	2.6	2.3	2.1	2.1	2.2	2.2
Manchester, NH	2.7	3.0	2.9	2.4	2.3	2.6	3.0	2.9	2.5	2.6	3.1	3.0
McAllen, TX	6.5	6.0	5.8	5.4	5.7	6.9	6.9	6.5	5.9	5.4	6.0	6.2

Table continued on following page.

Metro Area	2024											
	Jan.	Feb.	Mar.	Apr.	May	Jun.	Jul.	Aug.	Sep.	Oct.	Nov.	Dec.
Memphis, TN	4.0	3.7	3.8	3.4	3.7	4.9	5.0	4.8	4.4	4.5	4.5	4.4
Miami, FL[1]	1.9	2.0	2.3	2.3	2.3	2.6	2.8	2.9	2.4	2.4	2.4	2.4
Midland, TX	2.6	2.8	2.5	2.2	2.5	2.8	2.9	2.9	2.7	2.7	2.7	2.4
Milwaukee, WI	3.0	3.5	3.6	3.2	3.1	3.8	3.7	3.4	2.9	2.9	3.1	3.0
Minneapolis, MN	3.1	3.3	3.1	2.7	2.6	3.5	3.4	3.4	2.7	2.4	2.4	2.5
Nashville, TN	2.6	2.5	2.5	2.3	2.4	3.1	3.2	3.1	2.9	3.0	3.0	2.9
New Orleans, LA	4.6	4.3	4.2	3.8	3.9	5.0	5.0	4.9	4.7	4.7	4.5	4.2
New York, NY[1]	4.6	4.9	4.6	4.3	4.6	5.1	5.7	5.6	4.8	5.0	5.0	4.8
Oklahoma City, OK	3.3	3.4	3.0	2.6	3.0	3.3	3.3	3.2	3.0	3.0	3.0	2.8
Omaha, NE	3.1	3.2	2.9	2.7	2.9	3.3	3.4	3.1	2.8	3.0	2.9	2.8
Orlando, FL	3.2	3.1	3.1	2.9	3.1	3.6	3.8	3.8	3.4	3.4	3.5	3.1
Philadelphia, PA[1]	4.3	4.6	4.1	3.7	4.1	4.5	5.1	5.3	4.1	4.2	4.2	3.9
Phoenix, AZ	3.0	3.0	2.7	2.6	3.0	3.5	3.8	3.6	3.4	3.4	3.3	3.1
Pittsburgh, PA	3.9	4.1	3.6	3.1	3.3	3.9	4.2	4.4	3.1	3.4	3.3	3.4
Portland, OR	4.4	4.5	4.2	3.6	3.7	3.9	4.4	4.3	3.9	3.9	4.0	4.2
Providence, RI	4.8	5.2	4.5	3.8	4.1	4.3	4.9	5.0	4.0	4.2	4.4	4.4
Provo, UT	3.0	3.2	3.0	2.9	3.2	3.7	3.6	3.7	3.1	3.0	3.1	2.9
Raleigh, NC	3.3	3.4	3.2	2.9	3.1	3.4	3.6	3.5	2.9	2.9	3.1	2.9
Reno, NV	4.7	4.8	4.7	4.5	4.6	5.0	5.1	4.9	4.5	4.6	4.6	4.7
Richmond, VA	3.0	3.0	2.9	2.6	2.9	3.2	3.3	3.4	3.0	2.9	3.0	2.6
Rochester, MN	2.8	3.0	2.6	2.2	2.2	2.8	2.7	2.6	2.0	1.8	1.9	2.0
Sacramento, CA	4.9	4.9	4.7	4.2	4.0	4.8	5.1	5.2	4.6	4.7	4.8	4.6
Saint Louis, MO	3.9	4.1	3.9	3.4	3.7	4.0	4.2	3.9	3.2	3.3	3.3	3.2
Saint Paul, MN	3.1	3.3	3.1	2.7	2.6	3.5	3.4	3.4	2.7	2.4	2.4	2.5
Salem, OR	4.7	4.6	4.3	3.6	3.6	4.0	4.6	4.4	3.9	3.9	4.0	4.2
Salt Lake City, UT	3.0	3.4	3.2	3.0	3.1	3.5	3.5	3.6	3.0	3.1	3.0	2.9
San Antonio, TX	3.8	4.0	3.6	3.3	3.5	4.1	4.2	4.1	3.8	3.8	3.8	3.4
San Diego, CA	4.5	4.5	4.2	3.9	3.7	4.6	4.9	5.0	4.5	4.6	4.6	4.3
San Francisco, CA[1]	3.7	3.6	3.4	3.2	3.1	3.6	3.9	4.0	3.5	3.6	3.7	3.4
San Jose, CA	4.2	4.2	4.0	3.7	3.6	4.2	4.5	4.5	4.1	4.1	4.1	3.9
Santa Rosa, CA	4.3	4.2	4.0	3.6	3.4	4.1	4.4	4.5	3.9	4.1	4.2	4.0
Savannah, GA	2.9	3.0	3.0	2.5	3.1	3.5	3.4	3.7	2.9	3.0	2.9	2.8
Seattle, WA[1]	4.2	3.8	3.7	3.7	3.8	4.7	4.4	4.2	4.1	4.0	3.7	3.1
Sioux Falls, SD	1.8	2.1	1.6	1.6	1.6	1.8	1.5	1.8	1.3	1.5	1.5	1.8
Tampa, FL[1]	3.5	3.4	3.3	3.1	3.3	3.8	4.0	4.0	3.7	3.7	3.8	3.3
Tucson, AZ	3.3	3.3	3.0	2.8	3.3	4.0	4.3	4.0	3.7	3.7	3.6	3.4
Tulsa, OK	3.8	3.8	3.2	2.8	3.3	3.6	3.5	3.4	3.1	3.2	3.2	2.9
Virginia Beach, VA	3.0	3.0	2.9	2.6	3.0	3.2	3.4	3.4	3.1	3.0	3.1	2.7
Washington, DC[1]	3.9	4.1	3.9	3.4	3.7	4.4	4.6	4.7	4.0	4.1	4.1	3.8
Wichita, KS	3.6	3.8	3.7	3.4	3.7	4.2	5.0	4.6	3.8	4.2	4.3	3.8
Wilmington, NC	3.8	3.8	3.4	3.0	3.3	3.6	3.7	3.7	3.1	3.2	3.4	3.2
Winston-Salem, NC	3.6	3.7	3.6	3.1	3.4	3.9	4.1	4.0	3.3	3.3	3.6	3.2
U.S.	4.1	4.2	3.9	3.5	3.7	4.3	4.5	4.4	3.9	3.9	4.0	3.8

Note: Data is not seasonally adjusted and covers workers 16 years of age and older; All figures are percentages; (1) Figures cover the Metropolitan Statistical Area (MSA) except where noted; (1) Metropolitan Division
Source: Bureau of Labor Statistics, Local Area Unemployment Statistics

Average Hourly Wages: Occupations A – C

Metro Area	Accountants/ Auditors	Automotive Mechanics	Book-keepers	Carpenters	Cashiers	Computer Programmers	Computer Systems Analysts
Albuquerque, NM	40.90	25.69	23.51	26.42	14.93	43.80	46.83
Anchorage, AK	42.24	31.29	26.96	36.09	17.64	44.68	45.88
Ann Arbor, MI	41.19	27.70	24.68	30.96	15.32	39.67	53.91
Athens, GA	39.24	25.81	21.79	22.39	12.95	36.03	36.11
Atlanta, GA	46.20	28.17	24.88	24.84	13.99	49.60	53.95
Austin, TX	44.19	27.17	26.04	24.84	15.10	45.82	53.57
Baltimore, MD	44.96	27.65	26.87	28.13	16.18	52.85	56.04
Billings, MT	39.29	28.20	22.49	27.02	14.91	48.63	46.01
Boise City, ID	35.88	24.94	23.92	24.55	15.24	43.27	44.48
Boston, MA	49.79	29.49	28.51	38.40	17.37	57.83	60.98
Boulder, CO[2]	46.39	28.81	26.63	29.94	17.71	71.62	67.66
Cape Coral, FL	39.76	25.28	24.21	23.36	14.53	43.02	46.99
Cedar Rapids, IA	39.80	26.02	24.03	27.03	14.47	39.50	44.19
Charleston, SC	44.26	24.26	23.80	25.54	13.77	53.17	52.43
Charlotte, NC	47.13	27.27	24.68	25.51	14.02	44.72	57.50
Chicago, IL	44.28	28.71	25.75	38.11	16.33	46.08	48.09
Cincinnati, OH	41.81	24.64	24.76	27.72	14.23	56.17	52.48
Clarksville, TN	35.41	23.62	22.04	24.61	13.04	n/a	39.08
Cleveland, OH	41.49	26.14	24.08	29.35	14.16	44.94	47.53
College Station, TX	36.32	24.82	21.78	22.38	13.30	39.46	42.81
Colorado Springs, CO[2]	41.44	26.83	23.32	26.46	16.36	53.50	54.60
Columbia, MO	35.97	23.99	23.55	26.93	14.42	n/a	44.38
Columbia, SC	34.91	23.93	22.33	24.28	12.66	54.49	41.80
Columbus, OH	44.22	27.22	24.48	29.44	14.46	48.11	49.66
Dallas, TX	45.03	27.86	25.94	24.01	14.32	47.68	57.86
Davenport, IA	39.77	25.81	23.07	28.79	14.78	38.43	42.15
Denver, CO[2]	46.80	28.10	26.85	27.44	17.46	54.01	56.16
Des Moines, IA	40.26	26.59	24.64	28.46	14.74	45.02	47.37
Detroit, MI	43.77	27.01	25.39	31.70	14.88	39.07	50.95
Durham, NC	46.33	26.94	26.20	24.03	14.15	51.55	54.64
El Paso, TX	35.86	22.04	20.35	20.00	12.41	34.05	44.84
Eugene, OR	40.17	26.31	23.97	29.35	16.41	44.82	51.80
Fargo, ND	36.22	26.79	24.09	29.49	15.21	43.27	50.62
Fort Collins, CO[2]	43.11	27.93	24.64	26.93	16.61	54.48	53.23
Fort Wayne, IN	38.36	24.39	22.76	27.40	13.68	39.45	44.73
Fort Worth, TX	45.03	27.86	25.94	24.01	14.32	47.68	57.86
Gainesville, FL	38.54	24.87	23.70	23.37	14.25	44.12	41.84
Green Bay, WI	40.76	27.11	23.58	30.80	14.24	45.19	48.58
Greensboro, NC	41.27	25.40	22.80	21.70	13.29	43.91	50.14
Honolulu, HI	36.77	27.01	23.29	42.67	17.05	50.07	44.25
Houston, TX	45.33	27.12	24.69	24.93	14.10	n/a	56.46
Huntsville, AL	41.06	25.69	22.10	23.65	13.43	52.24	59.51
Indianapolis, IN	41.42	25.35	23.97	30.07	13.91	47.00	50.67
Jacksonville, FL	41.72	25.10	23.66	24.55	14.62	50.71	50.41
Kansas City, MO	41.41	26.51	24.38	31.38	15.02	46.73	48.94
Lafayette, LA	35.63	23.75	20.97	22.46	11.84	40.56	49.57
Las Vegas, NV	39.57	25.88	24.90	32.87	14.94	44.52	47.58
Lexington, KY	36.98	22.15	23.60	25.79	13.44	52.20	41.98
Lincoln, NE	34.67	25.66	22.74	25.07	14.50	43.25	40.47
Little Rock, AR	36.16	23.85	22.54	23.06	13.71	45.30	29.95
Los Angeles, CA	48.45	30.20	28.58	36.97	18.47	50.36	59.72
Louisville, KY	39.40	23.99	24.07	26.54	14.14	52.89	45.74
Madison, WI	41.87	28.99	25.40	32.44	15.63	42.40	46.04
Manchester, NH	42.84	28.99	25.41	28.98	14.89	41.19	52.98
McAllen, TX	33.75	22.30	19.81	18.97	12.40	38.07	37.09

Table continued on following page.

Metro Area	Accountants/ Auditors	Automotive Mechanics	Book-keepers	Carpenters	Cashiers	Computer Programmers	Computer Systems Analysts
Memphis, TN	39.28	25.26	23.48	25.20	13.30	43.86	48.38
Miami, FL	43.02	26.45	24.75	24.57	14.99	57.85	54.87
Midland, TX	47.51	26.20	25.44	24.81	14.69	42.10	57.62
Milwaukee, WI	43.31	28.74	24.38	32.43	14.53	43.19	50.52
Minneapolis, MN	45.40	29.52	26.89	35.62	16.35	50.83	53.62
Nashville, TN	41.77	26.05	24.43	25.67	14.57	n/a	42.96
New Orleans, LA	40.08	24.79	22.70	25.98	13.04	39.98	48.21
New York, NY	58.64	29.75	29.11	37.32	17.91	58.71	61.28
Oklahoma City, OK	41.96	23.62	22.88	25.29	13.24	57.04	47.08
Omaha, NE	37.98	26.58	24.02	26.11	14.93	46.38	46.14
Orlando, FL	42.38	25.24	23.73	24.25	15.21	46.42	49.67
Philadelphia, PA	46.34	27.57	26.12	32.62	15.31	46.77	51.52
Phoenix, AZ	42.29	28.52	25.59	28.74	16.53	40.51	51.41
Pittsburgh, PA	39.21	24.59	23.05	31.17	14.11	42.07	47.00
Portland, OR	44.95	29.63	26.60	35.28	17.91	57.44	60.32
Providence, RI	46.37	26.05	26.20	32.98	16.12	49.33	57.45
Provo, UT	38.12	23.63	23.58	25.60	15.11	43.63	48.54
Raleigh, NC	44.26	26.71	24.19	23.43	13.98	41.74	52.76
Reno, NV	41.47	27.04	25.86	32.80	15.27	49.79	47.77
Richmond, VA	42.37	27.70	24.33	24.90	15.01	46.29	51.27
Rochester, MN	46.22	27.15	27.32	32.24	15.88	n/a	n/a
Sacramento, CA	45.29	31.97	28.08	37.87	18.42	56.85	57.48
Saint Louis, MO	40.41	25.56	25.12	33.56	15.63	48.91	46.89
Saint Paul, MN	45.40	29.52	26.89	35.62	16.35	50.83	53.62
Salem, OR	42.14	27.01	26.35	27.76	16.54	52.83	53.95
Salt Lake City, UT	41.61	25.97	24.91	27.86	15.51	46.78	45.51
San Antonio, TX	41.41	25.74	23.19	23.06	14.39	62.03	51.53
San Diego, CA	50.36	29.84	28.01	36.37	18.50	60.74	57.81
San Francisco, CA	57.63	35.20	32.85	41.44	20.07	62.74	71.92
San Jose, CA	61.89	39.24	32.88	41.63	20.75	76.50	77.64
Santa Rosa, CA	47.74	31.99	29.51	40.36	19.48	48.16	55.29
Savannah, GA	40.41	27.16	23.06	24.58	13.64	46.30	52.25
Seattle, WA	51.01	30.63	28.45	39.76	20.63	80.47	66.53
Sioux Falls, SD	40.80	28.20	21.98	23.96	14.91	n/a	48.25
Tampa, FL	42.37	25.41	25.17	24.57	14.51	46.54	53.50
Tucson, AZ	39.27	26.22	24.08	25.46	15.74	46.55	51.81
Tulsa, OK	40.70	24.36	23.49	24.64	13.45	47.67	55.21
Virginia Beach, VA	41.24	26.43	23.13	24.88	14.28	50.07	50.99
Washington, DC	52.24	31.94	28.25	30.71	17.17	54.17	62.36
Wichita, KS	37.74	24.13	21.79	25.64	13.10	50.82	48.92
Wilmington, NC	37.67	23.96	22.76	24.06	13.23	37.74	46.73
Winston-Salem, NC	40.27	25.20	22.66	23.60	13.15	44.83	50.74

Notes: Figures cover the Metropolitan Statistical Area (MSA); (1) Data is from 2023 due to data quality issues in the state of Colorado and its substate areas in 2024; n/a not available
Source: Bureau of Labor Statistics, Metro Area Occupational Employment and Wage Estimates, May 2024

Average Hourly Wages: Occupations C – E

Metro Area	Comp. User Support Specialists	Construction Laborers	Cooks, Restaurant	Customer Service Reps.	Dentists	Electricians	Engineers, Electrical
Albuquerque, NM	24.18	20.58	16.62	20.23	92.52	28.48	71.65
Anchorage, AK	30.11	30.31	19.67	22.30	96.63	38.60	57.20
Ann Arbor, MI	27.63	24.45	18.17	20.90	n/a	37.90	52.52
Athens, GA	24.25	19.20	15.36	17.62	86.37	28.38	52.45
Atlanta, GA	31.11	20.30	16.66	21.35	102.19	30.62	56.08
Austin, TX	29.47	20.17	17.40	20.72	105.18	28.24	67.90
Baltimore, MD	33.50	22.42	18.38	21.60	108.70	33.58	59.60
Billings, MT	26.60	24.46	18.09	21.17	118.06	34.75	51.14
Boise City, ID	26.79	22.50	16.50	21.14	85.60	29.13	65.01
Boston, MA	37.62	33.95	21.98	25.48	n/a	40.10	64.82
Boulder, CO[1]	36.17	22.30	20.42	22.82	85.12	31.85	63.49
Cape Coral, FL	28.07	21.08	17.88	19.48	132.27	25.82	49.73
Cedar Rapids, IA	28.20	23.76	16.74	21.95	76.51	26.89	53.76
Charleston, SC	28.38	21.91	17.47	20.80	78.30	28.18	56.11
Charlotte, NC	30.08	21.52	17.64	21.55	106.87	27.55	58.48
Chicago, IL	30.31	34.99	18.66	23.30	89.54	44.39	57.06
Cincinnati, OH	28.23	26.28	15.92	21.20	103.59	30.46	51.81
Clarksville, TN	25.48	20.62	15.08	18.84	87.66	28.77	45.74
Cleveland, OH	28.26	27.82	17.24	22.13	81.41	32.62	49.77
College Station, TX	24.10	17.72	14.89	17.74	103.68	25.02	50.62
Colorado Springs, CO[1]	30.73	21.28	19.05	20.87	88.76	28.83	56.23
Columbia, MO	27.69	28.79	16.00	20.94	105.42	30.08	n/a
Columbia, SC	27.54	21.14	16.57	19.31	120.35	29.62	51.67
Columbus, OH	30.19	27.99	16.81	22.27	78.07	31.75	49.68
Dallas, TX	29.72	19.90	17.09	21.47	96.90	28.56	56.38
Davenport, IA	27.46	27.61	16.58	20.62	95.43	34.34	54.36
Denver, CO[1]	36.27	22.62	20.14	22.82	64.29	30.65	55.39
Des Moines, IA	29.14	24.89	17.75	24.02	93.83	32.28	69.53
Detroit, MI	29.25	26.26	18.06	22.70	93.92	36.41	53.76
Durham, NC	32.70	22.51	17.45	22.07	96.79	29.52	58.62
El Paso, TX	22.07	17.25	14.12	17.31	101.96	23.92	44.54
Eugene, OR	30.29	24.26	18.28	21.66	107.76	40.45	54.89
Fargo, ND	30.52	25.14	17.42	21.49	100.00	33.30	50.36
Fort Collins, CO[1]	32.68	21.53	18.75	20.21	100.41	29.77	55.88
Fort Wayne, IN	26.58	23.81	15.90	21.57	98.97	31.08	49.63
Fort Worth, TX	29.72	19.90	17.09	21.47	96.90	28.56	56.38
Gainesville, FL	25.88	19.68	16.92	19.63	98.53	25.55	51.00
Green Bay, WI	28.66	26.49	17.71	22.50	81.11	33.62	47.47
Greensboro, NC	26.94	20.44	16.19	20.71	85.23	26.42	53.13
Honolulu, HI	28.29	33.27	21.30	21.38	65.12	42.47	50.66
Houston, TX	29.02	20.13	15.99	20.40	115.55	28.39	57.48
Huntsville, AL	25.12	18.37	16.05	19.29	n/a	27.47	63.59
Indianapolis, IN	29.12	25.60	16.96	22.07	89.99	32.56	53.74
Jacksonville, FL	28.60	20.35	16.89	20.86	86.80	27.03	52.71
Kansas City, MO	28.37	26.74	18.07	21.64	89.46	35.72	51.97
Lafayette, LA	30.51	20.27	13.44	18.01	82.38	26.35	47.69
Las Vegas, NV	27.07	24.69	19.59	19.65	69.07	34.73	51.25
Lexington, KY	27.96	21.98	15.85	20.23	86.12	27.82	50.32
Lincoln, NE	28.07	21.86	17.81	19.65	85.28	29.82	47.88
Little Rock, AR	26.42	18.42	15.24	19.85	92.76	24.62	51.32
Los Angeles, CA	35.73	31.23	21.28	25.04	83.74	39.39	65.77
Louisville, KY	27.34	23.10	16.46	20.93	90.25	30.65	47.48
Madison, WI	29.81	27.12	18.70	23.53	98.38	36.51	51.89
Manchester, NH	34.06	22.66	18.60	23.92	77.22	30.59	70.89
McAllen, TX	21.73	15.75	13.57	17.73	106.72	21.99	46.39

Table continued on following page.

Metro Area	Comp. User Support Specialists	Construction Laborers	Cooks, Restaurant	Customer Service Reps.	Dentists	Electricians	Engineers, Electrical
Memphis, TN	28.25	22.21	16.20	21.10	91.70	27.81	53.37
Miami, FL	32.66	21.69	17.30	20.41	89.88	27.58	53.23
Midland, TX	27.70	20.63	16.62	20.78	n/a	28.92	61.86
Milwaukee, WI	30.47	28.30	18.61	23.48	97.31	35.83	50.13
Minneapolis, MN	33.76	30.67	20.11	24.54	108.57	41.70	54.81
Nashville, TN	29.95	22.45	18.35	21.72	97.05	29.83	55.61
New Orleans, LA	28.92	21.90	15.42	19.43	97.54	29.41	56.07
New York, NY	35.37	34.43	20.82	25.80	89.32	41.08	60.31
Oklahoma City, OK	26.99	20.63	17.14	20.02	112.93	30.47	53.72
Omaha, NE	29.50	23.84	18.03	21.38	103.65	31.36	48.89
Orlando, FL	28.57	21.13	18.25	19.99	85.11	26.17	56.13
Philadelphia, PA	31.66	28.19	17.84	23.03	87.74	38.14	61.83
Phoenix, AZ	32.43	23.17	19.56	22.50	98.52	29.58	59.00
Pittsburgh, PA	29.05	25.52	15.76	21.46	78.26	34.21	53.62
Portland, OR	31.89	27.95	20.13	23.78	94.71	46.08	57.53
Providence, RI	30.62	30.51	19.97	22.77	n/a	34.24	54.44
Provo, UT	28.65	22.38	17.58	19.85	66.32	29.16	60.54
Raleigh, NC	29.83	22.02	17.14	21.36	104.78	26.83	65.68
Reno, NV	28.19	27.64	18.27	20.68	74.31	32.97	57.15
Richmond, VA	29.64	19.84	17.56	20.92	103.90	29.24	56.26
Rochester, MN	33.24	28.42	18.68	23.08	122.85	39.75	50.77
Sacramento, CA	47.62	31.16	20.88	24.98	89.82	39.30	65.09
Saint Louis, MO	29.80	31.00	18.07	22.36	n/a	36.65	56.55
Saint Paul, MN	33.76	30.67	20.11	24.54	108.57	41.70	54.81
Salem, OR	31.51	25.90	18.91	22.72	104.28	40.07	55.99
Salt Lake City, UT	32.60	23.53	18.51	21.44	80.35	31.02	55.43
San Antonio, TX	27.32	19.44	15.83	20.34	78.33	26.69	55.23
San Diego, CA	35.01	30.44	21.15	24.53	87.88	39.61	65.99
San Francisco, CA	43.40	36.32	22.87	29.30	109.18	50.12	77.50
San Jose, CA	43.29	35.06	24.13	30.67	90.06	49.71	90.89
Santa Rosa, CA	37.08	32.20	21.98	25.04	82.86	42.00	63.20
Savannah, GA	31.48	19.01	16.30	18.64	98.92	28.43	57.20
Seattle, WA	37.28	31.08	22.67	27.52	97.55	48.19	67.55
Sioux Falls, SD	23.81	20.75	17.44	21.01	89.53	28.14	48.75
Tampa, FL	29.29	21.37	17.47	20.59	112.24	26.80	55.02
Tucson, AZ	28.35	21.11	17.71	19.74	92.54	28.60	62.08
Tulsa, OK	27.43	21.54	16.20	19.80	97.17	30.23	53.92
Virginia Beach, VA	29.01	19.76	17.15	19.47	87.77	29.26	53.55
Washington, DC	38.26	23.15	20.33	23.55	109.72	37.78	67.24
Wichita, KS	24.62	20.29	15.63	19.26	82.76	31.51	46.39
Wilmington, NC	28.36	21.81	16.50	19.57	104.98	26.12	54.21
Winston-Salem, NC	27.29	21.31	15.89	19.29	77.83	26.05	42.46

Notes: Figures cover the Metropolitan Statistical Area (MSA); (1) Data is from 2023 due to data quality issues in the state of Colorado and its substate areas in 2024; n/a not available
Source: Bureau of Labor Statistics, Metro Area Occupational Employment and Wage Estimates, May 2024

Appendix A: Comparative Statistics

Average Hourly Wages: Occupations F – J

Metro Area	Fast Food and Counter Workers	Financial Managers	First-Line Supervisors/ of Office Workers	General and Operations Managers	Hair- dressers/ Cosme- tologists	Home Health and Personal Care Aides	Janitors/ Cleaners
Albuquerque, NM	14.78	67.06	31.40	59.24	18.37	14.44	16.27
Anchorage, AK	16.07	66.10	34.12	67.82	n/a	18.20	19.57
Ann Arbor, MI	15.01	78.28	33.10	66.91	21.16	17.05	18.60
Athens, GA	12.25	70.43	29.73	48.33	20.63	13.58	14.96
Atlanta, GA	13.55	92.61	34.57	65.51	22.26	14.69	16.89
Austin, TX	14.09	89.92	36.88	68.18	20.93	13.82	16.90
Baltimore, MD	15.89	80.29	35.89	61.48	20.61	18.43	18.03
Billings, MT	14.42	73.01	31.75	52.57	21.23	16.16	18.70
Boise City, ID	13.54	68.45	30.86	47.05	15.23	16.17	16.90
Boston, MA	17.43	100.73	38.59	78.73	24.97	19.58	21.75
Boulder, CO[1]	17.78	93.87	36.12	81.98	25.46	19.56	19.68
Cape Coral, FL	14.23	82.00	32.80	57.19	17.77	16.30	16.54
Cedar Rapids, IA	13.79	67.28	31.58	49.70	22.37	17.35	17.85
Charleston, SC	13.83	72.75	33.77	59.32	18.76	15.46	15.59
Charlotte, NC	14.27	91.39	33.22	66.57	20.12	15.34	16.27
Chicago, IL	16.05	88.31	35.22	68.58	20.23	17.79	19.25
Cincinnati, OH	14.06	77.39	32.81	58.30	20.06	15.99	17.45
Clarksville, TN	12.79	65.73	29.27	48.25	16.23	15.17	15.39
Cleveland, OH	14.06	76.95	33.00	57.91	17.62	15.55	17.41
College Station, TX	12.43	70.24	29.93	51.36	16.38	12.18	15.33
Colorado Springs, CO[1]	15.91	84.63	32.60	70.11	22.98	17.68	17.57
Columbia, MO	14.25	67.68	31.10	46.12	20.40	17.18	16.98
Columbia, SC	12.71	64.62	33.15	54.00	16.41	14.20	15.80
Columbus, OH	14.24	75.71	33.43	60.59	18.45	15.89	17.74
Dallas, TX	13.48	83.96	36.12	67.98	17.46	13.45	16.43
Davenport, IA	14.11	69.21	30.67	52.32	21.43	16.37	17.91
Denver, CO[1]	16.95	93.78	36.61	79.34	23.38	18.27	18.56
Des Moines, IA	14.21	77.18	33.94	54.24	22.00	17.30	17.35
Detroit, MI	14.34	77.60	33.92	65.30	21.26	15.95	17.41
Durham, NC	14.66	87.22	34.76	68.52	24.56	15.58	17.12
El Paso, TX	11.61	67.83	27.70	46.07	15.79	11.14	13.49
Eugene, OR	16.00	72.01	33.88	52.88	21.53	19.39	18.09
Fargo, ND	14.66	75.72	33.25	56.75	20.05	18.76	18.02
Fort Collins, CO[1]	16.21	90.82	32.90	67.45	28.72	18.19	18.27
Fort Wayne, IN	13.24	65.40	33.46	64.53	16.40	15.55	16.97
Fort Worth, TX	13.48	83.96	36.12	67.98	17.46	13.45	16.43
Gainesville, FL	14.25	67.20	30.71	55.75	15.92	15.70	16.07
Green Bay, WI	13.45	72.06	32.86	64.79	18.07	15.70	16.94
Greensboro, NC	13.39	82.48	31.23	58.89	18.93	14.32	15.59
Honolulu, HI	16.01	67.37	32.34	60.89	24.25	17.39	18.20
Houston, TX	12.78	88.07	35.05	66.82	19.05	12.11	15.20
Huntsville, AL	13.10	78.84	31.88	74.54	15.09	13.34	15.09
Indianapolis, IN	14.01	75.66	36.11	72.23	17.77	15.78	16.98
Jacksonville, FL	13.94	80.15	33.12	59.57	17.54	15.94	16.39
Kansas City, MO	14.34	76.99	34.02	53.13	20.28	15.65	17.70
Lafayette, LA	12.06	57.76	27.80	57.89	12.82	10.36	13.40
Las Vegas, NV	14.78	68.81	30.93	60.08	16.64	14.71	18.25
Lexington, KY	13.35	70.52	31.52	48.11	21.66	16.98	16.37
Lincoln, NE	14.42	68.94	30.73	50.12	17.48	16.47	16.83
Little Rock, AR	13.24	60.66	28.31	42.89	14.46	13.31	15.15
Los Angeles, CA	18.75	96.29	37.23	81.25	27.74	17.43	19.78
Louisville, KY	13.57	71.03	33.66	51.34	24.77	17.39	16.81
Madison, WI	14.40	77.53	36.80	69.40	17.58	17.03	18.27
Manchester, NH	14.45	76.66	37.63	74.48	18.36	18.05	18.24

Table continued on following page.

Metro Area	Fast Food and Counter Workers	Financial Managers	First-Line Supervisors/ of Office Workers	General and Operations Managers	Hair-dressers/ Cosme-tologists	Home Health and Personal Care Aides	Janitors/ Cleaners
McAllen, TX	11.81	63.80	28.02	44.25	14.51	11.34	14.44
Memphis, TN	13.12	76.07	34.04	61.94	17.10	15.01	15.76
Miami, FL	14.62	85.42	34.06	64.93	18.78	16.09	15.94
Midland, TX	13.82	87.54	36.53	69.94	n/a	12.83	16.27
Milwaukee, WI	13.86	78.61	35.29	68.07	19.57	15.84	17.69
Minneapolis, MN	16.17	85.12	37.88	59.75	22.01	17.88	19.66
Nashville, TN	14.12	79.15	35.70	66.64	20.68	16.69	17.04
New Orleans, LA	13.66	67.51	30.04	62.93	14.33	11.68	14.73
New York, NY	17.50	119.16	39.92	89.97	24.83	19.02	21.61
Oklahoma City, OK	12.18	71.53	32.48	52.56	18.80	13.47	15.40
Omaha, NE	14.83	75.03	31.66	51.15	21.52	17.13	17.41
Orlando, FL	14.19	78.11	32.58	58.33	17.70	16.03	16.19
Philadelphia, PA	15.05	85.35	35.52	66.76	19.65	15.40	18.54
Phoenix, AZ	16.50	75.51	33.09	59.06	19.33	17.28	18.02
Pittsburgh, PA	13.48	73.83	32.42	57.41	17.44	14.92	17.29
Portland, OR	17.61	86.12	36.29	70.26	25.82	21.37	20.22
Providence, RI	15.96	82.12	36.46	63.72	19.74	19.36	19.58
Provo, UT	13.85	75.16	33.39	54.43	18.78	17.59	15.34
Raleigh, NC	14.64	85.21	31.78	66.79	22.26	15.48	16.07
Reno, NV	15.29	67.77	32.24	59.24	23.92	16.38	17.04
Richmond, VA	14.48	88.63	33.36	63.23	25.31	14.98	16.42
Rochester, MN	15.53	77.53	34.14	50.21	22.80	17.71	20.40
Sacramento, CA	19.02	82.16	37.86	67.60	20.39	16.89	20.72
Saint Louis, MO	15.19	76.57	34.31	53.75	20.57	15.72	17.54
Saint Paul, MN	16.17	85.12	37.88	59.75	22.01	17.88	19.66
Salem, OR	16.51	80.64	34.43	56.23	22.06	20.60	19.35
Salt Lake City, UT	13.99	78.19	35.75	60.12	21.89	18.64	16.02
San Antonio, TX	13.32	77.30	32.68	57.15	16.98	12.52	15.75
San Diego, CA	18.39	92.64	36.65	n/a	22.37	17.55	19.51
San Francisco, CA	20.67	117.20	43.48	85.95	23.49	18.28	23.06
San Jose, CA	20.83	142.60	46.77	94.44	21.94	18.62	21.80
Santa Rosa, CA	19.46	82.80	36.40	66.12	22.13	18.18	21.32
Savannah, GA	13.18	76.60	32.20	55.21	19.33	14.47	15.78
Seattle, WA	19.74	96.69	42.38	82.62	33.56	23.17	22.62
Sioux Falls, SD	15.01	86.95	31.03	76.69	23.12	18.16	16.68
Tampa, FL	14.40	81.07	32.48	65.80	18.35	16.19	16.47
Tucson, AZ	15.89	66.97	29.60	57.34	19.10	16.54	17.29
Tulsa, OK	12.63	71.47	31.71	53.60	17.42	13.24	15.65
Virginia Beach, VA	14.30	78.26	32.80	57.87	23.44	14.33	16.05
Washington, DC	16.65	93.22	38.57	77.26	25.20	18.26	18.52
Wichita, KS	12.56	75.40	30.36	48.65	17.46	14.72	15.77
Wilmington, NC	13.68	73.03	29.78	55.43	19.37	14.82	16.04
Winston-Salem, NC	13.91	77.03	30.59	59.42	18.68	14.44	15.37

Notes: Figures cover the Metropolitan Statistical Area (MSA); (1) Data is from 2023 due to data quality issues in the state of Colorado and its substate areas in 2024; n/a not available
Source: Bureau of Labor Statistics, Metro Area Occupational Employment and Wage Estimates, May 2024

Average Hourly Wages: Occupations L – N

Metro Area	Landscapers	Lawyers	Maids/House-keepers	Maintenance/Repairers	Marketing Managers	Network Admin.	Nurses, Licensed Practical
Albuquerque, NM	18.15	67.75	15.65	23.82	62.50	44.51	26.25
Anchorage, AK	21.86	65.58	18.49	27.18	60.07	45.18	37.16
Ann Arbor, MI	19.91	80.54	17.03	24.12	70.18	46.70	33.06
Athens, GA	17.53	49.61	13.10	20.51	72.47	40.57	27.62
Atlanta, GA	18.84	98.50	15.44	25.02	82.69	48.68	29.80
Austin, TX	18.93	83.20	15.47	24.12	79.43	50.49	30.98
Baltimore, MD	19.36	76.50	16.48	25.58	76.43	60.34	34.04
Billings, MT	19.81	52.20	17.08	22.86	66.97	39.58	26.99
Boise City, ID	20.23	67.91	16.90	24.14	62.17	49.66	30.70
Boston, MA	24.09	109.06	21.01	28.49	98.23	53.85	37.85
Boulder, CO[1]	23.16	120.91	18.76	28.09	89.78	53.52	32.93
Cape Coral, FL	17.78	72.21	16.09	23.30	65.95	46.21	29.34
Cedar Rapids, IA	18.72	61.80	15.71	26.12	66.98	41.23	29.02
Charleston, SC	18.21	62.85	15.15	23.84	66.50	46.44	29.19
Charlotte, NC	18.72	89.69	16.06	25.50	77.80	48.36	30.80
Chicago, IL	21.26	89.56	19.33	27.90	78.03	49.76	34.69
Cincinnati, OH	18.59	69.29	15.43	26.32	72.86	48.96	29.78
Clarksville, TN	17.20	67.51	13.62	22.72	56.80	57.61	26.97
Cleveland, OH	18.91	71.42	15.21	25.41	67.80	46.55	30.00
College Station, TX	16.48	67.99	13.30	20.21	61.86	38.10	26.76
Colorado Springs, CO[1]	20.66	69.39	16.92	23.63	81.56	49.17	30.52
Columbia, MO	17.79	71.41	15.77	22.42	59.28	43.70	28.34
Columbia, SC	17.37	65.86	13.97	23.42	63.36	43.01	28.97
Columbus, OH	19.22	72.24	15.53	25.88	70.72	48.31	30.09
Dallas, TX	18.42	85.71	15.45	24.02	74.76	50.61	30.36
Davenport, IA	18.79	67.21	15.51	25.55	69.88	40.45	28.99
Denver, CO[1]	21.35	95.55	18.17	26.82	89.00	51.25	31.94
Des Moines, IA	19.53	64.42	15.83	25.62	70.53	44.92	30.46
Detroit, MI	19.93	69.97	16.33	24.30	72.83	48.72	32.31
Durham, NC	19.05	73.55	17.00	25.50	82.71	53.21	30.26
El Paso, TX	15.24	61.03	12.61	19.68	55.59	39.84	27.06
Eugene, OR	19.74	68.79	17.08	24.77	64.41	45.54	35.15
Fargo, ND	20.93	60.13	16.65	25.20	66.41	40.53	28.38
Fort Collins, CO[1]	20.58	104.22	17.22	24.61	88.03	47.68	30.10
Fort Wayne, IN	17.85	65.81	14.93	25.25	n/a	39.62	29.69
Fort Worth, TX	18.42	85.71	15.45	24.02	74.76	50.61	30.36
Gainesville, FL	17.73	53.79	15.37	23.13	64.71	41.00	27.62
Green Bay, WI	19.50	69.46	16.12	25.64	75.74	41.79	28.26
Greensboro, NC	17.87	68.03	14.93	23.70	80.15	41.61	30.11
Honolulu, HI	20.46	58.87	25.07	27.07	63.78	48.37	32.75
Houston, TX	17.42	78.80	14.99	23.29	75.23	48.11	30.16
Huntsville, AL	17.69	69.83	13.23	22.69	67.44	48.12	25.96
Indianapolis, IN	18.81	82.32	15.57	25.58	64.61	43.51	30.93
Jacksonville, FL	17.93	62.65	15.49	23.93	69.06	44.92	28.41
Kansas City, MO	20.15	84.26	16.32	25.52	69.71	44.91	30.67
Lafayette, LA	15.75	66.98	12.04	19.43	52.19	45.64	24.52
Las Vegas, NV	19.84	n/a	20.07	26.40	59.85	49.09	34.18
Lexington, KY	18.10	57.22	14.59	22.68	59.96	41.66	28.18
Lincoln, NE	18.75	54.48	15.57	24.63	54.33	42.93	28.51
Little Rock, AR	16.67	65.50	13.80	22.43	55.96	40.49	26.10
Los Angeles, CA	21.42	130.10	21.39	27.74	87.09	53.71	37.14
Louisville, KY	18.54	58.69	15.46	25.41	68.75	43.31	29.46
Madison, WI	21.04	69.54	16.72	26.12	67.95	41.94	30.71
Manchester, NH	21.01	90.60	16.93	26.41	79.04	50.29	34.71
McAllen, TX	14.92	57.98	12.70	17.79	54.38	37.41	24.78

Table continued on following page.

Metro Area	Landscapers	Lawyers	Maids/House-keepers	Main-tenance/Repairers	Marketing Managers	Network Admin.	Nurses, Licensed Practical
Memphis, TN	18.30	71.60	15.17	23.77	70.27	43.88	25.70
Miami, FL	18.25	78.54	16.01	23.66	69.64	47.57	30.32
Midland, TX	18.44	95.87	14.15	23.89	73.71	47.24	30.11
Milwaukee, WI	19.82	86.63	17.09	26.01	71.02	46.35	30.73
Minneapolis, MN	22.32	79.57	19.15	28.72	85.36	48.14	30.75
Nashville, TN	19.47	80.00	15.97	24.27	70.23	54.49	28.30
New Orleans, LA	16.51	66.68	14.95	22.29	60.16	47.36	28.31
New York, NY	21.91	103.90	24.09	28.95	96.08	57.33	34.69
Oklahoma City, OK	17.06	59.75	13.86	21.81	69.08	41.11	26.98
Omaha, NE	20.04	68.96	16.54	25.08	63.75	45.55	29.24
Orlando, FL	17.82	68.56	16.98	23.02	75.25	45.79	28.81
Philadelphia, PA	19.86	82.76	16.94	26.00	81.62	49.02	32.87
Phoenix, AZ	19.42	81.05	17.66	25.41	74.34	46.72	35.33
Pittsburgh, PA	18.69	72.59	15.75	24.30	63.96	44.03	28.96
Portland, OR	21.90	76.99	19.20	28.31	81.04	50.92	38.94
Providence, RI	21.36	73.53	17.71	25.96	82.62	50.61	35.27
Provo, UT	20.19	70.82	16.07	24.23	70.63	46.73	28.85
Raleigh, NC	19.00	71.98	15.98	24.47	81.03	50.43	30.60
Reno, NV	21.79	96.52	18.19	25.86	73.52	48.59	35.06
Richmond, VA	18.50	80.01	15.53	25.46	84.07	49.36	30.78
Rochester, MN	21.83	65.23	18.18	26.25	80.62	52.13	29.80
Sacramento, CA	22.37	97.12	21.69	27.33	84.16	52.73	39.66
Saint Louis, MO	19.80	73.53	16.55	26.56	66.03	43.67	30.72
Saint Paul, MN	22.32	79.57	19.15	28.72	85.36	48.14	30.75
Salem, OR	20.37	76.23	19.11	25.44	64.66	52.82	35.99
Salt Lake City, UT	20.01	76.47	17.31	25.87	72.64	49.94	31.60
San Antonio, TX	17.39	73.65	14.28	22.06	67.10	43.87	29.23
San Diego, CA	21.52	93.11	20.83	27.48	93.41	50.55	37.47
San Francisco, CA	25.75	132.29	25.07	33.69	109.71	64.21	43.56
San Jose, CA	25.28	151.17	27.28	33.50	137.00	63.55	44.06
Santa Rosa, CA	23.68	124.30	22.21	28.52	80.50	50.04	41.93
Savannah, GA	17.56	67.70	13.59	23.15	75.38	45.56	27.56
Seattle, WA	24.35	88.39	20.95	30.02	94.44	55.61	39.88
Sioux Falls, SD	17.48	64.81	15.77	23.21	78.00	37.26	24.52
Tampa, FL	17.89	67.66	16.79	22.66	73.93	48.19	29.09
Tucson, AZ	18.04	67.35	16.29	22.70	65.42	44.42	34.81
Tulsa, OK	17.01	57.59	13.86	22.39	70.25	51.21	27.71
Virginia Beach, VA	17.88	71.39	15.26	24.23	77.38	47.60	29.68
Washington, DC	20.84	105.48	18.53	27.76	91.27	60.06	34.17
Wichita, KS	18.31	60.10	14.70	22.57	67.18	39.93	27.76
Wilmington, NC	17.61	60.44	14.71	22.36	72.18	42.11	29.97
Winston-Salem, NC	17.78	83.92	15.70	24.06	74.45	43.84	28.98

Notes: Figures cover the Metropolitan Statistical Area (MSA); (1) Data is from 2023 due to data quality issues in the state of Colorado and its substate areas in 2024; n/a not available
Source: Bureau of Labor Statistics, Metro Area Occupational Employment and Wage Estimates, May 2024

Average Hourly Wages: Occupations N – P

Metro Area	Nurses, Registered	Nursing Assistants	Office Clerks	Physical Therapists	Physicians	Plumbers	Police Officers
Albuquerque, NM	45.99	18.59	18.52	48.32	146.53	30.61	33.46
Anchorage, AK	54.49	22.44	25.42	54.28	n/a	40.27	52.82
Ann Arbor, MI	46.65	19.82	21.46	47.54	117.60	35.47	37.47
Athens, GA	40.42	17.28	20.80	45.86	148.79	26.20	28.56
Atlanta, GA	46.46	18.72	20.88	50.04	128.59	29.64	30.37
Austin, TX	44.74	18.68	21.24	50.22	140.23	30.87	40.67
Baltimore, MD	46.70	20.15	22.45	50.65	111.79	32.84	38.57
Billings, MT	43.06	20.43	21.25	46.45	n/a	37.35	35.12
Boise City, ID	44.68	18.92	21.13	46.02	150.09	28.71	36.96
Boston, MA	55.63	22.73	25.39	49.54	104.76	42.81	39.16
Boulder, CO[1]	47.77	22.19	27.23	47.73	157.65	33.25	43.85
Cape Coral, FL	41.84	18.75	22.60	46.75	178.53	25.11	36.26
Cedar Rapids, IA	37.78	19.56	21.03	42.76	148.31	33.30	35.70
Charleston, SC	42.57	18.63	20.56	47.07	142.06	26.91	30.52
Charlotte, NC	42.86	19.15	20.94	48.26	150.06	27.07	32.47
Chicago, IL	45.47	21.85	23.22	52.46	109.22	44.43	47.28
Cincinnati, OH	41.93	19.66	21.56	48.99	137.38	32.13	38.17
Clarksville, TN	37.88	17.59	18.67	45.46	154.95	31.80	26.37
Cleveland, OH	43.24	19.22	22.21	48.56	117.07	33.28	37.16
College Station, TX	40.15	16.34	n/a	49.86	118.72	26.89	36.08
Colorado Springs, CO[1]	41.57	20.55	25.08	47.11	145.41	29.44	40.85
Columbia, MO	39.72	18.73	20.78	43.86	149.57	30.64	28.96
Columbia, SC	40.80	17.13	19.07	45.02	172.10	25.12	32.54
Columbus, OH	42.87	19.72	22.35	47.24	129.01	32.38	42.38
Dallas, TX	46.50	18.80	21.12	52.68	105.52	30.24	41.90
Davenport, IA	36.47	18.90	20.19	45.91	133.88	34.59	34.22
Denver, CO[1]	44.80	21.50	27.01	47.63	148.66	32.33	44.76
Des Moines, IA	38.30	20.34	21.64	46.36	117.95	32.51	39.83
Detroit, MI	44.56	19.58	22.38	47.96	79.84	36.88	36.19
Durham, NC	n/a	19.70	21.79	44.30	69.93	28.13	30.46
El Paso, TX	42.08	16.41	16.95	46.74	120.70	25.72	36.19
Eugene, OR	54.25	23.01	22.54	47.48	165.85	40.25	42.81
Fargo, ND	39.76	19.70	24.78	43.52	165.27	31.67	36.83
Fort Collins, CO[1]	43.16	20.38	25.12	44.64	119.01	30.07	44.59
Fort Wayne, IN	39.85	18.10	21.10	46.11	144.14	35.26	36.57
Fort Worth, TX	46.50	18.80	21.12	52.68	105.52	30.24	41.90
Gainesville, FL	42.66	18.80	21.26	46.21	130.80	24.73	29.02
Green Bay, WI	41.77	19.98	21.47	47.00	196.56	39.90	39.06
Greensboro, NC	41.93	18.27	19.68	44.25	144.60	25.64	30.89
Honolulu, HI	60.17	21.81	21.33	48.19	152.85	40.69	45.53
Houston, TX	46.51	18.77	19.64	53.94	123.51	29.30	35.97
Huntsville, AL	35.22	16.31	16.03	47.20	140.44	26.63	30.79
Indianapolis, IN	42.93	18.85	22.26	47.40	154.93	33.46	38.34
Jacksonville, FL	41.31	18.27	21.57	46.05	130.38	26.34	33.29
Kansas City, MO	41.12	20.02	22.34	46.79	76.04	36.37	33.12
Lafayette, LA	38.87	14.75	15.09	45.77	127.73	26.64	26.21
Las Vegas, NV	49.23	21.32	21.50	55.52	108.49	31.52	41.22
Lexington, KY	40.98	19.39	19.89	44.65	134.53	31.89	32.13
Lincoln, NE	39.04	19.33	18.58	44.86	136.23	30.39	40.64
Little Rock, AR	39.00	16.82	19.51	45.58	113.68	25.08	28.58
Los Angeles, CA	66.35	23.03	23.99	56.57	82.19	37.49	52.17
Louisville, KY	42.06	19.38	18.96	44.32	137.23	33.07	31.32
Madison, WI	46.09	21.62	21.81	47.86	156.17	42.99	38.38
Manchester, NH	44.26	22.36	24.15	44.89	148.76	31.71	36.87
McAllen, TX	36.77	15.66	16.04	50.03	144.98	22.61	29.67

Table continued on following page.

Metro Area	Nurses, Registered	Nursing Assistants	Office Clerks	Physical Therapists	Physicians	Plumbers	Police Officers
Memphis, TN	40.79	17.76	19.17	48.19	143.52	28.45	32.26
Miami, FL	44.26	19.01	22.54	42.79	117.21	27.27	50.84
Midland, TX	42.82	18.39	23.20	54.19	n/a	27.83	40.49
Milwaukee, WI	43.77	21.00	21.09	48.16	115.37	41.81	41.03
Minneapolis, MN	49.42	22.60	24.20	47.65	159.99	42.95	42.99
Nashville, TN	42.71	19.32	20.60	47.86	134.22	29.46	30.96
New Orleans, LA	43.12	16.45	16.23	51.00	147.27	29.90	27.76
New York, NY	55.60	23.60	24.07	52.54	125.08	43.78	44.53
Oklahoma City, OK	41.29	17.28	19.03	48.05	113.07	27.59	35.39
Omaha, NE	40.84	20.08	19.65	45.26	132.45	34.64	39.22
Orlando, FL	41.57	17.96	21.36	47.77	152.34	26.02	32.01
Philadelphia, PA	46.88	20.72	22.87	50.29	103.98	38.73	41.45
Phoenix, AZ	46.26	21.03	24.26	50.72	101.37	33.45	42.24
Pittsburgh, PA	41.36	19.62	21.43	45.46	106.62	34.88	39.89
Portland, OR	59.41	24.32	24.99	51.26	145.16	46.10	45.23
Providence, RI	47.85	20.93	23.21	47.81	115.77	36.48	37.31
Provo, UT	40.74	18.10	20.61	47.91	138.71	27.75	34.98
Raleigh, NC	43.18	18.76	20.44	45.60	140.88	27.06	31.94
Reno, NV	49.60	21.66	22.82	51.17	119.36	34.61	40.69
Richmond, VA	43.52	19.49	22.18	49.10	124.83	28.27	33.25
Rochester, MN	50.31	21.62	23.84	46.20	142.26	41.69	38.02
Sacramento, CA	78.37	23.25	25.08	60.12	165.05	35.78	53.46
Saint Louis, MO	40.74	19.04	21.94	46.78	n/a	37.26	34.71
Saint Paul, MN	49.42	22.60	24.20	47.65	159.99	42.95	42.99
Salem, OR	58.70	24.31	23.22	46.55	156.96	38.33	41.55
Salt Lake City, UT	44.02	19.66	22.49	47.44	112.68	32.12	40.23
San Antonio, TX	42.93	17.50	19.72	48.60	148.25	28.13	33.62
San Diego, CA	67.00	23.07	23.88	52.74	133.58	36.03	53.06
San Francisco, CA	85.79	27.59	27.96	65.53	127.97	41.48	61.75
San Jose, CA	91.29	27.97	28.51	68.75	89.33	49.42	69.86
Santa Rosa, CA	82.45	23.29	26.18	62.99	96.04	38.02	53.85
Savannah, GA	41.90	17.49	19.60	47.93	140.56	29.86	30.08
Seattle, WA	57.82	25.24	26.95	50.63	142.83	45.49	53.76
Sioux Falls, SD	34.16	18.18	18.51	42.66	n/a	27.31	37.35
Tampa, FL	43.40	18.54	21.94	47.43	143.21	26.24	37.66
Tucson, AZ	44.18	20.24	22.28	47.48	134.43	27.72	37.95
Tulsa, OK	43.20	17.41	19.08	46.55	83.29	28.27	31.70
Virginia Beach, VA	42.13	18.43	21.17	48.12	125.27	27.83	32.02
Washington, DC	49.29	20.85	26.37	53.25	100.51	34.13	41.76
Wichita, KS	36.06	17.82	16.54	46.81	100.27	29.54	28.31
Wilmington, NC	39.17	18.20	18.96	41.99	129.60	25.08	26.40
Winston-Salem, NC	42.11	18.13	19.25	47.50	n/a	25.08	27.78

Notes: Figures cover the Metropolitan Statistical Area (MSA); (1) Data is from 2023 due to data quality issues in the state of Colorado and its substate areas in 2024; n/a not available
Source: Bureau of Labor Statistics, Metro Area Occupational Employment and Wage Estimates, May 2024

Appendix A: Comparative Statistics

Average Hourly Wages: Occupations P – S

Metro Area	Postal Mail Carriers	R.E. Sales Agents	Retail Salespersons	Sales Reps., Technical/ Scientific	Secretaries, Exc. Leg./ Med./Exec.	Security Guards	Surgeons
Albuquerque, NM	28.74	40.95	16.73	41.73	21.86	21.72	219.96
Anchorage, AK	27.61	43.45	19.57	40.10	21.78	26.71	n/a
Ann Arbor, MI	28.15	31.11	18.46	105.25	24.23	21.89	n/a
Athens, GA	28.08	27.38	14.88	n/a	17.77	21.83	n/a
Atlanta, GA	28.20	34.66	16.55	55.13	20.91	19.64	216.10
Austin, TX	29.21	41.46	17.04	45.57	22.22	19.26	n/a
Baltimore, MD	28.82	27.82	17.59	44.15	23.24	20.69	171.05
Billings, MT	28.52	37.77	17.80	49.31	21.21	19.51	n/a
Boise City, ID	28.72	n/a	18.06	59.59	20.77	20.32	n/a
Boston, MA	29.71	46.11	19.71	54.45	27.63	22.25	161.25
Boulder, CO[1]	29.62	37.36	20.20	68.73	23.54	25.69	n/a
Cape Coral, FL	29.05	37.59	16.92	57.39	20.71	17.45	n/a
Cedar Rapids, IA	28.91	21.00	16.36	49.65	21.59	19.04	n/a
Charleston, SC	29.37	n/a	16.45	50.27	21.83	18.35	n/a
Charlotte, NC	29.03	30.17	16.65	63.70	20.49	19.12	248.26
Chicago, IL	29.11	29.28	18.67	58.57	25.84	21.16	161.04
Cincinnati, OH	29.19	24.40	17.19	57.27	23.98	19.14	n/a
Clarksville, TN	27.83	25.11	16.33	34.76	19.85	19.00	n/a
Cleveland, OH	28.67	23.45	17.25	47.42	22.52	19.46	n/a
College Station, TX	27.95	29.01	15.01	41.37	19.66	16.89	n/a
Colorado Springs, CO[1]	27.18	33.25	18.80	53.78	21.04	19.20	n/a
Columbia, MO	28.47	24.50	16.22	46.86	20.78	18.70	n/a
Columbia, SC	27.58	25.47	15.69	55.80	20.60	16.75	n/a
Columbus, OH	29.11	25.57	17.40	54.37	23.47	19.81	n/a
Dallas, TX	29.14	35.39	16.85	49.39	22.33	19.16	172.43
Davenport, IA	28.67	31.72	16.82	46.92	21.95	19.78	n/a
Denver, CO[1]	29.38	n/a	20.04	57.52	23.31	22.24	n/a
Des Moines, IA	30.06	20.22	17.08	60.11	22.86	19.84	207.59
Detroit, MI	28.48	32.41	19.31	68.16	23.38	19.17	n/a
Durham, NC	29.34	28.62	16.63	57.68	23.09	21.40	n/a
El Paso, TX	28.75	31.06	14.45	41.79	18.76	14.38	n/a
Eugene, OR	27.06	26.12	18.58	52.14	23.51	19.91	186.25
Fargo, ND	30.03	34.07	18.57	54.80	21.50	20.01	n/a
Fort Collins, CO[1]	28.36	32.17	18.87	52.65	21.68	19.32	n/a
Fort Wayne, IN	28.41	37.39	16.08	52.60	20.58	20.23	n/a
Fort Worth, TX	29.14	35.39	16.85	49.39	22.33	19.16	172.43
Gainesville, FL	28.67	29.50	16.05	48.82	21.09	17.73	n/a
Green Bay, WI	29.14	28.56	17.47	31.64	22.49	20.67	n/a
Greensboro, NC	29.19	31.36	15.70	47.29	21.42	17.81	n/a
Honolulu, HI	27.98	33.03	19.06	58.17	25.07	20.40	n/a
Houston, TX	28.58	36.58	16.26	50.66	22.14	18.23	n/a
Huntsville, AL	27.93	22.98	16.48	52.53	21.47	19.04	n/a
Indianapolis, IN	29.29	36.12	16.89	55.71	21.53	21.17	222.23
Jacksonville, FL	29.28	35.39	16.85	47.51	21.36	17.65	n/a
Kansas City, MO	29.08	40.62	17.76	57.49	21.49	22.78	n/a
Lafayette, LA	28.33	20.17	14.62	53.76	19.61	15.29	n/a
Las Vegas, NV	28.67	32.12	17.32	51.43	22.21	19.00	n/a
Lexington, KY	28.80	31.80	16.41	45.46	21.53	17.37	n/a
Lincoln, NE	30.57	27.17	16.38	40.00	22.03	20.05	n/a
Little Rock, AR	29.24	n/a	15.97	38.95	19.79	18.85	n/a
Los Angeles, CA	29.11	36.15	20.52	56.19	26.51	21.76	181.61
Louisville, KY	28.87	25.01	16.47	51.44	22.05	18.78	n/a
Madison, WI	29.38	32.13	17.90	43.29	24.50	21.74	n/a
Manchester, NH	29.69	25.56	18.32	57.21	22.59	22.02	n/a
McAllen, TX	30.28	28.28	14.03	39.87	18.47	13.98	n/a

Table continued on following page.

Metro Area	Postal Mail Carriers	R.E. Sales Agents	Retail Salespersons	Sales Reps., Technical/ Scientific	Secretaries, Exc. Leg./ Med./Exec.	Security Guards	Surgeons
Memphis, TN	28.14	27.09	16.86	48.33	21.52	18.00	n/a
Miami, FL	28.58	35.78	17.72	72.39	22.74	19.47	n/a
Midland, TX	27.68	57.72	17.23	n/a	22.14	23.02	n/a
Milwaukee, WI	28.92	36.71	17.62	43.52	23.21	21.24	n/a
Minneapolis, MN	29.62	34.01	18.56	50.40	25.28	24.99	180.26
Nashville, TN	29.67	24.17	17.69	49.18	22.79	20.23	n/a
New Orleans, LA	28.47	24.83	15.83	70.24	20.08	17.58	n/a
New York, NY	28.97	50.92	21.03	71.17	25.44	21.96	153.50
Oklahoma City, OK	28.83	n/a	16.29	44.00	19.75	20.95	n/a
Omaha, NE	29.45	23.46	16.96	41.73	22.46	21.05	165.50
Orlando, FL	28.68	33.44	16.93	50.60	21.59	18.05	n/a
Philadelphia, PA	28.61	31.43	17.58	57.13	23.47	20.88	n/a
Phoenix, AZ	29.45	33.31	18.61	47.67	23.90	20.06	201.58
Pittsburgh, PA	28.52	31.38	16.07	51.43	20.70	18.83	n/a
Portland, OR	28.58	33.65	20.03	60.80	26.92	23.38	n/a
Providence, RI	29.03	31.86	18.21	51.21	24.94	19.43	n/a
Provo, UT	29.07	24.11	17.69	38.31	20.88	20.05	n/a
Raleigh, NC	29.38	33.92	16.98	55.52	22.71	20.01	n/a
Reno, NV	28.83	27.04	18.04	54.60	23.35	20.48	n/a
Richmond, VA	29.19	34.95	17.09	54.94	22.38	21.69	n/a
Rochester, MN	30.26	32.82	18.61	63.87	25.11	23.45	n/a
Sacramento, CA	29.98	35.09	20.50	56.67	26.05	21.11	n/a
Saint Louis, MO	28.63	22.92	17.47	49.86	21.95	21.78	n/a
Saint Paul, MN	29.62	34.01	18.56	50.40	25.28	24.99	180.26
Salem, OR	28.32	31.93	18.59	51.43	25.45	21.67	n/a
Salt Lake City, UT	29.32	31.26	19.37	49.93	22.46	21.09	n/a
San Antonio, TX	28.61	27.84	16.14	48.30	21.21	17.26	n/a
San Diego, CA	28.81	33.54	20.16	56.30	26.29	21.29	215.16
San Francisco, CA	29.93	39.65	22.87	70.21	31.24	24.81	n/a
San Jose, CA	29.61	49.32	23.09	78.15	31.07	24.80	n/a
Santa Rosa, CA	28.63	39.71	21.77	56.13	27.28	22.66	n/a
Savannah, GA	28.40	31.87	15.49	43.92	19.62	17.54	n/a
Seattle, WA	29.52	40.04	21.76	71.82	28.37	25.48	164.19
Sioux Falls, SD	29.60	44.83	20.29	72.14	19.77	19.11	n/a
Tampa, FL	28.84	34.03	16.81	55.31	22.08	18.32	210.11
Tucson, AZ	29.27	30.47	18.32	47.81	21.86	18.88	n/a
Tulsa, OK	29.17	29.25	16.41	43.73	19.75	19.04	n/a
Virginia Beach, VA	28.31	31.93	16.44	52.97	21.87	20.46	n/a
Washington, DC	29.66	34.90	18.96	54.33	26.32	26.46	178.95
Wichita, KS	28.32	n/a	16.72	58.23	19.03	18.73	n/a
Wilmington, NC	29.33	24.73	16.08	51.06	21.11	21.00	n/a
Winston-Salem, NC	28.87	23.59	15.88	51.83	21.50	20.24	n/a

Notes: Figures cover the Metropolitan Statistical Area (MSA); (1) Data is from 2023 due to data quality issues in the state of Colorado and its substate areas in 2024; n/a not available
Source: Bureau of Labor Statistics, Metro Area Occupational Employment and Wage Estimates, May 2024

Appendix A: Comparative Statistics

Average Hourly Wages: Occupations T – W

Metro Area	Teacher Assistants[2]	Teachers, Secondary School[2]	Telemarketers	Truck Drivers, Heavy	Truck Drivers, Light	Waiters/ Waitresses
Albuquerque, NM	15.58	32.70	33.59	25.68	20.59	18.83
Anchorage, AK	16.43	39.21	n/a	31.27	29.20	20.08
Ann Arbor, MI	16.34	35.96	n/a	28.12	23.79	20.05
Athens, GA	12.66	31.86	n/a	26.99	22.11	12.40
Atlanta, GA	14.65	35.49	16.14	28.06	23.97	13.74
Austin, TX	15.99	29.94	16.65	28.00	23.95	17.05
Baltimore, MD	18.88	36.16	16.80	28.16	23.74	19.68
Billings, MT	15.66	31.64	n/a	29.65	24.41	14.05
Boise City, ID	15.78	32.07	18.37	27.48	27.08	16.87
Boston, MA	20.03	42.74	18.61	29.10	25.46	22.07
Boulder, CO[1]	19.34	37.59	n/a	28.09	24.74	22.52
Cape Coral, FL	17.30	27.48	17.59	24.75	21.61	18.95
Cedar Rapids, IA	14.24	28.68	15.78	29.58	24.80	14.45
Charleston, SC	13.41	31.47	n/a	27.48	22.40	12.20
Charlotte, NC	14.49	27.70	19.21	27.14	21.73	16.65
Chicago, IL	18.41	42.55	17.05	31.25	25.40	16.76
Cincinnati, OH	17.09	33.20	16.50	30.56	24.16	18.39
Clarksville, TN	15.35	26.88	n/a	26.20	18.98	13.57
Cleveland, OH	17.13	37.67	15.51	28.14	21.75	18.81
College Station, TX	14.65	28.00	n/a	24.31	25.81	15.16
Colorado Springs, CO[1]	16.56	28.08	25.27	26.24	21.53	21.16
Columbia, MO	15.25	26.79	n/a	26.84	22.33	15.03
Columbia, SC	14.58	28.10	13.70	26.77	22.11	11.85
Columbus, OH	16.73	38.26	15.60	30.84	23.64	19.12
Dallas, TX	14.37	31.75	17.73	28.88	23.68	15.52
Davenport, IA	15.98	32.25	15.38	26.97	22.49	14.76
Denver, CO[1]	18.20	34.07	24.12	29.22	24.04	18.83
Des Moines, IA	15.17	29.25	15.86	29.34	22.55	15.00
Detroit, MI	15.96	34.65	16.11	27.01	21.91	19.88
Durham, NC	14.99	27.78	17.39	26.62	21.88	16.09
El Paso, TX	13.36	29.30	n/a	25.51	19.26	13.84
Eugene, OR	18.52	38.08	n/a	28.02	23.03	18.82
Fargo, ND	18.13	29.54	n/a	27.21	24.35	16.96
Fort Collins, CO[1]	17.53	31.75	n/a	26.38	22.67	21.70
Fort Wayne, IN	15.68	30.99	n/a	28.99	21.73	14.84
Fort Worth, TX	14.37	31.75	17.73	28.88	23.68	15.52
Gainesville, FL	15.81	33.04	n/a	24.90	21.27	18.15
Green Bay, WI	17.43	29.58	n/a	27.16	22.51	14.93
Greensboro, NC	13.56	25.65	16.15	26.84	21.55	15.80
Honolulu, HI	17.06	30.19	n/a	27.42	23.32	25.96
Houston, TX	14.01	31.15	18.64	27.49	23.30	15.23
Huntsville, AL	11.76	30.28	n/a	27.09	22.62	12.42
Indianapolis, IN	16.14	32.97	18.55	30.71	24.66	15.51
Jacksonville, FL	16.11	33.35	17.68	27.47	22.53	18.38
Kansas City, MO	15.24	29.47	18.48	28.62	23.71	17.04
Lafayette, LA	12.65	24.74	n/a	26.47	19.63	11.17
Las Vegas, NV	15.55	31.27	16.68	28.15	22.31	15.55
Lexington, KY	17.74	30.50	n/a	29.78	22.45	14.52
Lincoln, NE	13.52	29.94	14.12	38.54	22.72	19.50
Little Rock, AR	15.65	27.84	n/a	28.31	21.58	14.13
Los Angeles, CA	21.70	49.74	19.37	28.59	24.21	20.65
Louisville, KY	16.51	31.82	n/a	30.63	24.78	14.86
Madison, WI	18.13	30.40	17.61	27.62	23.52	17.52
Manchester, NH	18.04	34.04	15.89	27.49	22.94	21.07
McAllen, TX	13.28	30.53	n/a	24.00	19.17	13.40

Table continued on following page.

Metro Area	Teacher Assistants[2]	Teachers, Secondary School[2]	Telemarketers	Truck Drivers, Heavy	Truck Drivers, Light	Waiters/ Waitresses
Memphis, TN	14.32	28.90	13.76	29.58	29.29	13.80
Miami, FL	15.86	28.86	18.31	26.65	23.18	18.71
Midland, TX	15.30	31.99	n/a	28.32	23.98	15.93
Milwaukee, WI	17.98	34.09	17.30	28.14	22.92	16.18
Minneapolis, MN	20.05	35.70	22.16	31.39	25.01	13.95
Nashville, TN	14.83	29.56	15.16	28.95	23.69	15.99
New Orleans, LA	14.58	28.89	n/a	25.97	22.33	12.40
New York, NY	19.26	48.38	19.76	33.26	25.01	25.65
Oklahoma City, OK	14.11	27.06	16.04	27.43	20.70	14.43
Omaha, NE	14.60	29.23	14.96	27.64	23.61	19.47
Orlando, FL	15.02	27.08	17.71	26.28	22.34	18.62
Philadelphia, PA	16.42	37.57	18.66	29.70	23.32	19.57
Phoenix, AZ	17.41	33.10	25.15	27.04	25.25	23.73
Pittsburgh, PA	15.48	37.69	18.78	27.85	20.24	16.99
Portland, OR	19.63	42.02	19.64	31.98	24.55	22.74
Providence, RI	17.96	39.10	18.03	28.07	23.04	20.77
Provo, UT	15.72	32.55	19.36	27.39	21.30	16.73
Raleigh, NC	15.69	26.95	n/a	26.45	20.95	16.07
Reno, NV	17.00	36.97	16.27	31.35	24.02	13.93
Richmond, VA	16.87	30.92	n/a	29.88	21.77	19.74
Rochester, MN	18.97	34.45	n/a	30.88	23.86	12.89
Sacramento, CA	21.20	45.34	19.22	29.27	24.31	21.77
Saint Louis, MO	16.42	31.39	15.91	27.24	23.38	15.95
Saint Paul, MN	20.05	35.70	22.16	31.39	25.01	13.95
Salem, OR	18.55	36.88	n/a	29.67	22.75	20.45
Salt Lake City, UT	15.41	35.90	17.54	29.38	23.05	16.60
San Antonio, TX	12.78	29.49	16.58	25.47	21.43	15.16
San Diego, CA	20.95	54.30	19.47	28.38	23.68	22.56
San Francisco, CA	24.02	55.15	23.72	32.89	27.39	22.18
San Jose, CA	24.13	52.38	23.11	33.44	26.28	24.41
Santa Rosa, CA	22.92	47.05	n/a	29.46	25.70	21.12
Savannah, GA	13.88	32.08	13.85	27.26	24.37	13.65
Seattle, WA	24.88	47.37	21.66	33.99	26.42	27.97
Sioux Falls, SD	13.44	24.78	n/a	28.36	21.88	15.30
Tampa, FL	14.20	30.50	17.64	25.87	21.83	19.64
Tucson, AZ	16.88	25.54	n/a	25.42	23.43	20.95
Tulsa, OK	13.50	28.84	16.76	27.89	20.63	14.21
Virginia Beach, VA	18.39	34.95	20.17	24.69	20.85	19.88
Washington, DC	20.42	38.87	19.03	29.14	24.85	22.84
Wichita, KS	14.38	28.72	n/a	26.88	19.57	17.67
Wilmington, NC	14.70	25.61	16.58	24.77	19.92	14.23
Winston-Salem, NC	13.12	26.41	n/a	25.99	20.43	14.25

Notes: Figures cover the Metropolitan Statistical Area (MSA); (1) Data is from 2023 due to data quality issues in the state of Colorado and its substate areas in 2024; (2) Hourly wages were calculated from annual wage data based on a 40 hour work week; n/a not available
Source: Bureau of Labor Statistics, Metro Area Occupational Employment and Wage Estimates, May 2024

Means of Transportation to Work: City

City	Car/Truck/Van		Public Transportation			Bicycle	Walked	Other Means	Worked at Home
	Drove Alone	Car-pooled	Bus	Subway	Railroad				
Albuquerque, NM	73.2	8.8	1.2	0.0	0.1	0.9	1.9	1.2	12.8
Anchorage, AK	71.0	12.4	1.3	0.0	0.0	0.6	2.6	2.5	9.6
Ann Arbor, MI	45.6	5.0	7.3	0.1	0.0	2.4	13.1	0.5	26.2
Athens, GA	72.0	7.8	2.1	0.0	0.0	0.9	4.5	0.8	11.9
Atlanta, GA	55.2	4.6	3.6	2.5	0.1	0.7	4.2	2.4	26.6
Austin, TX	58.8	6.9	1.9	0.0	0.0	0.8	2.4	1.6	27.5
Baltimore, MD	56.8	6.9	9.3	1.0	0.8	0.6	5.6	3.1	15.9
Billings, MT	78.5	9.1	1.0	0.0	0.0	0.7	2.0	1.0	7.6
Boise City, ID	68.6	7.6	0.5	0.0	0.0	2.3	3.4	1.6	15.8
Boston, MA	34.1	5.4	8.6	13.6	1.2	2.1	13.8	2.4	18.8
Boulder, CO	41.9	3.6	5.8	0.0	0.0	7.6	8.6	0.9	31.6
Cape Coral, FL	76.0	8.1	0.2	0.0	0.0	0.1	1.0	1.4	13.1
Cedar Rapids, IA	77.0	6.5	0.6	0.0	0.0	0.3	2.2	0.8	12.6
Charleston, SC	68.1	6.5	0.9	0.0	0.0	1.5	4.1	1.2	17.6
Charlotte, NC	61.0	8.1	1.4	0.1	0.0	0.2	1.7	2.0	25.5
Chicago, IL	46.0	7.4	9.5	8.5	1.2	1.4	5.7	2.1	18.3
Cincinnati, OH	66.2	7.5	5.7	0.0	0.0	0.3	5.3	1.8	13.2
Clarksville, TN	81.0	8.7	0.5	0.0	0.0	0.0	1.2	1.5	7.1
Cleveland, OH	65.4	10.0	6.3	0.4	0.0	0.5	5.3	1.9	10.1
College Station, TX	70.8	8.0	2.3	0.0	0.0	1.9	3.9	1.1	12.1
Colorado Springs, CO	71.1	9.0	0.4	0.0	0.0	0.5	1.8	1.1	16.1
Columbia, MO	74.1	7.6	1.1	0.0	0.0	1.0	5.6	0.9	9.6
Columbia, SC	62.9	6.9	1.4	0.0	0.0	0.3	16.4	2.2	9.8
Columbus, OH	70.1	7.5	2.1	0.0	0.0	0.4	2.6	1.2	16.1
Dallas, TX	68.5	11.4	1.7	0.2	0.1	0.2	2.2	1.7	14.0
Davenport, IA	78.8	7.3	0.8	0.0	0.1	0.2	2.7	1.1	8.9
Denver, CO	57.7	6.5	2.8	0.3	0.1	1.6	3.9	2.7	24.4
Des Moines, IA	72.3	11.2	1.1	0.0	0.0	0.4	2.2	1.3	11.4
Detroit, MI	66.3	11.0	5.9	0.0	0.0	0.5	3.1	3.1	10.1
Durham, NC	65.2	8.0	2.2	0.0	0.0	0.5	2.3	1.4	20.6
El Paso, TX	76.5	11.1	1.0	0.0	0.0	0.1	1.1	2.3	7.8
Eugene, OR	63.0	7.9	2.6	0.0	0.0	4.7	5.3	1.1	15.3
Fargo, ND	78.7	6.6	0.7	0.0	0.1	0.3	3.5	2.0	8.1
Fort Collins, CO	63.3	5.6	1.4	0.0	0.0	4.2	4.2	1.0	20.2
Fort Wayne, IN	78.1	9.9	1.1	0.0	0.0	0.3	1.5	0.8	8.2
Fort Worth, TX	72.9	10.9	0.4	0.0	0.1	0.2	1.2	1.5	12.9
Gainesville, FL	62.9	9.0	4.9	0.0	0.0	3.5	5.0	2.3	12.4
Green Bay, WI	75.9	10.7	1.0	0.0	0.0	0.4	2.3	1.1	8.5
Greensboro, NC	73.7	8.2	2.4	0.0	0.0	0.2	2.3	1.4	11.8
Honolulu, HI	55.7	14.2	7.9	0.0	0.0	1.8	7.7	3.7	8.9
Houston, TX	69.7	10.1	2.9	0.1	0.0	0.4	1.9	3.1	11.7
Huntsville, AL	77.5	6.8	0.3	0.0	0.0	0.0	1.3	1.0	13.1
Indianapolis, IN	73.7	9.6	1.4	0.0	0.0	0.4	1.8	0.9	12.3
Jacksonville, FL	72.8	9.0	1.2	0.0	0.0	0.4	1.2	2.0	13.5
Kansas City, MO	72.7	7.4	1.9	0.0	0.0	0.2	1.5	1.5	14.8
Lafayette, LA	80.4	5.6	0.6	0.0	0.0	0.5	2.2	1.2	9.5
Las Vegas, NV	72.6	10.0	2.4	0.0	0.0	0.3	1.3	2.9	10.5
Lexington, KY	74.8	8.4	1.3	0.0	0.0	0.5	3.0	1.0	10.9
Lincoln, NE	75.7	8.6	0.9	0.0	0.0	0.9	3.2	0.8	10.0
Little Rock, AR	76.5	8.9	1.0	0.0	0.0	0.2	1.8	0.9	10.8
Los Angeles, CA	61.4	8.8	5.7	0.6	0.1	0.7	3.1	2.3	17.3
Louisville, KY	73.5	8.7	2.2	0.0	0.0	0.3	2.0	1.7	11.6
Madison, WI	57.6	5.9	5.6	0.0	0.1	3.1	8.2	1.3	18.2
Manchester, NH	74.2	9.1	0.4	0.1	0.0	0.3	2.4	1.5	12.1

Table continued on following page.

City	Car/Truck/Van		Public Transportation			Bicycle	Walked	Other Means	Worked at Home
	Drove Alone	Car-pooled	Bus	Subway	Railroad				
McAllen, TX	72.2	10.4	0.4	0.0	0.0	0.3	0.9	4.3	11.5
Memphis, TN	77.8	10.0	0.8	0.0	0.0	0.2	1.7	1.5	8.0
Miami, FL	61.7	7.9	5.4	1.1	0.1	0.8	5.4	3.5	14.2
Midland, TX	79.9	12.2	0.4	0.0	0.0	0.2	0.7	1.0	5.6
Milwaukee, WI	67.8	10.0	5.3	0.0	0.0	0.5	4.0	1.2	11.2
Minneapolis, MN	53.4	5.9	6.3	0.2	0.0	2.3	6.0	2.5	23.3
Nashville, TN	68.1	8.3	1.6	0.0	0.0	0.3	1.9	1.5	18.3
New Orleans, LA	63.2	8.7	3.8	0.1	0.0	1.9	5.6	3.0	13.7
New York, NY	21.9	4.3	9.8	34.4	1.0	1.5	9.4	2.7	15.0
Oklahoma City, OK	77.0	9.6	0.4	0.0	0.0	0.2	1.4	1.6	9.8
Omaha, NE	73.3	8.7	1.1	0.0	0.0	0.2	1.8	1.3	13.6
Orlando, FL	69.5	8.9	1.8	0.0	0.0	0.5	1.6	2.5	15.1
Philadelphia, PA	46.7	7.6	10.9	4.7	1.6	1.9	7.5	2.8	16.4
Phoenix, AZ	66.1	10.9	1.8	0.0	0.0	0.4	1.6	2.2	16.9
Pittsburgh, PA	48.2	6.2	11.6	0.3	0.0	1.1	9.8	2.3	20.4
Portland, OR	50.5	7.0	5.4	0.2	0.1	3.7	4.8	3.0	25.3
Providence, RI	62.6	9.8	3.1	0.0	1.1	0.8	7.3	2.6	12.7
Provo, UT	57.4	10.4	4.3	0.1	0.9	1.4	10.3	1.1	14.2
Raleigh, NC	65.1	6.6	1.3	0.0	0.0	0.4	1.6	1.6	23.4
Reno, NV	67.6	12.6	2.4	0.0	0.0	0.6	3.2	2.8	10.8
Richmond, VA	64.9	7.8	3.6	0.0	0.0	1.1	4.2	1.5	16.9
Rochester, MN	65.5	11.1	4.1	0.0	0.0	0.8	4.3	1.3	12.9
Sacramento, CA	65.5	9.0	1.0	0.2	0.1	1.4	2.7	2.4	17.7
Saint Louis, MO	66.6	6.7	4.4	0.4	0.1	0.9	4.0	1.9	15.0
Saint Paul, MN	59.3	10.0	5.0	0.1	0.0	0.8	3.7	2.7	18.3
Salem, OR	68.4	10.4	1.8	0.0	0.0	1.1	3.0	1.4	14.0
Salt Lake City, UT	60.2	8.1	3.1	0.3	0.3	1.6	4.8	2.9	18.5
San Antonio, TX	70.5	12.1	2.1	0.0	0.0	0.2	1.7	1.6	11.8
San Diego, CA	64.2	7.8	2.3	0.1	0.1	0.7	3.4	2.2	19.2
San Francisco, CA	28.6	6.0	14.1	4.8	1.1	3.3	10.0	4.5	27.5
San Jose, CA	64.6	10.5	1.6	0.2	0.5	0.5	1.8	1.7	18.5
Santa Rosa, CA	73.1	11.1	0.9	0.0	0.2	0.6	2.3	1.3	10.5
Savannah, GA	70.4	10.3	2.5	0.1	0.0	1.5	3.8	1.4	10.1
Seattle, WA	37.6	5.1	11.2	0.5	0.0	2.5	8.3	3.5	31.3
Sioux Falls, SD	79.4	7.7	0.7	0.0	0.0	0.2	1.9	0.9	9.4
Tampa, FL	66.1	8.2	1.3	0.0	0.0	0.8	2.3	2.1	19.3
Tucson, AZ	69.5	9.9	2.3	0.0	0.0	1.6	2.7	1.6	12.4
Tulsa, OK	75.4	10.2	0.5	0.0	0.0	0.3	1.7	1.8	10.1
Virginia Beach, VA	75.3	7.5	0.8	0.0	0.0	0.4	1.8	1.6	12.7
Washington, DC	28.2	4.3	8.1	13.8	0.3	3.3	10.0	2.7	29.4
Wichita, KS	80.0	9.6	0.6	0.0	0.0	0.4	0.9	1.5	6.9
Wilmington, NC	70.9	7.0	0.4	0.0	0.0	0.8	2.2	1.0	17.7
Winston-Salem, NC	73.2	9.5	1.1	0.0	0.0	0.3	2.0	1.6	12.3
U.S.	70.2	8.5	1.7	1.3	0.4	0.4	2.4	1.6	13.5

Note: Figures are percentages and cover workers 16 years of age and older
Source: U.S. Census Bureau, 2019-2023 American Community Survey 5-Year Estimates

Means of Transportation to Work: Metro Area

Metro Area	Car/Truck/Van		Public Transportation			Bicycle	Walked	Other Means	Worked at Home
	Drove Alone	Car-pooled	Bus	Subway	Railroad				
Albuquerque, NM	73.5	9.1	0.8	0.0	0.1	0.6	1.6	1.3	12.9
Anchorage, AK	71.3	11.7	1.1	0.0	0.0	0.5	2.4	3.1	9.8
Ann Arbor, MI	61.9	6.3	3.7	0.0	0.0	1.0	5.8	0.8	20.3
Athens, GA	74.7	7.3	1.3	0.0	0.0	0.6	3.3	0.9	12.1
Atlanta, GA	68.0	8.7	1.2	0.5	0.1	0.1	1.2	1.8	18.5
Austin, TX	63.4	7.7	1.0	0.0	0.0	0.4	1.8	1.4	24.2
Baltimore, MD	69.2	6.9	2.7	0.5	0.5	0.2	2.2	1.6	16.1
Billings, MT	76.5	10.5	1.0	0.0	0.0	0.5	2.3	1.0	8.2
Boise City, ID	71.7	8.3	0.3	0.0	0.0	1.1	2.2	1.4	15.1
Boston, MA	58.6	6.3	2.6	4.6	1.4	1.0	4.7	2.0	18.7
Boulder, CO	55.6	5.7	3.1	0.0	0.0	3.0	3.8	0.9	27.9
Cape Coral, FL	72.7	9.4	0.4	0.0	0.0	0.6	1.1	1.8	13.8
Cedar Rapids, IA	76.8	6.5	0.5	0.0	0.0	0.2	1.9	0.8	13.3
Charleston, SC	75.3	7.8	0.6	0.0	0.0	0.5	1.7	1.2	12.9
Charlotte, NC	69.3	8.1	0.7	0.1	0.0	0.1	1.2	1.5	19.0
Chicago, IL	63.6	7.8	3.3	2.9	2.0	0.6	2.8	1.6	15.6
Cincinnati, OH	75.0	7.7	1.3	0.0	0.0	0.2	1.8	1.1	12.9
Clarksville, TN	79.6	9.5	0.4	0.0	0.0	0.2	2.4	1.5	6.5
Cleveland, OH	74.3	7.4	1.9	0.1	0.0	0.2	2.1	1.3	12.6
College Station, TX	75.1	9.5	1.3	0.0	0.0	1.0	2.1	1.3	9.7
Colorado Springs, CO	70.5	9.0	0.3	0.0	0.0	0.4	3.3	1.1	15.4
Columbia, MO	76.0	8.8	0.7	0.0	0.0	0.7	3.8	1.0	8.9
Columbia, SC	76.2	8.1	0.5	0.0	0.0	0.1	3.5	1.7	9.9
Columbus, OH	72.2	6.8	1.1	0.0	0.0	0.2	1.9	1.1	16.6
Dallas, TX	71.2	9.4	0.5	0.1	0.1	0.1	1.2	1.5	15.9
Davenport, IA	80.1	7.2	0.8	0.0	0.0	0.1	2.4	0.9	8.4
Denver, CO	65.0	7.3	1.6	0.1	0.1	0.7	2.0	2.0	21.2
Des Moines, IA	74.3	7.9	0.4	0.0	0.0	0.2	1.6	1.2	14.3
Detroit, MI	74.8	7.6	1.0	0.0	0.0	0.2	1.3	1.2	13.8
Durham, NC	65.1	7.4	2.2	0.0	0.0	0.7	2.5	1.5	20.6
El Paso, TX	76.3	11.4	0.9	0.0	0.0	0.1	1.5	2.0	7.8
Eugene, OR	67.4	8.9	1.9	0.0	0.0	2.8	4.1	1.1	13.9
Fargo, ND	78.5	6.8	0.7	0.0	0.0	0.3	2.8	1.6	9.3
Fort Collins, CO	68.4	5.6	0.9	0.0	0.0	2.4	2.8	1.1	18.9
Fort Wayne, IN	79.9	9.1	0.7	0.0	0.0	0.3	1.2	0.7	8.1
Fort Worth, TX	71.2	9.4	0.5	0.1	0.1	0.1	1.2	1.5	15.9
Gainesville, FL	71.5	8.8	2.4	0.0	0.0	1.6	2.9	1.5	11.2
Green Bay, WI	78.7	7.8	0.4	0.0	0.0	0.2	1.7	0.9	10.4
Greensboro, NC	76.6	8.9	1.0	0.0	0.0	0.1	1.6	1.6	10.3
Honolulu, HI	64.0	13.7	5.2	0.0	0.0	1.0	5.0	2.6	8.4
Houston, TX	73.5	9.7	1.4	0.0	0.0	0.2	1.2	2.0	11.9
Huntsville, AL	78.3	6.8	0.2	0.0	0.0	0.0	0.8	1.1	12.7
Indianapolis, IN	74.5	8.4	0.6	0.0	0.0	0.3	1.3	0.9	14.0
Jacksonville, FL	72.1	8.2	0.7	0.0	0.0	0.4	1.1	1.8	15.6
Kansas City, MO	75.0	6.9	0.6	0.0	0.0	0.1	1.1	1.1	15.2
Lafayette, LA	82.4	6.3	0.3	0.0	0.0	0.3	1.8	1.3	7.7
Las Vegas, NV	72.6	10.3	2.3	0.0	0.0	0.2	1.2	2.6	10.7
Lexington, KY	76.1	8.6	0.9	0.0	0.0	0.4	2.5	0.8	10.7
Lincoln, NE	76.3	8.5	0.8	0.0	0.0	0.8	3.0	0.7	9.9
Little Rock, AR	79.2	8.8	0.5	0.0	0.0	0.1	1.2	1.0	9.1
Los Angeles, CA	67.1	9.2	2.9	0.3	0.1	0.6	2.3	1.9	15.5
Louisville, KY	76.0	8.4	1.1	0.0	0.0	0.2	1.5	1.2	11.6
Madison, WI	67.3	5.9	2.6	0.0	0.0	1.6	4.8	1.1	16.7
Manchester, NH	72.9	7.4	0.4	0.1	0.1	0.2	1.7	1.1	16.1

Table continued on following page.

Metro Area	Car/Truck/Van		Public Transportation			Bicycle	Walked	Other Means	Worked at Home
	Drove Alone	Car-pooled	Bus	Subway	Railroad				
McAllen, TX	75.8	10.3	0.2	0.0	0.0	0.1	1.2	3.7	8.6
Memphis, TN	79.5	9.2	0.4	0.0	0.0	0.1	1.0	1.1	8.6
Miami, FL	71.3	9.2	2.0	0.2	0.1	0.4	1.6	2.3	12.9
Midland, TX	79.8	12.0	0.3	0.0	0.0	0.2	1.1	1.3	5.2
Milwaukee, WI	73.8	7.1	2.1	0.0	0.0	0.3	2.2	0.9	13.5
Minneapolis, MN	67.7	7.1	2.2	0.0	0.0	0.5	2.0	1.4	19.0
Nashville, TN	72.4	8.2	0.7	0.0	0.0	0.1	1.1	1.2	16.3
New Orleans, LA	73.0	9.7	1.8	0.0	0.0	0.9	3.1	1.9	9.6
New York, NY	45.5	6.1	6.4	15.6	2.6	0.8	5.4	2.7	14.9
Oklahoma City, OK	78.1	9.0	0.3	0.0	0.0	0.2	1.6	1.3	9.5
Omaha, NE	75.8	7.8	0.6	0.0	0.0	0.1	1.5	1.1	13.0
Orlando, FL	70.8	9.2	1.0	0.0	0.1	0.3	1.2	1.8	15.6
Philadelphia, PA	64.4	7.0	3.4	1.5	1.3	0.6	3.2	1.7	16.8
Phoenix, AZ	66.9	9.7	1.0	0.0	0.0	0.5	1.4	2.0	18.5
Pittsburgh, PA	69.9	6.9	3.2	0.2	0.0	0.2	2.9	1.4	15.4
Portland, OR	62.7	7.7	2.6	0.2	0.1	1.4	3.1	2.0	20.4
Providence, RI	74.9	8.1	1.1	0.1	0.7	0.3	2.6	1.5	10.9
Provo, UT	66.7	10.1	1.2	0.0	0.6	0.5	2.9	1.0	17.1
Raleigh, NC	67.0	6.5	0.5	0.0	0.0	0.2	1.1	1.3	23.4
Reno, NV	70.2	12.5	1.8	0.0	0.0	0.4	2.2	2.1	10.8
Richmond, VA	71.6	7.3	1.0	0.0	0.1	0.3	1.7	1.2	16.7
Rochester, MN	69.6	9.9	2.4	0.0	0.0	0.6	3.5	1.1	12.8
Sacramento, CA	67.7	8.6	0.8	0.1	0.1	1.1	1.8	1.9	17.9
Saint Louis, MO	75.6	6.6	1.1	0.1	0.0	0.2	1.5	1.1	13.8
Saint Paul, MN	67.7	7.1	2.2	0.0	0.0	0.5	2.0	1.4	19.0
Salem, OR	70.9	11.0	1.1	0.0	0.0	0.7	2.4	1.3	12.6
Salt Lake City, UT	67.0	10.0	1.2	0.2	0.2	0.5	1.7	1.7	17.5
San Antonio, TX	71.5	10.9	1.3	0.0	0.0	0.2	1.5	1.5	13.0
San Diego, CA	67.6	8.2	1.6	0.1	0.1	0.5	3.1	2.0	16.9
San Francisco, CA	50.9	8.2	4.7	3.9	1.1	1.5	3.9	2.6	23.2
San Jose, CA	62.1	9.0	1.5	0.2	0.6	1.3	2.0	1.7	21.5
Santa Rosa, CA	71.0	9.2	0.7	0.1	0.2	0.7	2.4	1.4	14.4
Savannah, GA	76.6	9.4	1.0	0.0	0.0	0.7	1.7	1.5	9.0
Seattle, WA	59.1	8.2	4.7	0.1	0.3	0.8	3.3	1.8	21.6
Sioux Falls, SD	79.3	7.2	0.5	0.0	0.0	0.1	2.0	0.8	10.1
Tampa, FL	69.7	8.1	0.8	0.0	0.0	0.5	1.2	1.8	17.8
Tucson, AZ	70.7	9.6	1.5	0.0	0.0	1.0	1.9	1.5	13.8
Tulsa, OK	78.2	9.0	0.3	0.0	0.0	0.2	1.2	1.2	9.8
Virginia Beach, VA	75.8	8.2	1.0	0.0	0.0	0.3	2.4	1.6	10.7
Washington, DC	56.4	8.0	2.9	4.4	0.4	0.7	2.7	1.9	22.6
Wichita, KS	80.6	8.6	0.4	0.0	0.0	0.3	1.4	1.3	7.3
Wilmington, NC	73.9	7.8	0.2	0.0	0.0	0.3	1.2	1.1	15.5
Winston-Salem, NC	77.9	8.7	0.5	0.0	0.0	0.1	1.2	1.1	10.6
U.S.	70.2	8.5	1.7	1.3	0.4	0.4	2.4	1.6	13.5

Note: Figures are percentages and cover workers 16 years of age and older; Figures cover the Metropolitan Statistical Area (MSA)
Source: U.S. Census Bureau, 2019-2023 American Community Survey 5-Year Estimates

Travel Time to Work: City

City	Less Than 10 Minutes	10 to 19 Minutes	20 to 29 Minutes	30 to 44 Minutes	45 to 59 Minutes	60 to 89 Minutes	90 Minutes or More
Albuquerque, NM	11.7	36.0	27.6	17.3	3.0	2.5	1.9
Anchorage, AK	15.6	44.8	23.3	11.1	2.3	1.4	1.5
Ann Arbor, MI	12.9	45.8	18.9	13.6	5.8	2.3	0.7
Athens, GA	17.2	45.0	17.6	10.5	3.8	3.6	2.3
Atlanta, GA	7.8	29.8	25.5	22.5	6.3	5.1	3.0
Austin, TX	9.6	33.4	24.5	21.5	6.1	3.5	1.4
Baltimore, MD	7.2	24.8	24.3	24.3	8.5	6.9	4.0
Billings, MT	19.3	51.9	18.3	6.8	1.2	1.2	1.2
Boise City, ID	14.3	44.2	25.5	11.5	1.7	1.6	1.2
Boston, MA	6.9	21.3	20.7	28.8	11.4	8.6	2.3
Boulder, CO	20.2	44.2	16.9	9.4	5.0	2.9	1.3
Cape Coral, FL	7.8	24.9	22.7	24.9	10.5	6.5	2.7
Cedar Rapids, IA	19.8	47.9	17.9	8.7	1.8	2.5	1.4
Charleston, SC	11.8	32.8	24.8	19.0	7.2	2.5	1.8
Charlotte, NC	9.1	29.7	27.1	23.2	6.1	3.0	1.9
Chicago, IL	5.2	17.2	19.2	29.8	14.6	10.9	3.0
Cincinnati, OH	11.2	34.5	26.3	19.1	3.8	2.8	2.2
Clarksville, TN	10.5	32.6	25.9	13.1	7.3	8.3	2.3
Cleveland, OH	10.5	35.0	27.3	19.4	3.3	2.6	1.9
College Station, TX	17.5	54.7	15.3	7.9	1.4	1.8	1.5
Colorado Springs, CO	11.6	35.7	27.6	16.9	3.0	3.0	2.1
Columbia, MO	19.5	54.4	14.3	7.2	2.1	1.2	1.3
Columbia, SC	27.7	37.4	19.1	10.0	2.7	1.2	1.8
Columbus, OH	10.3	35.1	31.0	17.2	3.1	2.1	1.3
Dallas, TX	8.8	28.5	23.6	24.7	7.4	5.6	1.5
Davenport, IA	15.3	45.9	24.3	8.4	2.9	2.0	1.1
Denver, CO	8.6	28.3	25.3	25.9	6.5	3.9	1.5
Des Moines, IA	14.1	43.0	25.7	11.9	2.0	1.9	1.5
Detroit, MI	8.1	30.2	27.0	22.3	6.0	4.0	2.3
Durham, NC	10.2	37.8	25.1	17.8	4.8	2.6	1.6
El Paso, TX	9.3	33.5	28.5	20.1	4.3	2.4	1.9
Eugene, OR	16.3	50.9	19.5	7.2	2.2	2.1	1.9
Fargo, ND	20.1	56.1	15.1	4.6	1.5	1.7	0.9
Fort Collins, CO	15.6	45.7	19.3	10.1	4.6	3.3	1.4
Fort Wayne, IN	13.1	38.1	27.8	13.7	2.9	2.2	2.2
Fort Worth, TX	7.4	29.2	23.5	23.5	8.9	5.7	1.8
Gainesville, FL	16.1	43.8	23.4	11.6	2.6	1.6	0.9
Green Bay, WI	18.1	47.5	18.0	9.1	3.9	1.9	1.5
Greensboro, NC	13.4	40.9	22.3	14.6	3.5	3.0	2.4
Honolulu, HI	9.0	39.2	22.3	20.5	4.5	3.4	1.2
Houston, TX	7.5	25.3	23.6	27.7	8.6	5.5	1.8
Huntsville, AL	13.9	39.8	27.2	14.9	2.2	1.2	0.7
Indianapolis, IN	9.8	29.6	28.6	23.1	4.5	2.5	2.0
Jacksonville, FL	8.7	29.0	28.0	24.9	5.6	2.5	1.3
Kansas City, MO	11.7	35.0	28.3	18.3	3.5	1.8	1.4
Lafayette, LA	16.4	44.8	19.9	11.5	2.3	3.6	1.6
Las Vegas, NV	7.3	24.0	30.9	27.3	6.0	2.6	1.9
Lexington, KY	13.0	40.1	26.4	13.7	2.7	2.3	1.9
Lincoln, NE	16.8	46.0	22.5	8.9	2.9	2.1	1.0
Little Rock, AR	15.3	46.6	22.6	10.7	2.2	1.7	0.9
Los Angeles, CA	6.3	22.2	19.9	28.5	10.4	9.4	3.3
Louisville, KY	10.1	31.8	31.9	19.1	3.6	2.0	1.4
Madison, WI	14.4	40.3	25.5	14.3	3.2	1.7	0.6
Manchester, NH	12.9	35.1	23.0	16.0	6.2	5.1	1.9
McAllen, TX	14.6	39.5	23.9	15.2	2.9	2.1	1.7

Table continued on following page.

City	Less Than 10 Minutes	10 to 19 Minutes	20 to 29 Minutes	30 to 44 Minutes	45 to 59 Minutes	60 to 89 Minutes	90 Minutes or More
Memphis, TN	11.2	31.8	33.7	18.2	2.7	1.5	1.0
Miami, FL	6.4	24.1	25.7	27.6	8.7	6.0	1.5
Midland, TX	16.2	45.2	18.6	11.9	4.0	2.3	1.9
Milwaukee, WI	10.6	36.2	26.5	18.9	3.4	2.9	1.6
Minneapolis, MN	8.3	36.1	28.8	19.2	4.2	2.4	1.0
Nashville, TN	9.2	28.7	26.8	23.2	7.0	3.8	1.3
New Orleans, LA	11.9	35.1	24.3	18.7	5.2	3.1	1.7
New York, NY	4.4	12.7	14.0	27.0	16.1	18.7	7.1
Oklahoma City, OK	10.4	35.0	28.8	19.2	3.6	1.5	1.6
Omaha, NE	14.6	41.3	26.4	12.4	2.3	1.8	1.2
Orlando, FL	7.5	26.1	27.4	26.5	6.4	3.9	2.2
Philadelphia, PA	6.7	19.7	20.8	28.1	12.0	9.2	3.5
Phoenix, AZ	9.0	26.7	26.8	24.6	7.1	4.2	1.6
Pittsburgh, PA	10.3	34.0	26.0	20.5	4.6	3.2	1.5
Portland, OR	9.3	29.9	27.1	22.5	6.1	3.7	1.5
Providence, RI	11.0	36.1	20.6	16.8	6.7	6.1	2.7
Provo, UT	20.5	44.9	16.6	10.2	4.4	2.3	1.1
Raleigh, NC	10.3	33.4	26.8	19.9	5.4	2.5	1.7
Reno, NV	15.1	39.7	23.5	13.2	4.9	2.4	1.2
Richmond, VA	11.4	37.4	27.0	16.8	2.9	2.8	1.7
Rochester, MN	18.3	54.5	14.7	6.1	2.8	2.7	0.9
Sacramento, CA	8.9	32.2	25.8	21.3	5.1	3.5	3.2
Saint Louis, MO	9.9	36.2	27.2	19.5	3.2	2.5	1.6
Saint Paul, MN	10.5	35.0	27.6	19.0	4.4	2.1	1.4
Salem, OR	14.6	41.5	18.2	12.3	5.5	6.3	1.6
Salt Lake City, UT	14.6	45.2	20.6	12.7	3.5	2.1	1.3
San Antonio, TX	9.5	30.7	26.1	22.2	5.9	3.7	1.8
San Diego, CA	8.2	33.2	27.9	20.4	5.4	3.3	1.7
San Francisco, CA	5.3	21.2	22.1	28.8	10.6	8.9	3.1
San Jose, CA	5.9	26.5	25.5	25.0	8.6	5.7	2.7
Santa Rosa, CA	13.1	42.1	19.4	14.4	4.5	3.6	2.9
Savannah, GA	14.0	40.1	23.5	14.7	4.4	2.3	1.0
Seattle, WA	8.0	26.0	24.5	26.4	9.2	4.4	1.4
Sioux Falls, SD	15.9	52.2	22.0	6.2	1.5	1.0	1.2
Tampa, FL	10.8	31.4	22.8	22.5	6.5	4.2	1.8
Tucson, AZ	12.3	34.4	25.8	19.3	4.6	2.1	1.4
Tulsa, OK	14.0	46.0	25.7	9.8	1.8	1.4	1.3
Virginia Beach, VA	10.2	31.3	27.8	21.8	5.4	2.1	1.4
Washington, DC	5.2	19.2	22.5	33.1	11.8	6.3	1.9
Wichita, KS	14.0	46.0	25.9	9.5	1.8	1.4	1.4
Wilmington, NC	16.7	46.7	20.7	10.2	2.9	1.2	1.6
Winston-Salem, NC	14.4	39.6	23.0	14.0	4.1	2.9	2.0
U.S.	12.6	28.6	21.2	20.8	8.1	6.0	2.8

Note: Figures are percentages and include workers 16 years old and over
Source: U.S. Census Bureau, 2019-2023 American Community Survey 5-Year Estimates

Travel Time to Work: Metro Area

Metro Area	Less Than 10 Minutes	10 to 19 Minutes	20 to 29 Minutes	30 to 44 Minutes	45 to 59 Minutes	60 to 89 Minutes	90 Minutes or More
Albuquerque, NM	11.5	31.1	25.0	20.6	5.8	3.8	2.3
Anchorage, AK	14.7	40.5	21.8	11.4	5.1	4.0	2.6
Ann Arbor, MI	11.2	33.3	25.2	18.5	7.2	3.5	1.2
Athens, GA	13.4	38.2	22.3	13.7	5.2	4.1	3.0
Atlanta, GA	7.3	22.7	20.1	25.5	12.0	9.0	3.3
Austin, TX	9.5	27.1	21.8	24.0	9.7	6.0	1.9
Baltimore, MD	8.2	24.1	21.7	24.6	10.7	7.5	3.1
Billings, MT	18.7	42.7	20.8	11.0	2.7	2.1	2.0
Boise City, ID	13.4	31.8	25.2	19.9	5.8	2.3	1.5
Boston, MA	9.4	22.9	19.3	24.4	11.2	9.6	3.1
Boulder, CO	15.0	34.3	20.7	17.0	6.9	4.4	1.6
Cape Coral, FL	8.8	24.5	22.6	25.2	10.2	6.3	2.4
Cedar Rapids, IA	19.1	39.1	20.6	13.0	4.3	2.6	1.3
Charleston, SC	9.1	26.3	23.3	24.0	9.9	5.4	2.1
Charlotte, NC	9.8	27.9	22.9	23.4	9.2	4.9	2.0
Chicago, IL	8.9	22.3	19.5	25.3	11.9	9.3	2.9
Cincinnati, OH	10.7	28.7	25.2	23.3	6.9	3.4	1.7
Clarksville, TN	14.1	30.9	22.8	15.1	7.2	6.9	3.0
Cleveland, OH	12.0	28.7	25.7	22.7	6.4	2.8	1.7
College Station, TX	16.2	48.4	17.1	11.0	3.2	2.3	1.9
Colorado Springs, CO	12.1	32.3	26.6	19.0	4.3	3.5	2.2
Columbia, MO	17.1	44.0	20.2	11.8	3.4	1.7	1.8
Columbia, SC	12.7	28.9	23.6	22.0	7.3	3.2	2.3
Columbus, OH	11.7	29.8	27.5	20.7	5.8	3.1	1.5
Dallas, TX	8.8	25.5	21.7	25.3	10.2	6.5	2.0
Davenport, IA	18.0	35.9	26.0	12.4	3.7	2.6	1.4
Denver, CO	8.8	25.1	23.7	26.4	9.0	5.1	1.9
Des Moines, IA	15.2	35.6	26.7	15.6	3.8	1.7	1.3
Detroit, MI	10.0	27.0	23.7	24.2	8.5	4.8	1.7
Durham, NC	10.6	32.7	25.3	20.0	6.2	3.8	1.5
El Paso, TX	9.7	32.0	27.4	21.6	4.9	2.4	2.0
Eugene, OR	16.0	43.1	21.9	11.6	3.0	2.6	1.8
Fargo, ND	17.7	51.4	18.0	7.1	2.4	1.9	1.5
Fort Collins, CO	13.9	36.1	21.5	15.8	6.0	4.6	2.1
Fort Wayne, IN	13.8	34.9	28.2	15.9	3.4	1.9	2.0
Fort Worth, TX	8.8	25.5	21.7	25.3	10.2	6.5	2.0
Gainesville, FL	12.2	32.8	25.2	19.2	5.7	3.2	1.7
Green Bay, WI	16.8	39.6	22.4	13.1	4.3	2.1	1.7
Greensboro, NC	13.3	34.4	23.7	18.1	5.0	3.2	2.2
Honolulu, HI	9.9	27.1	20.0	25.2	9.1	6.5	2.1
Houston, TX	7.7	22.9	20.7	26.9	11.5	7.9	2.5
Huntsville, AL	10.8	30.8	28.1	22.2	4.9	1.9	1.2
Indianapolis, IN	11.3	27.6	24.2	24.6	7.2	3.3	1.9
Jacksonville, FL	9.2	26.2	24.8	26.0	8.2	3.9	1.7
Kansas City, MO	12.4	30.9	26.3	20.9	5.7	2.4	1.4
Lafayette, LA	13.7	32.9	21.8	19.4	5.2	3.8	3.2
Las Vegas, NV	7.9	27.2	29.2	25.9	5.3	2.6	2.0
Lexington, KY	14.4	35.7	24.4	16.8	4.4	2.5	1.8
Lincoln, NE	17.0	42.8	23.2	10.6	3.2	2.3	1.0
Little Rock, AR	13.2	32.4	22.2	21.1	6.6	3.1	1.5
Los Angeles, CA	7.3	25.0	20.8	25.4	9.7	8.5	3.3
Louisville, KY	10.6	29.6	28.4	20.9	6.1	2.9	1.5
Madison, WI	15.8	32.4	25.5	17.6	5.0	2.5	1.1
Manchester, NH	11.5	29.3	21.6	19.8	8.2	6.9	2.8
McAllen, TX	15.4	33.5	24.2	18.6	3.8	2.4	2.2

Table continued on following page.

Metro Area	Less Than 10 Minutes	10 to 19 Minutes	20 to 29 Minutes	30 to 44 Minutes	45 to 59 Minutes	60 to 89 Minutes	90 Minutes or More
Memphis, TN	11.0	26.8	27.9	23.6	6.6	2.6	1.4
Miami, FL	6.8	23.2	23.1	27.1	9.9	7.2	2.6
Midland, TX	15.7	40.3	20.4	14.4	4.2	2.3	2.7
Milwaukee, WI	12.3	32.4	26.0	20.7	4.7	2.5	1.4
Minneapolis, MN	11.1	29.6	25.3	22.3	6.9	3.5	1.4
Nashville, TN	9.6	26.0	21.1	24.2	10.7	6.6	1.8
New Orleans, LA	11.4	31.5	22.9	21.7	6.6	3.9	2.0
New York, NY	7.3	19.0	16.6	23.9	12.6	14.2	6.4
Oklahoma City, OK	12.2	31.4	25.4	21.2	5.6	2.6	1.7
Omaha, NE	14.0	36.2	27.4	15.9	3.5	1.8	1.2
Orlando, FL	7.1	23.4	22.2	27.8	10.6	6.3	2.5
Philadelphia, PA	10.0	24.4	20.8	24.1	10.6	7.3	2.8
Phoenix, AZ	10.2	26.0	24.3	23.7	8.7	5.3	1.8
Pittsburgh, PA	12.3	27.5	21.7	22.5	8.7	5.3	2.0
Portland, OR	11.5	29.0	23.7	21.7	7.7	4.5	1.8
Providence, RI	11.7	30.0	21.3	20.3	7.9	6.1	2.9
Provo, UT	17.2	34.7	19.9	17.0	6.2	3.7	1.3
Raleigh, NC	9.0	26.8	23.5	24.3	9.6	5.0	1.8
Reno, NV	12.8	34.1	24.2	17.6	6.0	3.6	1.6
Richmond, VA	9.7	28.3	26.8	23.2	6.5	3.2	2.2
Rochester, MN	18.1	41.6	18.7	12.5	4.6	2.9	1.6
Sacramento, CA	10.3	28.8	22.7	22.9	7.1	4.4	3.8
Saint Louis, MO	11.3	28.2	24.6	23.4	7.3	3.5	1.6
Saint Paul, MN	11.1	29.6	25.3	22.3	6.9	3.5	1.4
Salem, OR	15.0	32.4	19.8	17.1	7.4	6.5	1.8
Salt Lake City, UT	11.1	33.7	26.6	19.0	5.5	2.9	1.3
San Antonio, TX	9.5	27.1	24.0	23.8	8.3	5.1	2.3
San Diego, CA	8.5	29.3	25.1	23.4	7.1	4.5	2.1
San Francisco, CA	7.5	24.2	18.7	23.7	11.0	10.8	4.1
San Jose, CA	7.5	28.4	24.3	23.1	8.2	5.8	2.7
Santa Rosa, CA	14.0	34.1	19.3	17.3	6.3	5.6	3.4
Savannah, GA	10.5	29.3	23.7	22.8	8.5	3.7	1.5
Seattle, WA	8.7	23.7	21.6	24.7	10.5	7.8	3.0
Sioux Falls, SD	17.3	43.1	23.9	10.5	2.5	1.3	1.3
Tampa, FL	9.6	26.6	20.9	23.8	10.2	6.5	2.5
Tucson, AZ	11.0	29.4	25.2	23.2	6.8	2.6	1.7
Tulsa, OK	13.4	34.0	26.6	17.7	4.7	2.2	1.5
Virginia Beach, VA	10.5	31.2	24.1	21.7	6.9	3.9	1.8
Washington, DC	6.5	20.1	19.2	26.3	13.2	11.0	3.6
Wichita, KS	15.7	38.0	25.6	14.9	2.8	1.6	1.4
Wilmington, NC	12.4	35.0	23.4	18.2	5.8	3.0	2.3
Winston-Salem, NC	12.5	32.1	24.5	19.3	5.8	3.5	2.2
U.S.	12.6	28.6	21.2	20.8	8.1	6.0	2.8

Note: Figures are percentages and include workers 16 years old and over; Figures cover the Metropolitan Statistical Area (MSA)
Source: U.S. Census Bureau, 2019-2023 American Community Survey 5-Year Estimates

2024 Presidential Election Results

City	Area Covered	Trump (Rep.)	Harris (Dem.)	Stein (Green)	Kennedy (Ind.)	Oliver (Lib.)	Other
Albuquerque, NM	Bernalillo County	38.2	59.2	0.7	1.0	0.5	0.5
Anchorage, AK	State of Alaska	54.5	41.4	0.7	1.7	0.9	0.8
Ann Arbor, MI	Washtenaw County	26.5	70.7	1.3	0.4	0.4	0.7
Athens, GA	Clarke County	30.2	68.3	0.5	0.0	0.6	0.4
Atlanta, GA	Fulton County	26.8	71.3	0.6	0.0	0.5	0.8
Austin, TX	Travis County	29.2	68.3	1.0	0.0	0.8	0.6
Baltimore, MD	Baltimore City	12.1	84.6	1.4	0.8	0.4	0.7
Billings, MT	Yellowstone County	62.0	34.9	0.4	1.9	0.8	0.0
Boise City, ID	Ada County	53.8	43.4	0.4	1.3	0.6	0.5
Boston, MA	Suffolk County	22.2	74.3	1.1	0.0	0.4	2.0
Boulder, CO	Boulder County	20.8	76.5	0.8	0.9	0.6	0.4
Cape Coral, FL	Lee County	63.6	35.3	0.2	0.0	0.2	0.6
Cedar Rapids, IA	Linn County	44.1	54.0	0.0	0.8	0.5	0.6
Charleston, SC	Charleston County	46.3	51.9	0.5	0.0	0.8	0.6
Charlotte, NC	Mecklenburg County	32.5	65.2	0.7	0.0	0.5	1.1
Chicago, IL	Cook County	28.1	69.6	0.9	1.2	0.1	0.2
Cincinnati, OH	Hamilton County	41.7	56.5	0.4	0.0	0.6	0.8
Clarksville, TN	Montgomery County	58.3	39.9	0.3	0.8	0.0	0.7
Cleveland, OH	Cuyahoga County	33.6	64.7	0.5	0.0	0.4	0.8
College Station, TX	Brazos County	61.6	36.8	0.6	0.0	0.9	0.1
Colorado Springs, CO	El Paso County	53.5	43.7	0.5	1.1	0.8	0.4
Columbia, MO	Boone County	43.9	53.6	0.9	0.0	1.1	0.4
Columbia, SC	Richland County	31.8	66.4	0.4	0.0	0.5	0.9
Columbus, OH	Franklin County	34.9	63.0	0.6	0.0	0.6	0.9
Dallas, TX	Dallas County	37.8	59.9	1.1	0.0	0.7	0.5
Davenport, IA	Scott County	51.0	47.1	0.0	0.8	0.5	0.6
Denver, CO	Denver County	20.6	76.6	0.9	0.8	0.6	0.5
Des Moines, IA	Polk County	43.7	54.5	0.0	0.6	0.5	0.7
Detroit, MI	Wayne County	33.6	62.5	2.4	0.4	0.3	0.8
Durham, NC	Durham County	18.2	79.8	0.7	0.0	0.4	0.8
El Paso, TX	El Paso County	41.7	56.8	0.6	0.0	0.6	0.3
Eugene, OR	Lane County	36.6	59.5	0.9	1.5	0.4	1.1
Fargo, ND	Cass County	52.7	44.4	0.0	0.0	1.8	1.1
Fort Collins, CO	Larimer County	39.7	57.3	0.5	1.2	0.8	0.5
Fort Wayne, IN	Allen County	55.2	42.7	0.0	0.9	0.8	0.4
Fort Worth, TX	Tarrant County	51.8	46.7	0.7	0.0	0.7	0.1
Gainesville, FL	Alachua County	38.6	59.4	0.6	0.0	0.5	0.9
Green Bay, WI	Brown County	53.0	45.5	0.2	0.5	0.3	0.5
Greensboro, NC	Guilford County	38.3	60.0	0.5	0.0	0.4	0.8
Honolulu, HI	Honolulu County	38.3	59.9	0.7	0.0	0.5	0.5
Houston, TX	Harris County	46.4	51.9	1.0	0.0	0.6	0.1
Huntsville, AL	Madison County	53.4	44.4	0.3	0.8	0.5	0.6
Indianapolis, IN	Marion County	35.1	62.6	0.0	0.9	0.8	0.7
Jacksonville, FL	Duval County	49.9	48.5	0.5	0.0	0.4	0.7
Kansas City, MO	Jackson County	39.3	58.5	0.8	0.0	0.8	0.6
Lafayette, LA	Lafayette Parish	64.8	33.5	0.4	0.4	0.4	0.5
Las Vegas, NV	Clark County	47.8	50.4	0.0	0.0	0.4	1.4
Lexington, KY	Fayette County	39.8	57.9	0.7	0.9	0.5	0.2
Lincoln, NE	Lancaster County	46.8	51.0	0.4	0.0	0.8	1.1
Little Rock, AR	Pulaski County	37.7	59.8	0.6	1.1	0.5	0.3
Los Angeles, CA	Los Angeles County	31.9	64.8	1.1	1.2	0.3	0.6
Louisville, KY	Jefferson County	40.6	57.1	0.6	0.7	0.3	0.6
Madison, WI	Dane County	23.4	74.9	0.5	0.4	0.3	0.6
Manchester, NH	Hillsborough County	47.8	50.7	0.5	0.0	0.5	0.5
McAllen, TX	Hidalgo County	51.0	48.1	0.5	0.0	0.4	0.0

Table continued on following page.

City	Area Covered	Trump (Rep.)	Harris (Dem.)	Stein (Green)	Kennedy (Ind.)	Oliver (Lib.)	Other
Memphis, TN	Shelby County	36.2	61.5	0.6	0.8	0.0	1.0
Miami, FL	Miami-Dade County	55.2	43.8	0.3	0.0	0.2	0.5
Midland, TX	Midland County	79.6	19.2	0.2	0.0	0.6	0.3
Milwaukee, WI	Milwaukee County	29.7	68.2	0.7	0.4	0.2	0.7
Minneapolis, MN	Hennepin County	27.4	69.8	0.8	0.6	0.5	1.0
Nashville, TN	Davidson County	35.0	62.2	0.6	0.9	0.0	1.2
New Orleans, LA	Orleans Parish	15.2	82.2	0.9	0.3	0.5	1.0
New York, NY	New York City	30.0	68.1	0.9	0.0	0.0	1.0
New York, NY	Bronx County	27.0	71.9	0.6	0.0	0.0	0.5
New York, NY	Kings County	27.4	70.4	1.1	0.0	0.0	1.1
New York, NY	New York County	17.2	80.8	0.7	0.0	0.0	1.3
New York, NY	Queens County	37.0	61.1	1.2	0.0	0.0	0.7
New York, NY	Richmond County	63.9	34.6	0.9	0.0	0.0	0.6
Oklahoma City, OK	Oklahoma County	49.7	48.0	0.0	1.1	0.8	0.4
Omaha, NE	Douglas County	43.9	54.1	0.4	0.0	0.6	1.0
Orlando, FL	Orange County	42.4	55.9	0.7	0.0	0.3	0.7
Philadelphia, PA	Philadelphia County	19.9	78.6	0.9	0.0	0.3	0.3
Phoenix, AZ	Maricopa County	51.0	47.5	0.6	0.0	0.5	0.4
Pittsburgh, PA	Allegheny County	39.2	59.4	0.5	0.0	0.5	0.5
Portland, OR	Multnomah County	17.1	78.7	1.5	1.0	0.3	1.4
Providence, RI	Providence County	41.7	55.7	0.6	0.9	0.3	0.8
Provo, UT	Utah County	66.7	27.8	0.5	0.0	1.4	3.6
Raleigh, NC	Wake County	36.2	61.7	0.8	0.0	0.5	0.8
Reno, NV	Washoe County	48.3	49.3	0.0	0.0	0.5	1.8
Richmond, VA	Richmond City	64.7	34.5	0.2	0.0	0.2	0.3
Rochester, MN	Olmsted County	43.4	54.0	0.6	0.8	0.5	0.7
Sacramento, CA	Sacramento County	38.4	58.1	1.2	1.4	0.5	0.5
Saint Louis, MO	St. Louis City	16.5	80.7	1.2	0.0	0.7	0.8
Saint Paul, MN	Ramsey County	27.1	70.2	0.8	0.5	0.5	0.9
Salem, OR	Marion County	49.2	47.2	0.6	1.7	0.4	0.9
Salt Lake City, UT	Salt Lake County	42.9	52.9	0.7	0.0	1.0	2.5
San Antonio, TX	Bexar County	44.4	54.1	0.6	0.0	0.6	0.4
San Diego, CA	San Diego County	40.1	56.9	1.0	1.1	0.5	0.4
San Francisco, CA	San Francisco County	15.5	80.3	1.7	1.1	0.5	0.9
San Jose, CA	Santa Clara County	28.1	68.0	1.6	1.2	0.5	0.5
Santa Rosa, CA	Sonoma County	25.2	71.4	0.9	1.5	0.4	0.4
Savannah, GA	Chatham County	40.4	58.3	0.3	0.0	0.4	0.7
Seattle, WA	King County	22.3	73.6	1.2	1.0	0.4	1.4
Sioux Falls, SD	Minnehaha County	55.2	42.5	0.0	1.6	0.7	0.0
Tampa, FL	Hillsborough County	50.7	47.6	0.6	0.0	0.4	0.7
Tucson, AZ	Pima County	41.7	56.8	0.6	0.0	0.6	0.4
Tulsa, OK	Tulsa County	56.5	41.3	0.0	1.1	0.7	0.4
Virginia Beach, VA	Virginia Beach City	47.8	50.4	0.4	0.0	0.5	0.9
Washington, DC	District of Columbia	6.5	90.3	0.0	0.9	0.0	2.4
Wichita, KS	Sedgwick County	55.7	42.0	0.1	1.1	0.6	0.5
Wilmington, NC	New Hanover County	49.0	49.6	0.4	0.0	0.4	0.6
Winston-Salem, NC	Forsyth County	42.6	55.8	0.4	0.0	0.4	0.8
U.S.	U.S.	49.7	48.2	0.6	0.5	0.4	0.6

Note: Results are percentages and may not add to 100% due to rounding
Source: Dave Leip's Atlas of U.S. Presidential Elections

House Price Index (HPI)

Metro Area	National Ranking[2]	Quarterly Change (%)	One-Year Change (%)	Five-Year Change (%)	Since 1991Q1 (%)
Albuquerque, NM	152	0.28	4.68	60.38	291.99
Anchorage, AK	120	-2.19	5.44	38.20	272.70
Ann Arbor, MI	111	0.79	5.63	45.12	265.98
Athens, GA	145	0.95	4.82	77.54	363.29
Atlanta, GA	169	-0.09	4.19	66.19	310.49
Austin, TX	237	-1.06	-0.80	47.35	579.98
Baltimore, MD	113	0.13	5.59	41.90	246.61
Billings, MT	211	-0.95	2.58	54.45	434.47
Boise City, ID	156	0.77	4.58	63.16	546.52
Boston, MA[1]	123	0.36	5.29	50.28	365.78
Boulder, CO	218	0.54	2.49	40.60	618.40
Cape Coral, FL	240	-0.39	-2.44	67.84	353.01
Cedar Rapids, IA	204	-0.20	3.04	39.04	206.71
Charleston, SC	84	2.18	6.43	77.86	536.36
Charlotte, NC	175	0.39	4.07	71.74	349.74
Chicago, IL[1]	70	0.05	6.77	43.67	208.59
Cincinnati, OH	93	0.82	6.08	61.42	247.18
Clarksville, TN	(a)	n/a	3.55	67.67	n/a
Cleveland, OH	71	0.34	6.77	57.08	194.72
College Station, TX	(a)	n/a	1.96	50.70	n/a
Colorado Springs, CO	196	-0.38	3.24	49.58	453.42
Columbia, MO	24	0.09	8.46	58.84	279.40
Columbia, SC	61	0.87	6.97	64.02	248.40
Columbus, OH	63	1.20	6.96	61.81	293.84
Dallas, TX[1]	181	0.68	3.91	56.27	350.14
Davenport, IA	143	-0.86	4.87	39.11	236.99
Denver, CO	193	0.30	3.30	43.23	580.34
Des Moines, IA	174	-0.70	4.10	43.67	253.81
Detroit, MI[1]	40	0.25	7.71	52.17	227.11
Durham, NC	150	0.26	4.76	67.43	344.03
El Paso, TX	67	1.00	6.86	63.01	237.09
Eugene, OR	220	-1.37	2.45	48.27	459.38
Fargo, ND	214	-1.86	2.52	33.66	292.25
Fort Collins, CO	215	-0.72	2.52	44.72	544.83
Fort Wayne, IN	32	1.26	7.98	72.59	239.64
Fort Worth, TX[1]	194	0.54	3.30	53.69	324.24
Gainesville, FL	(a)	n/a	5.55	65.26	n/a
Green Bay, WI	103	-1.16	5.89	63.68	299.15
Greensboro, NC	65	0.24	6.92	68.92	226.57
Honolulu, HI	183	-0.33	3.85	35.89	242.48
Houston, TX	195	0.35	3.29	44.19	326.50
Huntsville, AL	76	-1.12	6.65	66.60	239.11
Indianapolis, IN	136	1.08	4.99	59.79	247.41
Jacksonville, FL	168	-0.18	4.19	65.48	401.54
Kansas City, MO	149	-0.76	4.78	56.68	300.63
Lafayette, LA	132	3.26	5.15	25.86	238.79
Las Vegas, NV	44	1.27	7.43	58.90	295.91
Lexington, KY	147	-0.02	4.79	58.94	282.27
Lincoln, NE	60	0.91	6.97	52.28	300.89
Little Rock, AR	197	-1.14	3.23	47.11	222.55
Los Angeles, CA[1]	114	0.65	5.59	48.41	341.40
Louisville, KY	81	0.59	6.45	50.59	291.73
Madison, WI	118	0.61	5.50	54.87	369.35
Manchester, NH	25	-0.15	8.25	67.31	310.83
McAllen, TX	(a)	n/a	8.58	59.26	n/a

Table continued on following page.

Metro Area	National Ranking[2]	Quarterly Change (%)	One-Year Change (%)	Five-Year Change (%)	Since 1991Q1 (%)
Memphis, TN	206	-0.64	2.99	49.80	207.31
Miami, FL[1]	19	2.12	8.69	89.36	668.91
Midland, TX	(a)	n/a	1.09	21.00	n/a
Milwaukee, WI	49	0.11	7.27	55.07	296.31
Minneapolis, MN	153	0.20	4.68	37.75	302.55
Nashville, TN	164	-0.12	4.28	65.94	467.10
New Orleans, LA	233	0.13	0.85	25.47	285.27
New York, NY[1]	34	0.62	7.86	43.82	309.75
Oklahoma City, OK	129	-0.57	5.22	50.62	294.07
Omaha, NE	154	0.12	4.63	51.76	295.39
Orlando, FL	56	2.87	7.06	70.73	377.10
Philadelphia, PA[1]	110	0.84	5.64	41.74	286.32
Phoenix, AZ	200	0.13	3.14	69.09	488.41
Pittsburgh, PA	104	0.17	5.87	45.46	262.85
Portland, OR	182	0.32	3.88	37.41	518.30
Providence, RI	41	0.25	7.70	64.34	289.70
Provo, UT	139	-1.41	4.94	59.50	545.94
Raleigh, NC	185	0.14	3.78	65.05	335.12
Reno, NV	121	0.31	5.40	49.95	361.77
Richmond, VA	98	0.07	5.98	59.60	306.38
Rochester, MN	160	-1.25	4.39	42.16	268.82
Sacramento, CA	198	0.32	3.19	42.05	255.25
Saint Louis, MO	92	1.02	6.12	48.75	237.26
Saint Paul, MN	153	0.20	4.68	37.75	302.55
Salem, OR	209	0.85	2.90	48.54	494.72
Salt Lake City, UT	115	0.53	5.58	59.66	644.94
San Antonio, TX	228	4.07	1.99	49.58	357.13
San Diego, CA	102	1.05	5.91	61.16	410.00
San Francisco, CA[1]	191	0.32	3.50	15.70	376.10
San Jose, CA	221	-0.52	2.35	36.42	433.00
Santa Rosa, CA	192	-0.37	3.47	28.24	304.85
Savannah, GA	225	-1.45	2.18	77.13	438.29
Seattle, WA[1]	91	-0.16	6.14	47.96	484.10
Sioux Falls, SD	224	0.06	2.21	52.27	347.79
Tampa, FL	229	-0.90	1.88	77.61	480.18
Tucson, AZ	223	-1.32	2.30	65.72	364.15
Tulsa, OK	116	1.84	5.52	56.84	272.73
Virginia Beach, VA	64	1.54	6.94	53.57	289.47
Washington, DC[1]	106	-0.50	5.79	38.73	288.38
Wichita, KS	170	-0.42	4.15	57.02	241.93
Wilmington, NC	137	0.32	4.98	74.07	421.24
Winston-Salem, NC	33	1.41	7.91	70.24	245.21
U.S.[3]	—	1.43	4.51	57.13	327.82

Note: The HPI is a weighted repeat sales index. It measures average price changes in repeat sales or refinancings on the same properties. This information is obtained by reviewing repeat mortgage transactions on single-family properties whose mortgages have been purchased or securitized by Fannie Mae or Freddie Mac since January 1975; all figures are for the period ended December 31, 2024; Figures cover the Metropolitan Statistical Area (MSA) unless noted otherwise; (1) Metropolitan Division; (2) Rankings are based on annual percentage change, for all MSAs containing at least 15,000 transactions over the last 10 years and ranges from 1 to 241; (3) Figures based on a weighted division average; (a) Not ranked because of increased index variability due to smaller sample size; n/a not available
Source: Federal Housing Finance Agency, Change in FHFA Metropolitan Area House Price Indexes, All Transactions Index, 2024Q4

Home Value: City

City	Under $100,000	$100,000 -$199,999	$200,000 -$299,999	$300,000 -$399,999	$400,000 -$499,999	$500,000 -$999,999	$1,000,000 or more	Median ($)
Albuquerque, NM	6.9	18.8	34.6	19.9	10.2	8.7	0.9	266,700
Anchorage, AK	5.3	7.4	17.7	25.8	19.8	21.8	2.2	375,900
Ann Arbor, MI	1.8	5.6	14.3	20.1	23.3	29.4	5.4	435,100
Athens, GA	8.3	18.2	31.4	20.3	9.1	11.0	1.8	271,800
Atlanta, GA	4.8	10.7	17.8	14.5	11.2	27.8	13.3	420,600
Austin, TX	2.9	2.8	11.0	14.7	17.1	39.2	12.2	512,700
Baltimore, MD	15.5	28.6	26.5	13.5	6.5	7.8	1.5	219,300
Billings, MT	6.6	10.2	30.1	25.7	15.5	10.6	1.3	311,800
Boise City, ID	4.2	3.9	12.0	18.2	21.0	33.8	6.9	456,000
Boston, MA	3.4	0.7	3.2	5.8	9.4	53.3	24.2	710,400
Boulder, CO	4.3	2.6	2.6	3.9	4.0	33.9	48.6	982,600
Cape Coral, FL	3.1	8.9	28.1	25.5	15.2	16.3	3.0	339,200
Cedar Rapids, IA	12.5	47.4	24.5	8.5	3.9	2.7	0.5	177,100
Charleston, SC	2.0	3.6	12.8	18.9	18.2	31.3	13.1	469,100
Charlotte, NC	4.4	13.0	22.8	19.2	12.6	20.8	7.2	351,500
Chicago, IL	6.6	16.0	24.7	17.7	11.1	18.1	5.8	315,200
Cincinnati, OH	14.9	31.5	20.8	12.4	7.1	10.7	2.6	215,300
Clarksville, TN	7.4	25.5	40.9	15.0	6.3	4.1	0.7	236,100
Cleveland, OH	53.4	31.8	8.1	3.0	1.6	1.7	0.5	94,100
College Station, TX	2.4	7.5	32.9	27.0	15.6	12.5	2.1	326,500
Colorado Springs, CO	4.1	3.5	14.0	23.8	22.3	29.5	2.8	420,700
Columbia, MO	6.6	23.2	30.2	18.4	10.8	10.1	0.8	268,300
Columbia, SC	12.4	26.0	23.5	11.7	8.3	14.7	3.5	243,500
Columbus, OH	11.3	27.4	31.0	18.0	6.6	4.9	0.8	234,500
Dallas, TX	9.9	20.3	20.7	12.2	8.8	19.9	8.2	295,300
Davenport, IA	18.4	45.7	19.6	9.4	3.8	2.8	0.3	162,900
Denver, CO	2.3	2.1	6.6	11.4	17.3	44.6	15.7	586,700
Des Moines, IA	13.7	44.2	27.4	8.7	2.6	2.7	0.7	183,700
Detroit, MI	63.8	21.8	7.7	3.4	1.3	1.6	0.4	76,800
Durham, NC	3.1	10.7	22.2	25.3	16.4	20.2	2.1	355,300
El Paso, TX	14.2	47.6	24.4	7.7	2.7	2.8	0.7	171,700
Eugene, OR	6.5	3.0	11.6	20.1	24.6	31.0	3.0	435,400
Fargo, ND	6.0	16.7	36.1	22.1	9.0	8.7	1.4	269,800
Fort Collins, CO	3.7	1.7	4.2	9.6	22.7	52.5	5.6	548,400
Fort Wayne, IN	19.8	42.0	25.3	7.7	2.8	2.0	0.3	169,700
Fort Worth, TX	8.5	18.0	31.0	21.0	10.5	8.9	2.0	277,300
Gainesville, FL	7.9	27.4	35.1	16.9	5.7	6.3	0.7	235,000
Green Bay, WI	8.5	46.2	29.0	8.4	4.0	3.6	0.3	191,500
Greensboro, NC	10.1	33.8	25.7	14.3	6.6	8.2	1.4	221,300
Honolulu, HI	2.1	1.6	3.1	8.6	10.6	35.0	39.0	834,100
Houston, TX	11.1	24.9	22.9	12.3	8.6	14.1	6.1	253,400
Huntsville, AL	11.8	23.6	22.4	17.3	9.3	12.8	2.7	263,100
Indianapolis, IN	14.2	33.3	28.5	11.6	5.2	6.1	1.1	207,000
Jacksonville, FL	11.0	20.4	27.6	19.5	10.1	9.1	2.2	266,100
Kansas City, MO	16.8	25.8	25.2	14.7	8.5	7.8	1.2	227,000
Lafayette, LA	11.2	23.8	28.6	14.9	9.3	10.0	2.2	251,300
Las Vegas, NV	3.9	4.5	17.2	25.6	19.7	24.9	4.2	395,300
Lexington, KY	5.4	22.4	29.2	18.8	10.0	11.8	2.4	272,100
Lincoln, NE	5.9	26.1	34.7	18.1	7.5	6.6	1.1	248,200
Little Rock, AR	15.5	28.7	22.6	12.2	8.1	10.2	2.6	221,200
Los Angeles, CA	2.5	1.2	1.2	2.5	5.7	47.7	39.2	879,500
Louisville, KY	11.8	32.0	25.5	13.2	7.6	8.4	1.5	221,500
Madison, WI	2.9	9.1	25.1	27.7	16.5	17.0	1.8	346,900
Manchester, NH	3.9	10.2	24.0	32.7	19.8	8.6	0.7	336,300
McAllen, TX	20.0	40.0	22.5	10.6	3.3	3.0	0.8	173,800

Table continued on following page.

City	Under $100,000	$100,000 -$199,999	$200,000 -$299,999	$300,000 -$399,999	$400,000 -$499,999	$500,000 -$999,999	$1,000,000 or more	Median ($)
Memphis, TN	31.7	28.3	18.4	8.8	4.5	6.3	1.9	157,100
Miami, FL	2.9	5.9	12.9	14.6	18.1	31.4	14.1	475,200
Midland, TX	7.8	12.9	29.7	24.9	10.4	11.8	2.5	298,600
Milwaukee, WI	19.7	43.3	25.1	5.9	2.6	2.6	0.8	172,000
Minneapolis, MN	2.9	10.4	25.0	25.6	14.0	18.1	4.0	345,600
Nashville, TN	3.4	6.6	21.4	22.5	16.9	22.1	7.1	383,100
New Orleans, LA	6.4	21.2	23.1	13.8	9.7	19.4	6.4	296,400
New York, NY	4.7	2.9	4.7	5.6	7.1	44.9	30.1	751,700
Oklahoma City, OK	14.8	30.5	27.8	13.1	5.7	6.6	1.6	215,100
Omaha, NE	9.8	29.2	31.6	14.2	7.4	6.7	1.2	230,100
Orlando, FL	3.5	15.0	19.9	19.6	14.5	22.0	5.4	359,000
Philadelphia, PA	14.0	26.4	26.8	14.6	6.6	9.5	2.0	232,400
Phoenix, AZ	5.7	6.6	20.5	21.1	16.0	24.9	5.2	381,900
Pittsburgh, PA	22.7	29.2	19.5	10.3	5.6	10.3	2.2	193,200
Portland, OR	2.5	1.5	4.8	11.9	21.2	50.0	8.1	557,600
Providence, RI	4.1	9.3	30.8	25.2	11.6	14.5	4.4	322,800
Provo, UT	5.1	1.8	10.4	24.4	22.4	31.3	4.6	437,100
Raleigh, NC	3.1	7.7	22.7	21.2	15.2	24.4	5.7	377,800
Reno, NV	6.1	3.0	6.9	14.9	19.3	42.7	7.1	498,600
Richmond, VA	4.9	17.9	22.4	17.1	13.0	19.0	5.7	328,100
Rochester, MN	4.4	16.0	33.6	19.2	12.2	13.4	1.1	287,500
Sacramento, CA	4.3	2.4	7.6	17.7	21.3	41.5	5.2	484,600
Saint Louis, MO	22.9	31.6	22.8	11.1	5.1	5.2	1.2	185,100
Saint Paul, MN	3.5	15.9	37.6	19.5	9.9	11.4	2.0	280,300
Salem, OR	6.8	5.2	14.1	29.1	22.7	21.4	0.8	382,400
Salt Lake City, UT	4.1	3.4	11.3	15.5	16.4	37.9	11.4	495,700
San Antonio, TX	13.7	29.8	29.2	14.1	6.3	5.9	1.0	219,700
San Diego, CA	2.6	1.2	1.5	3.4	7.1	48.7	35.6	848,500
San Francisco, CA	1.5	1.2	0.7	1.3	1.6	16.0	77.8	1,380,500
San Jose, CA	2.2	2.2	2.3	1.5	1.3	22.4	68.0	1,187,800
Santa Rosa, CA	3.7	2.8	2.7	3.8	7.2	65.4	14.3	685,000
Savannah, GA	12.1	29.9	27.2	12.5	6.6	9.4	2.4	225,200
Seattle, WA	1.1	0.6	1.2	3.6	5.2	47.4	40.8	912,100
Sioux Falls, SD	7.9	18.0	32.8	18.7	10.0	10.5	2.2	271,400
Tampa, FL	4.8	12.4	20.8	16.0	12.1	24.0	10.0	375,300
Tucson, AZ	12.9	21.2	34.4	17.5	7.6	5.4	1.1	242,200
Tulsa, OK	20.0	33.1	20.0	10.7	5.6	8.3	2.3	189,600
Virginia Beach, VA	3.1	7.5	23.9	23.4	16.1	21.5	4.5	366,300
Washington, DC	1.4	1.8	4.6	9.1	11.2	41.8	30.1	724,600
Wichita, KS	21.6	34.9	24.3	9.6	4.5	4.2	0.9	179,500
Wilmington, NC	3.3	13.2	23.0	21.1	14.2	19.1	6.2	350,300
Winston-Salem, NC	12.9	34.6	25.9	12.1	4.6	8.3	1.7	208,200
U.S.	12.1	17.8	19.5	14.4	10.5	19.1	6.5	303,400

Note: Figures are percentages except for median and cover owner-occupied housing units.
Source: U.S. Census Bureau, 2019-2023 American Community Survey 5-Year Estimates

Home Value: Metro Area

Metro Area	Under $100,000	$100,000-$199,999	$200,000-$299,999	$300,000-$399,999	$400,000-$499,999	$500,000-$999,999	$1,000,000 or more	Median ($)
Albuquerque, NM	9.6	19.3	31.5	17.9	9.9	10.1	1.6	263,500
Anchorage, AK	5.4	8.2	21.3	25.5	18.1	19.7	1.8	358,900
Ann Arbor, MI	7.1	11.0	21.8	19.2	16.2	21.4	3.4	353,000
Athens, GA	10.5	18.0	26.3	18.0	10.1	14.3	2.8	280,900
Atlanta, GA	5.5	13.6	23.9	19.8	13.6	19.9	3.6	335,100
Austin, TX	5.1	5.2	15.7	18.2	16.6	30.5	8.6	434,800
Baltimore, MD	5.5	10.2	19.7	19.9	15.1	25.5	4.1	373,300
Billings, MT	8.9	10.1	25.9	22.6	14.8	15.5	2.2	322,700
Boise City, ID	5.0	4.9	13.8	19.8	19.1	31.9	5.6	434,400
Boston, MA	2.6	1.9	5.8	10.4	15.0	48.7	15.6	610,900
Boulder, CO	3.9	1.2	2.5	6.2	10.6	49.6	25.9	713,900
Cape Coral, FL	8.7	12.9	23.1	19.9	12.6	17.6	5.1	326,300
Cedar Rapids, IA	11.7	37.7	25.8	12.6	6.1	5.0	1.0	202,100
Charleston, SC	8.4	11.0	22.2	18.2	12.1	19.8	8.1	345,400
Charlotte, NC	8.7	15.9	21.8	18.3	12.5	18.3	4.4	319,400
Chicago, IL	6.2	16.9	26.5	19.9	12.0	15.0	3.5	301,900
Cincinnati, OH	10.2	28.0	26.6	15.7	8.7	9.3	1.5	240,200
Clarksville, TN	13.8	25.6	31.2	14.6	7.2	6.3	1.2	229,400
Cleveland, OH	16.6	33.1	23.9	12.6	6.4	6.4	1.0	201,000
College Station, TX	15.0	18.5	26.1	17.3	9.5	11.2	2.3	261,900
Colorado Springs, CO	4.0	3.9	13.2	22.2	21.5	31.2	4.1	431,600
Columbia, MO	11.1	26.8	26.5	15.4	9.6	9.0	1.6	242,500
Columbia, SC	15.7	30.4	25.4	12.9	6.5	7.4	1.7	213,400
Columbus, OH	9.2	20.9	26.3	18.4	10.8	12.8	1.6	274,300
Dallas, TX	6.8	13.3	23.8	20.1	13.1	18.8	4.1	330,300
Davenport, IA	20.4	38.7	21.3	9.7	5.0	4.2	0.7	170,000
Denver, CO	3.2	1.7	5.1	11.3	18.6	49.8	10.3	570,300
Des Moines, IA	8.7	25.7	28.2	18.3	9.0	9.0	1.1	252,400
Detroit, MI	16.3	23.8	24.2	15.1	9.2	9.8	1.5	237,100
Durham, NC	6.8	12.7	19.0	19.3	14.3	23.7	4.1	359,400
El Paso, TX	17.9	45.6	23.7	7.1	2.7	2.4	0.6	167,000
Eugene, OR	7.7	4.1	16.6	22.5	19.7	25.8	3.5	395,800
Fargo, ND	6.0	16.9	33.8	21.7	10.4	9.8	1.5	276,600
Fort Collins, CO	4.8	1.6	4.6	11.8	22.6	47.6	6.9	532,200
Fort Wayne, IN	16.3	35.8	25.6	11.4	5.1	5.0	0.7	194,000
Fort Worth, TX	6.8	13.3	23.8	20.1	13.1	18.8	4.1	330,300
Gainesville, FL	13.9	23.8	25.3	16.2	9.0	10.1	1.6	245,800
Green Bay, WI	7.8	29.2	31.1	15.7	8.0	7.3	0.9	238,700
Greensboro, NC	15.0	33.0	23.9	13.1	6.3	7.9	1.0	207,600
Honolulu, HI	2.2	1.5	2.2	5.1	7.6	43.9	37.6	873,000
Houston, TX	9.2	18.8	28.6	17.5	10.0	12.4	3.6	275,200
Huntsville, AL	10.6	22.2	26.0	17.6	10.3	11.7	1.6	265,000
Indianapolis, IN	10.9	25.6	27.2	15.9	8.9	9.9	1.7	244,000
Jacksonville, FL	8.7	15.7	24.0	19.1	12.4	16.2	4.0	308,900
Kansas City, MO	10.8	22.1	25.5	17.5	10.4	11.8	1.8	265,400
Lafayette, LA	22.9	24.9	27.1	12.6	6.3	5.2	1.0	206,900
Las Vegas, NV	4.7	4.8	15.2	25.2	21.6	24.5	4.1	400,800
Lexington, KY	6.9	24.4	28.6	17.8	9.1	10.7	2.5	258,900
Lincoln, NE	5.8	24.3	32.7	18.0	8.9	8.9	1.3	257,500
Little Rock, AR	17.5	32.8	24.9	11.9	5.4	6.1	1.5	199,300
Los Angeles, CA	3.2	1.7	1.8	3.2	6.3	50.5	33.3	825,300
Louisville, KY	10.5	28.4	27.1	15.9	8.1	8.6	1.3	236,400
Madison, WI	3.7	11.6	24.1	23.9	16.0	18.4	2.3	344,600
Manchester, NH	3.8	6.2	18.2	25.4	21.4	23.3	1.5	385,500
McAllen, TX	39.7	34.5	16.0	5.7	2.2	1.6	0.4	124,000

Table continued on following page.

Metro Area	Under $100,000	$100,000 -$199,999	$200,000 -$299,999	$300,000 -$399,999	$400,000 -$499,999	$500,000 -$999,999	$1,000,000 or more	Median ($)
Memphis, TN	18.7	24.3	22.8	15.3	8.1	9.3	1.6	228,100
Miami, FL	6.3	9.6	15.7	17.5	16.5	26.1	8.3	405,600
Midland, TX	12.7	13.2	26.8	21.6	10.8	12.6	2.4	290,300
Milwaukee, WI	7.4	19.6	27.2	19.0	11.7	13.0	2.1	283,800
Minneapolis, MN	4.0	7.4	24.9	25.1	16.1	19.6	2.9	354,400
Nashville, TN	4.8	8.7	20.9	20.4	15.0	23.6	6.7	376,800
New Orleans, LA	8.9	25.9	28.3	15.3	7.8	10.8	3.0	248,000
New York, NY	3.6	3.3	7.3	11.1	14.3	44.4	16.0	587,400
Oklahoma City, OK	14.4	31.1	26.8	12.7	6.2	7.1	1.7	214,700
Omaha, NE	8.7	25.0	29.9	16.9	9.6	8.7	1.3	248,100
Orlando, FL	7.9	10.2	22.8	23.6	15.2	17.1	3.2	338,500
Philadelphia, PA	7.1	14.6	23.2	19.2	13.4	19.5	3.0	326,700
Phoenix, AZ	6.7	5.9	16.8	20.3	17.5	26.9	5.9	401,400
Pittsburgh, PA	19.2	29.5	23.7	12.0	6.6	7.6	1.3	204,500
Portland, OR	3.9	2.2	5.4	12.8	22.0	46.6	7.0	526,500
Providence, RI	3.3	4.7	20.9	24.5	18.9	24.2	3.4	385,900
Provo, UT	3.5	1.6	7.4	18.5	22.0	41.2	6.0	487,200
Raleigh, NC	5.3	9.2	19.3	20.0	16.2	26.2	3.9	381,000
Reno, NV	5.5	4.0	9.4	17.0	18.9	36.5	8.6	474,000
Richmond, VA	4.9	12.5	26.9	22.4	13.5	17.3	2.6	325,800
Rochester, MN	6.7	18.1	29.5	17.4	11.9	14.4	2.0	284,600
Sacramento, CA	4.1	2.1	5.1	12.0	18.3	49.6	8.8	559,000
Saint Louis, MO	14.9	26.3	25.0	14.9	8.2	8.9	1.8	232,100
Saint Paul, MN	4.0	7.4	24.9	25.1	16.1	19.6	2.9	354,400
Salem, OR	7.5	5.1	14.2	25.9	20.5	24.2	2.7	389,800
Salt Lake City, UT	4.0	2.6	9.9	17.6	20.3	38.7	6.9	478,200
San Antonio, TX	11.7	21.6	27.6	16.5	9.1	11.3	2.2	258,700
San Diego, CA	3.7	1.9	2.1	3.4	6.8	52.6	29.5	791,600
San Francisco, CA	2.1	1.4	1.3	1.7	3.4	31.8	58.4	1,113,800
San Jose, CA	2.1	1.7	1.8	1.3	1.2	19.3	72.6	1,342,700
Santa Rosa, CA	3.3	3.1	2.4	2.7	5.4	57.0	26.2	779,000
Savannah, GA	9.6	21.3	26.2	16.7	9.8	13.3	3.2	271,100
Seattle, WA	3.2	1.7	3.9	8.3	12.9	46.7	23.2	673,500
Sioux Falls, SD	8.4	18.3	30.7	18.5	10.4	11.8	1.9	274,800
Tampa, FL	11.5	14.4	22.9	19.3	12.1	16.0	3.8	306,100
Tucson, AZ	11.2	15.2	26.9	19.0	11.6	13.4	2.6	286,900
Tulsa, OK	17.5	31.2	25.4	12.1	5.9	6.5	1.4	204,400
Virginia Beach, VA	5.2	13.4	27.6	21.5	14.3	15.6	2.5	318,000
Washington, DC	2.5	2.4	8.4	14.5	16.2	42.5	13.4	553,000
Wichita, KS	20.1	33.8	25.4	10.2	4.8	4.9	0.8	188,200
Wilmington, NC	7.5	14.3	22.8	19.4	13.3	19.0	3.8	328,000
Winston-Salem, NC	14.0	32.0	26.0	13.0	6.5	7.3	1.2	213,300
U.S.	12.1	17.8	19.5	14.4	10.5	19.1	6.5	303,400

Note: Figures are percentages except for median and cover owner-occupied housing units; Figures cover the Metropolitan Statistical Area (MSA)
Source: U.S. Census Bureau, 2019-2023 American Community Survey 5-Year Estimates

Homeownership Rate

Metro Area	2017	2018	2019	2020	2021	2022	2023	2024
Albuquerque, NM	67.0	67.9	70.0	69.5	66.5	67.3	69.1	71.8
Anchorage, AK	n/a	n/a	n/a	n/a	n/a	n/a	n/a	n/a
Ann Arbor, MI	n/a	n/a	n/a	n/a	n/a	n/a	n/a	n/a
Athens, GA	n/a	n/a	n/a	n/a	n/a	n/a	n/a	n/a
Atlanta, GA	62.4	64.0	64.2	66.4	64.2	64.4	67.5	67.5
Austin, TX	55.6	56.1	59.0	65.4	62.2	62.4	60.3	56.2
Baltimore, MD	67.5	63.5	66.5	70.7	67.5	70.4	72.9	70.0
Billings, MT	n/a	n/a	n/a	n/a	n/a	n/a	n/a	n/a
Boise City, ID	n/a	n/a	n/a	n/a	n/a	n/a	n/a	n/a
Boston, MA	58.8	61.0	60.9	61.2	60.7	59.4	59.9	60.7
Boulder, CO	n/a	n/a	n/a	n/a	n/a	n/a	n/a	n/a
Cape Coral, FL	65.5	75.1	72.0	77.4	76.1	70.8	78.5	77.1
Cedar Rapids, IA	n/a	n/a	n/a	n/a	n/a	n/a	n/a	n/a
Charleston, SC	67.7	68.8	70.7	75.5	73.2	71.9	69.6	68.1
Charlotte, NC	64.6	67.9	72.3	73.3	70.0	68.7	64.8	62.7
Chicago, IL	64.1	64.6	63.4	66.0	67.5	66.8	67.3	68.0
Cincinnati, OH	65.7	67.3	67.4	71.1	72.1	67.1	69.6	72.3
Clarksville, TN	n/a	n/a	n/a	n/a	n/a	n/a	n/a	n/a
Cleveland, OH	66.6	66.7	64.4	66.3	64.7	63.0	63.1	65.6
College Station, TX	n/a	n/a	n/a	n/a	n/a	n/a	n/a	n/a
Colorado Springs, CO	n/a	n/a	n/a	n/a	n/a	n/a	n/a	n/a
Columbia, MO	n/a	n/a	n/a	n/a	n/a	n/a	n/a	n/a
Columbia, SC	70.7	69.3	65.9	69.7	69.4	70.9	69.2	73.4
Columbus, OH	57.9	64.8	65.7	65.6	64.6	61.5	58.6	61.5
Dallas, TX	61.8	62.0	60.6	64.7	61.8	60.4	61.7	61.1
Davenport, IA	n/a	n/a	n/a	n/a	n/a	n/a	n/a	n/a
Denver, CO	59.3	60.1	63.5	62.9	62.8	64.6	65.9	61.6
Des Moines, IA	n/a	n/a	n/a	n/a	n/a	n/a	n/a	n/a
Detroit, MI	70.2	70.9	70.2	71.8	71.6	71.9	73.5	72.0
Durham, NC	n/a	n/a	n/a	n/a	n/a	n/a	n/a	n/a
El Paso, TX	n/a	n/a	n/a	n/a	n/a	n/a	n/a	n/a
Eugene, OR	n/a	n/a	n/a	n/a	n/a	n/a	n/a	n/a
Fargo, ND	n/a	n/a	n/a	n/a	n/a	n/a	n/a	n/a
Fort Collins, CO	n/a	n/a	n/a	n/a	n/a	n/a	n/a	n/a
Fort Wayne, IN	n/a	n/a	n/a	n/a	n/a	n/a	n/a	n/a
Fort Worth, TX	61.8	62.0	60.6	64.7	61.8	60.4	61.7	61.1
Gainesville, FL	n/a	n/a	n/a	n/a	n/a	n/a	n/a	n/a
Green Bay, WI	n/a	n/a	n/a	n/a	n/a	n/a	n/a	n/a
Greensboro, NC	61.9	63.2	61.7	65.8	61.9	70.0	69.4	67.0
Honolulu, HI	53.8	57.7	59.0	56.9	55.9	57.7	60.4	58.5
Houston, TX	58.9	60.1	61.3	65.3	64.1	63.7	61.8	61.6
Huntsville, AL	n/a	n/a	n/a	n/a	n/a	n/a	n/a	n/a
Indianapolis, IN	63.9	64.3	66.2	70.0	70.1	68.8	70.2	69.6
Jacksonville, FL	65.2	61.4	63.1	64.8	68.1	70.6	72.9	67.0
Kansas City, MO	62.4	64.3	65.0	66.7	63.8	63.8	64.1	65.3
Lafayette, LA	n/a	n/a	n/a	n/a	n/a	n/a	n/a	n/a
Las Vegas, NV	54.4	58.1	56.0	57.3	57.7	58.7	58.9	58.5
Lexington, KY	n/a	n/a	n/a	n/a	n/a	n/a	n/a	n/a
Lincoln, NE	n/a	n/a	n/a	n/a	n/a	n/a	n/a	n/a
Little Rock, AR	61.0	62.2	65.0	67.7	64.6	64.4	62.6	61.7
Los Angeles, CA	49.1	49.5	48.2	48.5	47.9	48.3	48.0	48.3
Louisville, KY	71.7	67.9	64.9	69.3	71.4	71.7	68.3	67.0
Madison, WI	n/a	n/a	n/a	n/a	n/a	n/a	n/a	n/a
Manchester, NH	n/a	n/a	n/a	n/a	n/a	n/a	n/a	n/a
McAllen, TX	n/a	n/a	n/a	n/a	n/a	n/a	n/a	n/a
Memphis, TN	62.4	63.5	63.7	62.5	60.7	59.7	63.2	60.1

Table continued on following page.

Appendix A: Comparative Statistics   A-119

Metro Area	2017	2018	2019	2020	2021	2022	2023	2024
Miami, FL	57.9	59.9	60.4	60.6	59.4	58.3	58.6	60.8
Midland, TX	n/a	n/a	n/a	n/a	n/a	n/a	n/a	n/a
Milwaukee, WI	63.9	62.3	56.9	58.5	56.8	57.3	60.0	62.7
Minneapolis, MN	70.1	67.8	70.2	73.0	75.0	73.0	72.0	67.8
Nashville, TN	69.4	68.3	69.8	69.8	65.7	70.4	70.7	71.6
New Orleans, LA	61.7	62.6	61.1	66.3	66.2	66.3	63.2	63.2
New York, NY	49.9	49.7	50.4	50.9	50.7	50.5	50.2	49.4
Oklahoma City, OK	64.7	64.6	64.3	68.3	61.9	64.8	68.1	65.0
Omaha, NE	65.5	67.8	66.9	68.6	68.6	67.9	67.0	67.4
Orlando, FL	59.5	58.5	56.1	64.2	63.0	62.1	61.9	62.6
Philadelphia, PA	65.6	67.4	67.4	69.2	69.8	68.2	67.4	69.6
Phoenix, AZ	64.0	65.3	65.9	67.9	65.2	68.0	69.7	69.4
Pittsburgh, PA	72.7	71.7	71.5	69.8	69.1	72.7	72.4	71.7
Portland, OR	61.1	59.2	60.0	62.5	64.1	65.2	65.6	61.1
Providence, RI	58.6	61.3	63.5	64.8	64.1	66.3	65.4	63.2
Provo, UT	n/a	n/a	n/a	n/a	n/a	n/a	n/a	n/a
Raleigh, NC	68.2	64.9	63.0	68.2	62.7	65.1	68.8	65.0
Reno, NV	n/a	n/a	n/a	n/a	n/a	n/a	n/a	n/a
Richmond, VA	63.1	62.9	66.4	66.5	64.9	66.3	64.9	65.4
Rochester, MN	n/a	n/a	n/a	n/a	n/a	n/a	n/a	n/a
Sacramento, CA	60.1	64.1	61.6	63.4	63.2	63.5	64.4	63.0
Saint Louis, MO	65.6	65.8	68.1	71.1	73.8	69.9	69.4	68.2
Saint Paul, MN	70.1	67.8	70.2	73.0	75.0	73.0	72.0	67.8
Salem, OR	n/a	n/a	n/a	n/a	n/a	n/a	n/a	n/a
Salt Lake City, UT	68.1	69.5	69.2	68.0	64.1	66.6	62.9	61.0
San Antonio, TX	62.5	64.4	62.6	64.2	62.7	62.9	66.9	63.3
San Diego, CA	56.0	56.1	56.7	57.8	52.6	51.6	54.5	51.4
San Francisco, CA	55.7	55.6	52.8	53.0	54.7	56.4	55.0	56.4
San Jose, CA	50.4	50.4	52.4	52.6	48.4	53.1	53.5	52.3
Santa Rosa, CA	n/a	n/a	n/a	n/a	n/a	n/a	n/a	n/a
Savannah, GA	n/a	n/a	n/a	n/a	n/a	n/a	n/a	n/a
Seattle, WA	59.5	62.5	61.5	59.4	58.0	62.7	62.7	61.1
Sioux Falls, SD	n/a	n/a	n/a	n/a	n/a	n/a	n/a	n/a
Tampa, FL	60.4	64.9	68.0	72.2	68.3	68.4	66.9	68.9
Tucson, AZ	60.1	63.8	60.1	67.1	63.5	71.6	73.3	66.4
Tulsa, OK	66.8	68.3	70.5	70.1	63.8	63.7	62.8	65.3
Virginia Beach, VA	65.3	62.8	63.0	65.8	64.4	61.4	67.8	69.8
Washington, DC	63.3	62.9	64.7	67.9	65.8	66.2	65.1	64.0
Wichita, KS	n/a	n/a	n/a	n/a	n/a	n/a	n/a	n/a
Wilmington, NC	n/a	n/a	n/a	n/a	n/a	n/a	n/a	n/a
Winston-Salem, NC	n/a	n/a	n/a	n/a	n/a	n/a	n/a	n/a
U.S.	63.9	64.4	64.6	66.6	65.5	65.8	65.9	65.6

Note: Figures are percentages and cover the Metropolitan Statistical Area (MSA); n/a not available
Source: U.S. Census Bureau, Housing Vacancies and Homeownership Annual Statistics: 2017-2024

Year Housing Structure Built: City

City	2020 or Later	2010-2019	2000-2009	1990-1999	1980-1989	1970-1979	1960-1969	1950-1959	1940-1949	Before 1940	Median Year
Albuquerque, NM	0.7	6.9	16.2	14.2	14.1	19.2	9.5	12.3	3.9	3.0	1982
Anchorage, AK	0.2	6.6	12.1	11.6	24.8	27.5	9.7	5.8	0.9	0.8	1982
Ann Arbor, MI	1.3	6.5	6.8	11.2	9.9	16.0	17.9	10.6	4.8	15.2	1971
Athens, GA	1.6	8.9	19.0	16.3	14.5	14.3	12.0	5.8	2.7	4.9	1987
Atlanta, GA	2.3	15.8	21.0	8.9	7.8	7.8	10.2	8.8	5.3	12.1	1987
Austin, TX	2.5	20.7	17.2	13.0	17.3	13.7	7.2	4.1	2.0	2.3	1993
Baltimore, MD	0.3	4.3	4.1	4.1	4.6	5.8	8.6	15.3	11.6	41.1	1948
Billings, MT	2.3	12.7	10.6	11.9	11.3	16.3	9.0	13.1	5.5	7.4	1979
Boise City, ID	1.3	10.8	11.4	19.6	14.4	17.8	7.8	7.2	3.7	6.3	1985
Boston, MA	0.9	9.2	6.5	4.3	5.6	7.6	7.2	7.1	4.9	46.8	1947
Boulder, CO	0.5	8.5	8.8	12.4	15.5	19.8	16.2	9.0	1.5	7.7	1978
Cape Coral, FL	2.0	11.6	34.3	15.2	21.1	10.3	4.5	0.8	0.3	0.0	1999
Cedar Rapids, IA	0.8	9.6	11.3	10.9	7.5	14.7	13.9	12.4	4.3	14.7	1973
Charleston, SC	2.6	22.7	19.1	10.1	10.5	7.5	8.2	5.6	3.0	10.8	1994
Charlotte, NC	1.8	16.9	20.9	17.3	13.9	10.2	8.2	5.8	2.4	2.6	1994
Chicago, IL	0.4	5.1	8.2	4.9	5.0	7.9	9.7	11.6	8.2	39.1	1952
Cincinnati, OH	0.5	4.4	4.1	4.0	6.3	9.3	12.0	10.9	8.3	40.3	1951
Clarksville, TN	3.3	18.0	21.2	18.8	12.9	11.3	6.2	4.2	2.3	1.7	1996
Cleveland, OH	0.6	3.8	3.8	2.9	3.0	5.6	7.8	12.1	10.8	49.6	1940
College Station, TX	2.4	23.2	20.3	16.5	18.5	12.2	3.9	1.7	0.5	0.7	1998
Colorado Springs, CO	1.9	11.6	14.9	14.2	17.5	16.8	9.3	7.0	1.7	5.3	1986
Columbia, MO	0.8	17.5	20.3	17.0	12.3	9.9	10.3	4.5	2.4	5.0	1993
Columbia, SC	1.0	12.9	14.8	9.8	9.6	9.6	10.1	13.3	8.9	10.1	1978
Columbus, OH	1.0	9.6	11.8	13.7	13.3	14.4	10.7	9.6	4.0	12.0	1980
Dallas, TX	1.0	12.0	11.0	10.0	16.3	15.0	12.0	12.7	4.6	5.2	1980
Davenport, IA	0.6	4.8	9.1	8.4	6.9	15.3	12.8	11.8	6.0	24.2	1966
Denver, CO	2.3	15.5	10.9	6.6	7.4	12.0	9.9	13.0	5.2	17.2	1974
Des Moines, IA	0.6	6.9	7.3	6.8	6.4	12.8	9.5	14.6	7.3	27.8	1960
Detroit, MI	0.1	1.5	2.7	2.3	3.2	4.9	7.8	21.8	20.4	35.2	1947
Durham, NC	2.6	21.5	17.1	14.2	14.0	9.6	7.1	5.3	3.4	5.2	1994
El Paso, TX	0.9	14.1	13.5	11.7	14.9	15.9	10.2	10.9	3.2	4.7	1983
Eugene, OR	0.7	10.2	13.3	15.0	9.2	19.9	11.7	8.5	5.5	6.0	1979
Fargo, ND	1.3	20.3	14.9	14.5	11.5	13.7	5.8	7.7	2.5	7.9	1991
Fort Collins, CO	1.5	15.0	18.9	19.0	14.5	15.7	6.5	3.0	1.3	4.5	1992
Fort Wayne, IN	0.5	3.4	7.4	12.9	11.3	16.9	15.5	12.0	5.7	14.4	1971
Fort Worth, TX	2.4	17.7	20.8	11.1	13.2	8.7	6.9	9.3	4.5	5.6	1992
Gainesville, FL	1.3	6.5	14.0	14.2	19.5	20.2	11.8	7.0	2.7	2.9	1983
Green Bay, WI	0.4	3.2	7.3	9.8	12.5	17.9	12.6	16.1	5.9	14.4	1971
Greensboro, NC	0.8	9.8	14.7	14.5	15.6	13.9	11.0	10.1	3.8	5.7	1983
Honolulu, HI	0.5	7.5	6.7	7.8	10.5	25.9	19.6	11.6	5.1	4.8	1973
Houston, TX	1.4	14.0	13.0	9.3	14.1	19.0	12.1	9.4	3.7	4.1	1981
Huntsville, AL	2.3	15.6	12.4	10.8	14.8	11.9	20.1	7.8	1.8	2.6	1984
Indianapolis, IN	0.6	6.5	9.9	12.0	11.2	12.1	13.4	12.1	6.0	16.1	1972
Jacksonville, FL	2.4	10.6	17.4	13.1	15.9	11.9	9.3	10.3	4.1	5.0	1986
Kansas City, MO	1.0	8.2	10.1	8.5	8.6	11.4	12.0	13.2	5.5	21.6	1968
Lafayette, LA	0.8	12.4	11.5	9.3	18.6	21.5	12.8	8.7	2.7	1.6	1981
Las Vegas, NV	1.4	8.8	21.4	29.3	16.3	10.2	7.0	4.1	1.0	0.5	1994
Lexington, KY	1.1	10.0	14.5	15.6	13.0	14.5	13.4	8.5	2.7	6.7	1983
Lincoln, NE	1.0	11.9	14.2	13.6	10.1	14.5	8.7	10.3	3.2	12.4	1981
Little Rock, AR	0.4	9.7	11.7	11.8	13.1	17.9	14.7	8.5	4.9	7.2	1978
Los Angeles, CA	0.8	6.1	5.6	5.7	10.8	13.4	13.2	16.2	9.1	19.2	1964
Louisville, KY	0.8	7.7	11.8	10.4	6.9	13.0	12.7	14.2	6.6	15.9	1970
Madison, WI	0.9	11.8	14.3	11.8	9.5	12.8	11.9	9.2	4.3	13.4	1979
Manchester, NH	0.5	3.5	6.5	7.7	15.5	11.5	8.1	10.7	6.6	29.4	1964
McAllen, TX	1.2	13.0	24.8	16.8	18.5	15.3	5.0	2.3	1.2	1.9	1993

Table continued on following page.

City	2020 or Later	2010-2019	2000-2009	1990-1999	1980-1989	1970-1979	1960-1969	1950-1959	1940-1949	Before 1940	Median Year
Memphis, TN	0.5	3.6	6.5	9.7	12.4	17.3	14.6	20.0	7.7	7.7	1970
Miami, FL	1.8	15.4	17.0	6.0	7.4	11.9	10.0	13.5	9.1	7.9	1978
Midland, TX	2.2	21.9	10.1	9.7	17.3	10.9	7.7	16.6	2.5	1.1	1986
Milwaukee, WI	0.3	3.5	3.7	3.5	3.8	9.2	11.6	18.8	10.9	34.7	1952
Minneapolis, MN	1.0	8.8	6.2	4.2	6.8	8.2	6.8	8.2	6.2	43.6	1950
Nashville, TN	3.2	15.4	13.9	11.0	14.2	12.8	10.9	9.0	3.4	6.2	1985
New Orleans, LA	0.4	5.7	7.6	3.0	7.8	13.9	10.2	12.0	7.1	32.1	1959
New York, NY	0.4	5.5	5.5	3.7	5.0	7.0	12.2	12.8	9.4	38.4	1952
Oklahoma City, OK	1.6	13.7	13.3	9.3	13.4	15.6	11.3	9.2	5.0	7.4	1981
Omaha, NE	0.4	6.4	8.7	11.9	10.8	15.1	13.9	10.5	4.2	18.1	1972
Orlando, FL	1.3	16.1	21.0	13.1	15.1	12.7	7.2	8.4	2.6	2.6	1991
Philadelphia, PA	0.6	4.8	3.2	2.7	4.5	7.8	10.9	15.0	10.7	39.9	1949
Phoenix, AZ	1.1	8.6	16.4	14.3	17.3	18.9	9.5	9.6	2.4	1.9	1984
Pittsburgh, PA	0.5	4.8	3.7	3.4	4.2	6.5	7.9	13.0	7.6	48.4	1942
Portland, OR	0.9	11.0	10.1	7.3	6.4	10.5	8.4	11.0	7.2	27.1	1966
Providence, RI	0.4	2.2	4.9	4.5	5.6	7.8	5.4	7.5	6.3	55.6	1938
Provo, UT	1.1	7.6	11.6	18.7	14.7	17.7	9.7	7.3	5.0	6.6	1982
Raleigh, NC	1.6	17.5	23.5	17.1	16.0	9.6	6.8	3.7	1.3	2.9	1996
Reno, NV	3.0	11.6	19.1	15.0	13.3	17.7	8.5	5.7	3.1	2.9	1989
Richmond, VA	1.1	8.6	5.9	5.7	7.3	8.7	11.1	14.1	9.0	28.6	1959
Rochester, MN	1.2	12.9	18.5	14.1	11.1	12.4	9.9	9.0	3.7	7.2	1987
Sacramento, CA	0.9	6.3	15.0	7.8	15.2	13.3	11.3	11.9	7.2	11.0	1976
Saint Louis, MO	0.2	3.2	4.0	3.0	3.7	4.3	6.1	9.7	7.6	58.3	1938
Saint Paul, MN	0.7	4.5	5.1	3.5	7.3	9.8	9.4	11.7	6.7	41.2	1952
Salem, OR	1.8	9.1	13.5	15.9	9.5	18.5	9.3	9.3	4.5	8.6	1980
Salt Lake City, UT	1.8	10.6	6.8	5.5	7.4	11.4	9.8	12.2	8.2	26.3	1963
San Antonio, TX	1.6	11.9	15.2	11.3	16.2	13.8	10.1	9.5	5.2	5.2	1984
San Diego, CA	0.8	7.1	10.2	10.6	17.7	20.2	12.2	11.0	3.7	6.6	1978
San Francisco, CA	0.7	6.4	6.5	4.0	5.3	7.1	8.1	7.9	8.7	45.4	1945
San Jose, CA	0.6	7.3	9.6	9.6	12.1	23.6	18.5	10.9	2.7	5.2	1975
Santa Rosa, CA	1.0	6.2	12.3	12.5	17.9	20.9	11.9	8.1	4.4	4.9	1980
Savannah, GA	1.3	11.9	9.0	6.3	11.5	11.7	10.7	13.9	6.9	16.7	1971
Seattle, WA	1.2	17.6	12.0	7.4	7.5	7.2	7.7	8.4	7.4	23.4	1974
Sioux Falls, SD	2.0	19.1	18.4	13.3	10.6	10.4	6.5	8.0	3.0	8.6	1992
Tampa, FL	1.8	13.8	16.5	10.7	11.7	10.3	9.1	12.9	4.9	8.3	1984
Tucson, AZ	0.7	4.6	13.0	12.7	16.5	20.2	11.0	13.4	4.8	3.2	1979
Tulsa, OK	0.4	6.0	6.5	8.2	13.8	20.0	14.5	15.5	6.2	8.9	1972
Virginia Beach, VA	0.4	8.2	10.9	13.1	27.2	19.7	12.3	5.7	1.3	1.1	1984
Washington, DC	1.7	12.5	7.7	3.0	4.7	6.7	9.9	11.6	10.3	31.7	1957
Wichita, KS	0.7	6.9	10.1	11.2	12.8	13.3	9.1	18.0	7.7	10.3	1974
Wilmington, NC	2.3	13.1	14.9	16.2	15.2	11.1	6.2	6.3	5.7	9.1	1988
Winston-Salem, NC	1.1	8.6	13.2	12.5	15.0	14.4	11.0	12.2	4.1	7.7	1980
U.S.	1.2	8.9	13.6	12.8	13.0	14.4	10.0	9.7	4.5	11.9	1980

Note: Figures are percentages except for median year
Source: U.S. Census Bureau, 2019-2023 American Community Survey 5-Year Estimates

Year Housing Structure Built: Metro Area

Metro Area	2020 or Later	2010-2019	2000-2009	1990-1999	1980-1989	1970-1979	1960-1969	1950-1959	1940-1949	Before 1940	Median Year
Albuquerque, NM	0.9	7.5	17.4	16.2	15.7	17.7	8.6	9.5	3.3	3.2	1985
Anchorage, AK	0.5	9.5	16.8	12.5	23.9	22.9	7.8	4.6	0.8	0.7	1986
Ann Arbor, MI	1.2	6.4	13.0	16.0	10.5	15.4	12.3	9.1	4.3	11.8	1978
Athens, GA	1.8	10.2	19.4	18.1	15.0	14.1	9.5	4.6	2.2	5.1	1990
Atlanta, GA	1.7	11.8	23.5	19.3	16.7	11.5	6.8	4.2	1.7	2.8	1993
Austin, TX	4.0	25.5	21.4	14.6	14.3	9.7	4.5	2.8	1.3	2.0	2000
Baltimore, MD	0.6	7.2	9.6	13.0	13.4	12.8	10.3	12.4	6.0	14.6	1975
Billings, MT	2.1	12.3	12.8	12.9	11.6	16.7	7.7	10.1	4.8	9.1	1981
Boise City, ID	3.5	17.3	22.2	17.7	8.9	13.4	4.7	4.2	2.8	5.2	1996
Boston, MA	0.8	7.1	7.5	7.1	10.5	10.6	9.8	10.4	4.8	31.5	1963
Boulder, CO	1.5	11.2	12.5	18.7	14.7	19.1	9.9	5.0	1.4	6.2	1986
Cape Coral, FL	1.9	11.4	29.2	16.2	20.5	12.9	5.0	1.8	0.4	0.6	1995
Cedar Rapids, IA	0.9	10.2	13.2	12.8	7.4	13.6	11.6	10.2	3.6	16.6	1976
Charleston, SC	2.9	19.5	20.3	14.1	14.6	11.3	7.2	4.5	2.2	3.4	1995
Charlotte, NC	2.2	16.8	21.6	17.2	12.3	10.0	7.2	5.8	2.9	4.1	1994
Chicago, IL	0.5	4.6	11.5	10.7	9.2	13.9	11.6	12.4	5.5	20.1	1970
Cincinnati, OH	0.9	6.6	12.1	13.5	10.7	13.4	10.4	11.3	4.7	16.5	1975
Clarksville, TN	2.6	16.3	19.0	18.9	12.1	12.6	7.3	5.5	2.6	3.0	1994
Cleveland, OH	0.5	4.0	7.0	8.8	7.1	12.5	13.3	17.0	7.3	22.6	1962
College Station, TX	2.6	20.0	19.0	15.1	17.1	12.3	5.7	3.9	2.1	2.2	1994
Colorado Springs, CO	1.9	12.9	17.5	15.2	16.4	15.8	8.0	5.9	1.4	4.9	1988
Columbia, MO	1.0	14.0	17.9	16.8	13.2	13.1	9.7	4.6	2.4	7.3	1990
Columbia, SC	1.6	13.8	18.3	16.7	13.5	14.1	8.8	6.7	2.8	3.7	1990
Columbus, OH	1.4	9.5	14.1	14.9	11.5	13.7	10.1	9.2	3.5	12.1	1981
Dallas, TX	2.6	16.9	18.6	14.3	16.5	12.2	7.6	6.6	2.2	2.5	1992
Davenport, IA	0.6	5.3	8.4	7.9	7.0	16.0	13.7	12.1	6.9	22.1	1966
Denver, CO	1.9	13.0	15.6	13.8	13.5	16.4	8.7	8.4	2.4	6.3	1986
Des Moines, IA	2.2	15.6	15.3	12.1	7.8	12.5	7.5	8.3	3.5	15.3	1984
Detroit, MI	0.5	4.0	8.7	11.1	9.0	14.5	12.4	18.3	8.8	12.8	1968
Durham, NC	2.3	17.4	17.1	16.3	14.5	11.4	7.5	5.9	2.9	4.7	1992
El Paso, TX	1.4	16.4	15.2	12.8	14.7	14.6	8.7	9.3	2.8	4.1	1987
Eugene, OR	0.8	7.5	12.2	14.5	9.1	21.0	13.2	8.5	6.7	6.4	1977
Fargo, ND	1.9	19.2	17.1	13.2	9.8	14.3	6.5	7.4	2.2	8.2	1991
Fort Collins, CO	2.2	16.8	18.4	17.5	12.3	16.7	5.8	3.2	1.8	5.3	1993
Fort Wayne, IN	1.0	7.6	11.5	13.5	10.2	14.7	12.3	9.9	4.7	14.5	1976
Fort Worth, TX	2.6	16.9	18.6	14.3	16.5	12.2	7.6	6.6	2.2	2.5	1992
Gainesville, FL	1.8	9.8	17.7	17.7	18.9	16.6	8.4	4.7	1.9	2.5	1988
Green Bay, WI	1.0	8.5	13.4	15.1	11.6	15.5	9.9	9.3	4.0	11.7	1980
Greensboro, NC	0.9	9.0	15.8	16.5	14.4	14.3	10.1	8.9	4.1	6.0	1985
Honolulu, HI	0.6	7.7	9.6	11.4	12.8	23.9	17.3	10.0	3.8	3.0	1977
Houston, TX	2.3	18.1	19.6	12.8	14.7	15.1	7.6	5.4	2.1	2.3	1992
Huntsville, AL	2.9	16.7	18.5	15.2	14.9	9.8	12.7	5.5	1.4	2.3	1992
Indianapolis, IN	1.4	10.4	14.9	15.5	9.9	11.7	10.3	9.4	4.3	12.2	1982
Jacksonville, FL	3.2	13.5	20.2	14.3	16.1	11.4	7.3	7.2	2.9	3.8	1991
Kansas City, MO	1.2	8.8	13.5	13.3	12.0	14.1	11.2	10.6	4.0	11.4	1979
Lafayette, LA	1.4	15.7	15.9	12.0	15.0	15.9	9.4	8.3	3.2	3.4	1987
Las Vegas, NV	1.9	12.3	28.8	25.5	13.7	10.1	4.7	2.0	0.6	0.4	1997
Lexington, KY	1.2	10.3	15.9	16.7	13.1	14.2	10.8	7.5	2.8	7.5	1985
Lincoln, NE	1.1	11.9	14.3	13.5	9.6	14.7	8.9	9.5	3.2	13.1	1981
Little Rock, AR	1.3	13.5	17.7	15.3	13.9	15.3	9.9	6.3	3.2	3.7	1988
Los Angeles, CA	0.6	5.3	6.3	7.4	12.6	15.9	15.0	17.6	7.8	11.5	1969
Louisville, KY	1.1	8.4	13.5	13.4	9.3	14.8	11.1	11.7	5.1	11.6	1977
Madison, WI	1.2	11.5	15.9	14.2	10.4	13.6	9.2	7.5	3.3	13.1	1983
Manchester, NH	0.5	5.4	9.6	10.5	20.2	15.3	9.2	7.3	3.6	18.6	1977
McAllen, TX	1.6	18.0	27.8	19.0	15.8	9.7	3.9	2.1	1.1	1.1	1999

Table continued on following page.

Metro Area	2020 or Later	2010 -2019	2000 -2009	1990 -1999	1980 -1989	1970 -1979	1960 -1969	1950 -1959	1940 -1949	Before 1940	Median Year
Memphis, TN	0.9	7.4	15.0	16.1	13.3	15.3	10.5	11.7	4.8	4.9	1982
Miami, FL	1.0	7.4	12.8	13.8	19.0	20.4	11.5	9.6	2.6	2.0	1982
Midland, TX	2.4	24.0	11.8	9.7	17.4	10.3	6.8	13.7	2.4	1.3	1989
Milwaukee, WI	0.7	5.5	8.2	10.4	7.6	13.1	11.6	15.3	7.0	20.7	1966
Minneapolis, MN	1.3	8.6	13.3	13.4	13.8	13.9	9.3	9.1	3.6	13.6	1980
Nashville, TN	3.1	17.7	18.1	15.3	13.0	11.9	8.2	6.0	2.5	4.3	1993
New Orleans, LA	0.4	5.1	9.9	6.8	13.1	19.6	13.9	10.8	5.1	15.2	1973
New York, NY	0.5	5.3	6.6	5.9	7.8	9.6	13.3	15.3	8.3	27.3	1959
Oklahoma City, OK	1.7	13.5	14.4	10.3	13.8	16.5	11.2	8.6	4.3	5.6	1983
Omaha, NE	1.3	10.7	14.3	11.8	9.6	13.9	11.2	8.2	3.4	15.6	1978
Orlando, FL	2.1	15.3	21.5	17.9	18.5	11.6	5.5	4.9	1.1	1.5	1994
Philadelphia, PA	0.7	5.3	7.9	8.9	9.9	12.2	11.7	14.9	7.0	21.5	1966
Phoenix, AZ	1.9	12.2	23.7	17.9	16.2	14.9	6.3	4.8	1.1	0.9	1993
Pittsburgh, PA	0.6	4.6	6.4	7.3	7.7	11.8	11.3	16.3	8.2	25.8	1960
Portland, OR	1.4	11.1	14.0	16.3	10.9	16.0	8.0	6.7	4.2	11.3	1983
Providence, RI	0.4	3.6	6.3	7.6	11.6	11.9	10.3	11.6	5.9	30.8	1962
Provo, UT	3.7	22.3	22.9	16.1	8.5	11.7	4.3	4.2	2.6	3.9	1999
Raleigh, NC	2.9	20.7	23.7	19.4	13.7	8.2	4.8	3.0	1.2	2.5	1999
Reno, NV	2.3	10.8	21.1	16.9	14.2	17.6	7.9	4.6	2.3	2.3	1991
Richmond, VA	1.3	10.3	14.2	14.3	15.3	13.7	9.3	8.5	4.2	8.8	1984
Rochester, MN	1.2	10.4	18.3	13.5	10.5	13.0	8.9	7.5	3.4	13.3	1984
Sacramento, CA	1.2	6.8	17.1	14.0	16.3	17.3	10.4	9.3	3.3	4.2	1983
Saint Louis, MO	0.8	6.3	11.4	11.6	11.1	12.8	12.2	12.3	5.4	16.1	1973
Saint Paul, MN	1.3	8.6	13.3	13.4	13.8	13.9	9.3	9.1	3.6	13.6	1980
Salem, OR	1.6	8.1	14.1	16.7	9.7	21.1	9.8	7.1	3.9	7.9	1980
Salt Lake City, UT	1.9	14.7	14.4	14.0	11.3	16.8	8.3	8.1	3.2	7.2	1986
San Antonio, TX	3.0	18.3	18.5	12.4	13.9	11.8	7.6	6.7	3.7	4.0	1992
San Diego, CA	0.8	6.5	12.0	11.5	18.6	21.7	11.6	10.1	3.1	4.1	1980
San Francisco, CA	0.7	5.6	7.7	7.8	10.6	14.2	12.8	13.4	7.7	19.5	1967
San Jose, CA	0.9	8.8	9.2	9.6	11.7	20.4	17.4	13.7	3.4	4.8	1975
Santa Rosa, CA	1.0	5.3	10.1	13.2	18.0	19.8	11.8	8.5	4.2	8.0	1979
Savannah, GA	2.2	15.8	19.4	13.1	12.7	11.0	6.7	7.5	3.8	7.7	1990
Seattle, WA	1.3	12.4	14.7	14.0	13.7	12.9	10.5	6.8	3.9	9.7	1985
Sioux Falls, SD	1.9	17.3	17.9	13.6	9.2	11.2	6.3	7.4	3.1	12.2	1990
Tampa, FL	1.6	10.2	15.4	13.0	19.8	18.9	8.7	7.9	1.9	2.5	1985
Tucson, AZ	1.2	7.5	18.2	16.5	17.1	18.6	8.3	7.9	2.8	1.9	1986
Tulsa, OK	1.2	11.0	13.9	11.1	13.9	18.2	10.3	9.8	4.1	6.7	1981
Virginia Beach, VA	1.0	9.6	12.6	14.0	18.1	14.3	11.5	9.1	4.2	5.6	1983
Washington, DC	1.2	10.7	14.1	12.9	15.2	13.0	11.5	8.7	4.7	8.1	1983
Wichita, KS	0.9	7.8	12.0	12.8	12.5	13.0	8.1	15.9	6.1	10.7	1977
Wilmington, NC	2.7	17.1	23.5	18.8	14.4	9.9	4.4	3.2	2.4	3.6	1996
Winston-Salem, NC	1.0	8.7	15.6	15.9	14.5	15.5	10.1	9.0	3.7	6.1	1984
U.S.	1.2	8.9	13.6	12.8	13.0	14.4	10.0	9.7	4.5	11.9	1980

Note: Figures are percentages except for median year; Figures cover the Metropolitan Statistical Area (MSA)
Source: U.S. Census Bureau, 2019-2023 American Community Survey 5-Year Estimates

Gross Monthly Rent: City

City	Under $500	$500 -$999	$1,000 -$1,499	$1,500 -$1,999	$2,000 -$2,499	$2,500 -$2,999	$3,000 and up	Median ($)
Albuquerque, NM	5.3	37.7	35.1	16.1	3.9	0.8	1.1	1,085
Anchorage, AK	3.5	14.0	35.7	25.6	12.6	5.5	3.0	1,453
Ann Arbor, MI	3.0	11.6	32.6	26.6	14.6	4.9	6.7	1,552
Athens, GA	3.8	33.4	37.8	17.1	5.0	1.5	1.3	1,162
Atlanta, GA	9.7	10.8	22.9	28.6	16.1	6.4	5.6	1,617
Austin, TX	2.5	4.7	32.4	33.5	15.4	6.4	5.0	1,655
Baltimore, MD	13.0	15.9	35.9	21.5	8.9	2.8	2.0	1,290
Billings, MT	7.9	34.2	37.7	14.4	3.3	0.7	1.7	1,097
Boise City, ID	4.1	15.0	41.7	26.5	9.3	1.9	1.6	1,359
Boston, MA	12.2	9.1	9.8	15.4	18.7	13.2	21.6	2,093
Boulder, CO	2.9	4.3	17.5	29.8	18.2	10.7	16.5	1,924
Cape Coral, FL	0.8	4.6	24.6	39.7	20.2	6.3	3.7	1,751
Cedar Rapids, IA	7.5	49.3	31.3	8.7	0.9	0.3	2.0	925
Charleston, SC	4.4	7.5	29.8	31.4	16.4	4.4	6.1	1,632
Charlotte, NC	2.7	10.1	36.9	33.9	10.9	3.2	2.3	1,504
Chicago, IL	7.2	17.6	32.2	20.1	11.6	5.4	5.9	1,380
Cincinnati, OH	11.8	43.6	26.9	11.1	3.9	1.5	1.3	953
Clarksville, TN	2.4	26.4	43.4	20.7	6.1	0.8	0.3	1,215
Cleveland, OH	17.2	43.0	26.0	9.4	2.6	0.9	0.8	894
College Station, TX	2.3	31.8	36.6	18.4	6.6	3.1	1.1	1,168
Colorado Springs, CO	2.7	10.7	32.8	30.0	15.9	4.3	3.6	1,562
Columbia, MO	4.0	39.3	38.9	9.8	5.8	1.4	0.8	1,067
Columbia, SC	8.4	26.7	42.3	16.5	5.4	0.5	0.2	1,158
Columbus, OH	4.5	22.1	46.5	19.4	5.3	1.2	0.9	1,224
Dallas, TX	3.1	12.2	42.5	25.9	9.5	3.4	3.4	1,403
Davenport, IA	7.1	52.5	29.5	6.8	1.6	0.1	2.4	930
Denver, CO	5.7	6.3	22.4	28.8	19.9	9.0	7.9	1,770
Des Moines, IA	5.4	39.0	40.2	12.9	2.0	0.2	0.3	1,054
Detroit, MI	11.7	35.1	39.5	10.0	2.5	0.8	0.4	1,034
Durham, NC	4.9	15.5	37.1	29.7	8.9	2.1	1.8	1,412
El Paso, TX	8.8	37.4	37.3	12.4	3.1	0.6	0.5	1,041
Eugene, OR	4.5	22.0	34.3	25.4	8.7	2.5	2.6	1,347
Fargo, ND	4.3	56.5	27.7	8.1	1.6	0.7	1.1	916
Fort Collins, CO	2.5	10.8	26.1	33.0	19.7	6.0	1.9	1,661
Fort Wayne, IN	6.7	48.7	37.3	5.3	1.4	0.4	0.3	959
Fort Worth, TX	2.6	13.5	40.6	25.3	12.3	3.4	2.2	1,412
Gainesville, FL	3.6	27.6	37.8	20.0	7.3	2.2	1.6	1,214
Green Bay, WI	6.7	55.0	31.7	5.1	0.7	0.1	0.6	904
Greensboro, NC	4.8	31.8	45.3	12.5	3.2	0.8	1.5	1,114
Honolulu, HI	5.7	7.6	21.8	26.2	16.6	7.5	14.5	1,783
Houston, TX	2.7	21.1	39.5	23.4	8.1	2.6	2.7	1,313
Huntsville, AL	4.8	38.7	37.7	14.0	2.9	0.5	1.3	1,078
Indianapolis, IN	4.8	32.8	43.9	13.7	3.2	1.0	0.6	1,112
Jacksonville, FL	4.9	16.1	38.9	26.9	9.7	2.3	1.2	1,375
Kansas City, MO	6.7	25.9	41.6	18.6	4.6	1.5	1.2	1,186
Lafayette, LA	6.5	37.0	39.7	13.7	2.6	0.2	0.4	1,065
Las Vegas, NV	3.1	14.4	35.9	29.4	11.7	3.5	1.9	1,456
Lexington, KY	4.4	36.0	40.3	13.9	3.8	1.2	0.5	1,101
Lincoln, NE	4.7	41.3	37.3	12.0	3.0	0.5	1.4	1,045
Little Rock, AR	5.2	38.1	39.8	12.0	2.8	0.8	1.2	1,067
Los Angeles, CA	4.6	7.2	20.1	23.9	18.3	10.6	15.3	1,879
Louisville, KY	9.7	34.0	39.6	12.5	2.8	0.7	0.7	1,069
Madison, WI	3.6	15.5	41.6	26.0	8.2	2.4	2.7	1,364
Manchester, NH	5.5	12.8	34.2	31.7	12.5	1.9	1.3	1,465
McAllen, TX	8.3	40.3	37.2	11.2	2.0	0.9	0.0	1,017

Table continued on following page.

City	Under $500	$500-$999	$1,000-$1,499	$1,500-$1,999	$2,000-$2,499	$2,500-$2,999	$3,000 and up	Median ($)
Memphis, TN	4.9	32.5	43.3	15.2	2.8	0.7	0.6	1,123
Miami, FL	8.4	9.2	25.4	22.3	16.1	8.1	10.5	1,657
Midland, TX	3.2	15.5	38.6	24.4	11.7	4.2	2.3	1,407
Milwaukee, WI	7.0	39.6	38.2	10.7	2.4	1.0	1.1	1,033
Minneapolis, MN	8.7	16.4	35.0	22.5	10.8	3.3	3.3	1,329
Nashville, TN	6.2	10.7	34.1	28.4	12.8	4.5	3.3	1,486
New Orleans, LA	10.0	21.7	38.2	19.5	6.2	2.7	1.7	1,211
New York, NY	8.3	10.0	19.2	22.4	16.2	8.5	15.4	1,779
Oklahoma City, OK	5.3	36.3	40.4	13.3	2.8	1.1	0.7	1,083
Omaha, NE	4.4	29.7	43.5	16.1	4.3	0.8	1.3	1,150
Orlando, FL	3.1	6.0	30.0	36.5	17.1	4.7	2.6	1,650
Philadelphia, PA	8.5	18.1	35.8	22.6	8.7	3.1	3.2	1,323
Phoenix, AZ	3.5	13.5	36.2	29.1	12.0	3.7	2.0	1,458
Pittsburgh, PA	10.6	21.9	35.1	18.4	8.3	3.3	2.4	1,221
Portland, OR	4.6	9.6	30.1	29.6	15.0	6.3	4.8	1,596
Providence, RI	16.9	11.3	33.2	22.3	10.5	3.4	2.4	1,333
Provo, UT	5.6	28.6	40.3	16.6	6.4	1.9	0.5	1,152
Raleigh, NC	2.5	9.3	41.1	33.8	8.8	2.7	1.8	1,468
Reno, NV	4.9	15.0	33.3	26.7	13.4	4.0	2.7	1,453
Richmond, VA	9.4	14.9	41.0	24.1	7.9	1.9	0.8	1,314
Rochester, MN	6.3	23.1	32.8	23.3	8.8	1.7	4.0	1,316
Sacramento, CA	4.4	10.1	23.1	31.7	19.4	7.9	3.3	1,694
Saint Louis, MO	9.1	43.5	33.0	9.9	3.0	0.9	0.7	978
Saint Paul, MN	9.5	16.7	41.4	20.1	9.0	1.6	1.7	1,248
Salem, OR	5.6	16.1	43.1	24.0	8.2	1.8	1.2	1,323
Salt Lake City, UT	6.7	16.6	37.5	23.0	10.1	3.7	2.5	1,343
San Antonio, TX	4.8	21.4	43.5	21.8	5.7	1.6	1.2	1,258
San Diego, CA	2.3	3.9	11.3	22.8	21.9	16.0	21.8	2,223
San Francisco, CA	7.8	8.1	11.1	11.9	13.2	10.9	36.9	2,419
San Jose, CA	3.7	4.7	6.6	12.7	18.3	17.6	36.5	2,617
Santa Rosa, CA	4.1	5.1	12.9	24.0	23.2	15.4	15.3	2,084
Savannah, GA	6.6	17.0	41.8	23.1	7.7	1.9	2.0	1,302
Seattle, WA	5.0	4.2	15.6	25.4	21.5	13.0	15.5	1,998
Sioux Falls, SD	4.5	46.5	36.9	8.1	2.4	0.3	1.2	993
Tampa, FL	6.5	11.9	27.9	27.1	14.9	6.8	4.9	1,567
Tucson, AZ	4.5	38.5	36.3	15.0	3.5	0.8	1.3	1,079
Tulsa, OK	7.3	42.9	36.4	9.1	2.1	1.0	1.2	998
Virginia Beach, VA	1.9	5.3	31.3	38.7	14.9	3.9	4.0	1,649
Washington, DC	7.4	7.8	17.8	21.2	16.8	11.4	17.6	1,900
Wichita, KS	4.8	50.2	34.2	7.8	2.1	0.3	0.7	960
Wilmington, NC	6.3	17.3	40.7	25.1	7.1	1.9	1.5	1,311
Winston-Salem, NC	6.7	40.1	36.5	11.4	3.5	0.8	1.0	1,033
U.S.	6.5	22.3	29.5	20.2	10.8	4.8	5.9	1,348

Note: Figures are percentages except for Median; Gross rent is the contract rent plus the estimated average monthly cost of utilities (electricity, gas, and water and sewer) and fuels (oil, coal, kerosene, wood, etc.) if these are paid by the renter (or paid for the renter by someone else).
Source: U.S. Census Bureau, 2019-2023 American Community Survey 5-Year Estimates

Gross Monthly Rent: Metro Area

Metro Area	Under $500	$500 -$999	$1,000 -$1,499	$1,500 -$1,999	$2,000 -$2,499	$2,500 -2,999	$3,000 and up	Median ($)
Albuquerque, NM	5.5	36.2	35.3	16.7	4.3	0.9	1.1	1,102
Anchorage, AK	3.9	15.2	36.0	25.1	12.2	4.8	2.7	1,422
Ann Arbor, MI	4.3	14.9	39.0	23.1	10.3	3.5	4.7	1,400
Athens, GA	4.0	34.6	36.7	16.4	4.9	2.0	1.4	1,144
Atlanta, GA	3.5	10.4	31.9	33.0	14.4	4.1	2.7	1,563
Austin, TX	2.2	6.5	32.0	32.0	16.4	6.3	4.6	1,646
Baltimore, MD	6.9	10.5	29.1	28.1	15.8	5.6	3.9	1,562
Billings, MT	8.5	35.8	36.1	14.7	2.8	0.7	1.4	1,072
Boise City, ID	4.7	16.9	37.0	26.4	10.2	2.7	2.2	1,383
Boston, MA	9.4	8.3	13.6	21.1	19.8	12.2	15.5	1,940
Boulder, CO	3.0	4.7	17.7	31.3	20.8	10.0	12.5	1,893
Cape Coral, FL	2.9	8.6	31.7	34.5	14.0	4.2	4.1	1,597
Cedar Rapids, IA	7.8	50.9	29.5	8.0	1.3	0.3	2.2	899
Charleston, SC	3.1	11.1	36.7	27.9	13.4	4.0	3.8	1,488
Charlotte, NC	3.8	18.7	36.7	27.1	9.1	2.5	2.0	1,377
Chicago, IL	5.8	16.7	35.4	21.8	11.0	4.6	4.6	1,378
Cincinnati, OH	8.2	37.8	34.1	12.7	4.4	1.5	1.4	1,047
Clarksville, TN	4.4	33.0	39.4	17.7	4.4	0.6	0.5	1,141
Cleveland, OH	9.8	40.6	34.0	10.8	2.6	0.9	1.3	996
College Station, TX	4.0	32.0	38.0	16.6	5.7	2.2	1.4	1,146
Colorado Springs, CO	2.7	10.6	30.1	29.6	18.6	5.0	3.4	1,611
Columbia, MO	4.7	41.2	38.4	9.2	4.6	1.1	0.8	1,041
Columbia, SC	5.2	31.0	41.5	15.6	5.0	0.9	0.9	1,145
Columbus, OH	5.1	24.3	43.9	18.5	5.5	1.4	1.2	1,208
Dallas, TX	2.1	9.7	37.7	28.7	13.8	4.7	3.3	1,509
Davenport, IA	11.1	50.2	27.2	7.3	1.5	0.8	1.9	899
Denver, CO	3.6	5.3	21.2	32.6	21.1	9.5	6.7	1,805
Des Moines, IA	4.6	33.5	42.0	15.1	3.4	0.5	0.9	1,113
Detroit, MI	7.5	26.8	41.4	16.4	4.7	1.3	1.8	1,162
Durham, NC	5.0	18.6	36.6	26.5	8.7	2.4	2.3	1,374
El Paso, TX	8.7	37.2	37.0	13.0	3.1	0.5	0.4	1,045
Eugene, OR	5.4	23.6	36.5	23.0	7.6	1.9	1.9	1,287
Fargo, ND	4.7	52.7	29.3	9.2	2.5	0.8	0.9	940
Fort Collins, CO	2.6	10.0	25.7	33.1	18.9	6.6	3.1	1,677
Fort Wayne, IN	6.6	48.2	36.5	6.1	1.7	0.5	0.4	963
Fort Worth, TX	2.1	9.7	37.7	28.7	13.8	4.7	3.3	1,509
Gainesville, FL	3.9	27.5	36.4	20.0	7.2	2.6	2.3	1,219
Green Bay, WI	4.8	50.7	35.3	6.6	1.4	0.4	0.8	959
Greensboro, NC	7.6	37.7	39.7	10.5	2.6	0.7	1.2	1,045
Honolulu, HI	4.7	6.3	16.7	20.6	15.8	11.3	24.6	2,054
Houston, TX	2.6	17.5	39.1	24.9	10.1	3.2	2.6	1,378
Huntsville, AL	4.8	37.6	36.8	14.6	4.3	0.6	1.2	1,091
Indianapolis, IN	4.8	30.7	41.9	15.6	4.7	1.4	0.9	1,142
Jacksonville, FL	4.3	15.8	36.2	27.0	11.0	2.9	2.7	1,416
Kansas City, MO	5.4	25.3	41.7	18.9	5.6	1.4	1.6	1,201
Lafayette, LA	11.3	44.1	33.2	9.1	1.7	0.3	0.2	954
Las Vegas, NV	1.8	12.2	34.8	31.6	13.6	3.7	2.2	1,518
Lexington, KY	5.5	38.0	38.7	13.0	3.1	1.1	0.5	1,070
Lincoln, NE	4.8	41.4	37.2	11.8	2.9	0.5	1.4	1,043
Little Rock, AR	6.2	43.2	37.0	10.4	1.7	0.6	0.9	1,007
Los Angeles, CA	3.5	5.8	16.8	24.5	21.1	12.0	16.3	1,987
Louisville, KY	9.1	34.6	40.1	12.2	2.6	0.7	0.8	1,064
Madison, WI	3.9	19.6	41.6	23.8	6.9	1.9	2.2	1,300
Manchester, NH	5.5	11.2	31.2	31.7	14.5	3.8	2.0	1,532
McAllen, TX	11.1	48.5	30.9	7.4	1.4	0.5	0.2	925

Table continued on following page.

Metro Area	Under $500	$500 -$999	$1,000 -$1,499	$1,500 -$1,999	$2,000 -$2,499	$2,500 -2,999	$3,000 and up	Median ($)
Memphis, TN	4.9	30.4	42.2	16.0	4.3	1.2	1.0	1,153
Miami, FL	3.9	6.5	23.2	30.3	19.3	8.6	8.2	1,770
Midland, TX	3.7	17.8	38.4	23.7	10.7	3.8	2.0	1,377
Milwaukee, WI	6.0	33.5	39.6	14.3	3.8	1.5	1.3	1,105
Minneapolis, MN	6.6	14.0	36.6	25.6	10.8	3.3	3.2	1,396
Nashville, TN	5.4	15.0	34.3	27.1	11.6	3.7	2.8	1,434
New Orleans, LA	7.3	24.9	41.7	18.2	5.0	1.7	1.1	1,182
New York, NY	7.3	9.0	20.0	24.4	16.9	8.6	13.8	1,780
Oklahoma City, OK	5.3	36.8	39.1	13.4	3.1	1.1	1.1	1,081
Omaha, NE	5.0	29.1	42.6	16.6	4.3	0.9	1.5	1,152
Orlando, FL	2.1	8.2	28.7	34.6	18.0	5.3	3.0	1,659
Philadelphia, PA	6.4	14.6	35.3	25.2	11.2	3.7	3.7	1,413
Phoenix, AZ	2.7	10.8	31.5	30.9	15.3	5.2	3.5	1,581
Pittsburgh, PA	11.8	37.3	32.0	11.5	4.4	1.5	1.6	1,011
Portland, OR	3.4	7.7	28.4	33.9	16.2	6.3	4.1	1,654
Providence, RI	12.9	18.9	35.1	20.9	7.8	2.5	1.9	1,236
Provo, UT	3.1	16.5	34.5	27.9	12.6	3.7	1.8	1,434
Raleigh, NC	3.4	13.4	36.5	31.2	10.0	3.4	2.1	1,459
Reno, NV	4.2	14.7	31.6	27.3	14.8	4.0	3.4	1,491
Richmond, VA	5.5	14.0	39.6	27.9	9.1	1.8	2.0	1,388
Rochester, MN	7.9	29.2	31.6	19.9	7.1	1.3	3.0	1,195
Sacramento, CA	3.6	8.3	24.6	29.4	19.8	8.6	5.7	1,729
Saint Louis, MO	6.4	36.8	37.9	12.7	3.4	1.2	1.8	1,073
Saint Paul, MN	6.6	14.0	36.6	25.6	10.8	3.3	3.2	1,396
Salem, OR	4.9	16.5	43.8	24.6	7.3	1.8	1.1	1,324
Salt Lake City, UT	3.9	11.4	35.8	29.9	13.2	3.6	2.2	1,486
San Antonio, TX	4.4	19.8	41.8	22.8	7.7	2.0	1.4	1,299
San Diego, CA	2.2	4.0	12.0	24.8	22.5	14.8	19.6	2,154
San Francisco, CA	5.1	5.6	9.5	14.1	18.4	15.0	32.3	2,426
San Jose, CA	2.7	3.7	5.4	10.8	16.8	17.8	42.7	2,794
Santa Rosa, CA	4.1	6.8	13.4	21.5	22.3	14.4	17.4	2,093
Savannah, GA	4.2	17.2	38.3	28.2	8.4	1.9	1.8	1,370
Seattle, WA	4.0	4.8	16.7	28.3	22.6	11.5	12.2	1,932
Sioux Falls, SD	5.6	46.3	36.0	8.1	2.6	0.3	1.1	987
Tampa, FL	3.2	13.0	34.1	27.7	13.7	4.8	3.5	1,497
Tucson, AZ	4.3	32.8	35.8	18.7	4.9	1.4	2.1	1,154
Tulsa, OK	7.1	39.7	37.8	10.4	2.9	1.0	1.1	1,034
Virginia Beach, VA	5.0	13.8	37.7	28.0	10.3	2.6	2.7	1,416
Washington, DC	3.7	4.7	14.3	28.7	23.5	12.3	12.9	1,975
Wichita, KS	5.7	48.1	34.1	8.5	2.5	0.5	0.6	969
Wilmington, NC	5.1	19.5	40.4	23.1	7.7	2.0	2.3	1,313
Winston-Salem, NC	7.6	45.5	32.7	10.3	2.5	0.7	0.6	973
U.S.	6.5	22.3	29.5	20.2	10.8	4.8	5.9	1,348

Note: Figures are percentages except for Median; Gross rent is the contract rent plus the estimated average monthly cost of utilities (electricity, gas, and water and sewer) and fuels (oil, coal, kerosene, wood, etc.) if these are paid by the renter (or paid for the renter by someone else); Figures cover the Metropolitan Statistical Area (MSA)
Source: U.S. Census Bureau, 2019-2023 American Community Survey 5-Year Estimates

Highest Level of Education: City

City	Less than H.S.	H.S. Diploma	Some College, No Deg.	Associate Degree	Bachelors Degree	Masters Degree	Profess. School Degree	Doctorate Degree
Albuquerque, NM	9.1	21.6	21.2	9.5	20.9	12.0	2.8	2.9
Anchorage, AK	6.0	24.5	23.2	8.6	23.4	9.9	2.7	1.7
Ann Arbor, MI	2.4	7.0	8.9	4.0	30.5	26.4	8.7	12.1
Athens, GA	10.1	17.7	16.5	7.0	24.3	15.3	2.9	6.2
Atlanta, GA	7.0	16.0	13.6	5.0	32.8	16.8	5.7	3.0
Austin, TX	8.4	13.2	14.8	5.4	36.2	15.9	3.6	2.5
Baltimore, MD	12.8	27.9	18.4	5.5	18.1	11.7	3.1	2.5
Billings, MT	4.5	27.6	22.5	8.3	25.0	7.7	2.6	1.7
Boise City, ID	5.2	19.3	21.5	7.3	29.2	12.0	3.1	2.2
Boston, MA	11.1	18.3	11.6	4.9	28.5	16.4	5.2	3.9
Boulder, CO	3.1	6.4	10.2	3.5	36.9	25.7	5.1	9.1
Cape Coral, FL	6.8	35.3	22.6	9.5	16.7	6.0	1.7	1.3
Cedar Rapids, IA	5.9	25.9	22.4	12.9	22.2	7.8	2.1	0.8
Charleston, SC	4.1	15.4	16.0	6.8	35.5	13.8	5.2	3.2
Charlotte, NC	10.4	16.6	17.5	8.0	30.4	12.8	2.9	1.3
Chicago, IL	13.2	21.3	16.4	5.8	24.9	12.8	3.6	2.0
Cincinnati, OH	10.3	24.1	17.0	7.3	23.2	11.7	3.8	2.5
Clarksville, TN	5.8	27.4	24.2	12.0	18.9	9.4	1.2	1.1
Cleveland, OH	16.5	33.5	21.6	7.1	12.5	5.8	2.2	0.9
College Station, TX	5.4	14.4	16.9	6.2	29.5	16.1	2.0	9.5
Colorado Springs, CO	5.4	19.2	23.0	10.6	25.2	12.8	2.1	1.9
Columbia, MO	4.7	16.9	15.7	6.2	30.1	15.7	4.8	5.9
Columbia, SC	9.1	19.2	18.2	7.4	25.2	12.7	5.0	3.1
Columbus, OH	10.2	25.2	19.2	7.2	24.1	10.2	2.1	1.8
Dallas, TX	19.2	21.5	16.7	5.1	22.9	9.7	3.4	1.4
Davenport, IA	7.4	28.8	22.1	11.7	18.9	8.2	1.8	1.1
Denver, CO	8.6	14.8	15.7	5.3	33.8	15.0	4.7	2.2
Des Moines, IA	12.7	29.1	20.0	9.1	19.9	6.3	1.8	0.9
Detroit, MI	16.6	33.2	25.4	7.2	10.5	5.4	1.0	0.7
Durham, NC	8.6	15.4	13.7	6.6	28.8	16.9	4.5	5.5
El Paso, TX	18.1	24.4	21.3	8.8	18.3	6.7	1.4	1.0
Eugene, OR	5.2	17.4	24.3	8.8	23.7	13.5	3.6	3.5
Fargo, ND	4.7	18.7	20.7	12.7	29.0	9.9	2.0	2.3
Fort Collins, CO	2.4	13.5	16.1	8.2	34.3	18.9	2.8	3.9
Fort Wayne, IN	11.1	28.7	21.8	9.9	19.4	7.2	1.1	0.9
Fort Worth, TX	15.7	24.7	20.5	7.4	20.6	8.4	1.6	1.1
Gainesville, FL	5.7	17.7	14.9	10.0	25.7	15.1	4.2	6.8
Green Bay, WI	11.0	31.4	20.4	11.7	18.4	5.3	1.2	0.7
Greensboro, NC	9.9	21.5	20.1	8.7	24.2	11.3	2.3	2.1
Honolulu, HI	9.1	22.8	17.2	10.1	25.2	9.9	3.4	2.2
Houston, TX	19.7	21.5	16.6	6.2	21.3	9.6	3.2	1.9
Huntsville, AL	8.4	17.3	20.8	7.3	26.7	14.8	2.3	2.3
Indianapolis, IN	12.5	26.8	18.9	7.7	21.7	8.8	2.3	1.4
Jacksonville, FL	9.2	28.2	20.7	10.0	21.6	7.4	1.7	1.1
Kansas City, MO	8.2	25.0	21.6	7.4	23.8	10.1	2.7	1.2
Lafayette, LA	9.1	25.3	18.9	6.0	27.1	7.7	4.0	1.9
Las Vegas, NV	14.2	26.7	23.7	8.1	17.3	6.9	2.1	1.0
Lexington, KY	7.6	19.0	18.5	7.6	26.5	12.9	4.3	3.6
Lincoln, NE	7.0	20.4	20.3	11.4	26.4	9.8	2.3	2.5
Little Rock, AR	7.7	21.2	20.7	6.5	25.0	11.7	4.7	2.6
Los Angeles, CA	20.7	18.5	16.6	6.3	24.5	8.7	3.1	1.6
Louisville, KY	9.5	27.7	21.0	8.4	19.9	9.6	2.4	1.5
Madison, WI	4.3	14.6	14.4	7.5	33.5	16.0	3.7	6.0
Manchester, NH	11.3	29.1	18.1	8.0	22.5	8.8	1.3	0.9
McAllen, TX	20.1	20.7	20.6	6.5	20.3	7.6	2.9	1.2

Table continued on following page.

City	Less than H.S.	H.S. Diploma	Some College, No Deg.	Associate Degree	Bachelors Degree	Masters Degree	Profess. School Degree	Doctorate Degree
Memphis, TN	12.6	30.6	22.5	6.1	16.9	7.9	2.0	1.4
Miami, FL	20.0	25.2	11.6	7.5	21.5	8.8	4.1	1.3
Midland, TX	13.5	22.5	22.4	8.0	23.9	7.4	1.4	1.0
Milwaukee, WI	14.5	30.8	20.9	7.3	17.2	7.0	1.4	1.0
Minneapolis, MN	8.9	13.8	15.7	7.2	32.7	14.8	4.1	2.9
Nashville, TN	9.8	20.2	17.0	6.0	29.1	11.7	3.4	2.7
New Orleans, LA	10.9	21.3	20.7	5.2	22.5	12.0	4.8	2.6
New York, NY	16.3	23.0	13.2	6.5	23.6	12.4	3.3	1.7
Oklahoma City, OK	12.2	24.5	21.3	8.0	21.5	8.5	2.6	1.3
Omaha, NE	9.5	21.3	21.3	7.7	25.6	9.7	3.2	1.8
Orlando, FL	8.1	23.1	15.7	10.9	26.1	11.2	3.2	1.8
Philadelphia, PA	12.6	29.8	16.4	6.5	19.4	10.2	3.0	2.1
Phoenix, AZ	15.6	23.1	21.1	7.9	19.9	8.9	2.3	1.3
Pittsburgh, PA	5.7	23.7	14.7	8.0	24.6	14.1	4.5	4.6
Portland, OR	6.7	14.7	18.5	6.7	32.1	14.2	4.5	2.7
Providence, RI	18.1	27.5	14.8	4.9	18.3	9.7	3.5	3.3
Provo, UT	7.5	14.4	24.4	8.7	31.1	9.5	1.7	2.6
Raleigh, NC	7.5	15.9	16.2	7.4	32.5	14.3	3.5	2.6
Reno, NV	10.7	22.8	22.6	8.3	21.4	9.4	2.8	2.2
Richmond, VA	10.7	21.2	18.8	5.3	26.0	12.3	3.5	2.2
Rochester, MN	5.5	18.9	14.9	10.6	27.7	13.2	5.2	3.9
Sacramento, CA	13.1	20.5	21.6	8.4	22.9	8.7	3.3	1.6
Saint Louis, MO	9.5	24.5	19.7	6.1	22.0	12.1	3.4	2.7
Saint Paul, MN	11.1	20.8	16.9	7.7	25.2	12.3	3.3	2.8
Salem, OR	11.3	22.4	25.4	9.3	19.3	8.6	2.1	1.5
Salt Lake City, UT	8.4	17.1	16.9	6.7	28.9	13.6	4.7	3.7
San Antonio, TX	15.7	25.6	21.8	8.2	17.7	7.7	2.1	1.3
San Diego, CA	9.8	15.0	17.8	7.5	28.8	13.6	3.6	3.8
San Francisco, CA	11.2	11.3	12.0	5.3	35.1	16.7	4.9	3.4
San Jose, CA	14.5	16.4	15.5	7.1	26.2	15.1	2.1	3.1
Santa Rosa, CA	14.5	19.2	21.9	9.7	21.3	9.0	3.2	1.2
Savannah, GA	10.1	27.0	23.7	7.2	20.6	8.1	2.0	1.3
Seattle, WA	4.3	9.5	12.9	5.8	37.6	20.5	5.3	4.2
Sioux Falls, SD	6.9	24.3	20.1	11.2	25.4	8.2	2.5	1.3
Tampa, FL	10.2	22.5	14.7	8.0	26.3	11.7	4.4	2.2
Tucson, AZ	12.7	23.0	25.2	9.0	17.7	9.0	1.6	1.9
Tulsa, OK	12.4	25.0	21.2	8.2	20.8	8.0	3.0	1.5
Virginia Beach, VA	5.3	21.3	22.4	10.5	25.0	11.4	2.3	1.8
Washington, DC	7.2	14.5	11.8	2.9	26.1	22.7	10.3	4.6
Wichita, KS	12.0	26.0	23.0	8.1	19.7	8.5	1.6	1.1
Wilmington, NC	6.5	18.0	18.9	10.8	29.2	11.1	3.3	2.3
Winston-Salem, NC	11.6	23.7	19.5	7.9	21.6	10.2	2.8	2.6
U.S.	10.6	26.2	19.4	8.8	21.3	9.8	2.3	1.6

Note: Figures cover persons age 25 and over
Source: U.S. Census Bureau, 2019-2023 American Community Survey 5-Year Estimates

Highest Level of Education: Metro Area

Metro Area	Less than H.S.	H.S. Diploma	Some College, No Deg.	Associate Degree	Bachelors Degree	Masters Degree	Profess. School Degree	Doctorate Degree
Albuquerque, NM	9.7	23.6	22.0	9.7	19.2	11.0	2.4	2.5
Anchorage, AK	5.9	27.1	23.6	9.4	21.3	9.0	2.3	1.4
Ann Arbor, MI	4.2	14.2	16.8	6.7	27.1	19.4	5.1	6.5
Athens, GA	10.2	21.4	17.5	7.5	21.9	13.4	3.3	4.9
Atlanta, GA	9.2	23.0	18.4	7.9	25.4	11.7	2.6	1.8
Austin, TX	8.4	17.1	18.0	6.6	31.6	13.6	2.7	2.1
Baltimore, MD	7.9	23.6	18.2	7.0	23.4	14.4	3.1	2.5
Billings, MT	4.8	30.1	22.7	9.0	22.8	7.0	2.2	1.5
Boise City, ID	7.5	23.3	24.0	8.6	24.3	8.8	2.1	1.4
Boston, MA	7.7	20.8	13.3	7.0	27.5	16.4	3.6	3.7
Boulder, CO	4.5	11.0	14.5	6.1	34.5	20.0	3.8	5.6
Cape Coral, FL	9.6	30.0	19.8	9.8	18.8	8.2	2.3	1.4
Cedar Rapids, IA	4.8	27.8	20.7	13.9	22.2	8.0	1.7	0.9
Charleston, SC	8.1	22.9	19.8	9.3	24.9	10.7	2.8	1.6
Charlotte, NC	9.6	22.6	19.4	9.5	25.4	10.4	2.1	1.1
Chicago, IL	10.3	23.2	18.4	7.3	24.4	12.1	2.8	1.6
Cincinnati, OH	7.7	28.8	18.0	8.6	22.7	10.4	2.2	1.6
Clarksville, TN	7.7	29.5	23.6	11.2	17.4	8.2	1.3	1.1
Cleveland, OH	8.3	29.0	20.4	8.8	20.0	9.6	2.5	1.4
College Station, TX	11.7	23.8	18.7	6.8	22.2	10.2	1.7	5.0
Colorado Springs, CO	4.9	19.7	23.4	11.0	24.9	12.6	1.8	1.7
Columbia, MO	6.0	22.6	16.6	7.3	26.7	13.0	3.5	4.2
Columbia, SC	8.9	25.3	21.2	9.6	20.8	10.2	2.2	1.8
Columbus, OH	7.9	26.7	18.4	7.5	24.4	10.8	2.5	1.7
Dallas, TX	12.7	21.7	19.7	7.4	24.5	10.7	2.0	1.3
Davenport, IA	7.6	29.3	22.7	11.1	18.6	8.2	1.5	1.1
Denver, CO	7.7	18.4	18.2	7.3	30.3	13.3	2.9	1.9
Des Moines, IA	6.5	25.0	19.0	10.4	26.4	9.0	2.1	1.5
Detroit, MI	8.8	26.0	22.0	9.2	20.4	10.3	2.2	1.1
Durham, NC	8.9	17.0	14.3	7.5	26.3	15.5	4.8	5.6
El Paso, TX	19.4	24.9	21.1	9.2	17.1	6.1	1.2	0.9
Eugene, OR	6.9	22.8	27.0	9.9	19.7	9.4	2.3	2.1
Fargo, ND	4.4	19.1	20.8	13.5	28.4	9.7	1.9	2.3
Fort Collins, CO	3.4	16.8	19.3	8.8	31.0	14.9	2.7	3.1
Fort Wayne, IN	9.3	29.7	20.7	10.6	20.0	7.3	1.5	0.9
Fort Worth, TX	12.7	21.7	19.7	7.4	24.5	10.7	2.0	1.3
Gainesville, FL	7.3	24.2	16.4	11.1	20.3	11.8	4.0	4.8
Green Bay, WI	6.7	31.3	19.1	13.0	21.0	6.8	1.3	0.8
Greensboro, NC	11.7	26.5	20.8	9.6	20.0	8.5	1.5	1.4
Honolulu, HI	7.1	25.2	19.0	11.0	23.7	9.4	2.8	1.8
Houston, TX	14.9	22.7	19.5	7.5	22.1	9.3	2.3	1.7
Huntsville, AL	8.5	20.7	20.4	8.0	25.3	13.5	1.7	1.9
Indianapolis, IN	8.9	26.7	18.4	8.1	24.1	9.9	2.4	1.5
Jacksonville, FL	7.9	26.4	20.5	10.0	23.0	8.9	2.0	1.3
Kansas City, MO	6.9	24.9	21.1	7.9	24.4	11.0	2.5	1.3
Lafayette, LA	13.0	34.8	17.9	7.3	19.0	5.3	1.8	0.9
Las Vegas, NV	13.2	27.6	23.4	8.5	18.0	6.6	1.7	1.0
Lexington, KY	8.1	23.5	19.2	8.1	23.4	11.4	3.5	2.8
Lincoln, NE	6.4	20.9	20.1	11.9	26.2	9.8	2.1	2.4
Little Rock, AR	7.9	29.1	21.7	8.4	20.3	8.8	2.4	1.4
Los Angeles, CA	17.8	19.5	18.1	7.1	23.9	9.2	2.8	1.6
Louisville, KY	8.7	29.4	20.8	8.9	19.5	9.2	2.2	1.3
Madison, WI	4.1	20.2	16.6	9.7	29.9	12.7	2.9	3.8
Manchester, NH	7.0	25.6	17.2	9.6	25.4	12.1	1.6	1.5
McAllen, TX	30.7	25.2	18.3	5.6	13.9	4.8	1.0	0.6

Table continued on following page.

Metro Area	Less than H.S.	H.S. Diploma	Some College, No Deg.	Associate Degree	Bachelors Degree	Masters Degree	Profess. School Degree	Doctorate Degree
Memphis, TN	10.5	29.1	22.1	7.6	18.5	8.9	2.0	1.4
Miami, FL	13.1	25.7	16.0	9.5	21.8	9.0	3.4	1.4
Midland, TX	13.8	24.0	23.3	8.2	20.9	7.4	1.4	0.8
Milwaukee, WI	7.3	25.6	19.3	9.0	25.2	9.8	2.2	1.5
Minneapolis, MN	5.8	20.2	18.7	10.5	29.1	11.3	2.7	1.9
Nashville, TN	8.5	25.7	18.7	7.3	25.6	10.0	2.4	1.9
New Orleans, LA	12.5	26.2	21.5	6.7	19.6	8.7	3.1	1.6
New York, NY	12.4	23.2	14.0	6.8	24.9	13.3	3.5	1.8
Oklahoma City, OK	10.1	26.2	22.3	8.0	21.3	8.4	2.2	1.5
Omaha, NE	7.3	22.5	21.7	9.4	24.9	10.2	2.5	1.5
Orlando, FL	9.3	25.1	18.5	11.2	23.2	9.2	2.1	1.3
Philadelphia, PA	7.9	27.0	16.1	7.5	24.1	12.2	3.0	2.2
Phoenix, AZ	10.5	22.7	23.0	9.2	21.6	9.4	2.1	1.4
Pittsburgh, PA	5.1	31.4	15.5	10.6	22.6	10.6	2.3	1.9
Portland, OR	7.2	19.8	22.1	8.8	26.0	11.1	2.8	2.1
Providence, RI	11.6	27.8	17.2	8.4	21.3	9.9	2.1	1.7
Provo, UT	4.7	17.1	24.8	10.1	30.1	9.9	1.7	1.6
Raleigh, NC	7.1	17.3	16.6	8.8	30.8	14.4	2.6	2.4
Reno, NV	11.4	24.4	24.0	8.8	19.2	8.4	2.2	1.6
Richmond, VA	8.1	24.4	19.5	7.8	24.4	11.7	2.5	1.7
Rochester, MN	5.2	23.0	17.1	12.5	24.7	10.8	4.1	2.7
Sacramento, CA	9.9	20.6	23.3	9.9	23.0	8.7	3.0	1.6
Saint Louis, MO	6.7	25.5	21.0	9.3	22.3	11.2	2.3	1.7
Saint Paul, MN	5.8	20.2	18.7	10.5	29.1	11.3	2.7	1.9
Salem, OR	12.8	24.9	25.6	9.8	17.4	6.9	1.6	1.0
Salt Lake City, UT	8.2	22.7	22.1	9.2	24.1	9.7	2.3	1.7
San Antonio, TX	12.7	25.0	21.8	8.6	20.0	8.7	1.9	1.3
San Diego, CA	11.0	17.9	20.6	8.3	25.6	11.0	2.9	2.6
San Francisco, CA	10.5	15.0	15.5	6.6	30.0	15.1	3.9	3.4
San Jose, CA	10.9	13.9	13.9	6.5	27.8	19.3	2.9	4.8
Santa Rosa, CA	11.1	18.6	23.0	9.4	23.5	9.4	3.4	1.5
Savannah, GA	8.7	25.9	22.4	8.0	21.6	9.6	2.3	1.5
Seattle, WA	6.7	18.8	19.2	9.1	27.8	13.5	2.8	2.2
Sioux Falls, SD	6.3	25.7	19.7	12.6	24.8	7.7	2.0	1.2
Tampa, FL	9.1	27.4	19.4	10.0	21.5	8.9	2.2	1.3
Tucson, AZ	10.1	21.2	23.9	9.0	20.4	10.7	2.4	2.4
Tulsa, OK	9.9	28.6	22.4	9.4	19.7	7.0	1.9	1.1
Virginia Beach, VA	7.2	25.1	22.8	9.8	21.2	10.4	1.9	1.6
Washington, DC	8.5	17.3	14.6	5.8	27.0	18.7	4.7	3.4
Wichita, KS	9.7	26.4	23.4	9.0	20.2	8.8	1.5	1.0
Wilmington, NC	6.9	22.3	20.8	11.4	24.9	9.7	2.5	1.4
Winston-Salem, NC	10.8	28.4	21.4	9.8	18.9	7.3	1.9	1.5
U.S.	10.6	26.2	19.4	8.8	21.3	9.8	2.3	1.6

Note: Figures cover persons age 25 and over; Figures cover the Metropolitan Statistical Area (MSA)
Source: U.S. Census Bureau, 2019-2023 American Community Survey 5-Year Estimates

School Enrollment by Grade and Control: City

City	Preschool (%) Public	Preschool (%) Private	Kindergarten (%) Public	Kindergarten (%) Private	Grades 1 - 4 (%) Public	Grades 1 - 4 (%) Private	Grades 5 - 8 (%) Public	Grades 5 - 8 (%) Private	Grades 9 - 12 (%) Public	Grades 9 - 12 (%) Private
Albuquerque, NM	51.7	48.3	85.1	14.9	87.2	12.8	89.7	10.3	91.4	8.6
Anchorage, AK	53.5	46.5	89.2	10.8	84.1	15.9	87.8	12.2	91.8	8.2
Ann Arbor, MI	44.3	55.7	86.7	13.3	89.6	10.4	87.0	13.0	91.2	8.8
Athens, GA	65.1	34.9	95.8	4.2	88.4	11.6	86.4	13.6	89.2	10.8
Atlanta, GA	44.5	55.5	67.2	32.8	82.9	17.1	77.0	23.0	78.1	21.9
Austin, TX	51.1	48.9	85.1	14.9	87.7	12.3	86.7	13.3	90.3	9.7
Baltimore, MD	65.6	34.4	85.0	15.0	83.9	16.1	85.1	14.9	85.3	14.7
Billings, MT	39.2	60.8	80.1	19.9	84.7	15.3	84.3	15.7	86.1	13.9
Boise City, ID	34.8	65.2	80.0	20.0	85.7	14.3	89.3	10.7	86.4	13.6
Boston, MA	46.4	53.6	83.7	16.3	86.5	13.5	85.2	14.8	85.4	14.6
Boulder, CO	43.0	57.0	93.0	7.0	86.9	13.1	92.7	7.3	90.7	9.3
Cape Coral, FL	65.1	34.9	94.7	5.3	84.1	15.9	91.1	8.9	88.5	11.5
Cedar Rapids, IA	73.1	26.9	85.9	14.1	88.2	11.8	87.2	12.8	86.4	13.6
Charleston, SC	55.1	44.9	79.8	20.2	86.0	14.0	85.5	14.5	80.9	19.1
Charlotte, NC	50.8	49.2	86.8	13.2	88.6	11.4	87.4	12.6	88.8	11.2
Chicago, IL	56.4	43.6	81.6	18.4	82.8	17.2	83.6	16.4	85.2	14.8
Cincinnati, OH	60.9	39.1	77.2	22.8	78.5	21.5	78.9	21.1	81.8	18.2
Clarksville, TN	65.2	34.8	88.2	11.8	93.2	6.8	91.6	8.4	88.3	11.7
Cleveland, OH	68.9	31.1	68.7	31.3	78.2	21.8	77.9	22.1	77.6	22.4
College Station, TX	57.7	42.3	82.6	17.4	90.0	10.0	87.4	12.6	86.2	13.8
Colorado Springs, CO	64.6	35.4	88.0	12.0	87.3	12.7	88.4	11.6	90.7	9.3
Columbia, MO	49.7	50.3	85.6	14.4	87.0	13.0	89.5	10.5	91.0	9.0
Columbia, SC	33.0	67.0	81.8	18.2	76.7	23.3	85.6	14.4	84.0	16.0
Columbus, OH	64.5	35.5	79.2	20.8	84.3	15.7	85.7	14.3	87.2	12.8
Dallas, TX	69.0	31.0	88.5	11.5	89.5	10.5	91.1	8.9	89.8	10.2
Davenport, IA	52.6	47.4	86.2	13.8	79.3	20.7	86.4	13.6	92.5	7.5
Denver, CO	56.0	44.0	85.1	14.9	89.4	10.6	88.2	11.8	92.7	7.3
Des Moines, IA	76.4	23.6	88.0	12.0	90.8	9.2	91.8	8.2	93.8	6.2
Detroit, MI	81.6	18.4	91.8	8.2	93.4	6.6	92.1	7.9	92.4	7.6
Durham, NC	51.3	48.7	86.2	13.8	86.0	14.0	85.2	14.8	87.8	12.2
El Paso, TX	87.0	13.0	91.9	8.1	92.8	7.2	94.1	5.9	95.7	4.3
Eugene, OR	52.8	47.2	85.1	14.9	88.6	11.4	89.0	11.0	93.6	6.4
Fargo, ND	46.4	53.6	89.8	10.2	91.9	8.1	92.1	7.9	94.3	5.7
Fort Collins, CO	48.1	51.9	87.7	12.3	89.2	10.8	92.4	7.6	94.5	5.5
Fort Wayne, IN	45.6	54.4	70.8	29.2	78.5	21.5	82.0	18.0	79.2	20.8
Fort Worth, TX	61.4	38.6	86.8	13.2	90.9	9.1	91.0	9.0	91.3	8.7
Gainesville, FL	61.4	38.6	70.4	29.6	82.4	17.6	88.7	11.3	92.3	7.7
Green Bay, WI	71.0	29.0	86.2	13.8	87.3	12.7	89.8	10.2	90.4	9.6
Greensboro, NC	56.8	43.2	89.0	11.0	88.9	11.1	89.3	10.7	88.6	11.4
Honolulu, HI	36.4	63.6	74.0	26.0	79.9	20.1	76.4	23.6	69.1	30.9
Houston, TX	65.2	34.8	87.6	12.4	91.1	8.9	91.5	8.5	91.7	8.3
Huntsville, AL	63.7	36.3	80.9	19.1	81.8	18.2	78.2	21.8	84.2	15.8
Indianapolis, IN	61.1	38.9	85.4	14.6	82.9	17.1	83.7	16.3	85.2	14.8
Jacksonville, FL	56.5	43.5	83.5	16.5	83.4	16.6	80.0	20.0	83.7	16.3
Kansas City, MO	61.2	38.8	86.8	13.2	85.4	14.6	87.0	13.0	83.4	16.6
Lafayette, LA	55.1	44.9	71.4	28.6	76.8	23.2	72.2	27.8	78.4	21.6
Las Vegas, NV	68.6	31.4	91.1	8.9	87.6	12.4	89.3	10.7	91.2	8.8
Lexington, KY	29.5	70.5	81.0	19.0	82.3	17.7	85.7	14.3	85.4	14.6
Lincoln, NE	53.4	46.6	79.0	21.0	82.6	17.4	84.2	15.8	90.3	9.7
Little Rock, AR	66.2	33.8	86.5	13.5	78.2	21.8	76.0	24.0	77.5	22.5
Los Angeles, CA	55.2	44.8	85.7	14.3	87.7	12.3	87.5	12.5	88.0	12.0
Louisville, KY	50.3	49.7	77.2	22.8	81.9	18.1	81.0	19.0	78.2	21.8
Madison, WI	47.1	52.9	87.9	12.1	88.1	11.9	89.4	10.6	89.8	10.2
Manchester, NH	51.8	48.2	85.9	14.1	88.1	11.9	92.7	7.3	92.2	7.8
McAllen, TX	81.6	18.4	90.0	10.0	94.4	5.6	96.7	3.3	98.3	1.7

Table continued on following page.

City	Preschool (%)		Kindergarten (%)		Grades 1 - 4 (%)		Grades 5 - 8 (%)		Grades 9 - 12 (%)	
	Public	Private	Public	Private	Public	Private	Public	Private	Public	Private
Memphis, TN	60.2	39.8	87.7	12.3	88.1	11.9	88.5	11.5	85.6	14.4
Miami, FL	61.1	38.9	80.7	19.3	85.9	14.1	86.9	13.1	91.6	8.4
Midland, TX	57.2	42.8	67.9	32.1	78.9	21.1	76.4	23.6	84.3	15.7
Milwaukee, WI	77.0	23.0	73.9	26.1	75.5	24.5	73.9	26.1	79.9	20.1
Minneapolis, MN	53.1	46.9	86.3	13.7	86.2	13.8	87.0	13.0	88.8	11.2
Nashville, TN	51.0	49.0	82.7	17.3	82.9	17.1	78.2	21.8	81.2	18.8
New Orleans, LA	42.8	57.2	76.0	24.0	75.5	24.5	80.0	20.0	78.6	21.4
New York, NY	67.6	32.4	78.2	21.8	80.9	19.1	80.6	19.4	80.3	19.7
Oklahoma City, OK	69.7	30.3	86.9	13.1	87.9	12.1	86.4	13.6	86.9	13.1
Omaha, NE	54.5	45.5	79.9	20.1	82.7	17.3	82.7	17.3	83.3	16.7
Orlando, FL	60.7	39.3	81.8	18.2	85.9	14.1	90.0	10.0	88.0	12.0
Philadelphia, PA	54.5	45.5	78.0	22.0	79.4	20.6	79.1	20.9	77.6	22.4
Phoenix, AZ	62.6	37.4	86.7	13.3	88.9	11.1	91.5	8.5	92.2	7.8
Pittsburgh, PA	53.9	46.1	71.0	29.0	75.1	24.9	79.8	20.2	79.1	20.9
Portland, OR	36.8	63.2	84.3	15.7	87.0	13.0	86.9	13.1	85.7	14.3
Providence, RI	58.9	41.1	80.8	19.2	89.3	10.7	86.2	13.8	90.1	9.9
Provo, UT	64.9	35.1	88.2	11.8	91.6	8.4	95.6	4.4	91.6	8.4
Raleigh, NC	33.6	66.4	86.9	13.1	85.2	14.8	87.2	12.8	86.8	13.2
Reno, NV	54.6	45.4	96.7	3.3	89.2	10.8	88.3	11.7	93.6	6.4
Richmond, VA	53.2	46.8	90.2	9.8	87.7	12.3	84.7	15.3	82.7	17.3
Rochester, MN	43.6	56.4	90.6	9.4	86.3	13.7	84.5	15.5	90.2	9.8
Sacramento, CA	56.9	43.1	92.4	7.6	91.3	8.7	92.3	7.7	89.5	10.5
Saint Louis, MO	56.5	43.5	85.1	14.9	83.3	16.7	82.7	17.3	84.0	16.0
Saint Paul, MN	64.7	35.3	82.1	17.9	89.2	10.8	87.3	12.7	90.7	9.3
Salem, OR	70.2	29.8	88.8	11.2	88.5	11.5	91.6	8.4	97.2	2.8
Salt Lake City, UT	52.1	47.9	81.8	18.2	85.6	14.4	90.6	9.4	93.7	6.3
San Antonio, TX	73.0	27.0	89.7	10.3	90.7	9.3	92.1	7.9	91.8	8.2
San Diego, CA	47.0	53.0	84.6	15.4	88.6	11.4	91.3	8.7	90.8	9.2
San Francisco, CA	25.0	75.0	67.5	32.5	69.1	30.9	68.5	31.5	72.8	27.2
San Jose, CA	43.5	56.5	83.1	16.9	86.1	13.9	87.4	12.6	87.1	12.9
Santa Rosa, CA	55.2	44.8	90.3	9.7	92.4	7.6	88.6	11.4	92.8	7.2
Savannah, GA	76.3	23.7	85.4	14.6	88.1	11.9	88.2	11.8	88.6	11.4
Seattle, WA	35.0	65.0	76.0	24.0	77.9	22.1	74.8	25.2	78.3	21.7
Sioux Falls, SD	59.5	40.5	86.0	14.0	85.9	14.1	86.2	13.8	86.7	13.3
Tampa, FL	46.6	53.4	86.5	13.5	86.6	13.4	81.5	18.5	83.5	16.5
Tucson, AZ	71.7	28.3	90.3	9.7	88.2	11.8	88.1	11.9	91.9	8.1
Tulsa, OK	65.1	34.9	83.2	16.8	82.9	17.1	82.2	17.8	82.6	17.4
Virginia Beach, VA	39.5	60.5	77.6	22.4	88.8	11.2	88.5	11.5	91.2	8.8
Washington, DC	74.8	25.2	90.5	9.5	85.6	14.4	83.0	17.0	79.9	20.1
Wichita, KS	61.8	38.2	82.0	18.0	84.6	15.4	84.4	15.6	86.3	13.7
Wilmington, NC	55.8	44.2	84.8	15.2	79.3	20.7	75.6	24.4	87.1	12.9
Winston-Salem, NC	60.4	39.6	88.7	11.3	88.2	11.8	90.5	9.5	90.4	9.6
U.S.	58.7	41.3	85.2	14.8	87.2	12.8	87.9	12.1	89.0	11.0

Note: Figures shown cover persons 3 years old and over
Source: U.S. Census Bureau, 2019-2023 American Community Survey 5-Year Estimates

Appendix A: Comparative Statistics

School Enrollment by Grade and Control: Metro Area

Metro Area	Preschool (%) Public	Preschool (%) Private	Kindergarten (%) Public	Kindergarten (%) Private	Grades 1 - 4 (%) Public	Grades 1 - 4 (%) Private	Grades 5 - 8 (%) Public	Grades 5 - 8 (%) Private	Grades 9 - 12 (%) Public	Grades 9 - 12 (%) Private
Albuquerque, NM	60.4	39.6	84.3	15.7	86.3	13.7	88.4	11.6	90.3	9.7
Anchorage, AK	51.9	48.1	87.7	12.3	83.6	16.4	86.9	13.1	89.7	10.3
Ann Arbor, MI	53.0	47.0	89.6	10.4	85.0	15.0	84.6	15.4	91.8	8.2
Athens, GA	63.8	36.2	93.2	6.8	88.2	11.8	87.2	12.8	88.5	11.5
Atlanta, GA	56.1	43.9	84.1	15.9	88.3	11.7	87.2	12.8	88.5	11.5
Austin, TX	49.6	50.4	87.0	13.0	90.0	10.0	89.2	10.8	91.1	8.9
Baltimore, MD	47.0	53.0	82.9	17.1	84.6	15.4	84.0	16.0	84.2	15.8
Billings, MT	41.5	58.5	84.1	15.9	87.0	13.0	87.1	12.9	88.2	11.8
Boise City, ID	40.0	60.0	86.5	13.5	85.6	14.4	88.0	12.0	88.4	11.6
Boston, MA	45.6	54.4	87.8	12.2	90.3	9.7	89.1	10.9	85.9	14.1
Boulder, CO	48.1	51.9	87.6	12.4	88.7	11.3	91.5	8.5	93.0	7.0
Cape Coral, FL	61.4	38.6	86.9	13.1	88.2	11.8	88.7	11.3	90.3	9.7
Cedar Rapids, IA	74.7	25.3	87.6	12.4	88.4	11.6	88.3	11.7	89.7	10.3
Charleston, SC	47.5	52.5	82.7	17.3	86.5	13.5	87.9	12.1	87.7	12.3
Charlotte, NC	50.5	49.5	86.2	13.8	87.8	12.2	87.3	12.7	88.6	11.4
Chicago, IL	56.8	43.2	84.8	15.2	87.6	12.4	88.1	11.9	90.0	10.0
Cincinnati, OH	50.7	49.3	79.1	20.9	81.9	18.1	82.2	17.8	83.0	17.0
Clarksville, TN	62.8	37.2	85.3	14.7	86.8	13.2	86.0	14.0	87.6	12.4
Cleveland, OH	53.0	47.0	75.5	24.5	80.6	19.4	80.7	19.3	82.4	17.6
College Station, TX	61.4	38.6	87.5	12.5	90.5	9.5	87.7	12.3	90.5	9.5
Colorado Springs, CO	66.9	33.1	86.3	13.7	87.4	12.6	88.5	11.5	89.8	10.2
Columbia, MO	55.0	45.0	87.6	12.4	84.6	15.4	90.4	9.6	90.7	9.3
Columbia, SC	51.6	48.4	88.3	11.7	87.8	12.2	90.4	9.6	91.7	8.3
Columbus, OH	56.4	43.6	81.4	18.6	87.0	13.0	88.1	11.9	88.9	11.1
Dallas, TX	57.4	42.6	88.0	12.0	90.4	9.6	91.4	8.6	91.5	8.5
Davenport, IA	65.1	34.9	87.2	12.8	87.0	13.0	91.2	8.8	92.2	7.8
Denver, CO	58.5	41.5	86.4	13.6	89.3	10.7	89.9	10.1	91.6	8.4
Des Moines, IA	68.1	31.9	87.6	12.4	91.2	8.8	89.9	10.1	91.5	8.5
Detroit, MI	62.5	37.5	86.9	13.1	88.7	11.3	89.8	10.2	89.9	10.1
Durham, NC	43.5	56.5	80.2	19.8	85.4	14.6	85.0	15.0	89.7	10.3
El Paso, TX	87.0	13.0	94.1	5.9	93.1	6.9	94.4	5.6	96.2	3.8
Eugene, OR	54.2	45.8	84.1	15.9	87.0	13.0	89.6	10.4	91.4	8.6
Fargo, ND	65.0	35.0	90.0	10.0	89.1	10.9	90.7	9.3	91.7	8.3
Fort Collins, CO	52.8	47.2	85.7	14.3	85.4	14.6	86.7	13.3	88.2	11.8
Fort Wayne, IN	44.1	55.9	73.2	26.8	75.7	24.3	76.8	23.2	81.3	18.7
Fort Worth, TX	57.4	42.6	88.0	12.0	90.4	9.6	91.4	8.6	91.5	8.5
Gainesville, FL	53.9	46.1	72.0	28.0	76.7	23.3	78.1	21.9	86.5	13.5
Green Bay, WI	68.0	32.0	84.2	15.8	86.1	13.9	87.0	13.0	90.5	9.5
Greensboro, NC	56.8	43.2	86.7	13.3	85.9	14.1	85.7	14.3	87.9	12.1
Honolulu, HI	34.7	65.3	79.0	21.0	79.9	20.1	78.2	21.8	74.9	25.1
Houston, TX	57.2	42.8	88.1	11.9	90.9	9.1	92.0	8.0	91.7	8.3
Huntsville, AL	56.0	44.0	79.7	20.3	82.9	17.1	82.3	17.7	83.1	16.9
Indianapolis, IN	53.8	46.2	84.3	15.7	85.1	14.9	85.7	14.3	87.4	12.6
Jacksonville, FL	56.0	44.0	85.4	14.6	84.0	16.0	82.8	17.2	85.6	14.4
Kansas City, MO	60.8	39.2	86.2	13.8	87.9	12.1	88.5	11.5	88.5	11.5
Lafayette, LA	56.7	43.3	78.8	21.2	77.7	22.3	77.9	22.1	79.1	20.9
Las Vegas, NV	64.0	36.0	87.1	12.9	88.8	11.2	90.1	9.9	91.8	8.2
Lexington, KY	40.9	59.1	82.4	17.6	83.7	16.3	84.8	15.2	85.9	14.1
Lincoln, NE	54.3	45.7	79.6	20.4	81.9	18.1	84.4	15.6	90.5	9.5
Little Rock, AR	69.9	30.1	86.8	13.2	86.2	13.8	85.4	14.6	87.1	12.9
Los Angeles, CA	54.7	45.3	86.6	13.4	89.1	10.9	89.9	10.1	90.6	9.4
Louisville, KY	53.0	47.0	79.7	20.3	81.8	18.2	82.4	17.6	81.0	19.0
Madison, WI	64.6	35.4	89.5	10.5	88.4	11.6	90.8	9.2	93.5	6.5
Manchester, NH	45.6	54.4	81.4	18.6	85.2	14.8	87.5	12.5	89.8	10.2
McAllen, TX	93.3	6.7	96.4	3.6	97.7	2.3	98.1	1.9	98.7	1.3

Table continued on following page.

Metro Area	Preschool (%)		Kindergarten (%)		Grades 1 - 4 (%)		Grades 5 - 8 (%)		Grades 9 - 12 (%)	
	Public	Private	Public	Private	Public	Private	Public	Private	Public	Private
Memphis, TN	59.8	40.2	87.5	12.5	86.3	13.7	87.0	13.0	84.8	15.2
Miami, FL	50.2	49.8	80.4	19.6	84.2	15.8	85.0	15.0	85.7	14.3
Midland, TX	65.0	35.0	65.8	34.2	80.9	19.1	78.8	21.2	83.9	16.1
Milwaukee, WI	59.4	40.6	75.9	24.1	78.5	21.5	78.7	21.3	84.9	15.1
Minneapolis, MN	60.7	39.3	85.8	14.2	88.3	11.7	88.7	11.3	91.5	8.5
Nashville, TN	50.1	49.9	82.5	17.5	84.8	15.2	83.3	16.7	83.0	17.0
New Orleans, LA	50.8	49.2	76.7	23.3	76.5	23.5	78.6	21.4	75.1	24.9
New York, NY	58.7	41.3	80.9	19.1	83.9	16.1	84.6	15.4	83.7	16.3
Oklahoma City, OK	70.9	29.1	86.9	13.1	87.7	12.3	87.4	12.6	87.8	12.2
Omaha, NE	58.9	41.1	81.9	18.1	84.5	15.5	85.7	14.3	85.5	14.5
Orlando, FL	48.9	51.1	79.8	20.2	82.1	17.9	85.3	14.7	87.0	13.0
Philadelphia, PA	47.4	52.6	81.4	18.6	85.0	15.0	84.4	15.6	83.6	16.4
Phoenix, AZ	60.3	39.7	85.5	14.5	88.1	11.9	90.4	9.6	91.9	8.1
Pittsburgh, PA	52.6	47.4	81.9	18.1	87.4	12.6	89.1	10.9	89.6	10.4
Portland, OR	40.0	60.0	83.8	16.2	85.8	14.2	88.1	11.9	89.6	10.4
Providence, RI	57.9	42.1	85.5	14.5	89.4	10.6	88.9	11.1	88.7	11.3
Provo, UT	55.5	44.5	87.9	12.1	90.3	9.7	92.6	7.4	94.0	6.0
Raleigh, NC	33.6	66.4	82.6	17.4	85.2	14.8	85.7	14.3	87.6	12.4
Reno, NV	51.8	48.2	90.8	9.2	90.9	9.1	89.7	10.3	92.1	7.9
Richmond, VA	44.4	55.6	86.4	13.6	87.5	12.5	89.1	10.9	90.0	10.0
Rochester, MN	61.3	38.7	91.0	9.0	88.1	11.9	87.9	12.1	91.8	8.2
Sacramento, CA	55.0	45.0	87.3	12.7	89.8	10.2	90.5	9.5	90.7	9.3
Saint Louis, MO	53.9	46.1	82.1	17.9	82.1	17.9	83.2	16.8	84.7	15.3
Saint Paul, MN	60.7	39.3	85.8	14.2	88.3	11.7	88.7	11.3	91.5	8.5
Salem, OR	59.8	40.2	86.8	13.2	86.0	14.0	90.3	9.7	92.4	7.6
Salt Lake City, UT	57.4	42.6	84.7	15.3	89.9	10.1	93.4	6.6	93.9	6.1
San Antonio, TX	65.5	34.5	87.7	12.3	89.4	10.6	90.3	9.7	90.5	9.5
San Diego, CA	50.7	49.3	86.1	13.9	89.3	10.7	90.8	9.2	91.9	8.1
San Francisco, CA	38.9	61.1	81.4	18.6	84.7	15.3	83.8	16.2	85.8	14.2
San Jose, CA	36.2	63.8	80.1	19.9	84.7	15.3	85.9	14.1	86.5	13.5
Santa Rosa, CA	53.1	46.9	91.2	8.8	92.9	7.1	89.9	10.1	91.1	8.9
Savannah, GA	57.5	42.5	79.1	20.9	84.4	15.6	84.9	15.1	85.2	14.8
Seattle, WA	40.8	59.2	79.5	20.5	85.6	14.4	86.7	13.3	90.0	10.0
Sioux Falls, SD	64.5	35.5	86.8	13.2	86.8	13.2	87.8	12.2	87.7	12.3
Tampa, FL	54.3	45.7	82.4	17.6	84.7	15.3	84.3	15.7	86.4	13.6
Tucson, AZ	71.3	28.7	88.0	12.0	87.2	12.8	87.8	12.2	89.8	10.2
Tulsa, OK	67.2	32.8	84.6	15.4	84.2	15.8	85.3	14.7	85.5	14.5
Virginia Beach, VA	50.5	49.5	80.8	19.2	87.9	12.1	88.8	11.2	89.9	10.1
Washington, DC	45.5	54.5	82.8	17.2	86.8	13.2	87.5	12.5	88.2	11.8
Wichita, KS	63.2	36.8	80.5	19.5	85.1	14.9	86.3	13.7	87.5	12.5
Wilmington, NC	52.1	47.9	83.4	16.6	83.8	16.2	84.3	15.7	88.3	11.7
Winston-Salem, NC	48.5	51.5	85.5	14.5	87.3	12.7	89.0	11.0	86.7	13.3
U.S.	58.7	41.3	85.2	14.8	87.2	12.8	87.9	12.1	89.0	11.0

Note: Figures shown cover persons 3 years old and over; Figures cover the Metropolitan Statistical Area (MSA)
Source: U.S. Census Bureau, 2019-2023 American Community Survey 5-Year Estimates

Educational Attainment by Race: City

City	High School Graduate or Higher (%)					Bachelor's Degree or Higher (%)				
	Total	White	Black	Asian	Hisp.[1]	Total	White	Black	Asian	Hisp.[1]
Albuquerque, NM	90.9	94.6	94.0	88.3	84.4	38.7	45.2	38.8	51.0	25.4
Anchorage, AK	94.0	96.7	91.7	86.6	86.6	37.7	45.2	23.6	30.5	23.8
Ann Arbor, MI	97.6	98.6	92.7	97.2	92.8	77.7	79.7	44.8	85.2	75.5
Athens, GA	89.9	96.9	82.5	88.5	66.8	48.7	62.8	22.6	67.8	31.7
Atlanta, GA	93.0	98.5	87.9	97.7	86.1	58.4	81.2	34.6	86.7	50.5
Austin, TX	91.6	95.1	90.6	93.6	78.3	58.2	63.9	36.7	78.4	35.6
Baltimore, MD	87.2	92.9	85.7	92.2	70.0	35.4	62.2	20.0	73.3	31.3
Billings, MT	95.5	96.2	98.6	89.9	85.1	37.0	38.3	35.8	56.4	14.6
Boise City, ID	94.8	96.2	73.7	89.9	80.6	46.6	47.4	24.4	60.1	30.3
Boston, MA	88.9	96.4	86.4	80.9	72.8	54.1	72.5	26.7	57.4	26.6
Boulder, CO	96.9	98.3	95.0	95.1	78.4	76.8	79.1	43.7	79.9	48.6
Cape Coral, FL	93.2	94.9	87.7	90.2	87.3	25.7	26.8	21.3	50.2	18.9
Cedar Rapids, IA	94.1	95.5	81.1	88.4	90.0	32.9	33.6	15.5	55.7	25.0
Charleston, SC	95.9	98.3	86.7	92.1	87.9	57.7	65.3	22.9	67.6	39.8
Charlotte, NC	89.6	95.9	91.6	85.3	60.5	47.4	63.1	33.3	61.3	20.5
Chicago, IL	86.8	93.4	87.4	88.3	71.9	43.3	61.9	25.2	65.0	20.4
Cincinnati, OH	89.7	94.6	83.8	93.1	81.1	41.3	57.9	16.2	80.1	36.2
Clarksville, TN	94.2	95.8	95.2	84.5	84.8	30.6	33.8	27.3	27.8	19.9
Cleveland, OH	83.5	87.5	82.3	78.8	70.9	21.3	31.8	12.7	55.6	10.6
College Station, TX	94.6	97.4	88.7	95.6	83.0	57.1	60.8	24.5	79.1	40.4
Colorado Springs, CO	94.6	96.4	94.1	89.0	84.6	41.9	45.3	32.1	43.8	21.6
Columbia, MO	95.3	96.4	92.0	94.2	86.7	56.5	59.4	33.9	72.5	48.5
Columbia, SC	90.9	96.0	85.2	89.9	85.6	46.1	62.6	25.4	73.0	39.5
Columbus, OH	89.8	93.6	86.6	82.8	71.2	38.2	45.8	21.1	57.8	25.2
Dallas, TX	80.8	87.6	89.0	89.3	58.2	37.4	53.6	23.6	68.5	15.3
Davenport, IA	92.6	94.7	87.4	84.3	78.3	30.0	31.7	16.8	59.3	15.0
Denver, CO	91.4	96.4	91.5	87.1	72.5	55.6	66.7	31.4	58.1	23.3
Des Moines, IA	87.3	93.7	79.3	61.3	60.1	29.0	33.5	15.8	23.0	10.8
Detroit, MI	83.4	84.3	85.3	75.5	56.8	17.6	37.4	14.1	43.5	11.6
Durham, NC	91.4	96.1	91.7	92.8	59.7	55.7	70.7	39.4	76.8	22.1
El Paso, TX	81.9	87.0	94.8	88.4	78.7	27.5	31.5	30.8	52.7	23.9
Eugene, OR	94.8	95.7	98.0	92.9	86.2	44.2	44.8	37.2	59.1	33.3
Fargo, ND	95.3	96.6	82.3	87.0	95.2	43.2	44.3	20.1	69.9	31.7
Fort Collins, CO	97.6	98.4	87.7	95.1	91.1	59.9	62.0	34.6	76.2	37.0
Fort Wayne, IN	88.9	94.1	87.7	49.2	65.7	28.5	33.1	13.9	19.7	15.4
Fort Worth, TX	84.3	91.2	90.0	82.7	64.6	31.7	41.0	23.0	46.0	14.7
Gainesville, FL	94.3	96.5	87.4	96.9	94.7	51.7	57.0	28.8	77.5	61.4
Green Bay, WI	89.0	92.6	69.5	84.3	65.8	25.5	27.8	16.2	32.8	11.5
Greensboro, NC	90.1	95.2	89.5	75.7	70.2	39.9	52.3	28.0	46.5	19.4
Honolulu, HI	90.9	97.6	91.5	88.1	93.6	40.8	54.6	32.5	40.7	30.5
Houston, TX	80.3	88.5	89.9	86.6	60.7	36.0	50.8	27.4	61.7	16.7
Huntsville, AL	91.6	94.8	86.8	91.0	77.4	46.2	54.1	30.1	57.6	29.7
Indianapolis, IN	87.5	91.3	87.9	70.4	64.5	34.2	41.0	22.1	41.0	18.6
Jacksonville, FL	90.8	93.0	88.6	88.9	84.8	31.8	35.1	22.6	52.6	28.1
Kansas City, MO	91.8	94.9	89.8	89.9	73.9	37.8	47.4	17.5	49.5	20.7
Lafayette, LA	90.9	95.4	81.2	91.6	83.8	40.6	50.4	17.4	55.0	36.6
Las Vegas, NV	85.8	91.7	88.5	91.7	66.8	27.3	32.2	19.5	44.8	12.5
Lexington, KY	92.4	95.3	90.4	89.9	65.1	47.3	51.9	27.1	72.2	25.3
Lincoln, NE	93.0	95.2	86.6	81.2	70.7	41.0	42.7	25.0	43.3	21.1
Little Rock, AR	92.3	96.3	91.5	92.7	63.7	44.0	58.0	26.6	73.5	13.5
Los Angeles, CA	79.3	89.6	90.1	91.1	59.4	37.8	51.6	31.9	57.6	15.1
Louisville, KY	90.5	92.9	87.6	83.3	78.7	33.4	37.4	20.2	56.1	27.5
Madison, WI	95.7	97.7	91.9	92.5	78.5	59.2	62.9	25.6	70.4	37.4
Manchester, NH	88.7	91.3	75.7	81.2	68.7	33.5	35.4	22.8	35.6	13.5
McAllen, TX	79.9	85.7	99.5	89.7	77.2	32.0	35.4	31.6	64.7	28.6

Table continued on following page.

City	High School Graduate or Higher (%)					Bachelor's Degree or Higher (%)				
	Total	White	Black	Asian	Hisp.[1]	Total	White	Black	Asian	Hisp.[1]
Memphis, TN	87.4	93.9	87.8	86.8	52.0	28.2	49.9	17.9	60.0	17.8
Miami, FL	80.0	82.6	78.1	95.4	76.7	35.6	44.7	17.5	69.4	31.3
Midland, TX	86.5	91.9	90.5	70.2	74.6	33.7	40.3	20.1	39.1	22.1
Milwaukee, WI	85.5	92.8	86.0	74.3	64.6	26.6	41.0	13.7	32.7	12.0
Minneapolis, MN	91.1	97.2	74.9	86.3	71.6	54.5	65.6	19.1	62.7	31.0
Nashville, TN	90.2	93.9	89.5	83.4	61.8	46.9	56.0	29.8	55.1	20.5
New Orleans, LA	89.1	96.8	85.9	77.4	79.1	42.0	68.0	24.1	50.4	42.2
New York, NY	83.7	92.5	85.1	77.3	71.7	41.0	59.2	26.7	45.2	21.5
Oklahoma City, OK	87.8	91.4	90.7	81.6	61.7	34.0	38.4	26.1	48.0	12.8
Omaha, NE	90.5	95.1	86.9	71.7	61.9	40.3	45.7	18.6	50.2	15.0
Orlando, FL	91.9	95.6	84.1	93.4	90.9	42.2	53.5	21.7	59.3	33.9
Philadelphia, PA	87.4	93.5	88.1	74.3	72.6	34.6	51.0	20.4	42.0	19.5
Phoenix, AZ	84.4	91.2	89.2	89.2	66.9	32.3	38.9	27.3	62.6	13.6
Pittsburgh, PA	94.3	95.7	90.6	92.3	87.4	47.8	53.2	20.3	82.0	55.8
Portland, OR	93.3	96.2	88.6	81.7	80.0	53.5	58.1	29.8	47.3	35.7
Providence, RI	81.9	89.9	87.0	87.7	69.5	34.7	51.7	23.6	58.3	12.9
Provo, UT	92.5	95.3	99.6	84.9	75.2	45.0	49.0	29.9	52.7	20.8
Raleigh, NC	92.5	96.8	92.0	90.0	67.3	52.9	66.4	32.5	62.5	23.7
Reno, NV	89.3	94.9	91.5	90.5	65.3	35.7	39.9	26.6	49.2	15.2
Richmond, VA	89.3	96.6	85.0	90.3	61.4	44.1	70.1	16.1	64.9	25.2
Rochester, MN	94.5	97.2	73.9	86.1	78.6	50.1	51.6	25.7	61.6	34.9
Sacramento, CA	86.9	93.0	91.4	82.5	76.4	36.4	45.2	24.4	38.9	23.7
Saint Louis, MO	90.5	95.0	85.7	86.9	81.7	40.2	56.0	18.1	63.5	35.3
Saint Paul, MN	88.9	96.6	81.4	67.4	73.7	43.5	55.6	21.2	23.6	24.2
Salem, OR	88.7	93.5	94.1	86.4	63.7	31.4	35.1	27.7	46.3	12.8
Salt Lake City, UT	91.6	95.7	86.1	85.3	72.5	50.9	56.2	30.7	62.6	24.5
San Antonio, TX	84.3	88.4	91.0	85.7	78.0	28.7	33.7	25.0	56.5	19.4
San Diego, CA	90.2	95.2	90.0	90.2	76.2	49.9	57.6	31.3	57.3	25.4
San Francisco, CA	88.8	97.5	88.8	80.8	80.1	60.1	76.3	30.9	51.0	40.1
San Jose, CA	85.5	93.1	90.1	88.3	69.6	46.5	51.5	37.5	59.7	17.5
Santa Rosa, CA	85.5	94.7	85.7	83.6	63.0	34.8	42.5	21.8	45.8	14.6
Savannah, GA	89.9	95.3	86.3	81.6	86.9	32.0	47.8	17.9	46.9	32.4
Seattle, WA	95.7	98.4	89.9	91.2	87.8	67.5	72.6	33.8	69.8	49.3
Sioux Falls, SD	93.1	95.7	83.0	76.0	64.7	37.4	40.0	21.0	42.2	14.8
Tampa, FL	89.8	94.4	85.6	90.4	80.9	44.6	56.0	20.5	68.9	29.4
Tucson, AZ	87.3	91.8	87.3	88.4	76.7	30.2	35.6	17.5	51.9	17.3
Tulsa, OK	87.6	92.1	90.0	77.0	59.5	33.3	39.7	19.7	38.0	12.4
Virginia Beach, VA	94.7	96.4	92.7	89.4	89.9	40.4	44.2	27.9	46.6	32.5
Washington, DC	92.8	99.1	88.5	95.8	81.3	63.6	92.0	33.3	84.7	56.7
Wichita, KS	88.0	92.3	87.4	74.0	63.9	30.9	34.8	19.0	31.6	14.7
Wilmington, NC	93.5	96.4	84.9	87.8	77.5	45.8	51.7	23.0	61.8	30.2
Winston-Salem, NC	88.4	91.9	89.4	96.1	61.1	37.2	47.5	24.1	70.3	16.3
U.S.	89.4	92.9	88.1	88.0	72.5	35.0	37.7	24.7	57.0	19.9

Note: Figures shown cover persons 25 years old and over; (1) People of Hispanic origin can be of any race
Source: U.S. Census Bureau, 2019-2023 American Community Survey 5-Year Estimates

Educational Attainment by Race: Metro Area

Metro Area	High School Graduate or Higher (%)					Bachelor's Degree or Higher (%)				
	Total	White	Black	Asian	Hisp.[1]	Total	White	Black	Asian	Hisp.[1]
Albuquerque, NM	90.3	94.2	93.1	88.8	84.0	35.0	41.5	38.7	52.7	22.6
Anchorage, AK	94.1	96.2	91.7	86.6	87.7	34.0	38.9	23.5	29.7	23.9
Ann Arbor, MI	95.8	97.1	90.9	95.6	85.8	58.1	60.0	31.5	82.0	47.3
Athens, GA	89.8	94.2	82.4	85.0	66.0	43.5	49.5	21.4	64.9	30.8
Atlanta, GA	90.8	93.8	91.9	87.8	69.6	41.5	46.4	34.0	61.2	24.7
Austin, TX	91.6	94.9	93.3	93.8	78.2	49.9	54.2	36.5	76.1	29.0
Baltimore, MD	92.1	94.7	90.2	89.3	77.0	43.3	48.4	30.1	64.0	32.9
Billings, MT	95.2	95.8	99.0	87.5	84.4	33.5	34.3	31.1	47.3	15.7
Boise City, ID	92.5	94.9	80.7	90.9	72.9	36.6	38.2	24.7	55.8	19.1
Boston, MA	92.3	95.8	87.4	87.0	74.8	51.2	54.8	31.8	65.0	26.6
Boulder, CO	95.5	97.6	93.4	92.4	76.4	63.9	67.0	40.6	70.1	30.8
Cape Coral, FL	90.4	94.0	82.6	89.5	75.7	30.8	34.0	16.7	50.3	17.1
Cedar Rapids, IA	95.2	96.1	83.2	90.9	85.2	32.8	33.3	16.5	53.6	24.3
Charleston, SC	91.9	95.4	86.5	90.2	72.3	40.0	47.6	20.1	51.7	25.5
Charlotte, NC	90.4	93.4	90.6	88.0	67.0	39.0	42.6	30.0	61.9	21.4
Chicago, IL	89.7	94.4	89.4	91.3	71.8	40.9	47.4	25.8	67.0	18.6
Cincinnati, OH	92.3	93.5	87.9	88.6	76.7	36.9	38.1	22.8	63.4	31.1
Clarksville, TN	92.3	92.8	93.3	87.6	84.0	28.0	29.3	25.3	35.5	20.5
Cleveland, OH	91.7	93.6	87.0	87.8	78.0	33.4	36.9	18.3	63.6	19.0
College Station, TX	88.3	91.8	87.1	96.0	69.9	39.1	43.4	15.1	77.8	18.7
Colorado Springs, CO	95.1	96.6	95.2	90.1	86.4	41.0	43.8	32.5	44.9	23.2
Columbia, MO	94.0	94.6	91.5	92.8	87.6	47.5	48.9	28.5	71.0	38.4
Columbia, SC	91.1	93.5	88.9	91.0	75.3	35.0	39.2	27.3	64.1	22.7
Columbus, OH	92.1	94.2	87.4	86.3	75.0	39.4	41.8	23.9	62.6	27.7
Dallas, TX	87.3	92.0	92.2	90.0	66.3	38.5	42.8	31.6	65.4	17.8
Davenport, IA	92.4	94.5	83.5	82.5	77.4	29.4	30.4	14.2	61.6	16.8
Denver, CO	92.3	96.0	90.8	86.3	75.5	48.4	54.4	30.3	55.4	21.7
Des Moines, IA	93.5	96.3	82.0	73.9	69.3	39.1	40.8	20.1	44.7	17.4
Detroit, MI	91.2	92.9	88.4	89.5	76.9	34.1	36.5	19.4	66.4	26.5
Durham, NC	91.1	95.0	90.1	92.2	59.9	52.3	60.5	35.3	77.4	23.4
El Paso, TX	80.6	85.8	95.3	88.8	77.4	25.3	29.4	32.0	50.5	21.9
Eugene, OR	93.1	94.1	96.1	90.4	81.3	33.4	33.6	33.2	53.7	25.3
Fargo, ND	95.6	96.6	84.7	88.7	89.2	42.2	43.0	24.6	67.9	30.1
Fort Collins, CO	96.6	97.7	91.5	95.6	85.2	51.7	53.4	37.7	69.3	29.5
Fort Wayne, IN	90.7	93.8	88.5	59.3	68.5	29.7	32.0	15.8	29.2	16.9
Fort Worth, TX	87.3	92.0	92.2	90.0	66.3	38.5	42.8	31.6	65.4	17.8
Gainesville, FL	92.7	93.9	87.4	94.6	89.8	40.9	41.6	24.2	73.6	49.6
Green Bay, WI	93.3	95.2	74.2	85.9	69.6	29.9	30.8	18.3	44.5	15.5
Greensboro, NC	88.3	91.1	88.5	78.6	63.3	31.4	34.4	24.7	49.1	16.3
Honolulu, HI	92.9	97.2	95.8	90.6	94.5	37.7	51.2	32.8	39.2	29.2
Houston, TX	85.1	90.6	92.3	87.6	67.9	35.4	40.8	32.1	58.0	17.8
Huntsville, AL	91.5	93.3	88.5	91.9	77.4	42.4	45.2	33.2	63.5	30.7
Indianapolis, IN	91.1	93.5	88.2	81.4	70.5	37.8	40.4	24.9	54.4	24.0
Jacksonville, FL	92.1	93.8	88.5	89.6	87.1	35.1	37.9	23.6	52.4	30.2
Kansas City, MO	93.1	95.0	90.9	89.1	75.0	39.2	42.6	21.9	56.7	20.9
Lafayette, LA	87.0	90.1	79.6	72.7	76.8	27.0	30.1	15.1	36.6	27.1
Las Vegas, NV	86.8	91.8	90.6	90.6	69.6	27.3	31.1	21.2	42.9	12.7
Lexington, KY	91.9	93.9	90.6	89.7	65.7	41.1	43.4	25.4	67.8	23.0
Lincoln, NE	93.6	95.4	86.4	81.1	71.1	40.6	42.0	24.8	43.2	20.9
Little Rock, AR	92.1	93.9	91.4	89.9	68.2	32.9	35.4	25.8	55.9	17.4
Los Angeles, CA	82.2	90.4	91.1	89.2	65.7	37.4	46.4	31.8	55.5	16.2
Louisville, KY	91.3	92.7	87.7	86.4	77.4	32.1	33.7	20.6	60.2	25.4
Madison, WI	95.9	97.1	91.4	92.5	78.5	49.3	50.1	25.9	69.7	33.2
Manchester, NH	93.0	94.3	83.0	90.5	74.3	40.6	41.1	26.8	60.6	20.1
McAllen, TX	69.3	76.0	84.4	92.3	66.7	20.3	22.9	23.5	67.0	18.2

Table continued on following page.

Metro Area	High School Graduate or Higher (%)					Bachelor's Degree or Higher (%)				
	Total	White	Black	Asian	Hisp.[1]	Total	White	Black	Asian	Hisp.[1]
Memphis, TN	89.5	93.3	88.5	88.2	57.9	30.7	39.1	21.4	64.8	19.0
Miami, FL	86.9	90.6	84.2	88.6	81.7	35.6	42.4	22.4	56.3	31.2
Midland, TX	86.2	91.5	91.3	74.8	74.3	30.6	35.7	20.6	48.7	19.3
Milwaukee, WI	92.7	96.2	86.7	86.3	72.7	38.8	44.4	15.3	53.9	18.1
Minneapolis, MN	94.2	97.0	84.0	83.5	76.4	44.9	47.7	25.1	47.6	27.2
Nashville, TN	91.5	93.4	90.4	85.7	68.4	39.9	42.0	30.5	56.8	22.2
New Orleans, LA	87.5	92.2	85.3	80.0	74.8	33.0	41.2	22.5	47.7	25.0
New York, NY	87.6	93.7	86.9	84.4	74.1	43.5	52.7	28.4	57.0	22.8
Oklahoma City, OK	89.9	92.3	91.0	83.8	65.5	33.4	36.0	25.3	50.9	14.8
Omaha, NE	92.7	95.6	88.8	74.3	68.3	39.1	41.8	21.4	48.0	18.5
Orlando, FL	90.7	93.5	85.8	90.2	86.5	35.8	39.4	25.0	54.9	28.8
Philadelphia, PA	92.1	95.3	89.7	85.5	74.5	41.5	46.8	24.3	59.2	22.5
Phoenix, AZ	89.5	93.7	91.6	90.3	73.5	34.6	38.2	29.8	60.9	16.4
Pittsburgh, PA	94.9	95.4	91.7	87.5	86.9	37.4	37.8	21.5	69.8	39.9
Portland, OR	92.8	95.2	90.7	88.4	74.5	42.1	43.3	31.8	55.8	23.6
Providence, RI	88.4	90.8	85.6	88.6	72.1	35.0	37.5	25.4	56.3	16.8
Provo, UT	95.3	96.5	97.2	94.6	83.1	43.4	44.7	38.3	62.7	26.4
Raleigh, NC	92.9	96.0	92.2	93.3	69.1	50.2	55.5	33.9	76.2	22.7
Reno, NV	88.6	93.5	90.2	90.5	65.8	31.4	34.6	21.8	45.8	14.4
Richmond, VA	91.9	95.0	89.7	90.1	71.2	40.2	47.4	24.6	63.9	22.8
Rochester, MN	94.8	96.5	74.4	85.8	79.8	42.3	42.2	25.1	60.4	33.9
Sacramento, CA	90.1	94.4	91.4	85.1	78.1	36.3	39.2	26.0	45.0	22.0
Saint Louis, MO	93.3	94.7	88.8	90.9	82.6	37.6	40.1	22.0	68.6	31.0
Saint Paul, MN	94.2	97.0	84.0	83.5	76.4	44.9	47.7	25.1	47.6	27.2
Salem, OR	87.2	92.5	91.1	85.4	62.2	26.9	30.0	28.2	43.5	11.0
Salt Lake City, UT	91.8	95.2	84.3	86.9	74.6	37.8	40.9	25.4	52.0	18.6
San Antonio, TX	87.3	91.2	92.4	88.2	79.8	31.9	36.6	30.1	53.8	21.2
San Diego, CA	89.0	93.8	91.0	91.1	75.0	42.1	48.0	29.6	55.2	21.5
San Francisco, CA	89.5	96.2	91.4	88.4	73.3	52.4	61.6	32.3	59.9	25.1
San Jose, CA	89.1	94.7	92.0	91.9	72.1	54.8	57.5	42.1	69.5	20.2
Santa Rosa, CA	88.9	95.8	88.8	86.2	66.2	37.8	44.2	29.4	46.1	16.0
Savannah, GA	91.3	94.0	88.9	82.3	84.1	34.9	41.2	23.4	50.9	27.4
Seattle, WA	93.3	96.0	90.4	91.0	77.4	46.3	47.0	28.6	61.7	27.5
Sioux Falls, SD	93.7	95.6	83.4	76.1	66.5	35.7	37.4	20.1	40.3	16.0
Tampa, FL	90.9	93.1	89.2	86.4	82.3	34.0	35.4	26.6	54.2	25.9
Tucson, AZ	89.9	93.9	89.2	89.8	78.6	35.9	41.0	25.7	56.3	19.7
Tulsa, OK	90.1	92.7	90.7	77.9	66.0	29.8	32.6	21.1	33.6	15.1
Virginia Beach, VA	92.8	95.3	89.6	88.9	86.0	35.1	39.9	24.9	47.4	29.2
Washington, DC	91.5	96.2	92.8	91.8	70.7	53.8	64.4	39.1	67.2	29.3
Wichita, KS	90.3	93.5	87.6	75.1	67.1	31.5	34.2	19.0	32.5	16.4
Wilmington, NC	93.1	95.0	86.8	85.4	75.6	38.5	41.1	23.8	56.4	25.1
Winston-Salem, NC	89.2	91.0	90.0	88.5	63.8	29.6	31.4	24.6	54.1	14.7
U.S.	89.4	92.9	88.1	88.0	72.5	35.0	37.7	24.7	57.0	19.9

Note: Figures shown cover persons 25 years old and over; Figures cover the Metropolitan Statistical Area (MSA); (1) People of Hispanic origin can be of any race
Source: U.S. Census Bureau, 2019-2023 American Community Survey 5-Year Estimates

Cost of Living Index

Urban Area	Composite	Groceries	Housing	Utilities	Transp.	Health	Misc.
Albuquerque, NM	94.9	97.4	89.1	87.3	85.9	102.0	101.8
Anchorage, AK	122.8	126.5	133.1	112.4	113.6	147.1	114.1
Ann Arbor, MI	n/a	n/a	n/a	n/a	n/a	n/a	n/a
Athens, GA	98.9	100.4	97.3	99.4	95.0	96.7	100.8
Atlanta, GA	96.0	100.9	86.9	99.7	100.2	107.9	97.6
Austin, TX	97.3	96.6	104.1	98.6	94.9	98.6	92.2
Baltimore, MD	100.5	102.8	86.5	110.6	104.2	94.2	108.4
Billings, MT	99.8	103.5	95.3	82.7	120.0	114.8	98.9
Boise City, ID	102.1	103.7	101.0	77.8	109.9	98.2	106.6
Boston, MA	145.9	104.4	218.9	149.7	109.8	125.3	115.2
Boulder, CO	n/a	n/a	n/a	n/a	n/a	n/a	n/a
Cape Coral, FL	104.9	104.0	105.1	106.5	105.9	111.8	103.5
Cedar Rapids, IA	n/a	n/a	n/a	n/a	n/a	n/a	n/a
Charleston, SC	101.9	102.1	103.8	113.9	94.9	85.7	101.2
Charlotte, NC	98.9	101.1	84.8	101.3	94.4	99.6	110.0
Chicago, IL	115.1	103.9	140.1	96.7	107.3	107.9	107.0
Cincinnati, OH	96.0	100.7	87.3	99.6	96.2	94.8	100.4
Clarksville, TN	n/a	n/a	n/a	n/a	n/a	n/a	n/a
Cleveland, OH	91.4	99.8	81.2	85.5	96.7	92.2	96.1
College Station, TX	n/a	n/a	n/a	n/a	n/a	n/a	n/a
Colorado Springs, CO	101.9	101.9	110.2	75.7	95.1	95.5	104.0
Columbia, MO	90.0	96.2	79.7	96.8	84.8	98.8	94.3
Columbia, SC	89.2	99.1	69.2	117.6	80.6	75.6	98.3
Columbus, OH	95.3	100.6	96.5	104.2	87.5	82.3	93.6
Dallas, TX	101.7	98.9	95.1	115.6	91.2	104.5	107.4
Davenport, IA	90.1	97.4	76.8	83.2	105.1	97.3	94.6
Denver, CO	108.6	101.3	123.4	89.3	94.7	109.6	107.7
Des Moines, IA	85.8	99.6	66.1	80.8	93.2	87.2	94.9
Detroit, MI	103.3	101.0	106.0	100.6	103.7	107.0	102.0
Durham, NC	98.5	102.0	101.6	93.4	93.8	103.8	96.2
El Paso, TX	88.1	96.7	70.7	91.5	101.2	88.7	94.3
Eugene, OR	107.3	105.2	120.6	92.5	110.3	108.2	100.0
Fargo, ND	97.3	97.9	85.1	80.1	98.8	118.1	108.0
Fort Collins, CO	n/a	n/a	n/a	n/a	n/a	n/a	n/a
Fort Wayne, IN	90.3	99.0	77.5	91.0	100.4	97.4	93.1
Fort Worth, TX	96.0	99.3	85.8	116.7	94.7	105.7	97.0
Gainesville, FL	n/a	n/a	n/a	n/a	n/a	n/a	n/a
Green Bay, WI	90.5	97.9	80.9	82.0	102.8	95.1	93.4
Greensboro, NC	n/a	n/a	n/a	n/a	n/a	n/a	n/a
Honolulu, HI	186.8	130.4	310.0	197.6	133.6	120.8	130.4
Houston, TX	94.1	99.3	79.2	92.4	94.0	97.5	104.1
Huntsville, AL	90.8	100.2	72.3	88.7	96.5	92.5	100.7
Indianapolis, IN	88.8	98.0	76.9	88.4	98.0	86.9	92.5
Jacksonville, FL	92.9	104.0	87.1	89.7	87.2	85.2	96.0
Kansas City, MO	91.1	97.3	87.5	105.6	89.3	83.8	89.1
Lafayette, LA	87.2	97.1	64.5	84.1	97.9	80.7	100.5
Las Vegas, NV	98.5	103.7	104.6	113.8	115.0	85.2	85.1
Lexington, KY	91.9	100.5	77.2	84.4	97.3	97.6	99.7
Lincoln, NE	94.3	99.3	77.6	92.2	99.5	105.4	103.5
Little Rock, AR	93.4	97.3	77.6	84.2	94.5	84.6	107.8
Los Angeles, CA	149.4	109.3	232.5	107.2	136.1	101.1	118.9
Louisville, KY	94.1	99.1	80.1	83.2	96.7	114.9	102.4
Madison, WI	104.7	98.8	106.4	98.8	98.3	113.2	107.8
Manchester, NH	112.6	99.9	117.6	112.2	105.9	103.9	117.0
McAllen, TX	85.1	93.4	60.2	119.6	94.1	79.2	92.1
Memphis, TN	89.8	98.8	86.2	80.9	88.8	86.0	91.7

Table continued on following page.

Urban Area	Composite	Groceries	Housing	Utilities	Transp.	Health	Misc.
Miami, FL	120.9	110.8	157.4	104.9	100.6	98.1	107.4
Midland, TX	96.4	96.2	83.8	100.9	94.3	87.6	107.5
Milwaukee, WI	100.5	100.8	104.2	94.0	102.7	105.0	97.7
Minneapolis, MN	93.6	102.6	82.9	96.6	96.4	96.0	96.5
Nashville, TN	98.7	99.5	101.4	98.2	90.8	95.5	98.7
New Orleans, LA	112.4	99.2	148.7	71.6	95.6	102.6	104.0
New York, NY[2]	161.1	113.0	276.5	115.1	114.9	128.1	114.9
Oklahoma City, OK	82.2	94.9	60.1	96.8	91.3	103.9	86.0
Omaha, NE	91.9	99.1	82.5	84.2	94.4	94.0	97.5
Orlando, FL	96.4	104.7	91.7	103.7	97.4	91.9	95.2
Philadelphia, PA	103.2	104.1	99.2	105.5	105.3	96.2	106.0
Phoenix, AZ	106.3	102.8	115.6	106.6	105.4	91.6	102.2
Pittsburgh, PA	98.1	97.8	94.9	119.9	107.2	99.2	93.2
Portland, OR	116.6	107.2	146.0	86.6	127.4	110.5	101.9
Providence, RI	112.2	102.0	113.4	139.7	96.5	104.4	114.1
Provo, UT	102.5	96.7	111.3	93.2	107.4	89.9	100.5
Raleigh, NC	97.2	100.6	91.9	89.8	92.1	112.2	101.0
Reno, NV	104.0	102.9	110.9	93.4	123.5	88.5	98.6
Richmond, VA	94.2	99.9	84.6	96.2	95.3	91.1	99.2
Rochester, MN	n/a	n/a	n/a	n/a	n/a	n/a	n/a
Sacramento, CA	128.8	106.9	139.2	174.4	152.0	99.7	116.9
Saint Louis, MO	89.1	98.8	78.0	97.9	93.3	87.6	90.9
Saint Paul, MN	94.0	105.2	81.3	95.6	96.0	96.7	98.1
Salem, OR	n/a	n/a	n/a	n/a	n/a	n/a	n/a
Salt Lake City, UT	109.0	98.1	128.7	95.4	111.4	88.5	103.0
San Antonio, TX	91.2	94.5	79.0	81.8	94.3	111.3	98.5
San Diego, CA	145.3	111.1	212.1	139.4	140.9	102.2	113.9
San Francisco, CA	166.8	123.6	263.3	160.1	143.6	127.6	119.3
San Jose, CA	180.6	115.0	321.1	158.6	140.7	120.1	117.9
Santa Rosa, CA	n/a	n/a	n/a	n/a	n/a	n/a	n/a
Savannah, GA	93.8	102.5	78.1	99.5	102.7	113.7	96.4
Seattle, WA	145.1	110.3	212.2	101.4	128.4	128.5	122.4
Sioux Falls, SD	91.0	96.4	88.5	91.3	89.9	92.6	90.7
Tampa, FL	97.6	105.7	95.8	99.9	102.1	93.1	94.4
Tucson, AZ	n/a	n/a	n/a	n/a	n/a	n/a	n/a
Tulsa, OK	84.7	95.9	65.1	98.3	88.4	93.5	90.3
Virginia Beach, VA[3]	94.0	98.5	82.4	104.2	96.0	110.6	96.4
Washington, DC	141.9	105.9	222.4	102.4	107.9	117.0	113.2
Wichita, KS	88.8	94.9	65.9	98.2	97.5	94.3	99.6
Wilmington, NC	n/a	n/a	n/a	n/a	n/a	n/a	n/a
Winston-Salem, NC	93.4	97.0	77.5	101.7	92.1	105.8	101.5
U.S.	100.0	100.0	100.0	100.0	100.0	100.0	100.0

Note: The Cost of Living Index measures regional differences in the cost of consumer goods and services, excluding taxes and non-consumer expenditures, for professional and managerial households in the top income quintile. It is based on more than 50,000 prices covering almost 60 different items for which prices are collected three times a year by chambers of commerce, economic development organizations or university applied economic centers in each participating urban area. The numbers shown should be read as a percentage above or below the national average of 100. For example, a value of 115.4 in the groceries column indicates that grocery prices are 15.4% higher than the national average. Small differences in the index numbers should not be interpreted as significant. In cases where data is not available for the city, data for the metro area or for a neighboring city has been provided and noted as follows: (2) Brooklyn, NY; (3) Hampton Roads-SE Virginia
Source: The Council for Community and Economic Research, Cost of Living Index, 2024

Grocery Prices

Urban Area	T-Bone Steak ($/pound)	Frying Chicken ($/pound)	Whole Milk ($/half gal.)	Eggs ($/dozen)	Orange Juice ($/64 oz.)	Coffee ($/11.5 oz.)
Albuquerque, NM	14.86	1.51	4.61	3.01	4.27	5.45
Anchorage, AK	17.56	2.89	5.34	4.09	5.40	7.86
Ann Arbor, MI	n/a	n/a	n/a	n/a	n/a	n/a
Athens, GA	15.55	1.45	4.70	3.57	4.49	5.28
Atlanta, GA	15.52	1.44	4.67	3.38	4.47	5.59
Austin, TX	14.52	1.37	4.62	3.05	4.27	5.19
Baltimore, MD	15.52	1.44	4.64	3.35	4.34	5.56
Billings, MT	15.52	1.47	4.72	3.46	4.19	6.92
Boise City, ID	15.52	1.52	4.75	3.63	4.45	6.38
Boston, MA	15.52	1.51	4.76	3.03	4.54	5.39
Boulder, CO	n/a	n/a	n/a	n/a	n/a	n/a
Cape Coral, FL	15.51	1.46	4.69	3.46	4.51	5.45
Cedar Rapids, IA	n/a	n/a	n/a	n/a	n/a	n/a
Charleston, SC	15.51	1.64	4.54	3.41	4.43	5.46
Charlotte, NC	15.53	1.61	4.69	3.30	4.33	5.36
Chicago, IL	15.52	1.45	4.88	3.50	4.50	5.80
Cincinnati, OH	15.52	1.74	4.74	3.73	4.36	5.67
Clarksville, TN	n/a	n/a	n/a	n/a	n/a	n/a
Cleveland, OH	15.51	1.42	4.58	3.24	4.44	5.24
College Station, TX	n/a	n/a	n/a	n/a	n/a	n/a
Colorado Springs, CO	15.53	1.46	4.60	2.91	4.42	6.03
Columbia, MO	15.51	1.47	4.69	3.41	4.45	5.17
Columbia, SC	15.51	1.66	4.62	3.28	4.38	5.27
Columbus, OH	15.51	1.72	4.72	3.39	4.39	5.52
Dallas, TX	14.56	1.54	4.61	3.13	4.31	5.41
Davenport, IA	15.52	1.43	4.92	3.35	4.44	5.02
Denver, CO	15.52	1.45	4.62	2.98	4.42	6.16
Des Moines, IA	15.52	1.44	4.76	3.47	4.47	4.94
Detroit, MI	15.53	1.73	4.80	3.37	4.41	5.64
Durham, NC	15.53	1.48	4.61	3.25	4.39	5.40
El Paso, TX	14.86	1.41	4.63	2.97	4.27	5.42
Eugene, OR	15.53	1.92	4.92	3.47	4.49	6.40
Fargo, ND	15.51	1.46	4.85	3.12	4.28	5.46
Fort Collins, CO	n/a	n/a	n/a	n/a	n/a	n/a
Fort Wayne, IN	15.51	1.66	4.69	3.49	4.36	5.41
Fort Worth, TX	14.52	1.56	4.61	3.13	4.28	5.46
Gainesville, FL	n/a	n/a	n/a	n/a	n/a	n/a
Green Bay, WI	15.51	1.42	4.70	3.25	4.43	5.29
Greensboro, NC	n/a	n/a	n/a	n/a	n/a	n/a
Honolulu, HI	16.57	2.86	5.49	3.98	5.19	7.89
Houston, TX	14.53	1.62	4.64	3.18	4.33	5.40
Huntsville, AL	15.52	1.41	4.54	3.35	4.41	5.49
Indianapolis, IN	15.51	1.63	4.67	3.40	4.33	5.39
Jacksonville, FL	15.52	1.42	4.72	3.41	4.53	5.38
Kansas City, MO	15.52	1.45	4.70	3.17	4.38	5.06
Lafayette, LA	15.29	1.41	4.60	3.05	4.38	5.07
Las Vegas, NV	15.54	1.74	4.78	3.08	4.43	6.31
Lexington, KY	15.52	1.44	4.69	3.40	4.30	5.70
Lincoln, NE	15.51	1.44	4.68	3.13	4.43	5.17
Little Rock, AR	14.86	1.43	4.62	3.40	4.31	5.24
Los Angeles, CA	15.55	2.45	5.00	3.14	4.55	6.68
Louisville, KY	15.51	1.48	4.71	3.39	4.37	5.37
Madison, WI	15.51	1.43	4.77	3.34	4.44	5.60
Manchester, NH	15.51	1.42	4.71	2.98	4.42	5.31
McAllen, TX	14.52	1.28	4.54	2.96	4.22	5.08

Table continued on following page.

Urban Area	T-Bone Steak ($/pound)	Frying Chicken ($/pound)	Whole Milk ($/half gal.)	Eggs ($/dozen)	Orange Juice ($/64 oz.)	Coffee ($/11.5 oz.)
Memphis, TN	15.53	1.31	4.67	3.47	4.35	5.24
Miami, FL	15.52	1.45	4.80	3.77	4.78	5.91
Midland, TX	14.53	1.41	4.61	3.04	4.30	4.99
Milwaukee, WI	15.50	1.43	4.80	3.34	4.45	5.96
Minneapolis, MN	15.53	1.44	4.66	3.56	4.49	5.23
Nashville, TN	15.51	1.43	4.63	3.32	4.40	5.35
New Orleans, LA	15.51	1.36	4.66	3.19	4.38	4.94
New York, NY[2]	15.52	1.56	5.14	3.63	4.79	5.93
Oklahoma City, OK	15.34	1.46	4.55	2.97	4.28	5.16
Omaha, NE	15.51	1.44	4.87	3.22	4.43	5.50
Orlando, FL	15.52	1.45	4.63	3.47	4.53	5.53
Philadelphia, PA	15.46	1.52	4.70	3.48	4.41	5.43
Phoenix, AZ	15.53	1.77	4.76	2.95	4.40	6.24
Pittsburgh, PA	15.52	1.43	4.52	3.27	4.44	5.15
Portland, OR	15.52	1.89	4.93	3.57	4.49	6.85
Providence, RI	15.51	1.68	4.70	3.55	4.43	4.91
Provo, UT	15.52	1.54	4.57	2.91	4.17	5.79
Raleigh, NC	15.51	1.45	4.58	3.33	4.31	5.44
Reno, NV	15.53	2.26	4.66	2.91	4.36	5.88
Richmond, VA	15.51	1.43	4.65	3.38	4.37	5.55
Rochester, MN	n/a	n/a	n/a	n/a	n/a	n/a
Sacramento, CA	15.53	2.13	5.01	2.90	4.40	6.44
Saint Louis, MO	15.51	1.44	4.67	3.37	4.43	5.05
Saint Paul, MN	15.52	1.44	4.64	3.81	4.58	5.13
Salem, OR	n/a	n/a	n/a	n/a	n/a	n/a
Salt Lake City, UT	15.51	1.53	4.62	3.03	4.19	6.11
San Antonio, TX	14.53	1.33	4.57	2.98	4.25	5.05
San Diego, CA	15.56	2.40	5.07	3.17	4.63	6.78
San Francisco, CA	15.55	2.66	5.03	3.35	4.86	7.53
San Jose, CA	15.54	2.57	5.09	3.10	4.64	6.92
Santa Rosa, CA	n/a	n/a	n/a	n/a	n/a	n/a
Savannah, GA	15.52	1.43	4.72	3.53	4.53	5.62
Seattle, WA	15.51	1.98	4.94	3.87	4.58	7.06
Sioux Falls, SD	15.53	1.49	4.52	3.10	4.37	5.10
Tampa, FL	15.52	1.46	4.73	3.60	4.59	5.56
Tucson, AZ	n/a	n/a	n/a	n/a	n/a	n/a
Tulsa, OK	15.52	1.45	4.59	2.97	4.32	5.06
Virginia Beach, VA[3]	15.52	1.46	4.58	3.35	4.34	5.34
Washington, DC	15.51	1.42	4.62	3.47	4.44	5.77
Wichita, KS	15.50	1.43	4.66	3.16	4.30	5.36
Wilmington, NC	n/a	n/a	n/a	n/a	n/a	n/a
Winston-Salem, NC	15.51	1.46	4.60	3.19	4.30	5.15
Average[1]	15.42	1.55	4.69	3.25	4.41	5.46
Minimum[1]	14.50	1.16	4.43	2.75	4.00	4.85
Maximum[1]	17.56	2.89	5.49	4.78	5.54	7.89

Note: **T-Bone Steak** (price per pound); **Frying Chicken** (price per pound, whole fryer); **Whole Milk** (half gallon carton); **Eggs** (price per dozen, Grade A, large); **Orange Juice** (64 oz. Tropicana or Florida Natural); **Coffee** (11.5 oz. can, vacuum-packed, Maxwell House, Hills Bros, or Folgers); (1) Average, minimum, and maximum values for all 276 areas in the Cost of Living Index report; n/a not available; In cases where data is not available for the city, data for the metro area or for a neighboring city has been provided and noted as follows: (2) Brooklyn, NY; (3) Hampton Roads-SE Virginia
Source: The Council for Community and Economic Research, Cost of Living Index, 2024

Housing and Utility Costs

Urban Area	New Home Price ($)	Apartment Rent ($/month)	All Electric ($/month)	Part Electric ($/month)	Other Energy ($/month)	Telephone ($/month)
Albuquerque, NM	424,687	1,574	-	115.74	50.09	192.92
Anchorage, AK	758,772	1,670	-	108.68	138.69	193.41
Ann Arbor, MI	n/a	n/a	n/a	n/a	n/a	n/a
Athens, GA	483,427	1,622	-	113.87	91.54	192.87
Atlanta, GA	428,946	1,464	-	113.87	91.54	194.22
Austin, TX	500,842	1,849	-	137.02	59.06	203.47
Baltimore, MD	390,678	1,695	-	134.88	101.43	201.97
Billings, MT	517,409	1,317	-	94.77	60.66	185.25
Boise City, ID	514,076	1,611	-	83.70	59.41	179.42
Boston, MA	1,039,939	3,993	-	190.85	180.18	190.24
Boulder, CO	n/a	n/a	n/a	n/a	n/a	n/a
Cape Coral, FL	509,774	1,897	225.95	-	-	197.01
Cedar Rapids, IA	n/a	n/a	n/a	n/a	n/a	n/a
Charleston, SC	526,080	1,748	249.82	-	-	197.48
Charlotte, NC	398,825	1,562	213.43	-	-	189.47
Chicago, IL	566,384	3,240	-	113.94	70.31	212.43
Cincinnati, OH	443,467	1,416	-	116.95	90.88	189.55
Clarksville, TN	n/a	n/a	n/a	n/a	n/a	n/a
Cleveland, OH	391,639	1,431	-	83.27	78.55	189.85
College Station, TX	n/a	n/a	n/a	n/a	n/a	n/a
Colorado Springs, CO	557,240	1,828	-	86.01	42.49	192.15
Columbia, MO	451,668	1,041	-	114.12	78.36	199.61
Columbia, SC	328,383	1,205	-	119.24	143.41	195.98
Columbus, OH	482,718	1,613	-	146.60	76.69	189.10
Dallas, TX	477,656	1,572	-	171.06	80.72	203.47
Davenport, IA	387,652	1,218	-	85.51	62.12	200.43
Denver, CO	650,555	1,899	-	93.55	76.25	197.22
Des Moines, IA	359,756	846	-	84.52	63.10	188.12
Detroit, MI	568,077	1,560	-	134.21	78.36	187.38
Durham, NC	521,333	1,650	187.89	-	-	189.44
El Paso, TX	354,072	1,146	-	111.01	62.07	203.47
Eugene, OR	666,539	1,654	-	89.38	96.37	187.81
Fargo, ND	390,066	1,596	-	81.39	58.17	197.46
Fort Collins, CO	n/a	n/a	n/a	n/a	n/a	n/a
Fort Wayne, IN	364,871	1,370	-	109.31	68.72	192.42
Fort Worth, TX	422,585	1,470	-	170.29	80.72	210.13
Gainesville, FL	n/a	n/a	n/a	n/a	n/a	n/a
Green Bay, WI	447,400	1,055	-	90.06	61.14	188.34
Greensboro, NC	n/a	n/a	n/a	n/a	n/a	n/a
Honolulu, HI	1,681,170	4,424	529.02	-	-	187.39
Houston, TX	388,197	1,322	-	124.12	48.31	209.27
Huntsville, AL	361,221	1,123	172.74	-	-	189.28
Indianapolis, IN	360,369	1,336	-	99.46	70.12	192.42
Jacksonville, FL	391,862	1,714	170.55	-	-	197.76
Kansas City, MO	429,449	1,506	-	103.82	115.85	202.40
Lafayette, LA	306,872	1,150	-	96.15	60.82	190.09
Las Vegas, NV	554,723	1,576	-	160.52	94.44	188.64
Lexington, KY	380,651	1,239	-	82.51	72.69	194.48
Lincoln, NE	390,814	1,216	-	90.57	84.28	204.27
Little Rock, AR	407,536	1,155	-	76.85	69.20	208.40
Los Angeles, CA	1,311,286	2,988	-	163.45	65.93	194.86
Louisville, KY	388,161	1,369	-	82.51	72.69	188.14
Madison, WI	622,141	1,233	-	126.81	79.79	187.45
Manchester, NH	552,244	2,205	-	135.10	114.30	189.12
McAllen, TX	291,921	981	-	176.13	88.49	203.47

Table continued on following page.

Urban Area	New Home Price ($)	Apartment Rent ($/month)	All Electric ($/month)	Part Electric ($/month)	Other Energy ($/month)	Telephone ($/month)
Memphis, TN	404,407	1,598	-	105.22	38.46	195.12
Miami, FL	711,025	3,211	220.47	-	-	197.31
Midland, TX	400,707	1,483	-	150.59	53.85	202.34
Milwaukee, WI	541,477	1,627	-	123.28	67.66	187.62
Minneapolis, MN	405,152	1,419	-	98.70	98.25	191.53
Nashville, TN	519,432	1,670	-	105.42	77.00	223.33
New Orleans, LA	812,851	2,128	-	68.38	47.92	190.09
New York, NY[2]	1,411,780	3,995	-	157.71	92.60	203.07
Oklahoma City, OK	320,395	811	-	115.46	78.66	197.38
Omaha, NE	385,889	1,500	-	93.49	55.47	203.73
Orlando, FL	441,765	1,690	216.79	-	-	197.01
Philadelphia, PA	470,985	1,851	-	138.01	81.94	201.51
Phoenix, AZ	609,926	1,792	232.03	-	-	187.62
Pittsburgh, PA	478,461	1,602	-	137.23	130.44	200.01
Portland, OR	723,737	2,574	-	70.81	96.37	186.81
Providence, RI	474,141	2,453	-	171.99	161.54	198.12
Provo, UT	612,973	1,544	-	77.11	106.23	195.59
Raleigh, NC	466,683	1,514	-	107.05	69.13	189.30
Reno, NV	596,654	1,646	-	129.17	59.21	188.64
Richmond, VA	418,775	1,466	-	117.64	80.21	187.77
Rochester, MN	n/a	n/a	n/a	n/a	n/a	n/a
Sacramento, CA	718,604	2,241	-	397.28	53.75	191.51
Saint Louis, MO	427,558	1,128	-	100.98	92.58	203.68
Saint Paul, MN	404,109	1,358	-	92.16	101.15	192.06
Salem, OR	n/a	n/a	n/a	n/a	n/a	n/a
Salt Lake City, UT	717,422	1,758	-	96.56	93.13	196.83
San Antonio, TX	357,072	1,521	-	105.82	36.26	202.34
San Diego, CA	1,113,702	3,153	-	255.41	87.52	181.36
San Francisco, CA	1,383,739	3,749	-	264.12	131.73	205.06
San Jose, CA	1,860,932	3,311	-	267.58	131.25	192.30
Santa Rosa, CA	n/a	n/a	n/a	n/a	n/a	n/a
Savannah, GA	379,397	1,313	206.53	-	-	191.37
Seattle, WA	1,093,157	3,259	204.50	-	-	204.74
Sioux Falls, SD	509,371	977	-	103.68	71.55	198.68
Tampa, FL	455,535	1,796	203.80	-	-	197.76
Tucson, AZ	n/a	n/a	n/a	n/a	n/a	n/a
Tulsa, OK	339,822	935	-	118.37	80.52	197.22
Virginia Beach, VA[3]	389,841	1,484	-	120.02	103.90	187.93
Washington, DC	1,149,206	3,212	-	122.00	92.52	193.65
Wichita, KS	334,425	1,007	-	113.92	81.43	202.42
Wilmington, NC	n/a	n/a	n/a	n/a	n/a	n/a
Winston-Salem, NC	383,928	1,301	214.90	-	-	189.30
Average[1]	515,975	1,550	210.99	123.07	82.07	194.99
Minimum[1]	265,375	692	104.33	53.68	36.26	179.42
Maximum[1]	2,775,821	5,719	529.02	397.28	361.63	223.33

Note: **New Home Price** (2,400 sf living area, 8,000 sf lot, in urban area with full utilities); **Apartment Rent** (950 sf 2 bedroom/1.5 or 2 bath, unfurnished, excluding all utilities except water); **All Electric** (average monthly cost for an all-electric home); **Part Electric** (average monthly cost for a part-electric home); **Other Energy** (average monthly cost for natural gas, fuel oil, coal, wood, and any other forms of energy except electricity); **Telephone** (price includes the base monthly rate plus taxes and fees for three lines of mobile phone service); (1) Average, minimum, and maximum values for all 276 areas in the Cost of Living Index report; n/a not available; In cases where data is not available for the city, data for the metro area or for a neighboring city has been provided and noted as follows: (2) Brooklyn, NY; (3) Hampton Roads-SE Virginia

Source: The Council for Community and Economic Research, Cost of Living Index, 2024

Health Care, Transportation, and Other Costs

Urban Area	Doctor ($/visit)	Dentist ($/visit)	Optometrist ($/visit)	Gasoline ($/gallon)	Beauty Salon ($/visit)	Men's Shirt ($)
Albuquerque, NM	133.41	115.32	145.00	3.10	47.25	37.35
Anchorage, AK	243.83	173.17	265.00	3.68	50.00	45.44
Ann Arbor, MI	n/a	n/a	n/a	n/a	n/a	n/a
Athens, GA	123.75	128.33	97.63	3.12	56.40	40.51
Atlanta, GA	132.58	142.21	130.44	3.22	56.70	30.32
Austin, TX	109.05	135.58	126.98	2.98	67.39	27.11
Baltimore, MD	135.14	116.91	119.20	3.41	61.43	41.00
Billings, MT	215.23	110.57	164.07	3.33	38.78	36.85
Boise City, ID	169.88	102.77	145.10	3.61	52.55	48.06
Boston, MA	222.77	144.00	161.33	3.33	66.76	39.88
Boulder, CO	n/a	n/a	n/a	n/a	n/a	n/a
Cape Coral, FL	178.39	133.21	101.13	3.36	54.67	30.93
Cedar Rapids, IA	n/a	n/a	n/a	n/a	n/a	n/a
Charleston, SC	123.53	99.17	82.86	3.03	56.00	24.77
Charlotte, NC	157.61	120.57	92.08	3.12	79.44	57.64
Chicago, IL	179.67	126.00	113.83	3.55	62.23	34.52
Cincinnati, OH	158.21	98.92	97.57	3.18	39.43	41.70
Clarksville, TN	n/a	n/a	n/a	n/a	n/a	n/a
Cleveland, OH	117.00	111.33	110.47	3.21	40.20	39.79
College Station, TX	n/a	n/a	n/a	n/a	n/a	n/a
Colorado Springs, CO	134.99	106.17	132.00	3.04	50.14	30.58
Columbia, MO	182.67	95.67	138.50	3.10	45.42	37.14
Columbia, SC	150.00	58.67	67.33	3.12	38.83	34.56
Columbus, OH	115.70	94.35	93.20	3.19	49.51	36.47
Dallas, TX	138.26	133.49	135.65	3.07	72.78	43.45
Davenport, IA	167.17	105.92	108.62	3.41	39.87	34.38
Denver, CO	134.18	140.57	122.31	3.05	50.44	22.71
Des Moines, IA	119.38	101.96	128.70	3.15	42.46	37.61
Detroit, MI	183.09	126.33	95.64	3.42	60.83	52.14
Durham, NC	179.33	112.78	133.40	3.38	54.35	30.66
El Paso, TX	129.11	95.03	101.95	3.23	33.64	34.89
Eugene, OR	196.75	117.67	126.00	3.83	40.19	36.32
Fargo, ND	230.71	124.67	113.44	3.12	40.47	44.83
Fort Collins, CO	n/a	n/a	n/a	n/a	n/a	n/a
Fort Wayne, IN	137.75	106.33	122.67	3.32	33.28	39.34
Fort Worth, TX	138.71	136.11	137.89	3.03	52.39	37.44
Gainesville, FL	n/a	n/a	n/a	n/a	n/a	n/a
Green Bay, WI	167.58	112.11	84.28	3.14	30.42	26.22
Greensboro, NC	n/a	n/a	n/a	n/a	n/a	n/a
Honolulu, HI	201.94	127.00	258.67	4.58	75.33	58.48
Houston, TX	97.07	129.17	137.54	2.98	73.30	50.68
Huntsville, AL	121.00	115.28	99.56	3.04	58.56	30.30
Indianapolis, IN	112.66	105.53	77.80	3.35	39.07	43.61
Jacksonville, FL	106.53	98.40	97.76	3.34	79.67	30.27
Kansas City, MO	95.79	108.20	95.10	3.06	34.80	29.79
Lafayette, LA	95.33	95.87	120.20	3.01	40.73	44.86
Las Vegas, NV	110.44	99.25	100.78	4.13	48.86	25.05
Lexington, KY	144.23	113.73	92.42	3.19	60.23	44.97
Lincoln, NE	183.29	113.07	119.17	3.25	42.20	52.31
Little Rock, AR	133.00	83.67	105.53	2.95	52.55	47.99
Los Angeles, CA	130.00	133.17	127.53	4.85	94.00	38.64
Louisville, KY	152.10	159.00	107.05	3.21	43.89	48.00
Madison, WI	236.64	124.37	72.86	3.27	76.22	41.80
Manchester, NH	183.83	108.17	116.33	3.24	56.33	42.69
McAllen, TX	91.69	88.11	100.21	2.96	47.50	32.95

Table continued on following page.

Urban Area	Doctor ($/visit)	Dentist ($/visit)	Optometrist ($/visit)	Gasoline ($/gallon)	Beauty Salon ($/visit)	Men's Shirt ($)
Memphis, TN	112.80	97.80	83.95	3.00	46.92	27.44
Miami, FL	134.75	118.47	110.39	3.43	87.63	28.46
Midland, TX	97.50	108.17	132.67	3.13	69.08	43.45
Milwaukee, WI	174.22	122.03	86.17	3.30	44.20	32.41
Minneapolis, MN	170.09	100.86	120.48	3.16	40.96	41.19
Nashville, TN	122.71	110.37	114.45	3.08	48.65	32.66
New Orleans, LA	161.78	121.36	115.44	3.11	48.33	49.00
New York, NY[2]	192.84	171.93	152.60	3.43	68.80	44.04
Oklahoma City, OK	149.53	124.67	99.96	3.02	51.40	22.45
Omaha, NE	151.64	90.62	117.00	3.08	33.92	35.09
Orlando, FL	123.06	110.00	97.28	3.34	53.19	32.49
Philadelphia, PA	148.84	111.61	125.00	3.33	67.25	36.90
Phoenix, AZ	99.00	127.08	103.50	3.64	55.36	22.95
Pittsburgh, PA	96.56	128.63	105.71	3.67	44.32	28.77
Portland, OR	218.48	116.33	147.50	4.17	60.17	35.98
Providence, RI	168.33	117.58	111.08	3.28	50.22	31.37
Provo, UT	113.66	105.45	127.59	3.41	51.34	49.04
Raleigh, NC	146.67	153.61	109.33	3.23	55.17	32.17
Reno, NV	115.00	105.00	118.17	4.35	49.17	27.27
Richmond, VA	120.19	104.13	133.02	3.24	48.38	20.26
Rochester, MN	n/a	n/a	n/a	n/a	n/a	n/a
Sacramento, CA	151.58	121.82	173.55	5.28	71.49	36.48
Saint Louis, MO	92.32	115.88	95.55	3.38	41.97	28.19
Saint Paul, MN	169.08	101.40	118.46	3.16	41.44	42.25
Salem, OR	n/a	n/a	n/a	n/a	n/a	n/a
Salt Lake City, UT	129.02	100.40	125.47	3.38	56.68	44.66
San Antonio, TX	149.40	139.78	139.25	2.97	69.33	39.95
San Diego, CA	139.44	126.00	143.70	4.93	67.95	39.49
San Francisco, CA	183.65	160.37	168.34	5.07	86.22	48.81
San Jose, CA	212.00	131.83	166.92	5.00	65.28	32.93
Santa Rosa, CA	n/a	n/a	n/a	n/a	n/a	n/a
Savannah, GA	150.00	152.87	91.31	3.29	39.61	38.61
Seattle, WA	208.77	157.05	179.39	4.49	85.33	49.17
Sioux Falls, SD	116.42	116.32	140.94	3.04	40.11	30.74
Tampa, FL	126.57	112.70	118.00	3.36	48.00	27.91
Tucson, AZ	n/a	n/a	n/a	n/a	n/a	n/a
Tulsa, OK	109.57	109.83	111.11	2.95	35.40	29.28
Virginia Beach, VA[3]	144.92	148.93	69.03	3.20	42.70	32.71
Washington, DC	177.67	151.33	125.50	3.36	78.76	37.95
Wichita, KS	111.32	102.90	144.60	3.09	48.13	54.27
Wilmington, NC	n/a	n/a	n/a	n/a	n/a	n/a
Winston-Salem, NC	152.89	120.67	145.61	3.15	50.94	38.49
Average[1]	143.77	117.51	129.23	3.32	48.57	38.14
Minimum[1]	36.74	58.67	67.33	2.80	24.00	13.41
Maximum[1]	270.44	216.82	307.33	5.28	94.00	63.89

Note: **Doctor** (general practitioners routine exam of an established patient); **Dentist** (adult teeth cleaning and periodic oral examination); **Optometrist** (full vision eye exam for established adult patient); **Gasoline** (one gallon regular unleaded, national brand, including all taxes, cash price at self-service pump if available); **Beauty Salon** (woman's shampoo, trim, and blow-dry); **Men's Shirt** (cotton/polyester dress shirt, pinpoint weave, long sleeves); (1) Average, minimum, and maximum values for all 276 areas in the Cost of Living Index report; n/a not available; In cases where data is not available for the city, data for the metro area or for a neighboring city has been provided and noted as follows: (2) Brooklyn, NY; (3) Hampton Roads-SE Virginia

Source: The Council for Community and Economic Research, Cost of Living Index, 2024

Number of Medical Professionals

City	Area Covered	MDs[1]	DOs[1,2]	Dentists	Podiatrists	Chiropractors	Optometrists
Albuquerque, NM	Bernalillo County	503.5	30.6	87.4	9.4	24.9	17.7
Anchorage, AK	Anchorage Borough	384.5	55.4	134.9	5.9	65.7	31.5
Ann Arbor, MI	Washtenaw County	1,420.9	52.7	208.7	9.0	26.5	19.4
Athens, GA	Clarke County	392.7	17.7	50.0	3.8	21.5	16.2
Atlanta, GA	Fulton County	548.6	18.3	76.9	5.1	60.5	21.3
Austin, TX	Travis County	332.0	21.9	76.9	4.4	36.6	18.8
Baltimore, MD	Baltimore City	1,247.2	36.1	88.5	8.0	16.8	16.6
Billings, MT	Yellowstone County	379.2	40.0	101.3	9.4	38.6	26.9
Boise City, ID	Ada County	286.2	40.1	83.7	4.6	54.9	23.1
Boston, MA	Suffolk County	1,797.9	24.3	251.7	9.0	16.9	39.0
Boulder, CO	Boulder County	365.5	34.2	116.9	6.4	84.4	30.0
Cape Coral, FL	Lee County	198.8	29.9	56.1	7.9	28.8	13.3
Cedar Rapids, IA	Linn County	181.2	25.3	77.7	8.7	62.5	17.9
Charleston, SC	Charleston County	881.5	45.6	117.8	5.7	54.7	25.9
Charlotte, NC	Mecklenburg County	352.8	20.9	72.1	3.7	37.2	14.5
Chicago, IL	Cook County	472.9	34.3	100.5	12.9	30.1	22.5
Cincinnati, OH	Hamilton County	662.9	36.0	77.1	10.4	21.6	23.3
Clarksville, TN	Montgomery County	91.4	16.6	45.0	2.9	12.9	10.4
Cleveland, OH	Cuyahoga County	799.3	74.0	110.6	18.8	20.5	18.2
College Station, TX	Brazos County	254.5	20.2	58.0	3.3	19.6	18.0
Colorado Springs, CO	El Paso County	214.0	37.9	107.1	5.4	47.7	25.7
Columbia, MO	Boone County	864.2	95.9	78.6	5.8	41.2	28.0
Columbia, SC	Richland County	358.7	21.6	93.1	6.8	22.8	18.8
Columbus, OH	Franklin County	473.2	78.8	99.2	8.0	26.5	29.9
Dallas, TX	Dallas County	380.9	24.6	96.6	4.5	40.3	15.6
Davenport, IA	Scott County	256.4	56.3	85.5	5.2	190.5	16.6
Denver, CO	Denver County	610.0	36.3	84.8	6.8	40.6	17.3
Des Moines, IA	Polk County	221.1	118.9	80.8	12.3	63.7	21.2
Detroit, MI	Wayne County	348.3	61.0	80.1	9.8	19.1	12.4
Durham, NC	Durham County	1,206.3	21.9	77.2	4.2	21.1	13.7
El Paso, TX	El Paso County	231.2	22.1	49.5	4.7	9.2	10.8
Eugene, OR	Lane County	250.6	16.5	75.6	5.2	29.4	17.3
Fargo, ND	Cass County	401.6	26.5	78.4	5.1	75.9	33.6
Fort Collins, CO	Larimer County	251.9	39.3	85.2	6.5	57.4	21.3
Fort Wayne, IN	Allen County	272.1	33.5	72.7	5.6	23.8	26.6
Fort Worth, TX	Tarrant County	197.7	39.4	64.9	4.5	30.4	17.3
Gainesville, FL	Alachua County	1,059.4	68.3	193.4	5.6	26.9	19.2
Green Bay, WI	Brown County	265.5	25.6	80.7	3.3	50.5	19.9
Greensboro, NC	Guilford County	262.2	18.9	62.9	4.7	15.1	10.2
Honolulu, HI	Honolulu County	357.2	23.8	103.9	3.9	22.6	25.8
Houston, TX	Harris County	363.6	16.0	75.3	5.0	24.0	21.6
Huntsville, AL	Madison County	275.3	16.1	53.3	2.9	23.0	20.1
Indianapolis, IN	Marion County	475.0	31.6	95.4	6.9	17.5	22.1
Jacksonville, FL	Duval County	369.2	38.0	77.4	6.9	27.6	16.4
Kansas City, MO	Jackson County	343.6	110.1	94.5	7.1	49.3	20.2
Lafayette, LA	Lafayette Parish	383.7	17.3	71.3	4.0	33.6	14.4
Las Vegas, NV	Clark County	188.3	42.2	69.1	4.7	21.1	14.8
Lexington, KY	Fayette County	844.1	66.5	149.6	8.1	25.9	29.4
Lincoln, NE	Lancaster County	215.9	16.9	109.0	5.5	49.9	20.5
Little Rock, AR	Pulaski County	822.8	30.3	80.2	5.2	24.0	22.7
Los Angeles, CA	Los Angeles County	336.3	17.6	99.4	6.9	32.1	20.8
Louisville, KY	Jefferson County	506.3	25.2	107.8	8.5	28.2	17.9
Madison, WI	Dane County	669.0	28.0	77.3	5.2	45.9	21.9
Manchester, NH	Hillsborough County	235.1	26.7	85.2	6.6	26.9	22.5
McAllen, TX	Hidalgo County	145.8	4.7	31.4	1.6	8.0	7.2
Memphis, TN	Shelby County	429.3	17.8	78.8	4.0	15.5	33.0

Table continued on following page.

City	Area Covered	MDs[1]	DOs[1,2]	Dentists	Podiatrists	Chiropractors	Optometrists
Miami, FL	Miami-Dade County	415.2	27.2	81.5	10.0	20.1	16.3
Midland, TX	Midland County	154.1	6.4	60.4	2.3	14.1	11.9
Milwaukee, WI	Milwaukee County	431.6	36.6	92.8	7.1	22.0	12.1
Minneapolis, MN	Hennepin County	570.7	32.9	106.5	5.7	80.2	23.3
Nashville, TN	Davidson County	698.9	19.2	84.9	5.3	29.8	17.8
New Orleans, LA	Orleans Parish	1,005.0	33.8	86.5	4.9	10.2	8.8
New York, NY	New York City	545.5	24.3	90.9	13.8	16.8	19.8
Oklahoma City, OK	Oklahoma County	432.6	52.2	111.5	4.8	29.7	21.3
Omaha, NE	Douglas County	600.0	44.3	105.5	5.4	44.4	23.6
Orlando, FL	Orange County	349.3	28.9	54.1	4.1	29.8	14.1
Philadelphia, PA	Philadelphia County	663.2	66.9	86.4	16.3	15.6	20.8
Phoenix, AZ	Maricopa County	258.2	37.8	73.7	7.4	34.3	17.5
Pittsburgh, PA	Allegheny County	677.7	59.4	99.5	9.3	44.9	21.1
Portland, OR	Multnomah County	687.2	44.4	105.1	5.1	80.2	26.2
Providence, RI	Providence County	526.4	19.5	59.8	10.1	21.2	22.4
Provo, UT	Utah County	115.9	24.3	60.3	4.7	26.7	11.4
Raleigh, NC	Wake County	293.0	15.8	75.8	3.8	29.7	16.6
Reno, NV	Washoe County	310.2	25.2	72.1	4.4	30.7	23.7
Richmond, VA	Richmond City	822.6	63.6	155.7	13.5	7.4	15.7
Rochester, MN	Olmsted County	2,670.4	71.3	137.1	7.3	45.5	24.9
Sacramento, CA	Sacramento County	344.7	20.3	84.3	4.5	22.0	19.4
Saint Louis, MO	St. Louis City	1,491.0	56.9	71.0	4.3	23.4	21.7
Saint Paul, MN	Ramsey County	379.6	17.2	95.7	5.8	71.4	14.7
Salem, OR	Marion County	180.0	18.7	88.3	6.6	35.5	16.7
Salt Lake City, UT	Salt Lake County	422.6	23.4	83.1	6.6	29.7	15.1
San Antonio, TX	Bexar County	330.0	28.5	95.3	6.0	17.4	19.0
San Diego, CA	San Diego County	364.2	22.2	100.8	5.0	36.4	21.2
San Francisco, CA	San Francisco County	942.4	16.7	175.9	11.4	44.0	34.6
San Jose, CA	Santa Clara County	483.8	14.5	129.4	7.4	47.0	30.7
Santa Rosa, CA	Sonoma County	289.0	21.3	99.6	6.8	44.8	18.9
Savannah, GA	Chatham County	384.6	28.2	73.4	6.9	21.4	14.8
Seattle, WA	King County	521.6	19.0	118.3	6.4	48.4	24.3
Sioux Falls, SD	Minnehaha County	395.6	31.4	56.1	5.8	57.5	18.4
Tampa, FL	Hillsborough County	375.2	41.2	66.1	6.7	29.3	16.2
Tucson, AZ	Pima County	387.9	35.6	67.8	5.6	19.4	17.6
Tulsa, OK	Tulsa County	265.4	153.1	71.8	4.2	40.1	25.0
Virginia Beach, VA	Virginia Beach City	263.4	14.9	82.0	7.5	26.7	16.3
Washington, DC	District of Columbia	928.4	29.2	130.5	9.3	11.2	15.2
Wichita, KS	Sedgwick County	266.0	42.1	71.3	1.9	43.9	29.0
Wilmington, NC	New Hanover County	367.8	37.9	82.9	8.4	36.0	24.3
Winston-Salem, NC	Forsyth County	716.2	41.1	64.9	6.9	19.1	18.6
U.S.	U.S.	302.5	29.2	74.6	6.4	29.5	18.0

Note: All figures are the number of medical professionals per 100,000 population; Data as of 2023 unless noted; (1) Data as of 2022 and includes all active, non-federal physicians; (2) Doctor of Osteopathic Medicine
Source: U.S. Department of Health and Human Services, Health Resources and Services Administration, Bureau of Health Professions, Area Resource File (ARF) 2023-2024

Health Insurance Coverage: City

City	With Health Insurance	With Private Health Insurance	With Public Health Insurance	Without Health Insurance	Population Under Age 19 Without Health Insurance
Albuquerque, NM	91.7	60.1	45.1	8.3	5.0
Anchorage, AK	90.0	70.0	34.0	10.0	7.4
Ann Arbor, MI	97.2	86.7	20.9	2.8	2.1
Athens, GA	88.8	72.8	25.0	11.2	8.1
Atlanta, GA	89.5	70.4	27.2	10.5	6.2
Austin, TX	87.6	74.8	20.6	12.4	9.2
Baltimore, MD	94.2	58.5	46.8	5.8	3.8
Billings, MT	93.1	67.1	39.9	6.9	4.8
Boise City, ID	92.3	74.4	29.4	7.7	4.9
Boston, MA	97.0	69.9	35.8	3.0	1.9
Boulder, CO	96.5	83.8	21.0	3.5	1.0
Cape Coral, FL	88.4	65.5	38.4	11.6	10.1
Cedar Rapids, IA	95.5	71.1	36.8	4.5	1.6
Charleston, SC	93.6	79.0	27.0	6.4	2.0
Charlotte, NC	87.1	67.8	26.5	12.9	8.3
Chicago, IL	90.2	61.6	35.8	9.8	4.0
Cincinnati, OH	92.4	61.1	40.3	7.6	5.7
Clarksville, TN	90.7	72.1	34.3	9.3	4.3
Cleveland, OH	92.3	43.8	57.2	7.7	3.7
College Station, TX	91.9	83.0	16.5	8.1	4.7
Colorado Springs, CO	92.3	69.8	36.4	7.7	4.7
Columbia, MO	93.6	79.1	23.3	6.4	4.7
Columbia, SC	91.9	71.0	31.4	8.1	3.2
Columbus, OH	90.2	62.3	35.5	9.8	5.8
Dallas, TX	77.0	54.1	29.3	23.0	15.7
Davenport, IA	92.8	65.0	41.1	7.2	4.7
Denver, CO	91.2	68.3	30.8	8.8	5.3
Des Moines, IA	93.3	62.0	42.7	6.7	2.2
Detroit, MI	92.5	41.8	62.6	7.5	2.7
Durham, NC	88.4	70.6	27.4	11.6	8.6
El Paso, TX	79.0	53.1	34.9	21.0	11.9
Eugene, OR	94.5	68.2	39.0	5.5	2.3
Fargo, ND	93.9	79.5	26.0	6.1	4.5
Fort Collins, CO	94.4	78.3	25.0	5.6	4.8
Fort Wayne, IN	90.6	62.9	38.1	9.4	6.7
Fort Worth, TX	81.4	61.7	26.4	18.6	12.7
Gainesville, FL	91.8	76.6	23.8	8.2	5.0
Green Bay, WI	91.6	59.8	40.9	8.4	4.9
Greensboro, NC	90.9	65.5	35.7	9.1	4.1
Honolulu, HI	96.2	75.5	38.3	3.8	2.4
Houston, TX	76.0	52.1	30.3	24.0	16.0
Huntsville, AL	90.6	73.2	32.5	9.4	3.2
Indianapolis, IN	91.0	62.3	38.6	9.0	5.7
Jacksonville, FL	88.3	64.4	34.4	11.7	7.1
Kansas City, MO	88.7	68.3	29.8	11.3	7.4
Lafayette, LA	90.5	60.7	41.3	9.5	4.4
Las Vegas, NV	86.8	60.3	36.5	13.2	8.8
Lexington, KY	93.2	69.8	34.5	6.8	2.9
Lincoln, NE	93.3	76.3	28.6	6.7	3.9
Little Rock, AR	90.0	62.0	39.1	10.0	7.0
Los Angeles, CA	90.0	55.2	41.9	10.0	3.6
Louisville, KY	94.2	64.2	43.1	5.8	3.8
Madison, WI	95.7	81.9	24.1	4.3	2.9
Manchester, NH	91.2	66.6	35.0	8.8	4.9
McAllen, TX	74.2	48.4	32.3	25.8	14.9

Table continued on following page.

City	With Health Insurance	With Private Health Insurance	With Public Health Insurance	Without Health Insurance	Population Under Age 19 Without Health Insurance
Memphis, TN	85.2	55.1	41.3	14.8	8.6
Miami, FL	82.4	52.6	33.5	17.6	8.8
Midland, TX	85.2	72.0	21.3	14.8	11.7
Milwaukee, WI	90.9	52.2	46.7	9.1	3.6
Minneapolis, MN	94.1	69.5	32.8	5.9	2.8
Nashville, TN	87.4	69.0	29.0	12.6	9.0
New Orleans, LA	91.6	55.4	45.3	8.4	5.4
New York, NY	93.6	58.2	45.3	6.4	2.3
Oklahoma City, OK	86.0	63.0	34.4	14.0	7.6
Omaha, NE	90.3	69.2	31.0	9.7	6.9
Orlando, FL	86.1	64.6	27.6	13.9	8.0
Philadelphia, PA	92.8	58.8	45.9	7.2	4.5
Phoenix, AZ	85.5	58.6	34.6	14.5	9.8
Pittsburgh, PA	94.8	72.9	33.5	5.2	3.8
Portland, OR	94.5	71.5	33.1	5.5	2.1
Providence, RI	92.6	57.0	44.1	7.4	5.1
Provo, UT	90.6	78.6	17.5	9.4	9.8
Raleigh, NC	89.9	73.5	26.0	10.1	6.0
Reno, NV	89.5	67.9	31.5	10.5	7.0
Richmond, VA	90.2	63.3	36.9	9.8	7.2
Rochester, MN	95.7	79.7	30.5	4.3	3.7
Sacramento, CA	94.5	65.3	40.5	5.5	3.2
Saint Louis, MO	90.7	63.5	35.7	9.3	3.7
Saint Paul, MN	93.6	62.5	41.0	6.4	4.5
Salem, OR	92.6	63.9	41.9	7.4	1.9
Salt Lake City, UT	89.0	73.9	22.8	11.0	10.2
San Antonio, TX	82.5	58.4	33.8	17.5	9.8
San Diego, CA	93.7	71.9	31.7	6.3	3.6
San Francisco, CA	96.5	75.8	30.7	3.5	2.0
San Jose, CA	95.1	72.5	30.6	4.9	1.8
Santa Rosa, CA	93.6	67.8	39.1	6.4	3.9
Savannah, GA	86.2	59.3	36.7	13.8	5.7
Seattle, WA	95.6	80.5	23.5	4.4	1.8
Sioux Falls, SD	92.2	77.7	25.8	7.8	5.6
Tampa, FL	89.0	64.5	32.0	11.0	5.7
Tucson, AZ	89.0	57.0	42.7	11.0	7.4
Tulsa, OK	83.5	56.6	37.7	16.5	8.4
Virginia Beach, VA	93.5	78.0	30.8	6.5	3.8
Washington, DC	96.6	72.4	34.2	3.4	2.7
Wichita, KS	87.6	65.3	34.1	12.4	6.1
Wilmington, NC	88.4	69.5	32.5	11.6	8.0
Winston-Salem, NC	88.1	61.8	37.5	11.9	4.7
U.S.	91.4	67.3	36.3	8.6	5.4

Note: Figures are percentages that cover the civilian noninstitutionalized population
Source: U.S. Census Bureau, 2019-2023 American Community Survey 5-Year Estimates

Health Insurance Coverage: Metro Area

Metro Area	With Health Insurance	With Private Health Insurance	With Public Health Insurance	Without Health Insurance	Population Under Age 19 Without Health Insurance
Albuquerque, NM	91.9	59.2	47.2	8.1	5.0
Anchorage, AK	89.4	68.4	35.1	10.6	8.2
Ann Arbor, MI	96.7	81.5	28.7	3.3	2.0
Athens, GA	89.0	71.4	27.8	11.0	7.2
Atlanta, GA	87.8	69.1	28.2	12.2	7.2
Austin, TX	87.9	75.2	21.9	12.1	9.0
Baltimore, MD	95.1	74.5	34.4	4.9	3.6
Billings, MT	93.2	68.2	39.6	6.8	5.2
Boise City, ID	91.4	72.1	31.8	8.6	6.2
Boston, MA	97.2	76.4	33.5	2.8	1.6
Boulder, CO	95.6	79.6	26.6	4.4	2.0
Cape Coral, FL	87.5	62.0	43.6	12.5	9.7
Cedar Rapids, IA	96.3	74.8	35.1	3.7	1.4
Charleston, SC	90.3	71.9	32.2	9.7	6.8
Charlotte, NC	89.9	70.0	29.9	10.1	5.9
Chicago, IL	92.4	69.8	32.5	7.6	3.5
Cincinnati, OH	94.5	72.3	33.5	5.5	3.8
Clarksville, TN	90.7	69.7	36.3	9.3	6.7
Cleveland, OH	94.4	67.4	40.0	5.6	3.9
College Station, TX	88.1	73.2	24.7	11.9	7.6
Colorado Springs, CO	92.9	71.5	35.9	7.1	4.6
Columbia, MO	93.4	77.7	26.6	6.6	4.4
Columbia, SC	91.0	69.6	36.0	9.0	5.2
Columbus, OH	92.6	70.0	32.5	7.4	4.5
Dallas, TX	83.7	66.7	24.5	16.3	11.8
Davenport, IA	94.5	71.3	38.0	5.5	3.7
Denver, CO	92.2	72.2	29.4	7.8	5.0
Des Moines, IA	95.5	75.1	32.5	4.5	2.3
Detroit, MI	95.1	70.0	40.0	4.9	2.6
Durham, NC	90.2	72.6	29.5	9.8	6.1
El Paso, TX	78.1	52.1	34.3	21.9	12.9
Eugene, OR	94.1	63.9	44.5	5.9	2.9
Fargo, ND	94.8	80.6	25.8	5.2	4.2
Fort Collins, CO	94.3	74.9	31.0	5.7	3.8
Fort Wayne, IN	92.0	68.5	34.5	8.0	6.3
Fort Worth, TX	83.7	66.7	24.5	16.3	11.8
Gainesville, FL	90.9	71.2	30.8	9.1	5.2
Green Bay, WI	94.8	72.2	34.1	5.2	3.4
Greensboro, NC	90.2	64.1	37.2	9.8	4.2
Honolulu, HI	96.6	78.2	36.3	3.4	2.6
Houston, TX	81.3	61.4	27.1	18.7	12.6
Huntsville, AL	92.2	77.5	29.4	7.8	2.8
Indianapolis, IN	93.0	70.9	32.9	7.0	4.6
Jacksonville, FL	90.1	69.3	33.4	9.9	6.3
Kansas City, MO	91.1	74.1	27.9	8.9	5.6
Lafayette, LA	92.3	60.4	42.4	7.7	3.2
Las Vegas, NV	87.9	62.5	35.9	12.1	8.3
Lexington, KY	93.9	69.8	36.2	6.1	3.2
Lincoln, NE	93.7	77.6	28.1	6.3	3.8
Little Rock, AR	91.7	65.3	39.2	8.3	5.1
Los Angeles, CA	91.8	60.8	38.8	8.2	3.5
Louisville, KY	94.7	69.5	38.9	5.3	3.6
Madison, WI	96.3	82.6	26.5	3.7	2.8
Manchester, NH	94.0	77.1	29.3	6.0	4.0
McAllen, TX	70.3	37.7	37.5	29.7	15.7

Table continued on following page.

Metro Area	With Health Insurance	With Private Health Insurance	With Public Health Insurance	Without Health Insurance	Population Under Age 19 Without Health Insurance
Memphis, TN	88.9	64.1	36.1	11.1	6.4
Miami, FL	86.3	60.5	33.6	13.7	8.2
Midland, TX	84.7	70.7	21.7	15.3	12.1
Milwaukee, WI	94.6	70.6	35.5	5.4	2.8
Minneapolis, MN	95.7	77.3	30.9	4.3	2.7
Nashville, TN	90.6	72.8	28.6	9.4	5.8
New Orleans, LA	90.8	55.9	45.1	9.2	5.6
New York, NY	93.5	66.6	37.8	6.5	3.1
Oklahoma City, OK	87.7	66.8	33.5	12.3	7.3
Omaha, NE	92.9	74.5	29.2	7.1	4.7
Orlando, FL	88.7	66.6	31.4	11.3	6.3
Philadelphia, PA	94.7	72.5	35.5	5.3	3.4
Phoenix, AZ	89.3	66.2	34.1	10.7	8.6
Pittsburgh, PA	96.2	74.5	37.9	3.8	2.4
Portland, OR	94.2	72.3	34.0	5.8	3.2
Providence, RI	96.1	70.1	39.7	3.9	2.4
Provo, UT	92.3	82.1	17.4	7.7	6.0
Raleigh, NC	91.3	76.0	25.6	8.7	5.0
Reno, NV	90.4	69.0	32.8	9.6	6.8
Richmond, VA	93.2	73.3	33.5	6.8	5.0
Rochester, MN	95.6	79.5	31.1	4.4	4.0
Sacramento, CA	95.3	70.1	38.7	4.7	2.7
Saint Louis, MO	94.0	73.7	31.5	6.0	3.5
Saint Paul, MN	95.7	77.3	30.9	4.3	2.7
Salem, OR	92.0	63.0	42.6	8.0	3.3
Salt Lake City, UT	90.6	77.4	20.8	9.4	7.7
San Antonio, TX	85.0	64.6	31.8	15.0	9.1
San Diego, CA	93.2	69.6	34.3	6.8	3.8
San Francisco, CA	95.9	75.5	31.5	4.1	2.4
San Jose, CA	95.9	77.1	27.4	4.1	1.8
Santa Rosa, CA	94.6	71.3	38.3	5.4	3.2
Savannah, GA	88.0	67.8	32.8	12.0	6.6
Seattle, WA	94.4	75.5	29.6	5.6	2.7
Sioux Falls, SD	93.1	79.1	25.6	6.9	4.8
Tampa, FL	88.9	64.2	36.5	11.1	6.0
Tucson, AZ	91.1	62.8	42.8	8.9	7.0
Tulsa, OK	86.8	63.7	35.3	13.2	7.6
Virginia Beach, VA	93.3	73.2	35.8	6.7	4.0
Washington, DC	92.6	76.7	27.8	7.4	4.9
Wichita, KS	89.7	69.9	32.5	10.3	5.3
Wilmington, NC	90.4	71.3	38.0	9.6	6.8
Winston-Salem, NC	89.6	64.5	37.6	10.4	4.6
U.S.	91.4	67.3	36.3	8.6	5.4

Note: Figures are percentages that cover the civilian noninstitutionalized population; Figures cover the Metropolitan Statistical Area (MSA)
Source: U.S. Census Bureau, 2019-2023 American Community Survey 5-Year Estimates

Crime Rate: City

City	Total Crime	Violent Crime Rate				Property Crime Rate		
		Murder	Rape	Robbery	Aggrav. Assault	Burglary	Larceny -Theft	Motor Vehicle Theft
Albuquerque, NM	6,021.7	19.3	54.2	175.5	1,068.0	671.8	3,003.1	1,029.9
Anchorage, AK	3,953.3	7.7	150.2	161.7	742.0	334.0	2,132.4	425.2
Ann Arbor, MI	2,058.1	3.4	37.3	39.0	232.1	171.1	1,438.1	137.2
Athens, GA	2,950.7	3.9	60.2	61.7	305.6	238.4	2,063.4	217.6
Atlanta, GA	4,599.8	26.4	23.2	120.3	537.4	346.9	2,500.1	1,045.6
Austin, TX	3,804.7	6.7	50.3	93.3	348.8	468.0	2,125.2	712.4
Baltimore, MD	5,850.2	41.2	45.1	577.9	908.2	445.5	1,987.6	1,844.7
Billings, MT	4,487.3	7.4	83.2	123.6	674.0	346.1	2,723.2	529.8
Boise City, ID	1,512.1	2.1	67.9	21.9	177.7	131.7	971.9	138.8
Boston, MA	2,571.3	5.3	32.5	136.6	452.5	180.9	1,589.2	174.2
Boulder, CO	3,414.5	2.9	38.4	36.5	279.2	457.6	2,276.7	323.3
Cape Coral, FL	n/a	n/a	n/a	n/a	n/a	n/a	n/a	n/a
Cedar Rapids, IA	3,184.6	5.9	8.1	30.2	255.6	345.4	2,281.7	257.8
Charleston, SC	2,379.5	6.4	28.4	52.8	314.5	164.3	1,501.0	311.9
Charlotte, NC	4,562.0	9.4	25.4	128.4	563.0	430.0	2,578.2	827.7
Chicago, IL	4,038.7	19.0	47.3	412.3	128.1	280.1	2,145.0	1,006.8
Cincinnati, OH	4,956.6	22.0	71.4	208.4	426.2	617.2	2,416.3	1,195.2
Clarksville, TN	2,193.3	6.0	57.7	29.7	373.8	214.9	1,285.8	225.4
Cleveland, OH	6,515.8	38.8	119.5	448.1	1,096.8	894.3	2,475.2	1,443.0
College Station, TX	1,493.6	3.2	49.2	17.4	88.8	141.9	1,086.9	106.2
Colorado Springs, CO	4,386.7	4.9	104.2	76.4	506.5	521.6	2,354.6	818.4
Columbia, MO	2,897.3	7.7	59.4	33.2	285.5	307.1	1,859.5	344.9
Columbia, SC	4,223.4	7.8	45.2	107.4	596.5	455.8	2,537.2	473.5
Columbus, OH	3,089.1	10.5	115.3	117.5	141.8	412.2	1,553.0	738.9
Dallas, TX	4,701.5	18.5	36.8	157.8	458.4	470.3	2,126.6	1,433.1
Davenport, IA	4,501.0	9.0	102.1	91.1	488.4	688.6	2,601.3	520.5
Denver, CO	6,772.3	11.9	93.2	175.8	740.8	716.9	3,284.7	1,749.0
Des Moines, IA	4,056.1	4.3	69.2	90.6	542.8	451.2	2,271.3	626.7
Detroit, MI	6,785.7	40.6	109.3	225.5	1,676.7	756.9	2,485.8	1,490.8
Durham, NC	4,397.4	15.2	53.4	168.4	399.3	497.0	2,574.8	689.3
El Paso, TX	1,955.2	5.0	40.9	48.0	242.2	157.2	1,116.4	345.4
Eugene, OR	3,545.1	3.4	56.7	77.4	210.4	497.8	2,306.5	392.8
Fargo, ND	4,394.2	1.5	71.5	75.2	367.2	768.6	2,690.1	420.1
Fort Collins, CO	2,736.2	0.6	29.0	36.7	229.7	273.6	1,958.1	208.4
Fort Wayne, IN	2,623.8	9.6	43.7	64.9	153.1	251.0	1,800.3	301.0
Fort Worth, TX	3,135.9	8.7	69.1	71.2	340.8	391.4	1,763.5	491.2
Gainesville, FL	3,608.3	10.9	100.9	119.3	507.7	286.2	2,572.5	10.9
Green Bay, WI	1,915.3	5.7	66.3	31.3	283.4	215.1	1,029.2	284.3
Greensboro, NC	4,560.5	24.7	24.4	164.9	612.1	555.0	2,682.7	496.6
Honolulu, HI	2,128.6	0.6	28.0	51.7	105.8	193.1	1,377.3	372.0
Houston, TX	5,599.2	14.9	61.1	295.7	720.0	606.3	3,034.5	866.7
Huntsville, AL	834.6	2.7	15.1	17.4	94.8	101.9	521.4	81.4
Indianapolis, IN	4,653.4	18.9	55.9	174.2	782.0	615.8	2,229.9	776.8
Jacksonville, FL	n/a	n/a	n/a	n/a	n/a	n/a	n/a	n/a
Kansas City, MO	6,436.1	35.5	78.5	241.2	1,122.5	549.6	2,633.3	1,775.6
Lafayette, LA	5,421.0	23.1	24.7	98.1	672.4	1,017.6	3,291.8	293.3
Las Vegas, NV	3,551.8	8.0	49.8	77.6	334.6	524.7	1,681.3	875.9
Lexington, KY	3,004.7	4.4	56.6	76.9	115.9	337.8	2,022.9	390.3
Lincoln, NE	3,052.3	2.4	90.4	52.9	220.4	252.4	2,106.4	327.5
Little Rock, AR	7,228.6	30.5	122.2	223.2	1,425.2	925.7	4,003.7	498.1
Los Angeles, CA	3,666.8	8.6	51.4	230.1	530.0	406.4	1,764.3	676.0
Louisville, KY	4,385.4	22.9	32.7	148.2	561.8	498.8	2,104.4	1,016.8
Madison, WI	2,636.1	3.6	27.7	44.5	225.4	280.4	1,859.0	195.5
Manchester, NH	2,061.5	7.0	59.1	87.9	229.6	147.9	1,342.2	187.9

Table continued on following page.

Appendix A: Comparative Statistics

City	Total Crime	Violent Crime Rate				Property Crime Rate		
		Murder	Rape	Robbery	Aggrav. Assault	Burglary	Larceny-Theft	Motor Vehicle Theft
McAllen, TX	2,092.9	4.8	35.7	24.0	79.6	111.2	1,774.4	63.2
Memphis, TN	11,214.8	57.0	73.4	451.1	2,030.5	1,110.9	4,942.0	2,549.9
Miami, FL	3,436.7	7.1	28.3	109.7	346.9	254.1	2,223.1	467.6
Midland, TX	2,321.6	5.2	63.6	33.3	328.3	274.3	1,354.5	262.5
Milwaukee, WI	4,136.0	31.0	74.3	284.4	1,048.0	418.1	1,278.7	1,001.6
Minneapolis, MN	6,384.2	17.0	86.7	339.8	688.1	605.7	2,806.3	1,840.7
Nashville, TN	5,533.6	14.5	59.1	163.4	892.0	401.7	3,232.8	770.2
New Orleans, LA	6,450.6	53.0	187.0	180.1	941.0	478.3	2,770.8	1,840.5
New York, NY	3,066.4	4.2	25.3	200.0	438.8	167.2	2,006.8	224.2
Oklahoma City, OK	3,571.8	9.0	68.9	88.0	471.6	566.1	1,965.4	402.7
Omaha, NE[1]	4,029.5	6.0	61.6	69.5	424.0	259.6	2,514.4	694.4
Orlando, FL[1]	4,864.3	10.3	72.7	137.1	615.7	449.9	3,173.7	404.9
Philadelphia, PA	6,039.7	26.0	46.6	336.1	574.4	363.9	3,161.8	1,530.9
Phoenix, AZ	3,268.6	11.5	65.6	168.8	538.9	342.6	1,577.4	563.9
Pittsburgh, PA	n/a	n/a	n/a	n/a	n/a	n/a	n/a	n/a
Portland, OR	6,575.8	11.8	51.1	193.1	459.2	792.8	3,756.6	1,311.2
Providence, RI	2,215.3	5.8	34.3	59.6	209.9	157.2	1,482.7	265.8
Provo, UT	1,531.8	0.0	60.3	16.0	98.5	110.0	1,149.5	97.6
Raleigh, NC	3,117.6	5.4	32.1	87.2	403.4	306.3	1,891.3	391.8
Reno, NV	3,234.8	6.8	102.2	111.6	375.1	381.9	1,838.8	418.3
Richmond, VA	4,078.2	26.9	29.5	97.1	204.1	287.3	2,899.2	534.3
Rochester, MN	1,754.4	0.8	36.1	22.9	102.4	182.7	1,283.2	126.2
Sacramento, CA	3,692.9	7.7	32.1	225.3	535.6	520.1	1,672.4	699.8
Saint Louis, MO	7,844.8	56.4	70.3	260.3	1,058.2	751.1	3,434.0	2,214.5
Saint Paul, MN	3,714.1	9.0	67.3	126.8	420.8	434.5	1,962.9	692.8
Salem, OR	3,650.5	5.0	15.1	98.7	328.7	384.2	2,312.7	506.0
Salt Lake City, UT	6,514.5	7.7	159.7	175.6	524.9	555.4	4,504.8	586.4
San Antonio, TX	6,089.1	10.9	97.8	120.5	465.0	546.5	3,568.2	1,280.2
San Diego, CA	2,229.6	2.9	21.5	87.4	306.1	201.5	1,118.7	491.6
San Francisco, CA	6,422.7	6.6	37.3	349.7	316.5	720.8	4,135.3	856.4
San Jose, CA[1]	3,178.2	3.7	93.4	132.1	298.2	405.9	1,568.7	676.1
Santa Rosa, CA	1,799.8	5.7	65.0	63.9	196.2	257.8	1,004.2	206.9
Savannah, GA	n/a	n/a	n/a	n/a	n/a	n/a	n/a	n/a
Seattle, WA	5,789.3	9.0	36.2	221.7	510.2	1,126.3	2,662.2	1,223.7
Sioux Falls, SD	2,864.1	0.5	16.9	32.4	385.4	287.6	1,635.4	505.9
Tampa, FL	2,115.0	10.2	42.4	65.4	341.8	194.1	1,272.2	188.9
Tucson, AZ	n/a	n/a	n/a	n/a	n/a	n/a	n/a	n/a
Tulsa, OK	4,850.8	8.8	101.5	100.0	702.2	878.8	2,486.1	573.5
Virginia Beach, VA	1,751.8	3.7	22.0	29.5	40.1	86.6	1,431.3	138.5
Washington, DC	5,205.1	38.9	38.4	558.0	412.1	245.1	2,905.0	1,007.6
Wichita, KS	5,864.8	9.9	87.8	104.7	930.0	548.2	3,662.4	521.9
Wilmington, NC	3,995.9	8.2	31.0	99.4	348.9	455.7	2,763.4	289.4
Winston-Salem, NC	3,897.6	16.7	34.9	97.2	737.7	629.4	1,994.6	387.1
U.S.	2,290.9	5.7	38.0	66.5	264.1	250.7	1,347.2	318.7

Note: Figures are crimes per 100,000 population in 2023 except where noted; (1) 2022 data; n/a not available.
Source: FBI, Table 8, Offenses Known to Law Enforcement, by State by City, 2022, 2023

Temperature & Precipitation: Yearly Averages and Extremes

City	Extreme Low (°F)	Average Low (°F)	Average Temp. (°F)	Average High (°F)	Extreme High (°F)	Average Precip. (in.)	Average Snow (in.)
Albuquerque, NM	-17	43	57	70	105	8.5	11
Anchorage, AK	-34	29	36	43	85	15.7	71
Ann Arbor, MI	-21	39	49	58	104	32.4	41
Athens, GA	-8	52	62	72	105	49.8	2
Atlanta, GA	-8	52	62	72	105	49.8	2
Austin, TX	-2	58	69	79	109	31.1	1
Baltimore, MD	-7	45	56	65	105	41.2	21
Billings, MT	-32	36	47	59	105	14.6	59
Boise City, ID	-25	39	51	63	111	11.8	22
Boston, MA	-12	44	52	59	102	42.9	41
Boulder, CO	-25	37	51	64	103	15.5	63
Cape Coral, FL	26	65	75	84	103	53.9	0
Cedar Rapids, IA	-34	36	47	57	105	34.4	33
Charleston, SC	6	55	66	76	104	52.1	1
Charlotte, NC	-5	50	61	71	104	42.8	6
Chicago, IL	-27	40	49	59	104	35.4	39
Cincinnati, OH	-25	44	54	64	103	40.9	23
Clarksville, TN	-17	49	60	70	107	47.4	11
Cleveland, OH	-19	41	50	59	104	37.1	55
College Station, TX	-2	58	69	79	109	31.1	1
Colorado Springs, CO	-24	36	49	62	99	17.0	48
Columbia, MO	-20	44	54	64	111	40.6	25
Columbia, SC	-1	51	64	75	107	48.3	2
Columbus, OH	-19	42	52	62	104	37.9	28
Dallas, TX	-2	56	67	77	112	33.9	3
Davenport, IA	-24	40	50	60	108	31.8	33
Denver, CO	-25	37	51	64	103	15.5	63
Des Moines, IA	-24	40	50	60	108	31.8	33
Detroit, MI	-21	39	49	58	104	32.4	41
Durham, NC	-9	48	60	71	105	42.0	8
El Paso, TX	-8	50	64	78	114	8.6	6
Eugene, OR	-12	42	53	63	108	47.3	7
Fargo, ND	-36	31	41	52	106	19.6	40
Fort Collins, CO	-25	37	51	64	103	15.5	63
Fort Wayne, IN	-22	40	50	60	106	35.9	33
Fort Worth, TX	-1	55	66	76	113	32.3	3
Gainesville, FL	10	58	69	79	102	50.9	Trace
Green Bay, WI	-31	34	44	54	99	28.3	46
Greensboro, NC	-8	47	58	69	103	42.5	10
Honolulu, HI	52	70	77	84	94	22.4	0
Houston, TX	7	58	69	79	107	46.9	Trace
Huntsville, AL	-11	50	61	71	104	56.8	4
Indianapolis, IN	-23	42	53	62	104	40.2	25
Jacksonville, FL	7	58	69	79	103	52.0	0
Kansas City, MO	-23	44	54	64	109	38.1	21
Lafayette, LA	8	57	68	78	103	58.5	Trace
Las Vegas, NV	8	53	67	80	116	4.0	1
Lexington, KY	-21	45	55	65	103	45.1	17
Lincoln, NE	-33	39	51	62	108	29.1	27
Little Rock, AR	-5	51	62	73	112	50.7	5
Los Angeles, CA	27	55	63	70	110	11.3	Trace
Louisville, KY	-20	46	57	67	105	43.9	17
Madison, WI	-37	35	46	57	104	31.1	42
Manchester, NH	-33	34	46	57	102	36.9	63
McAllen, TX	16	65	74	83	106	25.8	Trace

Table continued on following page.

City	Extreme Low (°F)	Average Low (°F)	Average Temp. (°F)	Average High (°F)	Extreme High (°F)	Average Precip. (in.)	Average Snow (in.)
Memphis, TN	0	52	65	77	107	54.8	1
Miami, FL	30	69	76	83	98	57.1	0
Midland, TX	-11	50	64	77	116	14.6	4
Milwaukee, WI	-26	38	47	55	103	32.0	49
Minneapolis, MN	-34	35	45	54	105	27.1	52
Nashville, TN	-17	49	60	70	107	47.4	11
New Orleans, LA	11	59	69	78	102	60.6	Trace
New York, NY	-2	47	55	62	104	47.0	23
Oklahoma City, OK	-8	49	60	71	110	32.8	10
Omaha, NE	-23	40	51	62	110	30.1	29
Orlando, FL	19	62	72	82	100	47.7	Trace
Philadelphia, PA	-7	45	55	64	104	41.4	22
Phoenix, AZ	17	59	72	86	122	7.3	Trace
Pittsburgh, PA	-18	41	51	60	103	37.1	43
Portland, OR	-3	45	54	62	107	37.5	7
Providence, RI	-13	42	51	60	104	45.3	35
Provo, UT	-22	40	52	64	107	15.6	63
Raleigh, NC	-9	48	60	71	105	42.0	8
Reno, NV	-16	33	50	67	105	7.2	24
Richmond, VA	-8	48	58	69	105	43.0	13
Rochester, MN	-40	34	44	54	102	29.4	47
Sacramento, CA	18	48	61	73	115	17.3	Trace
Saint Louis, MO	-18	46	56	66	115	36.8	20
Saint Paul, MN	-34	35	45	54	105	27.1	52
Salem, OR	-12	41	52	63	108	40.2	7
Salt Lake City, UT	-22	40	52	64	107	15.6	63
San Antonio, TX	0	58	69	80	108	29.6	1
San Diego, CA	29	57	64	71	111	9.5	Trace
San Francisco, CA	24	49	57	65	106	19.3	Trace
San Jose, CA	21	50	59	68	105	13.5	Trace
Santa Rosa, CA	23	42	57	71	109	29.0	n/a
Savannah, GA	3	56	67	77	105	50.3	Trace
Seattle, WA	0	44	52	59	99	38.4	13
Sioux Falls, SD	-36	35	46	57	110	24.6	38
Tampa, FL	18	63	73	82	99	46.7	Trace
Tucson, AZ	16	55	69	82	117	11.6	2
Tulsa, OK	-8	50	61	71	112	38.9	10
Virginia Beach, VA	-3	51	60	69	104	44.8	8
Washington, DC	-5	49	58	67	104	39.5	18
Wichita, KS	-21	45	57	68	113	29.3	17
Wilmington, NC	0	53	64	74	104	55.0	2
Winston-Salem, NC	-8	47	58	69	103	42.5	10

Source: National Climatic Data Center, International Station Meteorological Climate Summary, 9/96; NOAA

Weather Conditions

City	Temperature			Daytime Sky			Precipitation		
	10°F & below	32°F & below	90°F & above	Clear	Partly cloudy	Cloudy	0.01 inch or more precip.	1.0 inch or more snow/ice	Thunder-storms
Albuquerque, NM	4	114	65	140	161	64	60	9	38
Anchorage, AK	n/a	194	n/a	50	115	200	113	49	2
Ann Arbor, MI	n/a	136	12	74	134	157	135	38	32
Athens, GA	1	49	38	98	147	120	116	3	48
Atlanta, GA	1	49	38	98	147	120	116	3	48
Austin, TX	< 1	20	111	105	148	112	83	1	41
Baltimore, MD	6	97	31	91	143	131	113	13	27
Billings, MT	n/a	149	29	75	163	127	97	41	27
Boise City, ID	n/a	124	45	106	133	126	91	22	14
Boston, MA	n/a	97	12	88	127	150	253	48	18
Boulder, CO	24	155	33	99	177	89	90	38	39
Cape Coral, FL	n/a	n/a	115	93	220	52	110	0	92
Cedar Rapids, IA	n/a	156	16	89	132	144	109	28	42
Charleston, SC	< 1	33	53	89	162	114	114	1	59
Charlotte, NC	1	65	44	98	142	125	113	3	41
Chicago, IL	n/a	132	17	83	136	146	125	31	38
Cincinnati, OH	14	107	23	80	126	159	127	25	39
Clarksville, TN	5	76	51	98	135	132	119	8	54
Cleveland, OH	n/a	123	12	63	127	175	157	48	34
College Station, TX	< 1	20	111	105	148	112	83	1	41
Colorado Springs, CO	21	161	18	108	157	100	98	33	49
Columbia, MO	17	108	36	99	127	139	110	17	52
Columbia, SC	< 1	58	77	97	149	119	110	1	53
Columbus, OH	n/a	118	19	72	137	156	136	29	40
Dallas, TX	1	34	102	108	160	97	78	2	49
Davenport, IA	n/a	137	26	99	129	137	106	25	46
Denver, CO	24	155	33	99	177	89	90	38	39
Des Moines, IA	n/a	137	26	99	129	137	106	25	46
Detroit, MI	n/a	136	12	74	134	157	135	38	32
Durham, NC	n/a	n/a	39	98	143	124	110	3	42
El Paso, TX	1	59	106	147	164	54	49	3	35
Eugene, OR	n/a	n/a	15	75	115	175	136	4	3
Fargo, ND	n/a	180	15	81	145	139	100	38	31
Fort Collins, CO	24	155	33	99	177	89	90	38	39
Fort Wayne, IN	n/a	131	16	75	140	150	131	31	39
Fort Worth, TX	1	40	100	123	136	106	79	3	47
Gainesville, FL	n/a	n/a	77	88	196	81	119	0	78
Green Bay, WI	n/a	163	7	86	125	154	120	40	33
Greensboro, NC	3	85	32	94	143	128	113	5	43
Honolulu, HI	n/a	n/a	23	25	286	54	98	0	7
Houston, TX	n/a	n/a	96	83	168	114	101	1	62
Huntsville, AL	2	66	49	70	118	177	116	2	54
Indianapolis, IN	19	119	19	83	128	154	127	24	43
Jacksonville, FL	< 1	16	83	86	181	98	114	1	65
Kansas City, MO	22	110	39	112	134	119	103	17	51
Lafayette, LA	< 1	21	86	99	150	116	113	< 1	73
Las Vegas, NV	< 1	37	134	185	132	48	27	2	13
Lexington, KY	11	96	22	86	136	143	129	17	44
Lincoln, NE	n/a	145	40	108	135	122	94	19	46
Little Rock, AR	1	57	73	110	142	113	104	4	57
Los Angeles, CA	0	< 1	5	131	125	109	34	0	1
Louisville, KY	8	90	35	82	143	140	125	15	45
Madison, WI	n/a	161	14	88	119	158	118	38	40
Manchester, NH	n/a	171	12	87	131	147	125	32	19

Table continued on following page.

City	Temperature			Daytime Sky			Precipitation		
	10°F & below	32°F & below	90°F & above	Clear	Partly cloudy	Cloudy	0.01 inch or more precip.	1.0 inch or more snow/ice	Thunder-storms
McAllen, TX	n/a	n/a	116	86	180	99	72	0	27
Memphis, TN	1	53	86	101	152	112	104	2	59
Miami, FL	n/a	n/a	55	48	263	54	128	0	74
Midland, TX	1	62	102	144	138	83	52	3	38
Milwaukee, WI	n/a	141	10	90	118	157	126	38	35
Minneapolis, MN	n/a	156	16	93	125	147	113	41	37
Nashville, TN	5	76	51	98	135	132	119	8	54
New Orleans, LA	0	13	70	90	169	106	114	1	69
New York, NY	n/a	n/a	18	85	166	114	120	11	20
Oklahoma City, OK	5	79	70	124	131	110	80	8	50
Omaha, NE	n/a	139	35	100	142	123	97	20	46
Orlando, FL	n/a	n/a	90	76	208	81	115	0	80
Philadelphia, PA	5	94	23	81	146	138	117	14	27
Phoenix, AZ	0	10	167	186	125	54	37	<1	23
Pittsburgh, PA	n/a	121	8	62	137	166	154	42	35
Portland, OR	n/a	37	11	67	116	182	152	4	7
Providence, RI	n/a	117	9	85	134	146	123	21	21
Provo, UT	n/a	128	56	94	152	119	92	38	38
Raleigh, NC	n/a	n/a	39	98	143	124	110	3	42
Reno, NV	14	178	50	143	139	83	50	17	14
Richmond, VA	3	79	41	90	147	128	115	7	43
Rochester, MN	n/a	165	9	87	126	152	114	40	41
Sacramento, CA	0	21	73	175	111	79	58	<1	2
Saint Louis, MO	13	100	43	97	138	130	109	14	46
Saint Paul, MN	n/a	156	16	93	125	147	113	41	37
Salem, OR	n/a	66	16	78	118	169	146	6	5
Salt Lake City, UT	n/a	128	56	94	152	119	92	38	38
San Antonio, TX	n/a	n/a	112	97	153	115	81	1	36
San Diego, CA	0	<1	4	115	126	124	40	0	5
San Francisco, CA	0	6	4	136	130	99	63	<1	5
San Jose, CA	0	5	5	106	180	79	57	<1	6
Santa Rosa, CA	n/a	43	30	n/a	365	n/a	n/a	n/a	2
Savannah, GA	<1	29	70	97	155	113	111	<1	63
Seattle, WA	n/a	38	3	57	121	187	157	8	8
Sioux Falls, SD	n/a	n/a	n/a	95	136	134	n/a	n/a	n/a
Tampa, FL	n/a	n/a	85	81	204	80	107	<1	87
Tucson, AZ	0	18	140	177	119	69	54	2	42
Tulsa, OK	6	78	74	117	141	107	88	8	50
Virginia Beach, VA	<1	53	33	89	149	127	115	5	38
Washington, DC	2	71	34	84	144	137	112	9	30
Wichita, KS	13	110	63	117	132	116	87	13	54
Wilmington, NC	<1	42	46	96	150	119	115	1	47
Winston-Salem, NC	3	85	32	94	143	128	113	5	43

Note: Figures are average number of days per year
Source: National Climatic Data Center, International Station Meteorological Climate Summary, 9/96; NOAA

Air Quality Index

Metro Area (Days[1])	Percent of Days when Air Quality was...					AQI Statistics	
	Good	Moderate	Unhealthy for Sensitive Groups	Unhealthy	Very Unhealthy	Maximum	Median
Albuquerque, NM (365)	26.6	72.3	0.8	0.0	0.3	207	60
Anchorage, AK (365)	81.1	18.6	0.3	0.0	0.0	102	25
Ann Arbor, MI (365)	46.0	50.4	2.5	0.5	0.5	218	52
Athens, GA (365)	47.4	51.8	0.8	0.0	0.0	147	52
Atlanta, GA (365)	26.6	67.7	4.9	0.8	0.0	172	57
Austin, TX (365)	40.3	56.7	3.0	0.0	0.0	122	54
Baltimore, MD (365)	55.1	40.3	3.6	0.8	0.3	205	49
Billings, MT (357)	85.7	13.2	0.8	0.3	0.0	191	29
Boise City, ID (365)	49.3	49.9	0.8	0.0	0.0	120	51
Boston, MA (365)	52.1	46.0	1.9	0.0	0.0	136	50
Boulder, CO (365)	52.6	45.8	1.1	0.5	0.0	181	50
Cape Coral, FL (363)	94.5	5.2	0.3	0.0	0.0	101	35
Cedar Rapids, IA (365)	35.6	59.5	3.8	0.8	0.3	207	54
Charleston, SC (365)	57.8	41.6	0.5	0.0	0.0	105	47
Charlotte, NC (365)	39.7	58.1	2.2	0.0	0.0	150	53
Chicago, IL (365)	20.8	67.4	9.0	2.2	0.5	246	60
Cincinnati, OH (365)	25.2	68.2	5.2	1.4	0.0	197	57
Clarksville, TN (365)	56.2	42.5	1.4	0.0	0.0	117	47
Cleveland, OH (365)	31.5	64.1	3.0	1.1	0.3	285	57
College Station, TX (348)	67.0	33.0	0.0	0.0	0.0	79	39
Colorado Springs, CO (365)	65.8	33.7	0.3	0.3	0.0	154	47
Columbia, MO (244)	79.9	18.0	2.0	0.0	0.0	143	42
Columbia, SC (365)	54.5	44.4	1.1	0.0	0.0	123	48
Columbus, OH (365)	37.0	59.5	2.5	0.8	0.3	210	54
Dallas, TX (365)	20.5	64.9	12.1	2.5	0.0	177	60
Davenport, IA (365)	37.3	56.4	5.2	0.8	0.3	232	54
Denver, CO (365)	19.7	72.3	7.4	0.5	0.0	179	64
Des Moines, IA (365)	46.0	49.9	3.3	0.8	0.0	166	52
Detroit, MI (365)	18.6	74.0	6.3	0.8	0.3	226	61
Durham, NC (361)	69.5	29.4	1.1	0.0	0.0	121	44
El Paso, TX (365)	18.9	75.9	4.9	0.3	0.0	155	64
Eugene, OR (365)	52.1	43.6	2.5	1.6	0.3	211	49
Fargo, ND (358)	50.3	46.4	2.8	0.6	0.0	175	50
Fort Collins, CO (365)	47.9	50.7	1.1	0.3	0.0	156	51
Fort Wayne, IN (365)	45.2	52.1	1.9	0.5	0.3	223	52
Fort Worth, TX (365)	20.5	64.9	12.1	2.5	0.0	177	60
Gainesville, FL (365)	74.0	25.8	0.3	0.0	0.0	104	40
Green Bay, WI (365)	57.0	38.1	3.3	1.6	0.0	182	46
Greensboro, NC (365)	50.1	48.8	1.1	0.0	0.0	131	50
Honolulu, HI (365)	92.3	7.4	0.3	0.0	0.0	117	31
Houston, TX (365)	9.9	74.5	12.3	3.0	0.3	205	65
Huntsville, AL (364)	56.0	43.1	0.8	0.0	0.0	135	49
Indianapolis, IN (365)	21.9	71.5	5.5	0.5	0.5	259	60
Jacksonville, FL (365)	41.6	57.8	0.5	0.0	0.0	124	52
Kansas City, MO (365)	34.0	58.1	6.8	1.1	0.0	166	55
Lafayette, LA (365)	56.7	43.0	0.3	0.0	0.0	112	47
Las Vegas, NV (365)	29.0	63.8	6.8	0.3	0.0	197	61
Lexington, KY (365)	63.3	35.9	0.5	0.3	0.0	167	45
Lincoln, NE (283)	69.6	29.3	0.7	0.4	0.0	160	42
Little Rock, AR (365)	33.4	65.2	1.1	0.3	0.0	174	55
Los Angeles, CA (365)	11.2	64.9	14.2	8.8	0.8	210	67
Louisville, KY (365)	32.1	62.2	5.5	0.3	0.0	182	55
Madison, WI (365)	49.6	43.6	5.5	0.5	0.8	268	51
Manchester, NH (365)	83.6	15.1	1.4	0.0	0.0	119	39

Table continued on following page.

Metro Area (Days[1])	Percent of Days when Air Quality was...					AQI Statistics	
	Good	Moderate	Unhealthy for Sensitive Groups	Unhealthy	Very Unhealthy	Maximum	Median
McAllen, TX (357)	57.7	42.3	0.0	0.0	0.0	95	44
Memphis, TN (365)	28.5	67.4	4.1	0.0	0.0	140	55
Miami, FL (365)	37.3	61.6	0.3	0.8	0.0	170	53
Midland, TX (n/a)	n/a	n/a	n/a	n/a	n/a	n/a	n/a
Milwaukee, WI (365)	43.6	48.8	6.6	0.3	0.8	270	53
Minneapolis, MN (365)	36.7	55.1	6.6	1.6	0.0	190	55
Nashville, TN (365)	34.8	62.5	2.7	0.0	0.0	133	54
New Orleans, LA (365)	38.1	59.2	2.7	0.0	0.0	126	53
New York, NY (365)	29.3	64.1	4.7	1.6	0.3	278	56
Oklahoma City, OK (365)	35.1	60.8	4.1	0.0	0.0	143	54
Omaha, NE (365)	50.4	42.7	6.3	0.5	0.0	169	50
Orlando, FL (365)	71.0	28.2	0.8	0.0	0.0	115	44
Philadelphia, PA (365)	17.8	75.3	5.2	1.1	0.3	331	59
Phoenix, AZ (365)	8.5	67.9	20.3	2.7	0.3	709	78
Pittsburgh, PA (365)	26.8	66.6	5.5	0.5	0.5	237	58
Portland, OR (365)	60.0	38.4	1.1	0.5	0.0	153	43
Providence, RI (365)	54.8	42.2	3.0	0.0	0.0	140	48
Provo, UT (365)	55.1	44.7	0.3	0.0	0.0	104	48
Raleigh, NC (365)	50.4	48.2	1.4	0.0	0.0	130	50
Reno, NV (365)	52.3	47.7	0.0	0.0	0.0	97	50
Richmond, VA (365)	55.9	42.7	0.5	0.8	0.0	159	48
Rochester, MN (365)	51.8	44.1	3.8	0.3	0.0	167	49
Sacramento, CA (365)	35.3	60.8	3.8	0.0	0.0	143	58
Saint Louis, MO (365)	14.0	79.5	5.8	0.8	0.0	185	60
Saint Paul, MN (365)	36.7	55.1	6.6	1.6	0.0	190	55
Salem, OR (365)	73.4	25.5	1.1	0.0	0.0	128	38
Salt Lake City, UT (365)	40.5	55.1	4.1	0.3	0.0	154	54
San Antonio, TX (365)	41.6	55.1	2.7	0.3	0.0	309	53
San Diego, CA (365)	16.7	71.2	12.1	0.0	0.0	150	67
San Francisco, CA (365)	34.0	62.5	3.6	0.0	0.0	130	54
San Jose, CA (365)	61.6	37.3	1.1	0.0	0.0	134	45
Santa Rosa, CA (365)	88.5	11.0	0.5	0.0	0.0	117	33
Savannah, GA (352)	56.0	43.5	0.6	0.0	0.0	108	48
Seattle, WA (365)	51.0	47.1	1.1	0.8	0.0	195	50
Sioux Falls, SD (365)	64.4	28.2	6.3	1.1	0.0	181	44
Tampa, FL (365)	39.5	59.2	1.4	0.0	0.0	114	52
Tucson, AZ (365)	33.7	64.4	1.9	0.0	0.0	147	54
Tulsa, OK (365)	37.8	56.7	4.9	0.5	0.0	197	53
Virginia Beach, VA (365)	62.7	36.4	0.5	0.3	0.0	174	44
Washington, DC (365)	43.3	51.2	4.4	0.8	0.3	222	52
Wichita, KS (365)	44.7	54.0	1.1	0.3	0.0	157	52
Wilmington, NC (362)	65.5	34.3	0.3	0.0	0.0	142	44
Winston-Salem, NC (365)	40.3	57.8	1.6	0.3	0.0	154	53

Note: The Air Quality Index (AQI) is an index for reporting daily air quality. EPA calculates the AQI for five major air pollutants regulated by the Clean Air Act: ground-level ozone, particle pollution (also known as particulate matter), carbon monoxide, sulfur dioxide, and nitrogen dioxide. The AQI runs from 0 to 500. The higher the AQI value, the greater the level of air pollution and the greater the health concern. There are six AQI categories: "Good" The AQI is between 0 and 50. Air quality is considered satisfactory; "Moderate" The AQI is between 51 and 100. Air quality is acceptable; "Unhealthy for Sensitive Groups" When AQI values are between 101 and 150, members of sensitive groups may experience health effects; "Unhealthy" When AQI values are between 151 and 200 everyone may begin to experience health effects; "Very Unhealthy" AQI values between 201 and 300 trigger a health alert; "Hazardous" AQI values over 300 trigger health warnings of emergency conditions; Figures cover the Metropolitan Statistical Area (MSA); (1) Number of days with AQI data in 2023
Source: U.S. Environmental Protection Agency, Air Quality Index Report, 2023

Air Quality Index Pollutants

Metro Area (Days[1])	Percent of Days when AQI Pollutant was...					
	Carbon Monoxide	Nitrogen Dioxide	Ozone	Sulfur Dioxide[2]	Particulate Matter 2.5	Particulate Matter 10
Albuquerque, NM (365)	0.0	0.3	53.2	–	23.8	22.7
Anchorage, AK (365)	0.8	0.0	0.0	–	70.1	29.0
Ann Arbor, MI (365)	0.0	0.0	33.2	–	66.8	0.0
Athens, GA (365)	0.0	0.0	26.8	–	73.2	0.0
Atlanta, GA (365)	0.0	0.8	31.5	–	67.7	0.0
Austin, TX (365)	0.0	1.1	29.3	–	69.6	0.0
Baltimore, MD (365)	0.0	1.1	54.5	–	44.4	0.0
Billings, MT (357)	0.0	0.0	0.0	–	100.0	0.0
Boise City, ID (365)	0.0	0.3	44.9	–	54.0	0.8
Boston, MA (365)	0.0	0.5	36.7	–	62.7	0.0
Boulder, CO (365)	0.0	0.0	74.5	–	25.5	0.0
Cape Coral, FL (363)	0.0	0.0	100.0	–	0.0	0.0
Cedar Rapids, IA (365)	0.0	0.0	23.6	–	76.4	0.0
Charleston, SC (365)	0.0	0.0	24.4	–	75.1	0.5
Charlotte, NC (365)	0.0	0.0	45.8	–	54.2	0.0
Chicago, IL (365)	0.0	1.6	27.1	–	67.7	3.6
Cincinnati, OH (365)	0.0	0.5	25.5	–	72.1	1.9
Clarksville, TN (365)	0.0	0.0	23.3	–	76.7	0.0
Cleveland, OH (365)	0.5	0.0	27.1	–	71.2	1.1
College Station, TX (348)	0.0	0.0	0.0	–	100.0	0.0
Colorado Springs, CO (365)	0.0	0.0	91.5	–	8.5	0.0
Columbia, MO (244)	0.0	0.0	100.0	–	0.0	0.0
Columbia, SC (365)	0.0	0.3	32.9	–	66.8	0.0
Columbus, OH (365)	0.0	0.0	26.6	–	71.2	2.2
Dallas, TX (365)	0.0	0.5	40.5	–	58.4	0.5
Davenport, IA (365)	0.0	0.0	30.4	–	62.2	7.4
Denver, CO (365)	0.0	5.5	66.6	–	23.3	4.7
Des Moines, IA (365)	0.0	0.8	22.2	–	77.0	0.0
Detroit, MI (365)	0.0	0.5	11.5	–	87.9	0.0
Durham, NC (361)	0.0	0.0	45.2	–	52.4	2.5
El Paso, TX (365)	0.0	1.4	29.9	–	56.4	12.3
Eugene, OR (365)	0.0	0.0	21.4	–	78.6	0.0
Fargo, ND (358)	0.0	0.3	31.3	–	68.4	0.0
Fort Collins, CO (365)	0.0	0.0	83.3	–	16.7	0.0
Fort Wayne, IN (365)	0.0	0.0	38.9	–	61.1	0.0
Fort Worth, TX (365)	0.0	0.5	40.5	–	58.4	0.5
Gainesville, FL (365)	0.0	0.0	38.1	–	61.9	0.0
Green Bay, WI (365)	0.0	0.0	35.9	–	64.1	0.0
Greensboro, NC (365)	0.0	0.0	31.8	–	66.8	1.4
Honolulu, HI (365)	0.0	0.0	47.7	–	51.2	1.1
Houston, TX (365)	0.0	0.3	31.5	–	62.7	5.5
Huntsville, AL (364)	0.0	0.0	25.3	–	74.7	0.0
Indianapolis, IN (365)	0.0	0.0	19.2	–	80.8	0.0
Jacksonville, FL (365)	0.0	0.0	17.0	–	83.0	0.0
Kansas City, MO (365)	0.0	1.4	39.5	–	55.6	3.6
Lafayette, LA (365)	0.0	0.0	54.8	–	44.7	0.5
Las Vegas, NV (365)	0.0	0.3	67.7	–	27.7	4.4
Lexington, KY (365)	0.0	1.1	40.0	–	58.9	0.0
Lincoln, NE (283)	0.0	0.0	74.9	–	25.1	0.0
Little Rock, AR (365)	0.0	0.0	16.4	–	83.6	0.0
Los Angeles, CA (365)	0.0	1.4	41.1	–	55.6	1.9
Louisville, KY (365)	0.0	0.5	28.2	–	71.2	0.0
Madison, WI (365)	0.0	0.0	31.5	–	68.5	0.0
Manchester, NH (365)	0.8	0.0	80.3	–	18.9	0.0

Table continued on following page.

	Percent of Days when AQI Pollutant was...					
Metro Area (Days[1])	Carbon Monoxide	Nitrogen Dioxide	Ozone	Sulfur Dioxide[2]	Particulate Matter 2.5	Particulate Matter 10
McAllen, TX (357)	0.0	0.0	5.3	–	94.7	0.0
Memphis, TN (365)	0.0	0.0	34.2	–	65.8	0.0
Miami, FL (365)	0.0	3.6	13.7	–	82.7	0.0
Midland, TX (n/a)	n/a	n/a	n/a	–	n/a	n/a
Milwaukee, WI (365)	0.0	1.4	31.5	–	67.1	0.0
Minneapolis, MN (365)	0.3	0.8	33.4	–	61.1	4.4
Nashville, TN (365)	0.0	0.5	26.0	–	73.4	0.0
New Orleans, LA (365)	0.0	0.3	37.5	–	62.2	0.0
New York, NY (365)	0.0	4.1	27.7	–	68.2	0.0
Oklahoma City, OK (365)	0.0	2.2	42.7	–	54.2	0.8
Omaha, NE (365)	0.0	0.0	48.2	–	47.4	4.4
Orlando, FL (365)	0.0	0.5	55.1	–	44.4	0.0
Philadelphia, PA (365)	0.0	0.3	22.5	–	77.3	0.0
Phoenix, AZ (365)	0.0	0.0	41.9	–	24.1	34.0
Pittsburgh, PA (365)	0.0	0.0	19.7	–	80.3	0.0
Portland, OR (365)	0.0	1.1	42.7	–	56.2	0.0
Providence, RI (365)	0.0	0.3	41.9	–	57.8	0.0
Provo, UT (365)	0.0	0.3	63.3	–	36.2	0.3
Raleigh, NC (365)	0.0	0.3	32.1	–	67.7	0.0
Reno, NV (365)	0.0	1.1	67.9	–	30.7	0.3
Richmond, VA (365)	0.0	4.4	34.8	–	60.8	0.0
Rochester, MN (365)	0.0	0.0	32.6	–	67.4	0.0
Sacramento, CA (365)	0.0	0.0	60.5	–	39.5	0.0
Saint Louis, MO (365)	0.0	0.0	27.7	–	67.4	4.9
Saint Paul, MN (365)	0.3	0.8	33.4	–	61.1	4.4
Salem, OR (365)	0.0	0.0	35.6	–	64.4	0.0
Salt Lake City, UT (365)	0.0	5.5	60.0	–	32.3	2.2
San Antonio, TX (365)	0.0	0.3	37.5	–	62.2	0.0
San Diego, CA (365)	0.0	0.3	50.7	–	41.4	7.7
San Francisco, CA (365)	0.3	4.4	17.8	–	77.5	0.0
San Jose, CA (365)	0.0	0.0	57.5	–	41.9	0.5
Santa Rosa, CA (365)	0.3	0.0	64.9	–	34.5	0.3
Savannah, GA (352)	0.0	0.0	14.8	–	85.2	0.0
Seattle, WA (365)	0.0	0.8	32.9	–	66.3	0.0
Sioux Falls, SD (365)	0.0	1.6	69.6	–	26.3	2.5
Tampa, FL (365)	0.0	0.0	27.7	–	71.5	0.8
Tucson, AZ (365)	0.0	0.0	49.0	–	33.7	17.3
Tulsa, OK (365)	0.0	0.0	45.2	–	52.9	1.9
Virginia Beach, VA (365)	0.0	1.6	33.7	–	64.7	0.0
Washington, DC (365)	0.0	1.4	44.1	–	54.2	0.3
Wichita, KS (365)	0.0	0.5	45.2	–	51.2	3.0
Wilmington, NC (362)	0.0	0.0	25.1	–	74.9	0.0
Winston-Salem, NC (365)	0.0	0.0	27.7	–	72.3	0.0

Note: The Air Quality Index (AQI) is an index for reporting daily air quality. EPA calculates the AQI for five major air pollutants regulated by the Clean Air Act: ground-level ozone, particle pollution (also known as particulate matter), carbon monoxide, sulfur dioxide, and nitrogen dioxide. The AQI runs from 0 to 500. The higher the AQI value, the greater the level of air pollution and the greater the health concern; Figures cover the Metropolitan Statistical Area (MSA); (1) Number of days with AQI data in 2023; (2) Sulfur dioxide is no longer included in this table because SO_2 concentrations tend to be very localized and not necessarily representative of broad geographical areas like counties and CBSAs
Source: U.S. Environmental Protection Agency, Air Quality Index Report, 2023

Air Quality Trends: Ozone

Metro Area	1990	1995	2000	2005	2010	2015	2020	2021	2022	2023
Albuquerque, NM	0.072	0.070	0.072	0.073	0.066	0.066	0.071	0.071	0.071	0.067
Anchorage, AK	n/a	n/a	n/a	n/a	n/a	n/a	n/a	n/a	n/a	n/a
Ann Arbor, MI	0.025	0.034	0.035	0.023	0.034	0.064	0.067	0.063	0.066	0.072
Athens, GA	n/a	n/a	n/a	n/a	n/a	n/a	n/a	n/a	n/a	n/a
Atlanta, GA	0.088	0.089	0.089	0.077	0.067	0.069	0.059	0.064	0.063	0.072
Austin, TX	0.088	0.089	0.088	0.082	0.074	0.073	0.066	0.066	0.073	0.074
Baltimore, MD	0.100	0.103	0.088	0.089	0.084	0.073	0.064	0.071	0.066	0.073
Billings, MT	n/a	n/a	n/a	n/a	n/a	n/a	n/a	n/a	n/a	n/a
Boise City, ID	n/a	n/a	n/a	n/a	n/a	n/a	n/a	n/a	n/a	n/a
Boston, MA	0.078	0.085	0.067	0.075	0.066	0.065	0.053	0.059	0.066	0.060
Boulder, CO	n/a	n/a	n/a	n/a	n/a	n/a	n/a	n/a	n/a	n/a
Cape Coral, FL	0.069	0.066	0.073	0.071	0.065	0.058	0.061	0.055	0.058	0.064
Cedar Rapids, IA	n/a	n/a	n/a	n/a	n/a	n/a	n/a	n/a	n/a	n/a
Charleston, SC	0.059	0.075	0.076	0.077	0.068	0.054	0.053	0.059	0.059	0.056
Charlotte, NC	0.094	0.091	0.099	0.089	0.082	0.071	0.060	0.067	0.068	0.072
Chicago, IL	0.074	0.094	0.073	0.084	0.070	0.066	0.076	0.071	0.070	0.081
Cincinnati, OH	0.083	0.082	0.074	0.075	0.069	0.069	0.067	0.065	0.068	0.072
Clarksville, TN	n/a	n/a	n/a	n/a	n/a	n/a	n/a	n/a	n/a	n/a
Cleveland, OH	0.084	0.090	0.079	0.084	0.074	0.069	0.069	0.066	0.068	0.071
College Station, TX	n/a	n/a	n/a	n/a	n/a	n/a	n/a	n/a	n/a	n/a
Colorado Springs, CO	n/a	n/a	n/a	n/a	n/a	n/a	n/a	n/a	n/a	n/a
Columbia, MO	n/a	n/a	n/a	n/a	n/a	n/a	n/a	n/a	n/a	n/a
Columbia, SC	0.091	0.079	0.089	0.082	0.069	0.058	0.053	0.061	0.061	0.064
Columbus, OH	0.090	0.091	0.085	0.084	0.073	0.066	0.062	0.061	0.061	0.066
Dallas, TX	0.094	0.103	0.096	0.096	0.079	0.078	0.070	0.076	0.072	0.081
Davenport, IA	0.065	0.072	0.064	0.065	0.057	0.060	0.063	0.066	0.061	0.079
Denver, CO	0.076	0.070	0.069	0.077	0.069	0.072	0.081	0.082	0.074	0.073
Des Moines, IA	n/a	n/a	n/a	n/a	n/a	n/a	n/a	n/a	n/a	n/a
Detroit, MI	0.083	0.088	0.076	0.083	0.074	0.068	0.072	0.069	0.068	0.074
Durham, NC	0.078	0.080	0.082	0.079	0.074	0.061	0.051	0.063	0.058	0.066
El Paso, TX	0.080	0.078	0.082	0.074	0.072	0.071	0.076	0.071	0.071	0.071
Eugene, OR	0.068	0.062	0.056	0.068	0.058	0.070	0.054	0.061	0.058	0.060
Fargo, ND	n/a	n/a	n/a	n/a	n/a	n/a	n/a	n/a	n/a	n/a
Fort Collins, CO	0.066	0.072	0.074	0.075	0.072	0.070	0.070	0.077	0.070	0.067
Fort Wayne, IN	0.086	0.094	0.086	0.081	0.067	0.061	0.064	0.062	0.064	0.067
Fort Worth, TX	0.094	0.103	0.096	0.096	0.079	0.078	0.070	0.076	0.072	0.081
Gainesville, FL	n/a	n/a	n/a	n/a	n/a	n/a	n/a	n/a	n/a	n/a
Green Bay, WI	n/a	n/a	n/a	n/a	n/a	n/a	n/a	n/a	n/a	n/a
Greensboro, NC	0.097	0.089	0.089	0.082	0.076	0.064	0.057	0.066	0.063	0.067
Honolulu, HI	0.034	0.049	0.044	0.042	0.046	0.048	0.044	0.045	0.044	0.046
Houston, TX	0.119	0.114	0.102	0.087	0.079	0.083	0.067	0.072	0.068	0.079
Huntsville, AL	0.079	0.080	0.088	0.075	0.071	0.063	0.057	0.061	0.065	0.064
Indianapolis, IN	0.085	0.095	0.081	0.081	0.070	0.065	0.065	0.067	0.070	0.073
Jacksonville, FL	0.080	0.068	0.072	0.076	0.068	0.060	0.057	0.061	0.062	0.060
Kansas City, MO	0.075	0.095	0.087	0.082	0.067	0.063	0.064	0.067	0.066	0.074
Lafayette, LA	n/a	n/a	n/a	n/a	n/a	n/a	n/a	n/a	n/a	n/a
Las Vegas, NV	n/a	n/a	n/a	n/a	n/a	n/a	n/a	n/a	n/a	n/a
Lexington, KY	0.078	0.088	0.077	0.078	0.070	0.069	0.060	0.064	0.065	0.070
Lincoln, NE	0.057	0.060	0.057	0.056	0.050	0.061	0.054	0.059	0.055	0.068
Little Rock, AR	0.080	0.086	0.090	0.083	0.072	0.063	0.062	0.066	0.063	0.067
Los Angeles, CA	0.128	0.109	0.090	0.086	0.074	0.082	0.096	0.076	0.077	0.081
Louisville, KY	0.082	0.091	0.087	0.083	0.076	0.071	0.063	0.064	0.063	0.072
Madison, WI	0.077	0.084	0.072	0.079	0.062	0.064	0.070	0.066	0.062	0.082
Manchester, NH	0.085	0.088	0.070	0.082	0.067	0.061	0.055	0.061	0.058	0.065
McAllen, TX	n/a	n/a	n/a	n/a	n/a	n/a	n/a	n/a	n/a	n/a
Memphis, TN	0.088	0.095	0.092	0.086	0.076	0.065	0.063	0.067	0.071	0.071

Table continued on following page.

Metro Area	1990	1995	2000	2005	2010	2015	2020	2021	2022	2023
Miami, FL	0.068	0.072	0.075	0.065	0.064	0.061	0.058	0.057	0.063	0.061
Midland, TX	n/a	n/a	n/a	n/a	n/a	n/a	n/a	n/a	n/a	n/a
Milwaukee, WI	0.095	0.106	0.082	0.092	0.079	0.069	0.074	0.072	0.073	0.077
Minneapolis, MN	0.068	0.084	0.065	0.074	0.066	0.061	0.060	0.067	0.057	0.077
Nashville, TN	0.089	0.092	0.084	0.078	0.073	0.065	0.061	0.064	0.065	0.071
New Orleans, LA	0.082	0.088	0.091	0.079	0.074	0.067	0.061	0.060	0.061	0.068
New York, NY	0.101	0.105	0.089	0.090	0.080	0.074	0.064	0.069	0.067	0.071
Oklahoma City, OK	0.080	0.087	0.083	0.077	0.071	0.067	0.066	0.068	0.071	0.072
Omaha, NE	n/a	n/a	n/a	n/a	n/a	n/a	n/a	n/a	n/a	n/a
Orlando, FL	0.081	0.075	0.080	0.083	0.069	0.060	0.059	0.061	0.062	0.066
Philadelphia, PA	0.102	0.109	0.099	0.091	0.083	0.074	0.065	0.069	0.067	0.071
Phoenix, AZ	0.080	0.086	0.082	0.077	0.075	0.072	0.079	0.079	0.074	0.077
Pittsburgh, PA	0.080	0.100	0.084	0.083	0.077	0.070	0.066	0.066	0.064	0.067
Portland, OR	0.081	0.065	0.059	0.059	0.056	0.064	0.058	0.058	0.059	0.062
Providence, RI	0.106	0.107	0.087	0.090	0.072	0.070	0.065	0.067	0.060	0.066
Provo, UT	n/a	n/a	n/a	n/a	n/a	n/a	n/a	n/a	n/a	n/a
Raleigh, NC	0.093	0.081	0.087	0.082	0.071	0.065	0.054	0.062	0.064	0.064
Reno, NV	0.074	0.069	0.067	0.069	0.068	0.071	0.073	0.078	0.064	0.065
Richmond, VA	0.083	0.089	0.080	0.082	0.079	0.062	0.054	0.061	0.060	0.063
Rochester, MN	n/a	n/a	n/a	n/a	n/a	n/a	n/a	n/a	n/a	n/a
Sacramento, CA	0.087	0.092	0.085	0.084	0.072	0.073	0.072	0.072	0.067	0.069
Saint Louis, MO	0.077	0.084	0.074	0.078	0.069	0.067	0.066	0.067	0.070	0.077
Saint Paul, MN	0.068	0.084	0.065	0.074	0.066	0.061	0.060	0.067	0.057	0.077
Salem, OR	n/a	n/a	n/a	n/a	n/a	n/a	n/a	n/a	n/a	n/a
Salt Lake City, UT	n/a	n/a	n/a	n/a	n/a	n/a	n/a	n/a	n/a	n/a
San Antonio, TX	0.090	0.095	0.078	0.084	0.072	0.079	0.069	0.070	0.076	0.074
San Diego, CA	0.110	0.085	0.079	0.074	0.073	0.068	0.078	0.068	0.067	0.072
San Francisco, CA	0.062	0.077	0.060	0.060	0.063	0.064	0.062	0.064	0.057	0.053
San Jose, CA	0.078	0.084	0.065	0.063	0.072	0.067	0.066	0.067	0.062	0.057
Santa Rosa, CA	n/a	n/a	n/a	n/a	n/a	n/a	n/a	n/a	n/a	n/a
Savannah, GA	n/a	n/a	n/a	n/a	n/a	n/a	n/a	n/a	n/a	n/a
Seattle, WA	0.082	0.062	0.056	0.053	0.053	0.059	0.056	0.061	0.065	0.056
Sioux Falls, SD	n/a	n/a	n/a	n/a	n/a	n/a	n/a	n/a	n/a	n/a
Tampa, FL	0.080	0.075	0.081	0.075	0.067	0.062	0.063	0.060	0.061	0.066
Tucson, AZ	0.073	0.078	0.074	0.075	0.068	0.065	0.070	0.068	0.069	0.069
Tulsa, OK	0.086	0.091	0.081	0.072	0.069	0.061	0.061	0.063	0.070	0.072
Virginia Beach, VA	0.085	0.084	0.083	0.078	0.074	0.061	0.053	0.057	0.057	0.059
Washington, DC	0.075	0.083	0.073	0.069	0.069	0.067	0.057	0.066	0.061	0.069
Wichita, KS	0.077	0.069	0.080	0.074	0.075	0.064	0.059	0.061	0.072	0.066
Wilmington, NC	0.082	0.079	0.080	0.075	0.062	0.057	0.054	0.062	0.058	0.067
Winston-Salem, NC	0.084	0.086	0.089	0.080	0.078	0.065	0.058	0.062	0.057	0.066
U.S.	0.087	0.089	0.081	0.080	0.072	0.068	0.066	0.067	0.067	0.070

Note: Figures cover the Metropolitan Statistical Area (MSA); n/a not available. The values shown are the composite ozone concentration averages among trend sites based on the highest fourth daily maximum 8-hour concentration in parts per million. These trends are based on sites having an adequate record of monitoring data during the trend period. Data from exceptional events are included.
Source: U.S. Environmental Protection Agency, Air Quality Monitoring Information, "Air Quality Trends by City, 1990-2023"

Maximum Air Pollutant Concentrations: Particulate Matter, Ozone, CO and Lead

Metro Area	PM 10 (ug/m³)	PM 2.5 Wtd AM (ug/m³)	PM 2.5 24-Hr (ug/m³)	Ozone (ppm)	Carbon Monoxide (ppm)	Lead (ug/m³)
Albuquerque, NM	182	7.5	23	0.069	2	n/a
Anchorage, AK	130	4.2	18	n/a	2	n/a
Ann Arbor, MI	n/a	10.6	33	0.073	n/a	n/a
Athens, GA	n/a	9.3	26	0.068	n/a	n/a
Atlanta, GA	60	10.6	28	0.077	2	n/a
Austin, TX	53	10.4	25	0.074	2	n/a
Baltimore, MD	42	10.1	32	0.075	1	n/a
Billings, MT	n/a	6.7	29	n/a	n/a	n/a
Boise City, ID	84	n/a	n/a	0.066	1	n/a
Boston, MA	47	7.8	22	0.071	1	n/a
Boulder, CO	39	6.8	19	0.071	n/a	n/a
Cape Coral, FL	n/a	n/a	n/a	0.064	n/a	n/a
Cedar Rapids, IA	68	9.9	25	0.08	n/a	n/a
Charleston, SC	70	8.1	20	0.062	n/a	n/a
Charlotte, NC	51	10	26	0.073	2	n/a
Chicago, IL	137	11.2	31	0.086	1	0.1
Cincinnati, OH	111	12.2	44	0.077	1	n/a
Clarksville, TN	n/a	8.6	22	0.07	n/a	n/a
Cleveland, OH	147	12.8	40	0.075	5	0.04
College Station, TX	n/a	8	20	n/a	n/a	n/a
Colorado Springs, CO	32	5.4	13	0.069	1	n/a
Columbia, MO	n/a	n/a	n/a	0.072	n/a	n/a
Columbia, SC	44	8.2	22	0.069	1	n/a
Columbus, OH	97	10.9	36	0.069	1	0
Dallas, TX	70	10.7	23	0.084	2	0.07
Davenport, IA	109	10.4	28	0.08	1	n/a
Denver, CO	89	8.7	24	0.077	2	n/a
Des Moines, IA	56	10.2	31	0.077	n/a	n/a
Detroit, MI	161	14.7	46	0.079	2	0.03
Durham, NC	42	8	24	0.066	n/a	n/a
El Paso, TX	180	8.6	23	0.074	2	n/a
Eugene, OR	118	10.1	46	0.06	n/a	n/a
Fargo, ND	n/a	11.5	39	0.07	n/a	n/a
Fort Collins, CO	n/a	n/a	n/a	0.071	1	n/a
Fort Wayne, IN	n/a	10	33	0.075	n/a	n/a
Fort Worth, TX	70	10.7	23	0.084	2	0.07
Gainesville, FL	n/a	6.3	17	0.058	n/a	n/a
Green Bay, WI	n/a	9.5	38	0.075	n/a	n/a
Greensboro, NC	39	9.8	25	0.067	n/a	n/a
Honolulu, HI	46	4.1	10	0.046	0	n/a
Houston, TX	161	13.1	28	0.09	2	n/a
Huntsville, AL	61	8.6	21	0.067	n/a	n/a
Indianapolis, IN	147	13.7	44	0.077	2	n/a
Jacksonville, FL	55	7.9	20	0.062	1	n/a
Kansas City, MO	256	9.6	27	0.077	1	n/a
Lafayette, LA	48	8.2	15	0.068	n/a	n/a
Las Vegas, NV	209	8.2	27	0.074	2	n/a
Lexington, KY	28	8.3	27	0.07	n/a	n/a
Lincoln, NE	n/a	n/a	n/a	0.068	n/a	n/a
Little Rock, AR	39	10.8	23	0.07	1	n/a
Los Angeles, CA	124	11.1	28	0.103	3	0.02
Louisville, KY	96	10.7	32	0.075	2	n/a
Madison, WI	208	10.7	39	0.082	n/a	n/a
Manchester, NH	n/a	4.5	20	0.067	1	n/a
McAllen, TX	47	n/a	n/a	0.051	n/a	n/a

Table continued on following page.

Metro Area	PM 10 (ug/m³)	PM 2.5 Wtd AM (ug/m³)	PM 2.5 24-Hr (ug/m³)	Ozone (ppm)	Carbon Monoxide (ppm)	Lead (ug/m³)
Memphis, TN	67	10.6	27	0.074	1	n/a
Miami, FL	65	9.4	24	0.066	2	n/a
Midland, TX	n/a	n/a	n/a	n/a	n/a	n/a
Milwaukee, WI	209	11	39	0.08	1	n/a
Minneapolis, MN	118	10.6	41	0.079	4	0.46
Nashville, TN	57	10.2	25	0.076	2	n/a
New Orleans, LA	49	9.4	19	0.071	2	0.02
New York, NY	41	10.5	40	0.076	2	n/a
Oklahoma City, OK	89	9.2	21	0.074	1	n/a
Omaha, NE	79	9.7	33	0.082	1	0.06
Orlando, FL	54	6.8	16	0.069	1	n/a
Philadelphia, PA	174	13.3	37	0.074	1	0
Phoenix, AZ	387	9.8	32	0.083	2	n/a
Pittsburgh, PA	168	12	36	0.071	3	0
Portland, OR	27	6.5	25	0.068	1	n/a
Providence, RI	29	8.2	29	0.075	2	n/a
Provo, UT	76	6.8	21	0.066	1	n/a
Raleigh, NC	60	9.2	31	0.064	1	n/a
Reno, NV	63	7.2	18	0.067	2	n/a
Richmond, VA	65	8.7	28	0.067	1	n/a
Rochester, MN	n/a	9.6	33	0.074	n/a	n/a
Sacramento, CA	57	9.4	28	0.077	n/a	n/a
Saint Louis, MO	160	11.3	26	0.082	2	0.1
Saint Paul, MN	118	10.6	41	0.079	4	0.46
Salem, OR	n/a	n/a	n/a	0.064	n/a	n/a
Salt Lake City, UT	79	8.6	31	0.076	1	n/a
San Antonio, TX	50	9	26	0.076	1	n/a
San Diego, CA	142	12.5	24	0.08	1	0.02
San Francisco, CA	48	9.9	23	0.069	4	n/a
San Jose, CA	59	8.2	25	0.067	1	0.02
Santa Rosa, CA	48	5	17	0.046	1	n/a
Savannah, GA	n/a	8.8	24	0.061	n/a	n/a
Seattle, WA	17	8.5	29	0.068	1	n/a
Sioux Falls, SD	80	n/a	n/a	0.082	n/a	n/a
Tampa, FL	76	7.8	16	0.069	1	0.05
Tucson, AZ	201	7.8	16	0.07	1	n/a
Tulsa, OK	101	9.3	20	0.078	1	n/a
Virginia Beach, VA	62	8.1	28	0.066	1	n/a
Washington, DC	142	9.7	33	0.076	2	n/a
Wichita, KS	99	n/a	n/a	0.068	n/a	n/a
Wilmington, NC	45	6.8	19	0.067	n/a	n/a
Winston-Salem, NC	72	9.5	31	0.069	n/a	n/a
NAAQS[1]	150	15.0	35	0.075	9	0.15

Note: Data from exceptional events are included; Figures cover the Metropolitan Statistical Area (MSA); (1) National Ambient Air Quality Standards; ppm = parts per million; ug/m³ = micrograms per cubic meter; n/a not available
Concentrations: Particulate Matter 10 (coarse particulate)—highest second maximum 24-hour concentration; Particulate Matter 2.5 Wtd AM (fine particulate)—highest weighted annual mean concentration; Particulate Matter 2.5 24-Hour (fine particulate)—highest 98th percentile 24-hour concentration; Ozone—highest fourth daily maximum 8-hour concentration; Carbon Monoxide—highest second maximum non-overlapping 8-hour concentration; Lead—maximum running 3-month average
Source: U.S. Environmental Protection Agency, Air Quality Monitoring Information, "Air Quality Statistics by City, 2023"

Maximum Air Pollutant Concentrations: Nitrogen Dioxide and Sulfur Dioxide

Metro Area	Nitrogen Dioxide AM (ppb)	Nitrogen Dioxide 1-Hr (ppb)	Sulfur Dioxide AM (ppb)	Sulfur Dioxide 1-Hr (ppb)	Sulfur Dioxide 24-Hr (ppb)
Albuquerque, NM	8	43	n/a	n/a	n/a
Anchorage, AK	n/a	n/a	n/a	n/a	n/a
Ann Arbor, MI	n/a	n/a	n/a	n/a	n/a
Athens, GA	n/a	n/a	n/a	n/a	n/a
Atlanta, GA	15	48	n/a	5	n/a
Austin, TX	13	n/a	n/a	n/a	n/a
Baltimore, MD	15	45	n/a	4	n/a
Billings, MT	n/a	n/a	n/a	19	n/a
Boise City, ID	8	38	n/a	3	n/a
Boston, MA	11	45	n/a	5	n/a
Boulder, CO	n/a	n/a	n/a	n/a	n/a
Cape Coral, FL	n/a	n/a	n/a	n/a	n/a
Cedar Rapids, IA	n/a	n/a	n/a	10	n/a
Charleston, SC	7	n/a	n/a	6	n/a
Charlotte, NC	11	37	n/a	2	n/a
Chicago, IL	17	54	n/a	79	n/a
Cincinnati, OH	18	49	n/a	21	n/a
Clarksville, TN	n/a	n/a	n/a	n/a	n/a
Cleveland, OH	9	44	n/a	27	n/a
College Station, TX	n/a	n/a	n/a	29	n/a
Colorado Springs, CO	n/a	n/a	n/a	5	n/a
Columbia, MO	n/a	n/a	n/a	n/a	n/a
Columbia, SC	3	28	n/a	2	n/a
Columbus, OH	9	43	n/a	4	n/a
Dallas, TX	14	46	n/a	17	n/a
Davenport, IA	n/a	n/a	n/a	4	n/a
Denver, CO	24	65	n/a	6	n/a
Des Moines, IA	n/a	n/a	n/a	n/a	n/a
Detroit, MI	14	50	n/a	55	n/a
Durham, NC	n/a	n/a	n/a	3	n/a
El Paso, TX	15	57	n/a	6	n/a
Eugene, OR	n/a	n/a	n/a	n/a	n/a
Fargo, ND	4	n/a	n/a	3	n/a
Fort Collins, CO	n/a	n/a	n/a	n/a	n/a
Fort Wayne, IN	n/a	n/a	n/a	n/a	n/a
Fort Worth, TX	14	46	n/a	17	n/a
Gainesville, FL	n/a	n/a	n/a	n/a	n/a
Green Bay, WI	n/a	n/a	n/a	n/a	n/a
Greensboro, NC	n/a	n/a	n/a	4	n/a
Honolulu, HI	3	23	n/a	60	n/a
Houston, TX	18	60	n/a	13	n/a
Huntsville, AL	n/a	n/a	n/a	n/a	n/a
Indianapolis, IN	13	44	n/a	3	n/a
Jacksonville, FL	10	40	n/a	40	n/a
Kansas City, MO	11	45	n/a	6	n/a
Lafayette, LA	n/a	n/a	n/a	n/a	n/a
Las Vegas, NV	20	52	n/a	5	n/a
Lexington, KY	6	39	n/a	7	n/a
Lincoln, NE	n/a	n/a	n/a	n/a	n/a
Little Rock, AR	3	13	n/a	4	n/a
Los Angeles, CA	21	61	n/a	8	n/a
Louisville, KY	13	47	n/a	13	n/a
Madison, WI	n/a	n/a	n/a	n/a	n/a
Manchester, NH	n/a	n/a	n/a	1	n/a
McAllen, TX	n/a	n/a	n/a	n/a	n/a

Table continued on following page.

Metro Area	Nitrogen Dioxide AM (ppb)	Nitrogen Dioxide 1-Hr (ppb)	Sulfur Dioxide AM (ppb)	Sulfur Dioxide 1-Hr (ppb)	Sulfur Dioxide 24-Hr (ppb)
Memphis, TN	9	38	n/a	2	n/a
Miami, FL	15	53	n/a	2	n/a
Midland, TX	n/a	n/a	n/a	n/a	n/a
Milwaukee, WI	11	46	n/a	3	n/a
Minneapolis, MN	12	45	n/a	14	n/a
Nashville, TN	13	52	n/a	6	n/a
New Orleans, LA	8	39	n/a	52	n/a
New York, NY	19	60	n/a	5	n/a
Oklahoma City, OK	12	29	n/a	1	n/a
Omaha, NE	n/a	n/a	n/a	39	n/a
Orlando, FL	n/a	n/a	n/a	4	n/a
Philadelphia, PA	15	48	n/a	5	n/a
Phoenix, AZ	24	58	n/a	4	n/a
Pittsburgh, PA	9	38	n/a	65	n/a
Portland, OR	9	29	n/a	n/a	n/a
Providence, RI	13	35	n/a	3	n/a
Provo, UT	8	39	n/a	n/a	n/a
Raleigh, NC	9	36	n/a	2	n/a
Reno, NV	11	49	n/a	3	n/a
Richmond, VA	13	47	n/a	3	n/a
Rochester, MN	n/a	n/a	n/a	n/a	n/a
Sacramento, CA	9	33	n/a	2	n/a
Saint Louis, MO	10	43	n/a	38	n/a
Saint Paul, MN	12	45	n/a	14	n/a
Salem, OR	n/a	n/a	n/a	n/a	n/a
Salt Lake City, UT	16	57	n/a	5	n/a
San Antonio, TX	8	37	n/a	2	n/a
San Diego, CA	14	49	n/a	n/a	n/a
San Francisco, CA	11	102	n/a	18	n/a
San Jose, CA	13	44	n/a	2	n/a
Santa Rosa, CA	3	25	n/a	n/a	n/a
Savannah, GA	n/a	n/a	n/a	44	n/a
Seattle, WA	15	50	n/a	3	n/a
Sioux Falls, SD	5	40	n/a	1	n/a
Tampa, FL	9	36	n/a	48	n/a
Tucson, AZ	13	39	n/a	1	n/a
Tulsa, OK	6	33	n/a	3	n/a
Virginia Beach, VA	8	37	n/a	3	n/a
Washington, DC	16	47	n/a	3	n/a
Wichita, KS	6	23	n/a	2	n/a
Wilmington, NC	n/a	n/a	n/a	n/a	n/a
Winston-Salem, NC	7	40	n/a	2	n/a
NAAQS[1]	53	100	30	75	140

Note: Data from exceptional events are included; Figures cover the Metropolitan Statistical Area (MSA); (1) National Ambient Air Quality Standards; ppb = parts per billion; n/a not available
Concentrations: Nitrogen Dioxide AM—highest arithmetic mean concentration; Nitrogen Dioxide 1-Hr—highest 98th percentile 1-hour daily maximum concentration; Sulfur Dioxide AM—highest annual mean concentration; Sulfur Dioxide 1-Hr—highest 99th percentile 1-hour daily maximum concentration; Sulfur Dioxide 24-Hr—highest second maximum 24-hour concentration
Source: U.S. Environmental Protection Agency, Air Quality Monitoring Information, "Air Quality Statistics by City, 2023"

Appendix B: Metropolitan Area Definitions

Includes Metropolitan Statistical Areas (MSA) and Metropolitan Divisions (MD) referenced in this book.

Note: On July 21, 2023, the Office of Management and Budget (OMB) announced changes to metropolitan and micropolitan statistical area definitions. The current definitions are shown below.

Albuquerque, NM MSA
Bernalillo, Sandoval, Torrance, and Valencia Counties

Anchorage, AK MSA
Anchorage Municipality and Matanuska-Susitna Borough

Ann Arbor, MI MSA
Washtenaw County

Athens-Clarke County, GA MSA
Clarke, Madison, Oconee, and Oglethorpe Counties

Atlanta, GA
Atlanta-Sandy Springs-Roswell, GA MSA
Barrow, Bartow, Butts, Carroll, Cherokee, Clayton, Cobb, Coweta, Dawson, DeKalb, Douglas, Fayette, Forsyth, Fulton, Gwinnett, Haralson, Heard, Henry, Jasper, Lumpkin, Meriwether, Morgan, Newton, Paulding, Pickens, Pike, Rockdale, Spalding, and Walton Counties

Atlanta-Sandy Springs-Roswell, GA MD
Barrow, Butts, Carroll, Clayton, Coweta, Dawson, DeKalb, Douglas, Fayette, Forsyth, Fulton, Gwinnett, Heard, Henry, Jasper, Lumpkin, Meriwether, Morgan, Newton, Pickens, Pike, Rockdale, Spalding, and Walton Counties

Austin-Round Rock-San Marcos, TX MSA
Bastrop, Caldwell, Hays, Travis, and Williamson Counties

Baltimore-Columbia-Towson, MD MSA
Baltimore city; Anne Arundel, Baltimore, Carroll, Harford, Howard, and Queen Anne's Counties

Billings, MT MSA
Carbon, Stillwater, and Yellowstone Counties

Boise City, ID MSA
Previously Boise City-Nampa, ID MSA
Ada, Boise, Canyon, Gem, and Owyhee Counties

Boston, MA
Boston-Cambridge-Newton, MA-NH MSA
Essex, Middlesex, Norfolk, Plymouth, and Suffolk Counties, MA; Rockingham and Strafford Counties, NH

Boston, MA MD
Norfolk, Plymouth, and Suffolk Counties

Boulder, CO MSA
Boulder County

Cape Coral-Fort Myers, FL MSA
Lee County

Cedar Rapids, IA, MSA
Benton, Jones, and Linn Counties

Charleston-North Charleston, SC MSA
Berkeley, Charleston, and Dorchester Counties

Charlotte-Concord-Gastonia, NC-SC MSA
Anson, Cabarrus, Gaston, Iredell, Lincoln, Mecklenburg, Rowan, and Union Counties, NC; Chester, Lancaster, and York Counties, SC

Chicago, IL
Chicago-Naperville-Elgin, IL-IN MSA
Cook, DeKalb, DuPage, Grundy, Kane, Kendall, Lake, McHenry, and Will Counties, IL; Jasper, Lake, Newton, and Porter Counties, IN

Chicago-Naperville-Schaumburg, IL MD
Cook, DuPage, Grundy, McHenry, and Will Counties

Cincinnati, OH-KY-IN MSA
Brown, Butler, Clermont, Hamilton, and Warren Counties, OH; Boone, Bracken, Campbell, Gallatin, Grant, Kenton, and Pendleton County, KY; Dearborn, Franklin, and Ohio Counties, IN

Clarksville, TN-KY MSA
Montgomery and Stewart Counties, TN; Christian and Trigg Counties, KY

Cleveland, OH MSA
Ashtabula, Cuyahoga, Geauga, Lake, Lorain, and Medina Counties

College Station-Bryan, TX MSA
Brazos, Burleson, and Robertson Counties

Colorado Springs, CO MSA
El Paso and Teller Counties

Columbia, MO MSA
Boone, Cooper, and Howard Counties

Columbia, SC MSA
Calhoun, Fairfield, Kershaw, Lexington, Richland, and Saluda Counties

Columbus, OH MSA
Delaware, Fairfield, Franklin, Hocking, Licking, Madison, Morrow, Perry, Pickaway, and Union Counties

Dallas, TX
Dallas-Fort Worth-Arlington, TX MSA
Collin, Dallas, Denton, Ellis, Hunt, Johnson, Kaufman, Parker, Rockwall, Tarrant, and Wise Counties

Dallas-Plano-Irving, TX MD
Collin, Dallas, Denton, Ellis, Hunt, Kaufman, and Rockwall Counties

Davenport-Moline-Rock Island, IA-IL MSA
Scott County, IA; Henry, Mercer, and Rock Island Counties, IL

Denver-Aurora-Centennial, CO MSA
Adams, Arapahoe, Broomfield, Clear Creek, Denver, Douglas, Elbert, Gilpin, Jefferson, and Park Counties

Des Moines-West Des Moines, IA MSA
Dallas, Guthrie, Jasper, Madison, Polk, and Warren Counties

Detroit, MI
Detroit-Warren-Dearborn, MI MSA
Lapeer, Livingston, Macomb, Oakland, St. Clair, and Wayne Counties

Detroit-Dearborn-Livonia, MI MD
Wayne County

Durham-Chapel Hill, NC MSA
Chatham, Durham, Orange, and Person Counties

El Paso, TX MSA
El Paso and Hudspeth Counties

Eugene-Springfield, OR MSA
Lane County

Fargo, ND-MN MSA
Cass County, ND; Clay County, MN

Fort Collins-Loveland, CO MSA
Larimer County

Fort Wayne, IN MSA
Allen, Wells, and Whitley Counties

Fort Worth, TX

Dallas-Fort Worth-Arlington, TX MSA
Collin, Dallas, Denton, Ellis, Hunt, Johnson, Kaufman, Parker, Rockwall, Tarrant, and Wise Counties

Fort Worth-Arlington-Grapevine, TX MD
Johnson, Parker, Tarrant, and Wise Counties

Gainesville, FL MSA
Alachua, Gilchrist, and Levy Counties

Green Bay, WI MSA
Brown, Kewaunee, and Oconto Counties

Greensboro-High Point, NC MSA
Guilford, Randolph, and Rockingham Counties

Honolulu, HI
See Urban Honolulu, HI

Houston-Pasadena-The Woodlands, TX MSA
Austin, Brazoria, Chambers, Fort Bend, Galveston, Harris, Liberty, Montgomery, San Jacinto, and Waller Counties

Huntsville, AL MSA
Limestone and Madison Counties

Indianapolis-Carmel-Greenwood, IN MSA
Boone, Brown, Hamilton, Hancock, Hendricks, Johnson, Madison, Marion, Morgan, Shelby, and Tipton Counties

Jacksonville, FL MSA
Baker, Clay, Duval, Nassau, and St. Johns Counties

Kansas City, MO-KS MSA
Johnson, Leavenworth, Linn, Miami, and Wyandotte Counties, KS; Bates, Caldwell, Cass, Clay, Clinton, Jackson, Lafayette, Platte, and Ray Counties, MO

Lafayette, LA MSA
Acadia, Lafayette, St. Martin, and Vermilion Parishes

Las Vegas-Henderson-North Las Vegas, NV MSA
Clark County

Lexington-Fayette, KY MSA
Bourbon, Clark, Fayette, Jessamine, Scott, and Woodford Counties

Lincoln, NE MSA
Lancaster and Seward Counties

Little Rock-North Little Rock-Conway, AR MSA
Faulkner, Grant, Lonoke, Perry, Pulaski, and Saline Counties

Los Angeles, CA

Los Angeles-Long Beach-Anaheim, CA MSA
Los Angeles and Orange Counties

Los Angeles-Long Beach-Glendale, CA MD
Los Angeles County

Louisville/Jefferson County, KY-IN MSA
Clark, Floyd, Harrison, and Washington Counties, IN; Bullitt, Henry, Jefferson, Meade, Nelson, Oldham, Shelby, and Spencer Counties, KY

Madison, WI MSA
Columbia, Dane, Green, and Iowa Counties

Manchester-Nashua, NH MSA
Hillsborough County

McAllen-Edinburg-Mission, TX
Hidalgo County

Memphis, TN-AR-MS MSA
Fayette, Shelby and Tipton Counties, TN; Crittenden County, AR; Benton, DeSoto, Marshall, Tate and Tunica Counties, MS

Miami, FL

Miami-Fort Lauderdale-West Palm Beach, FL MSA
Broward, Miami-Dade, and Palm Beach Counties

Miami-Miami Beach-Kendall, FL MD
Miami-Dade County

Midland, TX MSA
Martin and Midland Counties

Milwaukee-Waukesha, WI MSA
Milwaukee, Ozaukee, Washington, and Waukesha Counties

Minneapolis-St. Paul-Bloomington, MN-WI MSA
Anoka, Carver, Chisago, Dakota, Hennepin, Isanti, Le Sueur, Mille Lacs, Ramsey, Scott, Sherburne, Washington, and Wright Counties, MN; Pierce and St. Croix Counties, WI

Nashville-Davidson–Murfreesboro–Franklin, TN MSA
Cannon, Cheatham, Davidson, Dickson, Hickman, Macon, Maury, Robertson, Rutherford, Smith, Sumner, Trousdale, Williamson, and Wilson Counties

New Orleans-Metarie, LA MSA
Jefferson, Orleans, Plaquemines, St. Bernard, St. Charles, St. James, and St. John the Baptist Parishes

New York, NY

New York-Newark-Jersey City, NY-NJ MSA
Bergen, Essex, Hudson, Hunterdon, Middlesex, Monmouth, Morris, Ocean, Passaic, Somerset, Sussex, and Union Counties, NJ; Bronx, Kings, Nassau, New York, Putnam, Queens, Richmond, Rockland, Suffolk, and Westchester Counties, NY

New York-Jersey City-White Plains, NY-NJ MD
Bergen, Hudson, and Passaic Counties, NJ; Bronx, Kings, New York, Putnam, Queens, Richmond, Rockland, and Westchester Counties, NY

Oklahoma City, OK MSA
Canadian, Cleveland, Grady, Lincoln, Logan, McClain, and Oklahoma Counties

Omaha, NE-IA MSA
Harrison, Mills, and Pottawattamie Counties, IA; Cass, Douglas, Sarpy, Saunders, and Washington Counties, NE

Orlando-Kissimmee-Sanford, FL MSA
Lake, Orange, Osceola, and Seminole Counties

Appendix B: Metropolitan Area Definitions A-173

Philadelphia, PA

Philadelphia-Camden-Wilmington, PA-NJ-DE-MD MSA
New Castle County, DE; Cecil County, MD; Burlington, Camden, Gloucester, and Salem Counties, NJ; Bucks, Chester, Delaware, Montgomery, and Philadelphia Counties, PA

Philadelphia, PA MD
Delaware and Philadelphia Counties

Phoenix-Mesa-Chandler, AZ MSA
Maricopa and Pinal Counties

Pittsburgh, PA MSA
Allegheny, Armstrong, Beaver, Butler, Fayette, Lawrence, Washington, and Westmoreland Counties

Portland-Vancouver-Hillsboro, OR-WA MSA
Clackamas, Columbia, Multnomah, Washington, and Yamhill Counties, OR; Clark and Skamania Counties, WA

Providence-Warwick, RI MSA
Bristol County, MA; Bristol, Kent, Newport, Providence, and Washington Counties, RI

Provo-Orem-Lehi, UT MSA
Juab and Utah Counties

Raleigh-Cary, NC MSA
Franklin, Johnston, and Wake Counties

Reno, NV MSA
Lyon, Storey, and Washoe Counties

Richmond, VA MSA
Amelia, Charles City, Chesterfield, Dinwiddie, Goochland, Hanover, Henrico, King and Queen, King William, New Kent, Powhatan, Prince George, and Sussex Counties; Colonial Heights, Hopewell, Petersburg, and Richmond Cities

Rochester, MN MSA
Dodge, Fillmore, Olmsted, and Wabasha Counties

Sacramento-Roseville-Folsom, CA MSA
El Dorado, Placer, Sacramento, and Yolo Counties

Saint Louis, MO-IL MSA
Bond, Calhoun, Clinton, Jersey, Macoupin, Madison, Monroe, and St. Clair Counties, IL; St. Louis city; Crawford (part–Sullivan city), Franklin, Jefferson, Lincoln, St. Charles, St. Louis, and Warren Counties, MO

Saint Paul, MN
See Minneapolis-St. Paul-Bloomington, MN-WI MSA

Salem, OR MSA
Marion and Polk Counties

Salt Lake City-Murray, UT MSA
Salt Lake and Tooele Counties

San Antonio-New Braunfels, TX MSA
Atascosa, Bandera, Bexar, Comal, Guadalupe, Kendall, Medina, and Wilson Counties

San Diego-Chula Vista-Carlsbad, CA MSA
San Diego County

San Francisco, CA

San Francisco-Oakland-Fremont, CA MSA
Alameda, Contra Costa, Marin, San Francisco, and San Mateo Counties

San Francisco-San Mateo-Redwood City, CA MD
San Francisco and San Mateo Counties

San Jose-Sunnyvale-Santa Clara, CA MSA
San Benito and Santa Clara Counties

Santa Rosa-Petaluma, CA MSA
Sonoma County

Savannah, GA MSA
Bryan, Chatham, and Effingham Counties

Seattle, WA

Seattle-Tacoma-Bellevue, WA MSA
King, Pierce, and Snohomish Counties

Seattle-Bellevue-Kent, WA MD
King County

Sioux Falls, SD-MN MSA
Lincoln, McCook, Minnehaha, and Turner Counties, SD; Rock County, MN

Tampa, FL

Tampa-St. Petersburg-Clearwater, FL MSA
Hernando, Hillsborough, Pasco, and Pinellas Counties

Tampa, FL MD
Hernando, Hillsborough, and Pasco Counties

Tucson, AZ MSA
Pima County

Tulsa, OK MSA
Creek, Okmulgee, Osage, Pawnee, Rogers, Tulsa, and Wagoner Counties

Urban Honolulu, HI MSA
Honolulu County

Virginia Beach-Chesapeake-Norfolk, VA-NC MSA
Camden, Currituck, and Gates Counties, NC; Chesapeake, Hampton, Newport News, Norfolk, Poquoson, Portsmouth, Suffolk, Virginia Beach and Williamsburg cities, VA; Gloucester, Isle of Wight, James City, Mathews, Surry, and York Counties, VA

Washington, DC

Washington-Arlington-Alexandria, DC-VA-MD-WV MSA
District of Columbia; Calvert, Charles, Frederick, Montgomery, and Prince George's Counties, MD; Alexandria, Fairfax, Falls Church, Fredericksburg, Manassas, and Manassas Park cities, VA; Arlington, Clarke, Culpepper, Fairfax, Fauquier, Loudoun, Prince William, Rappahannock, Spotsylvania, Stafford, and Warren Counties, VA; Jefferson County, WV

Washington, DC-MD MD
District of Columbia; Charles and Prince George's Counties, MD

Wichita, KS MSA
Butler, Harvey, Sedgwick, and Sumner Counties

Wilmington, NC MSA
Brunswick, New Hanover and Pender Counties

Winston-Salem, NC MSA
Davidson, Davie, Forsyth, Stokes, and Yadkin Counties

Appendix C: Government Type and Primary County

This appendix includes the government structure of each place included in this book. It also includes the county or county equivalent in which each place is located. If a place spans more than one county, the county in which the majority of the population resides is shown.

Albuquerque, NM
Government Type: City
County: Bernalillo

Anchorage, AK
Government Type: Municipality
Borough: Anchorage

Ann Arbor, MI
Government Type: City
County: Washtenaw

Athens, GA
Government Type: Consolidated city-county
County: Clarke

Atlanta, GA
Government Type: City
County: Fulton

Austin, TX
Government Type: City
County: Travis

Baltimore, MD
Government Type: Independent city

Baton Rouge, LA
Government Type: Consolidated city-parish
Parish: East Baton Rouge

Billings, MT
Government Type: City
County: Yellowstone

Boise City, ID
Government Type: City
County: Ada

Boston, MA
Government Type: City
County: Suffolk

Boulder, CO
Government Type: City
County: Boulder

Cape Coral, FL
Government Type: City
County: Lee

Cedar Rapids, IA
Government Type: City
County: Linn

Charleston, SC
Government Type: City
County: Charleston

Charlotte, NC
Government Type: City
County: Mecklenburg

Chicago, IL
Government Type: City
County: Cook

Cincinnati, OH
Government Type: City
County: Hamilton

Clarksville, TN
Government Type: City
County: Montgomery

Cleveland, OH
Government Type: City
County: Cuyahoga

College Station, TX
Government Type: City
County: Brazos

Colorado Springs, CO
Government Type: City
County: El Paso

Columbia, MO
Government Type: City
County: Boone

Columbia, SC
Government Type: City
County: Richland

Columbus, OH
Government Type: City
County: Franklin

Dallas, TX
Government Type: City
County: Dallas

Davenport, IA
Government Type: City
County: Scott

Denver, CO
Government Type: City
County: Denver

Des Moines, IA
Government Type: City
County: Polk

Detroit, MI
Government Type: City
County: Wayne

Durham, NC
Government Type: City
County: Durham

El Paso, TX
Government Type: City
County: El Paso

Eugene, OR
Government Type: City
County: Lane

Fargo, ND
Government Type: City
County: Cass

Fort Collins, CO
Government Type: City
County: Larimer

Fort Wayne, IN
Government Type: City
County: Allen

Fort Worth, TX
Government Type: City
County: Tarrant

Gainesville, FL
Government Type: City
County: Alachua

Green Bay, WI
Government Type: City
County: Brown

Greensboro, NC
Government Type: City
County: Guilford

Honolulu, HI
Government Type: Census Designated Place (CDP)
County: Honolulu

Houston, TX
Government Type: City
County: Harris

Huntsville, AL
Government Type: City
County: Madison

Indianapolis, IN
Government Type: City
County: Marion

Jacksonville, FL
Government Type: City
County: Duval

Kansas City, MO
Government Type: City
County: Jackson

Lafayette, LA
Government Type: City
Parish: Lafayette

Las Vegas, NV
Government Type: City
County: Clark

Appendix C: Government Type and Primary County

Lexington, KY
Government Type: Consolidated city-county
County: Fayette

Lincoln, NE
Government Type: City
County: Lancaster

Little Rock, AR
Government Type: City
County: Pulaski

Los Angeles, CA
Government Type: City
County: Los Angeles

Louisville, KY
Government Type: Consolidated city-county
County: Jefferson

Madison, WI
Government Type: City
County: Dane

Manchester, NH
Government Type: City
County: Hillsborough

McAllen, TX
Government Type: City
County: Hidalgo

Memphis, TN
Government Type: City
County: Shelby

Miami, FL
Government Type: City
County: Miami-Dade

Midland, TX
Government Type: City
County: Midland

Milwaukee, WI
Government Type: City
County: Milwaukee

Minneapolis, MN
Government Type: City
County: Hennepin

Nashville, TN
Government Type: Consolidated city-county
County: Davidson

New Orleans, LA
Government Type: City
Parish: Orleans

New York, NY
Government Type: City
Counties: Bronx; Kings; New York; Queens; Staten Island

Oklahoma City, OK
Government Type: City
County: Oklahoma

Omaha, NE
Government Type: City
County: Douglas

Orlando, FL
Government Type: City
County: Orange

Philadelphia, PA
Government Type: City
County: Philadelphia

Phoenix, AZ
Government Type: City
County: Maricopa

Pittsburgh, PA
Government Type: City
County: Allegheny

Portland, OR
Government Type: City
County: Multnomah

Providence, RI
Government Type: City
County: Providence

Provo, UT
Government Type: City
County: Utah

Raleigh, NC
Government Type: City
County: Wake

Reno, NV
Government Type: City
County: Washoe

Richmond, VA
Government Type: Independent city

Riverside, CA
Government Type: City
County: Riverside

Rochester, MN
Government Type: City
County: Olmsted

Rochester, NY
Government Type: City
County: Monroe

Sacramento, CA
Government Type: City
County: Sacramento

Saint Louis, MO
Government Type: Independent city

Saint Paul, MN
Government Type: City
County: Ramsey

Salem, OR
Government Type: City
County: Marion

Salt Lake City, UT
Government Type: City
County: Salt Lake

San Antonio, TX
Government Type: City
County: Bexar

San Diego, CA
Government Type: City
County: San Diego

San Francisco, CA
Government Type: City
County: San Francisco

San Jose, CA
Government Type: City
County: Santa Clara

Santa Rosa, CA
Government Type: City
County: Sonoma

Savannah, GA
Government Type: City
County: Chatham

Seattle, WA
Government Type: City
County: King

Sioux Falls, SD
Government Type: City
County: Minnehaha

Tampa, FL
Government Type: City
County: Hillsborough

Tucson, AZ
Government Type: City
County: Pima

Tulsa, OK
Government Type: City
County: Tulsa

Virginia Beach, VA
Government Type: Independent city

Washington, DC
Government Type: City
County: District of Columbia

Wichita, KS
Government Type: City
County: Sedgwick

Wilmington, NC
Government Type: City
County: New Hanover

Winston-Salem, NC
Government Type: City
County: Forsyth

Appendix D: Chambers of Commerce

Albuquerque, NM
Albuquerque Chamber of Commerce
P.O. Box 25100
Albuquerque, NM 87125
Phone: (505) 764-3700
Fax: (505) 764-3714
www.abqchamber.com

Albuquerque Economic Development Dept
851 University Blvd SE, Suite 203
Albuquerque, NM 87106
Phone: (505) 246-6200
Fax: (505) 246-6219
www.cabq.gov/econdev

Anchorage, AK
Anchorage Chamber of Commerce
1016 W Sixth Avenue, Suite 303
Anchorage, AK 99501
Phone: (907) 272-2401
Fax: (907) 272-4117
www.anchoragechamber.org

Anchorage Economic Development Department
900 W 5th Avenue, Suite 300
Anchorage, AK 99501
Phone: (907) 258-3700
Fax: (907) 258-6646
aedcweb.com

Ann Arbor, MI
Ann Arbor Area Chamber of Commerce
115 West Huron, 3rd Floor
Ann Arbor, MI 48104
Phone: (734) 665-4433
Fax: (734) 665-4191
www.annarborchamber.org

Ann Arbor Economic Development Department
201 S Division, Suite 430
Ann Arbor, MI 48104
Phone: (734) 761-9317
www.annarborspark.org

Athens, GA
Athens Area Chamber of Commerce
246 W Hancock Avenue
Athens, GA 30601
Phone: (706) 549-6800
Fax: (706) 549-5636
www.aacoc.org

Athens-Clarke County Economic Development Department
246 W. Hancock Avenue
Athens, GA 30601
Phone: (706) 613-3233
Fax: (706) 613-3812
www.athensbusiness.org

Atlanta, GA
Metro Atlanta Chamber of Commerce
235 Andrew Young International Blvd NW
Atlanta, GA 30303
Phone: (404) 880-9000
Fax: (404) 586-8464
www.metroatlantachamber.com

Austin, TX
Greater Austin Chamber of Commerce
210 Barton Springs Road, Suite 400
Austin, TX 78704
Phone: (512) 478-9383
Fax: (512) 478-6389
www.austin-chamber.org

Baltimore, MD
Baltimore City Chamber of Commerce
P.O. Box 43121
Baltimore, MD 21236
443-860-2020
baltimorecitychamber.org

Baltimore County Chamber of Commerce
102 W. Pennsylvania Avenue, Suite 305
Towson, MD, 21204
Phone: (410) 825-6200
Fax: (410) 821-9901
www.baltcountychamber.com

Billings, MT
Billings Chamber of Commerce
815 S. 27th St
Billings, MT 59101
Phone: (406) 245-4111
Fax: (406) 245-7333
www.billingschamber.com

Boise City, ID
Boise Metro Chamber of Commerce
250 S. 5th Street, Suite 800
Boise City, ID 83701
Phone: (208) 472-5200
Fax: (208) 472-5201
www.boisechamber.org

Boston, MA
Greater Boston Chamber of Commerce
265 Franklin Street, 12th Floor
Boston, MA 02110
Phone: (617) 227-4500
Fax: (617) 227-7505
www.bostonchamber.com

Boulder, CO
Boulder Chamber of Commerce
2440 Pearl Street
Boulder, CO 80302
Phone: (303) 442-1044
Fax: (303) 938-8837
www.boulderchamber.com

Cape Coral, FL
Chamber of Commerce of Cape Coral
2051 Cape Coral Parkway East
Cape Coral, FL 33904
Phone: (239) 549-6900
www.capecoralchamber.com

Cedar Rapids, IA
Cedar Rapids Chamber of Commerce
424 First Avenue NE
Cedar Rapids, IA 52401
Phone: (319) 398-5317
Fax: (319) 398-5228
www.cedarrapids.org

Cedar Rapids Economic Development
50 Second Avenue Bridge, Sixth Floor
Cedar Rapids, IA 52401-1256
Phone: (319) 286-5041
Fax: (319) 286-5141
www.cedar-rapids.org

Charleston, SC
Charleston Metro Chamber of Commerce
P.O. Box 975
Charleston, SC 29402
Phone: (843) 577-2510
www.charlestonchamber.net

Charlotte, NC
Charlotte Chamber of Commerce
330 S Tryon Street
P.O. Box 32785
Charlotte, NC 28232
Phone: (704) 378-1300
Fax: (704) 374-1903
www.charlottechamber.com

Charlotte Regional Partnership
1001 Morehead Square Drive, Suite 200
Charlotte, NC 28203
Phone: (704) 347-8942
Fax: (704) 347-8981
www.charlotteusa.com

Chicago, IL
Chicagoland Chamber of Commerce
200 E Randolph Street, Suite 2200
Chicago, IL 60601-6436
Phone: (312) 494-6700
Fax: (312) 861-0660
www.chicagolandchamber.org

City of Chicago Department of Planning and Development
City Hall, Room 1000
121 North La Salle Street
Chicago, IL 60602
Phone: (312) 744-4190
Fax: (312) 744-2271
www.cityofchicago.org/city/en/depts/dcd.html

Cincinnati, OH
Cincinnati USA Regional Chamber
3 East 4th Street, Suite 200
Cincinnati, Ohio 45202
Phone: (513) 579-3111
www.cincinnatichamber.com

Clarksville, TN
Clarksville Area Chamber of Commerce
25 Jefferson Street, Suite 300
Clarksville, TN 37040
Phone: (931) 647-2331
www.clarksvillechamber.com

Cleveland, OH
Greater Cleveland Partnership
1240 Huron Rd. E, Suite 300
Cleveland, OH 44115
Phone: (216) 621-3300
www.gcpartnership.com

Appendix D: Chambers of Commerce

College Station, TX
Bryan-College Station Chamber of Commerce
4001 East 29th St, Suite 175
Bryan, TX 77802
Phone: (979) 260-5200
www.bcschamber.org

Colorado Springs, CO
Colorado Springs Chamber and EDC
102 South Tejon Street, Suite 430
Colorado Springs, CO 80903
Phone: (719) 471-8183
coloradospringschamberedc.com

Columbia, MO
Columbia Chamber of Commerce
300 South Providence Rd.
P.O. Box 1016
Columbia, MO 65205-1016
Phone: (573) 874-1132
Fax: (573) 443-3986
www.columbiamochamber.com

Columbia, SC
The Columbia Chamber
930 Richland Street
Columbia, SC 29201
Phone: (803) 733-1110
Fax: (803) 733-1113
www.columbiachamber.com

Columbus, OH
Greater Columbus Chamber
37 North High Street
Columbus, OH 43215
Phone: (614) 221-1321
Fax: (614) 221-1408
www.columbus.org

Dallas, TX
City of Dallas Economic Development Department
1500 Marilla Street, 5C South
Dallas, TX 75201
Phone: (214) 670-1685
Fax: (214) 670-0158
www.dallas-edd.org

Greater Dallas Chamber of Commerce
700 North Pearl Street, Suite 1200
Dallas, TX 75201
Phone: (214) 746-6600
Fax: (214) 746-6799
www.dallaschamber.org

Davenport, IA
Quad Cities Chamber
331 W. 3rd Street, Suite 100
Davenport, IA 52801
Phone: (563) 322-1706
quadcitieschamber.com

Denver, CO
Denver Metro Chamber of Commerce
1445 Market Street
Denver, CO 80202
Phone: (303) 534-8500
Fax: (303) 534-3200
www.denverchamber.org

Downtown Denver Partnership
511 16th Street, Suite 200
Denver, CO 80202
Phone: (303) 534-6161
Fax: (303) 534-2803
www.downtowndenver.com

Des Moines, IA
Des Moines Downtown Chamber
301 Grand Ave
Des Moines, IA 50309
Phone: (515) 309-3229
desmoinesdowntownchamber.com

Greater Des Moines Partnership
700 Locust Street, Suite 100
Des Moines, IA 50309
Phone: (515) 286-4950
Fax: (515) 286-4974
www.desmoinesmetro.com

Durham, NC
Durham Chamber of Commerce
P.O. Box 3829
Durham, NC 27702
Phone: (919) 682-2133
Fax: (919) 688-8351
www.durhamchamber.org

North Carolina Institute of Minority Economic Development
114 W Parish Street
Durham, NC 27701
Phone: (919) 956-8889
Fax: (919) 688-7668
www.ncimed.com

El Paso, TX
City of El Paso Department of Economic Development
2 Civic Center Plaza
El Paso, TX 79901
Phone: (915) 541-4000
Fax: (915) 541-1316
www.elpasotexas.gov

Greater El Paso Chamber of Commerce
10 Civic Center Plaza
El Paso, TX 79901
Phone: (915) 534-0500
Fax: (915) 534-0510
www.elpaso.org

Eugene, OR
Eugene Area Chamber of Commerce
1401 Williamette Street
Eugene, OR 97401
Phone: (541) 484-1314
Fax: (541) 484-4942
www.eugenechamber.com

Fargo, ND
Chamber of Commerce of Fargo Moorhead
202 First Avenue North
Fargo, ND 56560
Phone: (218) 233-1100
Fax: (218) 233-1200
www.fmchamber.com

Greater Fargo-Moorhead Economic Development Corporation
51 Broadway, Suite 500
Fargo, ND 58102
Phone: (701) 364-1900
Fax: (701) 293-7819
www.gfmedc.com

Fort Collins, CO
Fort Collins Chamber of Commerce
225 South Meldrum
Fort Collins, CO 80521
Phone: (970) 482-3746
Fax: (970) 482-3774
fortcollinschamber.com

Fort Wayne, IN
City of Fort Wayne Economic Development
1 Main Street
Fort Wayne, IN 46802
Phone: (260) 427-1111
Fax: (260) 427-1375
www.cityoffortwayne.org

Greater Fort Wayne Chamber of Commerce
826 Ewing Street
Fort Wayne, IN 46802
Phone: (260) 424-1435
Fax: (260) 426-7232
www.fwchamber.org

Fort Worth, TX
Fort Worth Chamber of Commerce
777 Taylor Street, Suite 900
Fort Worth, TX 76102-4997
Phone: (817) 336-2491
Fax: (817) 877-4034
www.fortworthchamber.com

City of Fort Worth Economic Development
City Hall
900 Monroe Street, Suite 301
Fort Worth, TX 76102
Phone: (817) 392-6103
Fax: (817) 392-2431
www.fortworthgov.org

Gainesville, FL
Greater Gainesville Chamber
300 East University Avenue, Suite 100
Gainesville, FL 32601
Phone: (352) 334-7100
Fax: (352) 334-7141
www.gainesvillechamber.com

Green Bay, WI
Greater Green Bay Chamber
300 N. Broadway, Suite 3A
Green Bay, WI 54303
Phone: (920) 593-3400
www.greatergbc.org

Greensboro, NC
Greensboro Chamber of Commerce
111 W. February One Place
Greensboro, NC 27401
Phone: (336) 387-8301
greensboro.org

Appendix D: Chambers of Commerce   A-179

Honolulu, HI
The Chamber of Commerce of Hawaii
1132 Bishop Street, Suite 402
Honolulu, HI 96813
Phone: (808) 545-4300
Fax: (808) 545-4369
www.cochawaii.com

Houston, TX
Greater Houston Partnership
1200 Smith Street, Suite 700
Houston, TX 77002-4400
Phone: (713) 844-3600
Fax: (713) 844-0200
www.houston.org

Huntsville, AL
Chamber of Commerce of
Huntsville/Madison County
225 Church Street
Huntsville, AL 35801
Phone: (256) 535-2000
www.huntsvillealabamausa.com

Indianapolis, IN
Greater Indianapolis Chamber of Commerce
111 Monument Circle, Suite 1950
Indianapolis, IN 46204
Phone: (317) 464-2222
Fax: (317) 464-2217
www.indychamber.com

Jacksonville, FL
Jacksonville Chamber of Commerce
3 Independent Drive
Jacksonville, FL 32202
Phone: (904) 366-6600
Fax: (904) 632-0617
www.myjaxchamber.com

Kansas City, MO
Greater Kansas City Chamber of Commerce
2600 Commerce Tower
911 Main Street
Kansas City, MO 64105
Phone: (816) 221-2424
Fax: (816) 221-7440
www.kcchamber.com

Kansas City Area Development Council
2600 Commerce Tower
911 Main Street
Kansas City, MO 64105
Phone: (816) 221-2121
www.thinkkc.com

Lafayette, LA
Greater Lafayette Chamber of Commerce
804 East Saint Mary Blvd.
Lafayette, LA 70503
Phone: (337) 233-2705
Fax: (337) 234-8671
www.lafchamber.org

Las Vegas, NV
Las Vegas Chamber of Commerce
6671 Las Vegas Blvd South, Suite 300
Las Vegas, NV 89119
Phone: (702) 735-1616
Fax: (702) 735-0406
www.lvchamber.org

Las Vegas Office of Business Development
400 Stewart Avenue
City Hall
Las Vegas, NV 89101
Phone: (702) 229-6011
Fax: (702) 385-3128
www.lasvegasnevada.gov

Lexington, KY
Greater Lexington Chamber of Commerce
330 East Main Street, Suite 100
Lexington, KY 40507
Phone: (859) 254-4447
Fax: (859) 233-3304
www.commercelexington.com

Lexington Downtown Development
Authority
101 East Vine Street, Suite 500
Lexington, KY 40507
Phone: (859) 425-2296
Fax: (859) 425-2292
www.lexingtondda.com

Lincoln, NE
Lincoln Chamber of Commerce
1135 M Street, Suite 200
Lincoln, NE 68508
Phone: (402) 436-2350
www.lcoc.com

Little Rock, AR
Little Rock Regional Chamber
One Chamber Plaza
Little Rock, AR 72201
Phone: (501) 374-2001
Fax: (501) 374-6018
www.littlerockchamber.com

Los Angeles, CA
Los Angeles Area Chamber of Commerce
350 South Bixel Street
Los Angeles, CA 90017
Phone: (213) 580-7500
Fax: (213) 580-7511
www.lachamber.org

Los Angeles County Economic
Development Corporation
444 South Flower Street, 34th Floor
Los Angeles, CA 90071
Phone: (213) 622-4300
Fax: (213) 622-7100
www.laedc.org

Louisville, KY
The Greater Louisville Chamber of
Commerce
614 West Main Street, Suite 6000
Louisville, KY 40202
Phone: (502) 625-0000
Fax: (502) 625-0010
www.greaterlouisville.com

Madison, WI
Greater Madison Chamber of Commerce
615 East Washington Avenue
P.O. Box 71
Madison, WI 53701-0071
Phone: (608) 256-8348
Fax: (608) 256-0333
www.greatermadisonchamber.com

Manchester, NH
Greater Manchester Chamber of Commerce
889 Elm Street
Manchester, NH 03101
Phone: (603) 666-6600
Fax: (603) 626-0910
www.manchester-chamber.org

Manchester Economic Development Office
One City Hall Plaza
Manchester, NH 03101
Phone: (603) 624-6505
Fax: (603) 624-6308
www.yourmanchesternh.com

McAllen, TX
McAllen Chamber of Commerce
1200 Ash Avenue
McAllen, TX 78501
Phone: (956) 682-2871
Fax: (956) 687-2917
mcallenchamber.com

Memphis, TN
Greater Memphis Chamber
22 North Front Street, Suite 200
Memphis, TN 38103-2100
Phone: (901) 543-3500
memphischamber.com

Miami, FL
Greater Miami Chamber of Commerce
1601 Biscayne Boulevard
Miami, FL 33132-1260
Phone: (305) 350-7700
Fax: (305) 374-6902
www.miamichamber.com

The Beacon Council
80 Southwest 8th Street, Suite 2400
Miami, FL 33130
Phone: (305) 579-1300
Fax: (305) 375-0271
www.beaconcouncil.com

Midland, TX
Midland Chamber of Commerce
303 W. Wall Street, Suite 200
Midland, TX 79701
Phone: (432) 683-3381
www.midlandtxchamber.com

Milwaukee, WI
Greater Milwaukee Chamber of Commerce
6815 W. Capitol Drive, Suite 300
Milwaukee, WI 53216
Phone: (414) 465-2422
www.gmcofc.org

Minneapolis, MN
Minneapolis Regional Chamber
81 South Ninth Street, Suite 200
Minneapolis, MN 55402
Phone: (612) 370-9100
Fax: (612) 370-9195
www.minneapolischamber.org

Minneapolis Community Development Agency
Crown Roller Mill
105 5th Avenue South, Suite 200
Minneapolis, MN 55401
Phone: (612) 673-5095
Fax: (612) 673-5100
www.ci.minneapolis.mn.us

Nashville, TN
Nashville Area Chamber of Commerce
211 Commerce Street, Suite 100
Nashville, TN 37201
Phone: (615) 743-3000
Fax: (615) 256-3074
www.nashvillechamber.com

TVA Economic Development
400 West Summit Hill Drive
Knoxville TN 37902
Phone: (865) 632-2101
www.tvaed.com

New Orleans, LA
New Orleans Chamber of Commerce
1515 Poydras Street, Suite 1010
New Orleans, LA 70112
Phone: (504) 799-4260
Fax: (504) 799-4259
www.neworleanschamber.org

New York, NY
New York City Economic Development Corporation
110 William Street
New York, NY 10038
Phone: (212) 619-5000
www.nycedc.com

The Partnership for New York City
One Battery Park Plaza
5th Floor
New York, NY 10004
Phone: (212) 493-7400
Fax: (212) 344-3344
www.pfnyc.org

Oklahoma City, OK
Greater Oklahoma City Chamber of Commerce
123 Park Avenue
Oklahoma City, OK 73102
Phone: (405) 297-8900
Fax: (405) 297-8916
www.okcchamber.com

Omaha, NE
Omaha Chamber of Commerce
1301 Harney Street
Omaha, NE 68102
Phone: (402) 346-5000
Fax: (402) 346-7050
www.omahachamber.org

Orlando, FL
Metro Orlando Economic Development Commission of Mid-Florida
301 East Pine Street, Suite 900
Orlando, FL 32801
Phone: (407) 422-7159
Fax: (407) 425.6428
www.orlandoedc.com

Orlando Regional Chamber of Commerce
75 South Ivanhoe Boulevard
P.O. Box 1234
Orlando, FL 32802
Phone: (407) 425-1234
Fax: (407) 839-5020
www.orlando.org

Philadelphia, PA
Greater Philadelphia Chamber of Commerce
200 South Broad Street, Suite 700
Philadelphia, PA 19102
Phone: (215) 545-1234
Fax: (215) 790-3600
www.greaterphilachamber.com

Phoenix, AZ
Greater Phoenix Chamber of Commerce
201 North Central Avenue, 27th Floor
Phoenix, AZ 85073
Phone: (602) 495-2195
Fax: (602) 495-8913
www.phoenixchamber.com

Greater Phoenix Economic Council
2 North Central Avenue, Suite 2500
Phoenix, AZ 85004
Phone: (602) 256-7700
Fax: (602) 256-7744
www.gpec.org

Pittsburgh, PA
Allegheny County Industrial Development Authority
425 6th Avenue, Suite 800
Pittsburgh, PA 15219
Phone: (412) 350-1067
Fax: (412) 642-2217
www.alleghenycounty.us

Greater Pittsburgh Chamber of Commerce
425 6th Avenue, 12th Floor
Pittsburgh, PA 15219
Phone: (412) 392-4500
Fax: (412) 392-4520
www.alleghenyconference.org

Portland, OR
Portland Business Alliance
200 SW Market Street, Suite 1770
Portland, OR 97201
Phone: (503) 224-8684
Fax: (503) 323-9186
www.portlandalliance.com

Providence, RI
Greater Providence Chamber of Commerce
30 Exchange Terrace, Fourth Floor
Providence, RI 02903
Phone: (401) 521-5000
Fax: (401) 351-2090
www.provchamber.com

Rhode Island Economic Development Corporation
Providence City Hall
25 Dorrance Street
Providence, RI 02903
Phone: (401) 421-7740
Fax: (401) 751-0203
www.providenceri.com

Provo, UT
Provo-Orem Chamber of Commerce
51 South University Avenue, Suite 215
Provo, UT 84601
Phone: (801) 851-2555
Fax: (801) 851-2557
www.thechamber.org

Raleigh, NC
Greater Raleigh Chamber of Commerce
800 South Salisbury Street
Raleigh, NC 27601-2978
Phone: (919) 664-7000
Fax: (919) 664-7099
www.raleighchamber.org

Reno, NV
Reno + Sparks Chamber of Commerce
449 S. Virginia Street, 2nd Floor
Reno, NV 89501
Phone: (775) 636-9550
www.thechambernv.org

Richmond, VA
Greater Richmond Chamber
600 East Main Street, Suite 700
Richmond, VA 23219
Phone: (804) 648-1234
www.grcc.com

Greater Richmond Partnership
901 East Byrd Street, Suite 801
Richmond, VA 23219-4070
Phone: (804) 643-3227
Fax: (804) 343-7167
www.grpva.com

Rochester, MN
Rochester Area Chamber of Commerce
220 South Broadway, Suite 100
Rochester, MN 55904
Phone: (507) 288-1122
www.rochestermnchamber.com

Sacramento, CA
Sacramento Metro Chamber
One Capitol Mall, Suite 700
Sacramento, CA 95814
Phone: (916) 552-6800
metrochamber.org

Saint Louis, MO
St. Louis Regional Chamber
One Metropolitan Square, Suite 1300
St. Louis, MO 63102
Phone: (314) 231-5555
www.stlregionalchamber.com

Saint Paul, OR
St. Paul Area Chamber
401 Robert Street N, Suite 150
St. Paul, MN 55101
Phone: (651) 223-5000
www.stpaulchamber.com

Salem, OR
Salem Area Chamber of Commerce
1110 Commercial Street NE
Salem, OR 97301
Phone: (503) 581-1466
www.salemchamber.org

Appendix D: Chambers of Commerce

Salt Lake City, UT
Salt Lake Chamber
175 E. University Blvd. (400 S), Suite 600
Salt Lake City, UT 84111
Phone: (801) 364-3631
www.slchamber.com

San Antonio, TX
The Greater San Antonio Chamber of Commerce
602 E. Commerce Street
San Antonio, TX 78205
Phone: (210) 229-2100
Fax: (210) 229-1600
www.sachamber.org

San Antonio Economic Development Department
P.O. Box 839966
San Antonio, TX 78283-3966
Phone: (210) 207-8080
Fax: (210) 207-8151
www.sanantonio.gov/edd

San Diego, CA
San Diego Economic Development Corp.
401 B Street, Suite 1100
San Diego, CA 92101
Phone: (619) 234-8484
Fax: (619) 234-1935
www.sandiegobusiness.org

San Diego Regional Chamber of Commerce
402 West Broadway, Suite 1000
San Diego, CA 92101-3585
Phone: (619) 544-1300
Fax: (619) 744-7481
www.sdchamber.org

San Francisco, CA
San Francisco Chamber of Commerce
235 Montgomery Street, 12th Floor
San Francisco, CA 94104
Phone: (415) 392-4520
Fax: (415) 392-0485
www.sfchamber.com

San Jose, CA
Office of Economic Development
60 South Market Street, Suite 470
San Jose, CA 95113
Phone: (408) 277-5880
Fax: (408) 277-3615
www.sba.gov

The Silicon Valley Organization
101 W Santa Clara Street
San Jose, CA 95113
Phone: (408) 291-5250
www.thesvo.com

Santa Rosa, CA
Santa Rosa Chamber of Commerce
1260 North Dutton Avenue, Suite 272
Santa Rosa, CA 95401
Phone: (707) 545-1414
www.santarosachamber.com

Savannah, GA
Savannah Chamber of Commerce
101 E. Bay Street
Savannah, GA 31402
Phone: (912) 644-6400
Fax: (912) 644-6499
www.savannahchamber.com

Seattle, WA
Greater Seattle Chamber of Commerce
1301 Fifth Avenue, Suite 2500
Seattle, WA 98101
Phone: (206) 389-7200
Fax: (206) 389-7288
www.seattlechamber.com

Sioux Falls, SD
Sioux Falls Area Chamber of Commerce
200 N. Phillips Avenue, Suite 102
Sioux Falls, SD 57104
Phone: (605) 336-1620
Fax: (605) 336-6499
www.siouxfallschamber.com

Tampa, FL
Greater Tampa Chamber of Commerce
P.O. Box 420
Tampa, FL 33601-0420
Phone: (813) 276-9401
Fax: (813) 229-7855
www.tampachamber.com

Tucson, AZ
Tucson Metro Chamber
212 E. Broadway Blvd
Tucson, AZ 85701
Phone: (520) 792-1212
tucsonchamber.org

Tulsa, OK
Tulsa Regional Chamber
One West Third Street, Suite 100
Tulsa, OK 74103
Phone: (918) 585-1201
www.tulsachamber.com

Virginia Beach, VA
Hampton Roads Chamber of Commerce
500 East Main Street, Suite 700
Virginia Beach, VA 23510
Phone: (757) 664-2531
www.hamptonroadschamber.com

Washington, DC
District of Columbia Chamber of Commerce
1213 K Street NW
Washington, DC 20005
Phone: (202) 347-7201
Fax: (202) 638-6762
www.dcchamber.org

District of Columbia Office of Planning and Economic Development
J.A. Wilson Building
1350 Pennsylvania Ave NW, Suite 317
Washington, DC 20004
Phone: (202) 727-6365
Fax: (202) 727-6703
www.dcbiz.dc.gov

Wichita, KS
Wichita Regional Chamber of Commerce
350 W Douglas Avennue
Wichita, KS 67202
Phone: (316) 265-7771
www.wichitachamber.org

Wilmington, NC
Wilmington Chamber of Commerce
One Estell Lee Place
Wilmington, NC 28401
Phone: (910) 762-2611
www.wilmingtonchamber.org

Winston-Salem, NC
Winston-Salem Chamber of Commerce
411 West Fourth Street, Suite 211
Winston-Salem, NC 27101
Phone: (336) 728-9200
www.winstonsalem.com

Appendix E: State Departments of Labor

Alabama
Alabama Department of Labor
P.O. Box 303500
Montgomery, AL 36130-3500
Phone: (334) 242-3072
adol.alabama.gov

Alaska
Dept of Labor and Workforce Development
P.O. Box 11149
Juneau, AK 99822-2249
Phone: (907) 465-2700
www.labor.state.ak.us

Arizona
Industrial Commission or Arizona
800 West Washington Street
Phoenix, AZ 85007
Phone: (602) 542-4661
www.azica.gov

Arkansas
Department of Labor
10421 West Markham
Little Rock, AR 72205
Phone: (501) 682-4500
www.labor.ar.gov

California
Labor and Workforce Development
445 Golden Gate Ave., 10th Floor
San Francisco, CA 94102
Phone: (916) 263-1811
www.labor.ca.gov

Colorado
Dept of Labor and Employment
633 17th St., 2nd Floor
Denver, CO 80202-3660
Phone: (888) 390-7936
cdle.colorado.gov

Connecticut
Department of Labor
200 Folly Brook Blvd.
Wethersfield, CT 06109-1114
Phone: (860) 263-6000
www.ctdol.state.ct.us

Delaware
Department of Labor
4425 N. Market St., 4th Floor
Wilmington, DE 19802
Phone: (302) 451-3423
dol.delaware.gov

District of Columbia
Department of Employment Services
614 New York Ave., NE, Suite 300
Washington, DC 20002
Phone: (202) 671-1900
does.dc.gov

Florida
Florida Department of Economic Opportunity
The Caldwell Building
107 East Madison St. Suite 100
Tallahassee, FL 32399-4120
Phone: (800) 342-3450
www.floridajobs.org

Georgia
Department of Labor
Sussex Place, Room 600
148 Andrew Young Intl Blvd., NE
Atlanta, GA 30303
Phone: (404) 656-3011
dol.georgia.gov

Hawaii
Dept of Labor & Industrial Relations
830 Punchbowl Street
Honolulu, HI 96813
Phone: (808) 586-8842
labor.hawaii.gov

Idaho
Department of Labor
317 W. Main St.
Boise, ID 83735-0001
Phone: (208) 332-3579
www.labor.idaho.gov

Illinois
Department of Labor
160 N. LaSalle Street, 13th Floor
Suite C-1300
Chicago, IL 60601
Phone: (312) 793-2800
www.illinois.gov/idol

Indiana
Indiana Department of Labor
402 West Washington Street, Room W195
Indianapolis, IN 46204
Phone: (317) 232-2655
www.in.gov/dol

Iowa
Iowa Workforce Development
1000 East Grand Avenue
Des Moines, IA 50319-0209
Phone: (515) 242-5870
www.iowadivisionoflabor.gov

Kansas
Department of Labor
401 S.W. Topeka Blvd.
Topeka, KS 66603-3182
Phone: (785) 296-5000
www.dol.ks.gov

Kentucky
Department of Labor
1047 U.S. Hwy 127 South, Suite 4
Frankfort, KY 40601-4381
Phone: (502) 564-3070
www.labor.ky.gov

Louisiana
Louisiana Workforce Commission
1001 N. 23rd Street
Baton Rouge, LA 70804-9094
Phone: (225) 342-3111
www.laworks.net

Maine
Department of Labor
45 Commerce Street
Augusta, ME 04330
Phone: (207) 623-7900
www.state.me.us/labor

Maryland
Department of Labor, Licensing & Regulation
500 N. Calvert Street
Suite 401
Baltimore, MD 21202
Phone: (410) 767-2357
www.dllr.state.md.us

Massachusetts
Dept of Labor & Workforce Development
One Ashburton Place
Room 2112
Boston, MA 02108
Phone: (617) 626-7100
www.mass.gov/lwd

Michigan
Department of Licensing and Regulatory Affairs
611 W. Ottawa
P.O. Box 30004
Lansing, MI 48909
Phone: (517) 373-1820
www.michigan.gov/lara

Minnesota
Dept of Labor and Industry
443 Lafayette Road North
Saint Paul, MN 55155
Phone: (651) 284-5070
www.doli.state.mn.us

Mississippi
Dept of Employment Security
P.O. Box 1699
Jackson, MS 39215-1699
Phone: (601) 321-6000
www.mdes.ms.gov

Missouri
Labor and Industrial Relations
P.O. Box 599
3315 W. Truman Boulevard
Jefferson City, MO 65102-0599
Phone: (573) 751-7500
labor.mo.gov

Montana
Dept of Labor and Industry
P.O. Box 1728
Helena, MT 59624-1728
Phone: (406) 444-9091
www.dli.mt.gov

Appendix E: State Departments of Labor

Nebraska
Department of Labor
550 S 16th Street
Lincoln, NE 68508
Phone: (402) 471-9000
dol.nebraska.gov

Nevada
Dept of Business and Industry
3300 W. Sahara Ave, Suite 425
Las Vegas, NV 89102
Phone: (702) 486-2750
business.nv.gov

New Hampshire
Department of Labor
State Office Park South
95 Pleasant Street
Concord, NH 03301
Phone: (603) 271-3176
www.nh.gov/labor

New Jersey
Department of Labor & Workforce Devel.
John Fitch Plaza, 13th Floor, Suite D
Trenton, NJ 08625-0110
Phone: (609) 777-3200
lwd.dol.state.nj.us/labor

New Mexico
Department of Workforce Solutions
401 Broadway, NE
Albuquerque, NM 87103-1928
Phone: (505) 841-8450
www.dws.state.nm.us

New York
Department of Labor
State Office Bldg. # 12
W.A. Harriman Campus
Albany, NY 12240
Phone: (518) 457-9000
www.labor.ny.gov

North Carolina
Department of Labor
4 West Edenton Street
Raleigh, NC 27601-1092
Phone: (919) 733-7166
www.labor.nc.gov

North Dakota
North Dakota Department of Labor and Human Rights
State Capitol Building
600 East Boulevard, Dept 406
Bismark, ND 58505-0340
Phone: (701) 328-2660
www.nd.gov/labor

Ohio
Department of Commerce
77 South High Street, 22nd Floor
Columbus, OH 43215
Phone: (614) 644-2239
www.com.state.oh.us

Oklahoma
Department of Labor
4001 N. Lincoln Blvd.
Oklahoma City, OK 73105-5212
Phone: (405) 528-1500
www.ok.gov/odol

Oregon
Bureau of Labor and Industries
800 NE Oregon St., #32
Portland, OR 97232
Phone: (971) 673-0761
www.oregon.gov/boli

Pennsylvania
Dept of Labor and Industry
1700 Labor and Industry Bldg
7th and Forster Streets
Harrisburg, PA 17120
Phone: (717) 787-5279
www.dli.pa.gov

Rhode Island
Department of Labor and Training
1511 Pontiac Avenue
Cranston, RI 02920
Phone: (401) 462-8000
www.dlt.state.ri.us

South Carolina
Dept of Labor, Licensing & Regulations
P.O. Box 11329
Columbia, SC 29211-1329
Phone: (803) 896-4300
www.llr.state.sc.us

South Dakota
Department of Labor & Regulation
700 Governors Drive
Pierre, SD 57501-2291
Phone: (605) 773-3682
dlr.sd.gov

Tennessee
Dept of Labor & Workforce Development
Andrew Johnson Tower
710 James Robertson Pkwy
Nashville, TN 37243-0655
Phone: (615) 741-6642
www.tn.gov/workforce

Texas
Texas Workforce Commission
101 East 15th St.
Austin, TX 78778
Phone: (512) 475-2670
www.twc.state.tx.us

Utah
Utah Labor Commission
160 East 300 South, 3rd Floor
Salt Lake City, UT 84114-6600
Phone: (801) 530-6800
laborcommission.utah.gov

Vermont
Department of Labor
5 Green Mountain Drive
P.O. Box 488
Montpelier, VT 05601-0488
Phone: (802) 828-4000
labor.vermont.gov

Virginia
Dept of Labor and Industry
Powers-Taylor Building
13 S. 13th Street
Richmond, VA 23219
Phone: (804) 371-2327
www.doli.virginia.gov

Washington
Dept of Labor and Industries
P.O. Box 44001
Olympia, WA 98504-4001
Phone: (360) 902-4200
www.lni.wa.gov

West Virginia
Division of Labor
749 B Building 6
Capitol Complex
Charleston, WV 25305
Phone: (304) 558-7890
labor.wv.gov

Wisconsin
Dept of Workforce Development
201 E. Washington Ave., #A400
P.O. Box 7946
Madison, WI 53707-7946
Phone: (608) 266-6861
dwd.wisconsin.gov

Wyoming
Department of Workforce Services
1510 East Pershing Blvd.
Cheyenne, WY 82002
Phone: (307) 777-7261
www.wyomingworkforce.org

Titles from Grey House

Visit www.GreyHouse.com for Product Information, Table of Contents, and Sample Pages.

Opinions Throughout History
Opinions Throughout History: Church & State
Opinions Throughout History: Conspiracy Theories
Opinions Throughout History: The Death Penalty
Opinions Throughout History: Diseases & Epidemics
Opinions Throughout History: Domestic Terrorism
Opinions Throughout History: Drug Use & Abuse
Opinions Throughout History: The Environment
Opinions Throughout History: Fame & Celebrity in America
Opinions Throughout History: Free Speech & Censorship
Opinions Throughout History: Gender: Roles & Rights
Opinions Throughout History: Globalization
Opinions Throughout History: Guns in America
Opinions Throughout History: Immigration
Opinions Throughout History: Law Enforcement in America
Opinions Throughout History: LGBTQ+ Rights
Opinions Throughout History: Mental Health
Opinions Throughout History: Nat'l Security vs. Civil & Privacy Rights
Opinions Throughout History: Presidential Authority
Opinions Throughout History: Refugees & Asylum Seekers
Opinions Throughout History: Robotics & Artificial Intelligence
Opinions Throughout History: Social Media Issues
Opinions Throughout History: Spies & Espionage
Opinions Throughout History: The Supreme Court
Opinions Throughout History: Truth & Lies in the Media
Opinions Throughout History: Voters' Rights
Opinions Throughout History: War & the Military
Opinions Throughout History: Workers Rights & Wages

General Reference
American Environmental Leaders
Constitutional Amendments
Encyclopedia of African-American Writing
Encyclopedia of Invasions & Conquests
Encyclopedia of Prisoners of War & Internment
Encyclopedia of the Continental Congresses
Encyclopedia of the United States Cabinet
Encyclopedia of War Journalism
The Environmental Debate
Environmental Sustainability: Skills & Strategies
Financial Literacy Starter Kit
From Suffrage to the Senate
The Gun Debate: Gun Rights & Gun Control in the U.S.
Historical Warrior Peoples & Modern Fighting Groups
Human Rights and the United States
Political Corruption in America
Privacy Rights in the Digital Age
The Religious Right and American Politics
Speakers of the House of Representatives, 1789-2021
US Land & Natural Resources Policy
The Value of a Dollar 1600-1865 Colonial to Civil War
The Value of a Dollar 1860-2024

This is Who We Were
This is Who We Were: Colonial America (1492-1775)
This is Who We Were: Civil War & Reconstruction
This is Who We Were: 1880-1899
This is Who We Were: In the 1900s
This is Who We Were: In the 1910s
This is Who We Were: In the 1920s
This is Who We Were: A Companion to the 1940 Census
This is Who We Were: In the 1940s (1940-1949)
This is Who We Were: In the 1950s
This is Who We Were: In the 1960s
This is Who We Were: In the 1970s
This is Who We Were: In the 1980s
This is Who We Were: In the 1990s
This is Who We Were: In the 2000s
This is Who We Were: In the 2010s

Working Americans
Working Americans—Vol. 1: The Working Class
Working Americans—Vol. 2: The Middle Class
Working Americans—Vol. 3: The Upper Class
Working Americans—Vol. 4: Children
Working Americans—Vol. 5: At War
Working Americans—Vol. 6: Working Women
Working Americans—Vol. 7: Social Movements
Working Americans—Vol. 8: Immigrants
Working Americans—Vol. 9: Revolutionary War to the Civil War
Working Americans—Vol. 10: Sports & Recreation
Working Americans—Vol. 11: Inventors & Entrepreneurs
Working Americans—Vol. 12: Our History through Music
Working Americans—Vol. 13: Education & Educators
Working Americans—Vol. 14: African Americans
Working Americans—Vol. 15: Politics & Politicians
Working Americans—Vol. 16: Farming & Ranching
Working Americans—Vol. 17: Teens in America
Working Americans—Vol. 18: Health Care Workers
Working Americans—Vol. 19: The Performing Arts

Grey House Health & Wellness Guides
Addiction Handbook & Resource Guide
Adolescent Mental Health Handbook & Resource Guide
Anxiety & Stress Handbook & Resource Guide
Attention Disorders Handbook & Resource Guide
The Autism Spectrum Handbook & Resource Guide
Autoimmune Disorders Handbook & Resource Guide
Breast Cancer Handbook & Resource Guide
Cardiovascular Disease Handbook & Resource Guide
Chronic Pain Handbook & Resource Guide
Dementia Handbook & Resource Guide
Depression Handbook & Resource Guide
Diabetes Handbook & Resource Guide
Nutrition, Obesity & Eating Disorders Handbook & Resource Guide

Consumer Health
Complete Mental Health Resource Guide
Complete Resource Guide for Pediatric Disorders
Complete Resource Guide for People with Chronic Illness
Complete Resource Guide for People with Disabilities
Older Americans Information Resource
Parenting: Styles & Strategies
Social Media & Your Mental Health
Teens: Growing Up, Skills & Strategies

Guide to Venture Capital & Private Equity Firms
Hudson's Washington News Media Contacts Guide
New York State Directory
Sports Market Place

Grey House Publishing | Salem Press | H.W. Wilson | 4919 Route 22, PO Box 56, Amenia NY 12501-0056

Grey House Imprints

Visit www.GreyHouse.com for Product Information, Table of Contents, and Sample Pages.

Grey House Titles, continued

Business Information
Business Information Resources
Complete Broadcasting Industry Guide: TV, Radio, Cable & Streaming
Directory of Mail Order Catalogs
Environmental Resource Handbook
Food & Beverage Market Place
Guide to Healthcare Group Purchasing Organizations
Guide to U.S. HMOs and PPOs

Education
Complete Learning Disabilities Resource Guide
Digital Literacy: Skills & Strategies

Statistics & Demographics
America's Top-Rated Cities
America's Top-Rated Smaller Cities
Profiles of California
Profiles of Florida
Profiles of Illinois
Profiles of Indiana
Profiles of Massachusetts
Profiles of Michigan
Profiles of New Jersey
Profiles of New York
Profiles of North Carolina & South Carolina
Profiles of Ohio
Profiles of Pennsylvania
Profiles of Texas
Profiles of Virginia
Profiles of Wisconsin

Canadian Resources
Associations Canada
Canadian Almanac & Directory
Canadian Environmental Resource Guide
Canadian Parliamentary Guide
Canadian Venture Capital & Private Equity Firms
Canadian Who's Who
Cannabis Canada
Careers & Employment Canada
Financial Post: Directory of Directors
Financial Services Canada
FP Bonds: Corporate
FP Bonds: Government
FP Equities: Preferreds & Derivatives
FP Survey: Industrials
FP Survey: Mines & Energy
FP Survey: Predecessor & Defunct
Health Guide Canada
Indigenous History & Culture in Canada
Libraries Canada
Major Canadian Cities: 50 Cities Compared, Ranked & Profiled

Books in Print Series
American Book Publishing Record® Annual
American Book Publishing Record® Monthly
Books In Print®
Books In Print® Supplement
Books Out Loud™
Bowker's Complete Video Directory™
Children's Books In Print®
El-Hi Textbooks & Serials In Print®
Forthcoming Books®
Law Books & Serials In Print™
Medical & Health Care Books In Print™
Publishers, Distributors & Wholesalers of the US™
Subject Guide to Books In Print®
Subject Guide to Children's Books In Print®

Weiss Financial Ratings
Financial Literacy Basics
Financial Literacy: How to Become an Investor
Financial Literacy: Planning for the Future
Weiss Ratings Consumer Guides
Weiss Ratings Guide to Banks
Weiss Ratings Guide to Credit Unions
Weiss Ratings Guide to Health Insurers
Weiss Ratings Guide to Life & Annuity Insurers
Weiss Ratings Guide to Property & Casualty Insurers
Weiss Ratings Investment Research Guide to Bond & Money Market Mutual Funds
Weiss Ratings Investment Research Guide to Exchange-Traded Funds
Weiss Ratings Investment Research Guide to Stock Mutual Funds
Weiss Ratings Investment Research Guide to Stocks

Titles from Salem Press

Visit www.SalemPress.com for Product Information, Table of Contents, and Sample Pages.

LITERATURE

Critical Insights: Authors

Louisa May Alcott
Sherman Alexie
Dante Alighieri
Isabel Allende
Maya Angelou
Isaac Asimov
Margaret Atwood
Jane Austen
James Baldwin
Saul Bellow
Roberto Bolano
Ray Bradbury
The Brontë Sisters
Gwendolyn Brooks
Albert Camus
Raymond Carver
Willa Cather
Geoffrey Chaucer
John Cheever
Kate Chopin
Joseph Conrad
Charles Dickens
Emily Dickinson
Frederick Douglass
T. S. Eliot
George Eliot
Harlan Ellison
Ralph Waldo Emerson
Louise Erdrich
William Faulkner
F. Scott Fitzgerald
Gustave Flaubert
Horton Foote
Benjamin Franklin
Robert Frost
Neil Gaiman
Gabriel Garcia Marquez
Thomas Hardy
Nathaniel Hawthorne
Robert A. Heinlein
Lillian Hellman
Ernest Hemingway
Langston Hughes
Zora Neale Hurston
Henry James
Thomas Jefferson
James Joyce
Jamaica Kincaid
Stephen King
Martin Luther King, Jr.
Barbara Kingsolver
Abraham Lincoln
C.S. Lewis
Mario Vargas Llosa
Jack London
James McBride
Cormac McCarthy
Herman Melville
Arthur Miller
Toni Morrison
Alice Munro
Tim O'Brien
Flannery O'Connor
Eugene O'Neill
George Orwell
Sylvia Plath
Edgar Allan Poe
Philip Roth
Salman Rushdie
J.D. Salinger
Mary Shelley
John Steinbeck
Amy Tan
Leo Tolstoy
Mark Twain
John Updike
Kurt Vonnegut
Alice Walker
David Foster Wallace
H. G. Wells
Edith Wharton
Walt Whitman
Oscar Wilde
Tennessee Williams
Virginia Woolf
Richard Wright
Malcolm X

Critical Insights: Works

Absalom, Absalom!
Adventures of Huckleberry Finn
The Adventures of Tom Sawyer
Aeneid
All Quiet on the Western Front
All the Pretty Horses
Animal Farm
Anna Karenina
As You Like It
The Awakening
The Bell Jar
Beloved
Billy Budd, Sailor
The Bluest Eye
The Book Thief
Brave New World
The Canterbury Tales
Catch-22
The Catcher in the Rye
The Color Purple
Crime and Punishment
The Crucible
Death of a Salesman
The Diary of a Young Girl
Dracula
Fahrenheit 451
A Farewell to Arms
Frankenstein; or, The Modern Prometheus
The Grapes of Wrath
Great Expectations
The Great Gatsby
Hamlet
The Handmaid's Tale
Harry Potter Series
Heart of Darkness
The Hobbit
The House on Mango Street
How the Garcia Girls Lost Their Accents
The Hunger Games Trilogy
I Know Why the Caged Bird Sings
In Cold Blood
The Inferno
Invisible Man
Jane Eyre
The Joy Luck Club
Julius Caesar
King Lear
The Kite Runner
Life of Pi
Little Women
Lolita
Lord of the Flies
The Lord of the Rings
Macbeth
The Merchant of Venice
The Metamorphosis
Midnight's Children
A Midsummer Night's Dream
Moby-Dick
Mrs. Dalloway
Native Son
Nineteen Eighty-Four
The Odyssey
Of Mice and Men
The Old Man and the Sea
On the Road
One Flew Over the Cuckoo's Nest
One Hundred Years of Solitude
Othello
The Outsiders
Paradise Lost
The Pearl
The Plague
The Poetry of Baudelaire
The Poetry of Edgar Allan Poe
A Portrait of the Artist as a Young Man
Pride and Prejudice
A Raisin in the Sun
The Red Badge of Courage
Romeo and Juliet
The Scarlet Letter
Sense and Sensibility
Short Fiction of Flannery O'Connor
Slaughterhouse-Five
The Sound and the Fury
A Streetcar Named Desire
The Sun Also Rises
A Tale of Two Cities
The Tales of Edgar Allan Poe
Their Eyes Were Watching God
Things Fall Apart
To Kill a Mockingbird
Twelfth Night, or What You Will
Twelve Years a Slave
War and Peace
The Woman Warrior
Wuthering Heights

Grey House Publishing | Salem Press | H.W. Wilson | 4919 Route 22, PO Box 56, Amenia NY 12501-0056

Titles from Salem Press

Visit www.SalemPress.com for Product Information, Table of Contents, and Sample Pages.

Critical Insights: Themes
The American Comic Book
American Creative Non-Fiction
The American Dream
American Multicultural Identity
American Road Literature
American Short Story
American Sports Fiction
The American Thriller
American Writers in Exile
Censored & Banned Literature
Civil Rights Literature, Past & Present
Coming of Age
Conspiracies
Contemporary Canadian Fiction
Contemporary Immigrant Short Fiction
Contemporary Latin American Fiction
Contemporary Speculative Fiction
Crime and Detective Fiction
Crisis of Faith
Cultural Encounters
Dystopia
Family
The Fantastic
Feminism Flash Fiction
Friendship
Gender, Sex and Sexuality
Going Into the Woods
Good & Evil
The Graphic Novel
Greed
Harlem Renaissance
The Hero's Quest
Historical Fiction
Holocaust Literature
The Immigrant Experience
Inequality
LGBTQ Literature
Literature in Times of Crisis
Literature of Protest
Love
Magical Realism
Midwestern Literature
Modern Japanese Literature
Nature & the Environment
Paranoia, Fear & Alienation
Patriotism
Political Fiction
Postcolonial Literature
Power & Corruption
Pulp Fiction of the '20s and '30s
Rebellion
Russia's Golden Age
Satire
The Slave Narrative
Social Justice and American Literature
Southern Gothic Literature
Southwestern Literature
The Supernatural
Survival
Technology & Humanity
Truth & Lies
Violence in Literature
Virginia Woolf & 20th Century Women Writers
War

Critical Insights: Film
Bonnie & Clyde
Casablanca
Alfred Hitchcock
Stanley Kubrick

Critical Approaches to Literature
Critical Approaches to Literature: Feminist
Critical Approaches to Literature: Moral
Critical Approaches to Literature: Multicultural
Critical Approaches to Literature: Psychological

Literary Classics
Recommended Reading: 600 Classics Reviewed

Novels into Film
Novels into Film: Adaptations & Interpretation
Novels into Film: Adaptations & Interpretation, Volume 2

Critical Surveys of Literature
Critical Survey of American Literature
Critical Survey of Drama
Critical Survey of Long Fiction
Critical Survey of Mystery and Detective Fiction
Critical Survey of Poetry
Critical Survey of Poetry: Contemporary Poets
Critical Survey of Science Fiction & Fantasy Literature
Critical Survey of Shakespeare's Film Adaptations
Critical Survey of Shakespeare's Plays
Critical Survey of Shakespeare's Sonnets
Critical Survey of Short Fiction
Critical Survey of World Literature
Critical Survey of Young Adult Literature

Critical Surveys of Graphic Novels
Heroes & Superheroes
History, Theme, and Technique
Independents & Underground Classics
Manga

Critical Surveys of Mythology & Folklore
Creation Myths
Deadly Battles & Warring Enemies
Gods & Goddesses
Heroes and Heroines
Legendary Creatures
Love, Sexuality, and Desire
World Mythology

Cyclopedia of Literary Characters & Places
Cyclopedia of Literary Characters
Cyclopedia of Literary Places

Grey House Publishing | Salem Press | H.W. Wilson | 4919 Route 22, PO Box 56, Amenia NY 12501-0056

Titles from Salem Press

Visit www.SalemPress.com for Product Information, Table of Contents, and Sample Pages.

Introduction to Literary Context
American Poetry of the 20th Century
American Post-Modernist Novels
American Short Fiction
English Literature
Plays
World Literature

Magill's Literary Annual
Magill's Literary Annual, Annual Editions 1977-2024

Masterplots
Masterplots, Fourth Edition
Masterplots, 2010-2018 Supplement

Notable Writers
Notable African American Writers
Notable American Women Writers
Notable Horror Fiction Writers
Notable Mystery & Detective Fiction Writers
Notable Writers of the American West & the Native American Experience
Notable Writers of LGBTQ+ Literature

HISTORY

The Decades
The 1900s in America
The 1910s in America
The Twenties in America
The Thirties in America
The Forties in America
The Fifties in America
The Sixties in America
The Seventies in America
The Eighties in America
The Nineties in America
The 2000s in America
The 2010s in America

Defining Documents in American History
Defining Documents: The 1900s
Defining Documents: The 1910s
Defining Documents: The 1920s
Defining Documents: The 1930s
Defining Documents: The 1950s
Defining Documents: The 1960s
Defining Documents: The 1970s
Defining Documents: The 1980s
Defining Documents: American Citizenship
Defining Documents: The American Economy
Defining Documents: The American Revolution
Defining Documents: The American West
Defining Documents: Business Ethics
Defining Documents: Capital Punishment
Defining Documents: Censorship
Defining Documents: Civil Rights
Defining Documents: Civil War
Defining Documents: Conservatism
Defining Documents: The Constitution
Defining Documents: The Cold War
Defining Documents: Dissent & Protest
Defining Documents: Domestic Terrorism & Extremism
Defining Documents: Drug Policy
Defining Documents: The Emergence of Modern America
Defining Documents: Environment & Conservation
Defining Documents: Espionage & Intrigue
Defining Documents: Exploration and Colonial America
Defining Documents: The First Amendment
Defining Documents: The Free Press
Defining Documents: The Great Depression
Defining Documents: The Great Migration
Defining Documents: The Gun Debate
Defining Documents: Immigration & Immigrant Communities
Defining Documents: The Legacy of 9/11
Defining Documents: LGBTQ+
Defining Documents: Liberalism
Defining Documents: Manifest Destiny and the New Nation
Defining Documents: Native Americans
Defining Documents: Political Campaigns, Candidates & Discourse
Defining Documents: Postwar 1940s
Defining Documents: Prison Reform
Defining Documents: The Salem Witch Trials
Defining Documents: Secrets, Leaks & Scandals
Defining Documents: Slavery
Defining Documents: Supreme Court Decisions
Defining Documents: Reconstruction Era
Defining Documents: The Vietnam War
Defining Documents: The Underground Railroad
Defining Documents: U.S. Involvement in the Middle East
Defining Documents: Voters' Rights
Defining Documents: Watergate
Defining Documents: Workers' Rights
Defining Documents: World War I
Defining Documents: World War II

Defining Documents in World History
Defining Documents: The 17th Century
Defining Documents: The 18th Century
Defining Documents: The 19th Century
Defining Documents: The 20th Century (1900-1950)
Defining Documents: The Ancient World
Defining Documents: Asia
Defining Documents: Genocide & the Holocaust
Defining Documents: Human Rights
Defining Documents: The Middle Ages
Defining Documents: The Middle East
Defining Documents: Nationalism & Populism
Defining Documents: The Nuclear Age
Defining Documents: Pandemics, Plagues & Public Health
Defining Documents: Religious Freedom & Religious Persecution
Defining Documents: Renaissance & Early Modern Era
Defining Documents: Revolutions
Defining Documents: The Rise & Fall of the Soviet Union
Defining Documents: Treason
Defining Documents: Women's Rights

Grey House Publishing | Salem Press | H.W. Wilson | 4919 Route 22, PO Box 56, Amenia NY 12501-0056

Titles from Salem Press

Visit www.SalemPress.com for Product Information, Table of Contents, and Sample Pages.

Great Events from History
Great Events from History: American History, Exploration to the Colonial Era, 1492-1775
Great Events from History: American History, Forging a New Nation, 1775-1850
Great Events from History: American History, War, Peace & Growth, 1850-1918
Great Events from History: The Ancient World
Great Events from History: The Middle Ages
Great Events from History: The Renaissance & Early Modern Era
Great Events from History: The 17th Century
Great Events from History: The 18th Century
Great Events from History: The 19th Century
Great Events from History: The 20th Century, 1901-1940
Great Events from History: The 20th Century, 1941-1970
Great Events from History: The 20th Century, 1971-2000
Great Events from History: Modern Scandals
Great Events from History: African American History
Great Events from History: The 21st Century, 2000-2016
Great Events from History: LGBTQ Events
Great Events from History: Human Rights
Great Events from History: Women's History

Great Lives from History
Great Athletes
Great Athletes of the Twenty-First Century
Great Lives from History: The 17th Century
Great Lives from History: The 18th Century
Great Lives from History: The 19th Century
Great Lives from History: The 20th Century
Great Lives from History: The 21st Century, 2000-2017
Great Lives from History: African Americans
Great Lives from History: The Ancient World
Great Lives from History: American Heroes
Great Lives from History: American Women
Great Lives from History: Asian and Pacific Islander Americans
Great Lives from History: Autocrats & Dictators
Great Lives from History: The Incredibly Wealthy
Great Lives from History: Inventors & Inventions
Great Lives from History: Jewish Americans
Great Lives from History: Latinos
Great Lives from History: LGBTQ+
Great Lives from History: The Middle Ages
Great Lives from History: The Renaissance & Early Modern Era
Great Lives from History: Scientists and Science

History & Government
American First Ladies
American Presidents
The 50 States
The Ancient World: Extraordinary People in Extraordinary Societies
The Bill of Rights
The Criminal Justice System
U.S. Court Cases
The U.S. Supreme Court

SOCIAL SCIENCES
Civil Rights Movements: Past & Present
Countries, Peoples and Cultures
Countries: Their Wars & Conflicts: A World Survey
Education Today: Issues, Policies & Practices
Encyclopedia of American Immigration
Ethics: Questions & Morality of Human Actions
Issues in U.S. Immigration
Principles of Sociology: Group Relationships & Behavior
Principles of Sociology: Personal Relationships & Behavior
Principles of Sociology: Societal Issues & Behavior
Racial & Ethnic Relations in America
Weapons, Warfare & Military Technology
World Geography

HEALTH
Addictions, Substance Abuse & Alcoholism
Adolescent Health & Wellness
Aging
Cancer
Community & Family Health Issues
Integrative, Alternative & Complementary Medicine
Genetics and Inherited Conditions
Infectious Diseases and Conditions
Magill's Medical Guide
Men's Health
Nutrition
Parenting: Styles & Strategies
Psychology & Behavioral Health
Social Media & Your Mental Health
Teens: Growing Up, Skills & Strategies
Women's Health

Principles of Health
Principles of Health: Allergies & Immune Disorders
Principles of Health: Anxiety & Stress
Principles of Health: Depression
Principles of Health: Diabetes
Principles of Health: Hypertension
Principles of Health: Nursing
Principles of Health: Obesity
Principles of Health: Occupational Therapy & Physical Therapy
Principles of Health: Pain Management
Principles of Health: Prescription Drug Abuse
Principles of Health: Whole Body Wellness

BUSINESS
Principles of Business: Accounting
Principles of Business: Economics
Principles of Business: Entrepreneurship
Principles of Business: Finance
Principles of Business: Globalization
Principles of Business: Leadership
Principles of Business: Management
Principles of Business: Marketing

Titles from Salem Press

Visit www.SalemPress.com for Product Information, Table of Contents, and Sample Pages.

SCIENCE
Ancient Creatures
Applied Science
Applied Science: Engineering & Mathematics
Applied Science: Science & Medicine
Applied Science: Technology
Biomes and Ecosystems
Digital Literacy: Skills & Strategies
Earth Science: Earth Materials and Resources
Earth Science: Earth's Surface and History
Earth Science: Earth's Weather, Water and Atmosphere
Earth Science: Physics and Chemistry of the Earth
Encyclopedia of Climate Change
Encyclopedia of Energy
Encyclopedia of Environmental Issues
Encyclopedia of Global Resources
Encyclopedia of Mathematics and Society
Environmental Sustainability: Skills & Strategies
Forensic Science
Notable Natural Disasters
The Solar System
USA in Space

Principles of Science
Principles of Aeronautics
Principles of Anatomy
Principles of Archaeology
Principles of Architecture
Principles of Astronomy
Principles of Behavioral Science
Principles of Biology
Principles of Biotechnology
Principles of Botany
Principles of Chemistry
Principles of Climatology
Principles of Computer-aided Design
Principles of Computer Science
Principles of Cybersecurity
Principles of Digital Arts & Multimedia
Principles of Ecology
Principles of Energy
Principles of Environmental Engineering
Principles of Fire Science
Principles of Food Science
Principles of Forestry & Conservation
Principles of Geology
Principles of Graphic Design & Typography
Principles of Information Technology
Principles of Marine Science
Principles of Mass Communication
Principles of Mathematics
Principles of Mechanics
Principles of Microbiology
Principles of Modern Agriculture
Principles of Pharmacology
Principles of Physical Science
Principles of Physics
Principles of Probability & Statistics
Principles of Programming & Coding
Principles of Robotics & Artificial Intelligence
Principles of Scientific Research
Principles of Sports Medicine & Exercise Science
Principles of Sustainability

Principles of Zoology

CAREERS
Careers: Paths to Entrepreneurship
Careers in Archaeology & Museum Services
Careers in Artificial Intelligence
Careers in the Arts: Fine, Performing & Visual
Careers in the Automotive Industry
Careers in Biology
Careers in Biotechnology
Careers in Building Construction
Careers in Business
Careers in Chemistry
Careers in Communications & Media
Careers in Criminal Justice
Careers in Culinary Arts
Careers in Cybersecurity
Careers in Earth Science
Careers in Education & Training
Careers in Engineering
Careers in Environment & Conservation
Careers in Financial Services
Careers in Fish & Wildlife
Careers in Forensic Science
Careers in Gaming
Careers in Green Energy
Careers in Healthcare
Careers in Heavy Equipment Operation, Maintenance & Repair
Careers in Hospitality & Tourism
Careers in Human Services
Careers in Illustration & Animation
Careers in Information Technology
Careers in Intelligence & National Security
Careers in Law, Criminal Justice & Emergency Services
Careers in Mass Communication
Careers in the Music Industry
Careers in Manufacturing & Production
Careers in Medical Technology
Careers in Nursing
Careers in Physics
Careers in Protective Services
Careers in Psychology & Behavioral Health
Careers in Public Administration
Careers in Sales, Insurance & Real Estate
Careers in Science & Engineering
Careers in Social Media
Careers in Sports & Fitness
Careers in Sports Medicine & Training
Careers in Technical Services & Equipment Repair
Careers in Transportation
Careers in Travel & Adventure
Careers in Writing & Editing
Careers Outdoors
Careers Overseas
Careers Working with Infants & Children
Careers Working with Animals

Titles from H.W. Wilson

Visit www.HWWilsonInPrint.com for Product Information, Table of Contents, and Sample Pages.

The Reference Shelf
Affordable Housing
Aging in America
Alternative Facts, Post-Truth and the Information War
The American Dream
Artificial Intelligence
Book Bans & Censorship
The Business of Food
Campaign Trends & Election Law
College Sports
Democracy Evolving
The Digital Age
Embracing New Paradigms in Education
Food Insecurity & Hunger in the United States
Future of U.S. Economic Relations: Mexico, Cuba, & Venezuela
Gene Editing & Genetic Engineering
Global Climate Change
Guns in America
Hacktivism
Hate Crimes
Health Conspiracies
Immigration & Border Control in the 21st Century
Income Inequality
Internet Abuses & Privacy Rights
Internet Law
Labor Unions
LGBTQ in the 21st Century
Marijuana Reform
Mental Health Awareness
Money in Politics
National Debate Topic 2020/2021: Criminal Justice Reform
National Debate Topic 2021/2022: Water Resources
National Debate Topic 2022/2023: Emerging Technologies & International Security
National Debate Topic 2023/2024: Economic Inequality
National Debate Topic 2024/2025: Intellectual Property Rights
National Debate Topic 2025/2026: The Arctic
New Developments in Artificial Intelligence
New Frontiers in Space
Policing in 2020
Pollution
Prescription Drug Abuse
Propaganda and Misinformation
Racial Tension in a Postracial Age
Reality Television
Renewable Energy
Representative American Speeches, Annual Editions
Reproductive Rights
Rethinking Work
Revisiting Gender
Russia & Ukraine
The South China Sea Conflict
Space Exploration
Sports in America
The Supreme Court
The Transformation of American Cities
The Two Koreas
UFOs
Vaccinations
Voting Rights
Whistleblowers

Core Collections
Children's Core Collection
Fiction Core Collection
Graphic Novels Core Collection
Middle & Junior High School Core
Public Library Core Collection: Nonfiction
Senior High Core Collection
Young Adult Fiction Core Collection

Current Biography
Current Biography Cumulative Index 1946-2025
Current Biography Magazine
Current Biography Yearbook

Readers' Guide to Periodical Literature
Abridged Readers' Guide to Periodical Literature
Readers' Guide to Periodical Literature

Indexes
Index to Legal Periodicals & Books
Short Story Index

Sears List
Sears List of Subject Headings
Sears List of Subject Headings, Online Database

History
American Game Changers: Invention, Innovation & Transformation
American Reformers
Speeches of the American Presidents

Facts About Series
Facts About the 20th Century
Facts About American Immigration
Facts About China
Facts About the Presidents
Facts About the World's Languages

Nobel Prize Winners
Nobel Prize Winners: 1901-1986
Nobel Prize Winners: 1987-1991
Nobel Prize Winners: 1992-1996
Nobel Prize Winners: 1997-2001
Nobel Prize Winners: 2002-2018

Famous First Facts
Famous First Facts
Famous First Facts About American Politics
Famous First Facts About Sports
Famous First Facts About the Environment
Famous First Facts: International Edition

American Book of Days
The American Book of Days
The International Book of Days

Grey House Publishing | Salem Press | H.W. Wilson | 4919 Route 22, PO Box 56, Amenia NY 12501-0056